W9-BSX-291

For more resources, visit the Web site for

The Making of the West

bedfordstmartins.com/hunt

FREE Online Study Guide

GET INSTANT FEEDBACK ON YOUR PROGRESS WITH

- Chapter self-tests
- Key terms review
- Map quizzes
- Timeline activities
- Note-taking outlines

FREE History research and writing help

REFINE YOUR RESEARCH SKILLS AND FIND PLENTY OF GOOD SOURCES WITH

- A database of useful images, maps, documents, and more at *Make History*
- A guide to online sources for history
- Help with writing history papers
- A tool for building a bibliography
- Tips on avoiding plagiarism

FOURTH EDITION

The Making of the West

PEOPLES AND CULTURES

FOURTH EDITION

The Making of the West

PEOPLES AND CULTURES

Volume C: Since 1750

Lynn Hunt
University of California, Los Angeles

Thomas R. Martin
College of the Holy Cross

Barbara H. Rosenwein
Loyola University Chicago

Bonnie G. Smith
Rutgers University

BEDFORD/ST. MARTIN'S
Boston ♦ New York

For Bedford/St. Martin's

Publisher for History: Mary Dougherty
Director of Development for History: Jane Knetzger
Developmental Editor: Danielle Slevens
Senior Production Editor: Karen S. Baart
Production Editor: Marcy Ross
Senior Production Supervisor: Jennifer L. Peterson
Senior Executive Marketing Manager: Jenna Bookin Barry
Associate Editor: Robin Soule
Production Assistants: Elise Keller and Victoria Royal
Copyeditor: Janet Renard
Indexer: Leoni Z. McVey, McVey & Associates, Inc.
Cartography: Mapping Specialists Limited
Photo Researcher: Bruce Carson
Permissions Manager: Kalina K. Ingham
Senior Art Director: Anna Palchik
Text Designer: Lisa Buckley
Page Layout: Boynton Hue Studio
Cover Designer: Billy Boardman
Cover Art: Vasili Semenovich Sadovnikov (1800–1879). *The Unveiling of the Nicholas I Memorial in St. Petersburg,* 1857. State Russian Museum, St. Petersburg, Russia. Bridgeman Art Library International, New York.
Composition: Jouve
Printing and Binding: RR Donnelley and Sons

President: Joan E. Feinberg
Editorial Director: Denise B. Wydra
Director of Marketing: Karen R. Soeltz
Director of Production: Susan W. Brown
Associate Director, Editorial Production: Elise S. Kaiser
Managing Editor: Elizabeth M. Schaaf

Library of Congress Control Number: 2011939727

Copyright © 2012, 2009, 2005, 2001 by Bedford/St. Martin's

All rights reserved. No part of this book may be reproduced, stored in a retrieval system, or transmitted in any form or by any means, electronic, mechanical, photocopying, recording, or otherwise, except as may be expressly permitted by the applicable copyright statutes or in writing by the Publisher.

Manufactured in the United States of America.

1 2 3 4 5 6 15 14 13 12 11

For information, write: Bedford/St. Martin's, 75 Arlington Street, Boston, MA 02116
(617-399-4000)

ISBN: 978–0–312–67268–3 (Combined Edition)
ISBN: 978–0–312–57571–7 (Loose-Leaf Edition)
ISBN: 978–0–312–58343–9 (High School Edition)
ISBN: 978–0–312–67269–0 (Volume I)
ISBN: 978–0–312–57569–4 (Loose-Leaf Edition, Volume I)
ISBN: 978–0–312–67271–3 (Volume II)
ISBN: 978–0–312–57570–0 (Loose-Leaf Edition, Volume II)
ISBN: 978–0–312–58340–8 (Volume A)
ISBN: 978–0–312–58341–5 (Volume B)
ISBN: 978–0–312–58342–2 (Volume C)

Acknowledgments: *Acknowledgments and copyrights are printed at the back of the book on pages C-1–C-2, which constitute an extension of the copyright page. It is a violation of the law to reproduce these selections by any means whatsoever without the written permission of the copyright holder. At the time of publication all Internet URLs published in this text were found to accurately link to their intended Web site. If you do find a broken link, please forward the information to* history@bedfordstmartins.com *so that it can be corrected for the next printing.*

Preface

History requires constant rethinking and rewriting, because current events make us see the past in a new light. The fall of the Berlin Wall in 1989; the attacks of September 11, 2001; and the world economic crisis that began in 2008 are dramatic examples of how events shift our perspective. As a result of these events, communism, Islam, and globalization all took on different meanings—not just for the present, but also in ways that compel us to reconsider the past. To take just one example, Islam has been part of the history of the West since its founding as a religion in the seventh century, and yet until the last two decades most textbooks of the history of the West gave it relatively little attention. No one would think of limiting its coverage now.

As this book goes into its fourth edition, we authors feel confident that our fundamental approach is well suited to incorporating changes in perspective. We have always linked the history of the West to wider developments in the world. A new edition gives us the opportunity to make those links even stronger and more global, and thereby help students better understand the world in which they live. Instructors who have read and used our book also confirm that the synthesis of approaches we offer—from military to gender history—enables them to bring the most up-to-date conceptualizations of the West into their classroom. We aim to integrate different approaches rather than privileging any one of them.

Our primary goal has been to create a text that demonstrates that the history of the West is the story of an ongoing process, not a finished result with one fixed meaning. We wanted also to make clear that there is no one Western people or culture that has existed from the beginning until now. Instead, the history of the West includes many different peoples and cultures. To convey these ideas, we have written a sustained story of the West's development in a broad, global context that reveals the cross-cultural interactions fundamental to the shaping of Western politics, societies, cultures, and economies. Indeed, the first chapter opens with a section on the origins and contested meaning of the term *Western civilization*.

Equally valuable to instructors has been the way our book is organized in a chronological framework to help students understand how political, social, cultural, and economic histories have influenced one another over time. We know from our own teaching that introductory students need a solid chronological framework, one with enough familiar benchmarks to make the material easy to grasp. Each chapter treats the main events, people, and themes of a period in which the West significantly changed; thus, students learn about political and military events and social and cultural developments as they unfolded. This chronological integration also accords with our belief that it is important, above all else, for students to see the interconnections among varieties of historical experience—between politics and cultures, between public events and private experiences, between wars and diplomacy and everyday life. Our chronological synthesis provides a unique benefit to students: it makes these relationships clear while highlighting the major changes of each age. For teachers, our chronological approach ensures a balanced account and provides the opportunity to present themes within their greater context. But perhaps best of all, this approach provides a text that reveals history as a process that is constantly alive, subject to pressures, and able to surprise us.

Cultural borrowing between the peoples of Europe and their neighbors has characterized Western civilization from the beginning. Thus, we have insisted on an expanded vision of the West that includes the United States and fully incorporates Scandinavia, eastern Europe, and the Ottoman Empire. Latin America, Africa, China, Japan, and India also come into the story. We have been able to offer sustained treatment of crucial topics such as Islam and provide a more thorough examination of globalization than any competing text. Study of Western history provides essential background to today's events, from debates over immigration to conflicts in the Middle East. Instructors have found this synthesis essential for helping students understand the West amid today's globalization.

In this edition, we have enhanced our coverage of Western interactions with other parts of the world and the cross-cultural exchanges that influenced the making of the West. Chapter 2, for example, demonstrates that despite the Dark Age, Greek civilization stayed in contact with civilization in the Near East as it reinvented itself—and that this cultural interaction produced a reemergence with profound differences from the social and political traditions that had existed in Greece before. Chapter 14 shows how the gold and silver discovered in the New World combined with growing confrontations over religion within Europe to reshape the long-standing rivalries among princes, treating these topics together to illustrate how earlier forms of globalization influenced daily life, religious beliefs, and the ways wars were fought. Chapter 27 features a revised, updated discussion of decolonization and the end of empire in Asia, Africa, and the Middle East, including a new document on torture in Algeria. Chapter 29 includes current coverage of recent events in the Middle East, the global economic crisis, the rise of economies in the Pacific and the Southern Hemisphere, and globalized culture and communications.

As always, we have also incorporated the latest scholarly findings throughout the book so that students and instructors alike have a text on which they can confidently rely. In the fourth edition, we have included new and updated discussions of topics such as fresh archaeological evidence for the possible role of religion in stimulating the major changes of the Neolithic Revolution; the dating of the Great Sphinx in Egypt, the scholarly debate that could radically change our ideas of the earliest Egyptian history; the newest thinking on the origins of Islam; the crucial issues in the Investiture Conflict between pope and emperor; the impact of the Great Famine of the fourteenth century; the slave trade, and especially its continuation into the nineteenth century; and, in a brand-new epilogue, the ways in which scholars are considering recent events within the context of the new digital world.

Aided by a fresh and welcoming design, new pedagogical aids, and new multimedia offerings that give students and instructors interactive tools for study and teaching (see "Versions and Supplements" on page xi), the new edition is, we believe, even better suited to today's Western civilization courses. In writing *The Making of the West: Peoples and Cultures*, we have aimed to communicate the vitality and excitement as well as the fundamental importance of history. Students should be enthusiastic about history; we hope we have conveyed some of our own enthusiasm and love for the study of history in these pages.

Pedagogy and Features

We know from our own teaching that students need all the help they can get in absorbing and making sense of information, thinking analytically, and understanding that history itself is often debated and constantly revised. With these goals in mind, we retained the class-tested learning and teaching aids that worked well in the previous editions, but we have also done more to help students distill the central story of each age and give them more opportunities to develop their own historical skills.

Compared with previous editions, the fourth edition incorporates more aids to help students sort out what is most important to learn while they read. Completely redesigned Chapter Review sections feature new, dynamic activities asking students to identify and discuss the chapter's key terms, encouraging students to go beyond rote memorization and consider each term's importance in context. We have also added questions in three different places: to the documents (which are described more fully below), to the end-of-chapter timelines, and to the Making Connections sections. Posed at the end of the documents, questions help focus students' attention on the main themes and concepts expressed in them. The questions at the end of the timelines encourage students to think about possible links between political, economic, social, and cultural events. We have added more questions to the Making Connections feature because instructors find these questions to be useful in prompting students to think across the sections of any given chapter. To further help students as they read, we have worked hard to ensure that chapter and section overviews outline the central points of each section in the clearest manner possible, and we have condensed some material to better illuminate key ideas.

The study tools introduced in the previous editions continue to help students check their understanding of the chapters and the periods they cover. Boldface key terms and names have been updated to concentrate on likely test items. Those terms and people are defined in a running glossary at the bottom of pages and collected in a comprehensive glossary at the end of the book. Review questions, strategically placed at the end of each major section, help students recall and assimilate core points in digestible increments. Vivid chapter-opening anecdotes, timelines, and conclusions further reinforce the central developments covered in the reading.

To reflect the richness of the themes in the text and offer further opportunities for historical investigation, we include a rich assortment of single-source documents (two to three per chapter), 30 percent of them new to this edition. Nothing can give students a more direct experience of the past than original voices, and we have endeavored to let those voices speak, whether it is Frederick

Barbarossa replying to the Romans when they offer him the emperor's crown, Marie de Sévigné's description of the French court, or an ordinary person's account of the outbreak of the Russian Revolution.

Accompanying these primary-source documents are our five unique skill-building features. Reviewed with users and revised for the fourth edition, these features extend the narrative by revealing the process of interpretation, providing a solid introduction to historical argument and critical thinking, and capturing the excitement of historical investigation.

- ***Seeing History*** features guide students through the process of reading images as historical evidence. Each of the ten features provides a pair of images for comparison and contrast, with background information and questions that encourage visual analysis. Examples include comparisons of pagan and Christian sarcophagi, Persian and Arabic coins, Romanesque and Gothic naves, pre- and post–French Revolution attire, and portrayals of soldiers in World War I.
- ***Contrasting Views*** features provide three or four often conflicting primary-source accounts of a central event, person, or development—such as Julius Caesar, Charlemagne, Magna Carta, Martin Luther, the English Civil War, and late-nineteenth-century migration—enabling students to understand history from a variety of contemporaneous perspectives.
- ***New Sources, New Perspectives*** features show students how historians continue to develop fresh insights using new kinds of evidence about the past, from tree rings to Holocaust museums.
- ***Terms of History*** features explain the meanings of some of the most important and contested terms in the history of the West—*civilization*, *nationalism*, and *progress*, for example—and show how those meanings have developed and changed over time.
- ***Taking Measure*** features introduce students to the intriguing stories revealed by quantitative analysis. Each feature highlights a chart, table, graph, or map of historical statistics that illuminates an important political, social, or cultural development.

The book's map program has been widely praised as one of the most comprehensive and inviting of any survey text. In each chapter, we offer three types of maps, each with a distinct role in conveying information to students. Four to five full-size maps show major developments, two to four "spot" maps—small maps positioned within the discussion right where students need them—serve as immediate locators, and "Mapping the West" summary maps at the end of each chapter provide a snapshot of the West at the close of a transformative period and help students visualize the West's changing contours over time. For this edition, we have added new maps and carefully considered each of the existing maps, simplifying where possible to better highlight essential information, and clarifying and updating borders and labels where needed.

We have striven to integrate art as fully as possible into the narrative and to show its value for teaching and learning. Over 430 illustrations—30 percent of which are new—were carefully chosen to reflect this edition's broad topical coverage and geographic inclusion, reinforce the text, and show the varieties of visual sources from which historians build their narratives and interpretations. All artifacts, illustrations, paintings, and photographs are contemporaneous with the chapter; there are no anachronistic illustrations. Substantive captions for the maps and art help students learn how to read visuals, and we have frequently included specific questions or suggestions for comparisons that might be developed. Specially designed visual exercises in the Online Study Guide supplement this approach. A new page design for the fourth edition supports our goal of intertwining the art and the narrative, and makes the new study tools readily accessible.

Acknowledgments

In the vital process of revision, the authors have benefited from repeated critical readings by many talented scholars and teachers. Our sincere thanks go to the following instructors, whose comments often challenged us to rethink or justify our interpretations and who always provided a check on accuracy down to the smallest detail.

Robert Beachy, *Goucher College*
William E. Burns, *George Washington University*
Kevin W. Caldwell, *Blue Ridge Community College*
Patricia G. Clark, *Westminster College*
Oliver Griffin, *St. John Fisher College*
Rebecca K. Hayes, *Northern Virginia Community College–Manassas*
Anne Huebel, *Franklin Pierce University*
Steven Kale, *Washington State University*
Jeff Kleiman, *University of Wisconsin–Marshfield*
John Leazer, *Carthage College*

Charles Levine, *Mesa Community College*
Mauro Magarelli, *William Paterson University*
Kelly Obernuefemann, *Lewis & Clark Community College*
Ann Ostendorf, *Gonzaga University*
Maryanne Rhett, *Monmouth University*
Sarah Shurts, *Montclair State University*
Mark Stephens, *Chabot College*
Frank Van Nuys, *South Dakota School of Mines and Technology*

Many colleagues, friends, and family members have made contributions to this work. They know how grateful we are. We also wish to acknowledge and thank the publishing team at Bedford/St. Martin's who did so much to bring this revised edition to completion: president Joan Feinberg, editorial director Denise Wydra, publisher for history Mary Dougherty, director of development for history Jane Knetzger, developmental editor Danielle Slevens, freelance editors Jim Strandberg and Debra Michals, associate editor Robin Soule, senior executive marketing manager Jenna Bookin Barry, senior production editor Karen Baart, freelance production editor Marcy Ross, managing editor Elizabeth Schaaf, art researcher Bruce Carson, text designer Lisa Buckley, page makeup artist Cia Boynton, cover designer Billy Boardman, and copyeditor Janet Renard.

Our students' questions and concerns have shaped much of this work, and we welcome all our readers' suggestions, queries, and criticisms. Please contact us at our respective institutions or via **history@bedfordstmartins.com**.

Versions and Supplements

Adopters of *The Making of the West* and their students have access to abundant extra resources, including documents, presentation and testing materials, the acclaimed Bedford Series in History and Culture volumes, and much much more. See below for more information, visit the book's catalog site at **bedfordstmartins.com/hunt/catalog**, or contact your local Bedford/St. Martin's sales representative.

Get the Right Version for Your Class

To accommodate different course lengths and course budgets, *The Making of the West* is available in several different formats, including three-hole punched loose-leaf Budget Books versions and e-books, which are available at a substantial discount.

- Combined edition (Chapters 1–29) — available in hardcover, loose-leaf, and e-book formats
- Volume 1: To 1750 (Chapters 1–17) — available in paperback, loose-leaf, and e-book formats
- Volume 2: Since 1500 (Chapters 14–29) — available in paperback, loose-leaf, and e-book formats
- Volume A: To 1500 (Chapters 1–13) — available in paperback format
- Volume B: 1340–1830 (Chapters 13–20) — available in paperback format
- Volume C: Since 1750 (Chapters 18–29) — available in paperback format

The online, interactive **Bedford e-Book** can be examined at **bedfordstmartins.com/hunt** or purchased at a discount there. Your students can also purchase *The Making of the West* in other popular e-book formats for computers, tablets, and e-readers.

Online Extras for Students

The book's companion site at **bedfordstmartins.com/hunt** gives students a way to read, write, and study, and to find and access quizzes and activities, study aids, and history research and writing help.

FREE **Online Study Guide.** Available at the companion site, this popular resource provides students with quizzes and activities for each chapter, including multiple-choice self-tests that focus on important concepts; flashcards that test students' knowledge of key terms; timeline activities that emphasize causal relationships; and map quizzes intended to strengthen students' geography skills. Instructors can monitor students' progress through an online Quiz Gradebook or receive email updates.

FREE **Research, Writing, and Anti-plagiarism Advice.** Available at the companion site, Bedford's **History Research and Writing Help** includes **History Research and Reference Sources**, with links to history-related databases, indexes, and journals; **More Sources and How to Format a History Paper**, with clear advice on how to integrate primary and secondary sources into research papers and how to cite and format sources correctly; **Build a Bibliography**, a simple Web-based tool known as The Bedford Bibliographer that generates bibliographies in four commonly used documentation styles; and **Tips on Avoiding Plagiarism**, an online tutorial that reviews the consequences of plagiarism and features exercises to help students practice integrating sources and recognize acceptable summaries.

Resources for Instructors

Bedford/St. Martin's has developed a wide range of teaching resources for this book and for this course. They range from lecture and presentation materials and assessment tools to course management options. Most can be downloaded or ordered at **bedfordstmartins.com/hunt/catalog**.

HistoryClass for The Making of the West. HistoryClass, a Bedford/St. Martin's Online Course Space, puts the online resources available with this textbook in one convenient and completely customizable course space. There, you and your students can access an interactive e-book and primary sources reader; maps, images, documents, and links; chapter review quizzes; interactive multimedia exercises; and research and writing help. In HistoryClass you can get all of our premium content and tools and assign, rearrange, and mix them with your own resources. For more information, visit **yourhistoryclass.com**.

Bedford Coursepack for Blackboard, WebCT, Desire2Learn, Angel, Sakai, or Moodle. We have free content to help you integrate our rich content into your course management system. Registered instructors can download coursepacks with no hassle and no strings attached. Content includes our most popular free resources and book-specific content for *The Making of the West.* Visit **bedfordstmartins.com/coursepacks** to see a demo, find your version, or download your coursepack.

Instructor's Resource Manual. The instructor's manual offers both experienced and first-time instructors tools for preparing for lecture and running discussions. It includes chapter review material, teaching strategies, and a guide to chapter-specific supplements available for the text.

Guide to Changing Editions. Designed to facilitate an instructor's transition from the previous edition of *The Making of the West* to the current edition, this guide presents an overview of major changes as well as changes in each chapter.

Computerized Test Bank. The test bank includes a mix of fresh, carefully crafted multiple-choice, matching, fill-in-the-blank, short-answer, and essay questions for each chapter. It also contains the Chapter Focus, Review, Important Events, and Making Connections questions from the textbook and model answers for each. The questions appear in Microsoft Word format and in easy-to-use test bank software that allows instructors to easily add, edit, re-sequence, and print questions and answers. Instructors can also export questions into a variety of formats, including WebCT and Blackboard.

PowerPoint Maps, Images, Lecture Outlines, and i>clicker Content. Look good and save time with *The Bedford Lecture Kit.* These presentation materials are downloadable individually from the Instructor Resources tab at **bedfordstmartins.com/hunt/catalog** and are available on *The Bedford Lecture Kit* Instructor's Resource CD-ROM. They include ready-made and fully customizable PowerPoint multimedia presentations built around lecture outlines with embedded maps, figures, and selected images from the textbook and detailed instructor notes on key points. Also available are maps and selected images in JPEG and PowerPoint formats; content for i>clicker, a classroom response system, in Microsoft Word and PowerPoint formats; the Instructor's Resource Manual in Microsoft Word format; and outline maps in PDF format for quizzing or handing out. All files are suitable for copying onto transparency acetates.

***Make History*—Free Documents, Maps, Images, and Web Sites.** *Make History* combines the best Web resources with hundreds of maps and images, to make it simple to find the source material you need. Browse the collection of thousands of resources by course or by topic, date, and type. Each item has been carefully chosen and helpfully annotated to make it easy to find exactly what you need. Available at **bedfordstmartins.com/makehistory**.

Videos and Multimedia. A wide assortment of videos and multimedia CD-ROMs on various topics in Western civilization is available to qualified adopters through your Bedford/St. Martin's sales representative.

Package and Save Your Students Money

For information on free packages and discounts up to 50%, visit **bedfordstmartins.com/hunt/catalog**, or contact your local Bedford/St. Martin's sales representative.

Bedford e-Book. The e-book for this title, described above, can be packaged with the print text at a discount.

***Sources of The Making of the West*, Fourth Edition.** This companion sourcebook provides written and visual sources to accompany each chapter of *The Making of the West.* Political, social, and cultural documents offer a variety of perspectives that complement the textbook and encourage students to make connections between narrative history and primary sources. Over thirty new documents and visual sources highlight the diversity of historical voices that shaped each period. To aid students in approaching and interpreting documents, each chapter contains an introduction, document headnotes, and questions for discussion. Available free when packaged with the print text.

***Sources of The Making of the West* e-Book.** The reader is also available as an e-book. When packaged with the print or electronic version of the textbook, it is available for free.

The Bedford Series in History and Culture. More than one hundred titles in this highly praised series combine first-rate scholarship, historical narrative, and important primary documents for undergraduate courses. Each book is brief, inexpensive, and focused on a specific topic or period. For a complete list of titles, visit **bedfordstmartins.com/history/series**. Package discounts are available.

Rand McNally Atlas of Western Civilization. This collection of over fifty full-color maps highlights social, political, and cross-cultural change and interaction from classical Greece and Rome to the postindustrial Western world. Each map is thoroughly indexed for fast reference. Available for $3.00 when packaged with the print text.

The Bedford Glossary for European History. This handy supplement for the survey course gives students historically contextualized definitions for hundreds of terms — from *Abbasids* to *Zionism* — that they will encounter in lectures, reading, and exams. Available free when packaged with the print text.

Trade Books. Titles published by sister companies Hill and Wang; Farrar, Straus and Giroux; Henry Holt and Company; St. Martin's Press; Picador; and Palgrave Macmillan are available at a 50% discount when packaged with Bedford/St. Martin's textbooks. For more information, visit **bedfordstmartins.com/tradeup**.

A Pocket Guide to Writing in History. This portable and affordable reference tool by Mary Lynn Rampolla provides reading, writing, and research advice useful to students in all history courses. Concise yet comprehensive advice on approaching typical history assignments, developing critical reading skills, writing effective history papers, conducting research, using and documenting sources, and avoiding plagiarism — enhanced with practical tips and examples throughout — have made this slim reference a best seller. Package discounts are available.

A Student's Guide to History. This complete guide to success in any history course provides the practical help students need to be effective. In addition to introducing students to the nature of the discipline, author Jules Benjamin teaches a wide range of skills, from preparing for exams to approaching common writing assignments, and explains the research and documentation process with plentiful examples. Package discounts are available.

The Social Dimension of Western Civilization. Combining current scholarship with classic pieces, this reader's forty-eight secondary sources, compiled by Richard M. Golden, hook students with the fascinating and often surprising details of how everyday Western people worked, ate, played, celebrated, worshipped, married, procreated, fought, persecuted, and died. Package discounts are available.

The West in the Wider World: Sources and Perspectives. Edited by Richard Lim and David Kammerling Smith, this first college reader to focus on the central historical question "How did the West become the West?" offers a wealth of written and visual source materials to reveal the influence of non-European regions on the origins and development of Western civilization. Package discounts are available.

Brief Contents

18 The Promise of Enlightenment, 1750–1789 587

19 The Cataclysm of Revolution, 1789–1799 619

20 Napoleon and the Revolutionary Legacy, 1800–1830 651

21 Industrialization and Social Ferment, 1830–1850 685

22 Politics and Culture of the Nation-State, 1850–1870 721

23 Empire, Industry, and Everyday Life, 1870–1890 759

24 Modernity and the Road to War, 1890–1914 797

25 World War I and Its Aftermath, 1914–1929 835

26 The Great Depression and World War II, 1929–1945 873

27 The Cold War and the Remaking of Europe, 1945–1960s 913

28 Postindustrial Society and the End of the Cold War Order, 1960s–1989 949

29 A New Globalism, 1989 to the Present 985

EPILOGUE The Making of the West Continues in the Digital Age E-1

Contents

Preface vii

Versions and Supplements xi

Brief Contents xiv

Maps and Figures xxiii

Special Features xxv

To the Student xxvii

CHAPTER 18

The Promise of Enlightenment

1750–1789 587

The Enlightenment at Its Height 588

Men and Women of the Republic of Letters 588
Conflicts with Church and State 591
The Individual and Society 592
Spreading the Enlightenment 596
The Limits of Reason: Roots of Romanticism and Religious Revival 598

Society and Culture in an Age of Enlightenment 599

The Nobility's Reassertion of Privilege 599
The Middle Class and the Making of a New Elite 600
Life on the Margins 603

State Power in an Era of Reform 605

War and Diplomacy 605
State-Sponsored Reform 607
Limits of Reform 609

Rebellions against State Power 610

Food Riots and Peasant Uprisings 610
Public Opinion and Political Opposition 611
Revolution in North America 612

Conclusion 614 Chapter 18 Review 616

DOCUMENT: Denis Diderot, "Encyclopedia" (1755) 590

CONTRASTING VIEWS: Women and the Enlightenment 594

TERMS OF HISTORY: Enlightenment 596

TAKING MEASURE: European Urbanization, 1750–1800 601

DOCUMENT: Thomas Jefferson, Declaration of Independence (July 4, 1776) 613

CHAPTER 19

The Cataclysm of Revolution

1789–1799 619

The Revolutionary Wave, 1787–1789 620
Protesters in the Low Countries and Poland 620
Origins of the French Revolution, 1787–1789 623

From Monarchy to Republic, 1789–1793 626
The Revolution of Rights and Reason 626
The End of Monarchy 628

Terror and Resistance 631
Robespierre and the Committee of Public Safety 632
The Republic of Virtue, 1793–1794 633
Resisting the Revolution 635
The Fall of Robespierre and the End of the Terror 636

Revolution on the March 638
Arms and Conquests 638
Poland Extinguished, 1793–1795 640
Revolution in the Colonies 640
Worldwide Reactions to Revolutionary Change 643

Conclusion 647 Chapter 19 Review 648

TERMS OF HISTORY: Revolution 621

DOCUMENT: The Rights of Minorities (1789) 627

DOCUMENT: Address on Abolishing the Slave Trade (February 5, 1790) 641

CONTRASTING VIEWS: Perspectives on the French Revolution 644

CHAPTER 20

Napoleon and the Revolutionary Legacy

1800–1830 651

The Rise of Napoleon Bonaparte 652
A General Takes Over 652
From Republic to Empire 654
The New Paternalism: The Civil Code 657
Patronage of Science and Intellectual Life 658

"Europe Was at My Feet": Napoleon's Conquests 659
The Grand Army and Its Victories, 1800–1807 659
The Impact of French Victories 661
From Russian Winter to Final Defeat, 1812–1815 664

The "Restoration" of Europe 667
The Congress of Vienna, 1814–1815 668
The Emergence of Conservatism 670
The Revival of Religion 671

Challenges to the Conservative Order 672
Romanticism 672
Political Revolts in the 1820s 675
Revolution and Reform, 1830–1832 678

Conclusion 681 Chapter 20 Review 682

SEEING HISTORY: The Clothing Revolution: The Social Meaning of Changes in Postrevolutionary Fashion 656

DOCUMENT: An Ordinary Soldier on Campaign with Napoleon (1812) 665

CONTRASTING VIEWS: Napoleon: For and Against 666

DOCUMENT: Wordsworth's Poetry (1798) 673

CHAPTER 21
Industrialization and Social Ferment

1830–1850 685

The Industrial Revolution 686
Roots of Industrialization 686
Engines of Change 688
Urbanization and Its Consequences 692
Agricultural Perils and Prosperity 695

Reforming the Social Order 696
Cultural Responses to the Social Question 696
The Varieties of Social Reform 698
Abuses and Reforms Overseas 701

Ideologies and Political Movements 703
The Spell of Nationalism 703
Liberalism in Economics and Politics 705
Socialism and the Early Labor Movement 706

The Revolutions of 1848 709
The Hungry Forties 709
Another French Revolution 710
Nationalist Revolution in Italy 711
Revolt and Reaction in Central Europe 712
Aftermath to 1848: Reimposing Authority 715

Conclusion 716 Chapter 21 Review 718

TAKING MEASURE: Railroad Lines, 1830–1850 688

NEW SOURCES, NEW PERSPECTIVES: Statistics and the Standard of Living of the Working Class 692

DOCUMENT: Marx and Engels, *The Communist Manifesto* (1848) 708

DOCUMENT: Alexis de Tocqueville Describes the June Days in Paris (1848) 713

CHAPTER 22
Politics and Culture of the Nation-State

1850–1870 721

The End of the Concert of Europe 722
Napoleon III and the Quest for French Glory 723
The Crimean War, 1853–1856: Turning Point in European Affairs 724
Reform in Russia 726

War and Nation Building 729
Cavour, Garibaldi, and the Process of Italian Unification 729
Bismarck and the Realpolitik of German Unification 731
Francis Joseph and the Creation of the Austro-Hungarian Monarchy 735
Political Stability through Gradual Reform in Great Britain 736
Nation Building in North America 737

Nation Building through Social Order 739
Bringing Order to the Cities 739
Expanding Government Bureaucracy 741
Schooling and Professionalizing Society 742
Spreading National Power and Order beyond the West 743
Challenging the Nation-State's Order at Home 745

The Culture of Social Order 748
The Arts Confront Social Reality 748
Religion and National Order 751
From the Natural Sciences to Social Science 753

Conclusion 754 Chapter 22 Review 756

DOCUMENT: Mrs. Seacole: The *Other* Florence Nightingale 726

DOCUMENT: Education of a Mathematical Genius in Russia 728

TERMS OF HISTORY: Nationalism 729

DOCUMENT: Bismarck Tricks the Public to Get His War 734

SEEING HISTORY: Photographing the Nation: Domesticity and War 738

CHAPTER 23
Empire, Industry, and Everyday Life

1870–1890 759

The New Imperialism 761
Taming the Mediterranean 761
The Scramble for Africa 762
Acquiring Territory in Asia 765
Japan's Imperial Agenda 766
The Paradoxes of Imperialism 766

The Industry of Empire 768
Industrial Innovation 769
Facing Economic Crisis 771
Revolution in Business Practices 772

Imperial Society and Culture 775
The "Best Circles" and the Expanding Middle Class 775
Working People's Strategies 776
National Fitness: Reform, Sports, and Leisure 780
Artistic Responses to Empire and Industry 781

The Birth of Mass Politics 783
Workers, Politics, and Protest 784
Expanding Political Participation in Western Europe 786
Power Politics in Central and Eastern Europe 788

Conclusion 791 Chapter 23 Review 794

DOCUMENT: An African King Describes His Government 764

TAKING MEASURE: European Emigration, 1870–1890 777

CONTRASTING VIEWS: Experiences of Migration 778

DOCUMENT: Henrik Ibsen, From *A Doll's House* 782

CHAPTER 24
Modernity and the Road to War

1890–1914 797

Public Debate over Private Life 798
Population Pressure 799
Reforming Marriage 801
New Women, New Men, and the Politics of Sexual Identity 801
Sciences of the Modern Self 803

Modernity and the Revolt in Ideas 806
The Opposition to Positivism 806
The Revolution in Science 806
Modern Art 807
The Revolt in Music and Dance 809

Growing Tensions in Mass Politics 810
The Expanding Power of Labor 810
Rights for Women and the Battle for Suffrage 811
Liberalism Tested 812
Anti-Semitism, Nationalism, and Zionism in Mass Politics 813

European Imperialism Challenged 817
The Trials of Empire 817
The Russian Empire Threatened 821
Growing Resistance to Colonial Domination 822

Roads to War 825
Competing Alliances and Clashing Ambitions 825
The Race to Arms 827
1914: War Erupts 828

Conclusion 830 Chapter 24 Review 832

TERMS OF HISTORY: Modern 799

NEW SOURCES, NEW PERSPECTIVES: Psychohistory and Its Lessons 804

DOCUMENT: Leon Pinsker Calls for a Jewish State 817

DOCUMENT: Turkish Nationalism 823

DOCUMENT: Vietnamese Resistance and the Importance of Becoming Modern 824

TAKING MEASURE: The Growth in Armaments, 1890–1914 828

CHAPTER 25
World War I and Its Aftermath

1914–1929 835

The Great War, 1914–1918 836
Blueprints for War 836
The Battlefronts 839
The Home Front 842

Protest, Revolution, and War's End, 1917–1918 845
War Protest 845
Revolution in Russia 846
Ending the War, 1918 849

The Search for Peace in an Era of Revolution 851
Europe in Turmoil 851
The Paris Peace Conference, 1919–1920 852
Economic and Diplomatic Consequences of the Peace 855

A Decade of Recovery: Europe in the 1920s 857
Changes in the Political Landscape 857
Reconstructing the Economy 860
Restoring Society 860

Mass Culture and the Rise of Modern Dictators 862
Culture for the Masses 862
Cultural Debates over the Future 863
The Communist Utopia 865
Fascism on the March in Italy 867

Conclusion 868 Chapter 25 Review 870

SEEING HISTORY: Portraying Soldiers in World War I 843
DOCUMENT: Outbreak of the Russian Revolution 847
TAKING MEASURE: The Victims of Influenza, 1918–1919 850
CONTRASTING VIEWS: The Middle East at the End of World War I: Freedom or Subjugation? 854
DOCUMENT: Memory and Battlefield Tourism 865

CHAPTER 26
The Great Depression and World War II

1929–1945 873

The Great Depression 874
Economic Disaster Strikes 874
Social Effects of the Depression 876
The Great Depression beyond the West 876

Totalitarian Triumph 878
The Rise of Stalinism 878
Hitler's Rise to Power 881
The Nazification of German Politics 883
Nazi Racism 885

Democracies on the Defensive 886
Confronting the Economic Crisis 886
Cultural Visions in Hard Times 888

The Road to Global War 890
A Surge in Global Imperialism 890
The Spanish Civil War, 1936–1939 892
Hitler's Conquest of Central Europe, 1938–1939 894

World War II, 1939–1945 896
The German Onslaught 896
War Expands: The Pacific and Beyond 897
The War against Civilians 897
Societies at War 900
From Resistance to Allied Victory 902
An Uneasy Postwar Settlement 907

Conclusion 908 Chapter 26 Review 910

DOCUMENT: A Family Copes with Unemployment 877
TERMS OF HISTORY: Fascism 879
CONTRASTING VIEWS: Nazism and Hitler: For and Against 882
DOCUMENT: The Greater East Asia Co-Prosperity Sphere 892
NEW SOURCES, NEW PERSPECTIVES: Museums and Memory 901

CHAPTER 27

The Cold War and the Remaking of Europe

1945–1960s 913

World Politics Transformed 914
- Chaos in Europe 915
- New Superpowers: The United States and the Soviet Union 916
- Origins of the Cold War 917
- The Division of Germany 920

Political and Economic Recovery in Europe 922
- Dealing with Nazism 922
- Rebirth of the West 923
- The Welfare State: Common Ground East and West 927
- Recovery in the East 928

Decolonization in a Cold War Climate 930
- The End of Empire in Asia 931
- The Struggle for Identity in the Middle East 932
- New Nations in Africa 933
- Newcomers Arrive in Europe 935

Daily Life and Culture in the Shadow of Nuclear War 936
- Restoring "Western" Values 937
- Cold War Consumerism and Shifting Gender Norms 939
- The Culture of Cold War 942
- The Atomic Brink 943

Conclusion 944 Chapter 27 Review 946

NEW SOURCES, NEW PERSPECTIVES: Government Archives and the Truth about the Cold War 918

DOCUMENT: The Schuman Plan on European Unity (1950) 926

DOCUMENT: Torture in Algeria 935

DOCUMENT: Popular Culture, Youth Consumerism, and the Birth of the Generation Gap 940

CHAPTER 28

Postindustrial Society and the End of the Cold War Order

1960s–1989 949

The Revolution in Technology 950
- The Information Age: Television and Computers 950
- The Space Age 952
- The Nuclear Age 953
- Revolutions in Biology and Reproductive Technology 953

Postindustrial Society and Culture 955
- Multinational Corporations 955
- The New Worker 956
- The Boom in Education and Research 957
- Changing Family Life and the Generation Gap 958
- Art, Ideas, and Religion in a Technocratic Society 959

Protesting Cold War Conditions 961
- Cracks in the Cold War Order 961
- The Growth of Citizen Activism 964
- 1968: Year of Crisis 965

The Testing of Superpower Domination and the End of the Cold War 970
- A Changing Balance of World Power 970
- The Western Bloc Meets Challenges with Reform 972
- Collapse of Communism in the Soviet Bloc 976

Conclusion 980 Chapter 28 Review 982

TAKING MEASURE: Postindustrial Occupational Structure, 1984 957

SEEING HISTORY: Critiquing the Soviet System: Dissident Art in the 1960s and 1970s 963

CONTRASTING VIEWS: Feminist Debates 966

DOCUMENT: Margaret Thatcher's Economic Vision 975

DOCUMENT: A Citizen's Experience of Gorbachev's Reforms 978

CHAPTER 29

A New Globalism

1989 to the Present 985

Collapse of the Soviet Union and Its Aftermath 986
The Breakup of Yugoslavia 987
The Soviet Union Comes Apart 990
Toward a Market Economy 992
International Politics and the New Russia 993

The Nation-State in a Global Age 994
Europe Looks beyond the Nation-State 995
Globalizing Cities and Fragmenting Nations 998
Global Organizations 999

An Interconnected World's New Challenges 999
The Problems of Pollution 999
Population, Health, and Disease 1001
North versus South? 1003
Radical Islam Meets the West 1003
The Promise and Problems of a World Economy 1006

Global Culture and Society in the Twenty-First Century 1008
Redefining the West: The Impact of Global Migration 1008
Global Networks and the Economy 1009
A New Global Culture? 1011

Conclusion 1015 Chapter 29 Review 1017

TERMS OF HISTORY: Globalization 988

DOCUMENT: Václav Havel, "Czechoslovakia Is Returning to Europe" 997

DOCUMENT: The Green Parties Unite Transnationally and Announce Common Goals (2006) 1001

TAKING MEASURE: World Population Growth, 1950–2010 1002

CONTRASTING VIEWS: The Dutch Debate Globalization, Muslim Immigrants, and Turkey's Admission to the EU 1010

EPILOGUE

The Making of the West Continues in the Digital Age

E-1

Social Transformation E-2

Economic Transformations E-2

War, Peace, and Politics E-4

Culture and Intellectual Creativity E-4

The West in the Digital World E-5

Conclusion E-5

Appendix: Useful Facts and Figures A-1

Glossary of Key Terms and People G-1

Index I-1

Map of Europe I-32

Map of the World I-34

Maps and Figures

Maps

Chapter 18

Map 18.1 The Seven Years' War, 1756–1763 606
Spot Map The First Partition of Poland, 1772 607
Spot Map The Pugachev Rebellion, 1773 611
Mapping the West Europe and the World, c. 1780 615

Chapter 19

Spot Map The Low Countries in 1787 622
Spot Map The Great Fear, 1789 626
Map 19.1 Redrawing the Map of France, 1789–1791 629
Spot Map The Vendée Rebellion, 1793 636
Map 19.2 French Expansion, 1791–1799 639
Map 19.3 The Second and Third Partitions of Poland, 1793 and 1795 640
Spot Map St. Domingue on the Eve of the Revolt, 1791 642
Mapping the West Europe in 1799 646

Chapter 20

Map 20.1 Napoleon's Empire at Its Height, 1812 660
Spot Map Consolidation of German and Italian States, 1812 662
Map 20.2 Europe after the Congress of Vienna, 1815 669
Spot Map Nationalistic Movements in the Balkans, 1815–1830 676
Map 20.3 Revolutionary Movements of the 1820s 678
Map 20.4 Latin American Independence, 1804–1830 678
Mapping the West Europe in 1830 680

Chapter 21

Map 21.1 Industrialization in Europe, c. 1850 689
Map 21.2 The Spread of Cholera, 1826–1855 694
Spot Map The Opium War, 1839–1842 702
Map 21.3 Languages of Nineteenth-Century Europe 704
Map 21.4 The Revolutions of 1848 710
Spot Map The Divisions of Italy, 1848 712
Mapping the West Europe in 1850 717

Chapter 22

Map 22.1 The Crimean War, 1853–1856 724
Map 22.2 Unification of Italy, 1859–1870 730
Map 22.3 Unification of Germany, 1862–1871 733
Spot Map The Austro-Hungarian Monarchy, 1867 736
Map 22.4 U.S. Expansion, 1850–1870 737
Spot Map Indian Resistance, 1857 743
Map 22.5 The Paris Commune, 1871 746
Mapping the West Europe and the Mediterranean, 1871 755

Chapter 23

Spot Map The Suez Canal and British Invasion of Egypt, 1882 761
Map 23.1 Africa, c. 1890 763
Spot Map British Colonialism in the Malay Peninsula and Burma, 1826–1890 765
Map 23.2 Expansion of Russia in Asia, 1865–1895 766
Spot Map The Union of Indochina, 1893 766
Map 23.3 Expansion of Berlin to 1914 789
Map 23.4 The Balkans, c. 1878 790
Spot Map Russia: The Pale of Settlement in the Nineteenth Century 791
Mapping the West The West and the World, c. 1890 793

Chapter 24

Spot Map Principal Ethnic Groups in Austria-Hungary, c. 1900 815

Map 24.1 Jewish Migrations in the Late Nineteenth Century 816
Spot Map The Struggle for Ethiopia, 1896 818
Map 24.2 Africa in 1914 819
Map 24.3 Imperialism in Asia, 1894–1914 820
Spot Map Russian Revolution of 1905 821
Map 24.4 The Balkans, 1908–1914 826
Mapping the West Europe at the Outbreak of World War I, August 1914 831

Chapter 25

Map 25.1 The Fronts of World War I, 1914–1918 838
Spot Map The Schlieffen Plan 839
Map 25.2 The Western Front 840
Map 25.3 The Russian Civil War, 1917–1922 849
Map 25.4 Europe and the Middle East after the Peace Settlements of 1919–1920 853
Spot Map The Little Entente 856
Spot Map National Minorities in Postwar Poland 858
Spot Map The Irish Free State and Ulster, 1921 859
Mapping the West Europe and the World in 1929 869

Chapter 26

Map 26.1 The Expansion of Japan, 1931–1941 891
Map 26.2 The Spanish Civil War, 1936–1939 893
Map 26.3 The Growth of Nazi Germany, 1933–1939 895
Spot Map The Division of France, 1940 896
Map 26.4 Concentration Camps and Extermination Sites in Europe 899
Map 26.5 World War II in Europe and Africa 903
Map 26.6 World War II in the Pacific 906
Mapping the West Europe at War's End, 1945 909

Chapter 27

Map 27.1 The Impact of World War II on Europe 916
Spot Map Yugoslavia after the Revolution 920
Map 27.2 Divided Germany and the Berlin Airlift, 1946–1949 921
Map 27.3 European NATO Members and the Warsaw Pact in the 1950s 921
Spot Map The Korean War, 1950–1953 931
Spot Map Indochina, 1954 932
Map 27.4 The Partition of Palestine and the Creation of Israel, 1947–1948 932
Map 27.5 The Decolonization of Africa, 1951–1990 934
Map 27.6 The Cuban Missile Crisis, 1962 944
Mapping the West The Cold War World, c. 1960 945

Chapter 28

Map 28.1 The Airbus Production System 956
Map 28.2 The Vietnam War, 1954–1975 962
Spot Map Prague Spring, 1968 968
Spot Map Israel after the Six-Day War, 1967 971
Spot Map Nationalist Movements of the 1970s 973
Mapping the West The Collapse of Communism in Europe, 1989–1990 981

Chapter 29

Map 29.1 Eastern Europe in the 1990s 987
Map 29.2 The Former Yugoslavia, c. 2000 989
Map 29.3 Countries of the Former Soviet Union, c. 2000 991
Map 29.4 The European Union in 2011 996
Map 29.5 The Middle East in the Twenty-First Century 1004
Spot Map Tigers of the Pacific Rim, c. 1995 1006
Mapping the West World's Top Fifteen Economies as of 2010 1016

Epilogue

The World in the New Millennium E-3

Figures

Figure 25.1 The Rising Cost of Living During World War I 845
Figure 26.1 Weapons Production of the Major Powers, 1939–1945 900
Figure 27.1 Military Spending and the Cold War Arms Race, 1950–1970 925
Figure 27.2 Women in the Workforce, 1950–1960 942
Figure 28.1 Fluctuating Oil Prices, 1955–1985 972

Special Features

Documents

Denis Diderot, "Encyclopedia" (1755) 590
Thomas Jefferson, Declaration of Independence (July 4, 1776) 613
The Rights of Minorities (1789) 627
Address on Abolishing the Slave Trade (February 5, 1790) 641
An Ordinary Soldier on Campaign with Napoleon (1812) 665
Wordsworth's Poetry (1798) 673
Marx and Engels, *The Communist Manifesto* (1848) 708
Alexis de Tocqueville Describes the June Days in Paris (1848) 713
Mrs. Seacole: The *Other* Florence Nightingale 726
Education of a Mathematical Genius in Russia 728
Bismarck Tricks the Public to Get His War 734
An African King Describes His Government 764
Henrik Ibsen, From *A Doll's House* 782
Leon Pinsker Calls for a Jewish State 817
Turkish Nationalism 823
Vietnamese Resistance and the Importance of Becoming Modern 824
Outbreak of the Russian Revolution 847
Memory and Battlefield Tourism 865
A Family Copes with Unemployment 877
The Greater East Asia Co-Prosperity Sphere 892
The Schuman Plan on European Unity (1950) 926
Torture in Algeria 935
Popular Culture, Youth Consumerism, and the Birth of the Generation Gap 940
Margaret Thatcher's Economic Vision 975
A Citizen's Experience of Gorbachev's Reforms 978
Václav Havel, "Czechoslovakia Is Returning to Europe" 997
The Green Parties Unite Transnationally and Announce Common Goals (2006) 1001

Contrasting Views

Women and the Enlightenment 594
Perspectives on the French Revolution 644
Napoleon: For and Against 666
Experiences of Migration 778
The Middle East at the End of World War I: Freedom or Subjugation? 854
Nazism and Hitler: For and Against 882

Feminist Debates 966
The Dutch Debate Globalization, Muslim Immigrants, and Turkey's Admission to the EU 1010

New Sources, New Perspectives

Statistics and the Standard of Living of the Working Class 692
Psychohistory and Its Lessons 804
Museums and Memory 901
Government Archives and the Truth about the Cold War 918

Terms of History

Enlightenment 596
Revolution 621
Nationalism 729
Modern 799
Fascism 879
Globalization 988

Seeing History

The Clothing Revolution: The Social Meaning of Changes in Postrevolutionary Fashion 656
Photographing the Nation: Domesticity and War 738
Portraying Soldiers in World War I 843
Critiquing the Soviet System: Dissident Art in the 1960s and 1970s 963

Taking Measure

European Urbanization, 1750–1800 601
Railroad Lines, 1830–1850 688
European Emigration, 1870–1890 777
The Growth in Armaments, 1890–1914 828
The Victims of Influenza, 1918–1919 850
Postindustrial Occupational Structure, 1984 957
World Population Growth, 1950–2010 1002

To the Student

This guide to *The Making of the West* introduces the tools and features designed to help you study and do well in your Western Civilization course.

In-text tools help you focus on what's important as you read.

CHAPTER 1

Early Western Civilization

4000–1000 B.C.E.

Kings in ancient Egypt believed that after they died the gods would judge them as rulers to decide their fate in the afterlife. In *Instructions for Merikare*, for example, written sometime around 2100–2000 B.C.E., an Egyptian king gives his son Merikare the following advice: "Make secure your place in the cemetery by being upright, by doing justice, upon which people's hearts rely. . . . When a man is buried and mourned, his deeds are piled up next to him as treasure." Being judged pure of heart led to an eternal reward; if the dead king reached the judges "without doing evil," he would be transformed so that he would "abide [in the afterlife] like a god, roaming [free] like the lords of time." A vital part of the justice demanded of an Egyptian king was to keep the country unified under a strong central authority to combat disorder.

Ordinary Egyptians, too, believed that they would win eternal rewards by living justly, which for them meant worshipping the gods and obeying the king and his officials. An illustrated guidebook containing instructions for mummies on how to travel safely in the underworld, com-

The Concept of Western Civilization 4
- Defining Western Civilization
- The Societies of Early Western Civilization

Mesopotamia, Home of the First Civilization, 4000–1000 B.C.E. 7
- The Emergence of Cities, 4000–2350 B.C.E.
- Metals and Empire Making: The Akkadians and the Ur III Dynasty, c. 2350–c. 2000 B.C.E.
- The Achievements of the Assyrians, the Babylonians, and the Canaanites, 2000–1000 B.C.E.

Egypt, the First Unified Country, 3050–1000 B.C.E. 16
- From the Unification of Egypt to the Old Kingdom, 3050–2190 B.C.E.
- The Middle and New Kingdoms in Egypt, 2061–1081 B.C.E.

Read the **chapter outlines** to preview the topics and themes to come.

ancient Italy's many peoples, but Greek literature, art, and philosophy influenced Rome's culture most of all. This cross-cultural contact that so deeply influenced Rome was a kind of competition in innovation between equals, not "inferior" Romans imitating "superior" Greek culture. Like other ancient peoples, Romans often learned from their neighbors, but they adapted foreign traditions to their own purposes and forged their own cultural identity.

The kidnapping legend belongs to Rome's earliest history, when kings ruled (753–509 B.C.E.). Rome's most important history comes afterward, divided into two major periods of about five hundred years each—the republic and the empire. Under the republic (founded 509 B.C.E.), male voters elected their officials and passed laws (although an oligarchy of the social elite controlled politics). Under the empire, monarchs once again ruled. Rome's greatest expansion came during the republic. Romans' belief in a divine destiny fueled this tremendous growth. They believed that the gods wanted them to rule the world by military might and law and improve it through social and moral values. Their faith in a divine destiny is illustrated by the legend of the Sabine women, in which the earliest Romans used a religious festival as a cover for kidnapping. Their conviction that values should drive politics showed in their determination to persuade the Sabine women that loyalty and love would outweigh the crime of kidnapping that turned them into Romans.

Roman values emphasized family loyalty, selfless political and military service to the community, individual honor and public status, the importance

sonal ambition before the good of the state, they destroyed the republic.

CHAPTER FOCUS: How did traditional Roman values affect both the rise and the downfall of the Roman republic?

Read the **Chapter Focus** questions at the start of each chapter to think about the main ideas you should look for as you read.

Roman Social and Religious Traditions

Roman social and religious traditions shaped the history of the Roman republic. Rome's citizens believed that eternal moral values connected them to one another and required them to honor the gods in return for divine support. Hierarchy affected all of life: people at all social levels were obligated to patrons or clients; in families, fathers dominated; in religion, people at all levels of society owed sacrifices, rituals, and prayers to the gods who protected the family and the state.

Roman Moral Values

Roman values defined relationships with other people and with the gods. Romans guided their lives by the *mos maiorum* ("the way of the elders"), or values handed down from their ancestors. The Romans

mos maiorum: Literally, "the way of the elders"; the set of Roman values handed down from the ancestors.

Consult the **running glossary** for definitions of the bolded **Key Terms and People**.

753 B.C.E. Traditional date of Rome's founding as monarc

509 B.C.E. Roman republic established

396 B.C.E. Defeat of Etruscan city of Veii; first great expansion of Roman territory

700 B.C.E. 600 B.C.E. 500 B.C.E. 400 B.C.E.

509–287 B.C.E. Struggle of the orders

451–449 B.C.E. Creation of Twelve Tables, Rome's first written law code

387 B.C.E. Gauls sack Rome

Preview chapter events and keep track of time with **chapter timelines**.

operate, the Greeks opened the way for the rise of a new power—the kingdom of Macedonia—that would end their independence in international politics. The Macedonian kings did not literally enslave the Greeks, as the Spartans did the helots, or usually even change their local governments. They did, however, abolish the city-states' freedom to control their foreign policy.

REVIEW QUESTION: How did daily life, philosophy, and the political situation change in Greece during the period 400–350 B.C.E.?

The Rise of Macedonia, 359–323 B.C.E.

The kingdom of Macedonia's rise to superpower status counts as one of the greatest surprises in an-

Use the **Review Questions** at the end of each major section to check your understanding of key concepts.

Special features introduce the way historians work and sharpen your critical-thinking skills.

Numerous **individual primary-source documents** offer direct experiences of the past and the opportunity to consider sources historians use.

Contrasting Views provides three or four often conflicting eyewitness accounts of a central event, person, or development to foster critical-thinking skills.

New Sources, New Perspectives shows how new evidence leads historians to fresh insights—and sometimes new interpretations.

Seeing History pairs two visuals with background information and probing questions to encourage analysis of images as historical evidence.

Terms of History identifies a term central to history writing and reveals how it is hotly debated.

Taking Measure data reveals how individual facts add up to broad trends and introduces quantitative analysis skills.

DOCUMENT

The Rape and Suicide of Lucretia

This story explaining why the Roman elite expelled the monarchy in 509 B.C.E., thus opening the way to the republic, centers on female virtue and courage, as do other stories about significant political changes in early Roman history. The values attributed to Lucretia obviously reflect men's wishes for women's behavior, but it would be a mistake to assume that women could not

Tarquinius said he loved her, begging and threatening her in turn, trying everything to wear her down. When she wouldn't give in, even in the face of threats of murder, he added another intimidation. "After I've murdered you, I am going to put the naked corpse of a slave next to your body, and everybody will say that you were killed during a disgraceful adultery." This

came to have his fun, to my despair, but it will also be his sorrow—if you are real men." They pledged that they would catch him, and they tried to ease her sadness, saying that the soul did wrong, not the body, and where there were no bad intentions there could be no blame. "It is your responsibility to ensure that he gets what he deserves," she said; "I am blameless, but I will not free myself from punishment. No dishonorable woman shall

CONTRASTING VIEWS

The Nature of Women and Marriage

Greeks believed that women had different natures from men and that both genders were capable of excellence, but in their own ways (Documents 1 and 2). Marriage was supposed to bring these natures together in a partnership of complementary strengths and obligations to each other (Document 3). Marriage contracts (Document 4), similar to modern prenuptial agreements, became common to define the partnership's terms.

praise of your excellence or blaming your faults.

Source: Thucydides, *History of the Peloponnesian War*, Book 2.45. Translation by Thomas R. Martin.

2. Melanippe Explains Why Men's Criticism of Women Is Baseless (late fifth century B.C.E.)

The Athenian playwright Euripides often por-

women make them flourish in every way. In this way women's role in religion is right and proper.

Therefore, should anyone put down women? Won't those men stop their empty fault-finding, the ones who strongly believe that all women should be blamed if a single one is found to be bad? I will make a distinction with the following argument: nothing is worse than a bad woman, but nothing is more surpassingly superior than a worthy one.

NEW SOURCES, NEW PERSPECTIVES

Papyrus Discoveries and Menander's Comedies

Fourth-century B.C.E. Greek playwrights invented a kind of comedy, called New Comedy, that is today's most popular entertainment—the situation comedy (sitcom). They wrote comedies that concentrated on

These comic plays inspired many imitations, especially Roman comedies, which inspired William Shakespeare (1564–1616) in England and Molière (1622–1673) in France. Their comedies, in turn, led to to-

day we can read most of *The Girl from Samos* and parts of other plays. In this way, Menander's characters, stories, and jokes have come back from the dead.

Recovering plays from papyrus is difficult. The handwriting is often difficult to make out, there are no gaps between

SEEING HISTORY

The Shift in Sculptural Style from Egypt to Greece

As Greek civilization revived during the Archaic Age (750–500 B.C.E.), artists took inspiration from the older civilizations of Egypt and the Near East, with sculpture in particular emerging as an important mode of cultural expression. Greek sculptors carved freestanding *kouros* ("young male") statues whose poses recalled the Egyptian style that remained unchanged for two thousand years: an erect posture, a striding leg, and a calm facial expression staring straight ahead. And yet important differences, both religious and stylistic, exist between Egyptian statuary and the Greek sculpture influenced by it.

Kaemheset (shown on the left) hold-

ralism and idealization of the human body that would characterize the later Greek classical style (see the illustration on page 93). What evidence do you see of that in the differences between the two sculptures?

Question to Consider

- **What cultural factors do you think could account for Egyptian statues keeping the same style over time, while the style of Greek statues changed?**

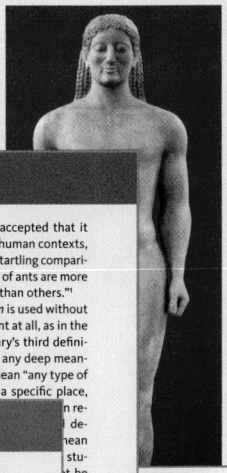

TERMS OF HISTORY

Civilization

Our word *civilization* comes from the ancient Roman word *civilis*, which meant "suitable for a private citizen" and "behaving like an ordinary, down-to-earth person." Historians connect civilization especially with urbanization and the ways of life that characterize city existence. Also, the word *civilization* often expresses the judgment that being civilized means

and intellectual refinement. **6.** cities or populated areas in general, as opposed to unpopulated or wilderness areas. **7.** modern comforts and conveniences, as made possible by science and technology.

All these definitions imply that *civilization* means an "advanced" or "refined" way of life compared to a "savage" or

lization has become so accepted that it can even be used in nonhuman contexts, such as in the following startling comparison: "some communities of ants are more advanced in civilization than others."[1]

Sometimes *civilization* is used without much definitional content at all, as in the Random House dictionary's third definition. Can the word have any deep meaning if it can be used to mean "any type of culture, society, etc. of a specific place,

TAKING MEASURE

European Emigration, 1870–1890

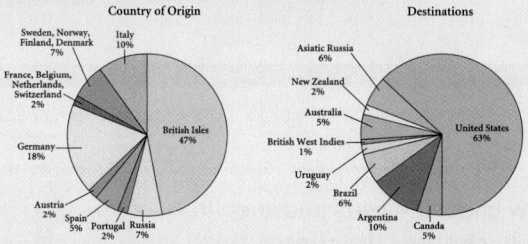

The suffering caused by economic change and by political persecution motivated people from almost every European country to leave their homes for greater secu-

and the United States. Both countries were known for following the rule of law and for providing economic opportunity in urban as well as rural areas.

Question for Consideration

- **Where did the majority of these migrants originate? What historical factors prompted them to leave their**

Art and maps help you to analyze images and think about events in their geographical context.

Full-size maps show major historical developments and carry informative captions.

MAP 24.3 Imperialism in Asia, 1894–1914

The established imperialists came to blows in East Asia as they struggled for influence in China and as they met a formidable new rival—Japan. Simultaneously, liberation groups like the Boxers were taking shape, committed to throwing off restraints imposed by foreign powers and eliminating these interlopers altogether. In 1911, revolutionary Sun Yat-sen overthrew the Qing dynasty, which had left China unprepared to resist foreign takeover, and started the country on a different course.

"Spot" maps offer geographic details right where you need them.

B.C.E., the Romans spent the next hundred years warring with the nearby Etruscan town of Veii. Their 396 B.C.E. victory doubled the Romans' territory. By the fourth century B.C.E., the Roman infantry legion of five thousand men had surpassed the Greek and Macedonian phalanx as an effective fighting force because its soldiers were trained to throw javelins from behind their long shields and then rush in to finish off the enemy with swords. A devastating sack of Rome in 387 B.C.E. by marauding Gauls (Celts) from beyond the Alps proved only a temporary setback, though it made Romans forever fearful of foreign invasion. By around 220 B.C.E., Rome controlled all of Italy south of the Po River, at the northern end of the

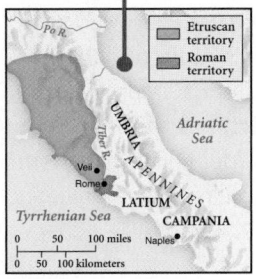

Rome and Central Italy, Fifth Century B.C.E.

Mapping the West summary maps provide a snapshot of the West at the close of each chapter.

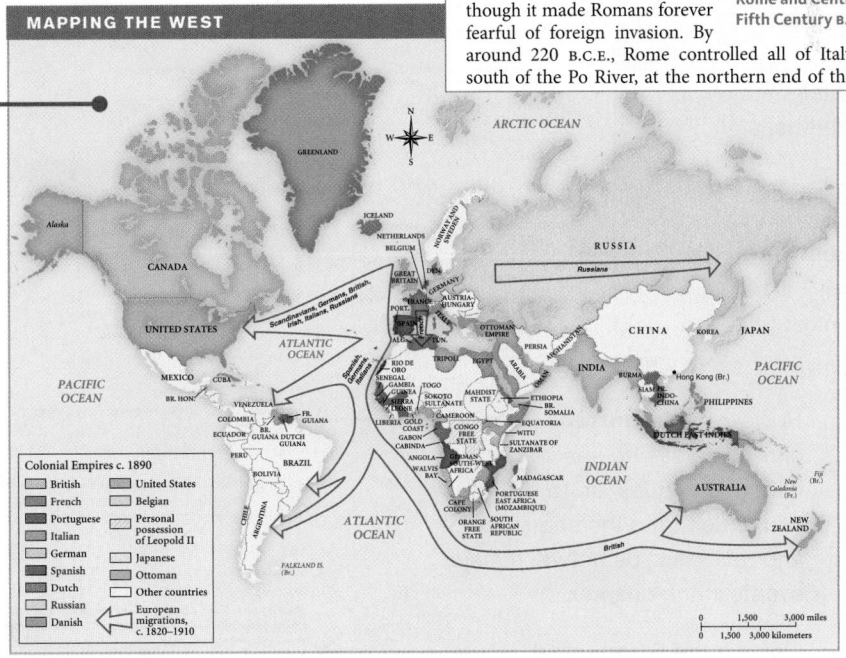

The West and the World, c. 1890

In the late nineteenth century, European trade and political reach spanned the globe. Needing markets for the vast quantities of goods that poured from European factories and access to raw materials to produce the goods, governments asserted that the Western way of life should be spread to the rest of the world and that resources would

End-of-chapter materials enable you to synthesize what you've learned and provide ideas for further research.

Read the **chapter conclusions** to review how the chapters' most important themes and topics fit together and learn how they connect to the next chapter.

Conclusion

The third-century civil wars brought the Roman Empire to a crisis that Diocletian's creation of the nd reorganization of government tem- eved, but Diocletian's reforms only de- vision of the empire. In the late fourth grations of non-Roman peoples fleeing ought intense pressures on the central . Emperor Theodosius I divided the em- stern and eastern halves in 395 to try to administration and defense. When Ro- ities bungled the task of integrating bar- s into Roman society, the newcomers created kingdoms that eventually replaced imperial government in the west. Roman history increasingly divided into two regional streams, even though ian in the sixth century niting the empire and re-

ration of barbarian tribes ransformed not only the society, and economy but , as they developed their le organizing themselves n territory. The economic weakness that accompa- changes destroyed the elite, which had been one erial stability, as wealthy icient country estates and

Consult the **For Further Exploration** boxes at the end of each chapter, which guide you to additional primary-source materials and related Web resources.

FOR FURTHER EXPLORATION

- **For additional primary-source material from this period**, see *Sources of the Making of the West*, Fourth Edition.
- **For Web sites, images, and documents related to topics in this chapter**, visit *Make History* at bedfordstmartins.com/hunt.

Visit the **free online study guide**, which provides quizzes and activities to help you master the chapter material.

Chapter 11 Review

Online Study Guide bedfordstmartins.com/hunt

Test your knowledge of the important concepts and historical figures in the **Key Terms and People** grids by identifying each term and explaining its significance.

Key Terms and People

In the grid below, identify the term or person and explain its historical significance. (To do this exercise online, go to bedfordstmartins.com/hunt.)

Term	Who or What & When	Why It Matters
Romanesque (p. 350)		
Gothic architecture (p. 351)		
Henry II (p. 354)		
common law (p. 357)		
Philip II (Philip Augustus) (p. 358)		
Magna Carta (p. 359)		
Frederick I (Barbarossa) (p. 362)		
troubadours (p. 366)		
chansons de geste (p. 368)		
chivalry (p. 369)		
Franciscans (p. 369)		
Fourth Crusade (p. 372)		

Answer the **Review Questions**, which repeat the chapter's end-of-section comprehension prompts.

Review Questions

1. What was new about education and architecture in the twelfth and early thirteenth centuries?
2. What new sources and institutions of power became available to rulers in the second half of the twelfth century?
3. What do the works of the troubadours and vernacular poets reveal about the nature of entertainment—its themes, its audience, its performers—in the twelfth century?
4. How did the idea of crusade change from the time of the original expedition to the Holy Land?

Answer the analytical **Making Connections** questions, which will help you link ideas within or across chapters.

Making Connections

1. What were the chief differences that se period 1150–1215 from those of the peri
2. How was the gift economy associated economy with the Gothic style?
3. How do political developments—the gr ment of strong monarchies, the growth and popularity of vernacular literature centuries?

Review the **Important Events** chronologies and answer the chronology question to make sure you understand the sequence of and relationships between major events in the chapter.

Important Events

Date	Event	Date	Event
1139–1153	Civil War in England	1202–1204	The Fourth Crusade
1152–1190	Reign of Frederick Barbarossa	1204	Fall of Constantinople to crusaders
1154–1189	Reign of King Henry II	1204	Philip takes Normandy, Anjou, Maine, Touraine, and Poitou from John
1176	Battle of Legnano	1209–1229	Albigensian Crusade
1180–1223	Reign of Philip II Augustus	1212	Battle of Las Navas de Tolosa; triumph of the *reconquista*
1182–1226	Francis of Assisi	1214	Battle of Bouvines
1189–1192	The Third Crusade	1215	Magna Carta

- Consider three events: **The Third Crusade (1189–1192)**, **The Fourth Crusade (1202–1204)**, and **the Albigensian Crusade (1209–1229)**. What were their various causes and results? How were they differently waged and led?

Consult the **Suggested References** to find additional Web and print sources for further research.

SUGGESTED REFERENCES

For the new schools, Abelard is a key primary source, while Clanchy provides perceptive background. Cultural and artistic developments are discussed in both Burl and Coldstream. Bartlett and Bradbury are essential for politics.

*Abelard's *The Story of My Misfortunes*: http://www.fordham.edu/halsall/source/abelard-sel.html

Aurell, Martin. *The Plantagenet Empire, 1154–1224*. Trans. David Crouch. 2007.

Bartlett, Robert. *England under the Norman and Angevin Kings, 1075–1225*. 2000.

Bouchard, Constance Brittain. *"Every Valley Shall Be Exalted": The Discourse of Opposites in Twelfth-Century Thought*. 2003.

Bradbury, Jim. *Philip Augustus: King of France*. 1998.

Burl, Aubrey. *Courts of Love, Castles of Hate: Troubadours and Trobairitz in Southern France, 1071–1321*. 2008.

Cheyette, Fredric L. *Ermengard of Narbonne and the World of the*

Coldstream, Nicola. *Medieval Architecture*. 2002.

**Crusade of Frederick Barbarossa: The History of the Expedition of the Emperor Frederick and Related Texts*. Trans. G. A. Loud. 2010.

Gaunt, Simon, and Sarah Kay. *The Troubadours: An Introduction*. 1999.

*Goldin, Frederick. *Lyrics of the Troubadors and Trouvères: Original Texts, with Translations*. 1973.

Gothic architecture: http://www.bc.edu/bc_org/avp/cas/fnart/arch/gothic_arch.html

Hudson, John. *The Formation of the English Common Law: Law and Society in England from the Norman Conquest to Magna Carta*. 1996.

Moore, R. I. *The Formation of a Persecuting Society: Power and Deviance in Western Europe, 950–1250*. 2nd ed. 2007.

Pegg, Mark Gregory. *A Most Holy War: The Albigensian Crusade and the Battle for Christendom*. 2008.

Robson, Michael. *The Franciscans in the Middle Ages*. 2006.

Stephensen, David. *Heavenly Vaults: From Romanesque to Gothic in Euro-*

Primary documents help you to understand history through the voices of those who lived it.

In each chapter of this textbook you will find many primary sources to broaden your understanding of the development of the West. Primary sources refer to firsthand, contemporary accounts or direct evidence about a particular topic. For example, speeches, letters, diaries, song lyrics, and newspaper articles are all primary sources that historians use to construct accounts of the past. Nonwritten materials such as maps, paintings, artifacts, and even architecture and music can also be primary sources. Both types of historical documents in this textbook — written and visual — provide a glimpse into the lives of the men and women who influenced or were influenced by the course of Western history.

To guide your interpretation of any source, you should begin by asking several basic questions, listed below, as starting points for observing, analyzing, and interpreting the past. Your answers should prompt further questions of your own.

1. **Who is the author?** Who wrote or created the material? What was his or her authority? (Personal? institutional?) Did the author have specialized knowledge or experience? If you are reading a written document, how would you describe the author's tone of voice? (Formal, personal, angry?)

2. **Who is the audience?** Who were the intended readers, listeners, or viewers? How does the intended audience affect the ways that the author presents ideas?

3. **What are the main ideas?** What are the main points that the author is trying to convey? Can you detect any underlying assumptions of values or attitudes? How does the form or medium affect the meaning of this document?

4. **In what context was the document created?** From when and where does the document originate? What was the interval between the initial problem or event and this document, which responded to it? Through what form or medium was the document communicated? (For example, a newspaper, a government record, an illustration.) What contemporary events or conditions might have affected the creation of the document?

5. **What's missing?** What's missing or cannot be learned from this source, and what might this omission reveal? Are there other sources that might fill in the gaps?

Now consider these questions as you read "Columbus Describes His First Voyage (1493)," the document on the next page. Compare your answers to the sample observations provided.

DOCUMENT

Columbus Describes His First Voyage (1493)

In this famous letter to Raphael Sanchez, treasurer to his patrons, Ferdinand and Isabella, Columbus recounts his initial journey to the Bahamas, Cuba, and Hispaniola (today Haiti and the Dominican Republic), and tells of his achievements. This passage reflects the first contact between native Americans and Europeans; already the themes of trade, subjugation, gold, and conversion emerge in Columbus's own words.

Indians would give whatever the seller required; . . . Thus they bartered, like idiots, cotton and gold for fragments of bows, glasses, bottles, and jars; which I forbad as being unjust, and myself gave them many beautiful and acceptable articles which I had brought with me, taking nothing from them in return; I did this in order that I might the more easily conciliate them, that they might be led to become Christians, and be inclined to entertain a regard for the King and Queen, our Princes and all Spaniards, and that I might induce them to take an interest in seeking out, and collecting, and delivering to us such things as they possessed in abundance, but which we greatly needed. They practise no kind of idolatry, but have a firm belief that all strength and power, and indeed all good things, are in heaven, and that I had descended from thence with these ships and sailors, and under this impression was I received after they had thrown aside their fears. Nor are they slow or stupid, but of very clear understanding; and those men who have crossed to the neighbouring islands give an admirable description of everything they observed; but they never saw any people clothed, nor any ships like ours. On my arrival at that sea, I had taken some Indians by force from the first island that I came to, in order that they might learn our language, and communicate to us what they know respecting the country; which plan succeeded excellently, and was a great advantage to us, for in a short time, either by gestures and signs, or by words, we were enabled to understand each other. These men are still travelling with me, and although they have been with us now a long time, they continue to entertain the idea that I have descended from heaven.

Source: Christopher Columbus, *Four Voyages to the New World*, trans. R. H. Major (New York: Corinth Books, 1961), 8–9.

Question to Consider

- **In what ways were Columbus's early impressions of native Americans both respectful and condescending?**

1. **Who is the author?** The title and headnote that precede each document contain information about the authorship and date of its creation. In this case, the Italian explorer Christopher Columbus is the author. His letter describes events in which he was both an eyewitness and a participant.
2. **Who is the audience?** Columbus sent the letter to Raphael Sanchez, treasurer to Ferdinand and Isabella — someone who Columbus knew would be keenly interested in the fate of his patrons' investment. Because the letter was also a public document written to a crown official, Columbus would have expected a wider audience beyond Sanchez. How might his letter have differed had it been written to a friend?
3. **What are the main ideas?** In this segment, Columbus describes his encounter with the native people. He speaks of his desire to establish good relations by treating them fairly, and he offers his impressions of their intelligence and naiveté — characteristics he implies will prove useful to Europeans. He also expresses an interest in converting them to Christianity and making them loyal subjects of the crown.
4. **In what context was the document created?** Columbus wrote the letter in 1493, within six months of his first voyage. He would have been eager to announce the success of his endeavor.
5. **What's missing?** Columbus's letter provides just one view of the encounter. We do not have a corresponding account from the native Americans' perspective nor from anyone else traveling with Columbus. With no corroborating evidence, how reliable is this description?

Note: You can use these same questions to analyze visual images. Start by determining who created the image — whether it's a painting, photograph, sculpture, map, or artifact — and when it was made. Then consider the audience for whom the artist might have intended the work and how viewers might have reacted. Consult the text for information about the time period, and look for visual cues such as color, artistic style, and use of space to determine the central idea of the work. As you read, consult the captions in this book to help you evaluate the images and to ask more questions of your own.

CHAPTER

The Promise of Enlightenment

18

1750–1789

The Enlightenment at Its Height 588
- Men and Women of the Republic of Letters
- Conflicts with Church and State
- The Individual and Society
- Spreading the Enlightenment
- The Limits of Reason: Roots of Romanticism and Religious Revival

Society and Culture in an Age of Enlightenment 599
- The Nobility's Reassertion of Privilege
- The Middle Class and the Making of a New Elite
- Life on the Margins

State Power in an Era of Reform 605
- War and Diplomacy
- State-Sponsored Reform
- Limits of Reform

Rebellions against State Power 610
- Food Riots and Peasant Uprisings
- Public Opinion and Political Opposition
- Revolution in North America

In the summer of 1766, Empress Catherine II ("the Great") of Russia wrote to Voltaire, one of the leaders of the Enlightenment:

> It is a way of immortalizing oneself to be the advocate of humanity, the defender of oppressed innocence. . . . You have entered into combat against the enemies of mankind: superstition, fanaticism, ignorance, quibbling, evil judges, and the powers that rest in their hands. Great virtues and qualities are needed to surmount these obstacles. You have shown that you have them: you have triumphed.

Over a fifteen-year period, Catherine corresponded regularly with Voltaire, a writer who, at home in France, found himself in constant conflict with authorities of church and state. Her admiring letter shows how influential Enlightenment ideals had become by the middle of the eighteenth century. Even an absolutist ruler such as Catherine endorsed many aspects of the Enlightenment call for reform; she, too, wanted to be an "advocate of humanity."

Catherine's letter aptly summed up Enlightenment ideals: progress for humanity could be achieved only by rooting out the wrongs left by superstition, religious fanaticism, ignorance, and outmoded forms of justice. Enlightenment writers used every means at their disposal—from encyclopedias to novels to personal interaction with rulers—to argue for reform. Everything had to be examined in the cold light of reason, and anything that did not promote the improvement of humanity was to be jettisoned. As a result, Enlightenment writers supported religious toleration, attacked the legal use of torture to extract confessions, and criticized censorship by state or church. The book trade and new places for urban socializing, such as coffeehouses and learned societies, spread these ideas within a new elite of middle- and upper-class men and women.

The lower classes had little contact with Enlightenment ideas. Their lives

Catherine the Great
In this portrait (c. 1762) by the Danish painter Vigilius Eriksen, the Russian empress Catherine the Great is shown on horseback, much like any male ruler of the time. Born Sophia Augusta Frederika of Anhalt-Zerbst in 1729, Catherine was the daughter of a minor German prince. When she married the future tsar Peter III in 1745, she promptly learned Russian and adopted Russian Orthodoxy. Peter, physically and mentally frail, proved no match for her; in 1762 she staged a coup against him and took his place when he was killed. *(Erich Lessing/Art Resource, NY.)*

were shaped more profoundly by an increasing population, rising food prices, and ongoing wars among the great powers. States had to balance conflicting social pressures: rulers pursued Enlightenment reforms that they believed might enhance state power, but they feared changes that might unleash popular discontent. For example, Catherine aimed to bring Western ideas, culture, and reforms to Russia, but when faced with a massive uprising of the serfs, she not only suppressed the revolt but also increased the powers of the nobles over their serfs. All reform-minded rulers faced similar potential challenges to their authority.

Even if the movement for reform had its limits, governments needed to respond to a new force: "public opinion." Rulers wanted to portray themselves as modern, open to change, and responsive to those who were reading newspapers and closely following political developments. Enlightenment writers appealed to public opinion, but they still looked to rulers to effect reform. Writers such as Voltaire expressed little interest in the future of peasants or the lower classes; they favored neither revolution nor political upheaval. Yet their ideas paved the way for something much more radical and unexpected. The American Declaration of Independence in 1776 showed how Enlightenment ideals could be translated into democratic political practice. After 1789, democracy would come to Europe as well.

CHAPTER FOCUS How did the Enlightenment influence Western politics, culture, and society?

The Enlightenment at Its Height

The Enlightenment emerged as an intellectual movement before 1750 but reached its peak in the second half of the eighteenth century. (See "Terms of History," page 596.) The writers of the Enlightenment called themselves **philosophes**; the word is French for "philosophers," but that definition is somewhat misleading. Whereas philosophers concern themselves with abstract theories, the philosophes were public intellectuals dedicated to solving the real problems of the world. They wrote on subjects ranging from current affairs to art criticism, and they wrote in every conceivable format. The Swiss philosophe Jean-Jacques Rousseau, for example, wrote political tracts, a treatise on education, a constitution for Poland, an analysis of the effects of the theater on public morals, a best-selling novel, an opera, and a notorious autobiography. The philosophes wrote for a broad educated public of readers who snatched up every Enlightenment book they could find at their local booksellers, even when rulers or churches tried to forbid such works. Between 1750 and 1789, the Enlightenment acquired its name and, despite heated conflicts between the philosophes and state and religious authorities, gained support in the highest reaches of government.

Men and Women of the Republic of Letters

Although *philosophe* is a French word, the Enlightenment was distinctly cosmopolitan; philosophes could be found from Philadelphia to St. Petersburg. The philosophes considered themselves part of a grand "republic of letters" that transcended national political boundaries. They were not republicans in the usual sense, that is, people who supported representative government and opposed monarchy. What united them were the ideals of reason, reform, and freedom. In 1784, the German philosopher

philosophes (fee luh SAWF): French for "philosophers"; public intellectuals of the Enlightenment who wrote on subjects ranging from current affairs to art criticism with the goal of furthering reform in society.

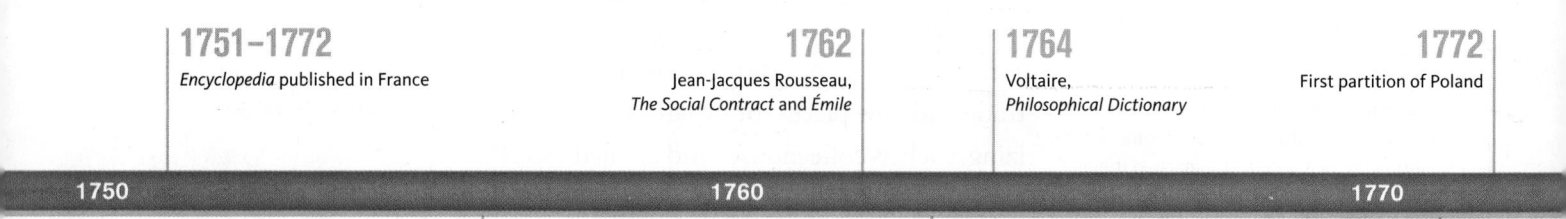

Immanuel Kant summed up the program of the Enlightenment in two Latin words: *sapere aude* ("dare to know") — have the courage to think for yourself.

The philosophes used reason to attack superstition, bigotry, and religious fanaticism, which they considered the chief obstacles to free thought and social reform. Voltaire took religious fanaticism as his chief target: "Once fanaticism has corrupted a mind, the malady is almost incurable. . . . The only remedy for this epidemic malady is the philosophical spirit." Enlightenment writers did not necessarily oppose organized religion, but they strenuously objected to religious intolerance. They believed that the systematic application of reason could do what religious belief could not: improve the human condition by pointing to needed reforms. Reason meant critical, informed, scientific thinking about social issues and problems. Many Enlightenment writers collaborated on the multivolume *Encyclopedia* (published 1751–1772), which aimed to gather together knowledge about science, religion, industry, and society. The ancestor of all modern encyclopedias from the *Encyclopædia Britannica* to Wikipedia online, the Enlightenment version differed by using knowledge to criticize defects in society. The chief editor of the *Encyclopedia*, Denis Diderot (1713–1784), explained the goal: "All things must be examined, debated, investigated without exception and without regard for anyone's feelings." (See Document, "Denis Diderot, 'Encyclopedia,'" page 590.)

The philosophes believed that the spread of knowledge would encourage reform in every aspect of life, from the grain trade to the penal system. Chief among their desired reforms was intellectual freedom — the freedom to use one's own reason to conduct studies and to publish the results. The philosophes wanted freedom of the press and freedom of religion, which they considered "natural rights" guaranteed by "natural law." In their view, progress depended on these freedoms.

Most philosophes, like Voltaire, came from the upper classes, yet Rousseau's father was a modest watchmaker in Geneva, and Diderot was the son of a cutlery maker. Rarely were women philosophes; one, however, was the French noblewoman Émilie du Châtelet (1706–1749), who wrote extensively

Science in Action

In September 1783 the Montgolfier brothers demonstrated their newly invented hot air balloon at Versailles with the royal family in attendance. The flight reached an altitude of 1500 feet, covered two miles, and lasted eight minutes. The passengers — a sheep, a duck, and a rooster — landed safely. Hydrogen balloons were developed at the same time and quickly replaced the hot air versions because they could fly higher and longer. Thousands of people flocked to see the launches. *(Private Collection / The Bridgeman Art Library International.)*

1775 Flour War in France

1776 American Declaration of Independence from Great Britain; Adam Smith, *The Wealth of Nations*

1784 Pierre-Augustin Caron de Beaumarchais, *The Marriage of Figaro*

1787 Delegates from the states draft the U.S. Constitution

1780 1790

1773 Pugachev rebellion of Russian peasants

1780 Joseph II of Austria undertakes a wide-reaching reform program

1781 Immanuel Kant, *The Critique of Pure Reason*

1785 Catherine the Great's Charter of the Nobility grants nobles exclusive control over their serfs in exchange for subservience to the state

DOCUMENT

Denis Diderot, "Encyclopedia" (1755)

Denis Diderot (1713–1784) led the multinational team that produced the Encyclopedia, *a work much more radical in its aims than its bland name suggests. Seventeen volumes of text and eleven volumes of illustrative plates were published between 1751 and 1772, despite the efforts of French authorities to censor the work. The volumes covered every branch of human knowledge from the tools of artisans to the finest points of theology. Diderot and his collaborators used the occasion to lay out the principles of the Enlightenment as an intellectual movement and to challenge the authority, in particular, of the Catholic church. The article "Encyclopedia" summarized the goals of the project.*

ENCYCLOPEDIA (Philosophy). This word means the *interrelation of all knowledge*; it is made up of the Greek prefix *en*, in, and the nouns *kyklos*, circle, and *paideia*, instruction, science, knowledge. In truth, the aim of an *encyclopedia* is to collect all the knowledge scattered over the face of the earth, to present its general outlines and structure to the men with whom we live, and transmit this to those who will come after us, so that the work of the past centuries may be useful to the following centuries, that our children, by becoming more educated, may at the same time become more virtuous and happier, and that we may not die without having deserved well of the human race. . . .

We have seen that our *Encyclopedia* could only have been the endeavor of a philosophical century; that this age has dawned, and that fame, while raising to immortality the names of those who will perfect man's knowledge in the future, will perhaps not disdain to remember our own names. . . .

I have said that it could only belong to a philosophical age to attempt an *encyclopedia*; and I have said this because such a work constantly demands more intellectual daring than is commonly found in ages of pusillanimous [timid] taste. All things must be examined, debated, investigated without exception and without regard for anyone's feelings. . . . We must ride roughshod over all these ancient puerilities [childish sillinesses], overturn the barriers that reason never erected, give back to the arts and sciences the liberty that is so precious to them. . . . We have for quite some time needed a reasoning age when men would no longer seek the rules in classical authors but in nature.

Source: Margaret C. Jacob, *The Enlightenment: A Brief History with Documents* (Boston: Bedford/St. Martin's, 2001), 157–58.

Question for Consideration

- **Why would the Catholic church and the French state find Diderot's vision for the *Encyclopedia* so threatening?**

about the mathematics and physics of Gottfried Wilhelm Leibniz and Isaac Newton. (Châtelet's lover Voltaire learned much of his science from her.) Few of the leading writers held university positions, except those who were German or Scottish. Universities in France were dominated by the Catholic clergy and unreceptive to Enlightenment ideals.

Enlightenment ideas developed instead through printed books and pamphlets; through hand-copied letters that were circulated and sometimes published; and through informal readings of manuscripts. Salons — informal gatherings, usually sponsored by middle-class or aristocratic women — gave intellectual life an anchor outside the royal court and the church-controlled universities. Seventeenth-century salons had been tame affairs. In the Parisian salons of the eighteenth century, in contrast, the philosophes could discuss ideas they might hesitate to put into print, testing public opinion and even pushing it in new directions. Best known was the Parisian salon of Madame Marie-Thérèse Geoffrin (1699–1777), a wealthy middle-class widow who had been raised by her grandmother and married off at fourteen to a much older man. (See the illustration on page 591.) She brought together the most exciting thinkers and artists of the time and provided a forum for new ideas and an opportunity to establish new intellectual contacts. Madame Geoffrin corresponded extensively with influential people across Europe, including Catherine the Great. One Italian visitor commented, "There is no way to make Naples resemble Paris unless we find a woman to guide us, organize us, *Geoffrinize* us."

Women's salons provoked criticism from men who resented their power. (See "Contrasting Views," page 594.) Nevertheless, the gatherings helped galvanize intellectual life and reform movements all over Europe. Wealthy Jewish women created nine of the fourteen salons in Berlin at the end of the eighteenth century, and Princess Zofia Czartoryska gathered around her in Warsaw the reform leaders of Poland-Lithuania. Some of the aristocratic women in Madrid who held salons had lived in France, and they combined an interest in French culture and ideas with their efforts to promote the new ideas in Spain. Salons could be tied

Madame Geoffrin's Salon in 1755
This 1812 painting by Anicet Charles Lemonnier claims to depict the best-known Parisian salon of the 1750s. Lemonnier was only twelve years old in 1755 and so could not have based his rendition on firsthand knowledge. Madame Geoffrin is the figure in blue on the right facing the viewer. The bust is of Voltaire. Rousseau is the fifth person to the left of the bust (facing right), and behind him (facing left) is Guillaume Raynal. *(Réunion des Musées Nationaux/Art Resource, NY.)*

closely to the circles of power: in France, for example, Louis XV's mistress, Jeanne-Antoinette Poisson, first made her reputation as hostess of a salon frequented by Voltaire and Montesquieu. When she became Louis XV's mistress in 1745, she gained the title marquise de Pompadour and turned her attention to influencing artistic styles by patronizing architects and painters.

Conflicts with Church and State

Madame Geoffrin did not approve of discussions that attacked the Catholic church, but elsewhere voices against organized religion could be heard. Criticisms of religion required daring because the church, whatever its denomination, wielded enormous power in society, and most influential people considered religion an essential foundation of good society and government. Defying such opinion, the Scottish philosopher David Hume (1711–1776) boldly argued in *The Natural History of Religion* (1755) that belief in God rested on superstition and fear rather than on reason. At a dinner party in Paris, Hume questioned whether there were really any atheists. His host responded that of the eighteen guests present, "fifteen were atheists, and three had not quite made up their minds."

Hume was right to be dubious because at the time most Europeans believed in God. After Newton, however, and despite Newton's own deep religiosity, people could conceive of the universe as an eternally existing, self-perpetuating machine, in which God's intervention was unnecessary. In short, such people could become either atheists (people who do not believe in God) or **deists** (people who believe in God but give him no active role in earthly affairs). For the first time, writers claimed the label *atheist* and disputed the common view that atheism led inevitably to immorality.

Deists continued to believe in a benevolent, all-knowing God who had designed the universe and set it in motion. But they usually rejected the idea that God directly intercedes in the functioning of the universe, and they often criticized the churches for their dogmatic intolerance of dissenters. Voltaire was a deist, and in his influential *Philosophical Dictionary* (1764) he attacked most of the claims of organized Christianity, both Catholic and Protestant. Christianity, he argued, had been the prime source of fanaticism and brutality among humans. Throughout his life, Voltaire's motto was *Écrasez l'infâme*—"Crush the infamous thing" (the "thing" being bigotry and intolerance). French authorities publicly burned his *Philosophical Dictionary.*

Criticism of religious intolerance involved more than simply attacking the churches. Critics also had to confront the states to which churches were closely tied. In 1762, a judicial case in Toulouse provoked an outcry throughout France that Voltaire soon joined. When the son of a local Calvinist was found hanged (he had probably committed suicide), magistrates accused the father, Jean Calas, of murdering him

deists: Those who believe in God but give him no active role in human affairs. Deists of the Enlightenment believed that God had designed the universe and set it in motion but no longer intervened in its functioning.

to prevent his conversion to Catholicism. (Since Louis XIV's revocation of the Edict of Nantes in 1685, it had been illegal to practice Calvinism publicly in France.) The all-Catholic parlement of Toulouse tried to extract the names of accomplices through torture—using a rope to pull up Calas's arm while weighing down his feet and then pouring water down his throat—but Calas refused to confess. The torturers then executed him by breaking every bone in his body with an iron rod. Voltaire launched a successful crusade to rehabilitate Calas's good name and to restore the family's properties, which had been confiscated after his death. Voltaire's efforts eventually helped bring about the extension of civil rights to French Protestants and encouraged campaigns to abolish the judicial use of torture.

Critics also assailed state and church support for European colonization and slavery. One of the most popular books of the time was the *Philosophical and Political History of European Colonies and Commerce in the Two Indies*, published in 1770 by the abbé Guillaume Raynal (1713–1796), a French Catholic clergyman. Raynal and his collaborators described in excruciating detail the destruction of native populations by Europeans and denounced the slave trade. Despite the criticism, the slave trade continued. So did European exploration. British explorer James Cook (1728–1779) charted the coasts of New Zealand and Australia, discovered New Caledonia, and visited the ice fields of Antarctica.

Cook's adventures captivated European readers. When he arrived on the Kona coast of Hawaii in 1779, Cook thought that the natives considered him godlike, but in a confrontation he fired his gun and killed a man, provoking an attack in which he and some of his men were killed. Like Cook, many Enlightenment writers held conflicting views of natives: to some, they were innocent because primitive, but to others they seemed untrustworthy because savage. Views of Africans could be especially negative. Hume, for example, judged blacks to be "naturally inferior to the whites," concluding, "There never was a civilized nation of any other complexion than white."

Nevertheless, the Enlightenment belief in natural rights helped fuel the antislavery movement, which began to organize political campaigns against slavery in Britain, France, and the new United States in the 1780s. Advocates of the abolition of slavery encouraged freed slaves to write the story of their enslavement. One such freed slave, Olaudah Equiano, wrote of his kidnapping and enslavement in Africa and his long effort to free himself. *The Interesting Narrative of the Life of Olaudah Equiano*, published in 1788, became an international best seller. Armed with such firsthand accounts of slavery, **abolitionists** began to petition their governments for the abolition of the slave trade and then of slavery itself.

Enlightenment critics of church and state usually advocated reform, not revolution. For example, though he resided near the French-Swiss border in case he had to flee, Voltaire made a fortune in financial speculations and ended up being celebrated in his last years as a national hero even by many former foes. Other philosophes also believed that published criticism, rather than violent action, would bring about necessary reforms. As Diderot said, "We will speak against senseless laws until they are reformed; and, while we wait, we will abide by them." The philosophes generally regarded the lower classes—"the people"—as ignorant, violent, and prone to superstition; as a result, they pinned their hopes on educated elites and enlightened rulers.

The Individual and Society

The controversy created by the conflicts between the philosophes and the various churches and states of Europe drew attention away from a subtle but profound transformation in worldviews. In previous centuries, questions of theological doctrine and church organization had been the main focus of intellectual and even political interest. The Enlightenment writers shifted attention away from religious questions and toward the secular (nonreligious) study of society and the individual's role in it. Religion did not drop out of sight, but the philosophes tended to make religion a private affair of individual conscience, even while rulers and churches still considered religion very much a public concern.

The Enlightenment interest in secular society produced two major results: it advanced the secularization of European political life that had begun after the French Wars of Religion of the sixteenth and seventeenth centuries, and it laid the foundations for the social sciences of the modern era. Not surprisingly, then, many historians and philosophers consider the Enlightenment to be the origin of modernity, which they define as the belief that human reason, rather than theological doctrine, should set the patterns of social and political life. This belief in reason as the sole foundation for secular authority has often been contested, but it has also proved to be a powerful force for change.

Although most of the philosophes believed that human reason could understand and even remake

abolitionists: Advocates of the abolition of the slave trade and of slavery.

society and politics, they disagreed about what reason revealed. Among the many different approaches were two that proved enduringly influential, those of the Scottish philosopher Adam Smith and the Swiss writer Jean-Jacques Rousseau. Smith provided a theory of modern capitalist society and devoted much of his energy to defending free markets as the best way to make the most of individual efforts. The modern discipline of economics took shape around the questions raised by Smith. Rousseau, by contrast, emphasized the needs of the community over those of the individual. His work, which led both toward democracy and toward communism, continues to inspire heated debate in political science and sociology.

Adam Smith | Adam Smith (1723–1790) optimistically believed that individual interests naturally harmonized with those of the whole society. To explain how this natural harmonization worked, he published *An Inquiry into the Nature and Causes of the Wealth of Nations* in 1776. Smith insisted that individual self-interest, even greed, was quite compatible with society's best interest: the laws of supply and demand served as an "invisible hand" ensuring that individual interests would be synchronized with those of the whole society. Market forces—"the propensity to truck, barter, and exchange one thing for another"—naturally brought individual and social interests in line.

Smith rejected the prevailing mercantilist views that the general welfare would be served by accumulating national wealth through agriculture or the hoarding of gold and silver. Instead, he argued that the division of labor in manufacturing increased productivity and generated more wealth for society and well-being for the individual. Using the example of the ordinary pin, Smith showed that when the manufacturing process was broken down into separate operations—one man to draw out the wire, another to straighten it, a third to cut it, a fourth to point it, and so on—workers who could make only one pin a day on their own could make thousands by pooling their labor.

To maximize the effects of market forces and the division of labor, Smith endorsed a concept called **laissez-faire** (that is, to leave alone) to free the economy from government intervention and control. He insisted that governments eliminate all restrictions on the sale of land, remove restraints on the grain trade, and abandon duties on imports. Free international trade, he argued, would stimulate production everywhere and thus ensure the growth of national wealth: "The natural effort of every individual to better his own condition, when suffered to exert itself with freedom and security, is so powerful a principle that it is alone, and without any assistance, not only capable of carrying the society to wealth and prosperity, but of surmounting a hundred impertinent obstructions with which the folly of human laws too often encumbers its operations." Governments, he continued, should restrict themselves to providing "security," that is, national defense, internal order, and public works. Smith recognized that government had an important role in providing a secure framework for market activity, but he placed most emphasis on freeing individual endeavor from what he saw as excessive government interference.

Jean-Jacques Rousseau
This eighteenth-century engraving of Rousseau shows him in his favorite place, outside in nature, where he walks, reads, and in this case collects plants. Rousseau claimed that he came to his most important insights while taking long walks, and in *Émile* he underlines the importance of physical activity for children. *(Private Collection/Roger Viollet, Paris, France/The Bridgeman Art Library International.)*

laissez-faire (LEH say FEHR): French for "leave alone"; an economic doctrine developed by Adam Smith that advocated freeing the economy from government intervention and control.

CONTRASTING VIEWS

Women and the Enlightenment

During the Enlightenment, women's roles in society became the subject of heated debates. Some men resented what they saw as the growing power of women, especially in the salons. Rousseau railed against their corrupting influence: "Every woman at Paris gathers in her apartment a harem of men more womanish than she." Rousseau's Émile *(Document 1) offered his own influential answer to the question of how women should be educated. The* Encyclopedia *ignored the contributions of salon women and praised women who stayed at home; in the words of one typical contributor, women "constitute the principal ornament of the world. . . . May they, through submissive discretion and through simple, adroit, artless cleverness, spur us [men] on to virtue." Many women objected to these characterizations. The editor of a prominent newspaper for women, Madame de Beaumer, wrote editorials blasting the masculine sense of superiority (Document 2). Many prominent women writers specifically targeted Rousseau's book because it proved to be the most influential educational treatise of the time (Document 3). Their ideas formed the core of nineteenth-century feminism.*

1. Jean-Jacques Rousseau, *Émile* (1762)

Rousseau used the character of Émile's wife-to-be, Sophie, to discuss his ideas about women's education. Sophie is educated for a domestic role as wife and mother, and she is taught to be obedient, always helpful to her husband and family, and removed from any participation in the public world. Despite his insistence on the differences between men's and women's roles, many women enthusiastically embraced Rousseau's ideas, for he placed great emphasis on maternal affections, breast-feeding, and child rearing. Rousseau's own children, however, suffered the contradictions that characterized his life. By his own admission, he abandoned to a foundling hospital all the children he had by his lower-class common-law wife because he did not think he could support them properly; if their fate was like that of most abandoned children of the day, they met an early death.

There is no parity between man and woman as to the importance of sex. The male is only a male at certain moments; the female all her life, or at least throughout her youth, is incessantly reminded of her sex and in order to carry out its functions she needs a corresponding constitution. She needs to be careful during pregnancy; she needs rest after childbirth; she needs a quiet and sedentary life while she nurses her children; she needs patience and gentleness in order to raise them; a zeal and affection that nothing can discourage. . . .

On the good constitution of mothers depends primarily that of the children; on the care of women depends the early education of men; and on women, again, depend their morals, their passions, their tastes, their pleasures, and even their happiness. Thus the whole education of women ought to be relative to men. To please them, to be useful to them, to make themselves loved and honored by them, to educate them when young, to care for them when grown, to counsel them, to console them, and to make life agreeable and sweet to them—these are the duties of women at all times, and should be taught them from their infancy.

Source: Susan Groag Bell and Karen M. Offen, *Women, the Family, and Freedom: The Debate in Documents*, vol. 1, *1750–1880* (Stanford: Stanford University Press, 1983), 46–49.

2. Madame de Beaumer, Editorial in *Le Journal des Dames* (1762)

Madame de Beaumer (d. 1766) was the first of three women editors of Le Journal des Dames *(The Ladies' Journal). She ran it for two years and published many editorials defending women against their male critics.*

The success of the *Journal des Dames* allows us to triumph over those frivolous persons who have regarded this periodical as a petty work containing only a few

Jean-Jacques Rousseau

Much more pessimistic about the relation between individual self-interest and the good of society was **Jean-Jacques Rousseau** (1712–1778). In Rousseau's view, society itself threatened natural rights or freedoms: "Man is born free, and everywhere he is in chains." Rousseau first gained fame by writing a prize-winning essay in 1749 in which he argued that the revival of science and the arts had corrupted social morals, not improved them. This startling conclusion seemed to oppose some of the Enlightenment's most cherished beliefs. Rather than improving society, he claimed, science and art raised artificial barriers between people and their natural state. Rousseau's works extolled the simplicity of rural life over urban society. Although he participated in the salons, Rousseau always felt ill at ease in high society, and he periodically withdrew to live in solitude far from Paris. Paradoxically, his solitude was often paid for by wealthy upper-class patrons

Jean-Jacques Rousseau (zhahn zhahk roo SOH): One of the most important philosophes (1712–1778); he argued that only a government based on a social contract among the citizens could make people truly moral and free.

bagatelles suited to help them kill time. In truth, Gentlemen, you do us much honor to think that we could not provide things that unite the useful to the agreeable. To rid you of your error, we have made our Journal historical, with a view to putting before the eyes of youth striking images that will guide them toward virtue. . . . An historical *Journal des Dames*! these Gentlemen reasoners reply. How ridiculous! How out of character with the nature of this work, which calls only for little pieces to amuse [ladies] during their toilette. . . . Please, Gentlemen *beaux esprits* [wits], mind your own business and let us write in a manner worthy of our sex; I love this sex, I am jealous to uphold its honor and its rights. If we have not been raised up in the sciences as you have, it is you who are the guilty ones.

Source: Susan Groag Bell and Karen M. Offen, *Women, the Family, and Freedom: The Debate in Documents*, vol. 1, *1750–1880* (Stanford: Stanford University Press, 1983), 27–28.

3. Catharine Macaulay, *Letters on Education* (1787)

Catharine Sawbridge Macaulay-Graham (1731–1791) was one of the best-known English writers of the 1700s. She wrote immensely popular histories of England and also joined in the debate provoked by Rousseau's Émile.

There is another prejudice . . . which affects yet more deeply female happiness, and female importance; a prejudice, which ought ever to have been confined to the regions of the east, because [of the] state of slavery to which female nature in that part of the world has been ever subjected, and can only suit with the notion of a positive inferiority in the intellectual powers of the female mind. You will soon perceive, that the prejudice which I mean, is that degrading difference in the culture of the understanding, which has prevailed for several centuries in all European societies. . . .

Among the most strenuous asserters of a sexual difference in character, Rousseau is the most conspicuous, both on account of that warmth of sentiment which distinguishes all his writing, and the eloquence of his compositions: but never did enthusiasm and the love of paradox, those enemies of philosophical disquisition, appear in more strong opposition to plain sense than in Rousseau's definition of this difference. He sets out with a supposition, that Nature intended the subjection of the one sex to the other; that consequently there must be an inferiority of intellect in the subjected party; but as man is a very imperfect being, and apt to play the capricious tyrant, Nature, to bring things nearer to an equality, bestowed on the woman such attractive graces, and such an insinuating address, as to turn the balance on the other scale. . . .

The situation and education of women . . . is precisely that which must necessarily tend to corrupt and debilitate both the powers of mind and body. From a false notion of beauty and delicacy, their system of nerves is depraved before they come out of the nursery; and this kind of depravity has more influence over the mind, and consequently over morals, than is commonly apprehended.

Source: Susan Groag Bell and Karen M. Offen, *Women, the Family, and Freedom: The Debate in Documents*, vol. 1, *1750–1880* (Stanford: Stanford University Press, 1983), 54–55.

Questions to Consider

1. **Why would women in the eighteenth century read Rousseau with such interest and even enthusiasm?**
2. **Why does Madame de Beaumer address herself to male readers if the *Journal des Dames* is intended for women?**
3. **Why would Macaulay focus so much of her analysis on Rousseau? Why does she not just ignore him?**
4. **In what ways did Enlightenment ideas appeal to women?**

who lodged him on their estates, even as his writings decried the upper-class privilege that made his efforts possible.

Rousseau explored the tension between the individual and society in a best-selling novel (*The New Heloise*, 1761); in an influential work on education (*Émile*, 1762); and in a treatise on political theory (*The Social Contract*, 1762). He wrote *Émile* in the form of a novel to make his educational theories easily comprehensible. Free from the supervision of the clergy, who controlled most schools, the boy Émile works alone with his tutor to develop practical skills and independent ways of thinking. After developing his individuality, Émile joins society through marriage to Sophie, who received the education Rousseau thought appropriate for women. (See "Contrasting Views," above.)

Whereas earlier Rousseau had argued that society corrupted the individual by taking him out of nature, in *The Social Contract* he aimed to show that the right kind of political order could make people truly moral and free. Individual moral freedom could be achieved only by learning to subject one's individual interests to "the general will," that is, the good of the community. Individuals did this by entering into a social contract not with their rulers,

TERMS OF HISTORY

Enlightenment

In 1784, in an essay titled "What Is Enlightenment?," the German philosopher Immanuel Kant gave widespread currency to a term that had been in the making for several decades. The term *enlightened century* had become common in the 1760s. The Enlightenment thus gave itself its own name, and the name clearly had propaganda value. The philosophes associated Enlightenment with philosophy, reason, and humanity; religious tolerance; natural rights; and criticism of outmoded customs and prejudices. They tied Enlightenment to "progress" and to the "modern," and it came into question, just as these other terms did, when events cast doubt on the benefits of progress and the virtues of modernity. Although some opposed the Enlightenment from the very beginning as antireligious, undermining of authority, and even atheistic and immoral, the French Revolution of 1789 galvanized the critics of Enlightenment who blamed every excess of revolution on Enlightenment principles.

For most of the nineteenth and twentieth centuries, condemnation of the Enlightenment came from right-wing sources. Some of the more extreme of these critics denounced a supposed "Jewish-Masonic conspiracy," believing that Jews and Freemasons benefited most from the spread of Enlightenment principles and worked in secret to jointly undermine Christianity and established monarchical authorities. Adolf Hitler and his followers shared these suspicions, and during World War II the Germans confiscated the records of Masonic lodges in every country they occupied. They sent the documents back to Berlin so that a special office could trace the links of this supposed conspiracy. They found nothing.

After the catastrophes of World War II, the Enlightenment came under attack from left-wing critics. They denounced the Enlightenment as "self-destructive" and even "totalitarian" because its belief in reason led not to freedom but to greater bureaucratic control. They asked why mankind was sinking into "a new kind of barbarism," and they answered, "Because we have trusted too much in the Enlightenment and its belief in reason and science." The Nazis used bureaucratic control and technology to kill millions of Jews and others they deemed inferior. Science gave us the atomic bomb and factories that pollute the atmosphere. These criticisms of the Enlightenment show how central the Enlightenment remains to the very definition of modern history.

but with one another. If everyone followed the general will, then all would be equally free and equally moral because they lived under a law to which they had all consented.

These arguments threatened the legitimacy of eighteenth-century governments. Like Hobbes and Locke before him, Rousseau derived his social contract from human nature, not from history, tradition, or the Bible. He went much further than Hobbes or Locke, however, when he implied that people would be most free and moral under a republican form of government with direct democracy. Neither Hobbes nor Locke favored republics. Moreover, Rousseau roundly condemned slavery: "To decide that the son of a slave is born a slave is to decide that he is not born a man." Not surprisingly, authorities in both Geneva and Paris banned *The Social Contract* for undermining political authority. Rousseau's works would become a kind of political bible for the French revolutionaries of 1789, and his attacks on private property inspired the communists of the nineteenth century such as Karl Marx. Rousseau's rather mystical concept of the general will remains controversial. The "greatest good of all," according to Rousseau, was liberty combined with equality, but he also insisted that the individual could be "forced to be free" by the terms of the social contract. His ideas provided no legal protections for individual rights. Rousseau's version of democracy did not preserve the individual freedoms so important to Adam Smith.

Spreading the Enlightenment

The Enlightenment flourished in places where an educated middle class provided an eager audience for ideas of constitutionalism and reform. (See "Terms of History," above.) It therefore found its epicenter in the triangle formed by London, Amsterdam, and Paris and diffused outward to eastern and southern Europe and North America. Where constitutionalism and guarantees of individual freedoms were most advanced, as in Great Britain and the Dutch Republic, the movement had less of an edge because there was, in a sense, less need for it. John Locke had already written extensively about constitutionalism in the 1690s. As a result, Scottish and English writers concentrated on economics, philosophy, and history rather than on politics or social relations. The English historian Edward Gibbon, for example, portrayed Christianity in a negative light in his immensely influential work *The History of the Decline and Fall of the Roman Empire* (1776–1788), but when he served as a member of Parliament he never even gave a speech. At the other extreme, in places with small middle classes, such as Spain and Russia, Enlightenment ideas did not get much traction because governments successfully suppressed writings they did not like. France was the Enlightenment hot spot because the French monarchy alternated between encouraging ideas for reform and harshly censuring criticisms it found too threatening.

The French Enlightenment

French writers published the most daring critiques of church and state, and they often suffered harassment and persecution as a result. Voltaire, Diderot, and Rousseau all faced arrest, exile, or even imprisonment. The Catholic church and royal authorities routinely forbade the publication of their books, and the police arrested booksellers who ignored the warnings. Yet the French monarchy was far from the most autocratic in Europe, and Voltaire, Diderot, and Rousseau all ended their lives as cultural heroes. France seems to have been curiously caught in the middle during the Enlightenment: with fewer constitutional guarantees of individual freedom than Great Britain, it still enjoyed much higher levels of prosperity and cultural development than most other European countries. In short, French elites had reason to complain, the means to make their complaints known, and a government torn between the desire to censor dissident ideas and the desire to appear open to modernity and progress. Publishing was controlled in France—where all books had to get official permissions—but not as tightly as in Spain, where the Catholic Inquisition made up its own list of banned books, or in Russia, where Catherine the Great allowed no opposition.

By the 1760s, the French government regularly ignored the publication of many works once thought offensive or subversive. In addition, a growing flood of works printed abroad poured into France and circulated underground. Private companies in Dutch and Swiss cities made fortunes smuggling illegal books into France over mountain passes and back roads. Foreign printers provided secret catalogs of their offerings and sold their products through booksellers who were willing to market forbidden books for a high price—among them not only philosophical treatises of the Enlightenment but also pornographic books and pamphlets (some by Diderot) lampooning the Catholic clergy and leading members of the royal court. In the 1770s and 1780s, lurid descriptions of sexual promiscuity at the French court helped undermine the popularity of the throne.

The German Enlightenment

Whereas the French philosophes often took a violently anticlerical and combative tone, their German counterparts avoided direct political confrontations with authorities. Gotthold Lessing (1729–1781) complained in 1769 that Prussia was still "the most slavish society in Europe" in its lack of freedom to criticize government policies. As a playwright, literary critic, and philosopher, Lessing promoted religious toleration for the Jews and spiritual emancipation of Germans from foreign, especially French, models of culture, which still dominated. Lessing also introduced the German Jewish writer Moses Mendelssohn (1729–1786) into Berlin salon society. Mendelssohn labored to build bridges between German and Jewish culture by arguing that Judaism was a rational and undogmatic religion. He believed that persecution and discrimination against the Jews would end as reason triumphed.

Reason was also the chief focus of the most influential German thinker of the Enlightenment, Immanuel Kant (1724–1804). A university professor who lectured on everything from economics to astronomy, Kant wrote one of the most important works in the history of Western philosophy, *The Critique of Pure Reason* (1781). Kant admired Adam Smith and especially Rousseau, whose portrait he displayed proudly in his lodgings. Just as Smith founded modern economics and Rousseau modern political theory, Kant in *The Critique of Pure Reason* set the foundations for modern philosophy. In this complex book, Kant established the doctrine of idealism, the belief that true understanding can come only from examining the ways in which ideas are formed in the mind. Ideas are shaped, Kant argued, not just by sensory information (a position central to empiricism, a philosophy based on John Locke's writings) but also by the operation on that information of mental categories such as space and time. In Kant's philosophy, these "categories of understanding" were neither sensory nor supernatural; they were entirely ideal and abstract and located in the human mind. For Kant, the supreme philosophical questions—Does God exist? Is personal immortality possible? Do humans have free will?—were unanswerable by reason alone. But like Rousseau, Kant insisted that true moral freedom could be achieved only by living in society and obeying its laws.

Major Works of the Enlightenment

1751	Beginning of publication of the French *Encyclopedia*
1755	David Hume, *The Natural History of Religion*
1762	Jean-Jacques Rousseau, *The Social Contract* and *Émile*
1764	Voltaire, *Philosophical Dictionary*
1770	Abbé Guillaume Raynal, *Philosophical and Political History of European Colonies and Commerce in the Two Indies*
1776	Adam Smith, *An Inquiry into the Nature and Causes of the Wealth of Nations*
1781	Immanuel Kant, *The Critique of Pure Reason*

The Limits of Reason: Roots of Romanticism and Religious Revival

As Kant showed, reason had its limits: it could not answer all of life's pressing questions. In reaction to what some saw as the Enlightenment's excessive reliance on the authority of human reason, a new artistic movement called **romanticism** took root. Although it would not fully flower until the early nineteenth century, romanticism traced its emphasis on individual genius, deep emotion, and the joys of nature to thinkers like Rousseau who had scolded the philosophes for ignoring those aspects of life that escaped and even conflicted with the power of reason. Rousseau's autobiographical *Confessions*, published posthumously in 1782, caused an immediate sensation because it revealed so much about his inner emotional life, including his sexual longings and his almost paranoid distrust of other Enlightenment figures.

A novel by the young German writer Johann Wolfgang von Goethe (1749–1832) captured the early romantic spirit with its glorification of emotion. *The Sorrows of Young Werther* (1774) told of a young man who loves nature and rural life and is unhappy in love. When the woman he loves marries someone else, he falls into deep melancholy and eventually kills himself. Reason cannot save him. The book spurred a veritable Werther craze: in addition to Werther costumes, engravings, embroidery, and medallions, there was even a perfume called Eau de Werther. The young Napoleon Bonaparte, who was to build an empire for France, claimed to have read Goethe's novel seven times.

romanticism: An artistic movement of the late eighteenth and early nineteenth centuries that glorified nature, emotion, genius, and imagination.

Religious revivals underlined the limits of reason in a different way. Much of the Protestant world experienced an "awakening" in the 1740s. In the German states, Pietist groups founded new communities; and in the British North American colonies, revivalist Protestant preachers drew thousands of fervent believers in a movement called the Great Awakening. In North America, bitter conflicts between revivalists and their opponents in the established churches prompted the leaders on both sides to set up new colleges to support their beliefs. These included Princeton, Columbia, Brown, and Dartmouth, all founded between 1746 and 1769.

Revivalism also stirred eastern European Jews at about the same time. Israel ben Eliezer (1698–1760) laid the foundation for Hasidism in the 1740s and 1750s. He traveled the Polish countryside offering miraculous cures and became known as the Ba'al Shem Tov ("Master of the Good Name") because he used divine names to effect healing and bring believers into closer personal contact with God. He emphasized mystical contemplation of the divine, rather than study of Jewish law, and his followers, the Hasidim (Hebrew for "most pious" Jews), often expressed their devotion through music, dance, and fervent prayer. Their practices soon spread all over Poland-Lithuania.

Most of the waves of Protestant revivalism ebbed after the 1750s, but in Great Britain one movement continued to grow through the end of the century. John Wesley (1703–1791), the Oxford-educated son of a cleric in the Church of England, founded **Methodism**, a term evoked by Wesley's insistence on strict self-discipline and a methodical approach to religious study and observance. In 1738, Wesley began preaching a new brand of Protestantism that emphasized an intense personal experience of salvation and a life of thrift, abstinence, and hard work. Traveling all over the British Isles, Wesley would mount a table or a box to speak to the ordinary people of the village or town. He slept in his followers' homes, ate their food, and treated their illnesses with various remedies, including small electric shocks for nervous diseases (Wesley eagerly followed Benjamin Franklin's experiments with electricity). In fifty years, Wesley preached forty thousand sermons, an average of fifteen a week. Not surprisingly, his preaching disturbed the Church of England's authorities, who refused to let him preach in the churches. In response, Wesley began to ordain his own clergy. While radical in religious views,

Methodism: A religious movement founded by John Wesley (1703–1791) that broke with the Church of England and insisted on strict self-discipline and a "methodical" approach to religious study and observance.

George Whitefield
This colored etching depicts one of the most prominent preachers of the Great Awakening in the British North American colonies, the English Methodist George Whitefield, preaching in the American colonies. Whitefield visited the North American colonies seven times, sometimes for long periods, and drew tens of thousands of people to his dramatic and emotional open-air sermons, which moved many listeners to tears of repentance. Whitefield was a celebrity in his time and is considered by many to be the founder of the Evangelical movement. *(The Granger Collection, New York—All rights reserved.)*

the Methodist leadership remained politically conservative during Wesley's lifetime; Wesley himself wrote many pamphlets urging order, loyalty, and submission to higher authorities.

REVIEW QUESTION **What were the major differences between the Enlightenment in France, Great Britain, and the German states?**

Society and Culture in an Age of Enlightenment

Religious revivals and the first stirrings of romanticism show that not all intellectual currents of the eighteenth century were flowing in the same channel. Some social and cultural developments manifested the influence of Enlightenment ideas, but others did not. The traditional leaders of European societies—the nobles—responded to Enlightenment ideals in contradictory fashion: many simply reasserted their privileges and resisted the influence of the Enlightenment, but an important minority embraced change and actively participated in reform efforts. The expanding middle classes saw in the Enlightenment a chance to make their claim for joining society's governing elite. They bought Enlightenment books, joined Masonic lodges, and patronized new styles in art, music, and literature. The lower classes were more affected by economic growth than by ideas. Trade boomed and the population grew, but people did not benefit equally. The ranks of the poor swelled, too, and with greater mobility, births to unmarried mothers also increased.

The Nobility's Reassertion of Privilege

Nobles made up about 3 percent of the European population, but their numbers and ways of life varied greatly from country to country. At least 10 percent of the population in Poland and 7 to 8 percent in Spain was noble, in contrast to only 2 percent in Russia and between 1 and 2 percent in the rest of western Europe. Many Polish and Spanish nobles lived in poverty; titles did not guarantee wealth. Still, the wealthiest European nobles luxuriated in almost unimaginable opulence. Many of the English peers, for example, owned more than ten thousand acres of land; invested widely in government bonds and trading companies; kept several country residences with scores of servants as well as houses in London; and occasionally even had their own private orchestras to complement libraries of expensive books, greenhouses for exotic plants, kennels of pedigreed dogs, and collections of antiques, firearms, and scientific instruments.

To support an increasingly expensive lifestyle in a period of inflation, European aristocrats sought to cash in on their remaining legal rights, called seigneurial dues (from the French *seigneur*, "lord"). Peasants felt the squeeze as a result. French landlords required their peasants to pay dues to grind grain at the lord's mill, bake bread in his oven, press grapes at his winepress, or even pass on their own land as inheritance. In addition, peasants had to work without compensation for a specified number of days every year on the public roads. They also paid taxes to the government on salt, an essential preservative, and on the value of their land; customs duties if they sold produce or wine in town; and the tithe on their grain (one-tenth of the crop) to the church.

In Britain, the landed gentry could not claim these same onerous dues from their tenants, but they tenaciously defended their exclusive right to hunt game. The game laws kept the poor from eating meat and helped protect the social status of the rich. The gentry enforced the game laws themselves by hiring gamekeepers who hunted down poachers and even set traps for them in the forests. According to the law, anyone who poached deer or rabbits while armed or disguised could be sentenced to death. After 1760, the number of arrests for breaking the game laws increased dramatically. In most other countries, too, hunting was the special right of the nobility, a cause of deep popular resentment.

Even though Enlightenment writers sharply criticized nobles' insistence on special privileges, most aristocrats maintained their marks of distinction. The male court nobility continued to sport swords, plumed hats, makeup, and elaborate wigs, while middle-class men wore simpler and more somber clothing. Aristocrats had their own seats in church and their own quarters in the universities. Frederick II ("the Great") of Prussia (r. 1740–1786) made sure that nobles dominated both the army officer corps and the civil bureaucracy. Russia's Catherine the Great (r. 1762–1796) granted the nobility vast tracts of land, the exclusive right to own serfs, and exemption from personal taxes and corporal punishment. Her Charter of the Nobility of 1785 codified these privileges in exchange for the nobles' political subservience to the state. In Austria, Spain, the Italian states, Poland-Lithuania, and Russia, most nobles consequently cared little about Enlightenment ideas; they did not read the books of the philosophes and feared reforms that might challenge their dominance of rural society.

In France, Britain, and the western German states, however, the nobility proved more open to the new ideas. Among those who personally corresponded with Rousseau, for example, half were nobles, as were 20 percent of the 160 contributors to the *Encyclopedia*. It had not escaped their notice that Rousseau had denounced inequality. In his view, it was "manifestly contrary to the law of nature . . . that a handful of people should gorge themselves with superfluities while the hungry multitude goes in want of necessities." The nobles of western Europe sometimes married into middle-class families and formed with them a new mixed elite, united by common interests in reform and new cultural tastes.

The Middle Class and the Making of a New Elite

The Enlightenment offered middle-class people an intellectual and cultural route to social improvement. The term *middle class* referred to the middle position on the social ladder; middle-class families did not have legal titles like the nobility above them, but neither did they work with their hands like the peasants, artisans, or laborers below them. Most middle-class people lived in towns or cities and earned their living in the professions—as doctors, lawyers, or lower-level officials—or through investment in land, trade, or manufacturing (see "Taking Measure," page 601). In the eighteenth century, the ranks of the middle class—also known as the bourgeoisie (from *bourgeois*, French for "city dweller")—grew steadily in western Europe as a result of economic expansion. In France, for example, the overall population grew by about one-third in the 1700s, but the bourgeoisie nearly tripled in size. Although middle-class people had many reasons to resent the nobles, they also aspired to be like them.

Lodges and Learned Societies

Nobles and middle-class professionals mingled in Enlightenment salons and joined the new Masonic lodges and local learned societies. The Masonic lodges began as social clubs organized around elaborate secret rituals of stonemasons' guilds. They called their members **Freemasons** because that was the term given to apprentice masons

Freemasons: Members of Masonic lodges, where nobles and middle-class professionals (and even some artisans) shared interest in the Enlightenment and reform.

TAKING MEASURE

European Urbanization, 1750–1800

The bar graph shows that northwestern Europe was the most urbanized region, followed by the Mediterranean countries. Central and eastern Europe were much less urbanized, which meant that they had much smaller middle classes.

Questions to Consider

1. **What are the possible consequences of these differences in urbanization?**
2. **What would urban consumers be more likely to purchase that rural consumers likely could not or would not?**
3. **How would urbanization contribute to the spread of the Enlightenment?**

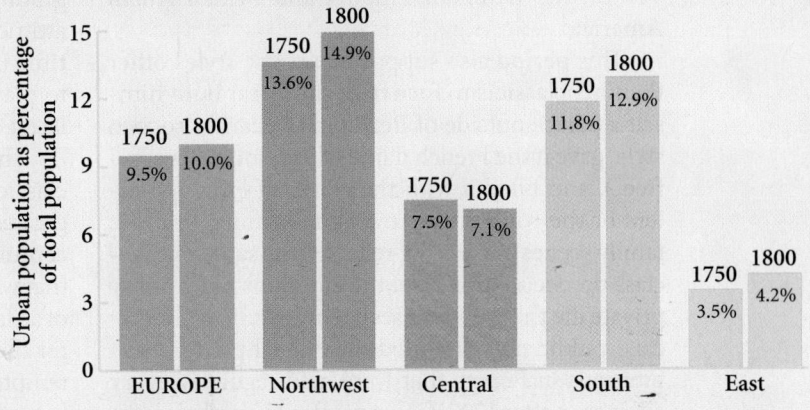

Source: Adapted from Andrew Lees and Lynn Hollen Lees, *Cities and the Making of Modern Europe, 1750–1914* (Cambridge: Cambridge University Press), 2008.

when they were deemed "free" to practice as masters of their guild. Although not explicitly political in aim, the lodges encouraged equality among members, and both aristocrats and middle-class men could join. Members wrote constitutions for their lodges and elected their own officers, thus promoting a direct experience of constitutional government.

Freemasonry arose in Great Britain and spread eastward: the first French and Italian lodges opened in 1726; Prussia's Frederick the Great founded a lodge in 1740; and after 1750, Freemasonry spread in Poland, Russia, and British North America. In France, women set up their own Masonic lodges. Despite the papacy's condemnation of Freemasonry in 1738 as subversive of religious and civil authority, lodges continued to multiply throughout the eighteenth century because they offered a place for socializing outside of the traditional channels and a way of declaring one's interest in the Enlightenment and reform. In short, Freemasonry offered a kind of secular religion. After 1789 and the outbreak of the French Revolution, conservatives would blame the lodges for every kind of political upheaval, but in the 1700s many high-ranking nobles became active members and saw no conflict with their privileged status.

Nobles and middle-class professionals also met in local learned societies, which greatly increased in number in this period. They gathered to discuss such practical issues as new scientific innovations or methods to eliminate poverty. The societies, sometimes called academies, brought the Enlightenment down from the realm of books and ideas to the level of concrete reforms. They sponsored essay contests, such as the one won by Rousseau in 1749 and the one set by the society in Metz in 1785 on the question "Are there means for making the Jews happier and more useful in France?" The Metz society approved essays that argued for granting civil rights to Jews.

New Cultural Styles Shared tastes in travel, architecture, the arts, and even reading helped strengthen the links between nobles and members of the middle class. "Grand tours" of Europe often led upper-class youths to recently discovered Greek and Roman ruins at Pompeii, Herculaneum, and Paestum in Italy. These excavations aroused enthusiasm for the neoclassical style in architecture and painting, which began pushing aside the rococo and the long-dominant baroque. Urban residences, government buildings, furniture, fabrics, wallpaper, and even pottery soon reflected the neoclassical emphasis on purity and clarity of forms. As one German writer noted, with considerable exaggeration, "Everything in Paris is in the Greek style." Employing neoclassical motifs, the English potter Josiah Wedgwood (1730–1795) almost single-handedly created a mass market for domestic crockery and appealed to middle-class desires to emulate the rich and royal. His designs of special tea sets for the British queen, for Catherine the Great of Russia, and for leading aristocrats allowed him to advertise his wares as fashionable. By 1767, he claimed that his Queensware pottery had "spread over the whole Globe," and indeed by then his pottery was being marketed in France, Russia, Venice, the Ottoman Empire, and British North America.

This period also supported artistic styles other than neoclassicism. Frederick the Great built himself a palace outside of Berlin in the earlier rococo style, gave it the French name of Sanssouci ("worry-free"), and filled it with the works of French masters of the rococo. A growing taste for moralistic family scenes in painting reflected the same middle-class preoccupation with the emotions of ordinary private life that could be seen in novels. The middle-class public now attended the official painting exhibitions in France that were held regularly every other year after 1737. Court painting nonetheless remained much in demand. Marie-Louise-Élizabeth Vigée-Lebrun (1755–1842), who painted portraits at the French court, reported that in the 1780s "it was difficult to get a place on my waiting list. . . . I was the fashion."

Although wealthy nobles still patronized Europe's leading musicians, music, too, began to reflect the broadening of the elite and the spread of Enlightenment ideals as classical forms replaced the baroque style. Complex polyphony gave way to melody, which made music more accessible to ordinary listeners. Large sections of string instruments became the backbone of professional orchestras, which now played to large audiences of well-to-do listeners in sizable concert halls. The public concert gradually displaced the private recital, and a new attitude toward "the classics" developed: for the first time in the 1770s and 1780s, concert groups began to play older music rather than simply playing the latest commissioned works.

This laid the foundation for what we still call classical music today—that is, a repertory of the greatest music of the eighteenth and early nineteenth centuries. Because composers now created works that would be performed over and over again as part of a classical repertory, rather than occasional pieces for the court or noble patrons, they deliberately attempted to write lasting works. As a result, the major composers began to produce fewer symphonies: the Austrian composer Franz Joseph Haydn (1732–1809) wrote more than a hundred symphonies, but his successor Ludwig van Beethoven (1770–1827) would create only nine.

The two supreme masters of the new musical style of the eighteenth century show that the transition from noble patronage to classical concerts was far from complete. Haydn and his fellow Austrian Wolfgang Amadeus Mozart (1756–1791) both wrote for noble patrons, but by the early 1800s their com-

Neoclassical Style
In this Georgian interior of Syon House on the outskirts of London, various neoclassical motifs are readily apparent: Greek columns, Greek-style statuary on top of the columns, and Roman-style mosaics in the floor. The Scottish architect Robert Adam created this room for the duke of Northumberland in the 1760s. Adam had spent four years in Italy and returned in 1758 to London to decorate homes in the "Adam style," meaning the neoclassical manner. *(Syon House, Middlesex, UK/The Bridgeman Art Library International.)*

Jean-Baptiste Greuze, *Broken Eggs* (1756)
Greuze made his reputation as a painter of moralistic family scenes. In this one, an old woman (perhaps the mother) confronts the lover of a young girl and points to the eggs that have fallen out of a basket, a symbol of lost virginity. Diderot praised Greuze's work as "morality in paint," but the paintings often had an erotic subtext. *(© Francis G. Mayer/Corbis.)*

positions had been incorporated into the canon of concert classics all over Europe. Incredibly prolific, both excelled in combining lightness, clarity, and profound emotion. Both also wrote numerous Italian operas, a genre whose popularity continued to grow: in the 1780s, the Papal States alone boasted forty opera houses. Haydn spent most of his career working for a Hungarian noble family, the Eszterházys. Asked once why he had written no string quintets (at which Mozart excelled), he responded simply: "No one has ordered any."

Interest in reading, like attending public concerts, took hold of the middle classes and fed a frenzied increase in publication. By the end of the eighteenth century, six times as many books were being published in the German states, for instance, as at the beginning. One Parisian author commented that "people are certainly reading ten times as much in Paris as they did a hundred years ago." Provincial towns in western Europe published their own newspapers; by 1780, thirty-seven English towns had local newspapers. Lending libraries and book clubs multiplied. Despite the limitations of women's education, which emphasized domestic skills, women benefited as much as men from the spread of print. As one Englishman observed, "By far the greatest part of ladies now have a taste for books." Women also wrote them. Catherine Macaulay (1731–1791) published best-selling histories of Britain, and in France Stéphanie de Genlis (1746–1830) wrote children's books—a genre that was growing in importance as middle-class parents became more interested in education. The universities had little impact on these new tastes. An Austrian reformer complained about the universities in his country: "Critical history, natural sciences—which are supposed to make enlightenment general and combat prejudice—were neglected or wholly unknown."

Life on the Margins

Booming foreign trade fueled a dramatic economic expansion—French colonial trade increased tenfold in the 1700s—but the results did not necessarily trickle all the way down the social scale. The population of Europe grew by nearly 30 percent, with especially striking gains in England, Ireland, Prussia, and Hungary. Even though food production increased, shortages and crises still occurred periodically. Prices went up in many countries after the 1730s and continued to rise gradually until the early nineteenth century; wages in many trades rose as well, but less quickly than prices. Some people prospered—for example, peasants who produced surpluses to sell in local markets and shopkeepers and artisans who could increase their sales to meet growing demand. But those at the bottom of the social ladder—day laborers in the cities and peasants with small holdings—lived on the edge of dire poverty, and when they lost their land or work, they either migrated to the cities or wandered the roads in search of food and work. In France alone, 200,000 workers left their homes every year in search of seasonal employment elsewhere. At least 10 percent of Europe's urban population depended on some form of charity.

The growing numbers of poor overwhelmed local governments. In some countries, beggars and vagabonds had been locked up in workhouses since the mid-1600s. The expenses for running these overcrowded institutions increased by 60 percent in England between 1760 and 1785. After 1740, most German towns created workhouses that were part workshop, part hospital, and part prison. Such institutions also appeared for the first time in Boston, New York, and Philadelphia. To supplement the inadequate system of religious charity, offices for the poor, public workshops, and workhouse hospitals, the French government created *dépôts de mendicité* ("beggar houses") in 1767. The government sent people to these new workhouses to labor in manufacturing, but most were too weak or sick to work, and 20 percent of them died within a few months of incarceration. The ballooning number of poor people created fears about rising crime. To officials, beggars seemed more aggressive than ever. The handful of police assigned to keep order in each town or district found themselves confronted with increasing incidents of rural banditry and crimes against property.

The Persistence of Popular Culture

Those who were able to work or keep their land fared better: an increase in literacy, especially in the cities, allowed some lower-class people to participate in new tastes and ideas. One French observer insisted, "These days, you see a waiting-maid in her backroom, a lackey in an anteroom reading pamphlets. People can read in almost all classes of society." In France, only 50 percent of men and 27 percent of women could read and write in the 1780s, but that was twice the rate of a century earlier. Literacy rates were higher in England and the Dutch Republic, much lower in eastern Europe. About one in four Parisians owned books, but the lower classes overwhelmingly read religious books, as they had in the past.

Whereas the new elite might attend salons, concerts, or art exhibitions, peasants enjoyed their traditional forms of popular entertainment, such as fairs and festivals, and the urban lower classes relaxed in cabarets and taverns. Sometimes pleasures were cruel. In Britain, bullbaiting, bearbaiting, dogfighting, and cockfighting were all common forms of entertainment that provided opportunities for organized gambling. "Gentle" sports frequented by the upper classes had their violent side, too, showing that the upper classes had not become as different as they sometimes thought. Cricket matches, whose rules were first laid down in 1744, were often accompanied by brawls among fans (not unlike soccer matches today, though on a much smaller scale). Many Englishmen enjoyed what one observer called a "battle royal with sticks, pebbles and hog's dung."

Changes in Sexual Behavior

As population increased and villagers began to move to cities to better their prospects, sexual behavior changed, too. The rates of births out of wedlock soared, from less than 5 percent of all births in the seventeenth century to nearly 20 percent at the end of the eighteenth. Historians have disagreed about the causes and meanings of this change. Some detect in this pattern a sign of sexual liberation and the beginnings of a modern sexual revolution: as women moved out of the control of their families, they began to seek their own sexual fulfillment. Others view this change more bleakly, as a story of seduction and betrayal: family and community pressure had once forced a man to marry a woman pregnant with his child, but now a man could abandon a pregnant lover by simply moving away.

Increased mobility brought freedom for some women, but it also aggravated the vulnerability of those newly arrived in cities from the countryside. Desperation, not reason, often ruled their choices. Women who came to the city as domestic servants had little recourse against masters or fellow servants who seduced or raped them. The result was a startling rise in abandoned babies. Most European cities established foundling hospitals in the 1700s, but infant and child mortality was 50 percent higher in such institutions than for children brought up at home. Some women tried herbs, laxatives, or crude surgical means of abortion; a few, usually servants who would lose their jobs if their employers discovered they had borne a child, resorted to infanticide.

European states had long tried to regulate sexual behavior; every country had laws against prostitution, adultery, fornication, sodomy, and infanticide. Reformers criticized the harshness of laws against infanticide, but they showed no mercy for "sodomites" (as male homosexuals were called), who in some places, in particular the Dutch Republic, were systematically persecuted and imprisoned or even executed. Male homosexuals attracted the attention of authorities because they had begun to develop networks and special meeting places. The stereotype of the effeminate, exclusively homosexual male seems to have appeared for the first time in the eighteenth century, perhaps as part of a growing emphasis on separate roles for men and women.

The Enlightenment's emphasis on reason, self-control, and childhood innocence made parents increasingly anxious about their children's sexuality. Moralists and physicians wrote books about the evils of masturbation, "proving" that it led to physical and mental degeneration and even madness.

While the Enlightenment thus encouraged excessive concern about children being left to their own devices, it nevertheless taught the middle and upper classes to value their children and to expect their improvement through education. Writers such as de Genlis and Rousseau drew attention to children, who were no longer viewed only as little sinners in need of harsh discipline. Paintings now showed individual children playing at their favorite activities rather than formally posed with their families. Books about and for children became popular. *The Newtonian System of the Universe Digested for Young Minds*, by "Tom Telescope," was published in Britain in 1761 and reprinted many times. Toys, jigsaw puzzles, and clothing designed for children all appeared for the first time in the 1700s. Children were no longer considered miniature adults.

REVIEW QUESTION What were the major differences in the impact of the Enlightenment on the nobility, the middle classes, and the lower classes?

State Power in an Era of Reform

Rulers turned to Enlightenment-inspired reforms to improve life for their subjects and to gain commercial or military advantage over rival states. Historians label many of the sovereigns of this time **enlightened despots** or enlightened absolutists, for they aimed to promote Enlightenment reforms without giving up their absolutist powers. Catherine the Great's admiring relationship with Voltaire showed how even the most absolutist rulers championed reform when it suited their own goals. Foremost among those goals was the expansion of a ruler's territory.

enlightened despots: Rulers—such as Catherine the Great of Russia, Frederick the Great of Prussia, and Joseph II of Austria—who tried to promote Enlightenment reforms without giving up their own supreme political power; also called enlightened absolutists.

War and Diplomacy

Europeans no longer fought devastating wars over religion that killed hundreds of thousands of civilians; instead, professional armies and navies battled for control of overseas empires and for dominance on the European continent. Rulers continued to expand their armies: the Prussian army, for example, nearly tripled in size between 1740 and 1789. Widespread use of flintlock muskets required deployment in long lines, usually three men deep, with each line in turn loading and firing on command. Military strategy became cautious and calculating, but this did not prevent the outbreak of hostilities. Between 1750 and 1775, the instability of the European balance of power resulted in a diplomatic reversal of alliances, a major international conflict, and the partition of Poland-Lithuania among Russia, Austria, and Prussia.

The Seven Years' War, 1756–1763

In 1756, a major reversal of alliances—what historians call the Diplomatic Revolution—reshaped relations among the great powers. Prussia and Great Britain signed a defensive alliance, prompting Austria to overlook two centuries of hostility and ally with France. Russia and Sweden soon joined the Franco-Austrian alliance. When Frederick the Great invaded Saxony, an ally of Austria, with his bigger and better-disciplined army, the long-simmering hostilities between Great Britain and France over colonial boundaries flared into a general war that became known as the **Seven Years' War** (1756–1763).

Fighting soon raged around the world (Map 18.1). The French and British battled on land and sea in North America (where the conflict was called the French and Indian War), the West Indies, and India. The two coalitions also fought each other in central Europe. At first, in 1757, Frederick the Great surprised Europe with a spectacular victory at Rossbach in Saxony over a much larger Franco-Austrian army. But in time, Russian and Austrian armies encircled his troops. Frederick despaired: "I believe all is lost. I will not survive the ruin of my country." A fluke of history saved him. Empress Elizabeth of Russia (r. 1741–1762) died and was succeeded by the mentally unstable Peter III, a fanatical admirer of Frederick and things Prussian. Peter withdrew Russia from the war. (This was practically his only accomplishment as tsar. He was soon mysteriously

Seven Years' War: A worldwide series of battles (1756–1763) between Austria, France, Russia, and Sweden on one side and Prussia and Great Britain on the other.

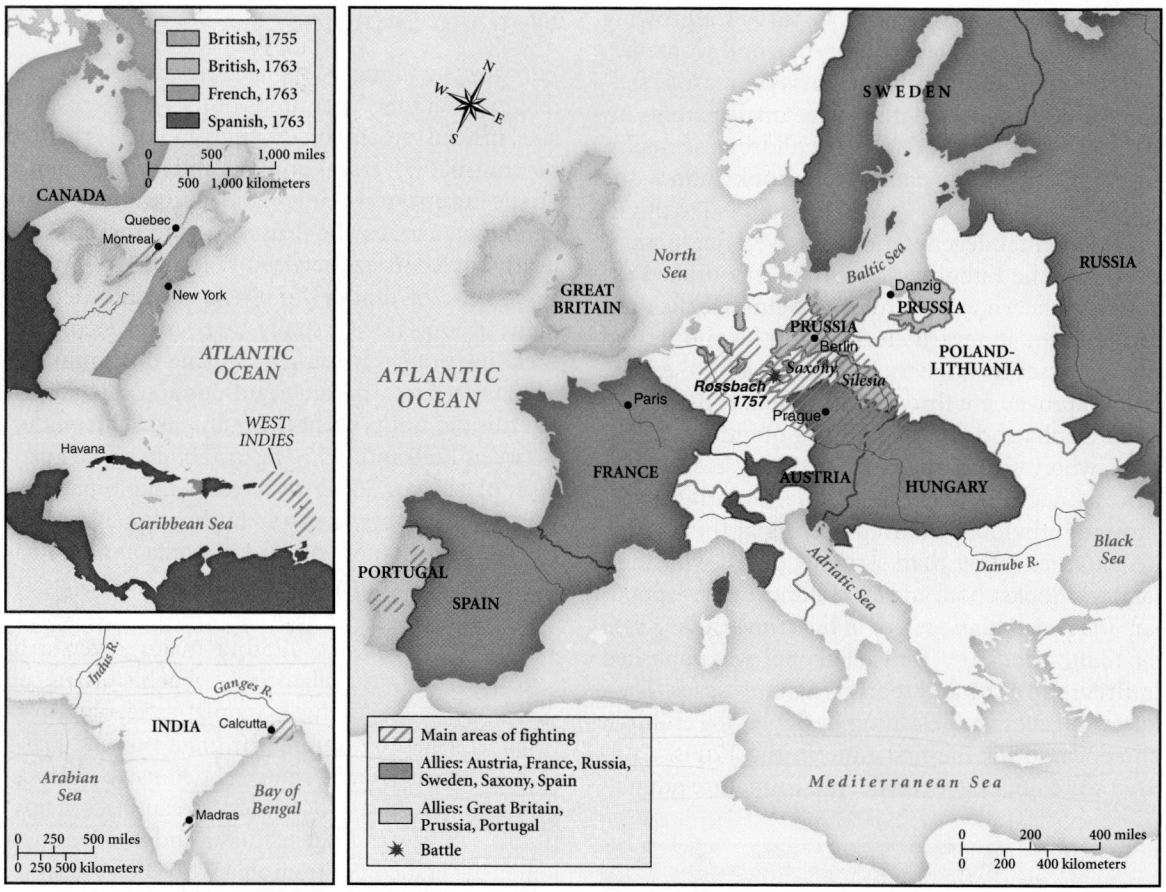

MAP 18.1 The Seven Years' War, 1756–1763

In what might justly be called the first worldwide war, the French and British fought each other in Europe, the West Indies, North America, and India. Skirmishing in North America helped precipitate the war, which became more general when Austria, France, and Russia allied to check Prussian influence in central Europe. The treaty between Austria and Prussia simply restored the status quo in Europe, but the changes overseas were much more dramatic. Britain gained control over Canada and India but gave back to France the West Indian islands of Guadeloupe and Martinique. Britain was now the dominant power of the seas.

murdered, probably at the instigation of his wife, Catherine the Great.) In a separate peace treaty Frederick kept all his territory, including Silesia, that had been conquered in the War of the Austrian Succession (1740–1748).

The Anglo-French overseas conflicts ended more decisively than the continental land wars. British naval superiority, fully achieved only in the 1750s, enabled Great Britain to rout the French in North America, India, and the West Indies. In the Treaty of Paris of 1763, France ceded Canada to Great Britain and agreed to remove its armies from India, in exchange for keeping its rich West Indian islands. Eagerness to avenge this defeat would motivate France to support the British North American colonists in their War of Independence just fifteen years later.

Prussia's Rise and the First Partition of Poland

Although Prussia suffered great losses in the Seven Years' War—some 160,000 Prussian soldiers died either in action or of disease—the army helped vault Prussia to the rank of leading powers. In 1733, Frederick II's father, Frederick William I, had instituted the "canton system," which enrolled peasant youths in each canton (or district) in the army, gave them two or three months of training annually, and allowed them to return to their family farms the rest of the year. They remained "cantonists" (reservists) as long as they were able-bodied. In this fashion, the Prussian military steadily grew in size; by 1740, Prussia had the third or fourth largest army in Europe even though it was tenth in population and thirteenth in land area. Under Frederick II, Prussia's military expenditures rose to two-thirds of the state's revenue. Virtually every nobleman served in the army, paying for his own support as officer and buying a position as company commander. Once retired, the officers returned to their estates, coordinated the canton system, and served as local of-

Dividing Poland, 1772
In this contemporary depiction, Catherine the Great, Joseph II, and Frederick the Great point on the map to the portion of Poland-Lithuania each plans to take. The artist makes it clear that Poland's fate rested in the hands of neighboring rulers, not its own people. Can you infer the sentiments of the artist from the content of this engraving? *(Hulton Archive/Getty Images.)*

The First Partition of Poland, 1772

ficials. In this way, the military permeated every aspect of rural society, fusing army and agrarian organization. The army gave the state great power, but the militarization of Prussian society also had a profoundly conservative effect: it kept the peasants enserfed to their lords and blocked the middle classes from access to estates or high government positions.

Prussia's power grew so dramatically that in 1772 Frederick the Great proposed that large chunks of Poland-Lithuania be divided among Austria, Prussia, and Russia. Although the Austrian empress Maria Theresa protested that the partition would spread "a stain over my whole reign," she agreed to the first **partition of Poland**, splitting one-third of Poland-Lithuania's territory and half of its people among the three powers. Austria feared growing Russian influence in Poland and in the Balkans, where Russia had been successfully battling the Ottoman Empire. Conflicts between Catholics, Protestants, and Orthodox Christians in Poland were used to justify this cynical move. Russia took over most of Lithuania, effectively ending the large but weak Polish-Lithuanian commonwealth.

partition of Poland: Division of one-third of Poland-Lithuania's territory between Prussia, Russia, and Austria in 1772.

State-Sponsored Reform

In the aftermath of the Seven Years' War, all the belligerents faced pressing needs for more money to fund their growing armies, to organize navies to wage overseas conflicts, and to counter the impact of inflation. To make tax increases more palatable to public opinion, rulers appointed reform-minded ministers and gave them a mandate to modernize government. As one adviser to the Austrian ruler Joseph II put it, "A properly constituted state must be exactly analogous to a machine . . . and the ruler must be the foreman, the mainspring . . . which sets everything else in motion." Such reforms always threatened the interests of traditional groups, however, and the spread of Enlightenment ideas aroused sometimes unpredictable desires for more change.

Administrative and Legal Reforms

Reforming monarchs did not invent government bureaucracy, but they did insist on greater attention to merit, hard work, and professionalism, which made bureaucrats more like modern civil servants. In this view, the ruler should be a benevolent, enlightened administrator who worked for the general well-being of his or her people. Frederick II of Prussia, who drove himself as hard as he drove his officials, boasted, "I am the first servant of the state." A freemason and supporter

Maria Theresa
Like Catherine the Great, Maria Theresa had herself painted on horseback to emphasize her sovereign position, which the crown over her head makes apparent. This portrait from 1757 does not make her seem warlike, however, as she carries no sword. She had sixteen children, two of whom became Holy Roman Emperor (Joseph II and Leopold II) and two of whom became queens (Marie-Antoinette of France and Maria Carolina of Naples). *(Scala/White Images/Art Resource, NY.)*

of religious toleration, Frederick abolished torture, reorganized taxation, and hosted leading French philosophes at his court. The Prussian king also composed more than a hundred original pieces of music.

Legal reform, both of the judicial system and of the often disorganized and irregular law codes, was central to the work of many reform-minded monarchs. Like Frederick the Great, Joseph II of Austria (r. 1780–1790) ordered the compilation of a unified law code, a project that required many years for completion. Catherine the Great began such an undertaking even more ambitiously. In 1767, she called together a legislative commission of 564 deputies and asked them to consider a long document called the *Instruction*, which represented her hopes for legal reform based on the ideas of Montesquieu and the Italian jurist Cesare Beccaria. Montesquieu had insisted that punishment should fit the crime; he criticized the use of torture and brutal corporal punishment. In his influential book *On Crimes and Punishments* (1764), Beccaria argued that justice should be administered in public, that judicial torture should be abolished as inhumane, and that the accused should be presumed innocent until proven guilty. He also advocated eliminating the death penalty. Despite much discussion and hundreds of petitions and documents about local problems, little came of Catherine's commission because the monarch herself—despite her regard for Voltaire and his fellow philosophes—proved ultimately unwilling to see through far-reaching legal reform.

The Church, Education, and Religious Toleration

Rulers everywhere wanted more control over church affairs, and they used Enlightenment criticisms of the organized churches to get their way. In Catholic countries, many government officials resented the influence of the Jesuits, the major Catholic teaching order. The Jesuits trained the Catholic intellectual elite, ran a worldwide missionary network, enjoyed close ties to the papacy, and amassed great wealth. Critics mounted campaigns against the Jesuits in many countries, and by the early 1770s the Society of Jesus had been dissolved in Portugal, France, and Spain. In 1773, Pope Clement XIV (r. 1769–1774) agreed under pressure to disband the order, an edict that held until a reinvigorated papacy restored the society in 1814. Joseph II of Austria not only applauded the suppression of the Jesuits but also required Austrian bishops to swear fidelity and submission to him. Joseph had become Holy Roman Emperor and co-regent with his mother, Maria Theresa, in 1765. After her death in 1780, he initiated a wide-ranging program of reform. Under him, the Austrian state supervised Catholic seminaries, abolished contemplative monastic orders, and confiscated monastic property to pay for education and poor relief.

Joseph II launched the most ambitious educational reforms of the period. In 1774, once the Jesuits had been disbanded, the General School Ordinance in Austria ordered state subsidies for local schools, which the state would regulate. By 1789, one-quarter of the school-age children attended school. In Prussia, the school code of 1763 required all children between the ages of five and thirteen to attend school. Although not enforced uniformly, the Prussian law demonstrated Frederick the Great's belief that modernization depended on education. Catherine the Great also tried to expand elementary education—and the education of women in particular—and founded engineering schools.

No ruler pushed the principle of religious toleration as far as Joseph II of Austria, who in 1781 granted freedom of religious worship to Protestants, Orthodox Christians, and Jews. For the first time, these groups were allowed to own property, build schools, enter the professions, and hold political and military offices. The efforts of other rulers to extend religious toleration proved more limited. Louis XVI signed an edict in 1787 restoring French Protestants' civil rights—but still, Protestants could not hold political office. Great Britain continued to deny Catholics freedom of open worship and the right to sit in Parliament. Most European states limited the rights and opportunities available to Jews. In Russia, only wealthy Jews could hold municipal office, and in the Papal States, the pope encouraged forced baptism. Even in Austria, where Joseph encouraged toleration, the laws forced Jews to take German-sounding names. The leading philosophes opposed persecution of the Jews in theory but often treated them with undisguised contempt. Diderot's comment was all too typical: the Jews, he said, bore "all the defects peculiar to an ignorant and superstitious nation."

Limits of Reform

When enlightened absolutist leaders introduced reforms, they often ran into resistance from groups threatened by the proposed changes. The most contentious area of reform was agricultural policy. Whereas Catherine the Great reinforced the authority of Russian nobles over their serfs, Joseph II tried to remove the burdens of serfdom in the Habsburg lands. In 1781, he abolished the personal aspects of serfdom: serfs could now move freely, enter trades, or marry without their lords' permission. Joseph abolished the tithe to the church, shifted more of the tax burden to the nobility, and converted peasants' labor services into cash payments.

The Austrian nobility furiously resisted these far-reaching reforms. When Joseph died in 1790, his brother Leopold II had to revoke most reforms to appease the nobles. Prussia's Frederick the Great, like Joseph, encouraged such agricultural innovations as planting potatoes and turnips (new crops that could help feed a growing population), experimenting with cattle breeding, draining swamplands, and clearing forests. But Prussia's noble landlords, called *Junkers* in German, continued to expand their estates at the expense of poorer peasants and thwarted Frederick's attempts to improve the status of serfs.

Reforming ministers also tried to stimulate agricultural improvement in France. Unlike most other western European countries, France still had about a hundred thousand serfs; though their burdens weighed less heavily on them than on those in eastern Europe, serfdom did not entirely disappear until 1789. A group of economists called the physiocrats urged the French government to deregulate the grain trade and make the tax system more equitable to encourage agricultural productivity. In the interest of establishing a free market, they also insisted that urban guilds be abolished because the guilds prevented free entry into the trades. Their proposed reforms applied the Enlightenment emphasis on individual liberties to the economy; Adam Smith took up many of the physiocrats' ideas in his writing in favor of free markets. The French government heeded some of this advice and gave up its system of price controls on grain in 1763, but it had to reverse the decision in 1770 when grain shortages caused a famine.

A conflict with the parlements, the thirteen high courts of law, prompted Louis XV to go even further in 1771. He replaced the parlements with courts in which the judges no longer owned their offices and thus could not sell them or pass them on as an inheritance. Justice would then presumably be more impartial. The displaced judges of the parlements succeeded in arousing widespread opposition to what they portrayed as tyrannical royal policy. The furor calmed down only when Louis XV died in 1774 and his successor, Louis XVI (r. 1774–1792), yielded to aristocratic demands and restored the old parlements.

Louis XVI tried to carry out part of the program suggested by the physiocrats, and he chose one of their disciples, Jacques Turgot (1727–1781), as his chief minister. A contributor to the *Encyclopedia*, Turgot pushed through several edicts that again freed the grain trade, suppressed guilds, converted the peasants' forced labor on roads into a money tax payable by all landowners, and reduced court expenses. He also began making plans to introduce a system of elected local assemblies, which would have increased representation in the government. Faced with broad-based resistance led by the parlements and his own courtiers, as well as with riots against rising grain prices, Louis XVI dismissed Turgot, and one of the last possibilities to overhaul France's government collapsed.

The failure of reform in France paradoxically reflected the power of Enlightenment thinkers; everyone now endorsed Enlightenment ideas but used them for different ends. The nobles in the parlements blocked the French monarchy's reform efforts using the very same Enlightenment language spoken by the crown's ministers. France's large and growing middle-class public felt increasingly frustrated by the failure to institute social change, a failure that ultimately helped undermine the monarchy itself. Where Frederick the Great, Catherine the Great, and even Joseph II used reform to bolster the efficiency of absolutist government, attempts at change in France backfired. French kings found that their ambitious programs for reform succeeded only in arousing unrealistic hopes.

REVIEW QUESTION What prompted enlightened absolutists to undertake reforms in the second half of the eighteenth century?

Rebellions against State Power

Although traditional forms of popular discontent had not disappeared, Enlightenment ideals and reforms changed the rules of the game in politics. Governments had become accountable for their actions to a much wider range of people than ever before. In Britain and France, ordinary people rioted when they perceived government as failing to protect them against food shortages. The growth of informed public opinion had its most dramatic consequences in the North American colonies, where a struggle over the British Parliament's right to tax turned into a full-scale war for independence. The American War of Independence showed that, once put into practice, Enlightenment ideals could have revolutionary implications.

Food Riots and Peasant Uprisings

Population growth, inflation, and the extension of the market system put added pressure on the already beleaguered poor. Seventeenth-century peasants and townspeople had rioted to protest new taxes. In the last half of the eighteenth century, the food supply became the focus of political and social conflict. Poor people in the villages and the towns believed that it was the government's responsibility to ensure they had enough food, and many governments did stockpile grain to make up for the occasional bad harvest. At the same time, in keeping with Adam Smith's and the French physiocrats' free-market proposals, governments wanted to allow grain prices to rise with market demand, because higher profits would motivate producers to increase the overall supply of food.

Free trade in grain meant selling to the highest bidder even if that bidder was a foreign merchant. In the short run, in times of scarcity, big landowners and farmers could make huge profits by selling grain outside their hometowns or villages. This practice enraged poor farmers, agricultural workers, and urban wageworkers, who could not afford the higher prices. Lacking the political means to affect policy, they could enforce their desire for old-fashioned price regulation only by rioting. Most did not pillage or steal grain but rather forced the sale of grain or flour at a "just" price and blocked the shipment of grain out of their villages to other markets. Women often led these "popular price fixings," as they were called in France, in desperate attempts to protect the food supply for their children.

Such food riots occurred regularly in Britain and France in the last half of the eighteenth century. One of the most turbulent was the so-called Flour War in France in 1775. Turgot's deregulation of the grain trade in 1774 caused prices to rise in several provincial cities. Rioting spread from there to the Paris region, where villagers attacked grain convoys heading to the capital city. Local officials often ordered merchants and bakers to sell at the price the rioters demanded, only to find themselves arrested by the central government for overriding free trade. The government brought in troops to restore order and introduced the death penalty for rioting.

Frustrations with serfdom and hopes for a miraculous transformation provoked the **Pugachev rebellion** in Russia beginning in 1773. An army deserter from the southeast frontier region, Emelian Pugachev (1742–1775) claimed to be Tsar Peter III, the dead husband of Catherine the Great. Pugachev's appearance seemed to confirm peasant hopes for a "redeemer tsar" who would save the people from oppression. He rallied around him Cossacks like himself who resented the loss of their old tribal independence. Now increasingly enserfed or forced to pay taxes and endure army service, these nomadic bands joined with other serfs, rebellious mine workers, and Muslim minorities. Catherine dispatched a large army to squelch the uprising, but Pugachev eluded them and the fighting spread. Nearly three million people eventually participated, making this the largest single rebellion in the history of tsarist Russia. When Pugachev urged the peasants to attack the nobility and seize their estates, hundreds of noble families perished. Foreign newspapers called it "the revolution in southern Russia" and offered fantastic stories about Pugachev's life history. Finally, the army captured the rebel leader and brought him in an iron cage to Moscow, where he was tortured and executed. In the aftermath, Catherine tightened the nobles' control over their serfs with the Charter of the Nobility and harshly punished those who dared to criticize serfdom.

The Pugachev Rebellion, 1773

Public Opinion and Political Opposition

Peasant uprisings might briefly shake even a powerful monarchy, but the rise of public opinion as a force independent of court society caused more enduring changes in European politics. Across much of Europe and in the North American colonies, demands for broader political participation reflected Enlightenment notions about individual rights. Aristocratic bodies such as the French parlements, which had no legislative role like that of the British Parliament, insisted that the monarch consult them on the nation's affairs, and the new educated elite wanted more influence, too. Newspapers began to cover daily political affairs, and the public learned the basics of political life, despite the strict limits on political participation in most countries. Monarchs turned to public opinion to seek support against aristocratic groups that opposed reform. Gustavus III of Sweden (r. 1771–1792) called himself "the first citizen of a free people" and promised to deliver the country from "insufferable aristocratic despotism." Shortly after com-

A Cossack

Emelian Pugachev and many of his followers were Cossacks, Ukrainians who set up nomadic communities of horsemen to resist outside control, whether from Turks, Poles, or Russians. This eighteenth-century painting captures the common view of Cossacks as horsemen always ready for battle but with a fondness for music, too. *(© Odessa Fine Arts Museum, Ukraine/The Bridgeman Art Library International.)*

Pugachev (poo guh CHAWF) rebellion: A massive revolt of Russian Cossacks and serfs in 1773 against local nobles and the armies of Catherine the Great; its leader, Emelian Pugachev, was eventually captured and executed.

ing to the throne, Gustavus proclaimed a new constitution that divided power between the king and the legislature, abolished the use of torture in the judicial process, and assured some freedom of the press.

The Wilkes affair in Great Britain showed that public opinion could be mobilized to challenge a government. In 1763, during the reign of George III (r. 1760–1820), John Wilkes, a member of Parliament, attacked the government in his newspaper, *North Briton*, and sued the crown when he was arrested. He won his release as well as damages. When he was reelected, Parliament denied him his seat, not once but three times.

The Wilkes episode soon escalated into a major campaign against the corruption and social exclusiveness of Parliament, complaints the Levellers had first raised during the English Revolution of the late 1640s. Newspapers, magazines, pamphlets, handbills, and cheap editions of Wilkes's collected works all helped promote his cause. Those who could not vote demonstrated for Wilkes. In one incident eleven people died when soldiers broke up a huge gathering of his supporters. The slogan "Wilkes and Liberty" appeared on walls all over London. Middle-class voters formed the Society of Supporters of the Bill of Rights, which circulated petitions for Wilkes; they gained the support of about one-fourth of all the voters. The more determined Wilkesites proposed sweeping reforms of Parliament, including more frequent elections, more representation for the counties, elimination of "rotten boroughs" (election districts so small that they could be controlled by one big patron), and restrictions of pensions used by the crown to gain support. These demands would be at the heart of agitation for parliamentary reform in Britain for decades to come.

Popular demonstrations did not always support reforms. In 1780, the Gordon riots devastated London. They were named after the fanatical anti-Catholic crusader Lord George Gordon, who helped organize huge marches and petition campaigns against a bill the House of Commons passed to grant limited toleration to Catholics. The demonstrations culminated in a seven-day riot that left fifty buildings destroyed and three hundred people dead. Despite the continuing limitation on voting rights in Great Britain, British politicians were learning that they could ignore public opinion only at their peril.

Political opposition also took artistic forms, particularly in countries where governments restricted organized political activity. A striking example of a play with a political message was *The Marriage of Figaro* (1784) by Pierre-Augustin Caron de Beaumarchais (1732–1799), who at one time or another worked as a watchmaker, a judge, a gunrunner in the American War of Independence, and a French spy in Britain. *The Marriage of Figaro* was first a hit at the French court, when Queen Marie-Antoinette had it read for her friends. But when her husband, Louis XVI, read it, he forbade its production on the grounds that "this man mocks at everything that should be respected in government." When finally performed publicly, the play caused a sensation. The chief character, Figaro, is a clever servant who gets the better of his noble employer. When speaking of the count, he cries, "What have you done to deserve so many rewards? You went to the trouble of being born, and nothing more." Two years later, Mozart based an equally famous but somewhat tamer opera on Beaumarchais's story. Looking back, Napoleon would say that the play was the "revolution in action."

Revolution in North America

Oppositional forms of public opinion came to a head in Great Britain's North American colonies, where the result was American independence and the establishment of a republican constitution that stood in stark contrast to most European regimes. Many Europeans saw the American War of Independence, or the American Revolution, as a triumph for Enlightenment ideas. As one German writer exclaimed in 1777, American victory would give "greater scope to the Enlightenment, new keenness to the thinking of peoples and new life to the spirit of liberty."

The American revolutionary leaders had been influenced by a common Atlantic civilization; they participated in the Enlightenment and shared political ideas with the opposition Whigs in Britain. Supporters demonstrated for Wilkes in South Carolina and Boston, and the South Carolina legislature donated a substantial sum to the Society of Supporters of the Bill of Rights. In the 1760s and 1770s, both British and American opposition leaders became convinced that the British government was growing increasingly corrupt and despotic. British radicals wanted to reform Parliament so that the voices of a broader, more representative segment of the population would be heard. The colonies had no representatives in Parliament, and colonists claimed that "no taxation without representation" should be allowed. Indeed, they denied that Parliament had any jurisdiction over the colonies, insisting that the king govern them through colonial legislatures and recognize their traditional British liberties. The failure of the "Wilkes and Liberty" campaign to produce concrete results convinced many Americans that Parliament was hopelessly tainted and that they

DOCUMENT

Thomas Jefferson, Declaration of Independence (July 4, 1776)

Although others helped revise the Declaration of Independence of the thirteen North American colonies from Great Britain, Jefferson wrote the original draft himself. A Virginia planter and lawyer, Jefferson went on to become governor of Virginia, minister to France, secretary of state, vice president, and president of the United States (1801–1809). The Declaration begins with a stirring expression of the belief in natural or human rights.

When in the Course of human events, it becomes necessary for one people to dissolve the political bands which have connected them with another, and to assume among the powers of the earth, the separate and equal station to which the Laws of Nature and of Nature's God entitle them, a decent respect to the opinions of mankind requires that they should declare the causes which impel them to the separation.

We hold these truths to be self-evident, that all men are created equal, that they are endowed by their Creator with certain unalienable Rights, that among these are Life, Liberty and the pursuit of Happiness.—That to secure these rights, Governments are instituted among Men, deriving their just powers from the consent of the governed,—That whenever any Form of Government becomes destructive of these ends, it is the Right of the People to alter or to abolish it, and to institute new Government, laying its foundation on such principles and organizing its powers in such form, as to them shall seem most likely to effect their Safety and Happiness. Prudence, indeed, will dictate that Governments long established should not be changed for light and transient causes; and accordingly all experience hath shewn, that mankind are more disposed to suffer, while evils are sufferable, than to right themselves by abolishing the forms to which they are accustomed. But when a long train of abuses and usurpations, pursuing invariably the same Object evinces a design to reduce them under absolute Despotism, it is their right, it is their duty, to throw off such Government, and to provide new Guards for their future security.—Such has been the patient sufferance of these Colonies; and such is now the necessity which constrains them to alter their former Systems of Government. The history of the present King of Great Britain is a history of repeated injuries and usurpations, all having in direct object the establishment of an absolute Tyranny over these States.

Source: U.S. National Archives and Records Administration, Washington, D.C.

Question for Consideration

- **In what ways does the Declaration of Independence express the ideas of the Enlightenment?**

would have to stand up for their rights as British subjects.

The British colonies remained loyal to the crown until Parliament's encroachment on their autonomy and the elimination of the French threat at the end of the Seven Years' War transformed colonial attitudes. Unconsciously, perhaps, the colonies had begun to form a separate nation; their economies generally flourished in the eighteenth century, and between 1750 and 1776 their population almost doubled. With the British clamoring for lower taxes and the colonists paying only a fraction of the tax rate paid by the Britons at home, Parliament passed new taxes, including the Stamp Act in 1765, which required a special tax stamp on all legal documents and publications. After violent rioting in the colonies, the British repealed the tax, but in 1773 the new Tea Act revived colonial resistance, which culminated in the so-called Boston Tea Party of 1773. Colonists dressed as Indians boarded British ships and dumped the imported tea (by this time an enormously popular beverage) into Boston's harbor.

Political opposition in the American colonies turned belligerent when Britain threatened to use force to maintain control. In 1774, the First Continental Congress convened, composed of delegates from the colonies, and unsuccessfully petitioned the crown for redress. The next year the Second Continental Congress organized an army with George Washington in command. After actual fighting had begun, in 1776, the congress issued the Declaration of Independence. An eloquent statement of the American cause written by the Virginia planter and lawyer Thomas Jefferson, the Declaration of Independence was couched in the language of universal human rights, which enlightened Europeans could be expected to understand. (See Document, "Declaration of Independence," above.) George III denounced the American "traitors and rebels." But European newspapers enthusiastically reported on every American response to "the cruel acts of oppression they have been made to suffer." In 1778, France boosted the American cause by entering on the colonists' side. Spain, too, saw an opportunity to

Resistance to British Rule

To demonstrate their resistance to the 1765 Stamp Act, Boston citizens tar and feather a tax collector. The Stamp Act is nailed upside-down to a tree. *(Private Collection/Peter Newark Pictures/The Bridgeman Art Library International.)*

check the growing power of Britain, though without actually endorsing American independence out of fear of the response of its Latin American colonies. Spain declared war on Britain in 1779; in 1780, Great Britain declared war on the Dutch Republic in retaliation for Dutch support of the rebels. The worldwide conflict that resulted was more than Britain could handle. The American colonies achieved their independence in the peace treaty of 1783.

The newly independent states still faced the challenge of republican self-government. The Articles of Confederation, drawn up in 1777 as a provisional constitution, proved weak because they gave the central government few powers. In 1787, a constitutional convention met in Philadelphia to draft a new constitution. It established a two-house legislature, an indirectly elected president, and an independent judiciary. The U.S. Constitution's preamble insisted explicitly, for the first time in history, that government derived its power solely from the people and did not depend on divine right or on the tradition of royalty or aristocracy. The new educated elite of the eighteenth century had now created government based on a "social contract" among male, property-owning, white citizens. It was by no means a complete democracy (women and slaves were excluded from political participation), but the new government represented a radical departure from European models. In 1791, the Bill of Rights was appended to the Constitution outlining the essential rights (such as freedom of speech) that the government could never overturn. Although slavery continued in the American republic, the new emphasis on rights helped fuel the movement for its abolition in both Britain and the United States.

Interest in the new republic was greatest in France. The U.S. Constitution and various state constitutions were published in French with commentary by leading thinkers. Even more important in the long run were the effects of the American war. Dutch losses to Great Britain aroused a widespread movement for political reform in the Dutch Republic, and debts incurred by France in supporting the American colonies would soon force the French monarchy to the edge of bankruptcy and then to revolution. Ultimately, the entire European system of royal rule would be challenged.

REVIEW QUESTION Why did public opinion become a new factor in politics in the second half of the eighteenth century?

Conclusion

When Thomas Jefferson looked back many years later on the Declaration of Independence, he said he hoped it would be "the signal of arousing men to burst the chains under which monkish ignorance

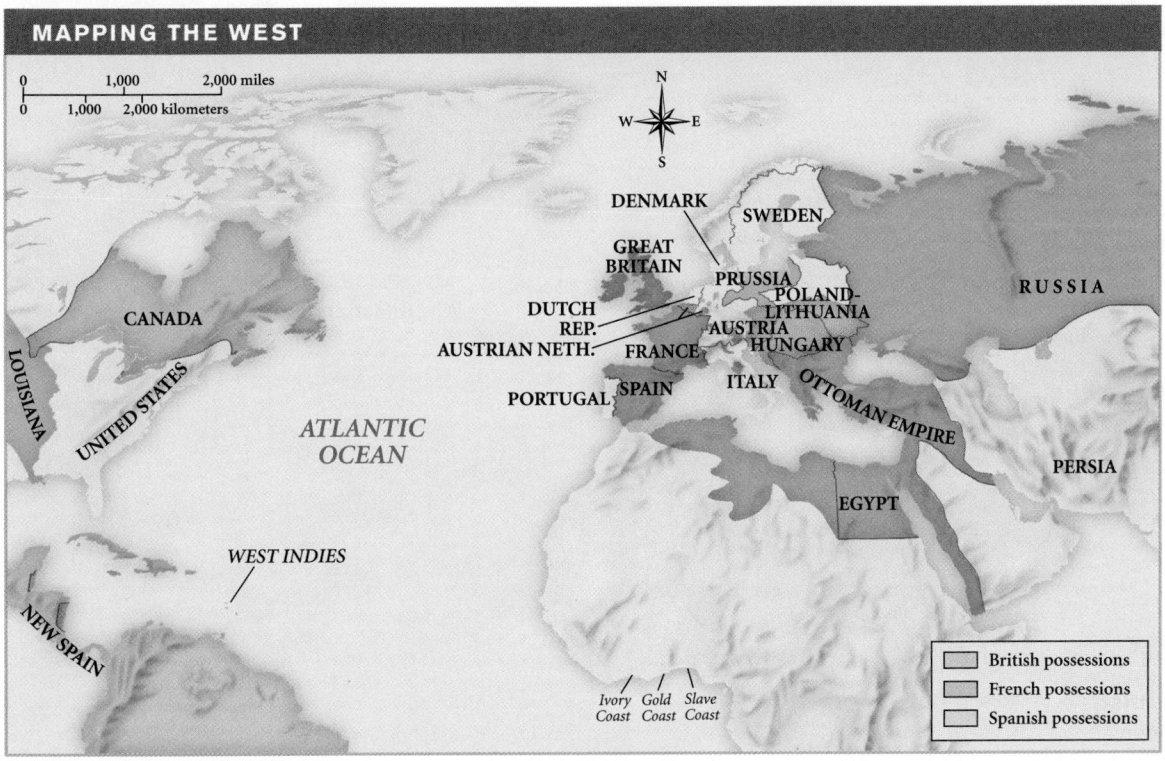

Europe and the World, c. 1780

Although Great Britain lost control over part of its North American colonies, which became the new United States, European influence on the rest of the world grew dramatically in the eighteenth century. The slave trade linked European ports to African slave-trading outposts and to plantations in the Caribbean, South America, and North America. The European countries on the Atlantic Ocean benefited most from this trade. Yet almost all of Africa, China, Japan, and large parts of India still resisted European incursion, and the Ottoman Empire, with its massive territories, still presented Europe with a formidable military challenge.

and superstition had persuaded them to bind themselves." What began as a cosmopolitan movement of a few intellectuals in the first half of the eighteenth century had reached a relatively wide audience among the educated elite of men and women by the 1770s and 1780s. The spirit of Enlightenment swept from the salons, coffeehouses, and Masonic lodges into the halls of government from Philadelphia to Vienna. Scientific inquiry into the causes of social misery and laws defending individual rights and freedoms gained adherents even among the rulers and ministers responsible for censoring Enlightenment works.

For most Europeans, however, the promise of the Enlightenment did not become a reality. Rulers such as Catherine the Great had every intention of retaining their full, often unchecked, powers, even as they corresponded with leading philosophes and entertained them at their courts. Moreover, would-be reformers often found themselves blocked by the resistance of nobles, by the priorities rulers gave to waging wars, or by popular resistance to deregulation of trade that increased the uncertainties of the market. Yet even the failure of reform contributed to the ferment in Europe after 1770. Peasant rebellions in eastern Europe, the "Wilkes and Liberty" campaign in Great Britain, the struggle over reform in France, and the revolution in America all occurred around the same time, and their conjunction convinced many Europeans that change was brewing. Just how much could change, and whether change made life better or worse, would come into question in the next ten years.

FOR FURTHER EXPLORATION

- **For additional primary-source material from this period**, see *Sources of the Making of the West*, Fourth Edition.
- **For Web sites, images, and documents related to topics in this chapter**, visit *Make History* at bedfordstmartins.com/hunt.

Chapter 18 Review

Online Study Guide bedfordstmartins.com/hunt

Key Terms and People

In the grid below, identify the term or person and explain its historical significance. (To do this exercise online, go to bedfordstmartins.com/hunt.)

Term	Who or What & When	Why It Matters
philosophes (p. 588)		
deists (p. 591)		
abolitionists (p. 592)		
laissez-faire (p. 593)		
Jean-Jacques Rousseau (p. 594)		
romanticism (p. 598)		
Methodism (p. 598)		
Freemasons (p. 600)		
enlightened despots (p. 605)		
Seven Years' War (p. 605)		
partition of Poland (p. 607)		
Pugachev rebellion (p. 611)		

Review Questions

1. What were the major differences between the Enlightenment in France, Great Britain, and the German states?
2. What were the major differences in the impact of the Enlightenment on the nobility, the middle classes, and the lower classes?
3. What prompted enlightened absolutists to undertake reforms in the second half of the eighteenth century?
4. Why did public opinion become a new factor in politics in the second half of the eighteenth century?

Making Connections

1. Why would rulers feel ambivalent about the Enlightenment, supporting reform on the one hand, while clamping down on political dissidents on the other hand?
2. Which major developments in this period ran counter to the influence of the Enlightenment?
3. In what ways had politics changed, and in what ways did they remain the same during the Enlightenment?
4. Explain how Catherine the Great of Russia could be taken as a symbol of both the promise and the limitations of the Enlightenment.

Important Events

Date	Event	Date	Event
1751–1772	*Encyclopedia* published in France	1775	Flour War in France
1756–1763	Seven Years' War fought in Europe, India, and the American colonies	1776	American Declaration of Independence from Great Britain; Adam Smith, *The Wealth of Nations*
1762	Jean-Jacques Rousseau, *The Social Contract* and *Émile*	1780	Joseph II of Austria undertakes a wide-reaching reform program
1763	Wilkes affair begins in Great Britain	1781	Immanuel Kant, *The Critique of Pure Reason*
1764	Voltaire, *Philosophical Dictionary*	1784	Pierre-Augustin Caron de Beaumarchais, *The Marriage of Figaro*
1771	Louis XV of France fails to break power of French law courts	1785	Catherine the Great's Charter of the Nobility grants nobles exclusive control over their serfs in exchange for subservience to the state
1772	First partition of Poland	1787	Delegates from the states draft the U.S. Constitution
1773	Pugachev rebellion of Russian peasants		

- Consider three events: ***Encyclopedia* published in France (1751–1772)**, **Wilkes affair begins in Great Britain (1763)**, and **American Declaration of Independence from Great Britain (1776)**. In what ways did the same Enlightenment ideals inform these events?

SUGGESTED REFERENCES

Gay's interpretive study of the Enlightenment remains useful, but the Kors volumes offer the most up-to-date views on the Enlightenment. Readers can find different perspectives in studies of individual rulers, their routes to power, and their reactions to the Enlightenment.

Beales, Derek. *Joseph II: In the Shadow of Maria Theresa: 1741–1780.* 2008.

Cash, Arthur H. *John Wilkes: The Scandalous Father of Civil Liberty.* 2006.

Catherine the Great: http://russia.nypl.org/home.html

Gay, Peter. *The Enlightenment: An Interpretation.* 2 vols. 1966, 1969.

Kors, Alan Charles, ed. *Encyclopedia of the Enlightenment.* 4 vols. 2003.

*Lessing, Gotthold Ephraim. *Nathan the Wise.* Ed. Ronald Schechter. 2004.

Mozart Project: http://www.mozartproject.org

Rounding, Virginia. *Catherine the Great: Love, Sex, and Power.* 2008.

*Rousseau, Jean-Jacques. *Discourse on the Origin and Foundations of Inequality among Men.* Ed. Helena Rosenblatt. 2011.

Schumann, Matt, and Karl W. Schweizer. *The Seven Years War: A Transatlantic History.* 2008.

Seven Years' War: http://www.historyworld.net/wrldhis/PlainTextHistories.asp?historyid=aa66

Venturi, Franco. *The End of the Old Regime in Europe, 1768–1776: The First Crisis.* Trans. R. Burr Litchfield. 1989.

Wilson, Peter H. *A Companion to Eighteenth-Century Europe.* 2008.

*Primary source.

CHAPTER

The Cataclysm of Revolution

19

1789–1799

On October 5, 1789, a crowd of several thousand women marched in a drenching rain from the center of Paris to Versailles, a distance of twelve miles. They demanded the king's help in securing more grain for the hungry and his reassurance that he did not intend to resist the emerging revolutionary movement. Joined the next morning by thousands of men who came from Paris to reinforce them, they broke into the royal family's private apartments, killing two of the royal bodyguards. To prevent further bloodshed, the king agreed to move his family and his government to Paris. A dramatic procession of the royal family guarded by throngs of ordinary men and women made its slow way back to the capital. The people's proud display of cannons and pikes underlined the fundamental transformation that was occurring. Ordinary people had forced the king of France to respond to their grievances. The French monarchy was in danger, and if such a powerful and long-lasting institution could come under fire, then could any monarch of Europe rest easy?

Although even the keenest political observer did not predict its eruption in 1789, the French Revolution had its immediate origins in a constitutional crisis provoked by a growing government deficit, traceable to French involvement in the American War of Independence. The constitutional crisis had come to a head on July 14, 1789, when armed Parisians captured the Bastille, a royal fortress and symbol of monarchical authority in the center of the capital. The fall of the Bastille, like the women's march to Versailles three months later, showed the determination of the common people to put their mark on events.

The French Revolution first grabbed the attention of the entire world because it seemed to promise universal human rights, constitutional government, and broad-based political participation. Its most famous slogan pledged "Liberty, Equality, and

Women's March to Versailles
Thousands of prints broadcast the events of the French Revolution to the public in France and elsewhere. This colored engraving shows a crowd of armed women marching to Versailles on October 5, 1789, to confront the king. The sight of armed women frightened many observers and demonstrated that the Revolution was not only a men's affair. Note the middle-class woman on the left being forced to join with the others. *(The Granger Collection, New York—All rights reserved.)*

The Revolutionary Wave, 1787–1789 620
- Protesters in the Low Countries and Poland
- Origins of the French Revolution, 1787–1789

From Monarchy to Republic, 1789–1793 626
- The Revolution of Rights and Reason
- The End of Monarchy

Terror and Resistance 631
- Robespierre and the Committee of Public Safety
- The Republic of Virtue, 1793–1794
- Resisting the Revolution
- The Fall of Robespierre and the End of the Terror

Revolution on the March 638
- Arms and Conquests
- Poland Extinguished, 1793–1795
- Revolution in the Colonies
- Worldwide Reactions to Revolutionary Change

Fraternity" for all. An enthusiastic German wrote, "One of the greatest nations in the world, the greatest in general culture, has at last thrown off the yoke of tyranny." The revolutionaries used a blueprint based on the Enlightenment idea of reason to remake all of society and politics: they executed the king and queen, established a republic for the first time in French history, abolished the nobility, and gave the vote to all adult men.

Even as the Revolution promised democracy, however, it also inaugurated a cycle of violence and intimidation. When the revolutionaries encountered resistance to their programs, they set up a government of terror to compel obedience. Some historians therefore see in the French Revolution the origins of modern totalitarianism—that is, governments that try to control every aspect of life, including daily activities, while limiting all forms of political dissent. As events unfolded after 1789, the French Revolution became the model of modern revolution; republicanism, democracy, terrorism, nationalism, and military dictatorship all took their modern forms during the French Revolution.

The Revolution might have remained a strictly French affair if war had not involved the rest of Europe. After 1792, huge French republican armies, fueled by patriotic nationalism, marched across Europe, promising liberation from traditional monarchies but often delivering old-fashioned conquest and annexation. French victories spread revolutionary ideas far and wide, from Poland to the colonies in the Caribbean, where the first successful slave revolt established the republic of Haiti.

The breathtaking succession of regimes in France between 1789 and 1799 and the failure of the republican experiment after ten years of upheaval raised disturbing questions about the relationship between rapid political change and violence: Do all revolutions inevitably degenerate into terror or wars of conquest? Is a regime democratic if it does not allow poor men, women, or blacks to vote? Such questions resonated in many countries because the French Revolution seemed to be only the most extreme example of a much broader political and social movement at the end of the eighteenth century.

CHAPTER FOCUS What was so revolutionary about the French Revolution?

The Revolutionary Wave, 1787–1789

Between 1787 and 1789, revolts in the name of liberty broke out in the Dutch Republic, the Austrian Netherlands (present-day Belgium and Luxembourg), and Poland as well as in France. At the same time, the newly independent United States of America was preparing a new federal constitution. Historians have sometimes referred to these revolts as the Atlantic revolutions because so many protest movements arose in countries on both shores of the North Atlantic. These revolutions were the product of long-term prosperity and high expectations, created in part by the spread of the Enlightenment. Europeans in general were wealthier, healthier, more numerous, and better educated than they had ever been before; and the Dutch, Belgian, and French societies were among the wealthiest and best educated within Europe. The French Revolution nonetheless differed greatly from the others. Not only was France the richest, most powerful, and most populous state in western Europe, but its revolution was also more violent, more long-lasting, and ultimately more influential. (See "Terms of History," page 621.)

Protesters in the Low Countries and Poland

Political protests in the Dutch Republic attracted European attention because Dutch banks still controlled a hefty portion of the world's capital at the

1787 Dutch Patriot revolt stifled by Prussian invasion

1788 Beginning of Austrian Netherlands resistance against reforms of Joseph II; opening of reform parliament in Poland

1789 French Revolution begins

1790 Internal divisions lead to collapse of resistance in Austrian Netherlands

1791 Beginning of slave revolt in St. Domingue (Haiti)

1787 1789 1791

TERMS OF HISTORY

Revolution

Revolution had previously meant cyclical change that brought life back to a starting point, as a planet makes a revolution around the sun. Revolutions could come and go, by this definition, and change nothing fundamental in the structure of society. After 1789, *revolution* came to mean a self-conscious attempt to leap into the future by reshaping society and politics and even the human personality. A revolutionary official analyzed the meaning of the word in 1793: "A revolution is never made by halves; it must either be total or it will abort. . . . *Revolutionary* means outside of all forms and all rules." In short, *revolution* soon had an all-or-nothing meaning; you were either for the revolution or against it. There could be no in between.

Revolution still has the same meaning given it by the French revolutionaries, but it is now an even more contested term because of its association with communist theory. In the nineteenth century, Karl Marx incorporated the French Revolution into his new doctrine of communism. In his view, the middle-class French revolutionaries had overthrown the monarchy and the "feudal" aristocracy to pave the way for capitalist development. In the future, the proletariat (industrial workers) would overthrow the capitalist middle class to install a communist government that would abolish private property. Since Marxists claimed the French Revolution as the forerunner of the communist revolution in the nineteenth and twentieth centuries, it was perhaps inevitable that those who opposed communism would also criticize the French Revolution.

The most influential example of this view is that of the French scholar François Furet. An ex-communist, Furet argued that the French Revolution can be seen as the origin of totalitarianism because it incarnated what Furet calls "the illusion of politics," that is, the belief that people can transform social and economic relationships through political revolution. The French revolutionaries became totalitarian, in Furet's view, because they wanted to establish a kind of political and social utopia (a perfect society), in which reason alone determined the shape of political and social life. Because this dream is impossible given human resistance to rapid change, the revolutionaries had to use force to achieve their goals. In other words, revolution itself was a problematic idea, according to Furet. *Revolution* as a term remains as contested as the events that gave rise to it.

end of the eighteenth century, even though the Dutch Republic's role in international politics had diminished. Revolts also broke out in the neighboring Austrian Netherlands and Poland. Although none of these movements ultimately succeeded, they showed how quickly political discontent could boil over in this era of rising economic and political expectations.

The Dutch Patriot Revolt, 1787

The Dutch Patriots, as they called themselves, wanted to reduce the powers of the prince of Orange, the kinglike stadholder who favored close ties with Great Britain. Government-sponsored Dutch banks owned 40 percent of the British national debt, and by 1796 they held the entire foreign debt of the United States. Relations with the British deteriorated during the American War of Independence, however, and by the middle of the 1780s, agitation in favor of the Americans had boiled over into an attack on the stadholder.

Building on support among middle-class bankers and merchants, the Dutch Patriots soon gained a more popular audience by demanding

1792
Beginning of war between France and rest of Europe; second revolution of August 10 overthrows monarchy

1794
Abolition of slavery in French colonies; Robespierre's government by terror falls

1797–1798
Creation of "sister republics" in Italian states and Switzerland

1793 1795 1797

1793
Second partition of Poland by Austria and Russia; Louis XVI of France executed for treason

1795
Third (final) partition of Poland; France annexes Austrian Netherlands

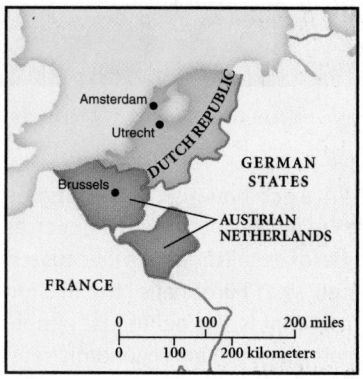

The Low Countries in 1787

political reforms and organizing armed citizen militias of men, called Free Corps. Town by town the Patriots forced local officials to set up new elections to replace councils that had been packed with Orangist supporters through patronage or family connections. Before long, the Free Corps took on the troops of the prince of Orange and got the upper hand. In response, Frederick William II of Prussia, whose sister had married the stadholder, intervened in 1787 with tacit British support. Thousands of Prussian troops soon occupied Utrecht and Amsterdam, and the house of Orange regained its former position.

Social divisions among the rebels paved the way for the success of this outside intervention. Many of the Patriots from the richest merchant families feared the growing power of the Free Corps. The Free Corps wanted a more democratic form of government, and to get it they encouraged the publication of pamphlets and cartoons attacking the prince and his wife, promoted the rapid spread of clubs and societies made up of common people, and organized crowd-pleasing public ceremonies, such as parades and bonfires, that sometimes turned into riots. In the aftermath of the Prussian invasion in September 1787, the Orangists got their revenge: lower-class mobs pillaged the houses of prosperous Dutch Patriot leaders, forcing many to flee to the United States, France, or the Austrian Netherlands. Those Patriots who remained nursed their grievances until the French republican armies invaded in 1795.

The Belgian Independence Movement If Austrian emperor Joseph II had not tried to introduce Enlightenment-inspired reforms, the Belgians of the ten provinces of the Austrian Netherlands might have remained tranquil. Just as he had done previously in his own crown lands (see Chapter 18), Joseph abolished torture, decreed toleration for Jews and Protestants (in this resolutely Catholic area), and suppressed monasteries. His reorganization of the administrative and judicial systems eliminated many offices that belonged to nobles and lawyers, sparking resistance among the upper classes in 1788.

Upper-class protesters intended only to defend historic local liberties against an overbearing government. Nonetheless, their resistance galvanized democrats, who wanted a more representative government and organized clubs to give voice to their demands. At the end of 1788, a secret society formed armed companies to prepare an uprising. By late 1789, each province had separately declared its independence, and the Austrian administration had collapsed. Delegates from the various provinces declared themselves the United States of Belgium, a clear reference to the American precedent.

Once again, however, social divisions doomed the rebels. When the democrats began to challenge noble authority, aristocratic leaders drew to their side the Catholic clergy and peasants, who had little sympathy for the democrats of the cities. Every Sunday in May and June 1790, thousands of peasant men and women, led by their priests, streamed into Brussels carrying crucifixes, nooses, and pitchforks to intimidate the democrats and defend the church. Faced with the choice between the Austrian emperor and "our current tyrants," the democrats chose to support the return of the Austrians under Emperor Leopold II (r. 1790–1792), who had succeeded his brother.

Polish Patriots A reform party calling itself the Patriots also emerged in Poland, which had been shocked by the loss of a third of its territory in the first partition of 1772. The Patriots sought to overhaul the weak commonwealth along modern western European lines and looked to King Stanislaw August Poniatowski (r. 1764–1795) to lead them. A nobleman who owed his crown solely to the dubious honor of being Catherine the Great's discarded lover but who was also a favorite correspondent of the Parisian salon hostess Madame Geoffrin, Poniatowski saw in moderate reform the only chance for his country to escape the consequences of a century's misgovernment and cultural decline. Ranged against the Patriots stood most of the aristocrats and the formidable Catherine the Great, determined to uphold imperial Russian influence.

Pleased to see Russian influence waning in Poland, Austria and Prussia allowed the reform movement to proceed. In 1788, the Patriots got their golden chance. Bogged down in war with the Ottoman Turks, Catherine could not block the summoning of a reform-minded parliament, which eventually enacted the constitution of May 3, 1791. It established a hereditary monarchy with somewhat strengthened authority, ended the veto power that each aristocrat had over legislation, granted townspeople limited political rights, and vaguely promised future Jewish emancipation. Abolishing serfdom was hardly mentioned. Within a year, however, Catherine II had turned her attention to Poland and engineered the downfall of the Patriots.

Origins of the French Revolution, 1787–1789

Many French enthusiastically greeted the American experiment in republican government and supported the Dutch, Belgian, and Polish Patriots. But they did not expect the United States and the Dutch Republic to provide them a model. Montesquieu and Rousseau, the leading political theorists of the Enlightenment, taught that republics suited only small countries, not big ones like France. After suffering humiliation at the hands of the British in the Seven Years' War (1756–1763), the French had regained international prestige by supporting the victorious Americans, and the monarchy had shown its eagerness to promote reforms. In 1787, for example, the French crown granted civil rights to Protestants. Yet by the late 1780s, the French monarchy faced a serious fiscal crisis caused by a mounting deficit. The fiscal crisis soon provoked a constitutional crisis of epic proportions.

Fiscal Crisis France's fiscal problems stemmed from the nation's support of the Americans against the British in the American War of Independence. About half of the French national budget went to paying interest on the debt that had accumulated. In contrast to Great Britain, which had a national bank to help raise loans for the government, the French government lived off relatively short-term, high-interest loans from private sources including Swiss banks, government annuities, and advances from tax collectors.

For years the French government had been trying unsuccessfully to modernize the tax system to make it more equitable. The peasants bore the greatest burden of taxes, whereas the nobles and clergy were largely exempt from them. Tax collection was also far from systematic: private contractors collected many taxes and pocketed a large share of the proceeds. With the growing support of public opinion, the bond and annuity holders from the middle and upper classes now demanded a clearer system of fiscal accountability.

In a monarchy, the ruler's character is always crucial. Many complained that **Louis XVI** (r. 1774–1792) showed more interest in hunting or in his hobby of making locks than in the problems of government. His wife, **Marie-Antoinette**, was blond, beautiful, and much criticized for her extravagant taste in clothes, elaborate hairdos, and supposed indifference to popular misery. It was reported that, when told the poor had no bread, the queen gave a reply that has come to epitomize oblivious coldheartedness: "Let them eat cake." "The Austrian bitch," as underground writers called her, had been the target of an increasingly nasty pamphlet campaign in the 1780s. By 1789, Marie-Antoinette had become an object of popular hatred. The king's ineffectiveness and the queen's growing unpopularity helped undermine the monarchy as an institution.

Faced with a mounting deficit, in 1787 Louis submitted a package of reforms to the Assembly of Notables, a group of handpicked nobles, clergymen, and officials. When this group refused to endorse his program, the king presented his proposals for a more uniform land tax to his old rival the parlement

Queen Marie-Antoinette (detail)
Marie-Louise-Élizabeth Vigée-Lebrun painted this portrait of the French queen Marie-Antoinette and her children in 1788. The queen appears in the most stylish and lavish fashions of the day. When her eldest son (not shown in this detail) died in 1789, her second son (on her lap here) became heir to the throne. Known to supporters of the monarch as Louis XVII, the child died in prison in 1795 and never ruled. Vigée-Lebrun fled France in 1789 and returned only in 1805. *(Chateau de Versailles, France/Giraudon/The Bridgeman Art Library International.)*

Louis XVI: French king (r. 1774–1792) who was tried for treason during the French Revolution; he was executed on January 21, 1793.

Marie-Antoinette: Wife of Louis XVI and queen of France who was tried for treason during the French Revolution and executed in October 1793.

of Paris. When it, too, refused, he ordered the parlement judges into exile in the provinces. Overnight, the judges (members of the nobility because of the offices they held) became popular heroes for resisting the king's "tyranny"; in reality, however, the judges, like the notables, wanted reform only on their own terms. Louis finally gave in to demands that he call a meeting of the Estates General, which had last met 175 years before.

The Estates General The calling of the Estates General electrified public opinion. Who would determine the fate of the nation? The **Estates General** was a body of deputies from the three estates, or orders, of France. The deputies in the First Estate represented some 100,000 clergy of the Catholic church, which owned about 10 percent of the land and collected a 10 percent tax (the tithe) on peasants. The deputies of the Second Estate represented the nobility, about 400,000 men and women who owned about 25 percent of the land, enjoyed many tax exemptions, and collected seigneurial dues and rents from their peasant tenants. The deputies of the Third Estate, mostly middle-class lawyers or officials, represented everyone else, at least 95 percent of the nation. Included in the Third Estate were the vast mass of peasants, some 75 percent of the population, and the *sans-culottes* ("without breeches") and middle classes of the cities. The sans-culottes were those who worked with their hands and wore long trousers rather than the knee breeches of the upper classes.

At the last meeting of the Estates General in 1614, each order had deliberated and voted separately. Before the elections to the Estates General in 1789, the king agreed to double the number of deputies for the Third Estate (making those deputies equal in number to the other two orders' combined), but he refused to mandate voting by individual head rather than by order. Voting by order, allowing each order to have one vote, would conserve the traditional powers of the clergy and nobility; voting by head, allowing each deputy one vote, would give the Third Estate an advantage since many clergymen and even some nobles sympathized with the Third Estate.

As the state's censorship apparatus broke down, pamphleteers by the hundreds denounced the traditional privileges of the nobility and clergy and called for voting by head rather than by order. In the most vitriolic of all the pamphlets, *What Is the Third Estate?*, the middle-class *abbé* ("abbot") Emmanuel-Joseph Sieyès charged that the nobility contributed nothing at all to the nation's well-being; they were, he said, "a malignant disease which preys upon and tortures the body of a sick man." In the winter and spring of 1789, villagers and townspeople alike held meetings to elect deputies and write down their grievances. The effect was immediate. Although educated men dominated the meetings at the regional level, the humblest peasants voted in their villages and burst forth with complaints, especially about taxes. As one villager lamented, "The last crust of bread has been taken from us." The long series of meetings raised expectations that the Estates General would help the king solve all the nation's ills.

These new hopes soared just at the moment France experienced an increasingly rare but always dangerous food shortage. Bad weather had damaged the harvest of 1788, causing bread prices to soar in many places in the spring and summer of 1789 and threatening starvation for the poorest people. In addition, a serious slump in textile production had been causing massive unemployment since 1786. Hundreds of thousands of textile workers were out of work and hungry, adding another volatile element to an already tense situation.

When some twelve hundred deputies journeyed to the king's palace of Versailles for the opening of the Estates General in May 1789, many readers avidly followed the developments in newspapers that sprouted overnight. Although most nobles insisted on voting by order, the deputies of the Third Estate refused to proceed on that basis. After six weeks of stalemate, on June 17, 1789, the deputies of the Third Estate took unilateral action and declared themselves and whoever would join them the National Assembly, in which each deputy would vote as an individual. Two days later, the clergy voted by a narrow margin to join them. Suddenly denied access to their meeting hall on June 20, the deputies met on a nearby tennis court and swore an oath not to disband until they had given France a constitution that reflected their newly declared authority. This "tennis court oath" expressed the determination of the Third Estate to carry through a constitutional revolution.

July 14, 1789: The Fall of the Bastille At first, Louis XVI appeared to agree to the new National Assembly, but he also ordered thousands of soldiers to march to Paris. The deputies who supported the Assembly feared a plot by the king and high-ranking nobles to arrest them and disperse the Assembly. "Everyone is convinced that the approach of the troops covers some violent design," one deputy wrote home. Their fears were

Estates General: A body of deputies from the three estates, or orders, of France: the clergy (First Estate), the nobility (Second Estate), and everyone else (Third Estate).

Fall of the Bastille
A central moment from the storming of the Bastille prison on July 14, 1789, is depicted in this colored print of a 1793 painting by Charles Thévenin. The insurgents have won the battle and are arresting the governor of the prison; in the next moments, they will cut off his head and parade it on a pike. The artist expresses his ambivalence about the violence by showing an insurgent in the right foreground brutally killing one of the defenders even though the battle is over. *(Réunion des Musées Nationaux/Art Resource, NY.)*

confirmed when, on July 11, the king fired Jacques Necker, the Swiss Protestant finance minister and the one high official regarded as sympathetic to the deputies' cause.

The popular reaction in Paris to Necker's dismissal and the threat of military force changed the course of the French Revolution. When the news spread, the sans-culottes in Paris began to arm themselves and attack places where either grain or arms were thought to be stored. A deputy in Versailles reported home: "Today all of the evils overwhelm France, and we are between despotism, carnage, and famine." On July 14, 1789, an armed crowd marched on the Bastille, a huge fortified prison that symbolized royal authority even though only a few prisoners were actually incarcerated there. After a chaotic battle in which a hundred armed citizens died, the prison officials surrendered.

The fall of the Bastille (an event now commemorated as the French national holiday) set an important precedent. The common people showed themselves willing to intervene violently at a crucial political moment. (See the illustration above.) All over France, food riots turned into revolts. Local governments were forced out of power and replaced by committees of "patriots" loyal to the revolutionary cause. The king's government began to crumble. To restore order, the patriots relied on newly formed

The Third Estate Awakens
This colored etching, produced after the fall of the Bastille (note the heads on pikes outside the prison), shows a clergyman (First Estate) and a noble (Second Estate) alarmed by the awakening of the commoners (Third Estate). The Third Estate breaks the chains of oppression and arms itself. In what ways does this print draw attention to the social conflicts that lay behind the political struggles in the Estates General? *(Réunion des Musées Nationaux/Art Resource, NY.)*

National Guard units composed of civilians. In Paris, the Marquis de Lafayette, a hero of the American War of Independence and a noble deputy in the National Assembly, became commander of the new National Guard. One of Louis XVI's brothers and many other leading aristocrats fled into exile. The Revolution thus had its first heroes, its first victims, and its first enemies.

REVIEW QUESTION How did the beginning of the French Revolution resemble the other revolutions of 1787–1789?

From Monarchy to Republic, 1789–1793

Until July 1789, the French Revolution followed a course much like that of the protest movements in the Low Countries. After July 1789, however, events in France escalated at a pace never before seen in history, leaving witnesses to them breathless with anticipation, anxiety, even shock. The French revolutionaries first tried to establish a constitutional monarchy based on the Enlightenment principles of human rights and rational government. This effort failed when the king attempted to flee and raise a counterrevolutionary army. When war broke out in 1792 and foreign soldiers invaded, a popular uprising on August 10, 1792, led to the arrest of the king and, for the first time in French history, the establishment of a republic.

The Revolution of Rights and Reason

Before drafting a constitution in 1789, the deputies of the National Assembly had to confront growing violence in the countryside. Most peasants could barely make ends meet but still had to pay taxes to the state, the tithe to the Catholic church, and a host of seigneurial dues to their lords, whether for using the lords' mills to grind wheat or to ensure their ability to give their land as inheritance to their children. As food shortages spread, peasants feared that the beggars and vagrants crowding the roads might be part of an aristocratic plot to starve the people by burning crops or barns. In many places, the **Great Fear** (the term used by historians to describe this rural panic) turned into peasant attacks on aristocrats or on the records of peasants' dues kept in the lord's château. Peasants now refused to pay dues to their lords, and the persistence of peasant violence raised alarms about the potential for a general peasant insurrection.

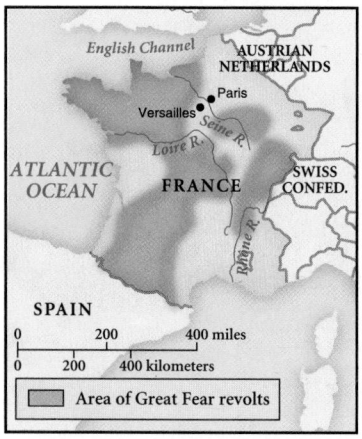

The Great Fear, 1789

The End of Feudalism

Alarmed by peasant unrest, the National Assembly decided to make sweeping changes. On the night of August 4, 1789, noble deputies announced their willingness to give up their tax exemptions and seigneurial dues. By the end of the night, amid wild enthusiasm, dozens of deputies had come to the podium to relinquish the tax exemptions of their own professional groups, towns, or provinces. The National Assembly decreed the abolition of what it called "the feudal regime"—that is, it freed the remaining serfs and eliminated all special privileges in matters of taxation, including all seigneurial dues on land. (A few days later the deputies insisted on financial compensation for some of these dues, but most peasants refused to pay.) Peasants had achieved their goals. The Assembly also mandated equality of opportunity in access to government positions. Talent, rather than birth, was to be the key to success. Enlightenment principles were beginning to become law.

The Declaration of the Rights of Man and Citizen

Three weeks later, the deputies to the National Assembly drew up the **Declaration of the Rights of Man and Citizen** as the preamble to a new constitution. In words reminiscent of the American Declaration of Independence, whose author, Thomas Jefferson, was in Paris at the time, it proclaimed, "Men are born and remain free and equal in rights." The Declaration granted freedom of religion, freedom of the press, equality of taxation, and equality before the law. It established the principle of national sovereignty: since "all sovereignty rests essentially in the nation," it said, the king derived his authority henceforth

Great Fear: The term used by historians to describe the French rural panic of 1789, which led to peasant attacks on aristocrats or on seigneurial records of peasants' dues.

Declaration of the Rights of Man and Citizen: The preamble to the French constitution drafted in August 1789; it established the sovereignty of the nation and equal rights for citizens.

DOCUMENT

The Rights of Minorities (1789)

When the National Assembly passed the Declaration of the Rights of Man and Citizen on August 26, 1789, it opened the way to discussion of the rights of various groups, from actors (considered ineligible for voting under the monarchy because they impersonated other people as part of their profession) to women, free blacks, mulattoes, and slaves. Count Stanislas de Clermont-Tonnerre, a nobleman and freemason, gave a speech on December 23, 1789, in which he advocated ending exclusions based on profession or religion, though not on gender or race. He was killed in the uprising of August 10, 1792, because he supported the monarchy.

Sirs, in the declaration that you believed you should put at the head of the French constitution you have established, consecrated, the rights of man and citizen. In the constitutional work that you have decreed relative to the organization of the municipalities, a work accepted by the King, you have fixed the conditions of eligibility that can be required of citizens. It would seem, Sirs, that there is nothing else left to do and that prejudices should be silent in the face of the language of the law; but an honorable member has explained to us that the *non-Catholics* of some provinces still experience harassment based on former laws, and seeing them excluded from the elections and public posts, another honorable member has protested against the effect of prejudice that persecutes some professions. This prejudice, these laws, force you to make your position clear. I have the honor to present you with the draft of a decree, and it is this draft that I defend here. I establish in it the principle that professions and religious creed can never become reasons for ineligibility. . . .

Every creed has only one test to pass in regard to the social body: it has only one examination to which it must submit, that of its morals. It is here that the adversaries of the Jewish people attack me. This people, they say, is not sociable. They are commanded to loan at usurious rates; they cannot be joined with us either in marriage or by the bonds of social interchange; our food is forbidden to them; our tables prohibited; our armies will never have Jews serving in the defense of the fatherland. The worst of these reproaches is unjust; the others are only specious. Usury is not commanded by their laws; loans at interest are forbidden between them and permitted with foreigners. . . .

But, they say to me, the Jews have their own judges and laws. I respond that is your fault and you should not allow it. We must refuse everything to the Jews as a nation and accord everything to Jews as individuals. We must withdraw recognition from their judges; they should only have our judges. We must refuse legal protection to the maintenance of the so-called laws of their Judaic organization; they should not be allowed to form in the state either a political body or an order. They must be citizens individually. But, some will say to me, they do not want to be citizens. Well then! If they do not want to be citizens, they should say so, and then, we should banish them. It is repugnant to have in the state an association of non-citizens, and a nation within the nation. . . . In short, Sirs, the presumed status of every man resident in a country is to be a citizen.

Source: *Archives parlementaires* 10 (Paris, 1878): 754–57. Translation by Lynn Hunt.

Question to Consider

- **To what extent is this speech in defense of minority rights a reflection of the revolutionary spirit?**

from the nation rather than from tradition or divine right.

By pronouncing all *men* free and equal, the Declaration immediately created new dilemmas. Did women have equal rights with men? What about free blacks in the colonies? How could slavery be justified if all men were born free? Did religious toleration of Protestants and Jews include equal political rights? Women never received the right to vote during the French Revolution, though Protestant and Jewish men did. Women were theoretically citizens under civil law but without the right to full political participation. (See Document, "The Rights of Minorities," above.)

Some women did not accept their exclusion, viewing it as a betrayal of the promised new order. In addition to joining demonstrations, such as the march to Versailles in October 1789 (see chapter opener), women wrote petitions, published tracts, and organized political clubs to demand more participation (see the illustration on page 628). In her Declaration of the Rights of Women of 1791, writer and political activist Olympe de Gouges (1748–1793) played on the language of the official Declaration to make the point that women should also be included. She announced in Article I, "Woman is born free and lives equal to man in her rights." She also insisted that since "woman has the right to mount the scaffold," she must "equally have the right to mount the rostrum." De Gouges linked her complaints to a program of social reform in which women would have equal rights to property and public office and equal responsibilities in taxes and criminal punishment.

A Women's Club

In this gouache by the Lesueur brothers, *The Patriotic Women's Club*, the club president urges the members to contribute funds for poor patriot families. Women's clubs focused on philanthropic work but also discussed revolutionary legislation. The colorful but sober dress indicates that the women are of the middle class. *(Snark/Art Resource, NY.)*

The Constitution and the Church

Unresponsive to calls for women's equality, the National Assembly turned to preparing France's first written constitution. As debates in the Assembly revealed deep political divisions, the deputies began to use terms—*left* and *right*—that would have an impact on political discussion to this day. The left—those who favored more far-reaching changes—sat on the left-hand side of the speaker's podium; the right—those who wanted to conserve elements of the old order and slow the pace of change—sat on the right-hand side. Left and right were evenly balanced in 1789, but left-wing politicians became increasingly prominent over time. The deputies gave voting rights only to white men who passed a test of wealth. Despite these limitations, France became a constitutional monarchy in which the king served as the leading state functionary. A one-house legislature was responsible for making laws. The king could postpone enactment of laws but not veto them. The deputies abolished all the old administrative divisions of the provinces and replaced them with a national system of eighty-three departments with identical administrative and legal structures (Map 19.1). All officials were elected; no offices could be bought or sold. The deputies also abolished the old taxes and replaced them with new ones that were supposed to be uniformly levied. The National Assembly had difficulty collecting taxes, however, because many people had expected a substantial cut in the tax rate. The new administrative system survived, nonetheless, and the departments are still the basic units of the French state today.

When the deputies turned to reforming the Catholic church, they created enduring conflicts. Convinced that monastic life encouraged idleness and a decline in the nation's population, the deputies outlawed any future monastic vows and encouraged monks and nuns to return to private life by offering state pensions. Motivated partly by the ongoing financial crisis, the National Assembly confiscated all the church's property and promised to pay clerical salaries in return. The Civil Constitution of the Clergy, passed in July 1790, set pay scales for the clergy and provided that the voters elect their own parish priests and bishops just as they elected other officials. The impounded property served as a guarantee for the new paper money, called assignats, issued by the government. The assignats soon became subject to inflation because the government began to sell the church lands to the highest bidders in state auctions. The sales increased the landholdings of wealthy city dwellers and prosperous peasants but cut the value of the paper money.

Faced with resistance to these changes, the National Assembly in November 1790 required all clergy to swear an oath of loyalty to the Civil Constitution of the Clergy. Pope Pius VI in Rome condemned the constitution, and half of the French clergy refused to take the oath. The oath of allegiance permanently divided the Catholic population, which had to choose between loyalty to the old church and commitment to the Revolution with its "constitutional" church. The revolutionary government lost many supporters by passing laws against the clergy who refused the oath and by forcing them into exile, deporting them forcibly, or executing them as traitors. Riots and demonstrations led by women greeted many of the oath-taking priests who replaced those who refused.

The End of Monarchy

The reorganization of the Catholic church offended Louis XVI and gave added weight to those pushing him to organize resistance. On June 20, 1791, the royal family escaped in disguise from Paris and fled toward the eastern border of France, where they hoped to gather support from Austrian emperor Leopold II, the brother of Marie-Antoinette. The plans went awry when a postmaster recognized the king from his portrait on the new French money, and the royal family was arrested at Varennes, forty miles from the Austrian Netherlands border. The National Assembly tried to depict the departure as a kidnapping, but the "flight to Varennes" touched off demonstrations in Paris against the royal family,

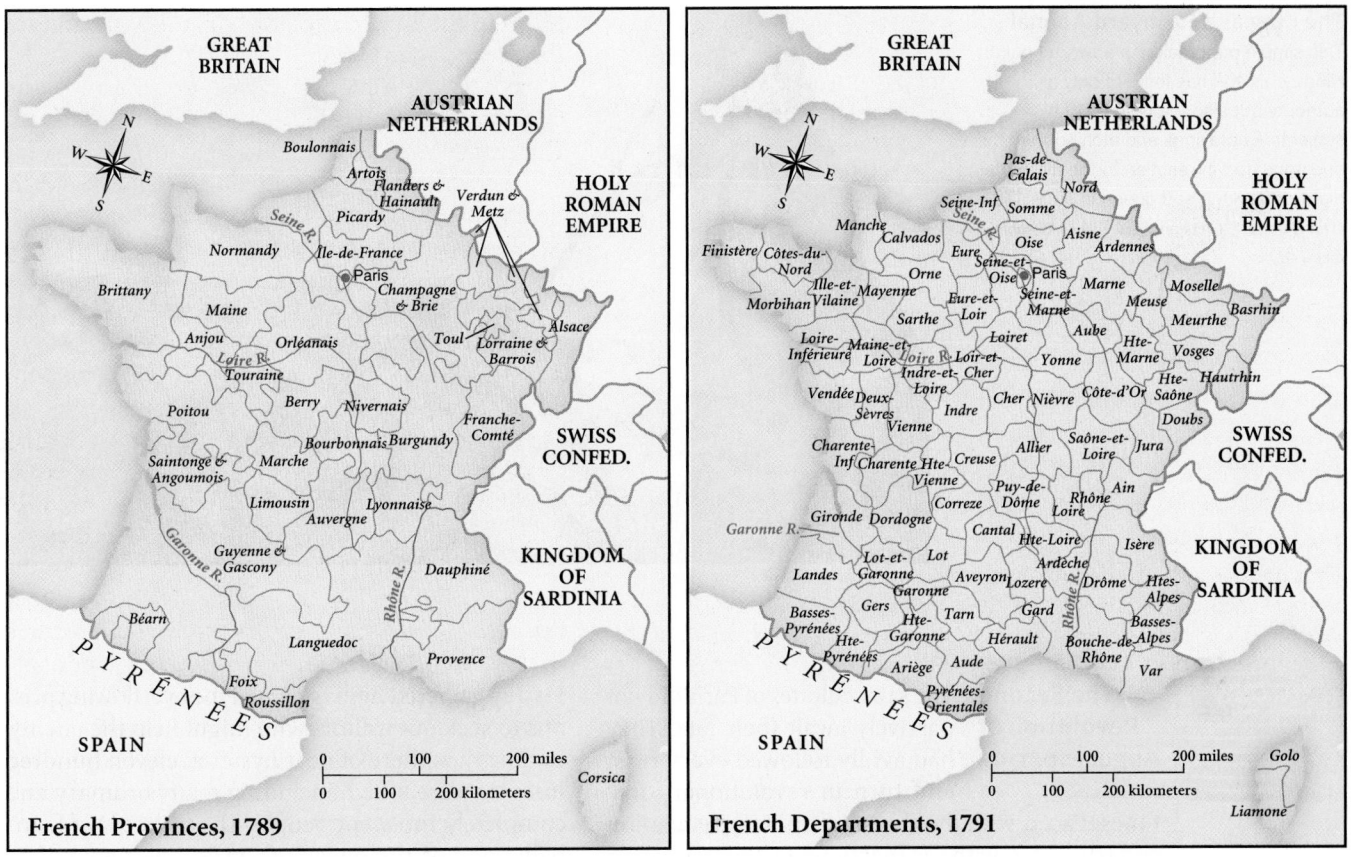

MAP 19.1 Redrawing the Map of France, 1789–1791

Before 1789, France had been divided into provinces named after the territories owned by dukes and counts in the Middle Ages. Many provinces had their own law codes and separate systems of taxation. As it began its deliberations, the new National Assembly determined to install uniform administrations and laws for the entire country. Discussion of the administrative reforms began in October 1789 and became law on February 15, 1790, when the Assembly voted to divide the provinces into eighty-three departments, with names based on their geographical characteristics: Basses-Pyrénées for the Pyrénées Mountains, Haute-Marne for the Marne River, and so on. | **How did this redrawing of the administrative map reflect the deputies' emphasis on reason over history?**

whom some now regarded as traitors. Cartoons circulated depicting the royal family as animals being returned "to the stable."

War with Austria and Prussia

The constitution, finally completed in 1791, provided for the immediate election of a new legislature. In a rare act of self-denial, the deputies of the National Assembly declared themselves ineligible for the new one. Those who had experienced the Revolution firsthand now departed from the scene, opening the door to men with little previous experience in national politics. The status of the king might have remained uncertain if war had not intervened, but by early 1792 everyone seemed intent on war with Austria. Louis and Marie-Antoinette hoped that such a war would lead to the defeat of the Revolution, whereas the deputies who favored a republic believed that war would lead to the king's downfall. On April 21, 1792, Louis declared war on Austria. Prussia immediately entered on the Austrian side. Thousands of French aristocrats, including two-thirds of the army officer corps, had already emigrated, including both the king's brothers, and they were gathering along France's eastern border in expectation of joining a counterrevolutionary army.

When fighting broke out in 1792, all the powers expected a brief and relatively contained war. Instead, it would continue despite brief interruptions for the next twenty-three years. War had an immediate radicalizing effect on French politics. When the French armies proved woefully unprepared for battle, the authority of the new legislature came under fire. In June 1792, an angry crowd invaded the hall of the legislature in Paris and threatened the royal family. The Prussian commander, the duke of Brunswick, issued a manifesto announcing that Paris would be totally destroyed if the royal family suffered any violence.

The King as a Farmyard Animal
This simple print makes a powerful point: King Louis XVI has lost not only his authority but also the respect of his subjects. Engravings and etchings like this one appeared in reaction to the attempted flight of the king and queen in June 1791. *(The Granger Collection, New York—All rights reserved.)*

The Second Revolution of August 10, 1792

The sans-culottes of Paris did not passively await their fate. They had avidly followed every twist and turn in revolutionary fortunes. Faced with the threat of military retaliation and frustrated with the inaction of the deputies, on August 10, 1792, the sans-culottes organized an insurrection and attacked the Tuileries palace, the residence of the king. The king and his family had to seek refuge in the meeting room of the legislature, where the frightened deputies ordered elections for a constitutional convention. By abolishing the property qualifications for voting, the deputies instituted universal male suffrage for the first time.

When it met, the National Convention abolished the monarchy and on September 22, 1792, established the first republic in French history. The republic would answer only to the people, not to any royal authority. Many of the deputies in the Convention belonged to the devotedly republican (and therefore left-wing) **Jacobin Club**, named after the former monastery in Paris where the club first met. The Jacobin Club in Paris headed a national political network of clubs that linked all the major towns and cities. Lafayette and other liberal aristocrats who had supported the constitutional monarchy fled into exile.

Violence soon exploded again when early in September 1792 the Prussians approached Paris. Hastily gathered mobs stormed the overflowing prisons to seek out traitors who might help the enemy. In an atmosphere of near hysteria, eleven hundred inmates were killed, including many ordinary and completely innocent people. The princess of Lamballe, one of the queen's favorites, was hacked to pieces and her mutilated body displayed beneath the windows where the royal family was kept under guard. These "September massacres" showed the dark side of popular revolution, in which the common people demanded instant revenge on supposed enemies and conspirators.

Jacobin Club: A French political club formed in 1789 that inspired the formation of a national network whose members dominated the revolutionary government during the Terror.

The Execution of the King

The National Convention faced a dire situation. It needed to write a new constitution for the republic while fighting a war with external enemies and confronting increasing resistance at home. Many thought the Revolution had gone too far when it confiscated the properties of the church, eliminated titles of nobility, and deposed the king. The French people had never known any government other than monarchy. Only half the population could read and write at even a basic level. In this situation, symbolic actions became very important. Any public sign of monarchy was at risk, and revolutionaries soon pulled down statues of kings and burned reminders of the former regime.

The fate of Louis XVI and the future direction of the republic divided the deputies elected to the National Convention. Most of the deputies were middle-class lawyers and professionals who had developed their ardent republican beliefs in the network of Jacobin Clubs. After the fall of the monarchy in August 1792, however, the Jacobins divided into

The Execution of King Louis XVI
Louis XVI was executed by order of the National Convention on January 21, 1793. In this print, the executioner shows the severed head to the National Guards standing in orderly silence around the scaffold. *(Mary Evans Picture Library.)*

two factions. The Girondins (named after a department in southwestern France, the Gironde, which provided some of its leading orators) met regularly at the salon of Jeanne Roland, the wife of a minister. They resented the growing power of Parisian militants and tried to appeal to the departments outside of Paris. The Mountain (so called because its deputies sat in the highest seats of the National Convention), in contrast, was closely allied with the Paris militants.

The first showdown between the Girondins and the Mountain occurred during the trial of the king in December 1792. Although the Girondins agreed that the king was guilty of treason, many of them argued for clemency, exile, or a popular referendum on his fate. After a long and difficult debate, the National Convention supported the Mountain and voted by a very narrow majority to execute the king. Louis XVI went to the guillotine on January 21, 1793, sharing the fate of Charles I of England in 1649. "We have just convinced ourselves that a king is only a man," wrote one newspaper, "and that no man is above the law."

REVIEW QUESTION **Why did the French Revolution turn in an increasingly radical direction after 1789?**

Terror and Resistance

The execution of the king did not solve the new regime's problems. The continuing war required even more men and money, and the introduction of a national draft provoked massive resistance in some parts of France. In response to growing pressures, the National Convention named the Committee of Public Safety to supervise food distribution, direct the war effort, and root out counterrevolutionaries. The leader of the committee, **Maximilien Robespierre** (1758–1794), wanted to go beyond these stopgap measures and create a "republic of virtue," in which the government would teach, or force, citizens to become virtuous republicans through a massive program of political reeducation. Thus began the **Terror**, in which the guillotine became the

Maximilien Robespierre (roh behs PYEHR): A lawyer from northern France who, as leader of the Committee of Public Safety, laid out the principles of a republic of virtue and of the Terror; his arrest and execution in July 1794 brought an end to the Terror.

Terror: The policy established under the direction of the Committee of Public Safety during the French Revolution to arrest dissidents and execute opponents in order to protect the republic from its enemies.

The Guillotine
Before 1789, only nobles were decapitated if condemned to death; commoners were usually hanged. Equalization of the death penalty was first proposed by J. I. Guillotin, a professor of anatomy and a deputy in the National Assembly. He also suggested that a mechanical device be constructed for decapitation, leading to the instrument's association with his name. The Assembly decreed decapitation as the death penalty in June 1791 and another physician, A. Louis, actually invented the guillotine. The executioner pulled up the blade by a cord and then released it. Use of the guillotine began in April 1792 and did not end until 1981, when the French government abolished the death penalty. The guillotine fascinated as much as it repelled. Reproduced in miniature, painted onto snuffboxes and china, worn as jewelry, and even serving as a toy, the guillotine became a part of popular culture. How could the guillotine be simultaneously celebrated as the people's avenger by supporters of the Revolution and vilified as the preeminent symbol of the Terror by opponents? *(Réunion des Musées Nationaux/Art Resource, NY.)*

most terrifying instrument of a government that suppressed almost every form of dissent (see the illustration above). These policies only increased divisions, which ultimately led to Robespierre's fall from power and to a dismantling of government by terror.

Robespierre and the Committee of Public Safety

The conflict between the more moderate Girondins and the more radical Mountain came to a head in spring 1793. Militants in Paris agitated for the removal of the deputies who had proposed a referendum on the king, and in retaliation the Girondins engineered the arrest of Jean-Paul Marat, a deputy allied with the Mountain who in his newspaper had been calling for more and more executions. Marat was acquitted, and Parisian militants marched into the National Convention on June 2, 1793, forcing the deputies to decree the arrest of their twenty-nine Girondin colleagues. The Convention consented to the establishment of paramilitary bands called "revolutionary armies" to hunt down political suspects and hoarders of grain. The deputies also agreed to speed up the operation of special revolutionary courts.

Setting the course for government and the war increasingly fell to the twelve-member Committee of Public Safety. When Robespierre was elected to the committee in July 1793, he became its guiding spirit and in effect the chief spokesman of the Revolution. A lawyer from northern France known as "the incorruptible" for his stern honesty and fierce dedication to democratic ideals, Robespierre remains one of the most controversial figures in world history because of his association with the Terror. Although he originally opposed the death penalty and the war, he was convinced that the emergency situation of 1793 required severe measures, including death for those, such as the Girondins, who opposed the committee's policies.

Like many other educated eighteenth-century men, Robespierre had read the classics of republicanism from the ancient Roman writers Tacitus and Plutarch to the Enlightenment thinkers Montesquieu and Rousseau. But he took them a step further. He defined "the theory of revolutionary government" as "the war of liberty against its enemies." He defended the people's right to democratic government, while in practice he supported many emergency measures that restricted their liberties. He personally favored a free-market economy, as did almost all middle-class deputies, but in this time of crisis he was willing to enact price controls and requisitioning. In an effort to stabilize prices, the National Convention established the General Maximum on September 29, 1793, which set limits on the prices of thirty-nine essential commodities and on wages. In a speech to the Convention, Robespierre explained the necessity of government by terror: "The first maxim of your policies must be to lead the people by reason and the people's enemies by terror. . . . Without virtue, terror is deadly; without terror, virtue is impotent." *Terror* was not an idle term; it seemed to imply that the goal of democracy justified what we now call totalitarian means, that is, the suppression of all dissent.

Through a series of desperate measures, the Committee of Public Safety set the machinery of the Terror in motion. It sent deputies out "on mission" to purge unreliable officials and organize the war effort. Revolutionary tribunals set up in Paris and provincial centers tried political suspects. In October 1793, the Revolutionary Tribunal in Paris convicted Marie-Antoinette of treason and sent her to the guillotine. The Girondin leaders and Jeanne Roland were also guillotined, as was Olympe de Gouges. The government confiscated all the property of convicted traitors.

The new republic won its greatest success on the battlefield. As of April 1793, France faced war with Austria, Prussia, Great Britain, Spain, Sardinia, and the Dutch Republic—all fearful of the impact of revolutionary ideals on their own populations. The execution of Louis XVI, in particular, galvanized European governments; according to William Pitt, the British prime minister, it was "the foulest and most atrocious act the world has ever seen." To face this daunting coalition of forces, the French republic ordered the first universal draft of men in history. Every unmarried man and childless widower between the ages of eighteen and twenty-five was declared eligible for conscription. The government also tapped a new and potent source of power—nationalist pride—in decrees mobilizing young and old alike:

> The young men will go to battle; married men will forge arms and transport provisions; women will make tents and clothing and serve in hospitals; children will make bandages; old men will get themselves carried to public places to arouse the courage of warriors and preach hatred of kings and unity of the republic.

Forges were set up in the parks and gardens of Paris to produce thousands of guns, and citizens everywhere helped collect saltpeter to make gunpowder. By the end of 1793, the French nation in arms had stopped the advance of the allied powers, and in the summer of 1794 it invaded the Austrian Netherlands and crossed the Rhine River. The army was ready to carry the gospel of revolution and republicanism to the rest of Europe.

The Republic of Virtue, 1793–1794

The program of the Terror went beyond pragmatic measures to fight the war and internal enemies to include efforts to "republicanize everything"—in other words, to effect a cultural revolution. While censoring writings deemed counterrevolutionary, the government encouraged republican art, set up civic festivals, and in some places directly attacked the churches in a campaign known as de-Christianization. In addition to drawing up plans for a new program of elementary education, the republic set about politicizing aspects of daily life, including even the measurement of space and time.

Republican Culture Refusing to tolerate opposition, the republic left no stone unturned in its endeavor to get its message across. Songs—especially the new national anthem, "La Marseillaise"—and placards, posters, pamphlets, books, engravings, paintings, sculpture, even everyday crockery, chamber pots, and playing cards conveyed revolutionary slogans and symbols. Foremost among the symbols was the figure of Liberty, which appeared on coins and bills, on letterheads and seals, and as statues in festivals. Hundreds of new plays were produced and old classics revised. To encourage the production of patriotic and republican works, the government sponsored state competitions for artists. Works of art were supposed to "awaken the public spirit and make clear how atrocious and ridiculous were the enemies of liberty and of the Republic."

At the center of this elaborate cultural campaign were the revolutionary festivals modeled on Rousseau's plans for a civic religion. The festivals first emerged in 1789 with the spontaneous planting of liberty trees in villages and towns. The Festival of Federation on July 14, 1790, marked the first anniversary of the fall of the Bastille. Under the National Convention, the well-known painter Jacques-Louis David (1748–1825), who was a deputy and an associate of Robespierre, took over festival planning. David aimed to destroy the mystique of monarchy and to make the republic sacred. His Festival of Unity on August 10, 1793, for example, celebrated the first

Representing Liberty
Liberty was represented by a female figure because in French the noun is feminine (*la liberté*). This painting from 1793–1794, by Jeanne-Louise (Nanine) Vallain, captures the usual attributes of Liberty: she is soberly seated, wearing a Roman-style toga and holding a pike with a Roman liberty cap on top. Her Roman appearance signals that she represents an abstract quality. The fact that she holds an instrument of battle suggests that women might be active participants. The Statue of Liberty in New York harbor, given by the French to the United States, is a late-nineteenth-century version of the same figure, but without any suggestion of battle. *(Nanine Vallain,* La Liberté, *Huile sur toile, 1794, Musée de la Révolution française, Vizille. © Conseil général de l'Isère/Domaine de Vizille.)*

anniversary of the overthrow of the monarchy. In front of the statue of Liberty built for the occasion, a bonfire consumed crowns and scepters symbolizing royalty while a cloud of three thousand white doves rose into the sky. This was all part of preaching the "moral order of the Republic . . . that will make us a people of brothers, a people of philosophers."

De-Christianization Some revolutionaries hoped the festival system would replace the Catholic church altogether. They initiated a campaign of **de-Christianization** that included closing churches (Protestant as well as Catholic), selling many church buildings to the highest bidder, and trying to force even those clergy who had taken the oath of loyalty to abandon their clerical vocations and marry. Great churches became storehouses for arms or grain, or their stones were sold off to contractors. The medieval statues of kings on the facade of Notre Dame cathedral were beheaded. Church bells were dismantled and church treasures melted down for government use.

In the ultimate step in de-Christianization, extremists tried to establish what they called the Cult of Reason to supplant Christianity. In Paris in the fall of 1793, a goddess of Liberty, played by an actress, presided over the Festival of Reason in Notre Dame cathedral. Local militants in other cities staged similar festivals, which alarmed deputies in the National Convention, who were wary of turning rural, devout populations against the republic. Robespierre objected to the de-Christianization campaign's atheism; he favored a Rousseau-inspired deistic religion without the supposedly superstitious trappings of Catholicism. The Committee of Public Safety halted the de-Christianization campaign, and Robespierre, with David's help, tried to institute an alternative, the Cult of the Supreme Being, in June 1794. Neither the Cult of Reason nor the Cult of the Supreme Being attracted many followers, but both show the depth of the commit-

de-Christianization: During the French Revolution, the campaign of extremist republicans against organized churches and in favor of a belief system based on reason.

ment to overturning the old order and all its traditional institutions.

Politicizing Daily Life In principle, the best way to ensure the future of the republic was through the education of the young. The deputy Georges-Jacques Danton (1759–1794), Robespierre's main competitor as theorist of the Revolution, maintained that "after bread, the first need of the people is education." The National Convention voted to make primary schooling free and compulsory for both boys and girls. It took control of education away from the Catholic church and tried to set up a system of state schools at both the primary and secondary levels, but it lacked trained teachers to replace those the Catholic religious orders had provided. As a result, opportunities for learning how to read and write may have diminished. In 1799, only one-fifth as many boys enrolled in the state secondary schools as had studied in church schools ten years earlier.

Although many of the ambitious republican programs failed, colors, clothing, and daily speech were all politicized. The tricolor—the combination of red, white, and blue that was to become the flag of France—was devised in July 1789, and by 1793 everyone had to wear a cockade (a badge made of ribbons) with the colors. Using the formal forms of speech—*vous* for "you"—or the title *monsieur* or *madame* might identify someone as an aristocrat; true patriots used the informal *tu* and *citoyen* or *citoyenne* ("citizen") instead. Some people changed their names or gave their children new kinds of names. Biblical and saints' names such as John, Peter, Joseph, and Mary gave way to names recalling heroes of the ancient Roman republic (Brutus, Gracchus, Cornelia), revolutionary heroes, or flowers and plants. Such changes symbolized adherence to the republic and to Enlightenment ideals rather than to Catholicism.

Even the measures of time and space were revolutionized. In October 1793, the National Convention introduced a new calendar to replace the Christian one. Its bases were reason and republican principles. Year I dated from the beginning of the republic on September 22, 1792. Twelve months of exactly thirty days each received new names derived from nature—for example, Pluviôse (roughly equivalent to February) recalled the rain (*la pluie*) of late winter. Instead of seven-day weeks, ten-day *décades* provided only one day of rest every ten days and pointedly eliminated the Sunday of the Christian calendar. The five days left at the end of the calendar year were devoted to special festivals called *sans-culottides*. The calendar remained in force for twelve years despite continuing resistance to it. More enduring was the new metric system based on units of ten that was invented to replace the hundreds of local variations in weights and measures. Other countries in Europe and throughout the world eventually adopted the metric system.

Revolutionary laws also changed the rules of family life. The state took responsibility for all family matters away from the Catholic church: people now registered births, deaths, and marriages at city hall, not the parish church. Marriage became a civil contract and as such could be broken and thereby nullified. The new divorce law of September 1792 was the most far-reaching in Europe: a couple could divorce by mutual consent or for reasons such as insanity, abandonment, battering, or criminal conviction. Thousands of men and women took advantage of the law to dissolve unhappy marriages, even though the pope had condemned the measure. (In 1816, the government revoked the right to divorce, and not until the 1970s did French divorce laws return to the principles of the 1792 legislation.) In one of its most influential actions, the National Convention passed a series of laws that created equal inheritance among all children in the family, including girls. The father's right to favor one child, especially the oldest male, was considered aristocratic and hence antirepublican.

Resisting the Revolution

By intruding into religion, culture, and daily life, the republic inevitably provoked resistance. Shouting curses against the republic, uprooting liberty trees, carrying statues of the Virgin Mary in procession, hiding a priest who would not take the oath, singing a royalist song—all these expressed dissent with the new symbols, rituals, and policies. Resistance also took more violent forms, from riots over food shortages or religious policies to assassination and full-scale civil war.

Women's Resistance Many women, in particular, suffered from the hard conditions of life that persisted in this time of war, and they had their own ways of voicing discontent. Long bread lines in the cities exhausted the patience of women, and police spies reported their constant grumbling, which occasionally turned into spontaneous demonstrations or riots over high prices or food shortages. Women also organized their fellow parishioners to refuse to hear Mass offered by the "constitutional" priests, and they protected the priests who would not sign the oath of loyalty.

Other forms of resistance were more individual. One young woman, Charlotte Corday, assassinated the outspoken deputy Jean-Paul Marat in July 1793.

Corday fervently supported the Girondins, and she considered it her patriotic duty to kill the deputy who, in the columns of his paper, had constantly demanded more heads and more blood. Marat was immediately eulogized as a great martyr, and Corday went to the guillotine vilified as a monster but confident that she had "avenged many innocent victims."

Rebellion and Civil War

Organized resistance broke out in many parts of France. The arrest of the Girondin deputies in June 1793 sparked insurrections in several departments. After the government retook the city of Lyon, one of the centers of the revolt, the deputy on mission ordered sixteen hundred houses demolished and the name of the city changed to Liberated City. Special courts sentenced almost two thousand people to death.

In the Vendée region of western France, resistance turned into a bloody and prolonged civil war. Between March and December 1793, peasants, artisans, and weavers joined under noble leadership to form a "Catholic and Royal Army." One rebel group explained its motives: "They [the republicans] have killed our king, chased away our priests, sold the goods of our church, eaten everything we have and now they want to take our bodies [in the draft]." The uprising took two different forms: in the Vendée itself, a counterrevolutionary army organized to fight the republic; in nearby Brittany, resistance took the form of guerrilla bands, which united to attack a target and then quickly melted into the countryside. Great Britain provided money and underground contacts for these attacks, which were almost always aimed at towns. In many ways this was a civil war between town and country, for the townspeople were the ones who supported the Revolution and bought church lands for themselves. The peasants had gained most of what they wanted in 1789 with the abolition of seigneurial dues, and they resented the government's demands for money and manpower and actions taken against their local clergy.

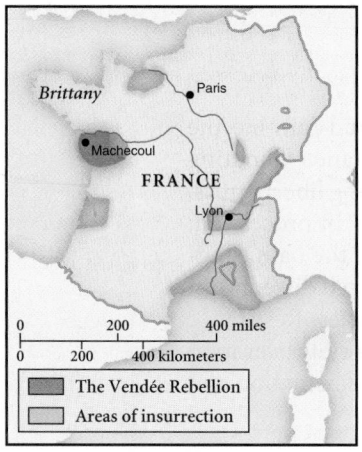

The Vendée Rebellion, 1793

For several months in 1793, the Vendée rebels stormed the largest towns in the region. Both sides committed horrible atrocities. At the small town of Machecoul, for example, the rebels massacred five hundred republicans, including administrators and National Guard members; many were tied together, shoved into freshly dug graves, and shot. By the fall, however, republican soldiers had turned back the rebels. A republican general wrote to the Committee of Public Safety claiming, "There is no more Vendée, citizens, it has perished under our free sword along with its women and children. . . . Following the orders that you gave me I have crushed children under the feet of horses, massacred women who at least . . . will engender no more brigands." His claims of complete victory soon turned hollow, however, as fighting continued.

"Infernal columns" of republican troops marched through the region to restore control, military courts ordered thousands executed, and republican soldiers massacred thousands of others. In one especially gruesome incident, the deputy Jean-Baptiste Carrier supervised the drowning of some two thousand Vendée rebels, including a number of priests. Barges loaded with prisoners were floated into the Loire River near Nantes and then sunk. Controversy still rages about the rebellion's death toll because no accurate count could be taken. Estimates of rebel deaths alone range from about 20,000 to higher than 250,000. Many thousands of republican soldiers and civilians also lost their lives in fighting that continued on and off for years. Even the low estimates reveal the carnage of this catastrophic confrontation between the republic and its opponents.

The Fall of Robespierre and the End of the Terror

In the atmosphere of fear of conspiracy that the outbreaks of rebellion fueled, Robespierre tried simultaneously to exert the National Convention's control over popular political activities and to weed out opposition among the deputies. As a result, the Terror intensified until July 1794, when a group of deputies joined within the Convention to order the arrest and execution of Robespierre and his followers. The Convention then ordered elections and drew up a new republican constitution that gave executive power to five directors. This "Directory government" maintained power during four years of seesaw battles between royalists and former Jacobins.

The Revolution Devours Its Own

In the fall of 1793, the National Convention cracked down on popular clubs and societies. First to be suppressed were women's political clubs. Founded in early 1793, the Society of Revolutionary Republican Women played a very active part in sans-culottes politics. The society urged harsher measures against the republic's enemies and insisted that women have a voice in politics even if they did not have the vote. Women had set up their own clubs in many provincial towns and also attended the meetings of local men's organizations. Using traditional arguments about women's inherent unsuitability for politics, the deputies abolished women's political clubs. The closing of women's clubs marked an important turning point in the Revolution. From then on, the sans-culottes and their political organizations came increasingly under the thumb of the Jacobin deputies in the National Convention.

In the spring of 1794, the Committee of Public Safety moved against its critics among leaders in Paris and deputies in the National Convention itself. First, a handful of "ultrarevolutionaries"—a collection of local Parisian politicians—were arrested and executed. Next came the other side, the "indulgents," so called because they favored a moderation of the Terror. Included among them was the deputy Danton, himself once a member of the Committee of Public Safety and a friend of Robespierre. Danton was the Revolution's most flamboyant orator and, unlike Robespierre, a high-living, high-spending, excitable politician. At every critical turning point in national politics, his booming voice had swayed opinion. Now, under pressure from the Committee of Public Safety, the Revolutionary Tribunal convicted him and his friends of treason and sentenced them to death.

"The Revolution," as one of the Girondin victims of 1793 had remarked, "was devouring its own children." Even after the major threats to the Committee of Public Safety's power had been eliminated, the Terror not only continued but worsened. A law passed in June 1794 denied the accused the right of legal counsel, reduced the number of jurors necessary for conviction, and allowed only two judgments: acquittal or death. The category of political crimes expanded to include "slandering patriotism" and "seeking to inspire discouragement." Ordinary people risked the guillotine if they expressed any discontent. The rate of executions in Paris rose from five a day in the spring of 1794 to twenty-six a day in the summer. The political atmosphere darkened even though the military situation improved. At the end of June, the French armies decisively defeated the main Austrian army and advanced through the Austrian Netherlands to Brussels and Antwerp. The emergency measures for fighting the war were working, yet Robespierre and his inner circle had made so many enemies that they could not afford to loosen the grip of the Terror.

The Terror hardly touched many parts of France, but overall the experience was undeniably traumatic. Across the country, the official Terror cost the lives of at least 40,000 French people, most of them living in the regions of major insurrections or near the borders with foreign enemies, where suspicion of collaboration ran high. As many as 300,000 French people—1 out of every 50—went to prison as suspects between March 1793 and August 1794. The toll for the aristocracy and the clergy was especially high. Many leading nobles perished under the guillotine, and thousands emigrated. Thirty thousand to forty thousand clergy who refused the oath left the country, at least two thousand (including many nuns) were executed, and thousands were imprisoned. The clergy were singled out in particular in the

Major Events of the French Revolution

May 5, 1789	The Estates General opens at Versailles
June 17, 1789	The Third Estate decides to call itself the National Assembly
June 20, 1789	"Tennis court oath" shows determination of deputies to carry out a constitutional revolution
July 14, 1789	Fall of the Bastille
August 4, 1789	National Assembly abolishes "feudalism"
August 26, 1789	National Assembly passes Declaration of the Rights of Man and Citizen
October 5–6, 1789	Women march to Versailles and are joined by men in bringing the royal family back to Paris
July 12, 1790	Civil Constitution of the Clergy
June 20, 1791	Louis and Marie-Antoinette attempt to flee in disguise and are captured at Varennes
April 20, 1792	Declaration of war on Austria
August 10, 1792	Insurrection in Paris and attack on Tuileries palace lead to removal of king's authority
September 2–6, 1792	Murder of prisoners in "September massacres" in Paris
September 22, 1792	Establishment of the republic
January 21, 1793	Execution of Louis XVI
March 11, 1793	Beginning of uprising in the Vendée
May 31–June 2, 1793	Insurrection leading to arrest of the Girondins
July 27, 1793	Robespierre named to the Committee of Public Safety
September 29, 1793	Convention establishes General Maximum on prices and wages
October 16, 1793	Execution of Marie-Antoinette
February 4, 1794	Slavery abolished in the French colonies
March 13–24, 1794	Arrest, trial, and executions of so-called ultrarevolutionaries
March 30–April 5, 1794	Arrest, trial, and executions of Danton and his followers
July 27, 1794	Arrest of Robespierre and his supporters (executed July 28–29); beginning of end of the Terror
October 26, 1795	Directory government takes office
April 1796–October 1797	Succession of Italian victories by Bonaparte

civil war zones: 135 priests were massacred at Lyon in November 1793, and 83 were shot in one day during the Vendée revolt. Yet many victims of the Terror were peasants or sans-culottes.

The final crisis of the Terror came in July 1794. Conflicts within the Committee of Public Safety and the National Convention left Robespierre isolated. On July 27, 1794 (the ninth of Thermidor, Year II, according to the revolutionary calendar), Robespierre appeared before the Convention with yet another list of deputies to be arrested. Many feared they would be named, and they shouted him down and ordered him arrested along with his followers on the committee, the president of the Revolutionary Tribunal in Paris, and the commander of the Parisian National Guard. An armed uprising led by the Paris city government failed to save Robespierre when most of the National Guard took the side of the Convention. Robespierre tried to kill himself with a pistol but only broke his jaw. The next day he and scores of followers went to the guillotine.

The Thermidorian Reaction and the Directory, 1794–1799

The men who led the attack on Robespierre in Thermidor (July 1794) did not intend to reverse all his policies, but that happened nonetheless because of a violent backlash known as the **Thermidorian Reaction**. As most of the instruments of terror were dismantled, newspapers attacked the Robespierrists as "tigers thirsting for human blood." The new government released hundreds of suspects and arranged a temporary truce in the Vendée. It purged Jacobins from local bodies and replaced them with their opponents. It arrested some of the most notorious "terrorists" in the National Convention, such as Carrier, and put them to death. Within the year, the new leaders abolished the Revolutionary Tribunal and closed the Jacobin Club in Paris. Popular demonstrations met severe repression. In southeastern France, in particular, the "White Terror" replaced the Jacobins' "Red Terror." Former officials and local Jacobin leaders were harassed, beaten, and often murdered by paramilitary bands who had tacit support from the new authorities. Those who remained in the National Convention prepared yet another constitution in 1795, setting up a two-house legislature and an executive body — the Directory, headed by five directors.

Thermidorian Reaction: The violent backlash against the rule of Robespierre that dismantled the Terror and punished Jacobins and their supporters.

The Directory regime tenuously held on to power for four years, all the while trying to fend off challenges from the remaining Jacobins and the resurgent royalists. The puritanical atmosphere of the Terror gave way to the pursuit of pleasure — low-cut dresses of transparent materials, the reappearance of prostitutes in the streets, fancy dinner parties, and "victims' balls" where guests wore red ribbons around their necks as reminders of the guillotine. Bands of young men dressed in knee breeches and rich fabrics picked fights with known Jacobins and disrupted theater performances with loud antirevolutionary songs. All over France, people petitioned to reopen churches closed during the Terror. If necessary, they broke into a church to hold services with a priest who had been in hiding or a lay schoolteacher who was willing to say Mass.

Although the Terror had ended, the revolution had not. In 1794, the most democratic and most repressive phases of the Revolution both ended at once. Between 1795 and 1799, the republic endured in France, but it directed a war effort abroad that would ultimately bring to power the man who would dismantle the republic itself.

REVIEW QUESTION What factors can explain the Terror? To what extent was it simply a response to a national emergency or a reflection of deeper problems within the French Revolution?

Revolution on the March

War raged almost constantly from 1792 to 1815. At one time or another, and sometimes all at once, France faced every principal power in Europe. The French republic — and later the French Empire under its supreme commander, Emperor Napoleon Bonaparte — proved an even more formidable opponent than the France of Louis XIV. New means of mobilizing and organizing soldiers enabled the French to dominate Europe for a generation. The influence of the French Revolution as a political model and the threat of French military conquest combined to challenge the traditional order in Europe and offer new prospects to the rest of the world as well.

Arms and Conquests

The powers allied against France squandered their best chance to triumph in early 1793, when the French armies verged on chaos because of the emigration of noble army officers and the problems of integrating new draftees. By the end of 1793, the French had a huge and powerful fighting force of 700,000 men. But the army still faced many problems in the field. As many as a third of the recent draftees deserted before or during battle. At times the soldiers were fed only moldy bread, and if their pay was late, they sometimes resorted to pillaging and looting. Generals might pay with their lives if they lost a key battle and their loyalty to the Revolution came under suspicion.

France nevertheless had one overwhelming advantage: those soldiers who agreed to serve fought for a revolution that they and their brothers and sisters had helped make. The republic was their government, and the army was in large measure theirs, too; many officers had risen through the ranks by skill and talent rather than by inheriting or purchasing their positions. One young peasant boy wrote to his parents, "Either you will see me return bathed in glory, or you will have a son who is a worthy citizen of France who knows how to die for the defense of his country."

When the French armies invaded the Austrian Netherlands and crossed the Rhine in the summer of 1794, they proclaimed a war of liberation. Middle-class people near the northern and eastern borders of France reacted most positively to the French invasion (Map 19.2). In the Austrian Netherlands, Mainz, Savoy, and Nice, French officers organized Jacobin Clubs that attracted locals. The clubs petitioned for annexation to France, and French legislation was then introduced, including the abolition of seigneurial dues. As the French annexed more and more territory, however, "liberated" people in many places began to view them as an army of occupation. Despite resistance, especially in the Austrian Netherlands, these areas remained part of France until 1815, and the legal changes were permanent.

The Directory government that came to power in 1795 launched an even more aggressive policy of creating semi-independent "sister republics" wherever the armies succeeded. When Prussia declared neutrality in 1795, the French armies swarmed into the Dutch Republic, abolished the stadholderate, and—with the revolutionary penchant for

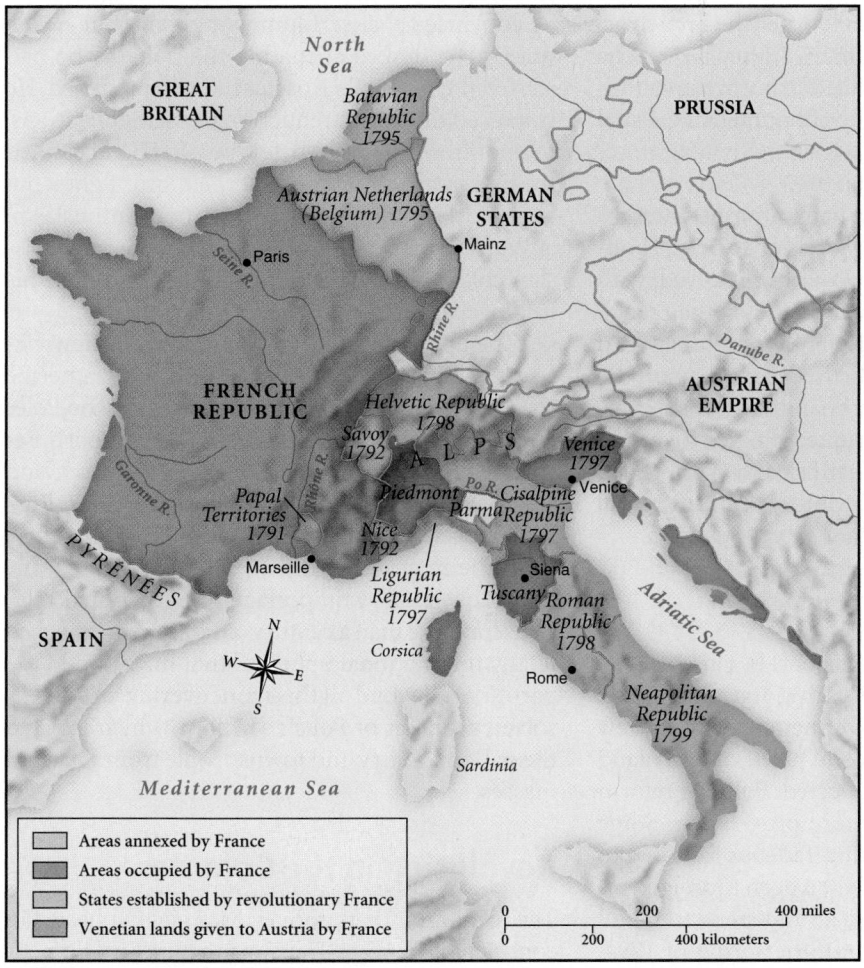

MAP 19.2 French Expansion, 1791–1799
The influence of the French Revolution on neighboring territories is dramatically evident in this map. The French directly annexed the papal territories in southern France in 1791, Nice and Savoy in 1792, and the Austrian Netherlands in 1795. They set up a series of sister republics in the former Dutch Republic and in various Italian states. Local people did not always welcome these changes. For example, the French made the Dutch pay a huge war indemnity, support a French occupying army of 25,000 soldiers, and give up some southern territories. The sister republics faced a future of subordination to French national interests.

MAP 19.3 The Second and Third Partitions of Poland, 1793 and 1795

In 1793, Prussia took over territory that included 1.1 million Poles while Russia gained 3 million new inhabitants. Austria gave up any claims to Poland in exchange for help from Russia and Prussia in acquiring Bavaria. In the final division of 1795, Prussia absorbed an additional 900,000 Polish subjects, including those in Warsaw; Austria incorporated 1 million Poles and the city of Cracow; Russia gained another 2 million Poles. The three powers determined never to use the term *Kingdom of Poland* again. | **How had Poland become such a prey to the other powers?**

renaming—created the new Batavian Republic, a satellite of France. The brilliant young general Napoleon Bonaparte gained a reputation by defeating the Austrian armies in northern Italy in 1797 and then created the Cisalpine Republic. Next he overwhelmed Venice and then handed it over to the Austrians in exchange for a peace agreement that lasted less than two years. After the French attacked the Swiss cantons in 1798, they set up the Helvetic Republic and curtailed many of the Catholic church's privileges. They conquered the Papal States in 1798 and installed a Roman Republic, forcing the pope to flee to Siena.

The revolutionary wars had an immediate impact on European life at all levels of society. Thousands of men died in every country involved, with perhaps as many as 200,000 casualties in the French armies alone in 1794 and 1795. More soldiers died in hospitals as a result of their wounds than on the battlefields. Constant warfare hampered world commerce and especially disrupted French overseas shipping. Times were now hard almost everywhere, because the dislocations of internal and external commerce provoked constant shortages.

Poland Extinguished, 1793–1795

France had survived in 1793 in part because its enemies were busy elsewhere. Fearing French influence, Prussia joined Russia in dividing up generous new slices of territory in the second partition of Poland (Map 19.3). As might be expected, Poland's reform movement became even more pro-French. Some leaders fled abroad, including Tadeusz Kościuszko (1746–1817), an officer who had been a foreign volunteer in the War of American Independence and who now escaped to Paris. In the spring of 1794, Kościuszko returned from France to lead a nationalist revolt.

The Polish cities of Cracow and Warsaw, and the old Lithuanian capital, Vilnius, responded with uprisings. Kościuszko faced an immediate, insoluble dilemma. He could win only if the peasants joined the struggle—highly unlikely unless villagers could be convinced that serfdom would end. But such a drastic step risked alienating the nobles who had started the revolt. So Kościuszko compromised. He promised the serfs a reduction of their obligations, but not freedom itself. A few peasant bands joined the insurrection, but most let their lords fight it out alone. Urban workers displayed more enthusiasm; at Warsaw, for example, a mob hanged several Russian collaborators, including an archbishop in his full regalia.

The uprising failed. Kościuszko won a few victories, but when the Russian empress Catherine the Great's forces regrouped, they routed the Poles and Lithuanians. Kościuszko and other Polish Patriot leaders languished for years in Russian and Austrian prisons. Taking no further chances, Russia, Prussia, and Austria wiped Poland completely from the map in the third partition (1795). "The Polish question" would plague international relations for more than a century as Polish rebels flocked to any international upheaval that might undo the partitions. Beyond all this maneuvering lay the unsolved problem of Polish serfdom, which isolated the nation's gentry and townspeople from the rural masses.

Revolution in the Colonies

The revolution that produced so much upheaval in continental Europe transformed life in France's

DOCUMENT

Address on Abolishing the Slave Trade (February 5, 1790)

Founded in 1788, the Society of the Friends of Blacks agitated for the abolition of the slave trade. Among its members were many who became leaders of the French Revolution. In a pamphlet titled Address to the National Assembly in Favor of the Abolition of the Slave Trade, *the Friends of Blacks denied that they wanted to abolish slavery altogether and argued only for the abolition of the slave trade. The pamphlet raised the prospect of a slave revolt, which in fact broke out in St. Domingue in 1791. As a consequence, many planters and their allies accused the society of fomenting the revolt.*

You have declared them, these rights; you have engraved on an immortal monument that all men are born and remain free and equal in rights; you have restored to the French people these rights that despotism had for so long despoiled; . . . you have broken the chains of feudalism that still degraded a good number of our fellow citizens; you have announced the destruction of all the stigmatizing distinctions that religious or political prejudices introduced into the great family of humankind. . . .

We are not asking you to restore to French blacks those political rights which alone, nevertheless, attest to and maintain the dignity of man; we are not even asking for their liberty. No; slander, bought no doubt with the greed of the shipowners, ascribes that scheme to us and spreads it everywhere; they want to stir up everyone against us, provoke the planters and their numerous creditors, who take alarm even at gradual emancipation. They want to alarm all the French, to whom they depict the prosperity of the colonies as inseparable from the slave trade and the perpetuity of slavery.

. . . The immediate emancipation of the blacks would not only be a fatal operation for the colonies; it would even be a deadly gift for the blacks, in the state of abjection and incompetence to which cupidity has reduced them. It would be to abandon to themselves and without assistance children in the cradle or mutilated and impotent beings.

It is therefore not yet time to demand that liberty; we ask only that one cease butchering thousands of blacks regularly every year in order to take hundreds of captives; we ask that henceforth cease the prostitution, the profaning of the French name, used to authorize these thefts, these atrocious murders; we demand in a word the abolition of the slave trade. . . .

In regard to the colonists, we will demonstrate to you that if they need to recruit blacks in Africa to sustain the population of the colonies at the same level, it is because they wear out the blacks with work, whippings, and starvation; that, if they treated them with kindness and as good fathers of families, these blacks would multiply and that this population, always growing, would increase cultivation and prosperity. . . .

If some motive might on the contrary push them [the blacks] to insurrection, might it not be the indifference of the National Assembly about their lot? Might it not be the insistence on weighing them down with chains, when one consecrates everywhere this eternal axiom: *that all men are born free and equal in rights.* So then therefore there would only be fetters and gallows for the blacks while good fortune glimmers only for the whites? Have no doubt, our happy revolution must reelectrify the blacks whom vengeance and resentment have electrified for so long, and it is not with punishments that the effect of this upheaval will be repressed. From one insurrection badly pacified will twenty others be born, of which one alone can ruin the colonists forever.

Source: *Adresse à l'Assemblée Nationale, pour l'abolition de la traite des noirs* (Paris: La Société des Amis des Noirs de Paris, February 1790), 1–4, 10–11, 17, 19–22. Translation by Lynn Hunt.

Question to Consider

- **Why did the authors of this pamphlet support an end to the slave trade but oppose an immediate, outright end to slavery itself? How do you respond to that aspect of their argument?**

Caribbean colonies, too. These colonies were crucial to the French economy. Twice the size in land area of the neighboring British colonies, they also produced nearly twice as much revenue in exports. The slave population had doubled in the French colonies in the twenty years before 1789. St. Domingue (present-day Haiti) was the most important French colony. Occupying the western half of the island of Hispaniola, it was inhabited not only by 465,000 slaves and 30,000 whites but also by 28,000 free people of color, whose primary job was to apprehend runaway slaves and ensure plantation security.

Despite the efforts of a Paris club called the Friends of Blacks, most French revolutionaries did not consider slavery a pressing problem. As one deputy explained, "This regime [in the colonies] is oppressive, but it gives a livelihood to several million Frenchmen. This regime is barbarous but a still greater barbarity will result if you interfere with it without the necessary knowledge." (See Document, "Address on Abolishing the Slave Trade," above.)

In August 1791, however, the slaves in northern St. Domingue, inspired by the slogan "Listen to the voice of Liberty which speaks in the hearts of all," organized a large-scale revolt. To restore authority over the slaves, the deputies in Paris granted civil and political rights to the free blacks. This action infuriated white planters and merchants, who in 1793 signed an agreement with Great Britain, now France's enemy in war, declaring British sovereignty over St. Domingue. To complicate matters further, Spain, which controlled the rest of the island and had entered on Great Britain's side in the war with France, offered freedom to individual slave rebels who joined the Spanish armies as long as they agreed to maintain the slave regime for the other blacks.

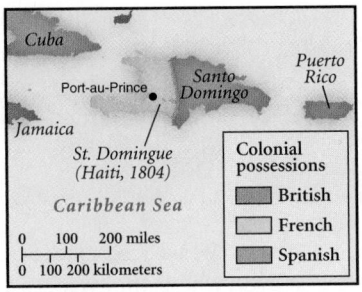

St. Domingue on the Eve of the Revolt, 1791

The few thousand French republican troops on St. Domingue were outnumbered, and to prevent complete military disaster, the French commissioner freed all the slaves in his jurisdiction in August 1793 without permission from the government in Paris. In February 1794, the National Convention formally abolished slavery and granted full rights to all black men in the colonies. These actions had the desired effect. One of the ablest black generals allied with the Spanish, the ex-slave François Dominique Toussaint L'Ouverture (1743–1803), changed sides and committed his troops to the French (see the illustration below). The French eventually appointed Toussaint governor of St. Domingue as a reward for his efforts. As former plantation owners fled to the new United States, slave owners there feared the prospect of spreading revolt.

The vicious fighting and the flight of whites left St. Domingue's economy in ruins. In 1800, the plantations produced one-fifth of what they had in 1789. In the zones Toussaint controlled, army officers or government officials took over the great estates and kept all those working in agriculture under military discipline. The former slaves were bound to their estates like serfs and forced to work the plantations in exchange for an autonomous family life and the right to maintain personal garden plots.

Toussaint remained in charge until 1802, when Napoleon sent French armies to regain control of the island. They arrested Toussaint and transported him to France, where he died in prison. His arrest prompted the English poet William Wordsworth to write of him:

> There's not a breathing of the common wind
> That will forget thee; thou hast great allies;
> Thy friends are exultations, agonies,
> And love, and man's unconquerable mind.

Toussaint L'Ouverture

The leader of the St. Domingue slave uprising appears on horseback, in his general's uniform, sword in hand. His depiction in this colored print from the early nineteenth century makes him seem much like other military heroes from the time, including Napoleon Bonaparte. *(Bibliothèque nationale, Paris, France/Archives Charmet/The Bridgeman Art Library International.)*

The English Rebuttal

In this caricature, James Gillray satirizes the French version of liberty. Gillray produced thousands of political caricatures. How would you interpret the message of this print? *(© The Trustees of the British Museum/Art Resource, NY.)*

Toussaint became a hero to abolitionists everywhere, a potent symbol of black struggles to win freedom. Napoleon attempted to restore slavery, as he had in the other French Caribbean colonies of Guadeloupe and Martinique, but the remaining black generals defeated his armies and in 1804 proclaimed the Republic of Haiti.

Worldwide Reactions to Revolutionary Change

As the example of the colonies shows, the French Revolution inflamed politics and social relations far beyond Europe. Citizens of the new United States witnessed more celebrations of the French Revolution between 1792 and 1796 than of Washington's birthday or even Independence Day, but the French Revolution soon became one of the most divisive issues in American politics. Thomas Jefferson wrote in January 1793 that "the liberty of the whole earth" depended on its success; John Adams, in contrast, believed that the French Revolution had set back human progress hundreds of years. In India, the ruler of the southern kingdom of Mysore, Tipu Sultan, planted a liberty tree and set up a Jacobin Club in the futile hope of gaining French allies against the British. Most other Muslim rulers, however, viewed the conflict as an obscure dispute between Christians. Views within Europe and the Americas evolved over time, and more and more people came to see the Revolution and especially the Terror as deeply problematic. (See "Contrasting Views," page 644.)

Many had greeted the events of 1789 with unabashed enthusiasm. The English Unitarian minister Richard Price had exulted, "Behold, the light . . . after setting AMERICA free, reflected to FRANCE, and there kindled into a blaze that lays despotism in ashes, and warms and illuminates EUROPE." Democrats and reformers from many countries flooded

CONTRASTING VIEWS

Perspectives on the French Revolution

Contemporaries instantly grasped the cataclysmic significance of the French Revolution and began to argue about its lessons for their own countries. A member of the British Parliament, Edmund Burke ignited a firestorm of controversy with his Reflections on the Revolution in France *(Document 1). He condemned the French revolutionaries for attempting to build a government on abstract reasoning rather than taking historical traditions and customs into account; his book provided a foundation for the doctrine known as conservatism, which argued for "conserving" the traditional foundations of society and avoiding the pitfalls of radical or revolutionary change. Burke's views provoked a strong response from the English political agitator Thomas Paine. Paine's pamphlet* Common Sense *(1776) had helped inspire the British North American colonies to demand independence from Great Britain. In* The Rights of Man *(Document 2), written fifteen years later, Paine attacked the traditional order as fundamentally unjust and defended the idea of a revolution to uphold rights. Joseph de Maistre, an aristocratic opponent of both the Enlightenment and the French Revolution, put the conservative attack on the French Revolution into a deeply religious and absolutist framework (Document 3). In contrast, Anne-Louise-Germaine de Staël, an opponent of Napoleon and one of the most influential intellectuals of the early nineteenth century, took the view that the violence of the Revolution had been the product of generations of superstition and arbitrary rule, that is, rule by an absolutist Catholic church and monarchical government (Document 4).*

1. Edmund Burke, *Reflections on the Revolution in France* (1790)

An Irish-born supporter of the American colonists in their opposition to the British Parliament, Edmund Burke (1729–1797) opposed the French Revolution. He argued the case for tradition, continuity, and gradual reform based on practical experience—what he called "a sure principle of conservation."

Can I now congratulate the same nation [France] upon its freedom? Is it because liberty in the abstract may be classed amongst the blessings of mankind, that I am seriously to felicitate a madman, who has escaped from the protecting restraint and wholesome darkness of his cell, on his restoration to the enjoyment of light and liberty? Am I to congratulate an highwayman and murderer, who has broke prison, upon the recovery of his natural rights? . . .

Government is not made in virtue of natural rights, which may and do exist in total independence of it; and exist in much greater clearness, and in a much greater degree of abstract perfection: but their abstract perfection is their practical defect. By having a right to every thing they want every thing. . . . The science of constructing a commonwealth, or renovating it, or reforming it, is, like every other experimental science, not to be taught *a priori* [based on theory rather than on experience]. Nor is it a short experience that can instruct us in that practical science; because the real effects of moral causes are not always immediate; but that which in the first instance is prejudicial may be excellent in its remoter operation; and its excellence may arise even from the ill effects it produces in the beginning. . . .

In the groves of *their* academy, at the end of every visto [vista], you see nothing but the gallows. Nothing is left which engages the affections on the part of the commonwealth. . . . To make us love our country, our country ought to be lovely.

Source: *Two Classics of the French Revolution:* Reflections on the Revolution in France *(Edmund Burke) and* The Rights of Man *(Thomas Paine)* (New York: Doubleday Anchor Books, 1973), 19, 71–74, 90–91.

2. Thomas Paine, The Rights of Man (1791)

In his reply to Burke, The Rights of Man, *which sold 200,000 copies in two years, Thomas Paine (1737–1809) defended the idea of reform based on reason, advocated a concept of universal human rights, and attacked the excesses of privilege and tradition in Great Britain. Elected as a deputy to the French National Convention in 1793 in recognition of his writings in favor of the French Revolution, Paine narrowly escaped condemnation as an associate of the Girondins.*

Before anything can be reasoned upon to a conclusion, certain facts, principles, or data, to reason from, must be established, admitted, or denied. Mr. Burke, with his usual outrage, abuses the *Declaration of the Rights of Man*, published by the National Assembly of France, as the basis on which the Constitution of France is built. This he calls "paltry and blurred sheets of paper about the rights of man."

Does Mr. Burke mean to deny that *man* has any rights? If he does, then he must mean that there are no such things as rights any where, and that he has none himself; for who is there in the world but man? . . .

Hitherto we have spoken only (and that but in part) of the natural rights of man. We have now to consider the civil rights of man, and to show how the one originates from the other. Man did not enter into society to become *worse* than he was before, nor to have fewer rights than he had before, but to have those rights better secured. His natural rights are the foundation of all his civil rights. . . .

A constitution is not a thing in name only, but in fact. It has not an ideal, but a real existence; and wherever it cannot be produced in a visible form, there is none. A constitution is a thing *antecedent* to a government, and a government is only the creature of a constitution. The constitution of a country is not the act of its government, but of the people constituting a government. . . .

Can then Mr. Burke produce the English Constitution? If he cannot, we may fairly conclude, that though it has been so much talked about, no such thing as a constitution exists, or ever did exist, and consequently that the people have yet a constitution to form.

Source: *Two Classics of the French Revolution:* Reflections on the Revolution in France *(Edmund Burke) and* The Rights of Man *(Thomas Paine)* (New York: Doubleday Anchor Books, 1973), 302, 305–6, 309.

3. Joseph De Maistre, *Considerations on France* (1797)

An aristocrat born in Savoy, Joseph de Maistre (1753–1821) believed in reform but he passionately opposed both the Enlightenment and the French Revolution as destructive to good order. He believed that Protestants, Jews, lawyers, journalists, and scientists all threatened the social order because they questioned the need for absolute obedience to authority in matters both religious and political. De Maistre set the foundations for reactionary conservatism, a conservatism that defended throne and altar.

This consideration especially makes me think that the French Revolution is a great epoch and that its consequences, in all kinds of ways, will be felt far beyond the time of its explosion and the limits of its birthplace. . . .

There is a satanic quality to the French Revolution that distinguishes it from everything we have ever seen or anything we are ever likely to see in the future. Recall the great assemblies, Robespierre's speech against the priesthood, the solemn apostasy [renunciation of vows] of the clergy, the desecration of objects of worship, the installation of the goddess of reason, and that multitude of extraordinary actions by which the provinces sought to outdo Paris. All this goes beyond the ordinary circle of crime and seems to belong to another world.

Source: Joseph de Maistre, *Considerations on France*, trans. Richard A. Lebrun (Cambridge: Cambridge University Press, 1994), 21, 41.

4. Anne-Louise-Germaine de Staël, *Considerations on the Main Events of the French Revolution* (1818)

De Staël published her views long after the Revolution was over, but she had lived through the events herself. She was the daughter of Jacques Necker, Louis XVI's Swiss Protestant finance minister. Necker's dismissal in July 1789 had sparked the attack on the Bastille. De Staël published novels, literary tracts, and memoirs and became one of the best-known writers of the nineteenth century. In her writings she defended the Enlightenment; though she opposed the violence unleashed by the Revolution, she traced it back to the excesses of monarchical government. (See her portrait on page 659.)

Once the people were freed from their harness there is no doubt that they were in a position to commit any kind of crime. But how can we explain their depravity? The government we are now supposed to miss so sorely [the former monarchy] had had plenty of time to form this guilty nation. The priests whose teaching, example, and wealth were supposed to be so good for us had supervised the childhood of the generation that broke out against them. The class that revolted in 1789 must have been accustomed to the privileges of feudal nobility which, as we are also assured, are so peculiarly agreeable to those on whom they weigh [the peasants]. How does it happen, then, that the seed of so many vices was sown under the ancient institutions? . . . What can we conclude from this, then?—That no people had been as unhappy for the preceding century as the French. If the Negroes of Saint-Domingue have committed even greater atrocities, it is because they had been even more greatly oppressed.

Source: Vivian Folkenflik, ed., *An Extraordinary Woman: Selected Writings of Germaine de Staël* (New York: Columbia University Press, 1987), 365–66.

Questions to Consider

1. **Which aspect of the French Revolution most disturbed these commentators?**
2. **How would you align each of these writers on a spectrum running from extreme right to extreme left in politics?**
3. **How would each of these writers judge the Enlightenment that preceded the French Revolution?**

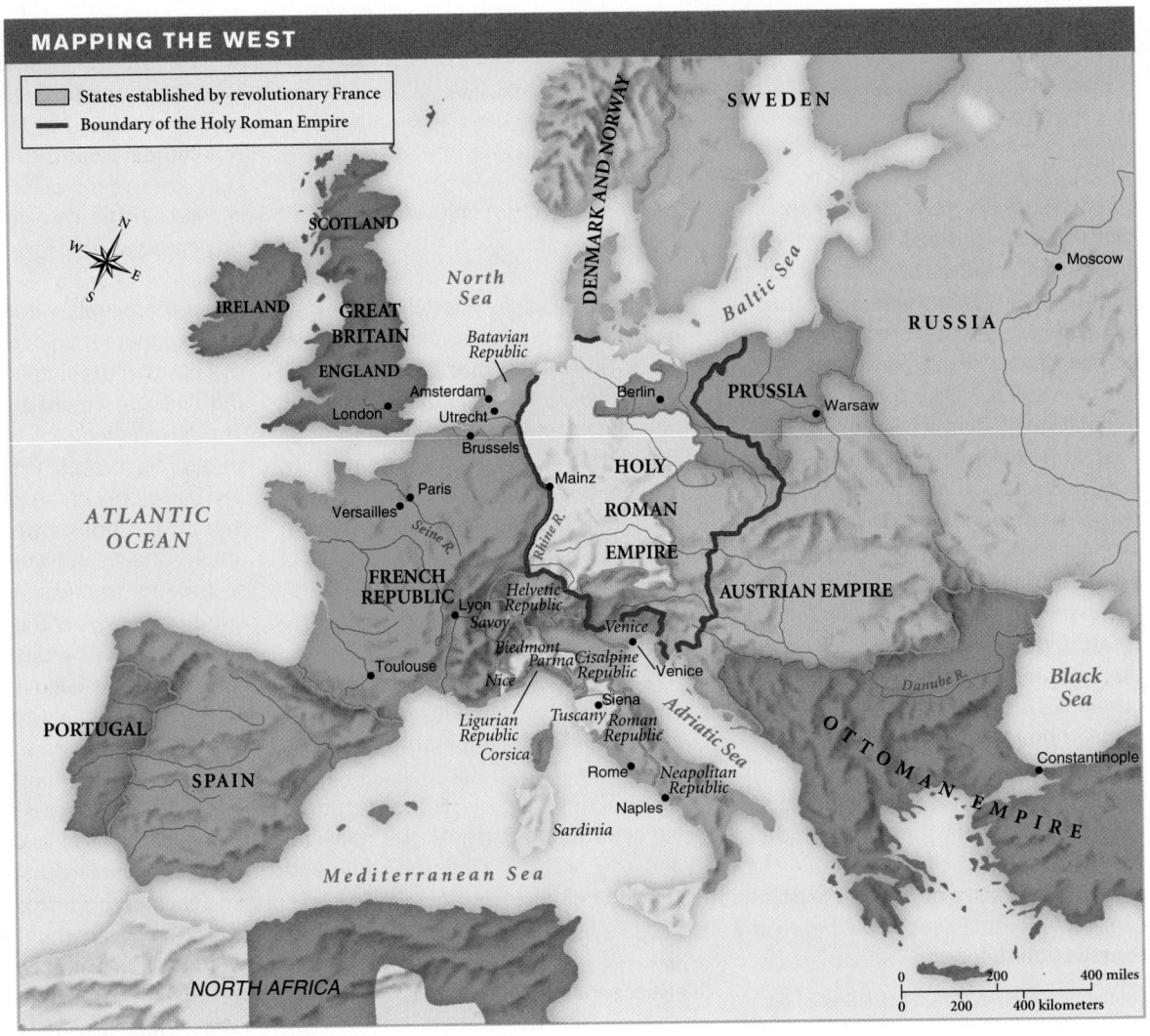

Europe in 1799

France's expansion during the revolutionary wars threatened to upset the balance of power in Europe. A century earlier, the English and Dutch had allied and formed a Europe-wide coalition to check the territorial ambitions of Louis XIV. Thwarting French ambitions after 1799 would prove to be even more of a challenge to the other European powers. The Dutch had been reduced to satellite status, as had most of the Italian states. Even Austria and Prussia would suffer devastating losses to the French on the battlefield. Only a new coalition of European powers could stop France in the future.

to Paris to witness events firsthand. Supporters of the French Revolution in Great Britain joined constitutional and reform societies that sprang up in many cities. Pro-French feeling ran even stronger in Ireland. Catholics and Presbyterians, both excluded from the vote, came together in 1791 in the Society of United Irishmen, which eventually pressed for secession from England.

European elites became alarmed when the French abolished monarchy and nobility and encouraged popular participation in politics. The British government, for example, quickly suppressed the corresponding societies and harassed their leaders, charging that their ideas and their contacts with the French were seditious. (See the illustration on page 643 for a negative English view.) When the Society of United Irishmen timed a rebellion to coincide with an attempted French invasion in 1798, the British mercilessly repressed them, killing thirty thousand rebels. To put down the rebellion, Britain required seventy thousand regular troops, twice as many as fought in any of the major continental battles.

Elites sometimes found allies in opposing the French. Peasants in the German and Italian states met the French occupation with resistance, often in the form of banditry. Because the French offered Jews religious toleration and civil and political rights wherever they conquered, anti-French groups sometimes attacked Jews. Many leading intellectuals in the German states, including the philosopher Immanuel Kant, initially supported the revolutionary cause, but after 1793 most of them turned against the popular violence and military aggressiveness of the Revolution. The German states, still run by many separate rulers, experienced a profound artistic and intellectual revival, which eventually connected with anti-French nationalism. This renaissance included a resurgence of intellectual life in the universities, a thriving press (1,225 journals were launched in the 1780s alone), and the multiplication of Masonic lodges and literary clubs.

Despite the turn in opinion, European rulers still dreaded the mere mention of revolution. Although Swedish king Gustavus III (r. 1771–1792) was assassinated by a nobleman, his son Gustavus IV (r. 1792–1809) was convinced that the French Jacobins had sanctioned the killing. Spain's royal government simply suppressed all news from France, fearing that it might ignite the spirit of revolt. Despite similar government controls on news in Russia, 278 outbreaks of peasant unrest occurred there between 1796 and 1798. A Russian landlord explained, "This is the self-same . . . spirit of insubordination and independence, which has spread through all Europe." When insubordination did turn revolutionary, as in Naples under French influence in 1799, the retribution could be awful: 100 republicans, including leading intellectuals, were executed when the royalists returned to power.

REVIEW QUESTION **Why did some groups outside of France embrace the French Revolution while others resisted it?**

Conclusion

Growing out of aspirations for freedom that also inspired the Dutch, Belgians, and Poles, the revolution that shook France permanently altered the political landscape of the Western world. Between 1789 and 1799, monarchy as a form of government gave way in France to a republic whose leaders were elected. Aristocracy based on rank and birth was undermined in favor of civil equality and the promotion of merit. The people who marched in demonstrations, met in clubs, and, in the case of men, voted in national elections for the first time insisted that government respond to them. Thousands of men held elective office. A revolutionary government tried to teach new values with a refashioned calendar, state festivals, and a civic religion. Its example inspired would-be revolutionaries everywhere.

But the French Revolution also had its darker side. The divisions created by the Revolution within France endured in many cases until after World War II. Even now, French public-opinion surveys ask if it was right to execute the king in 1793 (most believe that Louis XVI was guilty of treason but should not have been executed). The revolutionaries proclaimed human rights and democratic government as universal goals, but they also explicitly excluded women, even though they admitted Protestant, Jewish, and eventually black men. They used the new spirit of national pride to inspire armies and then used those armies to conquer other peoples. Their ideals of universal education, religious toleration, and democratic participation could not prevent the institution of new forms of government terror to persecute, imprison, and kill dissidents. These paradoxes created an opening for Napoleon Bonaparte, who rushed in with his remarkable military and political skills to push France — and with it all of Europe — in new directions.

FOR FURTHER EXPLORATION

- **For additional primary-source material from this period**, see *Sources of the Making of the West*, Fourth Edition.
- **For Web sites, images, and documents related to topics in this chapter**, visit *Make History* at bedfordstmartins.com/hunt.

Chapter 19 Review

Online Study Guide bedfordstmartins.com/hunt

Key Terms and People

In the grid below, identify the term or person and explain its historical significance. (To do this exercise online, go to bedfordstmartins.com/hunt.)

Term	Who or What & When	Why It Matters
Louis XVI (p. 623)		
Marie-Antoinette (p. 623)		
Estates General (p. 624)		
Great Fear (p. 626)		
Declaration of the Rights of Man and Citizen (p. 626)		
Jacobin Club (p. 630)		
Maximilien Robespierre (p. 631)		
Terror (p. 631)		
de-Christianization (p. 634)		
Thermidorian Reaction (p. 638)		

Review Questions

1. How did the beginning of the French Revolution resemble the other revolutions of 1787–1789?
2. Why did the French Revolution turn in an increasingly radical direction after 1789?
3. What factors can explain the Terror? To what extent was it simply a response to a national emergency or a reflection of deeper problems within the French Revolution?
4. Why did some groups outside of France embrace the French Revolution while others resisted it?

Making Connections

1. Should the French Revolution be viewed as the origin of democracy or the origin of totalitarianism (a government in which no dissent is allowed)? Explain.
2. Why did other European rulers find the French Revolution so threatening?
3. What made the French revolutionary armies so powerful in this period?
4. How was the French Revolution related to the Enlightenment that preceded it?

Important Events

Date	Event	Date	Event
1787	Dutch Patriot revolt stifled by Prussian invasion	1793	Second partition of Poland by Austria and Russia; Louis XVI of France executed for treason
1788	Beginning of Austrian Netherlands resistance against reforms of Joseph II; opening of reform parliament in Poland	1794	Abolition of slavery in French colonies; Robespierre's government by terror falls
1789	French Revolution begins	1795	Third (final) partition of Poland; France annexes Austrian Netherlands
1790	Internal divisions lead to collapse of resistance in Austrian Netherlands	1797–1798	Creation of "sister republics" in Italian states and Switzerland
1791	Beginning of slave revolt in St. Domingue (Haiti)		
1792	Beginning of war between France and rest of Europe; second revolution of August 10 overthrows monarchy		

- Consider three events: **Dutch patriot revolt stifled by Prussian invasion (1787)**, **French Revolution begins (1789)**, and **Beginning of slave revolt in St. Domingue (Haiti) (1791)**. How would you explain the relationships between these three uprisings? How were they similar and different in their inspirations, ideologies, tactics, and results?

SUGGESTED REFERENCES

The most influential book on the meaning of the French Revolution is still the classic study by Tocqueville, who insisted that the Revolution continued the process of state centralization undertaken by the monarchy. The revolutions in the colonies are now the subject of many new and important studies.

Andress, David. *The Terror: The Merciless War for Freedom in Revolutionary France.* 2006.

Armitage, David, and Sanjay Subrahmanyam, eds. *The Age of Revolutions in Global Context, c. 1760–1840.* 2010.

Censer, Jack R., and Lynn Hunt. *Liberty, Equality, Fraternity: Exploring the French Revolution* (includes CD-ROM of images and music). 2001. See also the accompanying Web site: http://www.chnm.gmu.edu/revolution

Chickering, Roger, and Stig Förster, eds. *War in an Age of Revolution, 1775–1815.* 2010.

Desan, Suzanne. *The Family on Trial in Revolutionary France.* 2006.

*Dubois, Laurent, and John D. Garrigus, eds. *Slave Revolution in the Caribbean, 1789–1804: A Brief History with Documents.* 2006.

Furet, François. *Interpreting the French Revolution.* Trans. Elborg Forster. 1981.

Godineau, Dominique. *The Women of Paris and Their French Revolution.* Trans. Katherine Streip. 1998.

*Hunt, Lynn, ed. *The French Revolution and Human Rights: A Brief Documentary History.* 1996.

*Levy, Darline Gay, Harriet Branson Applewhite, and Mary Durham Johnson, eds. *Women in Revolutionary Paris, 1789–1795.* 1979.

Palmer, R. R. *The Age of the Democratic Revolution: A Political History of Europe and America, 1760–1800.* Vol. 2, *The Struggle.* 1964.

*Popkin, Jeremy D. *Facing Racial Revolution: Eyewitness Accounts of the Haitian Insurrection.* 2007.

———. *You Are All Free: The Haitian Revolution and the Abolition of Slavery.* 2010.

Schechter, Ronald, ed. *The French Revolution: The Essential Readings.* 2001.

Scurr, Ruth. *Fatal Purity: Robespierre and the French Revolution.* 2007.

Tocqueville, Alexis de. *The Old Regime and the French Revolution.* Trans. Stuart Gilbert. 1856; repr. 1955.

*Primary source.

BONAPARTE

CHAPTER

Napoleon and the Revolutionary Legacy

20

1800–1830

In her novel *Frankenstein* (1818), the prototype for modern thrillers, Mary Shelley tells the story of a Swiss technological genius who creates a humanlike monster in his pursuit of scientific knowledge. The monster, "so scaring and unearthly in his ugliness," terrifies all who encounter him and ends by destroying Dr. Frankenstein's own loved ones. Despite desperate chases across deserts and frozen landscapes, Frankenstein never manages to trap the monster, who is last seen hunched over his creator's deathbed.

Frankenstein's monster can be taken as a particularly horrifying incarnation of the fears of the postrevolutionary era, but which fears did Shelley have in mind? Did the monster represent the French Revolution, which had devoured its own children in the Terror? Shelley was the daughter of Mary Wollstonecraft, an English feminist who had defended the French Revolution and died in childbirth when Mary was born in 1797. Mary Shelley was also the wife of the romantic poet Percy Bysshe Shelley, who often wrote against the ugliness of contemporary life and in opposition to the conservative politics that had triumphed in Great Britain after Napoleon's fall. Whatever the meaning—and Mary Shelley may well have intended more than one—*Frankenstein* makes the forceful point that humans cannot always control their own creations. The Enlightenment and the French Revolution had celebrated the virtues of human creativity, but Shelley's novel shows that innovation often has a dark and uncontrollable side.

Napoleon as Military Hero
In this painting from 1800–1801, *Napoleon Crossing the Alps at St. Bernard*, Jacques-Louis David reminds the French of Napoleon's heroic military exploits. Napoleon is a picture of calm and composure while his horse shows the fright and energy of the moment. David painted this propagandistic image shortly after one of his former students went to the guillotine on a trumped-up charge of plotting to assassinate the new French leader. The former organizer of republican festivals during the Terror had become a kind of court painter for the new regime. *(Réunion des Musées Nationaux/Art Resource, NY.)*

Those who witnessed Napoleon Bonaparte's stunning rise to European dominance might have cast him as either Frankenstein or his monster. Like the scientist Frankenstein, Bonaparte created something dramatically new: the French Empire with himself as emperor. Like the former kings of France, he ruled under his first name. This Corsican artillery

The Rise of Napoleon Bonaparte 652
- A General Takes Over
- From Republic to Empire
- The New Paternalism: The Civil Code
- Patronage of Science and Intellectual Life

"Europe Was at My Feet": Napoleon's Conquests 659
- The Grand Army and Its Victories, 1800–1807
- The Impact of French Victories
- From Russian Winter to Final Defeat, 1812–1815

The "Restoration" of Europe 667
- The Congress of Vienna, 1814–1815
- The Emergence of Conservatism
- The Revival of Religion

Challenges to the Conservative Order 672
- Romanticism
- Political Revolts in the 1820s
- Revolution and Reform, 1830–1832

officer who spoke French with an Italian accent ended the French Revolution even while maintaining some of its most important innovations. Bonaparte transformed France from a republic with democratically elected leaders to an empire with a new aristocracy based on military service. But he kept the revolutionary administration and most of the laws that ensured equal treatment of citizens. Although he tolerated no opposition at home, he prided himself on bringing French-style changes to peoples elsewhere.

Bonaparte continued his revolutionary policy of conquest and annexation until it reached grotesque dimensions. His foreign policies made many see him as a monster hungry for dominion; he turned the sister republics of the revolutionary era into kingdoms personally ruled by his relatives, and he exacted tribute wherever he triumphed. Eventually, resistance to the French armies and the ever-mounting costs of military glory toppled Napoleon. The powers allied against him met and agreed to restore the monarchical governments that had been overthrown by the French, shrink France back to its prerevolutionary boundaries, and maintain this settlement against future demands for change.

Although the people of Europe longed for peace and stability in the aftermath of the Napoleonic whirlwind, they lived in a deeply unsettled world. Profoundly affected by French military occupation, many groups of people organized to demand ethnic and cultural autonomy, first from Napoleon and then from the restored governments after 1815. In 1830, a new round of revolutions broke out in France, Belgium, Poland, and some of the Italian states. The revolutionary legacy was far from exhausted.

CHAPTER FOCUS How did Napoleon Bonaparte's actions force other European rulers to change their policies?

The Rise of Napoleon Bonaparte

In 1799, a charismatic young general took over the French republic and set France on a new course. Within a year, **Napoleon Bonaparte** (1769–1821) had effectively ended the French Revolution and steered France toward an authoritarian state. As emperor after 1804, he dreamed of European integration in the tradition of Augustus and Charlemagne, but he also mastered the details of practical administration. To achieve his goals, he compromised with the Catholic church and with exiled aristocrats willing to return to France. His most enduring accomplishment, the new Civil Code, tempered the principles of the Enlightenment and the Revolution with an insistence on the powers of fathers over children, husbands over wives, and employers over workers. His influence spread into many spheres as he personally patronized scientific inquiry and encouraged artistic styles in line with his vision of imperial greatness.

A General Takes Over

It would have seemed astonishing in 1795 that the twenty-six-year-old son of a noble family from the island of Corsica off the Italian coast would within four years become the supreme ruler of France and one of the greatest military leaders in world history. That year, Bonaparte was a penniless artillery officer, only recently released from prison as a presumed Robespierrist. Thanks to some early military suc-

Napoleon Bonaparte: The French general who became First Consul in 1799 and emperor (Napoleon I) in 1804; after losing the battle of Waterloo in 1815, he was exiled to the island of St. Helena.

1799 Coup against Directory government in France; Napoleon Bonaparte named First Consul

1801 Napoleon signs concordat with the pope

1804 Napoleon crowned emperor of France, issues new Civil Code

1805 British naval forces defeat French at the battle of Trafalgar; Napoleon wins his greatest victory at the battle of Austerlitz

1807–1814 French invade and occupy Spain and Portugal

1812 Napoleon invades Russia

1814–1815 Congress of Vienna

1815 Napoleon defeated at Waterloo and exiled to island of St. Helena, where he dies in 1821

1800 1805 1810 1815

cesses and links to Parisian politicians, however, he was named commander of the French army in Italy in 1796.

Bonaparte's astounding success in the Italian campaigns of 1796–1797 launched his meteoric career. With an army of fewer than fifty thousand men, he defeated the Piedmontese and the Austrians. In quick order, he established client republics dependent on his own authority, negotiated with the Austrians himself, and molded the army into his personal force by paying the soldiers in cash taken as tribute from the newly conquered territories. He pleased the Directory government by sending home wagonloads of Italian masterpieces of art, which were added to Parisian museum collections (most are still there) after being paraded in victory festivals.

In 1798, the Directory set aside its plans to invade England, gave Bonaparte command of the army raised for that purpose, and sent him across the Mediterranean Sea to Egypt. The Directory government hoped that French occupation of Egypt would strike a blow at British trade by cutting the route to India. Although the French immediately defeated a much larger Egyptian army, the British admiral Lord Horatio Nelson destroyed the French fleet while it was anchored in Aboukir Bay, cutting the French off from home. In the face of determined resistance and an outbreak of the bubonic plague, Bonaparte's armies retreated from a further expedition in Syria. But the French occupation of Egypt lasted long enough for that largely Muslim country to experience the same kinds of Enlightenment-inspired legal reforms that had been introduced in Europe: the French abolished torture, introduced equality before the law, eliminated religious taxes, and proclaimed religious toleration.

Even the failures of the Egyptian campaign did not dull Bonaparte's luster. Bonaparte had taken France's leading scientists with him on the expedition, and his soldiers had discovered a slab of black basalt dating from 196 B.C.E. written in both hieroglyphic and Greek. Called the Rosetta stone after a nearby town, it enabled scholars to finally decipher the hieroglyphs used by the ancient Egyptians.

With his army pinned down by Nelson's victory at sea, Bonaparte slipped out of Egypt and made his way secretly to southern France in October 1799. He arrived home at just the right moment: the war in Europe was going badly. The territories of the former Austrian Netherlands had revolted against French conscription laws, and deserters swelled the ranks of rebels in western France. Amid increasing political instability, generals in the field had become virtually independent, and the troops felt more loyal to their units and generals than to the republic. Disillusioned members of the government saw in Bonaparte's return an occasion to overturn the constitution of 1795.

On November 9, 1799, the conspirators persuaded the legislature to move out of Paris to avoid an imaginary Jacobin plot. But when Bonaparte stomped into the new meeting hall the next day and demanded immediate changes in the constitution, he was greeted by cries of "Down with the dictator!" His quick-thinking brother Lucien, president of the Council of Five Hundred (the lower house), saved Bonaparte's coup by summoning troops guarding the hall and claiming that some deputies had tried to assassinate the popular general. The soldiers ejected those who opposed Bonaparte and left the remaining ones to vote to abolish the Directory and establish a new three-man executive called the consulate.

Bonaparte became **First Consul**, a title revived from the ancient Roman republic. He promised to

---

First Consul: The most important of the three consuls established by the French Constitution of 1800; the title, given to Napoleon Bonaparte, was taken from ancient Rome.

1818
Mary Shelley, *Frankenstein*

1824
Ludwig van Beethoven, Ninth Symphony

1830
Greece gains its independence from Ottoman Turks; rebels overthrow Charles X of France and install Louis-Philippe; rebellion in Poland against Russia fails

1820 1825 1830 1835

1820
Revolt of liberal army officers against Spanish crown

1825
Russian army officers demand constitutional reform in Decembrist Revolt

1832
English Parliament passes Reform Bill; Johann Wolfgang von Goethe, *Faust*

be a man above party and to restore order to the republic. A new constitution—with no declaration of rights—was submitted to the voters. Millions abstained from voting, and the government falsified the results to give an appearance of even greater support to the new regime. Inside France, political apathy had overtaken the original enthusiasm for revolutionary ideals. Altogether it was an unpromising beginning; yet within five years, Bonaparte would crown himself Napoleon I, emperor of the French. The French armies would recover from their reverses of 1799 to push the frontiers of French influence even farther eastward.

From Republic to Empire

Napoleon had no long-range plans to establish himself as emperor and conquer most of Europe. The deputies of the legislature who engineered the coup d'état of November 1799 picked him as one of three provisional consuls only because he was a famous general. Napoleon immediately asserted his leadership over the other two consuls in the process of drafting another constitution—the fourth since 1789. He then set about putting his stamp on every aspect of French life, building monuments and institutions that in some cases have endured to the present day.

The End of the Republic

When the constitution of 1799 made Napoleon the First Consul, it gave him the right to pick the Council of State, which drew up all laws. He exerted control by choosing men loyal to him. Government was no longer representative in any real sense: the new constitution eliminated direct elections for deputies and granted no independent powers to the three houses of the legislature. Napoleon and his advisers chose the legislature's members out of a small pool of "notables." Almost all men over twenty-one could vote in the plebiscite (referendum) to approve the constitution, but their only option was to choose *yes* or *no*.

Napoleon's most urgent task was to reconcile to his regime Catholics who had been alienated by revolutionary policies. Although nominally Catholic, Napoleon held no deep religious convictions. "How can there be order in the state without religion?" he asked cynically. "When a man is dying of hunger beside another who is stuffing himself, he cannot accept this difference if there is not an authority who tells him: 'God wishes it so.'" In 1801, a concordat with Pope Pius VII (r. 1800–1823) ended a decade of church-state conflict in France. The pope validated all sales of church lands, and the government agreed to pay the salaries of bishops and priests who would swear loyalty to the state. Catholicism was officially recognized as the religion of "the great majority of French citizens." (The state also paid Protestant pastors' salaries.) Thus, the pope brought the huge French Catholic population back into the fold and Napoleon gained the pope's support for his regime.

Napoleon continued the centralization of state power that had begun under the absolutist monarchy of Louis XIV and resumed under the Terror. As First Consul, he appointed prefects who directly supervised local affairs in every department in the country. He created the Bank of France to facilitate government borrowing and relied on gold and silver coinage rather than paper money. He improved tax collection but balanced the budget only by exacting tribute from the territories he conquered.

To achieve order and end the upheavals of ten years of revolutionary turmoil, the regime severely limited political expression. Napoleon never relied on mass executions to maintain control, but he refused to allow those who opposed him to meet in clubs, influence elections, or publish newspapers. A decree reduced the number of newspapers in Paris from seventy-three to thirteen (and then finally to four), and the newspapers that remained became government organs. Government censors had to approve all operas and plays, and they banned "offensive" artistic works even more frequently than their royal predecessors had. The minister of police, Joseph Fouché, once a leading figure in the Terror of 1793–1794, imposed house arrest, arbitrary imprisonment, and surveillance of political dissidents. Political contest and debate shriveled to almost nothing. When a bomb attack on Napoleon's carriage failed in 1800, Fouché suppressed the evidence of a royalist plot and instead arrested hundreds of former Jacobins. More than one hundred of them were deported and seven hundred imprisoned.

When it suited him, Napoleon also struck against royalist conspirators. In 1804, he ordered his police to kidnap the duke d'Enghien from his residence in Germany. Napoleon had intelligence, which proved to be false, that d'Enghien had joined a plot in Paris against him. Even when he learned the truth, he insisted that a military tribunal try d'Enghien, a close relative of the dead king Louis XVI. After a summary trial, d'Enghien was shot on the spot.

By then, Napoleon's political intentions had become clear. He had named himself First Consul for life in 1802, and in 1804, with the pope's blessing, he crowned himself emperor. Once again, plebiscites approved his decisions but only yes/no alternatives

Napoleon's Coronation as Emperor
In this detail from *The Coronation of Napoleon and Josephine* (1805–1807), Jacques-Louis David shows Napoleon crowning his wife at the ceremony of 1804. Napoleon orchestrated the entire event and took the only active role in it: Pope Pius VII gave his blessing to the ceremony (he can be seen seated behind Napoleon), but Napoleon crowned himself. What is the significance of Napoleon crowning himself? *(Erich Lessing/Art Resource, NY.)*

were offered. Still, though the democratic political aims of the French Revolution had been trampled, some aspects of daily life continued to be affected by egalitarian ideals (see "Seeing History," page 656).

Imperial Rule Napoleon's outsize personality dominated the new regime. His face and name adorned coins, engravings, histories, paintings, and public monuments. His favorite painters embellished his legend by depicting him as a warrior-hero of mythic proportions even though he was short and physically unimpressive in person. Believing that "what is big is always beautiful," Napoleon embarked on ostentatious building projects that would outshine even those of Louis XIV. Government-commissioned architects built the Arc de Triomphe, the Stock Exchange, fountains, and even slaughterhouses. Most of the emperor's new construction reflected his neoclassical taste for monumental buildings set in vast empty spaces.

Napoleon worked hard at establishing his reputation as an efficient administrator with broad intellectual interests: he met frequently with scientists, jurists, and artists, and stories abounded of his unflagging energy. When not on military campaigns, he worked on state affairs, usually until 10:00 p.m., taking only a few minutes for each meal. "Authority," declared his adviser the abbé Sieyès, "must come from above and confidence from below." To establish his authority, Napoleon relied on men who had served with him in the army. His chief of staff Alexandre Berthier, for example, became minister of war, and the chemist Claude Berthollet, who had organized the scientific part of the expedition to Egypt, became vice president of the Senate in 1804. Napoleon's bureaucracy was based on a patron-client relationship, with Napoleon as the ultimate patron. Some of Napoleon's closest associates married into his family.

Combining aristocratic and revolutionary values in a new social hierarchy that rewarded merit and talent, Napoleon personally chose as senators the nation's most illustrious generals, ministers, prefects, scientists, rich men, and former nobles. Intending to replace both the old nobility of birth and the republic's strict emphasis on equality, in 1802 he

SEEING HISTORY

The Clothing Revolution: The Social Meaning of Changes in Postrevolutionary Fashion

Some revolutions take place in the realm of social life and culture rather than politics. One of the most striking of these social and cultural revolutions was the wearing of trousers. Before the French Revolution of 1789, men of the middle classes and nobility wore knee breeches, stockings, and buckled shoes, as can be seen in the colored engraving from 1778. Trousers (long pants) were worn only by working-class men, who needed them to protect themselves on the job and from the mud in the streets.

From Napoleon onward, a shift toward trousers took place across Europe, not all at once but slowly and surely. Napoleon himself wore close-fitting pantaloons (from which the word *pants* is derived) until he became too fat and reverted back to knee breeches. The colored engraving of a middle-class couple in 1830 shows how long pants had become the fashion for men. In line with political changes that installed equality under the law and careers open to merit rather than birth, men began to dress more alike; all men wore trousers. Taking a closer look at the men in both pictures, do you see any other changes in style and accessories that might reflect a less class-conscious society?

Women's dress, in contrast, maintained and even underlined social distinctions after the Revolution. In the nineteenth century, middle- and upper-class women continued to wear dresses with such long and full skirts that they could not possibly be imagined working. Working women wore simpler blouses and skirts that allowed the movements necessary to labor at home or in manufacturing.

Questions to Consider

1. **Compare the pre-Revolution fashion shown with that of the woman in the 1830 engraving. Does one outfit look more comfortable than the other? Why or why not? What other differences (or similarities) do you notice?**
2. **Why do you think women's fashion failed to become more uniform the way men's did in the decades following the Revolution?**

Gentleman Proposing to a Lady, 1778. *(Private Collection/The Stapleton Collection/The Bridgeman Art Library International.)*

Fashion for Men and Women, 1830. *(Musée de la Ville de Paris, Musée Carnavalet, Paris, France/Lauros/Giraudon/The Bridgeman Art Library International.)*

took the first step toward creating a new nobility by founding the Legion of Honor. (Members of the legion received lifetime pensions along with their titles.) Napoleon usually equated honor with military success; by 1814, the legion had thirty-two thousand members, only 5 percent of them civilians.

In 1808, Napoleon introduced a complete hierarchy of noble titles, ranging from princes down to barons and chevaliers. All Napoleonic nobles had served the state. Titles could be inherited but had to be supported by wealth — a man could not be a duke without a fortune of 200,000 francs or a chevalier without 3,000 francs. To go along with their new titles, Napoleon gave his favorite generals huge fortunes, often in the form of estates in the conquered territories.

Napoleon's own family reaped the greatest benefits. He made his older brother, Joseph, ruler of the newly established kingdom of Naples in 1806, the same year he installed his younger brother Louis as king of Holland. He proclaimed his twenty-three-year-old stepson, Eugène de Beauharnais, viceroy of Italy in 1805 and established his sister Caroline and brother-in-law General Joachim Murat as king and queen of Naples in 1808 when he moved Joseph to the throne of Spain. Napoleon wanted to establish an imperial succession, but he lacked an heir. In thirteen years of marriage, his wife, Josephine, had borne no children, so in 1809 he divorced her and in 1810 married the eighteen-year-old princess Marie-Louise of Austria. The next year Marie-Louise gave birth to a son, to whom Napoleon immediately gave the title king of Rome.

Emperor Napoleon in His Study
In this portrait painted by Jacques-Louis David in 1812, Napoleon is shown in his general's uniform, sword by his side. He stands by his desk covered with papers to show how hard he works for the country. *(Erich Lessing/Art Resource, NY.)*

The New Paternalism: The Civil Code

As part of his restoration of order, Napoleon brought a paternalistic model of power to his state. Previous governments had tried to unify and standardize France's multiple legal codes, but only Napoleon successfully established a new one, partly because he personally presided over the commission that drafted the new **Civil Code**, completed in 1804. Called the Napoleonic Code as a way of further exalting the emperor's image, it reasserted the Old Regime's patriarchal system of male domination over women and insisted on a father's control over his children, which revolutionary legislation had limited. For example, a child under age sixteen who refused to follow his or her father's commands could be sent to prison for up to a month with no hearing of any sort. Yet the code also required fathers to provide for their children's welfare. Moreover, the Civil Code protected many of the gains of the French Revolution by defining and ensuring property rights, guaranteeing religious liberty, and establishing a uniform system of law that provided equal treatment for all adult males and affirmed the right of men to choose their professions. Napoleon wanted to discourage abortion and infanticide, not uncommon among the poorest classes in the fast-growing urban areas, so he helped set up private charities to help indigent mothers and made it easier for women to abandon their children anonymously to a government foundling hospital.

Civil Code: The French legal code formulated by Napoleon in 1804; it ensured equal treatment under the law to all men and guaranteed religious liberty, but it curtailed many rights of women.

Although the code maintained the equal division of family property between all children, both male and female, it sharply curtailed women's rights in other respects. Napoleon wanted to restrict women to the private sphere of the home. One of his leading jurists remarked, "Women need protection because they are weaker; men are free because they are stronger." The law obligated a husband to support his wife, but the husband alone controlled any property held in common; a wife could not sue in court, sell or mortgage her own property, or contract a debt without her husband's consent. Divorce was severely restricted. A wife could petition for divorce only if her husband brought his mistress to live in the family home. In contrast, a wife convicted of adultery could be imprisoned for up to two years. The code's framers saw these discrepancies as a way to reinforce the family and make women responsible for private virtue, while leaving public decisions to men. The French code was imitated in many European and Latin American countries and in the French colony of Louisiana, where it had a similar negative effect on women's rights. Not until 1965 did French wives gain legal status equal to that of their husbands.

Napoleon took little interest in girls' education, believing that girls should spend most of their time at home learning religion, manners, and such "female occupations" as sewing and music. For boys, by contrast, the government set up a new system of lycées, state-run secondary schools in which students wore military uniforms and drumrolls signaled the beginning and end of classes. The lycées offered wider access to education and thus helped achieve Napoleon's goal of opening careers to those with talent, regardless of their social origins. (The lycées have dropped the military trappings and are now coeducational, but they are still the heart of the French educational system.)

The new paternalism extended to relations between employers and employees. The state required all workers to carry a work card attesting to their good conduct, and it prohibited all workers' organizations. The police considered workers without cards to be vagrants or criminals and could send them to a workhouse or prison. After 1806, arbitration boards settled labor disputes, but they took employers at their word while treating workers as minors, demanding that foremen and shop superintendents represent them. Occasionally strikes broke out, led by secret, illegal journeymen's associations, yet many employers laid off employees when times were hard, deducted fines from their wages, and dismissed them without appeal for being absent or making errors. These limitations on workers' rights won Napoleon the support of French business.

Patronage of Science and Intellectual Life

Napoleon did everything possible to promote French scientific inquiry, especially that which could serve practical ends. He closely monitored the research institutes established during the Revolution, sometimes intervening personally to achieve political conformity. An impressive outpouring of new theoretical and practical scientific work rewarded the state's efforts. Experiments with balloons led to the discovery of laws about the expansion of gases, and research on fossil shells prepared the way for new theories of evolutionary change later in the nineteenth century. The surgeon Dominique-Jean Larrey developed new techniques of battlefield amputation and medical care during Napoleon's wars, winning an appointment as an officer in the Legion of Honor and becoming a baron with a pension.

Napoleon aimed to modernize French society through science, but he could not tolerate criticism. Napoleon considered most writers useless or dangerous, "good for nothing under any government." Some of the most talented French writers of the time had to live in exile. The best-known expatriate was Anne-Louise-Germaine de Staël (1766–1817), the daughter of Louis XVI's finance minister, Jacques Necker. When explaining his desire to banish her, Napoleon exclaimed, "She is a machine in motion who stirs up the salons." While exiled in the German states, de Staël wrote *Corinne* (1807), a novel whose heroine is a brilliant woman thwarted by a patriarchal system, and *On Germany* (1810), an account of the important new literary currents east of the Rhine. Her books were banned in France.

Although Napoleon restored the strong authority of state and religion in France, many royalists and Catholics still criticized him as an impious usurper. (See "Contrasting Views," page 666.) François-René de Chateaubriand (1768–1848) admired Napoleon as "the strong man who has saved us from the abyss," but he preferred monarchy. In his view, Napoleon had not properly understood the need to defend Christian values against the Enlightenment's excessive reliance on reason. Chateaubriand wrote his *Genius of Christianity* (1802) to draw attention to the power and mystery of faith. He warned, "It is to the vanity of knowledge that we owe almost all our misfortunes. . . . The learned ages have always been followed by ages of destruction." Chateaubriand's book appeared during a rare lull in wars that soon engulfed much of Europe.

REVIEW QUESTION In what ways did Napoleon continue the French Revolution, and in what ways did he break with it?

Germaine de Staël
One of the most fascinating intellectuals of her time, Anne-Louise-Germaine de Staël seemed to irritate Napoleon more than any other person did. Daughter of Louis XVI's Swiss Protestant finance minister, Jacques Necker, and wife of a Swedish diplomat, Madame de Staël frequently criticized Napoleon's policies. She published best-selling novels and influential literary criticism, and whenever allowed to reside in Paris she encouraged the intellectual and political dissidents from Napoleon's regime. In this painting from 1809, Elisabeth Vigée-Lebrun depicts her as Corinne, the heroine of one of her novels. *(Musée d'Art et d'Histoire, Geneva, Switzerland/The Bridgeman Art Library International.)*

"Europe Was at My Feet": Napoleon's Conquests

Building on innovations introduced by the republican governments before him, Napoleon revolutionized the art of war with tactics and strategies based on a highly mobile army. By 1812, he ruled a European empire more extensive than any since ancient Rome (Map 20.1). Yet that empire had already begun to crumble, and with it went Napoleon's power at home. Napoleon's empire failed because it was based on a contradiction: Napoleon tried to reduce virtually all nations of Europe to the status of colonial dependents when Europe had long consisted of independent states. The result, inevitably, was a great upsurge in nationalist feeling that has dominated European politics to the present.

The Grand Army and Its Victories, 1800–1807

Napoleon attributed his military success "three-quarters to morale" and the rest to leadership and superiority of numbers at the point of attack. Conscription provided the large numbers: 1.3 million men ages twenty to twenty-four were drafted between 1800 and 1812, another 1 million in 1813–1814. Many willingly served because the republic had taught them to identify the army with the nation. Military service was both a patriotic duty and a means of social mobility. The men who rose through the ranks to become officers were young, ambitious, and accustomed to the new ways of war. Consequently, the French army had higher morale than the armies of other powers, most of which rejected conscription as too democratic and continued to restrict their officer corps to the nobility. Only in 1813–1814, when the military tide turned against Napoleon, did French morale plummet.

When Napoleon came to power in 1799, desertion was rampant and the generals competed with one another for predominance. Napoleon ended the squabbling by uniting all the armies into one Grand Army under his personal command. By 1812, he was commanding 700,000 troops; while 250,000 soldiers fought in Spain, others remained garrisoned in France. In any given battle, between 70,000 and 180,000 men, not all of them French, fought for France. Life on campaign was no picnic — ordinary soldiers slept in the rain, mud, and snow and often

MAP 20.1 Napoleon's Empire at Its Height, 1812

In 1812, Napoleon had at least nominal control of almost all of western Europe. Even before he made his fatal mistake of invading Russia, however, his authority had been undermined in Spain and seriously weakened in the Italian and German states. Still earlier, he had given up his dreams of a worldwide empire. French armies withdrew from Egypt in 1801 and from Saint Domingue (Haiti) in 1802. In 1803 Napoleon sold the Louisiana Territory to the United States.

had to forage for food—but Napoleon nonetheless inspired almost fanatical loyalty. He fought alongside his soldiers in some sixty battles and had nineteen horses shot from under him. One opponent said that Napoleon's presence alone was worth fifty thousand men.

A brilliant strategist who carefully studied the demands of war, Napoleon outmaneuvered virtually all his opponents. He had a pragmatic and direct approach to strategy: he went for the main body of the opposing army and tried to crush it in a lightning campaign. He gathered the largest possible army for one great and decisive battle and then followed with a relentless pursuit to break enemy morale altogether. His military command, like his rule within France, was personal and highly centralized. He essentially served as his own operations officer: "I alone know what I have to do," he insisted. This style worked as long as Napoleon could be on the battlefield, but he failed to train independent subordinates to take over in his absence. He also faced constant difficulties in supplying a rapidly moving army, which, because of its size, could not always live off the land.

One of Napoleon's greatest advantages was the lack of coordination among his enemies. Britain dominated the seas but did not want to field huge land armies. On the continent, the French republic had already set up satellites in the Netherlands and Italy, which served as a buffer against the big powers to the east—Austria, Prussia, and Russia. By maneuvering diplomatically and militarily, Napoleon could usually take these on one by one. After reorganizing the French armies in 1799, for example, Napoleon won striking victories against the Austrians at Marengo and Hohenlinden in 1800, forcing them to agree to peace terms. Once the Austrians had withdrawn, Britain agreed to the Treaty of Amiens in 1802, effectively ending hostilities on the continent. Napoleon considered the peace with Great Britain merely a truce, however, and it lasted only until 1803.

Napoleon used the breathing space not only to consolidate his position before taking up arms again but also to send an expeditionary force to the Caribbean colony of St. Domingue to regain control of the island. Continuing resistance among the black population and an epidemic of yellow fever forced Napoleon to withdraw his troops from St. Domingue and abandon his plans to extend his empire to the Western Hemisphere. As part of his retreat, he sold the Louisiana Territory to the United States in 1803.

When war resumed in Europe, the British navy once more proved its superiority by blocking an attempted French invasion and by defeating the French and their Spanish allies in a huge naval battle at Trafalgar in 1805. France lost many ships; the British lost no vessels, but their renowned admiral Lord Horatio Nelson died in the battle.

On land, Napoleon remained invincible. In 1805, Austria took up arms again when Napoleon demanded that it declare neutrality in the conflict with Britain. Napoleon promptly captured twenty-five thousand Austrian soldiers at Ulm, in Bavaria, in 1805. After marching on to Vienna, he again trounced the Austrians, who had been joined by their new ally, Russia. The battle of Austerlitz, often considered Napoleon's greatest victory, was fought on December 2, 1805, the first anniversary of his coronation.

After maintaining neutrality for a decade, Prussia now declared war on France. In 1806, the French routed the Prussian army at Jena and Auerstädt. In 1807, Napoleon defeated the Russians at Friedland. Personal negotiations between Napoleon and the young tsar Alexander I (r. 1801–1825) resulted in a humiliating settlement imposed on Prussia, which paid the price for temporary reconciliation between France and Russia; the Treaties of Tilsit turned Prussian lands west of the Elbe River into the kingdom of Westphalia under Napoleon's brother Jerome, and Prussia's Polish provinces became the duchy of Warsaw. Napoleon once again had turned the divisions among his enemies to his favor.

The Impact of French Victories

Wherever the Grand Army conquered, Napoleon's influence followed soon after. By annexing some territories and setting up others as satellite kingdoms with much-reduced autonomy, Napoleon attempted to colonize large parts of Europe (see Map 20.1, page 660). But even where he did not rule directly or through his relatives, his startling string of victories forced the other powers to reconsider their own methods of rule.

Rule in the Colonized Territories

Napoleon brought the disparate German and Italian states together so that he could rule them more effectively and exploit their resources for his own ends. In 1803, he consolidated the tiny German states by abolishing some of them and

Napoleon Visiting the Battlefield

Antoine-Jean Gros painted this scene of the battle of Eylau (now in northwestern Russia, then in East Prussia) shortly after Napoleon's victory against the Russian army in 1807. The painter aims to show the compassion of Napoleon for his men, but he also draws attention to the sheer carnage of war. Each side lost 25,000 men, killed or wounded, in this battle. What would you conclude from the way the ordinary soldiers are depicted here? *(Louvre, Paris, France/The Bridgeman Art Library International.)*

Consolidation of German and Italian States, 1812

attaching them to larger units. In July 1806, he established the Confederation of the Rhine, which soon included almost all the German states except Austria and Prussia. The Holy Roman Emperor gave up his title, held since the thirteenth century, and became simply the emperor of Austria. Napoleon established three units in Italy: the territories directly annexed to France and the satellite kingdoms of Italy and Naples. Italy had not been so unified since the Roman Empire.

Napoleon forced French-style reforms on both the annexed territories, which were ruled directly from France, and the satellite kingdoms, which were usually ruled by one or another of Napoleon's relatives but with a certain autonomy. French-style reforms included abolishing serfdom, eliminating seigneurial dues, introducing the Napoleonic Code, suppressing monasteries, and subordinating church to state, as well as extending civil rights to Jews and other religious minorities. Napoleon's chosen rulers often made real improvements in roads, public works, law codes, and education. The removal of internal tariffs fostered economic growth by opening up the domestic market for goods, especially textiles. By 1814, Bologna had five hundred factories and Modena four hundred. Yet almost everyone had some cause for complaint. Republicans regretted Napoleon's conversion of the sister republics into kingdoms. Tax increases and ever-rising conscription quotas fomented discontent as well. The annexed territories and satellite kingdoms paid half the cost of Napoleon's wars.

Almost everywhere, conflicts arose between Napoleon's desire for a standardized, centralized government and local insistence on maintaining customs and traditions. Sometimes his own relatives sided with the countries they ruled. Napoleon's brother Louis, for instance, would not allow conscription in the Netherlands because the Dutch had never had compulsory military service. When Napoleon tried to introduce an economic policy banning trade with Great Britain, Louis's lax enforcement infuriated the emperor, and Napoleon annexed the satellite kingdom in 1810.

Pressure for Reform in Prussia and Russia

Napoleon's victories forced defeated rulers to rethink their political and cultural assumptions. After the crushing defeat of Prussia in 1806 left his country greatly reduced in territory, Frederick William III (r. 1797–1840) appointed a reform commission, and on its recommendation he abolished serfdom and allowed non-nobles to buy and enclose land. Peasants gained their personal independence from their noble landlords, who could no longer sell them to pay gambling debts, for example, or refuse them permission to marry. Yet the lives of the former serfs remained bleak; they were left without land, and their landlords no longer had to care for them in hard times. The king's advisers also overhauled the army to make the high command more efficient and to open the way to the appointment of middle-class officers. Prussia instituted these reforms to try to compete with the French, not to promote democracy. As one reformer wrote to Frederick William, "We must do from above what the French have done from below."

Reform received lip service in Russia. Tsar Alexander I had gained his throne after an aristocratic coup deposed and killed his autocratic and capricious father, Paul (r. 1796–1801), and in the early years of his reign the remorseful young ruler created Western-style ministries, lifted restrictions on importing foreign books, and founded six new universities. In addition, reform commissions studied abuses, nobles were encouraged voluntarily to free their serfs (a few actually did so), and there was even talk of drafting a constitution. But none of these efforts reached beneath the surface of Russian life, and by the second decade of his reign Alexander began to reject the Enlightenment spirit that his grandmother Catherine the Great had instilled in him.

The Continental System

The one power always standing between Napoleon and total dominance of Europe was Great Britain. The British ruled the seas and financed anyone who would oppose Napoleon. In an effort to bankrupt this "nation of shopkeepers" by choking its trade, Napoleon inaugurated the **Continental System** in 1806. It prohibited all commerce between Great Britain and France or France's dependent states and allies. At first, the system worked: in 1807–1808, British exports dropped by 20 percent and manufacturing by 10 percent; unemployment

Continental System: The boycott of British goods in France and its satellites ordered by Napoleon in 1806; it had success but was later undermined by smuggling.

and a strike of sixty thousand workers in northern England resulted. The British retaliated by confiscating merchandise on ships, even those of powers neutral in the wars, that sailed into or out of ports from which the British were excluded by the system.

In the midst of continuing wars, moreover, the Continental System proved impossible to enforce, and widespread smuggling brought British goods into the European market. British growth continued, despite some setbacks; calico-printing works, for example, quadrupled their production, and imports of raw cotton increased by 40 percent. At the same time, French and other continental industries benefited from the temporary protection from British competition.

Resistance to French Rule, 1807–1812

Smuggling British goods was only one way of opposing the French. Almost everywhere in Europe, resistance began as local opposition to French demands for money or draftees but eventually prompted a more nationalistic patriotic defense. In southern Italy, gangs of bandits harassed the French army and local officials, who arrested thirty-three thousand Italian bandits in 1809 alone. But resistance continued via a network of secret societies called the *carbonari* ("charcoal burners"), which got its name from the practice of marking each new member's forehead with a charcoal mark. Throughout the nineteenth century, the carbonari played a leading role in Italian nationalism. In the German states, intellectuals wrote passionate defenses of the virtues of the German nation and of the superiority of German literature.

No nations bucked under Napoleon's reins more than Spain and Portugal. In 1807, Napoleon sent 100,000 troops through Spain to invade Portugal, Great Britain's ally. The royal family fled to the Portuguese colony of Brazil, but fighting continued, aided by a British army. When Napoleon got his brother Joseph named king of Spain in place of the senile Charles IV (r. 1788–1808), the Spanish clergy and nobles raised bands of peasants to fight the French occupiers. Even Napoleon's taking personal command of the French forces failed to quell the Spanish, who for six years fought a war of national

French Atrocities in Spain

In 1814 the Spanish painter Francisco Jose de Goya y Lucientes was inspired to depict a popular rebellion that took place in Madrid in 1808. The Spanish rebelled against the invading French when they learned that the French armies were forcing members of the Spanish royal family to leave Madrid. In this detail of the painting *The Second of May, 1808*, Mamelukes of the French army charge the rioting Spanish. (Mamelukes were Muslim soldiers who had originally been slaves.) *(Image © Francis G. Mayer/Corbis.)*

independence that pinned down thousands of French soldiers. Germaine de Staël commented that Napoleon "never understood that a war might be a crusade. . . . He never reckoned with the one power that no arms could overcome—the enthusiasm of a whole people."

More than a new feeling of nationalism was aroused in Spain. Peasants hated French requisitioning of their food supplies and sought to defend their priests against French anticlericalism. Spanish nobles feared revolutionary reforms and were willing to defend the old monarchy in the person of the young Ferdinand VII, heir to Charles IV, even while Ferdinand himself was congratulating Napoleon on his victories. The Spanish Catholic church spread anti-French propaganda that equated Napoleon with heresy. As the former archbishop of Seville wrote to the archbishop of Granada in 1808, "You realize that we must not recognize as king a freemason, heretic, Lutheran, as are all the Bonapartes and the French nation." In this tense atmosphere, the Spanish peasant rebels, assisted by the British, countered every French massacre with atrocities of their own. They tortured their French prisoners (boiling one general alive) and lynched collaborators.

From Russian Winter to Final Defeat, 1812–1815

Despite opposition, Napoleon ruled over an extensive empire by 1812. Only two major European states remained fully independent—Great Britain and Russia—but once allied they would successfully challenge his dominion and draw many other states to their side. Britain sent aid to the Portuguese and Spanish rebels, while Russia once again prepared for war. Tsar Alexander I made peace with Turkey and allied himself with Great Britain and Sweden. In 1812, Napoleon invaded Russia with 250,000 horses and 600,000 men, including contingents of Italians, Poles, Swiss, Dutch, and Germans. This daring move proved to be his undoing.

Invasion of Russia, 1812

Napoleon followed his usual strategy of trying to strike quickly, but the Russian generals avoided confrontation and retreated eastward, destroying anything that might be useful to the invaders. In September, on the road to Moscow, Napoleon finally engaged the main Russian force in the gigantic battle of Borodino (see Map 20.1, page 660). French casualties numbered 30,000 men, including 47 generals; the Russians lost 45,000. The French soldiers had nothing to celebrate around their campfires: as one soldier wrote, "Everyone . . . wept for some dead friend." Once again the Russians retreated, leaving Moscow undefended. Napoleon entered the deserted city, but the victory turned hollow because the departing Russians had set the wooden city on fire. Within a week, three-fourths of it had burned to the ground. Still Alexander refused to negotiate, and French morale plunged with worsening problems of supply. Weeks of constant marching in the dirt and heat had worn down the foot soldiers, who were dying of disease or deserting in large numbers (see Document, "An Ordinary Soldier on Campaign with Napoleon," page 665).

In October, Napoleon began his retreat; in November came the cold. A German soldier in the Grand Army described trying to cook fistfuls of raw bran with snow to make something like bread. For him, the retreat was "the indescribable horror of all possible plagues." Within a week the Grand Army lost 30,000 horses and had to abandon most of its artillery and food supplies. Russian forces harassed the retreating army, now more pathetic than grand. By December only 100,000 troops remained, one-sixth the original number, and the retreat had turned into a rout: the Russians had captured 200,000 soldiers, including 48 generals and 3,000 other officers.

Napoleon had made a classic military mistake that would be repeated by Adolf Hitler in World War II: fighting a war on two distant fronts simultaneously. The Spanish war tied down 250,000 French troops and forced Napoleon to bully Prussia and Austria into supplying soldiers of dubious loyalty for the Moscow campaign; those soldiers deserted at the first opportunity. The fighting in Spain and Portugal also exacerbated the already substantial logistical and communications problems involved in marching to Moscow.

The End of Napoleon's Empire

Napoleon's humiliation might have been temporary if the British and Russians had not successfully organized a coalition to complete the job. Napoleon still had resources at his command; by the spring of 1813, he had replenished his army with another 250,000 men. With British financial support, Russian, Austrian, Prussian, and Swedish armies met the French outside Leipzig in October 1813 and defeated Napoleon in the Battle of the Nations. One by one, Napoleon's German allies deserted him to join the German nationalist "war of liberation." The Confederation of the Rhine dissolved, and the Dutch revolted and restored the prince of Orange. Joseph Bonaparte fled Spain, and a combined Spanish-Portuguese army under British command invaded France. In only a few months, the allied powers crossed the Rhine and marched

DOCUMENT

An Ordinary Soldier on Campaign with Napoleon (1812)

Jakob Walter (1788–1864) recorded his experience as a soldier in the Napoleonic armies marching to Moscow in 1812. He wrote his account sometime after the events took place, though exactly when is not known. Walter was a German conscripted into military service from one of the many western German states controlled by Napoleon. The selection here describes the Napoleonic armies still on the offensive moving toward Moscow. But the seeds of future problems are already germinating.

On August 19, the entire army moved forward, and pursued the Russians with all speed. Four or five hours' farther up the river another battle started, but the enemy did not hold out long, and the march now led to Moshaisk [near Borodino], the so-called "Holy Valley." From Smolensk to Moshaisk the war displayed its horrible work of destruction: all the roads, fields, and woods lay as though sown with people, horses, wagons, burned villages and cities; everything looked like the complete ruin of all that lived. In particular, we saw ten dead Russians to one of our men, although every day our numbers fell off considerably. In order to pass through woods, swamps, and narrow trails, trees which formed barriers in the woods had to be removed, and wagon barricades of the enemy had to be cleared away. . . . The march up to there, as far as it was a march, is indescribable and inconceivable for people who have not seen anything of it. The very great heat, the dust which was like a thick fog, the closed line of march in columns, and the putrid water from holes filled with dead people and cattle brought everyone close to death; and eye pains, fatigue, thirst, and hunger tormented everybody. God! How often I remembered the bread and beer which I had enjoyed at home with such an indifferent pleasure! Now, however, I must struggle, half wild, with the dead and living. How gladly would I renounce for my whole life the warm food so common at home if I only did not lack good bread and beer now! I would not wish for more all my life. But these were empty, helpless thoughts. Yes, the thought of my brothers and sisters so far away added to my pain! Wherever I looked, I saw the soldiers with dead, half-desperate faces.

Source: Marc Raeff, ed., *Jakob Walter: The Diary of a Napoleonic Foot Soldier* (New York: Doubleday, 1991), 52–53.

Question to Consider

- **Do you think Walter's account of his experiences with Napoleon's army was clouded by the fact that he was a German conscript?**

toward Paris. In March 1814, the French Senate deposed Napoleon, who abdicated when his remaining generals refused to fight. Napoleon went into exile on the island of Elba off the Italian coast. His wife, Marie-Louise, refused to accompany him. The allies restored to the throne Louis XVIII (r. 1814–1824), the brother of Louis XVI, beheaded during the Revolution. (Louis XVI's son was known as Louis XVII even though he died in prison in 1795 without ever ruling.)

Because Louis XVIII lacked a solid base of support, Napoleon had one last chance to regain power. The new king tried to steer a middle course through a charter that established a British-style monarchy with a two-house legislature and guaranteed civil rights. But he was caught between nobles returning from exile, who demanded a complete restoration of their lands and powers, and the vast majority of ordinary people, who had supported either the republic or Napoleon during the previous twenty-five years. Sensing an opportunity, Napoleon escaped from Elba in early 1815 and, landing in southern France, made swift and unimpeded progress to Paris. Although he had left in ignominy, now crowds cheered him and former soldiers volunteered to serve him. The period eventually known as the Hundred Days (the length of time between Napoleon's escape and his final defeat) had begun. Louis XVIII fled across the border, waiting for help from France's enemies.

Napoleon quickly moved his reconstituted army of 74,000 men into present-day Belgium. At first, it seemed that he might succeed in separately fighting the two armies arrayed against him—a Prussian army of some 60,000 men and a joint force of 68,000 Belgian, Dutch, German, and British troops led by British general Sir Arthur Wellesley (1769–1852), duke of Wellington. The decisive **battle of Waterloo** took place on June 18, 1815, less than ten miles from Brussels. Napoleon's forces attacked Wellington's men first with infantry and then with cavalry, but the French failed to dislodge their opponents. Late in the afternoon, the Prussians arrived and the rout was complete. Napoleon had no

battle of Waterloo: The final battle lost by Napoleon; it took place near Brussels on June 18, 1815, and led to the deposed emperor's final exile.

CONTRASTING VIEWS

Napoleon: For and Against

After his final exile, Napoleon presented himself as a martyr to the cause of liberty whose goal was to create a European "federation of free people." Few were convinced by this "gospel according to St. Helena" (Document 1). Followers such as Emmanuel de Las Cases burnished the Napoleonic legend, but detractors such as Benjamin Constant viewed him as a tyrant (Document 2). For all his defects, Napoleon fascinated even those who were too young to understand his rise and fall. The French romantic poet Victor Hugo celebrated both the glory and the tragedy of Napoleonic ambitions (Document 3).

1. Napoleon's Own View from Exile

As might be expected, Napoleon put the most positive possible construction on his plans for France. In exile he wrote letters and talked at length to Emmanuel de Las Cases (1766–1842), an aristocratic officer in the royal navy who rallied to Napoleon in 1802, served in the Council of State, and later accompanied him to St. Helena. Much of what we know about Napoleon's views comes from a book published by Las Cases in 1821.

March 3, 1817:

In spite of all the libels, I have no fear whatever about my fame. Posterity will do me justice. The truth will be known; and the good I have done will be compared with the faults I have committed. I am not uneasy as to the result. Had I succeeded, I would have died with the reputation of the greatest man that ever existed. As it is, although I have failed, I shall be considered as an extraordinary man: my elevation was unparalleled, because unaccompanied by crime. I have fought fifty pitched battles, almost all of which I have won. I have framed and carried into effect a code of laws that will bear my name to the most distant posterity. I raised myself from nothing to be the most powerful monarch in the world. Europe was at my feet. I have always been of the opinion that the sovereignty lay in the people. In fact, the imperial government was a kind of republic. Called to the head of it by the voice of the nation, my maxim was, *la carrière est ouverte aux talents* ["careers open to talent"] without distinction of birth or fortune, and this system of equality is the reason that your oligarchy hates me so much.

Source: R. M. Johnston, *The Corsican: A Diary of Napoleon's Life in His Own Words* (Boston: Houghton Mifflin, 1921), 492.

2. Benjamin Constant, Spokesman for the Liberal Opposition to Napoleon

Benjamin Constant (1767–1830) came from an old French Calvinist family that had fled to Switzerland to escape persecution. Constant spent the early years of the French Revolution in a minor post at a minor German court. He moved to Paris in 1795 and became active in French politics during the Directory. Under Napoleon he went into exile, where he published a romantic novel, Adolphe *(1806), and pamphlets like this one attacking Napoleon. He reconciled to Napoleon during the Hundred Days and then opposed the restored Bourbon monarchy. In this selection, written during his exile, he expresses his hostility to Napoleon as a usurper dependent on war to maintain himself in power.*

Surely, Bonaparte is a thousand times more guilty than those barbarous conquerors who, ruling over barbarians, were by no means at odds with their age. Unlike them, he has chosen barbarism; he has preferred it. In the midst of enlightenment, he has sought to bring back the night. He has chosen to transform into greedy and bloodthirsty nomads a mild and polite people: his crime lies in this premeditated intention, in his obstinate effort to rob us of the heritage of all the enlightened generations who have preceded us on this earth. But why have we given him the right to conceive such a project?

When he first arrived here, alone, out of poverty and obscurity, and until he was twenty-four, his greedy gaze wandering over the country around him, why did we show him a country in which any religious idea was the object of irony? [Constant refers here to de-Christianization during the French Revolution.] When he listened to what was professed in our circles, why did serious thinkers tell him that man had no other motivation than his own interest? . . .

Because immediate usurpation was easy, he believed it could be durable, and

choice but to abdicate again. This time the victorious allies banished him permanently to the remote island of St. Helena, far off the coast of West Africa, where he died in 1821 at the age of fifty-two.

The cost of Napoleon's rule was high: 750,000 French soldiers and 400,000 others from annexed and satellite states died between 1800 and 1815. Yet his impact on world history was undeniable. (See "Contrasting Views," above.) Napoleon's plans for a united Europe, his insistence on spreading the legal reforms of the French Revolution, his social welfare programs, and even his inadvertent awakening of national sentiment set the agenda for European history in the modern era.

REVIEW QUESTION Why was Napoleon able to gain control over so much of Europe's territory?

once he became a usurper, he did all that usurpation condemns a usurper to do in our century.

It was necessary to stifle inside the country all intellectual life: he banished discussion and proscribed the freedom of the press.

The nation might have been stunned by that silence: he provided, extorted or paid for acclamation which sounded like the national voice. . . . War flung onto distant shores that part of the French nation that still had some real energy. It prompted the police harassment of the timid, whom it could not force abroad. It struck terror into men's hearts, and left there a certain hope that chance would take responsibility for their deliverance: a hope agreeable to fear and convenient to inertia. How many times have I heard men who were pressed to resist tyranny postponing this, during wartime till the coming of peace, and in peacetime until war commences!

I am right therefore in claiming that a usurper's sole resource is uninterrupted war. Some object: what if Bonaparte had been pacific? Had he been pacific, he would never have lasted for twelve years. Peace would have re-established communication among the different countries of Europe. These communications would have restored to thought its means of expression. Works published abroad would have been smuggled into the country. The French would have seen that they did not enjoy the approval of the majority of Europe.

Source: Benjamin Constant, "Further Reflections on Usurpation," in *Political Writings*, trans. Biancamaria Fontana (Cambridge: Cambridge University Press, 1988), 161–63.

3. Victor Hugo, "The Two Islands" (1825)

Victor Hugo (1802–1885) was France's greatest romantic poet and novelist, author of The Hunchback of Notre Dame *and* Les Misérables. *His father was a Napoleonic general, but his mother was an equally ardent royalist. In this early poem, Hugo compares Napoleon to one of Napoleon's favorite icons, the eagle, symbol of empire. The two islands of the title are Corsica, Napoleon's birthplace, and St. Helena, his place of final exile and death.*

These Isles, where Ocean's shattered spray
Upon the ruthless rocks is cast,
Seem like two treacherous ships of prey,
Made by eternal anchors fast.
The hand that settled bleak and black
Those shores on their unpeopled rack,
And clad in fear and mystery,
Perchance thus made them tempest-torn,
That Bonaparte might there be born,
And that Napoleon there might die. . . .
He his imperial nest hath built so far and high,
He seems to us to dwell within that tranquil sky,
Where you shall never see the angry tempest break.
'Tis but beneath his feet the growling storms are sped,
And thunders to assault his head
Must to their highest source go back.
The bolt flew upwards: from his eyrie [nest] riven,
Blazing he falls beneath the stroke of heaven;
Then kings their tyrant foe reward—
They chain him, living, on that lonely shore;
And earth captive giant handed o'er
To ocean's more resistless guard. . . .
Shame, hate, misfortune, vengeance, curses sore,
On him let heaven and earth together pour:
Now, see we dashed the vast Colossus low.
May he forever rue, alive and dead,
All tears he caused mankind to shed,
And all the blood he caused to flow.

Source: Henry Carrington, *Translations from the Poems of Victor Hugo* (London: Walter Scott, 1885), 34–41.

Questions to Consider

1. **Which of these views of Napoleon has the most lasting value as opposed to immediate dramatic effect?**
2. **According to these selections, what was Napoleon's greatest accomplishment? His greatest failure?**
3. **Victor Hugo called Napoleon "the vast Colossus." Why did he pick this larger-than-life metaphor even when writing lines critical of Napoleon's legacy of tears and bloodshed?**

The "Restoration" of Europe

Even while Napoleon was making his last desperate bid for power, his enemies were meeting in the Congress of Vienna (1814–1815) to decide the fate of postrevolutionary, post-Napoleonic Europe. Although interrupted by the Hundred Days, the **Congress of Vienna** settled the boundaries of European states, determined who would rule each nation, and established a new framework for international

Congress of Vienna: Face-to-face negotiations (1814–1815) between the great powers to settle the boundaries of European states and determine who would rule each nation after the defeat of Napoleon.

relations based on periodic meetings, or congresses, between the major powers. The doctrine of conservatism bolstered this post-Napoleonic order and in some places went hand in hand with a revival of religion.

The Congress of Vienna, 1814–1815

The Vienna settlement established a new equilibrium that relied on cooperation among the major powers while guaranteeing the status of smaller states. The revolutionary and Napoleonic wars had produced a host of potentially divisive issues. In addition to determining the boundaries of France, the congress had to decide the fate of Napoleon's duchy of Warsaw, the German province of Saxony, the Netherlands, the states once part of the Confederation of the Rhine, and various Italian territories. All had either changed hands or been created during the wars. These issues were resolved by face-to-face negotiations among representatives of the five major powers: Austria, Russia, Prussia, Britain, and France. With its aim to establish a long-lasting, negotiated peace endorsed by all parties, both winners and losers, the Congress of Vienna provided a model for the twentieth-century League of Nations and United Nations. The congress system, or "concert of Europe," helped prevent another major war until the 1850s, and no conflict comparable to the Napoleonic wars would occur again until 1914.

Austria's chief negotiator, Prince **Klemens von Metternich** (1773–1859), took the lead in devising the settlement and shaping the post-Napoleonic order. A well-educated nobleman who spoke five languages, Metternich served as a minister in the Austrian cabinet from 1809 to 1848. Although his penchant for womanizing made him a security risk in the eyes of the British Foreign Office (he even had an affair with Napoleon's younger sister), he worked with the British prime minister Robert Castlereagh (1769–1822) to ensure a moderate agreement that would check French aggression yet maintain France's great-power status. Metternich and Castlereagh believed that French aggression must be contained, because it had threatened the European peace since the days of Louis XIV, but at the same time that France must remain a major player to prevent any one European power from dominating the others. In this way, France could help Austria and Britain counter the ambitions of Prussia and Russia. Castlereagh hoped to make Britain the arbiter of European affairs, but he knew this could be accomplished only through adroit diplomacy because the British consti-

Klemens von Metternich (KLAY mehnts fawn MEH tur nihk): An Austrian prince (1773–1859) who took the lead in devising the post-Napoleonic settlement arranged by the Congress of Vienna (1814–1815).

Congress of Vienna

An unknown French engraver caricatured the efforts of the diplomats at the Congress of Vienna, complaining that they used the occasion to divide the spoils of European territory. What elements in this engraving make it a caricature? *(Photo: akg-images.)*

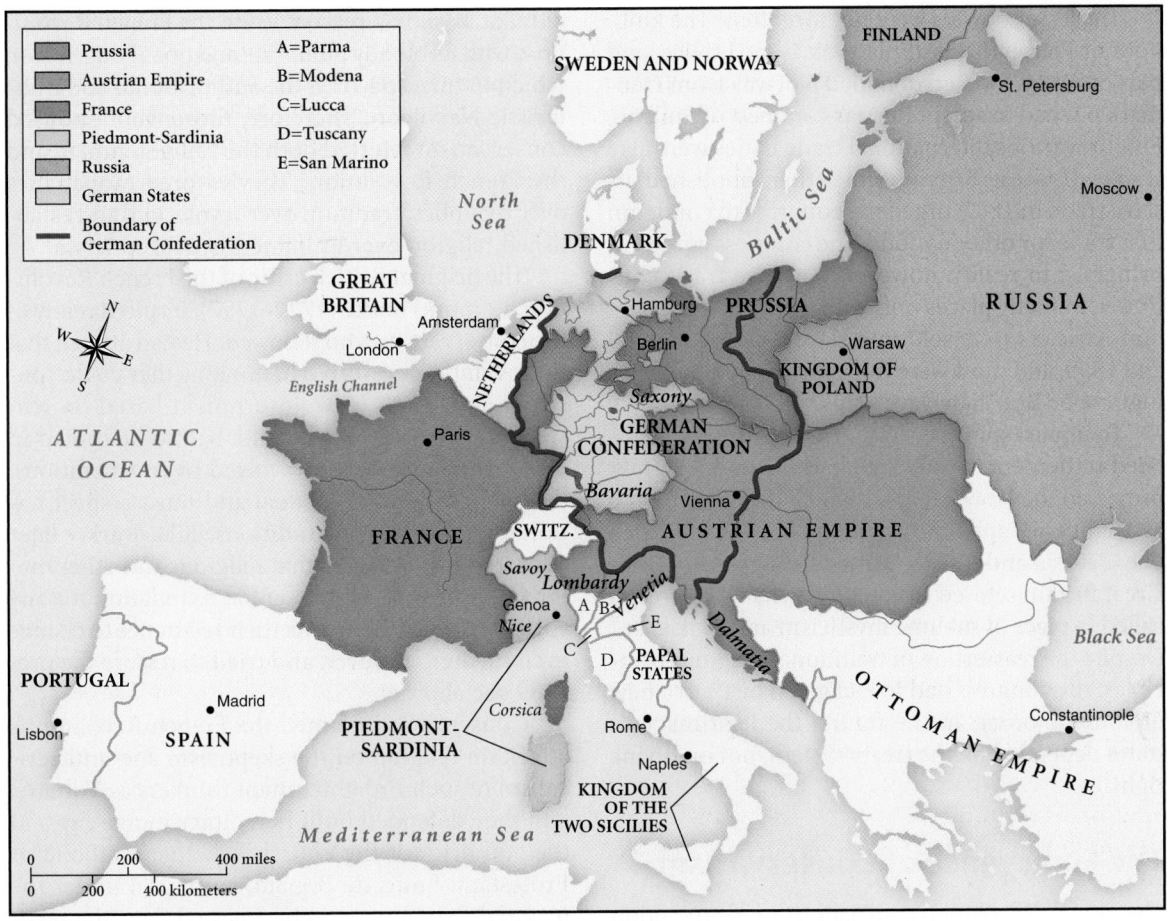

MAP 20.2 Europe after the Congress of Vienna, 1815

The Congress of Vienna forced France to return to its 1789 borders. The Austrian Netherlands and the Dutch Republic were united in a new kingdom of the Netherlands, the German states were joined in a German Confederation that built on Napoleon's Confederation of the Rhine, and Napoleon's duchy of Warsaw became the kingdom of Poland with the tsar of Russia as king. To compensate for its losses in Poland, Prussia gained territory in Saxony and on the left bank of the Rhine. Austria reclaimed the Italian provinces of Lombardy and Venetia and the Dalmatian coast.

tutional monarchy had little in common with most of its more absolutist continental counterparts.

The task of ensuring France's status at the Congress of Vienna fell to Prince Charles Maurice de Talleyrand (1754–1838), an aristocrat and former bishop who had embraced the French Revolution, served as Napoleon's foreign minister, and ended as foreign minister to Louis XVIII after helping arrange the emperor's overthrow. Informed of Talleyrand's betrayal, Napoleon called him "excrement in silk stockings." When the French army failed to oppose Napoleon's return to power in the Hundred Days, the allies took away all territory conquered since 1790, levied an indemnity against France, and required it to support an army of occupation until it had paid.

The goal of the Congress of Vienna was to achieve postwar stability by establishing secure states with guaranteed borders (Map 20.2). Because the congress aimed to "restore" as many regimes as possible to their former rulers, this epoch is sometimes labeled the **restoration**. But simple restoration was not always feasible, and in those cases the congress rearranged territory to balance the competing interests of the great powers. Thus, the congress turned the duchy of Warsaw into a new Polish kingdom but made the tsar of Russia its king. (Poland would not regain its independence until 1918.) The former Dutch Republic and the Austrian Netherlands, both annexed to France, were now united as the new kingdom of the Netherlands under the restored stadholder. Austria took charge of the German Confederation, which replaced the defunct Holy Roman Empire and also included Prussia.

---

restoration: The epoch after the fall of Napoleon, in which the Congress of Vienna aimed to "restore" as many regimes as possible to their former rulers.

The lesser powers were not forgotten. The kingdom of Piedmont-Sardinia took Genoa, Nice, and part of Savoy. Sweden obtained Norway from Denmark but had to accept Russia's conquest of Finland. Finally, various international trade issues were also resolved. Great Britain, which had abolished its slave trade in 1807, urged the congress to condemn that trade for other nations. The congress agreed in principle; in reality, however, the slave trade continued in many places until 1850. Nearly three million Africans were sold into slavery between 1800 and 1850, and most were transported on either Portuguese or Brazilian slave ships.

To impart spiritual substance to this very calculated settlement of political affairs, Tsar Alexander proposed the Holy Alliance, which called on divine assistance in upholding religion, peace, and justice. Prussia and Austria signed the agreement, but Great Britain refused to accede to what Castlereagh called "a piece of sublime mysticism and nonsense." Despite the reassertion of traditional religious principles, the congress had in fact given birth to a new diplomatic order: in the future, the legitimacy of states depended on the treaty system, not on divine right.

The Emergence of Conservatism

The French Revolution and Napoleonic domination of Europe had shown contemporaries that government could be changed overnight, that the old hierarchies could be overthrown in the name of reason, and that even Christianity could be written off or at least profoundly altered with the stroke of a pen. The potential for rapid change raised many questions about the proper sources of authority. Kings and churches could be restored and former revolutionaries locked up or silenced, but the old order no longer commanded automatic obedience. The old order was now merely *old*, no longer "natural" and "timeless." It had been ousted once and therefore might fall again. People insisted on having reasons to believe in their "restored" governments. The political doctrine that justified the restoration was **conservatism**.

Conservatives benefited from the disillusionment that permeated Europe after 1815. In the eyes of most Europeans, Napoleon had become a tyrant who ruled in his own interests. Conservatives saw a logical progression in recent history: the Enlightenment, based on reason, led to the French Revolution, with its bloody guillotine and horrifying Terror, which in turn spawned the authoritarian and militaristic Napoleon. Therefore, those who espoused conservatism rejected both the Enlightenment and the French Revolution. They favored monarchies over republics, tradition over revolution, and established religion over Enlightenment skepticism.

The original British critic of the French Revolution, Edmund Burke (1729–1797), inspired many of the conservatives who followed. He had argued that the revolutionaries erred in thinking they could construct an entirely new government based on reason. Government, Burke said, had to be rooted in long experience, which evolved over generations. All change must be gradual and must respect national and historical traditions. Like Burke, later conservatives believed that religious and other major traditions were an essential foundation for any society. Most of them took their resistance to change even further, however, and tried to restore the pre-1789 social order.

Conservatives blamed the French Revolution's attack on religion on the skepticism and anticlericalism of such Enlightenment thinkers as Voltaire, and they defended both hereditary monarchy and the authority of the church, whether Catholic or Protestant. Louis de Bonald, an official under the restored French monarchy, insisted that "the revolution began with the declaration of the rights of man and will only finish when the rights of God are declared." The declaration of rights, he asserted, represented the evil influence of Enlightenment philosophy and with it atheism, Protestantism, and freemasonry, which he lumped together. In this view, an enduring social order could be constructed only on the foundations provided by the church, the state, and the patriarchal family. Faith, sentiment, history, and tradition must fill the vacuum left by the failures of reason and excessive belief in individual rights. Across Europe, these views were taken up and elaborated by government advisers, professors, and writers. Not surprisingly, they had their strongest appeal in ruling circles and guided the politics of men such as Metternich in Austria, Alexander I in Russia, and the restored Bourbons in France.

The restored French monarchy provided a major test for conservatism because the returning Bourbons had to confront the legacy of twenty-five years of upheaval. Louis XVIII tried to ensure a measure of continuity by maintaining Napoleon's Civil Code. He also guaranteed the rights of ownership to church lands sold during the revolutionary period and created a parliament composed of the Chamber of Peers, nominated by the king, and the Chamber of Deputies, elected by very restricted suf-

---

conservatism: A political doctrine that emerged after 1789 and took hold after 1815; it rejected much of the Enlightenment and the French Revolution, preferring monarchies over republics, tradition over revolution, and established religion over Enlightenment skepticism.

frage (fewer than 100,000 voters in a population of 30 million). In making these concessions, the king tried to follow a moderate course of compromise, but the Ultras (ultraroyalists) pushed for complete repudiation of the revolutionary past. When Louis returned to power after Napoleon's final defeat, armed royalist bands attacked and murdered hundreds of Bonapartists and former revolutionaries. In 1816, the Ultras insisted on abolishing divorce and set up special courts to punish opponents of the regime. When an assassin killed Louis XVIII's nephew in 1820, the Ultras successfully demanded even more extreme measures.

The Revival of Religion

The experience of revolutionary upheaval and nearly constant warfare prompted many to renew their religious faith once peace returned. In France, the Catholic church sent missionaries to hold open-air "ceremonies of reparation" to express repentance for the outrages of revolution. In Rome, the papacy reestablished the Jesuit order, which had been disbanded during the Enlightenment. In the Italian states and Spain, governments used religious societies of laypeople to combat the influence of reformers and nationalists such as the Italian carbonari.

Revivalist movements, especially in Protestant countries, could on occasion challenge the status quo rather than supporting it. In parts of Protestant Germany and Britain, religious revival had begun in the eighteenth century with the rise of Pietism and Methodism, movements that stressed individual religious experience rather than reason as the true path to moral and social reform. The English Methodists followed John Wesley (1703–1791), who had preached an emotional, morally austere, and very personal "method" of gaining salvation.

The Methodists, or Wesleyans, gradually separated from the Church of England and in the early decades of the nineteenth century attracted thousands of members in huge revival meetings that lasted for days. Shopkeepers, artisans, agricultural laborers, miners, and workers in cottage industries, both male and female, flocked to the new denomination, even though at first Methodism seemed to emphasize conservative political views: Methodist statutes of 1792 had insisted that "none of us shall either in writing or in conversation speak lightly or irreverently of the government." In their hostility to rigid doctrine and elaborate ritual and their encouragement of popular preaching, however, the Methodists in England fostered a sense of democratic community and even a rudimentary sexual equality. From the beginning, women preachers traveled on horseback to preach in barns, town halls, and textile dye houses. The Methodist Sunday schools that taught thousands of poor children to read and write eventually helped create greater demands for working-class political participation.

The religious revival was not limited to Europe. In the United States, the second Great Awakening began around 1790 with huge camp meetings that brought together thousands of worshippers and scores of evangelical preachers, many of them Methodist. (The original Great Awakening took place in the 1730s and 1740s, sparked by the preaching of George Whitefield, a young English evangelist and follower of John Wesley.) Men and women danced to exhaustion, fell into trances, and spoke in tongues. During this period, Protestant sects began systematic missionary activity in other parts of the world. In the British colony of India, for example, Protestant missionaries pushed the British administration to abolish the Hindu custom of *sati*—the burning of widows on the funeral pyres of their

A Protestant Missionary in India
This colored engraving shows the English Baptist missionary William Carey (1761–1834) baptizing his first Hindu convert. Carey went to India in 1793 and spent forty years there as a teacher and a preacher. He led efforts to get the British governor general to outlaw the Hindu rite of *sati*, the burning of widows with their husbands. He became professor of Indian languages at Fort William College, established in Calcutta for training British officials, and supervised the translation of the Bible into more than forty local languages. *(The Granger Collection, New York—All rights reserved.)*

husbands—in 1829. The missionaries hoped such actions would make Indians more likely to embrace Christianity. Missionary activity by Protestants and Catholics would become one of the arms of European imperialism and cultural influence in the nineteenth century.

REVIEW QUESTION To what extent did the Congress of Vienna restore the old order?

Challenges to the Conservative Order

Conservatives hoped to clamp a lid on European affairs, but the lid kept threatening to fly off. Drawing on the turmoil in society and politics was romanticism, the burgeoning international movement in the arts and literature that dominated artistic expression in the first half of the nineteenth century. Although romantics shared with conservatives a distrust of the Enlightenment's emphasis on reason, romanticism did not translate into a unified political position. It did, however, heighten the general discontent with the conservative Vienna settlement. Isolated revolts threatened the hold of some conservative governments in the 1820s, but most of these rebellions were quickly bottled up. Then in 1830, successive uprisings briefly overwhelmed the established order. Across Europe, angry protesters sought constitutional guarantees of individual liberties and national unity and autonomy. The revolutionary legacy came back to life again.

Romanticism

As an artistic movement, romanticism encompassed poetry, music, painting, history, and literature. (See Chapter 18 for the origins of romanticism.) It glorified nature, emotion, genius, and imagination as antidotes to the Enlightenment and to classicism in the arts, challenging the reliance on reason, symmetry, and cool geometric spaces. Classicism idealized models from Roman history; romanticism turned to folklore and medieval legends. Classicism celebrated orderly, crisp lines; romantics sought out all that was wild, fevered, and disorderly. Chief among the arts of romanticism were poetry, music, and painting, which captured the deep-seated emotion characteristic of romantic expression. Romantics might take any political position, but they exerted the most political influence when they expressed nationalist feelings.

Romantic Poetry Romantic poetry celebrated overwhelming emotion and creative imagination. George Gordon, Lord Byron (1788–1824), explained his aims in writing poetry:

> For what is Poesy but to create
> From overfeeling, Good and Ill, and aim
> At an external life beyond our fate,
> And be the new Prometheus of new man.

Prometheus was the mythological figure who brought fire from the Greek gods to human beings. Byron did not seek the new Prometheus among political leaders or military men; he sought him within his own "overfeeling," his own intense emotions. Byron became a romantic hero himself when he rushed off to act on his emotions by fighting and dying in the Greek war for independence from

Romantic Painting
Johann Heinrich Fuseli painted *The Nightmare* in 1781, and it instantly became controversial because of the pose of the woman and the accompanying nightmarish figures. Are they actually present in the room, or are they only in the mind of the sleeper? Mary Shelley based a scene in *Frankenstein* on the painting; her parents were close friends of Fuseli. In what ways does this painting capture the themes of romanticism? *(Oil on canvas, 1781, Johann Heinrich Fussli [1741–1825]. Detroit Institute of Arts, USA/Founders Society purchase with Mr. and Mrs. Bert L. Smokler and Mr. and Mrs. Lawrence A. Fleischman funds/The Bridgeman Art Library International.)*

DOCUMENT

Wordsworth's Poetry (1798)

The son of a lawyer, William Wordsworth (1770–1850) studied at Cambridge University and then traveled to France during the early years of the French Revolution. He returned to England and began publishing the poetry that for many scholars marks the beginning of romanticism with its emphasis on the sublime beauties of nature. This excerpt from "Lines Composed a Few Miles above Tintern Abbey" (1798) shows the influence of his extensive walking tours through the English countryside. But the passage also captures the melancholy and nostalgia that characterized much of romantic poetry.

And now, with gleams of half-extinguished thought,
With many recognitions dim and faint,
And somewhat of a sad perplexity,
The picture of the mind revives again:
While here I stand, not only with the sense
Of present pleasure, but with pleasing thoughts
That in this moment there is life and food
For future years. And so I dare to hope,
Though changed, no doubt, from what I was when first
I came among these hills; when like a roe
I bounded o'er the mountains, by the sides
Of the deep rivers, and the lonely streams,
Wherever nature led: more like a man
Flying from something that he dreads, than one
Who sought the thing he loved. For nature then
(The coarser pleasures of my boyish days,
And their glad animal movements all gone by)
To me was all in all.—I cannot paint
What then I was. The sounding cataract
Haunted me like a passion: the tall rock,
The mountain, and the deep and gloomy wood,
Their colours and their forms, were then to me
An appetite; a feeling and a love,
That had no need of a remoter charm,
By thought supplied, nor any interest
Unborrowed from the eye.—That time is past.

Source: Paul Davis, ed., *Bedford Anthology of World Literature*. Book 5: *The Nineteenth Century*, 1800–1900 (Boston: Bedford/St. Martin's, 2003), 246–47.

Question to Consider

■ **In its specific imagery and overall message, how does Wordsworth's poem reflect a different sensibility about the world than writing associated with the Enlightenment?**

the Turks. An English aristocrat, Byron nonetheless claimed, "I have simplified my politics into a detestation of all existing governments."

Romantic poetry elevated the wonders of nature almost to the supernatural. In a poem that became one of the most beloved exemplars of romanticism, "Tintern Abbey" (1798), the English poet William Wordsworth (1770–1850) compared himself to a deer even while making nature seem filled with human emotions (see Document, "Wordsworth's Poetry," above). Like many poets of his time, Wordsworth greeted the French Revolution with joy; in his poem "French Revolution" (1809), he remembered his early enthusiasm: "Bliss was it in that dawn to be alive." But gradually he became disenchanted with the revolutionary experiment and celebrated British nationalism instead; in 1816, he published a poem to commemorate the "intrepid sons of Albion [England]" who died at the battle of Waterloo.

Their emphasis on authentic self-expression at times drew romantics to exotic, mystical, or even reckless experiences. Some romantics depicted the artist as possessed by demons and obsessed with hallucinations. This more nightmarish side was captured, and perhaps criticized, by Mary Shelley in *Frankenstein*. The aged German poet Johann Wolfgang von Goethe (1749–1832) likewise denounced the extremes of romanticism, calling it "everything that is sick." In his tragic play *Faust* (1808–1832), he seemed to warn of the same dangers Shelley portrayed in her novel. In Goethe's retelling of a sixteenth-century legend, Faust offers his soul to the devil in return for a chance to taste all human experience—from passionate love to the heights of power—in his effort to reshape nature for humanity's benefit. Faust's striving, like Frankenstein's, leaves a wake of suffering and destruction.

Romantic Painting and Music Romanticism in painting similarly idealized nature and the individual of deep feelings. The German romantic painter Caspar David Friedrich (1774–1840) depicted scenes—often far away in the mountains—that captured the romantic fascination with the sublime power of nature. His melancholy individual figures looked lost in the vastness of an overpowering nature. Friedrich hated the modern world. His landscapes

Eugène Delacroix, *Massacre at Chios* (1824)
More than any other painter associated with romanticism, Delacroix focused on dramatic events of his time. Here he shows sick and dying Greek civilians about to be massacred by the Turks. He aims to elicit sympathy for the Greek campaign for independence, a cause that had many followers in France and the rest of Europe.
(Oil on canvas, 1824/The Granger Collection, New York—All rights reserved.)

often had religious meaning as well, as in his controversial painting *The Cross in the Mountains* (1808), which showed a Christian cross standing alone in a mountain scene. It symbolized the steadfastness of faith but seemed to separate religion from the churches and attach it to mystical experience.

Many other artists developed similar themes. The English painter Joseph M. W. Turner (1775–1851) depicted his vision of nature in mysterious, misty seascapes, anticipating later artists by blurring the outlines of objects. The French painter Eugène Delacroix (1798–1863) chose contemporary as well as medieval scenes of great turbulence to emphasize light and color and break away from what he saw as "the servile copies repeated *ad nauseum* in academies of art." Critics denounced his techniques as "painting with a drunken broom." To broaden his experience of light and color, Delacroix traveled in the 1830s to North Africa and painted many exotic scenes in Morocco and Algeria.

The towering presence of the German composer **Ludwig van Beethoven** (1770–1827) in early-nineteenth-century music helped establish the direction for musical romanticism. His music, according to one leading German romantic, "sets in motion the lever of fear, of awe, of horror, of suffering, and awakens just that infinite longing which is the essence of Romanticism." Beethoven transformed the symphony into a connected work with recurring and evolving musical themes. Romantic symphonies conveyed the impression of growth, a metaphor for the organic process with an emphasis on the natural that was dear to the romantics. For example, Beethoven's Sixth Symphony, the *Pastoral* (1808), used a variety of instruments to represent sounds heard in the country. Beethoven's work—ranging from religious works to symphonies, sonatas, and concertos—showed remarkable diversity. Some of his work was explicitly political; his Ninth Symphony (1824) employed a chorus to sing the German poet Friedrich Schiller's verses in praise of universal human solidarity. Beethoven had admired Napoleon and even dedicated his Third Symphony, the *Eroica* (1804), to him, but when he learned of Napoleon's decision to name himself emperor, he tore up the dedication in disgust.

Romantic Nationalism

Should get at something deeper imo

If romantics had any common political thread, it was the support of nationalist aspirations, especially through the search for the historical origins of national identity. In the German states, the Austrian Empire, Russia and other Slavic lands, and Scandinavia, romantic poets and writers collected old legends and folktales that expressed a shared cultural and linguistic heritage stretching back to the Middle Ages. These collections showed that Germany, for example, had always existed even if it did not currently take the form of a single unified state. Italian nationalists took *The Betrothed* (1825–1827), a novel by Alessandro Manzoni (1785–1873), as a kind of bible. Manzoni, the grandson of the Italian Enlightenment hero Cesare Beccaria, set his novel in the seventeenth century, when Spain controlled Italy's destiny, but his readers understood that he intended to attack the Austrians who controlled northern Italy in his own day. By writing this book (the first historical novel in Italian literature) in the Tuscan dialect, Manzoni achieved two aims: he helped create a standard national language and popularized Italian history for a people long divided by different dialects and competing rulers.

Ludwig van Beethoven: The German composer (1770–1827) who helped set the direction of musical romanticism; his music used recurring and evolving themes to convey the impression of natural growth.

William Blake, *The Circle of the Lustful* (1824)
An English romantic poet, painter, engraver, and printmaker, Blake always sought his own way. Self-taught, he began writing poetry at age twelve and apprenticed himself to an engraver at fourteen. His works incorporate many otherworldly attributes; they are quite literally visionary—imagining other worlds. In this engraving of hell, the twisting, turning figures are caught up in a kind of spiritual ether. Can you find elements in this engraving that reflect a criticism of Enlightenment ideals? *(© Birmingham Museums and Art Gallery, Birmingham, UK/The Bridgeman Art Library International.)*

Manzoni had been inspired to write his novel by the most influential of all historical novelists, **Sir Walter Scott** (1771–1832). While working as a lawyer and then judge in Scotland, Scott first collected and published traditional Scottish ballads that he heard as a child. After achieving immediate success with his own poetry, especially *The Lady of the Lake* (1810), he switched to historical novels. His novels are almost all renditions of historical events, from *Rob Roy* (1817), with its account of Scottish resistance to the English in the early eighteenth century, to *Ivanhoe* (1819), with its tales of medieval England. One contemporary critic claimed, "There is more history in the novels of Walter Scott than in half of the historians." Scott captured the truths of human nature rather than sticking to the bare facts recorded by historians.

Political Revolts in the 1820s

The restoration of regimes after Napoleon's fall disappointed those who dreamed of constitutional freedoms and national independence. Membership grew in secret societies such as the carbonari, attracting tens of thousands of members, including physicians, lawyers, officers, and students. Revolts broke out in the 1820s in Spain, Italy, Russia, and Greece (see Map 20.3 on page 678), as well as across the Atlantic in the Spanish and Portuguese colonies of Latin America. Most revolts failed, but those in Greece and Latin America succeeded, largely because they did not threaten the conservative order in Europe.

Sir Walter Scott: A prolific author (1771–1832) of popular historical novels; he also collected and published traditional Scottish ballads and wrote poetry.

Uprisings in Spain and Italy

When Ferdinand VII regained the Spanish crown in 1814, he quickly restored the prerevolutionary nobility, church, and monarchy. He had foreign books and newspapers confiscated at the frontier and allowed the publication of only two newspapers. Not surprisingly, such repressive policies disturbed the middle class, especially the army officers who had encountered French ideas. Many responded by joining secret societies. In 1820, disgruntled soldiers demanded that Ferdinand proclaim his adherence to the constitution of 1812, which he had abolished in 1814. When the revolt spread, Ferdinand convened the *cortes* (parliament), which could agree on virtually nothing. Ferdinand bided his time, and in 1823 a French army invaded and restored him to absolute power. The French acted with the consent of the other great powers. The restored Spanish government tortured and executed hundreds of rebels; thousands were imprisoned or forced into exile.

Hearing of the Spanish uprising, rebellious soldiers in the kingdom of Naples joined forces with the carbonari and demanded a constitution. When a new parliament met, it too broke down over internal disagreements. The promise of reform sparked rebellion in the northern Italian kingdom of Piedmont-Sardinia, where rebels urged Charles Albert, the young heir to the Piedmont throne, to fight the Austrians for Italian unification. He vacillated; but in 1821, after the rulers of Austria, Prussia, and Russia met and agreed on intervention, the

Austrians defeated the rebels in Naples and Piedmont. Liberals were arrested in many Italian states, and the pope condemned the secret societies as "devouring wolves." Despite the opposition of Great Britain, which condemned the indiscriminate suppression of revolutionary movements, Metternich convinced the other powers to agree to his muffling of the Italian opposition to Austrian rule.

Metternich acted quickly to suppress any sign of dissent closer to home. University students had formed nationalist student societies called *Burschenschaften*, and in 1817 they held a mass rally at which they burned books they did not like, including Napoleon's Civil Code. Their leader was Friedrich Ludwig Jahn, who hoped to create a nationally unified Germany through education. He advocated gymnastics (he invented the parallel bars, the balance beam, gymnastics rings, the vaulting horse, and the horizontal bar) and study of all things German in order to create a stronger German "breed." Jahn favored the formation of a huge, racially pure German nation encompassing Switzerland, the Low Countries, Denmark, Prussia, and Austria. He also spouted such xenophobic (antiforeign) slogans as "If you let your daughter learn French, you might just as well train her to become a whore." Metternich did not mind the anti-French slant, but he was convinced — incorrectly — that the Burschenschaften in the German states and the carbonari in Italy were linked in an international conspiracy. In 1819, when a student assassinated the playwright August Kotzebue because he had ridiculed the student movement, Metternich convinced the leaders of the biggest German states to pass the Carlsbad Decrees, dissolving the student societies and more strictly censoring the press. Professors who criticized their rulers were immediately fired. Metternich considered any form of public criticism to be potentially subversive.

The Decembrist Revolt in Russia

Aspirations for constitutional government surfaced in Russia when Alexander I died suddenly in 1825. On a day in December when the troops assembled in St. Petersburg to take an oath of loyalty to Alexander's brother Nicholas as the new tsar, rebel officers insisted that the crown belonged to another brother, Constantine, whom they hoped would be more favorable to constitutional reform. Constantine, though next in the line of succession after Alexander, had refused the crown. The soldiers nonetheless raised the cry "Long live Constantine, long live the Constitution!" (Some troops apparently thought that "the Constitution" was Constantine's wife.) Soldiers loyal to Nicholas easily suppressed the Decembrist Revolt (so called after the month of the uprising), since the Decembrists were so outnumbered that they had no realistic chance to succeed. The subsequent trial, however, made the rebels into legendary heroes. Of their imprisonment at hard labor, the Russian poet Alexander Pushkin (1799–1837) wrote:

> The heavy-hanging chains will fall,
> The walls will crumble at a word,
> And Freedom greet you in the light,
> And brothers give you back the sword.

Pushkin would not live to see this freedom. For the next thirty years, Nicholas I (r. 1825–1855) used a new political police, the Third Section, to spy on potential opponents and stamp out rebelliousness.

Greek Independence from the Turks

The Ottoman Turks faced growing nationalist challenges in the Balkans, but the European powers feared that supporting such opposition would encourage a seditious spirit at home. The Serbs revolted against Turkish rule and won virtual independence by 1817. A Greek general in the Russian army, Prince Alexander Ypsilanti, tried to lead a revolt against the Turks in 1820 but failed when the tsar, urged on by Metternich, disavowed him. Metternich feared rebellion even by Christians against their Turkish rulers. A second revolt, this time by Greek peasants, sparked a wave of atrocities in 1821 and 1822. The Greeks killed every Turk who did not escape; in retaliation, the Turks hanged the Greek patriarch of Constantinople and, in the areas they still controlled, pillaged churches, massacred thousands of men, and sold the women into slavery.

Nationalistic Movements in the Balkans, 1815–1830

Western opinion turned against the Turks; Greece, after all, was the birthplace of Western civilization. While the great powers negotiated, Greeks and pro-Greece committees around the world sent food and military supplies; like the English poet Byron, a few enthusiastic European and American volunteers joined the Greeks. The Greeks

Greek Independence
From 1836 to 1839, the Greek painter Panagiotis Zographos worked with his two sons on a series of scenes from the Greek struggle for independence from the Turks. Response was so favorable that one Greek general ordered lithographic reproductions for popular distribution. Nationalistic feeling could be thus encouraged even among those who were not directly touched by the struggle. Here Turkish sultan Mehmet the Conqueror, exulting over the fall of Constantinople in 1453, views a row of Greeks under the yoke, a sign of submission. *(Visual Connection Archive.)*

held on until the great powers were willing to intervene. In 1827, a combined force of British, French, and Russian ships destroyed the Turkish fleet at Navarino Bay; and in 1828, Russia declared war on Turkey and advanced close to Constantinople. The Treaty of Adrianople of 1829 gave Russia a protectorate over the Danubian principalities in the Balkans and provided for a conference among representatives of Britain, Russia, and France, all of whom had broken with Austria in support of the Greeks. In 1830, Greece was declared an independent kingdom under the guarantee of the three powers; in 1833, the second son of King Ludwig of Bavaria became Otto I of Greece. Nationalism, with the support of European public opinion, had made its first breach in Metternich's system.

Wars of Independence in Latin America

Across the Atlantic, national revolts also succeeded after a series of bloody wars of independence. Taking advantage of the upheavals in Spain and Portugal that began under Napoleon, restive colonists from Mexico to Argentina rebelled. One leader who stood out was **Simón Bolívar** (1783–1830), born in Caracas (present-day Venezuela) to an aristocratic slave-owning family of Spanish descent. He was educated in Europe on the works of Voltaire and Rousseau. Although Bolívar fancied himself a Latin American Napoleon, he had to acquiesce to the formation of a series of independent republics between 1821 and 1823, even in Bolivia, which is named after him.

By 1825, Portugal had lost all its American colonies, including Brazil, and Spain was left with only Cuba and Puerto Rico (Map 20.4). Brazil declared its independence under the banner of the Portuguese king's own son and therefore maintained a monarchical form of government along with slavery. In contrast, the new republics freed those slaves who fought on their side, abolished the slave trade, and gradually eliminated slavery. Because the struggles for independence required arms and armed forces, the new Spanish American republics

Simón Bolívar (1783–1830): The Venezuelan-born, European-educated aristocrat who became one of the leaders of the Latin American independence movement in the 1820s. Bolivia is named after him.

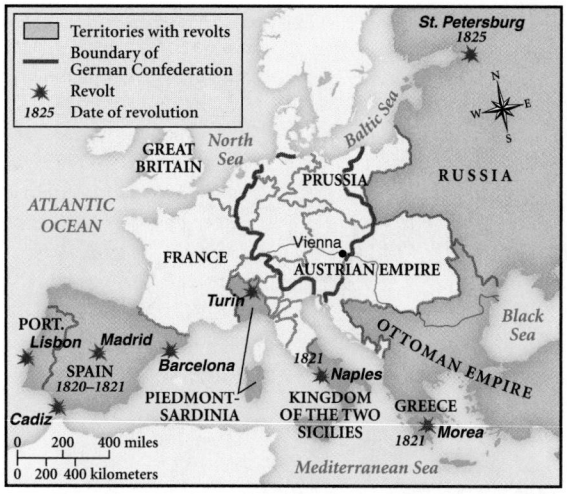

MAP 20.3 Revolutionary Movements of the 1820s
The revolts of the 1820s took place on the periphery of Europe, in Spain, Italy, Greece, Russia, and in the Spanish and Portuguese colonies of Latin America. Rebels in Spain and Russia wanted constitutional reforms. Although the Italian revolts failed, as did the uprisings in Spain and Russia, the Greek and Latin American independence movements eventually succeeded.

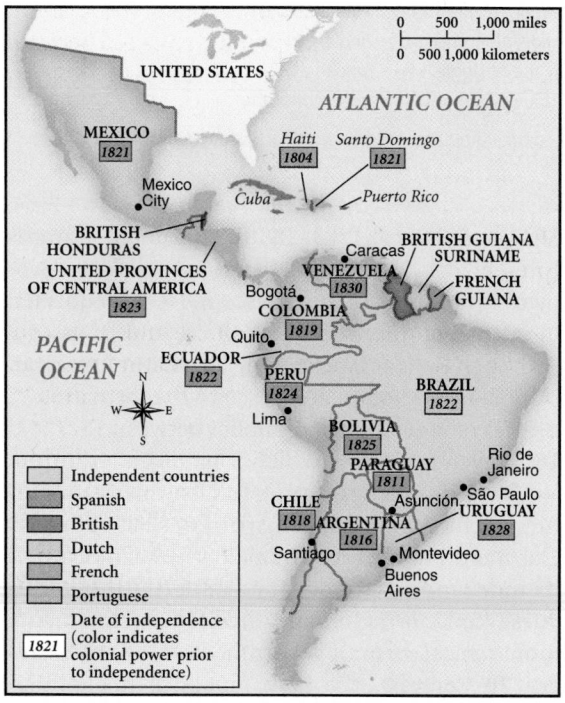

MAP 20.4 Latin American Independence, 1804–1830
Napoleon's occupation of Spain and Portugal seriously weakened those countries' hold on their Latin American colonies. Despite the restoration of the Spanish and Portuguese rulers in 1814, most of their colonies successfully broke away in a wave of rebellions between 1811 and 1830.

faced the prospect of internal violence for years afterward. Soldiers and militiamen refused to lay down their arms and sometimes fought on behalf of local interests against the new national governments. The United States and Great Britain recognized the new states, and in 1823 President James Monroe announced his Monroe Doctrine, closing the Americas to European intervention—a prohibition that depended on British naval power and British willingness to declare neutrality.

Revolution and Reform, 1830–1832

In 1830, a new wave of liberal and nationalist revolts broke against the bulwark of conservatism. The revolts of the 1820s had served as warning shots but had been largely confined to the peripheries of Europe. Now revolution once again threatened the established order in western Europe.

The French Revolution of 1830

Louis XVIII's younger brother and successor, Charles X (r. 1824–1830), brought about his own downfall by steering the monarchy in an increasingly repressive direction. In 1825, the Law of Indemnity compensated nobles who had emigrated during the French Revolution for the loss of their estates, and the Law of Sacrilege in the same year imposed the death penalty for such offenses as stealing religious objects from churches. Charles enraged liberals when he dissolved the legislature, removed many wealthy and powerful voters from the rolls, and imposed strict censorship. Spontaneous demonstrations in Paris led to fighting on July 26, 1830. After three days of street battles in which 500 citizens and 150 soldiers died, a group of moderate liberal leaders, fearing the reestablishment of a republic, agreed to give the crown to Charles X's cousin Louis-Philippe, duke of Orléans.

Charles X went into exile in England, and the new king extended political liberties and voting rights. Although the number of voting men nearly doubled, it remained minuscule—approximately 170,000 in a country of 30 million. Such reforms did little for the poor and working classes, who had manned the barricades in July. Dissatisfaction with the 1830 settlement boiled over in Lyon in 1831, when a silk-workers' strike over wages turned into a rebellion that died down only when the army arrived. Revolution had broken the hold of those who wanted to restore the pre-1789 monarchy and nobility, but it had gone no further this time than installing a more liberal, constitutional monarchy.

Simón Bolívar
This watercolor by Fernandez Luis Cancino celebrates Bolívar's promise to abolish slavery in territories he freed from Spanish rule. Although Bolívar liberated his own slaves in 1820, he was unable to persuade the legislators of the newly independent countries to act immediately. They insisted on gradual emancipation. *(Watercolor on paper by Luis Fernandez Cancino [nineteenth century], Casa-Museo 20 de Julio de 1810, Bogota, Colombia/Giraudon/The Bridgeman Art Library International.)*

Belgian Independence from the Dutch

News of the July revolution in Paris ignited the Belgians, whose country had been annexed to the kingdom of the Netherlands in 1815. Differences in traditions, language, and religion separated the largely Catholic Belgians from the Dutch. An opera about a seventeenth-century insurrection in Naples provided the spark, and students in Brussels rioted, shouting "Down with the Dutch!"

The riot turned into revolt. King William of the Netherlands appealed to the great powers to intervene; after all, the Congress of Vienna had established his kingdom. But Great Britain and France opposed intervention and invited Russia, Austria, and Prussia to a conference that guaranteed Belgium independence in exchange for its neutrality in international affairs. Belgian neutrality would remain a cornerstone of European diplomacy for a century. After much maneuvering, the crown of the new kingdom of Belgium was offered to a German prince, Leopold of Saxe-Coburg, in 1831. The choice, like that of Otto I of Greece, ensured the influence of the great European powers without favoring any one of them in particular. Belgium, like France and Britain, now had a constitutional monarchy.

Revolts in Italy and Poland

The Austrian emperor and the Russian tsar would have supported intervention in Belgium had they not been preoccupied with their own revolts. In the south, rebels in Naples and Palermo demanded constitutional government; in the north, rebels in Piedmont fought for an Italy independent of Austria. Metternich sent Austrian armies to quell the unrest.

The Polish revolt was more serious. When set up in 1815, the "congress kingdom" (so called because the Congress of Vienna had created it) was given a constitution that provided for an elected Polish parliament, a national army, and guarantees of free speech and a free press. But by 1818, its ruler, the Russian tsar Alexander I, had begun retracting these concessions. Polish students and military officers responded by forming secret nationalist societies to plot for change by illegal means. The government then cracked down, arresting student leaders and dismissing professors who promoted reforms. In 1830, in response to news of revolution in France, students raised the banner of rebellion. Polish aristocrats formed a provisional government, but it got no support from Britain or France and was defeated by the Russian army. In reprisal, Tsar Nicholas abolished the Polish constitution that his brother Alexander had granted and ordered thousands of Poles executed or banished. The independence movements in Poland and Italy went underground only to reemerge later.

The British Reform Bill of 1832

The British had long been preoccupied with two subjects: the royal family and elections for control of Parliament. In 1820, the domestic quarrels between the new king, George IV (r. 1820–1830), and his German wife, Caroline, seemed to threaten the future of the monarchy.

When George IV came to the throne, he tried to divorce Caroline, and he refused to have her crowned queen. He hoped to use rumors of her love affairs on the continent to win his case, but the divorce trial provoked massive demonstrations in support of Caroline. Women's groups gathered thousands of signatures on petitions supporting her, and popular songs and satires portrayed George as a fat, drunken libertine. Caroline's death a few months after George's coronation ended the Queen Caroline Affair. The monarchy survived, but with a tarnished reputation.

The demonstrations in the Queen Caroline Affair followed on the heels of a huge political rally held just the year before. In August 1819, sixty thousand people attended an illegal political meeting held in St. Peter's Fields in Manchester. They wanted reform of parliamentary elections, which had long been controlled by aristocratic landowners. When the local authorities sent the cavalry to arrest the speaker, panic resulted; eleven people were killed and many hundreds injured. Punsters called it the battle of Peterloo or the Peterloo massacre. An alarmed government passed the Six Acts, which forbade large political meetings and restricted press criticism.

In the 1820s, however, new men came into government. Sir Robert Peel (1788–1850), the secretary for home affairs, revised the criminal code to reduce the number of crimes punishable by death and introduced a municipal police force in London, called the Bobbies after him. In 1824, the laws prohibiting labor unions were repealed, and though restrictions on strikes remained, workers could now organize themselves legally to confront their employers collectively. In 1828, the appointment of the

Europe in 1830

By 1830, the fragilities of the Congress of Vienna settlement had become apparent. Rebellion in Poland failed, but Belgium won its independence from the kingdom of the Netherlands, and a French revolution in July chased out the Bourbon ruler and installed Louis-Philippe, who promised constitutional reform. Most European rulers held on to their positions in this period of ferment, but they had to accommodate new desires for constitutional guarantees of rights and growing nationalist sentiment.

duke of Wellington, the hero of Waterloo, as prime minister kept the Tories in power, and his government pushed through a bill in 1829 allowing Catholics to sit in Parliament and hold most public offices.

When in 1830, and again in 1831, the Whigs in Parliament proposed an extension of the right to vote, Tory diehards, principally in the House of Lords, dug in their heels and predicted that even the most modest proposals would doom civilization itself. Even though the proposed law would grant only limited, not universal, male suffrage, mass demonstrations in favor of it took place in many cities. One supporter of reform described the scene: "Meetings of almost every description of persons were held in cities, towns, and parishes; by journeymen tradesmen in their clubs, and by common workmen who had no trade clubs or associations of any kind." In this "state of diseased and feverish excitement" (according to its opponents), the **Reform Bill of 1832** passed, after the king threatened to create enough new peers to obtain its passage in the House of Lords.

Although the Reform Bill altered Britain's political structure in significant ways, the gains were not revolutionary. One of the bill's foremost backers, historian and member of Parliament Thomas Macaulay, explained, "I am opposed to Universal Suffrage, because I think that it would produce a destructive revolution. I support this plan, because I am sure that it is our best security against a revolution." Although the number of male voters increased by about 50 percent, only one in five Britons could now vote, and voting still depended on holding property. Nevertheless, the bill gave representation to new cities in the north for the first time and set a precedent for widening suffrage further. Exclusive aristocratic politics now gave way to a mixed middle-class and aristocratic structure that would prove more responsive to the problems of a fast-growing society. Those disappointed with the outcome would organize with renewed vigor in the 1830s and 1840s.

REVIEW QUESTION **Why were independence movements thwarted in Italy and Poland in this era, but not in Greece, Belgium, and Latin America?**

Reform Bill of 1832: A measure passed by the British Parliament to increase the number of male voters by about 50 percent and give representation to new cities in the north; it set a precedent for widening suffrage.

Conclusion

The agitations and uprisings of the 1820s and early 1830s showed that the revolutionary legacy still smoldered and might erupt into flames again at any moment. Napoleon Bonaparte had kept the legacy alive by insisting on fundamental reforms wherever his armies triumphed. His imperial rule galvanized supporters and opponents alike; no one could be indifferent to his impact on European and even world affairs. He reshaped French institutions and left a lasting imprint in many European countries. Moreover, like Frankenstein's monster, he seemed to bounce back from every reversal; between the French retreat from Moscow in 1812 and his final defeat at Waterloo in 1815, Napoleon lost many battles yet managed to raise an army again and again.

The French emperor's attempt to colonize much of Europe ultimately failed. Germans, Italians, Russians, and Spaniards all resisted and in the process discovered new national feelings that would have an impact throughout modern times. Unlike Frankenstein's monster, Napoleon could not hide from his enemies and was forced into exile until his death. The powers who eventually defeated Napoleon tried to maintain the European peace by shoring up monarchical governments and damping down aspirations for constitutional freedoms and national autonomy. They sometimes fell short. Belgium separated from the Netherlands, Greece achieved independence from the Turks, Latin American countries shook off the rule of Spain and Portugal, and the French installed a more liberal monarchy than the one envisioned by the Congress of Vienna. Yet Metternich's vision of a conservative Europe still held, and most efforts at revolt failed. In the next two decades, however, dramatic social changes would raise the stakes of political contests and prompt a new and much more deadly round of revolutions.

FOR FURTHER EXPLORATION

- **For additional primary-source material from this period**, see *Sources of the Making of the West*, Fourth Edition.
- **For Web sites, images, and documents related to topics in this chapter**, visit *Make History* at bedfordstmartins.com/hunt.

Chapter 20 Review

Online Study Guide bedfordstmartins.com/hunt

Key Terms and People

In the grid below, identify the term or person and explain its historical significance.
(For a printable version of this grid, visit bedfordstmartins.com/hunt.)

Term	Who or What & When	Why It Matters
Napoleon Bonaparte (p. 652)		
First Consul (p. 653)		
Civil Code (p. 657)		
Continental System (p. 662)		
battle of Waterloo (p. 665)		
Congress of Vienna (p. 667)		
Klemens von Metternich (p. 668)		
restoration (p. 669)		
conservatism (p. 670)		
Ludwig van Beethoven (p. 674)		
Sir Walter Scott (p. 675)		
Simón Bolívar (p. 677)		
Reform Bill of 1832 (p. 681)		

Review Questions

1. In what ways did Napoleon continue the French Revolution, and in what ways did he break with it?
2. Why was Napoleon able to gain control over so much of Europe's territory?
3. To what extent did the Congress of Vienna restore the old order?
4. Why were independence movements thwarted in Italy and Poland in this era, but not in Greece, Belgium, and Latin America?

Making Connections

1. What was the long-term significance of Napoleon for Europe?
2. What best explains Napoleon's fall from power: apathy at home, resistance to his rule, or military defeat?
3. In what ways did Metternich succeed in holding back the revolutionary legacy? In what ways did he fail?
4. How did the revolts and rebellions of the 1820s reflect the revolutionary legacy? In what ways did they move in new directions?

Important Events

Date	Event	Date	Event
1799	Coup against Directory government in France; Napoleon Bonaparte named First Consul	1818	Mary Shelley, *Frankenstein*
1801	Napoleon signs concordat with the pope	1820	Revolt of liberal army officers against Spanish crown
1804	Napoleon crowned emperor of France, issues new Civil Code	1824	Ludwig van Beethoven, Ninth Symphony
1805	British naval forces defeat French at the battle of Trafalgar; Napoleon wins his greatest victory at the battle of Austerlitz	1825	Russian army officers demand constitutional reform in Decembrist Revolt
1807–1814	French invade and occupy Spain and Portugal	1830	Greece gains its independence from Ottoman Turks; rebels overthrow Charles X of France and install Louis-Philippe; rebellion in Poland against Russia fails
1812	Napoleon invades Russia	1832	English Parliament passes Reform Bill; Johann Wolfgang von Goethe, *Faust*
1814–1815	Congress of Vienna		
1815	Napoleon defeated at Waterloo and exiled to island of St. Helena, where he dies in 1821		

- Consider three events: **Congress of Vienna (1814–1815)**, **Mary Shelley, *Frankenstein* (1818)**, and **Ludwig van Beethoven, Ninth Symphony (1824)**. How did the peace established by the Congress of Vienna help to foster these works? How might things have been different if Napoleon had not been defeated?

SUGGESTED REFERENCES

Napoleon and his wars have always been the subject of great interest, but recent scholars have devoted more attention to the long-term influence of the wars. The years between 1815 and 1830 have not attracted as much scholarship, even though those years are arguably even more significant than the Napoleonic era for their long-term cultural and political effects.

Bell, David A. *The First Total War: Napoleon's Europe and the Birth of Warfare as We Know It.* 2007.

Black, Jeremy. *The Battle of Waterloo.* 2010.

*Blaufarb, Rafe. *Napoleon: A Symbol for an Age. A Brief Biography with Documents.* 2008.

Breckman, Warren. *European Romanticism: A Brief History with Documents.* 2007.

Brewer, David. *The Greek War of Independence: The Struggle for Freedom from Ottoman Oppression and the Birth of the Modern Greek Nation.* 2003.

Cole, Juan. *Napoléon's Egypt: Invading the Middle East.* 2007.

Englund, Steven. *Napoleon: A Political Life.* 2004.

Fregosi, Paul. *Dreams of Empire: Napoleon and the First World War 1792–1815.* 1989.

Hobsbawm, E. J. *The Age of Revolution, 1789–1848.* 1996.

Johnson, Paul. *The Birth of the Modern: World Society, 1815–1830.* 1991.

Laven, David, and Lucy Riall, eds. *Napoleon's Legacy: Problems of Government in Restoration Europe.* 2000.

Napoleon Foundation: http://www.napoleon.org

Romantic Chronology: http://english.ucsb.edu:591/rchrono

Sandeman, G. A. C. *Metternich.* 2006.

Schroeder, Paul W. *The Transformation of European Politics 1763–1848.* 1996.

*Primary source.

CHAPTER

Industrialization and Social Ferment

21

1830–1850

The Industrial Revolution 686
- Roots of Industrialization
- Engines of Change
- Urbanization and Its Consequences
- Agricultural Perils and Prosperity

Reforming the Social Order 696
- Cultural Responses to the Social Question
- The Varieties of Social Reform
- Abuses and Reforms Overseas

Ideologies and Political Movements 703
- The Spell of Nationalism
- Liberalism in Economics and Politics
- Socialism and the Early Labor Movement

The Revolutions of 1848 709
- The Hungry Forties
- Another French Revolution
- Nationalist Revolution in Italy
- Revolt and Reaction in Central Europe
- Aftermath to 1848: Reimposing Authority

In 1830, the Liverpool and Manchester Railway Line opened to the cheers of crowds and the congratulations of government officials, including the duke of Wellington, the hero of Waterloo who had been named British prime minister. In the excitement, some of the dignitaries gathered on a parallel track. Another engine, George Stephenson's *Rocket*, approached at high speed—the engine could go as fast as twenty-seven miles per hour. Most of the gentlemen scattered to safety, but former cabinet minister William Huskisson fell and was hit. A few hours later he died, the first official casualty of the newfangled railroad.

Dramatic and expensive, railroads were the most striking symbol of the new industrial age. Industrialization and its by-product of rapid urban growth fundamentally changed political conflicts, social relations, cultural concerns, and even the landscape. So great were the changes that they are collectively labeled the Industrial Revolution. Although this revolution did not take place in a single decade like the French Revolution, the introduction of steam-driven machinery, large factories, and a new working class transformed life in the Western world. Peasants and workers streamed into the cities. London's population grew by 130,000 in the 1830s alone; Berlin's more than doubled between 1819 and 1849; and Paris's expanded by 120,000 just between 1841 and 1846. To many observers, overcrowding, disease, prostitution, crime, and alcohol consumption all seemed to be on the increase as a result.

The shock of industrial and urban growth generated an outpouring of commentary on the need for social reforms. Painters, poets, and especially novelists joined in the chorus warning about rising tensions. Many who wrote on social issues expected middle-class women to organize their homes as a domestic haven from the heartless process of upheaval. Yet despite the emphasis on domesticity, middle-class women participated in

Inauguration of the Railway Line from Naples to Portici, Italy, 1839
People of all classes flocked to the inauguration of new railway lines. This lithograph by the Italian artist Salvatore Fergola depicts the opening of the first railway line in Italy, which ran from Naples to Portici, a town five miles south of Naples. Portici housed a royal palace and offered access to Herculaneum, an important classical ruin visited by many foreigners. *(By Salvatore Fergola, Museum San Martino, Naples, photo © Roger Viollet/ The Image Works.)*

public issues, too: they set up reform societies that fought prostitution and helped poor mothers, they agitated for temperance (abstention from alcohol), and they joined the campaigns to abolish slavery. Middle-class men and women frequently denounced the lower classes' appetites for drink, tobacco, and cockfighting, but they remained largely silent when British traders received government support in forcing the Chinese to accept imports of the addictive drug opium.

Social ferment set the ideological pots to a boil. A word coined during the French Revolution, **ideology** refers to a coherent set of beliefs about the way the social and political order should be organized. The dual impact of the French Revolution and the Industrial Revolution prompted the development of a whole spectrum of ideologies to explain the meaning of the changes taking place. Nationalists, liberals, socialists, and communists offered competing visions of the social order they desired: they all agreed that change was necessary, but they disagreed about both the means and the ends of change. Their contest came to a head in 1848 when the rapid transformation of European society led to a new set of revolutionary outbreaks, more consuming than any since 1789. As in 1789, food shortages and constitutional crises fueled rebellions, but now class tensions and nationalist impulses fanned the flames in capitals across Europe, not only in Paris. Although the revolutionaries of 1848 eventually went down to defeat, the demands they raised shaped the political agenda for decades to come.

CHAPTER FOCUS How did the Industrial Revolution create new social and political conflicts?

ideology: A word coined during the French Revolution to refer to a coherent set of beliefs about the way the social and political order should be organized.

The Industrial Revolution

French and English writers of the 1820s invented the term **Industrial Revolution** to capture the drama of contemporary change and to draw a parallel with the French Revolution. The chief components of the Industrial Revolution, industrialization and urbanization, are long-term processes that have continued to the present; unlike the French upheaval, they do not have precise beginning and ending dates. The Industrial Revolution began in England in the 1770s and 1780s in textile manufacturing and spread from there across the continent. In the 1830s and 1840s, industrialization and urbanization both accelerated quite suddenly, as governments across Europe encouraged railroad construction and the mechanization of manufacturing. States exercised little control over the consequences of industrial and urban growth, however, and many officials, preachers, and intellectuals worried that unchecked growth would destroy traditional social relationships and create disorder. Some held out the constancy of rural life as an antidote to the ravages of industrialization and urbanization, but population growth produced new tensions in the countryside, too.

Roots of Industrialization

British inventors had been steadily perfecting steam engines for five decades before George Stephenson built his *Rocket*. A key breakthrough took place in 1776 when James Watt developed an efficient steam engine that could be used to pump water from coal mines or drive machinery in textile factories. Since

Industrial Revolution: The transformation of life in the Western world over several decades in the late eighteenth and early nineteenth centuries as a result of the introduction of steam-driven machinery, large factories, and a new working class.

1830–1832 Cholera epidemic sweeps across Europe

1832 George Sand, *Indiana*

1834 German *Zollverein* established under Prussian leadership

1839 Beginning of Opium War; invention of photography

1830 1835 1840

1830 France invades and begins conquest of Algeria

1833 Factory Act regulates work of children in Great Britain; abolition of slavery in British Empire

1835 Belgium opens first continental railway built with state funds coal fired the steam engines that drove new textile machinery, innovations tended to reinforce one another. This kind of synergy built on previous changes in the textile industry. In 1733, the Englishman John Kay had patented the flying shuttle, which enabled weavers to "throw" yarn across the loom rather than draw it back and forth by hand. When the flying shuttle came into widespread use in the 1760s, weavers began producing cloth more quickly than spinners could produce the thread. The resulting shortage of spun thread propelled the invention of the spinning jenny, a multispool spinning wheel that enabled one worker to run eight spools at once. In the following decades, increasingly mechanized forms of spinning yarn replaced thousands of women working at home by hand. The increased output of yarn then stimulated the mechanization of weaving. Using the engines produced by James Watt and his partner Matthew Boulton, Edmund Cartwright designed a mechanized loom in the 1780s that, when perfected, could be run by a small boy and yet yield fifteen times the output of a skilled adult working a handloom. By the end of the century, manufacturers were assembling new power machinery in large factories that hired semiskilled men, women, and children to replace skilled weavers.

Several factors interacted to make England the first site of the Industrial Revolution. Because population increased by more than 50 percent in England in the second half of the eighteenth century, manufacturers had an incentive to produce more and cheaper cotton cloth. England had a good supply of private investment capital from overseas trade and commercial profits, ready access to raw cotton from the plantations of its Caribbean colonies and the southern United States, and the necessary natural resources at home such as coal and iron. Good opportunities for social mobility and relative political stability in the eighteenth century provided an environment that fostered the pragmatism of the English and Scottish inventors who designed the machinery. These early industrialists shared a culture of informal scientific education through learned societies and popular lectures (one of the prominent forms of the Enlightenment in Britain). Manufacturers proved eager to introduce steam-driven machinery to increase output and gradually established factories to house the new machines and concentrate the labor of their workers. The agricultural revolution of the eighteenth century had enabled England to produce food more efficiently, freeing some agricultural workers to move to the new sites of manufacturing. Cotton textile production skyrocketed.

Elsewhere in Europe, textile manufacturing—long a linchpin in the European economy—expanded even without the introduction of new machines and factories because of the spread of the "putting-out," or "domestic," system. Under the putting-out system, manufacturers supplied the raw materials, such as woolen or cotton fibers, to families working at home. The mother and her children washed, carded, and combed the fibers. Then the mother and oldest daughters spun them into thread. The father, assisted by the children, wove the cloth. The cloth was then finished (bleached, dyed, smoothed, and so on) under the supervision of the manufacturer in a large workshop, located either in town or in the countryside. This system had existed in the textile industry for hundreds of years, but it grew dramatically in the eighteenth century, and the manufacture of other products—such as glassware, baskets, nails, and guns—followed suit. The spread of the putting-out system of manufacturing is sometimes called proto-industrialization to signify that the process helped pave the way for the full-scale Industrial Revolution. Because of the increase in textile production, ordinary people began to wear underclothes and nightclothes, both rare in the past. White, red, blue, yellow, green, and even pastel shades of cotton now replaced the black, gray, or brown of traditional wool.

1841
Charles Dickens, *The Old Curiosity Shop*

1848
Revolutions of 1848 throughout Europe; last great wave of Chartist demonstrations in Britain; Karl Marx and Friedrich Engels, *The Communist Manifesto*; abolition of slavery in French colonies; end of serfdom in Austrian Empire

1845 1850 1855

1846
Famine strikes Ireland; Corn Laws repealed in England; peasant insurrection in Austrian province of Galicia

1851
Crystal Palace exhibition in London

TAKING MEASURE

Railroad Lines, 1830–1850

Great Britain quickly extended its lead in the building of railroads. The extension of commerce and, before long, the ability to wage war would depend on the development of effective railroad networks. These statistics might be taken as predicting a realignment of power within Europe after 1850.

Source: B. R. Mitchell, *European Historical Statistics 1750–1970* (New York: Columbia University Press, 1975), F1.

Question to Consider

- **What do the numbers shown in this graph say about the relative positions of Germany (the German states, including Prussia but excluding Austria), the Austrian Empire, and France?**

Workers in the textile industry, whether in the putting-out system or in factories, enjoyed few protections against fluctuations in the market. Whenever demand for cloth declined, manufacturers simply did not buy from the families producing it. Hundreds of thousands of families might be reduced to bankruptcy in periods of food shortage or overproduction. Handloom weavers sometimes violently resisted the establishment of the factory power looms that would force them out of work. In England in 1811 and 1812, for example, bands of handloom weavers wrecked factory machinery and burned mills in the Midlands, Yorkshire, and Lancashire. To restore order and protect industry, the government sent in an army of twelve thousand regular soldiers and made machine wrecking punishable by death. The rioters were called Luddites after the fictitious figure Ned Ludd, whose signature appeared on their manifestos. (The term is still used to describe those who resist new technology.)

Engines of Change

Steam-driven engines took on a dramatic new form in the 1820s when the English engineer George Stephenson perfected an engine to pull wagons along rail tracks. In the 1830s and 1840s, every major country in Europe hurried to set up a railroad system, pushing industrialization from west to east across Europe (see "Taking Measure," above). Although the new industries employed only a small percentage of workers, the working class that took shape in them immediately attracted the attention of social commentators and government officials. Rulers could not afford to ignore the social problems that came from industrialization.

The Rise of the Railroad

The idea of a railroad was not new: iron tracks had been used since the seventeenth century to haul coal from mines in wagons pulled by horses. A railroad system as a mode of transport, however, developed only after Stephenson's invention of a steam-powered locomotive. Placed on the new tracks, steam-driven carriages could transport people and goods to the cities and link coal and iron deposits to the new factories. In the 1840s alone, railroad track mileage more than doubled in Great Britain, and British investment in railways jumped tenfold. The British also began to build railroads in India. Private investment that had been going into the building of thousands of miles of canals now went into railroads. Britain's success with rail transportation led other countries to develop their own projects. Railroads grew spectacularly in the United States in the 1830s and 1840s, reaching 9,000 miles of track by midcentury. In 1835, Belgium, newly independent in 1830, opened the first continental European railroad with state bonds backed by British capital. By 1850, the world had 23,500 miles of track, most of it in western Europe.

Railroad building spurred both industrial development and state power (Map 21.1). Governments everywhere participated in the construction of railroads, which depended on private and state funds to pay for the massive amounts of iron, coal, heavy machinery, and human labor required to build and run them. Demand for iron products accelerated industrial development. Until the 1840s, cotton had led industrial production; between 1816 and 1840, cotton output more than quadrupled in Great Britain. But from 1830 to 1850, Britain's output of iron and coal doubled (Table 21.1). Similarly, Austrian output of iron doubled between the 1820s and the 1840s. One-third of all investment in the German states in the 1840s went into railroads.

Steam-powered engines made Britain the world leader in manufacturing. By midcentury, more than half of Britain's national income came from manufacturing and trade. The number of steamboats in Great Britain rose from two in 1812 to six hundred in 1840. Between 1840 and 1850, steam-engine power doubled in Great Britain and increased even more rapidly elsewhere in Europe, as those adopting British inventions strove to catch up. The power applied in German manufacturing, for example, grew sixfold during the 1840s but still amounted to only a little more than a quarter of the British figure. German coal and iron outputs were only 6 or 7 percent of the British outputs.

Industrialization Moves Eastward

Although Great Britain consciously strove to protect its industrial supremacy, thousands of British engineers defied laws against the export of

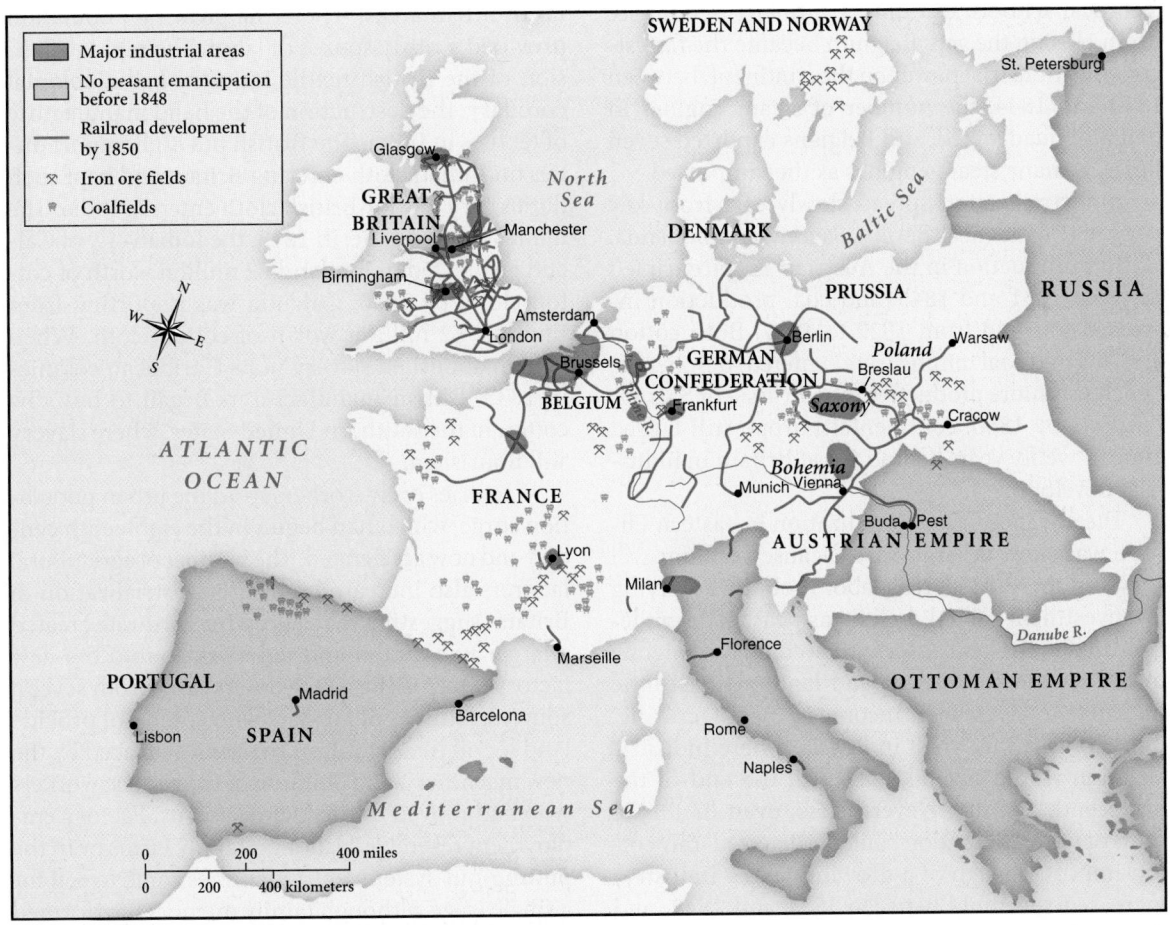

MAP 21.1 Industrialization in Europe, c. 1850

Industrialization (mainly mechanized textile production) first spread in a band across northern Europe that included Great Britain, northern France, Belgium, the northern German states, the region around Milan in northern Italy, and Bohemia. Although railroads were not the only factor in promoting industrialization, the map makes clear the interrelationship between railroad building and the development of new industrial sites of coal mining and textile production.

TABLE 21.1 Coal Output, 1830–1850*

Like the numbers for railroad mileage given in Taking Measure, page 688, these figures for coal production show the economic dominance of Great Britain throughout the period 1830–1850. As long as coal remained the essential fuel of industrialization, Britain enjoyed a clear advantage.

	Austria	Belgium	France	German States (including Prussia)	Great Britain
1830	214	**	1,863	1,800	22,800
1835	251	2,639	2,506	2,100	28,100
1840	473	3,930	3,003	3,200	34,200
1845	689	4,919	4,202	4,400	46,600
1850	877	5,821	4,434	5,100	50,200

*In thousands of metric tons.
**Data not available.

Source: B. R. Mitchell, *European Historical Statistics, 1750–1970* (New York: Columbia University Press, 1975), D2.

machinery or the emigration of artisans. Only slowly, thanks to the pirating of British methods and to new technical schools, did most continental countries begin closing the gap. Belgium became the fastest-growing industrial power on the continent: between 1830 and 1844, the number of steam engines in Belgium quadrupled, and Belgians exported seven times as many steam engines as they imported.

Industrialization spread slowly east from key areas in Prussia (near Berlin), Saxony, and Bohemia. Cotton production in the Austrian Empire tripled between 1831 and 1845, and coal production increased fourfold from 1827 to 1847. Both cotton growing and coal mining were centered in Bohemia, which was more productive than Prussia or Saxony. Even so, by 1850, continental Europe still lagged almost twenty years behind Great Britain in industrial development.

The advance of industrialization in eastern Europe was slow, in large part because serfdom still survived there, hindering labor mobility and tying up investment capital: as long as peasants were legally tied to the land as serfs, they could not migrate to the new factory towns and landlords felt little incentive to invest their income in manufacturing. The problem was worst in Russia, where industrialization would not take off until the end of the nineteenth century. Nevertheless, even in Russia signs of industrialization could be detected: raw cotton imports (a sign of a growing textile industry) increased sevenfold between 1831 and 1848, and the number of factories doubled along with the size of the industrial workforce.

Factories and Workers

Despite the spread of industrialization, factory workers remained a minority everywhere. In the 1840s, factories in England employed only 5 percent of the workers; in France, 3 percent; in Prussia, 2 percent. The putting-out system remained strong, employing two-thirds of the manufacturing workers in Prussia and Saxony, for example, in the 1840s. Many peasants kept their options open by combining factory work or putting-out work with agricultural labor. From Switzerland to Russia, people worked in agriculture during the spring and summer and in manufacturing in the fall and winter. Unstable industrial wages made such arrangements essential. In addition, some new industries idled periodically: for example, iron forges stopped for several months when the water level in streams dropped, and blast furnaces shut down for repairs several weeks every year.

Even though factories employed only a small percentage of the population, they attracted much attention. Already by 1830, more than a million people in Britain depended on the cotton industry for employment, and cotton cloth constituted 50 percent of the country's exports. Factories sprang up in urban areas, where the growing population provided a ready source of labor. The rapid expansion of the British textile industry had a colonial corollary: the destruction of the hand manufacture of textiles in India. The British put high import duties on Indian cloth entering Britain and kept such duties very low for British cloth entering India. The figures are dramatic: in 1813, the Indian city of Calcutta exported to England £2 million worth of cotton cloth; by 1830, Calcutta was importing from England £2 million worth of cotton cloth. When Britain abolished slavery in its Caribbean colonies in 1833, British manufacturers began to buy raw cotton in the southern United States, where slavery still flourished.

Factories drew workers from the urban population surge, which had begun in the eighteenth century and now accelerated. The number of agricultural laborers also increased during industrialization in Britain, suggesting that a growing birthrate created a larger population and fed workers into the new factory system. The new workers came from several sources: families of farmers who could not provide land for all their children, artisans displaced by the new machinery, and children of the earliest workers who had moved to the factory towns. Factory employment resembled labor on family farms or in the putting-out system: entire families came to toil for a single wage, although family members performed different tasks. Workdays of twelve to seventeen hours were typical, even for children, and the work was grueling.

As urban factories grew, their workers gradually came to constitute a new socioeconomic class with a distinctive culture and traditions. The term *working class*, like *middle class*, came into use for the first time in the early nineteenth century. It referred to the laborers in the new factories. In the past, urban workers had labored in isolated trades: water and wood carrying, gardening, laundry, and building. In contrast, factories brought working people together with machines, under close supervision by their employers. Soon developing a sense of common interests, they organized societies for mutual help and political reform. From these would come the first labor unions.

Factories produced wealth without regard to the pollution they caused or the exhausted state of their workers; industry created unheard-of riches and new forms of poverty all at once. "From this foul drain the greatest stream of human industry flows out to fertilize the whole world," wrote the French aristocrat Alexis de Tocqueville after visiting the new English industrial city of Manchester in the 1830s. "From this filthy sewer pure gold flows. Here humanity attains its most complete development and its most brutish, here civilization works its miracles and civilized man is turned almost into a savage." Studies by physicians set the life expectancy of workers in Manchester at just seventeen years (partly because of high rates of infant mortality), whereas the average life expectancy in England was forty years in 1840. (See "New Sources, New Perspectives," page 692.) One American visitor in Britain in the late 1840s described how "in the manufacturing town, the fine soot or *blacks* darken the day, give white sheep the color of black sheep, discolor the human saliva, contaminate the air, poison many plants, and corrode monuments and buildings." In some parts of Europe, city leaders banned factories, hoping to insulate their towns from the effects of industrial growth.

As factory production expanded, local and national governments collected information about the workers. Investigators detailed their pitiful condition. A French physician in the eastern town of Mulhouse described the "pale, emaciated women who walk barefooted through the dirt" to reach the factory. The young children who worked in the factory appeared "clothed in rags which are greasy with the oil from the looms and frames." A report to the city government in Lille, France, in 1832 described "dark cellars" where the cotton workers lived: "the air is never renewed, it is infected; the walls are plastered with garbage."

Government inquiries often focused on women and children. In Great Britain, the Factory Act of 1833 outlawed the employment of children under the age of nine in textile mills (except in the lace and silk industries); it also limited the workdays for those ages nine to thirteen to nine hours a day, and those ages thirteen to eighteen to twelve hours. Adults worked even longer hours. Investigating commissions showed that women and young children, sometimes under age six, hauled coal trucks through low, cramped passageways in coal mines. One nine-year-old girl, Margaret Gomley, described her typical day in the mines as beginning at 7:00 a.m. and ending at 6:00 p.m.: "I get my dinner at 12 o'clock, which is a dry muffin, and sometimes butter on, but have no time allowed to stop to eat it, I eat it while I am thrusting the load. . . . They flog us down in the pit, sometimes with their hand upon my bottom, which hurts me very much." In response to the investigations, the British Parliament in 1842 passed the Mines Act, which prohibited the employment of women and girls underground. In 1847, the Central Short Time Committee, one of Britain's many social reform organizations, successfully pressured Parliament to limit the workday of women and

Child Labor in Coal Mines

The passage of legislation in 1842 against women and girls working underground did nothing to prevent boys from continuing to perform essential tasks in cramped spaces in British coal mines. Lithographs such as this one from 1844 accompanied campaigns against these practices. *(akg-images.)*

NEW SOURCES, NEW PERSPECTIVES

Statistics and the Standard of Living of the Working Class

From the very beginning of industrialization, experts argued about whether industrialization improved or worsened the standard of living of the working class. There was a counterclaim for every claim, and most often these claims came in the form of statistics. Some experts argued that factories offered higher-paying jobs to workers; others countered that factories took work away from artisans such as handloom weavers and left them on the verge of starvation. Supporters of industrialization maintained that factories gave women paying work; opponents insisted that factories destroyed the family by taking women away from the home. Through mass production, industrialization made goods cheaper and therefore more available; by polluting the air, it destroyed health, lowered life expectancy, and ruined the environment. Karl Marx and Friedrich Engels would give the debate even more of an edge by tying it to the ideology of communism. In 1844, Engels described to Marx his aim in writing *The Condition of the Working Class in England*: "I shall present the English with a fine bill of indictment. At the bar of world opinion I charge the English middle classes with mass murder, wholesale robbery and all the other crimes in the calendar." The stakes of the argument were not small.

The controversy about the benefits and costs of industrialization has continued right down to the present, in part because it is an argument directly inspired by the ideologies—liberalism, socialism, communism—that emerged as explanations of and blueprints for economic and social change. In the 1830s and 1840s, liberals insisted that industrialization would promote greater prosperity for everyone, whereas conservatives complained that it destroyed traditional ways of life and socialists warned that it exaggerated inequality and class division. In the 1950s and 1960s, defenders of capitalist free enterprise still advanced the argument about prosperity, but now they were opposed by communists who argued that state control of production could sidestep the horrors of early capitalist exploitation. Newly developing countries looked to the history of the 1830s and 1840s for lessons about the likely impact of industrialization on their countries in the 1950s and beyond. The scholarly debates therefore attracted worldwide attention, and all sides called on statistics to make their competing cases.

Unfortunately, the statistics can be interpreted in many different ways. Did it matter more that wages for factory workers went up or that life expectancy went down? If an increase in sugar consumption in Great Britain from 207,000 tons in 1844 to 290,000 tons in 1847 meant an overall increase in the standard of living, how does that square with the hundreds of thousands of deaths in Ireland at the same time or the increasing disparity throughout Great Britain between rich and poor? Some convergence of opinion has taken place, however. Most now agree that by sometime between 1820 and 1845 (the exact date depending on the scholar), conditions in Great Britain had become better than before the Industrial Revolution. And there is no doubt that the debate itself has had one major positive effect: since making one's point depends on having statistics to prove it, the debate itself has encouraged a staggering amount

children to ten hours. The continental countries followed the British lead, but since most did not insist on government inspection, enforcement was lax.

Urbanization and Its Consequences

Industrial development spurred urban growth, yet even cities with little industry grew as well. **Urbanization** is the growth of towns and cities due to the movement of people from rural to urban areas. Here, too, Great Britain led the way: half the population of England and Wales was living in towns by 1850, while in France and the German states only about a quarter of the total population was urban. Both old and new cities teemed with rising numbers in the 1830s and 1840s; the population of Vienna ballooned by 125,000 between 1827 and 1847, and the new industrial city of Manchester grew by 70,000 just in the 1830s.

Massive rural emigration, rather than births to women already living in cities, accounted for this remarkable increase. Agricultural improvements had increased the food supply and hence the rural population, but the land could no longer support the people living on it. City life and new factories beckoned those faced with hunger and poverty, including immigrants from other lands: thousands of Irish emigrated to English cities, Italians went to

urbanization: The growth of towns and cities due to the movement of people from rural to urban areas, a trend that was encouraged by the development of factories and railroads.

of research into quantitative measures of just about everything imaginable, from measures of wages and prices to rates of mortality and even average heights (height being correlated, it is thought, to economic well-being). British soldiers in the nineteenth century were taller on average than those in any other country except the United States, and people who believe that industrialization improved the standard of living are happy to seize on this as evidence for their case.

The graph shown here, adapted from a recent study by Charles H. Feinstein, compares money earnings with the cost-of-living index to determine "real" earnings, that is, what the money earned would actually be able to buy in Great Britain. Feinstein developed an index of money earnings for both men and women for twenty different occupations and a cost-of-living index based on the price of twelve types of food as well as coal, candles, beer, footwear, clothing, and rent.

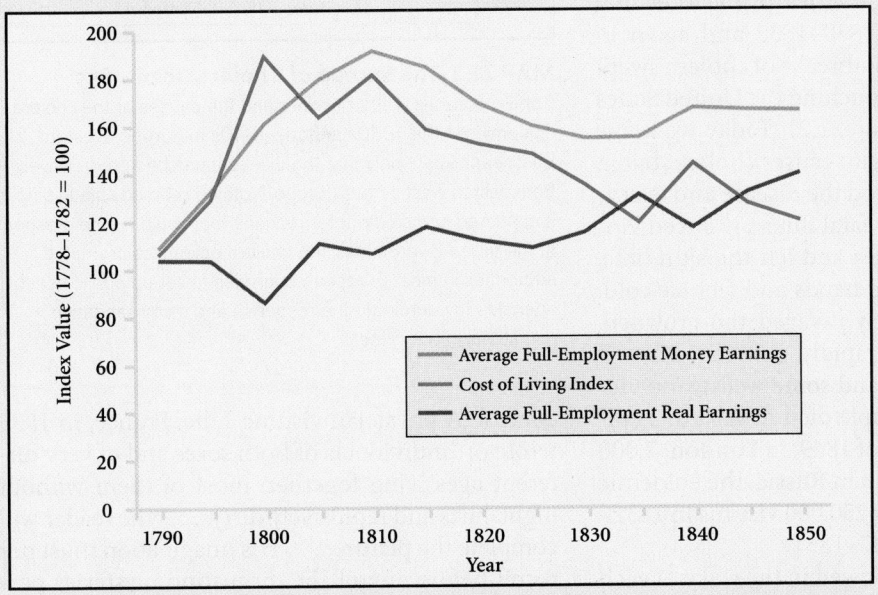

Annual Indexes of Money Earnings, the Cost of Living, and Real Earnings

(From Charles H. Feinstein, "Pessimism Perpetuated: Real Wages and the Standard of Living in Britain during and after the Industrial Revolution," Journal of Economic History *58, no. 3 [September 1998]: 625–58, table on 652–53.)*

Questions to Consider

1. **At what point according to this table did real earnings increase in significant fashion?**
2. **Looking back to Chapter 20, why might the cost of living have gone up so dramatically between 1800 and 1814?**
3. **What are the virtues of using statistical measures to determine the standard of living? What are the defects?**

Further Reading

Thompson, Noel W. *The Real Rights of Man: Political Economies for the Working Class, 1775–1850.* 1998.

Williamson, Jeffrey G., and Jeff Williamson. *Did British Capitalism Breed Inequality?* 2006.

French cities, and Poles flocked to German cities. Settlements sprang up outside the old city limits but gradually became part of the urban area. Cities incorporated parks, cemeteries, zoos, and greenways—all imitations of the countryside, which itself was being industrialized by railroads and factories. "One can't even go to one's land for the slightest bit of gardening," grumbled a French citizen, annoyed by new factories in town, "without being covered with a black powder that spoils every plant that it touches."

Overcrowding and Disease The rapid influx of people caused serious overcrowding in the cities because the housing stock expanded much more slowly than population growth and wages were not high enough for many workers to afford city rents. In Paris, thirty thousand workers lived in lodging houses, eight or nine to a room, with no separation of the sexes. In 1847 in St. Giles, the Irish quarter of London, 461 people lived in just twelve houses. Men, women, and children with no money for fuel huddled together for warmth on piles of filthy rotting straw or potato peels.

Severe crowding worsened already dire sanitation conditions. Residents dumped refuse into streets or courtyards, and human excrement collected in cesspools under apartment houses. At midcentury, London's approximately 250,000 cesspools were emptied only once or twice a year. Water was scarce and had to be fetched daily from nearby fountains. Despite the diversion of water from provincial rivers to Paris and a tripling of the number of public fountains, Parisians had enough water for only two baths annually per person (the upper classes enjoyed more baths, of course; the lower classes, fewer).

In London, private companies that supplied water turned on pumps in the poorer sections for only a few hours three days a week. In rapidly growing British industrial cities such as Manchester, one-third of the houses contained no latrines. Human waste ended up in the rivers that supplied drinking water. The horses that provided transportation inside the cities left droppings everywhere, and city dwellers often kept chickens, ducks, goats, pigs, geese, and even cattle, as well as dogs and cats, in their houses. The result was a "universal atmosphere of filth and stink," as one observer recounted.

Such conditions made cities prime breeding grounds for disease. In 1830–1832 and again in 1847–1851, devastating outbreaks of cholera swept across Asia and Europe, touching the United States as well in 1849–1850 (Map 21.2). Today we know that a waterborne bacterium causes cholera, but at the time no one understood the disease and everyone feared it. The usually fatal illness induced violent vomiting and diarrhea and left the skin blue, eyes sunken and dull, and hands and feet ice cold. While cholera particularly ravaged the crowded, filthy neighborhoods of rapidly growing cities, it also claimed many rural and some well-to-do victims. In Paris, 18,000 people died in the 1832 epidemic and 20,000 in that of 1849; in London, 7,000 died in each epidemic; and in Russia, the epidemic was catastrophic, claiming 250,000 victims in 1831–1832 and 1 million in 1847–1851.

Rumors and panic followed in the wake of each cholera epidemic. Everywhere the downtrodden imagined conspiracies: in Paris in April 1832, a crowd of workers attacked a central hospital, believing the doctors were poisoning the poor but using cholera as a hoax to cover up the conspiracy. Eastern European peasants burned estates and killed physicians and officials. Although devastating, cholera did not kill as many people as tuberculosis, Europe's number-one deadly disease. But tuberculosis took its victims gradually, one by one, and therefore had less impact on social relations.

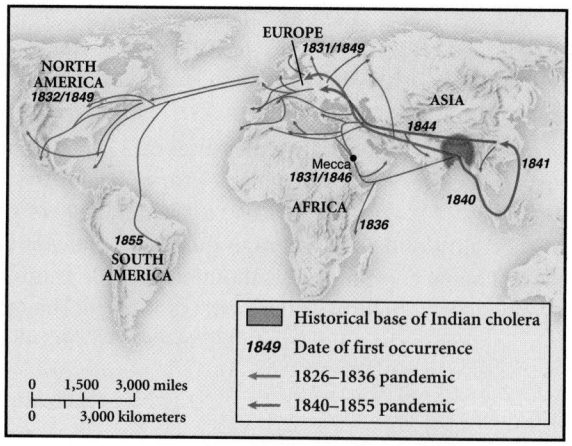

MAP 21.2 The Spread of Cholera, 1826–1855
Contemporaries did not understand the causes of the cholera epidemics in the 1830s and the 1840s in Europe. Western Europeans knew only that the disease marched progressively from east to west across Europe. Nothing seemed able to stop it. It appeared and died out for reasons that could not be grasped at the time. Nevertheless, the cholera epidemics prompted authorities in most European countries to set up public health agencies to coordinate the response and study sanitation conditions in the cities.

Middle-Class Fears Epidemics revealed the social tensions lying just beneath the surface of urban life. The middle and upper classes lived in large, well-appointed apartments or houses with more light, more air, and more water than in lower-class dwellings. But the lower classes lived nearby, sometimes in the cramped upper floors of the same apartment houses. Middle-class reformers often considered the poor to be morally degenerate because of the circumstances of urban life. In their view, overcrowding led to sexual promiscuity and illegitimacy. They depicted the lower classes as dangerously lacking in sexual self-control. A physician visiting Lille, France, in 1835 wrote of "individuals of both sexes and of very different ages lying together, most of them without nightshirts and repulsively dirty. . . . The reader will complete the picture. . . . His imagination must not recoil before any of the disgusting mysteries performed on these impure beds, in the midst of obscurity and drunkenness."

Officials collected statistics on illegitimacy that seemed to bear out these fears: one-quarter to one-half of the babies born in the big European cities in the 1830s and 1840s were illegitimate, and alarmed medical men wrote about thousands of infanticides. Between 1815 and the mid-1830s in France, thirty-three thousand babies were abandoned at foundling hospitals every year; 27 percent of births in Paris in 1850 were illegitimate, compared with only 4 percent of rural births. By collecting such statistics, physicians and administrators in the new public health movement hoped to promote legislation to better the living conditions for workers, but at the same time they helped stereotype workers as immoral and out of control.

Sexual disorder seemed to go hand in hand with drinking and crime. Beer halls and pubs dotted the urban landscape. By the 1830s, Hungary's twin cities of Buda and Pest had eight hundred beer and wine houses for the working classes. One London street boasted twenty-three pubs in three hundred yards. Police officials estimated that London had seventy thousand thieves and eighty thousand prostitutes. In many cities, nearly half the population lived at the level of bare subsistence, and increasing numbers depended on public welfare, charity, or criminality to make ends meet.

Everywhere reformers warned of a widening separation between rich and poor and a growing sense of hostility between the classes. The French poet Amédée Pommier wrote of "These leagues of laborers who have no work, / These far too many arms, these starving mobs." Clergymen joined physicians and humanitarians in making dire predictions. A Swiss pastor noted: "A new spirit has arisen among the workers. Their hearts seethe with hatred of the well-to-do; their eyes lust for a share of the wealth about them; their mouths speak unblushingly of a coming day of retribution." In 1848, it would seem that that day of retribution had arrived.

Agricultural Perils and Prosperity

Rising populations created increased demand for food and spurred changes in the countryside, too. Peasants and farmers planted fallow land, chopped down forests, and drained marshes to increase their farming capacity. Still, Europe's ability to feed its expanding population remained questionable: although agricultural yields increased by 30 to 50 percent in the first half of the nineteenth century, population grew by nearly 100 percent. Railroads and canals improved food distribution, but much of Europe—particularly in the east—remained isolated from markets and vulnerable to famines.

Most people still lived on the land, and the upper classes still dominated rural society. Successful businessmen bought land avidly, seeing it not only as the ticket to respectability but also as a hedge against hard times. Hardworking, crafty, or lucky commoners sometimes saved enough to purchase holdings that they had formerly rented or slowly acquired slivers of land from less fortunate neighbors. In France at midcentury, almost two million economically independent peasants tended their own small properties. But in England, southern Italy, Prussia, and eastern Europe, large landowners, usually noblemen, consolidated and expanded their estates by buying up the land of less successful nobles or peasants. As agricultural prices rose, the big landowners pushed for legislation to allow them to continue converting common land to private property.

Wringing a living from the soil under such conditions put pressure on traditional family life. For example, men often migrated seasonally to earn cash in factories or as village artisans, while their wives, sisters, and daughters did the traditional "men's work" of tending crops. In France, Napoleon's Civil Code provided for an equal distribution of inheritance among all heirs; as a result, land was divided over generations into such small parcels that less than 25 percent of all French landowners could support themselves. In the past, population growth had been contained by postponing marriage (leaving fewer years for childbearing) and by high rates of death in childbirth as well as infant mortality. Now, as child mortality declined outside the industrial cities and people without property began marrying earlier, Europeans became more aware of birth control methods. Contraceptive techniques improved; for example, the vulcanization of rubber in the 1840s improved the reliability of condoms. When such methods failed and population increase left no options open at home, people emigrated, often to the United States. Some 800,000 Germans had moved out of central Europe by 1850, while in the 1840s famine drove hundreds of thousands of Irish abroad. Between 1816 and 1850, five million Europeans left their home countries for new lives overseas. When France colonized Algeria in the 1830s and 1840s, officials tried to attract settlers by emphasizing the fertility of the land; they offered the prospect of agricultural prosperity in the colony as an alternative to the rigors of industrialization and urbanization at home.

Despite all the challenges to established ways of life, rural political power remained in the hands of traditional elites. The biggest property owners dominated their tenants, sharecroppers, and serfs, often demanding a greater yield without making improvements that would enhance productivity. They controlled the political assemblies as well and often personally selected local officials. Such power provoked resentment. One Italian critic wrote, "Great landowner is often the synonym for great ignoramus." Nowhere did the old rural social order seem more impregnable than in Russia. Most Russian serfs remained tied to the land, and troops easily suppressed serfs' uprisings in 1831 and 1842. Yet in the 1850s railroad construction would begin to transform life in Russia too, and the railroads would bring with them the same social problems—urbanization, the beginning of industrialization, and a growing awareness of social disparities—that threatened the social and political order in western Europe in the 1830s and 1840s. These new social problems demanded a response. But would that response be reform or revolution?

REVIEW QUESTION What dangers did the Industrial Revolution pose to both urban and rural life?

Reforming the Social Order

The experience of dramatic economic and social changes prompted artists and writers to focus on emerging social problems, even when they rejected the influence of the new industrial way of life. Their literary and artistic depictions of social problems helped inspire the creation of new organizations for social reform. Middle-class women often took the lead in establishing charitable organizations that tried to bring religious faith, educational uplift, and the reform of manners to the lower classes. The middle class, both men and women, expected women to soften the rigors of a rapidly changing society, but this expectation led to some confusion about women's proper role: Should they devote themselves to social reform in the world or to their own domestic spaces? Many hoped to apply the same zeal for reform to the colonial peoples living in places administered by Europeans.

Cultural Responses to the Social Question

The *social question*, an expression reflecting the widely shared concern about social changes arising from industrialization and urbanization, pervaded all forms of art and literature. The dominant artistic movement of the time, romanticism, generally took a dim view of industrialization. The English-born American painter Thomas Cole (1801–1848) complained in 1836: "In this age . . . a meager utilitarianism seems ready to absorb every feeling and sentiment, and what is sometimes called improvement in its march makes us fear that the bright and tender flowers of the imagination shall all be crushed beneath its iron tramp." Yet culture itself underwent important changes as the growing capitals of Europe attracted flocks of aspiring painters and playwrights; the 1830s and 1840s witnessed an explosion in culture as the number of would-be artists increased dramatically and new technologies such as photography and lithography (see the illustration on the top of page 698) brought art to the masses. Many of these new intellectuals would support the revolutions of 1848.

Romantic Concerns about Industrial Life

Because romanticism tended to glorify nature and reject industrial and urban growth, romantics often gave vivid expression to the problems created by rapid economic and social transformation. The English poet Elizabeth Barrett Browning, best known for her love poems, denounced child labor in "The Cry of the Children" (1843). Architects of the period sometimes sought to recapture a preindustrial world. When the British Houses of Parliament were rebuilt after they burned down in 1834, the architect Sir Charles Barry constructed them in a Gothic style reminiscent of the Middle Ages. This medievalism was taken even further by A. W. N. Pugin, who contributed some of the designs for the Houses of Parliament. In his polemical book *Contrasts* (1836), Pugin denounced modern conditions and compared them unfavorably with those in the 1400s. To underline his view, Pugin wore medieval clothes at home.

Romantic painters specialized in landscape as a way of calling attention to the sublime wonders of nature, but sometimes even landscapes showed the power of new technologies. In *Rain, Steam, and Speed: The Great Western Railway* (1844), the leading English romantic painter, Joseph M. W. Turner (1775–1851), portrayed the struggle between the forces of nature and the means of economic growth. Turner was fascinated by steamboats: in *The Fighting "Téméraire" Tugged to Her Last Berth to Be Broken Up* (1838; see the illustration on page 697), he featured the victory of steam power over more conventional sailing ships. An admirer described the painting as an "almost prophetic idea of smoke, soot, iron, and steam, coming to the front in all naval matters."

The Depiction of Social Conditions in Novels

Increased literacy, the spread of reading rooms and lending libraries, and serialization in newspapers and journals gave novels a large reading public. Unlike the fiction of the eighteenth century, which had focused on individual personalities, the great novels of the 1830s and 1840s specialized in the portrayal of social life in all its varieties. Manufacturers, financiers, starving students, workers, bureaucrats, prostitutes, underworld figures, thieves, and aristocratic men and women filled the pages of works by popular writers. Hoping to get out of debt, the French writer Honoré de Balzac (1799–1850) pushed himself to exhaustion and a premature death by cranking out ninety-five novels and many short stories. He aimed to catalog the social types that could be found in French society. Many of his characters, like himself, were driven by the desire to climb higher in the social order.

The English fiction writer Charles Dickens (1812–1870) worked with a similar frenetic energy and for much the same reason. When his father was imprisoned for debt in 1824, the young Dickens took a job in a shoe-polish factory. In 1836, he published a series of literary sketches of daily life in London to accompany a volume of caricatures by the

Joseph M. W. Turner, *The Fighting "Téméraire" Tugged to Her Last Berth to Be Broken Up* (1838)
In this painting a steamer belching smoke tows a wooden sailing ship to its last berth, where it will be destroyed. Turner muses about the passing of old ways but also displays his mastery of color in the final blaze of sunset, itself another sign of the passing of time. Turner was an avid reader of the romantic poets, especially Byron. British opinion polls have rated this painting the best of all British paintings. How does the painting capture the clash of old and new? *(© The National Gallery, London, UK/Art Resource, NY.)*

artist George Cruikshank. Dickens then produced a series of novels that appeared in monthly installments and attracted thousands of readers. In them, he paid close attention to the distressing effects of industrialization and urbanization. In *The Old Curiosity Shop* (1841), for example, he depicts the Black Country, the manufacturing region west and northwest of Birmingham, as a "cheerless region," a "mournful place," in which tall chimneys "made foul the melancholy air." In addition to publishing such enduring favorites as *Oliver Twist* (1838) and *A Christmas Carol* (1843), he ran charitable organizations and pressed for social reforms. For Dickens, the ability to portray the problems of the poor went hand in hand with a personal commitment to reform.

Novels by women often revealed the bleaker side of women's situations. Charlotte Brontë's *Jane Eyre* (1847) describes the difficult life of an orphaned girl who becomes a governess, the only occupation open to most single middle-class women. The French novelist Amandine-Aurore-Lucile Dupin Dudevant (1804–1876), writing under the pen name **George Sand**, took her social criticism a step further. She announced her independence in the 1830s by dressing like a man and smoking cigars. Though she published her work under a male pseudonym, as did many other women writers of the time, she created female characters who prevail in difficult circumstances through romantic love and moral idealism. Sand's novel *Indiana* (1832), about an unhappily married woman, was read all over Europe. Her notoriety — she became the lover of the Polish pianist and composer Frédéric Chopin, among others, and threw herself into socialist politics — made the term *George-Sandism* a common expression of disdain for independent women.

George Sand: The pen name of French novelist Amandine-Aurore-Lucile Dupin Dudevant (1804–1876), who showed her independence in the 1830s by dressing like a man and smoking cigars. The term *George-Sandism* became an expression of disdain for independent women.

George Sand

In this lithograph by Alcide Lorentz of 1842, George Sand is shown in one of her notorious male costumes standing on a cloud created by the cigar in her left hand. Sand published numerous works, including novels (*Indiana* is shown at her feet), plays, essays, travel writing, and an autobiography. She advocated setting up a Chamber of Mothers to go alongside the Chamber of Deputies (her right arm rests on sheets with those words on them), and she actively participated in the revolution of 1848 in France, writing pamphlets in support of the new republic. Disillusioned by the rise to power of Louis-Napoleon Bonaparte, she withdrew to her country estate and devoted herself exclusively to her writing. *(The Granger Collection, New York—All rights reserved.)*

The First Daguerreotype

Jacques Daguerre experimented extensively with producing an image on a metal plate before he came up with a viable photographic process in 1837. He called this first daguerreotype *Still Life*, a common title for paintings. In 1839, the French government bought the rights and made the process freely available. *(Louis Daguerre, Time & Life Pictures/Getty Images.)*

The Explosion of Culture

As artists became more interested in society and social relations, ordinary citizens crowded cultural events. Museums opened to the public across Europe, and the middle classes began collecting art. Popular theaters in big cities drew thousands from the lower and middle classes every night; in London, for example, some twenty-four thousand people attended eighty "penny theaters" nightly. The audience for print culture also multiplied. In the German states, for example, the production of new literary works doubled between 1830 and 1843, as did the number of periodicals and newspapers and the number of booksellers. Thirty or forty private lending libraries offered books in Berlin in the 1830s, and reading rooms in pastry shops stocked political newspapers and satirical journals. Young children and ragpickers sold cheap prints and books door-to-door or in taverns.

The advent of photography in 1839 provided an amazing new medium for artists. The daguerreotype, named after its inventor, French painter Jacques Daguerre (1787–1851), prompted one artist to claim that "from today, painting is dead." Although this prediction was highly exaggerated, photography did open up new ways of portraying reality. It did so only gradually, however, as early photographs required exposure times of twenty to thirty minutes, making it impossible to capture anything or anyone in movement.

Culture expanded its reach in part because the number of artists and writers swelled. Estimates suggest that the number of painters and sculptors in France, the undisputed center of European art at the time, grew sixfold between 1789 and 1838. Not everyone could succeed in this hothouse atmosphere, in which writers and artists furiously competed for public attention. Their own troubles made some of them more keenly aware of the hardships faced by the poor. A satirical article in one of the many bitingly critical journals and booklets published in Berlin proclaimed: "In Ipswich in England a mechanical genius has invented a stomach, whose extraordinary efficient construction is remarkable. This artificial stomach is intended for factory workers there and is adjusted so that it is fully satisfied with three lentils or peas; one potato is enough for an entire week."

The Varieties of Social Reform

Lithographs, novels, and even joke booklets helped drive home the need for social reform, but religious conviction also inspired efforts to help the poor. Moral reform societies, Bible groups, Sunday schools, and temperance groups aimed to turn the poor into respectable people. In 1844, for example, 450 different relief organizations operated in London alone. States supported these efforts by encouraging education and enforcing laws against the vagrant poor.

The Religious Impulse for Social Reform

Religiously motivated reformers first had to overcome the perceived indifference of the working classes. Protestant and Catholic clergy complained that workers had no interest in religion; less than 10 percent of the workers in the cities attended religious services. In a report on the state of religion in England and Wales in 1851, the head of the census commented that "the masses of our working population . . . are *unconscious secularists*. . . . These are never, or but seldom seen in our religious congregations." To combat such indifference, British religious groups launched the Sunday school movement, which reached its zenith in the 1840s. By 1851, more than half of all working-class children ages five to fifteen were attending Sunday school, even though very few of their parents regularly went to religious services. The Sunday schools taught children how to read at a time when few working-class children could go to school during the week.

Women took a more prominent role than ever before in charitable work. Catholic religious orders, which by 1850 enrolled many more women than men, ran schools, hospitals, leper colonies, insane asylums, and old-age homes. The Catholic church established new orders, especially for women, and increased missionary activity overseas. Protestant women in Great Britain and the United States established Bible, missionary, and female reform societies by the hundreds. Chief among their concerns was prostitution, and many societies dedicated themselves to reforming "fallen women" and castigating men who visited prostitutes. As a pamphlet of the Boston Female Moral Reform Society explained, "Our mothers, our sisters, our daughters are sacrificed by the thousands every year on the altar of sin, and who are the agents in this work of destruction: Why, our fathers, our brothers, and our sons."

Catholics and Protestants alike promoted the temperance movement. In Ireland, England, the German states, and the United States, temperance societies organized to fight the "pestilence of hard liquor." The first societies had appeared in the United States as early as 1813, and by 1835 the American Temperance Society claimed 1.5 million members. Temperance advocates saw drunkenness as a sign of moral weakness and a threat to social order. Industrialists pointed to the loss of worker productivity, and efforts to promote temperance often reflected middle- and upper-class fears of the lower classes' lack of discipline. One German temperance advocate insisted, "One need not be a prophet to know that all efforts to combat the widespread and rapidly spreading pauperism will be unsuccessful as long as the common man fails to realize that the principal source of his degradation and misery is his fondness of drink." Yet temperance societies also attracted working-class people who shared the desire for respectability.

Education and Reform of the Poor

Social reformers saw education as one of the main prospects for uplifting the poor and the working class. In addition to setting up Sunday schools, British churches founded organizations such as the British and Foreign School Society. More secular in intent were the Mechanics Institutes, which provided education for workers in the big cities. In 1833, the French government passed an education law that required every town to maintain a primary school, pay a teacher, and provide free education to poor boys. As the law's author, François Guizot, argued, "Ignorance renders the masses turbulent and ferocious." Girls' schools were optional, although hundreds of women taught at the primary level, most of them in private, often religious schools. Despite these efforts, only one out of every thirty children went to school in France, many fewer than in Protestant states such as Prussia, where 75 percent of children were in primary school by 1835. Popular education remained woefully undeveloped in most of eastern Europe. Peasants were specifically excluded from the few primary schools in Russia, where Tsar Nicholas I blamed the Decembrist Revolt of 1825 on education.

Above all else, the elite sought to impose discipline and order on working people. Popular sports, especially blood sports such as cockfighting and bearbaiting, suggested a lack of control, and longstanding efforts in Great Britain to eliminate these recreations now gained momentum through organizations such as the Society for the Prevention of Cruelty to Animals. By the end of the 1830s, bullbaiting had been abandoned in Great Britain. "This useful animal," rejoiced one reformer in 1839, "is no longer tortured amidst the exulting yells of those who are a disgrace to our common form and nature." The other blood sports died out more slowly, and efforts in other countries generally lagged behind those of the British.

When private charities failed to meet the needs of the poor, governments often intervened. Great Britain sought to control the costs of public welfare by passing a new poor law in 1834, called by its critics the Starvation Act. The law required that all able-bodied persons receiving relief be housed together in workhouses, with husbands separated from wives

Class Differences
In 1841 a new satirical weekly in London called *Punch* began publishing "cartoons" (humorous drawings). This one from 1843 depicts the dramatic differences between the life experiences of those with money ("Capital") and those who worked with their hands ("Labour"). *(From* Punch, *vol. 5, London, 1843, cartoon number 5/akg-images.)*

and parents from children. Workhouse life was designed to be as unpleasant as possible so that poor people would move on to regions of higher employment. British women from all social classes organized anti–poor law societies to protest the separation of mothers from their children in the workhouses.

Domesticity and the Subordination of Women

Many women viewed charitable work as the extension of their domestic roles: they promoted virtuous behavior and morality in their efforts to improve society. In one widely read advice book, Englishwoman Sarah Lewis suggested in 1839 that "women may be the prime agents in the regeneration of mankind." But women's social reform activities concealed a paradox. According to the ideology that historians call **domesticity**, women were to live their lives entirely within the domestic sphere, devoting themselves to their families and the home. The English poet Alfred, Lord Tennyson, captured this view in a popular poem published in 1847: "Man for the field and woman for the hearth; / Man for the sword and for the needle she. / . . . All else confusion." Many believed that maintaining proper and distinct roles for men and women was critically important to maintaining social order in general.

Most women had little hope of economic independence. The notion that they belonged in a separate, domestic sphere prevented women from pursuing higher education, work in professional careers, or participation in politics through voting or holding office—all activities deemed appropriate only to men. Laws everywhere codified the subordination of women. Many countries followed the model of Napoleon's Civil Code, which classified married women as legal incompetents along with children, the insane, and criminals. In Great Britain, which had no national law code, the courts upheld the legality of a husband's complete control. For example, a court ruled in 1840 that "there can be no doubt of the general dominion which the law of England attributes to the husband over the wife." In some countries, such as France and Austria, unmarried women enjoyed some rights over property, but elsewhere laws explicitly defined them as perpetual minors under paternal control.

Distinctions between men and women were most noticeable in the privileged classes. Whereas boys attended secondary schools, most middle- and upper-class girls still received their education at home or in church schools, where they were taught to be religious, obedient, and accomplished in music and languages. As men's fashions turned practical—long trousers and short jackets of solid, often dark colors; no makeup (previously common for aristocratic men); and simply cut hair—women continued to dress for decorative effect, now with tightly corseted waists that emphasized the differences between female and male bodies. Middle- and upper-class women favored long hair that required hours of brushing and pinning up, and they wore long, cumbersome skirts. Advice books written by women detailed the tasks that such women undertook in the home: maintaining household accounts, supervising servants, and organizing social events.

Scientists reinforced stereotypes. Once considered sexually insatiable, women were now described as incapacitated by menstruation and largely uninterested in sex, an attitude that many equated with moral superiority. Thus was born the "Victorian" woman (the epoch gets its name from England's

domesticity: An ideology prevailing in the nineteenth century that women should devote themselves to their families and the home.

Queen Victoria—see page 716), a figment of the largely male medical imagination. Physicians and scholars considered women mentally inferior. In 1839, Auguste Comte, an influential early French sociologist, wrote, "As for any functions of government, the radical inaptitude of the female sex is there yet more marked . . . and limited to the guidance of the mere family."

Some women denounced the ideology of domesticity and separate spheres; the English writer Ann Lamb, for example, proclaimed that "the duty of a wife *means* the obedience of a Turkish slave." Middle-class women who did not marry, however, had few options for earning a living; they often worked as governesses or ladies' companions for the well-to-do. Most lower-class women worked because of financial necessity; as the wives of peasants, laborers, or shopkeepers, they had to supplement the family's meager income by working on the farm, in a factory, or in a shop. Domesticity might have been an ideal for them, but rarely was it a reality. Families crammed into small spaces had no time or energy for separate spheres.

Abuses and Reforms Overseas

Like the ideal of domesticity, the ideal of colonialism often conflicted with the reality of economic interests. In the first half of the nineteenth century, those economic interests changed as European colonialism underwent a subtle but momentous transformation. Colonialism became **imperialism**—a word coined only in the mid-nineteenth century—as Europeans turned their interest away from the plantation colonies of the Caribbean and toward new colonies in Asia and Africa. Colonialism had most often led to the establishment of settler colonies, direct rule by Europeans, the introduction of slave labor from Africa, and the wholesale destruction of indigenous peoples; in contrast, imperialism usually meant more indirect forms of economic exploitation and political rule. Europeans still profited from their colonies, but now they also aimed to re-form colonial peoples in their own image—when it did not conflict too much with their economic interests to do so.

Abolition of Slavery Colonialism—as opposed to imperialism—rose and fell with the enslavement of black Africans. British religious groups, especially the Quakers, had taken the lead in forming antislavery societies. The contradiction between calling for more liberty at home and maintaining slavery in the West Indies seemed intolerable to them. One English abolitionist put the matter in these terms: "[God] has given to us an unexampled portion of civil liberty; and we in return drag his rational creatures into a most severe and perpetual bondage." Such groups as the London Society for Effecting the Abolition of the Slave Trade gained a first victory in 1807 when the British House of Lords voted to abolish the slave trade (though not the institution of slavery itself). The new Latin American republics abolished slavery in the 1820s and 1830s after they defeated the Spanish with armies that included many slaves. British missionary and evangelical groups continued to condemn the conquest, enslavement, and exploitation of native African populations and successfully blocked British annexations in central and southern Africa in the 1830s.

British reformers finally obtained the abolition of slavery in the British Empire in 1833. Antislavery petitions to Parliament bore 1.5 million signatures, including those of 350,000 women on one petition alone. In France, the new government of Louis-Philippe took strong measures against clandestine slave traffic, virtually ending French participation during the 1830s. Slavery was abolished in the remaining French Caribbean colonies in 1848.

Neither slavery nor the slave trade disappeared immediately just because the British and French had given it up. Because of increased participation by Spanish and Portuguese traders, almost as many slaves were traded in the 1820s as in the 1780s and the overall traffic did not dwindle until the 1850s. Human bondage continued unabated in Brazil, Cuba (still a Spanish colony), and the United States. Some American reformers supported abolition, but they remained a minority. Like serfdom in Russia, slavery in the Americas involved a quagmire of economic, political, and moral problems that worsened as the nineteenth century wore on.

Economic and Political Imperialism Despite the abolition of slavery, Britain and France had not lost interest in overseas colonies. Using the pretext of an insult to its envoy, France invaded Algeria in 1830 and, after a long military campaign, established political control over most of the country in the next two decades. By 1848, more than seventy thousand French, Italian, and Maltese colonists had settled there with government encouragement, often confiscating the lands of native peoples. In that year, the French government officially incorporated Algeria as part of France. Eventually, the French embarked on a policy of

imperialism: European dominance of the non-West through economic exploitation and political rule; the word (as distinct from *colonialism*, which usually implied establishment of settler colonies, often with slavery) was coined in the mid-nineteenth century.

Opium Den in London (c. 1870)
This woodcut by Gustave Doré shows that opium smoking persisted in Britain at least to the 1870s. Doré was a French book illustrator who came to London in 1869–1871 and produced illustrations of the poorer neighborhoods in the city. His taste for the grotesque is apparent in the figures watching the smokers. *(Snark/Art Resource, NY.)*

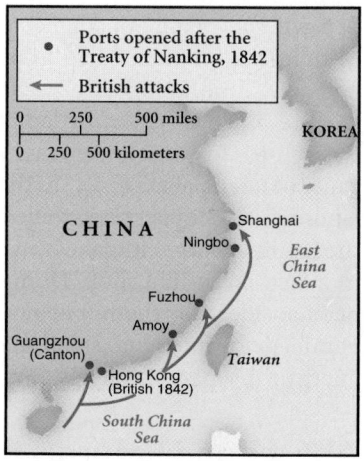

The Opium War, 1839–1842

assimilating the native population into French culture, but their efforts proved less than completely successful. France also imposed a protectorate government over the South Pacific island of Tahiti.

Although the British granted Canada greater self-determination in 1839, they extended their dominion elsewhere by annexing Singapore (1819), an island off the Malay peninsula, and New Zealand (1840). They also increased their control in India through the administration of the East India Company, a private group of merchants chartered by the British crown. The British educated a native elite to take over much of the day-to-day business of administering the country, and they used native soldiers to augment their military control. By 1850, only one in six soldiers serving Britain in India was European.

The East India Company also tried to establish a regular trade with China in opium, long known for its medicinal uses but increasingly bought in China as a recreational drug. The Chinese government forbade Western merchants to venture outside the southern city of Guangzhou (Canton) and banned the import of opium, but these measures failed. Through smuggling Indian opium into China and bribing local officials, British traders built up a flourishing market, and by the mid-1830s they were pressuring the British government to force an expanded opium trade on the Chinese. When the Chinese authorities expelled British merchants from southern China in 1839, Britain retaliated by bombarding Chinese coastal cities. The **Opium War** ended in 1842, when Britain dictated to a defeated China the Treaty of Nanking, by which four more Chinese ports were opened to Europeans and the British took sovereignty over the island of Hong Kong, received a substantial war indemnity, and were assured of a continuation of the opium trade. In this case, reform took a backseat to economic interest, despite the complaints of religious groups in Britain. In general, reform organizations aimed to improve the lives of the downtrodden, not overturn the basic structures of the political order or social hierarchy. Faced with continuing conflicts and unrest, some intellectuals and activists began to look for more systematic solutions to the social problems of the time.

REVIEW QUESTION **In which areas did reformers trying to address the social problems created by industrialization and urbanization succeed, and in which did they fail?**

Opium War: War between China and Great Britain (1839–1842) that resulted in the opening of four Chinese ports to Europeans and British sovereignty over Hong Kong.

Ideologies and Political Movements

Although reform organizations grew rapidly in the 1830s and 1840s, many Europeans found them insufficient to answer the questions raised by industrialization and urbanization. How did the new social order differ from the earlier one, which was less urban and less driven by commercial concerns? Who should control this new order? Should governments try to moderate or accelerate the pace of change? New ideologies such as liberalism and socialism offered competing answers to these questions and provided the platform for new political movements. Established governments faced challenges not only from liberals and socialists but also from the most potent of the new doctrines, nationalism. Nationalists looked past social problems to concentrate on achieving political autonomy and self-determination for groups identified by ethnicity rather than by class.

The Spell of Nationalism

According to the doctrine of **nationalism**, all peoples derive their identities from their nations, which are defined by common language, shared cultural traditions, and sometimes religion. When such nations do not coincide with state boundaries, nationalism can produce violence and warfare as different national groups compete for control over territory (Map 21.3).

Nationalist aspirations were especially explosive for the Austrian Empire, which included a variety of peoples united only by their enforced allegiance to the Habsburg emperor. The empire included three main national groups: the Germans, who made up one-fourth of the population; the Magyars of Hungary (which included Transylvania and Croatia); and the Slavs, who together formed the largest group in the population but were divided into different ethnic groups such as Poles, Czechs, Croats, and Serbs. The Austrian Empire also included Italians in Lombardy and Venetia, and Romanians in Transylvania. Efforts to govern such diverse peoples preoccupied Prince Klemens von Metternich, chief minister to the weak Habsburg emperor Francis I (r. 1792–1835). Metternich's domestic policy aimed to restrain nationalist impulses, and it largely succeeded until the 1840s. He set up a secret police organization on the Napoleonic model that opened letters of even the highest officials. Censorship in the Italian provinces was so strict that even the works of Dante were expurgated. Metternich announced that "the Lombards must forget that they are Italians."

Metternich's policies forced the leading Italian nationalist, **Giuseppe Mazzini** (1805–1872), into exile in France in 1831. There Mazzini founded Young Italy, a secret society that attracted thousands with its message that Italy would touch off a European-wide revolutionary movement. The conservative order throughout Europe felt threatened by Mazzini's charismatic leadership and conspiratorial scheming, but he lacked both European allies against Austria and widespread support among the Italian masses.

Since so many different ethnic groups lived within the borders of the Austrian Empire, neither the emperor nor Metternich favored aspirations for German unification. Economic unification in the German states nonetheless took a step forward with the foundation in 1834, under Prussian leadership, of the *Zollverein* ("customs union"). Austria was not part of the Zollverein. German nationalists sought a government uniting German-speaking peoples, but they could not agree on its boundaries: Would the unified German state include both Prussia and the Austrian Empire? If it included Austria, what about the non-German territories of the Austrian Empire? And could the powerful, conservative kingdom of Prussia coexist in a unified German state with other, more liberal but smaller states? These questions would vex German history for decades to come.

Polish nationalism became more self-conscious after the collapse of the revolt in 1830 against Russian domination. Ten thousand Poles, mostly noble army officers and intellectuals, fled Poland in 1830 and 1831. Most of them took up residence in western European capitals, especially Paris, where they mounted a successful public relations campaign for worldwide support. Their intellectual hero was the poet Adam Mickiewicz (1798–1855), whose mystical writings portrayed the Polish exiles as martyrs of a crucified nation with an international Christian mission: "Your endeavors are for all men, not only for yourselves. You will achieve a new Christian civilization."

Mickiewicz formed the Polish Legion to fight for national restoration, but rivalries and divisions among the Polish nationalists prevented united

nationalism: An ideology that arose in the nineteenth century and that holds that all peoples derive their identities from their nations, which are defined by common language, shared cultural traditions, and sometimes religion.

Giuseppe Mazzini: An Italian nationalist (1805–1872) who founded Young Italy, a secret society to promote Italian unity. He believed that a popular uprising would create a unified Italy.

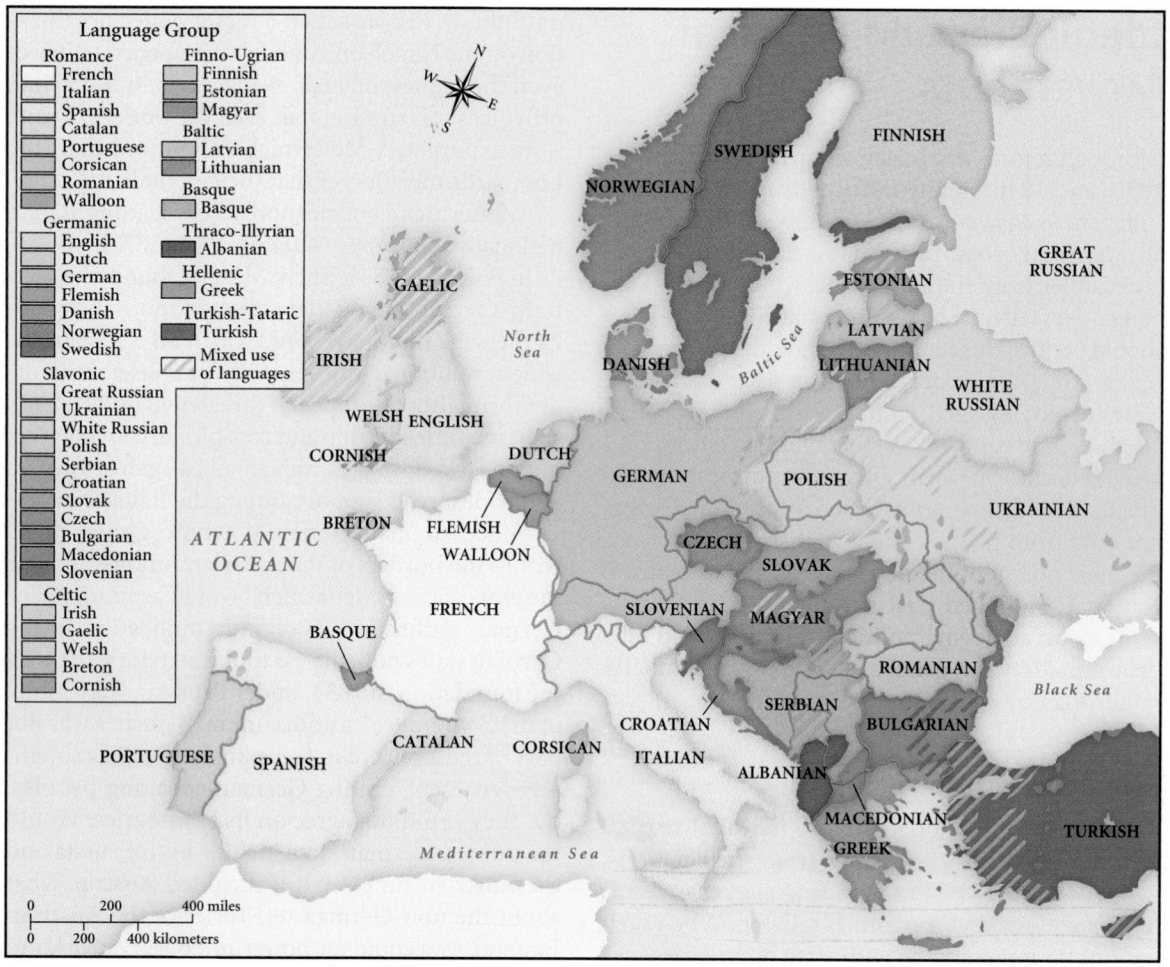

MAP 21.3 Languages of Nineteenth-Century Europe

Even this detailed map of linguistic diversity understates the number of different languages and dialects spoken in Europe. In Italy, for example, few people spoke Italian as their first language. Instead, they spoke local dialects such as Piedmontese or Ligurian, and some might speak better French than Italian if they came from the regions bordering France. How does the map underline the inherent contradictions of nationalism in Europe? What were the consequences of linguistic diversity within national borders? Keep in mind that even in Spain, France, and Great Britain, linguistic diversity continued right up to the beginning of the 1900s.

action until 1846, when Polish exiles in Paris tried to launch a coordinated insurrection for Polish independence. Plans for an uprising in the Polish province of Galicia in the Austrian Empire collapsed when peasants instead revolted against their noble Polish masters. Slaughtering some two thousand aristocrats, a desperate rural population served the Austrian government's end by defusing the nationalist challenge. Class interests and national identity worked against each other.

In Russia, nationalism took the form of opposition to Western ideas. Russian nationalists, or Slavophiles (lovers of the Slavs), opposed the Westernizers, who wanted Russia to follow Western models of industrial development and constitutional government. The Slavophiles favored maintaining rural traditions infused by the values of the Russian Orthodox church. Only a return to Russia's basic historical principles, they argued, could protect the country against the corrosion of rationalism and materialism. Slavophiles sometimes criticized the regime, however, because they believed the state exerted too much power over the church. The conflict between Slavophiles and Westernizers has continued to shape Russian cultural and intellectual life to the present day.

The most significant nationalist movement in western Europe could be found in Ireland. The Irish had struggled for centuries against English occupation, but Irish nationalists developed strong organizations only in the 1840s. In 1842, a group of writers founded the Young Ireland movement, which aimed to recover Irish traditions and preserve the Gaelic language (spoken by at least one-third of the peasantry). Daniel O'Connell (1775–1847), a Catholic lawyer and landowner who sat in the British House of Commons, hoped to force the British Parliament to repeal the Act of Union of 1801, which had made Ireland part of Great Britain. In 1843, London newspapers reported "monster meetings" that drew crowds of as many as 300,000 people in support of repeal of the union. In response, the British government arrested O'Connell and convicted him of conspiracy. As the Irish example shows, nationalism could turn social tensions into a political movement against an outside oppressor and make independence seem to be the only solution to social injustice. In 1848, when revolutions broke out all over Europe, nationalism often worked against the other political ideologies of the time.

Liberalism in Economics and Politics

As an ideology, **liberalism** had a longer lineage than nationalism but enjoyed less influence among the common people. Liberalism traced its origins to the writings of John Locke in the seventeenth century and the Enlightenment philosophy in the eighteenth. The adherents of liberalism defined themselves in opposition to conservatives on one end of the political spectrum and revolutionaries on the other. Unlike conservatives, liberals supported the Enlightenment ideals of constitutional guarantees of personal liberty and free trade in economics, believing that greater liberty in politics and economic matters would promote social improvement and economic growth. For that reason, they also generally applauded the social and economic changes produced by the Industrial Revolution, while opposing the violence and excessive state power promoted by the French Revolution. The leaders of the expanding middle class composed of manufacturers, merchants, and professionals favored liberalism.

British Liberalism

The rapid industrialization and urbanization of Great Britain created a receptive environment for liberalism. Its foremost proponent in the early nineteenth century was the philosopher and jurist Jeremy Bentham (1748–1832). He called his brand of liberalism utilitarianism because he held that the best policy is the one that produces "the greatest good for the greatest number" and is thus the most useful, or utilitarian. Bentham's criticisms spared no institution; he railed against the injustices of the British parliamentary process, the abuses of the prisons and the penal code, and the educational system. In his zeal for social engineering, Bentham proposed elaborate schemes for managing the poor and model prisons that would emphasize rehabilitation through close supervision rather than corporal punishment. British liberals like Bentham wanted government involvement, including deregulation of trade, but they shied away from any association with revolutionary violence.

British liberals wanted government to limit its economic role to maintaining the currency, enforcing contracts, and financing major enterprises like the military and the railroads. As historian and member of Parliament Thomas Macaulay (1800–1859) explained in 1830:

> Our rulers will best promote the improvement of the nation by strictly confining themselves to their own legitimate duties, by leaving capital to find its most lucrative course, commodities their fair price, industry and intelligence their natural reward, idleness and folly their natural punishment, by maintaining peace, by defending property, by diminishing the price of law, and by observing strict economy in every department of the State.

British liberals sought to lower or eliminate British tariffs, especially through repeal of the **Corn Laws**, which benefited landowners by preventing the import of cheap foreign grain while keeping the price of food artificially high for the workers. When landholders in the House of Commons thwarted efforts to lower grain tariffs, two Manchester cotton manufacturers set up the Anti–Corn Law League. The league appealed to the middle class against the landlords, who were labeled "a bread-taxing oligarchy" and "blood-sucking vampires," and attracted thousands of workers to its meetings. League members established local branches, published newspapers and the journal *The Economist* (founded in 1843 and now one of the world's most influential periodicals), and campaigned in elections. They

liberalism: An economic and political ideology that—tracing its roots to John Locke in the seventeenth century and Enlightenment philosophers in the eighteenth—emphasized free trade and the constitutional guarantees of individual rights such as freedom of speech and religion; its adherents stood between conservatives on the right and revolutionaries on the left in the nineteenth century.

Corn Laws: Tariffs on grain in Great Britain that benefited landowners by preventing the import of cheap foreign grain; they were repealed by the British government in 1846.

finally won the support of the Tory prime minister Sir Robert Peel, whose government repealed the Corn Laws in 1846.

Liberalism on the Continent Free trade had less appeal in continental Europe than in England because continental industries needed protection against British industrial dominance. As a consequence, liberals on the continent focused on constitutional reform. French liberals, for example, agitated for greater press freedoms and a broadening of the vote. Louis-Philippe's government brutally repressed working-class and republican insurrections in Lyon and Paris in the early 1830s and forced the republican opposition underground. The French king's increasingly restrictive governments also thwarted liberals' hopes for reforms by suppressing many political organizations and reestablishing censorship.

Repression muted criticism in most other European states as well. Nevertheless, liberal reform movements grew up in pockets of industrialization in Prussia, the smaller German states, and the Austrian Empire. Some state bureaucrats, especially university-trained middle-class officials, favored economic liberalism. Hungarian count Stephen Széchenyi (1791–1860) personally campaigned for the introduction of British-style changes. He introduced British agricultural techniques on his own lands, helped start up steamboat traffic on the Danube, encouraged the importation of machinery and technicians for steam-driven textile factories, and pushed the construction of Hungary's first railway line, from Budapest to Vienna.

In the 1840s, however, Széchenyi's efforts paled before those of the flamboyant Magyar nationalist Lajos Kossuth (1802–1894). After spending four years in prison for sedition, Kossuth grabbed every opportunity to publicize American democracy and British political liberalism, all in a fervent nationalist spirit. In 1844, he founded the Protective Association, whose members bought only Hungarian products; to Kossuth, boycotting Austrian goods was crucial to ending "colonial dependence" on Austria. Born of a lesser landowning family without a noble title, Kossuth did not hesitate to attack "the cowardly selfishness of the landowner class."

Even in Russia, signs of liberal opposition appeared in the 1830s and 1840s. Small circles of young noblemen serving in the army or bureaucracy met in cities, especially Moscow, to discuss the latest Western ideas and to criticize the Russian state: "The world is undergoing a transformation, while we vegetate in our hovels of wood and clay," wrote one. Out of these groups came such future revolutionaries as Alexander Herzen (1812–1870), described by the police as "a daring free-thinker, extremely dangerous to society." Tsar Nicholas I (r. 1825–1855) banned Western liberal writings as well as all books about the United States. He sent nearly ten thousand people a year into exile in Siberia as punishment for their political activities.

Socialism and the Early Labor Movement

The newest ideology, socialism, took up where liberalism left off: socialists believed that the liberties advocated by liberals benefited only the middle class—the owners of factories and businesses—not the workers. They sought to reorganize society totally rather than to reform it piecemeal through political measures. They envisioned a future society in which workers would share a harmonious, cooperative, and prosperous life. Building on the theoretical and practical ideas laid out in the early nineteenth century by thinkers and reformers such as Count Henri de Saint-Simon, Charles Fourier, and Robert Owen, the socialists of the 1830s and 1840s hoped that economic planning and working-class organization would solve the problems caused by industrial growth, including the threat of increasingly mechanical, unfeeling social relations.

Origins of Socialism Early socialists criticized the emerging Industrial Revolution for dividing society into two classes: the new middle class, or capitalists (who owned the wealth), and the working class, their downtrodden and impoverished employees. As their name suggests, the socialists aimed to restore harmony and cooperation through social reorganization. Robert Owen (1771–1858), a successful Welsh-born manufacturer, founded British socialism. In 1800, he bought a cotton mill in New Lanark, Scotland, and began to set up a model factory town, where workers labored only ten hours a day (instead of seventeen, as was common) and children between the ages of five and ten attended school rather than working. To put his principles once more into action, Owen moved to the United States in the 1820s and founded a community named New Harmony in Indiana. The experiment collapsed after three years, a victim of internal squabbling. But out of Owen's experiments

socialism: A social and political ideology, originating in the early nineteenth century, that advocated the reorganization of society to overcome the new tensions created by industrialization and restore social harmony through communities based on cooperation.

and writings, such as *The Book of the New Moral World* (1820), would come the movement for producer cooperatives (businesses owned and controlled by their workers), consumers' cooperatives (stores in which consumers owned shares), and a national trade union.

Claude Henri de Saint-Simon (1760–1825) and Charles Fourier (1772–1837) were Owen's counterparts in France. Saint-Simon was a noble who had served as an officer in the War of American Independence and lost a fortune speculating in national property during the French Revolution. Fourier traveled as a salesman for a Lyon cloth merchant. Both shared Owen's alarm about the effects of industrialization on social relations. Saint-Simon—who coined the terms *industrialism* and *industrialist* to define the new economic order and its chief animators—believed that work was the central element in the new society and that it should be controlled not by politicians but by scientists, engineers, artists, and industrialists themselves. To correct the abuses of the new industrial order, Fourier urged the establishment of communities that were part garden city and part agricultural commune; all jobs would be rotated to maximize happiness. Fourier hoped that a network of small, decentralized communities would replace the state.

Socialism and Women

The emancipation of women was essential to Fourier's vision of a harmonious community: "The extension of the privileges of women is the fundamental cause of all social progress." After Saint-Simon's death in 1825, some of his followers established a quasi-religious cult with elaborate rituals and a "he-pope" and "she-pope," or ruling father and mother. Saint-Simonians lived and worked together in cooperative arrangements and scandalized some by advocating free love. They set up branches in the United States and Egypt. In 1832, some Saint-Simonian women founded a feminist newspaper, *The Free Woman*, asserting that "with the emancipation of woman will come the emancipation of the worker."

In Great Britain, many women joined the Owenites and helped form cooperative societies and unions. They defended women's working-class organizations against the complaints of men in the new societies and trade unions. One woman wrote, "Do not say the unions are only for men. . . . 'Tis a wrong impression, forced on our minds to keep us slaves!" As women became more active, Owenites agitated for women's rights, marriage reform, and popular education. The French activist Flora Tristan (1801–1844) devoted herself to reconciling the interests of male and female workers. She had seen the "frightful reality" of London's poverty and made a reputation reporting on British working conditions. Tristan published a stream of books and pamphlets urging male workers to address women's unequal status, arguing that "the emancipation of male workers is *impossible* so long as women remain in a degraded state."

Collectivists and Communists

Even though most male socialists ignored Tristan's plea for women's participation, they did strive to create working-class associations. The French socialist Louis Blanc (1811–1882) explained the importance of working-class associations in his book *Organization of Labor* (1840), which deeply influenced the French labor movement. Similarly, the printer turned journalist Pierre-Joseph Proudhon (1809–1865) urged workers to form producers' associations so that the workers could control the work process and eliminate profits made by capitalists. His 1840 book *What Is Property?* argues that property is theft: labor alone is productive, and rent, interest, and profit unjust.

After 1840, some socialists began to call themselves **communists**, emphasizing their desire to replace private property by communal, collective ownership. The Frenchman Étienne Cabet (1788–1856) was the first to use the word *communist*. In 1840, he published *Travels in Icaria*, a novel describing a communist utopia in which a popularly elected dictatorship efficiently organized work, reduced the workday to seven hours, and made work tasks "short, easy, and attractive."

Out of the churning of socialist ideas of the 1840s emerged two men whose collaboration would change the definition of socialism and remake it into an ideology that would shake the world for the next 150 years. Karl Marx (1818–1883) had studied philosophy at the University of Berlin, edited a liberal newspaper until the Prussian government suppressed it, and then left for Paris, where he met Friedrich Engels (1820–1895). While working in the offices of his wealthy family's cotton manufacturing interests in Manchester, England, Engels had been shocked into writing *The Condition of the Working Class in England in 1844* (1845), a sympathetic depiction of industrial workers' dismal lives. In Paris, where German and eastern European intellectuals could pursue their political interests more freely than at home, Marx and Engels organized the Communist League, in whose name they published *The Communist Manifesto* in 1848 (see

communists: Those socialists who after 1840 (when the word was first used) advocated the abolition of private property in favor of communal, collective ownership.

DOCUMENT

Marx and Engels, *The Communist Manifesto* (1848)

Karl Marx (1818–1883) and Friedrich Engels (1820–1895) were both sons of prosperous German-Jewish families that had converted to Christianity. In the manifesto for the Communist League, they laid out many of the central principles that would guide Marxist revolution in the future: they insisted that all history is shaped by class struggle and that in future revolutions the working class would overthrow the bourgeoisie, or middle class, and replace capitalism and private property with a communist state in which all property is collectively rather than individually owned. As this selection shows, Marx and Engels always placed more emphasis on class struggle than on the state that would result from the ensuing revolution.

The history of all hitherto existing society is the history of class struggles.

Freeman and slave, patrician and plebeian, lord and serf, guild-master and journeyman, in a word, oppressor and oppressed, stood in constant opposition to one another, carried on an uninterrupted, now hidden, now open fight, a fight that each time ended, either in a revolutionary reconstitution of society at large, or in the common ruin of the contending classes. . . .

The modern bourgeois society that has sprouted from the ruins of feudal society has not done away with class antagonisms. It has but established new classes, new conditions of oppression, new forms of struggle in place of the old ones.

Our epoch, the epoch of the bourgeoisie, possesses, however, this distinctive feature: It has simplified the class antagonisms: Society as a whole is more and more splitting up into two great hostile camps, into two great classes directly facing each other: Bourgeoisie [middle class] and Proletariat [working class]. . . .

The weapons with which the bourgeoisie felled feudalism to the ground are now turned against the bourgeoisie itself.

But not only has the bourgeoisie forged the weapons that bring death to itself; it has also called into existence the men who are to wield those weapons—the modern working class—the proletarians. . . .

The essential condition for the existence, and for the sway of the bourgeois class, is the formation and augmentation of capital; the condition for capital is wage-labour. Wage-labour rests exclusively on competition between labourers. The advance of industry, whose involuntary promoter is the bourgeoisie, replaces the isolation of the labourers, due to competition, by their revolutionary combination, due to association. The development of Modern Industry, therefore, cuts from under its feet the very foundation on which the bourgeoisie produces and appropriates products. What the bourgeoisie, therefore, produces, above all, is its own gravediggers. Its fall and the victory of the proletariat are equally inevitable.

Source: Karl Marx and Friedrich Engels, *The Communist Manifesto*. Translated by Samuel Moore (*Manifesto of the Communist Party*; London: William Reeves, 1888).

Question to Consider

- **According to Marx and Engels, what are the consequences of "Modern Industry"?**

Document, "Marx and Engels, *The Communist Manifesto*," above).

It eventually became the touchstone of Marxist and communist revolutions all over the world. Communists, the *Manifesto* declared, must aim for "the downfall of the bourgeoisie [capitalist class] and the ascendancy of the proletariat [working class], the abolition of the old society based on class conflicts and the foundation of a new society without classes and without private property." Marx and Engels embraced industrialization because they believed it would eventually bring on the proletarian revolution and thus lead inevitably to the abolition of exploitation, private property, and class society.

Working-Class Organization

Socialism accompanied, and in some places incited, an upsurge in working-class organization in western Europe. British workers founded cooperative societies, local trade unions, and so-called friendly societies for mutual aid—all of which frightened the middle classes. A newspaper exclaimed in 1834, "The trade unions are, we have no doubt, the most dangerous institutions that were ever permitted to take root."

Many British workers joined in **Chartism**, which aimed to transform Britain into a democracy. In 1838, political radicals drew up the People's Charter, which demanded universal manhood suffrage, vote by secret ballot, equal electoral districts, annual elec-

Chartism: The British movement of supporters of the People's Charter (1838), which demanded universal manhood suffrage, vote by secret ballot, equal electoral districts, and other reforms.

tions, and the elimination of property qualifications for and the payment of stipends to members of Parliament. Chartists denounced their opponents as seeking "to keep the people in social slavery and political degradation." Many women took part by founding female political unions, setting up Chartist Sunday schools, organizing boycotts of unsympathetic shopkeepers, and joining Chartist temperance associations. Nevertheless, the People's Charter refrained from calling for woman suffrage because the movement's leaders feared that doing so would alienate potential supporters.

The Chartists organized a massive campaign during 1838 and 1839, with large public meetings, fiery speeches, and torchlight parades. Presented with petitions for the People's Charter signed by more than a million people, the House of Commons refused to act. In response to this rebuff from middle-class liberals, the Chartists allied themselves in the 1840s with working-class strike movements in the manufacturing districts and associated with various European revolutionary movements. But at the same time they—like their British and continental allies—distanced themselves from women workers.

Continental workers were less well organized because trade unions and strikes were illegal everywhere except Great Britain. Nevertheless, artisans and skilled workers in France formed mutual aid societies that provided insurance, death benefits, and education. In eastern and central Europe, socialism and labor organization—like liberalism—had less impact than in western Europe. Cooperative societies and workers' newspapers did not appear in the German states until 1848. In general, labor organization tended to flourish where urbanization and industrialization were most advanced; even though factory workers rarely organized, skilled artisans did so in order to resist mechanization and wage cuts. When revolutions broke out in 1848, artisans and workers played a prominent—and controversial—role.

REVIEW QUESTION **Why did ideologies have such a powerful appeal in the 1830s and 1840s?**

The Revolutions of 1848

Food shortages, overpopulation, and unemployment helped turn ideological turmoil into revolution. In 1848, demonstrations and uprisings toppled governments, forced rulers and ministers to flee, and offered revolutionaries an opportunity to put liberal, socialist, and nationalist ideals into practice (Map 21.4). In the end, the revolutions failed because the various ideological movements quarreled, leaving an opening for rulers and their armies to return to power. Rulers returned, but they now faced populations with greater expectations for political participation, national unification, and government responsiveness to social problems.

The Hungry Forties

Beginning in 1845, crop failures across Europe caused food prices to shoot skyward. In the best of times, urban workers paid 50 to 80 percent of their income for a diet consisting largely of bread; now even bread was beyond their means. Overpopulation hastened famine in some places, especially Ireland, where blight destroyed the staple crop, potatoes, first in 1846 and again in 1848 and 1851. Irish peasants had planted potatoes because a family of four might live off one acre of potatoes but would require at least two acres of grain. The Irish often sought security in large families, trusting that their children would help work the land and care for them in old age. By the 1840s, Ireland was especially vulnerable to the potato blight. Out of a population of

The Irish Famine
Contemporary depictions drew attention to the plight of the Irish peasants when a blight infected potato plants, destroying the single most important staple crop. The young girl on the left and the old woman on the right appear too weak with hunger even to move. *(The Granger Collection, New York—All rights reserved.)*

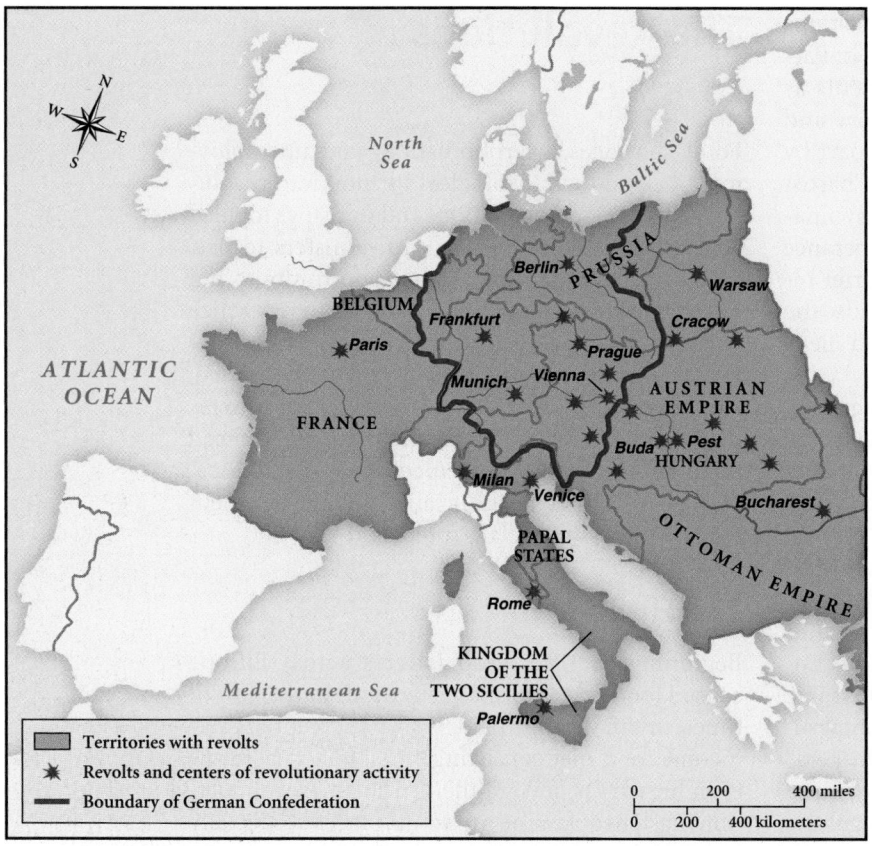

MAP 21.4 The Revolutions of 1848

The attempts of rulers to hold back the forces of change collapsed suddenly in 1848 when once again the French staged a revolution that inspired many others in Europe. This time, cities all over central and eastern Europe joined in as the spirit of revolt inflamed one capital after another. Although all of these revolutions eventually failed because of social and political divisions, the sheer scale of rebellion forced rulers to reconsider their policies.

eight million, as many as one million people died of starvation or disease. Corpses lay unburied on the sides of roads, and whole families were found dead in their cottages, half-eaten by dogs. Hundreds of thousands emigrated to England, the United States, and Canada.

Throughout Europe, famine jeopardized social peace. In age-old fashion, rumors circulated about farmers hoarding grain to drive up prices. Believing that governments should ensure fair prices, crowds took to the streets to protest, often attacking markets or bakeries. They threatened officials with retribution. "If the grain merchants do not cease to take away grains . . . we will go to your homes and cut your throats and those of the three bakers . . . and burn the whole place down." So went one threat from French villagers in the hungry winter of 1847. Although harvests improved in 1848, by then many people had lost their land or become hopelessly indebted.

High food prices also drove down the demand for manufactured goods, resulting in increased unemployment. Industrial workers' wages had been rising—in the German states, for example, wages rose by an average of 5.5 percent in the 1830s and 10.5 percent in the 1840s—but the cost of living rose by about 16 percent each decade, canceling out wage increases. Seasonal work and regular unemployment were already the norm when the crisis of the late 1840s exacerbated the uncertainties of urban life. "The most miserable class that ever sneaked its way into history" is how Friedrich Engels described underemployed and starving workers in 1847.

Another French Revolution

The specter of hunger amplified the voices criticizing established rulers. A Parisian demonstration in favor of reform turned violent on February 23, 1848, when panicky soldiers opened fire on the crowd, killing forty or fifty demonstrators. The next day, faced with fifteen hundred barricades and a furious populace, King Louis-Philippe abdicated and fled to England. A hastily formed provisional government declared France a republic once again.

The new republican government issued liberal reforms—an end to the death penalty for political crimes, the abolition of slavery in the colonies, and freedom of the press—and agreed to introduce universal adult male suffrage despite misgivings about political participation by peasants and unemployed workers. The government allowed Paris officials to organize a system of "national workshops" to provide the unemployed with construction work. When women protested their exclusion, the city set up a few workshops for women workers, albeit with wages lower than men's. To meet a mounting deficit, the provisional government then levied a 45 percent surtax on property taxes, alienating peasants and landowners.

While peasants grumbled, scores of newspapers and political clubs inspired grassroots democratic fervor in Paris and other cities. Meeting in concert halls, theaters, and government auditoriums, the clubs became a regular evening attraction for the citizenry. Women also formed clubs, published women's newspapers, and demanded representation in national politics.

This street-corner activism alarmed middle-class liberals and conservatives. To ensure its control, the republican government paid some unemployed youths to join a mobile guard with its own uniforms and barracks. Tension between the government and the workers in the national workshops rose. Faced with rising radicalism in Paris and other big cities, the voters elected a largely conservative National Assembly in April 1848; most of the deputies chosen were middle-class professionals or landowners who favored either a restoration of the monarchy or a moderate republic. The Assembly immediately appointed a five-man executive committee to run the government and pointedly excluded known supporters of workers' rights. Suspicious of all demands for rapid change, the deputies dismissed a petition to restore divorce and voted down woman suffrage by 899 to 1. When the numbers enrolled in the national workshops in Paris rocketed from a predicted 10,000 to 110,000, the government ordered the workshops closed to new workers, and on June 21 it directed that those already enrolled move to the provinces or join the army.

The workers exploded in anger. In the June Days, as the following week came to be called, the government summoned the army, the National Guard, and the newly recruited mobile guard to fight the workers. Alexis de Tocqueville breathed a sigh of relief: "The Red Republic [red being associated with demands for socialism] is lost forever; all France has joined against it. The National Guard, citizens, and peasants from the remotest parts of the country have come pouring in." (See Document, "Alexis de Tocqueville Describes the June Days in Paris," page 713.) The government forces crushed the workers: more than 10,000 people, most of them workers, were killed or injured; 12,000 were arrested; and 4,000 eventually were convicted and deported.

After the National Assembly adopted a new constitution calling for a presidential election in which all adult men could vote, the electorate chose **Louis-Napoleon Bonaparte** (1808–1873), nephew of the dead emperor. Bonaparte got more than 5.5 million votes out of some 7.4 million cast. He had lived most of his life outside of France, and the leaders of the republic expected him to follow their tune. In uncertain times, the Bonaparte name promised something to everyone. Even many workers supported him because he had no connection with the blood-drenched June Days.

In reality, Bonaparte's election spelled the end of the Second Republic, just as his uncle had dismantled the first one established in 1792. In 1852, on the forty-eighth anniversary of Napoleon I's coronation as emperor, Louis-Napoleon declared himself Emperor Napoleon III, thus inaugurating the Second Empire. (Napoleon I's son died and never became Napoleon II, but Napoleon III wanted to create a sense of legitimacy and so used the Roman numeral III.) Political division and class conflict had proved fatal to the Second Republic. Although the revolution of 1848 never had a period of terror like that in 1793–1794, it nonetheless ended in similar fashion, with an authoritarian government that tried to play monarchists and republicans off against each other.

French Women Activists in 1848
The French artist Honoré Daumier spared no one in his satires. In the early 1830s, one of his lithographs ridiculing the French king landed him in prison for six months. During the revolution of 1848, Daumier published several series mocking women activists. This one is from the series *The Divorcers*, and its caption proclaimed, "Lady Citizens . . . they say that divorce is about to be refused to us . . . let us continue meeting and declare that the country is in danger!" Divorce had been abolished in 1816 and was not reinstated in France until 1884. *(Bibliothèque nationale, Paris, France/Giraudon/The Bridgeman Art Library International.)*

Nationalist Revolution in Italy

In January 1848, a revolt broke out in Palermo, Sicily, against the Bourbon ruler. Then came the electrifying news of the February revolution in Paris. In

Louis-Napoleon Bonaparte (1808–1873): Nephew of Napoleon I; he was elected president of France in 1848, declared himself Emperor Napoleon III in 1852, and ruled until 1870.

The Violence of Revolution

Their red flag of revolt is all that is left to these victims at a barricade thrown up in Paris during the uprising of June 1848. What was the intention of artist Louis Adolphe Hervier when he chose to paint this scene? *(Oil on panel by Louis Adolphe Hervier, Private Collection/Archives Charmet/The Bridgeman Art Library International.)*

Milan, a huge nationalist demonstration quickly degenerated into battles between Austrian forces and armed demonstrators. In Venice, an uprising drove out the Austrians. Peasants in the south occupied large landowners' estates. Across central Italy, revolts mobilized the poor and unemployed against local rulers. Peasants demanded more land, and artisans and workers called for higher wages, restrictions on the use of machinery, and unemployment relief.

But class divisions and regional differences stood in the way of national unity. Property owners, businessmen, and professionals wanted liberal reforms and national unification under a conservative regime; intellectuals, workers, and artisans dreamed of democracy and social reforms. Some nationalists favored a loose federation; others wanted a monarchy under Charles Albert of Piedmont-Sardinia; still others urged rule by the pope; a few shared Mazzini's vision of a republic with a strong central government. Many leaders of national unification spoke standard Italian only as a second language; most Italians spoke regional dialects.

As king of the most powerful Italian state, Charles Albert (r. 1831–1849) inevitably played a central role. After some hesitation caused by fears of French intervention, he led a military campaign against Austria. It soon failed, partly because of dissension over goals and tactics among the nationalists. Although Austrian troops defeated Charles Albert in the north in the summer of 1848, democratic and nationalist forces prevailed at first in the south. In the fall, the Romans drove the pope from the city and declared Rome a republic. For the next few months, republican leaders, such as Giuseppe Mazzini and Giuseppe Garibaldi (1807–1882), congregated in Rome to organize the new republic. These efforts eventually faltered when foreign powers intervened. The new president of republican France, Louis-Napoleon Bonaparte, sent an expeditionary force to secure the papal throne for Pius IX. Mazzini and Garibaldi fled. Although revolution had been defeated in Italy, the memory of the Roman republic and the commitment to unification remained, and they would soon emerge again with new force.

Revolt and Reaction in Central Europe

News of the revolution in Paris also provoked popular demonstrations in central and eastern Europe. When the Prussian army tried to push back a crowd gathered in front of Berlin's royal palace on March 18, 1848, their actions provoked panic and street fighting. The next day the crowd paraded wagons loaded with dead bodies under the window of the Prussian king Frederick William IV (r. 1840–1860), forcing him to salute the victims killed by his own army. In a state of near collapse, the king promised to call an assembly to draft a constitution and adopted the German nationalist flag of black, red, and gold.

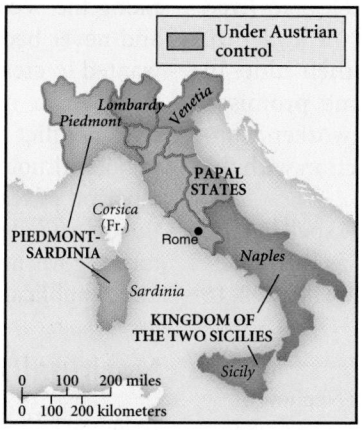

The Divisions of Italy, 1848

The goal of German unification soon took precedence over social reform or constitutional changes within the separate states. In March and April, most

DOCUMENT

Alexis de Tocqueville Describes the June Days in Paris (1848)

Alexis de Tocqueville (1805–1859) was a noble landowner, well-known writer, and deputy in the National Assembly elected in April 1848. As a political liberal, he supported the new republican government against the uprising of workers in the National Workshops. His description of the June Days comes from a memoir he wrote in 1850 about the events of the 1848 revolution. Although a fierce opponent of socialism, Tocqueville detected class struggle in the insurrection.

Now at last I have come to that insurrection in June which was the greatest and the strangest that had ever taken place in our history, or perhaps in that of any other nation: the greatest because for four days more than a hundred thousand men took part in it, and there were five generals killed; the strangest, because the insurgents were fighting without a battle cry, leaders, or flag, and yet they showed wonderful powers of co-ordination and a military expertise that astonished the most experienced officers.

Another point that distinguished it from all other events of the same type during the last sixty years was that its object was not to change the form of the government, but to alter the organization of society. In truth it was not a political struggle (in the sense in which we have used the word "political" up to now), but a class struggle, a sort of "Servile War." It stood in the same relation to the facts of the February Revolution as the theory of socialism stood to its ideas; or rather it sprang naturally from those ideas, as a son from his mother; and one should not see it only as a brutal and blind, but as a powerful effort of the workers to escape from the necessities of their condition, which had been depicted to them as an illegitimate depression, and by the sword to open up a road towards that imaginary well-being that had been shown to them in the distance as a right. It was this mixture of greedy desires and false theories that engendered the insurrection and made it so formidable. These poor people had been assured that the goods of the wealthy were in some way the result of a theft committed against themselves. They had been assured that inequalities of fortune were as much opposed to morality and the interests of society, as to nature. This obscure and mistaken conception of right, combined with brute force, imparted to it an energy, tenacity and strength it would never have had on its own.

One should note, too, that this terrible insurrection was not the work of a certain number of conspirators, but was the revolt of one whole section of the population against another. The women took as much part in it as the men. While the men fought, the women got the ammunition ready and brought it up. And when in the end they had to surrender, the women were the last to yield. . . .

Down all the roads not held by the insurgents, thousands of men were pouring in from all parts of France to aid us. Thanks to the railways, those from fifty leagues [150 miles] off were already arriving, although the fighting had begun only in the evening of the previous day. The next day and the days following, they were to arrive from one and two hundred leagues [300–600 miles] away. These men were drawn without distinction from all classes of society; among them there were great numbers of peasants, bourgeois, large landowners and nobles, all jumbled up together in the same ranks.

Source: Alexis de Tocqueville, *Recollections*, ed. J. P. Mayer and A. P. Kerr, trans. George Lawrence (Garden City, NY: Doubleday, 1970), 136–37, 152.

Question to Consider

- **Why is Tocqueville so dismissive of the goals of those who participated in the June Days revolt in Paris in 1848?**

of the German states agreed to elect delegates to a federal parliament at Frankfurt that would attempt to unite Germany. Local princes and even the more powerful kings of Prussia and Bavaria seemed to totter. Yet the revolutionaries' weaknesses soon became apparent. The eight hundred delegates to the Frankfurt parliament had little practical political experience and no access to an army. Unemployed artisans and workers smashed machines; peasants burned landlords' records and occasionally attacked Jewish moneylenders; women set up clubs and newspapers to demand their emancipation from "perfumed slavery."

The advantage lay with the princes, who bided their time. While the Frankfurt parliament laboriously prepared a liberal constitution for a united Germany—one that denied self-determination to Czechs, Poles, and Danes within its proposed German borders—Frederick William recovered his confidence. First, his army crushed the revolution in Berlin in the fall of 1848. Prussian troops then intervened to help other local rulers put down the last wave of democratic and nationalist insurrections in the spring of 1849. When the Frankfurt parliament finally concluded its work, offering the emperorship of a constitutional, federal Germany to the king of Prussia, Frederick William contemptuously refused this "crown from the gutter."

Events followed a similar course in the Austrian Empire. Just as Italians were driving the

Revolution of 1848 in Eastern Europe
This painting by an unknown artist shows a group of Romanian revolutionaries in Transylvania marching in opposition to Russian rule. Leading them is a woman identified as Ana Ipatescu. In April 1848, local landowners began to organize meetings. Paris-educated nationalists spearheaded the movement, which demanded the end of Russian control and various legal and political reforms. By August, the movement had split between those who wanted independence only and those who pushed for the end of serfdom and for universal manhood suffrage. In response, the Russians invaded Moldavia and the Turks moved into Walachia. By October, the uprising was over. Russia and Turkey agreed to control the provinces jointly. *(The Art Archive/National Museum, Bucharest/Collection Dagli Orti.)*

Austrians out of their lands in northern Italy and Magyar nationalists were demanding political autonomy for Hungary, a student-led demonstration for political reform on March 13, 1848, in Vienna turned into rioting, looting, and machine breaking. Metternich resigned, escaping to England in disguise. Emperor Ferdinand promised a constitution, an elected parliament, and the end of censorship. The beleaguered authorities in Vienna could not refuse Magyar demands for home rule, and Széchenyi and Kossuth both became ministers in the new Hungarian government. The Magyars were the largest ethnic group in Hungary but still did not make up 50 percent of the population, which included Croats, Romanians, Slovaks, and Slovenes, all of whom preferred Austrian rule to domination by local Magyars.

The ethnic divisions in Hungary foreshadowed the many political and social divisions that would doom the revolutionaries. Fears of peasant insurrection prompted the Magyar nationalists around Kossuth to abolish serfdom. This measure alienated the largest noble landowners. The new government alienated the other nationalities when it imposed the Magyar language on them. In Prague, Czech nationalists convened a Slav congress as a counter to the Germans' Frankfurt parliament and called for a reorganization of the Austrian Empire that would recognize the rights of ethnic minorities. Such assertiveness by non-German peoples provoked German nationalists to protest on behalf of German-speaking people in areas with a Czech or Magyar majority.

The Austrian government took advantage of these divisions. To quell peasant discontent and appease liberal reformers, it abolished all remaining peasant obligations to the nobility in March 1848. Rejoicing country folk soon lost interest in the revolution. Military force finally broke up the revolutionary movements. The first blow fell in Prague in June 1848; General Prince Alfred von Windischgrätz, the military governor, bombarded the city into submission when a demonstration led to violence (including the shooting death of his wife, watching from a window). After another uprising in Vienna a few months later, Windischgrätz marched seventy thousand soldiers into the capital and set up direct military rule. In December, the Austrian monarchy came back to life when the eighteen-year-old Francis Joseph (r. 1848–1916), unencumbered by promises extracted by the revolutionaries from his now feeble uncle Ferdinand, assumed the imperial crown after intervention by leading court officials. In the spring of 1849, General Count Joseph Radetzky defeated the last Italian challenges to Austrian power in northern Italy, and his army moved east, joining with Croats and Serbs to take on the Hungarian rebels. The Austrian army teamed up with Tsar Nicholas I, who marched into Hungary with more than 300,000 Russian troops. Hungary was put under brutal martial law. Széchenyi went mad, and Kossuth found refuge in the United States. Social conflicts and ethnic divisions weakened the revolutionary movements from the inside and gave the Austrian government the opening it needed to restore its position.

Aftermath to 1848: Reimposing Authority

Although the revolutionaries of 1848 failed to achieve their goals, their efforts left a profound mark on the political and social landscape. Between 1848 and 1851, the French served a kind of republican apprenticeship that prepared the population for another, more lasting republic after 1870. In Italy, the failure of unification did not stop the spread of nationalist ideas and the rooting of demands for democratic participation. In the German states, the revolutionaries of 1848 turned nationalism from an idea of professors and writers into a popular enthusiasm and even a practical reality. The initiation of artisans, workers, and journeymen into democratic clubs increased political awareness in the lower classes and helped prepare them for broader political participation. Almost all the German states had a constitution and a parliament after 1850. The spectacular failures of 1848 thus hid some important underlying successes.

The absence of revolution in 1848 was just as significant as its presence. No revolution occurred in Great Britain, the Netherlands, or Belgium, the three places where industrialization and urbanization had developed most rapidly. In Great Britain, the prospects for revolution actually seemed quite good: the Chartist movement took inspiration from the European revolutions in 1848 and mounted several gigantic demonstrations to force Parliament into granting all adult males the vote. But even though Parliament refused, no uprising occurred—in part because the government had already proved its responsiveness: the middle classes in Britain had been co-opted into the established order by the Reform Bill of 1832, and the working classes had won parliamentary regulation of children's and women's work.

The other notable exception to revolution among the great powers was Russia, where Tsar Nicholas I maintained a tight grip through police surveillance and censorship. The Russian schools, limited to the upper classes, taught Nicholas's three most cherished principles: autocracy (the unlimited power of the tsar), orthodoxy (obedience to the church in religion and morality), and nationality (devotion to Russian traditions). These provided no space for political dissent. Social conditions also fostered political passivity: serfdom continued in force, and the sluggish rate of industrial and urban growth created little discontent.

Although much had changed, the aristocracy remained the dominant power almost everywhere. As army officers, aristocrats put down revolutionary forces. As landlords, they continued to dominate the rural scene and control parliamentary bodies. They also held many official positions in the state bureaucracies. One Italian princess explained, "There are doubtless men capable of leading the nation . . . but their names are unknown to the people, whereas those of noble families . . . are in every memory." Aristocrats kept their authority by adapting to change: they entered the bureaucracy and professions, turned their estates into moneymaking enterprises, and learned how to invest shrewdly.

The reassertion of conservative rule hardened gender definitions. Women everywhere had participated in the revolutions, especially in the Italian states, where they joined armies in the tens of thousands and applied household skills toward making bandages, clothing, and food. As conservatives returned to power, all signs of women's political activism disappeared. The French feminist movement, the most advanced in Europe, fell apart when, after the June Days, the increasingly conservative republican government forbade women to form political clubs and arrested and imprisoned two of the most outspoken women leaders for their socialist activities. As rulers reimposed their authority in the years after 1848, many socialists, communists, and nationalists suffered a similar fate; if they did not fall in battle or go to prison, they fled into exile, waiting for another opportunity to voice their demands.

REVIEW QUESTION Why did the revolutions of 1848 fail?

Revolutions of 1848

1848	
January	Uprising in Palermo, Sicily
February	Revolution in Paris; proclamation of republic
March	Insurrections in Vienna, German cities, Milan, and Venice; autonomy movement in Hungary; Charles Albert of Piedmont-Sardinia declares war on Austrian Empire
May	Frankfurt parliament opens
June	Austrian army crushes revolutionary movement in Prague; June Days end in defeat of workers in Paris
July	Austrians defeat Charles Albert and Italian forces
November	Insurrection in Rome
December	Francis Joseph becomes Austrian emperor; Louis-Napoleon elected president in France
1849	
February	Rome declared a republic
April	Frederick William of Prussia rejects crown of united Germany offered by Frankfurt parliament
July	Roman republic overthrown by French intervention
August	Russian and Austrian armies combine to defeat Hungarian forces

The Crystal Palace, 1851
George Baxter's lithograph (above) shows the exterior of the main building for the Great Exhibition of the Works of Industry of All Nations in London. It was designed by Sir Joseph Paxton to gigantic dimensions: 1,848 feet long by 456 feet wide; 135 feet high; 772,784 square feet of ground-floor area covering no less than 18 acres. The lithograph by Peter Mabuse (below) offers a view of one of the colonial displays at the Great Exhibition. The tented room and carved ivory throne are meant to recall India, Britain's premier colony. *(Above: © Maidstone Museum and Art Gallery, Kent, UK/The Bridgeman Art Library. Below: Private Collection/The Stapleton Collection/The Bridgeman Art Library International.)*

Conclusion

In 1851, Europe's most important female monarch presided over a midcentury celebration of peace and industrial growth that helped dampen the still-smoldering fires of revolutionary passion. In the place of revolutionary fervor was a government-sponsored spectacle of what industry, hard work, and technological imagination could produce. Queen Victoria (r. 1837–1901), who herself promoted the notion of domesticity as women's sphere, opened the Great Exhibition of the Works of Industry of All Nations in London on May 1. A huge iron-and-glass building housed the display. Soon people referred to it as the Crystal Palace; its nine hundred tons of glass created an aura of fantasy, and the abundant goods from around the world inspired satisfaction and pride. One German visitor described the structure as "this miracle which has so suddenly appeared to dazzle the inhabitants of our globe." Many of the six million people who visited the Crystal Palace display came on the new railroads, the foremost symbol of the age of industrial transformation. Along with the railroads, the application of steam engines to textile manufacturing set in motion a host of economic and social changes: cities burgeoned with rapidly growing populations; factories concentrated laborers who formed a new working class; manufacturers now challenged landed elites for political leadership; and social problems galvanized reform organizations and governments alike. The Crystal Palace presented the rosy view of modern, industrial, urban life, but the housing shortages, in-

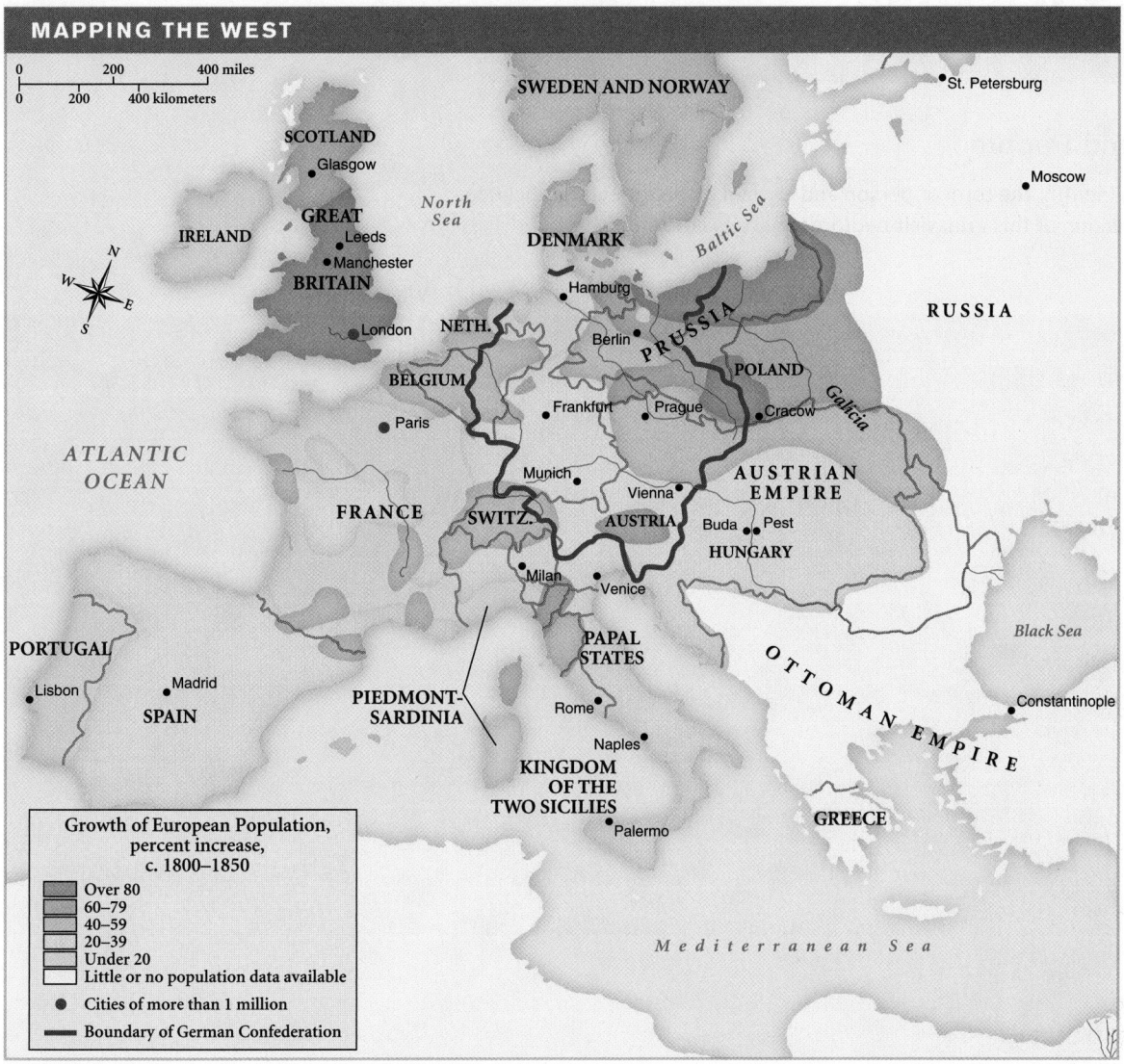

Europe in 1850

This map of population growth between 1800 and 1850 reveals important trends that would not otherwise be evident. Although population growth correlated for the most part with industrialization, population also grew in more agricultural regions such as East Prussia, Poland, and Ireland. Ireland's rapid population growth does not appear on this map because the famine of 1846–1851 killed more than 10 percent of the population and forced many others to emigrate. | **Compare this map to Map 21.1: Which areas experienced both industrialization and population increase?**

adequacy of water supplies, and recurrent epidemic diseases had not disappeared.

Although the revolutions of 1848 brought to the surface the profound tensions within a European society in transition toward industrialization and urbanization, they did not resolve those tensions. The Industrial Revolution continued, workers developed more extensive organizations, and liberals and socialists fought over the pace of reform. Confronted with the menace of revolution, conservative elites now sought alternatives that would be less threatening to the established order and still permit some change. This search for alternatives became immediately evident in the question of national unification in Germany and Italy. National unification would hereafter depend not on speeches and parliamentary resolutions, but rather on what the Prussian leader Otto von Bismarck would call "iron and blood."

FOR FURTHER EXPLORATION

- **For additional primary-source material from this period**, see *Sources of the Making of the West*, Fourth Edition.
- **For Web sites, images, and documents related to topics in this chapter**, visit *Make History* at bedfordstmartins.com/hunt.

Chapter 21 Review

Online Study Guide bedfordstmartins.com/hunt

Key Terms and People

In the grid below, identify the term or person and explain its historical significance. (For a printable version of this grid, visit bedfordstmartins.com/hunt.)

Term	Who or What & When	Why It Matters
ideology (p. 686)		
Industrial Revolution (p. 686)		
urbanization (p. 692)		
George Sand (p. 697)		
domesticity (p. 700)		
imperialism (p. 701)		
Opium War (p. 702)		
nationalism (p. 703)		
Giuseppe Mazzini (p. 703)		
liberalism (p. 705)		
Corn Laws (p. 705)		
socialism (p. 706)		
communists (p. 707)		
Chartism (p. 708)		
Louis-Napoleon Bonaparte (p. 711)		

Review Questions

1. What dangers did the Industrial Revolution pose to both urban and rural life?
2. In which areas did reformers trying to address the social problems created by industrialization and urbanization succeed, and in which did they fail?
3. Why did ideologies have such a powerful appeal in the 1830s and 1840s?
4. Why did the revolutions of 1848 fail?

Making Connections

1. Which of the ideologies of this period had the greatest impact on political events? How can you explain this?
2. In what ways might industrialization be considered a force for peaceful change rather than a revolution? (Hint: Think about the situation in Great Britain.)
3. In what ways did the revolutions of 1848 repeat elements of the French revolutions in 1789 and 1830, and in what ways did they break with those precedents?
4. Neither Great Britain nor Russia had a revolution in 1848. How is the absence of revolution in those two countries related to their history in the preceding decades?

Important Events

Date	Event	Date	Event
1830–1832	Cholera epidemic sweeps across Europe	1839	Beginning of Opium War; invention of photography
1830	France invades and begins conquest of Algeria	1841	Charles Dickens, *The Old Curiosity Shop*
1832	George Sand, *Indiana*	1846	Famine strikes Ireland; Corn Laws repealed in England; peasant insurrection in Austrian province of Galicia
1833	Factory Act regulates work of children in Great Britain; abolition of slavery in British Empire	1848	Revolutions of 1848 throughout Europe; last great wave of Chartist demonstrations in Britain; Karl Marx and Friedrich Engels, *The Communist Manifesto*; abolition of slavery in French colonies; end of serfdom in Austrian Empire
1834	German *Zollverein* established under Prussian leadership	1851	Crystal Palace exhibition in London
1835	Belgium opens first continental railway built with state funds		

- Consider three events: **Charles Dickens, *The Old Curiosity Shop* (1841)**, **Revolutions of 1848 throughout Europe (1848)**, and **Karl Marx and Friedrich Engels, *The Communist Manifesto* (1848)**. How do these events represent different responses to the changes wrought by the Industrial Revolution?

SUGGESTED REFERENCES

The spread of industrialization has elicited much more historical interest than the process of urbanization because the analysis of industrialization occupied a central role in Marxism. The Web site Gallica, produced by the National Library of France, offers a wealth of imagery and information on French cultural history.

Berend, Tibor Iván. *History Derailed: Central and Eastern Europe in the Long Nineteenth Century.* 2003.

Clark, Anna. *The Struggle for the Breeches: Gender and the Making of the British Working Class.* 1997.

Davidoff, Leonore, and Catherine Hall. *Family Fortunes: Men and Women of the English Middle Class, 1780–1850.* 2002.

Dickens Project: http://dickens.ucsc.edu/

Gallica: Images and Texts from Nineteenth-Century French-Speaking Culture: http://gallica.bnf.fr

Hanes, W. Travis, and Frank Sanello. *The Opium Wars: The Addiction of One Empire and the Corruption of Another.* 2004.

Hobsbawm, E. J. *The Age of Revolution, 1789–1848.* 1996.

Kahan, Alan S. *Liberalism in Nineteenth-Century Europe: The Political Culture of Limited Suffrage.* 2003.

Kinealy, Christine. *Repeal and Revolution: 1848 in Ireland.* 2009.

Kostantaras, Dean J. *Nationalism and Revolution in Europe, 1815–1848.* 2010.

Lees, Andrew, and Lynn Hollen Lees. *Cities and the Making of Modern Europe, 1750–1914.* 2007.

*Marx, Karl, and Frederick Engels. *The Communist Manifesto: With Related Documents.* Ed. John E. Toews. 1848; repr. 1999.

Mokyr, Joel. *The Enlightened Economy: An Economic History of Britain, 1700–1850.* 2009.

*Pollard, S., and C. Holmes. *Documents of European Economic History. Vol. 1, The Process of Industrialization, 1750–1870.* 1968.

Rapport, Mike. *1848, Year of Revolution.* 2009.

Thompson, E. P. *The Making of the English Working Class.* 1964.

*Primary source.

TEATRO LA FENICE
VENEZIA
IN OCCASIONE DEL CONGRESSO GEOGRAFICO INTERNAZIONALE
IMPRESA CESARE TREVISAN
DALL'11 AL 22 SETTEMBRE SI DARANNO 7 RAPPRESENTAZIONI DELLA GRANDIOSA OPERA-BALLO
AIDA
MUSICA DEL COMM.re GIUSEPPE VERDI
ESEGUITA DAI SEGUENTI ARTISTI
PRIME DONNE
EMMA TUROLLA — GIUSEPPINA PASQUA
PRIMO TENORE
GIOVANNI SANI
PRIMO BARITONO
COMM.re GOTTARDO ALDIGHIERI
PRIMI BASSI
ENRICO SERBOLINI * FRANCESCO PANARI
MAESTRO DIRETTORE D'ORCHESTRA
CAV.re FRANCO FACCIO
ALTRO MAESTRO
RAFAELE BRACALE
TENORE COMPRIMARIO GIUSEPPE CINQUANTA
M.o ISTRUTTORE DEI CORI LORENZO POLI
SUGGERITORE ANTONIO RENIER
COREOGRAFO
RINALDO ROSSI
N. 70 PROFESSORI D'ORCHESTRA, N. 80 CORISTI E CORISTE, N. 24 BALLERINE, N. 6 TROMBE EGIZIANE, BANDA
Direttore RINALDO ROSSI
Direttore delle masse GAETANO ARCHINTI
Pittore Scenografo CESARE RECANATINI
Direttore dei Macchinismi LUIGI CAPRARA
Vestiarista - proprietario L. ZAMPERONI della Scala di Milano
Attrezzista proprietario CROCE e FIGLIO della Scala di Milano
Fornitore della luce ANTONIO TREVISAN
Parrucchiere G. GASPEROTTO
Fornitrice delle Calzature R. MAVEROFFER della Scala di Milano
CIRCA N. 100 COMPARSE, 8 CORIFEE, CORIFEI, 12 PAGGI, 6 BALLERINI, STATISTI, STATISTE, ECC. ECC.
Biglietto d'ingresso alla platea e palchi (in sere ordinarie) L. 5.—
detto al loggione (id) 2.—
Poltrona a bracciuoli, oltre l'ingresso 10.—
Posti riservati in platea (scanni in velluto) 5.—
Posti riservati in Galleria (Loggione) 1.50
Abbonamento per le sette rappresent.re (compresa quella di gala) 25.—
detto limitato a N. 40 Poltrone 50.—
detto ai posti riservati (scanni) 25.—
Le suddette 7 rappresentazioni sono finora stabilite nelle sere dell'11-13-15-17-18-20-22 Settembre
Proprietà dello spartito Tito di Gio. Ricordi
Venezia 1 Agosto 1881
Stab. Tip. Lit. Vedr. E. Passero Udine

CHAPTER

Politics and Culture of the Nation-State

22

1850–1870

In 1859, the name *VERDI* suddenly appeared scrawled on walls across the disunited cities of the Italian peninsula. The graffiti seemed to celebrate the composer Giuseppe Verdi, whose operas thrilled crowds of Europeans. Among Italians, Verdi was a particular hero; his stories of downtrodden groups struggling against tyrannical government seemed to refer specifically to them. As his operatic choruses thundered out calls to rebellion in the name of the nation, Italian audiences were sure that Verdi was telling them to throw off Austrian and papal rule and unite in a newborn Roman Empire. The graffiti had a second political message: *VERDI* also formed an acronym for *V*ittorio *E*mmanuele *R*e *d'I*talia ("Victor Emmanuel, King of Italy"), and in 1859 it summoned Italians to unite under Victor Emmanuel II, king of Sardinia and Piedmont—the one Italian leader with a nationalist, modernizing profile. The graffiti was good publicity, for the very next year Italy united as a result of warfare and hard bargaining by political realists.

After the failed revolutions of 1848, European statesmen and the politically conscious public increasingly rejected idealism in favor of **Realpolitik**—a politics of tough-minded realism aimed at strengthening the state and tightening social order. Realpolitikers disliked the romanticism and high-minded ideas of the revolutionaries. Instead, they put their faith in power politics and even the use of violence to attain their goals. Two particularly skilled practitioners of Realpolitik, the Italian Camillo di Cavour and the Prussian Otto von Bismarck, succeeded in unifying Italy and Germany not by romantic slogans but by war and diplomacy. Most leading figures of the decades 1850–1870, enmeshed like

***Aïda* Poster**
Aïda (1871), Giuseppe Verdi's opera of human passion and state power among people of different nations, became a staple of Western culture, bringing people across Europe into a common cultural orbit. Written to celebrate the opening of the Suez Canal, *Aïda* also celebrated the improvement of Europe's access to Asian resources provided by the new waterway. The opera was a prime example of the surge of interest in Egyptian styles and objects that followed the opening of the canal. *(Madeline Grimoldi.)*

Realpolitik (ray AHL poh lih teek): Policies developed after the revolutions of 1848 and initially associated with nation building; they were based on realism rather than on the romantic notions of earlier nationalists. The term has come to mean any policy based on considerations of power alone.

The End of the Concert of Europe 722
- Napoleon III and the Quest for French Glory
- The Crimean War, 1853–1856: Turning Point in European Affairs
- Reform in Russia

War and Nation Building 729
- Cavour, Garibaldi, and the Process of Italian Unification
- Bismarck and the Realpolitik of German Unification
- Francis Joseph and the Creation of the Austro-Hungarian Monarchy
- Political Stability through Gradual Reform in Great Britain
- Nation Building in North America

Nation Building through Social Order 739
- Bringing Order to the Cities
- Expanding Government Bureaucracy
- Schooling and Professionalizing Society
- Spreading National Power and Order beyond the West
- Challenging the Nation-State's Order at Home

The Culture of Social Order 748
- The Arts Confront Social Reality
- Religion and National Order
- From the Natural Sciences to Social Science

Verdi's operatic heroes in power politics, strengthened their states by harnessing the forces of nationalism and liberalism that had led to earlier romantic revolts. Their achievements changed the face of Europe.

Making modern nation-states was complicated and called for more than winning wars. Economic development was crucial, as was using government policy and culture to create a sense of national identity and common purpose. As productivity and wealth increased, governments took vigorous steps to improve rapidly growing cities, promote public health, and boost national loyalty. State support for cultural institutions such as public schools helped establish a common fund of knowledge and even shared political beliefs. Authoritarian leaders like Bismarck and the new French emperor Napoleon III believed that a better quality of life would not only make the state more stable by calming revolutionary impulses of years past but also silence liberal critics.

Culture built a sense of belonging. Reading novels, attending operas and art exhibitions, and visiting the newly fashionable world's fairs gave ordinary people a stronger sense of being French or German or British and even of being European. Like politicians, artists and writers also came to reject romanticism, featuring instead harsher, more realistic aspects of everyday life. Artists painted nudes in shockingly blunt ways, eliminating romantic hues and dreamy poses. The Russian author Leo Tolstoy depicted the bleak life of soldiers in the Crimean War, which erupted in 1853 between the Russian and Ottoman Empires, while other authors wrote about ordinary people suffering poverty or turning to crime. Alongside the tough-minded nation-building policies there arose tough-minded art, not just mirroring Realpolitik but encouraging it.

In their quest to build strong nations, Western politicians did not shy away from using violence or causing harm. They sent armies to distant areas to stamp out resistance to their continuing global expansion. At home, governments uprooted neighborhoods to construct public buildings, roads, and parks. The process of nation building was often brutal, bringing foreign wars, arrests, and even civil war—all the centerpieces of many Verdi operas. In 1871, an uprising of Parisians challenged the central government's intrusion into everyday life and its failure to count the costs. Thus, for the most part, the powerful Western nation-state did not arise spontaneously. Instead, its growth and the tighter unification of peoples depended on shrewd policy, deliberate warfare, and new inroads into societies around the world. Realpolitik relied on all these factors, as well as on a general climate of modern opinion that valued realism, hard facts, and shrewd deeds.

CHAPTER FOCUS **How did the creation and strengthening of nation-states change European politics, society, and culture in the mid-nineteenth century?**

The End of the Concert of Europe

The revolutions of 1848 had weakened the concert of Europe, driving out its architect, Austrian foreign minister Klemens von Metternich, and allowing the forces of nationalism to flourish. It became more difficult for countries to control their competing ambitions and act together. In addition, the dreaded revival of Bonapartism in the person of Louis-Napoleon Bonaparte, the nephew of Napoleon I, added to European instability as France reasserted itself. One of Louis-Napoleon's targets was Russia, formerly a mainstay of the concert of Europe. To limit Russia's and Austria's grip on power, France helped engineer the Crimean War, which not only changed the distribution of European power but

1850s–1860s Positivism, Darwinism become influential

1853–1856 Crimean War

1861 Victor Emmanuel declared king of a unified Italy; abolition of serfdom in Russia

1850 1855 1860

1850s–1870s Realism in the arts

1857 British-led forces suppress Indian Rebellion

1861–1865 U.S. Civil War

Napoleon III and Eugénie Receive the Siamese Ambassadors, 1864
At a splendid gathering of their court, the emperor Napoleon III, his consort Eugénie, and their son and heir greet ambassadors from Siam, whose exoticism and servility before the imperial family are the centerpiece of this depiction by Jean-Léon Gerome. How might a middle-class French citizen react to this scene? *(Bridgeman-Giraudon/Art Resource, NY.)*

also resulted in the end of serfdom in Russia and the birth of new European nations.

Napoleon III and the Quest for French Glory

Louis-Napoleon Bonaparte, who declared himself Napoleon III in 1852, encouraged the revival of French grandeur and the cult of his famous uncle as part of nation building. "A man of destiny," he called himself. Napoleon III acted as Europe's schoolmaster, showing its leaders how to combine economic liberalism and nationalism with authoritarian rule. To the public, he claimed to represent "your families, your property—rich and poor alike," but he closed cafés where men might discuss politics and established a rubber-stamp legislature, the Corps législatif, that made representative government a charade. Imperial style replaced republican simplicity (see the illustration above). Napoleon's opulent court dazzled the public, and the emperor (like his namesake) cultivated a masculine image of strength and majesty by wearing military uniforms and by conspicuously maintaining mistresses. In contrast, Napoleon's wife, Empress Eugénie, followed middle-class norms by playing up her domestic role as devoted mother to her only son and supporting many charities. The authoritarian, apparently old-fashioned order imposed by Napoleon satisfied the many peasants that the radicalism of 1848 was under control.

Napoleon III was nonetheless a modernizer. He promoted a strong economy and public works

1867 Second Reform Bill in England; Austro-Hungarian monarchy

1868 Meiji Restoration begins in Japan

1869 Suez Canal opens

1869–1871 Women's colleges founded at Cambridge University

1870–1871 Franco-Prussian War

1871 German Empire proclaimed at Versailles; self-governing Paris Commune established

1865 1870 1875

programs, luring the middle and working classes away from radical politics with jobs. The magnificent rebuilding of Paris made France prosper as Europe recovered from the hard times of the late 1840s. Empress Eugénie wore lavish gowns, encouraging French silk production and keeping Paris at the center of the lucrative fashion trade. The regime also reached a free-trade agreement with Britain and backed the establishment of innovative investment banks. Such new institutions led the way in financing railroad expansion, and railway mileage increased fivefold during Napoleon III's reign. During the economic downturn of the late 1850s, he wooed support by allowing working-class organizations to form and introducing features of democratic government. Although some historians have judged Napoleon III to be devious because of these abrupt changes, he gave practical responses to economic change.

On the international scene, Napoleon III's main goals were to overcome the containment of France imposed by the Congress of Vienna and to acquire international glory like a true Bonaparte. To reshape European politics in France's favor, Napoleon pitted France first against Russia in the Crimean War, then against Austria in the War of Italian Unification (1860–1861), and finally against Prussia in the Franco-Prussian War (1870–1871). Beyond Europe, Napoleon's army continued to enforce French rule in Algeria and Southeast Asia. He attempted to install Maximilian, the brother of Habsburg emperor Francis Joseph, as emperor of Mexico and ultimately of all Central America. The attempt ended in a show of French weakness when Mexicans rebelled and executed Maximilian in 1867.

Despite this glaring failure, Napoleon successfully encouraged the construction of the Suez Canal to connect the Mediterranean and the Red Sea, and his foreign policy broke down the international order established at the Congress of Vienna. His push for worldwide influence eventually destroyed him, however: the French overthrew him after Prussia easily defeated his army in 1870.

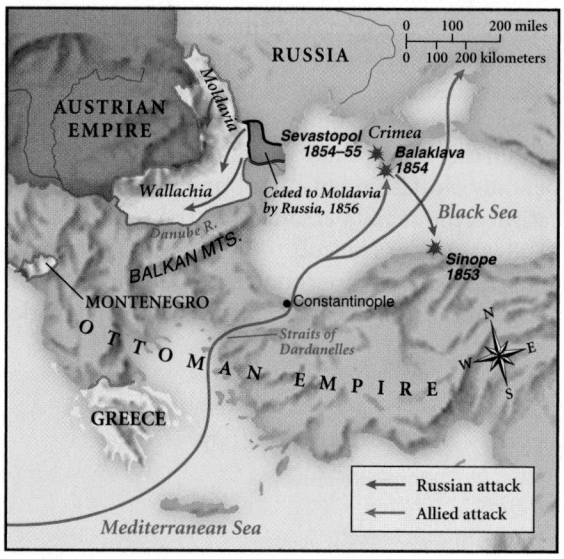

MAP 22.1 The Crimean War, 1853–1856
The most destructive war in Europe between the Napoleonic Wars and World War I, the Crimean War drew attention to the conflicting ambitions around territories of the declining Ottoman Empire. The war fractured the alliance of conservative forces from the Congress of Vienna, allowing Italy and Germany to come into being as unified states.

The Crimean War, 1853–1856: Turning Point in European Affairs

Napoleon III first flexed his diplomatic muscle in the Crimean War (1853–1856), which began as a conflict between the Russian and Ottoman Empires but ended as a war with long-lasting consequences for much of Europe. While professing to uphold the status quo, Russia had been expanding into Asia and the Middle East. In particular, Tsar Nicholas I wanted territory in the Ottoman Empire, fast becoming known as "the sick man of Europe" because of its disintegrating authority. Napoleon encouraged Nicholas to be even more aggressive in his expansionism—a maneuver that provoked war in October 1853 between the two eastern empires (Map 22.1). The war disrupted the united Austrian and Russian front that kept France in check. Other consequences would be the end of serfdom in Russia and the birth of new European nations.

The war drew in other states and upset Europe's balance of power as set in the Congress of Vienna. Napoleon III convinced Austria to remain neutral during the war, thus splitting the conservative Russian-Austrian coalition that had checked French ambitions since 1815. The Austrian government was concerned that the defeat of the Ottomans would bring Russian expansion into the Balkans. To protect its Mediterranean routes to East Asia, Britain prodded the Ottomans to stand up to Russia, but in the fall of 1853, the Russians blasted the Turkish wooden ships to bits at the Ottoman port of Sinope on the Black Sea. The Russians justified their actions as a necessary defense of Christians in the Ottoman Empire. In 1854, France and Great Britain, though enemies in war for more than a century, allied to declare war on Russia and defend the Ottoman Empire's sovereignty and territories.

Faced with attacking the massive Russian Empire, the British and French allies settled for the lim-

Nurse Tending Wounded Man
The Crimean War exposed the backward, and lethal, sanitary conditions of warfare—conditions that became intolerable to nation-states concerned with the well-being of their citizen soldiers. Women's contribution as nurses during both the Crimean War (shown in the image here) and the U.S. Civil War helped improve the situation, but voluntary assistance was not enough to prevent horrific death rates from disease and lack of coordinated medical attention. *(Private Collection/The Bridgeman Art Library International.)*

ited military goal of capturing the Russian naval base at Sevastopol, on the Crimea, a peninsula jutting into the Black Sea. Even so, the Crimean War was spectacularly bloody. British and French troops landed in the Crimea in September 1854 and waged a long siege at Sevastopol, which fell only after a year of savage and costly combat. Generals on both sides demonstrated their incompetence, and governments failed to provide combatants with even minimal supplies, sanitation, or medical care. Hospitals had no beds, no dishes, and no water. As a result, the war claimed a massive toll. A million men died, more than two-thirds from disease or starvation.

In the midst of this unfolding catastrophe, **Alexander II** (r. 1855–1881) ascended the Russian throne after the death of Nicholas I, his father. With casualties mounting, the new tsar asked for peace. As a result of the Treaty of Paris, signed in March 1856, Russia lost the right to base its navy in the Strait of Dardanelles and the Black Sea, which were declared neutral waters. Moldavia and Wallachia (which soon merged to form Romania) became autonomous Turkish provinces under the victors' protection, drastically reducing Russian influence in that region, too.

Some historians have called the Crimean War one of the most senseless conflicts in modern history because competing claims in southeastern Europe could have been settled by diplomacy had it not been for Napoleon III's driving ambition to disrupt the peace. Yet the war was full of consequence. New technologies were introduced into warfare: the railroad, shell-firing cannons, breech-loading rifles, and steam-powered ships. The relationship of the home front to the battlefront was beginning to change with the use of the telegraph and increased press coverage. Home audiences received news from the Crimean front lines more rapidly and in more detail than ever before. Reports of incompetence, poor sanitation, and the huge death toll outraged the public, inspiring some civilians, such as **Florence Nightingale**, to head for the front lines to help. Nightingale seized the moment to escape the confines of middle-class domesticity by organizing a battlefield nursing service to care for the British sick and wounded. Through her tough-minded organization of nursing units, she pioneered nursing as a profession and made sanitary conditions for soldiers a new and enduring priority. (See Document, "Mrs. Seacole: The *Other* Florence Nightingale," page 726.)

More immediately, the war accomplished Napoleon III's goal of severing the alliance between

Alexander II: Russian tsar (r. 1855–1881) who initiated the age of Great Reforms and emancipated the serfs in 1861.

Florence Nightingale: The Englishwoman who in the nineteenth century pioneered the professionalization of nursing and the use of statistics in the study of public health and the well-being of the military.

DOCUMENT

Mrs. Seacole: The *Other* Florence Nightingale

Another highly skilled medical worker besides Florence Nightingale made an impact on the battlefields in Crimea. Mary Seacole (1805–1881), daughter of a free black Jamaican woman and a Scottish army officer, had learned about medicine from her mother and from doctors who passed through Kingston, staying at the family's boardinghouse. In addition to a gift for healing, Mrs. Seacole (as she was always called) had a passion for travel—to Europe, the United States, and Panama—which she supported by tending other travelers. When the Crimean War broke out, she chafed—like Nightingale herself—to be at the battlefront. Arriving in Crimea in 1855, Mrs. Seacole saved many desperately ill soldiers who lacked all medical care. The text describes the mid-nineteenth century as an age of professionalization, domesticity for women, and lack of opportunity for many colonized people. Mrs. Seacole may be the exception that proves the rule, or it may be that society was more open and fluid than commonly believed.

[Sick soldiers] could and did get at my store sick-comforts and nourishing food, which the heads of the medical staff would sometimes find it difficult to procure. These reasons, with the additional one that I was very familiar with the diseases which they suffered most from and successful in their treatment (I say this in no spirit of vanity), were quite sufficient to account for the numbers who came daily to the British Hotel for medical treatment.

That the officers were glad of me as a doctress and nurse may be easily understood. When a poor fellow lay sickening in his cheerless hut and sent down to me, he knew very well that I should not ride up in answer to his message empty-handed. And although I did not hesitate to charge him with the value of the necessaries I took him, still he was thankful enough to be able to *purchase* them. When we lie ill at home surrounded with comfort, we never think of feeling any special gratitude for the sick-room delicacies which we accept as a consequence of our illness; but the poor officer lying ill and weary in his crazy hut, dependent for the merest necessaries of existence upon a clumsy, ignorant soldier-cook, who would almost prefer eating his meat raw to having the troubles of cooking it (our English soldiers are bad campaigners), often finds his greatest troubles in the want of those little delicacies with which a weak stomach must be humoured into retaining nourishment.

Source: Mary Grant Seacole, *Wonderful Adventures of Mrs. Seacole in Many Lands* (London: James Blackwood, 1857).

Question for Consideration

- **By her own account, why was Seacole successful in her profession? How might professionalizing medical people and city planners have viewed her?**

Austria and Russia, the two conservative powers on which the Congress of Vienna peace settlement had rested since 1815. It thus ended Austria's and Russia's grip on European affairs and undermined their ability to contain the forces of liberalism and nationalism. Russia's catastrophic defeat forced it to embark on some long-overdue reforms.

Reform in Russia

Defeat in the Crimean War not only blocked Russia's territorial ambition but also made clear the need for meaningful reform. Hundreds of peasant insurrections had erupted in the decade before the Crimean War. Serf defiance ranged from malingering at forced labor to boycotting vodka in protest of its heavy taxation. "Our own and neighboring households were gripped with fear," one aristocrat reported, because of potential serf violence. Although economic development spread in parts of eastern Europe, the Russian economy stagnated compared with that of western Europe. Old-fashioned farming techniques depleted soil and led to food shortages, and the nobility was often contemptuous of the suffering caused by malnutrition and hard labor.

Artists made their own call for reform with their sympathetic portrayals of serfs and condemnations of brutal masters, as in *A Hunter's Sketches* (1852) by novelist Ivan Turgenev. A Russian translation of American author Harriet Beecher Stowe's antislavery novel *Uncle Tom's Cabin* (1852) also hit home. When Russia lost the Crimean War, the educated public, including some government officials, found the poor performance of serf armies a disgrace and the system of serf labor a glaring problem.

Emancipation of the Serfs

Confronted with the need for change, Tsar Alexander II acted. Well educated and more widely traveled than his father, Alexander ushered in what came to be known as the Great Reforms, granting Russians new rights from above as a way of pre-

Emancipation of the Russian Serfs
This trading card was used as a marketing gimmick to promote canned meat. Cards like these were given away by the thousands and traded just as baseball cards are today. Historical scenes were popular subjects for the cards—this one shows the 1861 emancipation of the serfs in Russia. Note that the caption is in French, the language of the European upper classes, including those in Russia, who would have consumed this product. The emancipation is presented as a wholly beneficial act with no strings attached. *(Mary Evans Picture Library.)*

venting violent action from below that might force change. The most dramatic reform was the emancipation of almost fifty million serfs beginning in 1861. By the terms of emancipation, communities of newly freed serfs, headed by male village elders, received grants of land. The community itself, traditionally called a **mir**, had full power to allocate this land among individuals and to direct their economic activity. Although emancipation partially laid the groundwork for a modern labor force in Russia, communal landowning and decision making meant that individual peasants could not simply sell their parcel of land and leave their rural communities to work in factories, as laborers had been doing in western Europe.

The condition attached to the so-called land grants in Russia was that peasants were not *given* land along with their personal freedom: they were forced to "redeem" the land they farmed by paying off long-term loans from the government, which in land remained in the hands of the nobility, and most peasants ended up with less land than they had farmed as serfs. These conditions, especially the huge burden of debt and communal regulations, slowed Russian agricultural development for decades. Even so, idealistic reformers believed that the emancipation of the serfs, once treated by the nobility virtually as livestock, had produced miraculous results. As one of them put it, "The people are without any exaggeration transfigured from head to foot. . . . The look, the walk, the speech, everything is changed."

The state also reformed local administration, the judiciary, and the military. The government compensated the nobility for loss of peasant services and set up zemstvos—regional councils through which aristocrats could control local affairs such as education, public health, and welfare. Aristocratic control ensured that the zemstvos would remain conservative, but they became a new political force with the potential for challenging the authoritarian central government. Some aristocrats took advantage of newly relaxed rules on travel to see how the rest of Europe was governed. Their vision broadened as they observed different ways of solving social and economic problems. The principle of equality of all persons before the law, regardless of social rank, was introduced in Russia for the first time, as judicial reform gave all Russians access to modern civil courts. Even serfs were no longer left to the mercy of a landowner's version of justice. Military reform followed in 1874 when the government reduced the twenty-five-year period of service to a six-year term and began focusing on educating troops in an effort to match the efficiency and fitness of soldiers in western Europe.

From Reform to Rebellion

Alexander's reforms helped landowners be more effective in the market, just as enclosures and emancipation had done much earlier for landowners in western Europe. At the same time, the changes reduced the privileges of the nobility, weakening their authority and sparking family conflict. "An epidemic seemed to seize upon [noble] children . . . an

mir (mihr): A Russian farm community that provided for holding land in common and regulating the movements of any individual member by the group.

DOCUMENT

Education of a Mathematical Genius in Russia

Sofya Kovalevskaya (1850–1891) grew up in a privileged household with a governess and plenty of servants. Her education was supposed to include needlework, deportment, and other "womanly" subjects, but from childhood she developed tricks and practiced outright disobedience so that she could study math, a subject with which a favorite uncle helped her. Later, to get to universities in central and western Europe, she contracted a phony marriage with a young man with similar aspirations and then went to Göttingen and Berlin, where she had problems at first getting accepted as a student because she was a woman. Kovalevskaya finally found a university teaching position in Sweden and published some of the most important mathematical treatises of modern times. In this excerpt from her autobiographical sketch, she describes her girlhood determination to learn math.

Not until I grew somewhat more familiar with [algebra] did I begin to feel an attraction to mathematics so intense that I started to neglect my other studies. Observing the direction I was taking, my father—who in any case harbored a strong prejudice against learned women—decided that it was high time to put a stop to my mathematics lessons. . . . But somehow I managed to wheedle out of my teacher a copy of Bourdon's *Algebra Course* and began studying it with diligence.

Since I was under my governess's strict surveillance, I was forced to practice some cunning in this matter. At bedtime I used to put the book under my pillow and then, when everyone was asleep, I would read the night through under the dim light of the icon-lamp or the night lamp. . . .

My mathematical knowledge would likely have remained confined to the contents of Bourdon's *Algebra* if I had not been aided by the following incident, which motivated my father to reassess his views on my education to some degree.

One of our neighboring landowners, Professor Tyrtov, bought us the textbook of elementary physics he had written. I made an attempt to read it, but in the section on optics, to my chagrin, I encountered trigonometric formulas, sines, cosines and tangents.

Then trying to cope with the formulas contained in the book I tried to explain it for myself. *[Kovalevskaya's old teacher did not know these either.—Ed.]*

Some time later I was having a conversation with Professor Tyrtov about his book, and he expressed doubt at first that I could have understood it. To my declaration that I had read it with great interest he said, "Come, now—aren't you bragging?" But when I told him the means I had used to explain the trigonometric formulas he completely changed his tone. He went straight to my father, heatedly arguing the necessity of providing me with the most serious kind of instruction, and even comparing me to Pascal.

Source: Sofya Kovalevskaya, *A Russian Childhood* (New York: Springer-Verlag, 1978), 216–18.

Question to Consider

- **Describe Sofya Kovalevskaya's intellectual challenges. How does she address the prevailing idea that women should not study math?**

epidemic of fleeing from the parental roof," one observer noted. Rejecting aristocratic leisure, youthful rebels from the upper class valued practical activity and sometimes identified with peasants and workers instead of their own class. Some formed communes where they hoped to do humble manual labor; others turned to higher education, especially the sciences. Daughters of the nobility opposed their parents by cutting their hair short, wearing black, and escaping from home through phony marriages so they could study in western European universities. (See Document, "Education of a Mathematical Genius in Russia," above.) This rejection of traditional society led these young people to be labeled as nihilists (from the Latin for "nothing")—implying a lack of belief in any values whatsoever. In fact, they represented a defiant spirit percolating not just at the bottom but also at the top of Russian society.

Reform and an atmosphere of change also inspired resistance among the more than one hundred Russian-dominated ethnic groups in the Russian Empire. Aristocratic and upper-class nationalist Poles staged an uprising in 1863, demanding full national independence for their country. By 1864, however, Alexander II's army had regained control of the Russian section of Poland, using the promise of reform to win peasant help in defeating the rebels. The government then swiftly clamped down on other nationalist uprisings and enforced **Russification**—a tactic meant to reduce the threat of future rebellion by insisting that ethnic minorities within the empire adopt Russian language and culture. Despite these measures, the tsarist regime in this era of the

Russification: A program for the integration of Russia's many nationality groups that involved the forced learning of the Russian language and the practice of Russian Orthodox religion as well as the settlement of ethnic Russians among other nationality groups.

Great Reforms only partially succeeded in developing the administrative, economic, and civic institutions that made the nation-state strong elsewhere in Europe. The tsar and his inner circle tightly controlled the government, allowing few to share in power. In imperial Russia, autocracy and continued abuse of many in the population slowed the development of the sense of common citizenship forming elsewhere in the West, while the urge to revolt grew.

REVIEW QUESTION What were the main results of the Crimean War?

War and Nation Building

Dynamic leaders in the German and Italian states used the opportunity provided by the weakened concert of Europe to unify their fragmented countries through warfare. When national disunity threatened, the United States waged a bloody civil war to maintain its integrity, which opened the way for further expansion and vigorous economic growth. The rise of powerful **nation-states** such as Italy, Germany, and the United States was accompanied by a sense of pride in national identity—or nationalism—among their peoples (see "Terms of History," at right). This was not an inevitable or universal trend in the West, however. Millions of individuals in the Austrian Empire, Ireland, and elsewhere maintained a regional, local, or distinct ethnic identity even as the nation-state was strengthening and national sentiment was on the rise.

Cavour, Garibaldi, and the Process of Italian Unification

Despite the failure of the revolutions of 1848 in the Italian states, hope for national unification remained strong, aided by diplomatic instability across Europe. The kingdom of Piedmont-Sardinia, in the economically modernizing north of Italy, drove the unification process that came to be called the Risorgimento ("rebirth"). Italians rallied to the operas of Verdi, but it was railroads, a modern army, and the military support of France against the Austrian Empire, which still dominated the peninsula, that made political unification possible.

nation-state: An independent political unit of modern times based on representing a united people.

TERMS OF HISTORY

Nationalism

The word *nationalism* is associated with a sense of a common identity among people within geographically defined nation-states. Nationalism simultaneously promotes the nation-state around which that common identity develops. A phenomenon of the past two to three centuries, it became increasingly important to politics from the nineteenth century on. Strongly held feelings of a common national identity grew in the years after 1750, and this sense of national identification increasingly competed in people's minds with religious, regional, and local loyalties.

In an early version of nationalism, the eighteenth-century British took pride in the fact that as Protestants they had defeated the Catholic French king in the global trade wars in Asia and the New World. At about the same time, the German author Johann Gottfried Herder concluded from his studies that a common language—along with its folktales, history, and laws—also served as the basis for a shared national identity. Herder's emphasis on past accomplishments and traditions connects this kind of nationalism to themes in the romantic movement. In 1789, French revolutionary politicians set out in the Declaration of the Rights of Man and Citizen that all men were citizens—not subjects—and that as citizens they had rights. The Declaration thus proclaimed that common identity could be based on the rule of law. By the beginning of the nineteenth century, some of the major components of nationalism had developed: pride in military conquest (militaristic nationalism); pride in a common culture developed over centuries (sometimes called romantic nationalism); and belief in citizenship and the rule of law, with its guarantee of civil rights and other freedoms (civic nationalism).

In the nineteenth century, nationalism became a force in domestic and international politics. From the 1820s on, nationalistic politicians took to the battlefield, as in the fight for Greek independence or in the wars of Italian and German unification. Some Italian nationalists expected that unification would strengthen national identity by providing the kind of common citizenship and freedom that the Americans and French had won through their revolutions.

After 1848, realists like Bismarck and Cavour promoted nationalism as the work of "iron and blood"—national strength backed by military might. Nationalism became a matter of pride in a people's toughness and realism in a competitive world. After their wars of unification, both Germany and Italy continued to promote the vision of the nation triumphant in battle. This differed from the French revolutionary ideal of being triumphant in battle in order to bring rights and constitutions to oppressed peoples—a civic nationalism. By the end of the nineteenth century, the basis of nationalism had shifted from pride in democratic institutions to pride in a nation's military power. With growing racism in the nineteenth century, there came to be a form of nationalism based on purity of blood. Today, the word *nationalism* usually combines a wide array of ingredients, prompting politicians to appeal to common religion, laws, customs, language, ethnicity, race, and history to build national pride.

Cavour, Architect of the New Italy

The pragmatic **Camillo di Cavour** (1810–1861), prime minister of the kingdom of Piedmont-Sardinia from 1852 until his death, had a Realpolitiker's vision of how to unify the Italian states. A rebel in his youth, Cavour in his maturity organized steamship companies, played the stock market, and inhaled the heady air of modernization during his travels to Paris and London. He promoted economic development rather than idealistic uprisings as the means to achieve a united Italy. As a skilled prime minister, Cavour helped the less capable king, Victor Emmanuel II (r. Piedmont-Sardinia 1849–1861, r. Italy 1861–1878), achieve a strong Piedmontese economy, a modern army, and a liberal political climate as the foundation for Piedmont's claim to lead the unification process (Map 22.2).

Camillo di Cavour: Prime minister (1852–1861) of the kingdom of Piedmont-Sardinia and architect of a united Italy.

To unify Italy, however, Piedmont would have to confront Austria, which governed the provinces of Lombardy and Venetia and exerted strong influence over most of the peninsula. Cavour turned for help to Napoleon III, who at a meeting in the summer of 1858 promised French assistance in exchange for the city of Nice and the region of Savoy. Napoleon III additionally expected that France rather than Austria would influence the peninsula thereafter. Sure of French help, Cavour provoked the Austrians to invade northern Italy in April 1859. The cause of Piedmont-Sardinia's monarchy now became the cause of nationalist Italians everywhere, even those who had supported romantic republicanism in 1848, and they rose up on the side of Piedmont. The French and Piedmontese armies used the newly built Piedmontese railroad to move troops and thereby achieved rapid victories. Suddenly fearing the growth of Piedmont as a potential competing force, Napoleon independently signed a peace treaty with Austria that gave Lombardy,

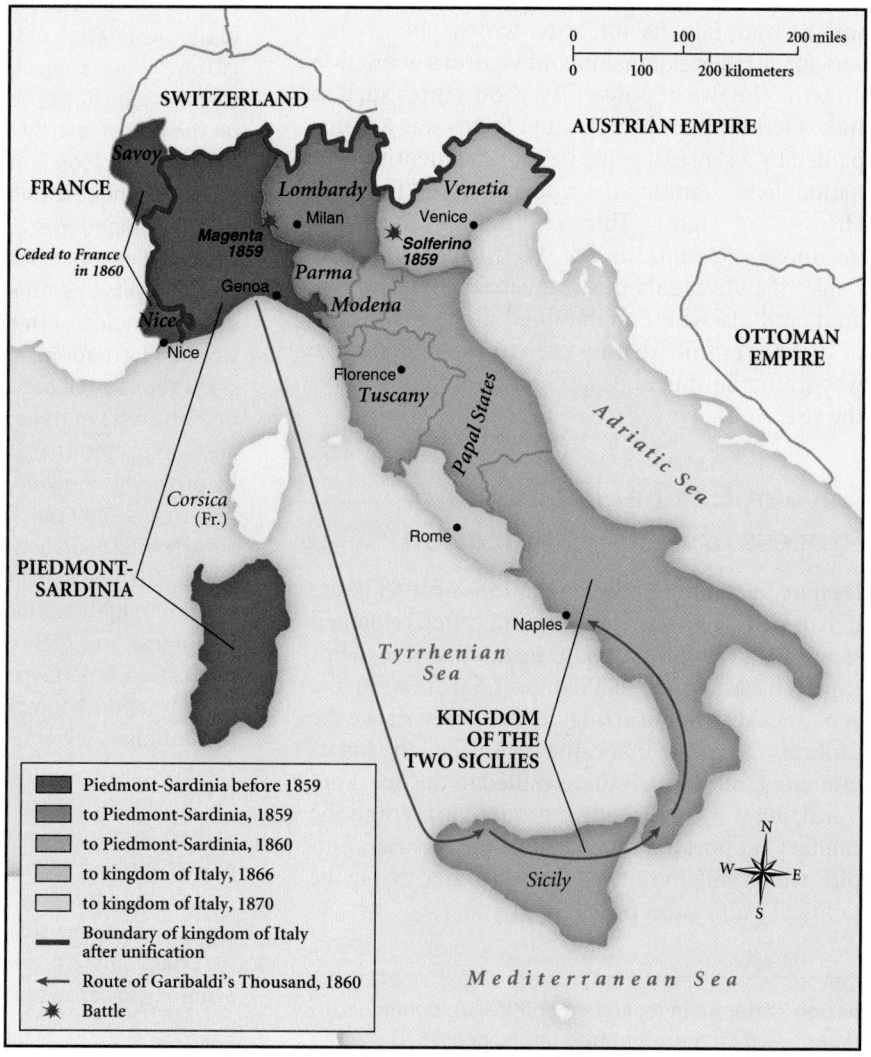

MAP 22.2 Unification of Italy, 1859–1870

The many states of the Italian peninsula had different languages, ways of life, and economic interests. The northern kingdom of Sardinia, which included the commercially advanced state of Piedmont, had much to gain from a unified market and a more extensive pool of labor. Although the armies of King Victor Emmanuel II and Giuseppe Garibaldi brought the Italian states together as a single country, it would take decades to construct a culturally, socially, and economically unified nation.

but not Venetia, to Piedmont. The rest of Italy remained disunited, leaving Cavour's nationalist ambitions not yet realized.

Garibaldi, Symbol of Italian Freedom

Napoleon III's plan to keep Italy disunited was soon derailed. Support for Piedmont continued to swell among Italians, while a financially strapped Austria stood by, unable to keep control of events on the peninsula. Citizens of the rest of the northern and central Italian states (except Rome, which French troops had occupied) ousted their leaders and elected to join Piedmont. Giuseppe Garibaldi (1807–1882), a committed republican and veteran of the revolutions of 1848, set sail from Genoa in May 1860 with a thousand red-shirted volunteers (many of them teenage boys) to liberate Sicily, where peasants were rebelling against their landlords and the corrupt government in anticipation of the Risorgimento. In the autumn of that year, Victor Emmanuel II's victorious forces descending from the north and Garibaldi's moving up from the south met in Naples. Although some of his followers still clamored for a republic, Garibaldi threw his support to the king. In 1861, the kingdom of Italy was proclaimed with Victor Emmanuel as its ruler.

Exhausted by a decade of overwork, Cavour died within months of leading the unification, leaving lesser men to organize the new Italy. The task ahead was enormous and complex: There was still no common Italian language; 90 percent of the peninsula's inhabitants spoke local dialects. Moreover, consensus among Italy's elected political leaders was often difficult to reach after the war, and admirers of Cavour, such as Verdi (who had been made senator), quit the quarrelsome political stage. Politicians from the wealthy commercial north and the impoverished agricultural south disagreed over issues like taxation and development, as they do even today. Finally, Italian borders did not yet seem complete because Venetia and Rome remained outside them, under Austrian and French control, respectively. Holding the new nation together amid these difficulties was the romanticized retelling of the Italian struggle for freedom from foreign and domestic tyrants, under the daring leadership of Garibaldi and his Red Shirts. The legend of Garibaldi papered over Cavour's economic and military Realpolitik, but the story became the centerpiece of a new and unifying national pride.

Bismarck and the Realpolitik of German Unification

The most momentous act of nation building for Europe and the world was the creation of a united Germany in 1871. This, too, was the product of Realpolitik, undertaken once the concert of Europe was smashed and the champions of the status quo defeated. Employing the old military caste to wage war, yet enjoying support from industrialists, merchants, and financiers who saw profits in a single national market, the Prussian state brought a vast array of cities and kingdoms under its control within a single decade. From then on, Germany prospered, continuing to consolidate its economic and political might. By the end of the nineteenth century, it would be the foremost continental power.

Seamstresses of the Red Shirts

Sewing uniforms and making battle flags, European women like these Italian volunteers saw themselves as contributors to the nation. Many nineteenth-century women participated in nation building as "republican mothers" by donating their domestic skills and raising the next generation of citizens to be patriotic. *(Oil on canvas, Florence / Private Collection / © Electa / akg-images / The Image Works.)*

King William I of Prussia and His Generals
Realpolitik politicians used warfare to create new nations like the unified Germany, which led other states in using up-to-date weaponry and transportation. Nonetheless, horses, swords, and flashing helmets such as those worn by King William I and the generals of Prussia were still a major feature of developing modern warfare. *(Reproduction of a painting by G. Koch/Mary Evans Picture Library/Everett Collection.)*

Bismarck's Rise to Power

The architect of the unified Germany was **Otto von Bismarck** (1815–1898). Bismarck came from a traditional Junker (Prussian landed nobility) family on his father's side; his mother's family included high-ranking bureaucrats and literati of the middle class. At university, the young Bismarck had gambled and womanized. After failing in the civil service, he worked to modernize operations on his landholdings while leading an otherwise decadent life. His marriage to a pious Lutheran woman gave him new seriousness. In the 1850s, his diplomatic service to the Prussian state made him increasingly angry at the Habsburg grip on German affairs. Establishing Prussia as the most respected and dominant German power became Bismarck's cause.

Otto von Bismarck (1815–1898): Leading Prussian politician and German chancellor who waged war in order to create a united German Empire, which was established in 1871.

In 1862, William I (king of Prussia, r. 1861–1888; German emperor, r. 1871–1888) appointed Bismarck prime minister in hopes that he would crush the growing power of the liberals in the Prussian parliament. The liberals, representing the prosperous professional and business classes, had gained parliamentary strength at the expense of conservative landowners during the decades of industrial expansion. Indeed, the liberals' wealth was crucial to the Prussian state's ability to augment its power, but liberals wanted Prussia to be like other parts of western Europe, with political rights for citizens and increased civilian control of the military. William I, along with members of the traditional Prussian elite such as Bismarck, rejected the western European model. Acting on his conservative beliefs, Bismarck rammed through programs to build the army and prevent civilian control. "Germany looks not to Prussia's liberalism, but to its power," he proclaimed. "The great questions of the day will not be settled by speeches and majority decisions—that was the great mistake of 1848 and 1849—but by iron and blood."

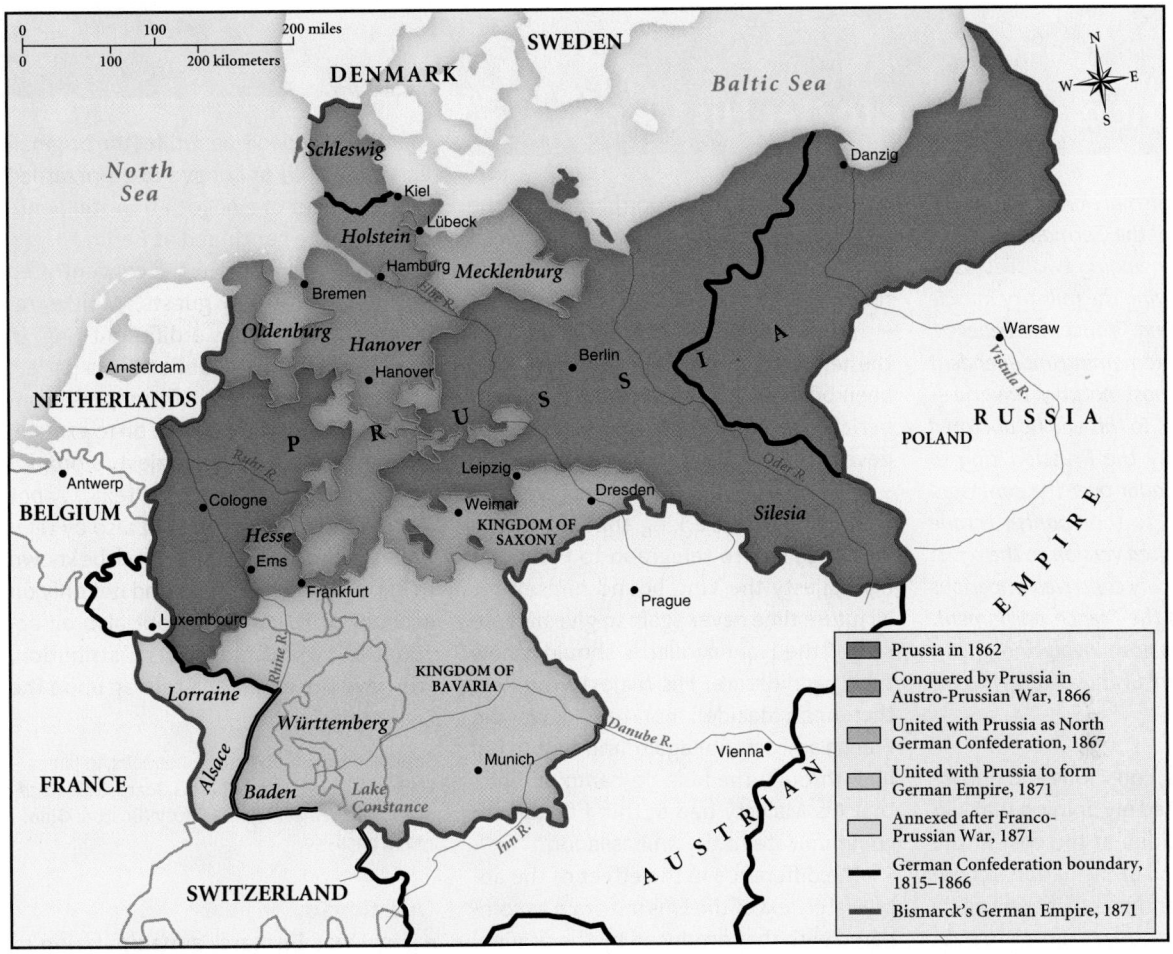

MAP 22.3 Unification of Germany, 1862–1871

In a complex series of diplomatic maneuvers, Prussian leader Otto von Bismarck welded disunited kingdoms and small states into a major continental power independent of the other dominant German dynasty, the Habsburg monarchy. That unity almost immediately unleashed the new nation's economic and industrial potential, but an aristocratic and agrarian elite remained firmly in power.

Prussia's Wars of Unification

After his triumph over the parliament, Bismarck led Prussia into a series of wars: against Denmark in 1864, Austria in 1866, and France in 1870. Using war as a political tactic, he kept the disunited German states from choosing Austrian leadership and instead united them around Prussia. Bismarck drew Austria into the 1864 war over Denmark's proposed incorporation of the provinces of Schleswig and Holstein, with their partially German population. The Prussian-Austrian victory resulted in an agreement that Prussia would administer Schleswig, and Austria, Holstein. That arrangement stretched Austria's geographic interests far from its central European base: "We were very honorable, but very dumb," Emperor Francis Joseph later said of being drawn into the Schleswig-Holstein debacle.

Austria proved weaker than Prussia, because the empire lagged in economic development and was beset by the discontent of its many national minorities. Bismarck, however, so encouraged Austria's pretensions to grandeur and influence that it disputed the administration of Schleswig and Holstein and in the summer of 1866 confidently declared war on Prussia itself. Within seven weeks, the modernized Prussian army, using railroads and breech-loading rifles against the outdated Austrian military, won a decisive victory that allowed Bismarck to drive Austria from the German Confederation and create the North German Confederation, led by Prussia (Map 22.3).

To bring the remaining German states into Prussia's expanding orbit, Bismarck next moved to provoke France into war. The atmosphere became charged when Spain proposed a Prussian prince to fill its vacant royal throne. This candidacy at once threatened France with Prussian rulers on two of its borders and inflated Prussian pride at the possibility of its princely lines ruling grand states. To get nationalist sentiments onto the news pages in

DOCUMENT

Bismarck Tricks the Public to Get His War

By 1870, Otto von Bismarck had gained the allegiance of most of the German states (excluding Austria) by waging two successful wars and thus showing the military muscle of Prussia. Defeating France, he believed, would pull in the remaining independent German states—most notably Bavaria—and unite Germany. To this end he doctored a document sent by the Prussian king to the French ambassador over the contested issue of succession to the Spanish throne and released the edited version to the press. He knew that its newly contrived imperious tone would offend the French parliament. Realpolitik, then as now, involved manipulating the press. Here Bismarck describes his actions.

All considerations, conscious and unconscious, strengthened my opinion that war could only be avoided at the cost of the honor of Prussia and of the national confidence in her. Under this conviction I made use of the royal authorization . . . to publish the contents of the telegram; and in the presence of my two guests [General Moltke and General Roon] I reduced the telegram by striking out words, but without adding or altering anything, to the following form:

"After the news of the renunciation of the hereditary prince of Hohenzollern had been officially communicated to the imperial government of France by the royal government of Spain, the French ambassador at Ems made the further demand of his Majesty the king that he should authorize him to telegraph to Paris that his Majesty the king bound himself for all future time never again to give his consent if the Hohenzollerns should renew their candidature. His Majesty the king thereupon decided not to receive the French ambassador again, and sent to tell him, through the aide-de-camp on duty, that his Majesty had nothing further to communicate to the ambassador."

The difference in the effect of the abbreviated text of the Ems telegram as compared with that produced by the original was not the result of stronger words, but of the form, which made this announcement appear decisive, while [the original] version would only have been regarded as a fragment of a negotiation still pending and to be continued at Berlin.

After I had read out the concentrated edition to my two guests, Moltke remarked: "Now it has a different ring; in its original form it sounded like a parley; now it is like a flourish of trumpets in answer to a challenge." I went on to explain: "If, in execution of his Majesty's order, I at once communicate this text, . . . not only to the newspapers, but also by telegraph to all our embassies, it will be known in Paris before midnight, and not only on account of its contents, but also on account of the manner of its distribution, will have the effect of a red rag upon the Gallic bull."

Source: Otto von Bismarck, *Memoirs*, in James Harvey Robinson and Charles Beard, eds., *Readings in Modern European History* (Boston: Ginn, 1909), 2:158–59.

Question to Consider

- **How was Bismarck's manipulation of the Ems telegram an example of Realpolitik at work?**

both countries, Bismarck edited a diplomatic communication (the so-called Ems telegram, named after the spa town in which it was issued) to make it look as if the king of Prussia had insulted France over the issue of the vacant throne. Publication of the revised telegram inflamed the French into demanding war. (See Document, "Bismarck Tricks the Public to Get His War," above.) The parliament gladly declared it on July 19, 1870, setting in motion the alliances Prussia had created with the other German states and launching the Franco-Prussian War. The Prussians captured Napoleon III with his army on September 2, 1870, and France's Second Empire fell two days later.

Birth of the German Empire

Prussian forces were still besieging Paris when, in January 1871 in the Hall of Mirrors at Versailles, King William of Prussia was proclaimed kaiser ("emperor") of the new German Reich ("empire"). The peace terms ending the Franco-Prussian War, signed in May, required France to cede the rich industrial provinces of Alsace and Lorraine to Germany and to pay a multibillion-franc indemnity. Without French protection for the papacy, Rome became part of Italy. Germany was now poised to dominate continental politics.

Prussian military might served as the foundation for German nation building, and a complex constitution for the German Empire ensured the continued political dominance of the aristocracy and monarchy—despite the growing wealth and influence of the liberal business classes. Kaiser William, who remained Prussia's king, controlled the military and appointed Bismarck to the powerful position of chancellor for the Reich. Individual German states were represented in a council called the Bundesrat, while the Reichstag was an assembly elected by universal male suffrage. The Reichstag ratified all budgets but had little power to initiate programs. In framing this political settlement, Bismarck accorded rights such as suffrage in the belief that the masses would uphold conservatism and the monarchy out of their fear of modernizing businessmen, whom Bismarck opposed as "liberal power." Taking no chances, he balanced this move with an electoral system in Prussia in which the votes from the upper classes counted more than those from the lower. He had little to fear from liberals, however. Dizzy with German military success, they came to support the blend of economic progress, constitutional government, and militaristic nationalism that Bismarck represented.

Francis Joseph and the Creation of the Austro-Hungarian Monarchy

The Austrian monarchy took a different approach to nation building, proving that there was no one blueprint for the modern nation-state. Just as the Crimean War left Russia searching for solutions to its social and political problems, so the confrontations with Cavour and Bismarck left the Habsburg Empire struggling to keep its standing in a rapidly changing Europe. The Habsburg Empire had emerged from the revolutions of 1848 renewed by the ascension of the young monarch Francis Joseph (r. 1848–1916), who favored absolutist rule. A tireless worker, Francis Joseph enhanced his authority through stiff court ceremonies, playing to the popular fascination with celebrity and power. Though the emperor stubbornly resisted reform, official standards of honesty and efficiency improved, and the government promoted local education. The administration used the German language and the schools taught it, but the government respected the rights of national minorities—Czechs and Poles, for instance—to receive education and communicate with officials in their native tongue. Above all, the government abolished most internal customs barriers, boosted railway construction, and attracted foreign capital. Like Paris, the capital city of Vienna underwent extensive rebuilding, and as industrialization progressed, if unevenly, people found jobs.

In the fast-moving nineteenth century, the absolutist Austrian emperor could not match Bismarck in nation building. Too much of the old regime remained as a roadblock: the Catholic church controlled education and civil institutions such as marriage, prosperous liberals lacked representation in such important policy matters as taxation and finance, and police informers swarmed around them. Wanting truly representative government and free speech, the liberals prevented measures—such as providing funds for modernizing the military—that would have strengthened the reactionary government. Unlike Bismarck in Prussia, there was no one to override the liberals to bring about change.

After Prussia's 1866 victory over Austria, the vast, wealthy kingdom of Hungary became the key to the Habsburg Empire's existence. The leaders of the Hungarian agrarian elites forced the Austrian

Muslim Quarter and Bazaar
Nineteenth-century Europeans were a diverse people, composed of many religions, ethnicities, and ways of life. In the Balkans, many were Muslims, as this marketplace in Sarajevo, Bosnia, illustrates. The goal of finding a common cultural ground eluded the peoples of the Balkans. The Habsburg monarchy, which annexed Bosnia-Herzegovina in 1908, exerted its influence in the area to keep peoples divided and to play one against the other. *(Albertina, Vienna.)*

emperor to accept a **dual monarchy**—that is, one in which the Magyars had home rule over the Hungarian kingdom within the Habsburg lands. This agreement restored the Hungarian parliament and gave it control of internal policy (including the right to decide how to treat Hungary's national minorities). Although the Habsburg emperor Francis Joseph was crowned king of Hungary and Austro-Hungarian foreign policy was coordinated from Vienna, the Hungarians mostly ruled themselves after 1867 and hammered out common policies such as tariffs with the government in Vienna. These negotiations were mostly bitter, weakening the process of nation building in the empire.

The Austro-Hungarian Monarchy, 1867

A second weakness in the compromise that created the dual monarchy was that, although designed specifically to address the Hungarian demands, the dual monarchy led to claims by Czechs, Slovaks, and other national groups in the Habsburg Empire for a similar kind of self-rule. Czechs who had helped the empire advance industrially, for example, wanted Hungarian-style liberties. More menacing, other leaders of dissatisfied ethnic groups turned to **Pan-Slavism**—that is, the transnational loyalty of all ethnic Slavs whose common heritage, they believed, transcended current national boundaries. Instead of looking toward Vienna, they turned to the largest Slavic country—Russia—as key to achieving the unity of all Slavs outside the Habsburg Empire. With so many competing ethnicities, the Austro-Hungarian monarchy remained a dynastic state in which people could show loyalty to the Habsburg dynasty but had increasing difficulty relating to one another as members of a single nation.

Political Stability through Gradual Reform in Great Britain

In contrast to the nations in turmoil on the continent, Britain appeared the ideal of liberal progress. By the 1850s, the monarchy symbolized domestic tranquillity and propriety. Unlike their predecessors, Queen Victoria (r. 1837–1901) and her husband, Prince Albert, portrayed themselves as models of morality, British stability, and middle-class virtues (see "Seeing History," page 738). Britain's parliamentary system steadily brought more men into the political process. Economic prosperity supported peaceful political reform, except that politicians did little to relieve Ireland's continued suffering. A flexible party system helped smooth governmental decision making: the Tories evolved into the Conservatives, who favored a more status-oriented politics but still went along with the emerging liberal consensus around economic development and representative government. The Whigs became the Liberals, so named for their commitment to the same values on which the term *liberal* had taken shape in the first place: progress and free, expansive trade, and appreciating active industrialists as much as the entrenched aristocracy. In 1867, the Conservatives, led by Benjamin Disraeli (1804–1881), passed the Second Reform Bill, which extended voting rights to a million more men. Disraeli proposed, like Bismarck somewhat later, that the working classes would choose "the most conservative interests in the country"—not the business ones. Thus more men voting and deferring to their aristocratic betters would build his party, not that of the Liberals.

Both political parties supported reforms because citizens had formed pressure groups to influence national policies. Women's groups advocated the Matrimonial Causes Act of 1857, which facilitated divorce, and the Married Women's Property Act of 1870, which allowed married women to own property and keep the wages they earned. The Reform League, another pressure organization, had held mass demonstrations in London to bring about passage of the Second Reform Bill. Plush royal ceremonies united critics and activists and masked political conflict but, more important, involved all social classes. Whereas previous monarchs' sexual infidelities had incited mobs to riot, Queen Victoria and Prince Albert, with their newly devised celebrations of royal marriages, anniversaries, and births, drew respectful crowds. Promoting the monarchy in this way was so successful that the term *Victorian* came to symbolize almost the entire nineteenth century and could refer to anything from manners to political beliefs.

The aristocracy, maintaining power despite the rising wealth of liberal businessmen, built gigantic country houses in traditional English architectural styles such as Queen Anne and Georgian, thus using the monarchical heritage to anchor the modern age. Yet Britain's politicians were as devoted to

---

dual monarchy: The shared power arrangement between the Habsburg Empire and Hungary after the Prussian defeat of the Austrian Empire in 1866–1867.

Pan-Slavism: The nineteenth-century movement calling for the unity of all Slavs across national and regional boundaries.

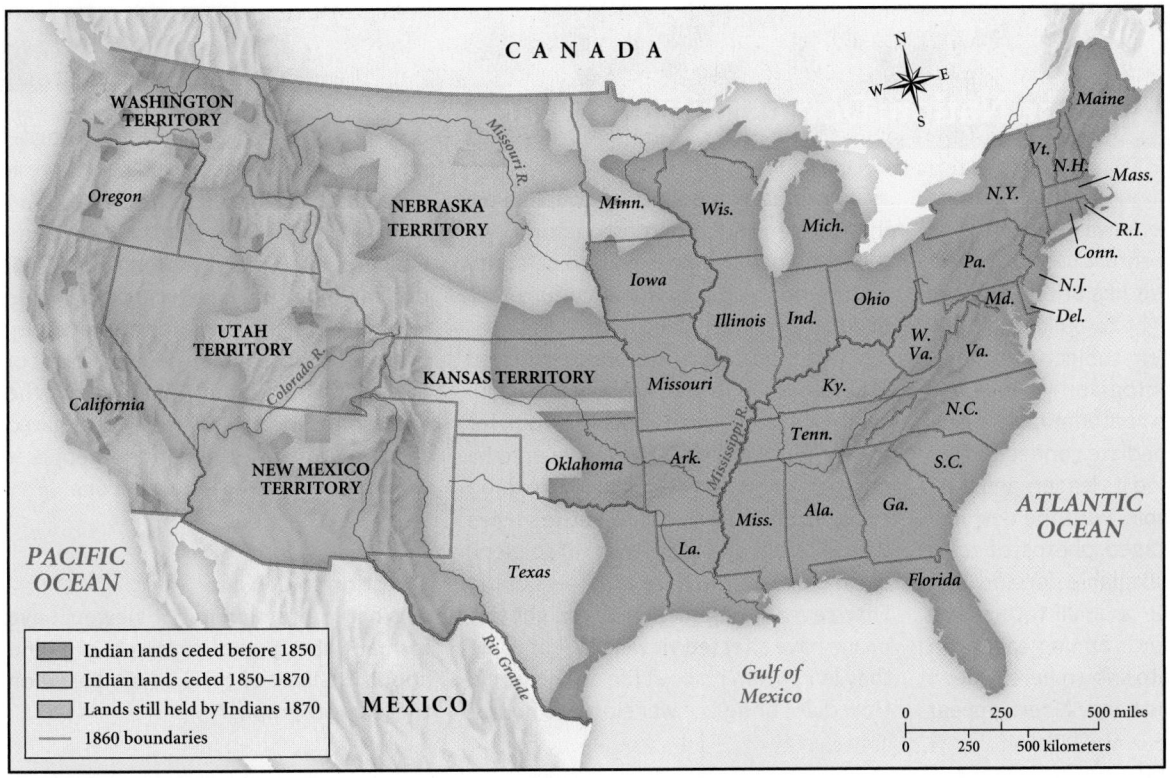

MAP 22.4 U.S. Expansion, 1850–1870

Like Russia, the United States expanded into adjacent regions to create a continental nation-state. In taking over territories, however, the United States differed from Russia by herding native peoples into small confined spaces called reservations so that settlers could acquire thousands of square miles for farming and other enterprises. The U.S. government granted full citizenship for all native Americans only in 1925.

Realpolitik as those in Germany, Italy, or France. Their policies included the use of violence to expand their overseas empire and, increasingly, to control Ireland, where reform stopped short. This violence occurred beyond the view of most British people, however, allowing them to imagine their nation as peaceful, advanced, and united.

Nation Building in North America

Nation building in the midcentury United States involved unprecedented and destructive upheaval. The young nation had a far more democratic political culture than that of Europe, and nationalism was on the rise. Virtually universal white male suffrage, a rambunctiously independent press, and mass political parties reflected a common belief that sovereignty derived from the people. From the beginning, a combative public politics shaped America.

The United States continued to expand westward (Map 22.4). In 1848, victory in the Mexican-American War almost doubled the size of the country: the United States officially annexed Texas, and large portions of California and the Southwest extended U.S. borders into formerly Mexican land. Politicians and citizens alike favored banning native Americans from these western lands and confining them to reservations. There was no agreement, however, on whether slavery would be allowed in the new western territories. The issue polarized the country. In the North, politicians in the new Republican Party ran on a platform of "free soil, free labor, free men," although few Republicans actually endorsed the abolitionists' demand to end slavery.

After Republican Abraham Lincoln was elected president in 1860, most of the slaveholding states seceded to form the Confederate States of America. Civil war broke out in 1861 when, under Lincoln's leadership, the North fought to preserve the Union. The future of nation building in the United States hung in the balance. Lincoln did not initially aim to abolish slavery, but his Emancipation Proclamation of January 1863, issued as a wartime measure, officially freed all slaves in the Confederacy and turned the war into a fight not only for union but also for an end to human bondage. After the summer of 1863, the North's superior industrial strength and military might overpowered and physically

SEEING HISTORY

Photographing the Nation: Domesticity and War

Fostering a common national identity among their citizens was important to many nineteenth-century European leaders, especially those, like Britain's Queen Victoria, who sought to build unity and loyalty among their subjects. The new technology of photography, developed in 1839, served this goal admirably by enabling a more immediate connection between the public and its leaders and their policies. For example, with the new medium, carefully staged photos of royal families became available for the first time, circulating in a small format like today's baseball cards among eager collectors. In the photo shown here, Queen Victoria and her husband, Albert, appear as an ordinary middle-class couple. Posing for many such photos, Victoria and Albert helped develop modern celebrity culture but also a national culture that transcended local identities.

The Crimean War was another shared experience for Britons, many of whom avidly collected photos from the front, for the conflict was one of the first ever to be photographed. Crowds flocked to exhibitions in major cities to view battle scenes (usually staged) and portraits of soldiers, like the one shown here of officers of the Fifty-seventh Regiment. How might this image have affected viewers? What could they learn from it about life on the front? How did it bring the war closer to home?

Both war photography and photography of national leaders, including U.S. president Abraham Lincoln with his wife, Mary Todd Lincoln, or France's Napoleon III and Eugénie, were major ingredients of nation building. The new technology made lofty leaders and the faraway wars they prosecuted accessible—indeed, a part of everyday life—to individuals across the West and beyond. As millions of eyes gazed on these images, the nation's people—wherever they lived—became one.

Question to Consider

- **What impression might viewers have formed about the royal couple and about the lives of the soldiers based on these photographs?**

Portrait of Queen Victoria and Prince Albert at Buckingham Palace, May 15, 1860. *(Hulton Archive / Getty Images.)*

Roger Fenton, Officers of the 57th Regiment, 1855. *(Library of Congress, Prints and Photographs Division. LC-USZC4-9132.)*

destroyed much of the South. By April 1865, the North had prevailed, though a Confederate sympathizer assassinated Lincoln. Constitutional amendments ended slavery and promised full political rights to African American men.

Northerners hailed their victory as the triumph of American values, but racism remained entrenched throughout the Union. By 1871, northern interest in promoting African American political rights was waning, and whites began regaining control of state politics in the South, often by organized violence and intimidation. The end of northern occupation of the South in 1877 was a setback in obtaining rights for blacks. Nonetheless, in ending slavery, the Union victory opened the way to stronger national government and to economic advancement no longer tied to the old Atlantic plantation system.

The North's triumph had profound effects elsewhere in North America. It allowed the reunited United States to contribute to Napoleon III's defeat in Mexico in 1867. The United States also threatened the annexation of Canada to punish Britain, whose dependence on cotton had led it to support the Confederacy. To prevent the loss of their largest territory, the British government allowed Canadians to form a united dominion — that is, a self-governing unit of the empire — in 1867. Dominion status answered Canadians' appeal for home rule, weakened the cause of those opposing Britain's control of Canada, and strengthened Canadian national unity.

REVIEW QUESTION What role did warfare play in the various nineteenth-century nation-building efforts?

Nation Building through Social Order

Government officials and reformers worked to establish social unity and order as a way of making political unity stronger. With new improvements, they also hoped to offset the violent changes of the nation-building process. Population rose dramatically and cities grew crowded as the nineteenth century progressed, leading officials across Europe to promote public health and safety. Many liberal theorists wanted a laissez-faire government that left social and economic life largely to private enterprise. In contrast, bureaucrats and reformers took direct action to improve citizens' lives and, along with missionaries and explorers, worked more actively to establish social order and to extend European power to the farthest reaches of the globe. Some of these efforts met violent resistance both within Europe and outside it.

Bringing Order to the Cities

European cities became the backdrop for displays of state power and accomplishment. Governments focused on improving capital cities such as Vienna and Rome, although many noncapital cities also acquired handsome parks, widened streets, stately museums, and massive city halls. In 1857, Austrian emperor Francis Joseph ordered the old Viennese city walls to be replaced with concentric boulevards lined with major public buildings such as the opera house and government offices (see the illustration on page 740). Opera houses and ministries were concrete evidence of national wealth and power, and the broad boulevards allowed crowds to observe royal pageantry. The wide roads were also easier for troops to navigate than the twisted, narrow medieval streets that in 1848 had concealed insurrectionists in cities like Paris and Vienna — an advantage that convinced some otherwise reluctant officials to approve the expense. Impressive parks and public gardens showed the state's control of nature, ordered people's leisure time, and inspired respect for the nation-state's achievements.

One effect of renovated cities was to highlight class differences. Construction first required destruction. Buildings and entire neighborhoods that had intermingled rich and poor disappeared, and thousands of city dwellers were dislocated. The boulevards often served as boundaries marking the newly built rich quarters from the poor sections of the city. In Paris, the process of urban change was called Haussmannization, named for the prefect Georges-Eugène Haussmann, who implemented a grand design that included eighty-five miles of new streets, many lined with showy dwellings for the wealthy. In London, the spaciousness and ornamentation of the many new banks and insurance companies, one architect believed, "help[ed] the impression of stability." The civic pride resulting from urban rebuilding would replace rebelliousness and disunity.

Yet amid redevelopment and beautification, serious problems menaced the urban population. Repeated epidemics of diseases such as cholera killed alarming numbers of city dwellers and gave the strong impression of social decay, not national power. Poor sanitation allowed typhoid bacteria to spread through sewage and into water supplies, infecting rich and poor alike. In 1861, Britain's Prince

Albert — the beloved husband of Queen Victoria — reputedly died of typhoid fever, commonly known as a "filth disease." Heaps of animal excrement in chicken coops, pigsties, and stables; unregulated urban slaughterhouses and tanneries; and piles of human waste alongside buildings were breeding grounds for disease. In cities the stench alone — not to mention the disorder it suggested — made sanitation a top priority.

Scientific research, increasingly undertaken in publicly financed laboratories and hospitals, provided the means to promote public health and control disease. France's Louis Pasteur, three of whose young daughters had also died of typhoid, advanced the germ theory of disease. Seeking a method to prevent wine from spoiling, Pasteur found that the growth of living organisms caused fermentation in wine, and he suggested that certain organisms — bacteria and parasites — might be responsible for human and animal diseases. Pasteur demonstrated that heating foods such as wine and milk to a certain temperature, a process that soon became known as pasteurization, killed these organisms and made food safe. English surgeon Joseph Lister applied Pasteur's germ theory of disease to infection and developed antiseptics for treating wounds and preventing puerperal fever, a condition, caused by the dirty hands of physicians and midwives, that killed innumerable women after childbirth.

Governments undertook projects to modernize sewer and other sanitary systems, including the straightening of rivers to eliminate marshes and other stagnant pools of water that could breed disease. Citizens often prized such improvements as signs of national superiority. In Paris, sewage flowed into newly built, watertight underground collectors (see the illustration on page 741). In addition, Haussmann piped in water from uncontaminated sources in the countryside to provide each household with a secure supply. These improvements were imitated across Europe: the Russian Empire's port city Riga (now in Latvia), for example, organized its first water company in 1863. To prevent devastating floods and to eliminate disease-ridden marshlands, governments rerouted and straightened rivers such as the Rhine and built canals. Improved sanitation testified to the activist state's ability to bring about progress.

Citizens responded positively to improvements in everyday life and came to expect that cities could and should change for the better. When sanitary public toilets for men became a feature of modern cities, women petitioned governments for similar facilities. More aware of dirt, disease, and smells, the

Museums and Nation Building

The Kunsthistorisches Museum (Museum of Fine Arts) in Vienna was part of a huge rebuilding project that adorned the city with wide boulevards and grand public buildings. Art museums such as Vienna's represented the cultural wealth of the state and allowed citizens to take pride in this wealth while they routinely gathered collectively to view it. *(ullstein—imagebroker.net.)*

Touring a National Treasure: The Sewers of Paris
The enlargement of sewage systems was so grand an undertaking in urban capitals that they attracted visitors. Many had a curiosity about what technology could achieve and flocked to the new sewers to enjoy tours—a pastime that continues to this day in cities like Paris. *(© Leonard de Selva/Corbis.)*

middle classes bathed more regularly, sometimes even once a week. One Russian city dweller complained to a Moscow newspaper of "an enormous cloud of white dust constantly over the city" that injured the eyes and lungs. Such individual concerns for refinement and health mirrored governments' pursuit of order.

Expanding Government Bureaucracy

Building an orderly national community meant a more active role for the state, and bureaucracies expanded in these years to direct nation building and the push for social order. The nation-state required citizens to follow a growing catalog of regulations as government authority reached further into everyday life. The censuses that Britain, France, and the United States had begun in the late eighteenth century became routine in most other countries as well. Censuses provided the state with personal details of citizens' lives such as age, occupation, residence, marital status, and number of children. Governments then used these data for everything from setting quotas for military conscription to predicting the need for new prisons. Reformers like Florence Nightingale, who gathered medical, public health, and other statistics to support sanitary reform, believed that such quantitative information would help government base decisions on facts rather than on influence peddling or ill-informed hunches, and thus make it less susceptible to corruption and inefficiency. In 1860, Sweden introduced the income tax, which opened private citizens' earnings from work or investment to government scrutiny.

To bring about their vision of social order, many governments also expanded the regulation of prostitution. Venereal disease, especially syphilis, was common, and like typhoid fever, it infected individuals and whole families. Officials blamed prostitutes, not their clients, for its spread. The police picked up suspect women, who were examined for syphilis and, if infected, confined for treatment. As states began monitoring prostitution and other social matters like public health and housing, they had to add departments and agencies. In 1867, Hungary's bureaucracy handled fewer than 250,000 individual cases ranging from health to poverty issues; twenty years later, it handled more than 1 million.

Schooling and Professionalizing Society

Emphasis on empirical knowledge and objective standards changed the professions and raised their status. Growing numbers of middle-class doctors, lawyers, managers, professors, and journalists employed solid information in their work. The middle classes argued that jobs in government should be awarded according to talent and skill rather than aristocratic birth or political connections. In Britain, a civil service law passed in 1870 required competitive examinations to ensure competency in government posts—a system long used in China. Governments began to allow professionals to influence state policy and to determine rules for admission to their fields. Such legislation had both positive and negative effects: groups could set high standards, but otherwise qualified people were sometimes prohibited from working because they lacked the established credentials. The medical profession, for example, gained the authority to license physicians, but it tried to block experienced midwives from attending childbirths. Science became the province of the trained specialist rather than the knowledgeable amateur. Newly employed at government-financed institutions, professors of science often viewed their work as part of a national struggle for prestige and superiority.

Nation building required major improvements in the education of all citizens, professional or not. "We have made Italy," one Italian official announced. "Now we have to make Italians." Education was one way of bringing citizens to hold common beliefs and values. Bureaucrats and professionals called for radical changes in the curriculum and faculty of schools—from kindergarten to university—to make the general population more fit for citizenship and able to further economic progress. Expansion of the electorate and lower-class activism prompted one British aristocrat to say of the common people, whom he feared as they gained influence, "We must now educate our masters!" Governments introduced compulsory schooling to reduce illiteracy rates, which were more than 65 percent in Italy and Spain in the 1870s and even higher in eastern Europe. As ordinary people were allowed to vote, books taught them about the responsibilities of citizenship and provided the practical knowledge necessary for contributing to industrial society.

Educational reform was not easy. At midcentury, religious authorities supervised schools and charged tuition, making primary education an option chosen only by prosperous or religious parents. After the 1850s, national politicians felt that their states could not afford masses of ignorant peasants, whose backwardness one French official blamed on parish priests, specifically "their lack of intelligence [and] the narrowness of their views." His statement was extreme, but more measured critics also questioned the relevance of religion in the curricula of modern schools. In 1861, an English commission on education concluded that instead of knowledge of the Bible, "the knowledge most important to a labouring man is that of the causes which regulate the amount of his wages, the hours of his work, the regularity of his employment, and the prices of what he consumes." To feel part of a nation, the young had to learn its language, literature, and history. Replacing religion was a challenge for the secular and increasingly knowledge-based state.

Enforcing school attendance was another challenge. Although the Netherlands, Sweden, and Switzerland had functioning primary-school systems before midcentury, rural parents in these and other countries resisted sending their children to school. Farm families depended on children to perform chores and believed that work in the fields or the household provided the best and most useful education. Urban homemakers from the lower classes needed their children to fetch water, dispose of waste, tend younger children, and scavenge for household necessities such as stale bread from bakers or soup from local missions. Yet some of the working poor developed a craze for learning, which made traveling lecturers, public forums, reading groups, and debating societies popular among the middle and working classes.

Secondary education also expanded through the creation of more lycées (high schools) and technical schools yet remained even more of a luxury. In authoritarian countries such as Russia, advanced knowledge, including education in science and technology, was suspect because it empowered the young with information and taught them to think for themselves. Reformers pushed for more advanced and more complex courses for young women as part of nation building. The rationale was that modern knowledge in history and science, for example, would make them more interesting wives and better mothers of future citizens. In Britain, the founders of two women's colleges—Girton (1869) and Newnham (1871)—at Cambridge University believed, and were later proved right, that exacting standards and a modern curriculum in women's higher education would inspire improvements in the men's colleges of Cambridge and Oxford. Nonetheless, higher education for women remained a hotly contested issue; the vast majority of people felt that knowledge of religion, sewing, and manners was adequate for women.

Education also opened professional doors to women, who came to attend universities—in particular, medical schools—in Zurich and Paris in the 1860s. Despite complaints by those who wanted to maintain separate spheres for men and women, women doctors argued that they could not only bring feminine values to health care but also get better results because women patients would be more open with them than with male doctors. The need for educated citizens also offered opportunities for large numbers of women to enter teaching, a field once dominated by men. Thousands of women founded nursery schools and kindergartens based on the Enlightenment idea that developmental processes start at an early age. In a newly unified Italy, women opened schools as a way to expand knowledge and teach lessons in citizenship. Yet many men opposed the idea of women teaching. "I shudder at philosophic women," wrote one critic of female kindergarten teachers. Seen as radical because it enticed middle-class women out of the home, the push for early childhood education was as controversial as other educational reforms.

Spreading National Power and Order beyond the West

In an age of nation building, colonies took on new importance because they seemed to add to the power of the nation-state. This benefit led Great Britain, France, and Russia to expand their political control and rule colonies directly instead of through trading companies. Sometimes the colonial powers offered social and cultural services, such as schools. For instance, in the 1850s and 1860s provincial governors and local officials promoted the extension of Russian borders to gain control over nomadic tribes in central and eastern Asia. Russian officials then instituted common educational and religious policies, such as instruction in the Russian language and in the principles of the Russian Orthodox church as a means to social order.

British Rule in India

Great Britain, the era's mightiest imperial power, made a dramatic change of course toward direct political rule abroad as part of nation building. Before the 1850s, British liberals desired commercial profits from colonies, but, believing in laissez-faire, they kept political involvement in colonial affairs minimal. Since the eighteenth century, the East India Company had been gaining control over various kingdoms on the Indian subcontinent, whose princes awarded the company trading and tax collection rights, and then began building railroads throughout the countryside to make commerce and revenue collecting more efficient. As commerce with Britain grew, many Indian businessmen, including traders and tax collectors for the company, became wealthy. Other local men served in the colonial army, which became one of the largest standing armies in the world.

European expansion, including Britain's, sometimes met resistance. In 1857, a contingent of Indian troops, both Muslim and Hindu, violently rebelled when a rumor spread that Britain would force them to use cartridges greased with cow and pig fat, which violated the Hindu ban on beef and the Muslim prohibition of pork. This was not their main grievance, however. The soldiers, more generally angered at widening British control such as the imposition of a heavy tax on salt, overran the old Moghul capital at Delhi and declared the independence of the Indian nation—an uprising that became known as the Indian Rebellion of 1857.

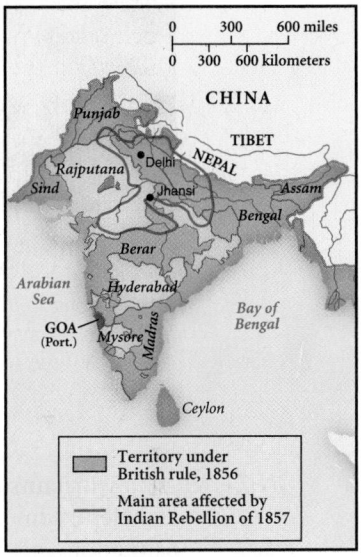

Indian Resistance, 1857

Simultaneously, uprisings erupted among displaced local rulers and their followers, who condemned "the tyranny and oppression of the infidel and treacherous English." Lakshmibai, the *rani* ("queen") of the state of Jhansi in central India, led a separate military revolt when the East India Company tried to take over her lands after her husband died. Even as the British brutally crushed the rebels, Indian nationalism was born. Victorious, the British government took direct control of India in 1858, and the British Parliament declared Queen Victoria the empress of India in 1876.

A system of rule took shape in which close to half a million South Asians, supervised by a few thousand British men, governed a region of once-independent states now called India. Local people continued to collect taxes and distribute patronage. Colonial rule meant both outright domination and subtle intervention in everyday life. For example, British taxes on high-quality Indian textiles aimed to divert the colonized Indian population away from domestically produced goods in favor of cheap British cottons. Artisans were directed instead to farm raw materials such as wheat, cotton, and jute to

An English View of the Indian Rebellion

Drawings such as this of the Indian Rebellion of 1857 show noble English families under savage attack by rebels. Artists emphasized the innocence of English victims and thus provided a rationale for the rule of superior Europeans over depraved non-Westerners. These drawings also united citizens around the expansion of the nation-state. *(The Granger Collection, New York—All rights reserved.)*

supply Britain's industry and feed its workers. Nevertheless, some Indians benefited from improved sanitation and medicine and chose to accept British arguments against Indian customs such as child marriage and *sati*—a widow who self-immolates on her husband's funeral pyre. Others found Europe's scientific values attractive and came to appreciate that British rule, ironically, brought a kind of unity to India's many separate princedoms, thus laying the foundation for an Indian nation. Soon the resulting nationalism would turn against British domination.

French Overseas Expansion

French political expansion was similarly complex. The French government pushed to establish its dominion over Cochin China (modern southern Vietnam) in the 1860s. Missionaries in the area, ambitious French naval officers, and even some local peoples—much like Indian merchants and financiers—pulled the French government farther into the region. Like the British, the French brought improvements such as the Mekong Delta project, which increased the amount of cultivable land and spurred growth in the food supply. Sanitation and public health programs proved a mixed blessing, because they led to a rise in population that strained resources. Furthermore, landowners and French imperialists siphoned off most of the profits from economic improvement. The French also undertook a cultural mission to transform cities like Saigon with tree-lined boulevards and other signs of Western life similar to those of Paris. French literature, theater, and art were popular not only with colonial officials but also with upper-class local people.

In this age of Realpolitik, the Crimean War had shown the great powers the importance of the Mediterranean basin. Napoleon III, remembering his uncle's campaign in Egypt, took an interest in building the Suez Canal, which would connect the Mediterranean with the Red Sea and the Indian Ocean and thus dramatically shorten the route from Europe to Asia. Following the canal's completion in 1869, "canal fever" spread: Verdi composed the opera *Aïda* (set in ancient Egypt), and people across the West applied Egyptian designs to textiles, furniture, art, and even public monuments in cities.

The rest of the Mediterranean and the Ottoman Empire felt the heightened presence of the European powers. The French army had occupied all of Algeria by 1870, when the number of European immigrants to the region reached one-quarter million. French rule in Algeria, as elsewhere, was aided by local people's attraction to European goods and technology and by the opportunity to make money. Merchants and local leaders cooperated in building railroads, sought trade with the French, and sent their children to European-style schools. Other local peoples, however, resisted the invasions by continuing to attack soldiers and settlers. European-spread diseases killed many others; by 1872, the native population in Algeria had declined by more than 20 percent from five years earlier.

European Inroads in China Its vastness allowed China to escape complete takeover, but the Qing Empire was rapidly losing its position as the world's most prosperous economy. Traders and Christian missionaries from Europe made inroads for the Western powers. Missionaries directed the Christian message to a population of 430 million, which had nearly doubled since the last century, but defeat in the Opium War caused an economic slump and helped generate the mass movement known as the Taiping ("Heavenly Kingdom"). Headed by a leader who claimed to be the brother of Jesus, the Taiping's millions of adherents wanted an end to the ruling Qing dynasty, the expulsion of foreigners, more equal treatment of women, and land reform. By the mid-1850s, the Taiping controlled half of China. The threatened Qing regime promised the British and French greater influence in exchange for aid in defeating the Taiping. More than 20 million Chinese died in the resulting civil war (compared with 600,000 dead in the U.S. Civil War). When peace finally came in 1864, Western governments controlled much of the Chinese customs service and had virtually unlimited access to the country.

The Meiji Restoration in Japan Japan alone in East Asia was able to escape Western domination, but it did not escape Western influence. Through Dutch traders at Nagasaki, the Japanese had become keenly aware of the industrial, military, and commercial innovations taking place in the West. In 1854, the Japanese agreed to open the country to foreign trade; contacts with Europe had already given the Japanese a healthy appetite for Western goods, including the West's superior weaponry. Japanese reformers in 1867 overthrew a government that resisted change and in 1868 enacted the Meiji Restoration. The word *Meiji* pointed to the "enlightened rule" of the new emperor whose power reformers had restored. The goal was to combine "Western science and Eastern values" as a way of "making new"—hence, a combination of restoration and innovation. The new regime set the stage for Japan to become a modern, technologically powerful state free from Western control.

Challenging the Nation-State's Order at Home

Europeans did not simply sit by as the growing nation-state changed and often disrupted their lives. A better-informed urban working class protested the upheavals in everyday life caused when cities were ripped apart for improvements and when the growth of factories destroyed artisans' livelihoods. Political theorists such as Pierre-Joseph Proudhon and Karl Marx analyzed what was wrong with society, and their ideas spread among disgruntled citizens. Unions sprang up, calling for strikes and other actions against both employers and the government. In the spring of 1871, the people of Paris, blaming the centralized state for the French surrender to the Prussians, declared Paris a commune—a community of equals without bureaucrats and politicians. Reacting to the Paris Commune, the middle classes and politicians feared for the stability of the rising nation-state.

The Rise of Marxism New theories arose to explain the growing power of the nation-state and the spread of industry on which the state depended. Increasingly educated by public schools, urban workers frequented cafés and pubs to hear news and discuss economic and political events. After the post-1848 repression of worker organizations, unions gradually started to take shape, sometimes in secret because of continuing opposition from governments. Many of the most outspoken labor activists were artisans struggling to survive in the new industrializing climate. They were attracted at first by the ideas of former printer Pierre-Joseph Proudhon (1809–1865). In the 1840s, Proudhon proclaimed, "Property is theft," suggesting that property ownership robbed people of their rightful share of the earth's benefits. He opposed the centralized state and proposed that society be organized instead around natural groupings of men in artisans' workshops. (Women, he believed, should work in seclusion at home for their husbands' comfort.) These workshops and a central bank crediting each worker for his labor would replace government and would lead to a "mutualist" social organization.

As the nation-state expanded its power, workers were also drawn to **anarchism**, which maintained that the existence of the state was the root of social injustice. According to Russian nobleman and anarchist leader Mikhail Bakunin (1814–1876), the slightest infringement on freedom, especially by the central state and its laws, was unacceptable. Anarchism thus advocated the destruction of all state power. Its appeal grew as government grew in the second half of the nineteenth century.

Political theorist and labor organizer Karl Marx (1818–1883) opposed both mutualism and anarchism. These doctrines, he insisted, were emotional and wrongheaded, lacking the sound, scientific basis of his own theory, subsequently called **Marxism**. Marx's analysis, appearing most notably in *Das Kapital* (*Capital*), adopted the liberal idea, dating back to John Locke in the seventeenth century, that human existence was defined by the necessity to work to fulfill basic needs such as food, clothing, and shelter. Published between 1867 and 1894, *Das Kapital* was based on mathematical calculations of production and profit that would justify Realpolitik for the working classes. Marx held that the fundamental organization of any society, including its politics and culture, derived from the relationships arising from work or production. This idea, known as *materialism*, meant that the foundation of a society rested on class relationships—such as those between serf and medieval lord, slave and master, or worker and capitalist. Marx called the class relationships that developed around work the *mode of production*—for instance, feudalism, slavery, or capitalism. He rejected the liberal focus on individual rights and emphasized instead the unequal class relations caused by those who had taken from workers control of the means of production—that is, the capital, land, tools, or factories that allowed basic human needs to be met.

anarchism: The belief that people should not have government; it was popular among some peasants and workers in the last half of the nineteenth century and the first decades of the twentieth.

Marxism: A body of thought about the organization of production, social inequality, and the processes of revolutionary change as devised by the philosopher and economist Karl Marx.

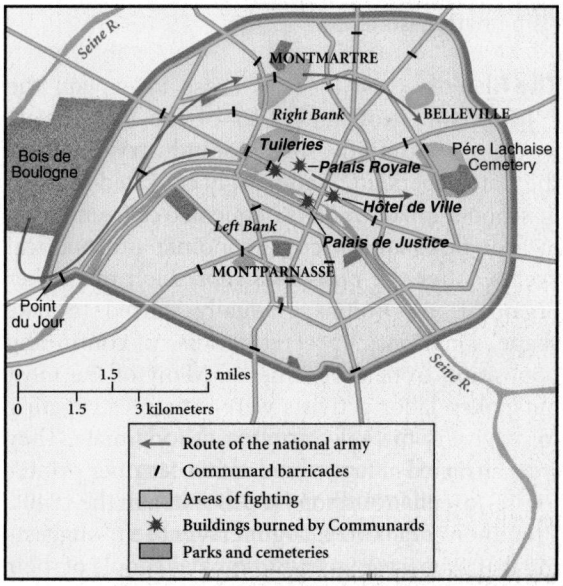

MAP 22.5 The Paris Commune, 1871
The war between the French government and the Paris Commune took place on the streets of Paris and resulted in widespread destruction of major buildings, most notably the Tuileries palace adjacent to the Louvre. Combatants destroyed many government records in what some saw as a civil war; bitterness, like destruction of property, was great on both sides.

Marx, like the politicians around him, took a tough-minded and realistic look at the economy, discarding the romantic views of the utopian socialists. Unlike them, he saw struggle, not warm-hearted cooperation, as the means for bringing about change. Workers' awareness of their oppression would produce class consciousness, he argued, leading them to revolt against their exploiters. Capitalism would be overthrown by these workers—the proletariat—who would then form a socialist society. Marx rejected the liberal Enlightenment view that society was basically harmonious, maintaining instead that social progress could occur only through conflict.

The Paris Commune versus the French State

As the Franco-Prussian War ended, revolution and civil war erupted not only in Paris but also in other French cities—catching the attention of Marx as a sign that his predictions were coming true. As the Prussians laid siege to Paris in the winter of 1870–1871, causing death from starvation and bitter cold, Parisians rose up and demanded new republican liberties, new systems of work, and a more balanced distribution of power between the central government and localities. On March 28, 1871, to counter what they saw as the despotism of the centralized government, they declared themselves a self-governing commune (Map 22.5). One issue behind the unrest was the nation-state's takeover of city life. As urban renovation had displaced tens of thousands of workers, homelessness and general chaos had embittered many Parisians against the state. Citizens in other French municipalities also orga-

The Commune
A sympathetic artist chose a ferocious woman to represent the Paris Commune. He shows her defending the people of France by driving off politicians who had negotiated the disastrous peace treaty with Germany and who wanted to bring back kings and emperors. The artist depicts those selling out the nation as wasps. *(© Bibliothèque nationale, Paris, France/Giraudon/The Bridgeman Art Library International.)*

nized themselves in an attempt to form a decentralized state of independent, confederated communes run by local citizens, not bureaucrats.

In the Paris Commune's two months of existence, its forty-member council, its National Guard, and its many other improvised offices found themselves at cross-purposes. Trying to maintain "communal" instead of "national" values, Parisians quickly developed a wide array of political clubs, local ceremonies, and self-managed workshops. Women workers, for example, banded together to make National Guard uniforms on a cooperative rather than a for-profit basis. Beyond liberal political equality, the Commune proposed to liberate the worker and ensure "the absolute equality of women laborers." Thus, a *commune*—in contrast to a *republic*—was meant to bring about social revolution. Communards, however, often disagreed on how to change society. Mutualism, anticlericalism, feminism, socialism, and anarchism were but a few of the proposed routes to social justice.

In the meantime, the provisional government that succeeded the defeated Napoleon III struck back to reinstitute national order. It quickly stamped out similar uprisings in other French cities. On May 21, the army entered Paris. In a week of fighting, both Communards and the army set the city ablaze (the Communards did so to slow the progress of government troops) and both sides executed hostages. Ultimately, the well-supplied national army won. In the wake of victory, the army shot tens of thousands of citizens on the streets. Parisian rebels, one citizen commented, "deserved no better judge than a soldier's bullet."

In an age of growing national power, the Communards had promoted a kind of antistate in an age of rising state power. Soon a different interpretation of the Commune emerged: it was the work of the *pétroleuse* ("woman incendiary")—a case of frenzied women running amok through the streets. While revolutionary men became heroes in the history books, writers were soon blaming the burning of Paris on women—"shameless slatterns, half-naked women, who kindled courage and breathed life into arson."

Defeat in the Franco-Prussian War, the rise of the Paris Commune, and the civil war were all horrendous blows to the French state. Key to restoring order in France after 1870 were instilling family virtues, fortifying religion, and claiming that the

Commune had resulted from the disorder women caused when they left the domestic sphere to influence politics. Karl Marx disagreed: he analyzed the Commune as a class struggle of workers attacking the propertied capitalists. The centralized state grew larger, in his mind, to protect the interests of those wealthy citizens alone. In the struggle against the Commune, the nation-state once again showed its strengthening muscle. Executions and deportations by the thousands followed, and fear of workers spread across Europe.

REVIEW QUESTION How did Europe's expanding nation-states attempt to impose social order within and beyond Europe, and what resistance did they face?

The Culture of Social Order

Artists and writers of the mid-nineteenth century had complex reactions to the state's expanding reach and the economic growth that sustained it. After 1848, many artists and writers criticized the resulting political repression as well as—paradoxically—the extension of the right to vote to working-class men. They saw daily life as filled with commercial values and organized by mindless officials. Ordinary people no longer appeared heroic, as they had during the revolutionary years. "How tired I am of the ignoble workman, the inept bourgeois, the stupid peasant, and the odious priest," wrote the French novelist Gustave Flaubert. Rejecting romanticism, he described ordinary people in a harsh new style called **realism**. Intellectuals of the time proposed scientific theories that also took a cold, hard look at human life in society and used their new insights to challenge fervent religious belief. Theirs was a detached point of view similar to that applied by statesmen to politics.

The Arts Confront Social Reality

Culture helped the cause of national unity. A hungry reading public devoured biographies of political leaders, past and present, and credited daring heroes with creating the triumphant nation-state. As the development of schooling spread literacy, all classes of readers responded to the mid-nineteenth-century novel and to an increasing number of artistic, scientific, and natural history exhibitions sponsored by the nation-state. While exalting hard-headed heroes of war and peace, citizens came to appreciate the artistic style called realism and, more generally, to embrace the shared national heritage they had begun learning about in school.

The Realist Novel In response to the craving for realism—that is, true-to-life portrayals of society without romantic or idealistic overtones—a well-financed press and commercially minded publishers produced an age of best sellers. Newspapers published the novels of Charles Dickens in serial form, and each installment attracted buyers eager for the latest plot twist. Drawn from contemporary English society, Dickens's characters included starving orphans, grasping lawyers, greedy bankers, and ruthless opportunists. *Hard Times* (1854) depicts the grinding poverty and ill health of workers alongside the heartlessness of businessmen. Novelist **George Eliot** (the pen name of Mary Ann Evans) deeply probed private, real-life dilemmas in *The Mill on the Floss* (1860) and *Middlemarch* (1871–1872). Describing rural society—high and low—Eliot allowed her readers to see one another's predicaments, wherever they lived. She knew the pain of ordinary life from her own experience: despite her fame, she was a social outcast because she lived with a married man. Popular novels that showed a hard reality helped form a shared culture among people in distant parts of a nation much as state institutions did.

French writers also scorned dreams of utopian, trouble-free societies and ideal beauty. Gustave Flaubert's novel *Madame Bovary* (1857) tells the story of a doctor's wife who longs to escape her provincial surroundings. Filled with romantic fantasies, she has two love affairs to escape her boredom, becomes hopelessly indebted buying gifts for her lovers, and commits suicide by swallowing arsenic. *Madame Bovary* scandalized French society with its frank picture of women's sexuality, but it attracted a wide readership. Poet Charles-Pierre Baudelaire, called satanic by his critics, wrote explicitly about sex. In his 1857 collection, *Les Fleurs du mal* (*Flowers of Evil*), he expressed drug- and alcohol-induced passions—some focused on the brown body of his

realism: An artistic style that arose in the mid-nineteenth century and was dedicated to depicting society realistically without romantic or idealistic overtones.

George Eliot: The pen name of English novelist Mary Ann Evans (1819–1880), who described the harsh reality of many ordinary people's lives in her works.

African mistress — and spun out visions that critics condemned as perverse. French authorities brought charges of obscenity against both Flaubert and Baudelaire. At issue was social and artistic order: "Art without rules is no longer art," maintained the prosecutor.

During the era of Alexander II's Great Reforms, Russian writers debated whether western European values were harming Russian culture. Adopting one viewpoint, Ivan Turgenev created a powerful novel of Russian life, *Fathers and Sons* (1862), a story of nihilistic children rejecting not only parental authority but also their parents' spiritual values in favor of science and facts. Fyodor Dostoevsky, in contrast, portrayed nihilists as dark, ridiculous, and neurotic. His novels made Turgenev look like a soft-headed romantic. The highly intelligent characters in Dostoevsky's *Crime and Punishment* (1866) are personally tormented and condemned to lead absurd, even criminal lives. Dostoevsky used antiheroes to emphasize spirituality and traditional Russian values but added a "realistic" spin by planting such values in ordinary, often seedy people. Just as people were drawn together by the innovations of the nation-state, the Russian public was drawn together in discussing these novels and the issues they raised about Russian identity.

Painting While writers of realism depended on sales to thousands of readers, painters usually depended on government support. Leaders such as Prince Albert of Great Britain actively patronized the arts and purchased works for official collections and for themselves. Having their artwork chosen for display at government-sponsored exhibitions was another way for artists to earn a living. Officially appointed juries selected works of art to be exhibited and then chose prizewinners from among them. Hundreds of thousands from all social classes attended, though not all could afford to buy the art.

After the revolutions of 1848, artists began rejecting the romantic idealizing of ordinary folk or grand historic events even though government purchasers continued to favor these topics. Instead, painters like Gustave Courbet portrayed groaning laborers at backbreaking work because, as he stated, an artist should "never permit sentiment to overthrow logic." The renovated city, artists found, had become a visual spectacle; its wide new boulevards served as a stage on which urban residents performed. *Universal Exhibition* (1867) by Édouard Manet used the world's fair of 1867 as its background; figures from all social classes promenaded in the foreground, gazing at the Paris scene and observing one another to learn correct modern behavior. Manet also broke with romantic conventions of the nude. His *Olympia* (1865) depicts a white courtesan lying on her bed, attended by a black woman (see the illustration on page 750). This disregard for the classical tradition of showing women in mythical or idealized settings was too much for the critics: "A sort of female gorilla," one wrote of *Olympia*, as debate raged. Shocking at first, graphic portrayals that shattered romantic illusions were a feature of realism and the subject of discussion among a broad public.

Opera Unlike most of the visual arts, opera was commercially profitable, accessible to most classes of society, and thus an effective means of reaching the nineteenth-century public. Verdi used musical theater to contrast noble ideals with the deadly effects of power and the lure of passion with the need for social order. The German Richard Wagner, the most musically innovative composer of the era, hoped to revolutionize opera by fusing music and drama to arouse the audience's fear, awe, and engagement with his productions. A gigantic cycle of four operas, *The Ring of the Nibelungen* reshaped ancient German myths into a modern, nightmarish story of a world doomed by its obsessive pursuit of money and power and saved only through unselfish love. His opera *The Mastersingers of Nuremberg* (*Die Meistersinger von Nürnberg*), composed between 1862 and 1867, was a tribute to German culture. The piece was said to be implicitly anti-Semitic because of its rejection of influences other than German ones in the arts. Wagner's flair for publicity and musical innovation made him a major force in philosophy, politics, and the arts across Europe. To his fellow citizens, however, his operas stood for Germany.

Age of Great Books

1851	Auguste Comte, *System of Positive Politics*
1852	Harriet Beecher Stowe, *Uncle Tom's Cabin*
1854	Charles Dickens, *Hard Times*
1857	Gustave Flaubert, *Madame Bovary*; Charles Baudelaire, *Les Fleurs du mal*
1859	Charles Darwin, *On the Origin of Species*; John Stuart Mill, *On Liberty*
1862	Ivan Turgenev, *Fathers and Sons*
1866	Fyodor Dostoevsky, *Crime and Punishment*
1867	Karl Marx, *Das Kapital*
1869	John Stuart Mill, *The Subjection of Women*
1871–1872	George Eliot, *Middlemarch*

Daumier, *The Burden*
Artists painted stark images of ordinary people as they struggled to survive in an industrializing age. Despite romantic views of a secluded separate sphere for women that was protected from life's realities, the majority of women hardly enjoyed such an existence, as shown by this depiction of a weighted-down working woman and her child. Daumier was one of the artists who captured that reality. *(National Gallery, Prague, Czech Republic/photo by Erich Lessing/Art Resource, NY.)*

A Realist View of the Nude
Manet's *Olympia* (1865) was one of the most shocking works of art of its day. The central woman is not glamorously dressed or posed erotically; rather, she stares candidly and boldly at the viewer. The black maid offers the woman—obviously a courtesan—flowers from an admirer. This scene was far too modern in its style and subject matter for most critics. *(Musée d'Orsay, Paris, France/Giraudon/The Bridgeman Art Library International.)*

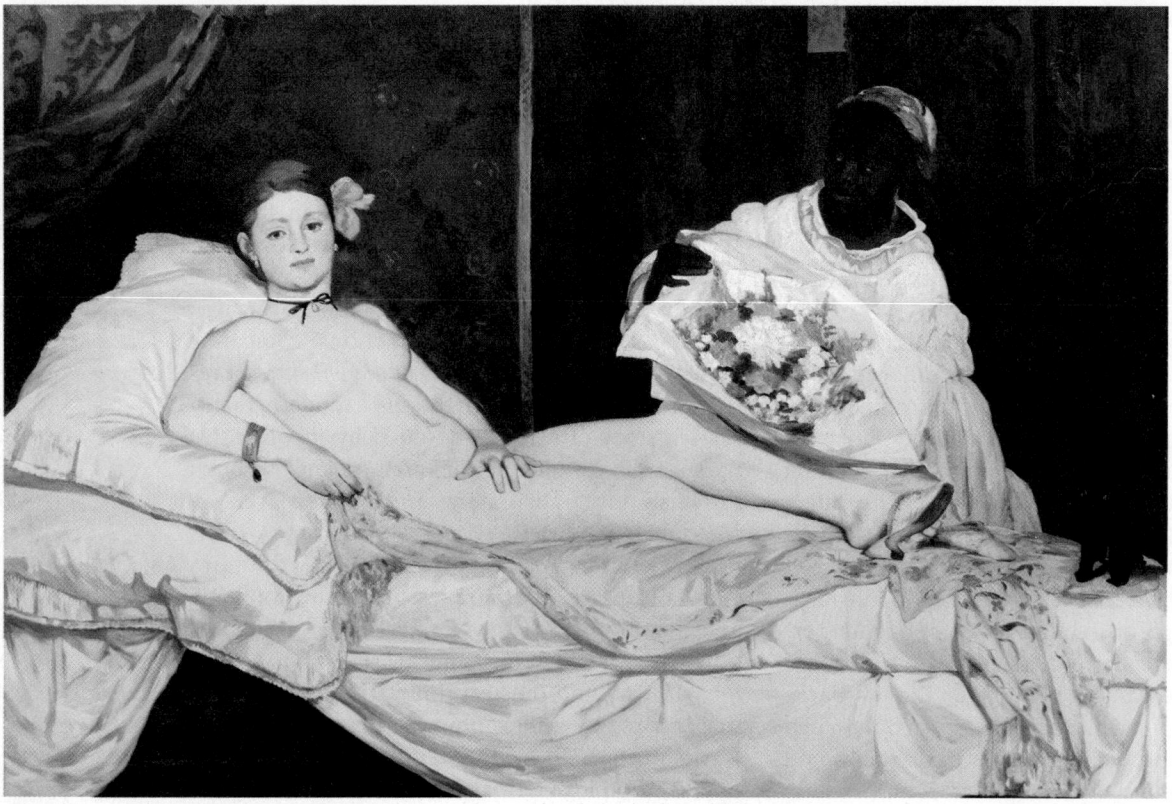

All of the arts, no matter how controversial, shaped the cultural attitudes of the decades 1850–1870. Employing the realist values of the nation builders, the arts provided visions that helped unite isolated individuals into a public with a shared, if debated, cultural experience. Artists both implicitly (like George Eliot) and more explicitly (like Richard Wagner) promoted nation building even as they experimented with new forms.

Religion and National Order

The expansion of state power set the stage for clashes over the role of organized religion in the nation-state. Should religion have the same hold on government and public life as in the past, thus competing with loyalty to the nation? In the 1850s, many politicians supported religious institutions and attended public church rituals because they were another source of order. Simultaneously, some nation builders, intellectuals, and economic liberals came to reject the religious worldview of established churches, particularly Roman Catholicism, as harmful to the nation because it was based in faith, not reason. Bismarck was one of those who believed that religious loyalties slowed the growth of nationalist sentiment.

Bismarck mounted a full-blown **Kulturkampf** ("culture war") against religion. The German government expelled the Jesuits from Germany in 1872, increased state power over the clergy in Prussia in 1873, and introduced a civil ceremony as an obligatory part of marriage in 1875. Bismarck had bragged, "I am the master of Germany in all but name," but he miscalculated his ability to manipulate politics. The pope fought back, sending a public letter to bishops to resist Bismarck's attack: "One must obey God more than men," he ordered. German Catholics rebelled against policies of religious repression as part of nation building, and even conservative Protestants thought Bismarck wrongheaded in attacking religion. Competition between church and state for power and influence heated up in the age of Realpolitik.

Catholic Reaction The Catholic church felt assaulted by the spread across Europe of rational and scientific thought that appeared to be replacing religious faith. It saw nation building in Italy and Germany as competition for people's traditional loyalty to Catholicism. In addition, nation builders had extended liberal rights to Jews, whom many Christians considered enemies. Attacking changing values, Pope Pius IX issued *The Syllabus of Errors* (1864), which found fault "with progress, with liberalism, and with modern civilization." In 1870, the First Vatican Council approved the dogma of papal infallibility. This teaching proclaimed that the pope spoke divinely revealed truth on issues of morality and faith. Eight years later, a new pope, Leo XIII, began reconciling the church to modern politics by encouraging up-to-date scholarship in Catholic institutes and universities and by accepting aspects of representative democracy. Leo's ideas marked a dramatic turn, ending the Kulturkampf between church and state and making it easier for the faithful to be both Catholic and patriotic.

Religion continued to have powerful popular appeal, but the place of organized religion in society was changing. While many in the upper and middle classes and most of the peasantry remained faithful, church attendance declined among workers and artisans. There was a religious gender gap, too. Women's spiritual beliefs became more intense, with both Roman Catholic and Russian Orthodox women's religious orders increasing in size and number; men, by contrast, were falling away from religious devotion. Many urban Jews abandoned religious practices and assimilated instead to secular, national cultures. The social composition of the faithful had come to take a distinctly different shape from the days when religion included everyone.

In 1854, the pope's announcement of the doctrine of the Immaculate Conception (stating that Mary, alone among all humans, had been born without original sin) was followed by an outburst of popular religious fervor, especially among women. In 1858, a young peasant girl, Bernadette Soubirous, began having visions of the Virgin Mary at Lourdes in southern France. In these visions, Mary told Soubirous to drink from the ground, at which point a spring appeared. Crowds, mostly of women, flocked to Lourdes, believing that its waters could cure their ailments. In 1867, less than ten years later, a new railroad line to Lourdes enabled millions of pilgrims to visit the shrine on church-organized trips. The Catholic church thus showed that it, too, could use such modern means as railroads, shopping centers, and medical verifications of miraculous cures to make the religious experience more up-to-date. Traditional institutions like churches began taking steps to make themselves as effective as the nation-state.

Kulturkampf: Literally, "culture war"; a term used in the 1870s by German chancellor Otto von Bismarck to describe his fight to weaken the power of the Catholic church.

The Challenge from Natural Science

At about the time of Soubirous's vision, the English naturalist **Charles Darwin** (1809–1882) published *On the Origin of Species* (1859). In this book and in later writings, Darwin argued that life had taken shape over countless millions of years before humans existed and that human life was but the result of this slow development, called evolution. For many, this theory directly challenged the Judeo-Christian dogma that humanity was the unique creation of God. Instead of God miraculously bringing the universe and all life into being in six days as described in the Bible, Darwin held that life developed from lower forms through a primal battle for survival and through the sexual selection of mates — a process he called natural selection. A respectable Victorian gentleman, Darwin shockingly announced in later writing that the Bible gave a "manifestly false history of the world." Darwin's theories also undermined certain liberal, secular beliefs. Enlightenment principles, for example, had not only glorified nature as tranquil and noble but also viewed human beings as essentially rational. The theory of natural selection, in which the fittest survive, suggested a different kind of human society, one composed of warlike individuals and groups constantly fighting one another to triumph over hostile surroundings.

Charles Darwin: The English naturalist (1809–1882) who popularized the theory of evolution by means of natural selection and thereby challenged the biblical story of creation.

Darwin's findings and other innovative biological research placed religious views of reproduction under attack. Working with pea plants in his monastery garden in the 1860s, the Austrian monk Gregor Mendel (1822–1884) discovered the principles of heredity, from which the science of genetics later developed. Investigation into the female reproductive cycle led German scientists to discover the principle of spontaneous ovulation — the automatic release of the egg by the ovary independent of sexual intercourse. This discovery caused theorists to conclude that men had strong sexual drives because reproduction depended on their

"Gentlemen, We Are Descended from Monkeys," Spain, Late Nineteenth Century

Darwin's scientific ideas aroused anger, admiration, and even mirth, as shown in this engraving some decades after the publication of his major works. As you consider this image, what message would you say the artist is trying to convey about evolution? *(The Art Archive / Bibliothèque des Arts Décoratifs / Alfredo Dagli Orti.)*

sexual arousal. In contrast, the spontaneous release of the egg each month independent of arousal indicated that women were passive and lacked sexual feeling.

Many other ideas disturbed the status quo. Even before Darwin, the influential writer Herbert Spencer (1820–1903) had written that the "unfit" should be allowed to perish in the name of progress—thus challenging the biblical teaching that the poor were valued. On these grounds Spencer opposed public education and any other attempt to soften the harshness of the struggle for existence. Darwin continued this line of argument when he claimed that white European men in the nineteenth century were wealthier and better because more highly evolved than white women or people of color. Despite recognizing a common ancestor for all humans, Darwin held that people of color, or "lower races," were far behind whites in intelligence and civilization. As for women, one could observe that they were in a lower state because any individual man achieved "a higher eminence in whatever he takes up." A school of thought known as Social Darwinism grew out of Darwin's and Spencer's ideas. In the years to come, Social Darwinists used their own version of evolutionary theory to lobby against traditional Christian charity and fairness and instead to promote racist, sexist, and other discriminatory policies as a way of strengthening the nation-state.

From the Natural Sciences to Social Science

In an age influenced by Realpolitik, Darwin's revolutionary thought was part of a quest to find alternatives to the idea that the social order was created by God. French thinker Auguste Comte (1798–1857) developed **positivism**—a theory claiming that careful study of facts would generate accurate and useful, or "positive," laws of society. Comte's *System of Positive Politics, or Treatise on Sociology* (1851) proposed that social scientists construct knowledge of the political order as they would an understanding of the natural world—that is, through observation and objective study. This idea inspired people to believe they could solve the problems resulting from economic and social changes. To accomplish this goal, tough-minded reformers founded study groups and scientifically oriented associations to dig up social facts such as statistics on poverty or the conditions of working-class life. Comte encouraged women's participation in reform because he deemed "womanly" compassion and love as fundamental to social harmony as scientific public policy was. Positivism led not only to women's increased public activism but also to the development of the social sciences in this period. Sociology was primary among the influential new disciplines that brought science and a new realism to the study of human society.

The celebrated English philosopher John Stuart Mill (1806–1873) used Comte's theories to advocate widespread reform and mass education. In his political treatise *On Liberty* (1859), Mill advocated the improvement of society generally, but he also expressed concern that superior people not be brought down by the will of the masses. Influenced not only by Comte but also by his wife, Harriet Taylor Mill, he argued for women's rights and introduced a woman suffrage bill into the House of Commons after her death. The bill's defeat led Mill to publish *The Subjection of Women* (1869), a work summarizing his studies with his wife. Translated into many languages and influential in eastern Europe, Scandinavia, and the Americas, *The Subjection of Women* showed the family as a despotic institution, lacking modern values such as rights and freedom. Mill called women's cheerful obedience in marriage a sham. To make a woman appear "not a forced slave, but a willing one," he said, she was trained from childhood not to value her own talent and independence but to welcome her own "submission" and "control" by men. Critiquing the century's basic beliefs about women's inferiority, *The Subjection of Women* became an internationally celebrated guide for a growing movement committed to obtaining basic rights for women.

The progressive side of Mill's social thought was soon lost in a flood of Social Darwinist theories and became one among several visions of social order believed to be scientific and thus true. The theories of Mill, Comte, Darwin, and others influenced later national debates over policy in the West. Inspired by the social sciences, policymaking came to rely on statistics and fact-gathering to produce realistic appraisals for the purpose of building strong, unified nations.

positivism: A theory developed in the mid-nineteenth century that the study of facts would generate accurate, or "positive," laws of society and that these laws could, in turn, help in the formulation of policies and legislation.

REVIEW QUESTION How did cultural expression and scientific and social thought help produce the hardheaded and realistic values of the mid-nineteenth century?

Conclusion

Throughout modern history, the development of nation-states has been neither inevitable nor uniform nor peaceful. This was especially true in the nineteenth century, when ambitious politicians, shrewd monarchs, and determined bureaucrats used a variety of methods and policies to transform very different countries into effective nation-states. Nation building was most dramatic in Germany and Italy, where states unified through military force and where people of opposing political opinions ultimately agreed that national unity should be the primary goal. Compelled by military defeat to shake off centuries of tradition, the Austrian and Russian monarchs instituted reforms as a way of keeping their systems in place. The Habsburg Empire became a dual monarchy, an arrangement that gave the Hungarians virtual home rule and raised the level of disunity. Reforms in Russia left the authoritarian monarchy intact and only partially transformed the social order.

After decades of romantic fervor, no-nonsense realism in politics—Realpolitik—became a much touted principle. Proponents of realism such as Darwin and Marx developed theories disturbing to those who maintained an Enlightenment faith in social and political harmony. Realist novels and artworks jarred polite society, and, like the operas of Verdi, portrayed dilemmas of the times. Growing government administrations set policies that were meant to bring order but often brought disorder, including the destruction of entire neighborhoods and violence toward people in far-off lands. In the long term, schooling taught the lower classes to be orderly citizens, and urban renewal ultimately improved cities and public health to complement nation building.

Objections arose to the expanding power of the nation-state. The Indian Rebellion of 1857 against Britain and the Paris Commune of 1871 against the French state were but two examples where violent actions raised difficult questions about nation-building methods. How far should the power of the state extend in both domestic and international affairs? Would nationalism be a force for war or for peace? In the face of state power, would ordinary people have any say in their destiny? As these issues ripened, the next decades saw extraordinary economic advances and an unprecedented surge in Europe's global power—much of it the result of successes in nation building.

FOR FURTHER EXPLORATION

- **For additional primary-source material from this period**, see *Sources of the Making of the West*, Fourth Edition.
- **For Web sites, images, and documents related to topics in this chapter**, visit *Make History* at bedfordstmartins.com/hunt.

Europe and the Mediterranean, 1871

European nation-states consolidated their power by building unified state structures and by developing the means for the diverse peoples within their borders to become socially and culturally integrated. Nation-states were also rapidly expanding outside their boundaries, extending their economic and political reach. North Africa and the Middle East—parts of the declining Ottoman Empire—particularly appealed to European governments because of their resources and their potential for further European settlement. They offered a gateway to the rest of the world. | **Compare this map of Europe with that from two decades earlier (page 717) to explain the progress of nation building. What aspects of nation building do not appear on this map?**

Chapter 22 Review

Online Study Guide bedfordstmartins.com/hunt

Key Terms and People

In the grid below, identify the term or person and explain its historical significance. (To do this exercise online, go to bedfordstmartins.com/hunt.)

Term	Who or What & When	Why It Matters
Realpolitik (p. 721)		
Alexander II (p. 725)		
Florence Nightingale (p. 725)		
mir (p. 727)		
Russification (p. 728)		
nation-state (p. 729)		
Camillo di Cavour (p. 730)		
Otto von Bismarck (p. 732)		
dual monarchy (p. 736)		
Pan-Slavism (p. 736)		
anarchism (p. 746)		
Marxism (p. 746)		
realism (p. 748)		
George Eliot (p. 748)		
Kulturkampf (p. 751)		
Charles Darwin (p. 752)		
positivism (p. 753)		

Review Questions

1. What were the main results of the Crimean War?
2. What role did warfare play in the various nineteenth-century nation-building efforts?
3. How did Europe's expanding nation-states attempt to impose social order within and beyond Europe, and what resistance did they face?
4. How did cultural expression and scientific and social thought help produce the hard-headed and realistic values of the mid-nineteenth century?

Making Connections

1. What were the main methods of nation building in the mid-nineteenth century, and how did they differ from those of state building in the early modern period?
2. How did realism in social thought break with Enlightenment values?
3. In what ways did religion emerge as an issue (both within and outside Europe) during the course of nation building?
4. How was the Paris Commune related to earlier revolutions in France? How did it differ from them? How was it related to nation building?

Important Events

Date	Event	Date	Event
1850s–1860s	Positivism, Darwinism become influential	1867	Second Reform Bill in England; Austro-Hungarian monarchy
1850s–1870s	Realism in the arts	1868	Meiji Restoration begins in Japan
1853–1856	Crimean War	1869	Suez Canal opens
1857	British-led forces suppress Indian Rebellion	1869–1871	Women's colleges founded at Cambridge University
1861	Victor Emmanuel declared king of a unified Italy; abolition of serfdom in Russia	1870–1871	Franco-Prussian War
1861–1865	U.S. Civil War	1871	German Empire proclaimed at Versailles; self-governing Paris Commune established

- Consider three events: **Positivism, Darwinism become influential (1850s–1860s)**, **Realism in the arts (1850s–1870s)**, and **German Empire proclaimed at Versailles (1871)**. How is this era's quest for practicality, order and stability shown in each of these events?

SUGGESTED REFERENCES

Nation building took many forms in the nineteenth century, including wars, urban improvement, mythmaking, and the development of scientific and realistic attitudes—all of these themes are found in the books below.

Barnes, David S. *The Great Stink of Paris and the Nineteenth-Century Struggle against Filth and Germs*. 2006.

Berra, Tim M. *Charles Darwin: The Concise Story of an Extraordinary Man*. 2009.

Blackbourn, David. *The Conquest of Nature: Water, Landscape, and the Making of Modern Germany*. 2006.

Gross, Michael B. *The War against Catholicism: Liberalism and the Anti-Catholic Imagination in Nineteenth-Century Germany*. 2005.

Heretz, Leonid. *Russia on the Eve of Modernity: Popular Religion and Traditional Culture under the Last Tsars*. 2008.

Kaufman, Suzanne. *Consuming Visions: Mass Culture and the Lourdes Shrine*. 2005.

Parker, Kate, and Julia Shone, eds. *The Austro-Hungarian Dual Monarchy, 1867–1918*. 2008.

Reid, Brian Holden. *The Civil War and the Wars of the Nineteenth Century*. 2006.

Riall, Lucy. *Garibaldi: The Invention of a Hero*. 2007.

Roy, Tapti. *The Raj of the Rani*. 2007.

*Seacole, Mary. *Wonderful Adventures of Mrs. Seacole in Many Lands*. 1857.

Unowsky, Daniel L. *The Pomp and Politics of Patriotism: Imperial Celebrations in Habsburg Austria, 1848–1916*. 2005.

The Victorian Web: http://www.victorianweb.org

Wetzel, David. *A Duel of Giants: Bismarck, Napoleon III, and the Origins of the Franco-Prussian War*. 2001.

Wirtschafter, Elise Kimerling. *Russia's Age of Serfdom 1649–1861*. 2008.

*Primary source.

CHAPTER

Empire, Industry, and Everyday Life

23

1870–1890

In the mid-1880s, Frieda von Bülow, a young German woman of aristocratic birth, joined several activist groups interested in promoting German colonial expansion in Africa. Like other women in these pro-imperial organizations, von Bülow was eager to help German settlers—and even some Africans—in East Africa, which Germany was in the process of colonizing. She also met adventurous men such as Carl Peters, a nationalist zealot and leading figure in imperialist circles. As Europeans competed to take over the African continent, von Bülow and Peters headed for Zanzibar and other distant cities not only to conquer them but also to carry on a passionate romance. Once in Africa, von Bülow basked in the freedom from her society's restrictions on women and developed an even stronger sense of German superiority in comparison to local African peoples. For his part, Peters followed his usual pattern of tricking Africans into giving up their lands and bullying them, using guns, rape, and other violence to get his way. Peters seduced one African woman and then had her executed because of her relationship with another man. Though Peters's womanizing caused von Bülow to break up with him, she maintained both her racism and her German nationalism, learning to shoot a gun on behalf of colonial conquest, writing popular novels about empire and white superiority, and setting up a plantation in Southeast Africa.

Von Bülow and Peters were just two of the tens of thousands of Europeans pursuing imperial adventure, as the search for lands to colonize reached a feverish pitch after the 1870s. Those involved in imperialism had a variety of motives and, like Peters, were often swaggering and violent. The rapid expansion of Western takeovers was called the "new imperialism" because the race for empire now aimed at political rather than mere economic power. Europeans had been acquiring global territory since the late

European Immigrants Arriving in New York
This calm image of an immigrant ship arriving in New York harbor hardly captures the emotions the immigrants had (as we know from their letters and diaries) on leaving their communities and facing an unknown life in the United States or other parts of the Western Hemisphere. Many came from agricultural regions and would soon be the labor behind the advance of industry; others would become settlers, driving out Native Americans and thus becoming agents of empire. *(The Granger Collection, New York—All rights reserved.)*

The New Imperialism 761
- Taming the Mediterranean
- The Scramble for Africa
- Acquiring Territory in Asia
- Japan's Imperial Agenda
- The Paradoxes of Imperialism

The Industry of Empire 768
- Industrial Innovation
- Facing Economic Crisis
- Revolution in Business Practices

Imperial Society and Culture 775
- The "Best Circles" and the Expanding Middle Class
- Working People's Strategies
- National Fitness: Reform, Sports, and Leisure
- Artistic Responses to Empire and Industry

The Birth of Mass Politics 783
- Workers, Politics, and Protest
- Expanding Political Participation in Western Europe
- Power Politics in Central and Eastern Europe

fifteenth century; the new imperialism was actually the final gulp in this process. In their rush for empire, Europeans like Frieda von Bülow and Carl Peters worked to control whole societies instead of dominating coastal trade until, by the beginning of the twentieth century, Western nations claimed jurisdiction over vast stretches of the world's surface. Beyond political control, Europeans tried to stamp other continents with European-style place-names, architecture, clothing, languages, and domestic customs. They used culture to secure their empires just as they used it to forge the nation-state.

Marianne North, *Pitcher Plant*
Wealthy Europeans increasingly traveled overseas in the quest for knowledge and adventure. As the West prospered, travel and world tourism did, too. An amateur artist, Marianne North initially gained an audience for her scientific drawings, reports, and specimens only because she traveled in the "best circles." Scientists later prized her drawings, like this one of a pitcher plant. *(Reproduced with the kind permission of the Director and the Board of Trustees, Royal Botanic Gardens, Kew.)*

Millions of people traveled vast distances in the nineteenth century—a time of greatly increased mobility and migration, much of which was made possible by an expansion of industry and colonization. Some migrated temporarily to serve in colonial governments or to find business opportunities. Others relocated permanently within Europe or outside it. In search of a better life, they migrated to Australia and to North and South America. Such migration changed the everyday life of both Europeans and non-Europeans: it uprooted tens of millions of people, disrupted social and family networks, and often inflicted terrible violence on native peoples dislocated by European migrants.

The decades from 1870 to 1890 were also an era of expanding industry in the West. Empire and industry fed on each other as raw materials from conquered areas supplied Western factories and as innovations in weaponry, transportation, medicine, and communication allowed imperialism to thrive. Manufacturing soared in the West as industrialization spread from Britain to central and eastern Europe and brought a continuous new supply of products to the market. A growing appetite for these products, many of them for household consumption, changed the fabric of everyday life for Europeans. New industry attracted people to cities, where common experiences of neighborhood and work life drew them closer together. As they became more educated and enjoyed a mushrooming variety of colonial goods, people learned to take pride in their nations' conquests. Urban workers began demanding greater participation in the political process. Proud Europeans brimmed with confidence and hope, while the grimmer aspects of empire and industrialization played themselves out in distant colonies, urban slums, and declining standards of living in rural areas.

1860s–1890s
Impressionism flourishes in the arts; absorption of Asian influences

1871
Franco-Prussian War ends

1876
British Parliament declares Victoria empress; invention of telephone

1879
Dual Alliance formed between Germany and Austria-Hungary

1860s 1870 1875 1880

1870s–1890s
Vast emigration from Europe continues; the new imperialism

1873
Extended economic recession begins with global impact

1878
Treaty of San Stefano

CHAPTER FOCUS How were imperial conquest and industrial advances related, and how did they affect Western society, culture, and politics in the late nineteenth century?

The New Imperialism

Imperialism surged in the last third of the nineteenth century. Industrial demand for raw materials and heated business rivalry for new markets fueled competition for territory in Africa and Asia, and European nations, the United States, and Japan now aimed to rule sizable portions of the world directly. The British government declared itself an empire in 1876 after taking control of India from the East India Company, and other governments followed the British model. National pride also grew with imperial expansion. "Nations are not great except for the activities they undertake," declared a French advocate of imperialism in 1885. Conquering foreign territory and developing wealth through industry appeared to heap glory on the nation-state. Although some missionaries and reformers involved in the new imperialism aimed to spread Western religions and culture as a benefit to colonized peoples, the expansion of the West increased the subjugation of those peoples, inflicted violence on them, and radically altered their lives.

Taming the Mediterranean

European countries had always viewed the African and Asian shores of the Mediterranean as areas where they could profit through trade and investment. In the late nineteenth century, they aimed for political control of the region as well. Egypt, a convenient and profitable stop on the way to Asia, was an early target. Modernizing rulers had made Cairo into a bustling metropolis with lively commercial and manufacturing enterprises. Egyptians also increased their production of raw materials, such as cotton for European textile mills. Europeans invested heavily in the region, first in ventures such as building the Suez Canal in the 1860s, then in laying thousands of miles of railroad track, improving harbors, creating telegraph systems, and finally and most important, loaning money at exorbitant rates of interest.

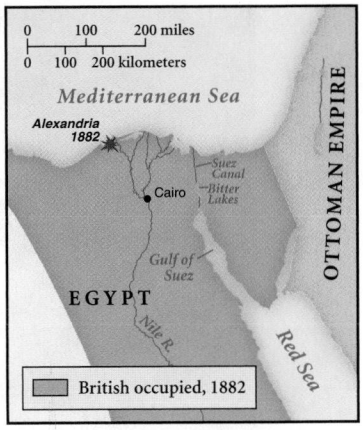

The Suez Canal and British Invasion of Egypt, 1882

In 1879, the British and the French took over the Egyptian treasury, allegedly to guarantee profits from their investments and the repayment of loans. In 1882, they invaded the country with the excuse of squashing Egyptian nationalists who protested the takeover of the treasury. The British next seized control of the government as a whole and forcibly reshaped the Egyptian economy from a system based on multiple crops that maintained the country's self-sufficiency to one that emphasized the production of a few crops—mainly cotton, raw silk, wheat, and rice—that cheaply fed both European manufacturing and the European working classes. Businessmen from the colonial powers, Egyptian landowners, and local merchants profited from these agricultural changes, while the bulk of the rural population barely eked out an existence.

Claiming a need to protect its stake in Algeria, France occupied neighboring Tunisia in 1881. Farther to the east, businessmen from Britain, France, and Germany flooded Asia Minor and the Middle East with cheap goods, driving artisans from their trades and into low-paid work building railroads or processing tobacco. Instead of basing wage rates on gender (as they did at home), Europeans used ethnicity and religion, paying Muslims less than Christians, and Arabs less than other ethnic

1882 Triple Alliance formed between Germany, Austria-Hungary, and Italy; Britain invades Egypt

1884 British Parliament passes the Reform Act, doubling size of male electorate

1885 Invention of workable gasoline engine; formation of Indian National Congress

1891 Construction of Trans-Siberian Railroad begins

1885 1890

1881 Tsar Alexander II assassinated; France occupies Tunisia

1882–1884 Bismarck sponsors social welfare legislation

1884–1885 European nations carve up Africa at Berlin conference

1889 Japan adopts constitution based on European models; socialists meet in Paris and establish Second International

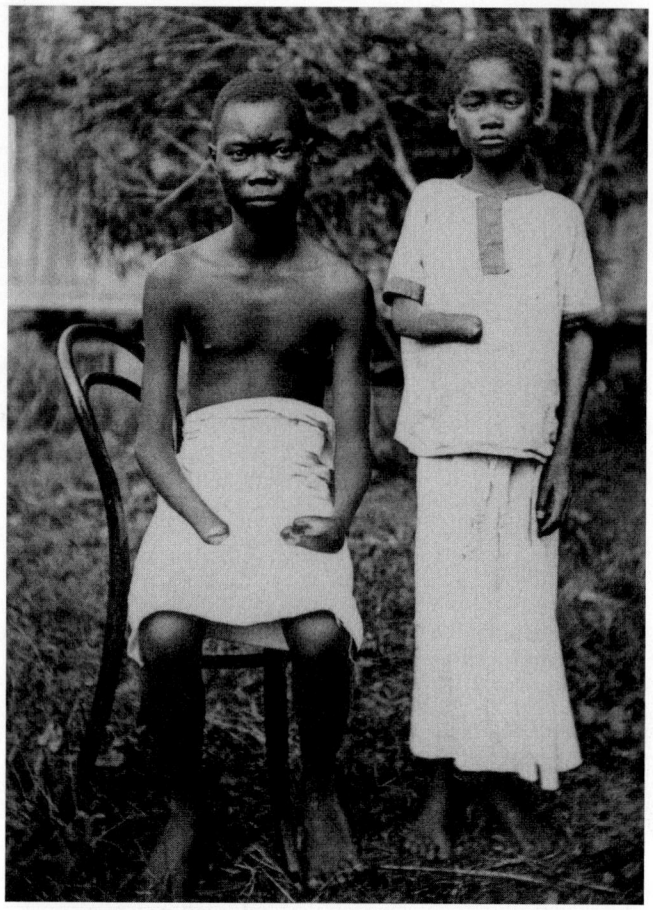

The Violence of Colonization
King Leopold II, ruler of the Belgian Congo, was so greedy and ruthless that his agents squeezed the last drop of rubber and other resources from local peoples. Missionaries reported and photographed such atrocities as the killing of workers whose quotas were even slightly short or the amputation of hands for the same offense. Belgian agents collected amputated hands and sent them to government officials to show Leopold that they were enforcing his kind of discipline. *(Anti-Slavery International.)*

groups. Such practices planted the seeds for anticolonial movements and long-lasting hatred.

The Scramble for Africa

After the British takeover of the Egyptian government, Europeans turned their attention to sub-Saharan Africa. In the past, contact between Europe and Africa had principally involved the trade of African slaves for manufactured goods from around the world. By this time, however, the European slave trade had virtually ended and the Europeans' objective had shifted to acquiring Africa's raw materials, such as palm oil, cotton, metals, diamonds, cocoa, and rubber. Additionally, Britain wanted the southern and eastern coasts of Africa for stopover ports on the route to Asia and its empire in India.

Except for the French conquest of Algeria, Europeans had rarely connected commerce with political control of Africa. Yet in the 1880s, European military forces conquered one African territory after another (Map 23.1). The British, French, Belgians, Portuguese, Italians, and Germans jockeyed to dominate peoples, land, and resources—"the magnificent cake of Africa," as King **Leopold II** of Belgium (r. 1865–1909) put it. Insatiable greed drove Leopold to claim the Congo region of central Africa, initiating competition with France for that territory and inflicting on its peoples unparalleled acts of cruelty (see the illustration on the left). German chancellor Otto von Bismarck, who saw colonies mostly as political bargaining chips, established German control over Cameroon and a section of East Africa, to which Frieda von Bülow and Carl Peters headed. Faced with competition, the British poured millions of pounds into conquering the continent "from Cairo to Cape Town," as the slogan went, and the French cemented their hold on large portions of western Africa.

The scramble for Africa escalated tensions in Europe and prompted Bismarck to call a conference of interested nations at Berlin. The European nations represented at the conference, held in a series of meetings in 1884 and 1885, decided that control of settlements along the African coast guaranteed rights to internal territory. This agreement led to the strictly linear dissection of the continent—a dissection that cut across indigenous boundaries of African culture and ethnic life. The Berlin conference also banned the sale of alcohol and controlled the flow of arms to indigenous peoples. In theory, the meeting was supposed to reduce bloodshed and ambitions for territory in Africa. In reality, the agreement simply accelerated conquest of the continent and left everyone on edge over the threat of more violence. Newspaper accounts depicted the struggle for foreign lands, whetting the popular appetite for more takeovers. Music hall audiences rose to their feet and cheered at the sound of popular songs about imperial heroes of the day.

The lust for conquest had perhaps its greatest effect in southern Africa, where farmers of European descent and immigrant prospectors, rather than military personnel, battled the Xhosa, Zulu, and other African peoples for control of their land. The Dutch had moved into the area in the seventeenth

Leopold II: King of Belgium (r. 1865–1909) who sponsored the takeover of the Congo in Africa, which he ran with great violence against native peoples.

century, but by 1815 the British had gained control. Thereafter, descendants of the Dutch, called Boers (Dutch for "farmers"), and British immigrants joined together in their fight to wrest farmland and mineral resources from local peoples. British businessman and politician Cecil Rhodes, sent to South Africa for his health just as diamonds were being discovered in 1870, cornered the diamond market and claimed a huge amount of African territory hundreds of miles into the interior. His ambition for Britain and for himself was boundless: "I contend that we are the finest race in the world," he

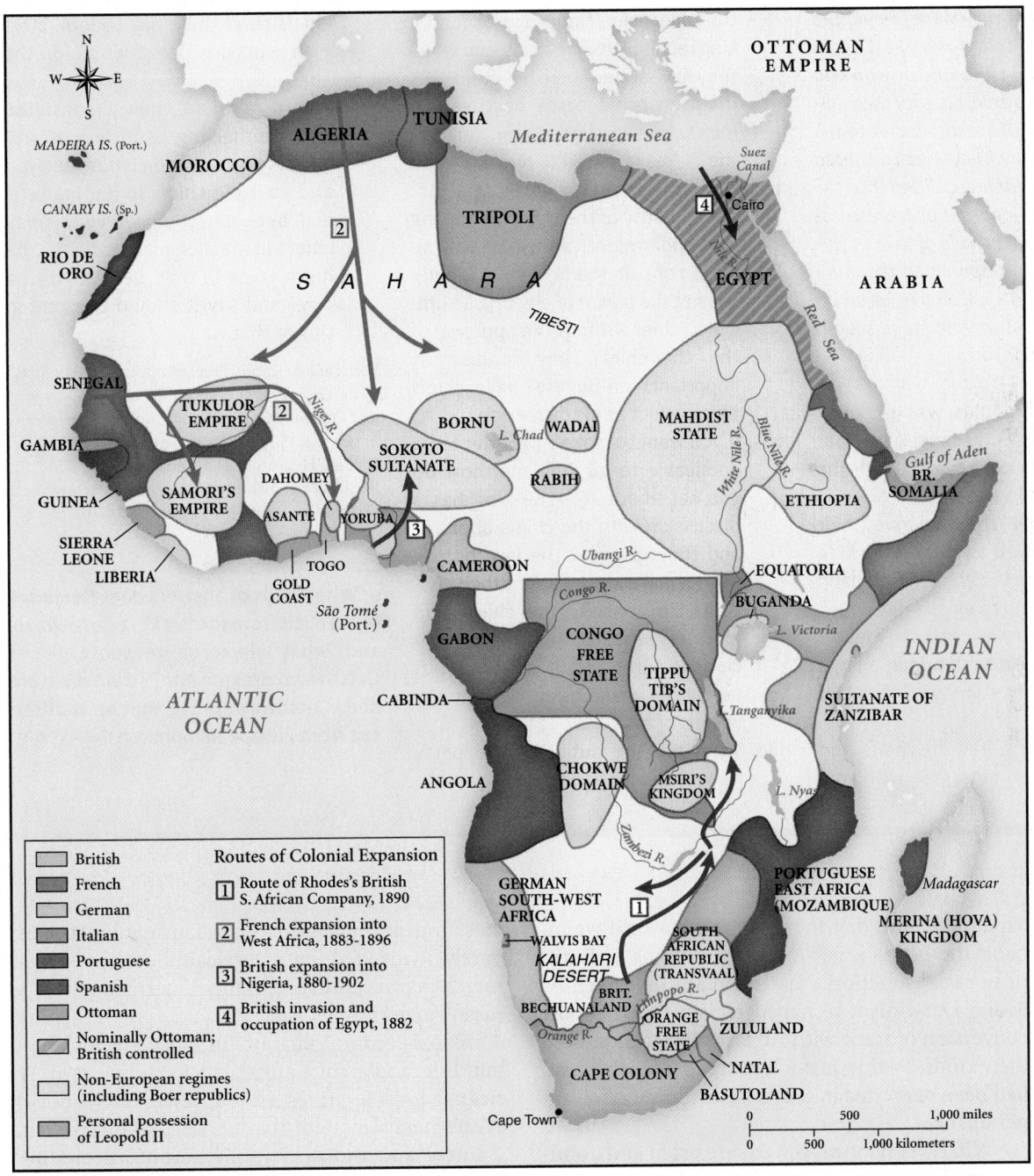

MAP 23.1 Africa, c. 1890

The scramble for Africa entailed a change in European trading practices, which generally had been limited to the coastline. Trying to penetrate economically and rule the interior ultimately resulted in a map of the continent that made sense only to the imperial powers, for it divided ethnic groups and made territorial unities that had nothing to do with Africans' sense of geography or patterns of settlement. This map shows the unfolding of that process and the political and ethnic groupings to be conquered.

DOCUMENT

An African King Describes His Government

The British engaged in bloody warfare against the king of Zulu society, Cetshwayo, on the grounds that they were freeing the Zulu from a cruel tyrant who kept them enslaved. Ultimately, the British won and sent Cetshwayo into exile, but they then subjected him to official questioning as to the nature of his tyranny. They were convinced that the Zulu were far less civilized than the British and utterly ignorant of representative government or the rule of law. In this passage Cetshwayo responds to the questions of the judge, Sir J. D. Barry, at an official hearing in 1881 as the judge sought proof of Zulu barbarism.

144. As king of the Zulus, was all power invested in you, as king, over your subjects?—In conjunction with the chiefs of the land.
145. How did the chiefs derive their power from you as king?—The king calls together the chiefs of the land when he wants to elect a new chief, and asks their advice as to whether it is fit to make such a man a large chief, and if they say "yes" the chief is made.
146. If you had consulted the chiefs, and found they did not agree with you, could you appoint a chief by virtue of your kingship?—In some cases, if the chiefs don't approve of it, the king requires their reasons, and when they have stated them he often gives it up. In other cases he tries the man to see whether he can perform the duties required of him or not.
147. In fact, you have the power to act independently of the chiefs in making an appointment, although you always consult them?—No, the king has not the power of electing an official as chief without the approval of the other chiefs. They are the most important men. But the smaller chiefs he can elect at his discretion. . . .
168. If you want to make a new law, to be applicable to all Zululand, how do you set about it?—The king has a discussion with the chiefs about it, and they give out the law, but he cannot make a law without their consent. He consults the chiefs and gives his reasons, and if they conclude to agree to it, it is the law, but he cannot make a law against the wishes of his chiefs. . . .
180. What are the duties of the petty [lower] chiefs?—They principally superintend work for their superior chiefs, and for the king. The larger chiefs send them out to look after men who are doing work for the king. . . .
183. The people are never consulted about either big or little matters? The only consultation is between you and your big chiefs in big matters, and between you and your small chiefs in smaller matters?—Yes, he has a voice in that; he can go to a chief and say it should be done in this or that way.

Source: *Report and Proceedings with Appendices of the Government Commission on Native Laws and Customs, Cape of Good Hope Parliamentary Paper*, G4, 1883, Part 1, 523–30, excerpted in William H. Worger et al., eds., *Africa and the West: A Documentary History*, 2 vols. (New York: Oxford University Press, 2010) 1:108–9.

Question to Consider

- **What kinds of answers does the judge try to elicit from former king Cetshwayo, and what kinds of responses does Cetshwayo provide him? To what extent does Cetshwayo prove that he is different from European monarchs?**

explained, "and that the more of the world we inhabit the better it is." Although notions of European racial superiority had been advanced before, Social Darwinism reshaped racism to justify the conversion of trade with Africans into conquest of their lands. Within just a few decades, Darwinism had been perverted into a racist justification for imperialism.

Wherever necessary to ensure profit and domination, Europeans either destroyed African economic and political systems or transformed them into instruments of their rule. A British governor of the West African region known as the Gold Coast put the matter succinctly in 1886: the British would "rule the country as if there were no inhabitants." Indeed, most Europeans considered Africans barely civilized, despite the wealth local rulers and merchants accumulated in their international trade in raw materials and slaves, and despite individual Africans' accomplishments in fabric dyeing, road building, and architecture (see Document, "An African King Describes His Government," above). Westerners claimed that Africans—unlike the Chinese and Indians, whom Europeans credited with a scientific and artistic heritage—were capable only of manual labor. They felt this justified their confiscation of land from Africans, who were then forced to work for them to pay European-imposed taxes. Agriculture to support families, often performed by women and slaves, declined in

Nigerian Brass Bust
This brass depiction of an *oni* or king in one region of what is now Nigeria shows the sophisticated skill of African artists. Although Westerners collected such statuary and proudly displayed it, many considered themselves to be far superior to Africans, whom they viewed as virtually without cultural talent and thus useful only for hard physical labor. *(The Granger Collection, New York—All rights reserved.)*

favor of mining and farming cash crops. Men were made to leave their homes to work in mines or to build railroads. Family and community networks, though upset by the new arrangements, helped support Africans during this upheaval in everyday life.

Acquiring Territory in Asia

Britain justified its invasion of African countries as strategically necessary for acquiring stopover ports to resupply Asian-bound ships and thus help to preserve its control over India's quarter of a billion people. In reality the expansion of imperial power from the 1870s on was occurring around the world, not just Africa. Much of Asia, with India as the centerpiece, was integrated into Western empires. At the same time, resistance to outside domination was also growing. Discriminated against but educated, the Indian elite in 1885 founded the Indian National Congress. Some of its members accepted British liberalism in economic and social policy, welcoming opportunities for trade, education, and social advancement. Others went further, however, challenging Britain's right to rule India at all. In the next century, the Congress would develop into a mass movement.

To the east, British military forces took control of the Malay peninsula in 1874 and of the interior of Burma in 1885. In both areas, political instability often threatened secure trade. The British depended on the region's tin, oil, rice, teak, and rubber as well as its access to the numerous interior trade routes of China. British troops guaranteed the order necessary to expand railroads for more efficient export of raw materials and the development of Western systems of communication. The British also built factories and hoped to use its Burmese and Malaysian base to expand industrially into China.

The British added to their holdings in Asia partly to counter Russian and French annexations. Since 1865, Russia had been absorbing the small Muslim states of central Asia, including provinces of Afghanistan (see Map 23.2). Besides extending into the Ottoman Empire, Russian tentacles reached into Persia, India, and China, often encountering British competition. The Trans-Siberian Railroad allowed

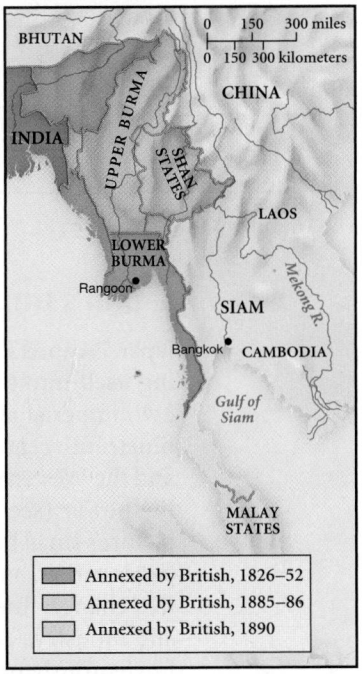

British Colonialism in the Malay Peninsula and Burma, 1826–1890

MAP 23.2 Expansion of Russia in Asia, 1865–1895

Russian administrators and military men continued enlarging Russia, bringing in Asians of many different ethnicities, ways of life, and religions. Land-hungry peasants in western Russia followed the path of expansion into Siberia and Muslim territories to the south. In some cases they drove native peoples from their lands, but in others they settled unpopulated frontier areas. As in all cases of imperial expansion, local peoples resisted any expropriation of their livelihood, while the central government tried various policies for integration.

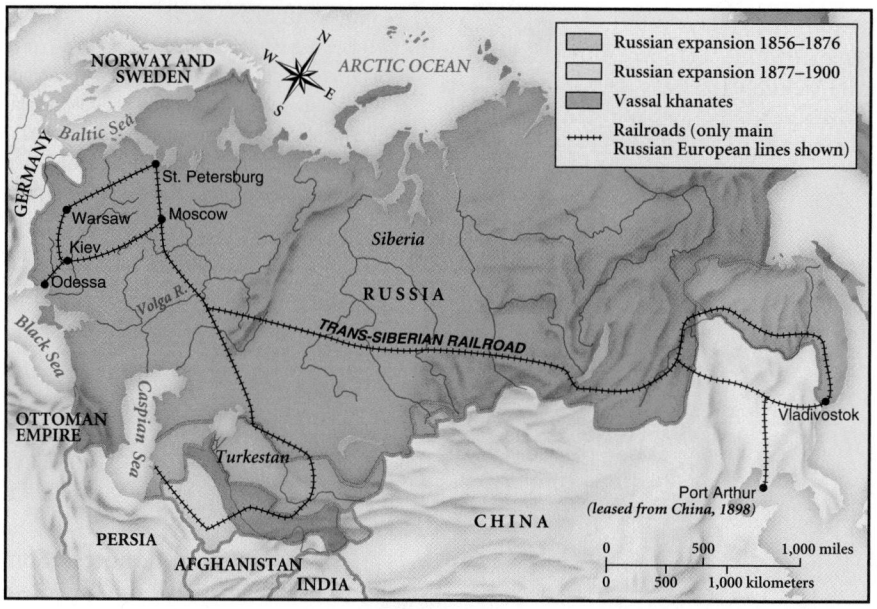

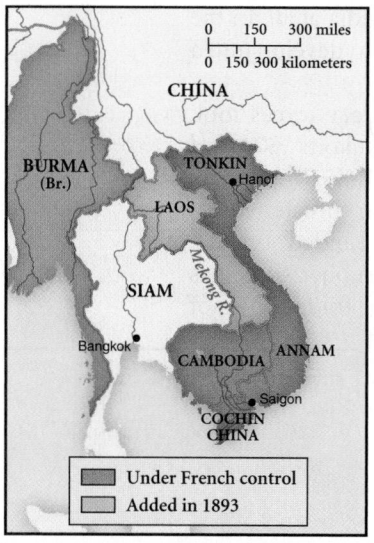

The Union of Indochina, 1893

Russia to begin integrating Siberia—considered a distant colony in the eighteenth and early nineteenth centuries. Hundreds of thousands of hungry peasants moved to the region, and trade routes to cities in the west expanded. France meanwhile used the threat of military action to negotiate favorable treaties with Indochinese rulers, creating the Union of Indochina from the ancient states of Cambodia, Tonkin, Annam, and Cochin China in 1887 (the latter three now constitute Vietnam). Laos was added to Indochina in 1893.

Japan's Imperial Agenda

Japan escaped European rule by rapidly transforming itself into a modern industrial nation with its own imperial agenda. A Japanese print of the late nineteenth century illustrates both traditional ways and the Western influence behind Japan's burgeoning power (see the illustration on page 767). The picture's small boats might have been rendered centuries earlier, but the steaming locomotive symbolizes change. The Japanese embraced foreign trade and industry. "All classes high and low shall unite in vigorously promoting the economy and welfare of the nation," ran one of the first pronouncements of the Meiji regime that had come to power in 1868. The Japanese government directed the country's turn toward modern industry, and state support led daring innovators like Iwasaki Yataro, founder of the Mitsubishi firm, to develop heavy industries such as mining and shipping. The Japanese sent students, entrepreneurs, and government officials to the West to bring back as much new knowledge as they could. Unlike China, Japan endorsed Western-style modernization in preparation for gaining its own empire.

Change was the order of the day in Japan. Japanese legal scholars, following German models, helped draft a constitution in 1889 that emphasized state power rather than individual rights. Western dress became the rule at the imperial court, and when fire destroyed Tokyo in 1872, a European planner directed the rebuilding in Western architectural style. The Japanese adapted samurai traditions such as spiritual discipline to create a large and technologically modern military. In the 1870s, Japan ordered naval ships from Britain and began conquering adjacent islands, including Okinawa. In the 1880s, it used its new naval strength to begin imposing favorable trade treaties on Korea, preliminary to a more complete takeover on the horizon.

The Paradoxes of Imperialism

Imperialism ignited constant, sometimes heated debate because of its many paradoxes. Although it was meant to make European nations more economically secure, imperialism intensified distrust in international politics and thus threatened everyone. Countries vied with one another for a share of world influence. In securing India's borders, for example, the British faced Russian expansion in Afghanistan and along the borders of China. Imperial competition even made areas of Europe more volatile than ever: Austria-Hungary, Russia, and rival ethnic groups disputed control of the Balkans as the Ottoman Empire's grip weakened in the region.

The Costs and Profits of Empire

Politicians claimed that empire would bring great riches, but the costs of empire were high. Opponents claimed that empire was more costly than profitable to societies as a whole. Britain, for example, spent enormous amounts of tax revenue to maintain its empire even as its industrial lead began to slip. Yet for certain businesses, colonies provided crucial markets and large profits: late in the century, French colonies bought 65 percent of France's exports of soap and 41 percent of its metallurgical exports. Imperialism provided huge numbers of jobs to people in European port cities, but taxpayers in all parts of a nation—whether they benefited or not—paid for colonial armies, increasingly costly weaponry, and administrators.

The Civilizing Mission

To those who opposed colonial expansion as "spending our money on distant adventures," advocates of imperialism pointed out that whites had a "civilizing mission." The French thus taught some of their colonial subjects French language, literature, and history. The emphasis was always on European, not local, culture. In Germany's African colonies, an exam for students in a school run by missionaries asked them to write on "Germany's most important mountains" and "the reign of William I and the wars he waged." The deeds of Africa's great rulers and the accomplishments of its kingdoms disappeared from the curriculum. While Europeans believed in instructing colonial subjects, they did not believe that Africans and Asians were as capable as Europeans of great achievements.

So imperialism's goal of "civilizing" was also in conflict. French advocates argued that their nation "must keep its role as the soldier of civilization." But it was unclear whether imperialism should emphasize soldiering (that is, the conquest and murder of local peoples) or civilizing (the education of local peoples in the European tradition). The French tried both in Indochina, building a legacy of resistance that continued unabated until the mid-twentieth century and another legacy of French culture among the people of that region.

Inferiority and Superiority

The paradoxes of imperialism extended to Europeans' study of other cultures. Western scholars and travelers had long studied Asian and African languages, art, and literature, and had gathered and used botanical and other scientific knowledge. Yet even the best scholars' appreciation of foreign cultures was tinged with bias, misinterpretation, and error. European scholars of Islam characterized Muhammad as an inferior imitation of Jesus, for example. Confident in their cultural superiority, many Europeans considered Asians and Africans as low types, variously characterizing them as lying, lazy, self-indulgent, or irrational. One English official proclaimed that "accuracy is abhorrent to the Oriental mind." At the height of imperialism, such beliefs offered still another justification for conquest: that inferior colonized peoples would ultimately be grateful for what Europe had brought them.

Modernization in Japan

Like the West, Japan bustled with commerce and industry thanks to improved and expanding transportation. Railroads, ships, and a range of new inventions such as the rickshaw speeded goods and individuals within cities, across the country, and ultimately to new, foreign destinations. The Japanese traveled widely to learn about ongoing technological innovation. *(Rue des Archives/The Granger Collection, New York—All rights reserved.)*

***An ABC for Baby Patriots* (1899)**
Pride in empire began at an early age, when learning the alphabet from this kind of book helped develop an imperial sensibility. The subject of geography became important in schools during the decades between 1870 and 1890 and helped young people know what possessions they could claim as citizens. In British schools, the young celebrated the holiday Empire Day with ceremonies and festivities emphasizing imperial power. *(Bodleian Library, University of Oxford. Mary F. Ames, shelfmark 2523 c. 24 [1899].)*

Hoping to spread the religion they believed superior, European missionaries ventured to newly secured areas of Africa and Asia with attitudes full of contradictions. A woman missionary reflected a common view when she remarked that the Tibetans with whom she worked were "going down, down into hell, and there is no one but me . . . to witness for Jesus amongst them." Many people under colonial rule did accept Christianity, often blending their local religious practices with Christian ones. Christianizing entire populations and making them obedient proved impossible, however. When native people resisted, "civilizers," including missionaries, often supported brutal military measures against them, willing to see them slaughtered in the name of imparting Christian values and Western order.

Yet other Europeans—from novelists to military men—held quite opposite views of conquered peoples, considering them better than Europeans because they were unspoiled by civilization. "At last some local color," enthused one colonial officer, fresh from the industrial cities of Europe, on seeing Constantinople. This romantic vision of an ancient center of culture, similar to eighteenth-century condescension toward the "noble savage," had little to do with the reality of conquered peoples' lives.

The paradoxes of imperialism are clear in hindsight, but at the time European self-confidence hid many of them. There was the belief that through imperialist ventures "a country exhibits before the world its strength or weakness as a nation," as one French politician announced. Some in government, however, worried that imperialism—because of its expense and the constant possibility of war—might weaken rather than strengthen the nation-state. The most glaring paradox of all was that Western peoples who believed in nation building and national independence invaded the territory of others thousands of miles away and refused them the right to rule themselves.

REVIEW QUESTION What were the goals of the new imperialism, and how did Europeans accomplish those goals?

The Industry of Empire

Behind the expansion of Western empires lay dramatic developments in economic and technological power. Fed by raw materials from around the world, industry turned out a cornucopia of new products, including the increasingly powerful guns that served imperial conquest, and many workers' wages increased. Beginning in 1873, however, downturns in business threatened both entrepreneurs and the working class. Businesspeople sought remedies in new technology, managerial techniques, and a revolutionary marketing institution—the department store. Governments played their part by changing business law and supporting the drive for raw materials and global profits. The steady advance of industry, global trade, and the consumer economy further transformed people's daily lives.

Industrial Innovation

In nineteenth-century Europe, an abundance of industrial, technological, and commercial innovation backed the ambitions of the nation-state and the drive for empire. Alongside the new inventions and discoveries that benefited European society and ultimately the world were innovations in medicines and firearms that speeded European conquest of Africa and Asia. Innovation remained uneven, however, as older leaders lagged and new leaders emerged in the contest for industrial prosperity.

In the last third of the nineteenth century, new products ranging from the bicycle, the typewriter, and the telephone to the internal combustion engine provided striking proof of industrial progress. In 1885, sophisticated German engineer Karl Benz devised a workable gasoline engine; six years later, France's Armand Peugeot constructed a car and tested it by chasing a bicycle race. Electricity became more widely used after 1880, providing power to light everything from private drawing rooms to government office buildings. Like the many bridges, skyscrapers, and railroad stations with their skeletal frames, the Eiffel Tower, constructed in Paris for the Universal Exposition of 1889, stood as a monument to the age's engineering wizardry. Visitors rode to the Eiffel Tower's summit in electric elevators.

To fuel the West's explosive industrial growth, the leading industrial nations mined and produced massive quantities of coal, iron, and steel in the 1870s and 1880s. Production of iron increased from 11 million to 23 million tons annually. Steel output in the industrial nations grew just as impressively, increasing from 500,000 to 11 million tons annually in these decades. Manufacturers used the metal to build the more than 100,000 locomotives that pulled trains—trains that transported two billion people a year.

The Spread of Factories and Innovations in Agriculture

Historians used to contrast a "second" Industrial Revolution, with a concentration on heavy industrial products like iron and steel, to the "first" one of the eighteenth and early nineteenth centuries, in which innovations in the manufacture of textiles and the use

The Invention of Electric Lighting

By the 1890s, residents of major European cities could see many fresh inventions in a single walk down the newly widened boulevards. In this illustration of Piccadilly in London, electric lighting illuminates the way for modern bicycles and automobiles as well as horse-drawn carriages. By the turn of the century, streets had also become crowded with electric trams. *(Mary Evans Picture Library.)*

of steam energy predominated. Many historians now believe this distinction mainly applies to Britain, where industrialization did rise in two stages. In countries where industrialization came later, the two developments occurred simultaneously. Numerous and increasingly advanced textile mills were installed on the European continent later than in Britain, for instance, at the same time that blast furnaces were being constructed. Although industrialization led to the decline of traditional crafts like weaving, home industry — or **outwork**, the process of having some aspects of industrial work done outside factories in individual homes (similar to the putting-out system described on page 687) — persisted in garment making, metalwork, and porcelain painting. Industrial production occurring simultaneously in homes, small workshops, and factories has continued through the entire history of modern manufacturing down to the present day.

Industrial innovations also changed agriculture. Chemical fertilizers boosted crop yields, and reapers and threshers mechanized harvesting. In the 1870s, Sweden produced a cream separator, a first step toward mechanizing dairy farming. Wire fencing and barbed wire replaced wooden fencing and stone walls, both of which required intensive labor to construct. Refrigeration, developed during this period, allowed fruits, vegetables, and meat to be transported without spoiling, thus diversifying and increasing the urban food supply. Tin from colonies facilitated large-scale commercial canning, which made many foods available year-round to people in the cities and thus improved their health.

The Tools of Empire

Industrial technology combined with scientific breakthroughs to provide the powerful guns, railroads, steamships, and medicines that accelerated Western penetration of Asia and Africa. The steam-powered gunboats that forced the Chinese to open their borders to opium in the 1830s continued to play a crucial role in European expansion. Improvements in steamboat technology helped in the conquest of the African interior, but the scientific development of quinine was also crucial. Before the development of medicinal quinine in the 1840s and 1850s, the deadly tropical disease malaria decimated many a European party embarking on exploration or military conquest, giving Africa the nickname "White Man's Grave." The use of quinine, extracted from cinchona bark from the Andes, radically cut deaths from malaria among soldiers, missionaries, adventurers, traders, and bureaucrats.

Drought and famine plagued large stretches of both Africa and Asia in these decades, thus weakening local peoples' ability to resist. Europeans kept their health, thanks to quinine, and then their weapons did the work of definitively destroying self-sufficiency and self-rule. Improvements to the breech-loading rifle and the development of the machine gun, or "repeater," between 1862 and the 1880s dramatically increased firepower. Europeans carried on a brisk trade selling outmoded guns at bargain prices to peoples needing protection both from their internal enemies and from the Europeans themselves. In contrast, Europeans crushed African resistance with rapid, accurate, and blazing gunfire: "The whites did not seize their enemy as we do by the body, but thundered from afar," claimed one local African resister. "Death raged everywhere — like the death vomited forth from the tempest."

Challenges to British Dominance

Despite innovation and global expansion, Britain's rate of industrial growth slowed as its entrepreneurs remained wedded to older technologies. Great Britain increased its trade, profited from its investments worldwide, and consolidated its global power in the late nineteenth century but shifted its focus to expanding both its global rule and the military means to protect it. Meanwhile, Germany and the United States began surpassing Britain in research, technical education, and innovation — and ultimately in overall rates of economic growth.

Following the Franco-Prussian War, Germany annexed Alsace and Lorraine, territories with both textile industries and rich iron deposits. Investing heavily in research, German businesses devised new industrial processes and began to mass-produce goods. Germany also spent as much money on education as on its military in the 1870s and 1880s. This investment resulted in highly skilled engineers and technical workers who sent German industrial productivity soaring. The United States began intensive exploitation of its vast natural resources, including coal, metal ores, gold, and oil. The value of U.S. industrial goods jumped from $5 billion in 1880 to $13 billion by 1900. Whereas German productivity rested more on state promotion of industrial efforts, U.S. growth often involved innovative entrepreneurs, such as Andrew Carnegie in iron and steel and John D. Rockefeller in oil. Most other countries trailed the three leaders in the pervasiveness of industry.

---

outwork: The nineteenth-century process of having some aspects of industrial work done outside factories in individual homes.

Sukharev Market, Moscow (c. 1890)
For all their modernization, cities also offered their products in dozens of centuries-old food and flea markets such as this one in Russia. Rural farmers brought fresh produce to the cities, while urban market women sold clothing and household items. *(© Austrian Archives/Corbis.)*

Areas of Slower Industrialization

French industry grew steadily, but French businesses remained smaller than those in Germany and the United States. In Spain, Austria-Hungary, and Italy, industrial development was primarily a local phenomenon. Austria-Hungary, for example, had densely industrialized areas around Vienna and in Styria and Bohemia, but the rest of the country remained tied to traditional, nonmechanized agriculture. Italy industrialized in the north while remaining rural and agricultural in the south. The Italian government spent more on building Rome into a grand capital than it invested in economic growth. A mere 1.4 percent of Italy's 1872 budget went to education and science, compared with 10.8 percent in Germany. Scandinavian countries, poor in coal and ore, lagged behind those with greater natural resources. The commercial use of electricity eventually helped them to industrialize in the last third of the nineteenth century and become leaders in the use of hydroelectric power.

Russia's road to industrialization was tortuous, slowed partly by its relatively small urban labor force. The terms of serf emancipation bound many Russian peasants, who may have wished to find opportunities in factory work, to the mir, or landed community. Some villages sent men and women to cities, but on the condition that they return for plowing and harvesting. Nevertheless, by the 1890s, Moscow, St. Petersburg, and a few other cities had substantial working-class populations. The Russian government attracted foreign capital, entrepreneurs, and engineers to help construct railroads, including the Trans-Siberian Railroad (1891–1916), which upon completion stretched 5,787 miles from Moscow to Vladivostok. Russia's industrial and military power increased, but its peasants bore the main burden of paying for the state's financing of industry, mostly in the form of higher taxes on vodka. Russia offered a prime example of the uneven benefits of industrialization: neither Russian peasants nor underpaid urban workers could afford to buy the goods their country produced.

Facing Economic Crisis

Economic conditions were far from rosy throughout the 1870s and 1880s despite industrial innovation. In 1873, prosperity suddenly gave way to a severe economic depression, followed by almost three decades of economic fluctuations, featuring sharp downturns. People of all classes lost their jobs or businesses and faced long stretches of unemployment or bankruptcy. Because economic ties bound industrialized western Europe to international markets, the downturns affected economies around the world: Australia, South Africa, California, Newfoundland, and the West Indies.

By the 1870s, as industry gained in influence, industrial and financial setbacks — not agricultural ones as in the past — were capable of sending the economy into a long tailspin. Innovation created new or modernized industries on an unprecedented scale, but economic uncertainty accompanied the forward march of Western industrial development, and businesspeople faced real problems. First, the start-up costs of new enterprises skyrocketed. The early textile mills had required relatively small amounts of capital in comparison to the new factories producing steel and iron. **Capital-intensive industry**, which required huge financial investment for the purchase of expensive machinery, replaced labor-intensive production, which relied on the hiring of more workers. Second, the distribution and consumption of goods failed to keep pace with industrial growth, in part because businessmen kept wages so low that workers could afford little besides food. For them, purchasing the new industrial goods was impossible. The series of slumps turned industrialists' attention to finding ways to enhance sales and distribution and to control markets and prices.

Governments took steps to address the economic crisis. New laws spurred the development of the **limited liability corporation**, which protected investors from personal responsibility for a firm's debt and thus encouraged investment. Before limited liability, owners or investors were personally responsible for the debts of a bankrupt business. In one case in England, a former partner who had failed to have his name removed from a legal document after leaving the business remained responsible to creditors when the company went bankrupt. He lost everything he owned except a watch and the equivalent of one hundred dollars. By reducing personal risk, limited liability made investors more confident about financing business ventures, which led to the growth of stock markets. These stock markets raised money from a larger pool of private capital than before and gave businesses the funds to innovate. At the center of an international economy linked by telegraph, telephone, railways, and steamships, the London Stock Exchange in 1882 traded industrial shares worth £54 million, a value that surged to £443 million by 1900.

capital-intensive industry: A mid- to late-nineteenth-century development in industry that required great investments of money for machinery and infrastructure to make a profit.

limited liability corporation: A legal entity, such as a factory or other enterprise, developed in the second half of the nineteenth century whose owners were liable for only restricted (limited) amounts of money owed to creditors in the case of financial failure.

Another way in which businesses met the crisis that began in 1873 was to band together in cartels and trusts. Cartels — combinations of industries formed to control prices and competition — flourished particularly in German chemical, iron, coal, and electric industries. A single German coal cartel, founded in the 1880s, eventually dominated more than 95 percent of coal production in Germany, allowing it to restrict output and set prices. Trusts — similar to cartels in their power to control prices but different in structure — appeared first in the United States in 1882, when John D. Rockefeller created the Standard Oil Trust by acquiring stock from many different oil companies and placing it under the direction of trustees. The trustees then controlled so much of the companies' stock that they could set prices for the entire industry and even dictate to the railroads the rates for transporting the oil. While expressing their belief in free trade, those who set up cartels and trusts were actually restricting the free market. Governments did the same by imposing import taxes, in the belief that doing so would help protect domestic industries.

Much of Europe had adopted free trade after midcentury, but during the recessions of the 1870s and 1880s the resulting huge trade deficits — caused when imports exceeded exports — soured many Europeans on the concept. Countries with trade deficits had less capital available to invest internally, slowing the growth of job opportunities and increasing the chance of social unrest. Farmers in many European countries suffered when improvements in transportation made it possible to import perishable food, such as cheap grain from the United States and Ukraine. With broad popular support, governments approved tariffs to make foreign goods more expensive. Farmers, capitalists, and even many workers backed taxes on imports to prevent competition from outside. By the early 1890s, all but Belgium, Britain, and the Netherlands had ended free trade.

Revolution in Business Practices

Industrialists also tried to minimize the damage of economic downturns by revolutionizing the everyday conduct of their businesses. A generation earlier, factory owners had been directly involved in every aspect of their businesses and often learned to run their firms through trial and error. In the late 1800s, industrialists began to hire managers to run their increasingly complex day-to-day operations. Managers who specialized in a particular aspect of a business — such as sales and distribution, finance, or the purchase of raw materials — made

Berlin Telephone Operators
Middle-class women needing jobs embraced the opportunities offered by the growing service sector in telephone, telegraph, and office work and other "respectable" employment. These Berlin telephone operators probably earned less than women factory workers, as service sector employers took advantage of an untapped educated pool of labor to advance industrial development. *(akg-images.)*

decisions in their area of expertise, assisted by workers in the new service sector.

The White-Collar Sector

A "white-collar" service sector, composed of workers with mathematical skills and literacy acquired in the new public primary schools, emerged as part of the development of management. Businesses employed secretaries, file clerks, and typists to guide the flow of business information. Banks that accepted savings from the general public and that invested those funds heavily in business needed tellers and clerks; railroads, insurance companies, and government-run telegraph and telephone companies all needed armies of office workers.

Women, responding to the availability of clean, respectable work, formed the bulk of service employees. At the beginning of the nineteenth century, middle-class women still tended businesses with their husbands. In the next few decades, however, the new ideology of domesticity became so strong that male employers were unwilling to hire married women, and women in the lower-middle and middle classes were themselves ashamed to work outside the home. But by the late nineteenth century, the costs of middle-class family life had increased, especially because children, who were now forced by law to get an education, were no longer working and contributing to family resources. Instead, the family needed more money to support them. Whether to help pay family expenses or to support themselves, both unmarried and married women of the respectable middle class increasingly took jobs despite the ideal of domesticity. Employers found, as one put it, a "quickness of eye and ear, and the delicacy of touch" in the new women workers.

By hiring women for newly created clerical jobs, business and government contributed to a dual labor market in which certain categories of jobs were predominantly male and others were overwhelmingly female. Since society had come to believe that women were not meant to work or even not fit to work, businesses made greater profits by paying women in the service sector chronically low wages—

Interior of Au Coin de la Rue (c. 1870)
This Parisian department store, not the grandest or first of its kind, shows the typical cascade of goods displayed on railings and balconies. The abundance of textiles and carpets sparked the shopper's imagination, inciting her to let go of thrift and wander wherever her fancy took her among the many counters and displays until she had overspent. *(© Stefano Bianchetti/Corbis.)*

much less than they would have had to pay men for doing the same tasks.

The Department Store

The drive to boost consumption led to a new development in merchandising—the emergence of the department store. Founded after mid-century in the largest cities, department stores gathered an impressive variety of goods in one place in imitation of the Middle Eastern bazaar. Created by daring entrepreneurs such as Aristide and Marguerite Boucicaut of the Bon Marché in Paris and John Wanamaker of Wanamaker's in Philadelphia, department stores eventually replaced stores selling single lines of goods such as dishware or fabrics.

Single-item stores that people entered knowing clearly what they wanted to purchase were often small, somber shops, miniature by comparison with the modern shopping palaces built of marble and filled with lights and mirrors. In the department store, luxurious silks, delicate laces, and richly embellished tapestries spilled over railings and counters, not in neat order reflecting rational, middle-class ideas, but in glorious disarray to stimulate consumer desires. Shoppers no longer limited their purchases to necessities but rather reacted to sales, a new marketing technique that could incite a buying frenzy. Because most men lacked the time for shopping expeditions, department stores became the domain of women, who came out of their domestic sphere into a new public role. Attractive salesgirls, another variety of service workers, were hired to inspire customers to buy. Department-store shopping also took place outside of cities: glossy mail order catalogs from the Bon Marché or Sears, Roebuck in Chicago arrived regularly in rural areas, with both necessities and exotic items from the faraway dream world of the city.

Consumerism was shaped by empire. Travelers like Frieda von Bülow and Carl Peters journeyed on speedier ocean liners, carrying quinine, antiseptics, and other medicines as well as cameras, revolvers, and the latest in rubber goods and apparel. Consumption of colonial products such as coffee, tea, sugar, tobacco, cocoa, and cola became more widespread for the stimulation they offered hardworking Westerners. Tons of palm oil from Africa were turned into both margarine and soap, allowing even ordinary people in the West to see themselves as cleaner and more civilized than those in other parts of the world, including areas from which those raw materials came. Empire and industry jointly shaped everyday life by exciting the desire to own things—whether industrial goods or products from the colonies.

REVIEW QUESTION What were the major changes in Western industry and business in the last third of the nineteenth century?

Imperial Society and Culture

The spread of empire not only made the world an interconnected marketplace but also transformed everyday culture and society. Success in manufacturing and foreign ventures created millionaires, and the expansion of a professional middle class and development of a service sector meant that more people were affluent enough to own property, see some of the world, and give their children a quality education. Many Europeans grew healthier, partly because of improved diet and partly because of government-sponsored programs aimed at promoting the fitness necessary for citizens of imperial powers. At the same time, the uncertainties of life in a rapidly changing society drove millions of poor Europeans to migrate in search of opportunities around the world—even in the colonies—while artists found exciting new subject matter in those same industrial and imperial changes around them.

The "Best Circles" and the Expanding Middle Class

Profits from empire and industrial growth added new members to the upper class, or "best circles," so called at the time because of their members' wealth, education, and social status. People in the best circles often came from the aristocracy, which remained powerful and was still widely seen as a model of style. Increasingly, however, aristocrats had to share their social position with new millionaires from the ranks of the upper middle class, or bourgeoisie. In fact, the very distinction between aristocrat and bourgeois became blurred, as monarchs gratefully bestowed aristocratic titles on wealthy businesspeople and as aristocrats financed global business ventures. Poorer aristocrats approved marriages between their children and those of the newly rich. Such arrangements brought much-needed money to old, established families and the glamour of an aristocratic title to newly wealthy families. Thus, Jeanette Jerome, daughter of a wealthy New York financier, married England's Lord Randolph Churchill (their son Winston later became England's prime minister). Millionaires discarded the thrifty ways of a century earlier to build palatial country homes and villas and engage in flashy displays of wealth. To justify their success, the wealthy often quoted Social Darwinist principles, maintaining that their prosperity resulted from their natural superiority over the poor.

Empire reshaped the way people in the best circles spent their leisure time. Upper-class men bonded over big-game hunting in Asia and Africa, which replaced age-old traditions of fox and bird hunting. European hunters forced native Africans, who had depended on hunting for income, food, and group unity, to work as guides, porters, and domestics on hunts. Collectors brought exotic specimens back to Europe for zoological exhibits, natural history museums, and traveling displays, all of which flourished during this period. Wealthy Europeans brought empire into their homes with displays of stags' heads, elephant tusks, and animal skins.

People in the best circles saw themselves as an imperial elite, and upper-class women devoted themselves to maintaining its standards of social conduct. Members of the upper class did their best to exclude inferiors by controlling their children's social lives, especially by preventing girls' sexual activity and relationships with the lower classes. Upper-class men regularly seduced lower-class women because a double standard saw promiscuity as normal for men and as immoral for women. Parents arranged many marriages directly, and "visiting days"—a kind of regulated open house—brought eligible young people together to help ensure correct matrimonial decisions.

Instead of working for pay, upper-class women devoted themselves to raising children and directing staffs of servants. They took their role seriously, keeping detailed accounts of their expenditures and monitoring their children's religious and intellectual development. Furnishings in fashionable homes displayed imperial treasures such as Persian-inspired textiles, Oriental carpets, bamboo furniture, and Chinese porcelains. With the importation of azaleas, rhododendrons, and other plants from around the world, lavish flower gardens replaced parks and lawns. Being an active consumer of fashionable clothing was also a time-consuming activity for women. In contrast to men's plain garments, upper-class women wore elaborate costumes—

Tiger Hunting in the Punjab
Big-game hunting became the imperial sport of choice, as this Indian work of art shows. European and American hunters took the place of local Asians and Africans who had previously depended on the hunt for their livelihood. Western manliness was coming to depend on such seemingly heroic feats as big-game hunting, and imperialists scorned those who continued the old aristocratic fox hunt as effeminate. Though not apparent in this illustration, some Western women enjoyed hunting, too. *(V & A Images, London/Art Resource, NY.)*

featuring constricting corsets, voluminous skirts, bustles, and low-cut necklines for evening wear—that made them symbols of elite leisure. Women offset the grim side of imperial and industrial society with the rigorous practice of art and music. One Hungarian observer wrote, "The piano mania has become almost an epidemic in Budapest as well as Vienna." Its keys made of ivory from Africa, the piano symbolized the imperial elite's accomplishments and superiority.

Below the best circles, or upper crust, the solid middle class of businesspeople and professionals such as lawyers was expanding, most notably in western and central Europe. In eastern Europe, this expansion did not happen naturally, and the Russian government often sought out foreigners to build its professional and business classes. Although middle-ranked businessmen and professionals could sometimes mingle with those at the top of society, their lives remained more modest. They did, however, employ at least one servant, which might give the appearance of leisure to the middle-class woman in the home. Professional men working at home did so from a well-appointed, if not lavish, room. Middle-class women did many household chores themselves, and middle-class domesticity substituted cleanliness and polish for the imperial grandeur of upper-class life.

Working People's Strategies

For centuries, working people had migrated from countryside to city and from country to country to make a living. After the middle of the nineteenth century, empire and industry were powerful factors in migration. Established European cities like Riga, Marseille, and Hamburg offered secure new industrial jobs and opportunities for work in global trade, while new colonies provided land, jobs for administrators, and the possibility of unheard-of wealth in diamonds, gold, and other natural resources.

Working People Leave Europe

Europeans who left their native lands moved for a variety of reasons (see "Contrasting Views," page 778). In parts of Europe, the land simply could not produce enough to support a rapidly expanding population. Greek shipbuilding in ancient times had stripped the vast forests of Sicily, leaving the soil eroded and nearly worthless. By the end of the nineteenth century, hundreds of thousands of Sicilians were leaving, often temporarily, to find work in the industrial cities of North and South America. One-third of all European immigrants came from the British Isles, especially Ireland between 1840 and 1920, first because of the potato famine and then because English landlords drove them from their farms to get higher rents by simply changing tenants. Between 1886 and 1900, half a million Swedes out of a population of 4.75 million quit their country (see "Taking Measure," page 777). Millions of rural Jews, especially from eastern Europe, left their villages for economic reasons, but Russian Jews also fled vicious anti-Semitism. Russian mobs brutally attacked Jewish communities, destroying homes and businesses and even murdering some Jews. These ritualized attacks, called pogroms, were scenes of horror. "People who saw such things never smiled anymore, no matter how long they lived," recalled one Russian Jewish woman who migrated to the United States in the early 1890s.

Commercial and imperial development determined destinations. Most migrants who left Europe

TAKING MEASURE

European Emigration, 1870–1890

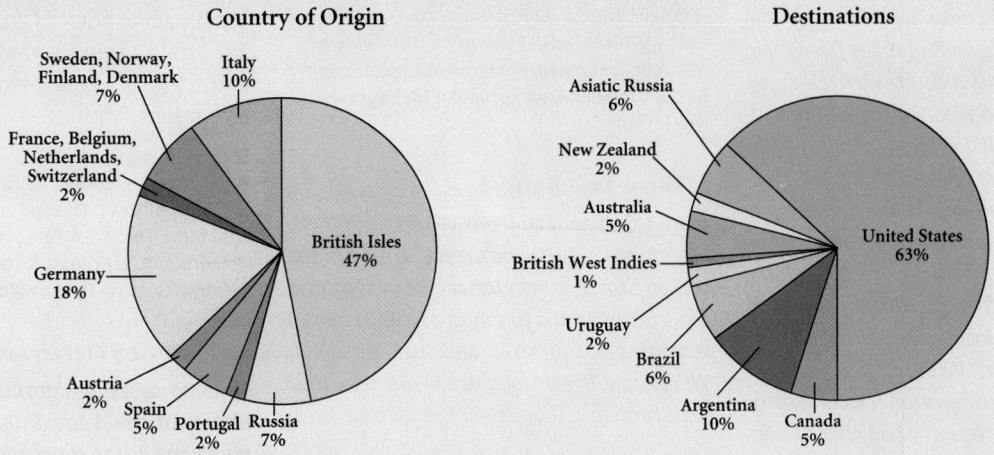

The suffering caused by economic change and by political persecution motivated people from almost every European country to leave their homes for greater security elsewhere. North America attracted more than two-thirds of these migrants, many of whom followed reports of vast quantities of available land in both Canada and the United States. Both countries were known for following the rule of law and for providing economic opportunity in urban as well as rural areas.

Source: Theodore Hamerow, *The Birth of New Europe: State and Society in the Nineteenth Century* (Chapel Hill: University of North Carolina Press, 1983), 169.

Question for Consideration

- **Where did the majority of these migrants originate? What historical factors prompted them to leave their homelands?**

went to North and South America, Australia, and New Zealand, as news of opportunity reached Europe. The railroad and steamship made journeys across and out of Europe more affordable and faster, though most workers traveled in steerage with few comforts. Once established elsewhere, migrants frequently sent money back home; the funds could be used to pay for education or to set up family members in small businesses, thus improving their condition. European farm families often received a good deal of their income from husbands or grown sons and daughters who had left. Cash-starved peasants in eastern and central Europe welcomed the arrival of "magic dollars" from their kin. Migrants themselves appreciated the chance to begin anew without the harsh conditions of the Old World. One settler in the United States was relieved to escape the meager peasant meal of rye bread and herring: "God save us from . . . all that is Swedish," he wrote home sourly.

Migration out of Europe often meant an end to the old way of life. Workers immediately had to learn new languages and compete for jobs in growing cities where they formed the cheapest pool of labor, often in factories or sweatshops. Emigrant women who worked as homemakers, however, tended to keep to themselves, preserving traditional ways. More insulated, they might never learn the new language or put their peasant dresses away. Their children and husbands more often left their past behind as they built a life in schools and factories of the New World.

More common than international migration was internal migration from rural areas to European cities, accelerating the urbanization of Europe. The most urbanized countries were Great Britain and Belgium, followed by Germany, France, and the Netherlands. In Russia, only 7 percent of the population lived in cities of ten thousand or more; in Portugal the figure was 12 percent. Many who moved to the cities were seasonal migrants who worked as masons, cabdrivers, or factory hands to supplement declining income from agriculture. When they returned to the countryside, they provided hands for the harvest. In villages across Europe, independent artisans such as handloom

CONTRASTING VIEWS

Experiences of Migration

In the nineteenth century, millions of migrants moved thousands of miles from their homelands. The vast distances traveled and the permanent relocation of these migrants were among the issues generating a wide range of responses. Among observers, government officials, migrants themselves, and those they left behind, reactions varied from acceptance and enthusiasm to opposition and anger. The conflicting reactions appeared in official reports, local newspapers, poems, and personal letters. While officials pointed to the benefits of emigration (Document 1), others in the home country had mixed views and opinions (Document 2). Migrants themselves had vastly differing experiences, adding to the debate over migration (Documents 3, 4, and 5).

1. The Government View

The preamble to the Hungarian census for 1890 was blunt and unambiguous on the subject of migration at a time when population growth was said to be a good thing. It offered a clear assessment of emigration.

Emigration has proved to be a veritable boom. The impoverished populace has been drawn off to where it has found lucrative employment; the position of those left behind, their work opportunities and standard of living, have undoubtedly improved thanks to the rise in wages, and thanks to the substantial financial aid coming into the country: sums of from 300,000 to 1,500,000 florints.

Source: Quoted in Julianna Puskas, "Consequences of Overseas Migration for the Country of Origin: The Case of Hungary," in Dirk Hoerder and Inge Blank, eds., *Roots of the Transplanted: Late 19th Century East Central and Southeastern Europe* (Boulder: East European Monographs, 1994), 1:397.

2. Those Left Behind

Teofila Borkowska, from Warsaw, Poland, reacted to her husband's resettlement in the United States in two letters from 1893 and 1894. Stripped of a family group, Borkowska struggled to survive, and her husband, Wladyslaw Borkowski, never did return or send for her.

1893. Dear Husband: Up to the present I live with the Rybickis. I am not very well satisfied, perhaps because I was accustomed to live for so many years quietly, with you alone. And today you are at one end of the world and I at the other, so when I look at strange corners [surroundings], I don't know what to do from longing and regret. I comfort myself only that you won't forget me, that you will remain noble as you have been. . . . I have only the sort of friends who think that I own thousands and from time to time someone comes to me, asking me to lend her a dozen roubles.

1894. Up to the present I thought and rejoiced that you would still come back to Warsaw, but since you write that you won't come I comply with the will of God and with your will. I shall now count the days and weeks [until you take me to America]. . . . Such a sad life! I go almost to nobody, for as long as you were in Warsaw everything was different. Formerly we had friends, and everybody was glad to see us, while now, if I go to anybody, they are afraid I need something from them and they show me beforehand an indifferent face.

Source: Letters from Teofila Borkowska to Wladyslaw Borkowski, July 21, 1893, and April 12, 1894, in William I. Thomas and Florian Znaniecki, *The Polish Peasant in Europe and America*, Vol. 2, Primary-Group Organization (Boston: Gorham Press, 1920), 348–49.

3. Migration Defended

In some cases, emigrants were said to be unpatriotic and cowardly for leaving their homeland just to avoid hard economic times. To charges against Swedish emigrants, journalist Isador Kjelberg responded with the following explanation.

Patriotism? Let us not misuse so fine a word! Does patriotism consist of withholding the truth from the workingman by claiming that "things are bad in America"? I want nothing to do with such patriotism! If patriotism consists of seeking, through lies, to persuade the poorest classes to remain under the yoke, like mindless beasts, so that we others should be so much better off, then I am lacking in patriotism. I love my country, as such, but even more I love and sympathize with the human being, the worker. . . . Among those who most sternly condemn emigration are those who least value the human and civic value of the workingman. . . . They demand that he remain here. What are they prepared to give him to compensate the deprivations this requires? . . . It is only cowardly, unmanly,

weavers often supported their unprofitable livelihoods by sending their wives and daughters to work in industrial cities.

Adaptation to Industrial Change Changes in technology and management practices eliminated outmoded jobs and often made factory work more stressful. Workers complained that new machinery speeded up the pace of work to an unrealistic level. For example, employers at a foundry in suburban Paris required workers using new furnaces to turn out 50 percent more metal per day than they had produced using the old furnaces. Stepped-up productivity demanded much more physical exertion, but workers received no additional pay for their extra efforts. Workers heartless, to let oneself become a slave under deplorable circumstances which one *can* overcome.

Source: Quoted in H. Arnold Barton, *A Folk Divided: Homeland Swedes and Swedish Americans, 1840–1940* (Carbondale: Southern Illinois University Press, 1994), 72–73.

This anonymous Swedish poem combined a political explanation of migration with an economic one.

I'm bound for young America,
Farewell old Scandinavia.
I've had my fill of cold and toil,
All for the love of mother soil.
You poets with your rocks and rills
Can stay and starve—on words, no frills.
There, out west, a man breathes free,
While here one slaves, a tired bee,
Gathering honey to fill the hive
Of wise old rulers, on us they thrive.
In toil we hover before their thrones,
While they take to slumber, like lazy drones.
Drunk with our nectar they've set us afright,
But opportunity has knocked, and we'll take our flight.

Source: Quoted in H. Arnold Barton, A *Folk Divided: Homeland Swedes and Swedish Americans, 1840–1940* (Carbondale: Southern Illinois University Press, 1994), 137.

4. The Perils of Migration

A contrasting view of emigration to the United States appeared in the following Slovak song.

My fellow countryman, Rendek from Senica, the son of poor parents
Went out into the wide world. In Pittsburgh he began to toil.
From early morning till late at night he filled the furnaces with coal.
Faster, faster, roared the foreman, every day. . . .
Rendek toiled harder
So as to see his wife.
But alas! He was careless
And on Saturday evening late
He received his injuries. At home his widow waited
For the card which would never come.
I, his friend, write this song
To let you know
What a hard life we have here.

Source: Quoted in Frantisek Bielik, Horst Hogh, and Anna Stvrtecka, "Slovak Images of the New World: 'We Could Pay Off Our Debts,'" in Dirk Hoerder and Inge Blank, eds., *Roots of the Transplanted: Late 19th Century East Central and Southeastern Europe* (Boulder: East European Monographs, 1994), 1:388.

5. The Lure of Latin America

The following letter, written in 1883 by an English migrant to his family, shows why, despite hardship, Europeans fled their homelands for places such as Argentina, where this immigrant settled. Original spelling has been preserved.

SAUCE GRANDE, SOUTH AMERICA, MARCH 28, 1883

MY DR BROTHER AND SISTERS

I received your kind and welcome letters and was glad to hear from you after so long a time. Since I last wrote you I have left my situation where I was for three years past and have sold my share of sheep which counted 300 at 34$ pr head I have also got my Wool and sheepskins for sale in Buenos Aires for which I expect to get about 8.000$. Last year I made about 13.000$ clear money.

I suppose you know that one thousand dollars amount to about 8£ in English money. Sheep are very cheap and plentiful in this country. Thousands are sold at 30$ pr head. I have the pleasure to inform you that I have got 1.500 sheep on thirds from Messrs Samuel & Bo. I am now living in a house alone with my flock of sheep and it is rather lonesome but as soon as I receive my wool money I intend to get married. My intended wife is a Miss Victoria Smith, who is born in this country but of English parents and speaks very good English. . . .

Hoping this will find you all well as, I am happy to say, it leaves me at presant I remain your Effectionate Brother

Willie X

Source: Fordham Modern History Sourcebook: Immigration. http://web.archive.org/web/19981203161408/www.signature.pair.com/letters/archive/argentina.html

Questions to Consider

1. **What are the different views of migration represented in these documents?**
2. **What interests and points of view do these contrasting opinions represent?**
3. **How do we draw an accurate view of migration from such contrasting views and experiences?**
4. **Given these differing views, why would people consider leaving Europe and why would governments promote it?**

also grumbled about the increased number of managers; many believed that foremen, engineers, and other supervisors interfered with their work. For women, supervision sometimes brought on-the-job harassment, as in the case of female workers in a German food-canning plant who kept their jobs only in return for granting sexual favors to the male manager.

Many in the urban and rural labor force continued to do outwork at home. In Russia, workers made bricks, sieves, shawls, lace, and locks during the slow winter season. Every branch of industry, from metallurgy to toy manufacturing to food processing, also employed urban women at home—and their work was essential to the family economy. They painted tin soldiers, wrapped chocolate, made cheese boxes, and polished metal. Factory owners liked the system because low piece rates made outworkers desperate for income under any conditions and thus willing to work extremely long days. A German seamstress at her new sewing machine reported that she "pedaled at a stretch from six o'clock in the morning until midnight. . . . At four o'clock I got up and did the housework and prepared meals." Owners could lay off women at home during slack times and rehire them whenever needed with little fear of organized protest.

Economic change and the periodic return of hard times had uneven consequences for people's everyday lives. In the late nineteenth century, joblessness and destitution threatened. Some city workers prospered by comparison to those in rural areas, though a growing number lost the steadiness of traditional artisanal work. By and large, however, urban workers were better informed and more connected to the progress of industry and empire than their rural counterparts were.

National Fitness: Reform, Sports, and Leisure

Many in the urban working class suffered from the stresses of industrial modernization and the upheaval of migration. In an age of Social Darwinist concerns about national fitness in the international struggle to survive, middle- and upper-class reformers founded organizations for social improvement. Officials also promoted competitive sports and healthy leisure-time activities to build national fitness and provide some relief from the stresses of daily life.

Reform for the Working Classes Settlement houses, clinics, and maternal and child health centers sprang up overnight in cities. Young middle- and upper-class men and women, often from universities, eagerly took up residence in poor neighborhoods to study and help the people there. Belief in the scientific approach to solving social problems, as well as compassion for the poor, led these reformers to seek the causes of social problems and their solutions. The Fabian Society, a small organization established in London in 1884, undertook studies to devise reforms based on planning rather than socialist revolution. In 1893, the Fabians helped found the Labour Party to make social improvement a political cause. Religious faith also shaped these efforts: "There is Christ's own work to be done," wrote one woman who volunteered to inspect workhouse conditions. Catholics and Protestants alike countered the decline in religious observance with missionary efforts among the working poor. The Catholic church in Hungary, for example, ministered to those experiencing rural poverty as agriculture came under the stresses of global competition.

To make the poor more fit in a competitive world, philanthropists and government officials intervened in the lives of working-class families. The worry was that the poor, as one reformer put it, "were permanently stranded on lower levels of evolution." Intervening more in the lives of poor families was seen as a way to "quicken evolution." Reformers sponsored health clinics and milk centers to provide good medical care and food for children and instructed mothers in child-care techniques, including breast-feeding to promote infant health. Some schools distributed free lunches, medicine, and clothing and inspected the health and appearance of their students. Yet the poor were also pressured to follow new standards they could ill afford, such as finding children respectable shoes, and reformers believed they had the right to enter working-class apartments whenever they chose to inspect them.

A few professionals began to distribute birth-control information in the belief that smaller families could better survive the challenges of urban life. In the 1880s, Aletta Jacobs (1851–1929), a Dutch physician, opened the first birth-control clinic, which specialized in promoting the new, German-invented diaphragm. Jacobs wanted to help women in Amsterdam slums who were worn out by numerous pregnancies and whose lives, she believed, would be greatly improved by limiting their fertility. Working-class women used these clinics, and knowledge of birth-control techniques spread by word of mouth among workers. The churches adamantly opposed this trend, and even reformers wondered whether birth control would increase the sexual exploitation of women if the threat of pregnancy were removed.

Another government reform effort consisted of measures said to protect women from certain kinds of work. Legislation across Europe barred women from night work and from such "dangerous" professions as florist and bartender—allegedly for health reasons. Additionally, medical statistics demonstrated that women in even the most strenuous jobs became sick less often than men. But lawmakers and workingmen claimed that women were not producing healthy enough children and were stealing jobs from men. Women who had worked in trades newly defined as dangerous were forced to find other, lower-paying jobs or remain at home. The new laws did not prevent women from holding jobs, but they made earning

Anglo-Indian Polo Team
Team sports underwent rapid development during the imperial years as spectators rooted for the success of their football team in the same spirit they rooted for their armies abroad. Some educators believed that team sports molded the male character so that men could be more effective soldiers against peoples of other races. In the instance of polo, as illustrated by the team photo here, the English learned from the Indians what would soon be seen as a typically English sport. *(Hulton Archive/Getty Images.)*

a living harder. Social Darwinists justified these measures as making the population fit for the struggle to survive.

Sports and Leisure | As nations competed for territory and global trade, male athletes turned away from village games and created sports teams. Soccer, rugby, and cricket drew mass followings that welded the lower and higher classes into a common, competitive culture. Large audiences drawn from all classes backed their favorite teams, and competitive sports began to be seen as signs of national strength and spirit. Newspapers reported the results of all sorts of new contests, whether they concerned nations vying for colonies or bicyclists participating in cross-country races such as the Tour de France, sponsored by tire makers who wanted to prove the superiority of their product. "The Battle of Waterloo was won on the playing fields of Eton," ran the wisdom of the day, suggesting that the games played in school could mold the strength of an army—an army that competed with those of other nations in pursuit of empire.

Team sports—like civilian military service—helped differentiate male and female spheres and thus promoted a social order based on distinction between the sexes. Reformers introduced exercise and gymnastics into schools for girls, often with the idea that these would strengthen them for motherhood and thus help build the nation-state. Some team sports for women emerged—soccer, field hockey, and rowing—but women generally were encouraged to engage in individual sports. "Riding [horses] improves the temper, the spirits and the appetite," wrote one sportswoman. As knowledge of the world developed, some women began to practice yoga.

The middle classes thought that leisure pursuits such as mountain climbing built mental and physical skills, and they even crossed the empire to challenge themselves. As a Swedish editor explained, "The passion for mountain-climbing can only be understood by those who realize that it is the step-by-step achievement of a goal which is the real pleasure of the world." Working-class people adopted middle-class habits by joining clubs for such pursuits as bicycling, touring, and hiking. Clubs that sponsored trips often had names like the Patriots or the Nationals, making a clear association between physical fitness and national strength. The emphasis on healthy recreation gave people a greater sense of individual might and promoted an imperial citizenship based less on constitutions and rights than on an individual nation's exercise of raw power. A farmer's son in the 1890s boasted that with a bicycle, "I was king of the road, since I was faster than a horse."

Artistic Responses to Empire and Industry

In the 1870s and 1880s, the arts explored the process of global expansion and economic innovation, often in the same gloomy Darwinistic terms that made reformers anxious. Darwin's theory held out the possibility that strong civilizations, if they failed to adapt to changing conditions, could weaken and collapse. French writer Émile Zola, influenced by fears of social decay, produced a series of novels set

DOCUMENT

Henrik Ibsen, From *A Doll's House*

Norwegian playwright Henrik Ibsen helped create the global marketplace of ideas with such plays as A Doll's House, *an 1879 work critical of traditional gender roles, as this conversation between Torvald Helmer and his wife, Nora, reveals. With women like Frieda von Bülow traveling the globe, Ibsen increasingly believed that the middle-class housewife did not develop as a full human being. His plays were performed in many countries—not only in Europe but also in Egypt, the United States, and as far away as Japan.* A Doll's House *sparked fierce debate around the world, especially about the condition of women. If European artists and writers borrowed from other cultures, Europe's cultural influence also spread beyond its borders.*

Helmer: Nora, how can you be so unreasonable and ungrateful? Haven't you been happy here?

Nora: No; never. I used to think I was; but I haven't ever been happy.

Helmer: Not—not happy?

Nora: No. I've just had fun. You've always been very kind to me. But our home has never been anything but a playroom. I've been your doll-wife, just as I used to be Papa's doll-child. And the children have been my dolls. I used to think it was fun when you came in and played with me, just as they think it's fun when I go in and play games with them. That's all our marriage has been, Torvald.

Helmer: There may be a little truth in what you say, though you exaggerate and romanticize. But from now on it'll be different. Playtime is over. Now the time has come for education.

Nora: Whose education? Mine or the children's?

Helmer: Both yours and the children's, my dearest Nora.

Nora: Oh, Torvald, you're not the man to educate me into being the right wife for you.

Helmer: How can you say that?

Nora: And what about me? Am I fit to educate the children?

Helmer: Nora!

Nora: Didn't you say yourself a few minutes ago that you dare not leave them in my charge?

Helmer: In a moment of excitement. Surely you don't think I meant it seriously?

Nora: Yes. You were perfectly right. I'm not fitted to educate them. There's something else I must do first. I must educate myself. And you can't help me with that. It's something I must do by myself. That's why I'm leaving you.

Helmer (jumps up): What did you say?

Nora: I must stand on my own feet if I am to find out the truth about myself and about life. So I can't go on living here with you any longer.

Helmer: Nora, Nora!

Nora: I'm leaving you now, at once. Christine will put me up for tonight—

Helmer: You're out of your mind! You can't do this! I forbid you!

Nora: It's no use your trying to forbid me any more. I shall take with me nothing but what is mine. I don't want anything from you, now or ever.

Helmer: What kind of madness is this?

Nora: Tomorrow I shall go home—I mean, to where I was born. It'll be easiest for me to find some kind of a job there.

Helmer: But you're blind! You've no experience of the world—

Nora: I must try to get some, Torvald.

Helmer: But to leave your home, your husband, your children! Have you thought what people will say?

Nora: I can't help that. I only know that I must do this.

Helmer: But this is monstrous! Can you neglect your most sacred duties?

Nora: What do you call my most sacred duties?

Helmer: Do I have to tell you? Your duties towards your husband, and your children.

Nora: I have another duty which is equally sacred.

Helmer: You have not. What on earth could that be?

Nora: My duty towards myself.

Source: Henrik Ibsen, *A Doll's House* (New York: Anchor, 1966), 96–97.

Question to Consider

- **How do Helmer's attempts to convince Nora to stay reveal his ideas about women and their proper roles in society?**

in industrializing France about a family plagued by alcoholism and madness. Zola's characters, who led violent strikes and in one case even castrated an oppressive grocer, raised questions about the future of civilization. Zola had a dark vision of how industrial society affected individuals: his novel *Women's Paradise* (1883) depicts the upper-class shopper who abandons rational decision making as a consumer for the frenzy of the new department stores. Other fictional heroines were equally upsetting because they violated other long-standing rules. The character Nora in the drama *A Doll's House* (1879) by Norwegian playwright Henrik Ibsen undermines civilized values and the health of society by leaving an oppressive marriage (see Document, "From *A Doll's House*," above).

Writers envisioned a widespread deterioration of behavior pervading urban and rural life. The stories of Emilia Pardo Bazán are tales of incest and murder among wealthy landowning families in rural Spain. The heroine of Olive Schreiner's *The Story of an African Farm* (1889) rejects the role of submissive wife in rural Africa, describing the British Empire as a "dirty little world, full of confusion." Schreiner became celebrated among opponents of empire for her grim portrayals. Novelists addressed the burning issues of their times and echoed the Social Darwinism that was in the air.

Decorative arts of this period featured a countertrend away from stark realism. Country people used mass-produced textiles to create traditional-looking costumes and developed ceremonies based on a mythical past. Such invented customs, romanticized as old and authentic, brought tourists from the cities to villages. So-called folk motifs caught the eye of modern urban architects and industrial designers, who copied rustic styles when creating household goods and decorative objects. The influence of empire is apparent in the traditional Persian and Indian motifs used by English designers William Morris (1834–1896) and his daughter May Morris (1862–1938) in their designs of fabrics, wallpaper, and household items based on such natural imagery as the silhouettes of plants. They wanted to replace "dead" and "ornate" styles of the early industrial years with the simple crafts of the past. Their work gave birth to the arts and crafts style, which paradoxically attracted consumers benefiting from the industrial age.

Industrial developments also influenced the work of painters, who by the 1870s felt intense competition from a popular industrial invention—the camera. Photographers could produce cheap copies of paintings and create more realistic portraits than painters could, at affordable prices. In response, painters altered their style, employing new and varying techniques to distinguish their art from the photographic realism of the camera. Claude Monet, for example, was fascinated by the way light transformed an object, and he often portrayed the same place—a bridge or a railroad station—at different times of day.

This daring style of art generally came to be called **impressionism**. It emphasizes the artist's attempt to capture a single moment by focusing on the ever-changing light and color found in ordinary scenes. Using splotches and dots, impressionists moved away from the precise realism of earlier painters and challenged artistic norms. Vincent Van Gogh used vibrant colors in great swirls to capture sunflowers, haystacks, and the starry evening sky. Distortions made the impressionists' visual style seem outrageous to those accustomed to realism, but a few enthusiastically greeted impressionism's luminous quality. Closely following the impressionists, French painter Georges Seurat depicted with thousands of dots and dabs the Parisian suburbs' newly created parks with their Sunday bicyclists and office workers in their store-bought clothing, carrying books or newspapers and parading like the well-to-do. Industry contributed to the new styles of painting, as factories produced a range of pigments that allowed artists to use a wider and more intense spectrum of colors than ever before. Both new industrial products such as the camera and chemically based paints gave birth to a rebellion in the arts.

An increasingly global vision also influenced painting in the age of empire. In both composition and style, impressionists borrowed heavily from Asian art and architecture. The impressionist goal of portraying the fleetingness of light or human situations came from an ancient Japanese concept—*mono no aware* ("sensitivity to the fleetingness of life"). The color, line, and delicacy of Japanese art (which many impressionists collected) is evident, for example, in Monet's later paintings of water lilies, his studies of wisteria, and even his re-creation of a Japanese garden at his home in France as the subject for artistic study. Similarly, the American expatriate Mary Cassatt used the two-dimensionality of Japanese art in *The Letter* (1890–1891) and other paintings. Van Gogh sometimes filled the background of portraits with copies of intensely colored Japanese prints, even imitating classic Japanese woodcuts. The graphic arts advanced the West's ongoing borrowing from around the globe, while responding to the changes brought about by industry.

REVIEW QUESTION How did empire and industry influence art and everyday life?

The Birth of Mass Politics

Ordinary people struggled for political voice, especially through the vote, as they watched the wealth and influence of industry and empire increase. By bringing more people into closer contact with one another in cities, the growth of industries helped

impressionism: A mid- to late-nineteenth-century artistic style that captured the sensation of light in images, derived from Japanese influences and in opposition to the realism of photographs.

Mary Cassatt, *The Letter* (c. 1890)
Mary Cassatt, an American artist who spent much of her time in Europe, was one of the many Western artists smitten by Japanese prints. Like many other Western artists of her day, she learned Japanese techniques for printmaking, but she also reshaped her painting style to follow Japanese conventions in composition, perspective, and the use of color. Cassatt is known for her many depictions of Western mothers and children and of individual women. In this painting, the woman herself even looks Japanese. *(Worcester Art Museum, Worcester, Massachusetts, USA / The Bridgeman Art Library International.)*

develop networks of political communication and a stronger national consciousness. The railroad, for example, took high-ranking officials such as British prime minister William Gladstone on campaigns to win votes before national audiences. Such events made workers more politically aware and active, leading western European governments to allow more men to vote. Although only men profited from electoral reform, the era's expanding franchise marked the beginning of mass politics—a major feature of the twentieth-century West. Women could not vote, but they participated in public life by forming auxiliary groups to support political parties. Among the authoritarian monarchies, Germany had male suffrage, but in more autocratic states to the east—for instance, Russia—violence and ethnic conflict shaped political systems. In such places, the harsh rule from above often resembled the control imposed on colonized peoples rather than participation of voting citizens.

Workers, Politics, and Protest

Workers in the 1870s–1890s joined together politically to exert pressure on governments and businesses. Strikes and worker activism were reactions to workplace hardships, but they depended on community bonds forged in neighborhoods. With the backing of their neighbors and fellow laborers, workers formed effective unions and powerful political parties—many of them based on a Marxist platform. Unions served to protect workers from the often brutal pace of industrial change and to guarantee that they received a fair wage. Workers banded together both in grassroots organizations, such as clubs and reading societies, and in transnational organizations, such as the Second International, across their individual nation-state's boundaries. Such organizations aimed to combat the growing nationalism and imperial competition that separated workers rather than binding them in a common cause.

Unions and Strikes As the nineteenth century entered its final decades, workers organized formal unions, which attracted the allegiance of millions. Unions demanded a say in working conditions and aimed, as one union's rule book put it, "to ensure that wages never suffer illegitimate reductions and that they always follow the rises in the price of basic commodities." Businessmen and governments viewed striking workers simply as rebels, threatening political unrest and destructive violence. Even so, strong unions appealed to some industrialists because a union could make strikes more predictable (or even prevent them) and present worker demands coherently instead of piecemeal by groups of angry workers.

From the 1880s on, the pace of collective action for better pay, lower prices, and better working conditions accelerated. In 1888, for example, hundreds of young women who made matches, the so-called London matchgirls, went on strike to end the fining system, under which they could be penalized an entire day's wage for being a minute or two late to work. The fines, the matchgirls maintained, helped companies reap profits of more than 20 percent. Newspapers and philanthropists picked up the strikers' story, condemning "respectable" owners "who suck wealth out of the starvation of helpless girls." In 1890, sixty thousand workers took to the streets of Budapest to agitate for safer working conditions and the vote; the next year, day laborers on Hungarian farms struck, too. Across Europe between 1888 and 1890, the number of strikes and major demonstrations rose by more than 50 percent, from 188 to 289.

Housewives, who often acted in support of strikers, carried out their own protests against high food prices. They confiscated merchants' goods and sold them at what they considered a fair price. "There should no longer be either rich or poor," argued Italian peasant women. "All should have bread for themselves and for their children. We should all be equal." They took other kinds of action as well: housewives often hid neighbors' truant children from school officials so that the children could continue to help with work at home. When landlords evicted tenants, women gathered in the streets to return the ousted families' household goods as fast as they were removed. Meeting on doorsteps or at fountains, laundries, and markets, women initiated rural newcomers into urban ways. In doing so, they helped cement the working-class unity created by workers in the factory.

Governments increasingly responded to strikes by calling out troops or armed police, even though most strikes were about working conditions and not about political revolution. Even in the face of government force, unions did not back down or lose their commitment to solidarity. Craft-based unions of skilled artisans, such as carpenters and printers, were the most active and cohesive, but from the mid-1880s on, a movement known as **new unionism** attracted transport workers, miners, matchgirls, and dockworkers. These new unions were nationwide groups with salaried managers who could plan a widespread general strike across the trades, focusing on such common goals as the eight-hour workday and also paralyzing an entire nation through work stoppages. Although the small, local workers' associations remained important, the large unions of the industrialized countries of western Europe had more potential for challenging large industries, cartels, and trusts.

Political Parties | Working-class political parties developed from unions. Workingmen helped create the Labour Party in England, the Socialist Party in France, and the Social Democratic Parties of Sweden, Hungary, Austria, and Germany — most of them inspired by Marxist theories. Germany was home to the largest socialist party in Europe after 1890. Socialist parties held out hope that newly enfranchised male working-class voters could become a collective force in national elections, even triumphing because of their numbers over the power of the upper class.

Those who accepted Marx's assertion that "workingmen have no country" also founded an international movement to address workers' common interests across national boundaries. In 1889, some four hundred socialists from across Europe met to form the **Second International**, a federation of working-class organizations and political parties that replaced the First International, founded by Marx before the Paris Commune. The Second International adopted a Marxist revolutionary program, but it also advocated suffrage (in countries where it still did not exist) and better working conditions.

Members of the Second International determined to rid the organization of anarchists, who flourished in the less industrial parts of Europe — Russia, Italy, and Spain. In these countries, anarchism drew strong support from peasants, small property owners, and agricultural day laborers, for whom Marxist theories of worker-controlled factories had less appeal. In an age of tough international competition in agriculture, many rural people sought a life free from the domination of large landowners and governments that backed the landowners' interests. Many advocated extreme tactics, including physical violence and even murder. "We want to overthrow the government . . . with violence since it is by the use of violence that they force us to obey," wrote one Italian anarchist. In the 1880s, anarchists bombed stock exchanges, parliaments, and businesses. Members of the Second International felt that such random violence was counterproductive.

Workingwomen joined unions and workers' political parties, but in much smaller numbers than men. Unable to vote in national elections and usually responsible for housework in addition to their

new unionism: A nineteenth-century development in labor organizing that replaced local craft-based unions with those that extended membership to all kinds of workers.

Second International: A transnational organization of workers established in 1889, mostly committed to Marxian socialism.

paying jobs, women had little time for party meetings. In addition, their low wages hardly allowed them to survive, much less pay party or union dues. Many workingmen also opposed women's presence in unions. Contact with women would mean "suffocation," one Russian workingman believed, and end male union members' sense of being "comrades in the revolutionary cause." Unions glorified the heroic struggles of a male proletariat against capitalism. Marxist leaders maintained that capitalism alone caused injustice to women and thus that the creation of a socialist society would automatically end gender inequality. As a result, although the new political organizations wanted women's support, they dismissed women's concerns about lower wages and sexual harassment.

Popular community activities that intertwined politics with everyday life also built worker solidarity. The gymnastics and musical societies that had once united Europeans in nationalistic fervor now served working-class goals. Socialist gymnastics, bicycling, and marching societies rejected competition and prizes as middle-class preoccupations, but they valued physical fitness because it could help workers in the "struggle for existence"—a reflection of the spread of Darwinian thinking to all levels of society. Workers also held festivals and cheerful parades, most notably on May 1—a centuries-old holiday that the Second International now claimed as a labor holiday. Like religious processions of an earlier time, parades fostered unity, and as a result, governments frequently banned such public gatherings, calling them a public danger.

Expanding Political Participation in Western Europe

Ordinary people everywhere in the West were becoming aware of politics through newspapers, which, combined with industrial and imperial progress, were important in developing a sense of citizenship in a nation. Western European countries moved toward mass politics more rapidly than did countries to the east. In western Europe, people's access to newspapers and their political participation meant that the will of the people was increasingly important and the power of small cliques relatively less so in determining election outcomes. In eastern Europe, in contrast, conservative elites opposed the integration of citizens as active participants in a national community that was the trend in western Europe.

Mass Journalism The rise of mass journalism after 1880 was the product of imperial and industrial development. The invention of automatic typesetting and the production of newsprint from wood pulp lowered the costs of printing; the telephone allowed reporters to communicate news to their papers almost instantly. Once literary in content, many daily newspapers now emphasized sensational news, using banner headlines, dramatic pictures, and gruesome or lurid details—particularly about murders and sexual scandals—to sell papers. In the hustle and bustle of industrial society, one editor wrote, "you must strike your reader right between the eyes." A series of articles in 1885 in London's *Pall Mall Gazette* on the "white slave trade" warned the innocent not to read further. The author then proceeded to describe how young women were "snared, trapped," and otherwise forced into prostitution in distant lands through sexual violation and drugs. Stories of imperial adventurers and exaggerated accounts of wasted women workers and their unborn babies similarly drew ordinary people to the mass press.

Journalism created a national community of up-to-date citizens, whether or not they could vote. Unlike the book, the newspaper was meant not for quiet reflection at home or in the upper-class club but for quick reading of attention-grabbing stories on mass transportation and on the streets. Elites complained that the sensationalist press was a sign of social decay, but for up-and-coming people from the working and middle classes, journalism provided an avenue to success. As London, Paris, Vienna, Berlin, and St. Petersburg became centers not only of politics but also of news, a number of European politicians got their start working for daily newspapers. In western Europe, increasing political literacy opened the political process to wider participation.

British Political Reforms A change in political campaigning was one example of this widening participation. In the fall of 1879, **William Gladstone** (1809–1898), leader of the British Liberals, whose party was then out of power, took a train trip across Britain to campaign for a seat in the House of Commons. During his campaign, Gladstone addressed thousands of workers, arguing for the people of India and Africa to have more rights and summoning his audiences to "honest, manful, humble effort" in the middle-class tradition of "hard work." Newspapers around the country reported on his trip and these accounts, along with mass meetings, fueled public interest in

William Gladstone (1809–1898): Liberal politician and prime minister of Great Britain who innovated in popular campaigning and who criticized British imperialism.

politics. Gladstone's campaign was successful, and he took the post of prime minister for the second of the four nonconsecutive terms he served between 1868 and 1894.

Other changes fostered the growth of mass politics in Britain. The Ballot Act of 1872 made voting secret, a reform that reduced the ability of landlords and employers to control how their workers voted. The **Reform Act of 1884** doubled the electorate to around 4.5 million men, enfranchising many urban workers and artisans and thus further diminishing traditional aristocratic influence in the countryside. To win the votes of the newly enfranchised, Liberal and Conservative parties alike established national political clubs to build party loyalty. These clubs competed with small cliques of parliamentary elites who had controlled party politics. Broadly based interest groups such as unions and national political clubs opened up politics by appealing to many more voters.

British political reforms immediately affected Irish politics by arming poor tenant farmers with the secret ballot. The political climate in Ireland was explosive mainly because of the repressive tactics of absentee landlords, many of them English and Protestant, who drove tenants from their land in order to charge higher rents to newcomers. In 1879, opponents of these landlords' attacks on Irish well-being formed the Irish National Land League and launched fiery protests. Irish tenants elected a solid bloc of nationalist representatives to the British Parliament.

The Irish members of Parliament began voting as a group, which gave them sufficient strength to defeat either the Conservatives or the Liberals. Irish leader **Charles Stewart Parnell** (1846–1891) demanded British support for **home rule**—a system giving Ireland its own parliament—in return for Irish votes. As prime minister, Gladstone accommodated Parnell with bills on home rule and tenant security. But Conservatives called home rule "a conspiracy against the honor of Britain," and when they were in power (1885–1886 and 1886–1892), they cracked down on Irish activism. Scandals reported in the press, some of them totally invented, weakened Parnell's influence. In 1890, the news broke of his affair with a married woman, and he died in disgrace soon after, as cultural values and the media determined politics. Irish home rule remained a heated political issue in the British Parliament, a powerful sign, some said, of the determination to end Ireland's colonial status.

Parnell Cartoon
Passions ran high among the English over demands for Irish home rule. A special target of outrage was the Irish leader Charles Stewart Parnell, whom the British government and media spied upon and lied about. Here Parnell is depicted as the evil murderer Mr. Hyde, from the popular tale of Dr. Jekyll and Mr. Hyde, out to destroy Prime Minister William Gladstone and by implication the well-being of the entire British Empire. *(Hulton Archive/Getty Images.)*

France's Third Republic

Prussia's defeat of Napoleon III in 1871 led to the creation of the **Third Republic** to replace the Second Empire. The republic was shaky at the start because the monarchist political factions—Bonapartist,

Reform Act of 1884: British legislation that granted the right to vote to a mass male citizenry.

Charles Stewart Parnell: Irish politician (1846–1891) whose advocacy of home rule was a thorn in the side of the British establishment.

home rule: The right to an independent parliament demanded by the Irish and resisted by the British from the second half of the nineteenth century on.

Third Republic: The French government that succeeded Napoleon III's Second Empire after its defeat in the Franco-Prussian War of 1870–1871. It lasted until France's defeat by Germany in 1940.

Orléanist, and Bourbon—all struggled to restore their respective families to power. But the republican form of government, which French supporters had been trying to solidify for almost a century, survived when the monarchists' compromise candidate for king, the comte de Chambord, stubbornly refused to accept the tricolored flag devised during the French Revolution. Associating the tricolor with the killing of Louis XVI, Chambord would accept only the white flag adorned with the fleur-de-lis of the Bourbons. He thus lost the chance to revive the monarchy, and in 1875 a new constitution created a ceremonial presidency and a premier (prime minister) dependent on support from the elected Chamber of Deputies. An alliance of businessmen, shopkeepers, professionals, and rural property owners hoped the new system would prevent the kind of strongman politics that had seen previous republics give way to the rule of emperors and the return of monarchs.

Fragile at birth, the Third Republic would remain so until World War II. Economic downturns, widespread corruption, and growing anti-Semitism, fueled by a highly partisan press, kept the Third Republic on shaky ground. Newspaper stories about members of the Chamber of Deputies selling their votes to business interests and about the alleged trickery of Jewish businessmen manipulating the economy added to the instability. As a result, the public also blamed Jews for the failures of republican government and the economy. With the support of those disgusted by the messiness of parliamentary politics, Georges Boulanger, a dashing and highly popular general, began a coup to take over the government. He soon lost his nerve, however, saving the French from rule by another strongman. Boulanger's popularity showed that in hard economic times, liberal values based on constitutions, elections, and the rights of citizens could be called into question by someone promising easy solutions.

Republican leaders attempted to strengthen citizen loyalty by instituting compulsory and free public education in the 1880s. In public schools, secular teachers who supported republicanism replaced the Catholic clergy, who usually favored a return to monarchy. A centralized curriculum—identical in every schoolhouse in the country—featured patriotic reading books and courses in French geography, literature, and history. To perpetuate republican ideals, the government established secular public high schools for young women, seen as the educators of future citizens. Mandatory military service for men in the republic's army inculcated national pride in place of regional and rural loyalties that were often centered on the Catholic church. In short, schools and the army both turned peasants into Frenchmen.

Political Liberalism Rejected

Although many western European leaders believed in economic liberalism, constitutions, and efficient government, these ideals did not always translate into universal male suffrage and citizens' rights in the less powerful western European countries. Spain and Belgium abruptly awarded suffrage to all men in 1890 and 1893, respectively, but both governments remained monarchies. An alliance of conservative landowners and the Catholic church dominated Spain, although there was increasingly lively urban activism in the industrial centers of Barcelona and Bilbao. Denmark and Sweden continued to limit political participation, and reform in the Netherlands increased male suffrage to only 14 percent by the mid-1890s. An 1887 law in Italy gave the vote to all men who had a primary school education, or 14 percent of the male population.

In Italy, the process of unification left a towering debt and huge pockets of discontented people, including Catholic supporters of the pope and impoverished citizens in the south. Without receiving the benefits of nation building—education, urban improvements, industrial progress, and the vote—the average Italian in the south felt less loyalty to the new nation than fear of the devastating effects of national taxes and the draft on the family economy. Italians' growing unhappiness with constitutional government would have dramatic implications in the twentieth century.

Power Politics in Central and Eastern Europe

Germany, Austria-Hungary, and Russia diverged from the political paths taken by western European countries in the decades 1870–1890. These countries industrialized at varying rates—Germany rapidly and Russia far more slowly. Literacy and the development of a civic, urban culture were more advanced in Germany and Austria-Hungary than in Russia. Even Russia, however, saw the development of a modern press, although with a far smaller readership than elsewhere. In all three countries, conservative large landowners remained powerful, often blocking improvements in transport, sanitation, and tariff policy that would support a growing urban population.

Bismarck's Germany

Bismarck had upset the European balance of power, first by humiliating France in the Franco-Prussian War and then by creating a powerful, unified Germany, with explosive economic growth and rapid development of every aspect of the nation-state, from transport to the thriving capital city of Berlin (Map 23.3). His goals achieved, Bismarck now desired stability built on diplomacy instead of war. Fearing that France would soon seek revenge against the new Reich and needing peace to consolidate the nation, he pronounced Germany "satisfied," meaning that it sought no new territory in Europe. To ensure Germany's long-term security, in 1873 Bismarck forged the Three Emperors' League — an alliance of Germany, Austria-Hungary, and Russia. The three conservative powers shared a commitment to maintaining the political status quo.

At home, Bismarck, who owned land and invested heavily in industry, joined with the liberals to create a variety of financial institutions, including a central bank to advance German commerce and industry. After religious leaders defeated his Kulturkampf against Catholicism, Bismarck turned to attacking socialists and liberals instead of Catholics as enemies of the regime. He used unsuccessful assassination attempts on Emperor William I as a pretext to outlaw the workers' Social Democratic Party in 1878. Hoping to lure the working class away from socialism, between 1882 and 1884 Bismarck sponsored an accident and disability insurance program — the first of its kind in Europe and an important step in broadening the role of government to encompass social welfare. In 1879, he put through tariffs protecting German agriculture and industry from foreign competition but also raising the prices of consumer goods for ordinary people. Ending his support for laissez-faire economics, Bismarck broke with political liberals while simultaneously increasing the power of the agrarian conservatives by attacking the interests of Germany's industrial sector.

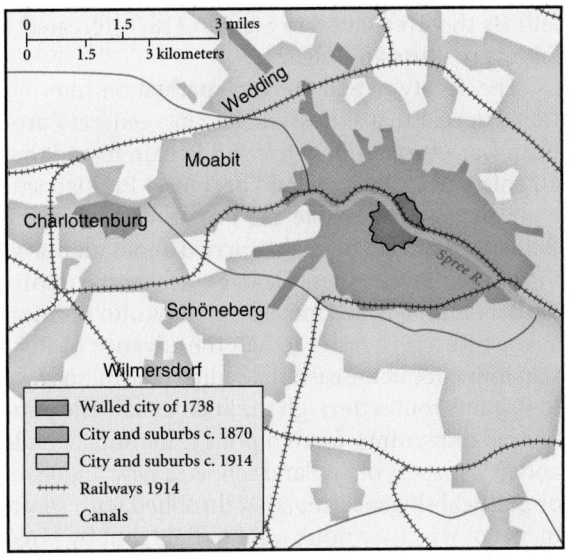

MAP 23.3 Expansion of Berlin to 1914
"A capital city is essential for the state to act as a pivot for its culture," the German historian Heinrich von Treitschke asserted. No other capital city grew as dramatically as Berlin after German unification in 1871. Industrialists and bankers set themselves up in the new capital, while workers migrated there for jobs, swelling the population. The city was newly dotted with military monuments and with museums to show off its culture.

Authoritarian Austria-Hungary

Austria-Hungary, like Germany, frequently employed liberal economic policies and practices. From the 1860s, liberal businessmen succeeded in industrializing parts of the empire, and the prosperous middle classes erected conspicuously large homes, giving themselves a prominence in urban life that rivaled the aristocracy's. They persuaded the government to enact free-trade provisions in the 1870s and to search out foreign investment to build up infrastructure, such as railroads.

Despite these measures, Austria-Hungary remained monarchist and authoritarian. Liberals in Austria — most of them ethnic Germans — saw their influence weaken under the leadership of Count Edouard von Taaffe, Austrian prime minister from 1879 to 1893. Building a coalition of clergy, conservatives, and Slavic parties, Taaffe used its power to weaken the liberals. In Bohemia, for example, he designated Czech as an official language of the bureaucracy and school system, thus breaking the German speakers' monopoly on officeholding. Reforms outraged individuals at whose expense other ethnic groups received benefits, yet those who won concessions, such as the Czechs, clamored for even greater autonomy. By playing nationalities off one another, the government ensured the monarchy's central role in holding together competing interest groups in an era of rapid change. Emperor Francis Joseph and his ministers still feared the influence of the most powerful Slavic nation — Russia — on the ethnic minorities living within Austria-Hungary.

Nationalists in the Balkans demanded independence from the declining Ottoman Empire, raising Austro-Hungarian fears and ambitions. In 1876, Slavs in Bulgaria and Bosnia-Herzegovina revolted against Turkish rule, killing Ottoman officials. As the Ottomans slaughtered thousands of Bulgarians in turn, two other small Balkan states, Serbia and Montenegro, rebelled against the sultan, too. Russian Pan-Slavic organizations sent aid to the Balkan rebels and so pressured the tsar's government that Russia declared war on Turkey in 1877 in the name of protecting Orthodox Christians. With help from Romania and Greece, Russia defeated the Ottomans and by the Treaty of San Stefano (1878) created a large, pro-Russian Bulgaria.

The Treaty of San Stefano sparked an international uproar that almost resulted in a general European war. Austria-Hungary and Britain feared that an enlarged Bulgaria would become a Russian satellite that would enable the tsar to dominate the Balkans. Austrian officials worried about an uprising of their own restless Slavs. British prime minister Benjamin Disraeli moved warships into position against Russia in order to halt the advance of Russian influence in the eastern Mediterranean, so close to Britain's routes through the Suez Canal. The public was drawn into foreign policy: the music halls and newspapers of England echoed a new jingoism, or political sloganeering, that throbbed with sentiments of war: "We don't want to fight, but by jingo if we do, / We've got the ships, we've got the men, we've got the money too!"

The other great powers, however, did not want a Europe-wide war, and in 1878 they attempted to revive the concert of Europe by meeting at Berlin under the auspices of Bismarck, who was a calming presence on the diplomatic scene. The Congress of Berlin rolled back the Russian victory by partitioning the large Bulgarian state that Russia had carved out of Ottoman territory and denying any part of Bulgaria full independence from the Ottomans (Map 23.4). Austria occupied (but did not annex) Bosnia and Herzegovina as a way of gaining clout in the Balkans; Serbia and Montenegro became fully independent. Nonetheless, the Balkans remained a site of political unrest, teeming ambition for independence, and great-power rivalries.

Following the Congress of Berlin, the European powers attempted to guarantee stability through a complex series of alliances and treaties. Anxious about the Balkans, Austria-Hungary forged a defensive alliance with Germany in 1879. The **Dual Alliance**, as it was called, offered protection against Russia and its potential for inciting Slav rebellions. In 1882, Italy joined this partnership (henceforth called the Triple Alliance), largely because of Italy's imperial rivalries with France. Tensions between Russia and Austria-Hungary remained high, so Bismarck replaced the Three Emperors League with the Reinsurance Treaty (1887) with Russia to

Dual Alliance: A defensive alliance between Germany and Austria-Hungary created in 1879 as part of Bismarck's system of alliances to prevent or limit war. It was joined by Italy in 1882 as a third partner and then called the Triple Alliance.

MAP 23.4 The Balkans, c. 1878
After midcentury, the map of the Balkans was almost constantly redrawn. This resulted in part from the weakness of the dominant Ottoman Empire, but also from the ambitions of inhabitants themselves and from great power rivalry. In tune with the growing sense of national identities based on shared culture, history, and ethnicity, various Balkan peoples sought to emphasize local, small-group identities rather than merging around a single dominant group such as the Serbs. Yet there was also a move by some intellectuals to transcend borders and create a southern Slav culture.

keep the Habsburgs from recklessly starting a war over Pan-Slavism.

Unrest in Russia | Besides its expansionist moves and setbacks, Russia was beset by domestic problems in the 1870s and 1880s. It remained almost the only European country without a constitutional government, and young Russians were turning to revolutionary groups for solutions to political and social problems. One such group, the Populists, wanted to rouse debt-ridden peasants to revolt. Other people formed terrorist bands with the goal of forcing change by assassinating public officials. The secret police, relying on informers, rounded up hundreds of members of one of the largest groups, Land and Liberty, and subjected them to brutal torture, show trials, and imprisonment. When in 1877 a young radical, Vera Zasulich, tried unsuccessfully to assassinate the chief of the St. Petersburg police, the people of the capital city applauded her act and acquittal, so great was their outrage at government treatment of young radicals from respectable families.

Russia: The Pale of Settlement in the Nineteenth Century

Writers added to the debate over Russia's future, often by specifically discussing these political issues and mobilizing public opinion. Novelists Leo Tolstoy, author of the epic *War and Peace* (1869), and Fyodor Dostoevsky, a former radical, believed that Russia above all required spiritual regeneration—not revolution. Tolstoy's novel *Anna Karenina* (1877) tells the story of an impassioned, adulterous love affair, but it also weaves in the spiritual quest of Levin, a former "progressive" landowner who, like Tolstoy, idealizes the peasantry's tradition of stoic endurance. Dostoevsky satirized Russia's radicals in *The Possessed* (1871), a novel in which a group of revolutionaries murders one of its own members. In Dostoevsky's view, the radicals were simply destructive, offering no solutions whatsoever to Russia's ills.

Despite the influential critiques published by Tolstoy and Dostoevsky, violent action rather than spiritual uplift remained the foundation of radicalism. In 1881, the People's Will, a splinter group of Land and Liberty impatient with its failure to mobilize the peasantry, killed Tsar Alexander II in a bomb attack. His death, however, failed to provoke the general uprising the terrorists expected. Alexander III (r. 1881–1894) unleashed a new wave of oppression against religious and ethnic minorities and gave the police virtually unchecked power. Popular books and drawings depicted Tatars, Poles, Ukrainians, and others as horrifying and uncivilized—and thus a menace to Russian culture. The five million Russian Jews, confined to the eighteenth-century Pale of Settlement (the name for the restricted territory in which they were permitted to live), endured particularly severe oppression. Local officials instigated pogroms against Jews, whose distinctive language, dress, and isolation in ghettos made them easy targets. Government administrators encouraged people to blame Jews for rising living costs—though the true cause was the high taxes levied on peasants to pay for industrialization.

As the tsar inflicted even greater repression across Russia, Bismarck's delicate system of alliances of the three conservative powers was coming apart. A brash but deeply insecure young kaiser, William II (r. 1888–1918), came to the German throne in 1888. William resented Bismarck's power, and his advisers flattered the young man into thinking that his own talent made Bismarck an unnecessary rival. William dismissed Bismarck in 1890 and let the Reinsurance Treaty with Russia lapse in favor of a pro-German relationship with Austria-Hungary. He thus destabilized the diplomatic scene just as imperial rivalries were intensifying antagonisms among the European nation-states and empires.

REVIEW QUESTION What were the major changes in political life from the 1870s to the 1890s, and which areas of Europe did they most affect?

Conclusion

The period from the 1870s to the 1890s has been called the age of empire and industry because Western society pursued both these ends in a way that rapidly transformed Europe and the world. Much of Europe thrived due to industrial innovation, becoming more populous and more urbanized. Using the innovative weapons streaming from Europe's factories, the great powers undertook a new imperialism that established political rule over foreign peoples. As they tightened connections with the rest

Torah Scrolls

After the assassination of Alexander II in 1881, the government unleashed pogroms against the Jews of the Russian Empire. The pogroms involved violent acts such as murder, beatings, and the destruction of property on a grand scale. In this image, Jewish men survey the damage done to the sacred texts of their religion during one such vicious attack.
(© From the Jewish Chronicle Archive/Heritage Images/The Image Works.)

of the globe, Europeans proudly spread their supposedly superior culture throughout the world and, like Frieda von Bülow and Carl Peters, sought out whatever distant peoples could offer in terms of power and wealth.

Imperial expansion and industrial change affected all social classes. The upper class attempted to maintain its position of social and political dominance, while an expanding middle class was gaining power and influence. Working-class people often suffered from the effects of rapid industrial change when their labor was replaced by machinery. Millions relocated to escape poor conditions in the countryside and to find new opportunities. Political reform, especially the expansion of suffrage, helped working-class men gain a political voice. Workers formed unions and political parties to protect their interests, but governments often responded to workers' activism with repression.

As workers struck for improved wages and conditions and the impoverished migrated to find a better life, Western society showed that troubles existed in the new imperial and industrial age. Newspapers informed people about disturbing national and international events overnight. By the 1890s, the advance of empire and industry was bringing unprecedented tensions to national politics, the international scene, and everyday life. Racism, anti-Semitism, and ethnic chauvinism were spreading, and many were questioning the costs of empire both to their own nation and conquered peoples. Politics in the authoritarian countries of central and eastern Europe was taking a more conservative turn, resisting participation and reform. The rising tensions of modern life would soon have grave consequences for the West as a whole.

FOR FURTHER EXPLORATION

- **For additional primary-source material from this period**, see *Sources of the Making of the West*, Fourth Edition.
- **For Web sites, images, and documents related to topics in this chapter**, visit *Make History* at bedfordstmartins.com/hunt.

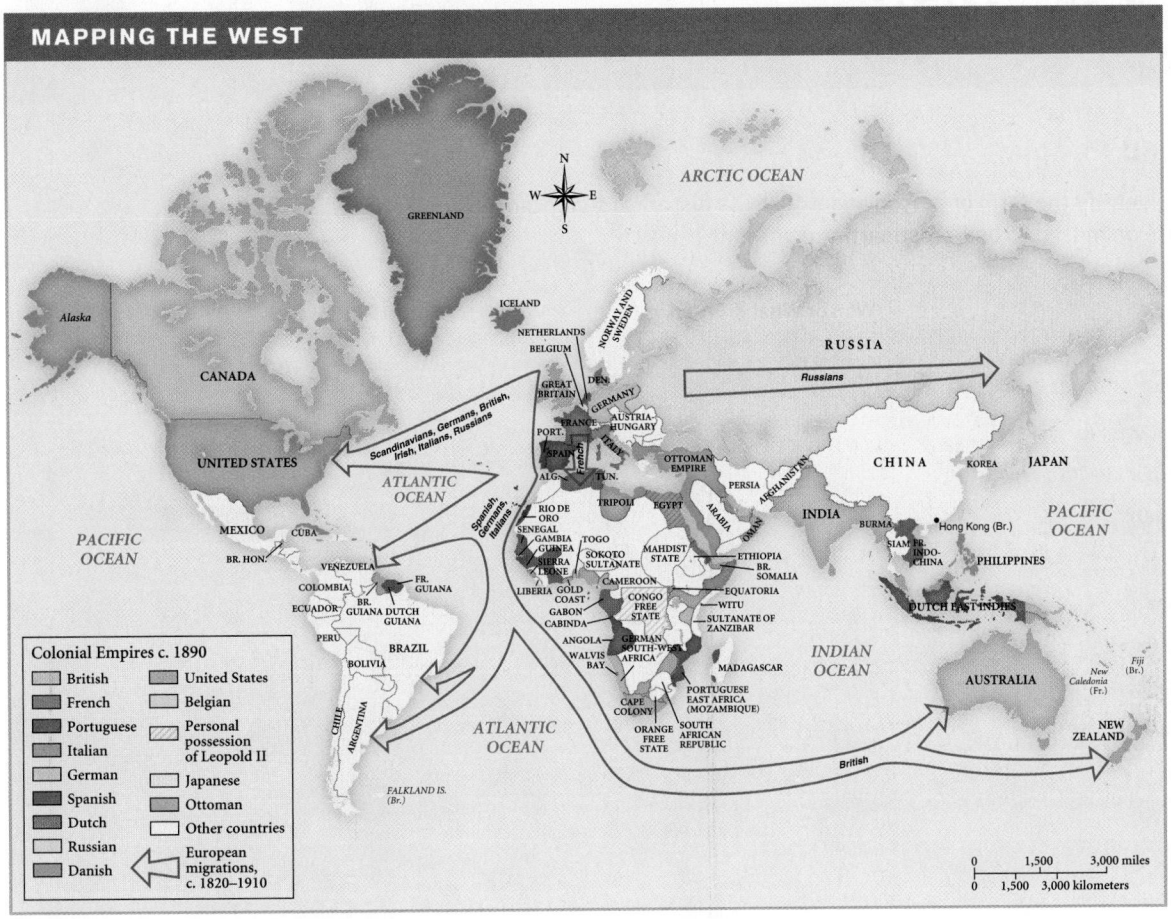

The West and the World, c. 1890

In the late nineteenth century, European trade and political reach spanned the globe. Needing markets for the vast quantities of goods that poured from European factories and access to raw materials to produce the goods, governments asserted that the Western way of life should be spread to the rest of the world and that resources would be best used by Europeans. Explorations and scientific discoveries continued both to build the knowledge base of Western nations and to enhance their ability for greater conquest. Simultaneously, millions of Europeans left their homes to find a better life elsewhere.

Chapter 23 Review

Online Study Guide bedfordstmartins.com/hunt

Key Terms and People

In the grid below, identify the term or person and explain its historical significance. (To do this exercise online, go to bedfordstmartins.com/hunt.)

Term	Who or What & When	Why It Matters
Leopold II (p. 762)		
outwork (p. 770)		
capital-intensive industry (p. 772)		
limited liability corporation (p. 772)		
impressionism (p. 783)		
new unionism (p. 785)		
Second International (p. 785)		
William Gladstone (p. 786)		
Reform Act of 1884 (p. 787)		
Charles Stewart Parnell (p. 787)		
home rule (p. 787)		
Third Republic (p. 787)		
Dual Alliance (p. 790)		

Review Questions

1. What were the goals of the new imperialism, and how did Europeans accomplish those goals?
2. What were the major changes in Western industry and business in the last third of the nineteenth century?
3. How did empire and industry influence art and everyday life?
4. What were the major changes in political life from the 1870s to the 1890s, and which areas of Europe did they most affect?

Making Connections

1. How did the new imperialism differ from European expansion of two centuries earlier? Of four centuries earlier?
2. Describe the effects of imperialism on European politics and society as a whole in 1870–1890.
3. Compare the political and social goals of the newly enfranchised male electorate with those of people from the "best circles."

Important Events

Date	Event	Date	Event
1860s–1890s	Impressionism flourishes in the arts; absorption of Asian influences	1882	Triple Alliance formed between Germany, Austria-Hungary, and Italy; Britain invades Egypt
1870s–1890s	Vast emigration from Europe continues; the new imperialism	1882–1884	Bismarck sponsors social welfare legislation
1871	Franco-Prussian War ends	1884	British Parliament passes the Reform Act, doubling size of male electorate
1873	Extended economic recession begins with global impact	1884–1885	European nations carve up Africa at Berlin conference
1876	British Parliament declares Victoria empress; invention of telephone	1885	Invention of workable gasoline engine; formation of Indian National Congress
1878	Treaty of San Stefano	1889	Japan adopts constitution based on European models; socialists meet in Paris and establish Second International
1879	Dual Alliance formed between Germany and Austria-Hungary	1891	Construction of Trans-Siberian Railroad begins
1881	Tsar Alexander II assassinated; France occupies Tunisia		

- Consider three events: **Impressionism flourishes in the arts (1860s–1890s)**, **Vast emigration from Europe continues (1870s–1890s)**, and **Bismarck sponsors social welfare legislation (1882–1884)**. How were all of these related to empire and industry?

SUGGESTED REFERENCES

The literature on imperialism is becoming increasingly exciting, especially as authors such as Burbank and Cooper show imperialism's relationship with the nation-state. Others show its confusions and chaotic nature.

Brewer, John, and Frank Trentmann, eds. *Consuming Cultures, Global Perspectives: Historical Trajectories, Transnational Exchanges*. 2006.

Burbank, Jane, and Frederick Cooper. *Empires in World History: Power and the Politics of Difference*. 2010.

Cain, P. J., and A. G. Hopkins, *British Imperialism, 1688–2000*. 2002.

Davis, Mike. *Late Victorian Holocausts: El Niño Famines and the Making of the Third World*. 2001.

Eley, Geoff. *Forging Democracy: A History of the Left in Europe, 1850–2000*. 2002.

Headrick, Daniel R. *Power over Peoples: Technology, Environments, and Western Imperialism 1400 to the Present*. 2010.

Lorcin, Patricia M. E., ed. *Algeria and France 1800–2000: Identity, Memory, Nostalgia*. 2006.

Manning, Patrick. *Migration in World History*. 2005.

Maynes, Mary Jo, et al. *Secret Gardens, Satanic Mills: Placing Girls in European History, 1750–1960*. 2005.

Rappaport, Erika. *Shopping for Pleasure: Women in the Making of London's West End*. 2000.

Reeder, Linda. *Widows in White: Migration and the Transformation of Rural Italian Women, Sicily, 1880–1920*. 2003.

Reid, Richard J. *A History of Modern Africa*. 2009.

Smith, Michael S. *The Emergence of Modern Business Enterprise in France, 1800–1930*. 2005.

Streets, Heather. *Martial Races: The Military, Race, and Masculinity in British Imperial Culture, 1857–1918*. 2004.

Weaver, Stewart, and Maurice Isserman. *Fallen Giants: A History of Himalayan Mountaineering from the Age of Empire to the Age of Extremes*. 2008.

Wildenthal, Lora. *German Women for Empire, 1884–1945*. 2001.

CHAPTER

Modernity and the Road to War

24

1890–1914

In the first decade of the twentieth century, a wealthy young Russian man traveled from one country to another to find relief from a common malady of the time called neurasthenia. Its symptoms included fatigue, lack of interest in life, depression, and sometimes physical illness. In 1910, the young man consulted Sigmund Freud, a Viennese physician whose unconventional treatment—eventually called psychoanalysis—took the form of a conversation about the patient's dreams, sexual experiences, and everyday life. Over the course of four years, Freud uncovered his patient's deeply hidden fear of castration, which was disguised as a fear of wolves—thus the name Wolf-Man, by which he is known to us. Freud worked his cure, as the Wolf-Man himself put it, "by bringing repressed ideas into consciousness" through extensive talking.

In many ways, the Wolf-Man could be said to represent his time. Born into a family that owned vast estates, he reflected Europe's growing prosperity, though on a grander scale than most. Countless individuals were troubled, even mentally disturbed like the Wolf-Man, and suicides were not uncommon. The Wolf-Man's own sister and father died from intentional drug overdoses. As the twentieth century opened, Europeans raised questions about family, gender relationships, empire, religion, and the consequences of technology. Every sign of imperial wealth brought on an apparently irrational sense of Europe's decline. British writer H. G. Wells saw in this era "humanity upon the wane . . . the sunset of mankind." Gloom filled the pages of many a book and upset the lives of individuals like the Wolf-Man.

Conflict rattled the world as a growing number of powers, including Japan and the United States, fought their way into even more territories. The nations of Europe had lurched from one diplomatic crisis to another

Edvard Munch, *The Scream* (1893)
In some of his paintings, Norwegian artist Edvard Munch captured a certain spirit of the turn of the century, depicting in soft pastel colors the newly leisured life of people strolling in the countryside. But modern life also had a tortured side, which Munch was equally capable of portraying. *The Scream* is taken as emblematic of the torments of modernity as the individual turns inward, beset by neuroses, self-destructive impulses, and even madness. It can also be suggested that the screamer, like Europe, travels the road to World War I. *(Scala/Art Resource, NY/© 2011 The Munch Museum/The Munch-Ellingsen Group/Artists Rights Society [ARS], New York.)*

Public Debate over Private Life 798
- Population Pressure
- Reforming Marriage
- New Women, New Men, and the Politics of Sexual Identity
- Sciences of the Modern Self

Modernity and the Revolt in Ideas 806
- The Opposition to Positivism
- The Revolution in Science
- Modern Art
- The Revolt in Music and Dance

Growing Tensions in Mass Politics 810
- The Expanding Power of Labor
- Rights for Women and the Battle for Suffrage
- Liberalism Tested
- Anti-Semitism, Nationalism, and Zionism in Mass Politics

European Imperialism Challenged 817
- The Trials of Empire
- The Russian Empire Threatened
- Growing Resistance to Colonial Domination

Roads to War 825
- Competing Alliances and Clashing Ambitions
- The Race to Arms
- 1914: War Erupts

over access to global resources and control of territory—both within Europe and outside it. As the great powers fought to dominate people around the world, competition for empire fueled an arms race that threatened to turn Europe—the most civilized region of the world, according to its leaders—into a savage battleground. In domestic politics, militant nationalism fueled ethnic hatreds and anti-Semitism, even leading to physical violence. Women suffragists along with politically disadvantaged groups such as the Slavs and Irish demanded full rights, even as political assassinations and public brutality swept away the liberal values of tolerance and human rights.

These were just some of the conflicts associated with modernity, a term often used to describe the rise of mass politics, the spread of technology, the faster pace of life, and the decline of a rural social order—all of which were visible in the West from the late nineteenth century on (see "Terms of History," page 799). The word *modern* was also applied to art, music, science, and philosophy of this period. Although many people today admire the brilliant, innovative qualities of modern art, music, and dance, people of the time were offended, even outraged, by the new styles and sounds. Freud's theory that sexual drives exist in even the youngest children shocked people. Every advance in science and the arts simultaneously undermined middle-class faith in the stability of Western civilization.

That faith was further tested when the heir to the Austro-Hungarian throne was assassinated in June 1914. Few gave much thought to the global significance of the event, least of all the Wolf-Man, whose treatment with Freud was just ending. He viewed the fateful day of June 28 simply as the day he "could now leave Vienna a healthy man." Yet the assassination put the spark to the powder keg of international discord that had been building for several decades. The resulting disastrous war, World War I, like the insights of Freud, would transform life in the West.

CHAPTER FOCUS How did developments in social life, art, intellectual life, and politics at the turn of the twentieth century produce instability and set the backdrop for war?

Public Debate over Private Life

At the beginning of the twentieth century, an increasing number of people could aspire to a comfortable family life because of Europe's improved standard of living. Yet as the twentieth century opened, traditional social norms such as heterosexual marriage and woman's domestic role as wife and mother came under attack by what were seen as the forces of modernity. The falling birthrate, rising divorce rate, and growing activism for marriage reform provoked heated accusations that changes in private life were endangering national health. Discussions about sexual identity became a political issue. Middle-class women took jobs and became active in public to such an extent that some feared the disappearance of distinct gender roles. Women's visibility in public life prompted one British songster in the late 1890s to write:

> Rock-a-bye baby, for father is near
> Mother is "biking" she never is here!
> Out in the park she's scorching all day
> Or at some meeting is talking away!

Discussions of gender roles and private life contributed to rising social tensions because they challenged so many traditional ideals. Freud and other scientists tried to be dispassionate in their study of such phenomena—sexuality, for example—and to formulate treatments for "modern" ailments such as those afflicting the Wolf-Man. Public discussions of private life, especially when they became inter-

1894–1895 Japan defeats China in Sino-Japanese War

1899–1902 South African War fought between Dutch descendants and British in South African states

1901 Irish National Theater established by Maud Gonne and William Butler Yeats; death of Queen Victoria

1904–1905 Japan defeats Russia in Russo-Japanese War

1895 1900

1894–1899 Dreyfus Affair exposes anti-Semitism in France

1900 Sigmund Freud publishes *The Interpretation of Dreams*

1903 Emmeline Pankhurst founds Women's Social and Political Union

TERMS OF HISTORY

Modern

The word *modernus* was introduced into Latin in the sixth century; after that, the claim to being modern occurred in many centuries and cultures. Shakespeare, for example, referred to "modern ideas" in his plays, and historians have long debated where "modern" history begins: with Abraham? with Charlemagne? with the Renaissance?

Despite the claims of many ages to being modern, the term has fastened itself most firmly on the period from the end of the nineteenth century through the first half of the twentieth. Its most specific historical use has been to describe the art, music, and dance that flourished at that time. When used in this sense, *modern* indicates a sharp break with lyrical, romantic music and dance and with the tradition of realism in the arts. The blurred images of the impressionists and the jarring music of Arnold Schoenberg are part of modern art because they break with accepted forms. The sexual rawness of Gustave Flaubert's *Madame Bovary* (see Chapter 22) or of Sigmund Freud's analysis of the Wolf-Man's dreams added to the multifaceted meanings of the word *modern*. Sometimes this intellectual break with the cultural past is referred to as modernism.

At the end of the nineteenth century, the word *modern* also referred to social phenomena. Women who went to work or entered universities or began careers were called modern women. They believed that, by showing themselves capable and rational, they could end restrictions placed on them. They lived different lives from those women who confined themselves to the domestic sphere. This departure from tradition also made them appear modern.

In seeking an education, these women were invoking a meaning of the words *modern* and *modernity* dating back to the Enlightenment. Rational thought and science have also been taken as the bedrock of the modern. *Modernization*—another derivative of the word *modern*—refers to the kind of scientific and technological progress that rational observation produced. Industry and its products—indoor plumbing, electricity, telephones, and automobiles—were signs of *modernity*. This focus on the term *modern* to indicate technological advance made it useful as a way to celebrate the West's modernity in contrast to other people's backwardness. Its association with new (and therefore superior) thinking and forward advancement became central to the justification for imperial rule, especially as Western empires were increasingly contested by 1900.

The many meanings of the word *modern* and those words deriving from it make it a multipurpose term. Complex, paradoxical, and dense with meaning, *modern* may not always be precise. But its very breadth explains why *modern* remains a much-debated term of history.

twined with politics, demonstrated the close connection of private and public concerns.

Population Pressure

From the 1890s on, European politicians and the public hotly discussed urgent concerns over trends in population, marriage, and sexuality. The staggering population increases of the eighteenth century continued through the nineteenth century, and rural people and migrants crowded into cities. Alarmed by the urban masses, Social Darwinists became louder in their warnings about racial decay. Reformers and politicians saw both the quantity and quality of population as looming national crises.

1905
Nicholas II establishes the Duma after revolution erupts in Russia; Albert Einstein publishes his special theory of relativity

1906
Women receive vote in Finland

1907
Pablo Picasso launches cubist painting with *Les Demoiselles d'Avignon*

1908
Young Turks revolt against rule by sultan in Ottoman Empire

1911–1912
Revolutionaries overthrow Qing dynasty and declare China a republic

1914
Assassination of Austrian archduke Francis Ferdinand and his wife by Serbian nationalist precipitates World War I

1905 1910 1915

Soaring Population

The European population continued to grow as the twentieth century opened. Germany increased in size from 41 million people in 1871 to 64 million in 1910, and tiny Denmark grew from 1.7 million people in 1870 to 2.7 million in 1911. Improvements in sanitation and public health that extended the human life span and reduced infant mortality contributed to the increase. Following the earlier examples of Vienna and Paris, planners tore apart and rebuilt Berlin, Budapest, and Moscow to house their swelling populations. The German government pulled down eighteenth-century Berlin and reconstructed the city with new roadways and mass-transport systems as the capital's population grew to over 4 million. Less-powerful states also rebuilt cities to absorb population growth: the Balkan capitals of Sofia, Belgrade, and Bucharest gained tree-lined boulevards and improved sanitation facilities. As the number of urban residents surpassed that of the rural population in a number of countries, ruling elites from the countryside protested the activism and unruliness of urban dwellers.

Alarm over the Falling Birthrate

While the absolute size of the population was rising in the West, the birthrate (measured in births per thousand people) was falling. The birthrate had been decreasing in France since the eighteenth century; other European countries began experiencing the decline late in the nineteenth century. The Swedish birthrate dropped from thirty-five births per thousand people in 1859 to twenty-four per thousand in 1911; Germany went from forty births per thousand in 1875 to twenty-seven per thousand in 1913.

Industrialization and urbanization helped bring about this change. Farm families needed fewer hands because new agricultural machinery was taking the place of human laborers. In cities, individual couples were free to make their own decisions about limiting family size, learning from neighbors or, for those with enough money and education, from pamphlets and advice books about birth-control practices, including coitus interruptus (the withdrawal method of preventing pregnancy). Industrial technology played a further role in curtailing reproduction: condoms, improved after the vulcanization of rubber in the 1840s, proved fairly reliable in preventing conception, as did the diaphragm. Abortions were also common.

The wider use of birth control stirred controversy. Critics accused middle-class women, whose fertility was falling most rapidly, of holding a "birth strike." Meeting early in the twentieth century, bishops in the Church of England condemned family limitation as "demoralizing to character and hostile to national welfare." Politicians worried that the drop in the birthrate was due to a crisis in masculinity, which would put military strength at risk. In the United States, Theodore Roosevelt, who became president in 1901, blamed middle-class women's selfishness for the population decline, calling family limitation "one of the most unpleasant and unwholesome features of modern life." The "quality" of those being born worried activists: If the "best" classes had fewer children, politicians asked, what would society look like if only the "worst" classes grew in number?

Racism and nationalism shaped the debate over population. The decline in fertility, one German nationalist warned, would fill the country with "alien peoples, above all Slavs and probably East European Jews as well." Nationalist groups promoting large, "racially fit" families sprang up in France, Germany, Britain, and elsewhere, and they inflamed the political climate with racial hatreds. Instead of building consensus to create an integrated political community, politicians won votes by rais-

Large Czech Family

This photograph of a rural family in Czechoslovakia shows the differences that were coming to distinguish urban from rural people. Although even a farm family, especially in eastern Europe, might proudly display technology such as a new phonograph, it might not practice family limitation, which was gradually reducing the size of urban households. In eastern Europe, several generations lived together more commonly in rural areas than in cities. How many generations do you see in this image? *(© Scheufler Collection/Corbis.)*

ing fears of ethnic minorities, the poor, and women who limited family size.

Reforming Marriage

Reformers thought that improving conditions within marriage would raise both the quality and quantity of children born. Many educated Europeans believed in eugenics — a set of ideas about producing "superior" people through selective breeding. A famed Italian criminologist declared that "lower" types of people were not humans but "orangutans." Eugenicists wanted increased childbearing for "the fittest" and decreased childbearing — even sterilization — for "degenerates": the disabled, criminals, and others deemed inferior. Women of the "better" classes, reformers also believed, would have more children if marriage were made more equal. One step would be to allow married women to keep their wages and to own property, both of which in the traditional system legally belonged to their husbands. Another step would be to allow women rights to their own children, and given the legal limits, reformers suggested, married women were reluctant to have more than one or two children.

Reformers worked to improve marriage laws in order to boost the birthrate, while feminists sought to improve the lot of mothers and their children. Sweden made men's and women's control over property equal in marriage and allowed married women to work without their husband's permission. Other countries, among them France (1884), legalized divorce and made it less complicated to obtain. Reformers reasoned that divorce would allow unhappy couples to separate and undertake more loving and thus more fertile marriages. By the early twentieth century, several countries had passed legislation that provided government subsidies for medical care and child support in order to encourage motherhood among the lower classes. Concerns regarding population partially laid the foundations for the welfare state — that is, a nation-state whose policies addressed not just military defense, foreign policy, and political processes but also the social and economic well-being of its people.

The conditions of women's lives varied across Europe. For example, a greater number of legal reforms occurred in western versus eastern Europe, but women could get university degrees in Austria-Hungary long before they could at Oxford or Cambridge. However, in much of rural eastern Europe, the father's power over the extended family remained almost dictatorial. According to a survey of family life in eastern Europe in the early 1900s, fathers married off their children so young that 25 percent of women in their early forties had been pregnant more than ten times. Yet reform of everyday customs did occur. For instance, in some Balkan villages a traditional family system called the *zadruga*, in which all individual families within an extended family shared a common great house, survived from earlier times. Yet by the late nineteenth century, individual couples gained privacy by building small sleeping dwellings surrounding the great house. In addition, among the middle and upper classes of eastern Europe, many grown children were coming to believe that they had a right to select a marriage partner instead of accepting the spouse their parents chose for them.

New Women, New Men, and the Politics of Sexual Identity

Rapid social change set the stage for even bolder behaviors among some middle-class women. Adventurous women traveled the globe on their own to promote Christianity, make money, or learn about other cultures. The increasing availability of white-collar jobs for educated women meant that more of them could adopt an independent way of life. The so-called **new woman** dressed more practically, with

new woman: A woman who, from the 1880s on, dressed practically, moved about freely, and often supported herself.

Sydney Grundy, *The New Woman* (1900)
By the opening of the twentieth century, the "new woman" had become a much-discussed phenomenon. Artists painted portraits of this independent creature, while novelists and playwrights like Henrik Ibsen depicted her ambition to throw off the wifely role — or at least to shape that role more to her own personality. In this lithograph, she also smokes. *(© Private Collection / The Stapleton Collection / The Bridgeman Art Library.)*

Maria Montessori
Maria Montessori, famous today for the global network of schools that bear her name, was the perfect example of a "new woman." Her work outside the home with children was controversial; she was also a highly skilled medical doctor and, secretly, an unwed mother. While she developed a set of sophisticated theories for the advancement of young children generally, others cared for her own son. *(akg-images/ullstein bild.)*

fewer petticoats and looser corsets, biked down city streets and country lanes, lived apart from her family in a women's club or an apartment, and supported herself (see the illustration on page 801). Italian educator Maria Montessori (1870–1952), the first woman in Italy to earn a medical degree and the founder of an educational system that still bears her name, secretly gave birth to an illegitimate child. Other new women lived openly with their lovers. The growing number of new women challenged accepted views of women's dependence and seclusion in the home. Not surprisingly, there was loud criticism: the new woman, German philosopher Friedrich Nietzsche wrote, had led to the "uglification of Europe."

Sexual identity also fueled debate. A popular book in the new field of "sexology," which studied sex scientifically, was *Sexual Inversion* (1896) by Havelock Ellis. Ellis, a British medical doctor, claimed that there was a new personality type—the homosexual—identifiable by such traits as effeminate behavior and attraction to the arts (in males) and physical affection for members of their own sex (in both males and females). Homosexuals joined the discussion, calling for recognition that they composed a natural "third sex" and were not just people behaving sinfully. Some maintained that homosexuals were members of an "intermediate sex," possessing both male and female traits and thus marking "a higher order" on the scale of human evolution. The discussion of homosexuality started the trend toward seeing sexuality in general as a basic part of human identity.

The issue became explosive in the spring of 1895, when Irish playwright Oscar Wilde (1854–1900) was convicted of indecency—a charge that referred to his sexual affairs with young men (see the illustration on the left)—and sentenced to two years in prison. "Open the windows! Let in the fresh air!" one newspaper rejoiced at the conviction. Between 1907 and 1909, German newspapers broadcast the courts-martial of military men in Kaiser William II's closest circle who were condemned for homosexuality and transvestitism. Amid growing concern over population and family values, the government had to assure the public that William's own family life

Oscar Wilde
The Irish-born writer Oscar Wilde symbolized the persecution experienced by homosexuals in the late nineteenth century. Convicted of indecency for having sexual relations with another man, Wilde served time in prison—a humiliation for the husband, father, acclaimed author, and witty playwright. *(Library of Congress, Prints and Photographs Division. LC-USZ62 914833.)*

was "a fine model" for the German nation. Heterosexuality thus took on patriotic overtones: accused homosexuals among the elite in Germany were said by journalists to be out to "emasculate our courageous master race." Despite the harsh judgments against homosexuals, these cases paved the way for growing sexual openness in the next generations. Yet they also made sexual issues regular weapons in politics.

Sciences of the Modern Self

Scientists and Social Darwinists found cause for alarm not only in the poor condition of the working class but also in modern society's mental complaints such as those of the Wolf-Man. Medical people decided that most mental illnesses originated in the "nerves," which were troubled by the hectic pace of urban living. New sciences of the mind such as psychology and psychoanalysis aimed to treat everyone, not just the insane.

New Approaches to Mental Ailments

A number of books in the 1890s presented arguments on causes and cures for modern nervous ailments. *Degeneration* (1892–1893), by Hungarian-born physician Max Nordau, blamed overstimulation for both individual and national deterioration. According to Nordau, male and female nervous complaints and the increasingly bizarre art world reflected a general downturn in the human species. The Social Darwinist remedy for such mental decline was imperial adventure for men and increased childbearing for both sexes because it would restore men's virility and women's femininity.

Investigations into the working of the mind led to new fields of study. Scientific study of the origins of criminal behavior developed into the field of criminology. French psychologist Alfred Binet designed intelligence tests he claimed could measure the capacity of the human mind more accurately than a schoolteacher could. In Russia, physiologist Ivan Pavlov proposed that behavior could be controlled by conditioning mental reflexes. Pavlov's experiments in changing behavior, especially his success in getting a dog to salivate upon hearing a bell, became part of the toolkit of modern psychology.

Freud and Psychoanalysis

Sigmund Freud (1856–1939) devised an approach to treating modern anxieties and mental problems that challenged the widespread liberal belief, dating from the Enlightenment, in a rational self that consistently acts in its own best interest. Dreams, he explained in *The Interpretation of Dreams* (1900), reveal an unseen, repressed, and powerful part of one's personality—the "unconscious"—where all sorts of desires are more or less hidden from one's rational understanding. Freud also believed that the human psyche is made up of

Sigmund Freud: Viennese medical doctor and founder, in the late nineteenth century, of psychoanalysis, a theory of mental processes and problems and a method of treating them.

Freud's Office and Collection
Sigmund Freud surrounded himself with imperial trophies such as Oriental rugs and African art objects in his study and therapy room in Vienna. Freud was fascinated by cures brought about through shamanism, trances, and other practices of non-Western medicine. Despite his successes, Freud, like other Jews, was a target of anti-Semitism from Nazis and others; he eventually escaped Vienna for exile in London in 1938.
(ullstein bild/The Granger Collection, NYC—All rights reserved.)

NEW SOURCES, NEW PERSPECTIVES

Psychohistory and Its Lessons

In the last fifty years, historians have radically changed the way they write history. In the nineteenth century, history books mostly recounted the deeds of kings and emperors, discussed royal genealogy, and listed wars and peace treaties. Determined to be factual, historians not only laid out the fine points of laws, charters, and treaties but also checked their sources in archives. They would often characterize historical actors as brave, evil, determined, or weak.

Much has changed since then, partly because of the rise of psychology and psychoanalysis as the twentieth century opened. Confronted with strikes, mass demonstrations, anarchist deeds, anti-Semitism, and other forms of political violence, some observers tried to explain a phenomenon they called crowd psychology. According to this view, psychological states are important factors in shaping some public events. Scholars began pursuing deeper insights and more systematic ways of analyzing the character and motivation of important people from the past.

Not surprisingly, Sigmund Freud studied great historic figures like Leonardo da Vinci from a psychoanalytic perspective, exploring the connection between repressed childhood fantasies and later towering accomplishments. Freud also explained the outbreak of World War I as more of a psychological than a diplomatic event. He saw the war as a collective death wish. He subjected both individuals and entire societies to psychoanalytic probing. Few historians followed Freud's lead.

In 1957, William Langer, president of the American Historical Association, charged his fellow scholars with being foolishly backward in their methods. Unlike scientists, he claimed, historians did not develop scientific systems or explore new techniques such as psychoanalysis that might advance their understanding of the past. Weren't such characterizations as ambition, greed, hate, and great intelligence simply commonsensical and not at all rigorously analytical? But what was the "scientific" depth in such characterizations? Another criticism by those interested in psychology and psychoanalysis was that historians often saw people as acting rationally in their self-interest. Trauma, irrational or uncontrollable drives, and unconscious motivations played no role in understanding historical figures.

Psychohistory was born of these discussions. Psychoanalyst Erik Erikson, in *Young Man Luther* (1958), announced that the Protestant Reformation originated in the childhood traumas of Martin Luther. Identity crises stemming from his relationship with his father caused Luther to search for and reject father figures, including the pope. Erikson's book caused a stir among historians, changing the way people understood Luther and starting an entirely new school of historical thought.

Some of the most compelling examples of psychohistory have focused on the lives of individuals whose leadership has appeared abnormal or even psychotic. Historians interested in psychoanalysis have examined Kaiser William II's childhood for explanations of his rejection of Bismarck, his turn to an aggressive foreign policy, and his participation in World War I. Analyses of Adolf Hitler's followers have attributed the blind worship of these dictators to mass psychic needs and traumas, while the brutality of Hitler's father and the adoration of his mother have been seen to play a role in the future dictator's development.

Psychohistory remains controversial. While its practitioners expand the field of historical explanation, its critics find that fitting the behavior of historical characters into Freud's schema can be a formulaic process. Other critics find that psychohistory is too imprecise and speculative because it is not based on the same kinds of hard, documentary evidence that

three competing parts: the ego, the part that is most in touch with the need to work and survive—that is, reality; the id (or libido), the part that contains instincts and sexual energies; and the superego, the part that serves as the conscience. Freud's theory of human mental processes and his method for treating their malfunctioning came to be called psychoanalysis.

Freud demanded that sexual life should be understood objectively, free from religious or moral judgments. He shocked many of his contemporaries by insisting, for example, that all children have sexual drives from the moment of birth. He believed that for the individual to attain maturity and for society to remain civilized, sexual desires—such as impulses toward incest—had to be rigorously repressed. Freud claimed that adult gender identity does not result from anatomy alone but rather develops over the course of a person's life experiences. Although gender is more complicated than biology alone would suggest, certain aspects of gender roles—such as motherhood—are normal. Freud's psychoanalytic theory maintained that girls and women have powerful sexual feelings, an idea that broke sharply with existing beliefs that women were passionless.

historians have been trained to use. Nonetheless, psychohistorians have made a good case that if we are going to look at personalities, character, and relationships, we should do so in the most informed way possible and not rely simply on clichés.

Questions to Consider

1. **What are the advantages and disadvantages of psychohistory?**
2. **How would you set out to investigate the psychological reasons for the actions of William II, Emmeline Pankhurst, Marie Curie, or Gavrilo Princip? Would you look at their social background, their childhood, their character, or other parts of their lives?**
3. **Can we write history without talking about the emotions, mental habits, and human relationships of major figures? To what extent should we either embrace or avoid psychologizing when thinking about the past?**

Further Reading

Binion, Rudolph. *Hitler among the Germans*. 1984.

Erikson, Erik. *Young Man Luther: A Study in Psychoanalysis and History*. 1958.

Kohut, Thomas A. *Wilhelm II and the Germans: A Study in Leadership*. 1991.

Kaiser William and Edward VII's Family

Psychotherapy aimed to cure troubled individuals in large part by discussing family relationships and the fantasies built around them. Psychohistory often draws its analyses from these same relationships. The royal families of Europe are ripe for such analysis because Russian, German, British, and other monarchs were closely related. (In this photo Britain's Edward VII is at right, and Germany's Kaiser William is second from right.) Psychohistorians may therefore view the outbreak of World War I as the work of complex family dynamics. *(Hulton Archive/Getty Images.)*

The influence of psychoanalysis became pervasive in the twentieth century (see "New Sources, New Perspectives," above). For example, Freud's "talking cure," as his method of treatment was quickly labeled, gave rise to a general acceptance of talking out one's problems. As psychoanalysis gained respect as a means of restoring mental health, terms such as *neurotic* and *unconscious* came into widespread use. Freud attributed girls' complaints about sexual harassment or abuse to fantasy caused by "penis envy," an idea that led members of the new profession of social work to believe that most instances of such abuse had not actually occurred. A meticulous scientist, Freud closely observed symptoms and paid attention to the most minute evidence from everyday life. Like Darwin, he rejected optimistic views of the world, claiming that humans were motivated by irrational drives toward death and destruction. These urges, he believed, shaped society's collective actions.

REVIEW QUESTION How did ideas about the self and about personal life change at the beginning of the twentieth century?

Modernity and the Revolt in Ideas

Toward the beginning of the twentieth century, intellectuals and artists so completely rejected longstanding beliefs and traditional artistic forms that they ushered in a new era. In science, the theories of Albert Einstein and other researchers established new truths in physics. Art and music became unrecognizable. Artists and musicians who produced deliberately shocking works were, like Freud, heavily influenced by advances in science and the progress of empire. Their blending of the scientific and the irrational, and of Western and non-Western styles, helped launch the disorienting revolution in ideas and creative expression that we now identify collectively as **modernism**.

The Opposition to Positivism

Late in the nineteenth century, many philosophers and social thinkers suddenly rejected the century-old belief that using scientific methods would uncover enduring social laws. This belief, called positivism, had emphasized the permanent nature of fundamental laws and had motivated reformers' attempts to perfect legislation based on studies of society. Challenging positivism, some critics declared that because human experience is ever changing, there are no constant or enduring social laws. German political theorist Max Weber (1864–1920) maintained that the sheer number of facts involved in policymaking would often make decisive action by bureaucrats impossible. In times of crisis, a charismatic leader might usurp power because of his ability to act simply on intuition. These turn-of-the-century thinkers, called relativists and pragmatists, influenced thinking about society and government throughout the twentieth century.

The most radical among the scholars was the German philosopher **Friedrich Nietzsche** (1844–1900), who distinguished between the "Apollonian," or rational, side of human existence and the "Dionysian" side, with its expression of more primal urges. Nietzsche believed that people generally prefer the rational, Apollonian explanations of life because the powerful Dionysian sense of death and love, such as that found in Greek tragedy, is too disturbing. He asserted that truth is not certain but rather a human representation of reality. Neither scientists nor other careful observers, he said, can have knowledge of nature that is not filtered through human perception.

Rather than writing the long, sustained type of argument common to traditional Western philosophy, Nietzsche used aphorisms—short, disconnected statements of truth or opinion—to convey the impression that his ideas were a single individual's unique perspective instead of a universal and absolute truth. Nietzsche was convinced that late-nineteenth-century Europe was witnessing the decline of absolute truths such as those found in religion. Thus, he announced, "God is dead, we have killed him." Far from arousing dread, however, the death of God, according to Nietzsche, would give birth to a joyful quest for new "poetries of life" to replace worn-out religious and middle-class rules. Nietzsche believed that an uninhibited, dynamic "superman," free from traditional religious and moral values, would replace the rule-bound middle-class person.

Nietzsche thought that each individual had within a vital life energy that he called "the will to power." The idea inspired many at the time, including his students. As a teacher, Nietzsche was so vibrant—like his superman—that his first students thought they were hearing another Socrates. Nietzsche's teaching career, however, was short-lived: he contracted syphilis and was insane in the last eleven years of his life, cared for by his sister. She edited his attacks on middle-class values into attacks on Jews, and after his death she revised his complicated concepts of the will to power and of superman to appeal to nationalists, anti-Semites, and militarists, all of whom he actually hated.

The Revolution in Science

While Nietzsche and other philosophers questioned the ability of traditional science to provide timeless truths, scientific inquiry itself flourished and the sciences gained in prestige. Around the turn of the century, however, discoveries by pioneering researchers shook the foundations of scientific certainty and challenged accepted knowledge. In 1896, French physicist Antoine Becquerel discovered radioactivity. He also suggested the mutability of elements by the rearrangement of their atoms. French chemist Marie Curie and her husband, Pierre Curie, isolated the elements polonium and radium, which

---

modernism: Artistic styles around the turn of the twentieth century that featured a break with realism in art and literature and with lyricism in music.

Friedrich Nietzsche: Late-nineteenth-century German philosopher who called for a new morality in the face of God's death at the hands of science and whose theories were reworked by his sister to emphasize militarism and anti-Semitism.

are more radioactive than the uranium Becquerel used. From these and other discoveries, scientists concluded that atoms are not solid, as had long been believed, but are composed of subatomic particles moving about a core. In a paper published in 1900, German physicist Max Planck announced his quantum theory, stating that energy is delivered not in a steady stream but in discrete packets, which he later called quanta.

In this atmosphere of discovery, physicist **Albert Einstein** (1879–1955) proclaimed his special theory of relativity in 1905. According to this theory, space and time are not absolute categories but instead vary according to the vantage point of the observer. Only the speed of light is constant. That same year, Einstein suggested that the solution to problems in Planck's theory lay in considering light both as little packets *and* as waves. Einstein later proposed yet another blurring of two distinct physical properties, mass and energy. He expressed this equivalence in the equation $E = mc^2$, or energy equals mass times the square of the speed of light. In 1916, Einstein published his general theory of relativity, which connected the force, or gravity, of an object with its mass and proposed a fourth mathematical dimension to the universe. Much more lay ahead once Einstein's theories of energy were applied to technology: television; nuclear power; and, within forty years, nuclear bombs.

The findings of Planck, Einstein, and others were not readily accepted, because long-standing scientific truths were at stake. Both Einstein and Planck struggled against mainstream science and its professional institutions. Other factors were at work: Marie Curie faced such resistance from the scientific establishment that even after she became the first person ever to receive a second Nobel Prize (1911), the prestigious French Academy of Science turned down her candidacy for membership. It claimed that a woman simply could not have done such outstanding work. Acceptance of these scientists' discoveries gradually came, and Max Planck Institutes were established in German cities, streets across Europe were named after Marie Curie, and Einstein's name became synonymous with *genius*. These scientists achieved what historians call a paradigm shift—that is, in the face of considerable resistance, they transformed the foundations of science as their findings and theories came to replace those of earlier pioneers.

Albert Einstein: Scientist whose theory of relativity (1905) revolutionized modern physics and other fields of thought.

Marie and Pierre Curie
Pierre and Marie Curie shared a Nobel Prize in Physics in 1903, and after Pierre's death in 1906, Marie went on to win a Nobel Prize in Chemistry in 1911. Their daughter Irène Joliot-Curie followed in her parents' footsteps; like her mother, she died of leukemia because of long exposure to radioactive material during experiments. *(Mary Evans Picture Library/AISA Media.)*

Modern Art

Conflicts between traditional values and new ideas also raged in the arts as artists distanced themselves further from classical Western styles. Some modern artists defied the historic and realistic scenes still favored, for example, by the powerful German monarchy and public museums. Modernism in the arts not only challenged time-honored standards but also led to an increase in competing artistic styles that continues today.

A Variety of Styles

Abandoning the soft colors of impressionism as too subtle for a dynamic industrial society, a group of Parisian artists exhibiting in 1905 combined blues, greens, reds, and oranges so intensely that they were called *fauves* ("wild beasts"). A leader of the short-lived fauvism, Henri Matisse soon struck out in a new direction, targeting the expanding class of white-collar workers. Matisse saw his art as meant "for every mental worker, be he businessman or writer, like an appeasing influence, like a mental soother, something like a good armchair in which to rest from physical fatigue." His colorful depictions of domestic interiors, North African scenes, and family life departed from strict realism, yet they appealed to viewers in part because of their calming qualities.

Duchamp's *Bicycle Wheel*
French artist Marcel Duchamp's *Bicycle Wheel* exemplifies the kind of modern art that outraged patrons and museumgoers. To many it appeared to mock the careful work of great Western artists in the past and to stand for nothing at all—that is, a kind of artistic nihilism. In fact, Duchamp closely studied Asian thought and religions, and many of his works reflect his engagement. In this case, the bicycle wheel stood for the wheel of dharma and thus represented an object of meditation. *(Marcel Duchamp [1887–1968]/The Israel Museum, Jerusalem, Israel/© DACS/Vera and Arturo Schwarz Collection of Dada and Surrealist Art/The Bridgeman Art Library International/© 2011 Artists Rights Society [ARS], New York/ADAGP, Paris/Succession Marcel Duchamp.)*

French artist Paul Cézanne initiated one of the most powerful trends in modern art by using rectangular daubs of paint to portray his geometric vision of dishes, fruit, drapery, and the human body. Cézanne's art accentuated structure—the lines and planes found in nature—instead of presenting nature as it appeared in everyday life. Following in Cézanne's footsteps, Spanish artist Pablo Picasso (1881–1973) developed a style called cubism. Its radical emphasis on planes and surfaces converted his models into bizarre, almost unrecognizable forms. Picasso's painting *Les Demoiselles d'Avignon* (1907), for example, showed the bodies of the *demoiselles* ("young ladies" or in this case "prostitutes") as fragmented and angular, with their heads modeled on African masks. Picasso's work showed the profound influences of African, Asian, and South American arts, but his use of these features was less decorative and more brutal than Matisse's, for example. Like imperialists who recounted their brutal exploits in speeches and memoirs, he brought knowledge of the empire home in a disturbing style that captured the jarring uncertainties of society and politics in these decades.

Art as Political Criticism

Across Europe, artists mixed political criticism, even outrage, with the stylistic changes in their work. "Show the people how hideous is their actual life," anarchists challenged. Picasso, who had spent his youth in working-class Barcelona, a hotbed of anarchist thought, aimed to present the plain truth about industrial society in his art. In 1912, Picasso and French painter Georges Braque devised a new kind of collage that incorporated bits of newspaper stories, string, and various useless objects. The effect was a work of art that appeared to be made of trash. The newspaper clippings Picasso included described battles and murders, suggesting that Western civilization was not as refined as it claimed to be. In eastern and central Europe, artists criticized the growing nationalism that determined royal purchases of sculpture and painting: "The whole empire is littered with monuments to soldiers and monuments to Kaiser William," one German artist complained. Groups of avant-garde artists in Vienna and Berlin produced other types of art, much of it critical of boastful nationalism.

Scandinavian and eastern European artists produced works expressing the torment many felt at the time. Like the ideas of Freud, their style of portraying inner feelings—called expressionism—broke with middle-class optimism. Norwegian painter

Edvard Munch aimed "to make the emotional mood ring out again as happens on a gramophone." His painting *The Scream* (1893), shown in the chapter opening illustration, used twisting lines and a tortured skeletal human form to convey the horror of modern life that many artists perceived. The Blue Rider group of artists, led by German painter Gabriele Münter and Russian painter Wassily Kandinsky, used geometric forms and striking colors to express an inner, spiritual truth. Kandinsky is often credited with producing the first fully abstract paintings around 1909; shapes in these paintings no longer bear any resemblance whatsoever to physical objects or reality but are meant to express deep feelings. The expressionism of Oskar Kokoschka, who worked in Vienna, was even more intense, displaying ecstasy, horror, and hallucinations. As a result, his work—like that of other expressionists and cubists before World War I—was a commercial failure in an increasingly complex marketplace run not only by museum curators but by professional dealers—"experts"—like the professionals in medicine and law.

Art Nouveau Objects
Alone among the new art at the turn of the twentieth century, art nouveau was a commercial success, producing objects such as this picture frame, mirror, and ashtray that well-to-do consumers bought in quantity. As it became a global style, art nouveau also influenced travel posters, stained-glass windows, and large pieces of furniture. *(Private Collection/The Bridgeman Art Library International.)*

Art Nouveau | Only one innovative style of this period was an immediate commercial success. That style, **art nouveau** ("new art"), won approval from government, critics, and the masses. Designers manufactured everything from dishes, calendars, and advertising posters to streetlamps and even entire buildings in this new style. As one French official said about the first art nouveau coins issued in 1895, "Soon even the most humble among us will be able to have a masterpiece in his pocket." Adapting elements from Asian design, art nouveau attempted to offset the harshness of industrial work and office routine with flowing lines and images depicting intertwined elements from nature. The impersonality of machines was replaced by vines and flowers and the softly curving bodies of female nudes intended to soothe the individual viewer. This idea directly contrasted with Picasso's artistic vision. Art nouveau was the notable exception to the public outcries over innovations in the visual arts.

The Revolt in Music and Dance

"Astonish me!" was the motto of modern dance and music, both of which shocked audiences in the concert halls of Europe. American dancer Isadora Duncan took Europe by storm at the turn of the century when, draped in a flowing garment, she appeared barefoot in one of the first performances of modern dance. Her sophisticated style was called "primitive" because it no longer followed the steps of classical ballet. Experimentation with forms of bodily expression animated the Russian Ballet's 1913 performance of *The Rite of Spring*, by Igor Stravinsky, the tale of an orgiastic dance to the death performed to ensure a plentiful harvest. The dance troupe struck awkward poses and danced to rhythms intended to sound primitive. At the work's premiere in Paris, one journalist reported that "the audience began shouting its indignation. . . . Fighting actually broke out among some of the spectators." Such controversy made *The Rite of Spring* a box-office hit, although critics called its choreographer a "lunatic" and the music itself "the most discordant composition ever written."

Composers had been rebelling against Western traditions for several decades, producing music that was disturbing rather than pretty. Having heard Asian musicians at international expositions, French composer Claude Debussy transformed his style to reflect non-European musical patterns and wrote

art nouveau: An early-twentieth-century artistic style in graphics, fashion, and household design that featured flowing, sinuous lines, borrowed in large part from Asian art.

articles in praise of Asian harmonies. Italian composer Giacomo Puccini used non-Western subject matter for his opera *Madame Butterfly*, which debuted in 1904. Listeners were jarred when they heard non-Western tonalities. Like the bizarre representation of reality in cubism, the works of Austrian composer Richard Strauss added to the revolution in music by using several musical keys simultaneously, thus distorting familiar musical patterns. Strauss's operas *Salome* (1905) and *Elektra* (1909) reflected the modern fascination with violence and obsessive passion. A newspaper critic claimed that Strauss's dissonant works "spit and scratch and claw each other like enraged panthers."

The early orchestral work of Austrian composer Arnold Schoenberg, who also wrote cabaret music to earn a living, shocked even Strauss. In *Theory of Harmony* (1911), Schoenberg proposed eliminating tonality altogether; a decade later, he devised a new twelve-tone scale. "I am aware of having broken through all the barriers of a dated aesthetic ideal," Schoenberg wrote of his music. But new aesthetic models distanced artists like Schoenberg from their audiences, who found this music unpleasant and incomprehensible. The artistic elite and the social elite parted ranks. "Anarchist! Nihilist!" shouted Schoenberg's audiences, using political terms to show their distaste for modernist music.

REVIEW QUESTION How did modernism transform the arts and the world of ideas?

Growing Tensions in Mass Politics

Alongside disturbances in intellectual life, the political atmosphere grew charged. On the one hand, liberal opinions led to political representation for workingmen. Networks of communication, especially the development of journalism, created a common fund of political knowledge that made mass politics possible. On the other hand, many political activists were no longer satisfied with the liberal rights such as the vote sought by earlier reformers, and some strenuously opposed them. Militant nationalists, anti-Semites, socialists, suffragists, and others demanded changes that challenged liberal values. Traditional elites, resentful of the rising middle classes and urban peoples, aimed to overturn constitutional processes and crush city life. Politics soon threatened national unity, especially in central and eastern Europe, where governments often answered reformers' demands with repression.

The Expanding Power of Labor

European leaders worried about the rise of working-class political power late in the nineteenth century. Laboring people's growing confidence came in part from expanding educational opportunities. Workers in England, for example, avidly read works by Shakespeare and took literally his calls for political action in the cause of justice that rang out in plays such as *Julius Caesar*. Unions gained members among factory workers, while the labor and socialist parties won seats in parliaments as men in the lower classes received the vote. In Germany, Kaiser William II had allowed antisocialist laws to lapse after dismissing Bismarck as chancellor in 1890. Through grassroots organizing at the local level, the Social Democratic Party, founded by German socialists in 1875, became the largest parliamentary group in the Reichstag by 1912. Other socialist parties across Europe helped elect workers' representatives into parliaments, where they focused on passing legislation that benefited workers and their families.

Winning elections actually raised problems among socialists. Some felt uncomfortable sitting in parliaments alongside the upper classes—in Marxism, the enemies of working people. Others worried that accepting high public offices would weaken socialists' commitment to the ultimate goal of revolution. These issues divided socialist organizations. Between 1900 and 1904, the Second International wrestled with the question of revisionism—that is, whether socialists should work from within governments to improve the daily lives of laborers or push for a violent revolution to overthrow governments. Powerful German Marxists argued that settling for reform rather than revolution would only buttress capitalism. The wealthy would continue to rule unchallenged while throwing small crumbs to a few working-class politicians. Stormy discussions divided these German purists, whom the German aristocracy held in contempt, from the socialist delegates of France, England, and Belgium who had gained influential government posts.

Police persecution forced some working-class parties to operate in exile. The Russian government, for instance, outlawed political parties, imprisoned activists, and gave the vote to only a limited number of men when it finally introduced a parliament in 1905. Thus, Russian activist V. I. Lenin (1870–1924), who would take power during the Russian Revolution of 1917 and whose brother was executed for plotting the tsar's assassination, was a journalist and Marxist theorist operating outside the country. Lenin advanced the theory that a highly disciplined socialist elite—rather than the working class as a whole—would lead a lightly industrialized Russia into socialism. At a 1903 party meeting of Russian Marxists, he maneuvered his opponents into walking out of the proceedings so that his supporters gained control of the party. Thereafter, his faction was known as the Bolsheviks, so named after the Russian word for "majority," which they had temporarily formed. They struggled to suppress the Mensheviks ("minority"), who had been the dominant voice in Russian Marxism until Lenin outmaneuvered them. Neither of these factions, however, had as large a constituency within Russia as the Socialist Revolutionaries, whose objective was to politicize peasants, rather than industrial workers, to bring about revolution. All of these groups prepared for the revolutionary moment through study, propaganda efforts, and secret organizing—not through the electoral politics successfully employed elsewhere in Europe.

During this same period, anarchists, along with some trade union members known as syndicalists, kept Europe in a panic with their terrorist acts. In the 1880s, anarchists had bombed stock exchanges, parliaments, and businesses; by the 1890s, they were assassinating heads of state: the Spanish premier in 1897, the empress of Austria-Hungary in 1898, the king of Italy in 1900, and the president of the United States in 1901, to name a few famous victims. Syndicalists advocated the use of direct action, such as general strikes and sabotage, to paralyze the economy and give labor unions more power. Not unexpectedly, the upper and middle classes watched these developments with alarm, while politicians from the old landowning and military elites of eastern and central Europe worked to reverse the trend toward constitutionalism and mass political participation.

Rights for Women and the Battle for Suffrage

Women continued to agitate for the benefits of liberalism such as the right to vote and to own their wages if married. Laws in France, Austria, and Germany even made women's attendance at political meetings a crime. There were many battlefields besides the one for legal rights. German women focused on widening opportunities for female education. Their activism aimed to achieve the German cultural ideal of *Bildung*—the belief that education can build character and that individual development has public importance. In several countries, women monitored the regulation of prostitution. Their goal was to prevent prostitutes from being imprisoned on suspicion of having syphilis when men with syphilis faced no such incarceration. Other women took up pacifism as their cause. Many of them were inspired by Bertha von Suttner's popular book *Lay Down Your Arms* (1889), which emphasized how war inflicted terror on women and families. (Later, von Suttner would influence Alfred Nobel to institute a peace prize and then win the prize herself in 1903.)

By the 1890s, many women activists decided to focus their efforts on a single issue—suffrage (the right to vote)—as the most effective way to correct the many problems caused by male privilege. Thereafter, suffragists created major organizations involving millions of activists, paid officials, and permanent offices out of the earlier reform groups and women's clubs. British suffrage leader Millicent Garrett Fawcett (1847–1929) pressured members of Parliament for women's right to vote and participated in national and international congresses on behalf of suffrage. Across the Atlantic, American Susan B. Anthony (1820–1906) traveled the country to speak at mass suffrage rallies, edited a suffragist newspaper, and founded the International Woman Suffrage Alliance in 1904. Its leadership argued that despite men's promises to protect women in exchange for their inequality, the system of male chivalry had led to exploitation and abuse. "So long as the subjection of women endures, and is confirmed by law and custom, . . . women will be victimized," a leading British suffragist claimed. Other activists believed that women had attributes needed to balance masculine qualities that dominated society. The characteristics associated with mothering, they asserted, were as necessary in shaping a country's destiny as were qualities that stemmed from industry and commerce.

Women's rights activists were predominantly, though not exclusively, from the middle class. Free from the need to earn a living, they simply had more time to be activists and to read the works of feminist theorists such as Harriet Taylor and John Stuart Mill. They attended theater productions of Norwegian playwright Henrik Ibsen's jarring plays about rebellious middle-class heroines, such as *A Doll's House* (see page 782). But working-class women also participated in the suffrage movement, though many distrusted the middle class and believed suffrage to be less crucial than women's pressing economic concerns. Textile workers of Manchester, England, for example, put together a vigorous movement for the vote, seeing it as essential to improved working conditions.

In 1906 in Finland, suffragists achieved their first major victory when the Finnish parliament granted women the vote. The failure of parliaments elsewhere in Europe to enact similar legislation pro-

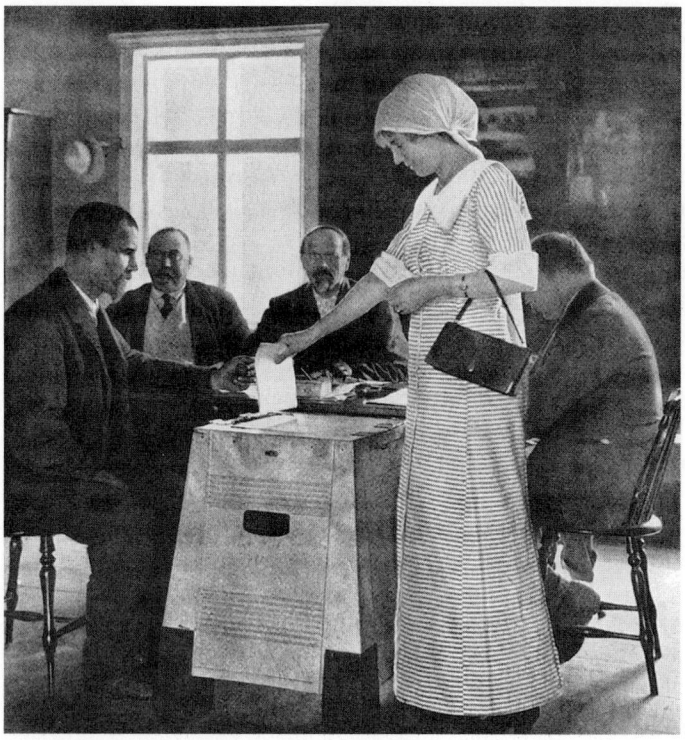

Woman Suffrage in Finland
In 1906, Finnish women became the first in Europe to receive the vote in national elections when the socialist party there—usually opposed to feminism as a middle-class rather than a working-class project—supported woman suffrage. The Finnish vote encouraged activists in the West, now linked together by many international organizations and ties, because it showed that more than a century of lobbying for reform could lead to gains. *(Mary Evans Picture Library.)*

voked some suffragists to violence. British suffragist **Emmeline Pankhurst** (1858–1928) and her daughters founded the Women's Social and Political Union (WSPU) in 1903 in the belief that women would accomplish nothing unless they threatened men's property. Starting in 1907, members of the WSPU held parades in English cities, and in 1909 they began a campaign of violence, blowing up railroad stations, slashing works of art, and chaining themselves to the gates of Parliament. Disguising themselves as ordinary shoppers, they carried little hammers in their hand warmers to smash the plate-glass windows of department stores and shops. Parades and demonstrations made suffrage a public spectacle, and outraged men responded by attacking the marchers. Arrested for disturbing the peace, the marchers went on hunger strikes in prison. Like striking workers, these women were willing to use confrontational tactics to obtain rights, and, like anarchists, they were not afraid to damage property or add to the tensions of urban life.

Liberalism Tested

Governments in western Europe, where liberal institutions were seemingly well entrenched, sought to control turn-of-the-century conflicts with pragmatic policies that often struck at liberalism's very foundations. Beyond ending the policy of free trade at the heart of economic liberalism, politicians decided that government needed to expand social welfare programs—another break with the liberal idea that societies should develop freely without government interference. Although the programs were few and addressed urban needs only in part, they added to the growing apparatus of the welfare state in which governments actively promoted social well-being.

Revising Liberalism in Britain

Political parties in Britain discovered that the recently enfranchised voter wanted solid benefits in exchange for his support. In 1905, the British Liberal Party won a majority in the House of Commons and pushed for social legislation aimed at the working class. "We are keenly in sympathy with the representatives of Labour," one Liberal politician announced. "We have too few of them in the House of Commons." The National Insurance Act of 1911 instituted a program of unemployment assistance funded by new taxes on the wealthy. When Conservatives in the House of Lords resisted the higher taxation, the Liberal government threatened to add to the number of lords and thus dilute the power of the nobility. The newcomers, unlike the defiant Conservatives, would be sure to vote for reform. Under this threat, the lords approved the Parliament Bill of 1911, which eliminated their veto power.

Emmeline Pankhurst (1858–1928): Organizer of a militant branch of the British suffrage movement, working actively for women's right to vote.

The Irish question further tested Britain's commitment to such liberal values as autonomy, opportunity, and individual rights. In the 1890s, new groups formed to foster Irish culture as a way of heightening the political challenge to what they saw as Britain's continuing colonization of the country. In 1901, the circle around poet William Butler Yeats and actress Maud Gonne founded the Irish National Theater to present Irish rather than English plays. Gonne took Irish politics into everyday life by opposing British efforts to gain the loyalty of the young. Every time an English monarch visited Ireland, he or she held special receptions for children. Gonne and other Irish volunteers sponsored competing events, handing out candies and other treats for patriotic youngsters. "Dublin never witnessed anything so marvelous," enthused one home rule supporter, "as the procession . . . of thirty thousand school children who refused to be bribed into parading before the Queen of England."

Promoters of an "Irish way of life" encouraged speaking Irish Gaelic instead of English, singing songs in Irish, and rallying in support of Catholicism instead of the Church of England. This cultural agenda gained political force with the founding in 1905 of Sinn Féin ("We Ourselves"), a group that strove for complete Irish independence. In 1913, Parliament approved home rule for Ireland. While the outbreak of World War I prevented the legislation from taking effect, it hardly killed dreams of independence.

Unrest in Italy Italian nation builders, left with a towering debt from unification and with widespread pockets of discontent, drifted rapidly from liberalism's moorings in solid industrial development and the rule of law. Corruption plagued Italy's constitutional monarchy, which had not yet developed either the secure parliamentary system of England or the authoritarian monarchy of Germany to guide its growth. To forge national unity in the 1890s, prime ministers used patriotic rhetoric and imperial adventure, notably a second unsuccessful attempt to conquer Ethiopia in 1896. Riots and strikes, followed by armed government repression, erupted, until Giovanni Giolitti, who served as prime minister for three terms between 1903 and 1914, adopted a policy known as *trasformismo* (from the word for "transform"). Following this policy, he used bribes, public works programs, and other benefits to localities to gain support from their deputies in parliament. Political opponents called Giolitti the "Minister of the Underworld" and accused him of preferring to buy the votes of local bosses rather than spending money to develop the Italian economy. In a wave of protest, urban workers in the industrial cities of Turin and Milan and rural laborers in the depressed agrarian south demanded change, especially of the suffrage laws that allowed only three million of more than eight million adult men to vote. Giolitti appeased the protesters by instituting social welfare programs and, in 1912, virtually complete manhood suffrage. These reforms, however, did not signal a full commitment either to a liberal constitutional system or to economic development across the nation.

Anti-Semitism, Nationalism, and Zionism in Mass Politics

The real crisis for liberal political values of equal citizenship and tolerance came in the two decades leading up to World War I when politicians used anti-Semitism and militant nationalism to win elections. They told voters that Jews were responsible for the difficulties of everyday life and that anti-Semitism and increased patriotism would fix all problems. Voters from many levels of society responded enthusiastically, agreeing that Jews were villains and the nation-state was the hero in the struggle to survive. In both republics and monarchies, anti-Semitism and militant nationalism played key roles in mass politics by providing those on the radical right with a platform to gain working-class votes and thus combat the radical left of social democracy. This new radical right shattered the older notion of nationalism based on liberal ideas of the rule of law and the equality of all citizens. Liberals had hoped that voting by the masses would make politics more harmonious as parliamentary debate and compromise smoothed out class and other differences. The new politics as shaped by right-wing leaders — usually representatives of the agrarian nobility, aristocrats who controlled the military, and highly placed clergy — dashed those hopes by making politics loud, emotional, and hateful and thus a distinct departure from liberal consensus and rational debate.

Authoritarianism in Russia A strong tradition of anti-Semitism existed in Russian politics. Russian tsar **Nicholas II** (r. 1894–1917) believed firmly in Russian orthodox religion, autocratic politics, and anti-Semitic social values. Taught as a child to hate Jews, Nicholas blamed them for any failure in Russian policy. Many high officials eagerly endorsed anti-

Nicholas II: Tsar of Russia (r. 1894–1917) who promoted anti-Semitism and resisted reform in the empire.

The Humiliation of Alfred Dreyfus
French captain Alfred Dreyfus was sent to a harsh exile after being convicted of spying for Germany. Before he was taken to Devil's Island, he was subjected to the extreme humiliation of having his officer's insignia and ribbons stripped from his uniform and his sword broken before hundreds of troops and a mob of screaming anti-Semites. We can only imagine what this meant to a man in his mid-thirties who, despite being Jewish, had worked his way through an elite military school and up the ranks of the army. What do you see in his bearing? *(The Granger Collection, New York.)*

Semitism to gain the tsar's favor. Pogroms became a regular threat to Russian Jews, especially as Nicholas was adamant that he would never order soldiers to "fire on Christians to protect Jews." Nicholas increasingly limited where Jews could live and how they could earn a living. This tradition of anti-Semitism was integral to Russian autocracy and religion.

The Dreyfus Affair in France

Principles of equal citizenship and tolerance were sorely tested in France, where the Dreyfus Affair marked the most notorious instance of anti-Semitism in mass politics. The fragile Third Republic was backed by a liberal alliance of businessmen, shopkeepers, professionals, and rural property owners but opposed by powerful forces in the aristocracy, the military, and the Catholic church. They hoped that this republic, like earlier ones, could be overthrown. Economic downturns, widespread corruption, and attempted coups made the republic more vulnerable, and the press attributed failures of almost any kind to Jews, who, it said, controlled all businesses and even the republic itself. Despite an excellent system of primary education promoting literacy and rational thinking, the public tended to agree, while the clergy and monarchists kept hammering the message that the republic was nothing but a conspiracy of Jews.

Amid rising anti-Semitism, a Jewish captain in the French army, Alfred Dreyfus, was charged with spying for Germany in 1894. From a well-respected family, Dreyfus had worked his way through the military, whose upper echelons were traditionally aristocratic, Catholic, and monarchist. The military produced manufactured "evidence" to gain Dreyfus's conviction and exile to the harsh fortress on Devil's Island. Even though the espionage continued after his arrest, the republican government stubbornly upheld Dreyfus's guilt. Then several newspapers received proof that the army had fabricated documents to convict Dreyfus. In 1898, the celebrated French novelist Émile Zola published an article titled *"J'accuse"* (I accuse) on the front page of a Paris daily, exposing the web of perjury that had created the impression of Dreyfus's guilt.

The article named the truly guilty parties and called for a return to government based on honesty and the rule of law. "I have but one passion, that of Enlightenment," wrote Zola. *"J'accuse"* led to public riots, quarrels among families and friends, and denunciations of the army, which eroded confidence in the republic and in French institutions. The government finally pardoned Dreyfus in 1899, dismissed the aristocratic and Catholic officers held responsible, and ended religious teaching orders to ensure a secular public school system that honored toleration and the rule of law. In the final analysis, however, the Dreyfus Affair made anti-Semitism and official lies a standard tool of politics by showing the effectiveness of hate-filled slogans on the public.

Nationalist and Anti-Semitic Politics in Germany

The ruling elites in Germany also used anti-Semitism to win support from those who feared the consequences of Germany's sudden and overwhelming industrialization. The agrarian elites, who still controlled the highest reaches of government, lost ground as agriculture (from which they drew their fortunes) declined as a force in Germany's economy. Its share of the gross national product fell from 37 percent in the 1880s to only 25 percent early in the 1900s. As industrialists grew wealthier and new opportunities drew rural workers to the cities, where they would be free from the landowner's grip, the agrarian elites came to loathe industry for challenging their traditional authority. A Berlin newspaper noted, "The agrarians' hate for cities . . . blinds them to the simplest needs and the most natural demands of the urban population."

In contrast to Bismarck's astute wooing of the masses through social programs, William II's aristocracy often encouraged anti-Semitism as its political tool. Conservatives and a growing radical right claimed that Jews, who made up less than 1 percent of the German population, were responsible for destroying traditional society. In the 1890s, nationalist and anti-Semitic political pressure groups flourished, hurling diatribes against Jews, new women, and Social Democrats, whom they branded as internationalist and unpatriotic. They played to the fears of small farmers by accusing Jews of causing agricultural booms and busts. Political campaigns came to feature hate-filled speeches and nationalist ranting rather than rational programs to meet the problems of economic change. This new right invented a modern politics that rejected the liberal value of parliamentary consensus, relying instead on inventing enemies and thus dividing what was supposed to be a unified nation-state.

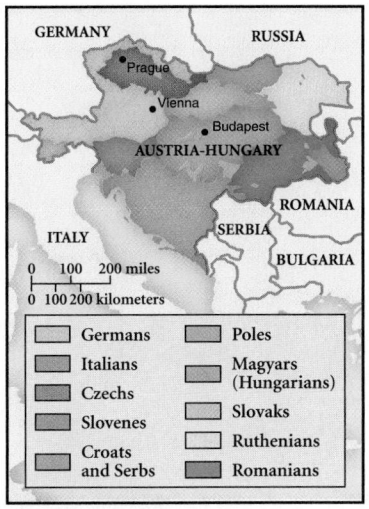

Principal Ethnic Groups in Austria-Hungary, c. 1900

Ethnic Politics in Austria-Hungary

Politicians in the dual monarchy of Austria-Hungary also used militant nationalism and anti-Semitism to win votes, but here the presence of many ethnic groups meant competing nationalisms and thus greater complexity in the politics of hate. Foremost among the nationalists were the Hungarians, who wanted autonomy for themselves while forcibly imposing Hungarian language and culture on all other, supposedly inferior, ethnic groups in Hungary. Nationalist claims for greater Hungarian influence (or Magyarization, from Magyars, the principal ethnic group) rested on two pieces of evidence: Budapest was a thriving industrial city, and the export of Hungarian grain from the vast estates of the Magyar nobility saved the monarchy's finances. The nationalists disrupted the Hungarian parliament so regularly that it weakened the orderly functioning of the government.

Although capable of causing trouble for the empire, Hungarian nationalists, who mostly represented agrarian wealth, were themselves vulnerable. Hungary's exploited ethnic groups—Slovaks, Romanians, and Ruthenians—resisted Magyarization. Industrial workers struck to protest horrendous labor conditions, and 100,000 activists gathered in the fall of 1905 in front of the Hungarian parliament to demonstrate for the vote. In response, Hungarians intensified Magyarization, even decreeing that all tombstones be engraved in Magyar. Emperor Francis Joseph temporarily quieted the Hungarian nationalists by threatening to introduce universal manhood suffrage, which would allow both the Magyars' lower-class and non-Magyar opponents to vote. Although many assimilated Magyar ways, discriminatory policies toward these groups and scorn for the imperial government in Vienna made for instability throughout Austria-Hungary.

Nationalities across the Dual Monarchy intensified their demands for rights. Croats, Serbs, and other Slavic groups in the south called for equality with the Hungarians. The central government allowed the Czechs a greater number of Czech officials in the government because of the growing industrial prosperity of their region. But every step favoring the Czechs provoked outrage from the traditionally dominant ethnic Germans. When Austria-Hungary decreed in 1897 that government officials in the Czech region of the empire would have to speak Czech as well as German, the Germans rioted—further straining unity in the empire.

Tensions mounted as German politicians in Vienna linked the growing power of Hungarians and Czechs to Jews. Karl Lueger, whose newly formed Christian Social Party attracted members from among the aristocracy, Catholics, artisans, shopkeepers, and white-collar workers, had great success with this new brand of politics. In hate-filled speeches that hurled abuse at Jews and other non-German groups, Lueger appealed to those for whom modern life meant a loss of privilege and security, and he was elected mayor of Vienna in 1895. Lueger's ethnic nationalism and anti-Semitism threatened the multinationalism on which Austria-Hungary was based. His attacks were so effective at getting votes, however, that a widening group of politicians made anti-Semitism an integral part of their election campaigns, calling Jews the "sucking vampire" of modernity and blaming them for the tumult of migration, the economy, and just about

MAP 24.1 Jewish Migrations in the Late Nineteenth Century
Pogroms in eastern Europe, increasingly violent anti-Semitism across the continent, and the search for opportunity motivated Jews to migrate to many parts of the world. Between 1890 and 1914, some five million Jews left Russia alone. They moved to European cities; to North and South America; and, as Zionism progressed, to Palestine.

anything else people found disturbing. Politics became a thing not of debate in parliaments but of violent racism in the streets.

The Jewish Response to Anti-Liberal Politics

Anti-Semites lumped Jewish people into one hated group, but like members of any other religion, Jews were divided by social class and education. Jews in western Europe had responded to increased legal tolerance in the nineteenth century by moving out of Jewish neighborhoods, intermarrying with Christians, and in some cases converting to Christianity — practices known as assimilation. Many well-educated Jews favored the classical culture of the German Empire because it seemed more rational and liberal than the ritualistic Catholicism of Austria-Hungary. Still, many accomplished and prosperous Jews, like the pioneer of psychoanalysis, Sigmund Freud, flourished amid the cosmopolitan urban culture of Vienna or Budapest despite escalating anti-Semitism. By contrast, less educated and less prosperous Jews, such as those in Russia and Romania, were increasingly singled out for persecution, legally disadvantaged, and forced to live in ghettos. Jews from these countries might seek refuge in the nearby cities of central and eastern Europe where they could eke out a living as day laborers or artisans. Jewish migration to the United States and other countries also swelled (Map 24.1). By 1900, many Jews were prominent in cultural and economic affairs in cities across the continent even as far more were discriminated against and victimized elsewhere.

Amid vast migration and continued persecution, a spirit of Jewish nationalism arose. "Why should we be any less worthy than any other . . . people?" one Jewish leader asked. "What about our nation, our language, our land?" Jews began organizing resistance to pogroms and anti-Semitic politics, and intellectuals drew on Jewish folklore, language, customs, and history to establish a national identity parallel to that of other Europeans. In the 1880s, the Ukrainian physician Leon Pinsker, seeing the Jews' lack of national territory as fundamental to the persecution heaped on them, advocated the migration of Jews to Palestine. (See Document, "Leon Pinsker Calls for a Jewish State," page 817.) In 1896, Theodor Herzl, strongly influ-

DOCUMENT

Leon Pinsker Calls for a Jewish State

In 1882, the Ukrainian physician Leon Pinsker published a pamphlet called Auto-Emancipation *in which he analyzed the situation of the Jews in Europe. This pamphlet convinced some in Europe—most notably Theodor Herzl—that Jews could never be assimilated into European culture no matter how many dropped their religion in favor of Christian ways. This pamphlet ultimately led some Jews to migrate to Palestine, despite Pinsker's own conviction that the Middle East was not necessarily the right place for creating a Jewish nation.*

This is the kernel of the problem, as we see it: *the Jews comprise a distinctive element among the nations under which they dwell, and as such can neither assimilate nor be readily digested by any nation. . . .*

A fear of the Jewish ghost has passed down the generations and the centuries. First a breeder of prejudice, later . . . it culminated in Judeophobia. Judeophobia is a psychic aberration. As a psychic aberration it is hereditary, and as a disease transmitted for two thousand years it is incurable. . . .

The Jews are aliens who can have no representatives, because they have no country. Because they have none, because their home has no boundaries within which they can be entrenched, their misery too is boundless. . . .

. . . If we would have a secure home, give up our endless life of wandering and rise to the dignity of a nation in our own eyes and in the eyes of the world, we must, above all, not dream of restoring ancient Judaea. We must not attach ourselves to the place where our political life was once violently interrupted and destroyed. The goal of our present endeavors must be not the "Holy Land," but a land of our own. We need nothing but a large tract of land for our poor brothers, which shall remain our property and from which no foreign power can expel us. There we shall take with us the most sacred possessions which we have saved from the shipwreck of our former country, the *God-idea* and the *Bible*. It is these alone which have made our old fatherland the Holy Land, and not Jerusalem or the Jordan. Perhaps the Holy Land will again become ours. If so, all the better, but *first of all*, we must determine—and this is the crucial point—what country is accessible to us, and at the same time adapted to offer the Jews of all lands who must leave their homes a secure and indisputed refuge, capable of productivization.

Source: Robert Chazan and Marc Lee Raphael, eds., *Modern Jewish History: A Source Reader* (New York: Schocken Books, 1974), 161, 163, 165–66, 169–71, 171–74.

Question to Consider

- **According to Pinsker, why must Jews find "a land of our own"? What is most important in determining the appropriate location for that homeland?**

enced by Pinsker, published *The Jewish State*, a book that called not simply for migration but for the creation of a Jewish nation-state, the goal of a movement known as **Zionism**. A Hungarian-born Jew, Herzl experienced anti-Semitism firsthand as a Viennese journalist and a writer in Paris during the Dreyfus Affair. He scoured Europe for financial backing, but many prosperous Jews who had assimilated thought his ideas mad. However, backed by poorer eastern European Jews, he organized the first International Zionist Congress (1897). By 1914, some eighty-five thousand Jews had moved into Palestine.

REVIEW QUESTION **What were the points of tension in European political life at the beginning of the twentieth century?**

Zionism: A movement that began in the late nineteenth century among European Jews to found a Jewish state.

European Imperialism Challenged

Anti-Semitism was only one sign that the conditions of modern life were deeply troubling and that the rule of law and other liberal values like tolerance were threatened. Militant nationalism across the West made it difficult for nations to calm international tensions. This nationalist atmosphere heated up, making imperial rivalries among the European powers alarmingly worse. As colonized peoples challenged European control, Japan's growth as an Asian power also threatened stability: in 1904–1905, Japanese expansionism came close to toppling the mighty Russian Empire.

The Trials of Empire

After centuries of global expansion, imperial adventure soured for Britain and France at the beginning of the twentieth century. Newcomers Italy and Germany now fought for a place at the imperial table, and the tense atmosphere among nations raised questions about the future. "Where thirty years ago there existed one sensitive spot in our relations with France, or Germany, or Russia," the British economist J. A. Hobson wrote in 1902, "diplomatic strains are of almost monthly occurrence between the Powers." Mounting tensions exploded violently when Japan and Russia went to war in 1904.

The South African War

Everyone was quick to violence when it came to empire, and Britain in its pursuit of the **South African War** (or Boer War) of 1899–1902 was no exception. In 1896, Cecil Rhodes, then prime minister of the Cape Colony in southern Africa, directed a raid into the neighboring territory of the Transvaal in hopes of stirring up trouble between the Boers, descendants of early Dutch settlers, and the more recent immigrants from Britain who had come to southern Africa in search of gold and other riches. In Rhodes's scheme, the turmoil caused by the raid would justify a British takeover of the Transvaal and the Orange Free State, which the Boers independently controlled. The Boers, however, easily routed the raiders, dealing Britain a bloody defeat and forcing Rhodes to resign in disgrace.

The stunned British government did not accept defeat easily, especially when other Europeans gloated over the British loss. In 1899, Britain began full-scale operations against the Boers. Foreign correspondents covering the South African War reported on appalling bloodshed, heavy casualties, and the unfit condition of the average British soldier. Most alarmingly to those who liked to think of Britain as the most civilized country in the world, news arrived back in London of rampant disease and inhumane treatment of South Africans herded into an unfamiliar institution—the concentration camp, which became the graveyard of tens of thousands, mostly women and children. Britain finally annexed the area after defeating the Boers in 1902, but the cost of war in money, destruction, demoralization, and loss of life was enormous (Map 24.2). Prominent citizens began to call imperialism not the work of civilization but an act of barbarism.

South African War: The war (1899–1902) between Britain and the Boer (originally Dutch) inhabitants of South Africa for control of the region; also called the Boer War.

Newcomers Face Setbacks

Nearly simultaneously with the South African War, the United States defeated Spain in the Spanish-American War in 1898 and took Cuba, Puerto Rico, and the Philippines as its trophies. Experienced in empire, the United States had successfully crushed native Americans, killing many and confining survivors to reservations. However, its imperial reach had generally been continental until its annexation of Hawaii in 1898. Both Cuba and the Philippines had begun vigorous efforts to free themselves from Spanish rule before the war. Urged on by the expansionist-minded Theodore Roosevelt (then assistant secretary of the navy) and the inflammatory daily press, the United States went to war against Spain, claiming it was doing so to help the independence movements. Instead of allowing the independence that victory promised, however, the U.S. government annexed Puerto Rico and Guam and bought the Philippines from Spain. Cuba was theoretically independent, but the United States monitored its activities.

Both Spain and the United States found the results of imperialism uncertain. Spain lost its territories, and the triumphant United States next had to wage a bloody war against the Filipinos, who wanted independence, not another imperial ruler. British poet Rudyard Kipling had encouraged the United States to "take up the white man's burden" by bringing the benefits of Western civilization to those liberated from Spain. However, reports of American brutality in the Philippines, where some 200,000 local people were slaughtered, disillusioned the Western public, who liked to imagine native peoples joyously welcoming the bearers of civilization.

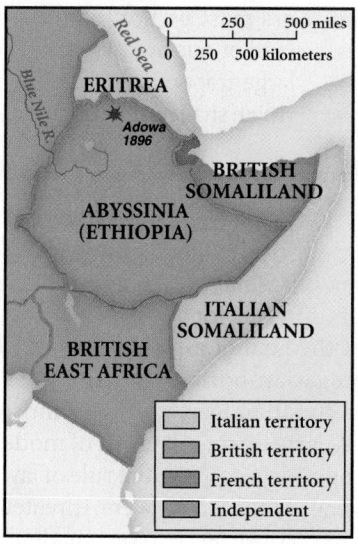

The Struggle for Ethiopia, 1896

Despite these setbacks, the newly unified countries had an emotional stake in gaining colonies. In the early twentieth century, Italian public figures bragged about Italians becoming Nietzschean supermen by conquering Africa and restoring Italy to its ancient position of world domination. After a disastrous war against Ethiopia in 1896, Italy won a costly victory over the Ottoman Empire in Libya. These wars stirred the military spirit in Italians, and hopes rose for imperial grandeur in the future.

Germany likewise joined the imperial contest, demanding an end to British-French domination as colonial powers. Under Bismarck, Germany had

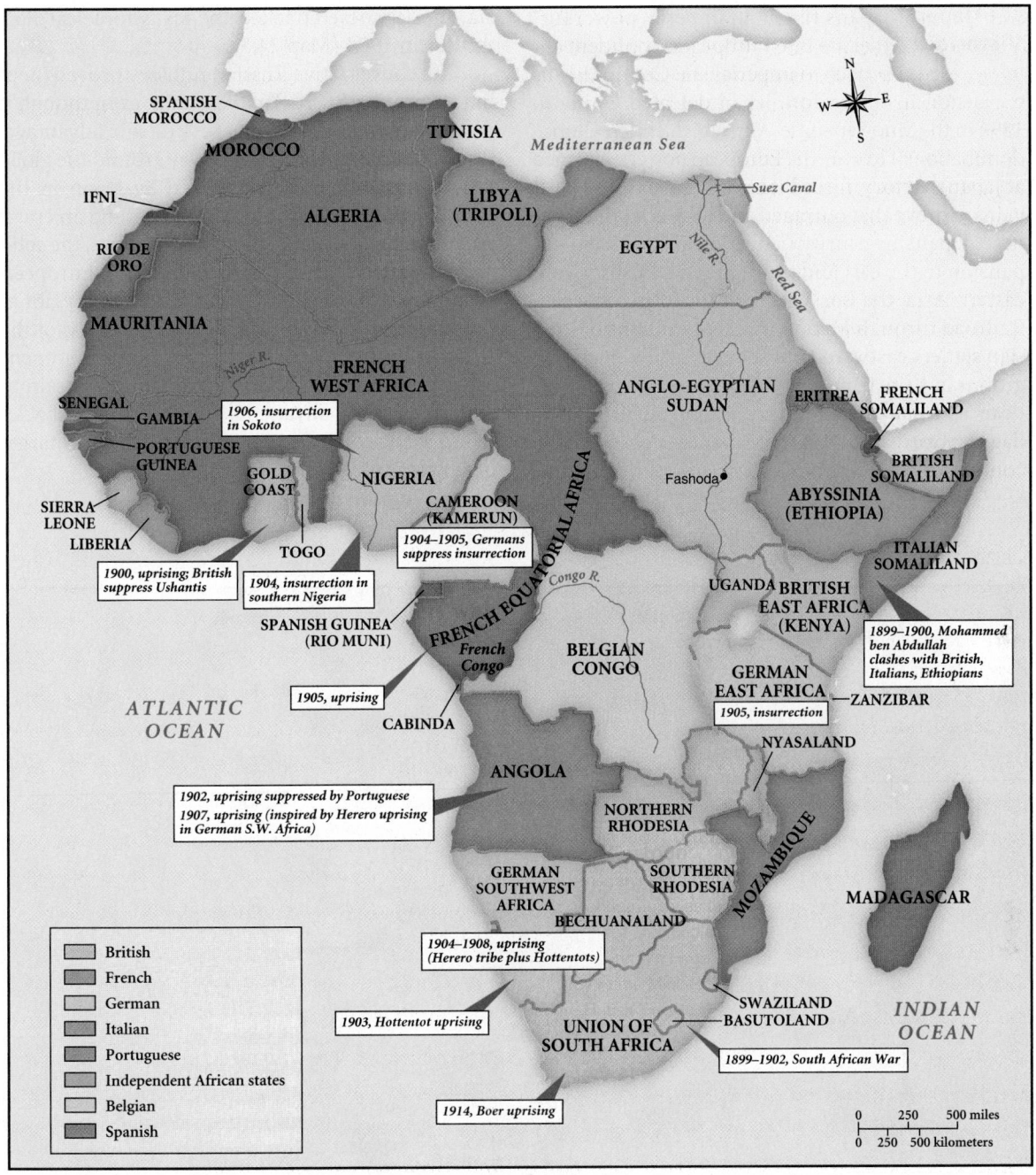

MAP 24.2 Africa in 1914

Uprisings intensified in Africa in the early twentieth century as Europeans tried both to consolidate their rule and to extract more wealth from the Africans. As Europeans were putting down rebellions against their rule, a pan-African movement arose, attempting to unite Africans as one people.

begun its imperial expansion, and German bankers and businessmen were active across Asia, the Middle East, and Latin America. By the turn of the century, Germany had colonies in Southwest Africa, the Cameroons, Togoland, and East Africa and sent linguists, ethnographers, and museum curators to study these cultures and obtain their treasures. Despite these successes, Germany, too, met humiliation and faced constant problems, especially in its dealings with Britain and France and with local peoples in Africa and elsewhere who resisted the German takeover. As Italy and Germany joined the aggressive pursuit of new territory, the confident rule-setting for imperialism at the Berlin Conference a generation earlier gave way to general anxiety, heated rivalry, and nationalist passion.

Japan Victorious

Japan's rise as an imperial power further ate into Europeans' confident approach to imperialism. Continuing its expansion in the region, Japan defeated China in 1894 in the Sino-Japanese War, which ended China's domination of Korea. The European powers, alarmed at Japan's victory, forced it to relinquish most of its gains, a move that outraged and affronted the Japanese. Japan's insecurity had risen with Russian expansion to the east and south in Asia. Pushing into eastern Asia, the Russians built the Trans-Siberian Railroad through Manchuria, sent millions of Russian settlers eastward, and sponsored anti-Japanese groups in Korea, making the Korean peninsula appear, as a Japanese military leader put it, like "a dagger thrust at the heart of Japan." Angered by the continuing presence of Russian troops in Manchuria, the Japanese attacked the tsar's forces at Port Arthur in 1904 (Map 24.3).

The conservative Russian military proved inept in the ensuing Russo-Japanese War, even though it often had better equipment or strategic advantage. Russia's Baltic Fleet sailed halfway around the globe only to be completely destroyed by Japan in the battle of Tsushima Strait (1905). Opening an era of Japanese domination in East Asian politics, the solid victory of a non-European nation over a European great power gave the West reason to worry about the future. As one English general observed of the Russian defeat: "I have today seen the most stupendous spectacle it is possible for the mortal brain to conceive—Asia advancing, Europe falling back." Japan annexed Korea in 1910 and began to target other areas for colonization.

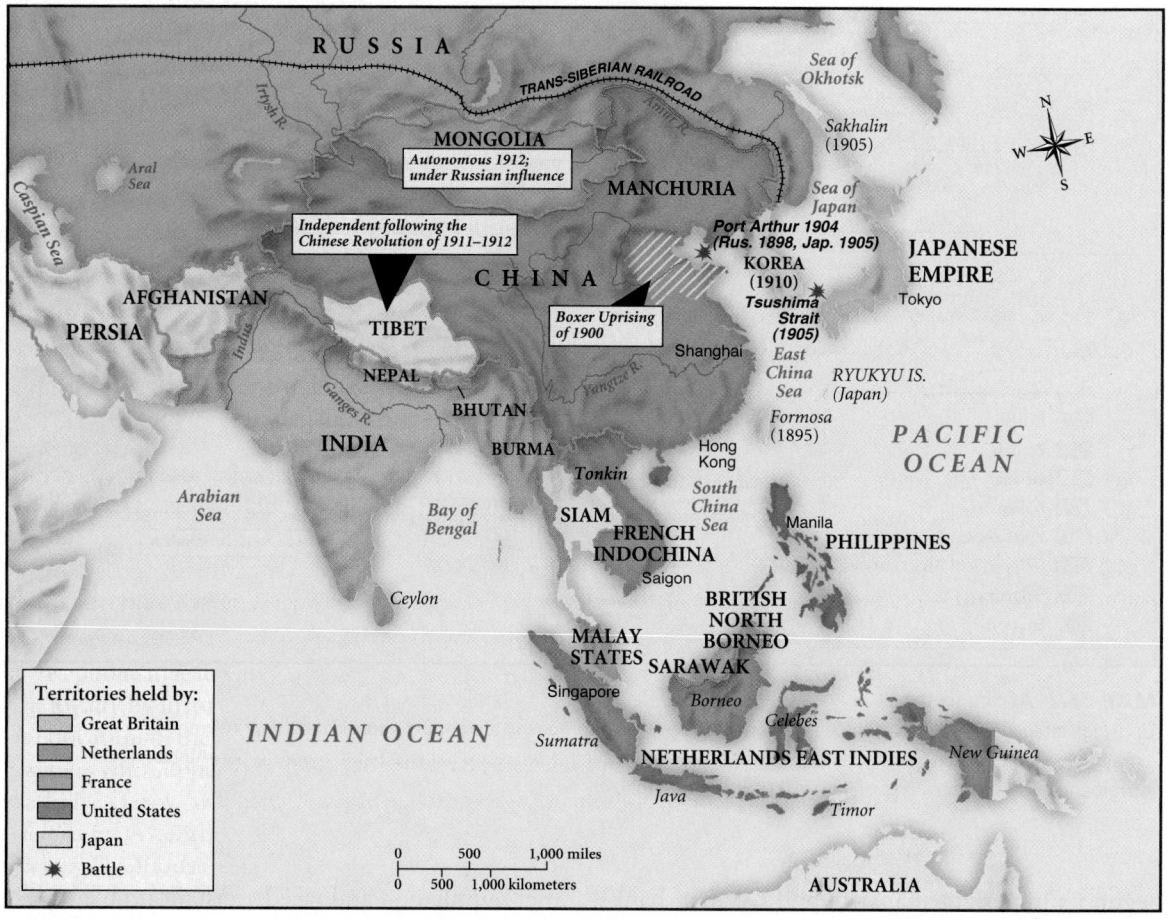

MAP 24.3 Imperialism in Asia, 1894–1914

The established imperialists came to blows in East Asia as they struggled for influence in China and as they met a formidable new rival—Japan. Simultaneously, liberation groups like the Boxers were taking shape, committed to throwing off restraints imposed by foreign powers and eliminating these interlopers altogether. In 1911, revolutionary Sun Yat-sen overthrew the Qing dynasty, which had left China unprepared to resist foreign takeover, and started the country on a different course.

The Russian Empire Threatened

Alongside the humiliating loss to Japan, revolution erupted in Russia in 1905, and the empire tottered on the brink of chaos. Having expanded southward in Asia and settled much of Siberia during the nineteenth century, the mighty Russian Empire had concealed its weaknesses well. State-sponsored industrialization in the 1890s had made the country appear modern to outside observers, and the Russification policy imitated Western-style nation building by attempting to impose a unified national culture on Russia's diverse population. Burdened by heavy taxes to pay for industrialization and by debts owed for the land they acquired during emancipation, peasants revolted in isolated uprisings at the turn of the century. Unrest occurred in the cities, too, as Marxist and union activists incited workers to demand better conditions. In 1903, skilled workers led strikes in Baku; the unity of Armenians and Tatars in these strikes showed how Russification made political cooperation possible among the various ethnicities. Growing worker activism, along with Japan's victory, challenged the autocratic regime.

The Revolution of 1905

On a Sunday in January 1905, a crowd gathered outside the tsar's Winter Palace in St. Petersburg to march in a demonstration to make Nicholas II aware of the brutal working conditions they suffered. Nicholas had often traveled the empire, displaying himself as the divinely ordained "father" of his people; therefore, his "children" thought it natural to appeal to him for aid. Leading the demonstration was a priest who, unknown to the crowd, was a police informant and agitator. Instead of allowing the marchers to pass, troops guarding the palace shot into the trusting crowd, killing hundreds and wounding thousands. Thus began the Revolution of 1905, as news of "Bloody Sunday" moved outraged workers elsewhere to rebel.

In almost a year of turmoil across Russia, urban workers struck over wages, hours, and factory conditions and demanded political representation in the government. Delegates from revolutionary parties such as the Social Democrats and the Socialist Revolutionaries encouraged more direct blows against the central government, but workers also organized their own councils, called soviets. In February, the uncle of the tsar was assassinated; in June, sailors on the battleship *Potemkin* mutinied; in October, a massive railroad strike brought rail transportation to a halt; and in November, uprisings broke out in Moscow. The tsar's forces kept killing protesters, but their deaths only produced more protest.

Anger at Nicholas II's absolute rule brought together an opposing group of artisans and industrial workers, peasants, professionals, and upper-class reformers. Women joined the fray, many demanding an end to discriminatory laws such as those firing women teachers who married. Using the unrest to press their goals, liberals from the zemstvos (local councils) and the intelligentsia (a Russian word for well-educated elites) demanded political reform, in particular the creation of a constitutional monarchy and representative legislature. They believed that the reliance on censorship and the secret police, characteristic of Russian imperial rule, marked the empire as backward. Nicholas's halfhearted responses triggered more street fighting. In the words of one protester, the tsar's attitude turned "yesterday's benighted slaves into decisive warriors."

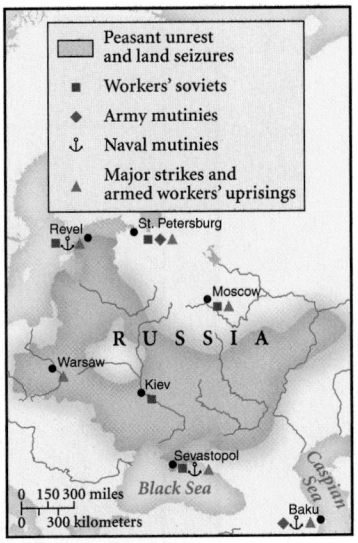

Russian Revolution of 1905

Attempts at Political Reform

The tsar finally yielded to the violence by creating a representative body called the **Duma**. Although very few Russians could vote for representatives to the Duma, its mere existence, along with the new right of open public debate, liberalized government and allowed people to present their grievances to a responsive body. Political parties committed to parliamentary rather than revolutionary programs also took shape during this time. When these newly formed constitutional parties backed the reforms, revolutionary activity finally stopped.

People soon wondered, however, if anything had really changed. From 1907 to 1917, the Duma convened, but twice when the tsar disliked its recommendations he simply sent the delegates home. Nicholas did have an able administrator in Prime Minister Pyotr Stolypin (1863–1911), who was determined to eliminate the sources of discontent. He ended the mir system of communal farming and canceled the land redemption payments that had burdened the peasants since their emancipation in

Duma: The Russian parliament set up in the aftermath of the outbreak of the Revolution of 1905.

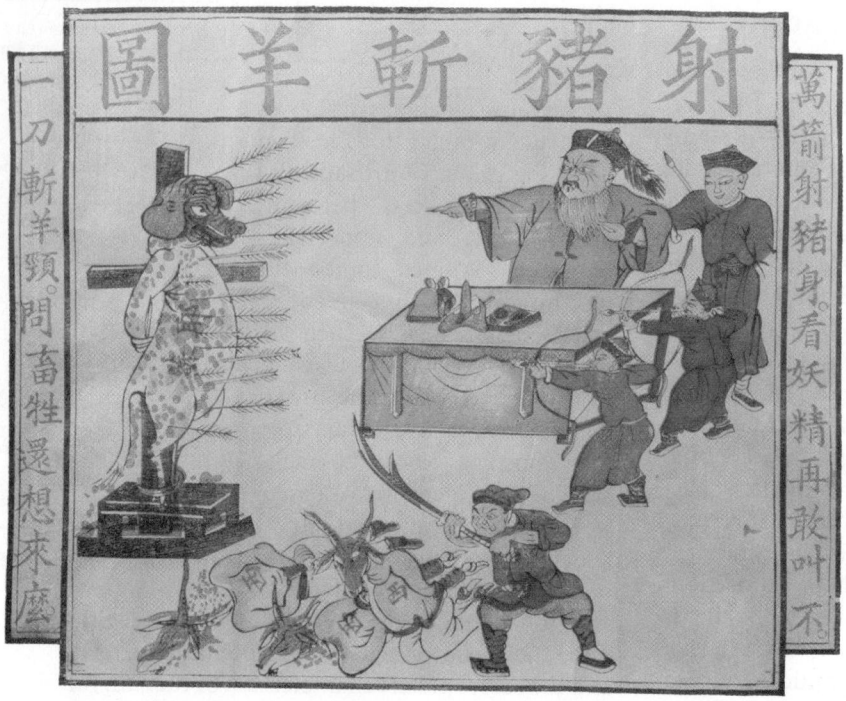

The Foreign Pig Is Put to Death
The Boxers used brightly colored placards to spread information about their movement in order to build wide support among the Chinese population. They felt that the presence of foreigners had caused a series of disasters, including the defection of the Chinese from traditional religion, the flow of wealth from the country, and a string of natural disasters such as famine. This depiction shows the harsh judgment of the Boxers toward foreigners and their Chinese allies—they are pigs to be killed. *(Private Collection/The Bridgeman Art Library International.)*

1861. He also made government loans available to peasants, who were then able to purchase land and thus to own farms outright. These reforms allowed people to move to the cities in search of jobs and created a larger group of independent peasants.

Stolypin was determined to restore law and order. He clamped down on revolutionary organizations, sentencing so many of their members to death by hanging that nooses were nicknamed "Stolypin neckties." The government urged more pogroms and stepped up Russification to crush ethnic dissent. But rebels continued to assassinate government officials—four thousand were killed or wounded in 1906–1907. Stolypin himself was assassinated in 1911. Stolypin's reforms promoted peasant well-being, which encouraged what one historian has called a "new peasant assertiveness." The industrial workforce also grew, but more strikes broke out, culminating in a general strike in St. Petersburg in 1914. The imperial government and the conservative nobility still had no solution to the ongoing activism in the streets, and their refusal to share power through the Duma left the way open to an even greater upheaval in 1917.

Growing Resistance to Colonial Domination

Japanese military victories over the Qing in China and the Romanovs in Russia upset the status quo in both countries. In addition, colonized peoples gained confidence from the Japanese victory to act more forcefully against imperialism. The ability of Russian revolutionaries to force a great European power to reform, however slightly, encouraged nationalist protests throughout the globe, further setting the West on edge.

Revolution in China

Uprisings began in China after its 1895 defeat by Japan led the Western powers to force more economic concessions from the Qing dynasty. Nonhuman factors also stepped in as drought and famine came to plague the empire. Despairing peasants organized into secret societies to expel the foreigners and restore Chinese dignity and power. One organization was the Society of the Righteous and Harmonious Fists, commonly called the Boxers, whose members maintained that ritual boxing would protect them from a variety of evils, including bullets. Encouraged by the Qing ruler, the dowager empress Tz'u-hsi (Cixi; 1835–1908), the Boxers rebelled in 1900, massacring the missionaries and Chinese Christians to whom they attributed China's troubles. Seven of the colonial powers united to put down the Boxer Uprising and encouraged their troops to devastate the areas in which the Boxers operated. Defeated once more, the Chinese had to pay a huge indemnity for damages done to foreign property and allow even greater foreign military occupation.

The Boxer Uprising thoroughly discredited the Qing dynasty, leading a group of revolutionaries to overthrow the dynasty in 1911 and to declare China a republic the next year. Their leader, Sun Yat-sen (1866–1925), who had been educated in Hawaii and Japan, combined Western ideas and Chinese values in his Three Principles of the People: "national-

DOCUMENT

Turkish Nationalism

Both old and new empires experienced waves of nationalist sentiment during the years 1890–1914. Turks dominated the Ottoman Empire and their newfound nationalism was directed at the European powers trying to encroach on Ottoman lands. Turkish nationalism, however, was also announced as the unifying force and dominant value of the multinational Ottoman empire and thus met with resistance from the many groups such as Slavs, Arabs, and others within the empire. The poem below, "Going to Battle," expresses Turkish nationalism and is now well known to children across Turkey. Mehmed Emin was twenty-eight when he published the work in 1897. His devotion to nationalism prompted him to adopt the name Yurdakul, meaning "slave to the homeland." After World War I, Mehmed Emin became a prominent politician in the new Turkish nation.

Going to Battle

I am a Turk, my religion, my race are great,
My breast, my soul are filled with fire.
He who is a man is the servant of his fatherland.
The Turkish child does not stay at home—I go.

I do not allow the book of Muhammad to be abolished,
I do not suffer the flag of Osman to be taken away,
I do not permit the enemy to attack my fatherland
The House of God will not be destroyed—I go.

The earth is the home of my ancestors;
My house, my village are a corner of this place.
Here is the homeland, here is the lap of God.
The fatherland needs sons—I go.

My god is witness that I will keep my word,
All my love for my country deep in my heart,
In my eyes nothing but my fatherland.
The enemy shall not take my native soil—I go.

I wipe my tears with a white shirt,
I whet my knife with a black stone.
I desire grandeur for my fatherland;
No one stays in this world forever—I go.

Source: Robert G. Landen, ed., *The Emergence of the Modern Middle East: Selected Readings* (New York: Van Nostrand Reinhold, 1970), 120.

Question to Consider

- **In what ways do the nationalist sentiments of the poem resemble those of Western nations, and in what ways do they differ?**

ism, democracy, and socialism." For example, Sun's socialism included the Chinese belief that all people should have enough food, and his Nationalist Party called for revival of the Chinese tradition of correctness in behavior between governors and the governed, modern economic reform, and an end to Western domination of trade. Sun's stirring leadership and the changes brought about by the 1911 revolution helped weaken Western imperialism.

Nationalists in India In India, the Japanese victory over Russia and the Revolution of 1905 stimulated politicians to take a more radical course than that offered by the Indian National Congress. The anti-British Hindu leader B. G. Tilak, less moderate than Congress reformers, urged noncooperation: "We shall not give them assistance to collect revenue and keep peace. We shall not assist them in fighting beyond the frontiers or outside India with Indian blood and money." Tilak promoted Hindu customs, asserted the distinctiveness of Hindu values from British ways, and inspired violent rebellion against the British. This brand of nationalism contrasted with that based on assimilating to British culture and promoting gradual change. Trying to stop Tilak, the British sponsored a rival nationalist group, the Muslim League, in a blatant attempt to divide Muslims from Hindus in the Congress.

Faced with political activism on many fronts, however, Britain conceded to Indians' representation in ruling councils and their right to vote based on property ownership. Because the independence movement had not fully reached the masses, some of these small concessions to the elites temporarily prevented an explosion of anger among colonized Indians as a whole. But discontent also mounted, sometimes silently, as did worries among the most clear-sighted imperialists about the future.

Young Turks in the Ottoman Empire Revolutionary nationalism was simultaneously weakening the Ottoman Empire, which for centuries had controlled much of the Mediterranean. Rebellions plagued Ottoman rule, and this resistance allowed European influence to grow even as Ottoman reformers aimed to strengthen the government. Sultan Abdul Hamid II (r. 1876–1909) tried to revitalize the multiethnic empire by using Islam to counteract the rising nationalism of

DOCUMENT

Vietnamese Resistance and the Importance of Becoming Modern

There was growing resistance to imperialism, using both weapons and words. Phan Boi Chau, an educated Vietnamese, chose words and formed one of the first important movements against the French in 1904. He wrote a torrent of pamphlets and essays describing the crimes of French occupiers of his homeland and proposing that the Vietnamese would become great and independent once they became more modern. Here is an excerpt from his essay "The New Vietnam" (1907). In 1925, the French condemned him to death for his ideas but ultimately allowed him to spend the rest of his life under police guard.

After a thousand kilometers of railroads have been laid, merchandise to be exchanged would reach its destination in hours; sprawling cities and large villages would promptly communicate with one another, then even if we were to relax in a sculpted house or if we were just to sit on a flowered mat, it would still feel as though we have scaled mountains and crossed rivers. What a wonderful sensation that will be! . . .

Ever since France came to protect us, Frenchmen hold every lever of power; they hold the power of life and death over everyone. The life of thousands of Vietnamese people is not worth that of a French dog; the moral prestige of hundreds of our officials does not prevail over that of a French woman. Look at those men with blue eyes and yellow beards. They are not our fathers, nor are they our brothers. How can they squat here, defecating on our heads? Are the men from Vietnam not ashamed of that situation? As long as our bodies remain able, we should try to flatten the crest of the open ocean; we should be determined to kill the enemy in order to raise the energy of the yellow race of ours.

After modernization we shall determine the domestic as well as foreign affairs of our country. The work of civilization will go on, day after day, and our country's status in the world will be heightened. We shall have three million infantrymen, as fierce as tigers, looking into the four corners of the universe. . . . All the shame and humiliation we have suffered previously . . . will become potent medicine to help us build up this feat of modernization. . . . The wind of freedom will blow fiercely, refreshing in one single sweep the entire five continents. Such will be the victory of our race.

Source: "The New Vietnam" (1907), quoted in Truong Buu Lam, *Colonialism Experienced: Vietnamese Writings on Colonialism 1900–1931* (Ann Arbor: University of Michigan Press, 2000), 105–8.

Question to Consider

- **What are Phan Boi Chau's charges against the French, and how does he see the future of Vietnam?**

the Serbs, Bulgarians, and Macedonians. Instead, he unintentionally provoked Turkish nationalism in Constantinople itself. Turkish nationalists rejected the sultan's pan-Islamic solution and built their movement on the uniqueness of their culture, history, and language, as many European ethnic groups were also doing (see Document, "Turkish Nationalism," page 823). They first traced the history and culture of the group they called Turks to change the word *Turk* from one of derision to one of pride. The Japanese defeat of Russia in 1904–1905 electrified these nationalists with the vision of a modern Turkey becoming "the Japan of the Middle East," as they called it. In 1908, a group of nationalists called the Young Turks took control of the government in Constantinople, which had been increasingly weakened by nationalist agitation and by the empire's growing indebtedness to Western financiers and businessmen.

The Young Turks' triumph motivated other ethnic groups in the Middle East and the Balkans to demand an end to Ottoman domination in their regions. These nationalists adopted Western values and political platforms, and some, such as the Egyptians, had strong contingents of feminist-nationalists who mobilized women to work for independence. The Young Turks, often aided by European powers with financial interests in the region, brutally repressed nationalist uprisings in Egypt, Syria, and the Balkans that their own success had encouraged.

The rebellions became part of the turmoil in global relations during the years just before World War I. Empires, whether old or young, were the scene of growing opposition in the wake of Japanese, Russian, and Turkish events. In German East Africa, colonial forces responded to native resistance in 1905 with a scorched-earth policy of destroying homes, livestock, food, and other resources, killing more than 100,000 Africans there. To maintain their grip on Indochina, the French closed the University of Hanoi, executed Indochinese intellectuals, and deported thousands of suspected nationalists (see Document, "Vietnamese Resistance and the Importance of Becoming Modern," above).

A French general stationed there summed up the fears of many colonial rulers: "The gravest fact of our actual political situation in Indochina is not the recent trouble in Tonkin [or] the plots undertaken against us but in the muted but growing hatred that our subjects show toward us." At home and abroad, Western political ambitions revolved around violence in speech and deed.

REVIEW QUESTION How and why did events in overseas empires from the 1890s on challenge Western faith in imperialism?

Roads to War

Internationally, competition intensified among the great powers and drove Western nationalists to become similarly more aggressive. In the spring of 1914, U.S. president Woodrow Wilson (1856–1924) sent his trusted adviser Colonel Edward House to Europe to observe the rising tensions there. "It is militarism run stark mad," House reported, adding that he foresaw an "awful cataclysm" ahead. Government spending on what people called the arms race had stimulated European economies. While stockpiles of arms temporarily promoted economic growth, however, they menaced the future. As early as the mid-1890s, one socialist had called the situation a "cold war" because the hostile atmosphere made war seem a certainty. By 1914, the air was even more charged, with militant nationalism in the Balkan states and politics—both at home and worldwide—propelling Europeans toward mass destruction.

Competing Alliances and Clashing Ambitions

As the twentieth century opened, the Triple Alliance that Bismarck had negotiated among Germany, Austria-Hungary, and Italy confronted an opposing alliance between France and Russia, created in the 1890s. The wild card in the diplomatic scenario was Great Britain, traditional enemy of France, especially in the contest for global power. Britain and France—constant rivals in Africa—edged to the brink of war in 1898 over competing claims to Fashoda, a town in the Sudan. The threat of conflict led France to withdraw, showing both nations as embracing a truce out of mutual self-interest. To prevent another Fashoda, they entered into secret agreements, the first of which (1904) recognized British claims in Egypt and French claims in Morocco. This agreement marked the beginning of the British-French alliance called the **Entente Cordiale**. Still, Britain's response to a future European war remained in question. Even French statesmen feared that, should war break out, their ally might decide to remain neutral.

Germany's Imperial Demands Kaiser William II inflamed the diplomatic atmosphere just as France and Britain were developing the Entente Cordiale. After victory in the Franco-Prussian War, Bismarck had proclaimed Germany a "satisfied" nation and worked to balance great-power interests in order to avoid further wars. William II, in contrast, was emboldened by Germany's growing industrial might and announced in 1901 that Germany needed greater global power to be achieved by "friendly conquests." His actions, however, were far from friendly. Believing in Britain's fundamental hostility toward France, William II used the opportunity presented by the defeat of France's ally Russia in 1904–1905 to contest French advances in Morocco. A boastful, blustery man who was easily prodded to rash actions by his advisers, William landed in Morocco in 1905 to block the French. To resolve what became known as the First Moroccan Crisis, an international conference met in Spain in 1906. Germany confidently expected to gain concessions and global influence, but instead the powers, now including the United States, upheld French claims in North Africa. France and Britain, seeing German interference in Morocco, drew closer together.

Germany found itself weak internationally and strong economically, a situation that made its leaders more determined to compete for territory abroad. When the French took over Morocco completely in 1911, Germany triggered the Second Moroccan Crisis by sending a gunboat to the port of Agadir and again demanding concessions from the French. This time no power—not even Austria-Hungary—backed Germany. No one acknowledged this dominant country's might or its right to influence in the region. The British and French now made binding military provisions for the deployment of their forces in case of war, thus strengthening the Entente Cordiale. Smarting from its setbacks on the world stage, Germany refocused its sights on its continental role and on its own alliances.

Entente Cordiale: An alliance between Britain and France that began with an agreement in 1904 to honor colonial holdings.

Crises in the Balkans

Germany's bold territorial claims, along with public uncertainty about the binding force of alliances, unsettled Europe, particularly the Balkans. German statesmen began envisioning the creation of a **Mitteleuropa**—a term that literally meant "central Europe" but that in their minds also included the Balkans and Turkey. The Habsburgs, firmly backed by Germany, judged that their own expansion into the Balkans and the resulting addition of even more ethnic groups would weaken the claims of any single ethnic minority in the Dual Monarchy. Russia, however, saw *itself* as the protector of Slavs in the region and wanted to replace the Ottomans as the dominant Balkan power, especially since Japan had crushed Russian hopes for expansion to the east. Austria's swift annexation of Bosnia-Herzegovina during the Young Turks' revolt in 1908 enraged not only the Russians but the Serbs as well, who wanted Bosnia as part of an enlarged Serbia. The Balkans thus whetted many appetites (Map 24.4).

Even without the greedy eyes cast on the Balkans, the situation would have been extremely volatile. The nineteenth century had seen the rise of nationalism and ethnicity as the basis for the unity of the nation-state, and by late in the century, ethnic loyalty challenged the dynastic rule of the Habsburgs and Ottomans in the Balkans. Greece, Serbia, Bulgaria, Romania, and Montenegro emerged as autonomous states, almost all of them composed of several ethnicities as well as several faiths: Or-

Mitteleuropa (miht el oy ROH pah): Literally, "central Europe," but used by military leaders in Germany before World War I to refer to land in both central and eastern Europe that they hoped to acquire.

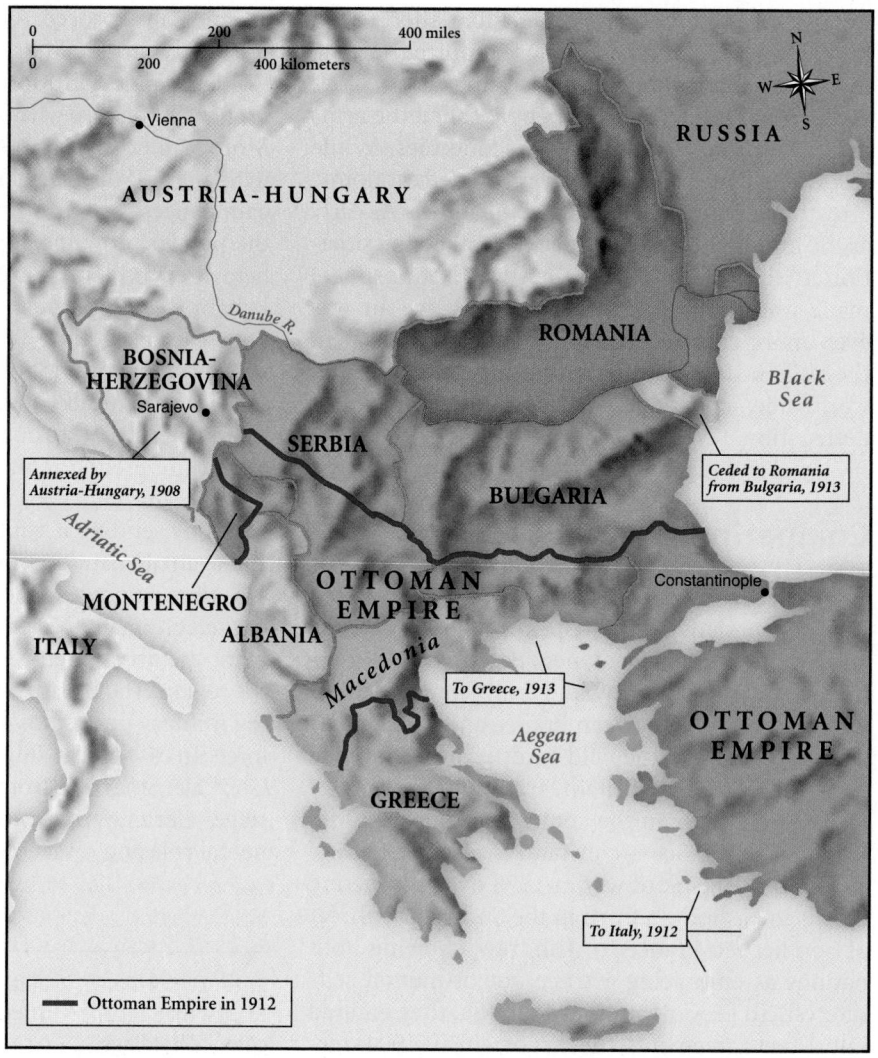

MAP 24.4 The Balkans, 1908–1914
Balkan peoples—mixed in religion, ethnicity, and political views—were successful in asserting their desire for independence, especially in the First Balkan War, which claimed territory from the Ottoman Empire. Their increased autonomy sparked rivalries among them and continued to attract attention from the great powers. Three empires in particular—the Russian, Ottoman, and Austro-Hungarian—simultaneously wanted influence for themselves in the region, which became a powder keg of competing ambitions.

thodox Christian, Roman Catholic, and Muslim. All these states sought more Ottoman and Habsburg territory to cement a common ethnicity—an impossible desire given the intermingling of ethnicities throughout the region. Nonetheless, war for territory was on these nationalists' agenda.

In the First Balkan War, in 1912, Serbia, Bulgaria, Greece, and Montenegro joined forces to gain Macedonia and Albania from the Ottomans. The victors divided up their booty, with Bulgaria gaining the most territory, but in the Second Balkan War, in 1913, Serbia, Greece, and Montenegro contested Bulgarian gains. The quick victory of these allies increased Austria's concern at Serbia's rising power. Grievances between the Habsburgs and the Serbs seemed stalemated as each aimed for greater influence in the Balkans. The region had become perilous: both Austria-Hungary (as ruler of many Slavs) and Russia (as their would-be protector) stationed increasing numbers of troops along the borders. The situation led strategists to think hopefully that a quick war there—something like Bismarck's wars—could resolve tension and uncertainty.

The Race to Arms

In the nineteenth century, global rivalries and aspirations for national greatness made constant readiness for war seem increasingly necessary. On the seas and in foreign lands, the colonial powers battled to establish control, and violence became an everyday occurrence in the drive for empire. The powers developed railroad, telegraph, and telephone networks everywhere to control their conquests and to move troops as well as to trade. Governments began to draft ordinary citizens for periods of two to six years into large standing armies, in contrast to the smaller forces that had served the more limited military goals of the eighteenth century. By 1914, escalating tensions in Europe boosted the annual intake of draftees: Germany, France, and Russia called up 250,000 or more troops each year. The per capita expenditure on the military rose in all the major powers between 1890 and 1914; the proportion of national budgets devoted to defense in 1910 was lowest in Austria-Hungary (at 10 percent) and highest in Germany (at 45 percent).

The modernization of weaponry also transformed warfare. Swedish arms manufacturer Alfred Nobel patented dynamite and developed a kind of gunpowder that improved the accuracy of guns and produced a clearer battlefield environment by reducing firearm smoke. Breakthroughs in the chemical industry led to improvements in long-range artillery, which by 1914 could fire on targets as far as six miles away. Munitions factories across Europe manufactured ever-growing stockpiles of howitzers, Mauser rifles, and Hotchkiss machine guns. Used in the Russo-Japanese and South African wars, these new weapons had shown that military offensives were more difficult to win than in the past because neither side could overcome such accurate firepower. Military leaders devised new strategies to protect their armies from the heavy firepower and deadly accuracy of the new weapons: in the Russo-Japanese War, trenches and barbed wire blanketed the front around Port Arthur.

Naval construction figured in both the arms race and the rising nationalism in politics. To defend against powerful weaponry, ships built after the mid-nineteenth century were made of metal rather than wood. Launched in 1905, HMS *Dreadnought*, a warship with unprecedented firepower, was the centerpiece of the British navy's plan to construct at least seven battleships per year. Germany also built up its navy and made itself a great land and sea power. Military men followed the writings of the American naval theorist Alfred Thayer Mahan, who argued that command of the seas determined international power. Germany thus planned naval bases as far away as the Pacific, but its drive to build battleships strengthened Britain's alliance with France in the Entente Cordiale and boosted the annual naval spending of those countries as well (see "Taking Measure," page 828). The Germans described their fleet buildup as "a peaceful policy," but, like British naval expansion, it only fed the hostile international climate and intense competition in weapons manufacture.

Public relations campaigns encouraged military buildup. When critics of the arms race suggested a temporary "naval holiday" to stop British and German building, British officials sent out news releases warning that such a cutback "would throw innumerable men on the pavement." Advocates of imperial expansion and nationalist groups lobbied for military spending as boosting national pride, while businessmen promoted large navies as beneficial to international trade and domestic industry. When Germany's Social Democrats questioned the use of taxes and their heavy burden on workers, the press criticized the party for lack of patriotism. The Conservative Party in Great Britain, eager for more battleships, made popular the slogan "We want eight and we won't wait." Public enthusiasm for arms buildups, militant nationalism, and growing international competition set the stage for war. The remarks of a French military leader were typical of sentiments at the time, even among the public at large. When asked in 1912 about his predictions for

TAKING MEASURE

The Growth in Armaments, 1890–1914

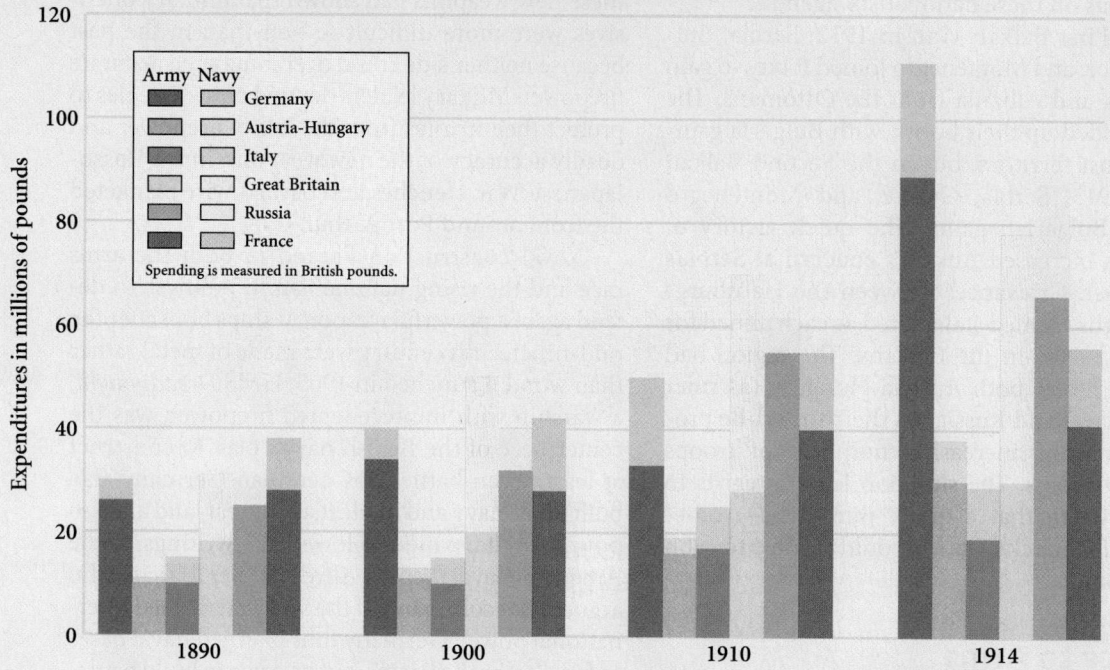

At the beginning of the twentieth century, the European powers engaged in a massive arms race that was part of industrial innovation. Even as sophisticated weaponry was one key to advancing global conquest, it also became part of national rivalries including economic, military, and imperial ones. Several comparisons offer themselves, not only in terms of the rates of increase but in terms of the military sectors that saw those increases. There is no doubt that the arms race stoked the fires of war, but historians often ask whether better diplomacy could have prevented the outbreak of the global conflict in 1914. The enormous military buildup, however, made some people living in the early twentieth century, as well as some later historians, see war as inevitable.

Source: *The Hammond Atlas of the Twentieth Century* (London: Times Books, 1996), 29.

Question to Consider

- **Which nations experienced the greatest rates of military buildup between 1890 and 1914, and which lagged behind? How do you account for the individual differences among the rates of military expansion?**

war and peace, he responded enthusiastically, "We shall have war. I will make it. I will win it."

1914: War Erupts

June 28, 1914, began as an ordinary, even happy day not only for Freud's patient the Wolf-Man but also for the Austrian archduke and heir to the Habsburg throne, Francis Ferdinand, and his wife, Sophie, as they ended a state visit to Sarajevo in Bosnia. The archduke, in full military regalia, was riding in a motorcade when a group of young Serb nationalists threw bombs in an unsuccessful assassination attempt. The danger did not register; after a stop, the archduke and his wife set out again. In the crowd was another nationalist, Gavrilo Princip, who had traveled in secret for several weeks to reach this destination, dreaming of reuniting his homeland of Bosnia-Herzegovina with Serbia and smuggling weapons with him to accomplish his end. Princip shot dead the unprotected and unsuspecting Austrian couple.

Some in the Habsburg government saw the assassination as an opportunity to put down the Serbians once and for all. Evidence showed that Princip had received arms and information from Serbian

Arrest of the Assassin
Gavrilo Princip belonged to the Young Bosnians, a group devoted to killing Habsburgs in revenge for the Austro-Hungarian monarchy's having sent workers to colonize their homeland. In June 1914, at the age of nineteen, Princip lived out his dream, killing the heir to the Habsburg throne and his wife. Here Princip is shown being apprehended. He spent the rest of his life in prison and was appalled at the carnage of World War I. *(© Bettmann/Corbis.)*

officials, who directed a terrorist organization from within the government. Endorsing a quick defeat of Serbia, German statesmen and military leaders urged the Austrians to be unyielding and promised support in case of war. The Austrians sent an ultimatum to the Serbian government, demanding suppression of terrorist groups and the participation of Austrian officials in an investigation of the crime, among other things. "You are setting Europe ablaze," the Russian foreign minister remarked of the Austrians' humiliating demands made on a sovereign state. Yet the Serbs were conciliatory, accepting all the terms except the presence of Austrian officials in the investigation. Kaiser William was pleased: "A great moral success for Vienna! All reason for war is gone." His relief proved unfounded. Austria-Hungary, confident of German backing, used the Serbs' resistance to one demand as the pretext for declaring war against them on July 28.

Some statesmen tried desperately to avoid war. The tsar and the kaiser sent pleading letters to one another not to start a European war. The British foreign secretary proposed an all-European conference, but without success. Germany displayed firm support for Austria in hopes of convincing the French and British to stay out of the war. The failure of either to fight, German officials believed, would keep Russia from mobilizing. Additionally, German military leaders had become fixed on fighting a short, preemptive war that would provide territorial gains leading toward the goal of a Mitteleuropa. As conservatives, they planned to impose martial law the minute war began, using it as an excuse for arresting the leadership of the German Social Democratic Party, which threatened their rule.

The European press caught the war fever of nationalist and pro-war organizations, and military leaders, especially in Germany and Austria-Hungary, promoted mobilization rather than diplomacy in the last days of July. The Austrians declared war and then ordered mobilization on July 31 in full confidence of German military aid, because as early as 1909 Germany had promised to defend Austria-Hungary, even if that country took the offensive. The thought was that Russia would not dare to intervene against an Austria-Hungary backed by Germany military power, but Nicholas II ordered the mobilization in defense of the Serbs—Russia's Slavic allies. Encouraging the Austrians to attack Serbia, the German general staff mobilized on August 1. France declared war by virtue of its agreement to aid its ally Russia, and when Germany violated Belgian neutrality on its way to invade France, Britain entered the war on the side of France and Russia.

REVIEW QUESTION What were the major factors leading to the outbreak of World War I?

Conclusion

Rulers soon forgot their last-minute hesitations when in some capitals celebration erupted with the declaration of war. "A mighty wonder has taken place," wrote a Viennese actor after watching the troops march off amid public enthusiasm. "We have become *young*." Both sides exulted, certain of victory as militant nationalism led many Europeans to favor war over peace. There were advantages to war: disturbances in private life and challenges to established truths would disappear, it was believed, in the crucible of war. A short conflict, people maintained, would resolve tensions ranging from the rise of the working class to political problems caused by global imperial competition. German military men saw war as an opportune moment to round up social democrats and reestablish the traditional power of an agrarian aristocracy. Liberal government based on rights and constitutions, some believed, had simply gone too far in allowing new groups full citizenship and political influence.

Modernity helped blaze the path to war. New technology, mass armies, and new techniques of persuasion supported the military buildup. *The Rite of Spring*, the ballet that opened in Paris on the eve of war in 1913, had taken as its theme humans' ritualistic attraction of death. Facing continuing violence in politics, chaos in the arts, and problems in the industrial order, there was a belief that war would save nations from the modern perils they faced. The nervous pessimism that characterized the years before 1914 would end, replaced by patriotism. "Like men longing for a thunderstorm to relieve them of the summer's sultriness," wrote an Austrian official, "so the generation of 1914 believed in the relief that war might bring." Tragically, any hope of relief soon faded. Instead of bringing the refreshment of summer rain, war opened an era of political turmoil, widespread suffering, massive human slaughter, and even greater doses of modernity.

FOR FURTHER EXPLORATION

- **For additional primary-source material from this period**, see *Sources of the Making of the West*, Fourth Edition.
- **For Web sites, images, and documents related to topics in this chapter**, visit *Make History* at bedfordstmartins.com/hunt.

Europe at the Outbreak of World War I, August 1914

All the powers expected a great, swift victory when war broke out. Many saw war as a chance to increase their territories; as rivals for trade and empire, almost all believed that war would bring them many advantages. But if European nations appeared well prepared and invincible at the start of the war, relatively few would survive the conflict intact.

Chapter 24 Review

Online Study Guide bedfordstmartins.com/hunt

Key Terms and People

In the grid below, identify the term or person and explain its historical significance. (To do this exercise online, go to bedfordstmartins.com/hunt.)

Term	Who or What & When	Why It Matters
new woman (p. 801)		
Sigmund Freud (p. 803)		
modernism (p. 806)		
Friedrich Nietzsche (p. 806)		
Albert Einstein (p. 807)		
art nouveau (p. 809)		
Emmeline Pankhurst (p. 812)		
Nicholas II (p. 813)		
Zionism (p. 817)		
South African War (p. 818)		
Duma (p. 821)		
Entente Cordiale (p. 825)		
Mitteleuropa (p. 826)		

Review Questions

1. How did ideas about the self and about personal life change at the beginning of the twentieth century?
2. How did modernism transform the arts and the world of ideas?
3. What were the points of tension in European political life at the beginning of the twentieth century?
4. How and why did events in overseas empires from the 1890s on challenge Western faith in imperialism?
5. What were the major factors leading to the outbreak of World War I?

Making Connections

1. How did changes in society at the turn of the twentieth century affect the development of mass politics?
2. How was culture connected to the world of politics in the years 1890–1914?
3. How had nationalism changed since the French Revolution?
4. In what ways were imperial wars from the 1890s to 1914 relevant to the outbreak of World War I?

Important Events

Date	Event	Date	Event
1894–1895	Japan defeats China in Sino-Japanese War	1905	Nicholas II establishes the Duma after revolution erupts in Russia; Albert Einstein publishes his special theory of relativity
1894–1899	Dreyfus Affair exposes anti-Semitism in France	1906	Women receive vote in Finland
1899–1902	South African War fought between Dutch descendants and British in South African states	1907	Pablo Picasso launches cubist painting with *Les Demoiselles d'Avignon*
1900	Sigmund Freud publishes *The Interpretation of Dreams*	1908	Young Turks revolt against rule by sultan in Ottoman Empire
1901	Irish National Theater established by Maud Gonne and William Butler Yeats; death of Queen Victoria	1911–1912	Revolutionaries overthrow Qing dynasty and declare China a republic
1903	Emmeline Pankhurst founds Women's Social and Political Union	1914	Assassination of Austrian archduke Francis Ferdinand and his wife by Serbian nationalist precipitates World War I
1904–1905	Japan defeats Russia in Russo-Japanese War		

- Consider three events: **Sigmund Freud publishes *The Interpretation of Dreams* (1900)**, **Emmeline Pankhurst founds Women's Social and Political Union (1903)**, and **Pablo Picasso launches cubist painting with *Les Demoiselles d'Avignon* (1907)**. How did these events help to bring about modernity?

SUGGESTED REFERENCES

The cultural ferment, social turmoil, and actual violence of the pre–World War I years come alive in the works listed here.

Adamson, Walter L. *Embattled Avant-Gardes: Modernism's Resistance to Commodity Culture in Europe*. 2007.

Anderson, Margaret L. *Practicing Democracy: Elections and Political Culture in Imperial Germany*. 2000.

Childs, Peter. *Modernism*. 2008.

Forth, Christopher E. *The Dreyfus Affair and the Crisis of French Manhood*. 2005.

Frevert, Ute. *A Nation of Barracks: Modern Germany, Military Conscription and Civil Society*. 2004.

Hull, Isabel. *Absolute Destruction: Military Culture and the Practices of War in Imperial Germany*. 2005.

Hunt, Nancy Rose. *A Nervous State: Violence, Sterility, and Healing Movements in Colonial Congo*. 2011.

Kaplan, Morris B. *Sodom on the Thames: Sex, Love, and Scandal in Wilde Times*. 2005.

Marchand, Suzanne, and David Lindenfeld, eds. *Germany at the Fin-de-Siècle*. 2004.

Meir, Natan M. *Kiev, Jewish Metropolis: A History, 1859–1914*. 2010.

Nolan, Michael E. *The Inverted Mirror: Mythologizing the Enemy in France and Germany, 1898–1914*. 2005.

Reagin, Nancy R. *Sweeping the German Nation: Domesticity and National Identity in Germany, 1870–1945*. 2006.

Stanford Encyclopedia of Philosophy: http://plato.stanford.edu

Stanislawski, Michael. *Zionism and the Fin-de-Siècle: Cosmopolitanism and Nationalism from Nordau to Jabotinsky*. 2001.

Thompson, J. Lee. *Theodore Roosevelt Abroad: Nature, Empire and the Journey of an American President*. 2010.

Willmott, H. P. *The Last Century of Sea Power: From Port Arthur to Chanak, 1894–1922*. 2009.

CHAPTER

World War I and Its Aftermath

25

1914–1929

Jules Amar found his true vocation as a result of war. A French expert on improving the efficiency of industrial work, Amar switched his focus after 1914. As hundreds of thousands of soldiers returned from the battlefront missing body parts, plastic surgery and the construction of masks and other devices to hide deformities developed rapidly. Amar devised artificial limbs that would allow the wounded soldier to return to normal life by "making up for a function lost, or greatly reduced." The artificial arms featured hooks, magnets, and other mechanisms with which veterans could hold a cigarette, play a violin, and, most important, work with tools such as typewriters. Those who had been mangled by the weapons of modern technological warfare would be made whole, it was thought, by technology such as Amar's.

Amar dealt with the human tragedy of the Great War, so named by contemporaries because of its staggering human toll—forty million wounded or killed in battle. The Great War did not settle problems or restore social order as the European powers hoped it would. Instead, the war produced political chaos, overturning the Russian, German, Ottoman, and Austro-Hungarian Empires. The burden of war crushed the European powers and accelerated the rise of the United States, while colonized peoples who served in the war intensified their demands for independence. In fact, the armistice in 1918 did not truly end conflict: many soldiers remained actively fighting long into what was supposed to be peacetime, and others had been so militarized that they longed for a life that was more like wartime.

World War I transformed society, too. A prewar feeling of doom and decline gave way to postwar cynicism. Many Westerners turned their backs on politics and in the Roaring Twenties attacked life with wild gaiety,

Grieving Parents
Before World War I, the German artist Käthe Kollwitz gained her artistic reputation with woodcuts of handloom weavers whose livelihoods were threatened by industrialization. From 1914 on, she depicted the suffering and death that swirled around her and never with more sober force than in these two monuments to her son Peter, who died on the western front in the first months of battle. Today one can still travel to his burial place in Vladslo, Belgium, to see this father and mother mourning their loss, like millions across Europe in those heartbreaking days.
(photo © John Parker Picture Library. © 2011 Artists Rights Society [ARS], New York/VG Bild-Kunst, Bonn.)

The Great War, 1914–1918 836
- Blueprints for War
- The Battlefronts
- The Home Front

Protest, Revolution, and War's End, 1917–1918 845
- War Protest
- Revolution in Russia
- Ending the War, 1918

The Search for Peace in an Era of Revolution 851
- Europe in Turmoil
- The Paris Peace Conference, 1919–1920
- Economic and Diplomatic Consequences of the Peace

A Decade of Recovery: Europe in the 1920s 857
- Changes in the Political Landscape
- Reconstructing the Economy
- Restoring Society

Mass Culture and the Rise of Modern Dictators 862
- Culture for the Masses
- Cultural Debates over the Future
- The Communist Utopia
- Fascism on the March in Italy

shopping for new consumer goods, enjoying once forbidden personal freedoms, and taking pleasure in the entertainment provided by films and radio. Others found reason for hope in the new political systems the war made possible: Soviet communism and Italian fascism. Modern communication technologies such as radio gave politicians the means to promote a utopian mass politics that, ironically, was antidemocratic, militaristic, and violent—like the war itself. Total war further weakened the gentlemanly political tone of British prime minister William Gladstone's day and perhaps even totally devastated it.

A war that was long anticipated and even welcomed in some quarters as a remedy for modernity destabilized Europe far into the following decades. From statesmen to ordinary citizens, many Europeans, including Jules Amar and those he helped, would spend the next decade dealing with the violent aftermath of war. While some tried to make war-ravaged society function normally, others kept alive the forces of militarism that the war had so glorified. It became clear that prewar normality was gone forever and that war and its values were shaping the 1920s.

CHAPTER FOCUS What political, social, and economic impact did World War I have during the conflict, immediately after it, and through the 1920s?

The Great War, 1914–1918

When war erupted in August 1914, two months after the assassination of the Austrian archduke and his wife at Sarajevo, there already existed long-standing alliances, well-defined strategies, and a stockpile of military technologies such as heavy artillery, machine guns, and airplanes. Most people felt that this would be a short, decisive conflict similar to Prussia's rapid victories in the 1860s and 1870–1871 and Japan's swift defeat of Russia in 1904–1905. In fact, the unexpected happened: the war lasted for more than four long years. It was also what historians call a **total war**, meaning one built on the full mobilization of entire societies—soldiers and civilians—and the industrial capacities of the nations involved. It was the war's unexpected and unprecedented horror that made World War I "great."

Blueprints for War

World War I's two sets of opponents were formed roughly out of the alliances developed during the previous fifty years. On one side stood the Central Powers (Austria-Hungary and Germany), which had evolved from Bismarck's Triple Alliance. On the other side were the Allies (France, Great Britain, and Russia), which had emerged as a bloc from the Entente Cordiale between France and Great Britain and the 1890s treaties between France and Russia. In 1915, Italy, originally part of the Triple Alliance, switched sides and joined the Allies in hopes of postwar gain. The war soon exploded globally: in late August 1914, Japan, eager to extend its empire into China, went over to the Allies, while in the fall the Ottoman Empire united with the Central Powers against its traditional enemy, Russia (Map 25.1).

Both sides fought with the same ferocious hunger for power, prestige, and prosperity that had inspired imperialism. Of the Central Powers, Germany wanted a bigger empire, to be gained by annexing Russian territory and incorporating parts of Belgium,

total war: A war built on the full mobilization of soldiers, civilians, and technology of the nations involved. The term also refers to a highly destructive war of ideologies.

1913–1925 Suffrage for women expands in much of Europe

1916 Irish nationalists stage Easter Uprising against British rule

1918 November: Armistice ends fighting of World War I; revolutionary turmoil throughout Germany; kaiser abdicates

1912 1915 1918

1914 August: World War I begins

1917 March: Revolution in Russia overturns tsarist autocracy; April: United States enters World War I; November: Bolshevik Revolution in Russia

1918–1922 Civil war in Russia

A French Regiment Leaves for the Front, August 1914
Bands played, crowds cheered, and bicyclists led the way as bayonet-equipped soldiers marched eagerly to war. Some viewed the outbreak of war more soberly, and this mood became more common as machine guns and poison chemicals brought the bravest men down. People in cities, working to provide munitions and supplies, soon felt the pinch of inflation; later, many lacked food. Countless men returned physically disabled or mentally deranged from their experience. *(Roger Viollet/Getty Images.)*

France, and Luxembourg. Some German leaders wanted to annex Austria-Hungary as well. Austria-Hungary hoped to keep its great-power status despite the competing nationalisms of ethnic groups within its borders. Among the Allies, Russia wished to reassert its status as a great power and as the protector of the Slavs by adding a reunified Poland to the Russian Empire and by taking formal leadership of other Slavic peoples. The French, too, craved territory, especially the return of Alsace and Lorraine, ceded to Germany after the Franco-Prussian War of 1870–1871. The British wanted to cement their hold on Egypt and the Suez Canal and keep the rest of their world empire secure. By the Treaty of London (1915), France and Britain promised Italy territory in Africa, Asia Minor, the Balkans, and elsewhere in return for joining the Allies.

The colonies participated too, providing massive assistance and serving as battlegrounds. Some one million Africans, one million Indians, and more than a million men from the British commonwealth countries fought on the battlefronts. The imperial powers also conscripted uncounted numbers of colonists as forced laborers: a million Kenyans and Tanzanians alone are estimated to have been conscripted for menial labor in the battle for East Africa. Colonial troops played a major role in the fighting across north and sub-Saharan Africa. Using Arab, African, and Indian troops, the British waged successful war in the Ottoman lands of the Middle East. In sub-Saharan Africa, the vicious campaign for East Africa cost many lives, not only among the African troops used against one another on behalf of the imperialist powers but also among the civilian population whose resources were confiscated and whose villages were burned. As one of the Allies, Japan seized German-controlled territories in China and imposed its rule there.

1919
Weimar Republic established

1922
Eliot, "The Waste Land"; Joyce, *Ulysses*

1924–1929
Period of general economic prosperity and stability

1921 1924 1927

1919–1920
Paris Peace Conference redraws map of Europe

1922
Ireland gains independence; Fascists march on Rome; Mussolini becomes prime minister; Hitler builds Nazi Party

1924
Lenin dies; Stalin and Trotsky contend for power

1929
October: Stock market crash in United States

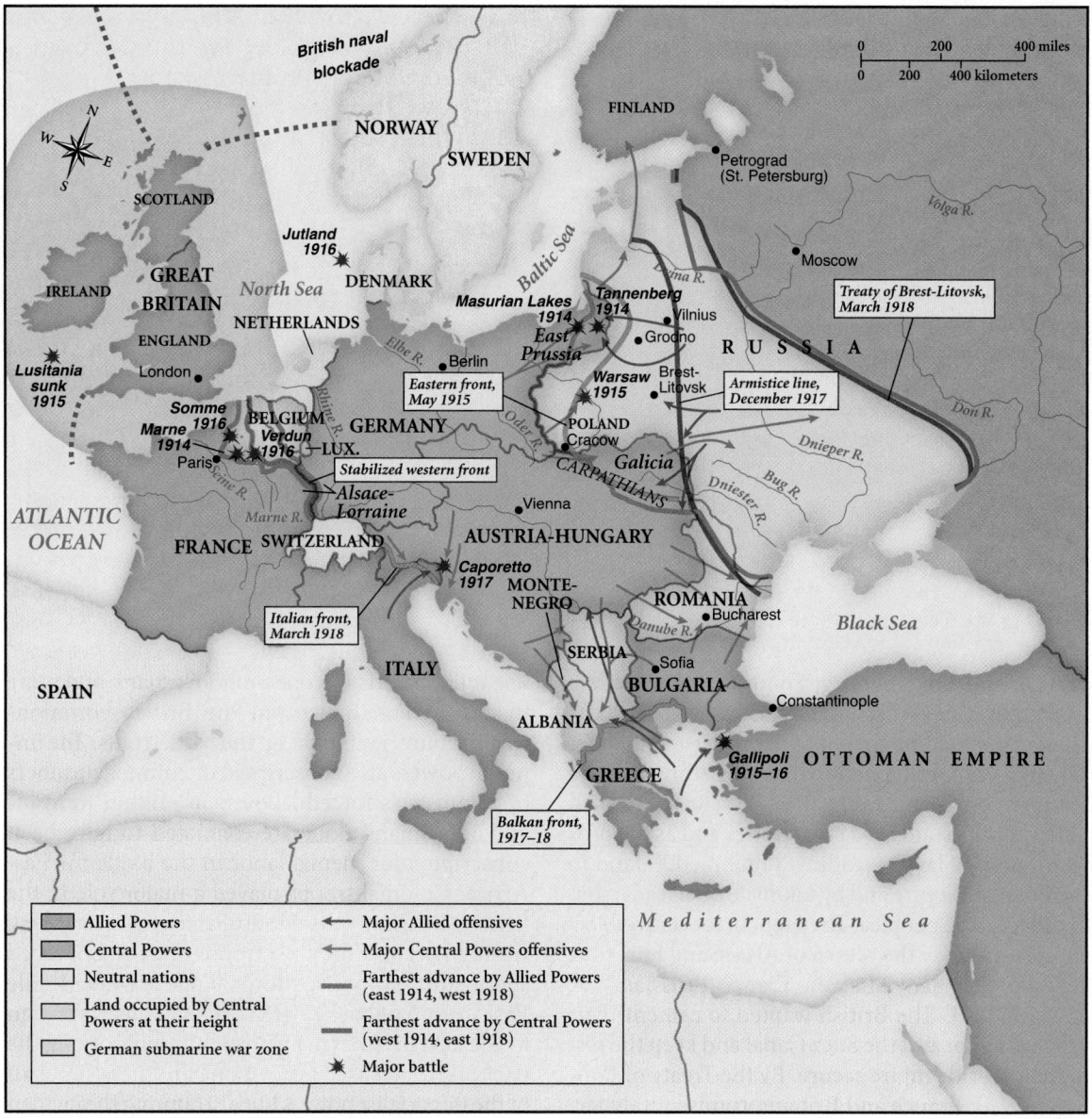

MAP 25.1 The Fronts of World War I, 1914–1918

Because the western front remained relatively stationary, devastation of land and resources was intense. All fronts, however, destroyed segments of Europe's hard-won industrial and agricultural capacity, while the immobile trenches increased military casualties whenever heavy artillery fire pounded them. Men long engaged in trench warfare developed an intense camaraderie based on their mutual suffering and deprivation.

Unprecedented use of machinery determined the course of war. In August 1914, machine guns, fast breech-loading rifles, and military vehicles such as airplanes, battleships, submarines, and motorized transport (cars and trains) were all at the armies' disposal. New technologies such as chlorine gas, tanks, and bombs developed between 1914 and 1918. Countries differed, however, in their experience with and access to large quantities of these technologies. British generals knew the destructive capacity of the weapons because of their colonial wars; the Germans were far more advanced in strategy and weaponry than either the Russians or the Austrians. The war itself became a lethal testing ground, as both new and old weapons were used, often ineffectively. Many officers on both sides believed in a **cult of the offensive**, which called for spirited attacks against the enemy and high troop

cult of the offensive: A military strategy of constantly attacking the enemy that was believed to be the key to winning World War I but that brought great loss of life while failing to bring decisive victory.

morale. Despite the availability of newer, more powerful war technology, an old-fashioned, heroic vision of war made many officers unwilling to abandon the more familiar sabers, lances, and bayonets. In the face of massive firepower, the cult of the offensive would cost millions of lives.

The Battlefronts

The first months of the war crushed any hope of a quick victory. All the major armies mobilized rapidly. The Germans were guided by the **Schlieffen Plan**, named after its author, Alfred von Schlieffen, a former chief of the general staff. The plan essentially outlined a way to combat enemies on two fronts by concentrating on one foe at a time. It called for a concentrated blow to the west against France, which would lead to that nation's defeat in six weeks, accompanied by a light holding action against Russia to the east. The attack on France was to proceed without resistance through neutral Belgium. Once France had fallen, Germany's western armies would move against Russia, which, it was believed, would mobilize far more slowly. None of the great powers expected that war would turn into the prolonged massacre of their nations' youth.

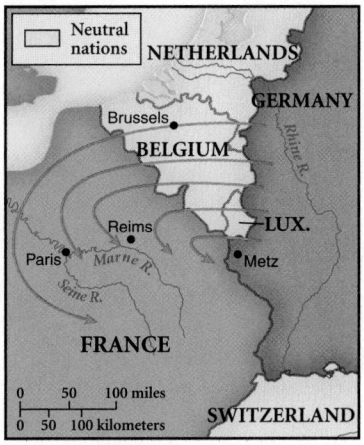

The Schlieffen Plan

Indecisive Offensives: 1914–1915 When German troops reached Belgium and Luxembourg at the beginning of August 1914, the Belgians surprisingly mounted a vigorous defense, which slowed the German advance. This allowed British and French troops, the latter based on France's eastern border, to reach the northern front. In September, the British and French armies engaged the Germans along the Marne River in France. Neither side could defeat the other, and casualties were shocking: in the first three months of war, more than 1.5 million men fell on the western front alone. Guns like the 75-millimeter howitzer, accurate at long range, turned what was supposed to be an offensive war of movement into a stationary standoff along a line that stretched from the North Sea through Belgium and northern France to Switzerland (Map 25.2). Deep within opposing lines of trenches dug along this front, millions of soldiers lived in nightmarish conditions.

On the eastern front, the Russian steam-roller—named thus because of the number of men mobilized, some twelve million in all—drove far more quickly than expected into East Prussia in mid-August. The Russians believed that no army could stand up to the massive number of their soldiers, regardless of how badly equipped and poorly trained those soldiers were. Their success was short-lived. The Germans overwhelmed the tsar's army in East Prussia and then turned south to Galicia. Victory made heroes of the German military leaders Paul von Hindenburg (1847–1934) and Erich Ludendorff (1865–1937), who demanded more troops for the eastern front. However, the German triumphs in the east had only temporarily halted the Russians and had also undermined the Schlieffen Plan by removing forces from the west before the western front had been won.

War at sea proved equally indecisive. Confident of Britain's superior naval power, the Allies blockaded ports to prevent supplies from reaching Germany and Austria-Hungary. Kaiser William and his advisers planned a massive U-boat (*Unterseeboot*, "underwater boat," or submarine) campaign against Allied and neutral shipping around Britain and France. In May 1915, U-boats sank the British passenger ship *Lusitania* and killed 1,198 people, including 124 Americans. Despite U.S. outrage, President Woodrow Wilson maintained a policy of neutrality; Germany, unwilling to provoke Wilson further, called off unrestricted submarine warfare. In May 1916, the navies of Germany and Britain finally clashed in the North Sea at Jutland. This inconclusive battle demonstrated that the German fleet could not master British seapower.

Ideas of a negotiated peace were discarded: "No peace before England is defeated and destroyed," William II stormed against his cousin King George V. "Only amidst the ruins of London will I forgive Georgy." French leaders called for a "war to the death." General staffs on both sides continued to prepare fierce attacks several times a year. Campaigns opened with heavy artillery pounding enemy trenches and gun emplacements. Troops then responded to the order to go "over the top" by scrambling out of their trenches and into battle, usually to be mowed down by machine-gun fire

Schlieffen Plan: The Germans' strategy in World War I that called for attacks on two fronts—concentrating first on France to the west and then turning east to attack Russia.

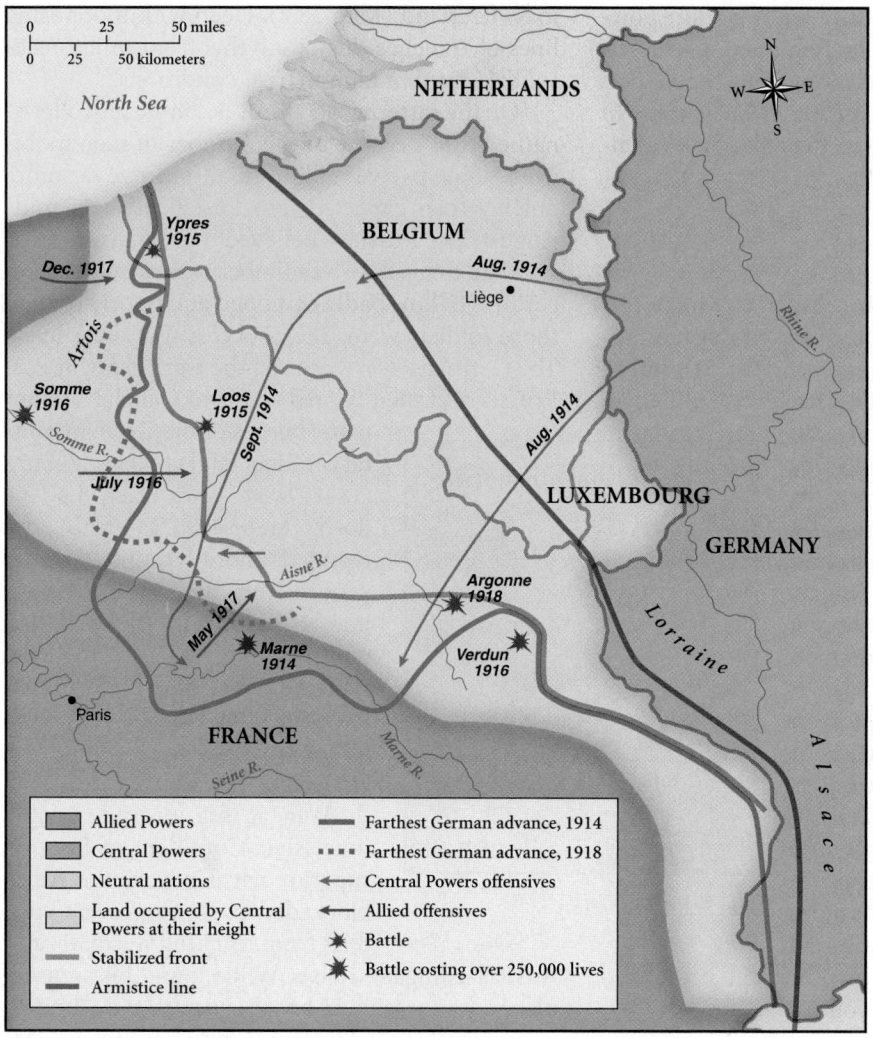

MAP 25.2
The Western Front
The western front occupied some of the richest parts of France, with long-lasting consequences. Destruction of French villages, roads, bridges, livestock, and property was the worst in Europe, while the trauma of the French people endured for generations. The effects of horrendous casualties, ever-present artillery fire, provisioning and hospital needs, and the demands of military and medical personnel changed everyone's way of life.

from defenders secure in their own trenches. On the western front, the French assaulted the Germans throughout 1915 to drive them from industrial regions. They accomplished little, and casualties of 100,000 and more for a single campaign became commonplace. On the eastern front, Russian armies captured parts of Galicia in the spring of 1915 and lumbered toward Hungary. The Central Powers struck back in Poland later that year, bringing the front closer to Petrograd (formerly St. Petersburg), the Russian capital.

Mounting Catastrophe: 1916

The next year's battles were even more disastrous and futile. To cripple French morale, the Germans launched massive assaults on the fortress at Verdun, firing as many as a million shells in a single day. Combined French and German losses totaled close to a million men. Nonetheless, the French held. Hoping to relieve their allies, the British unleashed an artillery pounding of German trenches in the Somme region in June 1916. In several months of battle at the Somme, 1.25 million men were killed or wounded, but the final result was stalemate. By the end of 1916, the French had suffered more than 3.5 million casualties. To help the Allies engaged at Verdun and the Somme, the Russians struck again, driving into the Carpathian Mountains, recouping territory, and menacing Austria-Hungary. The German army stopped the advance, as the German general staff decided it would take over Austrian military operations. The war was sapping Europe's strength and national independence.

The Soldiers' War

Had military leaders thoroughly dominated the scene, historians judge, all armies would have been utterly demolished by the end of 1915. Yet ordinary soldiers in this war were not automatons in the face of what seemed to them suicidal orders. Informal agreements among troops to avoid battles allowed some battalions to go for long stretches with hardly a casualty. Enemies facing each other across the trenches frequently ate their meals in peace, even though the trenches were within hand-

War in the Trenches
Men at the front developed close friendships while they lived with daily discomfort, death, and the horrors of modern technological warfare. Some of the complexities of trench warfare appear in this image showing soldiers rescuing their fallen comrades after fighting at Bagatelle in northern France. *(Hulton Archive/Getty Images.)*

War in the Skies (1914)
As the war started, aviators and the machines they piloted became symbols of the human potential to transcend time and space. The Great War, however, featured the airplane as the new weapon in what British writer H. G. Wells called the "headlong sweep to death." Daring pilots, or "aces," took the planes on reconnaissance flights and guided them in the totally new practice of aerial combat, as shown in this engraving from an Italian newspaper of a French airplane shooting down a German one. *(The Art Archive/Domenica del Corriere/Gianni Dagli Orti.)*

grenade reach. Throughout the war, soldiers on both fronts fraternized with one another. They played an occasional game of soccer, shouted across the trenches, and made gestures of agreement not to fight. A British veteran of the trenches explained to a new recruit that the Germans "don't want to fight any more than we do, so there's a kind of understanding between us. Don't fire at us and we'll not fire at you." Burying enemy dead in common graves with their own fallen comrades, many ordinary soldiers came to feel more warmly toward enemies who shared the trench experience than toward civilians back home.

Male camaraderie relieved some of the misery of trench life and aided survival. Sharing danger and deprivation on the front lines weakened traditional class distinctions. In some cases, upper-class officers and working-class recruits became friends in that "wholly masculine way of life uncomplicated by women," as another soldier put it. Soldiers picked lice from one another's bodies and clothes, tended one another's blistered feet, and came to love one another, sometimes even passionately. This sense of frontline community survived the war and influenced postwar politics.

Troops of colonized soldiers from Asia and Africa had different experiences. Often these soldiers were put in the very front ranks, where the risks were greatest. They suffered from the rigors of an unfamiliar climate and strange food as well as from Western war technology. Yet, like class divisions, racial barriers sometimes fell: a European might give extra blankets and clothing to soldiers from warmer regions. The perspectives of colonial troops changed, too: "What miserable crowned head was able to order such horrors?" wrote one corporal from West Africa. These troops saw their "masters" completely undone and "uncivilized," for when fighting did break out, trenches became a veritable hell of shelling and sniping, flying body parts, blinding gas, and rotting cadavers. Some soldiers became hysterical or shell-shocked through the stress and violence of battle. Some soldiers lost hope entirely: "It might be me tomorrow," a young British soldier wrote his mother in 1916. "Who cares?" Soldiers had gone to war to escape ordinary life in industrial society. They learned, however, as one German put it, "that in the modern war . . . the triumph of the machine over the individual is carried to its most extreme form." They took this hard-won knowledge into battle, pulling their comrades back when an offensive seemed lost or too costly.

The Home Front

World War I took place off the battlefield, too. Total war demanded the involvement of civilians in war industry: manufacturing the shells, the machine guns, the poisonous gases, the bombs, the airplanes, and eventually the tanks that were the backbone of technological warfare. Increased production of coffins, canes, wheelchairs, and artificial limbs (devised by the likes of Jules Amar) was also required. Because the war would have utterly failed without them, civilians had to work overtime, believe in, and sacrifice for victory. To keep the war machine operating smoothly, governments oversaw factories, transportation systems, and resources ranging from food to coal to textiles. Before the war, such tight government control would have outraged many liberals, but now it was accepted as necessary to win the war.

Politics Suspended At first, most political parties put aside their differences. Many socialists and working-class people who had formerly criticized the military buildup announced their support for the war. For decades, socialist parties had preached that "the worker has no country" and that nationalism was an ideology meant to keep workers disunited and subjected to the will of their employers. In August 1914, however, most socialists became as patriotic as the rest of society. Feminists divided over whether to maintain their traditional pacifism or to support the war. Although many feminists actively opposed the conflict, the British suffrage leader Emmeline Pankhurst and her daughter Christabel were among those who became militant nationalists, even changing the name of their suffrage paper to *Britannia.* Parties representing the middle classes dropped their distrust of the socialists and working classes. In the name of victory, national leaders wanted to end political division of all kinds: "I no longer recognize [political] parties," William II declared on August 4, 1914. "I recognize only Germans." Ordinary people, even those who had been at the receiving end of discrimination, came to believe that a new day of unity was dawning. One rabbi proudly echoed the kaiser: "In the German fatherland there are no longer any Christians and Jews, any believers and disbelievers, there are only Germans."

Mobilization of the People Governments mobilized the home front with varying degrees of success. All countries were caught without replacements for their heavy losses of military equipment and soon felt the shortage of food and labor as well. War ministries set up boards to allocate labor on both the home front and the battlefront and to give industrialists financial incentives to encourage productivity. The Russian bureaucracy, however, only cooperated halfheartedly with industrialists and other groups that could aid the war effort. In several countries, emergency measures allowed the drafting of both men and women for military or industrial service. Desperate for factory workers, the Germans forced Belgian citizens to move to Germany, housing them in prison camps. In the face of rationing, municipal governments set up canteens and day-care centers. Rural Russia, Austria-Hungary, Bulgaria, and Serbia, where youths, women, and old men struggled to sustain farms, had no such relief programs.

Governments throughout Europe passed sedition laws that made it a crime to criticize war-related policies. To ensure civilian acceptance of longer working hours and shortages of consumer goods, governments created propaganda agencies to advertise the war as a patriotic mission to resist villainous enemies (see "Seeing History," page 843). British propagandists fabricated some of the atrocities that the Germans, whom they called Huns (referring to the nomadic tribe of ancient times), supposedly committed against Belgians, and German propagandists warned that French African troops would rape German women if Germany were defeated. In Russia, Tsar Nicholas II had changed the German-sounding name of the capital St. Petersburg to the Russian Petrograd as a patriotic move. Maintaining that Armenians in the Ottoman Empire were plotting against the Central Powers, the Ottomans drove those Armenians living in Turkey from their homes, forcing them onto long marches or into concentration camps where they simply died or were murdered. The Allies also caused the deaths of civilians en masse by creating famines, blockading the Syrian provinces of the Ottoman Empire in hopes that the people there would rebel or die of starvation.

SEEING HISTORY

Portraying Soldiers in World War I

During World War I, photography captured the reality of life for soldiers in the trenches and riveted the public's attention. Because weaponry was so powerful, censorship in all combatant countries prevented the worst images—such as body parts lying around a battlefield or hanging from trees—from being printed. Some people created images that only suggested what war was like and tried to stir patriotism in heroic posters, while others, like Jules Amar, showed designs for prosthetics to add to veterans' bodies. Soldiers themselves also portrayed life at the front in a variety of artistic ways.

Visual propaganda was crucial in mobilizing civilian populations to join the military; work overtime on the home front; and willingly sacrifice food, health, and even their lives. Propaganda specialists who had promoted the arms buildups before the war now joined with graphic artists to produce emotionally compelling images, often of a savage enemy threatening helpless white women and their children. Celebrated Australian artist Norman Lindsay excelled in this genre as in others. The poster shown here, "The Trumpet Calls" (1918), suggested the transformation of ordinary men into muscular, brave soldiers. Indeed, Australian soldiers fought in large numbers in some of World War I's most celebrated battles, including the battle of Gallipoli (1915), and, like soldiers from every country, became symbols of patriotism and national strength as a result.

German artilleryman and artist Otto Dix was one of thousands of wartime volunteers, and his depictions of soldiers' reality was starkly different. Asked why he had signed up for the war, he replied: "I had to experience how someone beside me suddenly falls over and is dead and the bullet has hit him squarely. I had to experience that quite directly. I wanted it. I'm therefore not a pacifist at all—or am I? Perhaps I was an inquisitive person." His etching *Wounded Soldier* (completed in 1916 at the battle of the Somme and published in 1924) captures another side of war, one that many soldiers recalled in their postwar nightmares. Australian nurses described a similar reality for the wounded men in their diaries. As one put it more emotionally, "[I] shall not describe their wounds, they were too awful. One loses sight of all the honour and the glory in the work we are doing." Another said that she only wished the wounded who would eventually die had been "killed outright," so great was their agony. Competing visions of war shaped postwar culture and almost immediately influenced the course of politics.

Question to Consider

■ **Compare these visual depictions of soldiers, the motivations that might have led to their production, and the effects they might have had on the viewing public. Which image do you think more powerful, and why?**

Norman Lindsay, "The Trumpet Calls" (1918).
*(*The Trumpet Calls, *by Norman Lindsay. Library of Congress, Prints and Photographs Division, LC-USZC4-12164.)*

Otto Dix, *Wounded Soldier* (1924).
(Otto Dix [1891–1969], photo © ARS, NY. Wounded Man, Autumn 1916, Bapaume *from the portfolio* The War *[Verwundeter, Herbst 1916, Bapaume aus der Mappe Der Krieg]. 1924. Etching and aquatint from a portfolio of twenty etching, aquatint and drypoints, fourteen etching and aquatints, nine etching and drypoints, four etchings, and one drypoint and aquatint plate: 7¾ x 11 7/16" [19.7 x 29 cm.]; sheet: 13¾ x 18 11/16" [35 x 47.4 cm.]. Publisher: Karl Nierendorf, Berlin. Printer: Otto Felsing, Berlin. Gift of Abby Aldrich Rockefeller. [159.1934.6]. The Museum of Modern Art, New York, NY, USA. Digital Image © The Museum of Modern Art/Licensed by SCALA/Art Resource, NY/© 2011 Artists Rights Society [ARS], New York/VG Bild-Kunst, Bonn.)*

A New Workforce in Wartime

With men at the front, women (at right in this French photograph) moved into factory work at jobs from which they had been unofficially barred before the war. In addition, tens of thousands of forced laborers from the colonies were moved to Europe also to replace men sent to the front. The European experience of forced labor and service at the front politicized colonial subjects, fortifying independence movements in the postwar period. *(Roger Viollet/Getty Images.)*

Despite widespread popular support for the war, some individuals worked to bring about a negotiated peace. In 1915, activists in the international women's movement met in The Hague to call for an end to the war. "We can no longer endure . . . brute force as the only solution of international disputes," declared Dutch physician Aletta Jacobs. The women had no success, though many brought their cause to individual heads of state. In Austria-Hungary, nationalist groups agitating for ethnic self-determination hampered the empire's war effort. The Czechs undertook a vigorous anti-Habsburg campaign at home, while Croats, Slovenes, and Serbs in the Balkans formed a committee to plan a southern Slavic state independent of Austria-Hungary. The Allies encouraged such independence movements as part of their strategy to defeat Austria-Hungary.

The Civilians' War | The war upset the social order as well as the political one. In the war's early days, many women lost their jobs when luxury shops, textile factories, and other nonessential businesses closed. But governments and businesses soon recognized the amount of labor it would take to wage technological war. As more and more men left for the trenches, women who had lost their jobs elsewhere joined with low-paid domestic workers to take over higher-paying jobs in munitions and metallurgical industries. In Warsaw women drove trucks, and in London they conducted streetcars. Some young women drove ambulances and nursed the wounded near the front lines.

The press praised women's patriotism in adapting to the wartime emergency, but women's assumption of men's jobs looked to many like a sign of social disorder. In the words of one metalworker, women were "sending men to the slaughter." Men feared that women would remain in the workforce after the war, robbing men of the breadwinner role. Others, even some women, objected to women's loss of femininity. "The feminine in me decreased more and more, and I did not know whether to be sad or glad about this," wrote one Russian nurse about wearing rough male clothing near the battlefield. Others criticized young female munitions workers for squandering their pay on ribbons and jewelry. The heated prewar debates over the "new woman" and gender roles returned.

Although soldiers from different backgrounds often felt bonds of solidarity in the trenches, difficult wartime conditions increasingly pitted civilians

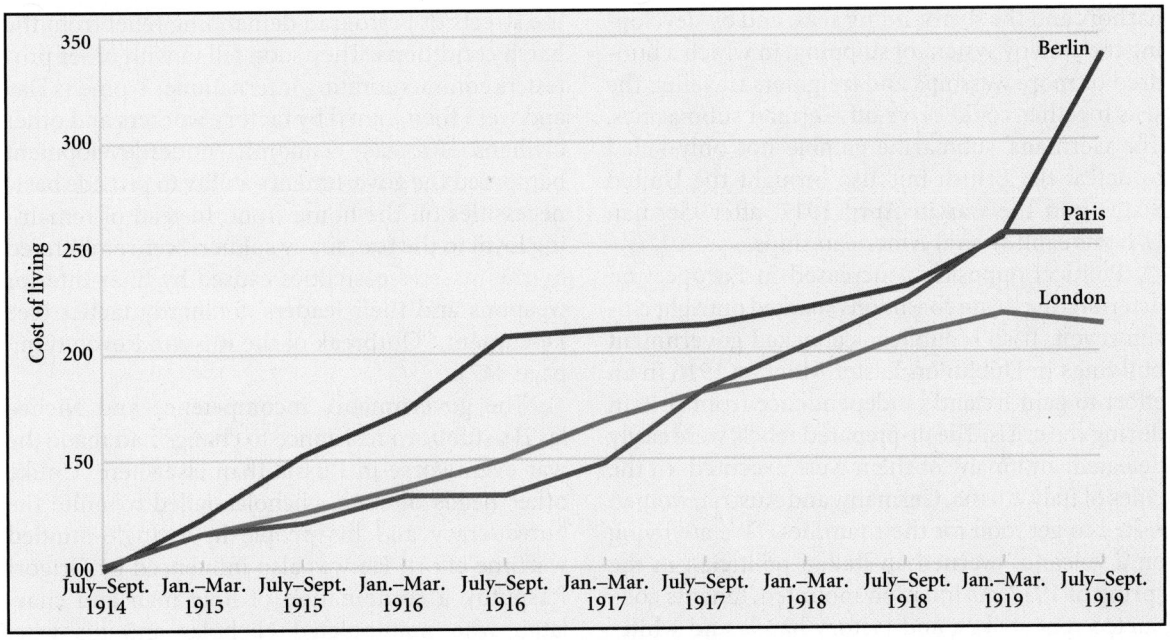

FIGURE 25.1 The Rising Cost of Living During World War I
The diversion of resources to the military resulted in a soaring cost of living for civilians. As men went to the front and as some remaining agricultural workers could find higher pay in factories, a decline in agricultural output led to scarcity and thus rising prices for food. Finally, housing came to be in short supply as resources were directed to the war effort rather than used to construct needed buildings. Even after the war, prices rose in Germany because the Allies maintained their blockade to keep the pressure on the peacemaking process. *(Jay Winter and Jean-Louis Robert,* Capital Cities at War: Paris, London, Berlin, 1914–1919 *[Cambridge: Cambridge University Press, 1997], 259.)*

against one another on the home front. Workers toiled long hours with less to eat, while many in the upper classes bought fancy food and fashionable clothing on the black market (outside the official system of rationing). Governments allowed many businesses high rates of profit, a policy that made the cost of living surge and thus contributed to social tensions (Figure 25.1). Shortages of staples like bread, sugar, and meat occurred across Europe. The Germans, in fact, called the brutal winter of 1916–1917 the turnip winter, because turnips were often the only food available. A German roof workers' association pleaded for relief: "We can no longer go on. Our children are starving." Reviving prewar anti-Semitism, some blamed Jews for the shortages. Colonial populations suffered oppressive conditions as well. The French forcibly transported some 100,000 Vietnamese to work in France for the war effort. Africans also faced grueling forced labor along with skyrocketing taxes and prices. Civilian suffering during the war, whether in the colonies or in Europe, laid the groundwork for ordinary people to take political action.

REVIEW QUESTION In what ways was World War I a total war?

Protest, Revolution, and War's End, 1917–1918

By 1917, the situation was becoming desperate for everyone—politicians, the military, and civilians. Discontent on the home front started shaping the course of the war. Neither patriotic slogans before the war nor propaganda during it had prepared people for wartime devastation. Civilians rebelled in cities across Europe. While soldiers in some armies mutinied, nationalist struggles continued to plague Britain and Austria-Hungary. Soon full-fledged revolution was sweeping Europe, toppling the Russian dynasty, and threatening not just war but civil war as well.

War Protest

On February 1, 1917, the German government, hard-pressed by the public clamor over mounting casualties and by the military's growing control, resumed full-scale submarine warfare. The military promised that this campaign would end the war in six months by cutting off food and military supplies to Britain and thus forcing the island nation to surrender. The British responded by mining their harbors and the surrounding seas, and by developing the convoy system of shipping, in which a hundred or more warships and freighters traveling the seas together could drive off German submarines. The Germans' submarine gamble not only failed to defeat the British but also brought the United States into the war in April 1917, after German U-boats sank several American ships.

Political opposition increased in Europe, and deteriorating living conditions sparked outright citizen revolt. Irish republicans attacked government buildings in Dublin on Easter Monday 1916 in an effort to gain Ireland's independence from Britain during the crisis. The ill-prepared rebels were easily defeated, and many of them were executed. In the cities of Italy, Russia, Germany, and Austria, women rioted to get food for their families. "We are living on a volcano," warned an Italian politician in the spring of 1917. As inflation mounted, tenants conducted rent strikes, and factory hands and white-collar workers alike walked off the job.

Amid these protests, Austria-Hungary secretly asked the Allies for a negotiated peace to avoid a total collapse of the empire. In the summer of 1917, the German Reichstag also made overtures for a "peace of understanding and permanent reconciliation of peoples." In January 1918, President Woodrow Wilson issued his **Fourteen Points**, a blueprint for a nonvindictive peace settlement held out to the war-weary citizens of the Central Powers. By that time, however, French soldiers had already mutinied against further bloody and useless offensives, and in Russia, protest had turned into outright revolution.

Revolution in Russia

Of all the warring nations, Russia sustained the greatest number of casualties—7.5 million by 1917. Slaughter on the eastern front drove hundreds of thousands of peasants into the Russian interior, spreading hunger, homelessness, and disease. In March 1917,[1] crowds of workingwomen swarmed the streets of Petrograd demanding relief from the harsh conditions. They soon fell in with other protesters commemorating International Women's Day and were then joined by factory workers and other civilians. Russia's economic underdevelopment hampered the government's ability to provide basic necessities on the home front. Instead of remaining loyal to the tsar, many soldiers were embittered by the massive casualties caused by their inferior weapons and their leaders' foolhardy tactics (see Document, "Outbreak of the Russian Revolution," page 847).

The government's incompetence and Nicholas II's stubborn resistance to change had made the war even worse in Russia than elsewhere. Unlike other heads of state, Nicholas failed to unite the bureaucracy and his people in a single-minded wartime effort. He was also influenced by Grigori Rasputin, a combination of holy man and charlatan who manipulated Nicholas and his wife, Alexandra, by claiming to control the hemophilia of their son and heir. Rasputin's disastrous impact on state matters led influential leaders to question rather than support the government. "Is this stupidity or treason?" one member of the Duma asked of the corrupt wartime administration. When the riots erupted in March 1917, Nicholas finally realized the situation was hopeless. He abdicated, bringing the three-hundred-year-old Romanov dynasty to a sudden end.

The Provisional Government

Aristocratic and middle-class politicians from the old Duma formed a new administration called the Provisional Government. At first, hopes were high that under the Provisional Government, as one revolutionary poet put it, "our false, filthy, boring, hideous life should become a just, pure, merry, and beautiful life." To survive, the Provisional Government had to pursue the war successfully, manage internal affairs better, and set the government on a firm constitutional footing. However, it did not rule alone, because other political forces had also strengthened during the revolution. Among them, the **soviets**—councils elected from workers and soldiers—competed with the government for political support. Born during the Revolution of 1905, the soviets in 1917 campaigned to end the deference usually given to the wealthy and to military officers, urged respect for workers and

[1]Until February 1918, Russia observed the Julian calendar, which was thirteen days behind the Gregorian calendar used by the rest of Europe. Hence, the first phase of the revolution occurred in March according to the Gregorian calendar (but February in the Julian calendar), the later phase in November on the Gregorian calendar (October according to the Julian). All dates used in this book follow the Gregorian calendar.

Fourteen Points: U.S. president Woodrow Wilson's World War I peace proposal; based on settlement rather than on conquest, it encouraged the surrender of the Central Powers.

soviets: Councils of workers and soldiers first formed in Russia in the Revolution of 1905; they were revived to represent the people in the early days of the 1917 Russian Revolution.

DOCUMENT

Outbreak of the Russian Revolution

It is clear only in retrospect when a full-fledged and sustainable revolution has broken out. Here an eighteen-year-old student describes what happened when news of the St. Petersburg revolt reached Moscow in the late winter of 1917. Crowds had already formed when the young man decided to see what was happening in the streets.

In the crowd were many students who explained that a revolution had begun in St. Petersburg. The news swept through them like a breeze and created an extraordinary atmosphere. People began to embrace and kiss; strangers became close friends; some wept for joy. In five to ten minutes people seemed reborn. A pretty girl came up to me and took me by the hand, as though we had known each other for ages. Then hand-in-hand, in a warm embrace, and without asking each other's name, we proceeded toward the Krutitskie barracks. . . .

The crowd grew bigger and bigger, and somewhere in the distance one could hear the well-known refrain of a revolutionary song. By this time it was so crowded that it was quite impossible to get to one side or the other. We continued to hold hands, as though we might get lost. Slowly, barely perceptibly, the human stream moved toward the Red Gates, where I knew there was another barracks. It was the same scene there, except that the soldiers were shouting loudly, waving and greeting us. We couldn't make out what they said. Near Pokrovka we ran into a group of police officers, but instead of greeting them with good-natured jokes, thousands of voices yelled fierce, threatening cries: "Pharaohs! Your time is up! Get away for your own good!"

. . . We moved slowly and could see neither the front nor the back of the crowd, for the street was blocked solid. For the first time in my life I sensed that atmosphere of joy, when everyone you meet seems close to you, your flesh and blood, when people look at one another with eyes full of love. To call it mass hypnosis is not quite right, but the mood of the crowd was transmitted from one to another like conduction, like a spontaneous burst of laughter, joy, or anger.

The majority of the crowd consisted of people who that morning had been praying for the good health of the imperial family. Now they were shouting, "Down with the Tsar!" and not disguising their joyful contempt. My companion was a good example. She showered me with questions: Where are we going? Why are we marching? Why is there a revolution? How will we manage without a tsar? It seemed like a mere holiday to her—Sunday's carnival procession, complete with mass participation. Tomorrow—Monday—humdrum working life would begin again, just as usual. Without asking a question, as though talking to herself, she suddenly said: "How good it would be if there was another revolution tomorrow!" What could I say? Tomorrow? Probably tomorrow the police would arrest us. But today there was a festival on the streets.

Source: Eduard Dune, *Notes of a Red Guard*, trans. and ed. Dianne Koenker and S. A. Smith (Champaign: University of Illinois Press, 1993), 32, 34.

Question to Consider

- **What is the mood of the crowd in Moscow? What was happening in Russia that would make them react this way to news of the revolt?**

the poor, and temporarily gave an air of celebration and carnival to the political upheaval. The peasants, also competing for power, began to confiscate landed estates and withhold produce from the market because there were no consumer goods for which to exchange food. As a result, urban food shortages worsened, threatening the Provisional Government.

In hopes of adding to the turmoil in Russia, the Germans in April 1917 provided safe rail transportation for **V. I. Lenin** (1870–1924) and other prominent Bolsheviks to return to Russia through German territory. Lenin had devoted his entire existence to bringing about socialism through the force of his small band of Bolsheviks. Upon his return to Petrograd, he issued the April Theses, a radical document that called for Russia to withdraw from the war, for the soviets to seize power on behalf of workers and poor peasants, and for all private land to be nationalized. As the Bolsheviks aimed to supplant the Provisional Government, they employed such slogans as "All power to the soviets" and "Peace, land, and bread."

The Bolshevik Takeover

Time was running out for the Provisional Government, which saw a battlefield victory as the only way to ensure its survival. On July 1, the Russian army attacked the Austrians in Galicia but was defeated once again. The new prime minister, Aleksandr Kerensky, used his commanding oratory to arouse patriotism, but he lacked the political skills needed to create an effective wartime government. Under the Provisional Government, the army itself

V. I. Lenin: Bolshevik leader who executed the Bolshevik Revolution in the fall of 1917, took Russia out of World War I, and imposed communism in Russia.

Revolution in Russia

1917	March 8	International Women's Day, strikes and demonstrations
	March 12	Establishment of Provisional Government
	March 15	Nicholas II abdicates
	April	Lenin and other Bolshevik leaders return to Russia
	May	Turmoil in the Provisional Government
	Late June–early July	Russian offensive against Germany fails
	Mid-July	Attempted popular uprising fails; Kerensky is prime minister
	September	Military coup fails
	November 6–7	Bolsheviks seize power on behalf of soviets
	November 25	Constituent assembly elections held
1918	January	Constituent assembly closed down by Bolsheviks
	March 2	Treaty of Brest-Litovsk
1918–1922		Civil war
1923		Union of Soviet Socialist Republics established
1924		Death of Lenin
1928–1929		Stalin takes full power

had become, as one critic put it, "a huge crowd of tired, poorly clad, poorly fed, embittered men"—eager for radical change.

The Bolshevik leadership, urged on by Lenin, attacked and overthrew the weakened Provisional Government in November 1917, an event called the **Bolshevik Revolution**. In January 1918, elections for a constituent assembly failed to give the Bolsheviks a plurality, so the party used troops to take over the new government completely. The Bolsheviks also seized town and city administrations, and in the winter of 1918–1919, their new government, observing Marxist doctrine, abolished private property and nationalized factories in order to stimulate production. The Provisional Government had allowed both men and women to vote in 1917, making Russia the first great power to legalize universal suffrage. This soon became a hollow privilege once the Bolsheviks limited the candidates to chosen members of the Communist Party.

The Bolsheviks asked Germany for peace and agreed to the Treaty of Brest-Litovsk (March 1918), which placed vast regions of the old Russian Empire under German occupation. Because the loss of millions of square miles to the Germans put Petrograd at risk, the Bolsheviks relocated the capital to Moscow and formally adopted the name Communists (taken from Karl Marx's writings) to distinguish themselves from the socialists/social democrats who had voted for the disastrous war in the first place. Lenin called the catastrophic terms of the treaty "obscene." However, he accepted them—not only because he had promised to bring peace to Russia but also because he believed that the rest of Europe would soon rebel against the war and overthrow the capitalist order.

Bolshevik Revolution: The overthrow of Russia's Provisional Government in the fall of 1917 by V. I. Lenin and his Bolshevik forces.

Civil War in Russia

A full-blown civil war now broke out in Russia, with the pro-Bolsheviks (or "Reds") pitted against an array of forces (the "Whites") who wanted to turn back the revolution (Map 25.3). Among the Whites were three distinct groups: the tsarist military leadership, composed mainly of landlords and supporters of aristocratic rule; the liberal educated class, including businessmen whose property had been nationalized; and non-Russian nationalities who had been brought into the empire through force and Russification and who fought the Bolsheviks because they saw their chance for independence. In addition, before World War I ended, Russia's former allies—notably the United States, Britain, France, and Japan—landed troops in the country both to block the Germans and to fight the Bolsheviks. The counterrevolutionary groups lacked a strong leader and unified goals, however. Instead, they competed with one another: the pro-tsarist forces, for example, alienated groups seeking independent nation-state status, such as the Ukrainians, Estonians, and Lithuanians, by stressing the goal of restoring the Russian Empire. Even with the presence of Allied troops, the opponents of revolution could not defeat the Bolsheviks without a common purpose or an effective, unified command.

The civil war shaped Russian communism. Leon Trotsky (1879–1940), Bolshevik commissar of war, built the highly disciplined army by ending democratic procedures, such as the election of officers, that had originally attracted soldiers to Bolshevism. Lenin and Trotsky introduced the policy of war communism, whereby urban workers and troops moved through the countryside, seizing grain from the peasantry to feed the civil war army and workforce. The Cheka (secret police) imprisoned political opponents and black marketers and often shot them without trial. As the bureaucracy, the Cheka, and the Red Army all grew in size and strength, the result was a more authoritarian government—a development that broke Marx's promise that revolution would bring a "withering away" of the state.

As the Bolsheviks clamped down on their opponents during the bloody civil war, they organized their supporters to foster revolutionary Marxism across Europe. In March 1919, they founded the

Third International, also known as the Communist International (Comintern), to replace the Second International with a centralized organization dedicated to preaching communism. By mid-1921, the Red Army had defeated the Whites in the Crimea, the Caucasus, and the Muslim borderlands in central Asia. After ousting the Japanese from Siberia in 1922, the Bolsheviks governed a state as multinational as the old Russian Empire had been. Although the revolution had turned out the inept Romanovs and the privileged aristocracy, the civil war and the resulting hunger and disease took millions of lives. Meanwhile, the Bolsheviks had made brutality their political style, one at odds with socialist promises for a humane and flourishing society.

Ending the War, 1918

With Russia out of the war, Europe's leaders faced a new balance of military forces. In the spring of 1918, the Central Powers made one final attempt to smash through the Allied lines using a new offensive strategy. It consisted of concentrated forces piercing single points of the enemy's defense lines and then wreaking havoc from the rear. Using these tactics, the Central Powers overwhelmed the Italian army at Caporetto in the fall of 1917, but a similar offensive on the western front in the spring of 1918

Lenin Addressing Soldiers

Lenin mobilized the masses with his oratory, but he also used traditional weapons of the Russian Empire such as secret police, imprisonment and torture, and executions. At the time of the civil war it was more than ever important to keep soldiers loyal. Understanding this, Lenin, with the crucial aid of Leon Trotsky, began building the Red Army into a formidable fighting force. *(Rue des Archives/The Granger Collection, New York—All rights reserved.)*

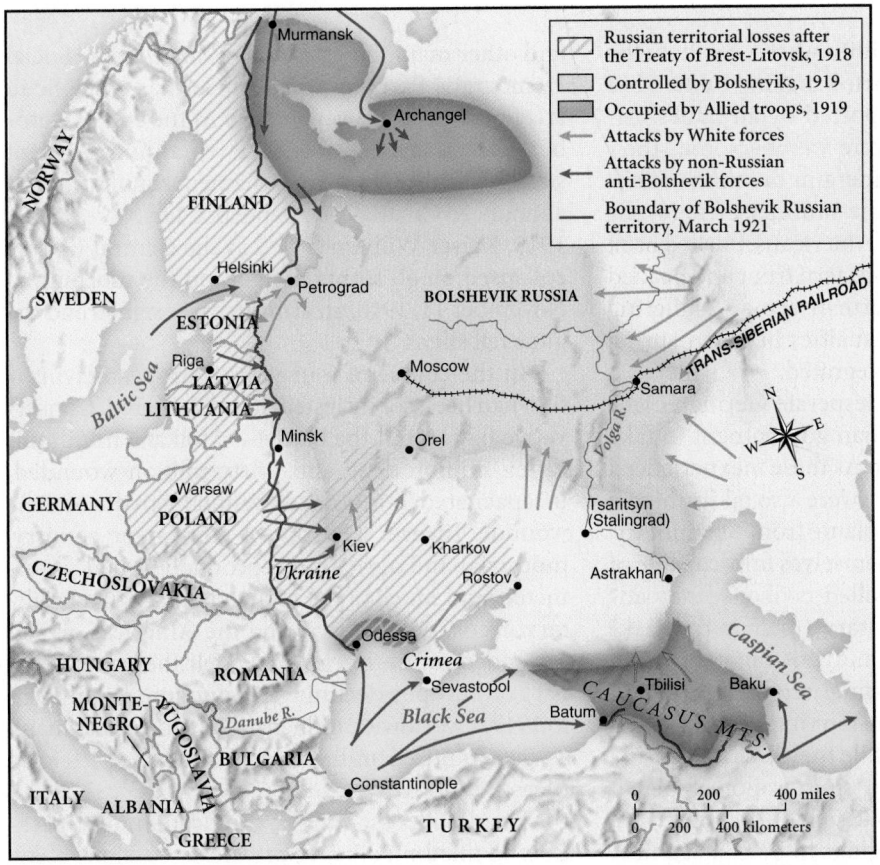

MAP 25.3 The Russian Civil War, 1917–1922

Nationalists, aristocrats, middle-class citizens, and property-owning peasants tried to combine their interests to defeat the Bolsheviks, but they failed to create an effective political consensus. As fighting covered the countryside, ordinary people suffered, especially when their grain was confiscated by armies on both sides. The Western powers and Japan also sent in troops to put down this threatening revolution.

TAKING MEASURE

The Victims of Influenza, 1918–1919

The influenza pandemic that broke out among soldiers and civilians during World War I was devastating, claiming between 50 and 100 million lives worldwide. Not only was the death toll unprecedented, but the victims of the flu differed significantly from those in the general population who had normally died from influenza and pneumonia. The graph at right, showing the "terrible W" shape of flu deaths, illustrates that difference. (*Specific death rate* refers to a method of calculating mortality rates from a specified cause.)

Question to Consider

- **What was the difference among victims of the flu pandemic during and immediately after World War I and those who had died of flu before the war? Why was this difference so alarming to officials and ordinary people alike?**

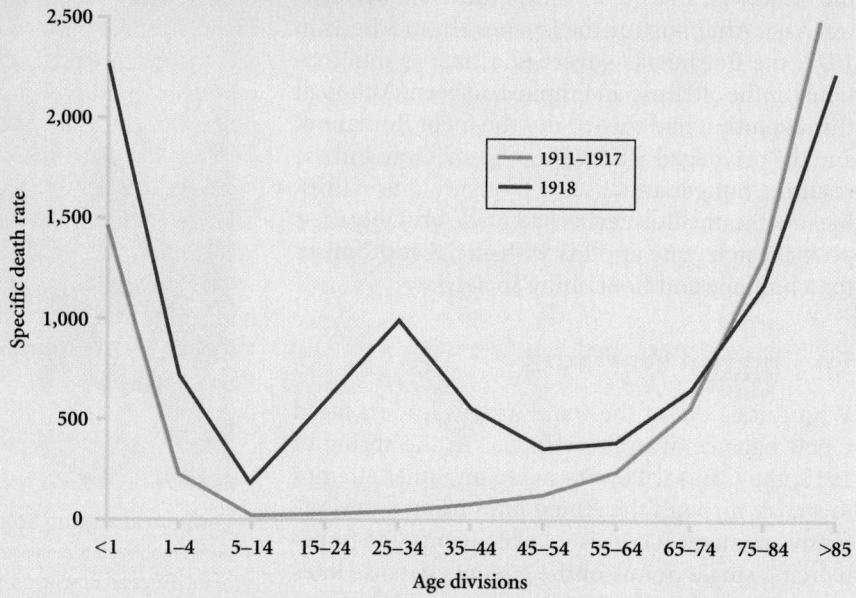

Source: Jeffrey K. Taubenberger and David Morens, "1918 Influenza: The Mother of All Pandemics," *Emerging Infectious Diseases* 12, no. 1 (2006): 15–22.

ground to a bloody halt within weeks. By then, the British and French had started making limited but effective use of tanks supported by airplanes. Although the first tanks were cumbersome, their ability to withstand machine-gun fire made offensive attacks winnable. In the summer of 1918, the Allies, now fortified by the Americans, pushed back the Germans all along the western front and headed toward Germany. The German armies, suffering more than two million casualties between spring and summer, rapidly disintegrated.

By October 1918, the desperate German command helped create a civilian government to take over rule of the home front. As these inexperienced politicians took power, they were also taking blame for the defeat. Shifting the blame from the military, the generals proclaimed themselves fully capable of winning the war. Weak-willed civilians, they announced, had dealt the military a "stab in the back" by forcing a surrender. Amid this outright lying, naval officers called for a final sea battle. Having spent years watching high-ranking officers enjoy champagne-filled meals while they themselves survived on turnips and thin soup, sailors rebelled against what they saw as a suicide mission. The sailors' revolt spread to workers in Berlin, Munich, and other major cities. The uprisings led the Social Democratic Party to declare a German republic in an effort to prevent revolution. At the end of October, Czechs and Slovaks declared an independent state, while the Croatian parliament simultaneously announced Croatia's independence. On November 9, 1918, Kaiser William II fled as the Central Powers collapsed on all fronts. Finally, on the morning of November 11, 1918, an armistice was signed and the guns fell silent.

In the course of four years, European civilization had been sorely tested, if not shattered. Conservative figures put the battlefield toll at a minimum of ten million dead and thirty million wounded, incapacitated, or doomed eventually to die of their wounds. In every European combatant country, industrial and agricultural production had plummeted, and much of the reduced output filled military needs. Asia, Africa, and the Americas, which depended on European trade, felt the painful impact of Europe's declining production. From 1918 to 1919, a worldwide influenza epidemic left as many as one hundred million more dead (see "Taking Measure," above).

Besides illness, hunger, and death, moral questioning filled media and private discussions alike.

Soldiers returning home in 1918 and 1919 flooded the book market with their memoirs, trying to give meaning to their experiences. Some twenty-five hundred war poets published in Britain alone. Whereas many had begun by emphasizing heroism and glory, others were cynical and bitter by war's end. They insisted that the fighting had been absolutely meaningless. Total war had not only drained society of resources and population but also sown the seeds of further catastrophe.

REVIEW QUESTION Why did people rebel during World War I, and what turned rebellion into outright revolution in Russia?

The Search for Peace in an Era of Revolution

World War I, like many other wars in the past, had unforeseen and dramatic consequences. Revolutionary fervor now swept the continent, especially in the former empires of Germany and Austria-Hungary. Until 1921, socialist victory seemed plausible; many of the newly independent peoples of eastern and central Europe strongly supported socialist principles. The revolutionary mood infected workers and peasants in Germany, too. In contrast, many activists on both the left and the right hoped for a political order based on military authority of the kind they had relied on during the war. Faced with both liberal and right-wing uprisings, diplomats from around the world arrived in Paris in January 1919 to negotiate the terms of peace, though without fully recognizing the fact that the war was still going on not only in city streets, where soldiers were bringing the war home, but also in people's hearts.

Europe in Turmoil

Urban citizens and returning soldiers ignited the protests that swept Europe in 1918 and 1919. In January 1919, the red flag of socialist revolution flew from the city hall in Glasgow, Scotland, while in cities of the collapsing Austro-Hungarian monarchy, workers set up councils to take over factory production and direct politics. Many soldiers did not disband at the armistice but formed volunteer armies, preventing the return to peacetime politics. Germany was especially unstable, partly because of the shock of defeat. Independent socialist groups and workers' councils fought for control of the government, and workers and veterans filled the streets, demanding food and back pay. Whereas in 1848, revolutionaries had marched to city hall or the king's residence, these protesters took over newspapers and telegraph offices to control the flow of information. One of the most radical socialist factions was the Spartacists, led by cofounders Karl Liebknecht (1871–1919) and Rosa Luxemburg (1870–1919). Unlike Lenin, the two leading Spartacists wanted any uprisings to give workers political experience instead of simply following an all-knowing party leadership on a set course.

German conservatives had believed that the war would put an end to Social Democratic influence; instead, it brought German socialists to power. Social Democratic leader Friedrich Ebert, who headed the new German government, rejected revolution and supported the creation of a parliamentary republic to replace the monarchy. He appeared to back the idea of settling political differences with military solutions by calling on the German army and the Freikorps — a roving paramilitary band of students, demobilized soldiers, and others — to suppress the workers' councils and demonstrators. "The enthusiasm is marvelous," wrote one young soldier. "No mercy's shown. We shoot even the wounded. . . . We were much more humane against the French in the field." Members of the Freikorps hunted down Luxemburg and Liebknecht, among others, and murdered them.

Violence continued even as an assembly meeting in the city of Weimar in February 1919 approved a constitution and founded a parliamentary republic called the **Weimar Republic**. This time the right rebelled, for the military leadership dreamed of a restored monarchy: "As I love Germany, so I hate the Republic," wrote one officer. To defeat a military coup by Freikorps officers, Ebert called for a general strike. This action cut short a takeover of the new republic by showing the clear lack of popular support for a military regime. But in so doing, the Weimar Republic had set a dangerous precedent: it had relied on street violence, paramilitary groups, and protests rather than parliaments to solve political problems.

Revolutionary activism surged and was smashed in many parts of Europe. Late in the winter of 1919, leftists proclaimed "soviet republics" — governments led by workers' councils — in Bavaria and Hungary. Volunteer armies and troops soon put the soviets down. The Bolsheviks tried to establish a Marxist regime in Poland in the belief that its people wanted a workers' revolution. Instead, the Poles resisted and drove the Red Army back in 1920, while the Allied powers rushed supplies and advisers to Warsaw.

Weimar Republic: The parliamentary republic established in 1919 in Germany to replace the monarchy.

Though they failed, the various revolts provided further proof that total war had let loose the forces of political chaos. War, it seemed, continued.

The Paris Peace Conference, 1919–1920

As political turmoil engulfed peoples from Berlin to Moscow, the Paris Peace Conference opened in January 1919. Visions of communism spreading westward haunted the deliberations, but the assembled statesmen were also focused on the reconstruction of a secure Europe and the status of Germany. Leaders such as French premier Georges Clemenceau had to satisfy angry citizens who were demanding revenge or, at the very least, money to rebuild and pay their nation's war debts. France had lost 1.3 million people — almost an entire generation of young men — and more than a million buildings, six thousand bridges, and thousands of miles of railroad lines and roads. Great Britain's representative, Prime Minister David Lloyd George, caught the mood of the British public by campaigning in 1918 with such slogans as "Hang the kaiser." The Italians arrived on the scene demanding the territory promised to them in the 1915 Treaty of London. Meanwhile, U.S. president Woodrow Wilson (1856–1924), head of the new world power that had helped achieve the Allied victory, had his own agenda. His Fourteen Points, on which the truce had been based, were steeped in the language of freedom and called for open diplomacy, arms reduction, and the right of nationality groups to determine their own government.

The Fourteen Points did not represent the mood of the victors. Allied propaganda had made the Germans seem like inhuman monsters, and many citizens demanded a harsh peace. In addition, some military experts feared that Germany was using the armistice only to regroup for more warfare. Indeed, Germans widely refused to admit that their army had lost the war. Eager for army support, Ebert had given returning soldiers a rousing welcome: "As you return unconquered from the field of battle, I salute you." Wilson's former allies campaigned to make him look naive and unrealistic. "Wilson bores me with his Fourteen Points," Clemenceau complained. "Why, the good Lord himself has only ten."

Nevertheless, Wilson's plan persuaded Germans that the settlement would not be vindictive. His commitment to *settlement* as opposed to *surrender* wisely recognized that Germany was still the strongest state on the continent, and he pushed for a treaty that balanced the strengths and interests of various European powers. Economists and other specialists accompanying Wilson to Paris agreed that, harshly dealt with and humiliated, Germany might soon become vengeful and chaotic — a lethal combination.

The Peace of Paris Treaties

After six months, the statesmen and their teams of experts produced the **Peace of Paris** (1919–1920), composed of a cluster of individual treaties that shocked the countries that had to accept them. The treaties separated Austria from Hungary, reduced Hungary by almost two-thirds of its inhabitants and three-quarters of its territory, broke up the Ottoman Empire, and treated Germany severely. They replaced the Habsburg Empire with a group of small, internally divided, and economically weak states: Czechoslovakia; Poland; and the Kingdom of the Serbs, Croats, and Slovenes (soon renamed Yugoslavia). After a century and a half of partition, Poland was reconstructed from parts of Russia, Germany, and Austria-Hungary — leaving one-third of its population ethnically non-Polish. The statesmen in Paris also created the Polish Corridor, which connected Poland to the Baltic Sea and separated East Prussia from the rest of Germany (Map 25.4). Austria and Hungary were both left reeling at their drastic loss of territory and resources.

The Treaty of Versailles, the centerpiece of the Peace of Paris, specifically dealt with Germany. In it, France recovered Alsace and Lorraine, and the Allies would temporarily occupy the left, or western, bank of the Rhine and the coal-bearing Saar basin. Wilson accepted his allies' expectations that Germany would pay substantial reparations for civilian damage during the war. The specific amount was set in 1921 at the crushing sum of 132 billion gold marks. Germany also had to reduce its army, almost eliminate its navy, stop manufacturing offensive weapons, and deliver a large amount of free coal each year to Belgium and France. Furthermore, it was forbidden to have an air force and had to give up its colonies. The average German saw in these terms an unmerited humiliation that was compounded by Article 231 of the treaty, which described Germany's "responsibility" for damage caused "by the aggression of Germany and her allies." Outraged Germans interpreted this as a **war guilt clause**, which blamed Germany for the war and allowed the victors to collect reparations from their economi-

---

Peace of Paris: The series of peace treaties (1919–1920) that provided the settlement of World War I. The Treaty of Versailles with Germany was the centerpiece of the Peace of Paris.

war guilt clause: The part of the Treaty of Versailles that assigned blame for World War I to Germany.

MAP 25.4 Europe and the Middle East after the Peace Settlements of 1919–1920

The political landscape of central, east, and east-central Europe changed dramatically as a result of the Russian Revolution and the Peace of Paris. The Ottoman, German, Russian, and Austro-Hungarian Empires were either broken up into multiple small states or territorially reduced. The settlement left resentments among Germans and Hungarians and created a group of weak, struggling nations in the heartland of Europe. The victorious powers took over much of the oil-rich Middle East. | **Why is it significant that the postwar geopolitical changes were so concentrated in one section of Europe?**

cally developed country rather than from ruined Austria. War guilt made Germans feel like outcasts in the community of nations.

The League of Nations | Besides redrawing the map of Europe, the Peace of Paris set up an organization called the **League of Nations,** whose members had a joint responsibility for maintaining peace—a principle called collective security. It was supposed to replace the divisive secrecy of prewar power politics. As part of Wilson's vision, the league would guide the world toward disarmament and arbitrate its members' disputes. The U.S. Senate, rejecting the idea of collective security, failed to ratify the peace settlement and refused to join the league. Moreover, Germany and Russia initially were excluded from the league and were thus blocked from working cooperatively with the league. The absence of these three important powers weakened the league as a global peacekeeper from the outset.

League of Nations: The international organization set up following World War I to maintain peace by arbitrating disputes and promoting collective security.

CONTRASTING VIEWS

The Middle East at the End of World War I: Freedom or Subjugation?

The end of World War I aroused hopes around the world. In Paris in 1919, representatives of the victorious powers were besieged by outsiders to Western government, each making a claim for special attention to their needs or for concrete action to realize the noble rhetoric of the Fourteen Points. The conquered and the colonized expected a fair-minded treaty based on a range of Allied agreements, and a variety of other peoples were encouraged by promises of self-determination. Yet it quickly became clear that there were contrasting views among the Allies themselves. Woodrow Wilson's Fourteen Points articulated one position on the future of colonized areas of the world, including the Ottoman Empire (Document 1). As the war drew to a close in November 1918, Britain and France seemed to endorse Wilson's position when it came to freedom for Ottoman subjects (Document 2). Other agreements, such as those dividing up oil between the British and French in the Middle East, gave a far different impression (Document 3). At the Paris Peace Conference in 1919–1920, Middle Eastern leaders lobbied for their independence. The emir Faisal was one of these, after having led pro-Allied troops to bring about freedom from the Ottomans and to achieve Arab unity (Document 4). When the mandate system was drawn up, however, it became clear that those under Ottoman rule would in fact remain unfree (Document 5).

1. Woodrow Wilson, Fourteen Points, January 8, 1918

President Woodrow Wilson's Fourteen Points, first presented in a speech to the U.S. Congress, raised hopes that the world would be fairer after the war than before. The fifth and twelfth points, presented here, spoke especially to those who had been held in colonial subjugation.

V. A free, openminded, and absolutely impartial adjustment of all colonial claims, based upon a strict observance of the principle that in determining all such questions of sovereignty the interests of the populations concerned must have equal weight with the equitable claims of the government whose title is to be determined.

XII. The Turkish portions of the present Ottoman Empire should be assured a secure sovereignty, but the other nationalities which are now under Turkish rule should be assured an undoubted security of life and an absolutely unmolested opportunity of autonomous development, and the Dardanelles should be permanently opened as a free passage to the ships and commerce of all nations under international guarantees.

Source: Woodrow Wilson, "Speech on the Fourteen Points," *Congressional Record*, 65th Congress, 2nd Session, 1918, 680–81.

2. The Anglo-French Declaration of November 7, 1918

As World War I reached its end in the autumn of 1918, the French and British issued this official declaration of their war aims.

The object aimed at by France and Great Britain in prosecuting in the East the War let loose by the ambition of Germany is the complete and definite emancipation of the peoples so long oppressed by the Turks and the establishment of national governments and administrations deriving their authority from the initiative and free choices of the indigenous populations.

Source: Parliamentary Debates, House of Commons, 5, cxlv, 351.

3. British-French Division of the Oil in Mesopotamia (Iraq)

Despite claims to favor Middle Eastern independence, the British and French made many agreements about their joint prerogatives in the region, this one concerning oil, which the war had shown to be an increasingly indispensable commodity.

The British Government undertake to grant to the French Government or its nominee twenty-five percent of the net

The League of Nations also organized the administration of the former colonies and territories of Germany and the Ottoman Empire—such as Togo, Cameroon, Syria, and Palestine—through systems of political control called mandates (see "Contrasting Views," above). The victorious powers exercised political control or mandates over these territories, while local leaders retained limited authority. The league justified the **mandate system** as providing governance by "advanced nations" over territories "not yet able to stand by themselves under the strenuous conditions of the modern world." But colonized people, many of whom had fought and received promises of political rights and independence for doing so, challenged these claims. They had seen how savage and degraded the people who claimed to be racially and politically superior could be. "Never again will the darker people of the world occupy just the place they had before," the African American leader W. E. B. Du Bois predicted in 1918. Yet the mandate system not only kept imperialism alive at a time when the powers were bankrupt and weak but also, like the Peace of Paris, aroused anger and resistance.

mandate system: The political control over the former colonies and territories of the German and Ottoman Empires granted to the victors of World War I by the League of Nations.

output of crude oil at current market rates which His Majesty's Government may secure from the Mesopotamian oilfields in the event of their being developed by Government action; or in the event of a private petroleum company being used to develop the Mesopotamian oilfields the British Government will place at the disposal of the French Government a share of twenty-five percent in such company.

Source: *Memorandum of Agreement between M. Philippe Berthelot, Directeur des Affaires Politiques et Commerciles au Ministère des Affaires Etrangères, and Professor Sir John Cadman, Director in Charge of His Majesty's Petroleum Department,* in Cmd. 675 of 1920 and in *U.S. Foreign Relations* 1920, ii, 655–58.

4. Claiming Independence for the Middle East

Arabs had hotly debated whether to assist the Allied colonizers in World War I, but promises of independence won them over. Some Arabs argued for independence of individual areas in the Middle East and for resolutions to competing claims of the Arabs and of new Jewish settlers in the region. Emir Faisal, who had commanded Arab forces in the war, presented the pan-Arab ideal.

The aim of the Arab nationalist movement is to unite the Arabs eventually into one nation. . . . I came to Europe on behalf of my father and the Arabs of Asia to say that they are expecting the powers at the Conference not to attach undue importance to superficial differences of condition among us and not to consider them only from the low ground of existing European material interests and supposed spheres of influence. They expect the powers to think of them as one potential people, jealous of their language and liberty, and they ask that no step be taken inconsistent with the prospect of an eventual union of these areas under one sovereign government.

Source: Stephen Bonsal, *Suitors and Suppliants: The Little Nations at Versailles* (Port Washington: Kennikat Press, 1969), 32–33.

5. Resolution of the Syrian Congress at Damascus, July 2, 1919

In 1919, a commission from the Paris Peace Conference was established to investigate the political conditions in the Middle East. The Syrian Congress met to prepare this statement for the commission.

Considering the fact that the Arabs inhabiting the Syrian area are not naturally less gifted than other more advanced races and that they are by no means less developed than the Bulgarians, Serbians, Greeks, and Roumanians at the beginning of their independence, we protest against Article 22 of the Covenant of the League of Nations placing us among the nations in their middle stage of development which stand in need of a mandatory power.

We oppose the pretentions of the Zionists to create a Jewish commonwealth in the southern part of Syria, known as Palestine, and oppose zionist migration to any part of our country. . . . Our Jewish compatriots shall enjoy our common rights and assume the common responsibilities.

We also have the fullest confidence that the Peace Conference will realize that we would not have risen against the Turks with whom we had participated in all civil, political, and representative privileges . . . and so will grant us our desires in full in order that our political rights may not be less after the war than they were before, since we have shed so much blood in the cause of our liberty and independence.

Source: Quoted in J. C. Hurewitz, ed., *The Middle East and North Africa in World Politics: A Documentary Record*, 2nd ed. 2 vols. (New Haven: Yale University Press, 1979), 2:180–81.

Questions to Consider

1. **Describe the various claims of the official combatant powers. How do you explain these differing positions?**
2. **How were the competing positions at the peace conference related to the politics and conditions of World War I?**
3. **Does any one or two of the demands seem more justifiable in addressing the peacetime needs of Europe and the world?**
4. **What was the position of the Arabs?**
5. **How do you explain the fact that the Arabs lost the argument so completely?**

Economic and Diplomatic Consequences of the Peace

Just as wartime conditions, including military action, continued long after the armistice, so the Peace of Paris posed problems into the 1920s and beyond. Western leaders faced two related issues in the aftermath of the war. The first was economic recovery and its relationship to war debts and German reparation payments. The second was ensuring that peace actually came about and lasted.

Economic Dilemmas

France, hardest hit by wartime destruction and billions of dollars in debt to the United States, estimated that Germany owed it at least $200 billion. Britain, by contrast, had not been physically devastated and was worried instead about maintaining its empire and restoring trade with Germany, not exacting huge reparations to rebuild. Nevertheless, both France and Britain were dependent on some German payments to settle their war debts to the United States because Europe's income from world trade had plunged during the war.

Germany claimed that the demand for reparations strained its government, already facing political upheaval. But Germany's economic problems had begun long before the Peace of Paris with the kaiser's policy of not raising taxes—especially on the rich—to pay for the war, leaving the new

Inflation and the German Elections
The extraordinary inflation that struck the German economy in 1923 haunted those who lived through it and lost their life savings as money became worthless. The disaster gravely affected both the social and political order, leaving a legacy of fear and outrage. In this poster, the German Democratic Party rouses terror with its highly charged image of inflation as a monstrous enemy of the nation in the election campaign of 1924. *(© Photo 12/The Image Works.)*

republic with a staggering debt. Now this republic, an experiment in democracy, needed to win over its citizens, and hiking taxes to pay Germany's debt would only anger them. In 1921, when Germans refused to present a realistic plan for paying reparations, the French occupied several cities in the Ruhr until a settlement was reached.

At odds with the powers to the west, the German government turned to eastern Europe for support. In the Treaty of Rapallo (1922), it reached an agreement establishing economic ties with Russia, which was desperate for Western trade. Meanwhile, Germany's relations with powers to the west continued to deteriorate. In 1923, after Germany defaulted on coal deliveries, the French and the Belgians sent troops into the Ruhr basin, planning to seize its resources to pay for wartime expenditures. Urged on by the government, Ruhr citizens shut down industry by staying home from work. The German government printed trillions of marks to support the workers and to pay its own war debts with practically worthless currency. The result was a staggering inflation in Germany that gravely threatened the international economy: at one point, a single U.S. dollar cost 4.42 trillion marks, and wheelbarrows of money were required to buy a turnip. Negotiations to resolve this economic chaos resulted in the Dawes Plan (1924) and the Young Plan (1929), which reduced reparations to more realistic levels and restored the value of German currency. Before that happened, however, the inflation had wiped out people's savings and turned many more Germans against their democratic government.

The Little Entente

Making Peace In addition to economic recovery, a second burning issue involved making the peace take hold and last. Statesmen determined that peace needed disarmament, a return of Germany to the community of nations, and security for the new countries of eastern Europe. Hard diplomatic bargaining produced two plans in Germany's favor. At the Washington Conference in 1921, the United States, Great Britain, Japan, France, and Italy agreed to reduce their number of battleships and to stop constructing new ones for ten years. Four years later, in 1925, the League of Nations sponsored a meeting of the great powers, including Germany, at Locarno, Switzerland. The Treaty of Locarno provided Germany with a seat in the league as of 1926. In return, Germany agreed not to violate the borders of France and Belgium and to keep the nearby Rhineland demilitarized—that is, unfortified by troops.

To the east, statesmen feared a German attempt to regain territory lost to Poland, to merge with Austria, or to launch any attack on states spun off from Austria-Hungary. To meet this threat, Czechoslovakia, Yugoslavia, and Romania formed the Little Entente in 1920–1921, a collective security agreement intended to protect them from Germany and Russia. Between 1924 and 1927, France allied itself with the Little Entente and with Poland. In 1928, sixty nations, including the major European powers, Japan, and the United States, signed the Kellogg-

Briand Pact, which formally rejected international violence. The pact lacked any mechanism for enforcement and thus resembled, as one critic put it, "an international kiss."

The publicity surrounding the international agreements of the 1920s sharply contrasted with old-style diplomacy, which had been conducted in secret and subject to little public scrutiny. The development of a system of open, collective security suggested a diplomatic revolution that would promote international peace. Yet openness allowed diplomats to feed the press information designed to provoke the masses. For example, the press and opposition parties whipped the German populace into a nationalist fury whenever Germany's diplomats appeared to compromise, even though these compromises worked to undo the Treaty of Versailles. Right-wing journalists who hated republican government used international meetings such as the one at Locarno to fire up political hatreds rather than promote peace or rational public discussion.

REVIEW QUESTION What were the major outcomes of the postwar peacemaking process?

A Decade of Recovery: Europe in the 1920s

Even after the armistice and the peace treaties, the wartime spirit endured. Towns and villages built their monuments to the fallen, and battlefield tourism sprang up for veterans and their families in search of a relative's final resting place. Words and phrases from the battlefield became part of everyday speech. Before the war the word *lousy* had meant "lice-infested," but English-speaking soldiers returning from the trenches now applied it to anything bad. Raincoats became *trenchcoats*, and terms like *bombarded* and *rank and file* entered civilian talk. Maimed, disfigured veterans were present everywhere, and while some received prostheses designed by Jules Amar, others without limbs were sometimes carried in baskets—hence the expression *basket case.*

Total war had generally strengthened the military spirit and authoritarian government. Four autocratic governments had collapsed as a result of the war, but whether these states would become workable democracies remained an open question. During the war, the European economy lost many of its international markets to India, Canada, Australia, Japan, and the United States. Now worldwide economic competition with these new players also threatened European recovery. Returning veterans crowded hospitals and mental institutions, and family life centered on their care. Although contemporaries referred to the 1920s as the Roaring Twenties or the Jazz Age, the sense of cultural excitement masked the serious problem of restoring stability and implementing democracy. The real challenge of the 1920s was coming to terms with the grim legacy of the war.

Women Gain Suffrage in the West

1906	Finland
1913	Norway
1915	Denmark, Iceland
1917	Netherlands, Russia
1918	Czechoslovakia, Great Britain (limited suffrage)
1919	Germany
1920	Austria, United States
1921	Poland
1925	Hungary (limited suffrage)
1945	Italy, France
1971	Switzerland

Changes in the Political Landscape

The collapse of autocratic governments and the widespread extension of suffrage to women brought political turmoil as well as the expansion of democracy. Women's suffrage resulted in part from decades of activism, but many men in government claimed that suffrage was a "reward" for women's war efforts. Women were voted into parliaments in the first postwar elections, and the impression grew that they had also made extraordinary gains in the workplace. French men pointedly denied women the vote, however, threatening that women voters would bring back the rule of kings and priests. (Only at the end of World War II would France and Italy extend suffrage to women.) The welfare state also expanded, with payments being made to veterans and victims of workplace accidents. These benefits stemmed from the belief that more evenly distributed wealth—sometimes called economic democracy—would prevent the outbreak of revolution.

The trend toward economic democracy was not easy to maintain, however, because the cycles of boom and bust that had characterized the late nineteenth century reemerged. A short postwar economic boom prompted by reconstruction and consumer spending was followed by an economic downturn that was most severe between 1920 and 1922. By the mid-1920s, many of the economic opportunities for women had disappeared and women made up a smaller percentage of the workforce than in 1913. Skyrocketing unemployment produced more discontent with governments. Veterans were especially angered by economic insecurity after their years of enduring the war's horrors, and unemployment resulted in more anger toward governments.

Eastern Europe The new republics of eastern Europe were unprepared for hard economic times and poorly equipped to compete in the world market. None but Czechoslovakia had a mature industrial sector, and agricultural techniques were often primitive. Additionally, vast migrations occurred as some 1 million citizens escaped the civil war in Russia and 800,000 soldiers from the defeated Whites searched for safety. Two million people fled Turkey, Greece, and Bulgaria because the postwar settlement called for the new nations to be built along "nationality" lines. One statesman called the chaotic postwar settlement "a great unmixing of populations." Hundreds of thousands landed in new nations with populations largely composed of their own ethnic group: Hungary, for example, had to receive 300,000 people of Magyar ethnicity who were no longer welcome in Romania, Czechoslovakia, or Yugoslavia. Most of these millions of refugees lacked land or jobs. They had nothing to do "but loaf and starve," one English journalist observed of refugees in Bulgaria. The influx of people brought more conflict in various parts of eastern Europe. Romania, Czechoslovakia, and the Kingdom of the Serbs, Croats, and Slovenes invaded Hungary, for instance, to gain more land.

National Minorities in Postwar Poland

Poland exemplified how postwar turmoil could destroy a new nation's parliamentary democracy. One-third of the reunified Poland consisted of Ukrainians, Belorussians, Germans, and other ethnic minorities—many of whom had grievances against the dominant Poles. Varying religious and cultural traditions also divided the Poles, who for 150 years had been split among Austria, Germany, and Russia. Polish reunification occurred without a common currency, political structure, or language—even the railroad tracks were not a standard size. Under a new constitution that professed equal rights for all ethnicities and religions, the Sejm (parliament) tried to redistribute large estates among the peasantry. However, declining crop prices and overpopulation (two-thirds of the population lived by subsistence farming) made life in the countryside difficult. The economic downturn brought strikes and violence in 1922–1923. Ultimately former military leader Jozef Pilsudski took power via a coup in 1926 because of the government's inability to bring about prosperity. In postwar east-central Europe, military solutions to economic hardship became common, demonstrating the endurance of war long after the peace had officially begun.

Central Europe Germany was a different case, though it, too, received a flood of refugees from the east. Although Germany's economy picked up and the nation became a center of experimentation in the arts, political life remained unstable because so many people, nostalgic for imperial glory, associated defeat with the new Weimar Republic. Extremist politicians heaped daily abuse on Weimar's parliamentary political system. A wealthy newspaper and film tycoon called anyone cooperating with the parliamentary system "a moral cripple." Right-wing parties favored violence rather than consensus building, and nationalist thugs murdered democratic leaders and Jews. Communists were not shy about jumping into street brawls, either.

Support for the far right came from wealthy landowners and businessmen, white-collar workers whose standard of living had dropped during the war, and members of the lower-middle and middle classes hurt by inflation. Bands of disaffected youth and veterans multiplied, among them a group called the Brown Shirts. Their leader was an ex-soldier and political newcomer named Adolf Hitler (1889–1945)—a favorite among antigovernment crowds. In the wake of the Ruhr occupation of 1923, Hitler and German military hero Erich Ludendorff launched a coup d'état—or *putsch* in German—from a beer hall in Munich. Government troops suppressed the Beer Hall Putsch and arrested its leaders, but Ludendorff was acquitted and Hitler spent less than a year in jail. To conservative judges, former aristocrats, and most of the prewar bureaucrats who still staffed the government, such men were national heroes.

Western Europe In France and Britain, parties on the right were less effective than in Germany because representative institutions were better established and the upper classes were not plotting to restore an authoritarian monarchy. In France, politicians from the conservative right and moderate left successively formed coalitions and rallied general support to rebuild war-torn regions and to force Germany to pay for the reconstruction. Hoping to stimulate population growth after the devastating loss of life, the French parliament made distributing birth-control information illegal and abortion a severely punished crime.

Britain encountered postwar boom-and-bust cycles and continuing conflict in Ireland. Ramsay

MacDonald (1866–1937), elected the first Labour prime minister in 1924, represented the political strength of workers. Like other postwar British leaders, he had to face the unpleasant truth that although Britain had the largest world empire, many of its industries were obsolete or in poor condition. A showdown came in the ailing coal industry, where prices fell and wages plunged once the Ruhr mines again offered tough postwar competition to British mines. On May 3, 1926, workers launched a nine-day general strike against wage cuts and dangerous conditions in the mines. The strike provoked unprecedented middle-class resistance. University students, homemakers, and businessmen shut down the strike by driving trains, working on docks, and replacing workers in other jobs. Citizens from many walks of life revived the wartime spirit to defeat those who appeared to them to be attacking the national economy.

In Ireland, the British government's continuing failure to implement home rule provoked bloody confrontations. In January 1919, republican leaders declared Ireland's independence and created a separate parliament. The British government refused to recognize the parliament and sent in the Black and Tans, a volunteer army of demobilized soldiers named for the color of their uniforms. Terror reigned in Ireland, as both the pro-independence forces and the Black and Tans waged guerrilla warfare, taking hostages, blowing up buildings, and even shooting into crowds at soccer matches. By 1921, public outrage forced the British to negotiate a treaty, one that reversed the Irish declaration of independence and made the Irish Free State a self-governing dominion owing allegiance to the British crown. Northern Ireland, a group of six northern counties containing a majority of Protestants, gained a separate status: it was self-governing but still had representation in the British Parliament. This settlement left bitter discontent, and violence soon erupted again.

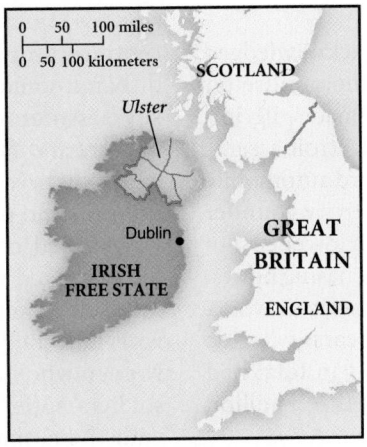

The Irish Free State and Ulster, 1921

The Colonies | War had also changed everything in the colonies. European politicians and military recruiters had promised colonized peoples the vote and other reforms, even independence, in exchange for their support during the war. However, these peoples' political activism — now enhanced by increasing education, trade, and experience with the West — mostly met with a brutal response. British forces massacred protesters at Amritsar, India, in 1919 and put down revolts against the mandate system in Egypt and Iran in the early 1920s. The Dutch jailed political leaders in Indonesia; the French punished Indochinese nationalists. For many Western governments, maintaining empires abroad was crucial to ensuring democracy at home, for any hint of declining national prestige fed antidemocratic forces.

Despite resistance, the 1920s marked the high tide of imperialism. Britain and France, enjoying new access to Germany's colonies in Africa and the territories of the fallen Ottoman Empire in the Middle East, were at the height of their global power. No matter how battered by the war, all the imperial powers took advantage of the growing profitability that enterprise around the world could bring. Middle Eastern and Indonesian oil, for instance, increasingly heated homes and fueled the West's growing number of automobiles, airplanes, trucks, ships, and buses. Products like chocolate and tropical fruit became regular items in Westerners' diets, and some Westerners built fortunes processing and selling products from the colonies.

The balance of power among the imperial nations was shifting, however. The most important change was Japan's surging competition for markets, resources, influence, and ultimately colonies. During the war, Japanese output of industrial goods such as metal and ships grew dramatically because the Western powers outsourced their wartime needs for such products. As Japan took business from Britain and France, its prosperity skyrocketed, allowing the country to become the dominant power in China. The Japanese government advertised its success as a sign of hope for non-Westerners. Japan's prosperity, the country's politicians claimed, would end the West's domination in the competition for land and resources. Ardently nationalist, the Japanese government was not yet strong enough to challenge the Western powers militarily. Thus, although outraged when the Western powers at Paris refused a nondiscrimination clause in the charter of the League of Nations, Japan cooperated in the Anglo-American–dominated peace. It agreed to the settlement at the naval conference in Washington that set the ratio of English, American, and Japanese shipbuilding at 5:5:3. "Rolls Royce, Rolls Royce, Ford," a Japanese official commented bitterly.

Reconstructing the Economy

The war had weakened European economies and allowed newcomers and rivals—Japan, India, the United States, Australia, and Canada—to flourish in their place. At the same time, the war had forced European manufacturing to become more efficient and had expanded the demand for automotive and air transport, electrical products, and synthetic goods. The prewar pattern of mergers and cartels continued after 1918, giving rise to gigantic food-processing firms such as Nestlé in Switzerland and petroleum enterprises such as Royal Dutch Shell. Owners of these large manufacturing conglomerates wielded more financial and political power than entire small countries. By the late 1920s, Europe had overcome the wild economic swings of the immediate postwar years and was enjoying renewed economic prosperity.

Some European businesspeople acknowledged that the United States had become the trendsetter in economic modernization, and they made pilgrimages to the Ford Motor Company's Detroit assembly line, which by 1929 produced a Ford automobile every ten seconds. Increased productivity, founder Henry Ford pointed out, resulted in a lower cost of living and thus increased workers' purchasing power. Rising productivity helped some American workers afford such expensive goods as cars: whereas French, German, and British citizens in total had fewer than two million cars, some seventeen million cars were on U.S. streets in 1925.

Scientific management also helped raise productivity. American efficiency expert Frederick Taylor (1856–1915) had developed methods to streamline workers' tasks and bodily motions for maximum productivity. European industrialists adopted Taylor's methods during the war and after, but they were also influenced by European psychologists who emphasized the mental aspects of productivity and thus the need to balance work and leisure activities. In theory, increased productivity not only produced prosperity for all but also united workers and management, avoiding Russian-style worker revolution. For many workers, however, the emphasis on efficiency seemed inhumane; in some businesses restrictions were so severe that workers were allowed to use the bathroom only on a fixed schedule. "When I left the factory, it followed me," wrote one worker. "In my dreams I was a machine."

The managerial sector in industry had expanded during the war and continued to do so thereafter. Workers' experience became devalued, with managers alone seen as creative and innovative. Managers reorganized work procedures and classified workers' skills. They categorized jobs held by women as requiring less skill—whether they did or not—and therefore deserving of lower wages. With male workers' jobs increasingly threatened by labor-saving machinery, unions usually agreed that women should receive lower wages to keep them from competing with men for scarce high-paying jobs. Like the managerial sector, a complex union bureaucracy had ballooned during World War I to help monitor labor's part in the war. Playing a key role in everyday political life, unions could mobilize masses of people, as evidenced by their actions against coups in Weimar Germany and by the general strike in Great Britain in 1926.

Restoring Society

Civilians met the returning millions of brutalized, incapacitated, and shell-shocked veterans with combined joy and apprehension—and that apprehension was often valid. Tens of thousands of German, central European, and Italian soldiers refused to disband; some British veterans vandalized university classrooms and assaulted women streetcar conductors and factory workers. Many veterans were angry that civilians had protested wartime conditions instead of enduring them. Patriotic when the war erupted, civilians, especially women, sometimes felt estranged from the returning warriors who had inflicted so much death and who had lived daily with filth, rats, and decaying human flesh. While women who had served on the front had seen the soldiers' suffering firsthand and could sympathize with them, many British suffragists, for instance, who had fought for equality in men's and women's lives before the war, now embraced separate spheres for men and women, so fearful were they of returning veterans.

For their part, veterans returned to a world that differed from the home they had left. They found that the war had blurred class distinctions, giving rise to expectations that life would be fairer afterward. Massive battlefield casualties had made it possible for commoners to move up to the ranks of officers, positions often monopolized by the prewar aristocracy. British author Rudyard Kipling, whose only son had been killed on the western front, was among those who influenced the decision that all memorials to individual soldiers would be the same for rich and poor, just as the experience of the trenches had been. Wealth, he maintained, should not allow some to "proclaim their grief above other people's grief" when rich and poor had died for the same cause. The identical, evenly spaced markers of military cemeteries kept all the dead equal, as did the mass "brothers' graves" at the battlefront where all ranks lay side by side in a single burial pit.

Despite their expectations, veterans often had few or no jobs open to them, and some found that their wives and sweethearts had abandoned them. Many found, too, that women's roles had gone through other changes: middle-class women did their own housework because former servants could earn more money in factories, and greater numbers of women worked outside the home. Women of all classes cut their hair short, wore sleeker clothes, smoked, and had money of their own because of war work.

Focusing on veterans' needs, governments tried to make civilian life as comfortable as possible to reintegrate men into society and reduce the appeal of communism. Politicians believed in the calming power of family life and supported social programs such as veterans' pensions and housing and benefits for out-of-work men. The new housing—"homes for heroes," as politicians called the program—was a considerable improvement over nineteenth-century working-class tenements. In Vienna, Frankfurt, Berlin, and Stockholm, modern housing projects provided common laundries, daycare centers, and rooms for socializing. They featured gardens, terraces, and balconies to provide a soothing, country ambience that offset the hectic nature of industrial life. Inside, they boasted modern kitchens and bathrooms, central heating, and electricity.

Despite government efforts to restore traditional family life, war had dissolved other middle-class conventions, among them attempts to keep unmarried young men and women apart. Freer relationships and more open discussions of sex characterized the 1920s. Middle-class youths of both sexes visited jazz clubs and attended movies together. Revealing bathing suits, short skirts, and body-hugging clothing emphasized women's sexuality, seeming to invite men and women to join together and replenish the postwar population. In the long run, however, the context for sexuality remained marriage. British scientist Marie Stopes published the best seller *Married Love* in 1918, and Dutch author Theodor van de Velde published the wildly successful *Ideal Marriage: Its Physiology and Technique* in 1927. Both authors described sex in glowing terms and offered precise information about birth control and sexual physiology. Changing ideas about sex were not limited to the middle and upper classes. One Viennese reformer described working-class marriage as "an erotic-comradely relationship of equals" rather than the economic partnership of past centuries. Meanwhile, such writers as the Briton D. H. Lawrence and the American Ernest Hemingway glorified men's sexual vigor in, respectively, *Women in Love* (1920) and *The Sun Also Rises* (1926). Mass culture's focus on heterosexuality encouraged the return to normality after the gender disorder that had troubled the prewar and war years.

As images of men and women changed, people paid more attention to bodily improvement. The increasing use of toothbrushes and toothpaste, safety and electric razors, and deodorants reflected new standards for personal hygiene and grooming. For

New Housing in Vienna
Politicians saw to the building of "homes for heroes" across postwar Europe, and Vienna was one leader in constructing modern housing for the working class. With many veterans enraged by the war experience and with socialist revolution a looming threat, new housing, it was hoped, would help return men to peaceful civilian life.
(© Bettmann/Corbis.)

The Flapper
This modern workingwoman smoking her cigarette stood for all that had changed—or was said to have changed—in the postwar world. Women had worked and had money of their own, they were out in public and could vote in many countries, and they were liberated from old constraints on their sexual and other behavior. *(Hulton Archive/Getty Images.)*

Western women, a multibillion-dollar cosmetics industry sprang up almost overnight. Women went to beauty parlors regularly to have their short hair cut, set, dyed, conditioned, straightened, or curled. They also tweezed their eyebrows, applied makeup, and even submitted to cosmetic surgery. Ordinary women "painted" their faces (something only prostitutes had done formerly) and competed in beauty contests. Instead of wanting to look plump and pale, people aimed to become thin and tan, often through exercise and playing sports. Consumers' new focus on personal health coincided with industry's need for a physically fit workforce.

As prosperity returned in the mid-1920s, people could afford to buy more consumer goods. Middle- and upper-class families snapped up sleek modern furniture, washing machines, and vacuum cleaners. Other modern conveniences such as electric irons and gas stoves appeared in better-off working-class households. Installment buying, popularized from the 1920s on, helped people finance these purchases. Housework became more mechanized, and family intimacy increasingly depended on machines of mass communication like radios, phonographs, and even automobiles. These new products not only transformed private life but also brought changes in the public world of mass culture and mass politics.

REVIEW QUESTION What were the major political, social, and economic problems facing postwar Europe, and how did governments attempt to address them?

Mass Culture and the Rise of Modern Dictators

Wartime propaganda had aimed to unite all classes against a common enemy. In the 1920s, new technology made the process of integrating diverse groups into a single Western or mass culture easier. The tools of mass culture—primarily radio, film, and newspapers—expanded their influence in the 1920s. Whereas some intellectuals urged elites to form an experimental avant-garde that refused to cater to "the drab mass of society," others wanted to use modern media and art to reach and even control the masses. The media had the potential for creating an informed citizenry and thus strengthening democracy. At the same time, it allowed authoritarian rulers and would-be dictators such as Benito Mussolini, Joseph Stalin, and Adolf Hitler to shape a uniform political thought and to control citizens' behavior far beyond what previous rulers had been able to do.

Culture for the Masses

The media received a big boost from the war. Bulletins from the battlefront whetted the public's craving for news and real-life stories, and sales of nonfiction books soared. After years of deprivation, people were driven to achieve material success, and they devoured books about how to gain it. A biography of Henry Ford, telling his story of upward mobility and technological accomplishment, became a best seller in Germany. With postwar readers avidly pursuing practical knowledge, institutes and night schools became popular, and school systems promoted the study of geography, science, and history. Phonographs, radio programs, and movies also widened the scope of national culture.

In the 1920s, film evolved from an experimental medium to a thriving international business in which large corporations set up theater chains and marketed movies worldwide. Specialization emerged, with directors, producers, marketers, film editors, and many others subdividing the process. A "star" system turned film personalities into celebrities who were promoted by publicists and lived like royalty.

Films of literary classics and political events developed people's sense of a common heritage and were often sponsored by governments. Bolshevik leaders backed the inventive work of director Sergei Eisenstein, whose films *Potemkin* (1925) and *Ten Days That Shook the World* (1927–1928) presented a Bolshevik view of history to Russian and international audiences.

Films incorporated familiar elements from everyday life. The piano accompaniment of silent films derived from music halls; comic characters and slapstick humor were borrowed from street or burlesque shows and from trends in postwar living. The popular comedies of the 1920s made the flapper more visible to the masses and poked fun at men's and women's inept attempts at marriage and emotional intimacy. Lavish cinema houses attracted some hundred million weekly viewers, the majority of them women. As popular films and books crossed national borders, a global culture for an international audience flourished.

Films also played to postwar fantasies and fears. In Germany, the influential hit *The Cabinet of Doctor Caligari* (1919) depicted frightening events in an insane asylum as horrifying symbols of state power. Popular detective and cowboy films portrayed heroes who could restore wholeness to the disordered world of murder, crime, and injustice. The plight of gangsters appealed to veterans, who had been exposed to the cheap value of modern life in the trenches. English comedian Charlie Chaplin (1889–1977) created the character of the Little Tramp, who won international popularity as the anonymous down-and-out hero trying to preserve his dignity in a mechanized world. Films featured characters from around the world and were often set in faraway deserts and mountain ranges; newsreels showed athletic, soldier-like bodies in sporting events like boxing.

Like film, radio evolved from an experimental medium to an instrument of mass culture during the 1920s. Developed from the wireless technology of Italian inventor Guglielmo Marconi, radio broadcasts in the first half of the 1920s were heard by mass audiences in public halls (much like movie houses) and featured orchestra performances and songs followed by audience discussion. The radio quickly became an affordable consumer item, allowing the public concert or lecture to penetrate the individual's private living space. Specialized programming for men (such as sports reporting) and for women (such as advice on home management) attracted listeners. Through radio, disabled veterans found ways to participate in public events and keep up-to-date. By the 1930s, radio helped politicians to reach the masses wherever they might be — even alone at home.

Cultural Debates over the Future

Cultural leaders in the 1920s either were obsessed with the horrendous experience of war or held high hopes for creating a fresh, utopian future that would have little relation to the past. German artists, especially, produced bleak or violent visions. The sculpture and woodcuts of German artist Käthe Kollwitz (1867–1945), whose son had died in the war, portrayed bereaved parents, starving children, and other heart-wrenching antiwar images (see page 834). Others thought that Europeans needed to search for answers in far-off cultures. Seeing Europe as decadent, some turned to the spiritual richness of Asian philosophies and religions. An "Asiatic fever" seemed to grip intellectuals, including the British writer Virginia Woolf, who drew on ideas of reincarnation in her novel *Orlando* (1928), and the filmmaker Sergei Eisenstein, who modeled the new techniques of juxtaposing film shots (montage) on Japanese calligraphy.

Other artists used satire and contempt to express postwar rage at civilization's wartime failure. George Grosz (1893–1959), stunned by the war's carnage, joined Dada, an artistic and literary movement that had emerged during the war. With a meaningless name, Dada produced works marked by nonsense and shrieking expressions of alienation. Grosz's paintings and cartoons of maimed soldiers and brutally murdered women reflected his wartime trauma and his self-proclaimed desire "to bellow back." In the postwar years, the modernist practice of shocking audiences became more savage and often more contemptuous of ordinary people. Portrayals of seedy everyday life flourished in cabarets and theaters in the 1920s and reinforced veterans' beliefs in civilian decadence.

The art world itself became a battlefield, especially in defeated Germany, where it paralleled the Weimar Republic's contentious politics. Popular writers such as veteran Ernst Jünger glorified life in the trenches and called for the militarization of society to restore order. In contrast, Erich Maria Remarque, also a veteran, cried out for an end to war in his controversial novel *All Quiet on the Western Front* (1928). This international best seller depicted the life shared by enemies on the battlefield, thus aiming to overcome the national hatred aroused by wartime propaganda. Remarque's novel was part of a flood of popular, and often bitter, literature appearing on the tenth anniversary of the war's end. It coincided with an interest in "Great War tourism" such as visiting battlefields. (See Document, "Memory and Battlefield Tourism," page 865.)

George Grosz, "Twilight" from the Series *Ecce Homo* (1922)
George Grosz's series of postwar art was named after a book by Friedrich Nietzsche, *Ecce Homo* (*Behold the Man*). The "man" to behold was the veteran, opportunistically called a hero by postwar politicians to get their votes but in fact living a grim reality, as Grosz saw it. Surrounded by prosperous businessmen, fashionable women, and strutting military officers, the veteran was pushed to the background, gray and lonely amid the colorful peacetime society. *(bpk, Berlin/Kunstbibliothek, Staaliche Museen, Berlin, Germany/photo by Kund Petersen/Art Resource, NY/Art © Estate of George Grosz/Licensed by VAGA, New York, NY.)*

Poets reflected on postwar conditions in more general terms, using styles that rejected the comforting rhymes or accessible metaphors of earlier verse. T. S. Eliot, an American-born poet who had studied Buddhism and Sanskrit and for a time worked as a banker in Britain, portrayed postwar life as petty and futile in "The Waste Land" (1922) and "The Hollow Men" (1925). The Irish poet William Butler Yeats joined Eliot in mourning the replacement of traditional society, with its religious and moral convictions, with a new, superficial generation gaily dancing to jazz and engaging in promiscuous sex. Both poets had an uneasy relationship with the modern world and at times advocated authoritarianism rather than democracy.

The postwar arts produced many a utopian fantasy turned upside down; dystopias of life in a war-traumatized Europe multiplied. In the bizarre stories of Franz Kafka, who worked by day in a large insurance company in Prague, the world is a vast, impersonal machine. His novels *The Trial* (1925) and *The Castle* (1926) show the hopeless condition of individuals caught between the cogs of society's relentlessly turning gears. His theme seemed to capture for civilian life the helplessness that soldiers had felt at the front. As an old social order collapsed in the face of political and technological innovation, other writers depicted the complex, sometimes nightmarish inner life of individuals.

Irish writer James Joyce portrayed this interior self built on memories and sensations, many of them from the war. Joyce's *Ulysses* (1922) illuminates the fast-moving inner lives of its characters in the course of a single day. In one of the most celebrated passages in *Ulysses*, a long interior monologue traces a woman's lifetime of erotic and emotional sensations. The technique of using a character's thoughts to propel a story was called stream of consciousness. Virginia Woolf, too, used this technique in her novel *Mrs. Dalloway* (1925). For Woolf, the war had dissolved the solid society from which absorbing stories and fascinating characters were once fashioned. Her characters experience fragmented conversations and incomplete relationships. Woolf's novel *Orlando* also reflected the postwar attention to women. In the novel, the hero Orlando lives hundreds of years and in the course of his long life is eventually transformed into a woman.

There was another side to the postwar story, however—one based not on the interior life of a traumatized society, but on the promise of technology. Before the war, avant-garde artists had celebrated the new, the futuristic, the utopian. After the war, like Jules Amar crafting prostheses for shattered limbs, many postwar artists were optimistic that technology could make an entire wounded society whole. The aim of art, observed one of them, "is not to decorate our life but to organize it." German artists, calling themselves the Bauhaus (after the idea of a craft association, or *Bauhütte*), created streamlined office buildings and designed functional furniture and utensils, many of them inspired by forms from "untainted" East Asia and Africa. Russian artists, temporarily caught up in the communist experiment, optimistically wrote novels about cement factories and created ballets about steel.

Artists fascinated by technology and machinery were drawn to the most modern of all countries—the United States. Hollywood films, glossy advertisements, and the bustling metropolis of New York tempted careworn Europeans. They loved films and

DOCUMENT

Memory and Battlefield Tourism

World War I left deep wounds in the survivors, including the families of those who had died, and memories of the war and their loved ones filled everyday life. Like the English writer Vera Brittain, many relatives roamed the battlefields of Europe, in hopes of cementing their memories and understanding what had happened to their loved ones—and to Western civilization as a whole. During the war, Brittain had served as a nurse while suffering the loss of her brother, fiancé, and friends. Whereas organized tours of battlefields had begun almost immediately after the war, in 1921 Brittain went on her own to find her brother's grave high up in the remote mountains of Italy. She recounted this visit in a memoir of her early life.

"How strange, how strange it is," I reflected, as I looked, with an indefinable pain stabbing my chest, for Edward's name among those neat rows of oblong stones, "that all my past years—the childhood of which I have no one, now, to share the remembrance, the bright fields at Uppingham, the restless months in Buxton, the hopes and ambitions of Oxford, the losses and long-drawn agonies of the War—should be buried in this grave on the top of a mountain, in the lofty silence, the singing unearthly stillness, of these remote forests! At every turn of every future road I shall want to ask him questions, to recall to him memories, and he will not be there. Who could have dreamed that the little boy born in such uneventful security to an ordinary provincial family would end his brief days in a battle among the high pine-woods of an unknown Italian plateau?"

Close to the wall, in the midst of a group of privates from the Sherwood Foresters who had all died on June 15th, I found his name: "Captain E. H. Brittain, M.C., 11th Notts. And Derby Regt. Killed in action June 15th, 1918. Aged 22." In Venice I had bought some rosebuds and a small asparagus fern in a pot; the shopkeeper had told me that it would last a long time, and I planted it in the rough grass beside the grave.

"How trivial my life has been since the War!" I thought, as I smoothed the earth over the fern. "How mean they are, these little strivings, these petty ambitions of us who are left, now that all of you are gone! How can the future achieve, through us, the sombre majesty of the past? Oh, Edward, you're so lonely up here; why can't I stay for ever and keep your grave company, far from the world and its vain endeavours to rebuild civilisation, on this Plateau where alone there is dignity and peace?"

Source: Vera Brittain, *Testament of Youth* (1933; repr. London: Virago, 1978), 525–27.

Question to Consider

- **In what ways are memory and historical facts important in this account of the postwar world? How do memory and facts shape Brittain's analysis of the future?**

stories about the Wild West or the carefree "modern girl." They were especially attracted to jazz, the improvisational music developed by African Americans. Performers like Josephine Baker (1906–1976) and Louis Armstrong (1900–1971) became international sensations when they toured Europe's capital cities. Like jazz, the New York skyscraper pointed to the future, not to the grim wartime past.

The Communist Utopia

Communism also promised a shining future and a modern, technological culture. As the Bolsheviks met powerful resistance, however, they became ever more ruthless and authoritarian. In the early 1920s, peasant bands called Green Armies revolted against the Bolshevik policy of war communism that confiscated their crops. Industrial production stood at only 13 percent of prewar levels, shortages of housing affected the entire population, and millions of refugees clogged the cities and roamed the countryside. In the early spring of 1921, workers in Petrograd and sailors at the naval base at Kronstadt revolted, protesting their short rations and the privileged standard of living that Bolshevik supervisors enjoyed. They called for "soviets without Communists"—that is, a worker state without elite leaders.

The Bolsheviks had many of the rebels shot, but the Kronstadt revolt pushed Lenin to institute reform. His New Economic Policy (NEP) returned parts of the economy to the free market, a temporary retreat to capitalist methods that allowed peasants to sell their grain and others to trade consumer goods freely. Although the state still controlled large industries and banking, the NEP encouraged people to produce, sell, and even, in the spirited slogan of one official, "get rich." As a result, consumer goods and more food became available. Although many people remained impoverished, some peasants and merchants prospered. The rise of these wealthy "NEPmen," who bought and furnished splendid homes, broke the Bolshevik promise of a classless utopia.

Further protests erupted within Communist ranks. At the 1921 party congress, a group called

The New Man
There was a sense in the postwar world that people were entering a new age after the horrors of war. Nowhere was this feeling stronger than among Communists in Russia, where it was also believed that communism would create the "new man." In this work by Eli Lissitsky, *Victory over the Sun: The New Man* (1923), note the energy in the figure as it stretches its reach in all directions. The use of pure lines and geometric forms symbolized the higher reality that the new man would reach once the messiness and corruption of ordinary reality had been eliminated. *(Tate, London/Art Resource, NY/© 2011 Artists Rights Society [ARS], New York/VG Bild-Kunst, Bonn.)*

the Worker Opposition objected to the party's takeover of economic control from worker organizations and pointed out that the NEP was not a proletarian program for workers. In response, Lenin suppressed the Worker Opposition and set up procedures for purging opponents—a policy that would become a deadly feature of Communist rule. Bolshevik leaders also worked to make the Communist revolution a cultural reality in people's lives and thinking. The Communist Party set up classes in a variety of political and social subjects throughout the countryside, and volunteers struggled to improve the literacy rate—which was only 40 percent on the eve of World War I. To create social equality between the sexes, which had been part of the Marxist vision of the future, the state made birth control, abortion, and divorce readily available. As commissar for public welfare, **Aleksandra Kollontai** (1872–1952) promoted birth-control education for adults and day care for children of working parents. To encourage literacy, she wrote simply worded novels about love and work in the new socialist state for ordinary readers.

The bureaucracy swelled to bring modern ways to every corner of life, and *hygiene* and *efficiency* became watchwords, as they were in the rest of Europe. Agencies such as the Zhenotdel ("Women's Bureau") taught women about sanitary housekeeping and their rights under communism. Efficiency experts aimed to replace tsarist backwardness with technological modernity based on American techniques. The short-lived government agency Proletkult tried to develop proletarian culture through such undertakings as workers' universities, a workers' theater, and workers' publishing. Russian artists experimented with blending high art and technology in mass culture. Poet Vladimir Mayakovsky wrote verse praising his Communist passport and essays promoting toothbrushing, while composers punctuated their music with the sound of train or factory whistles. The early days of Bolshevik rule saw interesting experiments in all of the arts and in mass culture.

As with war communism, many resisted efforts to change everyday life and culture. As Zhenotdel workers moved into the countryside, for example, they attempted to teach women to behave as men's equals. Peasant families, still strongly patriarchal, often resisted. In Islamic regions of central Asia, incorporated from the old Russian Empire into the new Communist one, Bolsheviks urged Muslim women to remove their veils, change their way of life by learning their rights, and generally to become more "modern," but fervent Muslims often attacked both Zhenotdel workers and women who followed their advice.

In the spring of 1922, Lenin suffered a debilitating stroke, and amid ongoing cultural experimentation and factional fighting, this architect of the Bolshevik Revolution died in January 1924. The party congress declared the day of his death a permanent holiday, changed the name of Petrograd to Leningrad, and elevated the deceased leader into a secular god. After Lenin's death, no one was allowed to criticize anything associated with his name, a situation that opened the way for future abuses of power by Communist leaders.

Joseph Stalin (1879–1953), who served in the powerful post of general secretary of the Communist Party, was the chief mourner at Lenin's funeral, using the occasion to hand out good jobs and other patronage. He advertised his role in joining Russian and non-Russian regions into the Union of Soviet Socialist Republics (USSR) in 1923 as an example of his leadership skills. Concerned with Stalin's influence and ruthlessness, Lenin in his last

Aleksandra Kollontai: A Russian activist and minister of public welfare in the Bolshevik government who promoted social programs such as birth control and day care for children of working parents.

Mussolini and the Black Shirts, 1922
Mussolini always struck a tough, military pose, even when not in uniform, as in this photo taken in 1922 with his Black Shirt supporters, many also without uniforms. Once in power, Mussolini continued the militarization of society that had begun during World War I, instilling a cult of obedience and submission to state authority that he viewed as more important than fancy theories of politics and government. *(The Granger Collection, New York—All rights reserved.)*

will and testament had asked that "the comrades find a way to remove Stalin." Stalin, however, prevented Lenin's will from being publicized and discredited his chief rival, Trotsky, as an unpatriotic internationalist. With the blessing of Trotsky's other rivals, Stalin had him exiled. Simultaneously, Stalin organized the Lenin cult, which included the public display of Lenin's embalmed corpse—still on view today. Bringing in several hundred thousand new party members who owed their positions in government and industry to him, Stalin had achieved virtually complete control of the USSR by 1929.

Fascism on the March in Italy

In Italy, the rise to power of a political journalist who had turned from socialism to the radical right—**Benito Mussolini** (1883–1945)—kept the war alive. Italians raged when the Allies at Paris refused to honor the territorial promises of the Treaty of London, and peasants and workers protested their economic plight during the slump of the early 1920s. Since the late nineteenth century, many Europeans had come to blame parliaments and constitutions for their troubles, so Italians backed Mussolini when he built a personal army (the Black Shirts) of veterans and the unemployed to overturn parliamentary government. In 1922, his supporters, known as the Fascists, started a march on Rome, forcing King Victor Emmanuel III (r. 1900–1946) to make Mussolini prime minister.

The Fascist movement flourished because of poverty and wounded national pride. Like the Bolsheviks, Mussolini promised an efficient military utopia and the restoration of men's warrior status. The Black Shirts attracted many young men who felt cheated of wartime glory and many veterans who missed the vigor of military life. The fasces, an ancient Roman symbol depicting a bundle of sticks wrapped around an ax with the blade exposed (representing both unity and force), served as the movement's emblem and provided its name: **fascism**. Unlike Marxism, fascism scoffed at coherent ideology: "Fascism is not a church," Mussolini announced upon taking power in 1922. "It is more like a training ground." The Fascist Party was defined by deeds—specifically its promotion of male

Benito Mussolini: Leader of Italian fascist movement and, after the March on Rome in 1922, dictator of Italy.

fascism: A doctrine that emphasizes violence and glorifies the state over the people and their individual or civil rights; in Italy, the Fascist Party took hold in the 1920s as Mussolini consolidated power.

violence and its attacks on parliamentary rule and the socialist movement.

Mussolini consolidated his power by criminalizing any criticism of the state and by using violence against opponents in parliament. Bands of men from the Fascist Party wrecked socialist newspaper offices, attacked striking workers, used their favorite tactic of forcing castor oil (which caused diarrhea) down the throats of socialists, and even murdered rivals. Yet this brutality and the sight of the Black Shirts marching through the streets like disciplined soldiers signaled to many Italians that their country was orderly and modern. Large landowners and businessmen approved the Fascists' attacks on strikers and therefore financed the movement. Their generous funding allowed Mussolini to build a large staff by hiring the unemployed, creating the illusion that Fascists could rescue the economy when no one else could.

Like a wartime leader, Mussolini used mass propaganda to build support for a kind of military campaign to remake Italy. Peasant men huddled around radios to hear him call for a "battle of wheat" to enhance farm productivity. Peasant women, responding to his praise for maternal duty, adored him for appearing to value womanhood. In the cities the government launched avant-garde architectural projects and used public relations promoters to advertise its achievements. The modern city became a stage set for Fascist spectacle: old residential neighborhoods fell to the wrecking machines, allowing room for broad avenues for Fascist parades, captured by newsreel cameras and broadcast by radio. Mussolini claimed that he made the trains run on time, and this triumph of modern technology fanned people's hopes that he could restore order, even if it was military order.

Mussolini added a strong dose of traditional values and prejudices to his modern order. Although an atheist himself, he recognized the importance of Catholicism in Italian life. In 1929, the Lateran Agreement between the Italian government and the church made the Vatican an independent state under papal sovereignty. The government recognized the church's right to determine marriage and family policy and supported its role in education. In return, the church ended its criticism of Fascist tactics. Mussolini also introduced a "corporate" state that denied individual political rights in favor of duty to the state, as in wartime. Corporatist decrees in 1926 outlawed labor unions, replacing them with organized groups or corporations of employers, workers, and professionals to settle grievances and determine conditions of work. Mussolini drew praise from business leaders when he announced cuts in women's wages; later he won the approval of civil servants, lawyers, and professors by banning women from those professions. Mussolini did not want women out of the workforce altogether, but he aimed to confine them to low-paying jobs as part of his scheme for reinvigorating men by boosting male privileges.

Mussolini's numerous admirers across the West included Adolf Hitler, who throughout the 1920s had been building a paramilitary group of storm troopers and a political organization called the National Socialist German Workers' Party (the Nazi Party). During his brief stint in jail for the 1923 Beer Hall Putsch, Hitler wrote *Mein Kampf* (My Struggle); in the book, he expressed both his vicious anti-Semitism and his political psychology for manipulating the masses. Hitler was fascinated by the details of Mussolini's success: the Black Shirts' dramatic march on Rome, Mussolini's legal accession to power, and his triumph over all opposition. Late in the 1920s, however, the conditions that had allowed Mussolini to rise to power in 1922 no longer existed in Germany. Although Hitler was welding the Nazi Party into a strong political instrument, the Weimar parliamentary government was actually functioning better as the decade wore on.

REVIEW QUESTION How did the postwar atmosphere influence cultural expression and encourage the trend toward dictatorship?

Conclusion

The year 1929 was to prove just as fateful as 1914 had been. In 1914, World War I began an orgy of death, causing tens of millions of casualties, the destruction of major dynasties, and the collapse of aristocratic classes. For four years, the war promoted military technology, fierce nationalism, and the control of everyday life by bureaucracy. While dynasties fell, the centralization of power increased the scope of the nation-state. The Peace of Paris treaties of 1919–1920 left Germans bitterly resentful, while in eastern and central Europe the intermingling of ethnicities, religions, and languages in the new states created by the treaties failed to guarantee a peaceful future. Massive migrations produced additional chaos, as some new nations expelled minority groups.

War furthered the development of mass society. It leveled social classes on the battlefield and in the graveyard, standardized political thinking through

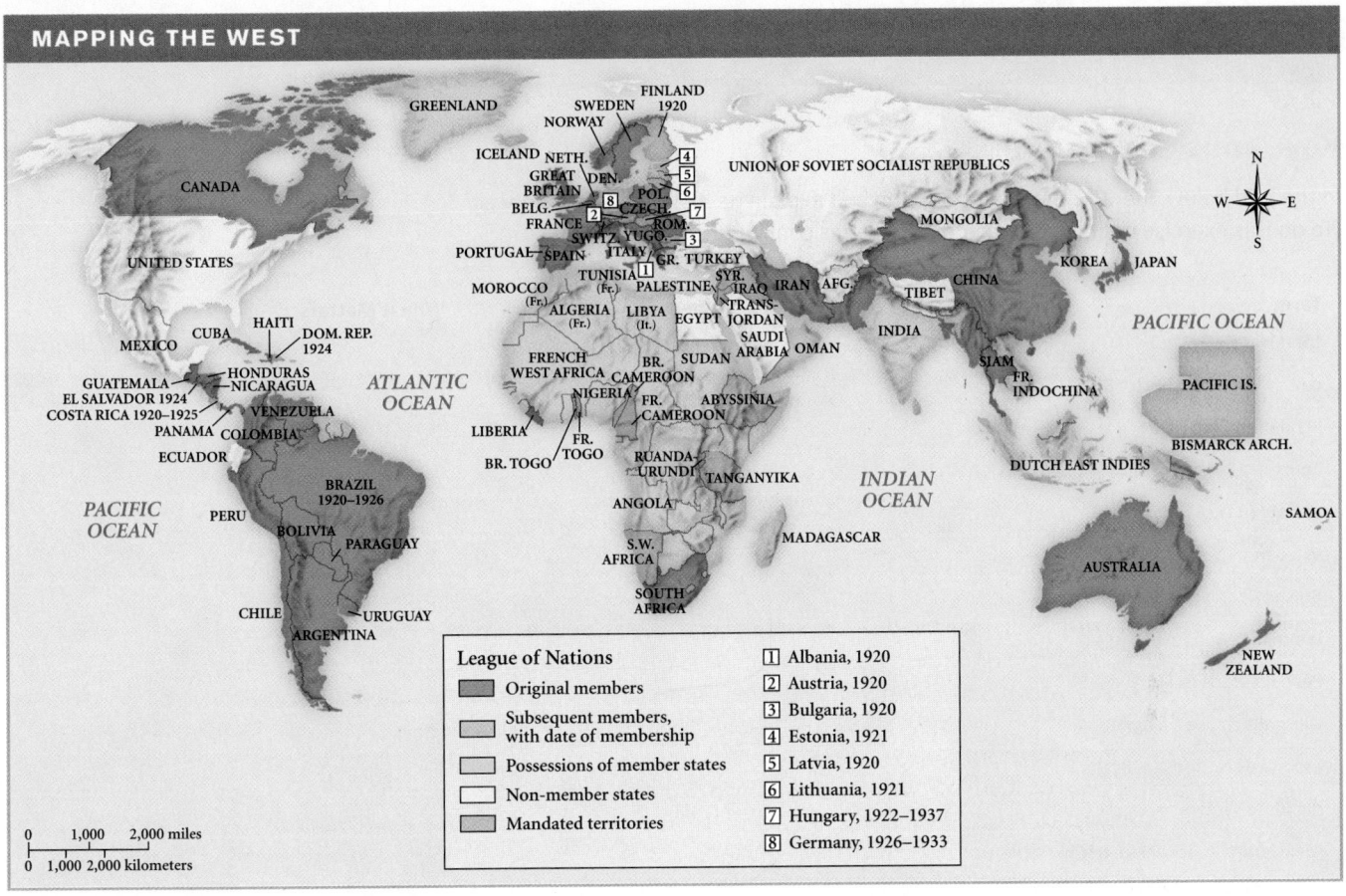

Europe and the World in 1929

The map reflects the partitions and nations that came into being as a result of war and revolution, while it obscures the increasing movement toward throwing off colonial rule. This was the true high point of empire: the drive for empire would diminish after 1929 except for Italy, which still craved colonies, and Japan, which continued searching for more land and resources to fuel its rapid growth. | **Observe the League of Nations membership as depicted in the map. What common bonds, if any, united these member nations?**

wartime propaganda, and extended many political rights to women. Production techniques, improved during wartime, were used in peacetime for manufacturing consumer goods. Technological innovations from the prostheses built by Jules Amar to air transport, cinema, and radio transmission became available to more people. Modernity in the arts intensified, probing the nightmarish war that continued to haunt the population.

By the end of the 1920s, the war had so militarized the population that strongmen had come to power in several countries, including the Soviet Union and Italy, with Adolf Hitler waiting in the wings in Germany. These strongmen and their followers kept alive the wartime commitment to violence. Many Westerners were impressed by the tough, modern efficiency of Fascists and Communists who made parliaments and citizen rule seem out of date, even effeminate. When the U.S. stock market crashed in 1929 and economic disaster circled the globe, authoritarian solutions and militarism continued to look appealing. What followed was a series of catastrophes even more devastating than those of World War I.

FOR FURTHER EXPLORATION

- **For additional primary-source material from this period**, see *Sources of the Making of the West*, Fourth Edition.
- **For Web sites, images, and documents related to topics in this chapter**, visit *Make History* at bedfordstmartins.com/hunt.

Chapter 25 Review

Online Study Guide bedfordstmartins.com/hunt

Key Terms and People

In the grid below, identify the term or person and explain its historical significance. (To do this exercise online, go to bedfordstmartins.com/hunt.)

Term	Who or What & When	Why It Matters
total war (p. 836)		
cult of the offensive (p. 838)		
Schlieffen Plan (p. 839)		
Fourteen Points (p. 846)		
soviets (p. 846)		
V. I. Lenin (p. 847)		
Bolshevik Revolution (p. 848)		
Weimar Republic (p. 851)		
Peace of Paris (p. 852)		
war guilt clause (p. 852)		
League of Nations (p. 853)		
mandate system (p. 854)		
Aleksandra Kollontai (p. 866)		
Benito Mussolini (p. 867)		
fascism (p. 867)		

Review Questions

1. In what ways was World War I a total war?
2. Why did people rebel during World War I, and what turned rebellion into outright revolution in Russia?
3. What were the major outcomes of the postwar peacemaking process?
4. What were the major political, social, and economic problems facing postwar Europe, and how did governments attempt to address them?
5. How did the postwar atmosphere influence cultural expression and encourage the trend toward dictatorship?

Making Connections

1. How did the experience of war shape postwar mass politics?
2. What social changes from World War I carried over into the postwar years and why?
3. How did postwar artistic and cultural innovations build on the modern movements that developed between 1890 and 1914?
4. What changes did the war bring to relationships between European countries and their colonies?

Important Events

Date	Event	Date	Event
1913–1925	Suffrage for women expands in much of Europe	1919	Weimar Republic established
1914	*August:* World War I begins	1919–1920	Paris Peace Conference redraws map of Europe
1916	Irish nationalists stage Easter Uprising against British rule	1922	Ireland gains independence; Fascists march on Rome; Mussolini becomes prime minister; Eliot, "The Waste Land"; Joyce, *Ulysses*; Hitler builds Nazi Party
1917	*March:* Revolution in Russia overturns tsarist autocracy *April:* United States enters World War I *November:* Bolshevik Revolution in Russia	1924	Lenin dies; Stalin and Trotsky contend for power
1918	*November:* Armistice ends fighting of World War I; revolutionary turmoil throughout Germany; kaiser abdicates	1924–1929	Period of general economic prosperity and stability
1918–1922	Civil war in Russia	1929	October: Stock market crash in United States

- Consider three events: **Eliot, "The Waste Land" (1922)**, **Fascists march on Rome (1922)**, and **Period of general economic prosperity and stability (1924–1929)**. How do these events illustrate the complexities of postwar life?

SUGGESTED REFERENCES

Readers of history and scholars continue to explore the gripping and tragic events of World War I. Martha Hanna's work captures the often heartrending relationship between the battlefront and home front.

Barry, John. *The Great Influenza: The Epic Story of the Greatest Plague in History.* 2004.

Hanna, Martha. *Your Death Would Be Mine: Paul and Marie Pireaud in the Great War.* 2006.

Healy, Maureen. *Vienna and the Fall of the Habsburg Empire: Total War and Everyday Life in World War I.* 2004.

Holquist, Peter. *Making War, Forging Revolution: Russia's Continuum of Crisis, 1914–1921.* 2002.

Horne, John, ed. *State, Society, and Mobilization in Europe during the First World War.* 2002.

Jensen, Eric N. *Body by Weimar: Athletes, Gender and German Modernity.* 2010.

Kent, Susan Kingsley. *Aftershocks: The Politics of Trauma in Britain, 1918–1931.* 2009.

Liulevicius, Vejas Gabriel. *War Land on the Eastern Front: Culture, National Identity and German Occupation in World War I.* 2000.

Makaman, Douglas, and Michael Mays, eds. *World War I and the Cultures of Modernity.* 2000.

Marks, Sally. *The Ebbing of European Ascendancy: An International History of the World.* 2002.

Northrup, Douglas. *Veiled Empire: Gender and Power in Stalinist Central Asia.* 2004.

Panchasi, Roxanne. *Future Tense: The Culture of Anticipation in France Between the Wars.* 2009.

Robb, George. *British Culture and the First World War.* 2002.

Roshwald, Aviel. *Ethnic Nationalism and the Fall of Empires: Central Europe, Russia and the Middle East, 1914–1923.* 2001.

Scales, Rebecca. "Radio Broadcasting, Disabled Veterans, and Politics of National Recovery in Interwar France." *French Historical Studies.* 2008.

Weitz, Eric D. *Weimar Germany: Promise and Tragedy.* 2009.

World War I Document Archive: http://www.lib.byu.edu/%7Erdh/wwi

CHAPTER

26

The Great Depression and World War II

1929–1945

When Etty Hillesum moved to Amsterdam from the Dutch provinces in 1932 to attend law school, an economic depression gripped the world. A resourceful young woman, Hillesum pieced together a living as a housekeeper and part-time language teacher so that she could continue her studies. Absorbed by the pressures and pleasures of her everyday life, she took little note of Adolf Hitler's spectacular rise to power in Germany, even when he demonized her fellow Jews as responsible for the economic slump and for virtually every other problem Germany faced. In 1939, the outbreak of World War II awakened her to the reality of what was happening. The German conquest of the Netherlands in 1940 led to the persecution of Dutch Jews, bringing Hillesum to a shattering realization, noted in her diary: "What they are after is our total destruction." The Nazis started relocating Jews to camps in Germany and Poland. Hillesum went to work for Amsterdam's Jewish Council, which was forced to organize the transport of Jews to the death camps in eastern Europe. Changing from self-absorbed student to heroine, she did what she could to help other Jews and began carefully recording the deportations. When she and her family were captured and deported in turn, she smuggled out letters from the transit camps along the route to Poland, describing the inhumane conditions and brutal treatment of the Jews. "I wish I could live for a long time so that one day I may know how to explain it," she wrote. Etty Hillesum never got her wish: she died at Auschwitz in November 1943.

The economic recovery of the late 1920s came to a halt with the U.S. stock market crash in 1929. Financial collapse in the United States was part of the worldwide Great Depression. Economic distress intensified social

Nazis on Parade
By the time Hitler came to power in 1933, Germany was mired in the Great Depression. Hated by Communists, Nazis, and conservatives alike, the Weimar Republic had few supporters. Hitler took his cue from Mussolini by promising an end to democracy and tolerance and by using the visual power of Nazi soldiers marching through the streets during the depression to win support for overthrowing the government. *(Hugo Jaeger/Time & Life Pictures/Getty Images.)*

The Great Depression 874
- Economic Disaster Strikes
- Social Effects of the Depression
- The Great Depression beyond the West

Totalitarian Triumph 878
- The Rise of Stalinism
- Hitler's Rise to Power
- The Nazification of German Politics
- Nazi Racism

Democracies on the Defensive 886
- Confronting the Economic Crisis
- Cultural Visions in Hard Times

The Road to Global War 890
- A Surge in Global Imperialism
- The Spanish Civil War, 1936–1939
- Hitler's Conquest of Central Europe, 1938–1939

World War II, 1939–1945 896
- The German Onslaught
- War Expands: The Pacific and Beyond
- The War against Civilians
- Societies at War
- From Resistance to Allied Victory
- An Uneasy Postwar Settlement

grievances. In Europe, many people turned to military-style strongmen for solutions to their problems. Among these dictators was Adolf Hitler, who called on the German masses to restore the national glory that had been damaged by defeat in 1918. He urged Germans to scorn democratic rights and root out those he considered to be inferior people: Jews, Slavs, and Sinti and Roma (often called Gypsies), among others. Militaristic and fascist regimes spread to Spain, Poland, Hungary, Japan, and countries of Latin America, crushing representative institutions. In the Soviet Union, Joseph Stalin justified the killing of millions of citizens as necessary for the USSR's industrialization and the survival of communism. For millions of hard-pressed people in the 1930s, dictatorship had great appeal.

Elected leaders in the democracies reacted cautiously to both economic depression and the dictators' aggression. In an age of mass media, leaders following democratic principles appeared timid, while dictators dressed in uniforms looked bold and decisive. Only the German invasion of Poland in 1939 pushed the democracies to strong action, as World War II erupted in Europe. By 1941, the war had spread across the globe with the United States, Great Britain, the Soviet Union, and many other nations united in combat against Germany, Italy, Japan, and their allies. Tens of millions would perish in this war because both technology and ideology had become more deadly than they had been just two decades earlier. More than half the dead were civilians, among them Etty Hillesum, whose only crime was being Jewish.

CHAPTER FOCUS **What were the main economic, social, and political challenges of the years 1929–1945, and how did governments and individuals respond to them?**

The Great Depression

The U.S. stock market crash of 1929 and economic developments around the world triggered the Great Depression of the 1930s. Rural and urban folk alike suffered as tens of millions lost their jobs and livelihoods. The whole world felt the depression's impact: commerce and investment in industry fell off, social life and gender roles were upset, and the birthrate plummeted. From peasants in Asia to industrial workers in Germany and the United States, the Great Depression shattered the lives of millions.

Economic Disaster Strikes

In the 1920s, U.S. corporations and banks as well as millions of individual Americans had not only invested all their money but also borrowed funds to invest in the stock market, which seemed to deliver endless profits. Confident that stock prices would continue to rise, they used easy credit to buy shares in popular companies based on electric, automotive, and other new technologies. By the end of the decade, the Federal Reserve Bank—the nation's central bank, which controlled financial policy—tried to slow speculation by limiting credit availability. To meet the new restrictions, brokers had to demand that their clients immediately pay back the money they had borrowed to buy stock. As stocks were sold to raise the necessary cash, the market collapsed. Between early October and mid-November 1929, the value of businesses listed on the U.S. stock exchange dropped from $87 billion to $30 billion. For individuals and for the economy as a whole, it was the beginning of catastrophe.

The crash helped bring on a global depression that unfolded over the course of several years. The

1929 U.S. stock market crashes; global depression begins; Soviet war against kulaks

1931 Japan invades Manchuria; Spanish republicans overthrow monarchy

1933 Hitler comes to power

1935 Nuremberg Laws; Italy invades Ethiopia

1936 Purges and show trials in USSR; Spanish Civil War begins

1937 Japan attacks China

1938 Germany annexes Austria; European leaders meet to negotiate with Hitler; Kristallnacht

1930 1935

United States had financed the international economic growth of the previous five years, so when the suddenly strapped U.S. banks cut back on loans and called in debts, they undermined businesses at home and abroad. As jobs dwindled, Europe and other parts of the world faced a decline in consumer buying, overproduction, and competition from low-cost U.S. and Japanese goods—all of which slowed the European economy, including the young businesses of eastern Europe.

The Great Depression left no sector of the world economy unscathed, but government actions made the depression worse. To try to spur their economies, governments cut budgets and set high tariffs against foreign goods; these policies discouraged the consumer spending and international trade needed to spark the economy. Officials in charge of global money flows that fostered commerce desperately guarded their own supplies of gold. Unemployment soared: Great Britain—with its outdated textile, steel, and coal industries—had close to three million unemployed in 1932. By 1933, almost six million German workers, or about one-third of the workforce, were unemployed. Even in France, which had a more self-sufficient economy based on small businesses, firms began to fail, and by the mid-1930s more than 800,000 French people had lost their jobs.

Agricultural prices had been declining for several years because of technological advances and abundant harvests around the world. With their incomes slashed, millions of small farmers had no money to buy the chemical fertilizers and motorized machinery they needed to remain competitive. Now creditors confiscated farms. Eastern and southern European peasants, who had pressed for the redistribution of land after World War I, could not afford to operate their newly acquired farms, and they, too, went under. In Poland, many of the

Unemployed in Germany (1932)
"I'm looking for work of any kind," this respectably dressed unemployed man announces on his sign. Germans were among those hardest hit by the Great Depression, and when demogogues pointed to such sights as evidence that democracy didn't work, it helped pull down the rule of constitutions, representative government, and guaranteed rights. *(ullstein bild/The Granger Collection, New York.)*

1940 France falls to German army

1941 Germany invades USSR; Japan attacks Pearl Harbor; U.S. enters war

1942–1943 Siege of Stalingrad

1945 Fall of Berlin; U.S. drops atomic bombs on Japan; World War II ends

1940 — 1945

1939 Germany invades Czechoslovakia, Poland; Spanish Civil War ends; Nazi-Soviet Pact; Britain, France declare war on Germany; World War II begins

1940–1941 Battle of Britain

1941–1945 The Holocaust

1944 Allied forces land at Normandy

700,000 new landowners fell into debt trying to upgrade their farms. Eastern European governments often ignored the farmers' plight while pouring available funds into industrialization—a policy that increased tensions in rural society.

Social Effects of the Depression

The Great Depression had complex effects on society. First, life was not uniformly bleak, and despite the slump, modernization continued. Bordering English slums, one traveler in the mid-1930s noticed, were "filling stations and factories that look like exhibition buildings, giant cinemas and dance halls and cafés, bungalows with tiny garages, cocktail bars, Woolworth's [and] swimming pools." Municipal and national governments continued road construction and sanitation projects. Running water, electricity, and sewage pipes were installed in many homes for the first time. New factories manufactured synthetic fabrics, automobiles, and electrical products such as stoves—all of them in demand. With government assistance, eastern European industry developed: Romanian industrial production, for example, increased by 55 percent between 1929 and 1939.

Second, the majority of Europeans and Americans had jobs throughout the 1930s, and people with steady employment benefited from a drastic drop in prices. Service workers, managers, and business magnates often prospered. In contrast, towns with heavy industry often saw more than half the population out of work. In England in the mid-1930s, close to 20 percent of the population lacked adequate food, clothing, or housing. In a 1932 school assignment, a German youth wrote: "My father has been out of work for two and a half years. He thinks that I'll never find a job." Despite the prosperity of many people, the Great Depression spread fear beyond the unemployed. (See Document, "A Family Copes with Unemployment," page 877.)

Economic catastrophe upset gender relations and weakened social ties. Women often found low-paying jobs doing laundry and cleaning house, while unemployed men sometimes stayed home all day and took over housekeeping chores. Some, however, felt that this "women's work" demeaned their masculinity, and as many women became breadwinners, albeit for low wages, men could be seen standing on street corners begging—a change in gender expectations that fed discontent. Young men in cities faced severe unemployment; with nothing to do but loiter in parks, they became ripe for movements like Nazism. As the number of farmworkers in western Europe decreased, rural men also faced a decline in male authority, once responsible for directing farm labor. Demagogues everywhere attacked democracy's failure to stop the collapse of traditional life. Their complaints helped clear the way for Nazi and Fascist politicians who promised to create jobs and thus restore male dignity.

Politicians drew attention to the declining birthrates during the slump as still another national problem. In difficult economic times, which had plagued the West on and off since World War I, people in the 1930s chose to have fewer children than ever before. In addition, compulsory education and more years of required schooling, enforced more strictly after the war, reduced the income once earned by children. Working-class children now cost their families money while they went to school. Family-planning centers opened, receiving many clients, and knowledge of birth control spread across the working and lower-middle classes. The situation, leaders believed, was ominous.

Politicians from all parties threatened that declining fertility along with a depressed economy would lead to a national collapse in morale and military readiness. Many politicians also used the population "crisis" to gain votes by igniting racism: "superior" peoples were selfishly failing to breed, politicians charged, while "inferior" peoples were just waiting to take their place. This racism took a particularly violent form in eastern Europe, where the rural population also rose because of increased life expectancy despite the declining birthrate. As financial hardships continued, political parties across eastern Europe blamed Jewish bankers for farm foreclosures and Jewish civil servants (of whom there were actually very few) for inadequate relief programs. Thus, population issues along with economic misery produced discord, especially in the form of ethnic hatred and anti-Semitism, opening the way still further for dictators who promised that eliminating "undesirables" would restore prosperity.

The Great Depression beyond the West

The effects of the depression extended beyond the West, spreading discontent in European empires. World War I and postwar investment had produced economic growth, a rising population, and explosive urbanization in Asia, Africa, and Latin America. Japan in particular had become a formidable industrial rival. The depression, however, cut the demand for copper, tin, and other raw materials and for the finished products made in urban factories worldwide. Rising agricultural productivity drove down the price of foodstuffs like rice and coffee, a disaster for colonial peoples who had been forced to grow a single cash crop. One French official in Algeria said that the collapse of agricultural prices

DOCUMENT

A Family Copes with Unemployment

Austria and Germany were incredibly hard hit by the depression. The trauma was made worse because of the catastrophic defeat and dismemberment of both the Austrian and German Empires. In 1931, sociologists visited a small industrial town called Marienthal, an hour outside of Vienna, to report on the psychological and physical condition of the hundreds of families left penniless by the closing of the textile mills.

The father was sitting on a low stool with a pile of worn-out children's shoes in front of him that he was trying to mend with roofing felt. The children were sitting together motionless on a box, in stockinged feet, waiting for their shoes to be finished. The father explained with embarrassment, ". . . On Sundays I have to patch the shoes up a bit so that the children can go to school again on Monday." He held up the completely dilapidated shoes of the eldest boy. "I just don't know what I can do with these. On holidays he can't go out of the house any more. . . ."

The youngest child caught our attention. His face was feverish and puffy and swollen around the nose. He breathed heavily with his mouth open. The mother explained: "He always has a cold. He ought to have his tonsils and adenoids out, but we can't afford the trip to the hospital. . . ." The father told us that things had been going terribly badly these last few days. All they had been able to buy was bread, and not enough of that. The children kept coming into the kitchen asking for another piece; they were always hungry. His wife sat in the kitchen crying.

Source: Marie Jahoda et al., eds., *Marienthal: The Sociography of an Unemployed Community*, trans. John Reginall and Thomas Elsaesser (1933; repr. Chicago: Aldine-Atherton, 1971), 87–88.

Question to Consider

- **How does the situation of this Austrian family illustrate why Europeans might have willingly followed Nazi and Fascist politicians in the 1930s?**

"endanger[ed] the entire colonial project." Just as in Europe, however, the economic picture in the colonies was uneven. For instance, established Indian industries such as the textile business gained strength, with India no longer needing British cloth.

Economic distress fueled anger, and anger led to action. Colonial farmers withheld produce like cocoa from imperial trade, and colonial workers went on strike to protest the wage cuts imposed by imperial landlords. Discontent ran deep. Millions of African and Asian colonial troops had fought for Britain and France in World War I, but the imperialist countries had given little back to their colonial populations. In fact, the League of Nations charter had pointedly omitted any reference to the principle of racial equality demanded by people of color at the Paris peace conference. Fortified by these wrongs, by the model of Japan's growing power, and by their own industrial development, more colonial peoples than ever before resolved to win independence.

In India, anger toward colonialism boiled over. Millions of working people, including hundreds of thousands of veterans, joined with the upper-class Indians, who had organized to gain rights from Britain in the late nineteenth century. Mohandas K. Gandhi (1869–1948), called Mahatma ("great-souled"), emerged as the charismatic leader for Indian independence. Trained in England as a Western-style lawyer, Gandhi preached Hindu self-denial and rejected British love of material wealth. He wore simple clothing made of thread he had spun himself and advocated **civil disobedience**—deliberately but peacefully breaking the law—a tactic he claimed to have taken from the British suffragists and from the teachings of spiritual leaders like Jesus and Buddha. Boycotting British-made goods and disobeying British laws, Gandhi aimed to end Indian deference to the British. The British jailed Gandhi repeatedly and tried to split the independence movement by promoting Hindu-Muslim antagonism. Instead, commitment to independence grew.

The end of the Ottoman Empire following World War I led to efforts to build new independent nations in the Middle East. Mustafa Kemal (1881–1938), who later took the name Atatürk ("first among Turks"), led the Turks to found an independent republic in 1923 and to craft a capitalist economy. In an effort to Westernize Turkish culture and promote the new Turkish state, Kemal moved the capital from Constantinople to Ankara in 1923, officially changed the name Constantinople to the Turkish name Istanbul in 1930, mandated Western dress for men and women, introduced the Latin alphabet, and abolished polygamy. In 1936, Turkish women

civil disobedience: The act of deliberately but peacefully breaking the law, a tactic used by Mohandas Gandhi in India and earlier by British suffragists to protest oppression and obtain political change.

Gandhi Speaks to Women and Children
Mohandas K. Gandhi, an English-trained lawyer, was central to making the Indian independence movement a mass phenomenon. He made Indians see the superior values in their own culture in contrast to those of the West. The West, he maintained, including the United States, valued only money. Gandhi riveted his audiences, addressing women and children as well as men. *(akg-images/Archiv Peter Rühe.)*

received the vote and were made eligible to serve in the parliament. Persia, which changed its name to Iran in 1935, similarly loosened the European grip on its economy by updating its government and by forcing the negotiation of oil contracts that kept Western countries from taking the oil for virtually nothing.

Anticolonial activism thrived in French colonies, too, but the government made few concessions. Like all imperial countries during the depression, France depended increasingly on the profits it could take from its empire; therefore, its trade with its colonies increased as trade with Europe lagged. France also depended on the colonies for sheer numbers of people, and the growing colonial population bolstered French optimism. One official estimated what colonial numbers could mean for national security: "One hundred and ten million strong, France can stand up to Germany." Ho Chi Minh, founder of the Indochinese Communist Party, rallied his people to protest French imperialism, but in 1930 the French government brutally crushed the peasant uprising he led. Needing their empires, Britain and France increased the number of their troops stationed around the world. As a result, fascism spread largely unchecked in Europe during the 1930s.

REVIEW QUESTION How did the Great Depression affect society and politics?

Totalitarian Triumph

Representative government collapsed in many countries under the sheer weight of social and economic crisis. After 1929, Mussolini in Italy, Stalin in the USSR, and Hitler in Germany were able to mobilize vast support for their regimes. Many admired Mussolini and Hitler for the discipline they brought to social and economic life. Desperate for economic relief, many citizens supported political violence as key to restoring well-being. Scholars have classified the Fascist, Nazi, and Communist regimes of the 1930s as totalitarian. The term *totalitarianism* refers to highly centralized systems of government that attempt to control society and ensure obedience through a single party and police terror. Born during World War I and gaining support in its aftermath, totalitarian governments broke with liberal principles of freedom and natural rights and came to wage war on their own citizens. But there were important differences among totalitarian states, especially between Fascist and Communist states. Whereas communism denounced private ownership of property and economic inequality, fascism supported them as crucial to national might (see Terms of History, page 879).

The Rise of Stalinism

In the 1930s, **Joseph Stalin** (1879–1953) led the transformation of the USSR from a rural society into an industrial power. Stalin ended Lenin's New Economic Policy, which had allowed individuals to profit from trade and agriculture, and in 1929 laid out the first of several ambitious five-year plans for industrializing the country. Coercion and violence were crucial components of this gigantic undertaking.

Transforming the Economy

Stalin's **five-year plans** outlined a program for huge increases in the output of coal, iron ore, steel, and industrial goods over successive five-year periods. Without an end to economic backwardness, Stalin warned, "the advanced countries . . . will crush us."

Joseph Stalin: Leader of the USSR who, with considerable backing, formed a brutal dictatorship in the 1930s and forcefully converted the country into an industrial power.

five-year plans: Centralized programs for economic development begun in 1929 by Joseph Stalin and copied by Adolf Hitler; these plans set production priorities and gave production targets for individual industries and agriculture.

TERMS OF HISTORY

Fascism

Fascism was, along with communism and liberalism, one of the dominant ideologies of the twentieth century. It began in the 1920s as Benito Mussolini's movement in Italy, taking its name from *fasces*—a Latin word for the bundle of rods with hatchet symbolizing Roman magisterial authority. Under Mussolini, the concept placed the value of the national community above that of individuals and the laws and rights that protected them.

The term was then broadened to apply generally to the various authoritarian political parties (such as the Nazis) and their leaders, who came to power in Italy, Germany, Spain, eastern Europe, and other parts of the world before World War II. As an outgrowth of World War I, fascism applauded violence and military struggle on the state's behalf and denied the value of peace and pacifism. Fascism was also explicitly and fundamentally antidemocratic: both Mussolini and Hitler loudly rejected democratic values, with Mussolini arguing that the twentieth century would be the century of "authority" and of the "state"—not the century of democracy and hard-won consensus, which he saw as outmoded.

The expansion of fascism as a general political concept passed through several phases, moving from a "rooting" stage of growth and mobilization, to the seizure and exercise of brutal state power, to a violent expansion that culminated in radical action such as war and genocide. The rooting stage required popular support, which Fascist leaders solicited through programs with mass appeal: just after World War I, Mussolini issued a First Fascist Program that included votes for women, the eight-hour day, taxation of war profits, confiscation of church lands, and workers' participation in industrial management. Once in power, however, Fascists cast aside the principles that had won them popular support. By 1935, fascism had come to focus on the powers of one charismatic leader: Hitler, Franco, and Mussolini, in their military-garbed persons, became living embodiments of the all-powerful state. Japan also joined the fascist Axis powers after its attack on the United States in 1941, in part because Japan's military had come to embrace the same violence-driven ambitions.

Underlying fascist actions was the core belief that racial superiority fostered a strong national community. Fascists argued that a regimented society would strengthen the "master race," with Germany and Japan slaughtering millions toward that end. Believing that militarization strengthens the state and transforms the people, fascists also eagerly pursued war as an important end in itself. Through regimentation, militarization, and violent action, fascists sought to eliminate those deemed inferior or subversive and cause the emergence of an idealized "man of steel."

This emphasis on inequality distinguished the fascist from the Soviet totalitarian state. While fascism valued inequality and the triumphs of the wealthy, Soviets did not. Thus, Germany and Italy supported the actions of the rebel chief Francisco Franco in the Spanish Civil War, seeing this as part of the drive to overthrow rights-based, equal-opportunity democracies in the name of an absolutist state where the wealthy and powerful flourished. Fascist ideology also affected areas such as Romania, Bulgaria, Albania, and Greece.

Today, the term *fascist* has lost its clear definition and is regularly used to characterize any opponent with whom one disagrees. In this regard, similar use is made of terms like *socialist* and *liberal*—words that once had a precise meaning, but now have become epithets among the uninformed.

He thus established economic planning—that is, government direction of the economy used on both sides in World War I and increasingly implemented around the world. Between 1928 and 1940, the number of Soviet workers in industry, construction, and transport grew from 4.6 million to 12.6 million and factory output soared. Stalin's first five-year plan helped make the USSR a leading industrial nation.

A new bureaucratic elite implemented the plans, and the number of managers—mostly party officials and technical experts—in heavy industry grew by almost 500 percent between 1929 and 1935. Despite limited rights to change jobs or even move from place to place, skilled workers benefited from the privileges that went along with their new industrial role. Compared with people working the land, both managers and industrial workers had better housing and wages. Communist officials received additional rewards such as country homes, good food, and luxurious vacations.

New or unskilled workers enjoyed no such benefits. Newcomers from the countryside were herded into barracks or tents and subjected to dangerous factory conditions. Despite the hardships, many took pride in their new skills. "We mastered this profession—completely new to us—with great pleasure," a female lathe operator recalled. More often, however, workers fresh from the countryside lacked the technical skills necessary to accomplish goals of the five-year plans. Because meeting these goals had top priority as a measure of progress toward a Communist utopia, official lying about productivity became part of the economic system. The attempt to turn an illiterate peasant society into an advanced industrial economy in a single decade brought intense suffering, but hardship was tolerated because, as one worker put it, Soviet workers believed in the need for "constant struggle, struggle, and struggle" to achieve a Communist society.

In country and city alike, politics influenced work. Stalin demanded more output from industry and more grain from peasants both to feed the urban workforce and to provide exports whose sale abroad would finance industrialization. Some peasants resisted government demands by withholding produce from the market, prompting Stalin to demand a "liquidation of the kulaks." The word *kulak*, which literally means "fist," was a negative term for prosperous peasants, but in practice it applied to anyone who opposed Stalin's plans to end independent farming. Party workers began searching villages, seizing grain, and forcing villagers to identify the kulaks among them. Propagandists followed to stir up hatred. One Russian remembered believing the kulaks were "bloodsuckers, cattle, swine, loathsome, repulsive: they had no souls; they stank." Denounced as "enemies of the state," whole families were robbed of their possessions, left to starve, or even murdered outright. Confiscated kulak land formed the basis for the new collective farms, or kolkhoz, where the remaining peasants were forced to share facilities and modern machinery. Traditional peasant life was brought to a violent end.

Transforming Society

Once the state had defined work life as central to communism, economic failure took on political meaning. Such failure was common because factory workers, farmers, and party officials alike were too inexperienced with advanced industrialization to meet quotas. The experiment with collectivization, combined with the murder of farmers, resulted in a drop in the grain harvest from 83 million tons in 1930 to 67 million in 1934. Soviet citizens starved. Blaming failure on "wreckers" deliberately plotting against communism, Stalin instituted **purges**—that is, state violence in the form of widespread arrests, imprisonments in labor camps, and executions—to rid society of these "villains." The purges touched all segments of society, beginning with engineers who were condemned for causing low productivity.

purges: The series of attacks on citizens of the USSR accused of being "wreckers," or saboteurs of communism, in the 1930s and later.

Beginning in 1936, the government charged prominent Bolshevik leaders with conspiring to overthrow Soviet rule. In a series of "show trials"—trials based on trumped-up charges, fabricated evidence, and coerced confessions—Bolshevik leaders were tortured and forced to confess in court. Most of those found guilty were shot. Some of the top leaders accepted their fate, seeing the purges as good for the future of socialism. Just before his execution, one Bolshevik loyalist and former editor of the party newspaper *Pravda* wrote to Stalin praising the "great and bold political idea behind the general purge." While there was resistance to Stalin, there were many sincere believers who sought to serve what they considered his noble work.

The spirit of purge swept through society, eventually reaching the Soviet power structure. One woman poet described the scene in towns and cities: "Great concert and lecture halls were turned into public confessionals. . . . People did penance for [everything]. . . . Beating their breasts, the 'guilty' would lament that they had 'shown political shortsightedness' and 'lack of vigilance' . . . and were full of 'rotten liberalism.'" In 1937 and 1938, military leaders were arrested and executed without public trials; some ranks were entirely wiped out. Although the massacre of military leaders appeared suicidal at a time when Hitler threatened war, thousands of high military posts became open to new talent. Stalin would not have to worry about an officer corps wedded to old ideas, as had happened in World War I. Simultaneously, the government expanded the system of prison camps, founded under Lenin, into an extensive network stretching several thousand miles from Moscow to Siberia. Called the Gulag—an acronym for the government department that ran the camps—the system held millions of prisoners under lethal conditions. Prisoners aided the economy by doing every kind of work from digging canals to building apartment buildings. Some one million died annually as a result of the harsh conditions, which included insufficient food, inadequate housing, and twelve- to sixteen-hour days of crushing physical labor. Regular beatings and murders of prisoners rounded out Gulag life, which became another aspect of totalitarian violence.

As social and sexual experimentation disappeared in the 1930s, toleration in Soviet social life ended. The birthrate in the USSR, like that in the rest of Europe, declined rapidly. The Soviet Union also needed to replace the millions of people lost since 1914. To meet this need, Stalin restricted access to birth-control information and abortion. Lavish wedding ceremonies came back into fashion, divorces became difficult to obtain, and the state made homosexuality a crime. Whereas Bolsheviks had once attacked the family as a capitalist institution, propaganda now referred to the family as a "school for socialism." At the same time, women in rural areas made gains in literacy and received improved health care. Positions in the lower ranks of the party opened to women as the purges continued, and more women were accepted into the professions. However, women in the industrial workforce faced increased stress. After long hours in factories, workingwomen stood in lines for scarce consumer goods and still performed all household and child-care tasks.

Avant-garde experimentation in the arts ended under Stalin. He called artists and writers "engineers of the soul" and, thus recognizing their influence, controlled their output through the Union of Soviet Writers. The union not only assigned housing, office space, equipment, and secretarial help but also determined the types of books authors could write. In return, the "comrade artist" adhered to the official style of "socialist realism," derived from the 1920s focus on the common worker as a hero. Although some writers and artists went underground, secretly creating works that are still coming to light, many others found ways to adjust their talents to the state's demands. The composer Sergei Prokofiev, for example, wrote music both for the delightful *Peter and the Wolf* and for Sergei Eisenstein's 1938 film *Alexander Nevsky*, a work that flatteringly compared Stalin to the medieval rulers of the Russian people. Aided by adaptable artists, workers, and bureaucrats, Stalin stood triumphant as the 1930s drew to a close. He was, as two different workers put it, "our beloved Leader" and "a god on earth."

Hitler's Rise to Power

A different but ultimately no less violent system emerged when **Adolf Hitler** (1889–1945) and his followers put an end to democracy in Germany. Since the early 1920s, Hitler had harangued the German masses to destroy the Weimar Republic and drummed at a message of anti-Semitism and the rebirth of the German "race." When the Great Depression struck Germany in 1929, his Nazi Party began to outstrip its rivals in elections, thanks in part to financial support from big business. Film and press tycoon Alfred Hugenberg helped, constantly slamming the Weimar government as responsible for the disastrous economy and for the loss of German pride after World War I. Nazi supporters took to the streets, attacking young Communist groups who agitated just as loudly on behalf of the new Soviet experiment. Hugenberg's newspapers always reported such incidents as the work of Communist thugs who had assaulted blameless Nazis, thus building sympathy for the Nazis among the middle classes.

Parliamentary government practically ground to a halt during the depression, adding to unrest and the sense of disorder. The Reichstag, or German assembly, failed to approve emergency plans to improve the economy, first because its members disagreed over policies and second because Nazi and Communist deputies disrupted its sessions. Its failure to act discredited democracy among the German people. Hitler's followers made parliamentary government look incapable of providing basic law and order by rampaging unchecked through the streets and attacking Jews, Communists, and Social Democrats. By targeting all these as a single, monolithic group of "Bolshevik" enemies, the Nazis won wide approval. They were seen as fearlessly confronting those within Germany responsible for the depression. Many thought it was time to replace democratic government with a bold new leader who would take on these enemies military-style, without concern for constitutions, laws, or individual rights. It was time for war at home.

Every age group and class of people supported Hitler, though like Stalin, he especially attracted young people. In 1930, 70 percent of Nazi Party members were under forty and many had never thought of war except as exciting games they played as children during World War I. They believed that a better world was possible under Hitler's command. The largest number of supporters came from the industrial working class, but many white-collar workers and members of the lower-middle class also joined the party in percentages out of proportion with their numbers in the population. The inflation that had wiped out savings left them especially bitter and open to Hitler's rhetoric. In the deepening economic crisis, the Nazi Party, which had received little more than 2 percent of the vote in 1928, won almost 20 percent in the Reichstag elections of 1930 and more than twice that in 1932 (see "Contrasting Views," page 882).

Hitler used modern propaganda techniques to build up his following. Nazi Party members passed

Adolf Hitler (1889–1945): Chancellor of Germany (1933–1945) who, with considerable backing, overturned democratic government, created the Third Reich, persecuted millions, and ultimately led Germany and the world into World War II.

CONTRASTING VIEWS

Nazism and Hitler: For and Against

Today Hitler is uniformly regarded as a dictator while his followers are seen as perpetrating great harm on German and other societies, especially by causing the deaths of tens of millions of people. In the 1930s, however, there was a division of opinion about Nazism and Hitler even before the coming of the Third Reich and its deadly programs.

1. An Author Opposes Nazism

Journalist, playwright, and novelist Lion Feuchtwanger was an early critic of Nazism, tagging it as a movement operating against the goals of democracy and clear thinking. Luckily, when the Nazis came to power in early 1933, Feuchtwanger was on a tour of the United States. The Nazis ransacked his house and burned his writings. On his return to Europe, Feuchtwanger went into exile but was temporarily imprisoned in France when the Nazis invaded. He eventually escaped to the United States, where he continued to write. This critique of Nazism dates from early 1931.

The war [World War I] liberated the barbarian instincts of the individual and society to a degree that was previously unimaginable. National Socialism has skillfully organized the barbarity. Among the intellectuals it is called OBG: Organized Barbarity of Germany.

Anti-logical and anti-intellectual in its being and ideology, National Socialism strives to depose reason and install in its place emotion and drive—to be precise, barbarity. Just because intellect and art are transnational, National Socialism distrusts and hates them to the extreme. . . .

Source: Lion Feuchtwanger, "How Do We Struggle against a Third Reich," January 21, 1931, in Anton Kaes et al., eds., *Weimar Republic Sourcebook* (Berkeley: University of California Press, 1994), 167.

2. Hitler Defends National Socialist Street Activism

Before and after the Nazis took power, storm troopers took to the streets at night, engaging in brawls, beating up Communists (who fought as well), and generally making their noisy presence felt. Their activism reassured some people that something was being done to protect Germany, while others believed that the Nazis were a menace. In this speech to the Industry Club in January 1932, Hitler explained the paramilitary activity and praised the storm troopers.

I know quite well, gentlemen, that when National Socialists march through the streets and suddenly in the evening a tumult and commotion arises, then the bourgeois draws back the window-curtain, looks out, and says: Once more my night's rest disturbed: no more sleep for me. Why must the Nazis always be so provocative and run about the place at night? Gentlemen, if everyone thought like that, then no one's sleep at night would be disturbed, it is true. But then the bourgeois today could not venture out into the street. If everyone thought in that way, if these young folk had no ideal to move them and drive them forward, then certainly they would gladly be rid of these nocturnal fights. But remember that it means sacrifice when today many hundreds of thousands of SA and SS men of the National Socialist movement every day have to mount their trucks, protect meetings, undertake marches, sacrifice themselves night after night, and then come back in the gray dawn either to workshop and factory or as unemployed to take the pittance of the dole. . . . Believe me, there is already in all this the force of an ideal—a great ideal! And if the whole German nation today had the same faith in its vocation as these hundreds of thousands, if the whole nation possessed

out thousands of recordings of Hitler's speeches and other Nazi mementos to German citizens. Teenagers painted their fingernails with swastikas, and soldiers flashed metal match covers with Nazi insignia. Nazi rallies were carefully planned displays in which Hitler captivated the crowds, who saw him as their strong, vastly superior *Führer* ("leader"). Frenzied and inspirational, he seemed neither a calculating politician nor a wooden bureaucrat but a "creative element," as one poet put it. In actuality, however, Hitler regarded the masses with contempt, and in *Mein Kampf* he discussed how to deal with them:

> The receptivity of the great masses is very limited, their intelligence is small. In consequence of these facts, all effective propaganda must be limited to a very few points and must harp on those in slogans until the last member of the public understands what you want him to understand.

Hitler's media techniques were so successful that they continue to influence political campaigns today, particularly in the use of sound bites and simple messages often filled with hate or threats.

In the 1932 elections, both Nazis and Communists did very well, making the leader of one of these two parties the logical choice as chancellor. Influential conservative politicians loathed the Communists for their opposition to private property and favored Hitler as someone they could easily con-this idealism, Germany would stand in the eyes of the world otherwise than she stands now!

Source: Adolf Hitler, "Address to the Industry Club," January 27, 1932, in Anton Kaes et al., eds., *The Weimar Republic Sourcebook* (Berkeley: University of California Press, 1994), 141.

3. A Professor against Hitler

Victor Klemperer was a professor of literature and a Protestant, though his father had been a Jewish rabbi. Once Hitler came to power, Klemperer, a veteran of World War I who was married to an "Aryan" woman, found himself unable to publish his writings and dismissed from his teaching position. During the Third Reich, he kept a journal tracking not only his own mounting difficulties but also the emigration, dismissals, poverty, and suicides of his family and friends. He had clear opinions about Hitler, whom he listened to on the radio, and firm beliefs about the Nazis and Communists.

November 11, 1933 . . . more than forty minutes of Hitler. A mostly hoarse, strained, agitated voice, long passages in the whining tone of the sectarian preachers. . . . "Jews!" want to set nations of millions at one another's throat. I want only peace, I have risen from the common people. I want nothing for myself. . . . etc. in no proper order, impassioned; every sentence mendacious, but I almost believe unconsciously mendacious. The man is a blinkered fanatic.

November 14, 1933 . . . All Germany prefers Hitler to the Communists. And I see no difference between either of the two movements; both are materialistic and lead to slavery.

Source: Victor Klemperer, *I Will Bear Witness: A Diary of the Nazi Years, 1933–1941*, trans. Martin Chalmers (New York: Random House, 1998), 41–42.

4. Praise for Nazis

A year after Hitler came to power, Paula Müller-Otfried, a former deputy to the Reichstag who had opposed both communism and liberalism, sent out this New Year's card.

When I wrote a year ago and saw only a glimmer of hope, I could not possibly have believed . . . my plea would be so richly fulfilled. . . . The vast majority of the *Volk* joyfully summoned the national regime, with its drive to purify public life, to combat unemployment, hunger, and need. . . . We prayed and the answer arrived. May God grant our rulers wisdom. May the "steel-hardened man" for whom we cried out a year ago . . . retain his power.

Source: Quoted in Claudia Koonz, *Mothers in the Fatherland: Women, the Family, and Nazi Politics* (New York: St. Martin's, 1987), 234.

5. Hitler in Prayers

Children in Germany recited the following bedtime prayer, addressed not to God but to Hitler. It expressed a clear view of who Hitler was and what he meant to Germany.

Führer, my Führer, sent to me from God, protect and maintain me throughout my life. Thou who has saved Germany from Deepest need, I thank thee today for my daily bread. Remain at my side and never leave me, Führer, my Führer. My Faith. My light. *Heil, mein Führer!*

Source: Quoted in Claudia Koonz, *Mothers in the Fatherland: Women, the Family, and Nazi Politics* (New York: St. Martin's, 1987), 287.

Questions to Consider

1. **What are the positive qualities attributed to Nazis and their leader?**
2. **What are the major criticisms of Hitler and the Nazis by the opposition?**
3. **To what do you attribute the different opinions about Hitler and the Nazis?**
4. **What aspects of pro-Nazi ideas made them so persuasive and appealing?**

trol. When Hitler was invited to become chancellor in January 1933, he accepted.

The Nazification of German Politics

Millions of Germans celebrated Hitler's ascent to power. "My father went down to the cellar and brought up our best bottles of wine. . . . And my mother wept for joy," one German recalled. "Now everything will be all right." Yet instead of being easy to control, Hitler took command brutally, quickly closing down representative government with an ugly show of force. Tens of thousands of his paramilitary supporters—the Stürmabteilung (SA), or "storm troopers"—paraded through the streets with blazing torches.

Terror in the Nazi State

Within a month of Hitler's taking power, the Nazi state was in place. When the Reichstag building was gutted by fire in February 1933, Nazis used the fire as the excuse for suspending civil rights, censoring the press, and prohibiting meetings of other political parties. Hitler had always claimed to hate democracy and diverse political opinions. "Our opponents complain that we National Socialists, and I in particular, are intolerant," he declared. "They are right, we are intolerant! I have set myself one task, namely to sweep those parties out of Germany."

Toys Depicting Nazis
As a totalitarian ideology, Nazism was part of everyday life. Nazi insignia decorated clothing, dishes, cigarette lighters, and even fingernails. Parents sent young people to Nazi clubs and organizations and bought Nazi toys like these for their children's playtime. Nazi songs, Nazi parades and festivals, and Nazi radio programs filled leisure hours. *(Imperial War Museum, London.)*

The storm troopers' violence became a way of life, silencing democratic politicians but also making those who participated in the violence feel part of a glorious whole. At the end of March, intimidated Reichstag delegates let pass the **Enabling Act**, which suspended the constitution for four years and allowed Nazi laws to take effect without parliamentary approval. Solid middle-class Germans approved the Enabling Act as a way to advance the creation of a *Volksgemeinschaft* ("people's community") of like-minded, racially pure Germans—Aryans, the Nazis named them. Heinrich Himmler headed the elite Schutzstaffel (SS), Hitler's "protection squadron," and he commanded the Reich's political police system. The Gestapo, the secret police force run by Hermann Goering, also enforced obedience to Nazism. These organizations had vast powers to arrest people and either execute them or imprison them in concentration camps, the first of which opened at Dachau, near Munich, in March 1933. The Nazis filled it and later camps with political enemies like socialists, and then with Jews, homosexuals, and others said to be enemies of the Volksgemeinschaft. As one Nazi leader proclaimed:

> [National socialism] does not believe that one soul is equal to another, one man equal to another. It does not believe in rights as such. It aims to create the German man of strength, its task is to protect the German people, and all . . . must be subordinate to this goal.

Hitler deliberately blurred authority in the government and party to encourage confusion and competition. He then settled disputes, often with violence. When Ernst Roehm, leader of the SA and Hitler's longtime collaborator, called for a "second revolution" to end the business and military elites' continuing influence on top Nazis, Hitler ordered Roehm's assassination. The bloody Night of the Long Knives (June 30, 1934), during which hundreds of SA leaders and innocent civilians were killed, strengthened the support of the conservative upper classes for the Nazi regime. They saw that Hitler would deal ruthlessly with those favoring a leveling-out of social privilege. Nazism's terrorist politics served as the foundation of Hitler's Third Reich—a German empire grandly advertised as the successor to the First Reich of Charlemagne and the Second Reich of Bismarck and William II.

Nazi Economic and Social Programs

Like violence, new economic programs, especially those putting people back to work, were crucial to the survival of Nazism. Economic revival built popular support, which in turn strengthened the call for German expansion. The Nazi government pursued **pump priming**—that is, stimulating the economy through government spending on tanks and airplanes and on public works programs such as building the Autobahn, or highway system. Unemployment declined from a peak of almost 6 million in 1932 to 1.6 million by 1936. As labor shortages appeared in some sectors, the government drafted single women into forced service as farmworkers and domestics. The Nazi Party closed down labor unions, and government managers determined work procedures and set pay levels, rating women's jobs lower than men's regardless of the level of expertise required. Imitating Stalin, Hitler announced a four-year plan in 1936 with the secret aim of preparing Germany for war by 1940. His programs produced large budget deficits, but he was already planning to conquer and loot neighboring countries to cover the costs.

Enabling Act: The legislation passed in 1933 suspending constitutional government for four years in order to meet the crisis in the German economy.

pump priming: An economic policy used by governments, including the Nazis in Germany, to stimulate the economy through public works programs and other infusions to public funds.

Nazi officials devised policies to control everyday life, including gender roles. In June 1933, a bill took effect that encouraged Aryans (those people defined as racially German) to marry and have children. The bill provided for loans to Aryan newlyweds, but only if the wife left the workforce. The loans were forgiven on the birth of the pair's fourth child. The ideal woman gave up her job, gave birth to many children, and completely surrendered her will to that of her husband, allowing him to feel powerful despite military defeat and economic depression. A good wife "joyfully sacrifices and fulfills her fate," one Nazi leader explained of women's contribution to rebuilding the community.

The government also controlled culture, destroying the rich creativity of the Weimar years. Although 70 percent of households had radios by 1938, programs were severely censored. Books like Erich Maria Remarque's *All Quiet on the Western Front* were banned, and in May 1933 a huge book-burning ceremony rid libraries of works by Jews, socialists, homosexuals, and modernist writers. Modern art in museums and private collections was either destroyed or confiscated. In the Hitler Youth, which boys and girls over age ten were required to join, children learned to report those adults they suspected of disloyalty to the Third Reich, even their own parents. People boasted that they could leave their bicycles out at night without fear of robbery, but their world was filled with informers—some 100,000 of them on the Nazi payroll. In general, the improved economy led many to inflate their belief in Hitler's powers. They saw him working an economic miracle while restoring pride in Germany and strengthening the Aryan community. For hundreds of thousands if not millions of Germans, however, Nazi rule in the 1930s brought anything but harmony and community.

Nazi Racism

The Nazis defined Jews as an inferior "race" dangerous to the superior Aryan "race" and responsible for most of Germany's problems, including defeat in World War I and the economic depression. The reasons for targeting Jews were, Hitler insisted, scientific. "National Socialism is a cool and highly reasoned approach to reality based on the greatest of scientific knowledge," he declared in a 1938 speech. Hitler attacked many ethnic and social groups, but he took anti-Semitism to new and frightening heights. In the rhetoric of Nazism, Jews were "vermin," "abscesses," and "Bolsheviks." They were enemies, biologically weakening the race and plotting Germany's destruction—all of this, given scientific knowledge then and now, utterly false. Thus building community meant eliminating as well as including. By branding Jews both as evil businessmen and as working-class Bolsheviks, Hitler fashioned an enemy for many segments of the population to hate.

Nazis insisted that terms such as *Aryan* and *Jewish* (a religious category) were scientific racial classifications that could be determined by physical characteristics such as the shape of the nose. In 1935, the government enacted the **Nuremberg Laws**, legislation that deprived Jews of citizenship and prohibited marriage between Jews and other Germans. Abortions and birth-control information were readily available to enemy outcast groups, including Jews, Slavs, Sinti and Roma, and mentally or physically disabled people, but were forbidden to women classified as Aryan. In the name of improving the Aryan race, doctors helped organize the T4 project, which used carbon monoxide poisoning and other means to kill large numbers of people—200,000 handicapped and elderly—late in the 1930s. The murder of the disabled aimed to eliminate those whose disability or "racial inferiority" endangered the Aryans. These murders prepared the way for even larger mass exterminations in the future.

Jews were forced into slave labor, evicted from their apartments, and prevented from buying most clothing and food. In 1938, a Jewish teenager, reacting to the harassment of his parents, killed a German official. In retaliation, Nazis and other Germans attacked some two hundred synagogues, smashed windows of Jewish-owned stores, ransacked apartments of known or suspected Jews, and threw more than twenty thousand Jews into prisons and camps. The night of November 9–10 became known as Kristallnacht, or the Night of Broken Glass. Faced with this relentless persecution, more than half of Germany's 500,000 Jews had emigrated by the outbreak of World War II in 1939. Their enormous emigration fees helped finance Germany's economic recovery, while neighbors and individual Nazis used anti-Semitism to justify stealing Jewish property and taking the jobs Jews were forced to leave. Identifying a group as a menacing foe had been an ideological tactic used to foster unity in wartime, but it now became a peacetime tactic that allowed those who stole from Jews to believe they were doing a patriotic service.

REVIEW QUESTION What role did violence play in the Soviet and Nazi regimes?

Nuremberg Laws: Legislation enacted by the Nazis in 1935 that deprived Jewish Germans of their citizenship and imposed many other hardships on them.

Democracies on the Defensive

Nazism, communism, and fascism offered bold new approaches to modern politics. These ideologies maintained that democracy was effeminate and that it wasted precious time in building consensus among all citizens. Totalitarian leaders' energetic military style of mobilizing the masses made representative government and the democratic values of the United States, France, and Great Britain appear feeble—a sign that these societies were on the decline. The appeal of totalitarianism to citizens around the world put democracies on the defensive as they aimed to restore the well-being of citizens while still upholding individual rights and the rule of law.

Confronting the Economic Crisis

As the depression wore on through the 1930s, some governments experimented with ways to solve social and economic crises democratically. The United States and Sweden were among the most successful in facing the double-barreled assault of economic depression and fascism. Other countries, such as France, had less consistently good results, but its short-lived Popular Front government made antifascism and the preservation of democracy its special cause. In the new nations of eastern Europe, however, the economic crisis took such a toll on individual lives that parliamentary government and the rule of law often gave way to dictatorship and worse.

The United States In the early days of the economic slump, U.S. president Herbert Hoover opposed direct help to the unemployed and even ordered the army to drive away jobless veterans who had marched on Washington, D.C. With unemployment close to fifteen million, Franklin Delano Roosevelt (1882–1945), the wealthy governor of New York, defeated Hoover in the presidential election of 1932 on the promise of relief and recovery. Roosevelt, or FDR as he became known, pushed through a torrent of legislation: relief for businesses, price supports for hard-pressed farmers, and public works programs for unemployed youth. The Social Security Act of 1935 set up a fund to which employers and employees contributed. It provided retirement benefits for workers, unemployment insurance, and payments to dependent mothers, their children, and people with disabilities.

These programs advanced a new kind of state taking shape not only in the United States but elsewhere across the West: the welfare state—that is, a state in which the government guarantees a certain level of economic well-being for individuals and businesses. Roosevelt's "New Deal" angered businesspeople and the wealthy, who saw it as socialist. Even though the depression remained severe, Roosevelt maintained widespread support. Like other successful politicians of the 1930s, he was an expert at using the new mass media, especially in his series of "fireside chats" broadcast by radio to the American people. Unlike Mussolini and Hitler, however, Roosevelt's public statements promoted rather than attacked faith in democratic rights and popular government. The participation of First Lady Eleanor Roosevelt sharply contrasted with the antiwoman ideology of Nazis and Fascists, and the Roosevelts insisted that justice and human rights for all must not be surrendered in difficult times. "We Americans of today . . . are characters in the living book of democracy," Roosevelt told a group of teenagers in 1939. "But we are also its author." Lynchings and other racial violence continued to cause great suffering in the United States during the Roosevelt administration, and the economy did not fully recover, yet the president's new programs and media success were able to keep most Americans' faith in democracy strong.

Sweden Sweden also developed a coherent program for solving economic and population problems, assigning the government a central role in promoting social welfare and economic democracy. Sweden devalued its currency to make Swedish exports more attractive on the international market. Thanks to pump-priming programs, Swedish productivity rose by 20 percent between 1929 and 1935, a time when other democracies were still experiencing decline.

Sweden addressed the population problem with government programs, but without the racism and coercion of Nazism. Alva Myrdal, a leading member of Sweden's parliament, believed that boosting childbirth depended both on the economy and on individual well-being. It was undemocratic, she maintained, that "the bearing of a child should mean economic distress" to parents. Acting on Myrdal's advice to promote "voluntary parenthood," the government introduced prenatal care, free childbirth in a hospital, a food relief program, and subsidized housing for large families. By the end of the decade, almost 50 percent of all mothers in Sweden received government aid, most effectively in the form of a **family allowance** to help cover the costs of raising children. Long a concern of feminists and other

family allowance: Government funds given to families with children to boost the birthrate in democratic countries (e.g., Sweden during the Great Depression) and totalitarian ones alike.

A Fireside Chat with FDR
President Franklin Delano Roosevelt was a master of words, inspiring Americans during the depression and World War II. Aware of its growing power in making politicians look dynamic, the press never showed that Roosevelt was actually confined to a wheelchair (after being paralyzed by polio). Instead, FDR became a symbol of U.S. resolve and might. Here he addresses the nation over a radio hookup on August 23, 1938, while First Lady Eleanor Roosevelt and the president's mother, Sara, observe—a far different image from that of Hitler and Mussolini. *(Hulton Archive/Getty Images.)*

social reformers, support of families became a new feature of the modern state, which now involved itself in promoting citizen well-being. Because all families—rural and urban, poor or prosperous—received these social benefits, there was widespread approval for developing a welfare state.

Britain and France

The most powerful democracy, the United States, had withdrawn from world leadership by refusing to participate in the League of Nations, leaving Britain and France with greater responsibility for international peace and well-being than their postwar resources could sustain. When the Great Depression hit, British prime minister Ramsay MacDonald faced a drop in government income. Though leader of the Labour Party, MacDonald reduced payments to the unemployed, and Parliament denied unemployment insurance to women even though they had contributed to the unemployment fund. To protect jobs, the government imposed huge tariffs on imported goods, but these only discouraged a revival of international trade and did not relieve British misery. Finally, in 1933, with the economy continuing to worsen, the government began to take effective steps with massive programs of slum clearance, new housing construction, and health insurance for the needy. British leaders rejected pump-priming methods of stimulating the economy as foolish and thus resorted to them only when all else had failed.

Depression struck later in France, but the country endured a decade of public strife in the 1930s due to postwar demoralization and stagnant population growth. Deputies with opposing solutions to the economic crisis frequently came to blows in the Chamber of Deputies, and administrations were voted in and out with dizzying speed. Parisians took to the streets to protest the government's budget cuts, and Nazi-style paramilitary groups flourished, attracting the unemployed, students, and veterans to the cause of ending representative government. In February 1934, the paramilitary groups joined Communists and other outraged citizens in riots around the parliament building. "Let's string up the deputies," chanted the crowd. "And if we can't string them up, let's beat in their faces, let's reduce them to a pulp." Hundreds of demonstrators were wounded and killed, but the right-wing enemies of democratic government lacked both substantial support outside Paris and a charismatic leader like Hitler or Mussolini to follow.

Shocked into action by fascist violence, French liberals, socialists, and Communists established an antifascist coalition known as the **Popular Front**. Until that time, such a merging of groups had been impossible because Stalin had directed Communists across Europe not to cooperate with other political parties. As fascism attracted followers around the world, however, Stalin reversed his earlier position and allowed Communists to join efforts to protect

Popular Front: An alliance of political parties (initially led by Léon Blum in France) in the 1930s to resist fascism despite philosophical differences.

democracy. For just over a year in 1936–1937 and again briefly in 1938, the French Popular Front led the government, with the socialist leader Léon Blum as premier. Like the American New Dealers and the Swedish reformers, the Popular Front instituted social-welfare programs, including family subsidies. Blum appointed women to his government (though women in France were still not allowed to vote). In June 1936, the government guaranteed workers two-week paid vacations, a forty-hour workweek, and the right to bargain collectively. Working people would long remember Blum as the man who improved their living standards and provided them with the right to vacations.

During its brief life, the Popular Front offered citizens a youthful but democratic political culture. "In 1936 everyone was twenty years old," one man recalled, evoking the atmosphere of idealism. To express their opposition to fascism, the French celebrated democratic holidays like Bastille Day with new enthusiasm. Not everyone liked the Popular Front, however, and despite support from workers, Léon Blum's government was politically weak. Bankers and industrialists sent their money out of the country in protest, leaving France financially strapped. "Better Hitler than Blum" was the slogan of the upper classes. Blum's government fell when it lost crucial support for refusing to aid the fight against fascism in Spain. Because of antiwar sentiment, France, like Britain, kept military budgets small and refused any form of military confrontation, even to help the new Spanish republic survive. The collapse of the antifascist Popular Front showed the difficulties that democratic societies had facing the revival of militarism during hard economic times.

Central and Eastern Europe

Fledgling democracies in central Europe, hit hard by the depression, also fought the twin struggle for economic survival and representative government, but with little success. In 1932, Engelbert Dollfuss came to power in Austria, dismissing the parliament and ruling briefly as a dictator. Despite his authoritarian stance, Dollfuss would not submit to the Nazis, who stormed his office and assassinated him in 1934 in an unsuccessful coup attempt. In Hungary, where outrage over the Peace of Paris remained intense, a crippled economy allowed right-wing general Gyula Gömbös to take over in 1932. Gömbös reoriented his country's foreign policy toward Mussolini and Hitler. He stirred up anti-Semitism and ethnic hatreds and left considerable pro-Nazi feeling after his death in 1936. In democratic Czechoslovakia, the Slovaks, who were both poorer and less educated than the urbanized Czechs, built a strong Slovak Fascist Party. In many of the new states created by the Peace of Paris, ethnic tensions simmered and the appeal of fascism grew during the Great Depression.

Cultural Visions in Hard Times

Responding to the crisis of hard times and political menace, cultural leaders produced art that captured the spirit of everyday struggle. Some sympathized with the situations of factory workers, homemakers, and shopgirls straining to support themselves and their families; others looked to interpret the lives of an ever-growing number of unemployed and destitute. Artists portrayed the inhuman, regimented, heartless side of modern life. In 1931, French director René Clair's film *Give Us Liberty* likened the routine of prison to work on a factory assembly line. In the film *Modern Times* (1936), the Little Tramp character created by **Charlie Chaplin** is a factory worker so molded by his monotonous job that he assumes anything he can see, even a coworker's body, needs mechanical adjustment.

Media sympathy poured out to other victims of the crisis, with women portrayed alternately as the cause and as the cure for society's problems. *The Blue Angel* (1930), a German film starring Marlene Dietrich, contrasted a powerfully seductive woman with an impractical, bumbling professor, showing how mixed-up gender roles could destroy men—and civilization. Such films worked to strengthen fascist claims. In comedies and musicals, by comparison, heroines behaved bravely, pulling their men out of the depths of despair and setting things right again. In such films as *Keep Smiling* (1938), the British comedienne Gracie Fields portrayed spunky working-class women who remained cheerful despite the challenges of living in hard times. Two years later, Chaplin mocked Hitler in his classic satire *The Great Dictator* (1940), which took a beleaguered Jewish woman as its heroine.

To drive home their antifascist, pacifist, or pro-worker beliefs, writers created realistic studies of human misery and the threat of war that haunted life in the 1930s. The British writer George Orwell described his experiences among the poor of Paris and London, wrote investigative pieces about the unemployed in the north of England, and published an account of atrocities committed by both sides during the Spanish Civil War (1936–1939). German writer Thomas Mann, a Christian, was so

Charlie Chaplin (1889–1977): Major entertainment leader, whose sympathetic portrayals of the common man and satires of Hitler helped preserve democratic values in the 1930s and 1940s.

Gracie Fields Keeps Smiling
Like Roosevelt and many cultural leaders during the Great Depression, British star Gracie Fields in the hit film *Shipyard Sally* (1939) urged viewers to be courageous and maintain their respect as workers and citizens despite hard times. This was in stark contrast to fascist advocacy of conquest, war, and violence toward neighbors at home and abroad. *(20th Century Fox/The Kobal Collection.)*

outraged at Hitler's ascent to power that he went into voluntary exile. Mann's series of novels based on the Old Testament hero Joseph convey the struggle between humane values and barbarism. The fourth volume, *Joseph the Provider* (1944), praised Joseph's welfare state, in which the granaries were full and the rich paid taxes so that the poor might live decent lives. In *Three Guineas* (1938), one of her last works, English writer Virginia Woolf attacked militarism, poverty, and the oppression of women, claiming they were interconnected parts of a single, devastating ethos undermining Europe in the 1930s.

While writers revived moral concerns, scientists in research institutes and universities pointed out limits to human understanding—limits that seemed at odds with the megalomaniacal pronouncements of dictators. Astronomer Edwin Hubble in California determined in the early 1930s that the universe was an expanding entity and thus an unpredictably changing one. Czech mathematician Kurt Gödel maintained that all mathematical systems contain some propositions that are undecidable. The German physicist Werner Heisenberg developed the uncertainty, or indeterminacy, principle in physics. Scientific observation of atomic behavior, according to this theory, itself disturbs the atom and thereby makes precise formulations impossible. Even scientists, Heisenberg asserted, had to settle for statistical probability. Approximation, probability, and limits to understanding were not concepts that military dictators welcomed, and even people in democracies had a difficult time reconciling these new ideas with science's reputation for certainty.

Religious leaders helped foster a spirit of resistance to dictatorship among the faithful. Some prominent clergymen hoped for a re-Christianization of ordinary people so that they might choose religious values rather than fascist ones. The Swiss theologian Karl Barth encouraged opposition to the Nazis, teaching that religious people had to take seriously biblical calls for resistance to oppression. In his 1931 address to the world on social issues, Pope Pius XI (r. 1922–1939) condemned the failure of modern societies to provide their citizens with a decent, moral life. To critics, the proclamation seemed an endorsement of the heavy-handed intervention of the fascists. In Germany, nonetheless, German Catholics opposed Hitler, and religious commitment inspired many other individuals to oppose the rising tide of fascism and protect Jews and other fellow citizens whose lives were now threatened.

REVIEW QUESTION How did the democracies' responses to the twin challenges of economic depression and the rise of fascism differ from those of totalitarian regimes?

The Road to Global War

The economic crash intensified competition among the major powers and made external colonies more important than ever. Governments did not let up on the collection of taxes in the colonies. As Britain, France, and other imperial powers guarded their holdings, Hitler, Mussolini, and Japan's military leaders believed that their nation's destiny was to rule a far larger territory. At first, statesmen in Britain and France hoped that sanctions imposed by the League of Nations would stop these aggressors. Other people, still traumatized by memories of the past war, wanted to turn a blind eye both to Japanese, Italian, and German expansionism and to the fascist attack on the Spanish republic. The unchecked brutality of these states in the 1930s led to another, more deadly global war.

A Surge in Global Imperialism

The global imperialism of the 1930s ultimately produced a thoroughly global war. The French, Dutch, British, and Belgians increased their control over their colonies, while in Palestine European Jews continued to arrive and claim the area from local peoples especially as Hitler enacted his harsh anti-Jewish policies in 1933. To prevent the arrival of Jews in their own countries, the major European states encouraged emigration to Palestine even as local leaders there regarded the soaring number of immigrants as a major threat. Straining like the colonial powers for resources, including food, at a time of modernization and growing need, Japan, Germany, and Italy escalated the competition for land and wealth—both close at hand and far away.

Japan's Expansionism

Japan, which had once borrowed from European institutions to become modern and powerful, now decided to chase Europeans from Asia. Japan's military and business leaders longed to control more of the continent and saw China, the Soviet Union, and the Western powers as obstacles to the empire's prosperity and the fulfillment of its destiny. Japan suffered from a weak monarchy in the person of Hirohito, just twenty-five years old when he became emperor in 1926, which led military and other groups to seek control of the government. Nationalists encouraged these leaders to pursue military success for Japan as the basis of a new world order. They viewed an expanded empire as key to pulling agriculture and small business from the depths of economic depression. A belief in racial superiority and in the right to take the lands of "inferior" peoples linked Japan with Germany and Italy in the 1930s. The groundwork was being laid for a powerful global alliance.

The Japanese army swung into action in 1931, when Japanese officers blew up a train in the Chinese province of Manchuria, where Japanese businesses had invested heavily. The army made the explosion look like a Chinese plot and used it as an excuse to take over the territory, set up a puppet government, and push farther into China (Map 26.1). The Japanese public agreed with journalistic calls for aggressive expansion, and from 1931 on, Japan continued to attack China, angering the United States, on which Japan depended for natural resources and markets. The Japanese military leadership saw its expansionism as fully justified because of unfair Western domination in East Asia. "Unequal distribution of land and resources causes war," an adviser to Hirohito announced to an enthusiastic Japanese public. Advocating Asian conquest as part of Japan's "divine mission," the military solidified its influence in the government. By 1936–1937, Japan was spending 47 percent of its budget on arms.

The situation in East Asia affected international politics. Japanese military success added to the threat Japan posed to the West, because the conquest of new regions gave Japanese goods bigger markets in Asia. The League of Nations condemned the invasion of Manchuria but imposed no sanctions. The league's condemnation outraged Japanese citizens and goaded the government to ally with Hitler and Mussolini. In 1937, Japan attacked China again, justifying its offensive as a first step toward liberating the region from Western imperialism. Hundreds of thousands of Chinese were massacred in the Rape of Nanjing—an atrocity so named because of the Japanese soldiers' brutality, especially toward girls and women. President Roosevelt immediately announced a U.S. embargo on the exportation of airplane parts to Japan and later drastically cut the flow of the crucial raw materials that supplied Japanese industry. Nonetheless, the Western powers, including the Soviet Union, did not effectively resist Japan's territorial expansion in Asia and the Pacific (see Document, "The Greater East Asia Co-Prosperity Sphere," page 892).

Germany and Italy Contest the Status Quo

Like Japanese leaders, Mussolini and Hitler called their countries "have-nots" and demanded land and resources more in line with the other imperial powers. Mussolini threatened "permanent conflict" to expand Italy's borders. Hitler's agenda included disregarding the Versailles treaty's restrictions and gaining

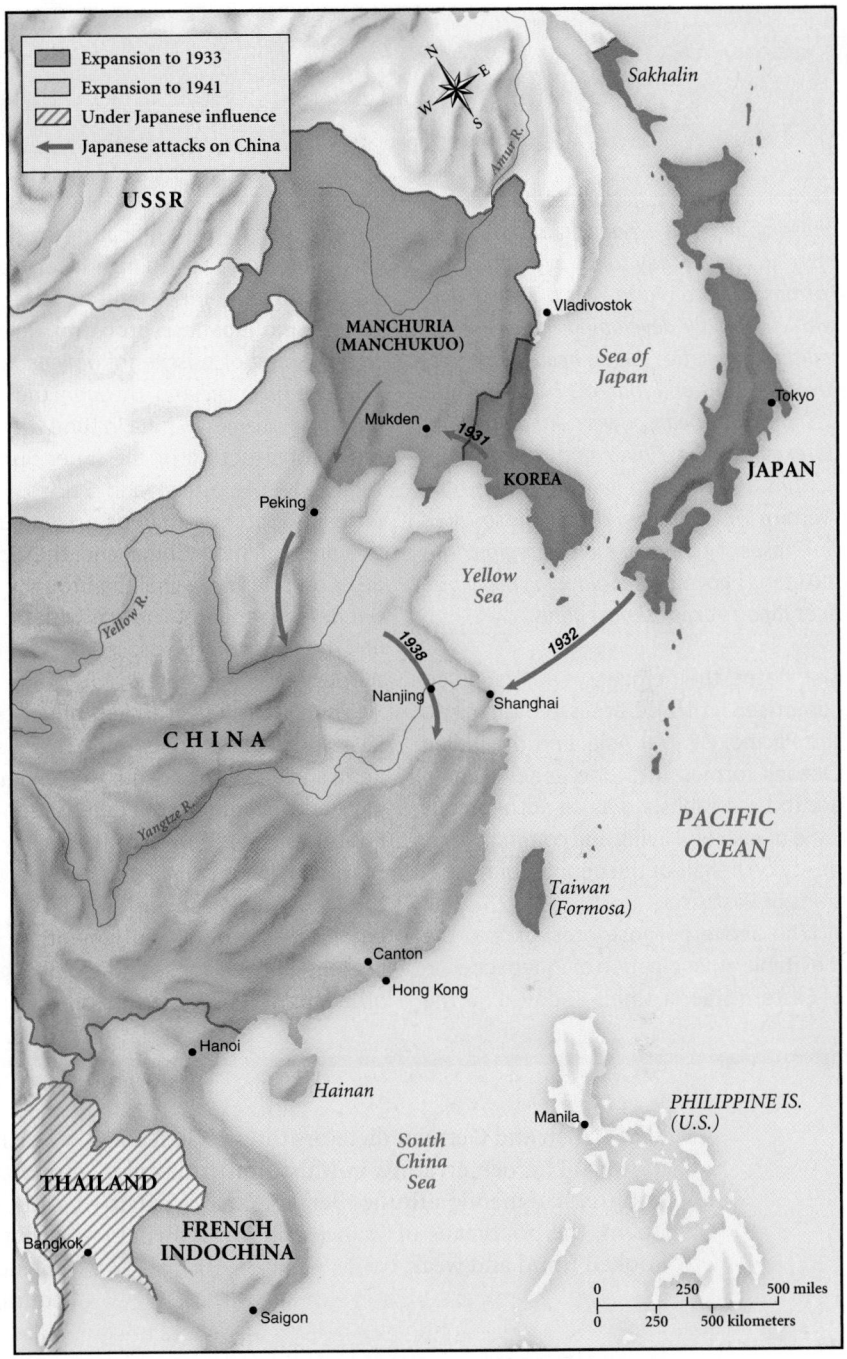

MAP 26.1 The Expansion of Japan, 1931–1941
Japanese expansion in the twentieth century approximated that of Russia and the United States in the nineteenth century; that is, it incorporated neighboring regions of Korea, Taiwan, and Manchuria with the vast area of China an inviting target. Japan's ambition upset the United States' own Pacific goals and made these two powers suddenly become deadly rivals.

Lebensraum, or living space, in which "superior" Aryans could thrive. This space would be taken from the "inferior" Slavic peoples and Bolsheviks, who would be moved to Siberia or would serve as slaves. The two dictators portrayed themselves as peace-loving men who resorted to extreme measures only to benefit their country and humanity. Their anticommunism appealed to statesmen across the West, and Hitler's anti-Semitism also had widespread support. Many thus favored these two dictators' demands to take land and resources that belonged to others.

Germany and Italy now moved to plunder other countries openly. In the autumn of 1933, Hitler announced Germany's withdrawal from the League of Nations. In 1935, he loudly rejected the clauses of the Treaty of Versailles that limited German military strength. Germany had been rearming in secret for years, but now it started doing so openly. Mussolini chose 1935 to invade Ethiopia, one of the few African states not overwhelmed by European imperialism. He wanted to demonstrate his regime's youth and vigor and to raise Italy's standing in the world. "The Roman legionnaires are again on the march," one soldier exulted. The poorly equipped Ethiopians resisted, but their capital, Addis Ababa, fell in the spring of 1936. Although the League of Nations voted to impose sanctions against Italy, Britain and France opposed an embargo with teeth in it—that is, one including oil—and thus kept the sanctions from being effective while also suggesting a lack of resolve to fight aggression. The fall of Ethiopia and Italy's boastful assertions of African racial inferiority strengthened the resolve of African nationalists.

While the world focused on Italy's Ethiopian campaign, in March 1936 Hitler defiantly sent his troops into what was supposed to be a permanently demilitarized zone in the Rhineland bordering France. The inhabitants greeted the arrival with wild enthusiasm, and the French, whose security was most endangered by this action, protested to the League of Nations instead of occupying the region, as they had done in the Ruhr in 1923. The British simply accepted the German military move.

Lebensraum: Literally, "living space"; the land that Hitler proposed to conquer so that the people he defined as true Aryans might have sufficient space to live their noble lives.

DOCUMENT

The Greater East Asia Co-Prosperity Sphere

During the 1930s, Japan entered a new phase of imperial expansion in the Pacific, after having already taken over Korea and Formosa before World War I. To keep pace with its rapidly developing industrial and military capacities, Japan needed access to raw materials and markets blocked by the U.S. and European powers. Japan justified its expansion in China and other Pacific nations as a move to liberate Asians from Western imperialism and form the so-called Co-Prosperity Sphere for the region. This secret 1942 government planning paper outlines Japan's expansionist goals.

The states, their citizens, and resources, comprised in those areas pertaining to the Pacific, Central Asia, and the Indian Oceans formed into one general union are to be established as an autonomous zone of peaceful living and common prosperity on behalf of the peoples of the nations of East Asia. . . .

The above purpose presupposes the inevitable emancipation or independence of Eastern Siberia, China, Indo-China, the South Seas, Australia, and India. . . . It is intended that the unification of Japan, Manchoukuo, and China in neighborly friendship be realized by the settlement of the Sino-Japanese problems through the crushing of hostile influences in the Chinese interior, and through the construction of a new China in tune with the rapid construction of the Inner Sphere. Aggressive American and British influences in East Asia shall be driven out of the area of Indo-China and the South Seas, and this area shall be brought into our defense sphere. The war with Britain and America shall be prosecuted for that purpose.

The Russian aggressive influence in East Asia will be driven out. Eastern Siberia shall be cut off from the Soviet regime and included in our defense sphere. For this purpose, a war with the Soviets is expected. It is considered possible that this Northern problem may break out before the general settlement of the present Sino-Japanese and the Southern problems if the situation renders this unavoidable. Next the independence of Australia, India, etc. shall gradually be brought about. For this purpose, a recurrence of war with Britain and her allies is expected. . . . Occidental individualism and materialism shall be rejected and a moral world view, the basic principle of whose morality shall be the Imperial Way, shall be established. The ultimate object to be achieved is not exploitation but co-prosperity and mutual help, not competitive conflict but mutual assistance and mild peace, not a formal view of equality but a view of order based on righteous classification, not an idea of rights but an idea of service, and not several world views but one unified world view.

Source: Ryusaku Tsunoda, William Theodore de Bary, and Donald Keene, *Sources of Japanese Tradition* (New York: Columbia University Press, 1958) 802–3, 805.

Question to Consider

- **Although the Japanese government claimed to be acting in the interest of other Asian countries, what language in this document suggests that it had different motives in mind?**

The Italian and German dictators thus appeared as powerful heroes, creating, in Mussolini's muscular phrase, a dynamic "Rome–Berlin Axis." Next to them, the politicians of France and Great Britain looked timid and weak.

The Spanish Civil War, 1936–1939

Spain seemed to be headed toward democracy early in the 1930s. In 1931, Spanish republicans overthrew the monarchy and the dictatorship that ruled in its name. For centuries, the Spanish state had backed the domination of large landowners and the Catholic clergy in the countryside. With some cities, like Barcelona and Bilbao, industrializing, these ruling elites kept an impoverished peasantry in their grip, making Spain a country of economic extremes. Urban people reacted enthusiastically to the end of the dictatorship and began debating the course of change, with constitutionalists, socialists, anarchists, Communists, and other splinter groups disagreeing on how to create a democratic nation. For republicans, the air was electric with promise. As public debate developed, one woman recalled, people sat for hours dreaming dreams: "We saw a backward country suddenly blossoming out into a modern state. We saw peasants living like decent human beings. We saw men allowed freedom of conscience. We saw life, instead of death, in Spain."

With little political experience, however, democratic groups so battled one another to get their way that the republic had a hard time putting in place a political program that would gain support in the countryside. Instead of building popular loyalty and reducing the strength of the right wing by enacting land reform, the various antimonarchist factions struggled among themselves to shape the new government. They wanted political and economic modernization, but they failed to mount a unified effort against their reactionary opponents. The republicans resorted instead to symbolic acts such as releasing political prisoners and handing out coveted mu-

Bombing of Barcelona, 1938
The Spanish Civil War gave fair warning that major wars to come would target civilians as well as soldiers. The forces aiming to overthrow the republic, with the aid of their Fascist allies in Germany and Italy, bombed cities large and small without regard to civilians. This indiscriminate bombing shocked the democracies, though not enough for any of them to intervene. *(AP Photo.)*

nicipal jobs to the urban unemployed. In 1936, growing monarchist opposition frightened the pro-republican forces into forming a Popular Front coalition to win elections and prevent the republic from collapsing.

In response to the Popular Front victory, the forces of the right drew closer together, using their considerable wealth to undermine the government. In 1936, a group of army officers led by General **Francisco Franco** (1892–1975) staged an uprising against the republic in Madrid. The rebels, who included monarchist landowners, the clergy, and the fascist Falange Party, soon had the help of fascists in other parts of Europe. Pro-republican citizens—male and female—fought back, forming armed volunteer units to meet the grave military challenge. In their minds, citizen armies symbolized republicanism, while professional troops followed the aristocratic rebels against democracy. As civil war gripped the country, the republicans generally held Madrid, Barcelona, and other commercial and industrial areas. The right-wing rebels took the agricultural west and south (Map 26.2).

Francisco Franco (1892–1975): Right-wing general who in 1936 successfully overthrew the democratic republic in Spain and instituted a repressive dictatorship.

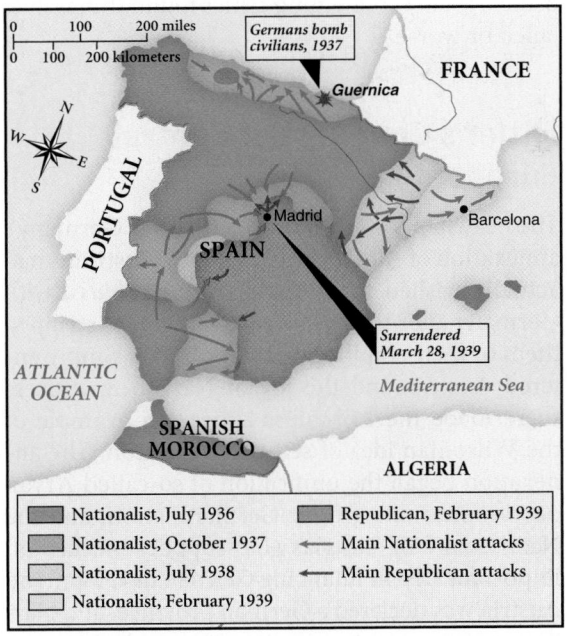

MAP 26.2 The Spanish Civil War, 1936–1939
Republican and antirepublican forces bitterly fought one another to determine whether Spain would be a democracy or an authoritarian state. Germany and Italy sent military assistance to the rebels, notably airplanes to experiment with bombing civilians, while volunteers from around the world arrived to fight for the republic. Defeating the ill-organized republican groups, General Francisco Franco instituted a pro-fascist government that sent many to jail and into exile.

Spain became a training ground for World War II. Hitler and Mussolini sent military personnel in support of Franco, gaining the opportunity to test new weapons and to practice the terror bombing of civilians. In 1937, German planes attacked the town of Guernica, mowing down civilians in the streets. This useless slaughter inspired Pablo Picasso's memorial mural to the dead, *Guernica* (1937), in which the intense suffering is starkly displayed in monochromatic grays and whites. The Spanish republic appealed everywhere for assistance, but only the Soviet Union answered. Stalin withdrew his troops and tanks in 1938 as the republican ranks floundered, however, while Britain and France refused to provide aid despite the outpouring of popular support for the cause of democracy. Instead, a few thousand volunteers from a variety of countries—including many students, journalists, and artists—fought for the republic. With Hitler and Mussolini on a rampage in Europe, "Spain was the place to stop fascism," these volunteers believed. The conflict was bitter and bloody, with widespread atrocities committed on both sides. The splinter groups and random armies with which the Republic defended itself could not hold, however. The aid Franco received helped his professional armies defeat the republicans in 1939, strengthening the cause of military authoritarianism in Europe. Tens of thousands fled Franco's brutal revenge; remaining critics found themselves jailed or worse.

Hitler's Conquest of Central Europe, 1938–1939

The next step toward World War II was Germany's annexation of Austria in 1938. Many Austrians had actually wished for a merger, or *Anschluss*, with Germany after the Paris peace settlement stripped them of their empire. So Hitler's troops simply entered Austria, and the joy of Nazi sympathizers there made the Anschluss appear an example of the Wilsonian idea of self-determination. The annexation began the unification of so-called Aryan peoples into one greater German nation, and the Nazi seizure of Austria's gold supplies marked an important step in financing German development. Austria was declared a German province, and Nazi thugs ruled once-cosmopolitan Vienna. An observer later commented on the scene:

> University professors were obliged to scrub the streets with their naked hands, pious white-bearded Jews were dragged into the synagogue by hooting youths and forced to do knee-exercises and to shout "Heil Hitler" in chorus.

Nazis gained additional support in Austria by attacking the stubborn problem of unemployment—especially among the young and out-of-work rural migrants to the cities. Factories sprang up overnight, mostly to foster rearmament, and new "Hitler housing" was made available to workers. "We were given work!" Austrians continued to say long afterward, defending their enthusiasm for the Third Reich. German policies eliminated some of the pain Austrians had suffered when their empire had been reduced to a small country after World War I.

With Austria firmly in his grasp, Hitler turned next to Czechoslovakia and its rich resources. Conquering this democracy looked more difficult, however, because Czechoslovakia had a large army, strong border defenses, and efficient armament factories—and most Czech citizens were prepared to fight for their country. The Nazi propaganda machine swung into action, accusing Czechoslovakia of persecuting its German minority. By October 1, 1938, Hitler warned, Czechoslovakia would have to grant autonomy (amounting to Nazi rule) to the German-populated border region, the Sudetenland, or face German invasion.

Hitler gambled correctly that the other Western powers would choose **appeasement**, the prevention of conflict by making concessions for grievances (in this case, the treatment of Germany in the Treaty of Versailles). As the October deadline approached, British prime minister Neville Chamberlain, French premier Edouard Daladier, and Mussolini met with Hitler at Munich and agreed not to oppose Germany's claim to the Sudetenland. Appeasement was widely seen as positive at the time, and the Munich Pact prompted Chamberlain to announce that he had secured "peace in our time." Having portrayed himself as a man of peace, Hitler waited until March 1939 to invade the rest of Czechoslovakia (Map 26.3). Britain and France responded by promising military support to Poland, Romania, Greece, and Turkey in case of Nazi invasion. In May 1939, Hitler and Mussolini countered this agreement by signing a pledge of mutual assistance called the Pact of Steel.

Some historians have sharply criticized the Munich Pact because it bought Hitler time to build his army and seemed to give him the green light for further aggression. They believe that a confrontation might have stopped Hitler and that even if war had resulted, the democracies would have triumphed at less cost than they later did. According to this view, each military move by Germany, Italy,

---

appeasement: Making concessions in the face of grievances as a way of preventing conflict.

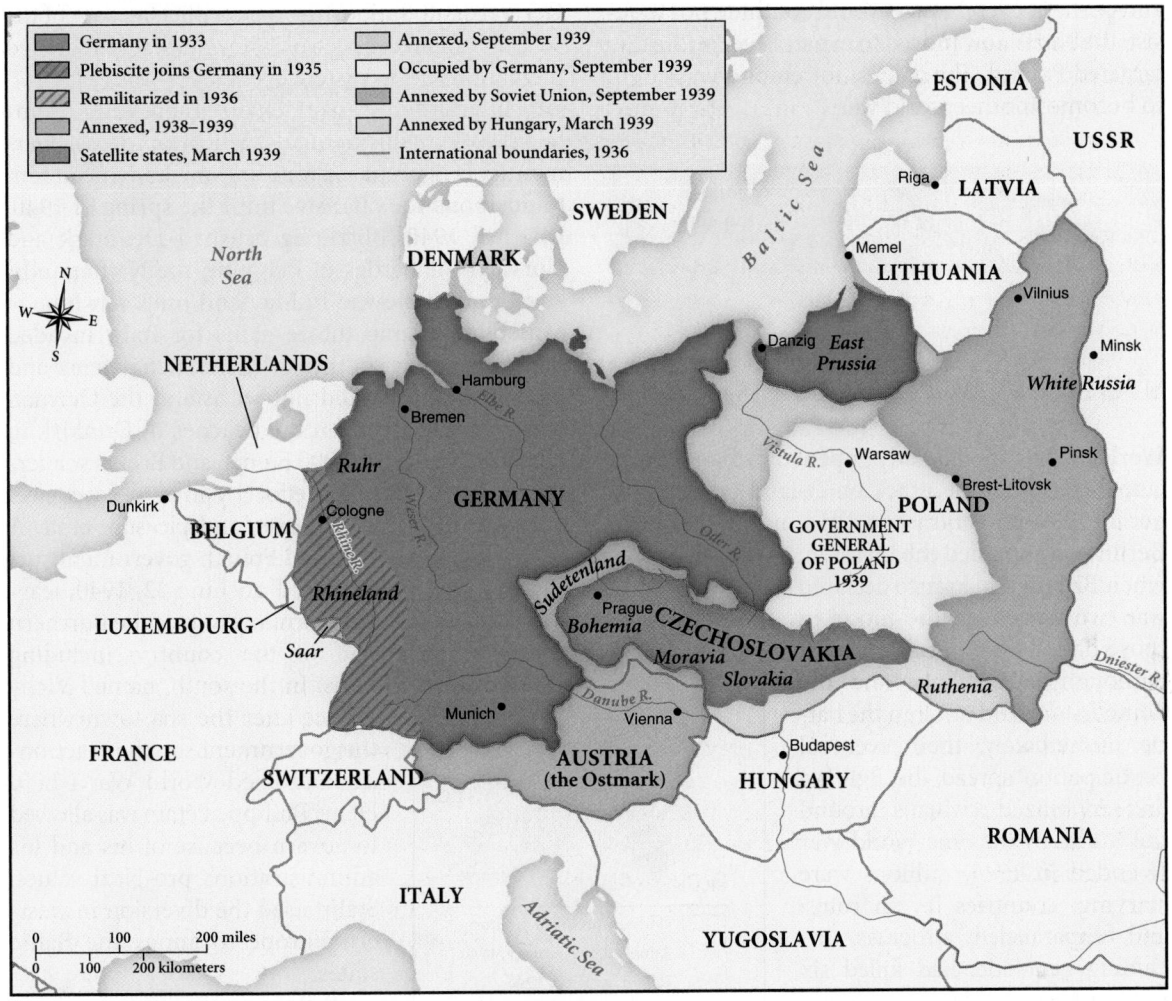

MAP 26.3 The Growth of Nazi Germany, 1933–1939

German expansion was rapid and surprising, as Hitler's forces and Nazi diplomacy achieved the annexation of several new states of central and eastern Europe. Although committed to defending the independence of these states through the League of Nations, French and British diplomats were more concerned with satisfying Hitler in the mistaken belief that doing so would prevent his claiming more of Europe. In the process, Hitler acquired the human and material resources of adjacent countries to support his Third Reich. | **What is the relationship between Germany's expansion during the 1930s and the terms of the Treaty of Versailles after World War I?**

and Japan should have been met with stiff opposition, and the Soviet Union should have been made a partner to this resistance. Others counter that appeasement provided France and Britain precious time to beef up their own armies, which the Munich Pact led them to do.

Stalin, excluded from the Munich deliberations, saw that the democracies were not going to fight to protect eastern Europe. He took action. To the astonishment of people in the West, on August 23, 1939, Germany and the USSR signed a nonaggression agreement. The **Nazi-Soviet Pact** provided that if one country became embroiled in war, the other country would remain neutral. Moreover, the two dictators secretly agreed to divide Poland and the Baltic states—Latvia, Estonia, and Lithuania—at some future date. The Nazi-Soviet Pact ensured that, should war come, the democracies would be fighting a Germany that feared no attack on its eastern borders. The pact also benefited the USSR. Despite Hitler's threats to wipe Bolshevism from the face of the earth, the pact allowed Stalin extra time to reconstitute his officer corps, which had been wiped out by the purges. In the belief that Great Britain

Nazi-Soviet Pact: The agreement reached in 1939 by Germany and the Soviet Union in which both agreed not to attack the other in case of war and to divide any conquered territories.

and perhaps even France would continue not to resist, the Nazis now moved to expand even more and targeted Poland. The contest for empire was about to become another world war.

REVIEW QUESTION How did the aggression of Japan, Germany, and Italy create the conditions for global war?

World War II, 1939–1945

World War II officially opened when Hitler launched an all-out attack on Poland on September 1, 1939. In contrast to 1914, no jubilation in Berlin accompanied the invasion; when Britain and France declared war two days later, the mood in those nations was similarly grim. Although Japan, Italy, and the United States did not join the battle immediately, their eventual participation spread the fighting and mobilized civilians around the world. By the time World War II ended in 1945, millions were starving; countries lay in ruins; and unparalleled atrocities, including genocide, had killed six million Jews and six million Slavs, Sinti and Roma, homosexuals, and other civilian targets of fascism.

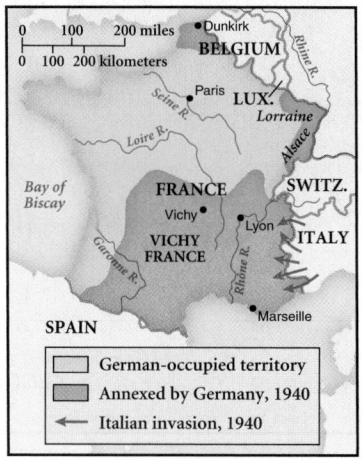

The Division of France, 1940

The German Onslaught

German forces quickly defeated the ill-equipped Polish troops by launching a **Blitzkrieg** ("lightning war"), in which they concentrated airplanes, tanks, and motorized infantry to encircle Polish defenders and capture the capital, Warsaw, with overpowering force and blinding speed. Allowing the army to conserve supplies, Blitzkrieg suggested to Germans at home that the costs of gaining Lebensraum would be low. On September 17, 1939, the Soviets invaded Poland from the east. By the end of the month, the Polish army was in shambles and the victors had divided the country according to the Nazi-Soviet Pact. Nazi propagandists frightened Germans into supporting the conflict because of the "warlike menace" of world Jewry that threatened the nation's very existence.

Hitler ordered an attack on France for November 1939, but his generals, who feared that Germany was ill prepared for total war, convinced him to postpone the offensive until the spring of 1940. In April 1940, Blitzkrieg crushed Denmark and Norway; the battles of Belgium, the Netherlands, and France followed in May and June. On June 5, Mussolini, eyeing future gains for Italy, invaded France from the southeast. The French defense and its British allies could not withstand the German onslaught. Trapped on the beaches of Dunkirk in northern France, 370,000 French and British soldiers were rescued in a heroic effort by an improvised fleet of naval ships, fishing boats, and pleasure craft. A dejected French government surrendered on June 22, 1940, leaving Germany to rule the northern half of the country, including Paris. In the south, named Vichy France after the spa town where the government sat, the reactionary and aged World War I hero Henri Philippe Pétain was allowed to govern because of his and his administration's pro-Nazi values. Stalin used the diversion in western Europe to annex the Baltic states.

Britain now stood alone. Blaming Germany's rapid victories on Chamberlain's policy of appeasement, the British swept him out of office and installed as prime minister Winston Churchill (1874–1965), an early campaigner for resistance to Hitler. After Hitler ordered the bombardment of Britain in the summer of 1940, Churchill rallied the nation by radio—now in millions of British homes—to protect the ideals of liberty with their "blood, toil, tears, and sweat." In the battle of Britain—or Blitz, as the British called it—the German Luftwaffe ("air force") bombed monuments, public buildings, weapons depots, and industry. Using the wealth of its colonies, Britain poured resources into antiaircraft weapons, its highly successful code-breaking group called Ultra, and further development of radar. At year's end, the British air industry was outproducing the Germans by 50 percent.

By the fall of 1940, German air losses forced Hitler to abandon his plan for a naval invasion of Britain. By forcing Hungary, Romania, and Bulgaria to join the Axis powers, Germany gained access to more food, oil, and other resources. He then made

Blitzkrieg: Literally, "lightning war"; a strategy for the conduct of war (used by the Germans in World War II) in which motorized firepower quickly and overwhelmingly attacks the enemy, leaving it unable to resist psychologically or militarily.

his fatal decision to attack the Soviet Union—the "center of judeobolshevism," he called it. In June 1941, the German army crossed the Soviet border, breaking the Nazi-Soviet Pact, and Hitler promised to "raze Moscow and Leningrad to the ground." Three million German and other troops quickly penetrated Soviet lines along a two-thousand-mile front, and by July, the German army had rolled to within two hundred miles of Moscow. Using a strategy of rapid encirclement, German troops killed, captured, or wounded more than half the 4.5 million Soviet soldiers defending the border.

Amid success, Hitler blundered. Considering himself a military genius and the Slavic people inferior, he proposed attacking Leningrad, the Baltic states, and the Ukraine simultaneously, even though his generals wanted to concentrate on Moscow. Hitler's grandiose strategy cost precious time without achieving a decisive victory, and driven by Stalin and local party members, the Soviet people fought back. The onset of winter turned Nazi soldiers into frostbitten wretches because Hitler had feared that equipping his army for Russian conditions would suggest to civilians that a long campaign lay ahead. Yet Hitler remained so convinced of a quick victory in the USSR that he switched German production from making tanks and artillery to making battleships and airplanes for war beyond the Soviet Union. Consequently, Germany's poorly supplied armies fell victim not only to the weather but also to a shortage of equipment. As the war became worldwide, Germany had an inflated view of its own power even though the Russian campaign demonstrated that this view was a fantasy.

War Expands: The Pacific and Beyond

With the outbreak of war in Europe, Japan occupied territories of the British Empire and invaded French Indochina to procure raw materials for its industrial and military expansion. The militarist Japanese government decided to settle matters once and for all with the United States, which was blocking Japan's access to technology and resources in an attempt to stop its expansionism. On December 7, 1941, it launched an all-out attack on the United States at Pearl Harbor in Hawaii. After bombing Pearl Harbor, Japanese planes then decimated a fleet of airplanes in the Philippines. Roosevelt immediately summoned the U.S. Congress to declare war on Japan. By the spring of 1942, the Japanese had conquered Guam, the Philippines, Malaya, Burma, Indonesia, Singapore, and much of the southwestern Pacific. Like Hitler's early conquests, the Japanese victories strengthened the military's confidence: "The era of democracy is finished," the foreign minister announced. Officials marketed Emperor Hirohito to conquered peoples as the pan-Asian monarch who would liberate Asians everywhere.

Germany quickly joined its Japanese ally and declared war on the United States—an enemy, Hitler proclaimed, that was "half Judaized and the other half Negrified." Mussolini followed suit. The United States was not prepared for a prolonged struggle at the time, partly because isolationist sentiment remained strong. Its armed forces numbered only 1.6 million, and no plan existed for producing the necessary guns, tanks, and airplanes. In addition, the United States and the Soviet Union mistrusted each other. Yet despite these obstacles to cooperation, Hitler's four enemies came together in the Grand Alliance of Great Britain, the Free French (an exile government in London led by General Charles de Gaulle), the Soviet Union, and the United States.

The Grand Alliance formed a larger coalition with twenty other countries—known collectively as the Allies. It had to overcome animosity and competing interests among its members in its struggle against the Axis powers—Germany, Italy, and Japan. Yet in the long run, the Allies had advantages: greater manpower and resources and access to goods from their global empires. The globalization of the war brought into play Britain's traditional naval strength and its leaders' and troops' experience in combat on many continents. Meeting frequently, Allied leaders worked hard to wage effective war against the Axis powers, whose rulers were fanatically committed to global conquest at any price.

The War against Civilians

Far more civilians than soldiers died in World War II. The Axis powers and Allies alike bombed cities simply to destroy civilian will to resist—a tactic that seemed to backfire by inspiring defiance rather than surrender. Two such Allied attacks were the firebombing of Dresden and Tokyo, which killed tens of thousands of civilians, though Axis attacks were more widespread. The British people, not British soldiers, were the target of the battle of Britain, and as the German army swept through eastern Europe, it slaughtered Jews, Communists, Slavs, and others Nazi ideology defined as "racial inferiors" and enemies. In Poland and Ukraine, the SS murdered hundreds of thousands of Polish citizens or relocated them to forced-labor camps. Confiscated Polish land and homes were given to "racially pure" Aryans from Germany and other central European countries. In the name of collectivization, Soviet

Life in the Warsaw Ghetto
The occupying Nazis resettled Warsaw's Jews into a minuscule area of the city in order, the Germans explained, to bring moral purification and to keep Germans from being infected by these "carriers of the bacteria of epidemics." Living with bare amounts of food, Warsaw's Jews died daily on the streets. Corpses were a regular sight for the average citizen—young or old. *(ullstein bild/The Granger Collection, New York.)*

forces perpetuated the same violence in the same area of eastern Europe, which has been called the Bloodlands for the millions who died there at the hands of both Nazis and Soviets.

Nazi and Soviet leaders saw literate people in the conquered areas as leading members of the civil society that they wanted to destroy. A ploy of the Nazis was to test captured people's reading skills, suggesting that those who could read would be given clerical jobs while those who could not would be relegated to hard labor. Those who could read, however, were lined up and shot. Because many in the German army initially rebelled at this inhuman mission, special Gestapo forces took up the charge of herding their victims into woods, to ravines, or even against town walls where they would be shot en masse. The Japanese did the same in China, in Southeast Asia, and on the islands in the Pacific. The number of casualties in China alone has been estimated at thirty million, with untold millions murdered elsewhere.

The Holocaust On the eve of war in 1939, Hitler had predicted "the destruction of the Jewish race in Europe." The Nazis' initial plan for reducing the Jewish population included driving Jews into urban ghettos, stripping them of their possessions, and making people live on minimal rations until they died of starvation or disease. There was also direct murder. Around Soviet towns, Jews were usually shot in pits, some of which they had been forced to dig themselves. After making people shed their clothes, which were put in ordered piles for later use, the Nazis killed ten thousand or more at a time, often with the help of local anti-Semitic volunteers. In Jedwabne, Poland, and surrounding towns in 1941, some eight hundred citizens on their own initiative beat and burned their Jewish neighbors to death and took their property—evidence that the Holocaust was not simply a Nazi initiative. However, the "Final Solution"—the Nazis' plan to murder all of Europe's Jews more systematically—was not yet fully under way.

An organized, technological system for rounding up Jews and transporting them to extermination sites had taken shape by the fall of 1941 and was formalized at a meeting in Wannsee, Germany, in January 1942. Although Hitler did not attend the meeting at Wannsee, his responsibility for the Holocaust is clear: he discussed the Final Solution's progress, issued oral directives for it, and made violent anti-Semitism a basis for Nazism from the beginning. Scientists, doctors, lawyers, government workers, and Nazi officials took initiative in making the Holocaust work. Six camps in Poland were developed specifically for the purposes of mass murder, though some, like Auschwitz-Birkenau, served as both extermination and labor camps (Map 26.4). Using techniques developed in the T4 project, which killed disabled and elderly people, the camp at Chelmno first gassed Christian Poles and Soviet prisoners of war. Specially designed crematoria for the mass burning of corpses started functioning in 1943. By then, Auschwitz had the capacity to burn

MAP 26.4 Concentration Camps and Extermination Sites in Europe

This map shows the major extermination sites and concentration camps in Europe, but the entire continent was dotted with thousands of lesser camps to which the victims of Nazism were transported. Some of these lesser camps were merely way stations on the path to ultimate extermination. In focusing on the major camps, historians often lose sight of the ways in which evidence of deportation and extermination blanketed Europe.

Children in Concentration Camps, c. 1945

When Germany undertook the Holocaust and ethnic cleansing, children of outcast groups were generally automatic victims, unless they seemed useful for medical experiments. Great numbers of children died of starvation in occupied and besieged areas or were killed when the Germans exacted reprisals for acts of resistance. Teenagers were used as slave laborers; the children in this picture may be older than they look because of starvation. *(Mary Evans/Alinari Archives.)*

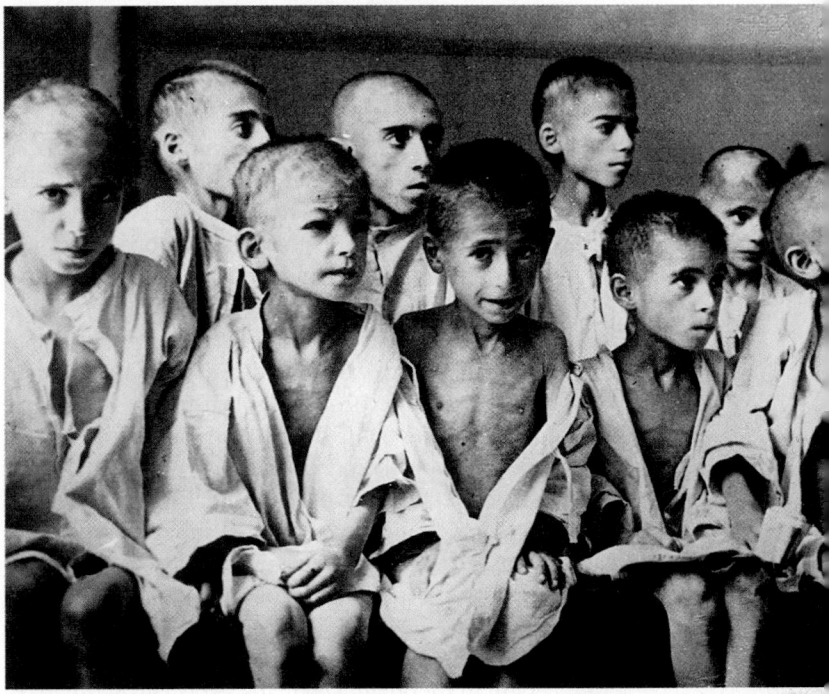

1.7 million bodies per year. About 60 percent of new arrivals—particularly children, women, and old people—were selected for immediate murder in the gas chambers; the other 40 percent labored until, utterly used up, they too were gassed.

Death and Life in the Camps

Victims from all over Europe were sent to extermination camps. In the ghettos of various European cities, councils of Jewish leaders, such as the one in Amsterdam where Etty Hillesum worked, were to choose those to be sent for "resettlement in the east"—a phrase used to mask the Nazis' true plans. For weakened, poorly armed ghetto inhabitants, open resistance meant certain death. When Jews rose up against their Nazi captors in Warsaw in 1943, they were mercilessly butchered. The Nazis also took pains to cloak the purpose of the extermination camps. Bands played to greet incoming trainloads of victims, and survivors later noted that the purpose of the camps was so unthinkable that potential victims could not begin to imagine their fate. Those not chosen for immediate murder had their heads shaved, were disinfected, and were then given prison garments—many of them used and so thin that they offered no protection against winter cold and rain. So began life in "a living hell," as one survivor wrote.

The camps were scenes of struggle for life in the face of torture and death. Instead of the minimum calories needed to keep an adult in good health, overworked inmates usually received less than five hundred calories per day, leaving them vulnerable to the diseases that swept through the camps. Prisoners sometimes went mad, as did many of the guards. In the name of advancing "racial science," doctors performed unbelievably cruel medical experiments with no anesthesia on pregnant women, twins, and other innocent people. Despite the harsh conditions, however, some people maintained their spirit: prisoners forged new friendships, and women in particular observed religious holidays and celebrated birthdays—all of which helped the struggle for survival. Thanks to those sharing a bread ration, wrote the Auschwitz survivor Primo Levi, "I managed not to forget that I myself was a man." In the end, six million Jews, the vast majority from eastern Europe—along with an estimated five to six million Slavs, Sinti and Roma, homosexuals, and countless others—were murdered in the Nazi genocidal fury. The bureaucratic organization of this vast crime perpetrated by apparently civilized people still shocks and outrages the world. (See "New Sources, New Perspectives," page 901.)

Societies at War

Even more than World War I, World War II depended on industrial productivity aimed at war and mass killings. The Axis countries remained at a disadvantage throughout the war despite their initial conquests, for the Allies simply outproduced them (Figure 26.1). Even while Germany occupied the Soviet industrial heartland and besieged many of its cities, the USSR increased its production of weapons. Both Japan and Germany made the most of their lower output, especially in the use of Blitzkrieg, but they faced other problems: Hitler had to avoid imposing wartime austerity because he had come to power promising prosperity, not more economic suffering. The use of vast quantities of stolen resources and of millions of slave laborers said to be inferior helped, but both Japan's and Germany's belief in their racial superiority worked against them by preventing them from accurately assessing the capabilities of an enemy they held in contempt.

Allied governments were overwhelmingly successful in mobilizing civilians, especially women. In Germany and Italy, where government policy particularly exalted motherhood and kept women from good jobs, officials began to realize that women were desperately needed in the workforce. Nazis changed their propaganda to emphasize the need for everyone to take a job, but their messages were not effective enough to convince women to take the low-paid work offered them. In contrast, Soviet women constituted more than half the workforce by war's end, and 800,000 volunteered for the military, even serving as pilots. As the Germans invaded, Soviet citizens moved entire factories eastward. In a dramatic about-face, the government encouraged devotion to the Russian Orthodox church as a way of boosting morale and patriotism.

Even more than in World War I, civilians faced huge amounts of propaganda when they listened to the radio or went to the movies. People were glued to their radios for war news, but much of it was tightly controlled. The totalitarian powers often withheld news of military defeats and large casualty numbers in order to keep civilian support. Wartime films focused on aviation heroes and infantrymen as well as on the self-sacrificing workingwomen and wives on the home front. Government agencies practiced censorship by allocating supplies only to films whose scripts they liked.

Between 1939 and 1945, governments organized many aspects of everyday life — a necessity because resources such as food had to be shifted away from civilians toward the military. In most countries, it

FIGURE 26.1 Weapons Production of the Major Powers, 1939–1945

World War II devoured people and weapons, necessitating dramatic changes in the workforce and everyday life. Because agricultural production was often hit hard by invading forces, people lived on reduced rations. Raw materials were channeled into the manufacture of weapons, and it was the real difference in productivity that spelled victory for the Allies: Germany and Japan were outproduced in almost every category. *(From* The Hammond Atlas of the Twentieth Century *[London: Times Books, 1996], 103.)*

	1939	1940	1941	1942	1943	1944	1945
Aircraft							
Great Britain	7,940	15,049	20,094	23,672	26,263	26,461	12,070
United States	5,856	12,804	26,277	47,826	85,998	96,318	49,761
USSR	10,382	10,565	15,735	25,436	34,900	40,300	20,900
Germany	8,295	10,247	11,776	15,409	24,807	39,807	7,540
Japan	4,467	4,768	5,088	8,861	16,693	28,180	11,066
Major Vessels							
Great Britain	57	148	236	239	224	188	64
United States	——	——	544	1,854	2,654	2,247	1,513
USSR	——	33	62	19	13	23	11
Germany (U-boats only)	15	40	196	244	270	189	0
Japan	21	30	49	68	122	248	51
Tanks							
Great Britain	969	1,399	4,841	8,611	7,476	5,000	2,100
United States	——	c. 400	4,052	24,997	29,497	17,565	11,968
USSR	2,950	2,794	6,590	24,446	24,089	28,963	15,400
Germany	c. 1,300	2,200	5,200	9,200	17,300	22,100	4,400
Japan	c. 200	1,023	1,024	1,191	790	401	142

NEW SOURCES, NEW PERSPECTIVES

Museums and Memory

Historical monuments and museums that house historical artifacts are testimonials to historical events because they provide records of those events and show that people were deeply moved by them. But is the impression conveyed by a tragic photo or the memory of an event the same as its history? For the most part, historians regard photographs and oral testimony as legitimate kinds of evidence. However, many judge institutions such as Holocaust museums to be only partially about the history of the Holocaust. Instead, a Holocaust museum tells a great deal about the nation or group that builds it. It tells about the "memory" that the nation or group wants people to have of the Holocaust.

The complicated development of Holocaust memorials is instructive to historians. Some Holocaust memory sites sprang up spontaneously in concentration camps as memorials constructed by survivors themselves. Stones, writings, plaques, flowers and plants, and other objects were used to testify to what had happened in the camp. In many cases, these initial memorials were replaced when local and national governments stepped in to take over the site, sometimes waiting years between destroying the spontaneous memorials and replacing them with an official one. The concentration camp at Dachau, near Munich, fell into disrepair until a group of survivors, including many Catholic clergy, demanded that the camp be made into a permanent museum and memorial, with the crematorium and other grisly features preserved. Although townspeople and local government resisted, Dachau and its crematorium became one of the most visited camps and indeed came to symbolize the Holocaust in all its horror. Yet Dachau was not primarily an extermination site for Jews, Slavs, and Sinti and Roma but rather a grim concentration camp where Hitler put political prisoners, many of them Catholic clergy. It is so often visited because it is on the tourist route, close to a beautiful city. Indeed, one of the plaques in this on-site museum invites visitors to tour other cultural institutions and scenery of the area while another asks them to remember that vast numbers of those interned at Dachau were Polish and Catholic. Historians need to take into account all of these factors in the politics of memories—official and unofficial, competing and contested.

In the case of Holocaust museums, official memories can clash with memories of actual survivors who, for instance, may not like what is often the most aesthetic or avant-grade in terms of art and architecture. Survivors have generally rejected abstract art, feeling that a more realistic depiction of their suffering is more authentic. The architectural design of the American Holocaust Museum was redone so that it would not look grimly out of place but would instead fit in with the tranquil style of the central museum mall in Washington, D.C., and thus be another tourist attraction. Historians question the way certain objects like shoes or eyeglasses are displayed to create a certain memory effect. They note that costume designers puff up prison uniforms to make them look more lifelike and to stir people emotionally.

Holocaust museums offer a powerful, vivid, and emotionally charged experience of history. In contrast, historians pride themselves on eliminating emotions and biases in ascertaining facts, calculating cause and effect, and reaching historical judgments. Though each provides an important representation of the past, the relationship between memory and history remains fraught with questions—and never more so than in the case of the Holocaust.

Questions to Consider

1. **What is the difference between a history textbook and a historical monument?**
2. **Do you trust a history book more than you trust a museum? How do people compare and evaluate the presentation of the past in either one?**
3. **Why might museums and public exhibitions of art and artifacts arouse more debate than history books might?**

Further Reading

Marcuse, Harold. *Legacies of Dachau: The Uses and Abuses of a Concentration Camp, 1933–2001*. 2001.

Sherman, Daniel J., and Irit Rogoff, eds. *Museum Culture: Histories, Discourses, Spectacles*. 1994.

Young, James Edward. *At Memory's Edge: After-Images of the Holocaust in Contemporary Art and Architecture*. 2000.

Jewish Museum Berlin

Among the latest of the museums dedicated to the Holocaust was this one, which opened in 2001 in Berlin—the heart of Nazi Germany. Architect Daniel Libeskind, a Polish Jew who lost many family members in the Holocaust, hoped the museum would serve not only as a memorial to Jewish deaths but also as a celebration of Jewish life and culture. What features on the museum's exterior stand out? *(© Jewish Museum Berlin. Photo: Jens Ziehe.)*

was simply taken for granted that civilians would not receive what they needed to survive in good health. Soviet children and old people were at the greatest risk, a high proportion of them among the one million residents who starved to death during the siege of Leningrad. Statisticians and other specialists in government regulated the production and distribution of food, clothing, and household products, all of which were rationed and generally of lower quality than before the war. They gave hints for meals without meat, sugar, and fat and urged women and children to embrace deprivation so that their fighting men would have more. With governments standardizing such items as food, clothing, and entertainment, World War II furthered the development of mass society in which people lived and thought in similar ways.

On both sides, propaganda and government policies promoted racial thinking. Since the early 1930s, the German government had published ugly caricatures of Jews and Slavs. Similarly, Allied propaganda during the war depicted Germans as perverts and the "Japs" as insectlike fanatics. The U.S. government forced citizens of Japanese origin into internment camps, while Muslims and minority ethnic groups in the Soviet Union were uprooted and relocated away from the front lines as potential Nazi collaborators. As in World War I, both sides drew colonized peoples into the war through forced labor and conscription into the armies. Some two million Indian men served the Allied cause, as did several hundred thousand Africans. As the Japanese swept through the Pacific and parts of East Asia, they, too, conscripted local men into their army.

Hidden Revolver

Resistance to Nazism took many forms, from the uprising in Warsaw to small acts of protest to assassinations of Nazi officers and collaborators. In a militarized state with informers everywhere, retaliation against Nazis sparked human ingenuity, whether in obtaining enough food or killing the enemy. Weapons were hidden in baby carriages, under clothing, or in books—as in this example from the Dutch resistance. *(Erich Lessing/Art Resource, NY.)*

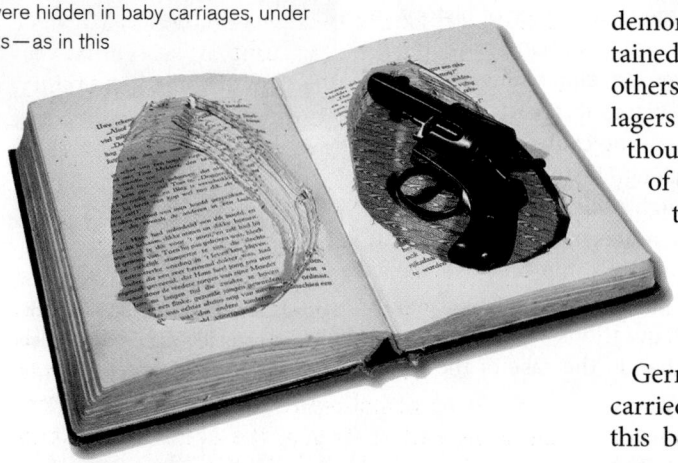

From Resistance to Allied Victory

Resistance to fascism began early in the war. Having escaped from France to London in 1940, General Charles de Gaulle directed from a distance the Free French government and its forces—a mixed organization of troops of colonized Asians and Africans, soldiers who had escaped via Dunkirk, and volunteers from other occupied countries. Meanwhile, Allied forces started tightening a noose around the Axis powers in mid-1942 (Map 26.5), and Allied victory began to look certain by 1943. At the same time, civilian resistance in the Nazi-occupied areas further pressured the Axis. Still, Hitler and Nazi officials continued to promote an unrealistic expectation of German victory, announcing, for example, that the United States was "a big bluff." Bluster could not win the war, however, and the Allies, squeezing Germany from east and west and crushing the Japanese in the Pacific, brought the war to an end in 1945.

Civilian Resistance Less well-known than the Free French, resisters in occupied Europe fought in Communist-dominated groups, some of which gathered information to aid the Allied invasion of the continent. Rural groups called partisans, or in France the *maquis*, planned assassinations of traitors and German officers and bombed bridges, rail lines, and military facilities. Although the Catholic church supported Mussolini in Italy and endorsed the Croatian puppet government's slaughter of a million Serbs, Catholic and Protestant clergy and their parishioners were among those who set up resistance networks, often hiding Jews and fugitives. The Polish resistance worked tirelessly against the Nazis, as did individuals such as Swedish diplomat Raoul Wallenberg, whose dealings with Nazi officials saved thousands of Hungarian Jews.

People also fought back through everyday activities. Homemakers circulated newsletters urging demonstrations at prisons where civilians were detained. In central Europe, hikers smuggled Jews and others over dangerous mountain passes. Danish villagers created vast escape networks, and countless thousands across Europe volunteered to be part of escape routes. Women resisters used stereotypes to good advantage, often carrying weapons to assassination sites in the correct belief that Nazis would rarely suspect or search them. They also seduced and murdered enemy officers. "Naturally the Germans didn't think that a woman could have carried a bomb," explained one Italian resister, "so this became the woman's task." Resistance kept

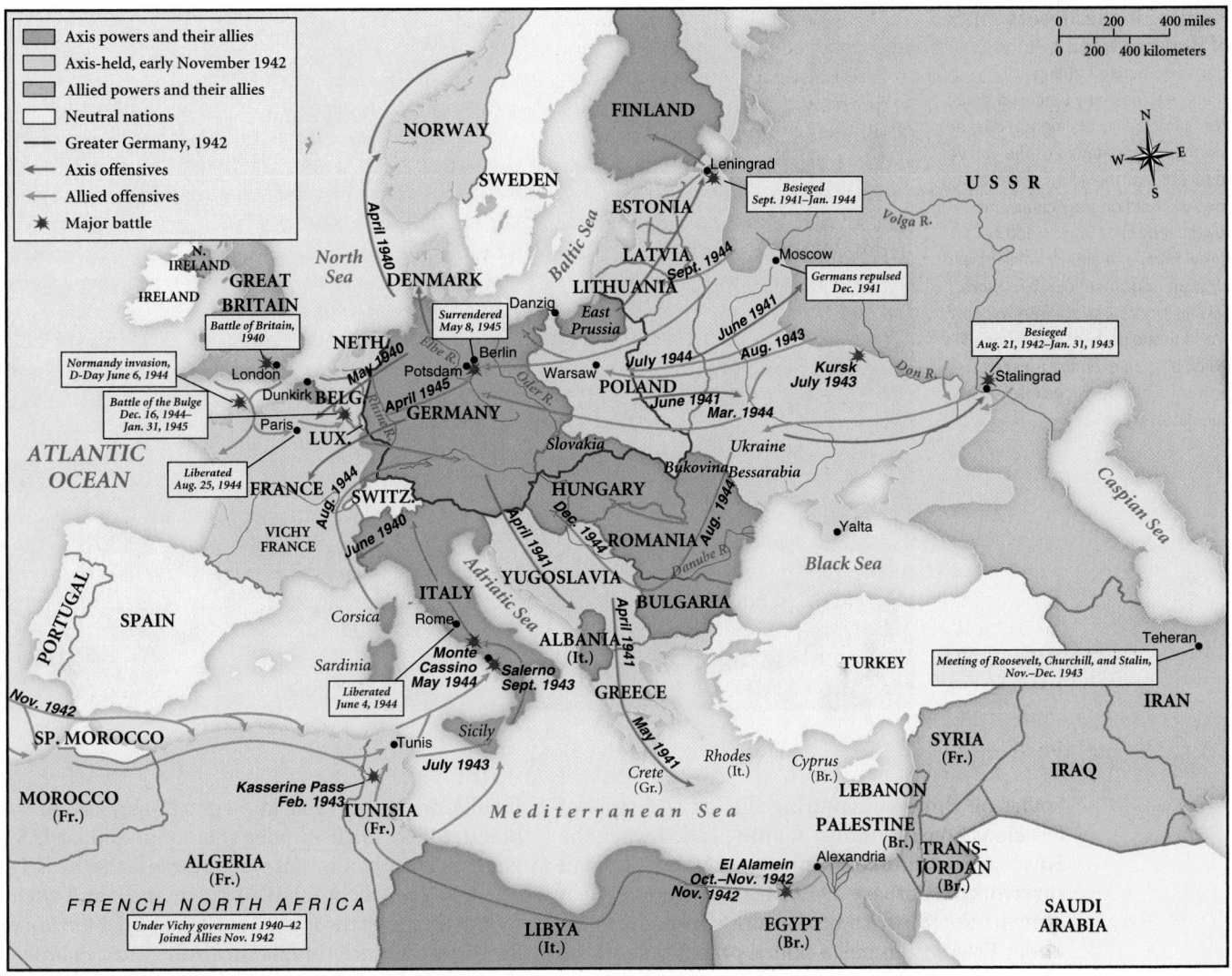

MAP 26.5 World War II in Europe and Africa

World War II inflicted massive loss of life and destruction of property on civilians, armies, and all the infrastructure—including factories, equipment, and agriculture—needed to wage total war. Thus, the war swept the European continent as well as areas in Africa colonized by or allied with the major powers. Ultimately the Allies crushed the Axis powers by moving from east, west, and south to inflict a total defeat.

alive the liberal ideal of individual action in the face of tyranny.

Both subtle and dramatically visible resistance took place in the fascist countries. Couples in Germany and Italy limited family size in defiance of pro-birth policies. German teenagers danced the forbidden American jitterbug, thus disobeying the Nazis and forcing the use of scarce manpower to police their groups. More spectacularly, in July 1944, a group of German military officers, fearing their country's military humiliation, tried but failed to assassinate Hitler—one of several such attempts. Wounded and shaken, Hitler mercilessly tortured and killed hundreds of conspirators, innocent friends, and family members. Some ask whether the assassination attempt came too late in the war to count as resistance. However, some five million Germans alone, and millions more of other nationalities, lost their lives in the last nine months of the war. Had Hitler died even as late as the summer of 1944, the relief to humanity would have been considerable.

The Axis Crushed in Europe

Amid civilian resistance, Allied forces turned the frontline war against the Axis powers beginning with the battle of Stalingrad in 1942–1943. The German army had as its goal the eventual access to

Fighting in the Streets of Budapest, 1945
House-to-house fighting characterized many battles in World War II (including Stalingrad) despite the "high-tech" nature of the war. As resisters saw the Allies undermining the Axis hold on their cities and towns, they shot from windows, threw bombs at enemy soldiers, and blew up or dismantled train tracks. The history of warfare from World War II to the present has thrown the invincibility of even the most powerful military forces into question. *(© Sovfoto.)*

Soviet oil through capturing this city. Months of ferocious house-to-house fighting ended when the Soviet army captured the ninety thousand German survivors in February 1943. Meanwhile, the British army in North Africa held against German troops under Erwin Rommel, a skilled practitioner of the new kind of mobile warfare who aimed to capture the Suez Canal and thus access to Middle Eastern oil. Although Rommel let his tanks improvise creatively, moving hundreds of miles from supply lines, the Allies' access to secret German communications because of their code-breaking capacity ultimately helped them block the capture of Egypt and take Morocco and Algeria in the fall of 1942. After driving Rommel out of Africa, the Allies landed in Sicily in July 1943, provoking a German invasion during which they took over the war effort from the Italians. A slow, bitter fight for the Italian peninsula followed, lasting until April 1945, when Allied forces finally triumphed. After Italy's liberation, partisans shot Mussolini and his mistress and hung their dead bodies for public display.

The victory at Stalingrad marked the beginning of the Soviet drive westward, during which the Soviets bore the brunt of the Nazi war machine. From the air, Britain and the United States bombed German cities, aiming to demoralize ordinary Germans and destroy war industries. But it was an invasion from the west that Stalin wanted from his allies. Finally, on June 6, 1944, known as D-Day, the combined Allied forces, under the command of U.S. general Dwight Eisenhower, attacked the heavily fortified French beaches of Normandy and then fought their way through the German-held territory of western France. In late July, Allied forces broke through German defenses and a month later helped liberate Paris. The Soviets meanwhile captured the Baltic states and entered Poland, pausing for desperately needed supplies. The Germans took advantage of the pause to put down an uprising of the Polish resistance in August 1944, which gave the Soviets a freer hand in eastern Europe after the war. Facing more than twice as many troops as on the western front, the Soviet army took Bulgaria and Romania at the end of August, then faced fierce German fighting in Hungary during the winter of 1944–1945. British, Canadian, U.S., and other Allied forces simultaneously fought their way eastward to join the Soviets in squeezing the Third Reich to its final defeat.

As the Allies advanced, Hitler decided that Germans were proving themselves unworthy of his greatness and deserved to perish in a total and bloody downfall. He thus refused all negotiations that might have spared them further death and destruction from the relentless bombing. As the Soviet army took Berlin, Hitler and his wife, Eva Braun, committed suicide. Although many soldiers remained loyal to the Third Reich, Germany finally surrendered on May 8, 1945.

The Atomic Bomb and the Defeat of Japan

The Allies had followed a "Europe first" strategy in conducting the war. They had nonetheless pursued the Japanese in the Pacific without pause. In 1940 and 1941, Japan had ousted the Europeans from many colonial holdings in Asia, but the Allies turned the tide in 1942 by destroying some of Japan's formidable navy in battles at Midway Island and Guadalcanal (Map 26.6). Japan had far less industrial capacity and manpower than the United States alone, to say nothing of the global resources of the Allies.

Allied forces stormed one Pacific island after another, where they found many inhabitants just as disillusioned by Japanese policies of forced labor and military conscription as they were by similar policies of the Western powers. This island-hopping gained the Allies bases from which to cut off the importation of supplies and to launch bombers toward Japan itself. Short of men and weapons, the Japanese military resorted to kamikaze tactics, in which pilots deliberately crashed their planes into Allied ships, killing themselves in the process. In response, the Allies stepped up their bombing of major cities, killing more than 100,000 civilians in their spring 1945 firebombing of Tokyo. The Japanese leadership still ruled out surrender.

Meanwhile a U.S.-based international team of more than 100,000 workers, including scientists and technicians, had been working on the Manhattan Project, the code name for a secret project to develop an atomic bomb. The Japanese practice of dying almost to the man rather than surrendering caused Allied military leaders to calculate that defeating Japan might cost the lives of hundreds of thousands of Allied soldiers (and even more Japanese). On August 6 and 9, 1945, the U.S. government therefore unleashed the new atomic weapons on Hiroshima and Nagasaki, killing 140,000 people

Hiroshima, 1945

This photo captures what little remained of the city of Hiroshima after the United States dropped an atomic bomb on August 6, 1945. Without the bomb, the U.S. military foresaw a long and costly struggle to defeat Japan, given that country's overall strategy of fighting to the last person and in the process inflicting the maximum number of enemy casualties. Some claim that the United States dropped the bomb to menace the Soviet Union, its opponent in the cold war just beginning. Others point to the fact that no such bomb was ever dropped on a Caucasian population. *(The Everett Collection, Inc.)*

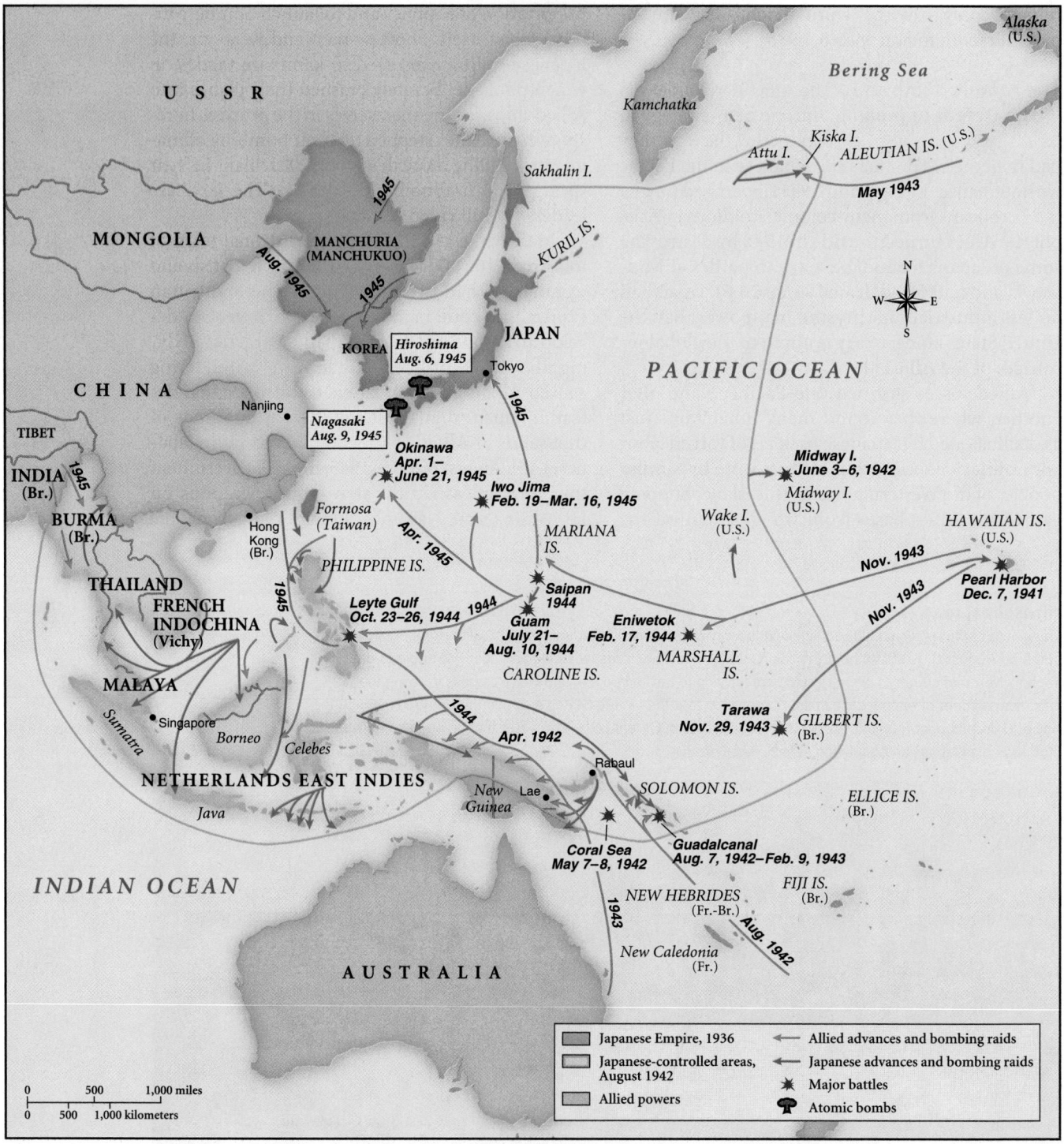

MAP 26.6 World War II in the Pacific

As in Europe, the early days of World War II gave the advantage to the Axis power Japan as it took the offensive in conquering islands in the Pacific and territories in Asia—many of them colonies of European states. Britain countered by mobilizing a vast Indian army, while the United States, after the disastrous losses at Pearl Harbor and in the Philippines, gradually gained the upper hand by costly assaults, island by island. The Japanese strategy of fighting to the last person instead of surrendering when a loss was in sight was one factor in President Truman's decision to drop the atomic bomb in August 1945.

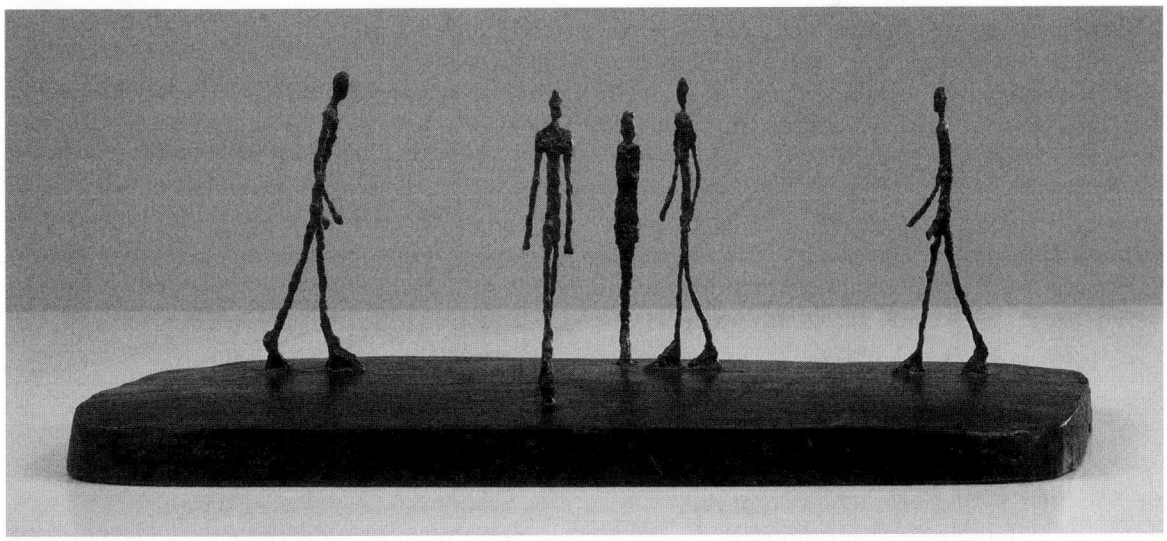

Alberto Giacometti, *The Square II* (1948–1949)
Swiss Artist Alberto Giacometti began making sculptures featuring thin, elongated figures in the 1940s. They appear to be moving forward, striving and active, but at the same time their spareness evokes the skeletal shape of concentration camp survivors. What kind of statement do you see Giacometti making about the times? *(bpk, Berlin/Nationalgalerie, Museum Berggruen, Staaliche Museen, Berlin, Germany/Art Resource, NY/© 2011 Succession Giacometti/Artists Rights Society [ARS], New York/ADAGP, Paris.)*

instantly; tens of thousands later died from burns, wounds, and other afflictions. Hardliners in the Japanese military wanted to continue the war, but on August 14, 1945, Japan surrendered.

An Uneasy Postwar Settlement

Throughout the war, Allied leaders had met not only to plan strategy but also to resolve postwar issues. Unlike World War I, however, there would be neither a celebrated peace conference nor a formal agreement among all the Allies about the final terms for peace. Yet peace and recovery were more important than ever: Europe lay in ruins, and tens of millions were starving, many of them wandering the continent in search of food, shelter, and personal safety. Because the victorious Allies distrusted one another to varying degrees, with the United States and the Soviet Union moving toward another war, the future looked grim.

Wartime Agreements about the Peace

Wartime agreements among members of the Grand Alliance about the future reflected their differences and became the subject of intense postwar debate. In 1941, Roosevelt and Churchill crafted the Atlantic Charter, which condemned aggression and endorsed collective security and the right of all people to choose their governments. Not only did the Allies come to support these ideals, but so did colonized peoples to whom, Churchill said, the charter was not meant to apply. In October 1944, Churchill and Stalin agreed on the postwar distribution of territories. The Soviet Union would control Romania and Bulgaria, Britain would control Greece, and they would jointly oversee Hungary and Yugoslavia. These agreements went against Roosevelt's faith in collective security, self-determination, and open doors in trade. In February 1945, the "Big Three"—Roosevelt, Churchill, and Stalin—met in the Crimean town of Yalta. Roosevelt advocated for the formation of the United Nations to replace the League of Nations as a global peace mechanism, and he supported future Soviet influence in Korea, Manchuria, and the Sakhalin and Kurile Islands. The last meeting of the Allied leaders, with President Harry S. Truman replacing Roosevelt, who had died in April, took place at Potsdam, Germany, in the summer of 1945. At Potsdam, they agreed to give the Soviets control of eastern Poland, to give a large stretch of eastern Germany to Poland, and to finalize a temporary four-way occupation of Germany that would include France as one of the supervising powers.

The War's Grim Legacy

The Great Depression had inflicted global suffering, while the Second World War left an estimated 100 million dead, more than 50 million refugees without homes, and one of the most abominable moral legacies in human history. Conscripted into armies or into labor camps for war production, colonial peoples in Vietnam, Algeria, India, and elsewhere were in full rebellion or close to it. For a second time in three decades, they had seen their imperial masters killing one another with the very technology that was supposed to prove European superiority. Deference to Europe was virtually finished, with independence a matter of time.

The war weakened and even destroyed standards of decency and truth. Democratic Europe had succumbed to continuous wartime values, and it was this Europe that George Orwell captured in his novel *1984* (1949). Orwell had worked for the wartime Ministry of Information (called the Ministry of Truth in the novel) and made up phony war news and threats for civilian audiences. Truth hardly mattered, and words changed meaning during the war to sound better: *battle fatigue* substituted for *insanity*, and *liberating* a country could mean invading it and slaughtering its civilians. Hungry, careworn people walking in ragged clothing along grimy streets characterized both wartime London and Orwell's fictional state of Oceania. Millions cheered the demise of Nazi evil in 1945, but Orwell saw the war as ending prosperity, deadening creativity, and bringing big government into everyday life. For Orwell, bureaucratic domination depended on continuing conflict, and fresh conflict was indeed brewing even before the war ended. As Allied powers competed for territory, a new struggle called the cold war was beginning.

REVIEW QUESTION How and where was World War II fought, and what were its major consequences?

Conclusion

The Great Depression, which brought fear, hunger, and joblessness to millions, created a setting in which dictators thrived because they promised to restore economic prosperity by destroying democracy and representative government. Desperate people believed the promises of these dynamic new leaders—Mussolini, Stalin, and Hitler—and often embraced the brutality of their regimes. In the USSR, Stalin's program of rapid industrialization cost the lives of millions as he inspired Communist believers to purge enemies—real and imagined. With the democracies preoccupied with economic recovery while preserving the rule of law and still haunted by memories of World War I, Hitler, Mussolini, and their millions of supporters went on to menace Europe unchallenged. At the same time, Japan embarked on a program of conquest aimed at ending Western domination in Asia and taking more of Asia for itself. The coalition of Allies that finally formed to stop the Axis powers of Germany, Italy, and Japan was an uneasy alliance among Britain, Free France, the Soviet Union, and the United States. World War II ended European dominance. Its economies were shattered, its colonies were on the verge of independence, and its peoples were starving and homeless.

The costs of a bloody war—one waged against civilians as much as armies—taught the victorious powers different lessons. The United States, Britain, and France were convinced that a minimum of citizen well-being was necessary to prevent a recurrence of fascism. The devastation of the USSR's population and resources made Stalin increasingly obsessed with national security and compensation for the damage inflicted by the Nazis. Britain and France faced the end of their imperial might, underscoring Orwell's insight that the war had utterly transformed society. The militarization of society and the deliberate murder of millions of innocent citizens like Etty Hillesum were tragedies that permanently injured the West's claims to being an advanced civilization. Nonetheless, backed by vast supplies of sophisticated weaponry, the United States and the Soviet Union used their opposing views on a postwar settlement to justify threatening one another—and the world—with another horrific war.

FOR FURTHER EXPLORATION

- **For additional primary-source material from this period**, see *Sources of the Making of the West*, Fourth Edition.
- **For Web sites, images, and documents related to topics in this chapter**, visit *Make History* at bedfordstmartins.com/hunt.

Europe at War's End, 1945

The damage of World War II left scars that would last for decades. Major German cities were bombed to bits, while the Soviet Union suffered an unimaginable toll of perhaps as many as forty-five million deaths due to the war alone. In addition to the vast civilian and military losses shown on this map, historians estimate that no less than twelve million people were murdered in the Nazi death camps. Everything from politics to family life needed rebuilding, adding to the chaos. *(From* The Hammond Atlas of the Twentieth Century *[London: Times Books, 1996], 102.)*

Chapter 26 Review

Online Study Guide bedfordstmartins.com/hunt

Key Terms and People

In the grid below, identify the term or person and explain its historical significance.
(To do this exercise online, go to bedfordstmartins.com/hunt.)

Term	Who or What & When	Why It Matters
civil disobedience (p. 877)		
Joseph Stalin (p. 878)		
five-year plans (p. 878)		
purges (p. 880)		
Adolf Hitler (p. 881)		
Enabling Act (p. 884)		
pump priming (p. 884)		
Nuremberg Laws (p. 885)		
family allowance (p. 886)		
Popular Front (p. 887)		
Charlie Chaplin (p. 888)		
Lebensraum (p. 891)		
Francisco Franco (p. 893)		
appeasement (p. 894)		
Nazi-Soviet Pact (p. 895)		
Blitzkrieg (p. 896)		

Review Questions

1. How did the Great Depression affect society and politics?
2. What role did violence play in the Soviet and Nazi regimes?
3. How did the democracies' responses to the twin challenges of economic depression and the rise of fascism differ from those of totalitarian regimes?
4. How did the aggression of Japan, Germany, and Italy create the conditions for global war?
5. How and where was World War II fought, and what were its major consequences?

Making Connections

1. Compare fascist ideas of the individual with the idea of individual rights that inspired the American and French Revolutions.
2. What are the major differences between World War I and World War II?
3. What explains the bleak view of writers like George Orwell after the Allied victory over the Axis powers?
4. What connections can you make between the Great Depression and the coming of World War II?

Important Events

Date	Event	Date	Event
1929	U.S. stock market crashes; global depression begins; Soviet leadership initiates "liquidation of the kulaks"; Stalin's first five-year plan officially begins	1940	France falls to German army
1931	Japan invades Manchuria; Spanish republicans overthrow monarchy	1940–1941	British air force fends off German attacks in the battle of Britain
1933	Hitler comes to power in Germany	1941	Germany invades Soviet Union; Japan attacks Pearl Harbor; United States enters war
1935	German government enacts Nuremberg Laws; Italy invades Ethiopia	1941–1945	The Holocaust
1936	Purges and show trials begin in USSR; Hitler remilitarizes Rhineland; Spanish Civil War begins	1942–1943	Siege of Stalingrad
1937	Japan attacks China	1944	Allied forces land at Normandy, France
1938	Germany annexes Austria; European leaders meet in Munich to negotiate with Hitler; Kristallnacht in Germany	1945	The fall of Berlin; United States drops atomic bombs on Hiroshima and Nagasaki; World War II ends
1939	Germany invades Czechoslovakia; Spanish Civil War ends; Nazi-Soviet Pact; Germany invades Poland; Britain and France declare war on Germany; World War II begins		

- Consider three events: **Global depression begins (1929)**, **Stalin's first five-year plan officially begins (1929)**, and **Hitler comes to power in Germany (1933)**. How did the global depression contribute to the success of these leaders?

SUGGESTED REFERENCES

This grim period in human history has yielded an ever-growing crop of excellent books, some of them coldly examining the worst aspects of the Great Depression and World War II and others looking at resistance, survival, and intellectual breakthroughs.

Alvarez, Luis. *The Power of the Zoot: Youth Culture and Resistance during World War II*. 2008.

Clavin, Patricia. *The Great Depression in Europe, 1929–1939*. 2000.

Collingham, Lizzie. *The Taste of War: World War II and the Battle for Food*. 2011.

Friedlander, Saul. *The Years of Extermination: Nazi Germany and the Jews, 1939–1945*. 2007.

*Gandhi, Mohandas. *Hind Swaraj and Other Writings*. 2009.

Gross, Jan. *Neighbors: The Destruction of the Jewish Community in Jedwabne, Poland*. 2001.

Hellbeck, Jochen. *Revolution on My Mind: Writing a Diary under Stalin*. 2006.

Imlay, Talbot C. *Facing the Second World War: Strategy, Politics, and Economics in Britain and France 1938–1940*. 2003.

Kaplan, Marion. *Between Dignity and Despair: Jewish Life in Nazi Germany*. 1998.

Maas, Ad, and Hans Hooijijers, eds. *Scientific Research in World War II: What Scientists Did in the War*. 2009.

Miner, Steven Merritt. *Stalin's Holy War: Religion, Nationalism, and Alliance Politics, 1941–1945*. 2003.

Naimark, Norman M. *Stalin's Genocides*. 2010.

Seidman, Michael. *Republic of Egos: A Social History of the Spanish Civil War*. 2002.

Snyder, Timothy. *Bloodlands: Europe between Hitler and Stalin*. 2010.

Stoltzfus, Nathan, et al., eds. *Courageous Resistance: The Power of Ordinary People*. 2007.

Tierney, Robert T. *Tropics of Savagery: The Culture of Japanese Empire in Comparative Frame*. 2010.

Viola, Lynn, ed. *Contending with Stalinism: Soviet Power and Popular Resistance in the 1930s*. 2003.

Weinberg, Gerhard. *A World at Arms: A Global History of World War II*. 2005.

Wildt, Michel. *An Uncompromising Generation: The Nazi Leadership of the Reich Security Main Office*. 2009.

*Primary source.

A LOVE CAUGHT IN THE FIRE OF REVOLUTION

Turbulent were the times
and fiery was
the love story
of Zhivago,
his wife...
and the
passionate,
tender
Lara.

METRO-GOLDWYN-MAYER PRESENTS A CARLO PONTI PRODUCTION

DAVID LEAN'S FILM OF BORIS PASTERNAK'S

DOCTOR ZHIVAGO

STARRING
GERALDINE CHAPLIN · JULIE CHRISTIE · TOM COURTENAY
ALEC GUINNESS · SIOBHAN McKENNA · RALPH RICHARDSON
OMAR SHARIF (AS ZHIVAGO) ROD STEIGER · RITA TUSHINGHAM

WINNER OF 6 ACADEMY AWARDS!

SCREEN PLAY BY ROBERT BOLT · DIRECTED BY DAVID LEAN

IN PANAVISION® AND METROCOLOR

MGM

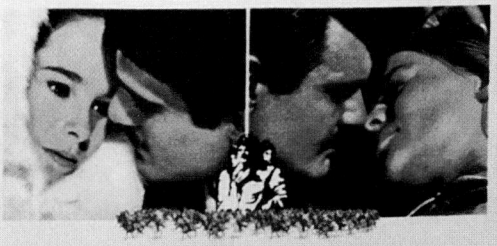

CHAPTER

27

The Cold War and the Remaking of Europe

1945–1960s

Late in 1945, with the USSR still reeling from the devastation of World War II, Soviet poet Boris Pasternak began a new project—*Doctor Zhivago*, a novel about a thoughtful medical man caught up in the whirlwind of the Russian Revolution. Like others in the USSR, Pasternak expected the postwar era to usher in, as he put it, "a great renewal of Russian life," ending the violence and famine of the past three decades. So he struggled on with his complex epic even as the cold war tensions between the United States and the USSR unfolded. In 1953, Joseph Stalin's sudden death raised Pasternak's hopes that a more tolerant political climate would allow his masterpiece to receive a warm reception; those hopes were dashed, however, when the Soviets forbade the book's publication.

A determined Pasternak bypassed the Soviet authorities and allowed *Doctor Zhivago* to come out first in 1957 in Italy—now an anti-Soviet ally of the United States in the cold war. The book became a best seller, showing its readers that the Russian Revolution was far from perfect and so angering the Soviet leadership that Stalin's successor, Nikita Khrushchev, forced Pasternak to decline the Nobel Prize for Literature awarded him in 1958. But if the cold war prompted the Soviets to denounce *Doctor Zhivago* and frighten people into denouncing its author, it was the cold war that allowed *Doctor Zhivago* to live on. Soon after the novel appeared, the famed Hollywood studio MGM bought the rights to the book and turned it into a blockbuster film (1965), seen by tens of millions. By that time, however, Pasternak was dead—a broken victim of cold war persecutions that haunted the world long after the calamitous years of war and genocide had ended.

***Doctor Zhivago* Poster**
As soon as Boris Pasternak's forbidden novel *Doctor Zhivago* was published in Italy in 1957, Hollywood's MGM studio went after the rights for the film. Finally completed in 1965, the movie was a cold war blockbuster—an epic of life and love in postrevolutionary Russia. The opening scene, invented for the movie, was a grim Soviet factory, while the story itself was more or less symbolized in this advertising poster highlighting two incredibly attractive people who fall in love and are torn apart by the crushing Bolshevik system. *(MGM/The Kobal Collection.)*

World Politics Transformed 914
- Chaos in Europe
- New Superpowers: The United States and the Soviet Union
- Origins of the Cold War
- The Division of Germany

Political and Economic Recovery in Europe 922
- Dealing with Nazism
- Rebirth of the West
- The Welfare State: Common Ground East and West
- Recovery in the East

Decolonization in a Cold War Climate 930
- The End of Empire in Asia
- The Struggle for Identity in the Middle East
- New Nations in Africa
- Newcomers Arrive in Europe

Daily Life and Culture in the Shadow of Nuclear War 936
- Restoring "Western" Values
- Cold War Consumerism and Shifting Gender Norms
- The Culture of Cold War
- The Atomic Brink

Following World War II, people in Europe, Japan, and much of East and Southeast Asia were starving and homeless. Evidence of genocide and other inhumanity was everywhere; and nuclear annihilation menaced the world. The old international order was gone, replaced by the rivalry of the United States and the Soviet Union for control of Europe, whose political, social, and economic order was shattered. The nuclear arsenals of these two superpowers—a term coined in 1947—grew massively in the 1950s, but they were enemies who did not fight outright. Thus, their terrifying rivalry was called the **cold war**. The cold war divided the West and led to political persecution in many areas, even in the wealthy and secure United States.

At the same time, the defeat of Nazism inspired cautious optimism and a revival of thoughtful reflection like Pasternak's. Heroic effort had defeated fascism, and that defeat raised hopes that a new age would begin. Atomic science promised advances in medicine, and nuclear energy was seen as a replacement for coal and oil. The creation of the United Nations in 1945 heralded an era of international cooperation. Around the globe, colonial peoples won independence from European masters, while in the United States the civil rights movement grew in strength. The welfare state expanded, and by the end of the 1950s, economic rebirth had made much of Europe more prosperous than ever before. An "economic miracle" had occurred; just a decade after the war, many Europeans and Americans were beginning to enjoy the highest standard of living they had ever known, which included the ability to buy quantities of consumer goods and to enjoy simple pleasures such as films like *Doctor Zhivago*.

cold war: The rivalry between the United States and the Soviet Union from 1945 to 1989 that led to massive growth in nuclear weapons on both sides.

The postwar period was one of open redefinition, as the experience of total war transformed both society and the international order. Gone was the definition of a West comprising Europe and its cultural offshoots such as the United States and of an East comprising Asian countries like India, China, and Japan. During the cold war, the word *West* came to stand for the United States and its dependent allies in western Europe, while *East* meant the Soviet Union and its tightly controlled bloc in eastern Europe. Still another set of terms arose in the 1950s, one that divided the globe into the first world, or capitalist bloc of countries; the second world, or socialist bloc; and the third world, or countries emerging from imperial domination. This last term was meant to compare favorably those rising nations to the Third Estate—that is, the rising citizens of the French Revolution—but is now considered an insulting term. As the world's people redefined themselves, the superpowers took the world to the brink of nuclear disaster when the United States discovered Soviet missile sites on the island of Cuba. From the dropping of the atomic bomb on Japan in 1945 to the Cuban missile crisis of 1962, fear and personal anguish like that suffered by Pasternak gripped much of the world, even in the midst of prosperity and Europe's rebirth.

CHAPTER FOCUS How did the cold war shape the politics, economy, social life, and culture of post–World War II Europe?

World Politics Transformed

World War II ended Europe's global leadership. Many countries lay in ruins in the summer of 1945, and conditions would deteriorate before they im-

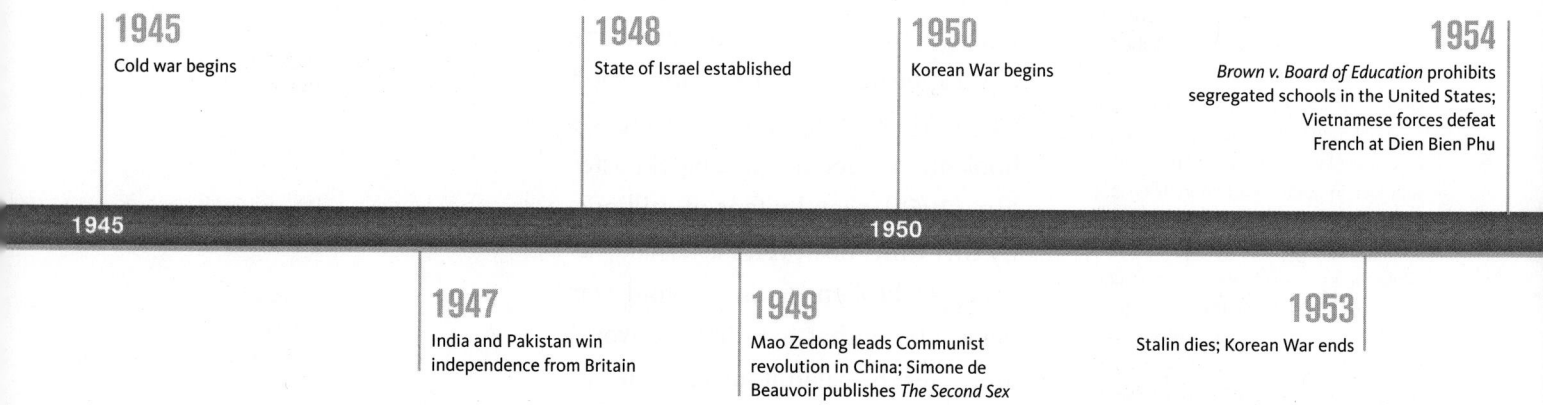

proved. Though victorious, bombed and bankrupt Britain could not feed its people, and continuing turmoil destroyed the lives of millions in central and eastern Europe. In contrast, the United States, whose territory was virtually untouched in the war, emerged as the world's sole economic giant, while the Soviet Union, despite suffering immense devastation, retained formidable military might. Occupying Europe as part of the victorious alliance against Nazism and fascism, the two superpowers used Germany—at the heart of the continent and its politics—to divide Europe in two. By the late 1940s, the USSR had imposed Communist rule throughout most of eastern Europe, as it gained control of the territory that the Nazis had desired for German settlement. Western Europeans found themselves at least partially controlled by the very U.S. economic power that helped them rebuild, especially because the United States maintained air bases and nuclear weapons sites on their soil. The new age of bipolar world politics made Europe its testing ground.

Chaos in Europe

In contrast to the often stationary trench warfare of World War I, armies in World War II had fought a war of movement on the ground and in the air. Massive bombing had leveled thousands of square miles of territory, and whole cities were clogged with rubble. On the Rhine River, almost no bridge remained standing; in the Soviet Union, seventy thousand villages and more than a thousand cities lay in shambles. Everywhere people were suffering. In the Netherlands, the severity of Nazi occupation left the Dutch population close to death, relieved only by a U.S. airlift of food. In Britain, many died in the bitterly cold winter of 1946–1947 because of a shortage of fuel. To control scarce supplies, Italian bakers sold bread by the slice. Allied troops in Germany were almost the sole source of food: "To see the children fighting for food," remarked one British soldier handing out supplies, "was like watching animals being fed in a zoo." There was social disarray, even chaos, at the war's end but no mass uprisings as after World War I. Until the late 1940s, people were too absorbed by the struggle for bare survival.

The tens of millions of refugees suffered the most, as they wandered a continent where resources were slim and the dangers of assault, robbery, and ethnic violence great. An estimated thirty million Europeans, many of German ethnicity, were forcibly expelled from Poland, Czechoslovakia, and Hungary. Many refugees fled to western Europe, but others ultimately found homes in countries that experienced little or no war damage, such as Denmark, Sweden, Canada, and Australia. Following the exodus of refugees from the east, western Europe became one of the world's most densely populated regions (Map 27.1). The USSR lobbied hard for the return of several million Soviet prisoners of war and forced laborers, and the Allies transported millions of Soviet refugees home. The Allies slowed the process when they discovered that Soviet leaders had ordered the execution of many of the returnees for being "contaminated" by Western ideas. Hundreds of thousands of Soviet citizens thus joined the ocean of destitute refugees.

Survivors of the concentration camps discovered that their suffering had not ended with Germany's defeat. Many returned home diseased and disoriented, while others had no home to return to, as property had been confiscated. Anti-Semitism—official policy under the Nazis—lingered in popular attitudes, and people used it to justify their claim to Jewish property and to jobs vacated by Jews. The fascist use of violence as a means of upward mobility remained common throughout eastern Europe. In the summer of 1946, a vicious crowd in Kielce, Poland, assaulted some 250 Jewish survivors, killing at least 40. Meanwhile, some officials across Europe

1957
Boris Pasternak publishes *Doctor Zhivago*; USSR launches *Sputnik*; Treaty of Rome establishes European Economic Community (Common Market)

1962
United States and USSR face off in the Cuban missile crisis

1955 1960 1965

1956
General Abdel Nasser nationalizes Suez Canal; uprising in Hungary against USSR

1958
Fifth Republic begins in France

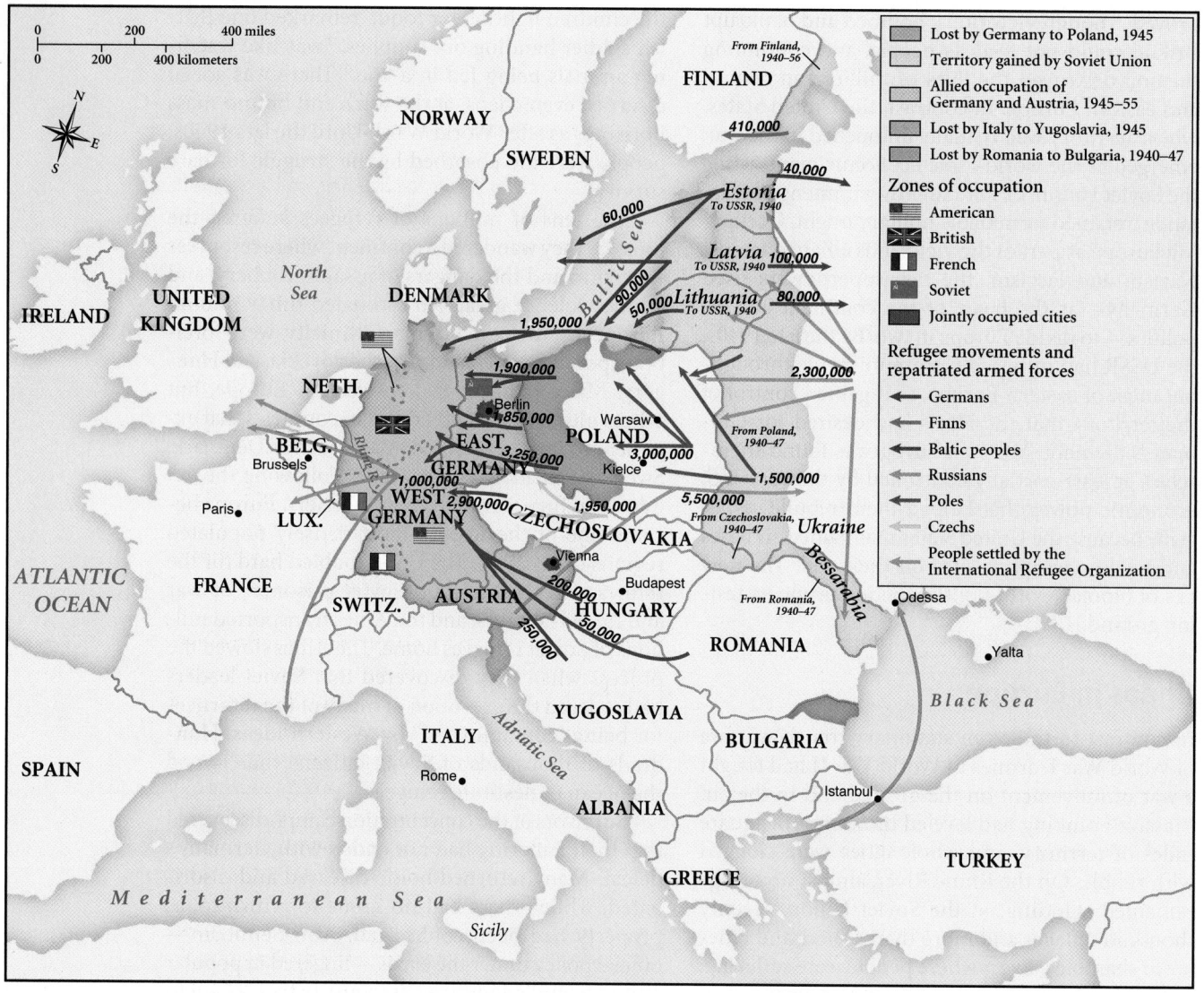

MAP 27.1 The Impact of World War II on Europe

European governments, many of them struggling to provide food and other necessities for their populations, found themselves responsible for hundreds of thousands, if not millions, of new refugees. Simultaneously, millions of prisoners of war, servicemen, and slave laborers were returned to the Soviet Union, many of them by force. This situation unfolded amid political instability and even violence. | **What does the movement of peoples shown on the map suggest about social conditions in post–World War II Europe?**

even denied that unprecedented atrocities had been committed and refused Jews any help. Survivors therefore fled to the port cities of Italy and other Mediterranean countries, eventually leaving Europe for Palestine, where Zionists had been settling for half a century. Unwilling to help Hitler's victims, many Europeans had simply lost their moral bearings.

New Superpowers: The United States and the Soviet Union

Only two countries were still powerful in 1945: the United States and the Soviet Union. The United States was now the richest nation in the world. Its industrial output had increased by a remarkable 15 percent annually between 1940 and 1944. By 1947, the United States controlled almost two-thirds of the world's gold bullion and launched more than half of the world's commercial shipping. Continued spending on industrial and military research added to postwar prosperity, bolstering the confident mood that now swept the United States. In contrast to the post–World War I policy of isolationism, Americans embraced global leadership. Many had learned about the world while tracking the war's progress; hundreds of thousands of soldiers, government officials, and relief workers had direct experience of Europe, Africa, and Asia. Despite the fear of nuclear annihilation that troubled many, a wave of suburban housing development and consumer spending kept the economy buoyant. Temporarily reversing the trend toward lower birthrates, a baby boom exploded from the late 1940s through the early 1960s in response to prosperity.

The Soviets also emerged from the war with a well-justified sense of accomplishment. Despite horrendous losses, they had resisted the most massive onslaught ever launched against a nation. Instead of being outcasts as they had been after World War I, Soviet officials expected to have influence on the world stage, and indeed many Europeans and Americans gratefully acknowledged the Soviet contribution to Hitler's defeat. Ordinary Soviet citizens believed that a victory that had cost the USSR as many as forty-five million lives would lead to improvement in everyday conditions and a continuation of the war's relatively relaxed politics. Rumors spread among the peasants that the collective farms would be divided and returned to them as individual property now that the war had been won and agriculture modernized. "Life will become pleasant," one writer prophesied. "There will be much coming and going, and a lot of contacts with the West." The Stalinist goals of industrialization and defense against Nazism had been won, and thus many Soviets, among them Boris Pasternak, anticipated an end to decades of hardship and repression.

Stalin took a different view and, despite his personal exhaustion from the wartime effort, moved ruthlessly to reassert control. In 1946, his new five-year plan set increased production goals and mandated more stringent collectivization of agriculture. For him, rapid recovery meant more work, not less, and more order, not greater freedom. Stalin cut back the army by two-thirds to beef up the labor force and also turned his attention to the low birthrate, a result of wartime male casualties and women's long, arduous working days, which discouraged them from adding child care to their already heavy responsibilities. He introduced an intense propaganda campaign emphasizing that women should hold down jobs and also fulfill their "true nature" by producing many children. A crackdown on freedom took place, and a new round of purges began in which people were told that enemies among them were threatening the state. Jews were especially targeted, and in 1953 the government announced that doctors — most of them Jews — had long been assassinating Soviet leaders, murdering newborns and patients in hospitals, and plotting to poison water supplies. Hysteria gripped the nation, as people feared for their lives. "I am a simple worker and not an anti-Semite," one Moscow resident wrote, "but I say . . . it's time to clean these people out." With this rebirth of Stalinism, an atmosphere of fear returned to feed the cold war.

Origins of the Cold War

The cold war between the United States and the Soviet Union, which began in 1945, would afflict the world for more than four decades. No peace treaty officially ended World War II to document what went wrong, as in the Peace of Paris of 1919–1920. As a result, the origins of the cold war remain a matter of debate, with historians faulting both sides for starting the dangerous rivalry (see "New Sources, New Perspectives," page 918). Some point to consistent U.S., British, and French hostility to the Soviets that began as far back as the Bolshevik Revolution of 1917 and continued through the depression and World War II. These powers opposed the Communists' abolition of private property and Russia's withdrawal from World War I. Others stress Stalin's aggressive policies, notably the 1939 Nazi-Soviet Pact and Stalin's quick claims on the Baltic states and Polish territory when World War II broke out. In this view, other countries naturally feared Soviet expansionism.

Suspicion ran deep among the Allied leadership during the war, and the alliance was always a troubled one. Stalin believed that Churchill and Roosevelt were deliberately letting the USSR bear the brunt of Hitler's rampage across the continent as part of their anti-Communist policy. He rightly viewed Churchill in particular as interested primarily in preserving Britain's imperial power, no matter what the cost in Soviet lives. At the time, some Americans believed that dropping the atomic bomb on Japan would also frighten the Soviets and discourage them from making any more land grabs. In addition, the new U.S. president, Harry Truman, was far tougher than Roosevelt with regard to Soviet needs. He cut off aid to the USSR almost the instant the last gun was fired, fueling Stalin's belief that the United States was aiming for the Soviet Union's utter collapse. Seeing a threat from the West, especially from a revived Germany, Stalin completed what he had begun in the war: the takeover of eastern Europe with the goal of collectivizing agriculture and providing the USSR with a permanent "buffer zone" of loyal European states. Across the Atlantic, Truman viewed the Soviet occupation of eastern Europe as opening an era of Communist takeovers around the world. Members of the U.S. State Department fueled U.S. fears by depicting Stalin as another in a long line of neurotic Asian tyrants thirsting for world domination.

The cold war thus became a series of moves and countermoves in the shared occupation of a rich European heartland that had fallen into chaos. In line with the view of its political needs, the USSR repressed democratic coalition governments of liberals, socialists, Communists, and peasant parties

NEW SOURCES, NEW PERSPECTIVES

Government Archives and the Truth about the Cold War

As the modern nation-state grew in the nineteenth century, historians came increasingly to rely on official government archives to answer questions arising from ideological disputes. The cold war was one such battle of charges and countercharges. Government archives have thrown light on the accusations of both sides. Participants and eyewitnesses, it is believed, are not reliable because of their bias. Instead, trained scholars, ridding themselves of bias, carefully examine government records, preserved in official repositories where tampering cannot take place.

The opening of the Soviet Union's archives in the late 1980s and 1990s after the fall of Soviet communism gave answers to many cold war questions. In 1956, in the midst of superpower rivalry, Nikita Khrushchev first threw official light on the slaughter connected with Stalin's regime. In Khrushchev's partial revelation of truths, V. I. Lenin and Joseph Stalin were presented as distinctly different political beings, with Lenin an ideologue and benefactor, and Stalin a creature of excess. The Soviet archives, however, revealed a more vicious Lenin, one who demanded from the start of the Bolshevik regime the kind of brutality that Khrushchev had pinned on Stalin alone. Lenin and his contemporaries started the reliance on wholesale massacre of the upper classes, peasants, dissenters, and even ordinary citizens. At the same time, the archives discredited the U.S. claim that the Soviet Union in the 1950s was out to conquer the world. Instead, scholars found both Stalin and Khrushchev fearful of a U.S. nuclear attack and eager to come to terms.

Much official U.S. archival material still remains closed to scholars, but the Freedom of Information Act (1966, amended 1974) allows historians to press for access and at times to obtain it. Official U.S. documents have opened up debate about the dropping of the atomic bomb, with some scholars concluding that it was not merely a matter of ending the war with Japan in the most expeditious way. Instead, brandishing atomic weapons served the United States' desire to scare the Soviets. Tapes released from John F. Kennedy's administration have shown the president differing from his generals, most of whom wanted a nuclear war during the Cuban missile crisis. Kennedy, far from being the consistent cold warrior he sought to portray, pulled back from the brink.

For all that new archival evidence can reveal, reliance on this material has many pitfalls. First, one train of thought leads to the mistaken belief that if an archive contains no written evidence of an event, the event is open to question. For instance, if there is no written order from Adolf Hitler to start the Holocaust, some have argued, it means that he did not know about the event or even that it did not occur. Second, archives are susceptible to evidence tampering, including forgery and document planting, as has happened with some Russian documents of the 1990s. Finally, excessive faith in archival documents, some critics say, skews history by suggesting that the most important kind of history comes from official government sources. Important historical evidence lies as well in sources ranging from newspapers, family account books, diaries, and personal letters to novels, paintings, and architecture, especially when many kinds of sources are used to verify one another.

Questions to Consider

1. **Are archives overseen by government officials more or less likely to be biased than other sources? How can we know the extent to which archives contain the truth?**
2. **What are the most reliable sources for discovering historical truth? Make a list and provide reasons for your counting these sources as reliable.**

Further Reading

Andrew, Christopher, and Vasili Mitrokhin. *The Mitrokhin Archive: The KGB in Europe and the West*. 1999.

Courtois, Stephane, et al. *The Black Book of Communism: Crimes, Terror, Repression*. Trans. Jonathan Murphy and Mark Kramer. 1999.

Zubok, Vladislav, and Constantine Pleshakov. *Inside the Kremlin's Cold War: From Stalin to Khrushchev*. 1996.

Russian Secret Archives

The opening of archives across the former Soviet bloc had many consequences. In the former East Germany, for instance, names of secret police informers were made public and many people had their reputations utterly tarnished. The opening of the archives also exposed the cases of those convicted with trumped-up evidence (some pictured here), most of them sent to camps and to their deaths long since. The probable existence of such secret archives around the world has made historians and the families of victims fight for access. Simultaneously, politicians in the democracies are struggling to keep their archives closed, especially to scholars trained to assess them. *(© Sovfoto.)*

in central and eastern Europe between 1945 and 1949. It imposed Communist rule almost immediately in Bulgaria and Romania. In Romania, Stalin cited citizen violence in 1945 as the excuse to demand an ouster of all non-Communists from the civil service and cabinet. In Poland, the Communists fixed the election results of 1945 and 1946 to create the illusion of approval for communism. Nevertheless, the Communists had to share power between 1945 and 1947 with the popular Peasant Party, which had a large constituency of rural workers and peasant landowners. The Allies protested many of these moves by the Communists as the cold war advanced.

The United States put its new interventionist spirit to work, promoting American influence. It acknowledged Soviet authority in USSR-occupied areas of central and eastern Europe but worried that Communist power would spread to western Europe. The Communists' promises of better conditions appealed to hungry workers, while memories of Communist leadership in the resistance to fascism gave it powerful appeal. In Greece, for example, Communist insurgents had enough of a following to threaten the right-wing monarchy the British had installed in 1944.

In March 1947, Truman reacted to the Communist threat in Greece by announcing what quickly became known as the **Truman Doctrine**, the use of economic and military aid to block communism. The president requested $400 million in military aid for Greece and Turkey, where the Communists were also exerting pressure. Fearing that Americans would balk at backing an un-democratic Greece, the U.S. Congress said it would agree to the program only if, as one congressman put it, Truman would "scare the hell out of the country." Truman thus publicized the expensive aid program as a necessary first step to prevent Soviet conquest of the world. The show of American support made the Communists back off, and in 1949 the Greek rebels declared a cease-fire.

In 1947, the United States also devised the **Marshall Plan**—a program of massive economic aid to Europe—to relieve the daily hardships that were making communism attractive to Europeans.

Truman Doctrine: The policy devised by U.S. president Harry Truman to limit communism after World War II by countering political crises with economic and military aid.

Marshall Plan: A post–World War II program funded by the United States to get Europe back on its feet economically and thereby reduce the appeal of communism. It played an important role in the rebirth of European prosperity in the 1950s.

The Cold War

1945–1949	USSR establishes satellite states in eastern Europe
1947	Truman Doctrine announces American commitment to contain communism; U.S. Marshall Plan provides massive aid to rebuild Europe
1948–1949	Soviet troops blockade Berlin; United States airlifts provisions to Berliners
1949	West Germany and East Germany formed; Western nations form North Atlantic Treaty Organization (NATO); Soviet bloc establishes Council for Mutual Economic Assistance (COMECON); USSR tests its first nuclear weapon
1950–1953	Korean War
1950–1954	U.S. senator Joseph McCarthy leads hunt for American Communists
1953	Stalin dies
1955	USSR and eastern bloc countries form military alliance, the Warsaw Pact
1956	Khrushchev denounces Stalin in "secret speech" to Communist Party Congress; Hungarians revolt unsuccessfully against Soviet domination
1959	Fidel Castro comes to power in Cuba
1961	Berlin Wall erected
1962	Cuban missile crisis

"The seeds of totalitarian regimes are nurtured by misery and want," Truman warned. Named after Secretary of State George C. Marshall, who proposed the plan, the program's direct aid would immediately improve everyday life, while its loans and financial credits would restart international trade. The government claimed that the Marshall Plan was not directed "against any country or doctrine but against hunger, poverty, desperation, and chaos." By the early 1950s, the United States had sent Europe more than $12 billion in food, equipment, and services, reducing communism's appeal in the countries of western Europe that received the aid.

Stalin saw the Marshall Plan as a U.S. political trick because the devastated USSR had little aid to offer client countries in eastern and central Europe. He thus clamped down still harder on eastern European governments, preventing them from responding to the U.S. offer of assistance and eliminating the last scraps of democracy in Hungary and Poland. In the autumn of 1947, a purge of non-Communist officials began in Czechoslovakia; by June 1948, Czechoslovakia's socialist president, Edvard Beneš, had resigned and been replaced by a Communist figurehead. The populace accepted the change so passively that Communist leaders said the takeover was "like cutting butter with a knife."

The only exception to the Soviet sweep in eastern Europe came in Yugoslavia, under the Commu-

Marshall Plan Poster
The Marshall Plan was a major factor in both western European recovery and the cold war. This poster in Italian advertises the plan as "Aid from America" and specifies that it includes "grain, coal, food, and medical supplies." Given both the image and the text, what would you judge the poster's effect to be? *(Archivio GBB/CONTRASTO/Redux.)*

nist ruler known as Tito (Josip Broz, 1892–1980). During the war, Tito had led the powerful anti-Nazi Yugoslav "partisans." After the war, he drew on support from Serbs, Croats, and Muslims to mount a Communist revolution. His revolution, however, was explicitly meant to avoid Soviet influence. Eager for Yugoslavia to develop industrially rather than simply serve Soviet needs, Tito remarked, "We study and take as an example the Soviet system, but we are developing socialism in our country in somewhat different forms." Stalin was furious; in his eyes, commitment to communism meant obedience to him. Nonetheless, Yugoslavia emerged from its Communist revolution as a culturally diverse federation of six republics and two independent provinces within Serbia. Tito's break with Stalin intensified the purges in the USSR because the Soviet government could point to Tito as a menacing example of the treachery supposedly at work even in the heart of the Communist world. Tito used his forceful personality and strong organization to hold diverse groups of southern Slavs together until his death in 1980 and to keep the Soviets at bay.

Yugoslavia after the Revolution

The Division of Germany

The superpower struggle for control of Germany took the cold war to a menacing level. The agreements reached at the Yalta and Potsdam conferences in 1945 provided for Germany's division into four zones, each of which was controlled by one of the four principal victors in World War II — the United States, the Soviet Union, Britain, and France — and occupied by troops from those nations. However, the superpowers disagreed on how to treat Germany. Many in the United States had come to believe that there was something wrong with the character of Germans — a permanently evil flaw responsible for two world wars and the Holocaust. After the war, the U.S. occupation forces undertook to reprogram German attitudes by controlling the press and censoring all media in the U.S. zone to ensure that they did not express fascist values. In contrast, Stalin believed that Nazism was an extreme form of capitalism. His solution was to confiscate the estates of wealthy Germans and redistribute them to ordinary people and supporters.

A second disagreement, concerning the economy, led to Germany's partition. According to the American plan for coordinating the various segments of the German economy, surplus crops from the Soviet-occupied areas would feed urban populations in the western zones; in turn, industrial goods would be sent to the USSR. The Soviets upset this plan. Following the Allied agreement that the USSR would receive reparations from German resources, the Soviets dismantled industries and seized German equipment on their own, shipping it all to the Soviet Union. They transported skilled German workers, engineers, and scientists to the USSR to work as forced laborers. The Soviets also manipulated the currency in their zone, enabling the USSR to buy German goods at unfairly low prices.

The struggle between the superpowers escalated still more when the western Allies agreed to merge their zones into a West German state. Instead of limiting German power, as wartime agreements called for, the United States began an economic buildup of the western zone under the Marshall Plan in order to make that zone a strong buffer against the Soviets. By 1948, notions of a permanently weakened Germany had ended, and the United States enlisted many former Nazi officials as spies and bureaucrats to jump-start the economy and pursue the cold war.

On July 24, 1948, Stalin retaliated by using Soviet troops to blockade Germany's capital, Berlin. Like Germany as a whole, the city—located more than one hundred miles deep into the Soviet zone and thus cut off from western territory—had been divided into four occupation zones. Expecting the United States and its allies to give up on Berlin, the Soviets declared that the city was now part of their zone of occupation and refused to allow western vehicles to travel through the Soviet zone to reach it. The United States responded decisively with the Berlin airlift—Operation Vittles, as U.S. pilots called it—flying in millions of tons of provisions to Berliners. During the winter of 1948–1949, the Berlin airlift even funneled in coal to warm some two million isolated citizens (Map 27.2). Given the limited number of available transport planes, pilots kept the plane engines on to achieve a rapid turnaround that would ensure the delivery of enough provisions. The Soviets ended their blockade in May 1949, but cold war rhetoric made the divided capital an enduring symbol of the capitalist-communist divide—of good versus evil.

The creation of competing institutions, military alliances, and entirely new countries added to cold war tensions (Map 27.3). A few months after the establishment of the West German state in 1948, the USSR formed an East German state. In 1949, the United States, Canada, and their allies in western Europe and Scandinavia formed the **North Atlantic Treaty Organization (NATO)**, which provided a unified military force for its member countries. In 1955, after the United States forced France and Britain to invite West Germany to join NATO, the Soviet Union retaliated by establishing with its satellite countries the military organization commonly called the **Warsaw Pact**. By that time, both the United States and the USSR had accelerated arms buildups: the Soviets had exploded their own atomic bomb in 1949, and both nations then tested increasingly powerful nuclear weapons. These two

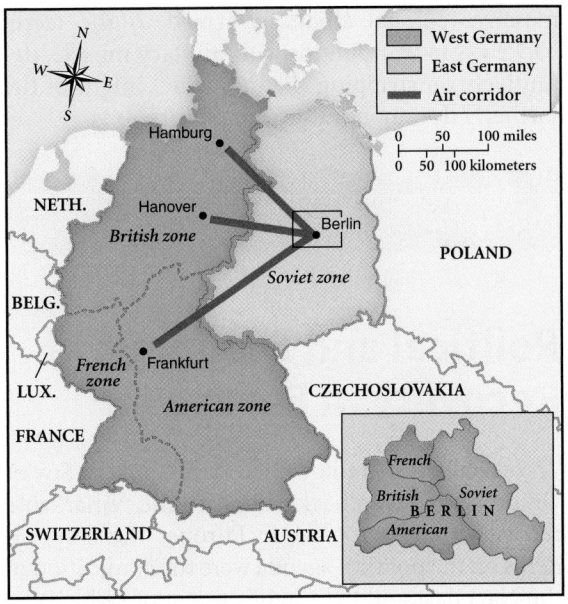

MAP 27.2 Divided Germany and the Berlin Airlift, 1946–1949

Berlin—controlled by the United States, Great Britain, France, and the Soviet Union—was deep in the Soviet zone of occupation and became a major point of contention among the former allies. When the USSR blockaded the western half of the city, the United States responded with a massive airlift. To stop movement between the two zones, the USSR built a wall in 1961 and used troops to patrol it.

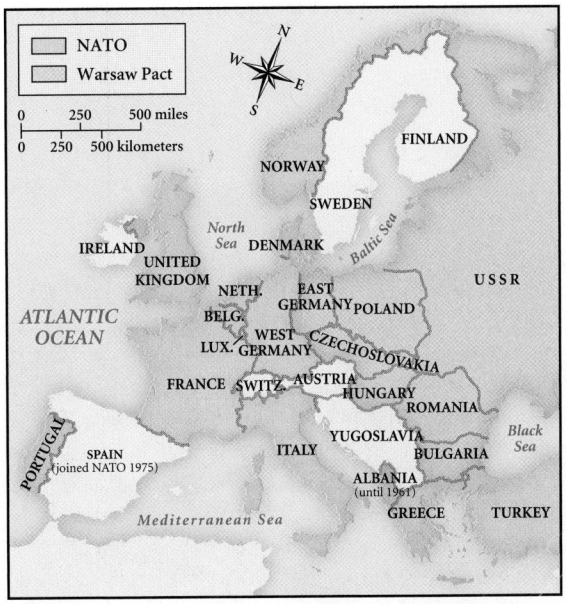

MAP 27.3 European NATO Members and the Warsaw Pact in the 1950s

The two superpowers intensified their rivalry by creating large military alliances: NATO, formed in 1949, and the Warsaw Pact, formed in 1955 after NATO invited West German membership. International politics revolved around these two alliances, which faced off in the heart of Europe. War games for the two sides often assumed a massive war concentrated in central Europe over control of Germany.

North Atlantic Treaty Organization (NATO): The security alliance formed in 1949 to provide a unified military force for the United States, Canada, and their allies in western Europe and Scandinavia.

Warsaw Pact: A security alliance of the Soviet Union and its allies formed in 1955, in retaliation for NATO's admittance of West Germany.

massive regional alliances, armed to the teeth, backed cold war politics with military muscle, definitively outstripping the individual might of the formerly dominant European powers.

REVIEW QUESTION What were the major events in the development of the cold war?

Political and Economic Recovery in Europe

The clash between the United States and the Soviet Union served as a background to the remarkable recovery that took place in Europe. The first two items on the political agenda were the eradication of the Nazi past and the establishment of stable governments. While western Europe revived its democratic political structures, its individualistic culture, and its productive capabilities, eastern Europe was far less prosperous and far more repressive under the Stalinism of the immediate postwar period. Even to the east, however, the conditions of everyday life improved as peasant societies were forced to modernize and some consumer goods industries and basic health services were restored. By 1960, people across the continent were enjoying a higher standard of living than ever before in their history. Governments took increasing responsibility for the health and well-being of citizens, making the cold war era also the age of the welfare state.

Dealing with Nazism

In May 1945, Europeans lived under a confusing system in which local resistance leaders, Allied armies of occupation, international relief workers, and the remnants of bureaucracies—among them Nazi sympathizers—vied for authority. The goals of feeding civilians, dealing with millions of refugees, purging Nazis, and setting up peacetime governments all needed attention. Governments-in-exile returned to reclaim power, but they often ran up against occupying armies that were a law unto themselves. The Soviets were especially feared for inflicting rape and robbery on Germans—abuses they justified by pointing to the tens of millions of worse atrocities committed by the Nazis. Adding to the sense of disorder was the lively trade in sex for food among starving civilians and well-supplied soldiers in all armies. The desire for revenge against Nazis hardened with the discovery of the death camps' skeletal survivors and the remains of the millions murdered there. Employing swift vigilante justice, civilians released pent-up rage and punished collaborators for their participation in genocide and occupation crimes. In France, villagers often shaved the heads of women suspected of associating with

Polish Refugees
These refugees, a handful among millions, are waiting for a train that might carry them to a safer destination. The refugee situation was appalling, as ethnic Poles, Germans, Hungarians, Croats, Czechs, and others were driven from areas where in some cases their families had lived for centuries. The goal of many postwar governments was to "ethnically cleanse" regions along the line of thought that grew up with Wilson's Fourteen Points: that national ethnicities should determine the kind of society and government they would have. *(Photo by Fred Ramage/Keystone/Getty Images.)*

Women Clearing Berlin
The amount of destruction caused by World War II was staggering, requiring the mobilization of the civilian population in Berlin, where women were conscripted to sort the rubble and clear it away. Scenes like this were ultimately used as propaganda in the cold war to make it seem as if the Germans were the victims rather than the perpetrators of the war. That German soldiers held in Soviet camps were only slowly repatriated added to the image of Soviet rather than German aggression in World War II. *(akg-images.)*

Germans and made some of them parade naked through the local streets. Members of the resistance executed tens of thousands of Nazi officers and collaborators on the spot and without trial.

Allied representatives undertook what they claimed to be a systematic "denazification" that ranged from forcing German civilians to view the death camps to investigating and bringing to trial suspected local collaborators. The trials conducted at Nuremberg, Germany, by the victorious Allies in the fall of 1945 used the Nazis' own documents to reveal a horrifying panorama of crimes by Nazi leaders. Although international law lacked any definition of genocide as a crime, the judges at Nuremberg found sufficient cause to impose death sentences on half of the twenty-four defendants, among them Hitler's closest associates, and to give prison terms to the remainder. The Nuremberg trials introduced today's notion of prosecution for crimes against humanity.

Allied prosecution of the Axis leadership was hardly thorough, however. Some of those most responsible for war crimes disappeared and were not pursued, leaving many Germans skeptical about Allied intentions. As women in Germany faced violence at the hands of occupying troops, endured starvation, and were forced to do the rough manual labor of clearing rubble, Germans came to believe that they themselves were the main victims of the war. German civilians also interpreted the trials of Nazis as simple payback by victors rather than a just punishment of the guilty. Distrust mounted when Allied officials, eager to restore government services and make western Europe more efficient than Soviet-controlled eastern Europe, began to hire former high-ranking Fascists and Nazis. Soon the new West German government proclaimed that the war's real casualties were the German prisoners of war still held in Soviet camps.

Rebirth of the West

Following the immediate postwar chaos, Europe's revival accelerated in the 1950s. In western Europe, reform-minded civilian governments reflected the broad coalitions of the resistance movements and other opposition to the Axis powers. They conspicuously emphasized democratic values to show their rejection of the totalitarian regimes that had earlier attracted so many Europeans. Rebuilding devastated towns and cities spurred industrial recovery, while bold projects for economic cooperation—like the European Common Market and the conversion of wartime technology to peacetime use—produced a brisk trade in consumer goods and services in western Europe by the late 1950s. Memories of the war remained vivid, but prosperity restored confidence and hope for a better future.

Democratic Politics Restored

Resistance leaders made the first claims on political office in postwar western Europe. In France, the leader of the Free French, General Charles de Gaulle, governed briefly as chief of state, and the French approved a constitution in 1946 that established the Fourth Republic and finally granted the vote to French women. De Gaulle wanted a more conservative political system with a strong executive and, failing to achieve that, soon resigned in favor of centrist and left-wing parties. Meanwhile, Italy replaced its constitutional monarchy with a republic that also allowed women the vote for the first time. As in France, a resistance-based government initially took control. Then, late in 1945, the socialist and labor politicians were replaced by a coalition headed by the conservative **Christian Democrats**, descended from the traditional Catholic centrist parties of the prewar period. Other countries likewise saw the growing influence of Christian politicians because of their participation in the resistance.

Still other voters in western Europe favored the Communist Party. Symbol of the common citizen, the Soviet soldier was a hero to many western Europeans outside occupied Germany. So were the resistance leaders, who were themselves often Communist. Some establishment politicians had decided late in the war to join what looked to be a certain resistance victory, and they, too, received credit. People still remembered the hardships of the depression of the 1930s. Therefore, in Britain, despite the wartime successes of Winston Churchill's Conservative Party leadership, the government of longtime Labour Party leader Clement Attlee—though not Communist—appeared most likely to fulfill promises to share prosperity equitably among the classes. The extreme difficulties of the immediate postwar years provided further support for governments that would represent the millions of ordinary citizens who had suffered, fought, and worked incredibly hard during the war.

In West Germany, however, with the Communist takeovers occurring directly to the east and with memories of the millions of German soldiers who had died at the hands of the Red Army, communism and the left in general had little appeal. In 1949, centrist politicians came to power in the new state, officially named the German Federal Republic, whose constitution aimed to prevent the emergence of a dictator and to guarantee individual rights. West Germany's first chancellor was the seventy-three-year-old Catholic anti-Communist Konrad Adenauer, who allied himself with the economist Ludwig Erhard. Erhard stabilized the postwar German currency so that people would have enough confidence in its soundness to resume normal trade, manufacturing, and other economic activity crucial to society's revival. Successfully guiding Germany away from both fascism and communism and using large amounts of U.S. Marshall Plan aid, the economist and the politician restored the representative government that Hitler had overthrown.

Paradoxically, given its leadership in the fight against fascism, the United States was a country in which individual freedom and democracy were imperiled after the war. Two events in 1949—the Soviet Union's successful test of an atomic bomb and the Communist revolution in China—brought to the fore Joseph McCarthy, a U.S. senator foreseeing a reelection struggle. To strengthen his following and win the election, McCarthy warned of a great conspiracy to overthrow the U.S. government. As during the Soviet purges, people of all occupations—including government workers, film stars, and union leaders—were called before congressional panels to confess, testify against friends, and say whether they had ever had Communist sympathies. The atmosphere was electric with confusion, for only five years before, the mass media had run glowing stories about Stalin and the Soviet system. During the war, the American public was told to think of Stalin as a friendly "Uncle Joe." By 1952, however, millions of Americans had been investigated, imprisoned, or fired from their jobs. McCarthy had works like Thomas Paine's *Common Sense*, written in the eighteenth century to support the American Revolution, removed from U.S. agency shelves at home and abroad, and he personally oversaw book burnings. Although the Senate finally voted to censure McCarthy in the winter of 1954, the assault on freedom had been devastating. Even as democracy was restored, fearfulness and anticommunism had come to dominate political life.

An Economic Surge

Given the wartime destruction, the economic rebirth of western Europe was even more surprising than the revival of democracy. In the first weeks and months after the war, the job of rebuilding often involved menial physical labor that mobilized entire populations for such jobs as clearing the

---

Christian Democrats: Powerful center to center-right political parties that evolved in the late 1940s from former Catholic parties of the pre–World War II period.

massive urban rubble by hand. Initially, governments diverted labor and capital into rebuilding infrastructure—transportation, communications, industrial capacity—and away from producing consumer goods. However, the scarcity of household goods sparked unrest. Communism held some attraction because it seemed less interested in the revival of big business and more concerned with ensuring ordinary people a decent standard of living. In the midst of this growing discontent, the Marshall Plan suddenly boosted recovery with American dollars; food and consumer goods became more plentiful; and demand for automobiles, washing machines, and vacuum cleaners accelerated economic growth. Increased productivity wiped out most unemployment.

Helping the postwar recovery was the continuation of military spending for the cold war and the adaptation of wartime technology to meet consumer needs. Civilian travel expanded as nations organized their own airlines based on improved airplane technology. Developed to relieve wartime shortages, synthetic goods such as nylon now became part of peacetime civilian life. Factories churned out a vast assortment of plastic products, ranging from pipes to rainwear. In the climate of cold war, however, military needs remained high: governments ordered bombs, fighter planes, tanks, and missiles (Figure 27.1) and sponsored military research. The outbreak of the Korean War in 1950 (see page 931) increased U.S. orders for manufactured goods to wage that war, further sustaining economic growth in Europe. Ultimately, the cold war prevented a repeat of the 1920s, when reduced military spending threw people out of jobs and fed the growth of fascism.

Large and small states alike developed and redeveloped modern economies in short order. In the twelve principal countries of western Europe, the annual rate of economic growth had been 1.3 percent per inhabitant between 1870 and 1913. Those countries almost tripled that rate between 1950 and 1973, attaining an annual per capita growth rate of 3.8 percent. Among the larger powers, West Germany surprisingly became the economic leader, achieving by the 1960s a stunning revival called the "economic miracle." The smaller Scandinavian countries also achieved a notable recovery: Sweden succeeded in the development of automobile, truck, and shipbuilding industries. Finland modernized its industry in order to pay the reparations demanded by the Soviet Union for resisting its invasion. It also modernized its agriculture, which in turn forced the surplus farm population to seek factory work. Scandinavian women joined the workforce in record numbers, which also boosted economic growth and expanded prosperity. The thirty years after World War II were a golden age of European economic growth.

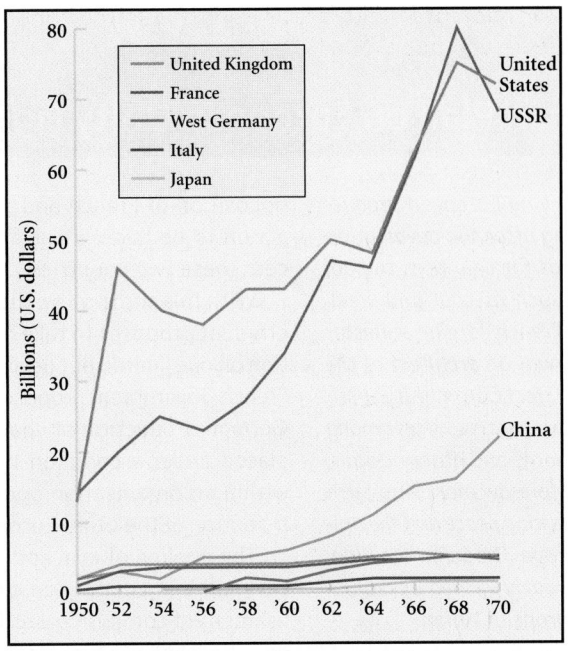

FIGURE 27.1 Military Spending and the Cold War Arms Race, 1950–1970
As soon as the war ended, the United States and the Soviet Union started a massive arms buildup that would continue into the 1980s. Because it had not suffered destruction during the war, the United States could afford to spend hundreds of billions of dollars on weapons. The Soviet Union could not, so its military expenditures deprived Soviet citizens of consumer goods. By the end of the twentieth century, the United States and Russia held vast arsenals of nuclear and other weapons and, along with France, led the way in selling arms that fueled war and genocide around the world.

Birth of the Common Market

The creation of the Common Market, which evolved over time to become the European Union, was the final ingredient in the postwar recovery. The Marshall Plan demanded as a condition for assistance that recipient nations undertake far-reaching economic cooperation. In 1951, Italy, France, West Germany, Belgium, Luxembourg, and the Netherlands took a major step toward cooperation when they formed the European Coal and Steel Community (ECSC)—an organization to manage the joint production of basic resources. Importantly, it arranged for West Germany's abundant output of coal and steel to benefit all of western Europe. According to the ECSC's principal architect, Robert

DOCUMENT

The Schuman Plan on European Unity (1950)

One method of reviving European productivity and well-being after the devastation of World War II was for countries to pool natural resources such as coal and steel. Robert Schuman, French foreign minister from 1948 to 1953, was an architect of the European Coal and Steel Community, instituted after the war to share resources among France, West Germany, and other nations. Schuman, however, foresaw more long-term benefits, including lasting peace and the unification of all of Europe. The Schuman Plan, excerpted here, is widely viewed as a blueprint for today's European Union.

World peace can only be safeguarded if constructive efforts are made proportionate to the dangers which threaten it. . . . Europe will not be made all at once, nor according to a single, general plan. It will be formed by taking measures which work primarily to bring about real solidarity. The gathering of the European nations requires the elimination of the age-old opposition of France and Germany. The action to be taken must first of all concern these two countries.

With this aim in view, the French Government proposes to take immediate action on one limited but decisive point. The French Government proposes that Franco-German production of coal and steel be placed under a common high authority within an organisation open to the participation of the other European nations.

The pooling of coal and steel production will immediately ensure the establishment of common bases for economic development as a first step in the federation of Europe, and will change the destinies of those regions which have long been devoted to the manufacture of arms, to which they themselves were the constant victims.

The common production thus established will make it plain that any war between France and Germany becomes not only unthinkable, but materially impossible. The establishment of this powerful entity, open to all countries willing to take part, and eventually capable of making available on equal terms the fundamental elements of industrial production, will give a real foundation to their economic unification. . . .

By pooling basic production and by creating a new high authority whose decisions will be binding on France, Germany and the other countries that may subsequently join, these proposals will lay the first concrete foundation for a European Federation which is so indispensable to the preservation of peace.

Source: U.S. Department of State Bulletin, June 12, 1959, 936–37. Reprinted in A. G. Harryvan and J. van der Harst, eds., *Documents on European Union* (New York: St. Martin's, 1997), 61–62.

Question to Consider

- **What are the goals of the Schuman Plan and how realistic do they seem in retrospect?**

Schuman, the cooperation created by the organization would make another war "materially impossible." Simply put, ties created by joint productivity and trade would keep France and Germany from another cataclysmic war. (See Document, "The Schuman Plan on European Unity," above.)

The success of the ECSC led to the next momentous step: in 1957, the six ECSC members signed the Treaty of Rome, which provided for a more general trading partnership called the **European Economic Community (EEC)**, known popularly as the **Common Market**. The EEC reduced tariffs among the six partners and developed common trade policies. It brought under one cooperative economic umbrella more than two hundred million consumers and would eventually add several hundred million more. According to one of its founders, the EEC aimed to "prevent the race of nationalism, which is the true curse of the modern world." Increased cooperation produced great economic rewards for the six members, whose rates of economic growth soared.

Britain pointedly refused to join the partnership at first, since membership would have required it to surrender certain imperial trading rights among its Commonwealth partners such as Australia and Canada. Since 1945, British politicians had shunned the developing continental trading bloc because, as one of them put it, participation would make Britain "just another European country." Even without Britain, the rising prosperity of a new western Europe joined in the Common Market was striking.

Economic planning and coordination by specialists (as developed during wartime) shaped the Common Market. Called technocrats, specialists working for the Common Market were to base decisions on expertise rather than on personal interest and on the goals of the organization as a whole

European Economic Community (EEC or Common Market): A consortium of six European countries established in 1957 to promote free trade and economic cooperation among its members; its membership and activities expanded over the years, and it later evolved into the European Union (EU).

rather than on the demands of any one nation. The aim was to reduce the potential for irrationality and violence in politics, both domestic and international. Administered by a commission of technocrats based in Brussels, Belgium, the Common Market transcended the borders of the nation-state and thus exceeded the power of elected politicians. Some critics insisted (and some still insist today) that expert planning would diminish democracy by transferring decision making from legislators to a transnational bureaucracy. Defenders were just as insistent that planning and cooperation would be the surest tools of prosperity and lasting peace.

The Welfare State: Common Ground East and West

On both sides of the cold war divide, governments channeled new resources into state-financed programs such as pensions, disability insurance, and national health care. These social programs taken as a whole became known as the **welfare state**, indicating that states were no longer interested solely in maintaining order and augmenting their power. Veterans' pensions and programs were primary, but the welfare state extended beyond those who had sacrificed in wartime and in part became a weapon in the cold war. Because the European population had declined during the war, almost all countries now desperately wanted to boost the birthrate and thus gave couples direct financial aid for having children. Imitating the social security programs initiated under Bismarck and the more sweeping Swedish programs of the 1930s, nations expanded or created family allowances, health care and medical benefits, and programs for pregnant women and new mothers. The French gave larger family allowances for each birth after the first; for many French families, this allowance provided as much as a third of the household income. Countries east and west vied to show their support of citizens.

Some welfare-state policies had a strong gender bias against women. Britain's maternity benefits and child allowances favored women who did not work outside the home by providing little coverage for workingwomen. The West German government passed strict legislation that forced employers to give women maternity leave, thus discouraging them from hiring women. It also cut back or eliminated pensions and benefits to married women. In fact, West Germans bragged about removing women from the workforce, claiming that doing so distinguished democratic practices from Communist ones. The refusal to build day-care centers or to allow stores to remain open in the evening so that workingwomen could buy food for their families led West Germany to have among the lowest rates of female employment of any industrial country. Another result of West Germany's discriminatory policies was a high rate of female poverty in old age.

By contrast, in eastern Europe and the Soviet Union, where wartime loss of life had been enormous, women worked nearly full-time and usually

The Welfare State in Action, 1947
The Danish creche, or day-care center, here shows the welfare state in action. Government programs to maintain the well-being of citizens became almost universally available in Europe, Canada, and (to a lesser extent) the United States. Children were seen as particularly important, given the loss of life in the war, so governments encouraged couples to reproduce through up-to-date health care systems, day-care centers, and generous family allowances to support family growth. *(Hulton Archive/Getty Images.)*

welfare state: A system (developed on both sides during the cold war) comprising government-sponsored social programs to provide health care, family allowances, disability insurance, and pensions for veterans and retired workers.

outnumbered men in the workforce. As in many western European countries, however, child-care programs, family allowances, and maternity benefits were designed to encourage pregnancies by workingwomen. A national health program provided medical services, as in most countries to the west, but the hardships of everyday life undermined the drive to increase population. The scarcity of consumer goods, the housing shortages, and the lack of household conveniences discouraged workingwomen in Communist countries from having large families no matter what the government wanted. Because women bore the sole burden of domestic duties under such conditions on top of their paying jobs, they rarely wanted more children. As a result, birthrates in the eastern bloc stagnated.

Across Europe, welfare-state programs aimed to improve people's health. State-funded health care systems covered medical needs in most industrial nations except the United States. The combination of better material conditions and state provision of health care dramatically extended life expectancy and lowered rates of infant mortality. Contributing to the overall progress, the number of doctors and dentists more than doubled between the end of World War I and 1950, and vaccines greatly reduced the death toll from such diseases as tuberculosis, diphtheria, measles, and polio. In England, schoolchildren stood an inch taller, on average, than children the same age had a decade earlier.

State initiatives in other areas played a role in raising the standard of living. A growing network of government-built atomic power plants brought more thorough electrification of eastern Europe and the Soviet Union. Governments legislated more leisure time for workers. Beginning in 1955, Italian workers received twenty-eight paid holidays annually; in Sweden, workers received twenty-nine vacation days, a number that grew in the 1960s. Housing shortages brought on by three decades of economic depression and destructive war meant that postwar Europeans often lived with three generations sharing one or two rooms. To rebuild, governments sponsored a postwar housing boom. New suburbs and even entire cities formed around the edges of major urban areas in both East and West. Many buildings went up slapdash, and although some suburbs ultimately were seen as a blight on the environment, they dramatically improved living conditions for postwar refugees, workers, and immigrants.

Recovery in the East

To create a Soviet bloc according to Stalin's vision, Communists revived the harsh methods that had transformed peasant economies earlier in the century. In eastern Europe, Stalin not only continued to collectivize agriculture but also brought about badly needed industrialization through the nationalization of private property. In Hungary, for example, Communists seized and reapportioned all estates over twelve hundred acres. Having gained

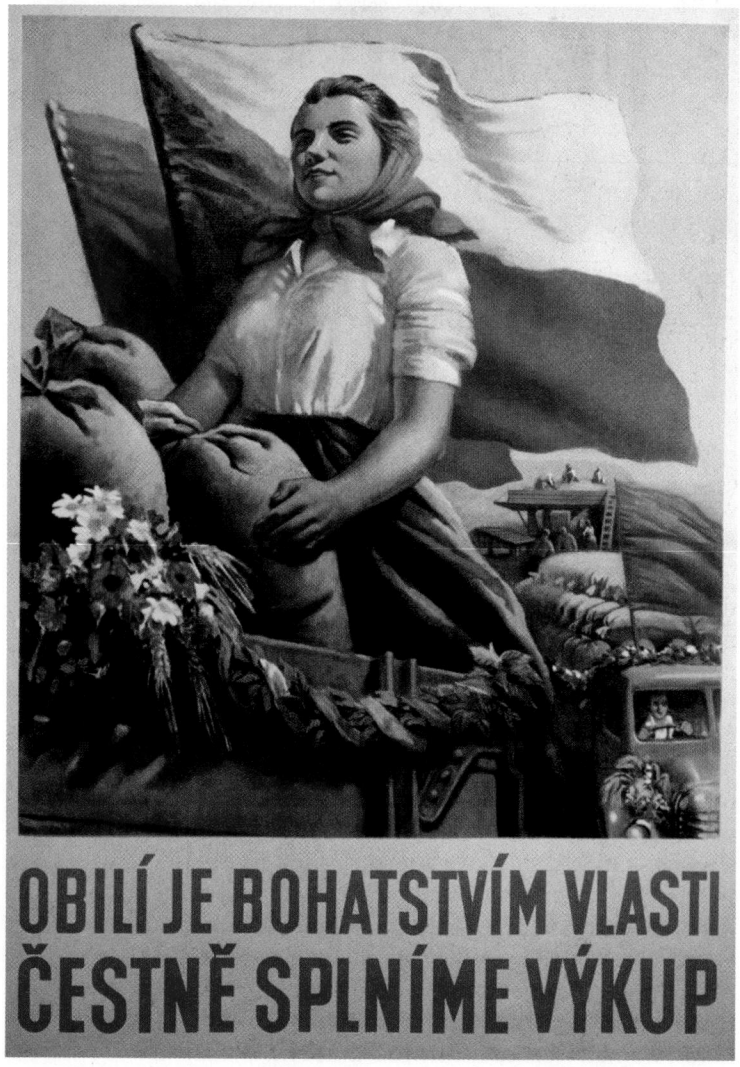

Propaganda for Collective Farming
Dramatic changes were in store for people in eastern Europe who fell under Communist control after World War II. Most objectionable was the policy of collective farming, which stripped farmers of their lands and forced them to farm state property as a group. The poster aims to show Czechs that farming will bring huge benefits, including personal satisfaction. How do you interpret this poster, and why does a woman figure so prominently? *(The Art Archive/German Poster Museum, Essen/Marc Charmet.)*

support of the poorer peasants through this redistribution, the Communists later dispossessed those peasants of their prized lands and pushed them into cooperative farming, though less thoroughly than in the USSR. In Poland, a substantial number of private farms remained.

The process of collectivization was brutal, and rural people later looked back on the 1950s as dreadful. But some workers in the countryside felt that ultimately their lives and their children's lives had improved. "Before we peasants were dirty and poor, we worked like dogs. . . . Was that a good life? No sir, it wasn't. . . . I was a miserable sharecropper and my son is an engineer," said one Romanian peasant. Despite modernization, government investment in agriculture was never high enough to produce the bumper crops of western Europe, and even the USSR depended on produce from the small plots that enterprising farmers cultivated on the side.

Constructing the Soviet Bloc

Stalin admired American industrial know-how and prodded the Communist economies to match U.S. productivity. The Soviet Union formed regional organizations like those in the West, instituting the Council for Mutual Economic Assistance (COMECON) in 1949 to coordinate economic relations among the satellite countries and Moscow. The terms of the COMECON relationship worked against the satellite states, however, for the USSR was allowed to buy goods from its clients at bargain prices and sell goods to them at exorbitant ones. Nonetheless, these formerly peasant states became oriented toward technology and industrial economies directed by bureaucrats, who touted the virtues of steel plants and modern transport.

To escape collectivization, rural people moved to cities, where they received education, health care, and ultimately jobs, albeit at the price of repression. The Roman Catholic church often protested the imposition of communism, but the government crushed it as much as possible or used agents to infiltrate it. The government also discriminated against former members of the elite, including professionals, and even imprisoned them or forced them into hard labor in uranium and other dangerous mines. This policy cleared away opposition—real and imagined—to the Communist takeover of eastern Europe.

Culture, along with science, was a building block of Stalinism in both the USSR and satellite countries. State-instituted programs aimed to build loyalty to the modernizing regime; thus, citizens were obliged to attend adult education classes, women's groups, and public ceremonies. An intense program of Russification and de-Christianization forced non-Russian students in eastern Europe to read histories of the war that ignored their own country's resistance and gave the Red Army sole credit for fighting the Nazis. Rigid censorship resulted in what even one Communist writer in the USSR characterized as "a dreary torrent of colorless, mediocre literature." Stalin also purged prominent wartime leaders to ensure obedience and conformity. Marshal Zhukov, a popular leader of the Soviet armed forces, was shipped to a distant command, while Anna Akhmatova, the widely admired poet who championed wartime resistance to the Nazis, was confined to a crowded hospital room because she refused to glorify Stalin in her postwar poetry.

The Death of Stalin

In March 1953, amid growing repression, Stalin died, and it soon became clear that the old ways would not hold. Political prisoners in the labor camps rebelled, leading to the release of more than a million people from the Gulag. In June 1953, workers in East German cities, many of them socialists and antifascist activists from before the war, protested the rise of privileged Communists in a series of strikes that spread like wildfire. At the other end of the social order, Soviet officials, despite enjoying luxury goods and plentiful food, had come to distrust Stalinism and now favored change. To calm protests across the Soviet bloc, governments stepped up the production of consumer goods—a policy called goulash communism (after the Hungarian stew) because it resulted in more food for ordinary people. The future after Stalin remained uncertain, however.

In 1955, **Nikita Khrushchev** (1894–1971), an illiterate coal miner before the Bolshevik Revolution, outmaneuvered other rivals to become the undisputed leader of the Soviet Union—but he did so without the Stalinist practice of executing his opponents. Khrushchev listened to popular complaints in both city and countryside and then made the surprising move of attacking Stalin. At a party congress in 1956, Khrushchev denounced the "cult of personality" Stalin had built about himself and announced that Stalinism did not equal communism. Khrushchev thus cleverly attributed problems with communism to a single individual. The "secret speech"—it was not published in the USSR but became known fairly quickly—was a bombshell. People experienced, in the words of one writer, "a

---

Nikita Khrushchev (nyih KEE tuh kroosh CHAWF): Leader of the USSR from c. 1955 until his dismissal in 1964; known for his speech denouncing Stalin, creation of the "thaw," and participation in the Cuban missile crisis.

holiday of the soul." Debates broke out in public, and books appeared championing the ordinary worker against the party bureaucracy. The climate of relative tolerance for free expression after Stalin's death was called the thaw.

Protest erupted once more in early summer 1956, when discontented Polish railroad workers struck for better wages. Inspired by the Polish example and angry at living under communism, Hungarians rebelled against forced collectivization in October 1956—"the golden October," they would call their uprising. As in Poland, economic issues, especially announcements of reduced wages, and reports of Stalin's crimes contributed to the outbreak of violence that soon targeted the entire Communist system. Tens of thousands of protesters filled the streets of Budapest and succeeded in returning a popular hero, Imre Nagy, to power. When Nagy announced that Hungary might leave the Warsaw Pact, however, Soviet troops moved in, killing tens of thousands and causing hundreds of thousands more to flee to the West. Nagy was hanged. Crushing the Hungarian Revolution vividly displayed the limits to the thaw. Despite a rhetoric of democracy, the United States refused to intervene in Hungary, choosing not to risk World War III by challenging the Soviet sphere of influence.

The failure of eastern European uprisings overshadowed significant changes since Stalin's death. While defeating his rivals, Khrushchev ended the Stalinist purges and reformed the courts, which came to function according to procedures instead of staging the show trials of the past. The secret police lost many of its arbitrary powers. "It has become more interesting to visit and see people," Boris Pasternak said of the changes. "It has become easier to work." In 1957, the Soviets successfully launched the first artificial earth satellite, *Sputnik*, and in 1961 they put the first cosmonaut, Yuri Gagarin, in orbit around the earth. The Soviets' edge in space technology shocked the western bloc and motivated the creation of the U.S. National Aeronautics and Space Administration (NASA). For Soviet citizens, such successes indicated that the USSR had achieved Stalin's goal of modernization and might inch further toward freedom.

Khrushchev, however, was inconsistent, showing himself open to changes in Soviet culture at one moment and then bullying honest writers at another. After assaulting Pasternak because his novel *Doctor Zhivago* cast doubt on communism and affirmed the value of the individual, in 1961 he allowed the publication of Aleksandr Solzhenitsyn's *One Day in the Life of Ivan Denisovitch*. This chilling account of life in the Gulag was useful, however, in underscoring Khrushchev's denunciation of Stalin's crimes and excesses. Under the thaw, Khrushchev made several trips to the West and was more widely seen by the public than Stalin. More confident and more affluent, the Soviets took steps to reduce their diplomacy's paranoid style and to expand communism's appeal in the new nations of Asia, Africa, and Latin America emerging from colonialism. Despite the USSR's more relaxed posture, however, the cold war advanced and the superpowers moved closer to the nuclear brink.

REVIEW QUESTION What factors drove recovery in western Europe and in eastern Europe?

Decolonization in a Cold War Climate

After World War II, activists in colonized regions in Asia, Africa, and the Middle East used the postwar chaos in Europe and the uncertainties of the cold war to achieve their long-held goal of liberation. At war's end, the colonial powers repressed nationalist groups and futilely attempted to reimpose their control as if they were still dominant around the world. Yet colonized peoples had been on the front lines defending the West; and as in World War I, they had witnessed the full barbarism of Western warfare. Like African American soldiers in the U.S. army, they experienced discrimination even while saving the West. Excluded from victory parades so that the great powers could maintain the illusion of white and Western supremacy, colonial veterans returning home did not receive the rights of citizenship promised them. Moreover, successive wars had allowed local industries in the colonies to develop, while industry in the imperial homelands fell into decline. As a result of the war, colonized peoples, often steeped in Western values and experienced in war and business, were committed to independence.

The path to independence—a process called **decolonization**—was paved with difficulties. In Africa, a continent whose peoples spoke more than five thousand languages and dialects, the European creation of convenient administrative units such as Nigeria and Rhodesia had cut across ethnic lines and undermined local cultures. Religion played a divisive role in independence movements. In India,

decolonization: The process—whether violent or peaceful—by which colonies gained their independence from the imperial powers after World War II.

Hindus and Muslims battled one another even though they shared the goal of eliminating the British. In the Middle East and North Africa, pan-Arab and pan-Islamic movements — that is, those wanting to bring together all Arabs or all Muslims as the basis for decolonization — might seem to have been unifying forces. Yet many Muslims were not Arab, not all Arabs were Muslim, and Islam itself encompassed a range of beliefs. Differences among religious beliefs, ethnic groups, and cultural practices — many of them invented or promoted by the colonizers to divide and rule — worked against political unity. Despite these complications, various peoples in what was coming to be called the third world succeeded in overthrowing imperialism, while the United States and the Soviet Union rushed in to co-opt them for the cold war.

The End of Empire in Asia

At the end of World War II, leaders in Asia succeeded in mobilizing mass discontent to drive out foreign rulers. Declining from an imperial power to a small island nation, Britain was the biggest loser. In 1947, it parted with India, whose independence it had promised in the 1930s. While some two million Indian men were mobilized to fight in the Middle East and Asia, local Indian industry became an important supplier of war goods, and Indian business leaders bought out British entrepreneurs short of cash. Now, armed with economic might and an effective military, Indians began to face off with the British in strikes and other protests.

Britain quickly faced reality. So great was the mistrust it had incited between the Indian National Congress and the Muslim League that Britain decreed that two countries should emerge from the old colony. The partition of 1947 created India for Hindus and Pakistan (itself later divided into two parts) for Muslims. During the independence year, political tensions exploded among opposing members of the two religions. Still another religious group, the Sikhs, felt totally ignored in the settlement and therefore also contributed to the violence. Hundreds of thousands of people overall were massacred in the great shift of populations between India and Pakistan. In 1948, a radical Hindu assassinated Gandhi, who though a Hindu himself had continued to champion religious reconciliation. Elsewhere, as some half a billion Asians gained their independence, Britain's sole remaining Asian colony of note was Hong Kong.

In 1949, after prolonged fighting, a Communist takeover in China brought in a government led by Mao Zedong (1893–1976). Chinese communism in the new People's Republic of China emphasized above all that the country was no longer the plaything of the colonial powers and that its goal was the welfare of the peasantry rather than the industrial proletariat — a departure from both Marxism and Stalinism. At the same time, Mao instituted reforms such as civil equality for women but also imposed Soviet-style collectivization, rapid industrialization, and brutal repression of the privileged classes.

The United States and the Soviet Union were deeply interested in East Asia, the United States because of the region's economic importance and the USSR because of its shared borders. The victory of the Chinese Communists spurred both to increase their involvement in Asian politics. The superpowers faced off first in Korea, which had been split at the thirty-eighth parallel after World War II. In 1950, the North Koreans, with the support of the Soviet Union, invaded U.S.-backed South Korea, whose agents had themselves been stirring up tensions with raids across the border. The United States maneuvered the Security Council of the United Nations into approving a "police action" against the North, and its forces quickly drove well into North Korean territory, where they were met by the Chinese army. After two and a half years of a horribly destructive stalemate, the opposing sides finally agreed to a settlement in 1953: Korea would remain split at its prewar border, the thirty-eighth parallel. As a result of the Korean War, the United States increased its military spending from almost $11 billion in 1948 to almost $60 billion in 1953. The expansion of the cold war to Asia prompted the creation of an Asian counterpart to NATO: the U.S.-backed Southeast Asia Treaty Organization (SEATO), established in 1954. Another effect of the Korean War was the rapid reindustrialization of Japan to provide the United States with supplies.

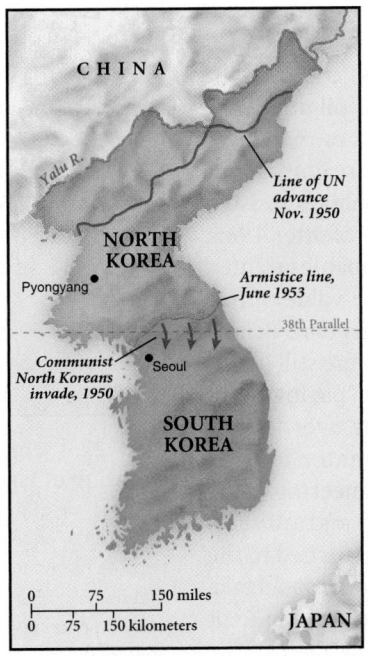

The Korean War, 1950–1953

The cold war then spread to Indochina, where nationalists had been struggling against the postwar revival of French imperi-

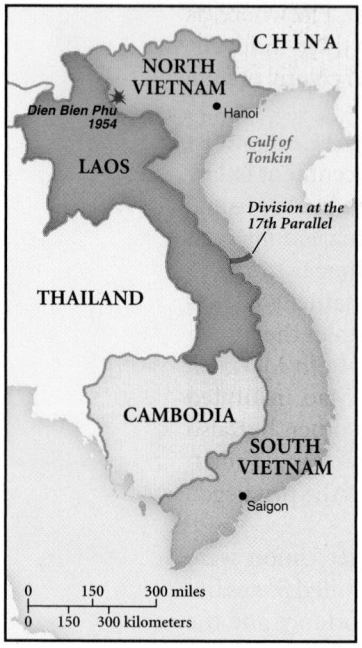

Indochina, 1954

alism. Their leader, the European-educated Ho Chi Minh (1890–1969), built a powerful organization, the Viet Minh, to fight colonial rule. He advocated the redistribution of land held by big landowners, especially in the rich agricultural area in southern Indochina where some six thousand owners possessed more than 60 percent of the land. Viet Minh peasant guerrillas ultimately defeated the technologically superior French army, which was receiving aid from the United States, in the bloody battle of Dien Bien Phu in 1954. Later that year, the Geneva Conference carved out an independent Laos and divided Vietnam along the seventeenth parallel into North and South, each free from French control. The Communist-backed Viet Minh, under Ho Chi Minh as president, ruled in the north, while the United States supported the landowner-backed regime of Ngo Dinh Diem (1901–1963) in the south. Continued superpower intervention undermined the peace agreement, as the two countries fought the cold war in small foreign nations—conflicts now referred to as proxy wars.

The Struggle for Identity in the Middle East

Independence struggles in the Middle East highlighted the world's growing need for oil and often showed the ability of small countries to maneuver between the superpowers. As in other regions dominated by the West, Middle Eastern peoples resisted attempts to reimpose imperial control after 1945. Weakened by the war, British oil companies wanted to tighten their grip on profits as the value of this energy source soared. To achieve this end, British leaders arrogantly behaved as if they were still dominant. For example, Winston Churchill, paying a visit to Saudi Arabia during negotiations over the renewal of Britain's oil rights in the country, insisted that he be served drinks and cigars, sneering at the Islamic prohibitions against alcohol and tobacco. Outraged by this insult, Saudi Arabia turned to the United States, saying that the superpower could take over the oil consortium so long as Britain was kept out. By playing the Western countries against one another, Middle Eastern leaders gained their independence and simultaneously renegotiated higher payments for drilling rights.

The legacy of the Holocaust complicated the Middle Eastern political scene. Since early in the century Western backing for a Jewish settlement in the Middle East had stirred up Arabs' determination not to be pushed out of their ancient homeland. When World War II broke out, 600,000 Jewish settlers and twice as many Arabs lived, tensely, in British-controlled Palestine. In 1947, an exhausted Britain ceded Palestine to the newly created United Nations, which voted to partition Palestine into an Arab region and a Jewish one (Map 27.4). Hostility turned to open war, which Jewish military forces won, and on May 14, 1948, the state of Israel came into being. "The dream had come true," Golda Meir, the future prime minister of Israel, remembered, but "too late to save those who had perished in the Holocaust." Israel opened its gates to immigrants, pitting its expansionist ambitions against those of its Arab neighbors.

One of those neighbors, Egypt, gained its independence from Britain at the end of the war. Britain, however, still dominated shipping to Asia through its control of the Suez Canal, which was owned by a

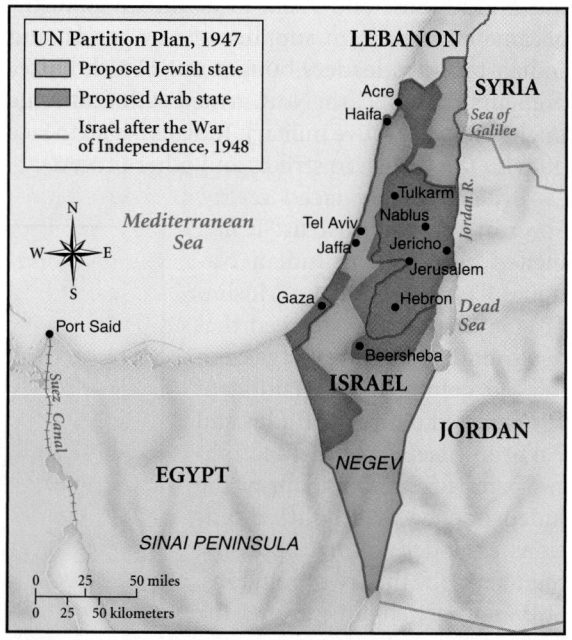

MAP 27.4 The Partition of Palestine and the Creation of Israel, 1947–1948

The creation of the Jewish state of Israel in 1948 against a backdrop of ongoing wars among Jews and indigenous Arab peoples turned the Middle East into a powder keg, a situation that has lasted until the present day. The struggle for resources and for securing the borders of viable nation-states was at the heart of these bitter contests, threatening to pull the superpowers into a third world war.

British-run company. In 1952, Colonel Gamal Abdel Nasser (1918–1970) became Egypt's president on a platform of economic modernization and true national independence—meaning Egyptian control of the canal. In July 1956, Nasser nationalized the canal: "I am speaking in the name of every Egyptian Arab," he remarked in his speech explaining the takeover, "and in the name of all free countries and of all those who believe in liberty and are ready to defend it." Nasser became a heroic figure to Arabs in the region, especially when Britain, supported by Israel and France, attacked Egypt, bringing the Suez crisis to a head while the Hungarian Revolution (see page 930) was in full swing. The British branded Nasser another Hitler and hoped that the events in Hungary would distract the superpowers. The United States, however, fearing that Egypt would turn to the USSR, made the British back down. Nasser's triumph inspired confidence that colonized peoples around the world could gain true independence.

Emerging Nations in the Cold War
Emerging nations could be the playthings of the superpowers during the cold war, but they could also benefit from the rivalry. When Egyptian president Gamal Abdel Nasser refused U.S. military aid in the 1950s because of the supervision the U.S. demanded, Nasser turned to the Soviets and received not only military support but also a low-interest loan for the Aswan Dam—the kind of development project undertaken by emerging nations to provide power and water for both agriculture and industry. In 1964, Nasser (right), Soviet leader Nikita Krushchev, and Algerian president Ahmed Ben Bella inaugurated the opening of the dam. *(Rue des Archives/The Granger Collection, New York—All rights reserved.)*

New Nations in Africa

In sub-Saharan Africa, nationalist leaders roused their people to challenge Europe's increasing demands for resources and labor—demands that resulted in poverty for African peoples. "The European Merchant is my shepherd, and I am in want," went one African version of the Twenty-third Psalm. During World War II, many Africans had flocked to urban shantytowns, where they kept themselves alive by doing menial labor for whites and by scavenging. At the war's end, veterans returned home and protest mounted. Kwame Nkrumah (1909–1972), for example, led the inhabitants of the British-controlled West African Gold Coast in Gandhi-inspired civil disobedience, finally driving the British to withdraw and bringing the state of Ghana into being in 1957. Nigeria, the most populous African region, achieved independence in 1960, and many other African states also became free (Map 27.5).

In mixed-race territory with large settler populations the independence struggle was often fierce and bloody. The eastern coast and southern and central areas of Africa had numerous European settlers, who resisted giving up their control. In British East Africa, where white settlers ruled in splendor and where blacks lacked both land and economic opportunity, fighting erupted in the 1950s. African men formed rebel groups named the Land Freedom Army but nicknamed Mau Mau. With women serving as provisioners, messengers, and weapon stealers, Mau Mau bands, composed mostly of war veterans from the Kikuyu ethnic group, tried to recover land from whites. In 1964, the Land Freedom Army's resistance helped Kenya gain formal independence, but only after the British had put hundreds of thousands of Kikuyus in concentration camps—called a "living hell" and a "British gulag" by those tortured there. The British slaughtered tens of thousands more.

France—although eager to regain its great-power status after its humiliating defeat and occupation in World War II—followed the British pattern of granting independence with relatively little bloodshed to territories such as Tunisia, Morocco, and West Africa, where there were few white settlers. In Algeria, however, which had one million settlers of European descent, the French fought bitterly to keep control. In the final days of World War II, the French army massacred tens of thousands of Algerian nationalists seeking independence; however, the liberation movement resurfaced with new intensity in 1954 as the Front for National Liberation

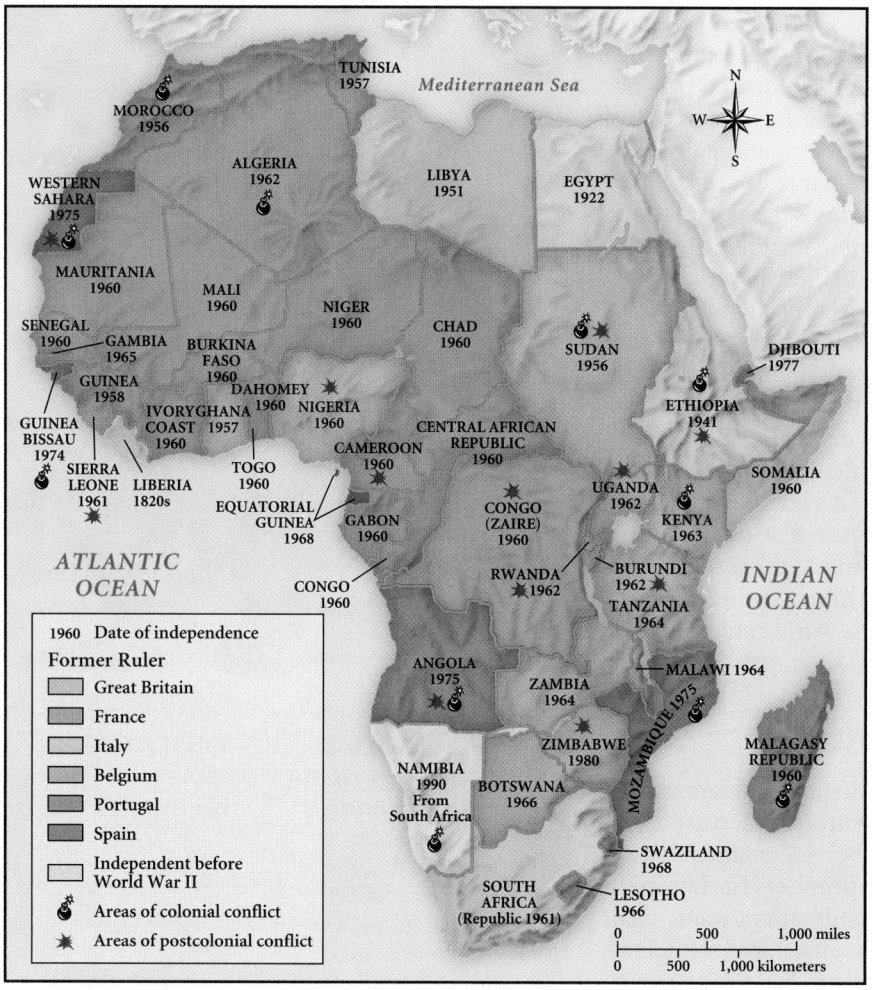

MAP 27.5 The Decolonization of Africa, 1951–1990
The liberation of Africa from European rule was an uneven process, sometimes occurring peacefully and at other times demanding armed struggle to drive out European settlers, governments, and armies. The difficult—and costly—process of nation building following liberation involved setting up state institutions, including educational and other services. Creating national unity out of many ethnicities also took work, except where the struggle against colonialism had already brought people together.

(FNL). The French dug in, sending more than 400,000 troops. Neither side fought according to the rules of warfare: the French savagely tortured Algerian Arabs; Algerian women, shielded from suspicion by gender stereotypes, planted bombs in European cafés and carried weapons to assassination sites. "The loss of Algeria," warned one statesman, defending French savagery, "would be an unprecedented national disaster," while the FNL, far less powerful and smaller in number, took its case to the court of world opinion. Reports of the French army's barbarous practices against Algeria's Muslim population prompted protests in Paris and around the globe. (See Document, "Torture in Algeria," page 935.)

France's Fourth Republic collapsed over Algeria, and wartime leader Charles de Gaulle returned to power in 1958. While promising an end to the Algerian nightmare, he demanded the creation of a new republican government, one with a strong president who chose the prime minister and could exercise emergency power. As de Gaulle's plans to decolonize Algeria unfolded, the French military launched a campaign of terrorism within France itself. By 1962, de Gaulle had negotiated independence with the Algerian nationalists, and hundreds of thousands of *pieds noirs* ("black feet")—as the French condescendingly called Europeans in Algeria—as well as their Arab supporters fled to France.

Violent resistance to the reimposition of colonial rule also ended the empires of the Dutch and Belgians. As newly independent nations emerged in Asia, Africa, and the Middle East, structures arose to promote international security and worldwide deliberations that included representation from the new states. Foremost among these was the **United Nations (UN)**, convened for the first time in 1945. One notable change ensured the UN a greater chance of success than the League of Nations: both the United States and the Soviet Union were active

United Nations (UN): An organization set up in 1945 for collective security and for the resolution of international conflicts through both deliberation and the use of force.

DOCUMENT

Torture in Algeria

Torture was common in the Algerian War, and both the French and the pro-independence forces advertised the brutality of the other side. The French had the greatest means available to pick up and torture not just suspected opponents to their rule but also their neighbors, families, and even bystanders in buildings and on the street. The Algerians printed accounts by the score and circulated them around the world, eventually prompting a broad segment of global public opinion, some of it already shocked by the record of Axis torture and genocide, to oppose French colonialism. As the cases were verified, many more came to light. Here is a published account of the torture of a young woman, Djamila Boupacha, from her sworn deposition against the French. We have edited out some of the most horrific acts done to her.

On the night of 10th and 11th of February 1960, the police, Arab collaborators, and police inspectors—about fifty in all—got out of their jeeps and military trucks . . . and stopped at my parents' house where I lived in Algiers. . . .

On the spot and without being taken away, I was beaten savagely. My brother-in-law Abedelli Ahmed who was also there, suffered the same fate as did my father Boupacha Abdelaziz, 70 years of age.

We were taken to the triage center El-Biar. There I received terrible blows which made me fall to the ground. That was when the soldiers, led by a parachutist captain, crushed my ribs with their boots. I still suffer today from deviated ribs on the left.

After four or five days, I was transferred to Hussein-Dey. It was, they told me, to receive "the second degree." I soon found out what that meant: electric torture to begin with (the electrodes placed on my breasts did not stick so one of the torturers glued them to my skin with scotch tape), then they burned me in the same way on my legs, groin, genitals, and face. Electric torture alternated with cigarette burns, punches with fists, and water torture: suspended over a full bathtub, I was made to drink until suffocating.

Source: Sworn testimony, published in *El Moudjahid* 66 (June 20, 1960), reprinted in *La Femme algerienne dans la revolution. Textes et témoignages inédits* (Alger: ENAG/EDITIONS), 68–69. Translated by Bonnie G. Smith.

Question to Consider

- **What might have been the reaction of various groups, ethnicities, political parties, and regions of European and U.S. society to this testimony?**

members from the outset. The UN's charter outlined a collective global authority that would resolve conflicts and provide military protection if any members were threatened by aggression. In 1955, the Indonesian president Sukarno, who had succeeded in wrenching Indonesian independence from the Dutch, sponsored the Bandung Convention of nonaligned nations to set a common policy for achieving modernization and facing the superpowers. Newly independent countries viewed the future with hope but still had to contend with the high costs of nation building and problems left from decades of colonial exploitation. Both UN deliberations and meetings such as the Bandung Conference began raising major global issues such as human rights and inequities between the countries of the north, which had prospered through colonial plunder, and those of the south, which had been plundered.

Newcomers Arrive in Europe

Amid the uncertainties of wars of independence, people from the former colonies began migrating to Europe—a reversal of the nineteenth-century trend of migration out of Europe. The first non-Europeans came from Britain's Caribbean possessions right after the war. Next, labor shortages in Germany, France, Switzerland, and elsewhere drove governments to negotiate with southern European countries for temporary workers. The German situation was particularly dire; in 1950, the working-age population (people between the ages of fifteen and sixty-four) was composed of 15.5 million men and 18 million women. In an ideological climate that wanted women out of the workforce, the government desperately needed immigrants. Germany and France next turned to North African and then to sub-Saharan countries in the 1960s. Countries in the Soviet bloc took refugees from war-torn Southeast Asia. Scandinavia received immigrants from around the world who flocked there because of reportedly greater opportunity and social programs to integrate newcomers. By the 1980s, some 8 percent of the European population was foreign-born, compared with 6 percent in the United States.

According to negotiated agreements, immigrant workers would have only temporary resident status, with a regular process of return to their homeland. Turks and Algerians would arrive in Germany or France, for example, to work for a set period of

Newcomers to Europe
World War II disrupted everyday life and patterns of trade not only in Europe but also around the globe. Some of the first people to immigrate to Europe in search of postwar opportunity were from the Caribbean (like these men photographed in London in 1956) and South Asia. An expanding welfare state hired some of them to do menial work in hospitals, clinics, and construction, no matter what their qualifications. Governments and businesses in western Europe needed these new laborers to rebuild after World War II, and though some objected, many of these workers—and their wives and children—became not only citizens but political, economic, and cultural leaders as well. *(© Hulton-Deutsch Collection/Corbis.)*

time, return home temporarily to see their families, then head back to Europe for another period as guest workers. Initially, these workers were housed in barracks and few Europeans paid any attention to the quality of their lives. They were welcomed because they took few social services, not even needing education because they came as adults. For businesspeople and policymakers alike, temporary workers made good economic sense. Virtually none of the welfare-state benefits would apply to them; often their menial work was off the books. "As they are young," one French business publication explained, "the immigrants often pay more in taxes than they receive in allowances." Most immigrants did jobs that people in the West were not likely to want: they collected garbage, built roads, and cleaned homes. Although men predominated among migrant workers, women performed similar chores for even less pay.

Immigrants came to see Europe as a land of relatively good government, wealth, and opportunity. Living conditions, too, seemed decent to many. As one Chinese immigrant to Spain put it: "If you want to be a millionaire, you must go to Singapore; if you want to be rich, you must go to Germany; but if you want good weather and an easy life, go to Spain." The advantages of living in Europe, especially the higher wages, made many decide to stay and soon attracted clandestine workers. In the late 1970s, clandestine workers from Africa and Asia began entering countries like Italy that had formerly exported labor. As empires collapsed, European populations became more diverse in terms of race, religion, ethnicity, and social life. Across Europe and North America, many newcomers eventually became citizens and their children achieved good positions in government, business, education, and the professions.

REVIEW QUESTION What were the results of decolonization?

Daily Life and Culture in the Shadow of Nuclear War

Both World War II and the cold war shaped postwar culture. People engaged in heated debate over responsibility for Nazism, ethnic and racial justice, and the merits of the two superpowers. During this period of intense self-scrutiny, Europeans discussed the Americanization that seemed to accompany the influx of U.S. dollars, consumer goods, and cultural media. The quality of private life, so torn by war and totalitarianism, gained attention across the cold war divide. As Europeans examined their war-filled past and their newfound prosperity, the cold war menaced hopes for peace and stability. In 1961, the USSR demanded the construction of a massive wall that physically divided the city of Berlin in half. In October 1962, the world held its breath while the leaders of the Soviet Union and the United States nearly provoked nuclear conflagration over the issue of missiles on the island of Cuba. In hindsight, the existence of extreme nuclear threat in an age of unprecedented prosperity seems utterly bewildering, but for those who lived with the threat of global annihilation, the dangers were all too real.

Restoring "Western" Values

After the depravity of fascism, cultural currents in Europe and the United States reemphasized universal values and spiritual renewal. Some saw the churches as central to the restoration of values through an active commitment to re-Christianizing both the West and the world without concern for national boundaries or imperial competition. Responding to what he saw as a crisis in faith caused by affluence and secularism, Pope John XXIII (r. 1958–1963) in 1962 convened the Second Vatican Council. Known as **Vatican II**, this council modernized the liturgy, democratized many church procedures, and at the last session in 1965 renounced church doctrine that condemned the Jewish people as guilty of killing Jesus. Vatican II promoted ecumenism—that is, mutual cooperation among the world's faiths—and outreach to the world different from the old practice of missionary crusading to expand empires.

The trend toward a more secular culture continued despite reform in the churches. In the early postwar years, people in the U.S. bloc emphasized the triumph of a Western heritage, a Western civilization, and Western values over fascism, and they characterized the war as one "to defend civilization [from] a conspiracy against man." This definition of *West* often emphasized the heritage of Greece and Rome and the rise of national governments in England, France, and western Europe as they encountered "barbaric" forces, a concept that included nomadic tribes, Nazi armies, Communist agents, or national liberation movements in Asia and Africa. Many white Europeans looked back nostalgically on their imperial history and produced exotic films and novels about conquest and its pageantry. University courses in Western civilization flourished after the war to reaffirm these values.

Holocaust and Resistance Literature

Readers around the world snapped up memoirs of the death camps and tales of the resistance. Rescued from the Third Reich in 1940, Nelly Sachs won the Nobel Prize for Literature in 1966 for her poetry about the Holocaust. Anne Frank's *Diary of a Young Girl* (1947), the moving record of a teenager hidden with her family in the back of an Amsterdam house, showed the survival of Western values in the face of Nazi persecution. Amid the menacing evils of Nazism, Frank, who died near the end of the war in the Bergen-Belsen camp, wrote that she never stopped believing that "people are really good at heart." Governments erected permanent plaques at spots where resisters had been killed, and organizations of resisters publicly commemorated their role in winning the war, hiding the fact of widespread collaboration in the heroism of resistance. Thus, French filmmakers, for instance, avoided the subject for decades after the war. Many a politician with a Nazi past returned easily to the new cultural mainstream even as the stories of resistance took on mythical qualities.

Existential Philosophy

At the end of the 1940s, **existentialism** became the rage among the cultural elites and students in universities. This philosophy explored the meaning of human existence in a world where evil flourished. Two of existentialism's leaders, Albert Camus and Jean-Paul Sartre, had written for the resistance during the war, and in its aftermath they confronted the question of "being," given what they perceived as the absence of God and the tragic breakdown of morality. Their answer was that being, or existing, was not the automatic process either of God's creation or of birth into the natural world. One was not born with spiritual goodness in the image of a creator, but instead created an "authentic" existence through action and choice. Camus's novels, such as *The Stranger* (1942) and *The Plague* (1947), pondered the responsibility of humans living under an evil and corrupt political order. Sartre's writings emphasized political activism and resistance under totalitarianism. Even though they had never confronted the enormous problems of making choices while living under fascism, young people in the

Vatican II: A Catholic Council held between 1962 and 1965 to modernize some aspects of church teachings (such as condemnation of Jews), to update the liturgy, and to promote cooperation among the faiths (i.e., ecumenism).

existentialism: A philosophy prominent after World War II developed primarily by Jean-Paul Sartre to stress the importance of action in the creation of an authentic self.

Jean-Paul Sartre and Simone de Beauvoir
The postwar period saw the rise of glossy, richly illustrated weekly magazines featuring news and pop culture. The faces of even the most complex philosophers became well known to the public, while their private lives intrigued readers. The public story of these two existentialists, who were seen to promote the revival of human values after the nightmare of fascism, hid the twisted relationship Sartre and Beauvoir actually had. *(David E. Sherman/Time & Life Pictures/Getty Images.)*

1950s found existentialism compelling and made it the most fashionable philosophy of the day.

In 1949, **Simone de Beauvoir**, Sartre's lifetime companion, published the twentieth century's most important work on the condition of women, *The Second Sex*. Beauvoir believed that most women had failed to take the kind of action necessary to lead authentic lives. Instead, they lived in the world of biological necessity, devoting themselves exclusively to having children. Failing to create an authentic self through action and accomplishment, they had become its opposite—an object, or "Other." Moreover, instead of struggling to define themselves and assert their freedom, women passively accepted their lives as defined by men. Beauvoir's now classic book was a smash hit, and people wrote her thousands of letters asking for advice. Both Sartre and Beauvoir became celebrities, for the media spread the new commitment to humane values just as it had previously spread support for Nazism or for other political ideas.

Simone de Beauvoir (see MAWN duh bohv WAHR): Author of *The Second Sex* (1949), a globally influential work that created an interpretation of women's age-old inferior status from existentialist philosophy.

Race and Human Rights

People of color in Africa and Asia contributed new theories of humanity by exploring the topics of liberation and racial difference. During the 1950s, Frantz Fanon, a black psychiatrist from the French colony of Martinique, began analyzing liberation movements, gaining his insights from his participation in the Algerian war of liberation and other struggles at the time. He wrote that the mental functioning of the colonized person was "traumatized" by the brutal imposition of an outside culture. Ruled by guns, the colonized person knew only violence and would thus naturally decolonize by means of violence. Translated into many languages, Fanon's *Black Skin, White Masks* (1952) and *The Wretched of the Earth* (1961) posed the question of how to decolonize one's culture and mind.

Simultaneous with decolonization, the commitment to the cause of civil rights of such longstanding organizations as the National Association for the Advancement of Colored People (NAACP), founded in 1909, intensified in the 1950s. African Americans had fought in World War II to defeat the Nazi idea of white racial superiority; as civilians, they now hoped to advance that ideal in the United States. With its ruling in *Brown v. Board of Education* (1954), the U.S. Supreme Court declared that segregated education violated the U.S. Constitution. The next step in the civil rights movement came in December 1955, in Montgomery, Alabama, when Rosa Parks, a seamstress and part-time secretary for the local branch of the NAACP, boarded a city bus and took the first available seat in the "colored" section. When a white man found himself without a seat, the driver screamed at Parks, "Nigger, move back." She refused to move, and her studied use of civil disobedience led to a boycott of public transportation in Montgomery and eventually to widespread nonviolent disobedience among African Americans throughout the South.

Civil rights groups boycotted discriminatory businesses, held sit-ins at segregated facilities, and registered black voters disfranchised by local regulations. Talented leaders emerged, foremost among them the great orator Martin Luther King Jr. (1929–1968), a Baptist pastor from Georgia, whose speeches roused activists to nonviolent resistance despite brutal white retaliation. Strongly influenced by Gandhi's life and practice of nonviolent resistance, King advocated "soulforce"—Gandhi's *satyagraha* ("holding to truth")—to counter aggression. The postwar culture of nonviolence shaped the early years of the civil rights movement until the influence of Fanon and other third world activists turned it toward more violent activism in pursuit of rights.

Frantz Fanon
Caribbean psychiatrist Frantz Fanon fought in the French army and studied medicine in Paris; he was also influenced by the existential thinking of his time. His experiences with the French put him on the side of those fighting for national liberation, especially in Algeria. Fanon died of leukemia at age thirty-six, but in his brief lifespan he became a towering intellectual figure for his explanation of the need to decolonize the mind and to use violence to defeat the colonial powers. *(© Everett Collection Inc./Alamy.)*

Cold War Consumerism and Shifting Gender Norms

Government spending on Europe's reconstruction and welfare after World War II helped prevent the kind of upheaval that had followed World War I. Meanwhile, the rising birthrate and bustling youth culture led to an upsurge in consumer spending—a contrast to wartime, during which the lack of consumer goods had made for an absence of spending. Increased emphasis on consumer needs created jobs for veterans. Nonetheless, the war had affected men's roles and sense of themselves. Young men who had missed World War II adopted the rough, violent style of soldiers, and roaming gangs posed as tough military types. While Soviet youth admired aviator aces, elsewhere groups such as the "teddy boys" in England (named after their Edwardian style of dressing) and the *gamberros* ("hooligans") in Spain took their cues from pop culture in rock-and-roll music and film. (See Document, "Popular Culture, Youth Consumerism, and the Birth of the Generation Gap," page 940.)

The leader of rock-and-roll style was the American singer Elvis Presley. Sporting slicked-back hair and an aviator-style jacket, Presley bucked his hips and sang sexual lyrics to screaming and devoted fans. Rock-and-roll concerts and movies galvanized youth across Europe, including the Soviet bloc, where teens demanded the production of blue jeans and leather jackets. In a German nightclub late in the 1950s, members of a British rock group of Elvis fans called the Quarrymen performed, yelling at and fighting with one another as part of their show. They would soon become known as the Beatles. Rebellious young American film stars like James Dean in *Rebel Without a Cause* (1955) and Marlon Brando in *The Wild One* (1953) created the beginnings of a postwar youth culture in which the ideal was to be a bad boy.

Zbigniew Cybulski, the Polish James Dean
Zbigniew Cybulski depicted a tortured young resistance fighter in the film *Ashes and Diamonds* (1958) by Andrzej Wajda. Cybulski's character is to assassinate a Communist resistance leader on what turns out to be the last day of World War II, and his human dilemma around the act is set amid the chaos in Poland at war's end. Like existentialist philosophers and other film directors at the time, Wajda captured the debate over human values and the interest in young heroes of the postwar era. *(Photofest.)*

The rebellious and rough masculine style appeared also in literature, for example in James Watson's autobiography, *The Double Helix* (1968), in which he described how he and Francis Crick had discovered the structure of the DNA molecule

DOCUMENT

Popular Culture, Youth Consumerism, and the Birth of the Generation Gap

A new development put young people at the cutting edge of consumerism and other aspects of Americanization and economic revival. The generation gap, so much talked about in the 1960s, took shape in the preceding decade because of youthful openness on matters of the body and sexuality. Not so mired in the war as their parents, the young were ready for adventure—and adults worried about the consequences. Here an Austrian working-class woman (born in 1933) who sewed for a living describes her consumerism and youth more generally around 1955.

I bought myself records, American blues and jazz, Benny Goodman and Louis Armstrong. I was happy dancing the boogie-woogie. . . .

In fashion I was always very much in opposition to my mother. First, there was the craze around nylon stockings, which were very expensive, and which almost everyone bought. We wore long checked skirts, not made of sheep's wool but of a "mixed" wool that was produced out of rags. Then came a short skirt, just above the knee. When I went dancing, however, everyone wore tight, fashionable skirts. One really had to get oneself into them with a shoehorn, and one's backside stood out. I then sewed a kind of cascade on one side, and thus attired, I proudly went dancing.

At first one wore hair long. But my boss was at me so much about it that I had it cut. Then with the new permanents from America one got a totally new look which was flat in the back with a garland of curls around the rest. But fashion changed fast, at one minute such a hairdo was modern, but then one had to put a comb in to push it up higher.

My home was very nice, with a great deal of love, and because of that my parents gave me a lot of freedom although my mother was always concerned. Above everything she always worried: "What will the neighbors think?"

We only spoke about sex with our schoolmates. Certainly nothing about it came from my parents, nothing either from the school. No, one could not ask about such things. . . . Everything was taboo. And boys and girls were strictly segregated from one another in the school. I remember at carnival time a boy came to school dressed as a girl and was sent right home.

Source: Birgit Bolognese-Leuchtenmüller et al., eds., *Frauen der ersten Stunde 1945–1955* (Vienna: Medieninhaber Europaverlag, 1985), 20–21. Translation by Bonnie G. Smith.

Question to Consider

- **How does this woman's account reflect the clash of ideas between the older and younger generations?**

by stealing other people's findings. The German novelist Heinrich Böll, who decades later admitted to having been a Nazi soldier, protested that West Germany's postwar goal of respectability had allowed the reappearance of the types of people who had produced Nazism. In Böll's novel *The Clown* (1963), the young middle-class hero leaves home and takes up life as a vagabond clown, amusing audiences with clever pantomimes about the folly of their lives. Not a breadwinner but a bum, he ends up a model bad boy begging in a railroad station. American "beat" poets and writers vehemently rejected the traditional ideals of the upright male breadwinner and family man.

Both high and low culture revealed that two horrendous world wars had upset the Enlightenment view of men as rational, responsible achievers. The 1953 inaugural issue of the American magazine *Playboy*, and the hundreds of magazines that came to imitate it across Europe, ushered in a startling depiction of a changed male identity. This new media presented modern man as sexually aggressive and independent of dull domestic life—just as he had been in the war. Breadwinning for a family destroyed a man's freedom and sense of self, this new male culture claimed. The definition of men's citizenship had come to include not just political and economic rights but also sexual freedom outside the restrictions of marriage.

In contrast, Western society promoted a postwar model for women that differed from their wartime roles, adopting instead the fascist notion of women's inferiority. Rather than being essential workers and heads of families in the absence of their men, postwar women were to symbolize the return to normalcy by leading a domestic and submissive life at home. Late in the 1940s, the fashion house of Christian Dior launched a clothing style called the "new look." It featured pinched waists, tightly fitting bodices, and voluminous skirts. This restoration of the nineteenth-century female silhouette invited a renewal of clearly defined gender roles. Women's magazines publicized the new look and urged women to give up ambitions for themselves. Even in the hard-pressed Soviet Union, domesticity flourished; recipes for homemade face creams, for

Rock and Roll
Rock and roll, born in the 1950s, swept cities around the world with unprecedented energy and speed. Teen women wore the voluminous skirts that the "new look" had made fashionable in the late 1940s, and young men sported hairdos like those of Elvis Presley or Zbigniew Cybulski. East and west, teens thronged and even rioted to attend rock concerts and would continue to do so despite public criticism and even police action against the movement. *(ullstein bild/The Granger Collection, New York—All rights reserved.)*

example, passed from woman to woman, and beauty parlors did a brisk business. In the West, household products such as refrigerators and washing machines raised standards for housekeeping by giving women the means to be "perfect" housewives.

However, new-look propaganda did not necessarily mesh with reality or even with all social norms. Dressmaking fabric was still being rationed in the late 1940s; even in the next decade, women could not always get enough of it to make voluminous skirts. In Europe, where people had barely enough to eat, the underwear needed for new-look contours simply did not exist—although for many, unfortunately, the semistarved look was not achieved by choice. In Spain, women were said to perform their role best by being religious and concerned with the spiritual well-being of their families. Spanish advertising, however, emphasized the physical beauty available through cosmetics and clothing; it urged women to buy things that would make their families look better, too.

Despite welfare-state policies intended to promote childbearing, European women continued to work outside the home after the war; indeed, mature women and mothers were working more than ever before—especially in the Soviet bloc (Figure 27.2). Across the Soviet sphere consumer goods were always in short supply, but opinion makers stressed to these women the importance of a tasteful and up-to-date domestic interior. East and West, the female workforce was going through a profound revolution as it gradually became populated by wives and mothers who would hold jobs all their lives despite being bombarded with images of nineteenth-century femininity.

The advertising business presided over the creation of these cultural messages as part of both the return of consumerism and the cold war. Guided by marketing experts, western Europeans imitated Americans by drinking Coca-Cola; using American detergents, toothpaste, and soap; and driving some forty million motorized vehicles, including motorbikes, cars, buses, and trucks. While many Europeans embraced American business practices, the cold war was ever present: the Communist Party in France led a successful campaign to ban Coca-Cola for a time in the 1950s, and tastemakers in the Soviet sphere initiated competing products and styles.

Radio remained the most influential medium in the 1950s, carrying much of the postwar consumer advertising and making the connection between cold war and consumerism. Even as the number of radios in homes grew steadily, television loomed on the horizon. In the United States, two-thirds of the population had TV sets in the early 1950s, while in Britain only one-fifth did. Only in the 1960s did television become an important consumer item for most Europeans. In radio and television, though, both East and West tried to exceed the other in advertising their values. Russian programs stressed a uniform Communist culture, often emphasizing the importance of family values and practical, if aesthetically pleasing, household tips for women. The United States, by contrast, emphasized diverse programming, promoted debate about current affairs, and filled the airwaves with

	Member Countries of Council of Mutual Economic Assistance[1]		Member Countries of European Economic Community[2]	
	1950	1960	1950	1960
Female as % of total population	54.9	53.9	51.8	51.6
Female labor force as % of total labor force	48.5	48.7	31.1	31.4
Distribution of female labor force (%):				
Agriculture	63.3	50.0	26.1	16.8
Industry	16.9	22.6	29.3	31.3
Services	19.8	27.4	44.6	51.9

[1]Albania, Bulgaria, Czechoslovakia, East Germany, Hungary, Poland, Romania, and USSR

[2]Belgium, Denmark, France, West Germany, Ireland, Italy, Luxembourg, Netherlands, and United Kingdom

FIGURE 27.2 Women in the Workforce, 1950–1960

In contrast to the situation after World War I, women did not leave the workforce in great numbers after World War II. In fact, Europe faced labor shortages. In Soviet-bloc countries, women vastly outnumbered men because so many men had died in the war, and the task of rebuilding demanded every available worker. In western Europe, women's workforce participation was lower, and countries like West Germany tried to keep women out of the labor pool to distinguish themselves from the Communist bloc. Note the increase in women's service-sector employment in just one decade. *(From* World Employment 1996–1997: National Policies in a Global Context *[Geneva: International Labour Office, 1996], 7.)*

The Three Graces

French artist Niki de Saint Phalle's compositions often tried to capture the vibrancy of non-Western art, especially that created by women, whose spirit and style she hoped to duplicate in her own work. Saint Phalle's sculptures decorate public places across the West. *(*Washington Post*/Getty Images.)*

advertising for consumer goods. The cold war was thus a consumer as well as a military phenomenon.

The Culture of Cold War

Films, books, and other cultural productions also promoted the cold war even when they conveyed an antiwar message. Books like George Orwell's *1984* (1949) were claimed by both sides in the cold war as supporting their position. Ray Bradbury's popular *Fahrenheit 451* (1953), whose title refers to the temperature at which books would burn, condemned restrictions on intellectual freedom on both sides of the cold war divide. In the USSR, official writers churned out spy stories, and espionage novels topped best-seller lists in the West. *Casino Royale* (1953), by the British author Ian Fleming, introduced the fictional British intelligence agent James Bond, who tested his wit and physical prowess against Communist and other political villains. Soviet pilots would not take off for flights when the work of Yulian Simyonov, the Russian counterpart of Ian Fleming, was playing on radio or television. Reports, fictional and real, of Soviet- and U.S.-bloc characters facing one another down became part of everyday life.

High culture also operated in a cold-war climate. Europe's major cities rebuilt their war-ravaged opera houses and museums, and both sides tried to win the cold war by pouring vast sums of money into high culture. The United States did so by secretly channeling government money into foundations to award fellowships to artists or promote favorable journalism around the world. As leadership of the art world passed to the United States, art became part of the cold war. Abstract expressionists such as American artist Jackson Pollock produced nonrepresentational works by dripping and spattering paint; they also spoke of the importance of the artist's self-discovery in the process of painting. "If I stretch my arms next to the rest of myself and wonder where my fingers are, that is all the space I need as a painter," commented Dutch-born artist Willem de Kooning on his relationship with his canvas. Said to exemplify Western freedom, such painters were awarded commissions at the secret direction of the U.S. Central Intelligence Agency.

The USSR more openly promoted an official Communist culture. When a show of abstract art opened in the Soviet Union, Khrushchev yelled that it was "dog shit." Pro-Soviet critics in western Europe saw U.S.-style abstract art as "an infantile sickness" and supported socialist realist art with "human content," showing the condition of the workers and the oppressed races in the United States. The Italian filmmakers Roberto Rossellini, in *Open City* (1945), and Vittorio De Sica, in *The Bicycle Thief* (1948), developed the neorealist technique that challenged lush Hollywood-style sets and costumes by using ordinary characters living in devastated, impoverished cities. By depicting stark conditions, neorealist directors conveyed their distance both from middle-class prosperity and from fascist bombast. "We are in rags? Let's show everyone our rags," said one Italian director. Many of these left-leaning directors associated support for the suffering masses with the Communist cause, while on the pro-American side, the film *Doctor Zhivago* became a hit celebrating individualism and condemning the Communist way of life. Overtly or covertly, the cold war affected virtually all aspects of cultural life.

The Atomic Brink

The 1950s were a time of emotional terror for people at the center of the cold war. Radio bombarded the public with messages about the threat of nuclear annihilation at the hands of the villainous superpower enemy. As superpower rivalry heated up, radio's propaganda function remained as strong as it had been in wartime, and it was soon joined by television. During the late 1940s and 1950s, the Voice of America, with its main studio in Washington, D.C., broadcast in thirty-eight languages from one hundred transmitters and provided an alternative source of news as well as menacing messages for people in eastern Europe. Its Soviet counterpart broadcast in Russian around the clock but initially spent much of its wattage jamming U.S. programming. The public also heard reports of nuclear build-ups, and tests of emergency power facilities sent them scurrying for cover. Children rehearsed at school for nuclear war, while at home families built bomb shelters in their backyards. Fear gripped people's emotions in these decades.

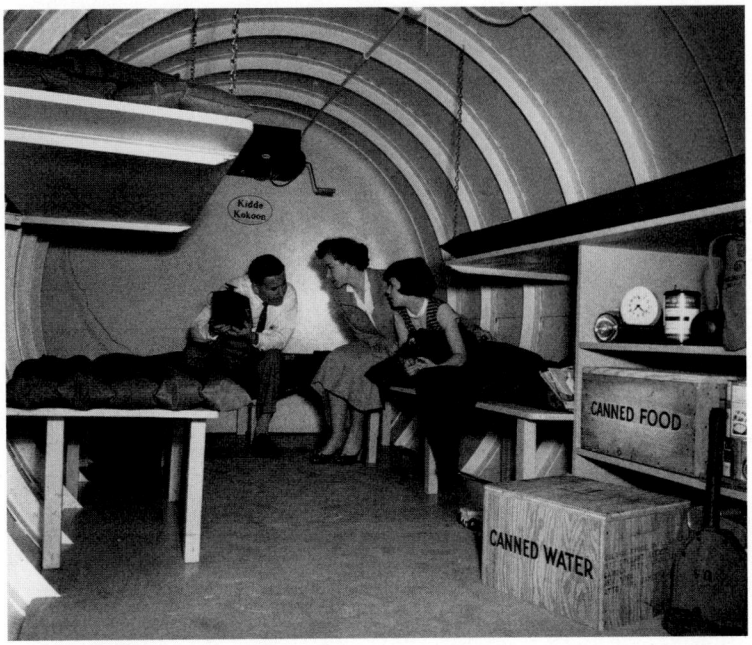

Bomb Shelter
Americans expressed their fear of nuclear annihilation by building tens of thousands of individual bomb shelters. Stocked with several months' supply of canned food and other goods, the shelters were to protect a family from the nuclear blast itself and from the disorder that might follow nuclear war. The government also prepared shelters to shield top officials and to ensure the continuation of civil society despite vast casualties and massive destruction. *(© Bettman/Corbis.)*

In this upsetting climate of cold war, **John Fitzgerald Kennedy** (1917–1963) was elected U.S. president in 1960. Kennedy represented American affluence and youth, yet he also confirmed the nation's commitment to the cold war. Kennedy's media advisers recognized how perfect a match their articulate, good-looking president was for the power of television. A war hero and an early fan of the fictional cold war spy James Bond, Kennedy par-

John Fitzgerald Kennedy: U.S. president (1961–1963) who faced off with Soviet leader Nikita Khrushchev in the Cuban missile crisis.

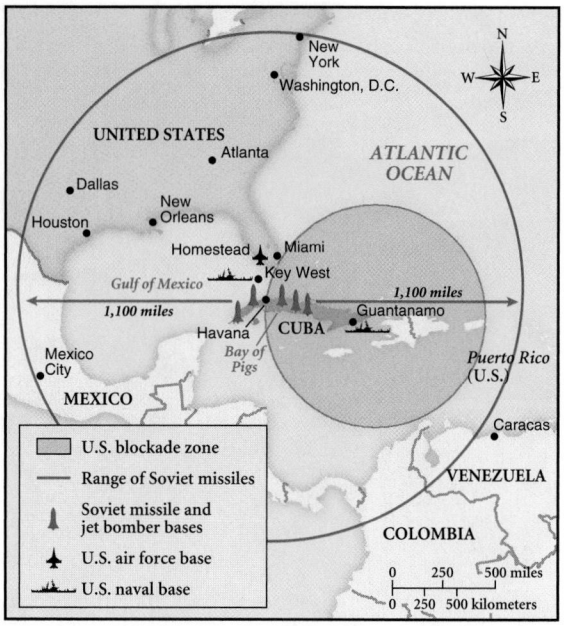

MAP 27.6 The Cuban Missile Crisis, 1962
Just off the coast of the southeastern United States, Cuba posed a threat to North American security once the Soviet Union began stocking the island with silos for missiles. The United States reacted vigorously, insisting that the USSR dismantle the missile sites. Although his generals were prepared for nuclear war with the Soviet Union, President Kennedy refused to take this step, and Soviet premier Khrushchev similarly backed down from a military confrontation. | **Explain the placement of missiles in Cuba and the U.S. reaction to it.**

ticipated in the escalating cold war. Some of this escalation occurred over the nearby island of Cuba, where in 1959 the Communist leader Fidel Castro (1926–) had come to power by overthrowing the corrupt government of the dictator Fulgencio Batista. After being rebuffed by the United States, Castro aligned his new government with the Soviet Union. In the spring of 1961, Kennedy, assured by the Central Intelligence Agency (CIA) of success, launched an invasion of Cuba at the Bay of Pigs intended to overthrow Castro. The invasion failed miserably and humiliated the United States.

Cold war tensions increased. In the summer of 1961, the East German government directed workers to stack bales of barbed wire across miles of the city's east–west border as the beginning of the Berlin Wall. The divided city had served as an escape route by which some three million people, including skilled workers and professionals, had fled to the West. Kennedy responded by calling for more defense spending. In October 1962, tensions came to a head in the **Cuban missile crisis**, when the CIA reported the installation of silos to house Soviet medium-range missiles in Cuba (Map 27.6). Kennedy acted forcefully, ordering a naval blockade of ships headed for Cuba and demanding removal of the installations. For several days, the world stood on the brink of nuclear war. Then, between October 25 and 27, Khrushchev and Kennedy negotiated an end to the crisis. Kennedy spent the remainder of his short life working to improve nuclear diplomacy; Khrushchev did the same. In the summer of 1963, less than a year after the shock of the Cuban missile crisis, the United States and the Soviet Union signed a test-ban treaty outlawing the explosion of nuclear weapons in the atmosphere and in the seas. Allowing the superpowers to back away from the brink, the treaty held out hope that the cold war and its culture would give way to something better.

REVIEW QUESTION How were everyday culture and social life part of the cold war?

Conclusion

Nikita Khrushchev was ousted in 1964 for his erratic policies and for the Cuban missile crisis. In his forced retirement, he expressed regret at his brutal treatment of Boris Pasternak: "We shouldn't have banned [*Doctor Zhivago*]. There's nothing anti-Soviet in it." But the postwar decades were grim times. Two superpowers — the Soviet Union and the United States — each controlling atomic arsenals, overshadowed European leadership and engaged in a menacing cold war, complete with the threat of nuclear annihilation. The cold war saturated everyday life, giving birth to bomb shelters, spies, purges, and witch hunts — all of them creating a culture of anxiety that kept people in constant fear of imminent war. Cold war diplomacy divided Europe into an eastern bloc dominated by the Soviets and a freer western bloc mostly allied with the United States. In this bleak atmosphere, starving, homeless, and refugee people joined the task of rebuilding a devastated Europe.

Despite the chaos at the end of 1945, both halves of Europe recovered almost miraculously in little more than a decade. Eastern Europe, where wartime devastation and ongoing violence were greatest, experienced less prosperity. In the West, wartime technology served as the basis for new consumer

Cuban missile crisis: The confrontation in 1962 between the United States and the USSR over Soviet installation of missile sites off the U.S. coast in Cuba.

MAPPING THE WEST

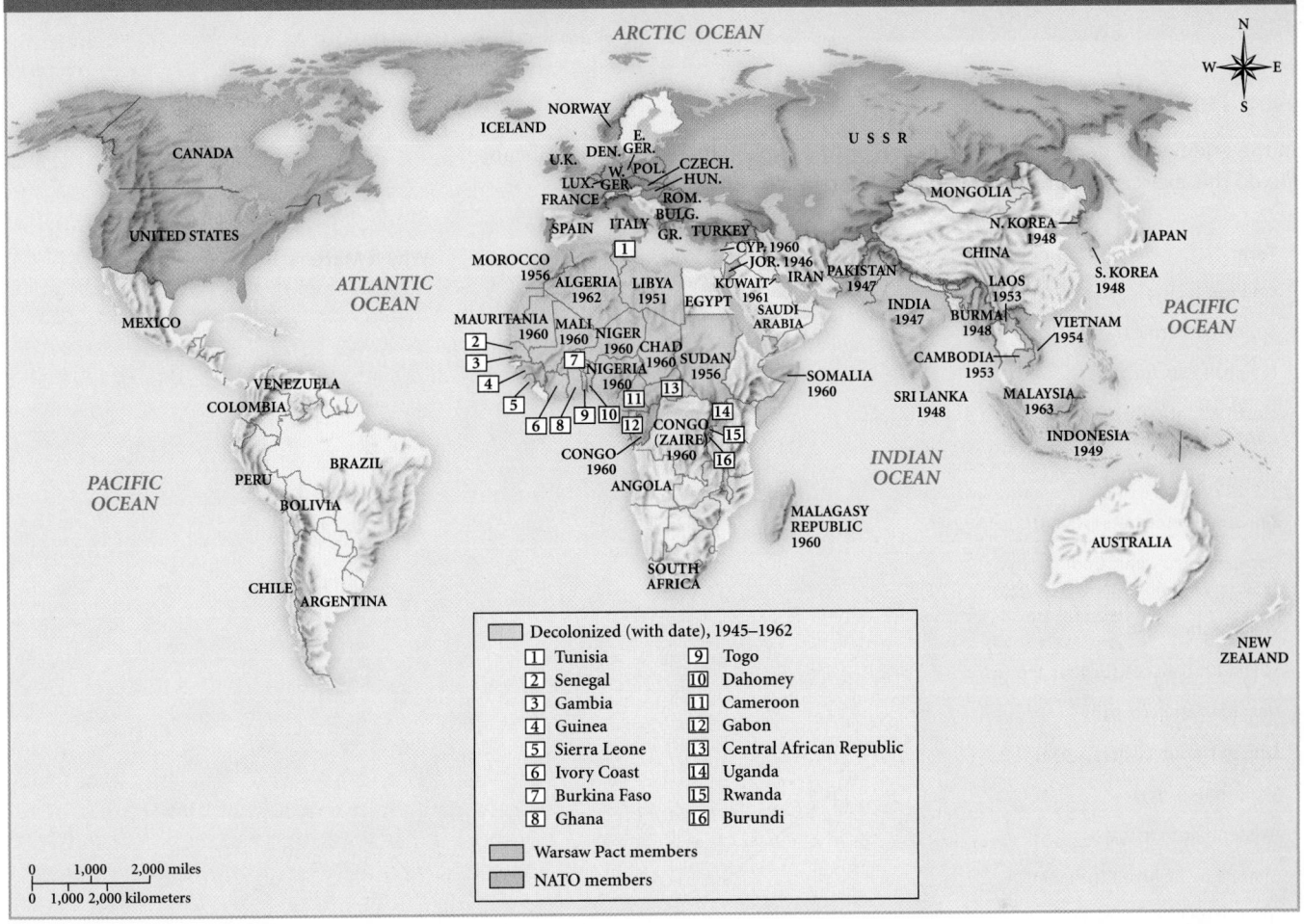

The Cold War World, c. 1960

Superpower rivalry between the United States and the Soviet Union resulted in the division of much of the industrial world into cold war alliances. Simultaneously, the superpowers vied for the allegiance of the newly decolonized countries of Asia and Africa by providing military, economic, and technological assistance. Wars such as those in Vietnam and Korea were also products of the cold war. | **How might this map be said to convey the idea that a first world, a second world, and a third world existed? How does this map differ from the map on page 793?**

goods and welfare-state planning improved health. Spurred on by aid from the United States, western Europe formed the successful Common Market, which became the foundation for greater European unity in the future. As a result of World War II and the cold war, Germany recovered as two countries, not one. The war so weakened the European powers that they lost their colonies to thriving independence movements. Newly independent nations emerged in Asia and Africa, leaving in question whether there would be further change in the balance of global power. These new countries were often caught in the competition for cold war allies and faced the additional problems of creating stable political structures and a sound economic future. As the West as a whole grew in prosperity, its cultural life focused paradoxically on reviving Western values while enjoying the new phenomenon of mass consumerism. Above all, the West—and the rest of the world—had to survive the atomic rivalry of the superpowers.

FOR FURTHER EXPLORATION

- **For additional primary-source material from this period**, see *Sources of the Making of the West*, Fourth Edition.
- **For Web sites, images, and documents related to topics in this chapter**, visit *Make History* at bedfordstmartins.com/hunt.

Chapter 27 Review

Online Study Guide bedfordstmartins.com/hunt

Key Terms and People

In the grid below, identify the term or person and explain its historical significance. (To do this exercise online, go to bedfordstmartins.com/hunt.)

Term	Who or What & When	Why It Matters
cold war (p. 914)		
Truman Doctrine (p. 919)		
Marshall Plan (p. 919)		
North Atlantic Treaty Organization (NATO) (p. 921)		
Warsaw Pact (p. 921)		
Christian Democrats (p. 924)		
European Economic Community (EEC or Common Market) (p. 926)		
welfare state (p. 927)		
Nikita Khrushchev (p. 929)		
decolonization (p. 930)		
United Nations (UN) (p. 934)		
Vatican II (p. 937)		
existentialism (p. 937)		
Simone de Beauvoir (p. 938)		
John Fitzgerald Kennedy (p. 943)		
Cuban missile crisis (p. 944)		

Review Questions

1. What were the major events in the development of the cold war?
2. What factors drove recovery in western Europe and in eastern Europe?
3. What were the results of decolonization?
4. How were everyday culture and social life part of the cold war?

Making Connections

1. What was the political climate after World War II, and how did it differ from the political climate after World War I?
2. What were the relative strengths of the two European blocs in the cold war?
3. What were the main developments of postwar cultural life?
4. Why did decolonization follow World War II so immediately?

Important Events

Date	Event	Date	Event
1945	Cold war begins	1954	*Brown v. Board of Education* prohibits segregated schools in the United States; Vietnamese forces defeat French at Dien Bien Phu
1947	India and Pakistan win independence from Britain	1956	General Abdel Nasser nationalizes Suez Canal; uprising in Hungary against USSR
1948	State of Israel established	1957	Boris Pasternak publishes *Doctor Zhivago*; USSR launches *Sputnik*; Treaty of Rome establishes European Economic Community (Common Market)
1949	Mao Zedong leads Communist revolution in China; Simone de Beauvoir publishes *The Second Sex*	1958	Fifth Republic begins in France
1950	Korean War begins	1962	United States and USSR face off in the Cuban missile crisis
1953	Stalin dies; Korean War ends		

- Consider three events: **India and Pakistan win independence from Britain (1947)**, **Simone de Beauvoir publishes *The Second Sex* (1949)**, and ***Brown v. Board of Education* prohibits segregated schools in the United States (1954)**. How did colonized peoples, women, and African Americans use the experience of war to seek liberation and civil rights?

SUGGESTED REFERENCES

New nationhood and the postwar era are charted in exciting new books that study veterans, youth, and daily life in the aftermath of Nazism and an age of cold war. Historians are also focusing on the complexities of decolonization.

Chin, Rita, et al., eds. *After the Nazi Racial State: Difference and Democracy in Germany and Europe*. 2009.

De Grazia, Victoria. *Irresistible Empire: America's Advance through 20th-Century Europe*. 2005.

Edele, Mark. *Soviet Veterans of World War II: A Popular Movement in an Authoritarian Society, 1941–1991*. 2008.

Frommer, Benjamin. *National Cleansing: Retribution against Nazi Collaborators in Postwar Czechoslovakia*. 2005.

Gaddis, John. *The Cold War: A New History*. 2006.

Grossman, Atina. *Jews, Germans, and Allies: Close Encounters in Occupied Germany, 1945–1949*. 2007.

Jobs, Richard I. *Riding the New Wave: Youth and the Rejuvenation of France after World War II*. 2007.

Milward, Alan S. *The United Kingdom and the Economic Community*. 2002.

Moeller, Robert. *War Stories: The Search for a Usable Past in the Federal Republic of Germany*. 2001.

Nord, Philip. *France's New Deal: From the Thirties to the Postwar Era*. 2010.

Pence, Katherine, and Paul Betts, eds. *Socialist Modern: East German Everyday Culture and Politics*. 2008.

Poiger, Uta. *Jazz, Rock, and Rebels: Cold War Politics and American Culture in a Divided Germany*. 2000.

Shepard, Todd. *The Invention of Decolonization: The Algerian War and the Remaking of France*. 2006.

Shipway, Martin. *Decolonization and Its Impact: A Comparative Approach to the End of the Colonial Empires*. 2008.

Smith, Andrea L., ed. *Europe's Invisible Migrants*. 2003.

Smith, Mark B. *Property of Communists: The Urban Housing Program from Stalin to Khrushchev*. 2010.

Statler, Andrea, and Andrew Johns, eds. *The Eisenhower Administration, the Third World, and the Globalization of the Cold War*. 2006.

M. Jan Hus, Velký výklad víry, kap. V., 1420
Bojuj pro ty až do smrti, neboť pravda tě vysvobodí
ZARMOUCENI OZNAMUJEME, ŽE DNE 19. LEDNA 1969 OD NÁS
NAVŽDY ODEŠEL NÁŠ SYN A BRATR, STUDENT
FILOSOFICKÉ FAKULTY UNIVERSITY KARLOVY
PALACH
NEJCISTŠÍMI A NEJHUMÁNNĚJŠÍMI LIDSKÝMI
IDEÁLY OBĚTOVAL SEBE SAMA SVÉMU LIDU A SVÉ ZEOUŠENÉ
VLASTI.
TĚLESNÝ POZŮSTATEK NAŠEHO JANA BUDOU V SOBOTU DNE
ZE LEDNA 1969 V 16 HODIN ULOŽENY DO ZEMĚ
ŽELEZNICKÉHO BRODU
Pan Prezident
Václav Havel
DNES 9.1.1990
Týden Časem
NEZAPOMENEM
Tvůj
NÁROD

CHAPTER

28

Postindustrial Society and the End of the Cold War Order

1960s–1989

In January 1969, Jan Palach, a twenty-one-year-old philosophy student, drove to a main square in Prague, doused his body with gasoline, and set himself ablaze. Before that, he had put aside his coat with a message in it demanding an end to Communist repression in Czechoslovakia. It promised more such suicides unless the government lifted state censorship. The manifesto was signed "Torch No. 1." Jan Palach's suicide stunned his nation. Black flags hung from windows, and close to a million people flocked to his funeral. In the next months, more Czech youth followed Palach's grim example and became torches for freedom.

Before his self-immolation, Jan Palach was an ordinary, well-educated citizen of an increasingly technological society. Having recovered from World War II, the West shifted from a manufacturing economy based on heavy industry to a service economy that depended on technical knowledge in such fields as engineering, health care, and finance. This new service economy has been labeled "postindustrial." To staff it, institutions of higher education sprang up at a dizzying rate and attracted more students than ever before. Young men like Jan Palach—along with women, minorities, and many other activists in the 1960s and 1970s—far from being satisfied with their rising status, struck out against war and cold war, inequality and repression, and even against technology itself. From Czechoslovakia to the United States and around the world, protesters warned that postindustrial nations in general and the superpowers in particular were becoming technological and political monsters. Before long, countries in both the Soviet and U.S. blocs were on the verge of political revolution.

Shrine to Jan Palach
Jan Palach was a martyr to the cause of an independent Czechoslovakia. His self-immolation on behalf of that cause roused the nation. As makeshift shrines sprang up and multiplied throughout the 1970s and 1980s, they served as common rallying points that ultimately contributed to the overthrow of Communist rule. Václav Havel, the future president of a liberated Czechoslovakia, was arrested early in the momentous year of 1989 for commemorating Palach's sacrifice at a shrine. In light of so many other deaths in the Soviet bloc, why did Jan Palach's death become so powerful a force?
(© Marc Garanger/Corbis.)

The Revolution in Technology 950
- The Information Age: Television and Computers
- The Space Age
- The Nuclear Age
- Revolutions in Biology and Reproductive Technology

Postindustrial Society and Culture 955
- Multinational Corporations
- The New Worker
- The Boom in Education and Research
- Changing Family Life and the Generation Gap
- Art, Ideas, and Religion in a Technocratic Society

Protesting Cold War Conditions 961
- Cracks in the Cold War Order
- The Growth of Citizen Activism
- 1968: Year of Crisis

The Testing of Superpower Domination and the End of the Cold War 970
- A Changing Balance of World Power
- The Western Bloc Meets Challenges with Reform
- Collapse of Communism in the Soviet Bloc

The challenges posed by young reformers came at a bad time for the superpowers and other leading European states. An agonizing war in Vietnam weakened the United States, and China confronted the Soviet Union on its borders. In a dramatic turn of events, the oil-producing states of the Middle East formed a cartel and reduced the export of oil to the leading Western nations in the 1970s. The resulting price increases helped bring on a recession, threatening the ballooning postindustrial economy. Extremists turned to terrorism to achieve their goals, while despite their wealth and military might, the superpowers could not guarantee that they would emerge victorious in this age of increasingly global competition. As the USSR experienced decay in a climate of postindustrial innovation across the West, a reform-minded leader—Mikhail Gorbachev—directed his nation to change course and initiated new policies of economic and political freedom. It was too late: in 1989, the Soviet bloc collapsed, an event brought about in part by countless acts of protest, not least of them the individual heroism of Jan Palach and his fellow human torches.

CHAPTER FOCUS How did technological, economic, and social change contribute to increased activism, and what were the political results of that activism?

The Revolution in Technology

The protests of the 1960s began in the midst of astonishing technological advances. These advances steadily boosted prosperity and changed daily life in the West, where people awoke to instantaneous radio and television news, worked with computers, and used new forms of contraceptives to control reproduction. Satellites orbiting the earth relayed telephone signals and collected military intelligence, while around the world nuclear energy powered economies. Smaller gadgets—electric popcorn poppers, portable radios and tape players, automatic garage door openers—made life more pleasant. The increased use of machines led one philosopher to insist that people were no longer self-sufficient individuals, but rather cyborgs—that is, humans who needed machines to sustain ordinary life processes.

The Information Age: Television and Computers

Information technology powered change in the postindustrial period that began in the 1960s, just as innovations in textile making and the spread of railroads had in the nineteenth century. This technology's ability to transmit knowledge, culture, and political information globally made it even more revolutionary. In the first half of the twentieth century, mass journalism, film, and radio had begun to forge a more uniform society based on shared information and images. In the last third of the century, television, computers, and telecommunications made information even more accessible and, some critics said, made culture more standardized. Once-remote villages were linked to urban capitals on the other side of the world thanks to videocassettes, satellite television, and telecommunications. Because of technology, protests became media events worldwide.

Television Americans embraced television in the 1950s; following the postwar recovery, it was Europe's turn. Between the mid-1950s and the mid-1970s, Europeans rapidly adopted television as a major entertainment and communications medium. In 1954, just 1 percent of French households had television; by 1974, almost 80 percent did. With the average viewer tuning in about

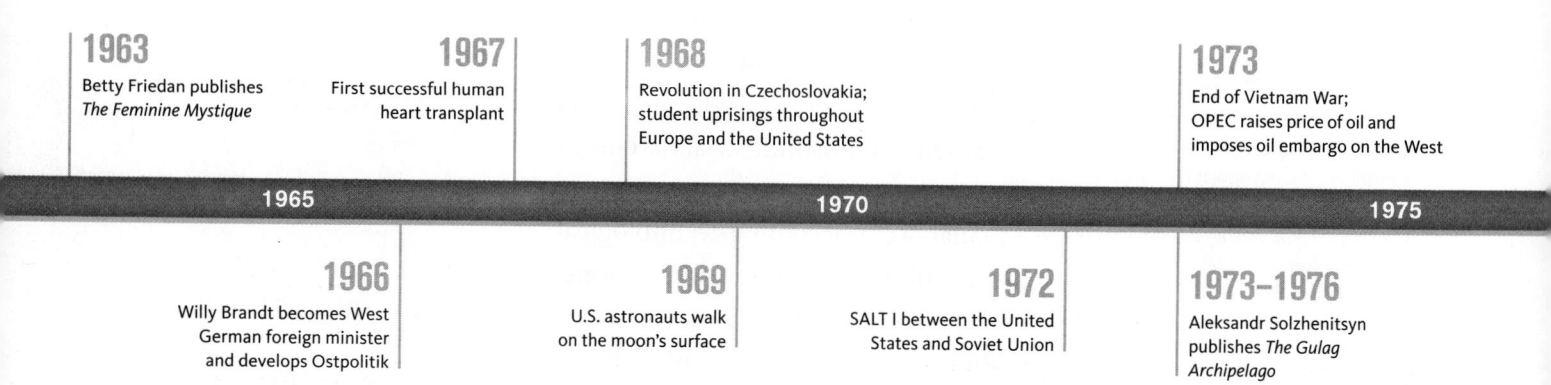

four and a half hours a day, the audience for newspapers and theater declined. "We devote more . . . hours per year to television than [to] any other single artifact," one sociologist commented in 1969. As with radio, European governments funded television broadcasting with tax dollars and controlled TV programming to avoid what they perceived as the substandard fare offered by American commercial TV; instead they featured drama, ballet, concerts, variety shows, and news. The welfare state, in Europe at least, thereby gained more power to shape daily life.

The emergence of communications satellites and video recorders in the 1960s brought competition to state-sponsored television. Worldwide audiences enjoyed broadcasts from throughout the West as satellite technology allowed for the global transmission of sports broadcasts and other programming. What statesmen and intellectuals considered the junk programming of the United States—soap operas, game shows, sitcoms—arrived dubbed in the native language. Feature films on videotape became readily available to television stations (although not yet to individuals) and competed with made-for-television movies and other programs. The competition increased in 1969 when the Sony Corporation introduced the first affordable color videocassette recorder to the consumer market. Critics complained that, although TV provided more information than had ever been available before, the resulting shared culture represented the lowest common denominator.

East and west, television exercised a powerful political and cultural influence. Even in a rural area of the Soviet Union, more than 70 percent of the inhabitants watched television regularly in the late 1970s. Educational programming united the far-flung population of the USSR by broadcasting shows designed to advance Soviet culture. At the same time, with travel impossible or forbidden to many, shows about foreign lands were among the most popular—as were postcards from these lands, which became household decorations. Heads of state could usually bump regular programming. In the 1960s, French president Charles de Gaulle appeared frequently on television, using the grandiose gestures of an imperial ruler to stir patriotism. As electoral success in western Europe increasingly depended on cultivating a successful media image, political staffs needed media experts as much as they did policy experts.

Computers Just as revolutionary as television, the computer reshaped work in science, defense, and ultimately industry. Computers had evolved dramatically since the first electronic ones, like the Colossus used by the British in 1943 to decode Nazi military and diplomatic messages. Several countries had devised these machines, all of them primitive by later standards in being gigantic, slow, noisy, and able only to decode. From the 1940s to the 1980s, computing machines shrank from the size of a gymnasium to that of an attaché case. They also became both far less expensive and fantastically more powerful, thanks to the development of increasingly sophisticated digital electronic circuitry implanted on tiny silicon chips, which replaced clumsy radio tubes. Within a few decades, the computer could perform hundreds of millions of operations per second and the price of the integrated circuit at the heart of computer technology would fall to less than a dollar.

Computers changed the pace and patterns of work not only by speeding up tasks but also by performing many operations that workers had once done themselves. In garment making, for example, experienced workers no longer painstakingly figured out how to arrange patterns on cloth for maximum economy. Instead, a computer specified instructions for the best positioning of pattern pieces, and trained workers, usually women, followed the machine's directions. Soon, like outworkers of the eighteenth

1978
The first test-tube baby is born in England

1981
Ronald Reagan becomes U.S. president

1985
Mikhail Gorbachev becomes Soviet premier

1986
Explosion at Chernobyl nuclear plant; Spain joins the Common Market

1980 1985 1990

1978–1979
Islamic revolution in Iran; hostages taken at U.S. embassy in Teheran

1980
Solidarity organizes resistance to Polish communism; British prime minister Margaret Thatcher begins dismantling the welfare state

1989
Chinese students revolt in Tiananmen Square; Communist governments ousted in eastern Europe; Berlin Wall demolished

The Space Age

1957	Soviet Union launches the first artificial satellite, *Sputnik*
1961	Soviet cosmonaut Yuri Gagarin orbits the earth; capsule carrying Alan Shepard Jr. makes first U.S. suborbital flight
1965	United States launches first commercial communications satellite, *Intelsat I*
1969	U.S. astronauts Neil Armstrong and Edwin "Buzz" Aldrin walk on moon's surface
1970s–present	Soviet Union and United States individually and in collaboration with various countries perform space station maneuvers, lunar probes, and other scientific experiments
1971	Soviet Union attempts unsuccessfully to put the space station *Salyut 1* into orbit
1973	United States puts the experimental space station *Skylab* into orbit
1976	*Viking* spacecraft explores Mars
1979–1986	Spacecraft *Voyager* makes successful flybys of Jupiter, Saturn, and Uranus

Valentina Tereshkova, Russian Cosmonaut
People sent into space were heroes, representing modern values of courage, strength, and well-honed skills. Insofar as the space age was part of the cold war race for superpower superiority, the USSR held the lead during the first decade. The Soviets trained both women and men, and the 1963 flight of Valentina Tereshkova—the first woman in space—supported Soviet claims of gender equality in contrast to the all-male superstar image of the early U.S. space program.
(Hulton Archive/Getty Images.)

century, people could work for large industries at home, connected to a central mainframe. In 1981, the French phone company launched a public Internet server, the Minitel—a forerunner of the World Wide Web—through which individuals could make reservations, perform stock transactions, and obtain information.

Whereas during the Industrial Revolution mechanical power replaced humans' physical energy, the computer technology of the information revolution added to brainpower and thus advanced the postindustrial age. Many observers believed that computers would profoundly expand mental capacity, providing, in the words of one scientist, "boundless opportunities . . . to resolve the puzzles of cosmology, of life, and of the society of man." Others countered that computers programmed people, reducing human initiative and the ability to solve problems. The information revolution was under way.

The Space Age

The "space race" between the United States and the Soviet Union, also made possible by computers, began when the Soviets launched the satellite *Sputnik* in 1957. The competition led to increasingly complex space flights that tested humans' ability to survive the process of space exploration, including weightlessness. Astronauts walked in space, endured weeks (and later months) in orbit, docked with other craft, fixed satellites, and carried out experiments for the military and private industry. In addition, a series of unmanned rockets launched weather, television, intelligence, and other communications satellites into orbit around the earth. In July 1969, a worldwide television audience watched as U.S. astronauts Neil Armstrong and Edwin "Buzz" Aldrin walked on the moon's surface—the climactic moment in the space race.

The space race also influenced Western culture. Astronauts and cosmonauts were perhaps the era's most admired heroes: Yuri Gagarin, John Glenn, and Valentina Tereshkova—the first woman in space—topped the list. A whole new fantasy world developed. Children's toys and games revolved increasingly around space. Films such as *2001: A Space Odyssey* (1968) portrayed space explorers answering questions about life that were formerly the domain of church leaders. Polish author Stanislaw Lem's popular novel *Solaris* (1961), later made into a film, described space-age individuals engaged in personal quests and drew readers and ultimately viewers into a futuristic fantasy.

The space age grew out of cold war concerns, and advances in rocket technology not only launched vehicles into space but also powered destructive missiles. At the same time, the space age promoted and even depended on global cooperation. From the 1960s on, U.S. spaceflights often involved the participation of other countries. In 1965, an international consortium headed by the United States launched the first commercial communications satellite, *Intelsat I*—a feat envisioned since early in the postwar period. By the 1970s, some 150 countries were working together at more than four hundred stations worldwide to maintain global satellite communications. Although some 50 percent of satellites were for spying purposes, the rest made international communication and the global transmission of data possible. Transnational collaboration was more than ever a necessity.

Pure science flourished amid the space race. Astronomers used mineral samples from the moon to calculate the age of the solar system with unprecedented precision. Unmanned spacecraft provided data on cosmic radiation, magnetic fields, and infrared sources. Although the media depicted the space age as one of warrior astronauts conquering space, breakthroughs depended on the products of technology, including the radio telescope, which depicted space by receiving, measuring, and calculating nonvisible rays. These findings reinforced the so-called big bang theory of the origin of the universe, first outlined in the 1930s by American astronomer Edwin Hubble and given crucial support in the 1950s by the discovery of low-level radiation permeating the universe in all directions. The big bang theory proposes that the universe originated from the explosion of superdense, superhot matter some ten to twenty billion years ago.

The Nuclear Age

Scientists, government officials, and engineers put the force of the atom to economic use, especially in the form of nuclear power, and the dramatic boost in available energy helped continue postwar economic expansion into the 1960s and beyond. The USSR built the first nuclear plant to produce electricity in Obinsk in 1954, followed by Britain and the United States. During the 1960s and 1970s, nuclear power for industrial and household use multiplied a hundredfold—a growth that did not include the nuclear-powered submarines and aircraft carriers, which also multiplied in this period.

Because of the vast costs and complex procedures involved in building, supplying, running, and safeguarding nuclear reactors, governments provided substantial aid and even financed nuclear power plants almost entirely. "A state does not count," announced French president Charles de Gaulle, "if it does not . . . contribute to the technological progress of the world." The watchword for all governments building nuclear reactors was technological development—a new function for the modern state. The USSR sponsored plants throughout the Soviet bloc as part of the drive to modernize, but it was not alone—Western nations, too, continued to rely on nuclear power. In 2006, France produced some 80 percent of its energy, and the United States 20 percent, via nuclear power plants. More than thirty countries had substantial nuclear installations in the twenty-first century, with new ones under construction.

Revolutions in Biology and Reproductive Technology

A revolution in the life sciences brought about dramatic health benefits and ultimately changed reproduction itself. In 1952, scientists Francis Crick, an Englishman, and James Watson, an American, discovered the structure of deoxyribonucleic acid **(DNA)**, the material in a cell's chromosomes that carries hereditary information. Simultaneously, other scientists were working on "the pill"—an oral contraceptive for women that capped more than a century of scientific work in the field of birth control. Still other breakthroughs in biology lay ahead, including ones that revolutionized conception and made possible the scientific duplication of species (cloning).

Understanding DNA Crick and Watson solved the mystery of biological inheritance when they demonstrated the structure of DNA. They showed how the double helix of the DNA molecule splits in cellular reproduction to form the basis of each new cell. This genetic material, biologists concluded, provides a chemical pattern for an individual organism's life. Beginning in the 1960s, genetics and the new field of molecular biology progressed rapidly. Growing understanding of nucleic acids and proteins not only led to increased knowledge about viruses and bacteria but also effectively ended in the West such diseases as polio, mumps, measles, tetanus, and syphilis through the development of new vaccines.

Scientists used their understanding of DNA to alter the makeup of plants and to bypass natural

DNA: The genetic material that forms the basis of each cell; the discovery of its structure in 1952 revolutionized genetics, molecular biology, and other scientific and medical fields.

Thalidomide Children
In the last third of the twentieth century, increasingly destructive side effects of powerful medicines became apparent. Women who had taken the drug thalidomide gave birth to children with severe disabilities, a result of the race to profit from scientific and technological developments. Children affected by thalidomide, once they became adults, were among those who launched the disability rights movement. *(DPA/LANDOV.)*

animal reproduction in a process called cloning—obtaining the cells of an organism and dividing or reproducing them in an exact copy in a laboratory. In 1997, the process had so evolved that one group of British researchers produced a cloned sheep named Dolly, though she suffered an array of disabilities and died six years later. Cloning raised questions about whether scientists should interfere with so basic and essential a process as reproduction. Similarly, the possibility of genetically altering plant and animal species and even creating new ones (for instance, to control agricultural pests) led to concern about how such actions would affect the balance of nature.

In 1967, Dr. Christiaan Barnard of South Africa performed the first successful heart transplant. Other researchers later developed both immunosuppressants (to prevent rejection of the transplant) and an artificial heart. As major advances like these occurred, commentators began to ask whether the enormous cost of new medical technology to save a few people would be better spent on helping the many who lacked even basic medical care.

Transforming Reproduction

Technology also influenced the most intimate areas of human relations—sexuality and procreation. Matching family size to agricultural productivity no longer shaped sexual behavior in the industrialized and urbanized West. With reliable birth-control devices more readily available, young people began sexual relations earlier, with less risk of pregnancy. These trends accelerated in the 1960s when the birth-control pill, the result of research around the world, was first marketed in the United States. The pill was initially tested on American medical students in Puerto Rico and then on a larger scale among Puerto Rican nurses, many of whom were eager for reliable contraception. By 1970, the pill's use was spreading around the world. Millions also sought out voluntary surgical sterilization through tubal ligations and vasectomies. New techniques brought abortion, traditionally performed by amateurs, into the hands of medical professionals, making it a safe procedure for the first time.

Childbirth and conception were similarly transformed. Whereas only a small minority of Western births took place in hospitals in 1920, more than 90 percent did by 1970. Obstetricians now performed much of the work midwives had once done. As pregnancy and birth became a medical process, new procedures and equipment made it possible to monitor women and fetuses throughout pregnancy, labor, and delivery. The number of medical interventions such as cesarean births rose.

In 1978, the first "test-tube baby," Louise Brown, was born to an English couple. She had been conceived when her mother's eggs were fertilized with her father's sperm in a laboratory dish and then implanted in her mother's uterus—a complex process called **in vitro fertilization**. If a woman could

in vitro fertilization: A process developed in the 1970s by which human eggs are fertilized with sperm outside the body and then implanted in a woman's uterus.

not carry a child to term, the laboratory-fertilized embryo could be implanted in the uterus of a surrogate, or substitute, mother. Researchers even began working on an artificial womb to allow for reproduction entirely outside the body—from storage bank to artificial embryonic environment. In reproductive technology, as in other areas, the revolution in biology was dramatically changing human life, improving health, and even making new life possible.

REVIEW QUESTION What were the technological and scientific advances of the 1960s and 1970s, and how did they change human life and society?

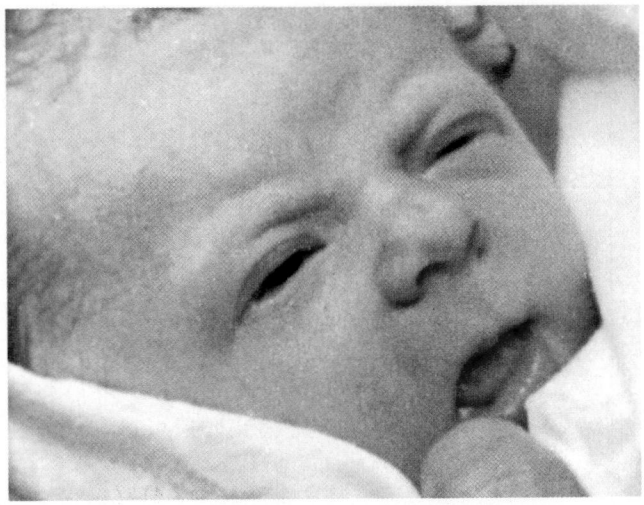

The First Test-Tube Baby
The birth in Britain in 1978 of Louise Brown, the first baby conceived by in vitro fertilization, caused a sensation worldwide. The new procedure was just one of the many medical breakthroughs of the late twentieth century and gave hope to would-be parents around the world that science might make infertility a thing of the past. *(Getty Images.)*

Postindustrial Society and Culture

Soaring investments in science and the spread of technology put Western countries on what has been labeled a postindustrial course. Instead of being centered on manufacturing and heavy industry, a postindustrial economy emphasized the distribution of services such as health care and education. The service sector was the leading force in the economy, and this meant that intellectual work, not industrial or manufacturing work, was central to creating jobs and profits. Moreover, all parts of society and industry interlocked, forming a system constantly in need of complex analysis, as in the nuclear industry. These characteristics of postindustrial society and culture would carry over from the 1960s and 1970s into the next century.

Multinational Corporations

A major development of the postindustrial era was the growth of the **multinational corporation**. Multinationals produced goods and services for a global market and conducted business worldwide, but unlike older kinds of international firms, they established major factories and managerial centers in countries other than their home base. For example, of the five hundred largest businesses in the United States in 1970, more than one hundred did over a quarter of their business abroad, with IBM operating in more than one hundred countries. Although U.S.-based corporations led the way, European and Japanese multinationals like Volkswagen, Shell, Nestlé, and Sony also had a broad global reach.

Some multinational corporations had bigger revenues than entire nations. They appeared to burst the bounds of the nation-state as they set up shop in whatever part of the world offered cheap labor. In the first years after World War II, multinationals preferred European employees, who constituted a highly educated labor pool and had well-developed consumer habits. Then, beginning in the 1960s, multinationals moved more of their operations to the emerging economies of formerly colonized states to reduce labor costs and avoid taxes. Although multinational corporations provided jobs in developing areas, profits usually went out of those areas to enrich foreign stockholders. Multinational corporations lacked the interest in the well-being of localities or nations that earlier industrialists had often shown. Thus, this system of business looked to some like imperialism in a new form.

Firms believed that they could stay competitive only by expanding, merging with other companies, or partnering with governments. In France, for example, a massive glass conglomerate merged with a metallurgical company to form a new group specializing in all phases of construction—a wise move given the postwar building boom. Firms also increased their investment in research and used international cooperation to produce major new products. Beginning with its first commercial flight in 1976, the British-French Concorde supersonic aircraft flew from London to New York in under four

multinational corporation: A business that operates in many foreign countries by sending large segments of its manufacturing, finance, sales, and other business components abroad.

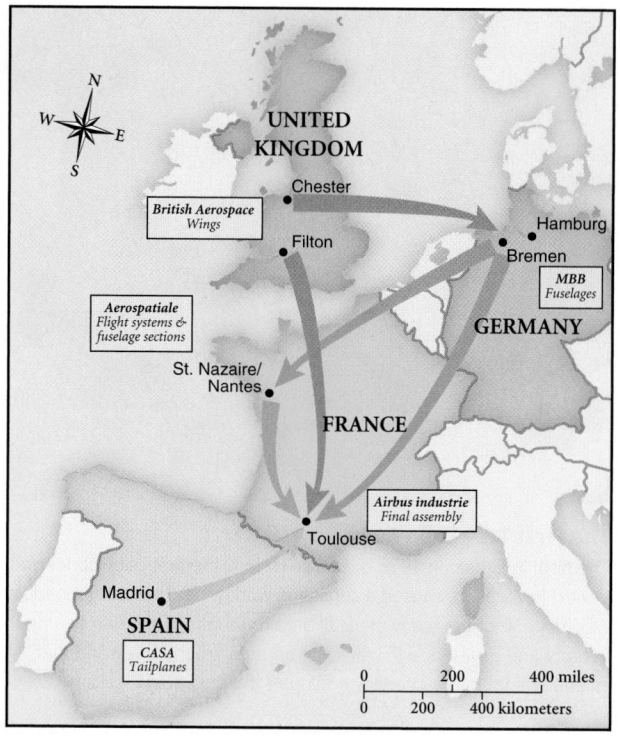

MAP 28.1 The Airbus Production System

Aircraft manufacturer Airbus began as an international consortium, marking an important step in the economic and industrial integration of Europe and the revitalization of its national economies. Today, Airbus is a global enterprise with locations offering parts and service around the world, including the United States, China, and India. Its orders for and deliveries of planes have exceeded those of its top competitor over the past few years.

hours. Another venture was the Airbus, a more practical series of passenger jets inaugurated in 1972 by a consortium of European firms. Both projects grew from the strong relationships among government, business, and science as well as from the international cooperation in manufacturing among members of the Common Market (Map 28.1). Such relationships allowed European businesses to compete successfully with U.S.-based and other multinational giants.

The New Worker

In the early years of industry, workers often labored to exhaustion and lived in poor conditions. These conditions changed fundamentally in postwar Europe with the reduction of the blue-collar workforce, the growth of off-shore manufacturing, and increased automation of industrial work. Manufacturing was simply cleaner and less dangerous than ever before. Within firms, the relationship of workers to bosses shifted as management started grouping workers into teams that set their own production quotas, determined and assigned tasks, and competed with other teams to produce more. As workers took on responsibilities once assigned to managers, union membership declined.

In both the U.S. and Soviet blocs, a new working class of white-collar service personnel emerged. Its rise undermined economic distinctions based on the way a person worked, for those who performed service work or had managerial titles were not necessarily better paid than blue-collar laborers. The ranks of service workers swelled with researchers, planners, health care and medical staff, and government functionaries. As emphasis on service grew, entire categories of employees such as flight attendants devoted much of their skill to the psychological well-being of customers. The consumer economy provided more jobs in restaurants and personal health, fitness and grooming, and hotels and tourism. By 1969, the percentage of service-sector employees had passed that of manufacturing workers in several industrial countries: 61.1 percent versus 33.7 percent in the United States, and 48.8 percent versus 41.1 percent in Sweden (see "Taking Measure," page 957).

Postindustrial work life differed somewhat in the Soviet bloc. There, the percentage of farmers remained higher than in western Europe. A huge difference between professional occupations and those involving physical work also remained in socialist countries because of declining investment in advanced machinery and cleaner work processes. Men in both blocs generally earned higher pay and had better jobs than women. Uniquely in the Soviet bloc, however, women's badly paying jobs included street cleaning, garbage collection, heavy labor on farms, general medicine, and dentistry. Somewhere between 80 and 95 percent of women in socialist countries worked, mostly under difficult conditions.

Farming changed as well, consolidating and becoming more scientific. Small landowners sold family plots to farmers and corporations engaged in agribusiness — that is, vast acreage devoted to commercial rather than peasant farming. Governments, farmers' cooperatives, and planning agencies shaped the decision making of the individual farmer; they set production quotas and handled an array of marketing transactions. Genetic research that yielded pest-resistant seeds and the skyrocketing use of pesticides, fertilizers, and machinery contributed to economic growth. Between 1965 and 1979, the number of tractors in Germany more than tripled from 384,000 to 1.34 million.

Technical planners played a crucial role in transforming agriculture. For example, in the 1970s, a woman named Fernande Pelletier owned a hundred-acre farm in southwestern France in the new set-

TAKING MEASURE

Postindustrial Occupational Structure, 1984

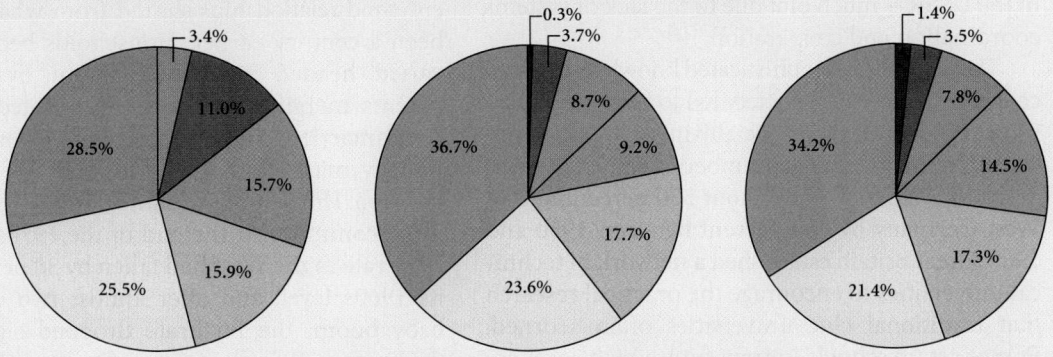

Striking changes occurred in the composition of the workforce in the postwar period. Agriculture continued to decline as a source of jobs; by the 1980s, the percentage of agricultural workers in the most advanced industrial countries had dropped well below 10 percent. The most striking development was the expansion of the service sector, which came to employ more than half of all workers. In the United States, the agricultural and industrial sectors (represented by production and transportation workers), which had dominated a century earlier, now offered less than a third of all jobs.

Source: *Yearbook of Labour Statistics* (Geneva: International Labour Office, 1992), Table 2.7.

Question to Consider

- **What difference does it make to ordinary people that jobs in service work predominate? What does the rise of the service sector mean for the economy and society as a whole?**

- Production and transport workers, laborers
- Sales and service workers
- Clerical and related workers
- Professional, technical, and related workers
- Administrative and managerial workers
- Agricultural workers
- Other

[1]Austria, Belgium, West Germany, Denmark, Spain, Finland, Greece, Ireland, Netherlands, Norway, Portugal, and Sweden.

ting of international agribusiness. On the advice of a government expert to produce whatever foods might sell competitively in the Common Market, Pelletier switched from lamb and veal to foie gras and walnuts, and she joined with other farmers in her region to buy heavy machinery and to bring products to market. Agricultural prosperity required as much managerial and technical know-how as did success in other parts of the economy.

The Boom in Education and Research

Education and research were key to running postindustrial society and had now become the means by which nations maintained their economic and military might. In the West, common sense, hard work, and creative intuition had launched the earliest successes of the Industrial Revolution. By the late twentieth century, success in business or government demanded a wide variety of expertise and ever-growing staffs of researchers—"the accumulation of knowledge, not of wealth," as one official put it.

Investment in research fueled military and industrial leadership. The United States funneled more than 20 percent of its gross national product (a measure of the total value of goods and services a nation produced in a year) into research in the 1960s, attracting many of Europe's leading intellectuals and technicians to move to the United States in a so-called brain drain. Complex systems required intricate coordination and professional oversight—nuclear power generation, for example, included scientific conceptualization, plant construction, and the publicly supervised disposal of radioactive waste. Scientists and bureaucrats frequently made more crucial decisions than did elected politicians in the realm of space programs, weapons development, and economic policy. Here east–west differences became important: Soviet-bloc nations proved less adept at linking their considerable achievements in science to real-life applications because of bureaucratic red tape. In the 1960s, some 40 percent of scientific findings in the Soviet bloc became obsolete before the government approved them for application to technology. An invisible backsliding from superpower effectiveness and leadership had begun in the USSR—much of it due to the lack of systems coordination and cooperation.

The centrality of sophisticated knowledge to success in postindustrial society led to unprecedented growth in education, especially in universities and scientific institutes. The number of university students in Sweden rose by about 580 percent and in West Germany by 250 percent between 1950 and 1969. Great Britain established a network of technical universities to encourage the practical research that traditional elite universities often scorned. France set up schools to train future high-level experts in administration. The scientific establishment in the Soviet Union grew so rapidly that Soviet advanced researchers outnumbered those in the United States by the late 1970s. Meanwhile, institutions of higher learning, particularly in the United States and western Europe, added courses in business management, information technology, and systems analysis designed for the new pool of postindustrial workers.

Changing Family Life and the Generation Gap

Just as education changed to meet the needs of postindustrial society, family structures and parent-child relationships shifted from what they had been a century earlier. Households became more varied, headed by a single parent, by remarried parents merging two sets of unrelated children, by unmarried couples cohabitating, or by traditionally married couples who had few—or no—children. Households of same-sex partners became more common. At the end of the 1970s, the marriage rate in the West had fallen by 30 percent from its 1960s level, and after almost two decades of baby boom, the birthrate dropped significantly. On average, Belgian women, for example, bore 2.6 children in 1960 but only 1.8 by the end of the 1970s. In the Soviet bloc, the birthrate was even lower. Although the birthrate fell, the percentage of children born outside of marriage soared.

Daily life within the family also changed. Technological consumer items filled the home, with radio and television often forming the basis of the household's common social life. Appliances such as dishwashers, washing machines, and clothes dryers became more affordable and more widespread, especially in the western bloc, raising standards of cleanliness and reducing (in theory) the time women had to devote to household work. More women worked outside the home during these years to pay for the prolonged economic dependence of children, but working mothers still did the housework and provided child care almost entirely themselves.

Whereas earlier the family had organized labor, taught craft skills, and monitored reproductive behavior of young people, the modern family seemed to have a primarily psychological mission, providing emotional nurturance for children who acquired their intellectual skills in school. Parents turned to psychologists, social workers, and other social service experts for advice on rearing their children. Television and other media also offered much-heeded instruction and models of how people should deal with life in postindustrial society.

The Rolling Stones (1976)
The Rolling Stones were more energetic, sexual, and flamboyant than the earlier British rock sensation, the Beatles. Astute marketing experts for big record companies helped such rock groups target youth successfully. What exactly was the appeal of the Beatles, the Rolling Stones, and the other celebrated rock stars who followed in their wake? *(Getty Images.)*

Postindustrial society changed teenagers' lives most dramatically, creating strong differences between adolescents and adults. A century earlier, teens had been full-time wage earners like their parents; now, in the new knowledge-based society, most were students and some were financially dependent on their parents into their twenties. Despite teenagers' longer financial childhood, sexual activity began at an ever younger age, and people talked more openly about sex, prompting the Western media to announce the arrival of a "sexual revolution."

With rising prosperity after the war, youth simultaneously gained new roles as consumers. Seeing baby boomers as a multibillion-dollar market, advertisers and industrialists wooed them with consumer items associated with rock music—records, portable radios, and stereos. Rock music celebrated youthful rebellion against adult culture in biting, critical, and often explicitly sexual lyrics. Sex roles for the young did not change, however. Despite the popularity of a few individual women rockers, promoters focused on groups of male musicians, whom they depicted as heroic, surrounded by worshipping female "groupies." The new models for youth such as the Beatles were themselves the products of advanced technology and savvy marketing for mass consumption. "What's your message for American teenagers?" the Beatles were asked. "Buy some more Beatles records," they responded. The mixture of high-tech music, pop-star marketing, and the sexual openness of fans contributed to a sense that there was a unique youth culture separating the young from their parents—the so-called generation gap.

Art, Ideas, and Religion in a Technocratic Society

Cultural trends developed alongside the march of consumer society and technological breakthroughs. Artists and scholars of the postindustrial age addressed the growing consumerism and the new world of space, electronics, and computers in their art and thought. As colonies threw off the imperialist yoke and became new nations, the influence of their culture on the West remained strong. Like the new multinational corporations, many artists and scholars enjoyed increasing international recognition and reached global markets. Social scientists gained influence by employing complex statistical and other scientific methods made possible by increasingly sophisticated and powerful computers.

The Visual Arts A new style in the visual arts was called **pop art**. It featured images from everyday life and employed the glossy techniques and products of what these artists called admass, or mass advertising. Like advertising itself, art leadership passed from Europe to the United States. U.S. pop artist Robert Rauschenberg, for example, made collages from comic strips, magazine clippings, and fabric to fulfill his vision that "a picture is more like the real world when it's made out of the real world." Maverick American artists such as Andy Warhol (1928–1987) made pop art a financial success with their parodies of modern commercialism. Through images of actress Marilyn Monroe and former first lady Jacqueline Kennedy, Warhol showed, for example, how depictions of women were used to sell everything mass culture had to offer in the 1960s and 1970s. He depicted Campbell's soup cans as they appeared in advertisements and sold these works as elite artistic creations.

Swedish-born artist Claes Oldenburg (1929–) portrayed the grotesque aspects of ordinary consumer products in *Giant Hamburger with Pickle Attached* (1962) and *Lipstick Ascending on Caterpillar Tractor* (1967). Capturing this mocking world of

Pop Art
Claes Oldenburg excelled in highlighting objects of everyday life, such as this hamburger (*Floor Burger*, 1962). He also modeled vacuum cleaners, shuttlecocks, telephones, and many other much-used things—a feature of pop art, which often contained humor in addition. Can you spot the humor in this creation? *(Claes Oldenburg,* Floor Burger, *1962. Canvas filled with foam rubber and cardboard boxes, painted with latex and Liquitex, 4 ft. 4 in. [1.32 m] high; 7 ft. [2.13 m] diameter. Collection Art Gallery of Ontario, Toronto, Canada, Purchase 1967. Photo courtesy the Oldenburg van Bruggen Studio. Copyright © 1962 Claes Oldenburg. Photo provided by The Bridgeman Art Library International.)*

pop art: A style in the visual arts that mimicked advertising and consumerism and that used ordinary objects as a part of paintings and other compositions.

art, German artist Sigmar Polke did cartoon-like drawings of products and of those who craved them. Others practicing this "high art" added "low" objects such as scraps of metal, cigarette butts, dirt, and even excrement to their work. The Swiss sculptor Jean Tinguely used rusted parts of old machines—the junk of industrial society—to make fountains that could move. His partner Niki de Saint Phalle (1930–2002) then decorated them with huge, gaudy figures—many of them inspired by the folk traditions of the Caribbean and Africa (see Chapter 27, page 942). Their colorful, mobile fountains adorned main squares in Stockholm, Paris, and other cities.

Music The American composer John Cage (1912–1992) worked in a similar vein when he added to his musical scores sounds produced by such everyday items as combs, pieces of wood, and radio noise. Buddhist influence led Cage to incorporate silence in music and to compose by randomly tossing coins and then choosing notes by the corresponding numbers in the ancient Chinese *I Ching* (Book of Changes). These techniques continued the trend away from classical melody that had begun with modernism. Other composers, called minimalists, simplified music by featuring repetition and sustained notes instead of producing the lush melodies of nineteenth-century symphonies and piano music. Estonian composer Arvo Pärt wrote minimalist pieces in the 1970s using only three or four notes in total; he called this style "starvation" music to emphasize the lack of both freedom and goods in the Soviet bloc. Such innovation in classical music continued to produce sounds that many listeners found unpleasant. Yet improved recording technology and mass marketing brought music of all varieties to a wider home audience than ever before.

Social Science The social sciences reached the peak of their prestige in the postindustrial era, often because of the increasing use of statistical models made possible by advanced electronic computations. Sociologists and psychologists produced detailed studies that claimed to demonstrate rules for understanding individual and group behavior. Those who gained knowledge of such rules over the course of their university education would thus be fit to govern an increasingly complex postindustrial population. Anthropology was among the most exciting of the social sciences, for it brought young university students information about societies that seemed untouched by modern technology and industry. Colorful ethnographic films revealed different lifestyles and seemingly exotic practices. While studying people who came to be called "the other," students had their sense of freedom reinforced by the vision of going back to nature. Whatever their discipline, social scientists announced that, like technicians and engineers, their specialized methods and factual knowledge were key to managing the complexities of postindustrial society and setting policy for developing nations.

At the same time, the social sciences undermined Enlightenment beliefs that individuals had true freedom. French anthropologist Claude Lévi-Strauss (1908–2009) developed a theory called structuralism, which insisted that all societies function within controlling structures—kinship and exchange, for example. While challenging existentialism's claim that humans could create a free existence, structuralism also attacked the social sciences' faith in rationality. Lévi-Strauss's book *The Savage Mind* (1966) demonstrated that people outside the West, even though they did not use scientific methods, had their own extremely effective systems of problem solving. In the 1960s and 1970s, the findings of some social scientists additionally echoed concerns that technology and highly managed bureaucratic systems were creating a society in which people lacked individuality and freedom.

Religion Religious leaders and parishioners responded to the changing times in a variety of ways. Pope Paul VI (r. 1963–1978) opposed artificial birth control as it became more prevalent, while also becoming the first pontiff to carry out the global vision of Vatican II by visiting Africa, Asia, and South America. In some places, grassroots religious fervor surged in the face of advancing science and the threat of nuclear annihilation. Growing numbers of U.S. Protestants, for example, joined sects that stressed the literal truth of the Bible and denied the validity of past scientific discoveries such as the age of the universe and the evolution of the species. In western Europe, however, Christian churchgoing remained at a low ebb. In the 1970s, for example, only 10 percent of the British population went to religious services—about the same number that attended live soccer matches. Most striking was the changing composition of the Western religious public. Immigration of people from former colonies and other parts of the world increased the strength of non-Christian religions such as Islam and varieties of Hindu faiths. Mosques, Buddhist temples, and shrines to other creeds appeared in a greater number of cities and towns. New religious values sometimes mixed tensely with western European Judeo-Christianity and the antireligious culture of the Soviet bloc.

REVIEW QUESTION How did Western society and culture change in the postindustrial age?

Protesting Cold War Conditions

The United States and the Soviet Union reached new heights of power in the 1960s, but trouble was brewing for the superpowers. By 1965, the six-nation Common Market had temporarily replaced the United States as the leader in worldwide trade, and its members often acted in their own self-interest, not in the interests of the superpowers. In 1973, Britain's membership in the Common Market, followed by Ireland and Denmark, boosted the market's exports to almost three times those of the United States. The USSR faced challenges, too. Communist China, along with countries in eastern Europe, contested Soviet leadership, and many decolonizing regions refused to ally with either of the superpowers. The struggle for an independent Vietnamese nation continued, too, and by the mid-1960s, the United States was waging a devastating war in Vietnam in order to block the Communist independence movement there. Rising citizen discontent, sometimes expressed in dramatic acts of protest like that of Jan Palach, presented another serious challenge to the cold war order. From the 1960s until 1989, people rose up against technology, the lack of fundamental rights, and the potential for nuclear holocaust.

Cracks in the Cold War Order

Across the social and political spectrum came calls to reduce cold war tensions in this age of unprecedented technological advance. In the Soviet Union, the new middle class of bureaucrats and managers demanded a better standard of living and a reduction in the cold war hostility that made everyday life so menacing. Voters in western European countries elected politicians who promoted an increasing array of social programs designed to ensure the economic democracy of the welfare state and to promote technological development. A significant minority of voters shifted their allegiance from the centrist Christian Democratic coalitions that supported U.S. political goals to Socialist, Labor, and Social Democratic parties that endorsed policies to bridge the cold war divide.

Germany and France

The German and French governments both made solid and highly visible changes in policy, which, though different, upset the cold war order. In Germany, Social Democratic politicians had enough influence to shift money from cold war defense spending to domestic programs. Willy Brandt (1913–1992), the Socialist mayor of West Berlin, became foreign minister in 1966 and worked to improve frigid relations with Communist East Germany in order to open up trade. This anti–cold war policy, known as **Ostpolitik**, gave West German business leaders what they wanted: "the depoliticization of Germany's foreign trade," as one industrialist put it, and an opening of consumerism in the Soviet bloc. West German trade with eastern Europe grew rapidly, but it left the relatively poorer countries of the Soviet bloc strapped with mounting debt — some $45 billion annually by 1970. Nonetheless, commerce began building bridges across the U.S.-Soviet cold war divide.

To break the superpowers' stranglehold on international politics, French president Charles de Gaulle poured huge sums into French nuclear development, withdrew French forces from NATO, and signed trade treaties with the Soviet bloc. Communist China and France also drew closer through trade and diplomatic ties. However, de Gaulle protected France's good relations with Germany to prevent further encroachments from the Soviet bloc. At home, de Gaulle's government sponsored the construction of modern housing and ordered the exterior cleaning of all Parisian buildings — a massive project taking years — to wipe away more than a century of industrial grime and to demonstrate community, not cold war, values. With his haughty pursuit of French grandeur, de Gaulle offered the European public an alternative to obeying the superpowers.

The Soviet Union

Brandt's Ostpolitik and de Gaulle's independence had their echoes in Soviet-bloc reforms. After the ouster of Soviet premier Nikita Khrushchev in 1964, the new leadership of Leonid Brezhnev (1909–1982) and Alexei Kosygin (1904–1980) initially continued attempts at reform, encouraging plant managers to turn a profit and allowing the production of televisions, household appliances, and cheap housing to alleviate the discontent of an increasingly better-educated and better-informed citizenry. The government also allowed more cultural and scientific meetings with Westerners, another move that relaxed the cold war atmosphere in the mid-1960s. Like the French, the Soviets set up "technopoles" — new cities devoted to research and technological innovation. The Soviet satellites in eastern Europe seized the economic opportunity presented by Moscow's relaxed posture. For example, Hungarian leader János Kádár introduced elements of a market system into the national economy by encouraging

Ostpolitik: A policy initiated by West German foreign minister Willy Brandt in the late 1960s in which West Germany sought better economic relations with the Communist countries of eastern Europe.

small businesses and trade to develop outside the Communist-controlled state network.

Soviet-bloc writers sought to break the hold of socialist realism on the arts and reduce their praise for the Soviet past. Dissident artists' paintings rejected brightly colored scenes and heroic figures and instead depicted Soviet citizens as worn and tired in grays and other monochromatic color schemes (see "Seeing History," page 963). Ukrainian poet Yevgeny Yevtushenko exposed Soviet complicity in the Holocaust in *Babi Yar* (1961), a passionate protest against the slaughter of tens of thousands of Jews near Kiev during World War II. East Berlin writer Christa Wolf challenged the celebratory nature of socialist art when she showed a couple tragically divided by the Berlin Wall in her novel *Divided Heaven* (1965). Repression of artistic expression returned in the later 1960s and 1970s, as the Soviet government took to bulldozing outdoor art shows, thereby forcing visual artists to hold secret exhibitions, announced at the very last minute by word of mouth. For their part, writers relied on **samizdat** culture, a form of protest activity in which individuals reproduced government-suppressed publications by hand and passed them from reader to reader, thus building a foundation for the successful resistance of the 1980s.

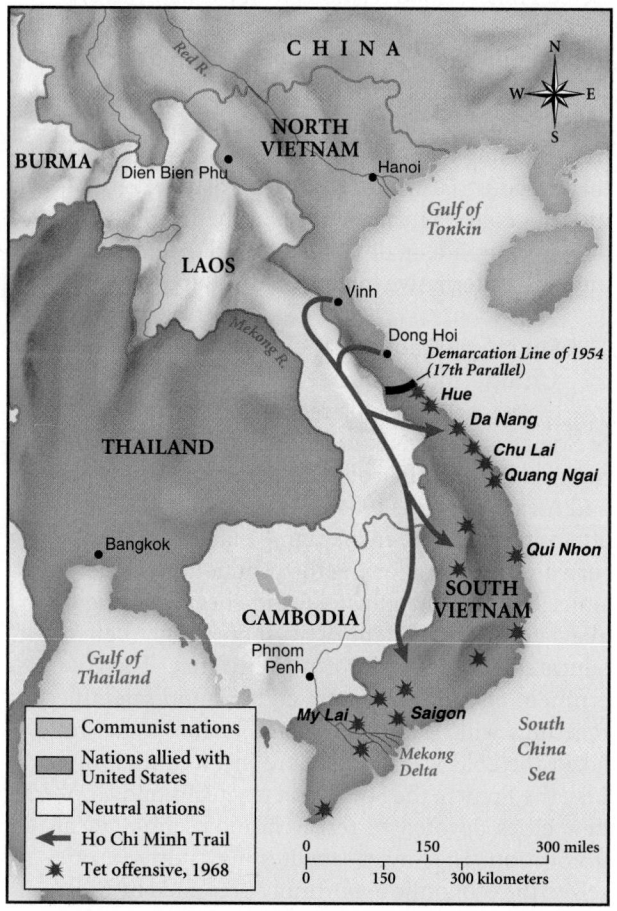

MAP 28.2 The Vietnam War, 1954–1975
The local peoples of Southeast Asia had long resisted incursions by their neighbors. The Vietnamese beat the French colonizers in the battle of Dien Bien Phu in 1954. But the Americans soon became involved, trying to stem what they saw as the tide of Communist influence behind the Vietnamese liberation movement. The ensuing war in Vietnam in the 1960s and 1970s spread into neighboring countries, making the region the scene of vast destruction.

The United States

Other issues challenged U.S. leadership of the western bloc during the cold war. The assassination of President John F. Kennedy in November 1963 shocked the nation and the world, but only momentarily did it halt the escalating demands for civil rights for African Americans and other minorities. White segregationists murdered and brutalized those attempting to integrate lunch counters, register black voters, or simply march on behalf of freedom. This violent racism was a weak point in the American claim to moral superiority in the cold war. In response to the murders and destruction, Kennedy had introduced civil rights legislation and forced the desegregation of schools and universities. Lyndon B. Johnson (1908–1973), Kennedy's successor, steered the Civil Rights Act through Congress in 1964. This legislation forbade segregation in public facilities and created the Equal Employment Opportunity Commission (EEOC) to fight job discrimination based on "race, color, national origin, religion, and sex." Southern conservatives had tacked on the provision outlawing discrimination against women in the vain hope that it would doom the bill. Modeling himself on his hero Franklin Roosevelt, Johnson envisioned what he called the Great Society, in which new government programs would improve the lot of the forty million Americans living in poverty. Johnson's many reform programs included Project Head Start for educating disadvantaged preschool children and the Job Corps for training youth. Black novelist Ralph Ellison called Johnson "the greatest American president for the poor and the Negroes."

Still, the cold war did not go away, and the United States became increasingly embroiled in Vietnam (Map 28.2). After the Geneva Conference of 1954, which divided Vietnam into North and South, the United States increased its support for the corrupt leaders of non-Communist South Vietnam. North

samizdat: A key form of dissident activity across the Soviet bloc in which individuals reproduced government-suppressed publications by hand and passed them from reader to reader, thus building a foundation for the successful resistance of the 1980s.

SEEING HISTORY

Critiquing the Soviet System: Dissident Art in the 1960s and 1970s

Artists, writers, composers, and performers in the USSR were supposed to follow Communist Party directives, creating uplifting works that spread Communist ideals, despite the political repression and economic hardships that plagued the system. Numerous dissident artists sought to undermine the Communist message and criticize the regime through their work, thus helping to prepare the ground for a full-scale revolt against the Soviet system in the late 1980s. The Soviet government persecuted these artists and their families and often destroyed subversive works that were displayed in public. Yet dissident artists bravely forged ahead, displaying their art and even selling it to foreign dealers to smuggle out of the country.

Dissident artists employed a range of techniques, both subtle and explicit, to critique the Soviet regime. Eric Bulatov often made use of the officially approved Soviet style of socialist realism in his works to slyly criticize the system. His painting *Krasikov Street*, shown here, shows Lenin walking forward and refers to Lenin's much-repeated motto meant to inspire Soviet citizens: "Always forward, never backward." How does Bulatov use motion and color here to comment on both Soviet society and the Communist establishment? What messages is he conveying?

In his work *The General*, Boris Orlov used sculpture to lampoon one of the mainstays of Soviet society during the cold war. As the heroes of World War II and protectors of communism, generals were officially revered, parading on Soviet holidays and at commemorative events. Their uniforms feature oak and laurel leaves—common symbols of strength and victory. What are the general's main features as portrayed by Orlov? What adjectives would you use to describe this work? How would you characterize the tone and purpose of Orlov's depiction?

Question to Consider

■ **As you reflect on these two works of art, what in your opinion would have made them dangerous to the survival of Soviet communism?**

Boris Orlov, *The General*, 1970. *(Collection of the Jane Voorhees Zimmerli Art Museum, Rutgers, The State University of New Jersey, The Norton and Nancy Dodge Collection of Nonconformist Art from the Soviet Union. Photograph by Jack Abraham. 14194 © Boris Orlov/RAO, Moscow/VAGA, New York, NY.)*

Eric Bulatov, *Krasikov Street*, 1977. *(Erik Bulatov, Krasikov Street, 1977. Oil on canvas 150 x 198.5 cm. Collection of the Zimmerli Art Museum at Rutgers University, Norton and Nancy Dodge Collection of Nonconformist Art from the Soviet Union, 1991.0877/05125. Photograph by Jack Abraham. © 2011 Artists Rights Society [ARS], New York/ADAGP, Paris.)*

Vietnam, China, and the Soviet Union backed the rebel Vietcong, or South Vietnamese Communists. By 1966, the United States had more than half a million soldiers in South Vietnam, yet the strength of the Vietcong seemed to grow daily. Despite massive bombings by the United States, the insurgents, who had struggled against colonialism for decades, rejected a negotiated peace even as Johnson's advisers regularly appeared on television claiming that the United States was winning the war. Faced with mounting casualties, growing antiwar sentiment, and increasing military costs, Johnson announced in March 1968 that he would not run for president again.

The Growth of Citizen Activism

In the midst of cold war conflict and technological advance, a new activism emerged. Prosperity and the rising benefits of a postindustrial, service-oriented economy made people ever more eager for peace. University students did not want their lives to end on faraway battlefields. Other activists — among them minorities, women, and homosexuals — simply wanted a fair chance at education, jobs, and some political voice. Students, blacks and other minorities, Soviet-bloc citizens, women, environmentalists, and homosexuals brought various Western societies to the brink of revolution during what became increasingly fiery protests in the late 1960s.

Civil Rights The U.S. civil rights movement broadened, as other minorities joined African Americans in demanding fair treatment. In 1965, César Chávez (1927–1993) led Mexican American migrant workers in the California grape agribusiness to strike for better wages and working conditions. Meanwhile, beginning in 1965, urban riots erupted across the United States out of African Americans' frustration in their struggle for equal rights. The issue blacks faced was one they felt they had in common with decolonizing peoples: how to shape an identity different from that imposed on them by white oppressors. Some chose to celebrate their race under the banner "black is beautiful," and some urged a push for "black power" to reclaim rights forcefully instead of "begging" for them nonviolently. Separatism, not integration, became the goal of others. Small cadres of militants like the Black Panthers took up arms, believing that, like decolonizing peoples elsewhere, they needed to protect themselves against the violent whites around them.

From the 1950s on, homosexuals had also lobbied for the decriminalization of their sexual lives and practices. Propaganda equated male homosexuality with a lack of militaristic manliness needed to protect the nation-state on either side of the cold war divide. In June 1969, gay men in the Stonewall area of Greenwich Village, New York, rioted against the police and more general persecution, as had African Americans, both to assert their civil rights and to affirm their identity. The gay liberation movement born in that time came to span the globe and to include not only men but gay women, too.

Student Activism As a result of the new turn in black efforts for change, white American university students who had participated in the early stages of the civil rights movement found themselves excluded from leadership positions. Many of them soon joined the swelling protests against technological change, consumerism, and the Vietnam War. European youth were also feverish for reform. In the mid-1960s, university students in Rome occupied an administration building after right-wing opponents assassinated one of their number during a protest against the 200-to-1 student–teacher ratio. In 1966, Prague students, chanting "The only good Communist is a dead one," held carnival-like processions to commemorate the tenth anniversary of the 1956 Hungarian uprisings. The "situationists" in France used shocking graffiti and street theater to call on students to wake up from the slumbering pace of consumer society.

Throughout the 1960s, students criticized the traditional university curriculum and flaunted their own countercultural values. They questioned how studying Plato or Dante would help them after graduation. "How to Train Stuffed Geese" was French students' satirical version of the teaching methods inflicted on them. "No professors over forty" and "Don't trust anyone over thirty" were powerful slogans of the day. Long hair, communal living, scorn for personal cleanliness, and ridicule for sexual chastity were part of students' rejection of middle-class values. Widespread use of the pill and open promiscuity made the sexual revolution explicit and public. Marijuana use became common among students, and amphetamines and barbiturates added to the drug culture, which had its own rituals, music, and gathering places. Hated by students, big business nonetheless made billions of dollars by selling everything from blue jeans to natural foods as well as by packaging and managing the rock stars of the counterculture.

The Women's Movement Women's activism erupted across the political spectrum (see "Contrasting Views," page 966). Working for reproductive rights, women in France helped end the nation's ban on birth control in 1965. More

Second-Wave Feminists on the March
Like turn-of-the-century feminists, women in the 1960s and 1970s took to the streets to protest their condition. This march in Paris features signs showing a clock fixed at 7:30 and a list of chores including "breakfast for husband," "wake the children," and "hurry." For many citizens, the sight of "unladylike" women demonstrating in public was a shock—which was the point for many activists. *(© Rue des Archives/AGIP/The Granger Collection, New York—All rights reserved.)*

politically conventional middle-class women eagerly responded to the international best seller *The Feminine Mystique* (1963) by American journalist Betty Friedan. Pointing to the stagnating talents of many housewives, Friedan helped organize the National Organization for Women (NOW) in 1966 "to bring women into full participation in the mainstream of American society now." NOW advocated equal pay for equal work and a variety of other legal and economic reforms. In Sweden, women lobbied to make tasks both at home and in the workplace less gender-segregated, and in these same years a few Soviet women began speaking out against their low-paid and unpaid work that kept the USSR running.

Women engaged in the civil rights and student movements soon realized that many protest organizations devalued women just as society at large did. Male activists adopted the leather-jacketed machismo style of their film and rock heroes, but women in the movements were often judged by the status of their male-protester lovers. "A woman was to 'inspire' her man," African American activist Angela Davis complained, adding that women seeking equality were accused of wanting "to rob [male activists] of their manhood." West German women students tossed tomatoes at male protest leaders in defiance of male domination of the movement and of standards set by society for ladylike behavior.

1968: Year of Crisis

Calls for reform finally boiled over in 1968. In January, on the first day of Tet, the Vietnamese New Year, the Vietcong and the North Vietnamese attacked more than one hundred South Vietnamese towns and American bases, inflicting heavy casualties. The Tet offensive, as it came to be called, led many in the United States and across the West to conclude that the war might be unwinnable and fueled the antiwar movement around the world. Students in Paris, Tokyo, Mexico City, and other major capitals took to the streets against the war, often in violent protest. Meanwhile, in Czechoslovakia, a quieter movement against Soviet cold war domination had taken shape, but the atmosphere in that country, as elsewhere, became explosive when the Soviets invaded to put down reform.

The Outbreak of Violence

On April 4, 1968, a white racist assassinated civil rights leader Martin Luther King Jr. Riots erupted in more than a hundred cities in the United States as African Americans vented their anguish and rage. Rejecting King's policy of nonviolence, black leaders turned to violence: "Burn, baby, burn," chanted rioters as they rampaged through grim inner cities. On campuses, bitter clashes over the inter-

CONTRASTING VIEWS

Feminist Debates

The feminist movement of the late twentieth century provoked the most pronounced and widespread debate over gender in recorded history. Discussion often reached a heated pitch, as it did in other reform movements of the day. Feminists had a variety of concerns, often depending on their nationality, ethnicity, race, religion, sexual orientation, and class. Opinion on these issues could produce conflict among activists and serious divisions on goals and policies, as the authors of the Combahee River Statement demonstrated (Document 1). At times, concerns over issues like equal opportunity in the workplace were directed at government policies, as in the case of the Soviet worker (Document 2). Italian feminists saw all the disabilities imposed by government as characteristic of larger problems (Document 3), while Germans explicitly connected the cause of feminism to that of environmentalism (Document 4). With the advances in global travel and televised news, comparisons came to the fore as well (Document 5).

1. Criticizing White Feminism

In the United States, black women, like several other minority groups, found themselves marginalized in both the feminist and civil rights movements. In 1977, some of them issued the Combahee River Statement.

Black, other third world, and working women have been involved in the feminist movement from its start, but both outside reactionary forces and racism and elitism within the movement itself have served to obscure our participation. . . .

Black feminist politics also have an obvious connection to movements for Black liberation, particularly those of the 1960s and 1970s. . . . It was our experience and disillusionment within these liberation movements, as well as experience on the periphery of the white male left, that led to the need to develop a politics that was antiracist, unlike those of white women, and antisexist, unlike those of Black and white men. . . .

Above all else, our politics initially sprang from the shared belief that Black women are inherently valuable, that our liberation is a necessity not as an adjunct to somebody else's but because of our need as human persons for autonomy.

Source: "The Combahee River Collective Statement," in *Feminism in Our Time: The Essential Writings, World War II to the Present*, ed. Miriam Schneir (New York: Vintage, 1994), 177–79.

2. Criticizing Socialism

Official policy in the Soviet Union stated that socialism had brought women full equality, eliminating the need for feminism. In the 1970s, however, clusters of Russian women announced their dissatisfaction with so-called equality under socialism. Tatyana Mamonova, the editor of a collection of Russian women's writings such as this from a railroad worker, was ultimately expelled from the USSR.

It is becoming increasingly clear that the current equality means only giving women the right to perform heavy labor. . . . [I]n our day the woman, still not freed from the incredible burden of the family, strains herself even harder in the service of society. The situation . . . is true not only in large cities but also in villages. On collective and state farms, women do the hardest and most exhausting work while the men are employed as administrators, agronomists, accountants, warehouse managers, or high-paid tractor and combine drivers. In other words, men do the work that is more interesting and more profitable and does not damage their health.

Source: Tatyana Mamonova, ed., *Women and Russia: Feminist Writings from the Soviet Union* (Boston: Beacon Press, 1984), 8.

3. Policy and Patriarchy

In Italy, as in the Soviet Union, feminism had an underground quality involving mimeographed tracts and graffiti on buildings; women formed their own bookshops and published small newspapers. But others lobbied hard to get legislation on divorce and abortion changed, while in 1976 the Feminist Movement of Rome issued this article in its paper.

Patriarchal society is based on authoritarian-exploitative relationships, and its sexuality is sadomasochistic. The values of power, of the domination of man over the other [woman], are reflected in sexu-

twined issues of war, technology, racism, and sexism closed down classes.

Similar student unrest erupted across the globe, most dramatically in France. In January, students at the university in Nanterre, outside of Paris, had gone on strike, invading administration offices to protest what they saw as a second-rate education. They called themselves a proletariat — an exploited working class — as worker activists had done for more than a century. They did not embrace Soviet communism but rather considered themselves part of the New Left, not the old Communist or Socialist left. When students at the prestigious Sorbonne in Paris also took to the streets in protest, police assaulted them. The Parisian middle classes reacted with unexpected, if temporary, sympathy to the student uprising because of their own resentment of bureaucracy. They were also horrified at seeing the police force beating middle-class students and even passersby who expressed their support.

French workers joined in the protest. Some nine million went on strike, occupying factories and callality, where historically woman is given to man for his use. . . .

The idea of woman as man's property is fundamental to her oppression and she is often the only possession that dominant men allow exploited men to keep. . . .

In other words woman is given to the (exploited) man as compensation for his lack of possessions. . . .

We denounce as the latest form of woman's oppression the idea of a "sexual revolution" where woman is forced to go from being one man's object to being everybody's object, and where sadomasochistic pornography in films, in magazines, in all the forms of mass media that brutalize and violate woman, is bandied about as a triumph of sexual liberty.

Source: "Male Sexuality—Perversion," *Movimento Femminista Romano* (1976), quoted in *Italian Feminist Thought: A Reader*, eds. Paola Bono and Sandra Kemp (Oxford: Blackwell, 1991), 68–69.

4. Feminism and Environmentalism

Environmentally aware feminists took a different approach, such as announced in this "Manifesto of the 'Green' Women." It was originally a 1975 speech made in West Germany in the context of the moon landing and other accomplishments in space.

Man has actually landed on the moon—an admirable feat. . . . We "Green" women . . . believe that men belong to our environment. In order to rescue that environment for our children, we want to confront this man, this adventurer and moon explorer. A female cosmonaut from a so-called socialist republic doesn't justify this energy-wasting enterprise for us at a time when three-fourths of the earth's population is suffering from malnutrition.

Our inability to solve immediate problems may tempt us into escape—to the moon, into careerism, escape into ideologies, into alcohol or other drugs. But one group cannot escape completely: women, society's potential mothers, who must give birth to children, willingly or unwillingly, in this polluted world of ours.

Source: Delphine Brox-Brochot, "Manifesto of the 'Green' Women," in *German Feminism: Readings in Politics and Literature*, eds. Edith Hoshino Altbach et al. (Albany: State University of New York Press, 1984), 314.

5. Comparing the Situation of European and African Women

In an age when communications technology was bringing greater knowledge of conditions around the world, there were more frequent comparisons of situations faced by Western women with those faced by women in distant regions. The Malian politician Awa Thiam offered such an analysis in her Speak Out, Black Sisters *(1986).*

In any European country, when a husband goes in for that form of semi-condoned polygamy that consists of taking a mistress—or several—the wife can have recourse to the law by instituting action for divorce, or at least obtain support for better treatment from him. Such a course of action is not possible for a Muslim woman, who grows up in a system of institutionalized polygamy, where this is not permitted. What is more, such action would appear aberrant in a Black African context, in which marriage is generally religious, not civil. And this is the main basis for our claim that the Black woman's struggle is of a different nature from that of her White sister. The majority of European women do not lack essentials, whereas Black women are fighting for survival as much in the field of institutions as in the manner of her daily existence.

Source: Awa Thiam, *Speak Out, Black Sisters: Feminism and Oppression in Black Africa*, quoted in *Daughters of Africa: An International Anthology of Words and Writings by Women of African Descent from Ancient Egypt to the Present*, ed. Margaret Busby (New York: Ballantine Books, 1994), 477–78.

Questions to Consider

1. **What was the relationship between ideas within the feminist movement of the 1960s and 1970s and the thinking of other reform movements of the day?**
2. **In what ways was feminism in these decades a unified movement in terms of its thinking, and in what ways was it a set of multiple movements?**
3. **What issues do these activists raise?**
4. **What possibilities for consensus do you see in the differing positions?**

ing not only for higher wages but also for participation in everyday decision making. The combined revolt of youth and workers looked as if it might spiral into another French revolution, so unified were the expressions of political anger. The normally decisive president Charles de Gaulle seemed paralyzed at first, but he soon sent tanks into Paris. In June, he announced a raise for workers, and businesses offered them more involvement in decision making. Many citizens, having grown tired of the street violence, the destruction of so much private property, and the breakdown of services such as garbage collection, began to sympathize with the government instead of the students. Although demonstrations continued throughout June, the student movement in France at least had been closed down. The revolutionary moment had passed.

The Prague Spring By contrast, the 1968 revolt in Prague began within the Czechoslovak Communist Party itself. At a party congress in the autumn of 1967, Alexander Dubček,

Invasion Puts Down the Prague Spring
When the Soviet Union and other Warsaw Pact members cracked down on the Prague Spring, they met determined citizen resistance. People refused assistance of any kind to the invaders and personally talked to them about the Czech cause. Despite the repression, protests small and large continued until the final fall of Communist rule two decades later. *(© Bettmann/Corbis.)*

Prague Spring, 1968

head of the Slovak branch of the party, had called for more social and political openness. Attacked as an inferior Slovak by the Communist leadership, Dubček nonetheless struck a chord among frustrated party officials, technocrats, and intellectuals. Czech citizens began to dream of creating a new society—one based on "socialism with a human face." Reform-minded party delegates elevated Dubček to the top position, and he quickly changed the Communist style of government by ending censorship, instituting the secret ballot for party elections, and allowing competing political groups to form. "Look!" one little girl in the street remarked as the new government took power. "Everyone's smiling today." The Prague Spring had begun—"an orgy of free expression," one Czech journalist called it. People bought uncensored publications, packed uncensored theater productions, and engaged in nonstop political debate.

Dubček faced the enormous problem of negotiating policies acceptable to the USSR, the party bureaucracy, and reform-minded citizens. His government handed down reforms with warnings about maintaining "discipline" and showing "wise behavior." Fearing change, the Polish, East German, and Soviet regimes threatened the reform government daily. When Dubček failed to attend a meeting of Warsaw Pact leaders, Soviet threats intensified until finally, in August 1968, Soviet tanks rolled into Prague in a massive show of force. Citizens tried to halt the return to Communist orthodoxy through sabotage: they painted graffiti on the tanks and removed street signs to confuse invading troops. Illegal radio stations broadcast testimonials of resistance, and merchants refused to sell food or other commodities to Soviet troops. These actions did not stop the determined Soviet leadership, which gradually removed reformers from power. Jan Palach and other university students immolated themselves the following January, but the moment of reform-minded change eventually ended here, too. Around the world, governments worked to stamp out criticism of the cold war order.

The Superpowers Restore Order

The protests of 1968 challenged the political direction of Western societies, but little turned out the way reformers hoped as governments turned to conservative solutions. In November 1968, the Soviets announced the Brezhnev Doctrine, which stated that reform movements, as a "common problem" of all socialist countries, would face swift repression. In the early 1970s, the hard-liner Brezhnev clamped down on critics, crushing the morale of dissidents in the USSR. "The shock of our tanks crushing the Prague Spring . . . convinced us that the Soviet colossus was invincible," explained one pessimistic liberal. Other voices persisted, however. In 1974, Brezhnev expelled author Aleksandr Solzhenitsyn from the USSR after the publication of the first volume of *The Gulag Archipelago* (1973–1976) in the U.S.-led bloc. Solzhenitsyn documented the story of the Gulag (the Soviet system of internment and forced-labor camps) with firsthand reports and other sources of information about the deadly conditions prisoners endured. More than any other single work, *The Gulag Archipelago* disillusioned loyal Communists around the world.

The USSR and other Communist countries used both persecution of ordinary citizens and the "soft" power of the new medium of television to reestablish order. Soviet psychologists, working with the government, certified the "mental illness" of people who did not play by the rules; thus, dissidents wound up as virtual prisoners in mental institutions. In a revival of tsarist Russia's anti-Semitism, Jews faced educational restrictions (especially in university admissions), severe job discrimination, and constant assault on their religious practice. Soviet officials commonly accused Jews of being "unreliable." One said, "They think only of emigrating. . . . It's madness to give them an education, because it's state money wasted." Simultaneously the new medium of television was enlisted to restore calm. In Czechoslovakia, where by 1970 some 80 percent of households had TV, government writers created a new batch of soap operas after the uprisings. These featured heroines who taught their families to replace activism in the public sphere with the contentment of private life. Heroes selflessly traveled to the West for their jobs, only to return disillusioned by its faults.

Despite these efforts, the brain drain of eastern European intellectuals to the West and of Jews to Israel or the United States increased into the 1970s and beyond. The modernist composer György Ligeti had left Hungary in 1956, after which his work was celebrated in concert halls and in such classic films as *2001: A Space Odyssey*. From exile in Paris, Czech writer Milan Kundera enthralled audiences with *The Book of Laughter and Forgetting* (1979) and *The Unbearable Lightness of Being* (1984). His novels chronicled his own path from enthusiasm for communism to despair shaped by bitter humor. Kundera claimed that the Soviet regime in Czechoslovakia depended on making people forget. The memory of fallen leaders was ruthlessly erased from history books, for instance, and individuals tried to block out grim reality by engaging in lots of sexual activity. Like the migrants from fascist Germany and Italy in the 1930s, newcomers — from noted intellectuals to skilled craftspeople and dancers — enriched the culture of those countries in the West that welcomed them.

In the United States, the reaction against activists was different, though restoring order ultimately succeeded there, too. Elected in 1968, President **Richard Nixon** (1913–1994) promised to bring peace to Southeast Asia, but in 1970 he ordered U.S. troops to invade Cambodia, the site of North Vietnamese bases. Campuses erupted again in protest, and on May 4 the National Guard killed four students and wounded eleven others at a demonstration at Kent State University in Ohio. Nixon called the victims "bums," and a growing reaction against the counterculture led many Americans to agree with one citizen who declared that the guardsmen "should have fired sooner and longer." The United States and North Vietnam agreed to peace in January 1973, but warfare continued. In 1975, a determined North Vietnamese offensive defeated South Vietnam and its U.S. allies and forcibly reunified the country. The United States reeled from the defeat, having suffered loss of young lives, turbulence at home, vast military costs, and a weakening of its reputation around the world. Yet a strong current of public opinion turned against activists, born of the sense that somehow they — not the war, government corruption, or the huge war debt — had brought down the United States. Both superpowers were being tested, almost to the limits, creating a climate of uncertainty not only about politics but also about the future of postindustrial prosperity.

REVIEW QUESTION What were the main issues for protesters in the 1960s, and how did governments address them?

Richard Nixon: U.S. president (1969–1974) who escalated the Vietnam War, worked for accommodation with China, and resigned from the presidency after trying to block free elections.

The Testing of Superpower Domination and the End of the Cold War

Protesters like Jan Palach left a lasting legacy that continued to motivate those seeking political change, particularly in the Soviet bloc. As order was restored, some disillusioned reformers in the West turned to open terrorism, and like every other political occurrence in these days, television broadcast the events. New forces also emerged from beyond Europe and the United States to challenge superpower dominance. The 1970s brought an era of détente — a lessening of tensions — during which both superpowers limited the nuclear arms race in order to deal with crises at home. Even so, internal corruption, the threat of terrorism, competition from the oil-producing states, and the pursuit of warfare beyond their borders all threw the superpowers and their allies off balance, allowing reform-minded heads of state to come to the fore. The two most famous innovators were Margaret Thatcher in Britain and Mikhail Gorbachev in the USSR, who introduced drastic new policies in the 1980s to keep their economies moving forward. But in the Soviet bloc, postindustrial prosperity was simply unattainable by trying to refine the old system. Gorbachev's reforms actually contributed to the collapse of the Soviet system and the end of the cold war in 1989.

A Changing Balance of World Power

After being tested by protest at home, the superpowers found themselves facing a changing balance in world power. In 1972, the United States pulled off a foreign policy triumph over the USSR when it opened relations with the other Communist giant — China. But it was hit hard by a Middle Eastern oil embargo that followed on the heels of that victory. As the situation in the Middle East grew ever bloodier, militants in Iran took U.S. embassy personnel hostage. The relationship of the United States to the Middle East began to weaken the U.S. bloc and to compete with the cold war as a major global issue.

From Nixon in China to Détente In the midst of turmoil at home and the draining war in Vietnam, Henry Kissinger, Nixon's secretary of state and a believer — like Otto von Bismarck — in Realpolitik, decided to take advantage of the ongoing rivalry between the USSR and China. After the Communist Revolution in 1949, Mao Zedong, China's new leader, undertook foolish experiments in both manufacturing and agriculture that caused famine and massive suffering. In the Cultural Revolution of the 1960s, Mao encouraged students to attack officials, teachers, and other authorities to prevent — he claimed — the development of a Soviet-style bureaucracy. As internal problems grew in both the Soviet Union and China, the two Communist giants skirmished along their shared borders and in diplomatic arenas. In 1972, President Nixon visited China, linking, if only tentatively, two very different great nations both facing disorder at home. Within China, Nixon's visit helped slow the brutality and excesses of Mao's Cultural Revolution. It also advanced the careers of Chinese pragmatists who were interested in technology, trade, and relations with the West and who laid the groundwork for China's boom that started later in the century.

The diplomatic success of the visit also sped up the process of détente between the United States and the Soviet Union. Fearful of the Chinese diplomatic advantage and similarly confronted by popular protest, the Soviets made their own overtures to the U.S.-led bloc. In 1972, the superpowers signed the first Strategic Arms Limitation Treaty (SALT I), which set a cap on the number of antimissile defenses each country could have. In 1975, in the Helsinki accords on human rights, the western bloc officially acknowledged Soviet territorial gains in World War II in exchange for the Soviet bloc's guarantee of basic human rights.

Despite these diplomatic successes, the war in Vietnam left the United States billions of dollars in debt to other countries. The international currency system collapsed under the weight of this imbalance. In the face of the resulting global economic chaos, Common Market countries united to force the United States to relinquish its single-handed direction of Western economic strategy. Another blow to U.S. leadership followed when it was revealed that Nixon's office had threatened the U.S. system of free elections by authorizing the burglary and wiretapping of Democratic Party headquarters at Washington's Watergate building during the 1972 presidential campaign. The Watergate scandal forced Nixon to resign in disgrace in the summer of 1974 — the first U.S. president ever to do so. Nixon's downfall was one more weak spot in U.S. superpower status in the 1960s and 1970s.

Oil and Stagflation Amid the instability in the United States in the 1960s and 1970s, the Middle East's oil-producing nations dealt Western dominance still another major blow. Tensions between Israel and the Arab world pro-

The Middle East and the Politics of Oil
When Middle Eastern countries took control of the price and volume of oil they sold, Western leaders were taken aback, so thoroughly accustomed were the United States and its allies to setting the conditions of trade. OPEC leaders were lampooned in cartoons as the global economic crisis unfolded. Stagflation hit Western economies hard, while everyone came to terms with the new force of oil in international politics. *(© Copyright 1977 by Hy Rosen/Albany Times-Union, Albany, New York.)*

vided the catalyst. In 1967, Israeli forces, responding to Palestinian guerrilla attacks, quickly seized Gaza and the Sinai peninsula from Egypt, the Golan Heights from Syria, and the West Bank from Jordan. Israel's stunning victory in this action, which came to be called the Six-Day War, was followed in 1973 by a joint Egyptian and Syrian attack on Israel on Yom Kippur, the most holy day in the Jewish calendar. Israel, with material assistance from the United States, stopped the assault.

Israel after the Six-Day War, 1967

Having failed militarily, the Arabs turned to economic clout. They struck at the West's weakest point—its dependence on Middle Eastern oil for its advanced industries and postindustrial lifestyle. Arab nations in the **Organization of Petroleum Exporting Countries (OPEC)**, a relatively loose consortium before the Yom Kippur War, combined to quadruple the price of their oil and impose an embargo, cutting off all exports of oil to the United States and its allies because they backed Israel. For the first time since imperialism's heyday, the producers of raw materials—not the industrial powers—controlled the flow of commodities and set prices to their own advantage. The West was now mired in an oil crisis.

Throughout the 1970s, oil-dependent Westerners watched in astonishment as OPEC upset the balance of economic power and helped provoke a recession in the West (Figure 28.1). The oil embargo and price hike not only caused unemployment to rise by more than 50 percent in Europe and the United States but also caused inflation to soar. By the end of 1973, the inflation rate jumped to over 8 percent in West Germany, 12 percent in France, and 20 percent in Portugal. Eastern-bloc countries, dependent on Soviet oil, fared little better because the West could no longer afford their products and the Soviets boosted the price of their own oil. Skyrocketing interest rates discouraged both industrial investment and consumer buying. With prices, unemployment, and interest rates all rising—an unusual combination of economic conditions called **stagflation**—some in the West came to realize that both energy resources and economic growth had limits. Western Europe drastically cut back on its oil dependence by undertaking conservation, enhancing public trans-

Organization of Petroleum Exporting Countries (OPEC): A consortium that regulated the supply and export of oil and that acted with more unanimity after the United States supported Israel against the Arabs in the wars of the late 1960s and early 1970s.

stagflation: The combination of a stagnant economy and soaring inflation; a period of stagflation occurred in the West in the 1970s as a result of an OPEC embargo on oil.

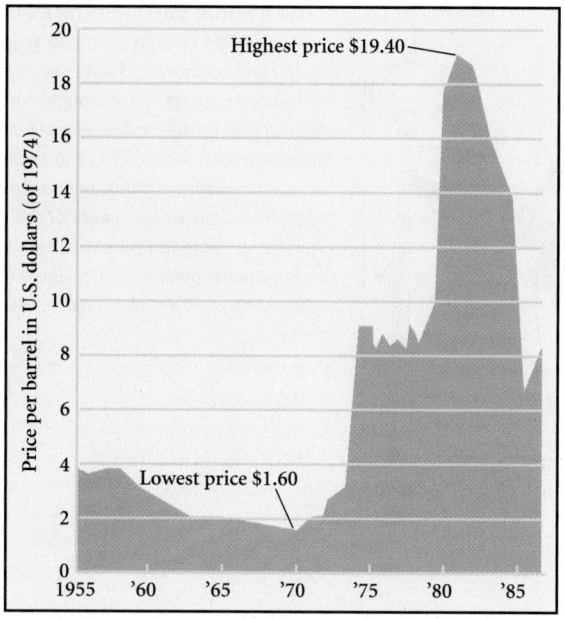

FIGURE 28.1 Fluctuating Oil Prices, 1955–1985
Colonization allowed the Western imperial powers to obtain raw materials at advantageous prices or even without paying at all. OPEC's oil embargo and price hikes of the 1970s were signs of change, which included the exercise of decolonized countries' control over their own resources. OPEC's action led to a decade of painful economic downturn, but it also encouraged some European governments to improve public transportation, encourage the production of fuel-efficient cars, and make individual consumers cut back their dependence on oil.

portation, and raising the price of gasoline to encourage the development of fuel-efficient cars.

The U.S. bloc took further blows. Elected U.S. president in 1976, Jimmy Carter—a successful peanut farmer and governor of Georgia—was unable to return the economy to its pre–Vietnam War and pre–oil embargo prosperity. His administration also faced an insurmountable crisis in the Middle East. In the late 1970s, students, clerics, shopkeepers, and unemployed men in Iran began a religious uprising that brought to power the Islamic ayatollah (a Shi'ite religious leader) Ruhollah Khomeini (1902–1989). Using the new medium of audiocassette recordings to spread his message, Khomeini called for a transformation of Iran into a truly Islamic society, which meant the renunciation of the Western ways advocated by the American-backed shah, who as a result was deposed. In the autumn of 1979, revolutionary supporters of Khomeini took hostages at the U.S. embassy in Teheran and held them for 444 days, even as images of the captives' stricken faces were sent around the globe via satellites. The United States was essentially paralyzed in the face of Islamic militancy, further OPEC price hikes, and a downwardly spiraling economy.

The Western Bloc Meets Challenges with Reform

As the 1980s opened, the first agenda item for non-Communist governments in the West was to put their economic houses in order. Second was to confront the growing phenomenon of terrorism—that is, coordinated and targeted political violence by opposition groups. The mix of terrorism, the energy crisis, soaring unemployment, and double-digit inflation sparked the election of conservative politicians, who maintained that decades of supporting a welfare state were at the heart of economic problems. Across the West, people came to feel that the unemployed and new immigrants from around the world were responsible for the downturn in the postindustrial economy. Nineteenth-century emphases on competitiveness, individualism, and revival of privilege for the "best circles" replaced the twentieth-century trend toward advancing economic democracy to combat totalitarianism. Postindustrial society changed political course.

Terrorism The terrorism at the U.S. embassy in Iran was part of a trend that had actually begun in the West. In the 1970s, terrorist bands of young people in Europe responded to the suppression of activism and the worsening economic conditions with kidnappings, bank robberies, bombings, and assassinations. In West Germany, the Red Army Faction—eager to bring down the Social Democratic coalition that had led the country through the 1970s—assassinated prominent businessmen, judges, and other public officials. Practiced in assassinations of public figures and random shootings of pedestrians, Italy's Red Brigades kidnapped and then murdered the head of the dominant Christian Democrats in 1978. Advocates of independence for the Basque nation in northern Spain assassinated Spanish politicians and police officers.

In the 1970s, Catholics in Northern Ireland pitted themselves against the dominant Protestants to protest job discrimination and a lack of civil rights. Demonstrators urged union with the Irish Republic, and with protest escalating, the British government sent in troops. On January 30, 1972, which became known as Bloody Sunday, British troops fired at demonstrators and killed thirteen, setting off a cycle of violence that left five hundred dead in that year alone. Protestants fearful of losing their dominant position combated a reinvigorated Irish Republican Army (IRA), which carried out bombings and assassinations to press for the union of the two Irelands and an end to the oppression of Catholics.

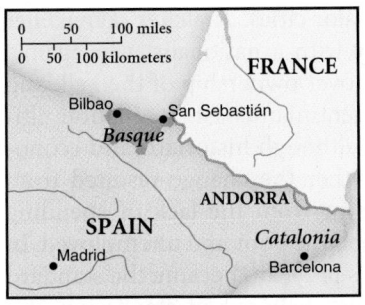

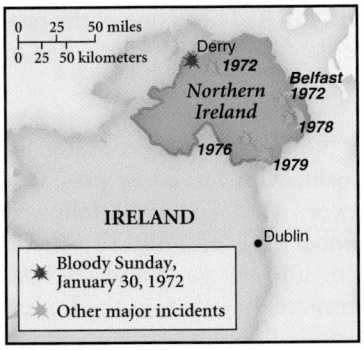

Nationalist Movements of the 1970s

Soldiers and Civilians in Northern Ireland

Separatist, civil rights, and terrorist movements increasingly directed their violence against ordinary people, following the lead of soldiers in World War II. In Northern Ireland, British troops fought to put down the Irish Republican Army, but civilians were also their target. However, this image from Derry in 1969 shows that civilians resisted, fighting with homemade weapons. It was only late in the 1990s that both sides called a halt to the killing and agreed to negotiate. *(Getty Images.)*

Terrorists failed in their goal of overturning the existing democracies, and, battered as it was, parliamentary government scored a few important successes in the 1970s. Spain and Portugal, suffering under dictatorships since the 1930s, set out on a course of political openness and greater prosperity. The death of Spain's Francisco Franco in 1975 ended more than three decades of dictatorial rule. Franco's handpicked successor, King Juan Carlos, surprisingly steered his nation to Western-style constitutional monarchy, facing down threatened military coups. Portugal and Greece also ousted right-wing dictators, thus paving the way for their integration into western Europe and for economic growth. Despite these democratic advances, economic crisis and political terrorism weighed on the West.

Thatcher Reshapes Politics

More than anyone else, **Margaret Thatcher**, the leader of Britain's Conservative Party and prime minister from 1979 to 1990, reshaped the West's political and economic ideas to meet the crisis. Coming to power amid continuing economic decline, revolt in Northern Ireland, and labor unrest, the combative prime minister rejected the politics of consensus building. She believed that only business could revive the sluggish British economy, so she lashed out at union leaders, Labour Party politicians, and people who received welfare-state benefits, calling them enemies of British prosperity. Her policies against the welfare state sounded a revolutionary chord, and she called herself "a nineteenth-century liberal" in reference to the economic individualism of that age. In her view, business leaders were the key members of society. She characterized immigrants, whose low wages contributed greatly to business profits, as inferior. Under Thatcher, even workers blamed labor leaders or newcomers for Britain's troubles.

The policies of "Thatcherism" were based on monetarist, or supply-side, economic theory. According to monetarist theory, inflation results when government pumps money into the economy at a rate higher than the nation's economic growth rate. Monetarists thus believe that the government should keep a tight rein on the money supply to prevent prices from rising rapidly. Supply-side economists maintain that the economy as a whole flourishes when businesses grow and their prosperity "trickles down" throughout society. To implement these

Margaret Thatcher: Prime minister of Britain (1979–1990) who set a new tone for British politics by promoting neoliberal economic policies and criticizing poor people, union members, and racial minorities as worthless, even harmful citizens.

On the World Stage: Margaret Thatcher and Mohammed Anwar al-Sadat

Margaret Thatcher, Great Britain's conservative prime minister, and Egyptian president Mohammed Anwar al-Sadat met in London in August 1981, just two months before Sadat was assassinated for participating in the Egyptian-Israeli peace accord. Thatcher's term in office was as memorable as Sadat's: she went on to launch a new conservatism in politics and economics that would sweep the world in the 1980s and 1990s. *(Mary Evans Picture Library/Marx Memorial Library.)*

theories, the British government cut income taxes on the wealthy as a way of encouraging investment and increased sales taxes to compensate for the lost revenue. The result was a greater burden on working people, who bore the brunt of the higher sales tax. Thatcher also vigorously cut government's role in the economy: she sold publicly owned businesses and utilities such as British Airways, refused to prop up "outmoded" industries such as coal mining, and slashed education and health programs. As Thatcher's package of economic policies spread through the West and the world, it came to be known as **neoliberalism** (see Document, "Margaret Thatcher's Economic Vision," page 975).

In the first three years of Thatcher's government, the British economy did not respond well to her shock treatment. The quality of universities, public transportation, highways, and hospitals deteriorated, and leading scholars and scientists left the country in a renewal of the brain drain. In addition, social unity fragmented as she pitted the lower classes against one another. In 1981, blacks and Asians rioted in major cities. Thatcher revived her sagging popularity with a nationalist war against Argentina in 1982 over ownership of the Falkland Islands off the Argentinian coast. Stagflation ultimately dissipated, although historians and economists debated whether the change resulted from Thatcher's policies or from the lack of spending power that burdened the poor and unemployed. In any case, Thatcher's program became the standard for those facing the challenge of stagflation and economic decline. Britain had been one of the pioneers of the welfare state, and now it pioneered in changing course.

neoliberalism: A theory first promoted by British prime minister Margaret Thatcher, calling for a return to liberal principles of the nineteenth century, including the reduction of welfare-state programs and the cutting of taxes for the wealthy to promote economic growth.

In Thatcher's Footsteps

In the United States, Ronald Reagan, who served as president between 1981 and 1989, followed a similar road to combat the economic crisis there. Dividing U.S. citizens into the good and the bad, Reagan vowed to promote the values of the "moral majority," which included commitment to Bible-based religion, dedication to work, and unquestioned patriotism. He blasted so-called spendthrift and immoral "liberals" when introducing "Reaganomics"—a program of whopping income tax cuts for the wealthy combined with massive reductions in federal spending for student loans, school lunch programs, and mass transit. Like Thatcher, Reagan believed that cutting programs for the poor and taxes for the wealthy would help the economy. Federal funding of social programs, he felt, only encouraged bad Americans to be lazy.

In foreign policy, Reagan warned of the Communist threat from the Soviet Union—which he called the "evil empire"—and thus rolled back détente. He demanded huge military budgets to counter the Soviets and announced the Strategic Defense Initiative (SDI), known popularly as Star Wars, a costly plan to put lasers in space to defend the United States against a nuclear attack. The combination of tax cuts and military expansion had pushed the federal budget deficit to $200 billion by 1986. As in Britain, inflation was brought under control and business picked up.

Other western European leaders also limited welfare-state benefits in the face of stagflation, though without Thatcher's and Reagan's socially divisive rhetoric. West German leader Helmut Kohl, who took power in 1982, reduced welfare spending, froze government wages, and cut corporate taxes. By 1984, the inflation rate was only 2 percent and West Germany had acquired a 10 percent share of world trade. Unlike Thatcher, Kohl did not fan class and racial hatreds. Such a strategy would have been particularly unwise in Germany, where terrorism on the left and on the right continued to flourish.

DOCUMENT

Margaret Thatcher's Economic Vision

Margaret Thatcher, Britain's longest-serving prime minister, changed Western thinking about the welfare state. Many Europeans saw the welfare state as a mainstay of democracy, which would alleviate the hardships that had turned workers toward either socialism, from Bismarck's time onward, or toward Mussolini's and Hitler's fascism during the difficult interwar years. Thatcher, however, believed that programs to provide health care, education, and housing coddled the lazy. She thought the money for such programs should be invested in private industry, to produce a profit and to encourage more investment and greater productivity. Here she outlines her thoughts on public spending to members of the Conservative Party.

I and my colleagues say that to add to public spending takes away the very money and resources that industry needs to stay in business, let alone to expand. Higher public spending, far from curing unemployment, can be the very vehicle that loses jobs and causes bankruptcies in trade and commerce. That is why we warned local authorities that since rates [taxes] are frequently the biggest tax that industry now faces, increases in them can cripple local businesses. . . .

That is why I stress that if those who work in public authorities take for themselves large pay increases, they leave less to be spent on equipment and new buildings. That in turn deprives the private sector of the orders it needs, especially some of those industries in the hard pressed regions. Those in the public sector have a duty to those in the private sector not to take out so much in pay that they cause others' unemployment. That is why we point out that every time high wage settlements in nationalised monopolies lead to higher charges for telephones, electricity, coal, and water, they can drive companies out of business and cost other people their jobs.

If spending money like water was the answer to our country's problems, we would have no problems right now. If ever a nation has spent, spent, spent, and spent again, ours has. Today that dream is over. All of that money has got us nowhere, but it still has to come from somewhere. Those who urge us to relax the squeeze, to spend yet more money indiscriminately in the belief that it will help the unemployed and the small businessman, are not being kind or compassionate or caring. They are not the friends of the unemployed or the small business. They are asking us to do again the very things that caused the problems in the first place. . . .

I am accused of lecturing or preaching about this. I suppose it is a critic's way of saying, "Well, we know it is true, but we have to carp at something." I do not care about that. But I do care about the future of free enterprise, the jobs and exports it provides, and the independence it brings to our people.

Source: Juliet S. Thompson and Wayne C. Thompson, ed., *Margaret Thatcher: Prime Minister Indomitable* (Boulder: Westview, 1994), 230–31.

Question to Consider

- **According to Thatcher, how does public spending harm the private sector and the citizens of Great Britain as a whole?**

Moreover, the legacy of Nazism loomed menacingly. When an unemployed German youth said of immigrant Turkish workers, "Let's gas 'em," the revival of Nazi hate speech appalled many in Germany's middle class.

By 1981, stagflation had put more than 1.5 million people out of work in France, but the French took a different political path to deal with the economic crisis. They elected a Socialist president, François Mitterrand, who nationalized banks and certain industries and increased wages and social spending to stimulate the economy—the opposite of Thatcherism. New public buildings like museums and libraries arose along with new subway lines and improved public transport. When conservative Jacques Chirac succeeded Mitterrand as president in 1995, he adopted neoliberal policies. Socially divisive politics that had unfolded during hard economic times grew in appeal. From the 1980s on, the racist National Front Party won 10 percent and sometimes more of the French vote with promises to deport African and Middle Eastern immigrants.

Prosperity in Smaller States

At the same time, smaller European states without heavy defense commitments began to thrive, some of them by slashing welfare programs. Spain joined the Common Market in 1986 and used Common Market investment and tourist dollars to help rebuild its sagging infrastructure as in the southern cities of Granada and Córdoba. In Ireland, new investment in education for high-tech jobs combined with low wage rates attracted business to the country in the 1990s. Prosperity and the rising death toll led to a political rapprochement between Ireland and Northern Ireland in 1999. Austria prospered, too, in part by reducing government pensions and aid to business. Austrian chancellor Franz Vranitsky summed up the changed focus of government in the 1980s and 1990s: "In Austria, the shelter that the state has given to almost everyone—employee as well as entrepreneur—has led . . . a lot of people [to] think not only what they can do to solve a problem but what the state can do. . . . This needs to change." The century-long growth of the welfare state slowed by the 1990s as new economic and political theories took hold.

Almost alone, Sweden maintained a full array of social programs for everyone. The government offered each immigrant a choice of subsidized housing in neighborhoods inhabited primarily by Swedes or primarily by people from the immigrant's native land. Such programs were expensive: the tax rate on income over $46,000 was 80 percent. Despite a highly productive workforce, Sweden dropped from fourth to fourteenth place among nations in per capita income by 1998. Although the Swedes reduced their costly dependence on foreign oil by cutting consumption in half between 1976 and 1986, their welfare state came to seem extreme to many citizens. As elsewhere, immigrants were cast as the source of the country's problems—past, present, and future: "How long will it be before our Swedish children will have to turn their faces toward Mecca?" ran one politician's campaign speech in 1993.

Collapse of Communism in the Soviet Bloc

Beginning in 1985, reform came to the Soviet Union as well, but instead of fortifying the economy, it helped bring about the collapse of the Soviet bloc. The need for reform was evident. In 1979, the USSR became embroiled against Islam in Afghanistan when it supported a coup by a Communist faction against the government: casualties were 800,000 for the Soviets alone and 3 million for Afghans. Further, global communications technology, international trade, and the ongoing protests of workers, artists, and intellectuals showed Soviet citizens that another way of life was possible. Citizens could see that the Soviet system of corrupt economic management produced a deteriorating standard of living. After working a full day, Soviet homemakers stood in long lines to obtain basic commodities. Shortages necessitated the three-generation household, in which grandparents took over tedious homemaking tasks from their working children and grandchildren. "There is no special skill to this," a seventy-three-year-old grandmother and former garbage collector remarked. "You just stand in line and wait." Even so, people often went away empty-handed as basic household supplies like soap disappeared instantly from stores. One cheap and readily available product—vodka—often formed the center of people's social lives. Alcoholism reached crisis levels, diminishing productivity and tremendously straining the nation's morale.

Mikhail Gorbachev, Soviet Reformer

In 1985, a new leader, **Mikhail Gorbachev**, unexpectedly opened an era of change in hopes of remedying all these ills. The son of peasants, Gorbachev had risen through Communist Party ranks as an agricultural specialist and had traveled abroad to observe life in the West. At home, he saw the consequences of that economic stagnation: in much of the USSR, ordinary people decided not to have children. The Soviet Union was forced to import massive amounts of grain because 20 to 30 percent of the grain that was produced in the USSR rotted before it could be harvested or shipped to market, so great was the inefficiency of the state-directed economy. Industrial pollution had reached scandalous proportions because state-run enterprises cared only about meeting production quotas. A massive and privileged party bureaucracy feared innovation and failed to achieve socialism's professed goal of a decent standard of living for working people. To match U.S. military growth, the Soviet Union diverted 15 to 20 percent of its gross national product (more than double the U.S. proportion) to armaments, further crippling the economy's chances of raising living standards. As these problems grew, a new cynical generation was coming of age that had no memory of World War II or Stalin's purges. "They believe in nothing," a mother said of Soviet youth in 1984.

Gorbachev knew from experience and from his travels to western Europe that the Soviet system was completely inadequate, and he quickly proposed several unusual programs. A crucial economic reform, **perestroika** ("restructuring"), aimed to reinvigorate the Soviet economy by improving productivity, increasing investment, encouraging the use of up-to-date technology, and gradually introducing such market features as prices and profits. The complement to economic change was the policy

Mikhail Gorbachev: Leader of the Soviet Union (1985–1991) who instituted reforms such as glasnost and perestroika, thereby contributing to the collapse of Communist rule in the Soviet bloc and the USSR.

perestroika: Literally, "restructuring"; an economic policy instituted in the 1980s by Soviet premier Mikhail Gorbachev calling for the introduction of market mechanisms and the achievement of greater efficiency in manufacturing, agriculture, and services.

of **glasnost** (usually translated as "openness" or "publicity"), which called for disseminating "wide, prompt, and frank information" and for allowing Soviet citizens new measures of free speech. When officials complained that glasnost threatened their status, Gorbachev replaced more than a third of the Communist Party's leadership in the first months of his administration. The pressing need for glasnost became most evident after the Chernobyl catastrophe in 1986, when a nuclear reactor exploded and spewed radioactive dust into the atmosphere. Bureaucratic cover-ups delayed the spread of information about the accident, with lethal consequences for people living near the plant.

After Chernobyl, even the Communist Party and Marxism-Leninism were opened to public criticism. Party meetings suddenly included complaints about the highest leaders and their policies. Television shows adopted the outspoken methods of American investigative reporting; one program exposed the plight of Leningrad's homeless children — an admission of communism's failings. Instead of publishing made-up letters praising the great Soviet state, newspapers were flooded with real ones complaining of shortages and abuse. One outraged "mother of two" protested that the cost-cutting policy of reusing syringes in hospitals was a source of AIDS. "Why should little kids have to pay for the criminal actions of our Ministry of Health?" she asked. Debate and factions arose across the political spectrum (see Document, "A Citizen's Experience of Gorbachev's Reforms," page 978). In the fall of 1987, one of Gorbachev's allies, Boris Yeltsin, quit the government after denouncing perestroika as insufficient to produce real reform. Yeltsin's political daring, which in the past would have consigned him to oblivion (or Siberia), inspired others to organize in opposition to crumbling Communist rule. In the spring of 1989, in a remarkably free balloting in Moscow's local elections, not a single Communist was chosen.

Glasnost and perestroika dramatically changed superpower relations. Recognizing how severely the cold war arms race was draining Soviet resources, Gorbachev almost immediately began scaling back missile production. His unilateral actions gradually won over Ronald Reagan. In 1985, the two leaders initiated a personal relationship and began defusing the cold war. "I bet the hard-liners in both our countries are bleeding when we shake hands," said the jovial Reagan at the conclusion of one meeting. In early 1989, Gorbachev withdrew the last of his country's forces from the debilitating war in Afghanistan, and the United States started to cut back its own vast military buildup.

Mikhail and Raisa Gorbachev
Mikhail Gorbachev and his wife, Raisa, gave a fresh look to Soviet politics. They traveled, made friends abroad, and were fashionable and modern. While the Gorbachevs became part of Western celebrity culture, however, average citizens back home in the USSR saw the Gorbachevs' privileged lifestyle as simply the continuation of the Communist government's disregard for ordinary people. *(© Peter Turnley/Corbis.)*

Rebellion in Poland

As Gorbachev's reforms in the USSR started spiraling out of his control, dissent was rising across the Soviet bloc, beginning in Poland, where resistance to the Soviet takeover had existed for decades. In the summer of 1980, Poles had gone on strike to protest government-increased food prices. As the protest spread, workers at the Gdańsk shipyards, led by electrician Lech Walesa and crane operator Anna Walentynowicz, created an independent labor movement called **Solidarity**. The organization soon embraced much of the adult population, including a million members of the Communist Party. Both intellectuals and the Catholic church, long in the forefront of opposition to antireligious communism,

glasnost: Literally, "openness" or "publicity"; a policy instituted in the 1980s by Soviet premier Mikhail Gorbachev calling for greater openness in speech and in thinking, which translated to the reduction of censorship in publishing, radio, television, and other media.

Solidarity: A Polish labor union founded in 1980 by Lech Walesa and Anna Walentynowicz that contested Communist Party programs and eventually succeeded in ousting the party from the Polish government.

DOCUMENT

A Citizen's Experience of Gorbachev's Reforms

Some people—especially in the U.S. bloc—interpreted Gorbachev's reforms as noble and enlightened, opening the way to free markets and free speech. In particular, the policy of glasnost offered the possibility of free speech, leading to lively television programming and newspaper investigations. In 1987 the weekly Ogonyok, *whose name means "A Small Fire," began publishing letters to the editor from actual readers. Before that, most letters to newspapers and magazines in the Soviet Union had been written by editors to tow the proper political line. The feature became so popular that within two years the magazine was receiving as many as 150,000 letters a year covering every situation imaginable—from corruption to waiting in line, from privileges given to officials to the shortcomings of Gorbachev's reforms themselves. Presented here is a letter from a schoolteacher writing in 1988 about her own experience of glasnost.*

As a member of the "Knowledge" Society and a deputy to the local soviet, I was asked to prepare a speech for the evening in honor of the Seventieth Anniversary of the October Revolution. I studied M. S. Gorbachev's speech, "the October Revolution and *Perestroika*: The Revolution Continues," thoroughly and collected material about exemplary production workers in our village. In my speech I pointed out not only the successes, but also the shortcomings of our village, district and school. I gave the speech on November 6, and a week later I was called into the Executive Committee of the village society. I was accused of being apolitical [disloyal] and told that I would not be allowed onto the podium . . . because I was airing dirty linen in public.

. . . [A]fter a rebuke like that I have lost my desire to tell the truth, especially since the Party organization of the Cheremkhovsky collective farm and the chairman of the village soviet have suffered because of me. They were both reprimanded for not checking my speech, and for letting me onto the podium. Apparently, *glasnost* and *perestroika* have not reached us yet.

Source: Letter of Z. I. Kupriyanova, January 1988, in *Small Fires: Letters from the Soviet People to* Ogonyok *Magazine 1987–1990*, ed. Christopher Cerf and Marina Albee (New York: Summit Books, 1990), 60.

Question to Consider

- **What aspects of Gorbachev's policy does the speaker address in her letter, and what is the letter's tone?**

supported Solidarity workers as they occupied factories in protest against the deteriorating conditions of everyday life. The members of Solidarity waved Polish flags and paraded giant portraits of the Virgin Mary and Pope John Paul II—a Polish native.

Global media coverage encouraged Solidarity leaders to demand government recognition of the union's legitimacy. As food became scarce and prices rose, tens of thousands of women joined in with marches, crying "We're hungry!" They also protested working conditions, but as both workers and the only caretakers of home life, it was the scarcity of food that sent them into the streets. The Communist Party teetered on the edge of collapse, until the police and the army, with Soviet support, imposed a military government and in the winter of 1981 outlawed Solidarity. The stern and puritanical head of the new regime, Wojciech Jaruzelski, could not push repression too far: he needed new loans from the U.S.-led bloc to keep the sinking Polish economy afloat. Using world communications networks, dissidents kept Solidarity alive both inside and outside of Poland. Workers kept meeting, creating a new culture outside the official Soviet arts and newscasts. Poets read dissident verse to overflow crowds, and university professors lectured to Solidarity members on such forbidden topics as Polish resistance in World War II. Activism in Poland and the news about it set the stage for communism's downfall across the Soviet bloc.

The Revolutions of 1989

The year 1989 saw the sudden and unexpected disintegration of Communist power in eastern Europe, but uprisings were occurring around the world—in Chile, the Philippines, Haiti, South Africa, and China, for example. In 1980 the global news network CNN was established, linking many individual movements for democratic change through its twenty-four-hour coverage of world events. The most surprising and widely covered of these was the attack on the Communist state in China. Inspired by Gorbachev's visit to Beijing, in the spring of 1989 thousands of Chinese students massed in the city's Tiananmen Square, the world's largest public square, to demand democracy. They used telex machines and e-mail to rush their messages to the international community, and they effectively conveyed their goals through the cameras that Western television, broadcasting via satellite, trained on them. China's aged Communist leaders, while pushing economic modernization, refused to consider the introduction of democracy. As workers began joining the pro-democracy forces, the government crushed the movement and executed as many as a thousand rebels.

News of the protests in Tiananmen Square was galvanizing to those in eastern Europe, who were inspired in their long-standing tradition of resistance. In June 1989, the Polish government, weakened by its own bungling of the economy and lacking Soviet support for further repression, held free parliamentary elections. Solidarity candidates overwhelmingly defeated the Communists, and Walesa became president in early 1990, hastening Poland's rocky transition to a market economy. Gorbachev openly reversed the Brezhnev Doctrine, refusing to interfere in the political course of another nation. When it became clear that the Soviet Union would not intervene in Poland, the fall of communism repeated itself across the Soviet bloc.

Communism collapsed first in Poland and then in Hungary, in part because of those countries' early introduction of free-market measures. In Hungary, which had experimented with "market socialism" since the 1960s, even officials began to realize that political democracy had to accompany economic freedom. Citizens were already protesting the government, lobbying, for example, against ecologically unsound projects like the construction of a new dam. They encouraged boycotts of Communist holidays, and on March 15, 1989, they boldly commemorated the anniversary of the Hungarian uprising. Finally, these popular demands for liberalization led the Parliament in the fall of 1989 to dismiss the Communist Party as the official ruling institution; people across the country tore down Soviet and Communist symbols.

The most potent symbol of a divided Europe—the Berlin Wall—stood in the midst of a divided Germany. East Germans had attempted to escape over the wall for decades, and since the early 1980s dissidents had held peace vigils in cities across East Germany. In the summer of 1989, crowds of East Germans flooded the borders to escape the crumbling Soviet bloc, and hundreds of thousands of protesters rallied throughout the fall against the regime. Satellite television brought them visions of postindustrial prosperity and of free and open public debate in West Germany. Crowds of demonstrators greeted Gorbachev, taken as a hero by many, when he visited the country in October. On November 9, guards at the Berlin Wall allowed free passage to the west, turning protest into a festive holiday: West Berliners greeted the Easterners with bananas, a consumer good that had been in short supply in the Eastern zone, and that fruit became the unofficial symbol of a newfound liberation. As they strolled freely in the streets, East Berliners saw firsthand the goods available in a successful postindustrial society.

November 1989: East Germany Meets West Germany
The fall of the Berlin Wall and the "iron curtain" separating the Soviet from the western bloc was a joyous occasion across Europe, but nowhere more so than in Germany. Divided from one another into two countries after World War II, Germans would later find that reunification was a problem, bringing unemployment and social dislocation. In November 1989, however, West Germans lined up to welcome their fellow citizens traveling from the east to see what life was like beyond the Soviet sphere. *(ullstein bild/Bildarchiv/The Granger Collection, New York—All rights reserved.)*

Soon thereafter, citizens—east and west—released years of frustration by assaulting the Berlin Wall with sledgehammers. The government finished the wall's destruction in 1990.

In Czechoslovakia, where both Soviet-style "softer" cultural policies aimed to maintain order since 1968, people also watched televised news of glasnost expectantly. Persecuted dissidents had maintained their critique of Communist rule. In an open letter to the Czechoslovak Communist Party leadership, playwright Václav Havel accused Marxist-Leninist rule of making people materialistic and indifferent to civic life. In 1977, Havel, along with a group of fellow intellectuals and workers, signed Charter 77, a public protest against the regime that resulted in the arrest of the signers. In the mid-1980s, they and the wider population heard Gorbachev on television calling for free speech, though never mentioning reform in Czechoslovakia. Protesters clamored for democracy, but the government turned the police on them, arresting activists in January 1989 for commemorating the death of Jan Palach. The turning point came in November 1989 when, in response to police beatings of students, Alexander Dubček, leader of the Prague Spring of 1968, addressed the crowds in Prague's Wenceslas Square with a call to oust the Stalinists from the government. Almost immediately, the Communist leadership resigned. Capping what became known as the "velvet revolution" for its lack of bloodshed, the formerly Communist-dominated parliament elevated Havel to the presidency.

The world's attention next fastened on the unfolding political drama in Romania. From the mid-1960s on, Nicolae Ceaușescu had ruled as the harshest dictator in Communist Europe since Stalin. In the name of modernization, he destroyed whole villages; to build up the population, he outlawed contraceptives and abortions, a restriction that led to the abandonment of tens of thousands of children. He preached the virtues of a very slim body so that he could cut rations and use the savings on his pet projects such as buying up private castles and other property. Most Romanians lived in utter poverty as Ceaușescu channeled almost all the country's resources into building himself an enormous palace in Bucharest. To this end, he tore down entire neighborhoods and dozens of historical buildings and crushed opponents of the gaudy project to make it appear popular. Yet in early December 1989, an opposition movement rose up: workers demonstrated against the dictatorial government, and the army turned on Ceaușescu loyalists. On Christmas Day, viewers watched on television as the dictator and his wife were tried by a military court and then executed. For many, the death of Ceaușescu meant that the very worst of communism was over.

Homeless Romanian Children (1995)
These children were among the many who lived without families around the railroad station in Romania's capital city, Bucharest. Nicolae Ceaușescu's regime prohibited birth control and abortion in order to increase the supply of workers while simultaneously cutting back on food rations. Children were the victims of this policy, even after Ceaușescu was overthrown, as families simply abandoned children they could not support. In order to survive, the children scavenged, stole, and begged. *(© Barry Lewis/Corbis.)*

REVIEW QUESTION How and why did the balance of world power change during the 1980s?

Conclusion

The fall of the Berlin Wall in 1989 symbolized the end of the cold war, even though the USSR still stood as a bulwark of communism. Collapse of communism in the Soviet satellites was an utter surprise around the world, for U.S.-bloc analysts had reported throughout the 1980s that the Soviet empire was in dangerously robust health. But no one should have been unaware of dissent or economic discontent. Since the 1960s, rebellious youth, ethnic and racial minorities, and women had all been condemning conditions across the West, along with criticizing the threat posed by the cold war. By the early 1980s, wars in Vietnam and Afghanistan, protests against privations in the Soviet bloc, the power of oil-producing states, and the growing political force of Islam had cost the superpowers their resources and reputations. Margaret Thatcher in Britain, Ronald Reagan in the United States, and Mikhail Gorbachev in the Soviet Union tried with varying degrees of success to put their postindustrial and cold war houses in order. The first two were successful, while Gorbachev's policies of glasnost and perestroika — aimed at political and economic improvements — brought on collapse.

Glasnost and perestroika were supposed to bring about the high levels of postindustrial prosperity enjoyed outside the Soviet bloc. Across the West, including the USSR, an unprecedented set of technological developments had transformed businesses, space exploration, and the functioning of government. Technological advances also had an enormous impact on everyday life. Work changed as society reached a stage called postindustrial, in which the service sector predominated. New patterns of family life, new relationships among the generations, and revised standards for sexual behavior also characterized these years, leading to youth rebellions. It was only in the United States and western Europe, however, that the full consumer benefits of postindustrialization reached ordinary people, for the attainment of a thoroughgoing consumer, service, and high-tech society demanded levels of efficiency, coordination, and cooperation unknown in the Soviet bloc.

The Collapse of Communism in Europe, 1989–1990

The 1989 overthrow of the Communist Party in the USSR satellite countries of eastern Europe occurred with surprising rapidity. The transformation began when Polish voters tossed out Communist Party leaders in June 1989, and then accelerated in September when thousands of East Germans fled to Hungary, Poland, and Czechoslovakia. Between October and December, Communist regimes were replaced in East Germany, Czechoslovakia, Bulgaria, and Romania. Within three years, the Baltic states would declare their independence, the USSR itself would dissolve, and the breakup of Yugoslavia would lead to war in the Balkans.

Many complained, nonetheless, about the dramatic changes resulting from postindustrial development. The protesters of the late 1960s addressed postindustrial society's stubborn problems: concentrations of bureaucratic and industrial power (often enabled by technology), social inequality, environmental degradation, and even uncertainty about humankind's future. In the Soviet sphere, protests were continuous but were little heeded until the collapse of Soviet domination of eastern Europe in 1989. Soon communism would be overturned in the USSR itself. However, the triumph of democracy in the former Soviet empire opened an era of painful adjustment, impoverishment, and even violence for hundreds of millions of people. Amid this rapid political change was the growing awareness—via technology's instantaneous coverage of the fall of repressive governments across the globe—that the world's peoples were more tightly connected than ever before.

FOR FURTHER EXPLORATION

- **For additional primary-source material from this period**, see *Sources of the Making of the West*, Fourth Edition.
- **For Web sites, images, and documents related to topics in this chapter**, visit *Make History* at bedfordstmartins.com/hunt.

Chapter 28 Review

Online Study Guide bedfordstmartins.com/hunt

Key Terms and People

In the grid below, identify the term or person and explain its historical significance. (To do this exercise online, go to bedfordstmartins.com/hunt.)

Term	Who or What & When	Why It Matters
DNA (p. 953)		
in vitro fertilization (p. 954)		
multinational corporation (p. 955)		
pop art (p. 959)		
Ostpolitik (p. 961)		
samizdat (p. 962)		
Richard Nixon (p. 969)		
Organization of Petroleum Exporting Countries (OPEC) (p. 971)		
stagflation (p. 971)		
Margaret Thatcher (p. 973)		
neoliberalism (p. 974)		
Mikhail Gorbachev (p. 976)		
perestroika (p. 976)		
glasnost (p. 977)		
Solidarity (p. 977)		

Review Questions

1. What were the technological and scientific advances of the 1960s and 1970s, and how did they change human life and society?
2. How did Western society and culture change in the postindustrial age?
3. What were the main issues for protesters in the 1960s, and how did governments address them?
4. How and why did the balance of world power change during the 1980s?

Making Connections

1. What were the differences between industrial society of the late nineteenth century and postindustrial society of the late twentieth century?
2. Why were there so many protests, acts of terrorism, and uprisings across the West in the decades between 1960 and 1990?
3. What have been the long-term consequences of Communist rule in the Soviet bloc between 1917 and 1989?
4. How did technology shape politics over the course of the twentieth century?

Important Events

Date	Event	Date	Event
1963	Betty Friedan publishes *The Feminine Mystique*	1978	The first test-tube baby is born in England
1966	Willy Brandt becomes West German foreign minister and develops Ostpolitik	1978–1979	Islamic revolution in Iran; hostages taken at U.S. embassy in Teheran
1967	First successful human heart transplant	1980	Solidarity organizes resistance to Polish communism; British prime minister Margaret Thatcher begins dismantling the welfare state
1968	Revolution in Czechoslovakia; student uprisings throughout Europe and the United States	1981	Ronald Reagan becomes U.S. president
1969	U.S. astronauts walk on the moon's surface	1985	Mikhail Gorbachev becomes Soviet premier
1972	SALT I between the United States and Soviet Union	1986	Explosion at Chernobyl nuclear plant; Spain joins the Common Market
1973	End of Vietnam War; OPEC raises price of oil and imposes oil embargo on the West	1989	Chinese students revolt in Tiananmen Square; Communist governments ousted in eastern Europe; Berlin Wall demolished
1973–1976	Aleksandr Solzhenitsyn publishes *The Gulag Archipelago*		

- Consider three events: **Betty Friedan publishes *The Feminine Mystique* (1963)**, **Aleksandr Solzhenitsyn publishes *The Gulag Archipelago* (1973–1976)**, and **British prime minister Margaret Thatcher begins dismantling the welfare state (1980)**. How can all of these be considered responses to postindustrial society?

SUGGESTED REFERENCES

The history-changing events of the 1960s to 1989 ran the gamut from life-changing technology to dramatic political upheavals—all of them chronicled in the innovative books below. The story of television in post-uprising Czechoslovakia illustrates that even dictatorships used this new technology to "soften" its control.

Bauer, Martin W., and George Gaskell, eds. *Biotechnology: The Making of a Global Controversy*. 2002.

Bren, Paulina. *The Greengrocer and His TV: The Culture of Communism after the 1968 Prague Spring*. 2010.

Carter, David. *Stonewall: The Riots That Sparked the Gay Rights Movement*. 2011.

Chaplin, Tamara. *Turning on the Mind: French Philosophers on Television*. 2007.

Dahl, Henne Marlene, and Tine Rask Eriksen, eds. *Dilemmas of Care in the Nordic Welfare State: Continuity and Change*. 2005.

Fink, Carole, et al. *1968: The World Transformed*. 1998.

*Freedman, Estelle B. *The Essential Feminist Reader*. 2007.

Green Parties Worldwide: http://www.greens.org

Hadley, Louisa, and Elizabeth Ho, eds. *Thatcher & After: Margaret Thatcher and Her Afterlife in Contemporary Culture*. 2011.

Harvey, Brian. *Europe's Space Program: To Ariane and Beyond*. 2003.

Horn, Gerd-Rainer. *The Spirit of 68: Rebellion in Western Europe and North America, 1956–1976*. 2007.

Kenney, Padraic. *Carnival of Revolution: Central Europe, 1989*. 2002.

Kotkin, Steven. *Armageddon Averted: Soviet Collapse, 1970–2000*. 2008.

Martin Luther King Jr. Papers Project at Stanford University: http://mlk-kpp01.stanford.edu/

Natalicchi, Giorgio. *Wiring Europe: Reshaping the European Telecommunications Regime*. 2001.

Ouimet, Matthew J. *The Rise and Fall of the Brezhnev Doctrine in Soviet Foreign Policy*. 2003.

Siani-Davies, Peter. *The Romanian Revolution of December 1989*. 2005.

Suri, Jeremy. *Power and Protest: Global Revolution and the Rise of Détente*. 2003.

Varon, Jeremy. *Bringing the War Home: The Weather Underground, the Red Army Faction, and Revolutionary Violence in the Sixties and Seventies*. 2004.

*Primary source.

CHAPTER

A New Globalism

29

1989 to the Present

Collapse of the Soviet Union and Its Aftermath 986
- The Breakup of Yugoslavia
- The Soviet Union Comes Apart
- Toward a Market Economy
- International Politics and the New Russia

The Nation-State in a Global Age 994
- Europe Looks beyond the Nation-State
- Globalizing Cities and Fragmenting Nations
- Global Organizations

An Interconnected World's New Challenges 999
- The Problems of Pollution
- Population, Health, and Disease
- North versus South?
- Radical Islam Meets the West
- The Promise and Problems of a World Economy

Global Culture and Society in the Twenty-First Century 1008
- Redefining the West: The Impact of Global Migration
- Global Networks and the Economy
- A New Global Culture?

Thérèse is a Congolese immigrant to Paris who arrived there in the late 1970s with the help of a brother who worked for an airline. Thérèse had been well-known in Africa as the teenage girlfriend of pop singer Bozi Boziana, who wrote a hit song about her. But Congo's political instability made her search for safety in Paris. Once there, Thérèse remained famous among African immigrants because she ran *nganda*, or informal bars, for them. Like Thérèse, the immigrants who frequent her nganda are often Congolese and other Africans who have settled in Paris, many of them illegally. They flock to her nganda because they like her stylish dress, the African food she cooks, the African music she plays, and the African products she sells. Many of Thérèse's small bars and eateries have flourished, only to be closed down by landlords who want more of her handsome profits or who object to her running an unlicensed café. Despite such obstacles, Thérèse keeps business going by moving her faithful clientele around her Paris neighborhood from basement to shop front to spare room. Thérèse is a new global citizen, counting on networks back home for supplies, constantly on the move because she lives on the margins of legality, and always striving to make a good living for herself and her family.

Thérèse is just one concrete example of the ways in which people in the post–cold war world crossed national boundaries while maintaining crucial ties around the globe. The end of the cold war rivalry between the superpowers and their allies paved the way for a more intimately connected world. In the 1990s, globalization advanced further with the dramatic collapse of communism in Yugoslavia and then of the Soviet Union itself. The world was no longer divided in two by the heavily guarded borders and hostile cold war propaganda. Now, instead of being forced to follow one superpower or the other, nations and individuals around the

Global Citizens
The world's migrants at the turn of the millennium sought safety, education, or jobs in the West's manufacturing and service occupations. Like these young immigrants from Senegal who are sharing a meal at a café in Paris, they also appreciated Western amenities. Children of immigrants were sometimes disillusioned, however, not wanting the life of extreme sacrifice that their parents had lived. Their frustrations at not being accepted as full citizens occasionally erupted into protest and even violence.
(© Directphoto.org / Alamy.)

world had more opportunity to trade and interact freely. The Common Market transformed itself into the European Union, which from 2004 on admitted many states from the former Soviet bloc. The telecommunication systems put in place in the 1960s advanced **globalization**, binding peoples and cultures together in an ever more complicated social and economic web.

The global age brought the vast national and international migration of tens of millions of people, an expanding global marketplace, and rapid cultural exchange of popular music, books, films, and television shows. On the negative side, the new globalization also brought lethal disasters such as epidemic diseases, environmental deterioration, genocide, and terrorism. Nations in the West faced competition from the rising economic power of Japan, China, India, and Latin America. International business mergers accelerated in the 1990s, advancing efficiencies but often threatening jobs. As millions of workers found new but sometimes unsatisfying jobs in an interlinked economy, they discovered that the global age was one of opportunities but also insecurities (see "Terms of History," page 988).

While the end of superpower rivalry made global exchange easier, it also resulted in the dominance of a single power, the United States, in world affairs. As the United States sought to exercise global power through warfare, however, the West itself seemed to fragment. European states started to resist the United States just as the Soviet satellites had pulled away from the USSR. New forces arose to rival those of the West: not only did the economic power of Asian, Middle Eastern, and other countries create new centers of influence, but so did the cultural might of Islam. Some observers predicted a huge "clash of civilizations" because of sharp differences between Western civilization and cultures beyond the West. Others, however, saw a different clash — one between a Europe reborn after decades of disastrous wars as a peace-seeking group of nations confronting an imperial United States that, like Europe in the nineteenth century, was increasingly at war around the world. Instead of bringing connections and understanding, globalization in either of these scenarios could bring global splintering, even catastrophic warfare.

Such a dire future was not on most Westerners' minds, but globalization did bring economic struggles for many. Beginning in 2007, the global economy collapsed, resulting in widespread hardship. As Asia and other non-Western parts of the world recovered beginning in 2010, it became apparent that a reenergizing of Western capacities was needed. Illegal immigrants began leaving Europe and the United States as unemployment climbed. Whether Thérèse was among them, we do not know.

globalization: The interconnection of labor, capital, ideas, services, and goods around the world. Although globalization has existed for hundreds of years, the late twentieth and early twenty-first centuries are seen as more global because of the speed with which people, goods, and ideas travel the world.

CHAPTER FOCUS How has globalization been both a unifying and a divisive influence on the West in the twenty-first century?

Collapse of the Soviet Union and Its Aftermath

Following the fall of communist regimes in eastern Europe, rejection of communism spread in the 1990s, turning events in unpredictable, even violent directions. Yugoslavia and then the Soviet Union itself fell apart, as nationality groups in the USSR began to demand independence. The USSR had held together more than one hundred ethnic groups,

1989 Chinese students revolt in Tiananmen Square; fall of the Berlin Wall

1990–1991 War in Persian Gulf

1990s Internet revolution

1991 Civil war erupts in former Yugoslavia; failed coup by Communist hard-liners in Soviet Union

1992 Soviet Union is dissolved

1993 Toni Morrison wins Nobel Prize for Literature; Czechoslovakia splits into Czech Republic and Slovakia

1994 Nelson Mandela elected president of South Africa; Russian troops invade Chechnya; European Union (EU) officially formed

1999 European Union introduces the euro; world population reaches six billion

1990 1995

MAP 29.1 Eastern Europe in the 1990s
In the 1990s, the countries of eastern Europe tried to forge their own destiny free from the direction of either Russia or the United States. The transition was far from easy. States like Czechoslovakia fragmented, and many state borders were contested. Turning from Russia, the leadership of these countries began to look to western Europe, most of them eventually opting for membership in the European Union.

and the five republics of Soviet Central Asia were home to fifty million Muslims. For more than a century, successive governments had attempted to instill Russian and Soviet culture, although some cultural autonomy was allowed. The policy of Russification failed to build any heartfelt allegiance, leading to a swift collapse of the USSR. In Yugoslavia, Communist rulers had also enforced unity among religious and ethnic groups, and intermarriage among them occurred regularly. Beginning in the unstable years of the early 1990s, however, ambitious politicians seeking to build a following whipped up ethnic hatreds (Map 29.1). Throughout the decade, the use of ethnic violence as a political tool made it unclear whether peaceful, democratic nations would emerge. The additional uncertainty of who would control the massive Soviet arsenal of nuclear weapons posed an even more dangerous threat.

The Breakup of Yugoslavia

Ethnic nationalism shaped the post-Communist future in Yugoslavia. Tensions erupted there in 1990 after Serbia's president **Slobodan Milosevic** began to promote control of the entire Yugoslav federation by ethnic Serbs as a replacement for communism. Other ethnic groups in Yugoslavia resisted Milosevic's militant pro-Serb nationalism and called for secession. "Slovenians . . . have one more reason to say they are in favor of independence," warned one of them in the face of rising

Slobodan Milosevic: President of Serbia (1989–1997) who pushed for Serb control of post-Communist Yugoslavia; in 2002, he was tried for crimes against humanity in the ethnic cleansing that accompanied the dissolution of the Yugoslav state.

2000
Vladimir Putin becomes president of Russia

2001
September 11 terrorist attacks; United States declares "war against terrorism," attacks Afghanistan

2003
United States invades Iraq; the West divides on this policy

2004
Ten countries join European Union

2005
Emissions reductions of Kyoto Protocol go into effect

2007
Bulgaria and Romania admitted to European Union; world economic crisis begins

2009
Barack Obama becomes the first African American president of the United States

2010
China overtakes Japan to become world's second largest economy

2000 2005 2010

TERMS OF HISTORY

Globalization

Globalization refers to the worldwide connections linking peoples, economies, cultures, and politics. A globalized world today means a world without borders, in which human activities flow without—or in spite of—official restrictions. The current definition of *globalization* includes economic policies such as free trade and outsourcing of work, collective security mechanisms such as the United Nations, and environmental agreements such as the Kyoto Protocol. Flows of information, migration, disease, and fashions also make up globalization.

When globalization began is a matter of opinion. Commonly the idea is that globalization began some twenty years ago when the Internet allowed economic activity to operate more globally. The rise of economic competitors to the West is seen as a recent phenomenon. This view also holds that the fall of the Soviet Union contributed to globalization because it stopped the division of the world into two competing spheres of influence. The cold war blocked the free exchange not only of ideas but also of goods and services. It hindered cooperation in politics as well as effective activity by nongovernmental organizations (NGOs) and the United Nations.

Historians, however, tend to date globalization in the distant past: some put it in the fifteenth century when Europeans crossed the Atlantic and began exploiting their new connections with the Western Hemisphere. Other historians look back further, to large-scale regional exchanges: the Indus Valley civilizations, the Hellenistic Age, the Islamic Golden Age, and the reign of the Mongol khans have all been cited as examples of globalization. In both these longer views, large-scale, high-speed exchanges are not defining factors in globalization; rather, constant dealings outside of a specific political and economic center are key.

In the broadest definition of *globalization*, the phenomenon has had mixed results for the West. Early globalization promoted enriched diets and biological diversity as plants and animals spread from the Middle East and North Africa to Europe. Goods traveled across Asia to Europe via the early Silk Road, and Christianity and Judaism were notable non-Western religions that changed European culture. Migrants from Asia and Africa also appeared in the West before European pathfinders set out on their voyages. In fact, knowledge of African gold and Asian riches inspired those voyages in the first place. On the negative side, plagues also traveled these routes before the age of Columbus, devastating populations in and beyond Europe. Groups of Asian nomads often wreaked havoc on European centers, and Europeans later brought devastation to them.

Globalization even in ancient times included attempts to see the world as a whole. From the ancient Hellenic author Polybius, who traveled the Mediterranean, to the English scholar Arnold Toynbee, historians have tried to write universal history and to rise above the parochial, local, and temporary with the goal of viewing humanity altogether. The end of the cold war provided the most recent incentive to achieve a universal perspective. For some thinkers, the search for a broader view seems part of a new millennium aiming toward cosmopolitanism, as expressed in the slogan "Think globally, act locally." Globalization is founded on the condition of plural and often conflicting values, aims, and outcomes. Whether in debates over outsourcing, migration, or the role of the World Bank, globalization means complexity, contradictions, and a willingness to deal with the advantages and disadvantages of relationships at a great distance. It is a difficult concept, but one that appears permanently to be with us.

Serb claims for domination of the small republics that made up Yugoslavia (Map 29.2). In the summer of 1991, two of these republics, Slovenia and Croatia, countered Milosevic's call for a Serb-dominated centralized state by seceding. Croatia, however, lost almost a quarter of its territory when the Yugoslav army, eager to enforce Serbian supremacy, invaded. A devastating civil war broke out in Bosnia-Herzegovina when the republic's Muslim majority tried to create a multicultural and multiethnic state. With the covert military support of Milosevic's government, Bosnian Serb men formed a guerrilla army and gained the upper hand. A United Nations (UN) arms embargo prevented the Bosnian Muslims from equipping their forces adequately to defend themselves even though the Serbs at the time were massacring them.

Violence in the Balkans was relentless—inflicted on neighbors in the name of creating "ethnically pure" states in a region where ethnic mixture, not ethnic purity, was the norm. During the 1990s, civilians died by the tens of thousands, as Serbs under Milosevic's leadership pursued a policy they called **ethnic cleansing**—that is, genocide—against the other ethnicities or nationalities. They raped women

ethnic cleansing: The mass murder—genocide—of people according to ethnicity or nationality; it can also include eliminating all traces of the murdered people's past. Examples include the post–World War I elimination of minorities in eastern and central Europe and the rape and murders that resulted from the breakup of Yugoslavia in the 1990s.

MAP 29.2 The Former Yugoslavia, c. 2000
After a decade of destructive civil war, UN forces and UN-brokered agreements attempted to protect the civilians of the former Yugoslavia from the brutal consequences of post-Communist rule. Ambitious politicians, most notably Slobodan Milosevic, used the twentieth-century Western strategy of fostering ethnic and religious hatred as a powerful tool to build support for themselves while making those favoring peace look softhearted and unfit to rule. | **What issues of national identity does the breakup of Yugoslavia indicate?**

to leave them pregnant with Serb babies as another form of conquest. In 1995, Croatian forces murdered Serbs who had helped seize land from Croatia. That same year, the Serbs retaliated by slaughtering eight thousand Muslim boys and men in the town of Srebrenica. "Kill the lot," the commander of the Serb forces ordered at Srebrenica. The Serbs buried the bodies in mass graves, then reburied them to conceal the massacre. Military units on all sides destroyed libraries and museums, architectural treasures like the Mostar Bridge, and cities rich with history such as Dubrovnik. Ethnic cleansing thus entailed eliminating both actual people and all traces of their complex past. Many in the West explained violence in the Balkans as part of "age-old" blood feuds typical of a backward, "almost Asian" society. Others saw using genocide to achieve national power as nothing more than a modern political practice that had been employed by the imperial powers and by other politicians, including Adolf Hitler.

Destruction of the Mostar Bridge in Yugoslavia, 1990
In modern history, the construction of a nation-state has depended on the growth of institutions such as armies and bureaucracies and the promotion of a common national culture. In an effort to dominate Bosnia and Croatia, Serbs in the 1990s destroyed non-Serb art, books, and architecture, including such symbols as the sixteenth-century bridge. *(Top and bottom: © Cardinale Stephane/ Corbis-Sygma.)*

As with German, Italian, and Japanese aggression in the 1930s, no one stepped in to stop the violence in the former Yugoslavia. Peacekeepers were put in place, but they turned their backs on such atrocities as the Srebrenica massacre and let them proceed to their horrific end. Late in the 1990s, Serb forces moved to attack Muslims of Albanian ethnicity living in the Yugoslav province of Kosovo. From 1997 to 1999, crowds of Albanian Kosovars fled their homes as Serb militias and the Yugoslav army slaughtered the civilian population. North Atlantic Treaty Organization (NATO) pilots bombed the region to drive back the army and Serb militias. UN peacekeeping forces finally intervened to enforce an interethnic truce, but people throughout the world felt that this intervention came far too late to protect human rights and human lives.

Alongside the independent republics of Bosnia and Croatia, a new regime emerged in Serbia, and Milosevic was turned over to the International Court of Justice, or World Court, in the Netherlands to be tried for crimes against humanity. In 2003, Milosevic loyalists, many of them due to be rounded up for trial in the World Court, assassinated the new Serbian prime minister. Across a fragmenting eastern Europe, hateful racial, ethnic, and religious rhetoric influenced political agendas in the post-Communist states.

The Soviet Union Comes Apart

In less than three years after the overthrow of communism in its eastern European satellites, the once powerful Soviet Union itself fell apart. Perestroika had failed to revitalize the Soviet economy; people confronted corruption, soaring prices, the specter of unemployment, and even greater scarcity of goods than in the past. Although Soviet leader Mikhail Gorbachev announced late in 1990 that there was "no alternative to the transition to the market [economy]," his plan satisfied no one. In 1991, the Russian parliament elected Boris Yeltsin as president of the Russian Republic over a Communist candidate.

Yeltsin's election was the last straw for a group of eight antireform hard-liners, including the powerful head of the Soviet secret police, or KGB, who attempted a coup to overthrow the government. As coup leaders held Gorbachev under house arrest and claimed to be rescuing the Soviet Union from the "mortal danger" posed by "extremist forces," Yeltsin defiantly stood atop a tank outside the Russian parliament building and called for mass resistance. Residents of Moscow and Leningrad filled the streets, and units of the army defected to protect Yeltsin's headquarters. People used fax machines and computers to coordinate internal resistance and send messages to the rest of the world. Citizen action defeated the coup and prevented a return to the Communist past.

Yeltsin Defeats the Communists

After the failed coup, the Soviet Union disintegrated. People tore down statues of Soviet heroes; Yeltsin outlawed the Communist Party newspaper, *Pravda*, and sealed the KGB's files. At the end of August 1991, the Soviet parliament suspended operations of the Communist Party itself. The Baltic states of Estonia, Latvia, and Lithuania declared their independence in September; other republics within the USSR followed their lead. Bloody ethnic conflicts erupted in the disintegrating Soviet world. In the Soviet republic of Tajikistan, native Tajiks rioted against Armenians living there; in the Baltic states, anti-Semitism revived as a political tool. The USSR finally dissolved on January 1, 1992. Twelve of the fifteen former Soviet republics banded together as the Commonwealth of Independent States (CIS), but that hardly ended the disintegration of Russian power (Map 29.3).

Weakened by the coup attempt, Gorbachev abandoned politics. Yeltsin stepped in and accelerated the change to a market economy, introducing new problems as he did so. Plagued by corruption, the Russian economy entered an ever-deepening crisis. Yeltsin's political allies bought up national resources, stripped them of their value, and sent billions of dollars out of the country, as a new class of superwealthy Russians called oligarchs was born. Managers, military officers, and bureaucrats took whatever goods they could lay their hands on, including weaponry, and sold it.

By 1999, Yeltsin's own family appeared to be deeply implicated in stealing the wealth once seen as belonging to all the people. To build support by appealing to nationalist anti-ethnic sentiments in Russia, Yeltsin launched a destructive military action against the resource-rich province of Chechnya, which wanted independence. Meanwhile social disorder prevailed as organized criminals interfered in the distribution of goods and services and assassinated legitimate entrepreneurs, legislators, and anyone who criticized them. The Russian parliament pursued an investigation into the business dealings of Yeltsin, his family, and his allies, leading Yeltsin to resign on December 31, 1999. He appointed a new protégé, **Vladimir Putin**, as interim president.

Vladimir Putin: President of Russia elected in 2000 and prime minister as of 2008; he has worked to reestablish Russia as a world power through control of the country's resources and military capabilities.

MAP 29.3 Countries of the Former Soviet Union, c. 2000
Following an agreement of December 1991, twelve of the countries of the former Soviet Union formed the Commonwealth of Independent States (CIS). Dominated by Russia and with Ukraine often disputing this domination, the CIS worked to bring about common economic and military policies. As nation-states dissolved rapidly in the late twentieth century, regional alliances and coordination were necessary to meet the political and economic challenges of the global age.

Vladimir Putin Takes Charge

Putin was a little-known functionary in Russia's new security apparatus, which had evolved from the old KGB. In the presidential elections of spring 2000, Putin surprised everyone when the electorate voted him in. Though associated with the Yeltsin family corruption, he declared himself committed to legality. "Democracy," he announced, "is the dictatorship of law." With a solid mandate, Putin proceeded to drive from power the biggest figures in regional and central government, usually the henchmen of the oligarchs. Faced with a desperate economic situation, Putin claimed he would restore "strong government" and end the influence of a "handful of billionaires with only egotistical concerns." Putin's popularity rose even higher when the government arrested the billionaire head of the Yukos Oil Company in 2003. The pillaging of the country—the source of ordinary citizens' recent suffering—was finally being punished. According to critics, however, Putin was merely transferring Russia's natural resources and other assets to himself and his own cronies. He also continued the destructive war in Chechnya, causing casualties, atrocities, disease, and the physical devastation of Chechen cities.

Toward a Market Economy

Developing free markets and republican governments initially brought misery to Russia and the rest of eastern Europe. The conditions of everyday life grew increasingly dire as salaries went unpaid, food remained in short supply, and essential services disintegrated. In 1994, inflation soared at a rate of 14 percent a month in Russia, while industrial production dropped by 15 percent. People took drastic steps to stay alive. Hotel lobbies became clogged with prostitutes because women were the first people fired as governments privatized industry and cut service jobs. Unpaid soldiers sold their services to the Russian Mafia. Ordinary citizens lined the sidewalks of major cities selling their household possessions. "Anything and everything is for sale," one critic noted at the time. Simultaneously, pent-up demand was unleashed for items never before available. An enormous underground economy existed in goods such as automobiles stolen from people in other countries and then driven or shipped to Russia.

There were, of course, many pluses to the new system of government. People with enough money were able to travel freely for the first time, and the media were initially more open than ever before. Some workers, many of them young and highly educated, profited from contacts with technology and business. However, their frequent emigration to more prosperous parts of the world further depleted the human resources of the former Communist states. At the same time, as the different republics that had once composed the Soviet Union became independent, the hundreds of thousands of ethnic Russians who had earlier been sent by the state to colonize these regions returned to Russia as refugees, putting further demands on the chaotic Russian economy but occasionally reuniting families. The dismantling of communism was more complicated and painful than anyone had imagined it would be.

The Economic Agenda For many in the former Soviet bloc, the first priority was getting their economies running again—but on new terms. Replacing a state-controlled economy with a market one could not happen naturally or automatically, but rather required government guidance. Given the spiraling misery, however, many opposed the introduction of new market-oriented measures. In Russia, members of collective farms fought to preserve them as a means of security in a rapidly changing world. With the farms up for sale, most collective farmers faced landlessness and starvation. The countries that experienced the most success were those in which administrators had already introduced ingredients of free trade, such as allowing farmers to sell their produce on the open market or encouraging independent entrepreneurs or even government factories to deal in international trade. Hungary and Poland thus emerged from the transition with less strain, because both had adopted some free-market practices early on and had hired advisers to speed the transformation of the economy. They set up business schools and worked to attract foreign capital, anchoring themselves securely to the world economy.

Elsewhere the transition to a market economy happened differently. The former Soviet Union itself became, in the words of one critic, a vast "kleptocracy" in the 1990s as the country's resources—theoretically the property of all the people—were stolen for individual gain. An economist described the new scene as "piratization" rather than privatization. In this regard, one Polish adviser noted, democracy and a successful economic transition went hand in hand, for without a powerful representative government, former officials would simply operate as criminals. Corruption fed on the Soviet system of off-the-books dealing, tax evasion, bribery, and outright theft. In addition to corruption, the Soviet policy of removing the economy from global developments further hindered the transition. Industry had not benefited from technological change. Because plants and personnel were hopelessly out of date, the introduction of competition and free trade often meant closing factories and firing all the workers.

Talent Flees the Region A final element in post-Soviet economic difficulties was a region-wide brain drain. The economic chaos that followed the fall of communism set off a rush of migration from eastern Europe to western Europe, often involving those with marketable skills. Mi-

Post-Soviet Shopping
The economy of the former Soviet bloc changed dramatically after the fall of communism. Insiders and Western firms bought up out-of-date factories and natural resources for very little money, often installing modern labor-saving equipment. As prosperity grew, megastores and luxury malls sprang up for eager consumers. Located in the suburbs of Moscow, the megastore shown here is part of Europe's largest shopping mall. *(© TASS/Sovoto.)*

grants left for several reasons, including the lack of jobs, the upsurge of ethnic hatreds, and the availability of higher salaries for well-educated workers in other countries. "I knew in my heart that communism would collapse," said one Romanian ex-dissident, commenting sadly on the exodus of youth from his country, "but it never crossed my mind that the future would look like this." Escaping anti-Semitism also played a role. Post-Communist politicians used the rallying cry of hatred of Jews to build a following, just as Hitler and many others had done so effectively in the past. Unchecked banditry and violence inflicted by organized crime added to the disadvantages of remaining in eastern Europe.

The everyday advantages of living in western Europe included safe water, better housing, personal safety, and at least a minimal level of social services. Although western Europe was now on a firm neoliberal course of reducing spending on welfare state programs, most benefits had disappeared entirely in former Communist countries. Pensions for veterans and retired workers were rarely paid, and even when paid were often worthless given the soaring inflation. Day-care centers, kindergartens, and homes for the elderly closed their doors, and health care deteriorated. In these circumstances, the benefits of citizenship in western European countries were a powerful attraction.

International Politics and the New Russia

Although Gorbachev had pulled the Soviet Union out of its disastrous war with Afghanistan, his successors opened another war to prevent the secession of oil-rich Chechnya and to provide a nationalist rallying cry to build domestic support for the administration during the difficult transition. For decades, Chechens had been integrated into the Soviet bureaucracy and military, but in the fall of 1991, the National Congress of the Chechen People took over the government of the region from the USSR to gain the same kind of independence achieved by other former Soviet states. In June 1992, Chechen rebels got control of massive numbers of Russian weapons, including airplanes, tanks, and some forty thousand automatic weapons and machine guns.

In December 1994, the Russian government sealed the Chechen borders and invaded. A high Russian official defended the war as crucial to bolstering Yeltsin's position: "We now need a small victorious war. . . . We must raise the President's rating." Despite the Russian population's opposition to the war, Chechnya's capital city of Grozny was pounded to bits. Casualties mounted not only among Chechen civilians but also among Russians. In 2002, Chechen loyalists took hundreds of hostages in a Moscow theater; Chechen suicide bombers blew up airplanes, buses, and apartment buildings. Putin pursued the Chechen war into the twenty-first century, weakening the reputation of the post-Communist government.

Putin expanded Soviet influence in Ukraine, Belarus, India, and China as well by taking advantage of the politics of energy. Russia had the commodities — especially oil and gas — needed to sustain the fantastic growth of emerging industries around the world, and by 2005 surging commodity prices were making Russia once again a real player in global politics — now because of its economic strength. Democratic values, however, were not put

Chechnya, 1999
Russia justified its war in Chechnya in the 1990s and early 2000s as part of a struggle against Muslim terrorists. During the war, the Russian military kidnapped and murdered Chechen rebels while pummeling cities with gunfire and harassing the population, as this photo of civilians being checked shows. In retaliation, Chechens brought terrorism to Russia, setting off bombs and blowing up planes. Even with the new administration of Vladimir Putin, the bloodshed continued. *(© Reuters/Corbis.)*

Assassination in Moscow
In 2009, Russian citizens honored journalist and human rights activist Anna Politkovskaya, assassinated three years earlier in her Moscow apartment building. Politkovskaya relentlessly investigated the atrocities during the war in Chechnya as well as the corruption in the Putin government. Honest journalism in post-Soviet Russia was dangerous; scores of journalists were murdered in the twenty years following the collapse of communism, and many of Politkovskaya's collaborators were also killed. Several men were arrested, tried, and acquitted in the Politkovskaya case. *(AP Photo/Pavel Golovkin.)*

into practice. Putin's critics were mercilessly assassinated, newspapers and broadcast media were closed down, and a general distrust of politics grew among people who had never really experienced sustained political exchange of views. Yet Putin's popularity was steady, especially as the Russian government used its new wealth to refurbish cities and everyday life grew easier.

REVIEW QUESTION What were the major issues facing the former Soviet bloc in the 1990s and early 2000s?

The Nation-State in a Global Age

Although the end of the Soviet system fractured one large regional economy, it gave a boost to European unification. In the 1990s and early 2000s, the European Economic Community (Common Market), which renamed itself the European Community in 1993, was healthy compared with other regions of the world, especially those plagued with civil wars and violence. It was also economically robust compared with former Soviet-bloc countries, many of which applied for membership to benefit from tying themselves to a powerful transnational organization. The relatively harmonious operation of the European Community and its economic success provoked the formation of the North American Free Trade Agreement (NAFTA), which established a free-trade zone of the United States, Canada, and Mexico. The nationalist function of cities diminished as major urban areas like London and Paris became packed with people from other countries, who brought with them new ideas and new customs. Organizations for world governance grew in influence alongside the strength of large regional economic blocs. There was resistance to these trends from those who wanted to preserve their own traditions and who felt the loss of a secure, face-to-face, local way of life.

The Euro
The euro went into circulation on January 1, 2002. The euro bills' designer used architectural imagery of windows and bridges to suggest openness, light, connectedness, and boundary crossing. Reflecting the compromise between Europe and individual states, the head sides of euro coins bear a common image, while the tail sides contain symbols chosen by individual nations within the euro zone. *(Royalty Free/Corbis.)*

Europe Looks beyond the Nation-State

From the 1990s on, Europeans worked to strengthen their shared institutions beyond those of the traditional nation-state, first by expanding the range of their common efforts. The Common Market of the 1950s had opened the pathway to unified supranational policy in economic matters; its evolution into the European Community and then the European Union (EU) in the 1990s extended cooperation in political and cultural matters. Then, in 2004 and 2007, nations from the former Soviet bloc joined the EU, suggesting that power might shift eastward if some of these new EU members built thriving economies, too.

From Common Market to European Union

The Common Market changed dramatically after the demise of European communism. In 1992, the twelve countries of the Common Market ended national distinctions in certain business activities, border controls, and transportation, effectively closing down passport controls at their shared borders. Citizens of the member countries carried a uniform burgundy-colored passport, and governments, whether municipal or national, had to treat all member nations' firms the same. In 1994, by the terms of the **Maastricht Treaty**, the European Community (EC) became the **European Union (EU)**, and in 1999 a common currency—the **euro**—came into being, first for transactions among financial institutions and then in 2002 for general use by the public. Common policies governed everything from the number of American soap operas aired on television to pollution controls on automobiles to the health warnings on cigarette packages. The EU parliament convened regularly in Strasbourg, France, while subgroups met to negotiate further cultural, economic, and social policies. With the adoption of a common currency, an EU central bank came into being to guide interest rates and economic policy.

The EU was seen as the key to a peaceful Europe. "People with the same money don't go to war with one another," said a French nuclear scientist about the introduction of the euro. Greece pushed for the admission of its traditional enemy Turkey in 2002 and 2003 despite the warnings of a former president of France that a predominantly Muslim country could never fit in with the Christian traditions of EU members. Both Greece and Turkey stood to benefit by having their disputes adjudicated by the larger body of European members, principally because they would be able to cut that part of

Maastricht Treaty: The agreement among the members of the European Community to have a closer alliance, including the use of common passports and eventually the development of a common currency; by the terms of this treaty, the European Community became the European Union (EU) in 1994.

European Union (EU): Formerly the European Economic Community (EEC, or Common Market), and then the European Community (EC); formed in 1994 by the terms of the Maastricht Treaty. Its members have political ties through the European parliament as well as long-standing common economic, legal, and business mechanisms.

euro: The common currency in seventeen member states of the European Union (EU) and of EU institutions. It went into effect gradually, used first in business transactions in 1999 and entering public circulation in 2002.

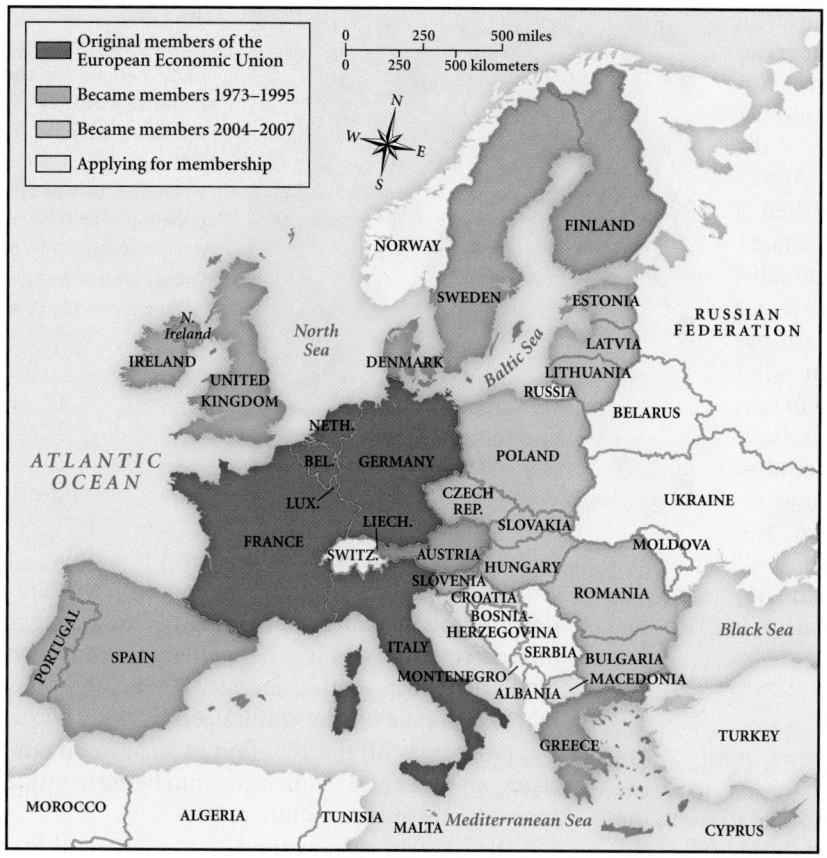

MAP 29.4 The European Union in 2011
The European Union (EU) appeared to increase the economic health of its members despite the rocky start of its common currency, the euro. The EU helped end the traditional competition between its members and facilitated trade and worker migration by providing common passports and business laws, and open borders. But many critics feared a loss of cultural distinctiveness among peoples in an age of mass communications.

their defense budget used for weapons directed against each other. Like the rivalry between Germany and France, that between Turkey and Greece, it was hoped, would dissolve if bound by the strong economic and political ties of the EU. As of 2011, however, Turkey was still awaiting progress on its application.

Drawbacks to EU membership remained. The EU enforced no common regulatory practices, and the common economic policies demanding cooperation among its members were not always observed. Individual governments set up hurdles and barriers for businesses, such as obstructing transnational mergers they did not like. One government might block the acquisition of a company based on its own soil no matter what the advantages to shareholders, the economy, the workforce, or the consumers of unified Europe. Nonetheless, countries of eastern Europe clamored to join, working hard to meet not only the EU's fiscal requirements but also those pertaining to human rights and social policy (Map 29.4).

East Joins West | That the EU became attractive to eastern Europe is demonstrated in the case of Greece, long considered the poor relative of the other member countries. Greece joined the European Community in 1981; its per capita gross domestic product was 64 percent of the European average in 1985. However, Greek leaders and the EU made a real effort during the 1990s to bring the country closer to EU norms. Hoping for similar gains, the countries to the east moved toward EU membership throughout the 1990s. The collapse of the Soviet system advanced privatization of eastern European industry, as governments sold basic services to the highest bidder. Often, only companies in the wealthy western countries of the EU could afford to purchase eastern European assets. For example, the Czech Republic in 2001 sold its major energy distributor Transgaz and eight other regional distributors for 4.1 billion euros to a German firm. Lower wages and costs of doing business in eastern Europe attracted foreign investment, especially to Poland, the Czech Republic, Hungary, and Slovenia—the most developed state spun off from Yugoslavia. There were hopes that membership would encourage further investment and advance modernization. (See Document, "Václav Havel,'Czechoslovakia Is Returning to Europe,'" page 997.)

In 2004, the EU admitted ten new members—the Czech Republic, Cyprus, Estonia, Hungary, Latvia, Lithuania, Malta, Poland, Slovakia, and

DOCUMENT

Václav Havel, "Czechoslovakia Is Returning to Europe"

Czech playwright and longtime anti-Communist activist Václav Havel became the first president of his country after the Communist Party was ousted in 1989. Havel was an idealist who believed that the people of eastern Europe had gained important insights from their experience of Soviet domination. This speech provides a backdrop to the admission of eastern European countries to the European Union in 2004. Despite fears among more prosperous EU countries that the lower standard of living in eastern Europe will drag the EU down, there is also a strong sense that the EU is incomplete without them. Havel details what eastern Europeans have to offer, even to those who have long enjoyed greater freedom and prosperity, including the Congress of the United States, before which the speech was given.

Czechoslovakia is returning to Europe. . . . We are doing what we can so that Europe will be capable of really accepting us, its wayward children. Which means that it may open itself to us, and may begin to transform its structures—which are formally European but de facto Western European. . . .

The Communist type of totalitarian system has left . . . all the nations of the Soviet Union and the other countries the Soviet Union subjugated in its time, a legacy of countless dead, an infinite spectrum of human suffering, profound economic decline, and above all enormous human humiliation. It has brought us horrors that fortunately you have not known.

At the same time, however—unintentionally, of course—it has given us something positive: a special capacity to look, from time to time, somewhat further than someone who has not undergone this bitter experience. A person who cannot move and live a somewhat normal life because he is pinned under a boulder has more time to think about his hopes than someone who is not trapped that way. . . .

For this reason, the salvation of the human world lies nowhere else than in the human heart, in the human power to reflect, in human meekness and in human responsibility. . . . If we are no longer threatened by world war, or by the danger that the absurd mountains of accumulated nuclear weapons might blow up the world, this does not mean that we have definitively won. We are in fact far from the final victory. . . .

In other words, we still don't know how to put morality ahead of politics, science and economics. We are still incapable of understanding that the only genuine backbone of all our actions—if they are to be moral—is responsibility. Responsibility to something higher than my family, my country, my company, my success. Responsibility to the order of Being, where all our actions are indelibly recorded. . . .

I end where I began: history has accelerated. I believe that once again it will be the human mind that will notice this acceleration, give it a name, and transform those words into deeds.

Source: From speech delivered to the Joint Session of Congress, Washington, D.C., on February 21, 1990. Reprinted in *Vital Speeches of the Day*, March 15, 1990, 329–30.

Question to Consider

- **What argument is Havel making, and why did he choose to make it to politicians in the United States?**

Slovenia—and in 2007 it welcomed Bulgaria and Romania. Just before Poland's admission to the EU, its standard of living was 39 percent of EU standards, up from 33 percent in 1995. The Czech Republic and Hungary were at 55 and 50 percent, respectively. In all three cases these figures masked the discrepancy between the ailing countryside and thriving cities. Citizens in eastern Europe were not always happy at the prospect of joining the EU. A retiree foresaw the cost of beer going up and added, "If I wanted to join anything in the West, I would have defected." Still others felt that having just established an independent national identity, they should not allow themselves to be swallowed up once again. People in older member states were having second thoughts, too: in the spring of 2005, a majority of voters in France and the Netherlands rejected a complex draft constitution that would have strengthened EU ties. Commentators attributed the rejection to popular anger at the EU bureaucracy's failure to consult ordinary people in this and other decision making.

Although still weak by comparison with most of western Europe, the economic life of eastern Europe had in fact picked up considerably by 2000. In contrast to the massive layoffs, soaring inflation, and unpaid salaries of the first post-Communist years, in 2002 residents of Poland, Slovenia, and Estonia had purchasing power some 40 percent higher than in 1989. Outsourcing by international companies began to flourish across the region, increasing opportunities for those with language and commercial skills. Even in countries with the weakest economies—Latvia, Bulgaria, and Romania—a greater number of residents enjoyed such modern conveniences as freezers, computers, and portable telephones. Shopping malls sprang up mostly around capital cities, testifying both to the urban nature of the benefits of the free economy and to the allure of this great new market of 100 million customers. Superstores like the furniture giant IKEA and the electronics firm Electroworld were a consumer's paradise to those long starved of goods. "When Electroworld opened in Budapest [April 2002], it provoked a riot. Two hundred thousand people crowded to get in the doors," reported one amazed observer. Critics worried that eastern Europeans had fallen prey to "consumania," that is, uncontrolled materialism and frenzied shopping. Consumers themselves, however, saw shopping as "a social act, indicating that one had joined consumer society," as one eastern European businessman put it. Learning to read labels and to compare prices offered by superstores was a sign of belonging to a global community of those free and prosperous enough to consume. Proudly, many believed they had left Communist poverty behind.

Globalizing Cities and Fragmenting Nations

After the collapse of communism, the West changed still further. One notable change was the globalization of major cities. These were cities whose institutions, functions, and visions were overwhelmingly global rather than regional or national. They contained stock markets, legal firms, insurance companies, financial service organizations, and other enterprises that operated worldwide and that were linked to similar enterprises in other global cities. Within these cities, high-level decision makers set global economic policy and enacted global business. The presence of high-powered and high-income global businesspeople made urban life extremely costly, driving middle managers and engineers to lower-priced living quarters in the suburbs, which nonetheless provided good schools and other amenities for well-educated white-collar earners. Crowded into the slums of global cities and the poorer suburbs were the lowest paid of service providers — the maintenance, domestic, and other workers whose menial labor was essential around the clock to the needs and comfort of those at the top.

Global cities often had the best transport or telecommunication facilities and thus became centers for migration for highly skilled and more modest workers alike. Paris, London, Moscow, and New York were not just cosmopolitan but global spaces in direct and constant contact with institutions, businesses, and governments around the world. In contrast, citizens of more locally oriented cities took pride in maintaining a distinctive national culture or local sense of community and often denounced global cities as rootless. Critics also pointed out that their concentrated wealth came at the expense of poorer people in southern countries and that their citizens lacked patriotic focus on national causes. Global cities were often the base for diasporas of prosperous migrants, such as the estimated ninety thousand Japanese in England in the mid-1990s who staffed Japan's thriving global businesses. Because these migrants did not aim to become citizens, they made no economic or political claims on the adopted country and were thus sometimes called invisible migrants. As a result, global cities were said to produce a "deterritorialization of identities" — meaning that many city dwellers lacked both a national and a local sense of themselves, so much did they travel the world or deal worldwide.

Ironically, as globalization took hold economically and culturally, there came to be more nation-states in Europe in 2000 than there had been in 1945. Claims of ethnic distinctiveness caused individual nation-states to break apart and separatist movements — like that in Chechnya — to grow. Despite two centuries aimed at unification of the Slavs, for example, Slavs separated themselves from one another in the 1990s and early twenty-first century. Yugoslavia came apart into several states, as discussed earlier in this chapter, and in 1993, Czechoslovakia split into the Czech Republic and Slovakia (see Map 29.1, page 987).

Activists launched movements for regional independence in France, Italy, and Spain. Some Bretons (residents of the historical French province of Brittany) and Corsicans demanded independence from France, the Corsicans violently attacking national officials. Sharp cultural differences threatened to split Belgium in two. Basque nationalists in northern Spain assassinated tourists, police, and other public servants in an effort to gain autonomy, and although in 2005 they publicly renounced terrorism, violence often resurfaced. The push for an independent northern Italy began somewhat halfheartedly, but when politicians saw its attractiveness to voters, they loudly publicized the urgent need for secession. As cities globalized and nations fragmented, new combinations of local, national, and global identities took shape. Basque separatists in Spain promoted a common identity with Basques in France and other parts of the world — not with other Spaniards. Nganda manager Thérèse simultaneously enjoyed her neighborhood in Paris, her identity as a migrant to France, and contact with friends and family in Congo. Such changing identities, plus the overall expansion of the EU, called the nation-state into question.

Global Organizations

Supranational organizations, some of them regulating international politics and others addressing finance and social issues, had been in place for decades. By the twenty-first century, the interconnectedness of industry, finance, and government had made these organizations both more plentiful and influential. The World Bank, the International Monetary Fund (IMF), and the World Trade Organization (WTO) raised money from national governments and dealt, for example, with the terms of trade among countries and the economic well-being of individual peoples. The IMF made loans to developing countries on the condition that they restructure their economies according to neoliberal principles. Other supranational organizations were charitable foundations, think tanks, or service-based organizations acting independently of governments, many of them based in Europe and the United States; they were called **nongovernmental organizations (NGOs)**. Because some—the Rockefeller Foundation, the Ford Foundation, and the Open Society Foundation, for example—controlled so much money, NGOs often had considerable international power. After the fall of the Soviet bloc, NGOs used their resources to shape economic and social policy and even the course of political transformation. Some charitable and activist NGOs, like the French-based Doctors Without Borders, depended on global contributions and used them to provide medical attention in such places as the former Yugoslavia, where people facing war had no other medical help. Small, locally based NGOs excelled at inspiring grassroots activism. All of these organizations, small and large, were in tune with the globalization process. As with the EU, the larger NGOs were often criticized for influencing government policies with no regard for democratic processes.

Not everyone supported or was pleased with the process of globalization; some people formed activist groups to attack globalization or to influence its course. In 1998, the Association for the Taxation of Financial Transactions and Aid to Citizens (ATTAC) worked to block the control of globalization by the forces of high finance, declaring: "Commercial totalitarianism is not free trade." ATTAC had as its major policy goal to tax international financial transactions (just as the purchase of household necessities was taxed) and to create with the tax a fund for people living in poor countries. With members from more than forty nations, the organization held well-attended conferences to find new directions for countries suffering from global development. French farmer José Bové, a globally known activist, protested the opening of McDonald's chains in France and destroyed stocks of genetically modified seeds: "The only regret I have now," Bové claimed at his trial in 2003, "is that I didn't destroy more of it." Bové went to jail, but he remained a hero to anti-globalism activists who saw him as an enemy of standardization and an honest champion, in his own words, of "good food."

nongovernmental organizations (NGOs): Charitable foundations and activist groups such as Doctors Without Borders that work outside of governments, often on political, economic, and relief issues; also, philanthropic organizations such as the Rockefeller, Ford, and Open Society Foundations that shape economic and social policy and the course of political reform.

REVIEW QUESTION What trends suggest that the nation-state was a declining institution at the beginning of the twenty-first century?

An Interconnected World's New Challenges

The rising tide of globalization ushered in as many challenges as opportunities. First, the health of the world's peoples and their environment came under a multipronged attack from nuclear disaster, acid rain, and surging population. Second, economic prosperity and physical safety continued to elude great masses of people, especially in the southern half of the globe. Third, as suprastate organizations developed, transnational allegiances and religious and ethnic movements vied for power and influence. Growing prosperity in some regions outside the West and a devastating economic crisis that rippled from Wall Street across the globe challenged the traditional economic leadership of the United States and Europe. The crisis, along with their newfound wealth, led leaders in Asia, the Middle East, and Latin America to suggest that the West give up its claims to dominance.

The Problems of Pollution

By the early years of the twenty-first century, many people had become aware of the dangers of industrial growth—once seen as an unqualified blessing. Despite growing ecological awareness, technological development continued to threaten the environment. In the aftermath of the 1986 nuclear explosion at Chernobyl, which killed thirty-one people instantly, levels of radioactivity rose for hundreds of miles in all directions and some fifteen thousand

Smart Cars in Europe
The havoc caused by the oil crisis of the 1970s and the growing awareness of climate change in the latter part of the twentieth century spurred many European states to encourage the development of alternate sources of energy and transportation. Thus, by the twenty-first century, the landscape was dotted not only with windmills but also with tiny, highly fuel-efficient automobiles like the Smart car shown here. European governments also heavily taxed gasoline with the result that it cost twice as much or more than in the United States, thus further encouraging people to buy the Smart car rather than an SUV—a far rarer sight in Europe than in the United States.
(© David Cooper/Toronto Star/ZUMA/Corbis.)

people perished over time from the effects of radiation. Moreover, as Russia opened up, it became clear that Soviet managers and officials had thrown toxic waste into thousands of square miles of lakes and rivers. Used nuclear fuel had been dumped in neighboring seas, and many nuclear and other tests had left entire regions of Asia unfit for human, animal, and plant life.

Other environmental problems had devastating global effects. Pollutants from fossil fuels such as natural gas, coal, and oil mixed with atmospheric moisture to produce acid rain, a poisonous brew that destroyed forests in industrial areas. In eastern Europe, the unchecked use of fossil fuels turned trees into brown skeletons and inflicted ailments such as chronic bronchial disease on children. In other areas, clearing the world's rain forests to develop the land for cattle grazing or for cultivation of cash crops depleted the global oxygen supply. By the late 1980s, scientists determined that the use of chlorofluorocarbons (CFCs), chemicals found in aerosol and refrigeration products, had blown a hole in the earth's ozone layer, the part of the blanket of atmospheric gases that prevents harmful ultraviolet rays from reaching the planet. Simultaneously, automobile and industrial emissions of chemicals were infusing that thermal blanket. The buildup of CFCs, carbon dioxide, and other atmospheric pollutants produced what is known as a greenhouse effect that results in **global warming**, an increase in the temperature of the earth's lower atmosphere. Already in the 1990s, the Arctic pack ice was breaking up, allowing Finland by 2002 to ship oil along a once-iced-over route. Scientists predicted dire consequences: the rate of global ice melting, which had more than doubled since 1988, would raise sea levels by more than ten inches by 2100, flooding coastal areas, disturbing fragile ecosystems, and harming the freshwater supply. Other results of the greenhouse effect included not only climatic extremes such as alternating periods of drought and drenching rain but also dramatic weather events such as severe storms.

Activism against unbridled industrial growth took decades to develop as an effective political force. An escapee from Nazi Germany, E. F. "Fritz" Schumacher, produced one of the bibles of the environmental movement, *Small Is Beautiful* (1973), which spelled out how technology and industrialization threatened the earth and its inhabitants. Rachel Carson's powerful critique, *Silent Spring* (1962), advocated the immediate rescue of rivers, forests, and the soil from the ravages of factories and chemical farming in the United States. In West Germany, environmentalism united members of older and younger generations around a political tactic called citizen initiatives, in which groups of people blocked plans for urban growth that menaced forests and farmland. In 1979, the **Green Party** was founded in West Germany; soon the emergence of Green Party candidates across Europe forced other politicians to voice their concern for the environment. (See Document, "The Green Parties Unite Transnationally and Announce Common Goals," page 1001.)

global warming: An increase in the temperature of the earth's lower atmosphere resulting from a buildup of chemical emissions.

Green Party: A political party first formed in West Germany in 1979 to bring about environmentally sound policies. It spread across Europe and around the world thereafter.

DOCUMENT

The Green Parties Unite Transnationally and Announce Common Goals (2006)

In 1993, members of Green Parties across Europe formed the European Federation of Green Parties, which came to include members from twenty-nine European countries. The federation also made global connections with parties in Australia, Taiwan, the United States, and elsewhere in the world. In 2004, the federation formally became the European Green Party, which in 2006 adopted a charter endorsing not only environmental responsibility but a range of other values as well. Following is the opening statement of the charter. Even as it was written, the charter became outdated, for in 2006 China passed the United States as the world's leading emitter of greenhouse gases.

The European Greens proudly stand for the sustainable development of humanity on planet Earth, a mode of development respectful of human rights and built upon the values of environmental responsibility, freedom, justice, diversity and non-violence.

Green political movements emerged in Europe while the continent was divided by the Cold War and amidst the energy crises of the mid-seventies. At that time, it became clear that the pattern of economic development was unsustainable and was putting the planet and its inhabitants in grave environmental, social and economic dangers. Existing political parties were incapable of dealing with this challenge.

Our origins lie in many social movements: environmentalists and anti-nuclear activists concerned with the growing damages to our planet; non-violent peace activists promoting alternative ways to resolve conflicts; feminists, struggling for real equality between women and men; freedom and human rights movements fighting against dictatorial and authoritarian regimes; third-world solidarity movements supporting the end of colonization and more economically balanced relations between the North and the South of our planet; activists campaigning against poverty and for social justice within our own societies.

Question to Consider

- **What examples about the social and political situations around the world do the charter's authors provide to show the importance of their cause?**

Spurred by successful Green Party campaigns, Europeans attacked environmental problems on local and global levels. Some European cities—Frankfurt, for example—developed car-free zones, and in Paris, whenever automobile emissions reached dangerous levels, cars were banned from city streets until the emission levels receded. The Smart, a very small car using reduced amounts of fuel, became fashionable in Europe. European cities also developed bicycle lanes on major city streets, and the United States did the same in the twenty-first century. To reduce dependence on fossil fuels, parts of Europe developed wind power to such an extent that 20 percent of some countries' electricity was generated by wind. Many cities in the West undertook extensive recycling of waste materials. These were success stories, involving changing habits and dependencies in some of the most industrialized countries in the world. By 1999, some eighty-four countries, including EU members, had signed the Kyoto Protocol, an international treaty whose signatories agreed to reduce their levels of emissions and other pollutants to specified targets. However, the United States, the world's second leading polluter after China, rejected this partnership. The Kyoto emissions reductions finally went into effect in February 2005, but the United States' refusal to join its former allies to protect the environment suggested that the West was fragmenting around basic values.

Population, Health, and Disease

The issue of population was as difficult in the early twenty-first century as it had been in the 1930s. Nations with less-developed economies struggled with the pressing problem of surging population, while Europe experienced negative growth (that is, more deaths than births) after 1995. The less industrially developed countries accounted for 98 percent of worldwide population growth, in part because the spread of Western medicine enabled people there to live much longer than before. By late 1999, the earth's population had reached six billion, with a doubling forecast for 2045 (see "Taking Measure," page 1002). Yet because many European countries were not replacing their population, they were facing problems related to an aging citizenry and a shortage of younger people to bring new ideas and promote change. In fact, Europe as a region had the lowest fertility in the world. The fertility rate in Italy and Spain was only 1.3 children per woman of reproductive age, far below the replacement level of 2.1 needed to maintain a steady population number.

TAKING MEASURE

World Population Growth, 1950–2010

A major question in the twenty-first century is whether the global environment can sustain billions of people indefinitely. In the early modern period, local communities had lived according to unwritten rules that balanced population size with the productive capacities of individual farming regions. Centuries later, the same need for balance had reached global proportions. As fertility dropped around the planet because of contraception, population continued to grow because of improved health.

Question to Consider

- **Which areas have the strongest rate of growth? What are the potential causes and implications of this growth?**

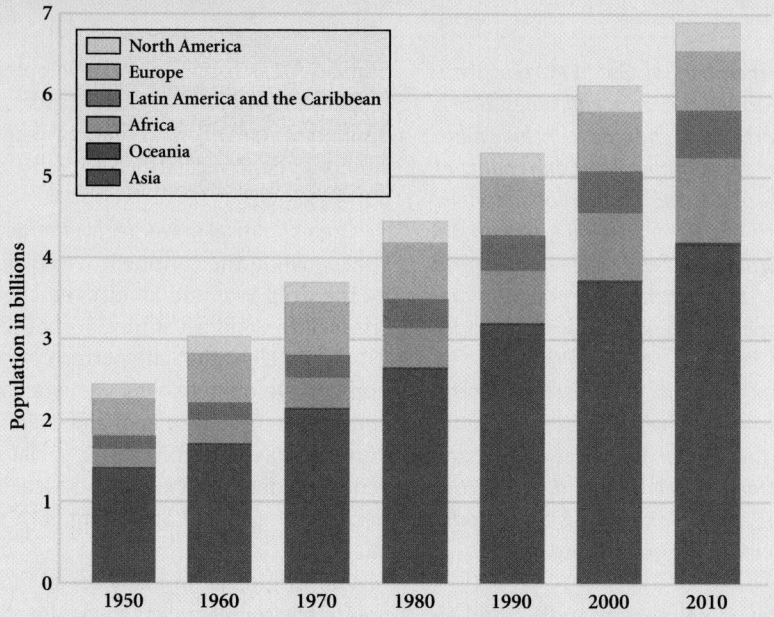

Some forecasters predicted that this low rate meant that by 2050 the population of Europe would fall from 725 to 600 million. Economists saw as a consequence fewer young workers paying into the social security system to fund retirees' pensions and health care.

Population problems were especially urgent in Russia, where life expectancy was declining at a catastrophic rate from a peak of seventy years for Russian men in the mid-1970s to fifty-one years at the beginning of the twenty-first century. Heart disease and cancer were the leading causes of male death, and these stark death rates were generally attributed to increased drinking (one in seven men was an alcoholic in Russia), smoking, drug use, poor diet, and general stress. Between 1992 and 2010, the Russian population declined from 149 to 142 million, with predictions that by 2050 it would fall below 100 million. Meanwhile, fertility rates in the former Soviet bloc were also declining: the lowest levels of fertility in 2003 were in the Czech Republic and Ukraine (1.1 children per woman of reproductive age), and children in eastern Europe lived on average twelve years less than their counterparts in western Europe.

Good health was spread unevenly around the world. Western medicine brought better health to many in the less-developed world through the increased use of vaccines and drugs for diseases such as malaria and smallpox. However, half of all Africans lacked the basic ingredients of well-being such as safe drinking water. Drought and poverty, along with the corruption of politicians in some cases, spread famine in Sudan, Somalia, Ethiopia, and elsewhere. Around the world, the poor and the unemployed suffered more chronic illnesses than those who were better off, but they received less care. Whereas in many parts of the world people still died from malnutrition and infectious diseases, in the West noncontagious illnesses (heart disease, autoimmune diseases, stroke, cancer, and depression) were more lethal. The distribution of health services—for example, heart transplants for the wealthy versus preventive health care for a wider range of clients—became a hotly debated issue.

Disease, like population and technology, operated on a global terrain, though there were many regional differences. In the early 1980s, both Western values and Western technological expertise were challenged by the spread of a global epidemic disease: acquired immunodeficiency syndrome (AIDS). An incurable, highly virulent killer that effectively shuts down the body's entire immune system, AIDS initially afflicted heterosexuals in central Africa; the disease later turned up in Haitian immigrants to the United States and in homosexual men worldwide. Within a decade, AIDS became a global epidemic. The disease spread especially quickly and widely among the heterosexual populations of Africa and Asia, passed mainly by men to and through women, but in 2010 the U.S. capital, Washington D.C., had a rate of infection as high as that in Africa. By 2010, a cure seemed to be on the medical horizon; in the meantime protease-inhibiting drugs helped alleviate the symptoms. The mounting global death toll made some equate AIDS with the Black Death. Treatment was often not provided to poor people living in sub-Saharan Africa and the slums of Asian cities, but global NGOs worked to get life-saving drugs to these people. In addition to the AIDS pandemic, the deadly Ebola virus and dozens of other viruses smoldered like a global conflagration in the making. In the twenty-first century, an avian flu virus called severe acute respiratory syndrome (SARS) and swine flu — both potentially deadly to humans — traveled the world even as health professionals worked to contain them. Diseases as much as environmental dangers underscored the interconnectedness of the world's peoples.

North versus South?

During the 1980s and 1990s, world leaders tried to address the differences between the earth's northern and southern regions. Other than Australians and New Zealanders, southern peoples generally suffered lower living standards and measures of health than northerners. Emerging from colonial rule and economic exploitation by northerners, citizens in the southern regions could not yet count on their governments to provide welfare services or education. Funding for such programs generally came from the wealth of the northern countries; international organizations like the World Bank and the International Monetary Fund provided loans for economic development. However, the conditions tied to those loans, such as cutting government spending for education and health care, led to criticism that ordinary citizens gained no real benefit. Some twenty-first-century leaders from both North and South advocated that wealthy countries simply give southern countries the money they needed as reparation for centuries of imperial plunder.

Southern regions experienced different kinds of barriers to economic development. Latin American nations grappled with government corruption, multibillion-dollar debt, widespread crime, and grinding poverty, though some countries — prominent among them Brazil — began to strengthen their economies by marketing their oil and other natural resources more effectively and by valuing administrative expertise among government officials. In contrast, Africa suffered from drought, famine, and civil war. In countries such as Rwanda, Somalia, and Sudan, the military rule, ideological factionalism, and ethnic antagonism encouraged under imperialism produced a lethal mixture of conflict and genocide in the 1990s and early 2000s. Millions perished; others were left starving and homeless due to kleptocracies that drained revenues. In Africa, too, nations began turning away from violence and military dictatorship toward constitutional government at the same time that uneven economic development and the scourge of AIDS and other unchecked diseases added to the weight of the continent's problems.

Radical Islam Meets the West

North–South antagonisms became evident in the rise of radical Islam, which often flourished where democracy and prosperity for the masses were missing. The Iranian hostage crisis that began in 1979 and commanded the world's attention revealed the nationalism and anti-Western sentiment among Islamic fundamentalists. The charismatic leaders of the 1980s and 1990s — the ayatollah Ruhollah Khomeini in Iran; Libya's Muammar Qaddafi; Iraq's Saddam Hussein; and **Osama bin Laden**, a Saudi Arabian by birth and leader of the transnational terrorist organization al-Qaeda — variously promoted a pan-Islamic or (outside Iran) pan-Arabic world order that gathered increasing support. Khomeini's program — "Neither East, nor West, only the Islamic Republic" — had wide appeal. Renouncing the Westernization that had flourished under the shah, Khomeini's regime in Iran (whose population is predominantly Persian, not Arabic) required women once again to cover their bodies almost totally in special clothing, restricted their access to divorce, and eliminated a range of other rights for men and women alike. Buoyed by the prosperity that oil had brought, Islamic revolutionaries believed that a strict theocracy would restore the pride and Islamic identity that imperialism had stripped from Middle Eastern men. Khomeini built widespread support among Shi'ite Muslims by proclaiming the ascendancy of the Shi'ite clergy. Although they were numerous, even constituting the majority in parts

---

Osama bin Laden: Wealthy leader of the militant Islamic group al-Qaeda, which executed terrorist plots, including the September 11, 2001, attacks on the United States, to end the presence of U.S. forces in his home country, Saudi Arabia.

of the Middle East, the Shi'ites had long been discriminated against by the Sunnis.

Power in the Middle East remained fragmented, however, and Islamic leaders did not achieve their unifying goals. Instead, war plagued the region. In 1980, Saddam Hussein, fearing a rebellion from Shi'ites in Iraq, attacked Iran, in hopes of channeling Shi'ite discontent with a patriotic crusade against non-Arab Iranians. The United States provided Iraq with massive aid in the struggle against Iran, but eight years of combat, with extensive loss of life on both sides, ended in stalemate. In 1990, Saddam tested the post–cold war waters by invading neighboring Kuwait in hopes of annexing the oil-rich country to debt-ridden Iraq. A United Nations coalition led by the United States stopped the invasion and defeated the Iraqi army, but discontent mounted in the region (Map 29.5).

To the east, the Taliban—a militant Islamic group initially funded by the United States, China, Saudi Arabia, and Pakistan during the cold war—took over the government of Afghanistan in the late 1990s. Its leaders imposed a regime that forbade girls from attending schools and women from leaving their homes without a male escort and demanded from men strict adherence to its rules for dress.

To the west, conflict between the Israelis and the Palestinians continued. As Israeli settlers took more Palestinian land, Palestinian suicide bombers

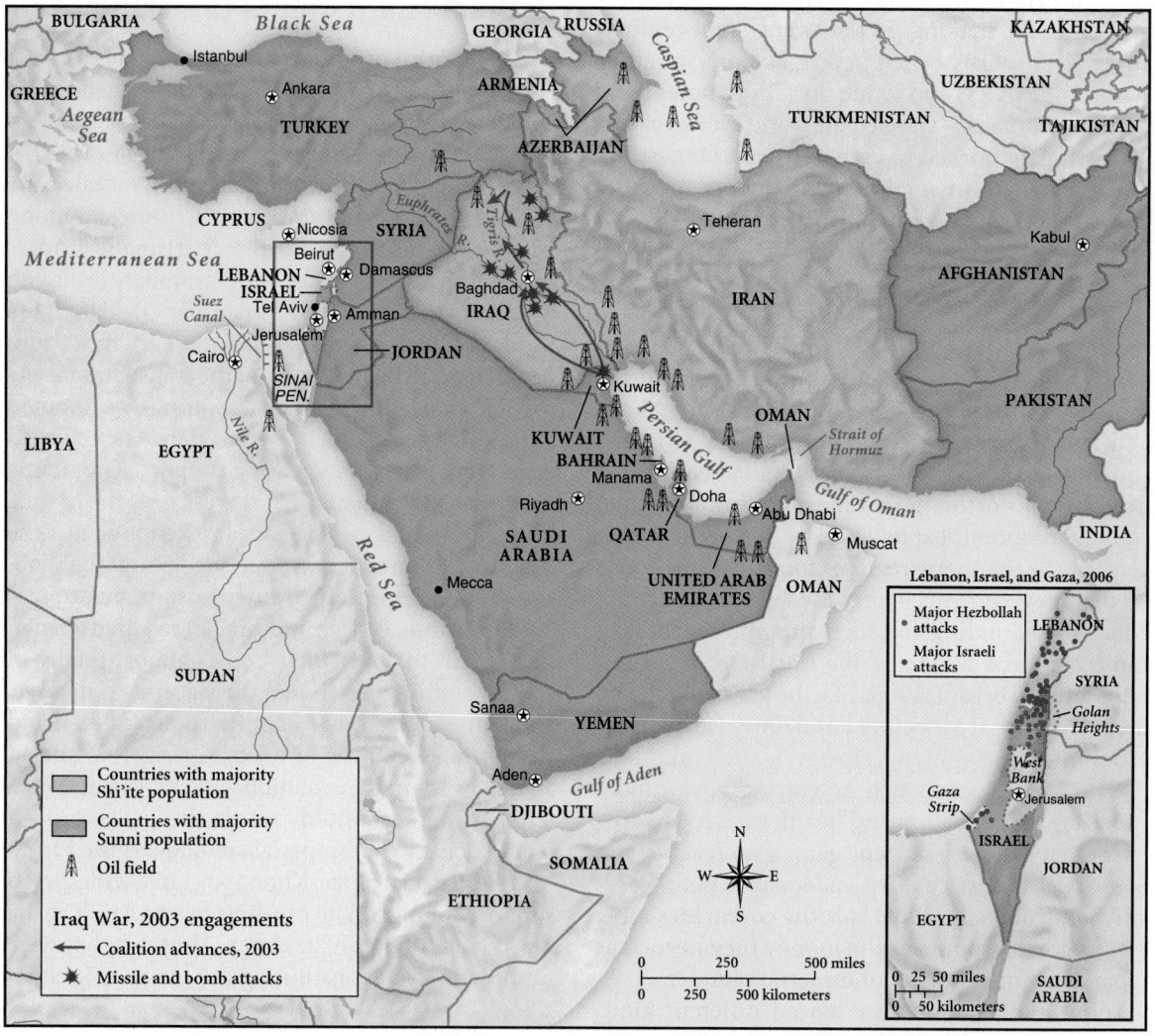

MAP 29.5 The Middle East in the Twenty-First Century

Tensions among states in the Middle East, especially the ongoing conflict between the Palestinians and Israelis and animosities among Shi'ites and Sunnis, became more complicated from the 1990s on. The situation in the Middle East grew more uncertain in 2003 when a U.S.- and British-led invasion of Iraq deteriorated into escalating violence among competing religious and ethnic groups in the country. Additionally, for thirty-four days in the summer of 2006, Israel bombed Lebanon, including its capital city and refugee camps, with fire returned by Hezbollah and Hamas forces in the region.

began murdering Israeli civilians in the late 1990s. The Israeli government retaliated with missiles, machine guns, and tanks, often killing Palestinian civilians in turn. In 2006, the Israelis, responding to the political militia Hezbollah's kidnapping of Israeli soldiers, attacked Lebanon, destroying infrastructure, sending missiles into its capital city of Beirut, and killing hundreds of civilians. In 2009, Israel's invasion and bombing of Gaza had similar results.

Beginning in the 1980s and continuing into the 2000s, terrorists from the Middle East and North Africa planted bombs in European cities, blew airplanes out of the sky, and bombed the Paris subway system. These attacks, causing widespread destruction and loss of life, were said to be punishment for the West's support both for Israel and for the dictatorships in the other Middle Eastern countries.

On September 11, 2001, the ongoing terrorism in Europe and around the world caught the full attention of the United States. In an unprecedented act, Muslim militants hijacked four planes in the United States and flew two of them into the World Trade Center in New York City and one into the Pentagon in Virginia. The fourth plane, en route to the Capitol, crashed in Pennsylvania when passengers forced the hijackers to lose control of the aircraft. The hijackers, most of whom were from Saudi Arabia, were inspired by the wealthy radical leader of al-Qaeda, Osama bin Laden, who sought to end the presence of U.S. forces in Saudi Arabia. They had trained in bin Laden's terrorist camps in Afghanistan and learned to pilot planes in the United States. The loss of more than three thousand lives led the United States to declare a "war against terrorism." In the wake of the September 11 attacks, the administration of U.S. president George W. Bush forged a multinational coalition, which included the vital cooperation of Islamic countries such as Pakistan, with the main goals of driving the ruling Taliban out of Afghanistan. After some initial coalition success, the war dragged on inconclusively and, as of 2011, the Taliban was making a comeback.

At first, the September 11 attacks and other lethal terrorist attacks around the world promoted global cooperation. European countries rounded up suspected terrorists and conducted the first successful trials of them in the spring of 2003. Ultimately, however, the West became divided when the United States claimed that Saddam Hussein was concealing weapons of mass destruction in Iraq and suggested ties between him and bin Laden's terrorist group. Great Britain, Spain, and Poland were among those who joined the coalition of invading forces, but powerful European states, including Germany, Russia, and France, refused, sparking the anger of many Americans, some of whom sported bumper stickers with the demand "First Iraq, Next France" or participated in happy hours devoted to "French bashing."

Europeans React to September 11 Terror Attacks
On September 11, 2001, terrorists killed thousands of people from dozens of countries in airplane attacks on the World Trade Center and the Pentagon. Throughout the world, people expressed their shock and sorrow in vigils, and like this British tourist in Rome, they remained glued to the latest news. Terrorism, which had plagued Europeans for several decades, easily traveled the world in the days of more open borders, economic globalization, and cultural exchange. *(© Alberto Pizzoli/Corbis-Sygma.)*

U.S. war fever mounted with the suggestion that Syria and Iran should also be invaded, while the rest of the world condemned what seemed a sudden American blood lust. Europeans in general, including the British public, accused the United States of becoming a world military dictatorship in order to preserve its only remaining value — wasteful consumerism. The United States countercharged that the Europeans were too selfishly enjoying their democracy and creature comforts to help fund the military defense of freedom under attack. The Spanish withdrew from the U.S. occupation of Iraq after terrorists linked to al-Qaeda bombed four Madrid commuter trains on March 11, 2004. The British, too, reeled when terrorists exploded bombs in three subway cars and a bus in central London in July 2005. Barack Obama, who was elected the first African American U.S. president in 2008, promised to bring home all the troops. As of 2011, however, the United States still maintained a military presence in Iraq, though alone among western nations since others in the initial coalition had all withdrawn their forces.

Terrorist Attacks on Spanish Commuter Trains, 2004
Terrorism became more widespread from the 1970s onward, taking many forms and espousing many causes. Although terrorists of the 1970s and early 1980s often targeted prominent individuals, later ones engineered wider attacks on random citizens to increase the loss of life. On March 11, 2004, foreign terrorists who opposed Spain's participation in the U.S.-led invasion of Iraq used bombs planted on commuter trains to kill 191 people and injure more than 2,000. Spanish voters ousted the prime minister and installed one who pulled Spanish forces out of Iraq. *(Christophe Simon/AFP/Getty Images.)*

The Promise and Problems of a World Economy

Amid the violence, an incredible rise in industrial entrepreneurship and technological development took place outside the West. Just as economic change in the early modern period had redirected European affairs from the Mediterranean to the Atlantic, so explosive productivity from Japan to Singapore in the 1980s and 1990s spread economic power from the Atlantic region to the Pacific. By the twenty-first century the economies of Brazil, Russia, India, and China—sometimes called the BRICs—were also developing rapidly, bringing new prosperity to their people. When the world economic collapse began in 2007, these newcomers were less indebted and less threatened than the West.

The Pacific Economic Surge

The rise of the Pacific was almost imperceptible from one year to the next, but in 1982, the Asian-Pacific nations accounted for 16.4 percent of global gross domestic product, a figure that had doubled since the 1960s. By 1989, East Asia's share of world production had grown to more than 25 percent as that of the West declined. By 2006, China alone was achieving economic growth rates of over 10 percent per year, and in 2010 it overtook Japan as the second largest national economy after the United States, with Germany falling to fourth place.

South Korea, Taiwan, Singapore, and Hong Kong were popularly called **Pacific tigers** for the ferocity of their growth in the 1980s and 1990s. By the 1990s, China, pursuing a policy of economic modernization and market orientation, had joined the surge in productivity and even surpassed all the others. Japan, however, led the initial charge of Asian economies with investment in high-tech consumer industries driving the Japanese economy. For example, in 1982, Japan had thirty-two thousand industrial robots in operation; western Europe employed only nine thousand, and the United States had seven thousand. In 1989, the Japanese government and private businesses invested $549 billion to modernize industrial capacity, a full $36 billion more than in the United States. Such spending paid off substantially, as buyers around the world snapped up automobiles, televisions, videocassette recorders, and computers from Japanese or other Asian-Pacific companies. As the United States poured vast sums into its military budgets and a series of wars, Asian and

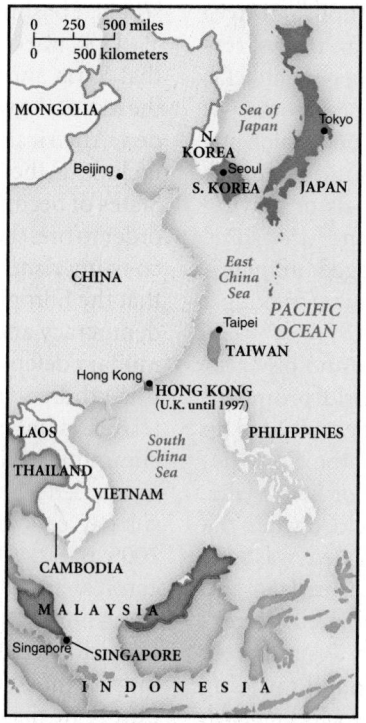

Tigers of the Pacific Rim, c. 1995

Pacific tigers: Countries of East Asia so named because of their massive economic growth, much of it from the 1980s on; foremost among these were Japan and China.

Middle Eastern governments purchased U.S. government bonds, thus financing America's ballooning national debt. Forty years after its total defeat in World War II, Japan was bankrolling its former conqueror. By 2000, China had become the largest creditor of the United States.

Despite rising national prosperity, individual workers, particularly outside of Japan, often paid dearly for this newly created wealth. For example, safety standards in China were abominable, leading to horrendous mining disasters among other catastrophes. Women in South Korea, Taiwan, and Central America labored in sweatshops to produce clothing for U.S.-based companies. Using the lure of a low-paid and docile female workforce, governments were able to attract electronics and other industries. However, educational standards rose, along with access to birth control and other medical care for these women, and many valued the escape from rural poverty.

Other Emerging Economies

Other emerging economies in the Southern Hemisphere as a whole continued to increase their share of the world's gross domestic product during the 1980s and 1990s, and some achieved political gains as well. In South Africa, native peoples began winning the struggle for political rights when, in 1990, the moderate government of F. W. de Klerk released political leader Nelson Mandela, imprisoned for almost three decades because of his anti-apartheid activism. After holding free elections in 1994, which Mandela won, South Africa—like Brazil, Russia, Iran, Saudi Arabia, Nigeria, and Chile—profited from the need for vast quantities of raw materials such as oil and ores to feed global expansion. India made strides in education, women's rights, and local cooperation (calming bitter rivalries), but assassinations of prime ministers raised the question of whether India would be able to attract investment and thus to continue modernization. After the brief rule of a Hindu nationalist government that often blocked development, India's economy also achieved soaring growth early in the twenty-first century, taking business from Western firms and making global acquisitions that gave it, for example, the world's largest steel industry. Although Western firms faced the challenge of competition, they also profited from prosperity that was more widely spread around the world by the 1990s.

World Economic Collapse

There was a downside to global economic interconnectedness. Beginning in 1997, when speculators brought down the Thai baht, and continuing with the collapse of the Russian ruble in 1998 and the bursting of the technology bubble in the early 2000s, the global economy suffered a series of shocks. Then in 2008, the real estate bubble burst in the United States, setting in motion a financial crisis of enormous proportions. For several years, lenders had been making home mortgages available to U.S. consumers who could not afford them. The boom in housing made the economy as a whole look robust. Bankers then sold their bad housing debt around the world to those who hoped to make handsome profits based on rate increases written into the mortgage contracts. When people were unable to make their monthly mortgage payments and pay their ballooning credit card debt, credit became unavailable both to ordinary people and to banks and industry. A credit collapse followed, just as it had in the stock market crash of

Protesting Reform amid Economic Crisis

By 2010 and 2011, global economic crisis and the attempts to repair the damage had led to massive government debt. To remedy the situation, governments cut back on jobs, benefits, and services while giving banks and businesses huge bailouts. Here, on the island of Cyprus, unions and NGOs sponsored this demonstration against the policy of simultaneously heaping money on banks and taking it from ordinary citizens. *(EPA/Katia Christodouloul/Landov.)*

1929. Beginning in the United States and continuing around the world, banks and industries became insolvent, forcing governments to set common policies to prop up failing banks with billions of dollars. Unemployment rose as businesses and consumers alike stopped purchasing goods.

By 2011, their more prudent management helped Asian economies as well as that of Brazil to recover, even as governments in the West faced bankruptcy and horrific rates of unemployment, such as the 20 percent of Spain's population who were out of work. It looked to some as if the European Union itself might collapse as the richer nations such as Germany and France were threatened by backing the debt of the poorer ones such as Greece, Ireland, Portugal, and even Italy. The globalization of economic crises was another of the perils faced by the world's population.

REVIEW QUESTION What were the principal challenges facing the West at the beginning of the twenty-first century?

Global Culture and Society in the Twenty-First Century

Amid warfare, booms, and crises, increased migration and growing global communications were changing culture and society, prompting many to ask what would become of national cultures and Western civilization itself. Would the world become a homogeneous mass with everyone wearing the same kind of clothing, eating the same kind of food, watching the same films, and communicating with the same smartphones? Some critics predicted a clash of civilizations in which increasingly incompatible religions and cultures would lead to a global holocaust. Others asked whether the West would fragment as the United States wore itself down waging war while much of Europe distanced itself from its former ally.

The migration that had accelerated since the 1990s, the spread of disease, global climate change, the information revolution, and the global sharing of culture argued against the cultural purity of any group, Western or otherwise. "Civilizations," Indian economist and Nobel Prize winner Amartya Sen wrote after the terrorist attacks of September 11, "are hard to partition . . . given the diversities within each society as well as the linkages among different countries and cultures."

Through global communication and migration, Western society changed even more rapidly in the 1980s and 1990s than it had hundreds of years earlier when it came into intense contact with the rest of the globe. In addition, national boundaries in the traditional European center of the West were weakening, given the open borders within the EU and the influx of migrants. Culture knew no national boundaries, as East, West, North, and South became saturated with one another's cultural products via satellite television, films, telecommunications, and computer technology. Consequently some observers labeled the new century an era of denationalization — meaning that national cultures as well as national boundaries were becoming less distinct. There is no denying that even while the West absorbed peoples and cultures, it continued to exercise not only economic but also cultural influence over the rest of the globe. Yet Western influence was also being contested as Westerners absorbed the cultures of other regions.

Redefining the West: The Impact of Global Migration

The global movement of people was massive in the last third of the twentieth century and into the twenty-first. Uneven economic development, political persecution, and warfare (which claimed more than 100 million victims after 1945) sent tens of millions in search of opportunity and safety. By 2010, France had between five and eight million Muslims within its borders and Europe as a whole had between thirty-five and fifty million. Other parts of the world were as full as the West of migrants from other cultures. The oil-producing nations of the Middle East employed millions of foreign workers, who generally constituted one-third of the labor force. Violence in Africa sent Rwandans, Congolese, and others to South Africa, as its government abandoned all-white rule. Wars in Afghanistan increased the number of refugees to Iran to nearly two million in 1995, while the Iraq-Iran War and the U.S. invasion of Iraq in 2003 sent millions more fleeing. In 2010, there were more than 200 million migrants worldwide, with many of them headed to the West.

Migrants often earned desperately needed income for family members who remained in the native country, and in some cases they propped up the economies of entire nations. In countries as different as the Yugoslav republics, Egypt, Spain, Mexico, and Pakistan, money sent home from abroad constituted up to 60 percent of national income. Sometimes migration was coerced: many eastern European and Asian prostitutes were held in international sex rings that controlled their passports, wages, and lives. Others came to the West voluntarily, seeking op-

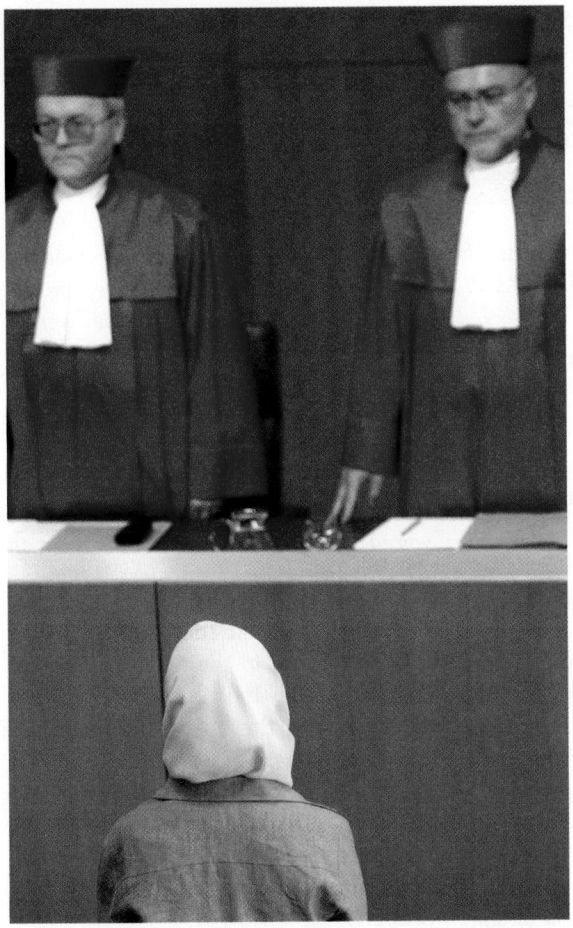

Headscarf Controversy in Germany
Western countries have long debated the relationship between religion and the nation-state, especially in public education. In an age of global migration, the issue of religion in the schools resurfaced, this time focusing on the headscarves worn by many Muslim women. In 2003, a German court upheld the right of teacher Fereshta Ludin, pictured here, to wear her headscarf while teaching on the grounds of religious freedom. Note the justices' own different clothing. *(© Vincent Kessler/Reuters/Corbis.)*

portunity and a better life: "I do not want to go back to China," said one woman restaurant owner in Hungary in the 1990s. "Some of my relatives there also have restaurants. . . . They have to have good relations with officials, . . . and sometimes they have to bribe somebody. . . . I would not be happy living like that." Like the illegal Congolese café proprietor Thérèse, whose story opens this chapter, many lived on the margins of the law, supporting networks of family and maintaining global economic ties from a new base in the West.

Foreign workers were often scapegoats for native peoples suffering from economic woes such as unemployment caused by downsizing. On the eve of EU enlargement in 2004, the highly respected weekly magazine *The Economist* included an article entitled "The Coming Hordes," which warned of Britain's being overrun by Roma (Gypsies) from eastern Europe. Political parties with racist programs sprang to life in Europe, aided by celebrities: the Moscow rock band Corroded Metals campaigned for anti-immigrant candidates with hate-filled songs and chants in English of "Kill, kill, kill, kill the bloody foreigners" running in the background. Even citizens of immigrant descent often had a difficult time being accepted. In Austria, France, the Netherlands, Sweden, and many other Western countries, thriving anti-immigrant and white supremacist politicians challenged centrist parties. In Austria and the Netherlands, anti-immigration candidates were elected to head the government. (See "Contrasting Views," page 1010.) Nonetheless, because employers sought out illegal immigrants for the low wages they could be paid, the West remained a place of opportunity.

Global Networks and the Economy

Like migration, rapid technological change also weakened traditional political, cultural, and economic borders and to some extent even made borders obsolete. In 1969, the U.S. Department of Defense developed a computer network to carry communications in case of nuclear war. This system and others like it in universities, government, and business grew into an unregulated system of more than ten thousand networks worldwide. These came to be known as the Internet—shorthand for *internetworking*. By 1995, users in more than 137 countries were connected to the Internet, creating new "communities" via the World Wide Web based on business needs, shared cultural interests, or other factors that transcended common citizenship in a particular nation-state. By 2011, some two billion people—one-third of the world's population—used the Internet, creating an online marketplace that offered goods and services ranging from advanced weaponry to organ transplants. While enthusiasts claimed that the Internet could promote world democracy, critics charged that communications technology favored elites and disadvantaged those without computer skills or the financial resources needed to access computers. In fact, wealthy North America, Europe, and Australia/Oceania had the highest percentage of users.

By 2000, as postindustrial skills spread, the Internet had brought service jobs to countries that had heretofore suffered unemployment and real poverty. One of the first countries to recognize the possibilities of computing and help-desk services was Ireland, which pushed computer literacy to attract business. In 2003, U.S. firms spent $8.3 bil-

CONTRASTING VIEWS

The Dutch Debate Globalization, Muslim Immigrants, and Turkey's Admission to the EU

Early in the twenty-first century, Westerners debated a series of intertwined issues springing from conditions created by the new globalized world. The issue of immigration and the accommodation of peoples from outside the West was one of them. The Netherlands was one of the European countries that began debating whether globalization hadn't gone too far in this direction. The debate came to the fore in the Netherlands after an animal rights activist in 2002 assassinated Pim Fortuyn, a candidate for prime minister who ran on a popular anti-immigrant platform and proclaimed, "Holland is full." When, in 2004, a Muslim radical assassinated filmmaker Theo van Gogh, who took special pride in insulting Islam, the Dutch debate over globalization fixated on the presence of foreigners, especially Muslims, in the Netherlands and the admission of Turkey to the European Union.

1. The View from Everyday Life

Leon was a Rotterdam window cleaner who did not want his last name revealed. Here is his opinion of the main problem of Dutch life brought about by globalization.

There are too many people coming here who don't want to work. Before long there will be more foreigners than Dutch people, and Dutch people won't be the boss of their own country. That's why this has to be stopped.

Source: Jennifer Ehrlich, "Liberal Netherlands Grows Less So on Immigration," *Christian Science Monitor*, December 19, 2003.

2. Too Much Islamic Architecture

Many immigrants and their descendants, all of whom could become Dutch citizens, often lived in cities where there was economic opportunity. Although mosques existed in many cities, most were tucked away in obscure and shabby parts of town near the ghettos where many Muslim immigrant families lived. When the Muslim community in Rotterdam proposed building a stately mosque with 164-foot minarets, many in Rotterdam opposed the project. Ronald Sorenson, a member of Rotterdam's city council, objected in particular to the design of the proposed mosque and its cultural connotations.

There's no reason the minarets have to be that high—it will not be Rotterdam; it will be Mecca on the Maas [River].

Source: Jennifer Ehrlich, "Liberal Netherlands Grows Less So on Immigration," *Christian Science Monitor*, December 19, 2003.

3. Opposing Immigration and Turkey's Membership in the European Union

Acceptance of new members has made the EU the largest economic power in the world. In the first decade of the twenty-first century, some Europeans looked to the integration of Turkey into the EU as further expansion of EU influence. Others, however, opposed it, as the issue of EU enlargement had implications for immigration. Geert Wilders, member of Dutch parliament, voiced his opposition. In 2010, he was put on trial for inciting hatred against Muslims.

Turkey is an Islamic country and as such doesn't belong in the EU. The flow [of Turks] is already too big. . . . There is a big problem with the integration of immigrants already in Holland. They top the list in terms of criminality, unemployment, welfare payments, domestic violence. . . . Let us concentrate on solving the problems with the immigrants already here properly.

Source: *Expatica*, October 5, 2004.

4. A Student's Thoughts on Muslims in the Netherlands

Loubna el Morabet, a PhD candidate in social science at Leiden University, gave this reaction to Geert Wilders's pronouncements on Muslims and to the media's coverage of him and his political party.

lion on outsourcing to Ireland and $7.7 billion on outsourcing to India. In that same year, the United States bought $77.38 billion in services from foreign countries and sold $131.01 billion to them, meaning in fact that more was insourced than outsourced. Thus, the Internet allowed for jobs to be apportioned anywhere. Moroccans did help-desk work for French or Spanish speakers, and in the twenty-first century Estonia, Hungary, and the Czech Republic as well as India and the Philippines were rebuilding their economies successfully by providing call-center and other business services. The Internet allowed service industries to globalize just as the manufacturing sector had done much earlier through multinational corporations.

Globalization of the economy affected the West in complex ways. Those who worked in outsourcing enterprises were more likely than those in domestic firms to participate in the global consumer economy, much of it for Western goods. Benefiting from the booming global economy of the 1990s, the Irish and eastern Europeans became integrated into the Western consumer economy, and by the 2000s Asians and South Americans were integrated, too. Their new disposable income allowed them to purchase luxury automobiles, CD players, and per-

This is an ongoing process. Muslims in the Netherlands are already very Dutch. I have done research in the Netherlands and England and learnt that Muslim students here have adopted the Dutch mentality. This is their country.

Of course I feel threatened when I hear Wilders speaking. But if I take a step back, I realize he will never be able to carry out his ideas. Taxing headscarves is nonsense and halting immigration from Islamic countries is discrimination. The principle of equality is deeply embedded in Dutch law.

I think it is ridiculous that media pay so much attention to a party that has garnered a handful of seats in the municipal elections. [Left-wing liberal party] D66 was the real winner of the local elections and that happens to be the one party that tells Wilders: "You are shutting people out, you discriminate." That gets relatively little attention.

Source: "Muslims Quietly Take Wilders' Abuse," Radio Netherlands Worldwide, March 25, 2010.

5. An Evaluation of Dutch Values

Popular Amsterdam actress Funda Müjde admitted to being called a "filthy Turk" during the debates over immigration and ethnic violence in the city.[1] *In her online stage performances and journalism, she gave sharp-witted responses to the anti-immigration furor around her.*

"Do aliens actually love Holland?" This question woke me up with a start. After work (a workshop at the Employment Office) I traveled back [home from the job] with a colleague because he needed to be in Amsterdam. We have been working together for a while now and I notice that our conversations are always about something substantial.

Now it seemed as if he was even bolder in asking all kinds of questions.

Hurray! Do we aliens (read: mainly the first-generation Moroccans and Turks) really love Holland? Immediately I want to answer this question with another question. "Does Holland really love aliens?" Just in time, I bite my tongue.

Source: Funda Müjde Web site, http://www.fundam.nl/English/fundas-column-telegraaf-daily-newspaper-04.htm.

6. Encouragement for Religious Tolerance in the EU

On July 21, 2004, Dutch prime minister Jan Peter Balkenende gave a speech before the European Parliament that called on Europeans to reconsider their position on immigration.

We must not allow ourselves to be guided by fear, for example, of Islam. The raising of barriers to any particular religion is not consistent with Europe's shared values. Our opposition should be directed not against religions, but against people and groups misusing their religion to get their way by force. Islam is not the problem.

Source: European Stability Initiative, "Speech by the President, Jan Peter Balkenende, to the European Parliament, in Strasbourg on 21 July 2004," http://www.esiweb.org.

Questions to Consider

1. **What are the main points of view in the debate over Muslims, immigration, and the admission of Turkey to the European Union?**
2. **How do you evaluate the strength of each position?**
3. **Given that globalization brought about a wide variety of changes, why would Muslim immigration and Turkish EU membership become such heated issues?**
4. **What sense do you get of the Muslim reaction to hostility and discrimination?**

[1] Ian Buruma, *Murder in Amsterdam: The Death of Theo van Gogh and the Limits of Tolerance* (New York: Penguin, 2006), 175.

sonal computers that would have been far beyond their means a decade earlier. Non-Westerners may have taken jobs from the West, but they often sent funds back. For example, a twenty-one-year-old Indian woman, working for a service provider in Bangalore under the English name Sharon, used her salary to buy Western consumer items, such as a cell phone from the Finnish company Nokia. "As a teenager I wished for so many things," she said. "Now I'm my own Santa Claus." Ordinary Western workers often discovered that this global revolution threatened their jobs. In Germany, where taxes for social security and other welfare-state financing comprised 42 percent of payroll costs in 2003, the incentive for businesses to downsize or to move to countries with lower costs was strong. Globalization redistributed jobs across the West and reworked economic networks to operate worldwide.

A New Global Culture?

Despite the sense that national boundaries are weakening, cultural exchange flowing in many directions goes back millennia. In the ancient world, Greek philosophers and traders knew distant Asian religious beliefs, and Middle Eastern religions such as

Judaism and Christianity were influenced by them. In the eighteenth and nineteenth centuries, Western scholars immersed themselves in Asian philosophy and languages. By the early 1990s, visitors from around the world had made tourism the largest single industry in Britain and in many other Western countries, promoting cultural exchange. Chinese students in Tiananmen Square in 1989 testified to the power of the West in the world's imagination when in the name of freedom they rallied around their own representation of the Statue of Liberty (which itself was a gift from France to the United States). In Japan, businesspeople wore Western-style clothing and watched soccer, baseball, and other Western sports using English terms, while Europeans and Americans wore flip-flops, carried umbrellas, and practiced yoga — all imports from beyond the West.

Remarkable innovations in communications integrated cultures and made the earth seem a much smaller place, though possibly one with a Western flavor. Videotapes and satellite-beamed telecasts transported American television shows to Hong Kong and Japanese movies to Europe and North America. American rock music sold briskly in Russia and elsewhere in the former Soviet bloc. When more than 100,000 Czechoslovakian rock fans, including President Václav Havel, attended a Rolling Stones concert in Prague in 1990, it was clear that despite half a century of supposed isolation under communism, Czechs and Slovaks had been well tuned in to the larger world. Young black immigrants forged transnational culture when they created hip-hop and other pop music styles by combining elements of Africa, the Caribbean, Afro-America, and Europe. Athletes like the Brazilian soccer player Ronaldo and Japanese baseball star Ichiro Suzuki became better known to countless people than their own national leaders were. Film entrepreneurs marketed such international blockbusters as the Chinese *Crouching Tiger, Hidden Dragon* (2000). With their messages conveyed around the world, even today's moral leaders — the Nobel Peace Prize winners Nelson Mandela, former president of South Africa; the Dalai Lama, the spiritual leader of Tibet; and Aung San Suu Kyi, opposition leader in Burma — are global figures.

Culture from beyond the West

As it had done for centuries, the West continued to devour material from other cultures — whether Hong Kong films, African textiles, Indian music, or Latin American pop culture. One of the most important influences in the West came from what was called the boom in Latin American literature. Latin American authors developed a style known as magical realism that melded everyday events with Latin American history and geography, while also incorporating elements of myth, magic, and religion. The novels of Colombian-born Nobel Prize winner Gabriel García Márquez were translated into dozens of languages. His lush fantasies, including *One Hundred Years of Solitude* (1967), *Love in the Time of Cholera* (1988), and many later works, portray people of titanic ambitions and passions who endure war and all manner of personal trials. García Márquez narrated the tradition of dictators in Latin America, but he also paid close attention to the effects of global business. *One Hundred Years of Solitude*, for example, closes with the machine-gunning in 1928 of thousands of workers for the American United Fruit company because they asked for one day off per week and breaks to use the toilet. Wherever they lived, readers snapped up the book, which sold thirty million copies worldwide. García Márquez's work inspired a host of other outstanding novels in the magical realism tradition, including Laura Esquivel's *Like Water for*

Tourism, Migration, and the Mixing of Cultures
Tourism was a major economic boon to the West, and Western countries were the top tourist destinations in the world. Spreading prosperity allowed for greater leisure and travel to distant spots. Curiosity grew about other cultures. This Scottish bagpiper in London clearly arouses the interest of passersby, whether visitors from afar or citizens of his own country. *(© Will van Overbeek. All Rights Reserved.)*

Chocolate (1989). In the 1990s, the work was translated into two dozen languages and became a hit film because of its setting in a Mexican kitchen during the revolution of 1910, where cooking, sexuality, and brutality are intertwined. The Latin American boom continued into the early twenty-first century, with innumerable authors in the West adopting aspects of García Márquez's style.

Magical realism influenced a range of Western writers, including those migrating to Europe. Some described how the experience of Western culture felt to the transnational person. British-born Zadie Smith, daughter of a Jamaican mother, became a prizewinning author with her novel *White Teeth* (2000), which describes postimperial Britain through the lives of often bizarre and larger-than-life characters from many ethnic backgrounds. Odd science fiction technology, deep emotional wounds, and weird but hilarious situations guide a plot full of heartbreak. Equally drawn to aspects of the magical realist style, Indian-born **Salman Rushdie** published the novel *The Satanic Verses* (1988), which outraged Muslims around the world because it appeared to blaspheme the Prophet Muhammad. From Iran, the ayatollah Khomeini issued a fatwa (decree) promising both a monetary reward and salvation in the afterlife to anyone who would assassinate the writer. Rushdie's Italian and Japanese translators were murdered, while his Norwegian publisher survived an assassination attempt. In a display of Western cultural unity, international leaders took bold steps to protect Rushdie until the threat to his life was lifted a decade later.

As groups outside the accepted circles engaged in artistic production, battles over culture erupted. U.S. novelist **Toni Morrison** became, in 1993, the first African American woman to win the Nobel Prize for Literature. In works such as *Beloved* (1987), *Jazz* (1992), and *A Mercy* (2008), Morrison describes the nightmares, daily experiences, achievements, and dreams of those who were brought as slaves to the United States and their descendants. But some parents objected to the inclusion of Morrison's work in school curricula alongside Shakespeare and other authors of the accepted canon. Critics charged that unlike Shakespeare's universal Western truth, the writing of African Americans, Native Americans, and women represented only propaganda, not great literature. In both the United States and Europe, politicians on the right saw the presence of multiculturalism as a sign of national decay similar to that brought about by immigration.

Toni Morrison, Recipient of the Nobel Prize
Toni Morrison, shown here receiving the Nobel Prize for Literature in 1993, was the first African American woman to receive the Nobel Prize. Morrison uses her literary talent to depict the condition of blacks under slavery and after emancipation. She also publishes insightful essays on social, racial, and gender issues. *(AP Photo.)*

Building Post-Soviet Culture

In the former Soviet bloc, artists and writers faced unique challenges. After the Soviet Union collapsed, celebrated writers like Mikhail Bulgakov (1891–1940), famous in the West for his novel *The Master and Margarita* (published posthumously in 1966–1967), became known in his homeland. At the same time, the collapse put literary dissidents out of business. In helping bring down the Soviet regime, they had lost their subject matter—the critique of a tyrannical system. State-supported authors suddenly lost their jobs. Eastern-bloc writers who formerly found both critical and financial success in the West seemed less heroic—and less talented—in the wide-open post-Soviet world. The work of Czech writer Milan Kundera, for example, lost its luster. It had been, according to one critic, merely about Western publishers' hype, not literature but merely a "line of business." To make matters worse, there was no idea of what the post-Communist arts should be.

New literature aimed at rethinking the communist experience and eastern Europe's cultural relationship to western Europe and the West more

Salman Rushdie: Immigrant British author, whose novel *The Satanic Verses* (1988) led the ayatollah Ruhollah Khomeini of Iran to issue a fatwa calling for Rushdie's murder.

Toni Morrison: The first African American woman to win the Nobel Prize for Literature; her works include *Beloved* (1987), *Jazz* (1992), and *A Mercy* (2008).

generally. Andrei Makine, an expatriate Russian author, became popular worldwide for his poignant yet disturbing novels of the collapse of communism. He described the attraction of western European culture and the role of the war and the Gulag on the imaginations of eastern-bloc people, including teenagers. Both *Dreams of My Russian Summers* (1995) and *Once Upon the River Love* (1994) describe young people bred to fantasize about the wealth, sexiness, and material goods of western Europe and America. Victor Pelevin wrote more satirically and bitingly in such works as *The Life of Insects* (1993), in which insect-humans buzz around Russia trying to discover who they are in the post-Soviet world. Pelevin, a Buddhist and former engineer, wrote hilarious send-ups of politicians and the almost sacred Soviet space program, depicting it as a media sham run from the depths of the Moscow subway system in which hundreds of cosmonaut-celebrities are killed to prevent the truth from getting out. For him, "any politician is a TV program, and this doesn't change from one government to another." So one simply judged them by haircuts, ties, and other aspects of personal style, as he showed in his novel *Homo Zapiens* (1999), in which politicians are all "virtual"—that is, produced by technical effects and scriptwriters.

In music and the other arts, much energy was spent on recovering and absorbing all the underground works that had been hidden since 1917. For example, music lovers were astonished as the work of first-rate composers emerged. Those composers had written their classical works in private for fear that they might contain phrasings, sounds, and rhythms that would be called subversive. Meanwhile, they had often earned a living writing for films, as did Giya Kancheli, who wrote immensely popular music for more than forty films but was in addition a gifted composer of classical music. Other work could now become even better known. Alfred Schnittke (1934–1998) produced dozens of operas, symphonies, chamber music pieces, concertos, and other works that were extremely sad, punctuated with anger in loud bursts of dissonance, and set in a somber bass register. Alongside great artists, ordinary people in eastern Europe rethought the past, creating ceremonies honoring Gulag victims and those purged by Stalin, all the while trying to sort out what Communism had meant to their lives and to history.

U.S. Cultural Dominance Even as the cold war ended and as the post-Soviet world tried to rethink its cultural values, the global power of the United States gave its culture an edge. The United States's success in marketing its culture, along with the legacy of British imperialism, helped make English the dominant international language by the end of the twentieth century. Such English words as *stop*, *shopping*, *parking*, *okay*, *weekend*, and *rock* infiltrated dozens of non-English vocabularies. English became one of the official languages of the European Union; across Europe, it served as the main language of higher education, science, and tourism. Already in the 1960s, French president Charles de Gaulle, fearing the corruption of the French language, had banned such new words as *computer* in government documents, and succeeding administrations followed his path. The ban did not stop the influx of English into scientific, diplomatic, and daily life. Nonetheless, in another sign of cultural divide, the EU's parliament and national cultural ministries regulated the amount of American programming on television and in cinemas.

American influence in film was dominant: films such as *The Matrix Reloaded* (2003) and *Avatar* (2009) earned hundreds of millions of dollars from global audiences. Simultaneously, however, the United States itself welcomed films from around the world—whether the Mexican *Y Tu Mamá También* (2001) or the British *Slumdog Millionaire* (2009). "Bollywood" films—happy, lavish films from the Indian movie industry—had a huge following in all Western countries, even influencing the plots of some American productions. The fastest-growing media sector in the United States in the twenty-first century was Spanish-language television, just one more indication that even in the United States culture was based on mixture and global exchange.

Postmodernism Some have called the global culture of the late twentieth and early twenty-first centuries **postmodernism**, defined in part as intense stylistic mixing in the arts without following an elite set of standards. Striking examples of postmodern art abounded in Western society, including the AT&T Building (now known as the Sony Building) in New York City, which looks sleek and modern. Its entryway, however, is a Roman arch, and its cloud-piercing top suggests eighteenth-century Chippendale furniture. Postmodern buildings used elements from the past, drawing from cultural styles that spanned millennia and continents without valuing one style above others. The Guggenheim Museum in Bilbao, Spain, designed by American Frank Gehry and considered bizarre

postmodernism: A term applied in the late twentieth century to both an intense stylistic mixture in the arts without a central unifying theme or elite set of standards and a critique of Enlightenment and scientific beliefs in rationality and the possibility of certain knowledge.

by classical or even modern standards, includes forms, materials, and perspectives that, by rules of earlier decades, did not belong together. Architects from around the world working in a variety of hybrid styles completed the postunification rebuilding of Berlin. One crowning achievement was the rebuilding of the Reichstag, whose traditional facade was given a modern dome of glass and steel. To add to the changing reality, all of these postmodern buildings could be visited virtually on the World Wide Web.

Some intellectuals defined postmodernism in political terms as part of the decline of the eighteenth-century Enlightenment ideals of human rights, individualism, and personal freedom, which were seen as modern (see page 799). This political postmodernism included the decline of the Western nation-state. A structure like the Bilbao Guggenheim was simply an international tourist attraction rather than an institution reflecting Spanish traditions or national purpose. It embodied consumption, global technology, mass communications, and international migration rather than citizenship, nationalism, and rights. These qualities made it a rootless structure, unlike the Louvre in Paris, for example, which was built by the French monarchy to serve its own purposes. Critics saw the Bilbao Guggenheim as drifting, more like the nomadic businesswoman Thérèse, who moved between nations and cultures with no set identity. Cities and nations alike were losing their function as places providing social roots, personal identity, or human rights. For postmodernists of a political bent, computers had replaced the autonomous, free self and bureaucracy had rendered representative government obsolete.

REVIEW QUESTION What social and cultural questions has globalization raised?

The German Reichstag: Reborn and Green
Nothing better symbolizes the end of the postwar era and the new millennium than the restoration of the Reichstag, the parliament building in Berlin. Like other manifestations of postmodernism, the restoration—designed by a British architect—preserves the old, while adding a new dome of glass, complete with solar panels that make the building self-sufficient in its energy needs. Visitors can walk around the glass dome, looking at their elected representatives deliberating below. *(© Svenja-Foto/Corbis.)*

Conclusion

Postmodernist thinking has not eclipsed humane values in the global age. The urge to find practical solutions to the daunting problems of contemporary life—population explosion, scarce resources, pollution, global warming, ethnic hatred, North–South inequities, and terrorism—through the careful assessment of facts still guides public policy. Some of these global problems were briefly overshadowed by the collapse of the Soviet empire, which initially produced human misery, rising criminality, and the flight of population during the 1990s and even into the 2000s. Reformers who sought improved conditions of life by bringing down Soviet and Yugoslav communism saw unexpected bloodshed and even genocide. What appeared an economic boom resulting from globalization and the collapse of communism itself had disadvantages, as a series of crises beginning in Thailand in 1997 and finally exploding in the more sustained crisis from 2007 on cost jobs and harmed human well-being.

Yet the past twenty-five years have also seen great improvements. Events from South Africa and Latin America, for example, indicated that there could be progress toward democracy, prosperity, and an end to oppression. Human health gradually improved even as scientists sought to cure the victims of global pandemics and even to prevent them altogether. The global age ushered in by the Soviet collapse unexpectedly brought denationalization to many regions of the world, leading to weakening of borders and cooperation among former enemies. The expansion of the European Union and the tight-

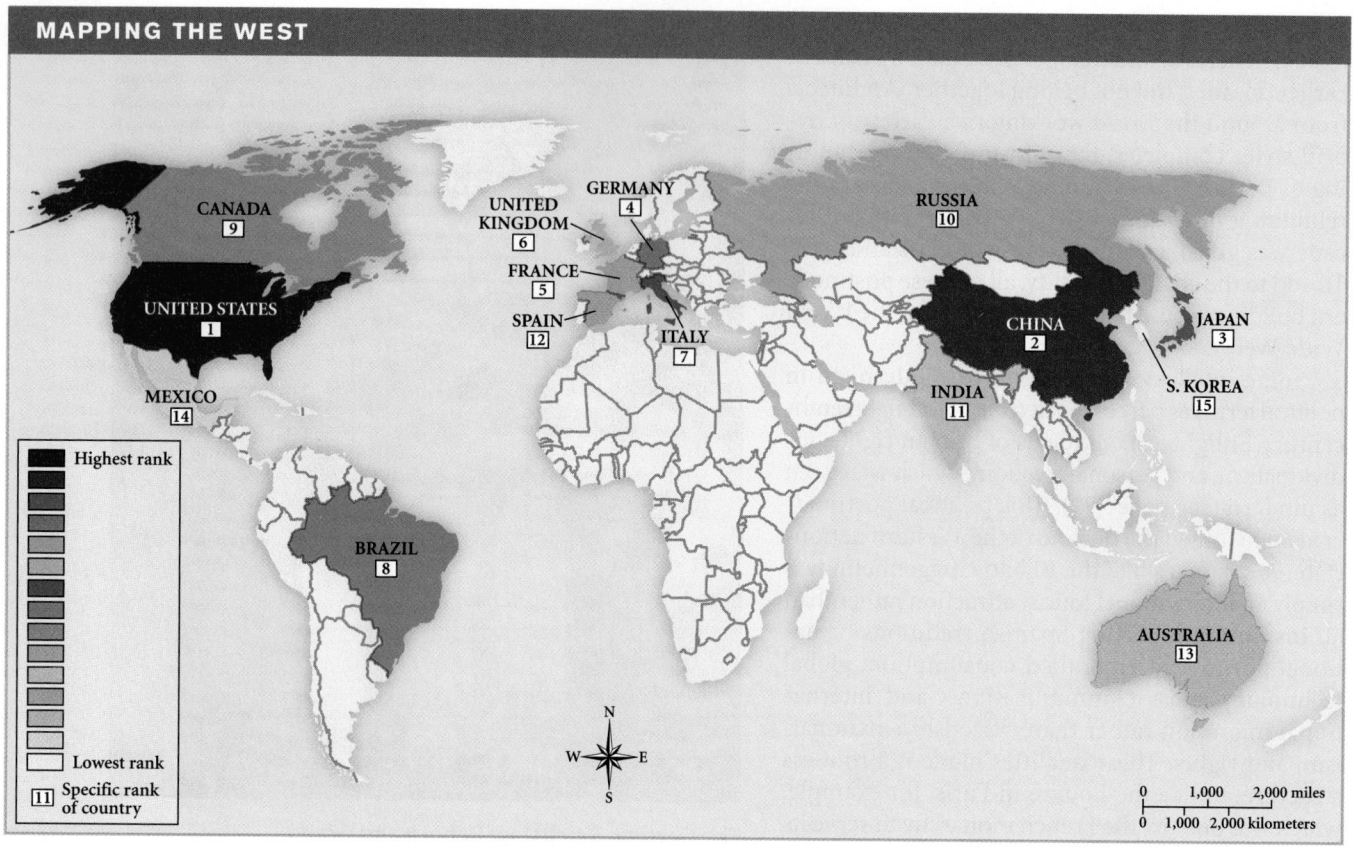

The World's Top Fifteen Economies as of 2010

From the nineteenth to the twenty-first centuries, the comparative economic strength of individual nations changed considerably. In the nineteenth century, India and China had the largest economies; they were eclipsed by the European powers as the Industrial Revolution progressed. The European powers in turn were eventually overtaken by the United States. By the end of the twentieth century, the reemergence of non-Western economic powerhouses marked another transformation. | **How would you describe economic dynamism in the twenty-first century as shown in the map?**

ening of relationships within it are the best example of this development.

Some consequences of increasing globalization are still being determined. The Internet and migration suggest that people's empathy for one another grew worldwide. One commentator claimed that there was little bloodshed in the collapse of the Soviet empire because fax machines and television circulated images of events globally, which discouraged the excessive violence often associated with political revolution. At the same time, militants from Saudi Arabia, Egypt, Indonesia, the Philippines, North Africa, Britain, and elsewhere unleashed unprecedented terrorism on the world in an attempt to push back global forces. Nor did powerful countries hesitate to wage wars against Chechnya, Kuwait, Iraq, Afghanistan, Lebanon, and other nations around the world. On a different level, even as globalization raised standards of living and education in many parts of the world, in other areas—such as poorer regions in Africa and Asia—people faced disease and the dramatic social and economic crises specifically associated with the global age. In contrast, the most hopeful development in recent globalization was communication in the arts and in culture more generally—most visible in the exchange of books, music, and ideas around the world—and the cooperation that nations undertook with one another in the realm of health, economics, and politics. Events from the recent past thus show that both opportunities and challenges lie ahead for citizens of the West and of the world as they make the transition to what some are calling the digital age.

FOR FURTHER EXPLORATION

- **For additional primary-source material from this period**, see *Sources of the Making of the West*, Fourth Edition.
- **For Web sites, images, and documents related to topics in this chapter**, visit *Make History* at bedfordstmartins.com/hunt.

Chapter 29 Review

Online Study Guide bedfordstmartins.com/hunt

Key Terms and People

In the grid below, identify the term or person and explain its historical significance. (To do this exercise online, go to bedfordstmartins.com/hunt.)

Term	Who or What & When	Why It Matters
globalization (p. 986)		
Slobodan Milosevic (p. 987)		
ethnic cleansing (p. 988)		
Vladimir Putin (p. 990)		
Maastricht Treaty (p. 995)		
European Union (EU) (p. 995)		
euro (p. 995)		
nongovernmental organizations (NGOs) (p. 999)		
global warming (p. 1000)		
Green Party (p. 1000)		
Osama bin Laden (p. 1003)		
Pacific tigers (p. 1006)		
Salman Rushdie (p. 1013)		
Toni Morrison (p. 1013)		
postmodernism (p. 1014)		

Review Questions

1. What were the major issues facing the former Soviet bloc in the 1990s and early 2000s?
2. What trends suggest that the nation-state was a declining institution at the beginning of the twenty-first century?
3. What were the principal challenges facing the West at the beginning of the twenty-first century?
4. What social and cultural questions has globalization raised?

Making Connections

1. In what ways were global connections at the beginning of the twenty-first century different from the global connections at the beginning of the twentieth century?
2. How did the Western nation-state of the early twenty-first century differ from the Western nation-state at the opening of the twentieth century?
3. Migration has been a major factor across the human past. How has it affected the West differently in the twenty-first century?
4. Economic crises caused by changes in weather, the spread of disease, and trade and financial disturbances have been constants throughout history. How does the economic crisis that began in 2007 compare with earlier crises?

Important Events

Date	Event	Date	Event
1989	Chinese students revolt in Tiananmen Square; fall of the Berlin Wall	2000	Vladimir Putin becomes president of Russia
1990s	Internet revolution	2001	September 11 terrorist attacks; United States declares "war against terrorism," attacks Afghanistan
1990–1991	War in Persian Gulf	2003	United States invades Iraq; the West divides on this policy
1991	Civil war erupts in former Yugoslavia; failed coup by Communist hard-liners in Soviet Union	2004	Ten countries join European Union
1992	Soviet Union is dissolved	2005	Emissions reductions of Kyoto Protocol go into effect
1993	Toni Morrison wins Nobel Prize for Literature; Czechoslovakia splits into Czech Republic and Slovakia	2007	Bulgaria and Romania admitted to European Union; world economic crisis begins
1994	Nelson Mandela elected president of South Africa; Russian troops invade Chechnya; European Union (EU) officially formed	2009	Barack Obama becomes the first African American president of the United States
1999	European Union introduces the euro; world population reaches six billion	2010	China overtakes Japan to become world's second largest economy

- Consider three events: **Internet revolution (1990s)**, **Soviet Union is dissolved (1992)**, and **European Union (EU) officially formed (1994)**. How did each of these events help to bring about a more interconnected, globalized world?

SUGGESTED REFERENCES

Studies of the globalized world describe both hopeful efforts to cure disease and survive migration and devastating effects of terrorism and ethnic conflict. Interesting works portray politics and everyday life in post-Soviet Russia and eastern Europe.

Bass, Gary J. *Freedom's Battle: The Origins of Humanitarian Intervention*. 2008.

Bess, Michael. *The Light-Green Society: Economic and Technological Modernity in France*. 2003.

Brier, Jennifer. *Infectious Ideas: U.S. Political Response to the AIDS Crisis*. 2009.

Bucur, Maria. *Heroes and Victims: Remembering the War in Twentieth-Century Romania*. 2009.

Burleigh, Michael. *Blood and Rage: A Cultural History of Terrorism*. 2008.

Burrett, Tina. *Television and Presidential Power in Putin's Russia*. 2010.

*Emecheta, Buchi. *The New Tribe*. 1996.

*Gorbachev, Mikhail. *Memoirs*. 1996.

Hoerder, Dirk. *Cultures in Contact: World Migrations in the 2nd Millennium*. 2002.

Hsu, Roland, ed. *Ethnic Europe: Mobility, Identity, and Conflict in a Globalized World*. 2010.

Humphrey, Caroline. *The Unmaking of Soviet Life: Everyday Economies after Socialism*. 2002.

Kavoori, Anandam P., and Aswin Punathambekar, eds. *Global Bollywood*. 2008.

Kenney, Padraic. *The Burdens of Freedom: Eastern Europe since 1989*. 2006.

MacGaffey, Janet, et al. *Congo-Paris: Transnational Traders on the Margins of the Law*. 2000.

Osumare, Halifu. *The Africanist Aesthetic in Global Hip-Hop: Power Moves*. 2007.

Ried, T. R. *The United States of Europe: The New Superpower and the End of American Supremacy*. 2005.

Rosefielde, Steven. *Russia in the 21st Century: The Prodigal Superpower*. 2006.

Sinno, Abdulkader H., ed. *Muslims in Western Politics*. 2008.

United Nations. *Overcoming Barriers: Human Mobility and Development*. 2009.

United Nations population data: http://www.unfpa.org/swp/swpmain.htm

*Primary source.

Epilogue

The Making of the West Continues in the Digital Age

Social Transformation E-2

Economic Transformations E-2

War, Peace, and Politics E-4

Culture and Intellectual Creativity E-4

The West in the Digital World E-5

Were you born digital? If you are reading this book between 2012 and 2015, the answer to this question for many of you is most likely yes. You have been able to access the Internet since you were four or five years old; you probably keep in touch with friends through Facebook and are a skillful and frequent texter; and you are likely to download music and videos onto a range of digital equipment, including your iPod, iPhone, or iPad. Online research is easy for you, and you may even be accessing this book online.

We refer to your own possible life experience to ask whether the West and the world have entered a new age comparable to the Stone Age, the Iron Age, the Commercial Revolution of the Middle Ages, the Agricultural Revolution, the Industrial Revolution, or the Global Age—all of these distinct times in history characterized by profound, if sometimes invisible, transformations in the way humans live. Many suspect that we in the West, and to a large extent the world, have entered such a transformative period—a new and distinct episode in human history. That new age is the Digital Age, and you are a major player in it. Let's use this brief epilogue to consider how this development relates to events and trends that you have studied in this book.

For historians, understanding trends in the recent past is a challenge in itself. Every day is filled with news, and never more so than after September 11, 2001. Global communication technology makes reporting virtually instantaneous—but unlike journalists, who are pressed for an immediate story, historians try to judge which items from the unfiltered mass of instant news will be important in the long run. Historians identify social, cultural, and political events that are uniquely important or generally significant for people's everyday lives, and they need time to collect facts from multiple sources. They make the most reliable evaluations when events are no longer news—that is, after a substantial amount of time has shown the events' lasting influence and importance.

When we wrote the first edition of this book, we held our breath in the face of rapidly changing events and judged that the fall of communism and the increasing interconnectedness of the world's peoples and cultures were the challenges not only of the moment but also of history.

Today we persist in that judgment, knowing that the fall of communism and the coming of globalism have brought even greater opportunities and perils than we saw only a few years earlier. Now, after we made our first selections of important trends, we judge the potential for the unification of the entire European continent as momentous. We also see both the rising economic development around the world and the forces of terrorism as still important historical influences. As an experiment in history, you might note the important events during the months in which you take this course, put your list away for several years or more, and then see if those events — along with the events discussed in this epilogue — stand the test of time.

We imagine that you would probably put that list of important events away digitally rather than on hard copy. From there you can share it with friends on a social networking site. In contrast, previous generations would have written their list on paper and put it in a drawer, where it would exist privately. In our first version of this book on the West, we missed the transformative effects of the Digital Age, and it has only slowly dawned on us in watching our students and doing our research that a major revolution in human life may be under way. The Internet has been around for more than forty years, and the World Wide Web for nearly twenty, but only recently has the full import of digitization become apparent: entire cultures are being changed, beginning most thoroughly with the current generation, by this process. Let's consider how the Digital Age may be yielding new patterns in some of the major categories that help us describe the past. We encourage you to add to the list.

Social Transformation

In studying the history of the West, we see how social structures have frequently been transformed by technological innovations. Developments in stone and iron capacity, for example, revolutionized human life and consequently reshaped social patterns. The Industrial Revolution prompted another massive social shift: in preindustrial society, those who controlled both agriculture and labor were, on the whole, the people able to cultivate learning and participate in politics. Those who worked the land, whether slave or free, often (though not always) led difficult lives with little social or political influence. The coming of manufacturing altered that social situation, as we saw in the rise of industrial society and the more democratic politics that often made it a success. Increasingly, education and knowledge determined social structure, giving influence, power, and wealth to those who had the intellectual tools to innovate — or at least the knowledge to coordinate or operate — technology and services.

The Digital Age is no less filled with meaning for society. Today, social status and social class are determined largely by access to digital technology. One's ability to secure a good job often depends on one's skill with this technology — but one can only acquire such skill with the proper equipment and access. In this regard, the West remains a privileged place to be born. As a principal site of wealth and technology, the West has more "digital natives" than other parts of the world do — though people in places like South Korea, Japan, China, Egypt, and Libya are rapidly accessing digital technology, and those with digital skills are advancing in their societies. A large gap remains — similar to older wealth-, class-, and status-based differences — between those who are adept with digital media and those who are not.

The Digital Age also allows for social identities that are more fluid than ever before. Fundamental characteristics such as gender, age, and appearance — as well as other traits such as skills and abilities, likes and dislikes, or professional experience — can be manipulated, refashioned, or fabricated in new and hard-to-detect ways. Moreover, with digitization, people's identities have become public in entirely new ways. Those with access to digital technology can create social networks and participate in various types of information sharing. Concerns for privacy and individuality that developed in the West from the seventeenth century onward may no longer be relevant when many aspects of people's identity are available to corporations, governments, online pirates, and a significant portion of the population.

Finally, although gender discrimination is rampant around the world — evidenced especially by the fact that 80 percent of the world's poor are women and children — digital skills seem to know no gender. Many of the first computer programmers in Europe were women. Then computers took off, and programming became an essential, highly paid job primarily held by men. The gender-neutral potential of the Digital Age has not yet been fully realized.

Economic Transformations

Over the last two chapters of this book, we have looked at the economic impact of digitization. As explained earlier, computer technology has allowed for a great advance in the globalization of economies in all parts of the world. The surprising rise of economies in Brazil, Russia, India, and China, for example, has appeared as a challenge to the West's overwhelming lead in the modern global economy (see the map below). Oddly enough, although the Digital Age began in the West and although many of the world's foremost digital innovators are also Westerners, the emerging nations may be the powerhouses of the future, especially as they increasingly develop their digital capabilities. Companies and individuals alike are investing in emerging markets and are seeing the first industrial nations as falling behind.

The Digital Age has thus had mixed effects on economic well-being. Service jobs demanding literacy and technological skills have migrated to new places such as Ireland and eastern Europe. Jobs have also left the West, finding new homes in areas where skills are high and wages low—for example, in India and Southeast Asia. Thus, skills are being built around the world, especially as non-Westerners become polylingual and technologically adept. The number of highly educated engineers, lawyers, and other top members of the service sector is soaring outside the West even as the building of modern skills across the population is declining in the center of technological innovation. In this respect one wonders whether digital technology is fundamentally changing the Western economy—which remains predominantly capitalist—as much as it is changing skill levels, boosting human capacities everywhere.

Digitization has also affected worldwide patterns of commerce, as new jobs have helped the number of consumers buying the products of Western innovation to soar. At the same time, commercial behavior has been changing: On a micro level, individuals are banking online, engaging in real-time stock trading, changing their consumption patterns in ways that impact business massively (consider, for example, the amount of e-commerce that now takes place during holiday seasons), and becoming the subjects of ever more targeted advertising campaigns. On a more global scale, online transactions—from an eBay purchase by a New

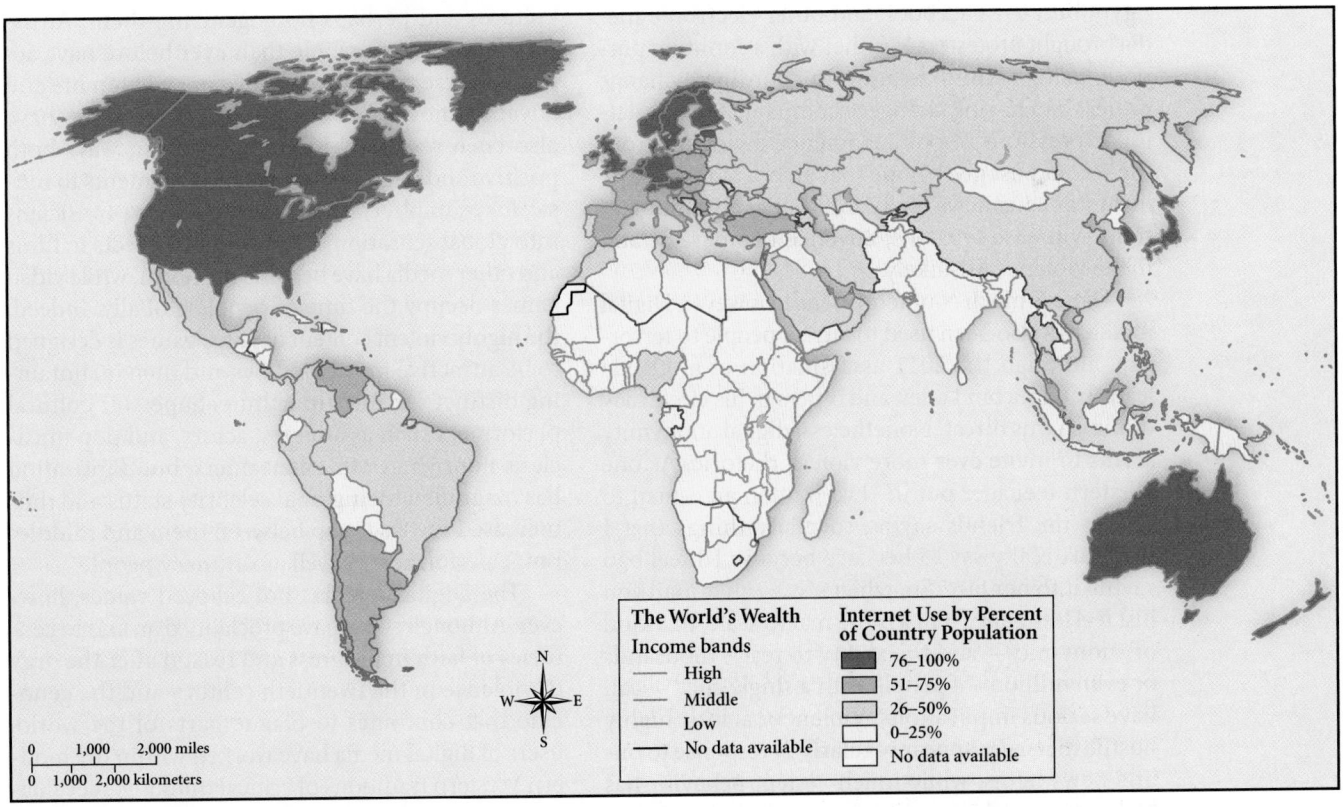

The World in the New Millennium

By the twenty-first century, the Internet had transformed communications and economic organization into an interconnected global network. Observers now think in terms of a North/South divide rather than an East/West one. People in the North had greater access to the communications network and for the most part enjoyed greater wealth than those in the South. But despite greater inequalities and lower Internet usage (compared with those in the North), Africa, the Middle East, and Latin America have seen an acceleration of Internet access. | **In what ways does this map indicate a closely connected world?**

Yorker of an antique poster in Australia to the trade in foreign currencies—are facilitating the immediate purchase of anything, anywhere, at any time, linking global economies in a way never before possible.

War, Peace, and Politics

Whether digitization will lead to a more peaceful world remains an open question. The evidence is mixed. There is the positive example from the relatively calm revolutions, mobilized in part by new communications, that overthrew communism across eastern Europe. In comparison with the civil war that erupted during the English Revolution, the Terror during the French Revolution, and the horrific civil war following the Russian Revolution of 1917, the events of 1989 were pacific—except for the civil war in Yugoslavia in the 1990s, where there was less Internet access and other communication infrastructure than elsewhere. In 2011, governments were overturned relatively peacefully in Tunisia and Egypt because Facebook and other electronic media brought protesters together with a common purpose, using communication to coordinate change rather than having change accompanied by escalating expressions of public violence. Evidence from the recent past gives hope that an era of even more instantaneous news feeds and digital communications will ease tensions, advance democracy, and make violence less likely.

There is much counterevidence, however. Digital media has also been used to attract people to terrorism, although the 2011 assassination of al-Qaeda leader Osama bin Laden and others in his circle may diminish this threat. Nonetheless, digital anonymity seems to invite ever more violent rhetoric. As one Western teenager put it: "I've written an e-mail to one of my friends saying so many things that I wouldn't really say to her face because I'd feel bad saying it to her face. So, when it's . . . an e-mail you just feel less guilty." On a more macro scale, this kind of anonymity—and the ability to reach thousands or even millions of people with a single click—can have serious implications. Violent or at least highly hostile messages appear regularly in response to online news items, while much violent behavior has been previewed in warnings on Web sites and elsewhere from young and older perpetrators.

Questions also arise about the Digital Age and the evolution of politics. It has become apparent around the world that digitization has altered politics, bringing in young people—especially those who were born digital. Whereas the selection of political leaders once took place among a select few in England or France, followed by mass campaigning by train and increasingly in the print media, today politics appears to be in the process of transformation. Digital media played a significant role in twenty-first-century political campaigns in Ukraine and other parts of eastern Europe, elections in the United States, and reform movements in the Middle East—to name a few. Protests are launched, supporters meet in chat forums, speeches are livestreamed, and money is raised via the Internet, shaping public opinion on a near constant basis and uniting ordinary people across nations and around the world.

Culture and Intellectual Creativity

Simultaneously, our culture itself has become digitized. Digitization has allowed cultural products such as film, music, art, and sports to travel the world with unprecedented speed, uniting the world's cultures and perhaps homogenizing them. At the same time, more people than ever before have access to these products, which can brighten life and advance knowledge. The products themselves have also been reworked by digitization, in ways both positive and negative: digital enhancements to music, for example, can transform mediocre musicians into global sensations. Superhuman effects in films and other media have become the norm, while video games occupy the time of people globally. Indeed, the highly violent content of video games is designed to be attractive mostly to boys and men, maintaining distinct sex roles in culture. Superstar cultural performers such as athletes, actors, and pop musicians flourish as our entertainers, but digitization has magnified their global celebrity status and thus increased the wage gap between them and middle-range performers as well as ordinary people.

The Digital Age has not eclipsed values, however. Although some have proclaimed an end to centuries of faith in progress and reason after the orgy of violence in the twentieth century and the genocide that continues to plague parts of the world, users of digital media have worked within the modern Western traditions of critical thinking, reevaluation, and problem solving. Digital media, and their enabling of widespread information sharing and fact checking, have allowed individuals and organizations to spread awareness of the daunting problems of contemporary life—population explosion, scarce resources, North–South inequities, global pollution, ethnic hatred, and global terrorism—which demand, more than ever, the exercise of humane values and rational thought. Yet through digitization we have become ever more aware that attempts at rational decision making fall short because of the issue of unintended consequences—that is, one cannot know in advance the consequences of an act. Who would have predicted, for example, the human misery and rising criminality resulting initially from the fall of communism across eastern Europe?

The West in the Digital World

Indeed, it is during the Digital Age that we have been made aware of the paradoxes in the momentous events around us. The collapse of communism signaled the eclipse of an ideology that was perhaps noble in its theory of making life better for the average person but deadly in practice. Events in South Africa and Northern Ireland have indicated that certain long-feuding groups can rationally put aside decades of bloodshed and work toward peace; in contrast, those reformers rationally seeking improved conditions by bringing down Soviet and Yugoslav communism unleashed bloodshed, sickness, unprecedented corruption, assassinations, and even genocide. The globalization ushered in by both the Digital Age and the Soviet collapse has unexpectedly brought denationalization to many regions of the world.

What, then, will become of Western traditions in an increasingly digitized world? A 2010 poll suggested that the places where the Digital Age has settled in the fastest have the *lowest* level of optimism about the future: only 31 percent of Britons, 30 percent of Americans, and 26 percent of French citizens believe that their nations are moving in the right direction and are content with their lot. In contrast, 87 percent of Chinese, 50 percent of Brazilians, and 45 percent of Indians have higher expectations for the future of their country.[1] Despite relative discontent among Europeans and Americans, Western traditions of democracy, human rights, and economic well-being still have much to offer. Although these were initially intended for a limited number of people—white men in powerful Western nations—global debates about their value and relevance are more widespread than ever, thanks in large part to digitization. The nation-state, which protected those values for the privileged and denied them to many others, is another legacy of the West that is being rethought in an age of transnationalism and instant communication. Migrants, for example, demand the dignity of national citizenship, but opponents of immigration often use the Internet to resist those demands. Moreover, it is often supranational organizations, rather than the nation-state, that have advocated for the expansion of citizenship, prosperity, and humane values in electronic forums and political activism.

At the same time, the West faces questions of its own unity and cultural identity—an identity that more than ever includes people from Asia, Africa, and the Americas—areas far from Europe, the traditional center of the West. Will the Digital Age help resolve the tensions and problems brought on by the West's greater complexity? Throughout history, non-Westerners of all kinds have challenged, criticized, refashioned, and made enormous contributions to Western culture; they have also served the West's citizens as slaves, servants, and menial workers. One of the greatest challenges to the West and the world in this global millennium is to determine how diverse peoples and cultures can live together on terms that are fair for everyone. We hope that the growing capacities of the Digital Age will provide answers. As we saw in the final chapter of this book, supranational organizations, both governmental and nongovernmental, have attempted to meet the challenges created by increased globalism, but the long-term effects of their efforts to achieve such benefits as human rights are not yet known.

The consequences of increasing globalization are still being determined. While the Internet and migration suggest that people will and often do have empathy for one another worldwide, militants—using the most advanced technology to build global networks—have unleashed unprecedented terrorism on the world in an attempt to push back global forces. Even as globalization has raised standards of living and education in many parts of the world, in other areas—such as poorer regions in Africa and Asia—people face disease and the dramatic social and economic deterioration associated with the global age. Rational results of planning and inexplicable consequences coexist in our present, global, digitized world.

Conclusion

A final challenge to the West involves the inventive human spirit. Over the past five hundred years, the West has benefited from its scientific and technological advances and perhaps never more so than

[1]Pew Research Council, quoted in *The Economist*, December 18, 2010, 13.

in the Digital Age. Longevity and improved material well-being have spread to many places, and in the past century, communication and information technology have brought people closer to one another than ever before. However, through the use of technology, the period from the last century to the present one has also become the bloodiest era in human history—and one during which the use of technology has threatened, and still threatens, the future of the earth as a home for the human race. Technology has facilitated war, genocide, terrorism, and environmental deterioration, all of which pose great challenges to the West and to the world. The use of digital media to promote violent causes, inflame others, and network with and recruit new followers has made some of these challenges even more significant. Yet digitization has simultaneously made us more aware than ever of the dangers we face. The making of the West has been a constantly inventive undertaking, but also a deadly one. The question is, How will the human race adapt to the creativity the Digital Age has unleashed? How will the West and the world manage both the promises and the challenges of Digital Age technology to protect the human race in the years ahead?

Appendix

Useful Facts and Figures

Prominent Roman Emperors A-1
Prominent Byzantine Emperors A-2
Prominent Popes A-3
The Carolingian Dynasty A-3
German Kings Crowned Emperor A-3
Rulers of France A-4
Monarchs of England and Great Britain A-4
Prime Ministers of Great Britain A-5
Rulers of Prussia and Germany A-6
Rulers of Austria and Austria-Hungary A-6
Leaders of Post–World War II Germany A-6
Rulers of Russia, the USSR, and the Russian Federation A-7
Rulers of Spain A-7
Rulers of Italy A-7
Secretaries-General of the United Nations A-8
United States Presidential Administrations A-8
Major Wars of the Modern Era A-8

Prominent Roman Emperors

Julio-Claudians

27 B.C.E.–14 C.E.	Augustus
14–37	Tiberius
37–41	Gaius (Caligula)
41–54	Claudius
54–68	Nero

Flavian Dynasty

69–79	Vespasian
79–81	Titus
81–96	Domitian

Golden Age Emperors

96–98	Nerva
98–117	Trajan
117–138	Hadrian
138–161	Antoninus Pius
161–180	Marcus Aurelius

Severan Emperors

193–211	Septimius Severus
211–217	Antoninus (Caracalla)
217–218	Macrinus
222–235	Severus Alexander

Period of Instability

235–238	Maximinus Thrax
238–244	Gordian III
244–249	Philip the Arab
249–251	Decius
251–253	Trebonianus Gallus
253–260	Valerian
270–275	Aurelian
275–276	Tacitus
276–282	Probus
283–285	Carinus

Dominate

284–305	Diocletian
306	Constantius
306–337	Constantine I
337–340	Constantine II
337–350	Constans I
337–361	Constantius II
361–363	Julian
363–364	Jovian
364–375	Valentinian I
364–378	Valens
367–383	Gratian
375–392	Valentinian II
378–395	Theodosius I (the Great)

The Western Empire

395–423	Honorius
406–407	Marcus
407–411	Constantine III
409–411	Maximus
411–413	Jovinus
412–413	Sebastianus
423–425	Johannes
425–455	Valentinian III
455–456	Avitus
457–461	Majorian
461–465	Libius Severus
467–472	Anthemius
473–474	Glycerius
474–475	Julius Nepos
475–476	Romulus Augustulus

Prominent Byzantine Emperors

Dynasty of Theodosius

395–408	Arcadius
408–450	Theodosius II
450–457	Marcian

Dynasty of Leo

457–474	Leo I
474	Leo II
474–491	Zeno
475–476	Basiliscus
484–488	Leontius
491–518	Anastasius

Dynasty of Justinian

518–527	Justin
527–565	Justinian I
565–578	Justin II
578–582	Tiberius II
578–582	Tiberius II (I) Constantine
582–602	Maurice
602–610	Phocas

Dynasty of Heraclius

610–641	Heraclius
641	Heraclonas
641	Constantine III
641–668	Constans II
646–647	Gregory
649–653	Olympius
669	Mezezius
668–685	Constantine IV
685–695	Justinian II (banished)
695–698	Leontius
698–705	Tiberius III (II)
705–711	Justinian II (restored)
711–713	Bardanes
713–716	Anastasius II
716–717	Theodosius III

Isaurian Dynasty

717–741	Leo III
741–775	Constantine V Copronymus
775–780	Leo IV
780–797	Constantine VI
797–802	Irene
802–811	Nicephorus I
811	Strauracius
811–813	Michael I
813–820	Leo V

Phrygian Dynasty

820–829	Michael II
821–823	Thomas
829–842	Theophilus
842–867	Michael III

Macedonian Dynasty

867–886	Basil I
869–879	Constantine
887–912	Leo VI
912–913	Alexander
913–959	Constantine VII Porphrogenitos
920–944	Romanus I Lecapenus
921–931	Christopher
924–945	Stephen
959–963	Romanus II
963–969	Nicephorus II Phocas
976–1025	Basil II
1025–1028	Constantine VIII (IX) alone
1028–1034	Romanus III Argyrus
1034–1041	Michael IV the Paphlagonian
1041–1042	Michael V Calaphates
1042	Zoe and Theodora
1042–1055	Constantine IX Monomachus
1055–1056	Theodora alone
1056–1057	Michael VI Stratioticus

Prelude to the Comnenian Dynasty

1057–1059	Isaac I Comnenos
1059–1067	Constantine X (IX) Ducas
1068–1071	Romanus IV Diogenes
1071–1078	Michael VII Ducas
1078–1081	Nicephorus III Botaniates
1080–1081	Nicephorus Melissenus

Comnenian Dynasty

1081–1118	Alexius I
1118–1143	John II
1143–1180	Manuel I
1180–1183	Alexius II
1183–1185	Andronieus I
1183–1191	Isaac, Emperor of Cyprus

Dynasty of the Angeli

1185–1195	Isaac II
1195–1203	Alexius III
1203–1204	Isaac II (restored) with Alexius IV
1204	Alexius V Ducas Murtzuphlus

Lascarid Dynasty in Nicaea

1204–1222	Theodore I Lascaris
1222–1254	John III Ducas Vatatzes
1254–1258	Theodore II Lascaris
1258–1261	John IV Lascaris

Dynasty of the Paleologi

1259–1289	Michael VIII Paleologus
1282–1328	Andronicus II
1328–1341	Andronicus III
1341–1391	John V
1347–1354	John VI Cantancuzenus
1376–1379	Andronicus IV
1379–1391	John V (restored)
1390	John VII
1391–1425	Manuel II
1425–1448	John VIII
1449–1453	Constantine XI (XIII) Dragases

Prominent Popes

314–335	Sylvester
440–461	Leo I
590–604	Gregory I (the Great)
687–701	Sergius I
741–752	Zachary
858–867	Nicholas I
1049–1054	Leo IX
1059–1061	Nicholas II
1073–1085	Gregory VII
1088–1099	Urban II
1099–1118	Paschal II
1159–1181	Alexander III
1198–1216	Innocent III
1227–1241	Gregory IX
1243–1254	Innocent IV
1294–1303	Boniface VIII
1316–1334	John XXII
1447–1455	Nicholas V
1458–1464	Pius II
1492–1503	Alexander VI
1503–1513	Julius II
1513–1521	Leo X
1534–1549	Paul III
1555–1559	Paul IV
1585–1590	Sixtus V
1623–1644	Urban VIII
1831–1846	Gregory XVI
1846–1878	Pius IX
1878–1903	Leo XIII
1903–1914	Pius X
1914–1922	Benedict XV
1922–1939	Pius XI
1939–1958	Pius XII
1958–1963	John XXIII
1963–1978	Paul VI
1978	John Paul I
1978–2005	John Paul II
2005–	Benedict XVI

The Carolingian Dynasty

687–714	Pepin of Heristal, Mayor of the Palace
715–741	Charles Martel, Mayor of the Palace
741–751	Pepin III, Mayor of the Palace
751–768	Pepin III, King
768–814	Charlemagne, King
800–814	Charlemagne, Emperor
814–840	Louis the Pious

West Francia

840–877	Charles the Bald, King
875–877	Charles the Bald, Emperor
877–879	Louis II, King
879–882	Louis III, King
879–884	Carloman, King

Middle Kingdoms

840–855	Lothair, Emperor
855–875	Louis (Italy), Emperor
855–863	Charles (Provence), King
855–869	Lothair II (Lorraine), King

East Francia

840–876	Ludwig, King
876–880	Carloman, King
876–882	Ludwig, King
876–887	Charles the Fat, Emperor

German Kings Crowned Emperor

Saxon Dynasty

962–973	Otto I
973–983	Otto II
983–1002	Otto III
1002–1024	Henry II

Franconian Dynasty

1024–1039	Conrad II
1039–1056	Henry III
1056–1106	Henry IV
1106–1125	Henry V
1125–1137	Lothair II (Saxony)

Hohenstaufen Dynasty

1138–1152	Conrad III
1152–1190	Frederick I (Barbarossa)
1190–1197	Henry VI
1198–1208	Philip of Swabia
1198–1215	Otto IV (Welf)
1220–1250	Frederick II
1250–1254	Conrad IV

Interregnum, 1254–1273: Emperors from Various Dynasties

1273–1291	Rudolf I (Habsburg)
1292–1298	Adolf (Nassau)
1298–1308	Albert I (Habsburg)
1308–1313	Henry VII (Luxemburg)
1314–1347	Ludwig IV (Wittelsbach)
1347–1378	Charles IV (Luxemburg)
1378–1400	Wenceslas (Luxemburg)
1400–1410	Rupert (Wittelsbach)
1410–1437	Sigismund (Luxemburg)

Habsburg Dynasty

1438–1439	Albert II
1440–1493	Frederick III
1493–1519	Maximilian I
1519–1556	Charles V
1556–1564	Ferdinand I
1564–1576	Maximilian II
1576–1612	Rudolf II
1612–1619	Matthias
1619–1637	Ferdinand II
1637–1657	Ferdinand III
1658–1705	Leopold I
1705–1711	Joseph I
1711–1740	Charles VI
1742–1745	Charles VII (not a Habsburg)
1745–1765	Francis I
1765–1790	Joseph II
1790–1792	Leopold II
1792–1806	Francis II

Rulers of France

Capetian Dynasty

987–996	Hugh Capet
996–1031	Robert II
1031–1060	Henry I
1060–1108	Philip I
1108–1137	Louis VI
1137–1180	Louis VII
1180–1223	Philip II (Augustus)
1223–1226	Louis VIII
1226–1270	Louis IX (St. Louis)
1270–1285	Philip III
1285–1314	Philip IV
1314–1316	Louis X
1316–1322	Philip V
1322–1328	Charles IV

Valois Dynasty

1328–1350	Philip VI
1350–1364	John
1364–1380	Charles V
1380–1422	Charles VI
1422–1461	Charles VII
1461–1483	Louis XI
1483–1498	Charles VIII
1498–1515	Louis XII
1515–1547	Francis I
1547–1559	Henry II
1559–1560	Francis II
1560–1574	Charles IX
1574–1589	Henry III

Bourbon Dynasty

1589–1610	Henry IV
1610–1643	Louis XIII
1643–1715	Louis XIV
1715–1774	Louis XV
1774–1792	Louis XVI

After 1792

1792–1799	First Republic
1799–1804	Napoleon Bonaparte, First Consul
1804–1814	Napoleon I, Emperor
1814–1824	Louis XVIII (Bourbon Dynasty)
1824–1830	Charles X (Bourbon Dynasty)
1830–1848	Louis Philippe
1848–1852	Second Republic
1852–1870	Napoleon III, Emperor
1870–1940	Third Republic
1940–1944	Vichy government, Pétain regime
1944–1946	Provisional government
1946–1958	Fourth Republic
1958–	Fifth Republic

Monarchs of England and Great Britain

Anglo-Saxon Monarchs

829–839	Egbert
839–858	Ethelwulf
858–860	Ethelbald
860–866	Ethelbert
866–871	Ethelred I
871–899	Alfred the Great
899–924	Edward the Elder
924–939	Ethelstan
939–946	Edmund I
946–955	Edred
955–959	Edwy
959–975	Edgar
975–978	Edward the Martyr
978–1016	Ethelred the Unready
1016–1035	Canute (Danish nationality)
1035–1040	Harold I
1040–1042	Hardicanute
1042–1066	Edward the Confessor
1066	Harold II

Norman Monarchs

1066–1087	William I (the Conqueror)
1087–1100	William II
1100–1135	Henry I

House of Blois

1135–1154	Stephen

House of Plantagenet

1154–1189	Henry II
1189–1199	Richard I
1199–1216	John
1216–1272	Henry III
1272–1307	Edward I
1307–1327	Edward II
1327–1377	Edward III
1377–1399	Richard II

House of Lancaster

1399–1413	Henry IV
1413–1422	Henry V
1422–1461	Henry VI

House of York

1461–1483	Edward IV
1483	Edward V
1483–1485	Richard III

House of Tudor

1485–1509	Henry VII
1509–1547	Henry VIII
1547–1553	Edward VI
1553–1558	Mary
1558–1603	Elizabeth I

House of Stuart

1603–1625	James I
1625–1649	Charles I

Commonwealth and Protectorate (1649–1660)

1653–1658	Oliver Cromwell
1658–1659	Richard Cromwell

House of Stuart (Restored)

1660–1685	Charles II
1685–1688	James II
1689–1694	William III and Mary II
1694–1702	William III (alone)
1702–1714	Anne

House of Hanover

1714–1727	George I
1727–1760	George II
1760–1820	George III
1820–1830	George IV
1830–1837	William IV
1837–1901	Victoria

House of Saxe-Coburg-Gotha

1901–1910	Edward VII

House of Windsor

1910–1936	George V
1936	Edward VIII
1936–1952	George VI
1952–	Elizabeth II

Prime Ministers of Great Britain

Term	Prime Minister	Government
1721–1742	Sir Robert Walpole	Whig
1742–1743	Spencer Compton, Earl of Wilmington	Whig
1743–1754	Henry Pelham	Whig
1754–1756	Thomas Pelham-Holles, Duke of Newcastle	Whig
1756–1757	William Cavendish, Duke of Devonshire	Whig
1757–1761	William Pitt (the Elder), Earl of Chatham	Whig
1761–1762	Thomas Pelham-Holles, Duke of Newcastle	Whig
1762–1763	John Stuart, Earl of Bute	Tory
1763–1765	George Grenville	Whig
1765–1766	Charles Watson-Wentworth, Marquess of Rockingham	Whig
1766–1768	William Pitt, Earl of Chatham (the Elder)	Whig
1768–1770	Augustus Henry Fitzroy, Duke of Grafton	Whig
1770–1782	Frederick North (Lord North)	Tory
1782	Charles Watson-Wentworth, Marquess of Rockingham	Whig
1782–1783	William Petty FitzMaurice, Earl of Shelburn	Whig
1783	William Henry Cavendish Bentinck, Duke of Portland	Whig
1783–1801	William Pitt (the Younger)	Tory
1801–1804	Henry Addington	Tory
1804–1806	William Pitt (the Younger)	Tory
1806–1807	William Wyndham Grenville (Baron Grenville)	Whig
1807–1809	William Henry Cavendish Bentinck, Duke of Portland	Tory
1809–1812	Spencer Perceval	Tory
1812–1827	Robert Banks Jenkinson, Earl of Liverpool	Tory
1827	George Canning	Tory
1827–1828	Frederick John Robinson (Viscount Goderich)	Tory
1828–1830	Arthur Wellesley, Duke of Wellington	Tory
1830–1834	Charles Grey (Earl Grey)	Whig
1834	William Lamb, Viscount Melbourne	Whig
1834–1835	Sir Robert Peel	Tory
1835–1841	William Lamb, Viscount Melbourne	Whig
1841–1846	Sir Robert Peel	Tory
1846–1852	John Russell (Lord)	Whig
1852	Edward Geoffrey–Smith Stanley Derby, Earl of Derby	Whig
1852–1855	George Hamilton Gordon Aberdeen, Earl of Aberdeen	Peelite
1855–1858	Henry John Temple Palmerston, Viscount Palmerston	Tory
1858–1859	Edward Geoffrey–Smith Stanley Derby, Earl of Derby	Whig
1859–1865	Henry John Temple Palmerston, Viscount Palmerston	Tory
1865–1866	John Russell (Earl)	Liberal
1866–1868	Edward Geoffrey–Smith Stanley Derby, Earl of Derby	Tory
1868	Benjamin Disraeli, Earl of Beaconfield	Conservative
1868–1874	William Ewart Gladstone	Liberal
1874–1880	Benjamin Disraeli, Earl of Beaconfield	Conservative
1880–1885	William Ewart Gladstone	Liberal
1885–1886	Robert Arthur Talbot, Marquess of Salisbury	Conservative
1886	William Ewart Gladstone	Liberal
1886–1892	Robert Arthur Talbot, Marquess of Salisbury	Conservative
1892–1894	William Ewart Gladstone	Liberal
1894–1895	Archibald Philip–Primrose Rosebery, Earl of Rosebery	Liberal
1895–1902	Robert Arthur Talbot, Marquess of Salisbury	Conservative
1902–1905	Arthur James Balfour, Earl of Balfour	Conservative
1905–1908	Sir Henry Campbell-Bannerman	Liberal
1908–1915	Herbert Henry Asquith	Liberal
1915–1916	Herbert Henry Asquith	Coalition
1916–1922	David Lloyd George, Earl Lloyd-George of Dwyfor	Coalition
1922–1923	Andrew Bonar Law	Conservative
1923–1924	Stanley Baldwin, Earl Baldwin of Bewdley	Conservative
1924	James Ramsay MacDonald	Labour
1924–1929	Stanley Baldwin, Earl Baldwin of Bewdley	Conservative
1929–1931	James Ramsay MacDonald	Labour
1931–1935	James Ramsay MacDonald	Coalition
1935–1937	Stanley Baldwin, Earl Baldwin of Bewdley	Coalition
1937–1940	Neville Chamberlain	Coalition
1940–1945	Winston Churchill	Coalition
1945	Winston Churchill	Conservative
1945–1951	Clement Attlee, Earl Attlee	Labour
1951–1955	Sir Winston Churchill	Conservative
1955–1957	Sir Anthony Eden, Earl of Avon	Conservative
1957–1963	Harold Macmillan, Earl of Stockton	Conservative
1963–1964	Sir Alec Frederick Douglas-Home, Lord Home of the Hirsel	Conservative
1964–1970	Harold Wilson, Lord Wilson of Rievaulx	Labour
1970–1974	Edward Heath	Conservative
1974–1976	Harold Wilson, Lord Wilson of Rievaulx	Labour
1976–1979	James Callaghan, Lord Callaghan of Cardiff	Labour
1979–1990	Margaret Thatcher (Baroness)	Conservative
1990–1997	John Major	Conservative
1997–2007	Tony Blair	Labour
2007–2010	Gordon Brown	Labour
2010–	David Cameron	Conservative

Rulers of Prussia and Germany

1701–1713	*Frederick I
1713–1740	*Frederick William I
1740–1786	*Frederick II (the Great)
1786–1797	*Frederick William II
1797–1840	*Frederick William III
1840–1861	*Frederick William IV
1861–1888	*William I (German emperor after 1871)
1888	Frederick III
1888–1918	*William II
1918–1933	Weimar Republic
1933–1945	Third Reich (Nazi dictatorship under Adolf Hitler)
1945–1952	Allied occupation
1949–1990	Division of Federal Republic of Germany in west and German Democratic Republic in east
1990–	Federal Republic of Germany (reunited)

*King of Prussia.

Rulers of Austria and Austria-Hungary

1493–1519	*Maximilian I (Archduke)
1519–1556	*Charles V
1556–1564	*Ferdinand I
1564–1576	*Maximilian II
1576–1612	*Rudolf II
1612–1619	*Matthias
1619–1637	*Ferdinand II
1637–1657	*Ferdinand III
1658–1705	*Leopold I
1705–1711	*Joseph I
1711–1740	*Charles VI
1740–1780	Maria Theresa
1780–1790	*Joseph II
1790–1792	*Leopold II
1792–1835	*Francis II (emperor of Austria as Francis I after 1804)
1835–1848	Ferdinand I
1848–1916	Francis Joseph (after 1867 emperor of Austria and king of Hungary)
1916–1918	Charles I (emperor of Austria and king of Hungary)
1918–1938	Republic of Austria (dictatorship after 1934)
1945–1956	Republic restored, under Allied occupation
1956–	Free Republic

*Also bore title of Holy Roman Emperor.

Leaders of Post–World War II Germany

West Germany (Federal Republic of Germany), 1949–1990

Years	*Chancellor*	*Party*
1949–1963	Konrad Adenauer	Christian Democratic Union (CDU)
1963–1966	Ludwig Erhard	Christian Democratic Union (CDU)
1966–1969	Kurt Georg Kiesinger	Christian Democratic Union (CDU)
1969–1974	Willy Brandt	Social Democratic Party (SPD)
1974–1982	Helmut Schmidt	Social Democratic Party (SPD)
1982–1990	Helmut Kohl	Christian Democratic Union (CDU)

East Germany (German Democratic Republic), 1949–1990

Years	*Communist Party Leader*
1946–1971	Walter Ulbricht
1971–1989	Erich Honecker
1989–1990	Egon Krenz

Federal Republic of Germany (reunited), 1990–

Years	*Chancellor*	*Party*
1990–1998	Helmut Kohl	Christian Democratic Union (CDU)
1998–2005	Gerhard Schroeder	Social Democratic Party (SPD)
2005–	Angela Merkel	Christian Democratic Union (CDU)

Rulers of Russia, the USSR, and the Russian Federation

c. 980–1015	Vladimir
1019–1054	Yaroslav the Wise
1176–1212	Vsevolod III
1462–1505	Ivan III
1505–1553	Vasily III
1553–1584	Ivan IV
1584–1598	Theodore I
1598–1605	Boris Godunov
1605	Theodore II
1606–1610	Vasily IV
1613–1645	Michael
1645–1676	Alexius
1676–1682	Theodore III
1682–1689	Ivan V and Peter I
1689–1725	Peter I (the Great)
1725–1727	Catherine I
1727–1730	Peter II
1730–1740	Anna
1740–1741	Ivan VI
1741–1762	Elizabeth
1762	Peter III
1762–1796	Catherine II (the Great)
1796–1801	Paul
1801–1825	Alexander I
1825–1855	Nicholas I
1855–1881	Alexander II
1881–1894	Alexander III
1894–1917	Nicholas II

Union of Soviet Socialist Republics (USSR)*

1917–1924	Vladimir Ilyich Lenin
1924–1953	Joseph Stalin
1953–1964	Nikita Khrushchev
1964–1982	Leonid Brezhnev
1982–1984	Yuri Andropov
1984–1985	Konstantin Chernenko
1985–1991	Mikhail Gorbachev

Russian Federation

1991–1999	Boris Yeltsin
1999–2008	Vladimir Putin
2008–	Dmitry Medvedev

*USSR established in 1922.

Rulers of Spain

1479–1504	Ferdinand and Isabella
1504–1506	Ferdinand and Philip I
1506–1516	Ferdinand and Charles I
1516–1556	Charles I (Holy Roman Emperor Charles V)
1556–1598	Philip II
1598–1621	Philip III
1621–1665	Philip IV
1665–1700	Charles II
1700–1746	Philip V
1746–1759	Ferdinand VI
1759–1788	Charles III
1788–1808	Charles IV
1808	Ferdinand VII
1808–1813	Joseph Bonaparte
1814–1833	Ferdinand VII (restored)
1833–1868	Isabella II
1868–1870	Republic
1870–1873	Amadeo
1873–1874	Republic
1874–1885	Alfonso XII
1886–1931	Alfonso XIII
1931–1939	Republic
1939–1975	Fascist dictatorship under Francisco Franco
1975–	Juan Carlos I

Rulers of Italy

1861–1878	Victor Emmanuel II
1878–1900	Humbert I
1900–1946	Victor Emmanuel III
1922–1943	Fascist dictatorship under Benito Mussolini (maintained in northern Italy until 1945)
1946 (May 9–June 13)	Humbert II
1946–	Republic

Secretaries-General of the United Nations

Years	Secretary-General	Nationality
1946–1952	Trygve Lie	Norway
1953–1961	Dag Hammarskjöld	Sweden
1961–1971	U Thant	Myanmar
1972–1981	Kurt Waldheim	Austria
1982–1991	Javier Pérez de Cuéllar	Peru
1992–1996	Boutros Boutros-Ghali	Egypt
1997–2006	Kofi A. Annan	Ghana
2007–	Ban Kimoon	South Korea

United States Presidential Administrations

Term(s)	President	Political Party
1789–1797	George Washington	No party designation
1797–1801	John Adams	Federalist
1801–1809	Thomas Jefferson	Democratic-Republican
1809–1817	James Madison	Democratic-Republican
1817–1825	James Monroe	Democratic-Republican
1825–1829	John Quincy Adams	Democratic-Republican
1829–1837	Andrew Jackson	Democratic
1837–1841	Martin Van Buren	Democratic
1841	William H. Harrison	Whig
1841–1845	John Tyler	Whig
1845–1849	James K. Polk	Democratic
1849–1850	Zachary Taylor	Whig
1850–1853	Millard Filmore	Whig
1853–1857	Franklin Pierce	Democratic
1857–1861	James Buchanan	Democratic
1861–1865	Abraham Lincoln	Republican
1865–1869	Andrew Johnson	Republican
1869–1877	Ulysses S. Grant	Republican
1877–1881	Rutherford B. Hayes	Republican
1881	James A. Garfield	Republican
1881–1885	Chester A. Arthur	Republican
1885–1889	Grover Cleveland	Democratic
1889–1893	Benjamin Harrison	Republican
1893–1897	Grover Cleveland	Democratic
1897–1901	William McKinley	Republican
1901–1909	Theodore Roosevelt	Republican
1909–1913	William H. Taft	Republican
1913–1921	Woodrow Wilson	Democratic
1921–1923	Warren G. Harding	Republican
1923–1929	Calvin Coolidge	Republican
1929–1933	Herbert C. Hoover	Republican
1933–1945	Franklin D. Roosevelt	Democratic
1945–1953	Harry S. Truman	Democratic
1953–1961	Dwight D. Eisenhower	Republican
1961–1963	John F. Kennedy	Democratic
1963–1969	Lyndon B. Johnson	Democratic
1969–1974	Richard M. Nixon	Republican
1974–1977	Gerald R. Ford	Republican
1977–1981	Jimmy Carter	Democratic
1981–1989	Ronald W. Reagan	Republican
1989–1993	George H. W. Bush	Republican
1993–2001	William J. Clinton	Democratic
2001–2009	George W. Bush	Republican
2009–	Barack Obama	Democratic

Major Wars of the Modern Era

1546–1555	German Wars of Religion
1526–1571	Ottoman wars
1562–1598	French Wars of Religion
1566–1609, 1621–1648	Revolt of the Netherlands
1618–1648	Thirty Years' War
1642–1648	English Civil War
1652–1678	Anglo-Dutch Wars
1667–1697	Wars of Louis XIV
1683–1697	Ottoman wars
1689–1697	War of the League of Augsburg
1702–1714	War of Spanish Succession
1702–1721	Great Northern War
1714–1718	Ottoman wars
1740–1748	War of Austrian Succession
1756–1763	Seven Years' War
1775–1781	American Revolution
1796–1815	Napoleonic wars
1846–1848	Mexican-American War
1853–1856	Crimean War
1861–1865	United States Civil War
1870–1871	Franco-Prussian War
1894–1895	Sino-Japanese War
1898	Spanish-American War
1904–1905	Russo-Japanese War
1914–1918	World War I
1939–1945	World War II
1946–1975	Vietnam wars
1950–1953	Korean War
1990–1991	Persian Gulf War
1991–1997	Civil War in the former Yugoslavia
2001–	War in Afghanistan
2003–	Iraq War

Glossary of Key Terms and People

This glossary contains definitions of terms and people that are central to your understanding of the material covered in this textbook. Each term or person in the glossary is in boldface in the text when it is first defined, then listed again in the corresponding Chapter Review section to signal its importance. We have also included the page number on which the full discussion of the term or person appears so that you can easily locate the complete explanation to strengthen your historical vocabulary.

For words or names not defined here, two additional resources may be useful: the index, which will direct you to many more topics discussed in the text, and a good dictionary.

abolitionists (592): Advocates of the abolition of the slave trade and of slavery.

Alexander II (725): Russian tsar (r. 1855–1881) who initiated the age of Great Reforms and emancipated the serfs in 1861.

anarchism (746): The belief that people should not have government; it was popular among some peasants and workers in the last half of the nineteenth century and the first decades of the twentieth.

appeasement (894): Making concessions in the face of grievances as a way of preventing conflict.

art nouveau (809): An early-twentieth-century artistic style in graphics, fashion, and household design that featured flowing, sinuous lines, borrowed in large part from Asian art.

battle of Waterloo (665): The final battle lost by Napoleon; it took place near Brussels on June 18, 1815, and led to the deposed emperor's final exile.

Beauvoir, Simone de (938): Author of *The Second Sex* (1949), a globally influential work that created an interpretation of women's age-old inferior status from existentialist philosophy.

Beethoven, Ludwig van (674): The German composer (1770–1827) who helped set the direction of musical romanticism; his music used recurring and evolving themes to convey the impression of natural growth.

bin Laden, Osama (1003): Wealthy leader of the militant Islamic group al-Qaeda, which executed terrorist plots, including the September 11, 2001, attacks on the United States, to end the presence of U.S. forces in his home country, Saudia Arabia.

Bismarck, Otto von (732): 1815–1898. Leading Prussian politician and German chancellor who waged war in order to create a united German Empire, which was established in 1871.

Blitzkrieg (896): Literally, "lightning war"; a strategy for the conduct of war (used by the Germans in World War II) in which motorized firepower quickly and overwhelmingly attacks the enemy, leaving it unable to resist psychologically or militarily.

Bolívar, Simón (677): 1783–1830. The Venezuelan-born, European-educated aristocrat who became one of the leaders of the Latin American independence movement in the 1820s. Bolivia is named after him.

Bolshevik Revolution (848): The overthrow of Russia's Provisional Government in the fall of 1917 by V. I. Lenin and his Bolshevik forces.

Bonaparte, Louis-Napoleon (711): 1808–1873. Nephew of Napoleon I; he was elected president of France in 1848, declared himself Emperor Napoleon III in 1852, and ruled until 1870.

Bonaparte, Napoleon (652): The French general who became First Consul in 1799 and emperor (Napoleon I) in 1804; after losing the battle of Waterloo in 1815, he was exiled to the island of St. Helena.

capital-intensive industry (772): A mid- to late-nineteenth-century development in industry that required great investments of money for machinery and infrastructure to make a profit.

Cavour, Camillo di (730): Prime minister (1852–1861) of the kingdom of Piedmont-Sardinia and architect of a united Italy.

Chaplin, Charlie (888): 1899–1977. Major entertainment leader, whose sympathetic portrayals of the common man and satires of Hitler helped preserve democratic values in the 1930s and 1940s.

Chartism (708): The British movement of supporters of the People's Charter (1838), which demanded universal manhood suffrage, vote by secret ballot, equal electoral districts, and other reforms.

Christian Democrats (924): Powerful center to center-right political parties that evolved in the late 1940s from former Catholic parties of the pre–World War II period.

Civil Code (657): The French legal code formulated by Napoleon in 1804; it ensured equal treatment under the law to all men and guaranteed religious liberty, but it curtailed many rights of women.

civil disobedience (877): The act of deliberately but peacefully breaking the law, a tactic used by Mohandas Gandhi in India and earlier by British suffragists to protest oppression and obtain political change.

cold war (914): The rivalry between the United States and the Soviet Union from 1945 to 1989 that led to massive growth in nuclear weapons on both sides.

communists (707): Those socialists who after 1840 (when the word was first used) advocated the abolition of private property in favor of communal, collective ownership.

Congress of Vienna (667): Face-to-face negotiations (1814–1815) between the great powers to settle the boundaries of European states and determine who would rule each nation after the defeat of Napoleon.

conservatism (670): A political doctrine that emerged after 1789 and took hold after 1815; it rejected much of the Enlightenment and the French Revolution, preferring monarchies over republics, tradition over revolution, and established religion over Enlightenment skepticism.

Continental System (662): The boycott of British goods in France and its satellites ordered by Napoleon in 1806; it had success but was later undermined by smuggling.

Corn Laws (705): Tariffs on grain in Great Britain that benefited landowners by preventing the import of cheap foreign grain; they were repealed by the British government in 1846.

Cuban missile crisis (944): The confrontation in 1962 between the United States and the USSR over Soviet installation of missile sites off the U.S. coast in Cuba.

cult of the offensive (838): A military strategy of constantly attacking the enemy that was believed to be the key to winning World War I but that brought great loss of life while failing to bring decisive victory.

Darwin, Charles (752): The English naturalist (1809–1882) who popularized the theory of evolution by means of natural selection and thereby challenged the biblical story of creation.

de-Christianization (634): During the French Revolution, the campaign of extremist republicans against organized churches and in favor of a belief system based on reason.

Declaration of the Rights of Man and Citizen (626): The preamble to the French constitution drafted in August 1789; it established the sovereignty of the nation and equal rights for citizens.

decolonization (930): The process — whether violent or peaceful — by which colonies gained their independence from the imperial powers after World War II.

deists (626): Those who believe in God but give him no active role in human affairs. Deists of the Enlightenment believed that God had designed the universe and set it in motion but no longer intervened in its functioning.

DNA (953): The genetic material that forms the basis of each cell; the discovery of its structure in 1952 revolutionized genetics, molecular biology, and other scientific and medical fields.

domesticity (700): An ideology prevailing in the nineteenth century that women should devote themselves to their families and the home.

Dual Alliance (790): A defensive alliance between Germany and Austria-Hungary created in 1879 as part of Bismarck's system of alliances to prevent or limit war. It was joined by Italy in 1882 as a third partner and then called the Triple Alliance.

dual monarchy (736): The shared power arrangement between the Habsburg Empire and Hungary after the Prussian defeat of the Austrian Empire in 1866–1867.

Duma (821): The Russian parliament set up in the aftermath of the outbreak of the Revolution of 1905.

Einstein, Albert (807): Scientist whose theory of relativity (1905) revolutionized modern physics and other fields of thought.

Eliot, George (748): The pen name of English novelist Mary Ann Evans (1819–1880), who described the harsh reality of many ordinary people's lives in her works.

Enabling Act (884): The legislation passed in 1933 suspending constitutional government for four years in order to meet the crisis in the German economy.

enlightened despots (605): Rulers — such as Catherine the Great of Russia, Frederick the Great of Prussia, and Joseph II of Austria — who tried to promote Enlightenment reforms without giving up their own supreme political power; also called enlightened absolutists.

Entente Cordiale (825): An alliance between Britain and France that began with an agreement in 1904 to honor colonial holdings.

Estates General (624): A body of deputies from the three estates, or orders, of France: the clergy (First Estate), the nobility (Second Estate), and everyone else (Third Estate).

ethnic cleansing (988) The mass murder — genocide — of people according to ethnicity or nationality; it can also include eliminating all traces of the murdered people's past. Examples include the post–World War I elimination of minorities in eastern and central Europe and the rape and murders that resulted from the breakup of Yugoslavia in the 1990s.

euro (995): The common currency in seventeen member states of the European Union (EU) and of EU institutions. It went into effect gradually, used first in business transactions in 1999 and entering public circulation in 2002.

European Economic Community (EEC or Common Market) (926): A consortium of six European countries established in 1957 to promote free trade and economic cooperation among its members; its membership and activities expanded over the years, and it later evolved into the European Union (EU).

European Union (EU) (995): Formerly the European Economic Community (EEC, or Common Market), and then the European Community (EC); formed in 1994 by the terms of the Maastricht Treaty. Its members have political ties through the European parliament as well as long-standing common economic, legal, and business mechanisms.

existentialism (937): A philosophy prominent after World War II developed primarily by Jean-Paul Sartre to stress the importance of action in the creation of an authentic self.

family allowance (886): Government funds given to families with children to boost the birthrate in democratic countries (e.g., Sweden during the Great Depression) and totalitarian ones alike.

fascism (867): A doctrine that emphasizes violence and glorifies the state over the people and their individual or civil rights; in Italy, the Fascist Party took hold in the 1920s as Mussolini consolidated power.

First Consul (653): The most important of the three consuls established by the French Constitution of 1800; the title, given to Napoleon Bonaparte, was taken from ancient Rome.

five-year plans (878): Centralized programs for economic development begun in 1929 by Joseph Stalin and copied by Adolf Hitler; these plans set production priorities and gave production targets for individual industries and agriculture.

Fourteen Points (846): U.S. president Woodrow Wilson's World War I peace proposal; based on settlement rather than on conquest, it encouraged the surrender of the Central Powers.

Franco, Francisco (893): 1892–1975. Right-wing general who in 1936 successfully overthrew the democratic republic in Spain and instituted a repressive dictatorship.

Freemasons (600): Members of Masonic lodges, where nobles and middle-class professionals (and even some artisans) shared interest in the Enlightenment and reform.

Freud, Sigmund (803): Viennese medical doctor and founder, in the late nineteenth century, of psychoanalysis, a theory of mental processes and problems and a method of treating them.

Gladstone, William (786): 1809–1898. Liberal politician and prime minister of Great Britain who innovated in popular campaigning and who criticized British imperialism.

glasnost (977): Literally, "openness" or "publicity"; a policy instituted in the 1980s by Soviet premier Mikhail Gorbachev calling for greater openness in speech and in thinking, which translated to the reduction of censorship in publishing, radio, television, and other media.

global warming (1000): An increase in the temperature of the earth's lower atmosphere resulting from a buildup of chemical emissions.

globalization (986): The interconnection of labor, capital, ideas, services, and goods around the world. Although globalization has existed for hundreds of years, the late twentieth and early twenty-first centuries are seen as more global because of the speed with which people, goods, and ideas travel the world.

Gorbachev, Mikhail (976): Leader of the Soviet Union (1985–1991) who instituted reforms such as glasnost and perestroika, thereby contributing to the collapse of Communist rule in the Soviet bloc and the USSR.

Great Fear (626): The term used by historians to describe the French rural panic of 1789, which led to peasant attacks on aristocrats or on seigneurial records of peasants' dues.

Green Party (1000): A political party first formed in West Germany in 1979 to bring about environmentally sound policies. It spread across Europe and around the world thereafter.

Hitler, Adolf (881): 1899–1945. Chancellor of Germany (1933–1945) who, with considerable backing, overturned democratic government, created the Third Reich, persecuted millions, and ultimately led Germany and the world into World War II.

home rule (787): The right to an independent parliament demanded by the Irish and resisted by the British from the second half of the nineteenth century on.

ideology (686): A word coined during the French Revolution to refer to a coherent set of beliefs about the way the social and political order should be organized.

imperialism (783): European dominance of the non-West through economic exploitation and political rule; the word (as distinct from *colonialism*, which usually implied establishment of settler colonies, often with slavery) was coined in the mid-nineteenth century.

impressionism (783): A mid- to late-nineteenth-century artistic style that captured the sensation of light in images, derived from Japanese influences and in opposition to the realism of photographs.

in vitro fertilization (954): A process developed in the 1970s by which human eggs are fertilized with sperm outside the body and then implanted in a woman's uterus.

Industrial Revolution (686): The transformation of life in the Western world over several decades in the late eighteenth and early nineteenth centuries as a result of the introduction of steam-driven machinery, large factories, and a new working class.

Jacobin Club (630): A French political club formed in 1789 that inspired the formation of a national network whose members dominated the revolutionary government during the Terror.

Kennedy, John Fitzgerald (943): U.S. president (1961–1963) who faced off with Soviet leader Nikita Khrushchev in the Cuban missile crisis.

Khrushchev, Nikita (929): Leader of the USSR from c. 1955 until his dismissal in 1964; known for his speech denouncing Stalin, creation of the "thaw," and participation in the Cuban missile crisis.

Kollontai, Aleksandra (866): A Russian activist and minister of public welfare in the Bolshevik government who promoted social programs such as birth control and day care for children of working parents.

Kulturkampf (751): Literally, "culture war"; a term used in the 1870s by German chancellor Otto von Bismarck to describe his fight to weaken the power of the Catholic church.

laissez-faire (593): French for "leave alone"; an economic doctrine developed by Adam Smith that advocated freeing the economy from government intervention and control.

League of Nations (853): The international organization set up following World War I to maintain peace by arbitrating disputes and promoting collective security.

Lebensraum (891): Literally, "living space"; the land that Hitler proposed to conquer so that the people he defined as true Aryans might have sufficient space to live their noble lives.

Lenin, V. I. (847): Bolshevik leader who executed the Bolshevik Revolution in the fall of 1917, took Russia out of World War I, and imposed communism in Russia.

Leopold II (762): King of Belgium (r. 1865–1909) who sponsored the takeover of the Congo in Africa, which he ran with great violence against native peoples.

liberalism (705): An economic and political ideology that—tracing its roots to John Locke in the seventeenth century and Enlightenment philosophers in the eighteenth—emphasized free trade and the constitutional guarantees of individual rights such as freedom of speech and religion; its adherents stood between conservatives on the right and revolutionaries on the left in the nineteenth century.

limited liability corporation (772): A legal entity, such as a factory or other enterprise, developed in the second half of the nineteenth century whose owners were liable for only restricted (limited) amounts of money owed to creditors in the case of financial failure.

Louis XVI (623): French king (r. 1774–1792) who was tried for treason during the French Revolution; he was executed on January 21, 1793.

Maastricht Treaty (995): The agreement among the members of the European Community to have a closer alliance, including the use of common passports and eventually the development of a common currency; by the terms of this treaty, the European Community became the European Union (EU) in 1994.

mandate system (854): The political control over the former colonies and territories of the German and Ottoman Empires granted to the victors of World War I by the League of Nations.

Marie-Antoinette (623): Wife of Louis XVI and queen of France who was tried for treason during the French Revolution and executed in October 1793.

Marshall Plan (919): A post–World War II program funded by the United States to get Europe back on its feet economically and thereby reduce the appeal of communism. It played an important role in the rebirth of European prosperity in the 1950s.

Marxism (746): A body of thought about the organization of production, social inequality, and the processes of revolutionary change as devised by the philosopher and economist Karl Marx.

Mazzini, Giuseppe (703): An Italian nationalist (1805–1872) who founded Young Italy, a secret society to promote Italian unity. He believed that a popular uprising would create a unified Italy.

Methodism (598): A religious movement founded by John Wesley (1703–1791) that broke with the Church of England and insisted on strict self-discipline and a "methodical" approach to religious study and observance.

Metternich, Klemens von (668): An Austrian prince (1773–1859) who took the lead in devising the post-Napoleonic settlement arranged by the Congress of Vienna (1814–1815).

Milosevic, Slobodan (987): President of Serbia (1989–1997) who pushed for Serb control of post-Communist Yugoslavia; in 2002, he was tried for crimes against humanity in the ethnic cleansing that accompanied the dissolution of the Yugoslav state.

mir (727): A Russian farm community that provided for holding land in common and regulating the movements of any individual member by the group.

Mitteleuropa (826): Literally, "central Europe," but used by military leaders in Germany before World War I to refer to land in both central and eastern Europe that they hoped to acquire.

modernism (806): Artistic styles around the turn of the twentieth century that featured a break with realism in art and literature and with lyricism in music.

Morrison, Toni (1013): The first African American woman to win the Nobel Prize for Literature; her works include *Beloved* (1987), *Jazz* (1992), and *A Mercy* (2008).

multinational corporation (955): A business that operates in many foreign countries by sending large segments of its manufacturing, finance, sales, and other business components abroad.

Mussolini, Benito (867): Leader of Italian fascist movement and, after the March on Rome in 1922, dictator of Italy.

nationalism (703): An ideology that arose in the nineteenth century and that holds that all peoples derive their identities from their nations, which are defined by common language, shared cultural traditions, and sometimes religion.

nation-state (729): A sovereign political unit of modern times based on representing a united people.

Nazi-Soviet Pact (895): The agreement reached in 1939 by Germany and the Soviet Union in which both agreed not to attack the other in case of war and to divide any conquered territories.

neoliberalism (974): A theory first promoted by British prime minister Margaret Thatcher, calling for a return to liberal principles of the nineteenth century, including the reduction of welfare-state programs and the cutting of taxes for the wealthy to promote economic growth.

new unionism (785): A nineteenth-century development in labor organizing that replaced local craft-based unions with those that extended membership to all kinds of workers.

new woman (801): A woman who, from the 1880s on, dressed practically, moved about freely, and often supported herself.

Nicholas II (813): Tsar of Russia (r. 1894–1917) who promoted anti-Semitism and resisted reform in the empire.

Nietzsche, Friedrich (806): Late-nineteenth-century German philosopher who called for a new morality in the face of God's death at the hands of science and whose theories were reworked by his sister to emphasize militarism and anti-Semitism.

Nightingale, Florence (725): The Englishwoman who in the nineteenth century pioneered the professionalization of nursing and the use of statistics in the study of public health and the well-being of the military.

Nixon, Richard (969): U.S. president (1969–1974) who escalated the Vietnam War, worked for accommodation with China, and resigned from the presidency after trying to block free elections.

nongovernmental organizations (NGOs) (999): Charitable foundations and activist groups such as Doctors Without Borders that work outside of governments, often on political, economic, and relief issues; also, philanthropic organizations such as the Rockefeller, Ford, and Open Society Foundations that shape economic and social policy and the course of political reform.

North Atlantic Treaty Organization (NATO) (921): The security alliance formed in 1949 to provide a unified military force for the United States, Canada, and their allies in western Europe and Scandinavia.

Nuremberg Laws (885): Legislation enacted by the Nazis in 1935 that deprived Jewish Germans of their citizenship and imposed many other hardships on them.

Opium War (702): War between China and Great Britain (1839–1842) that resulted in the opening of four Chinese ports to Europeans and British sovereignty over Hong Kong.

Organization of Petroleum Exporting Countries (OPEC) (971): A consortium that regulated the supply and export of oil and that acted with more unanimity after the United States supported Israel against the Arabs in the wars of the late 1960s and early 1970s.

Ostpolitik (961): A policy initiated by West German foreign minister Willy Brandt in the late 1960s in which West Germany sought better economic relations with the Communist countries of eastern Europe.

outwork (770): The nineteenth-century process of having some aspects of industrial work done outside factories in individual homes.

Pacific tigers (1006): Countries of East Asia so named because of their massive economic growth, much of it from the 1980s on; foremost among these were Japan and China.

Pankhurst, Emmeline (812): 1858–1928. Organizer of a militant branch of the British suffrage movement, working actively for women's right to vote.

Pan-Slavism (736): The nineteenth-century movement calling for the unity of all Slavs across national and regional boundaries.

Parnell, Charles Stewart (787): Irish politician (1846–1891) whose advocacy of home rule was a thorn in the side of the British establishment.

partition of Poland (607): Division of one-third of Poland-Lithuania's territory between Prussia, Russia, and Austria in 1772.

Peace of Paris (852): The series of peace treaties (1919–1920) that provided the settlement of World War I. The Treaty of Versailles with Germany was the centerpiece of the Peace of Paris.

perestroika (976): Literally, "restructuring"; an economic policy instituted in the 1980s by Soviet premier Mikhail Gorbachev calling for the introduction of market mechanisms and the achievement of greater efficiency in manufacturing, agriculture, and services.

philosophes (588): French for "philosophers"; public intellectuals of the Enlightenment who wrote on subjects ranging from current affairs to art criticism with the goal of furthering reform in society.

pop art (959): A style in the visual arts that mimicked advertising and consumerism and that used ordinary objects as a part of paintings and other compositions.

Popular Front (887): An alliance of political parties (initially led by Léon Blum in France) in the 1930s to resist fascism despite philosophical differences.

positivism (753): A theory developed in the mid-nineteenth century that the study of facts would generate accurate, or "positive," laws of society and that these laws could, in turn, help in the formulation of policies and legislation.

postmodernism (1014): A term applied in the late twentieth century to both an intense stylistic mixture in the arts without a central unifying theme or elite set of standards and a critique of Enlightenment and scientific beliefs in rationality and the possibility of certain knowledge.

Pugachev rebellion (611): A massive revolt of Russian Cossacks and serfs in 1773 against local nobles and the armies of Catherine the Great; its leader, Emelian Pugachev, was eventually captured and executed.

pump priming (884): An economic policy used by governments, including the Nazis in Germany, to stimulate the economy through public works programs and other infusions to public funds.

purges (880): The series of attacks on citizens of the USSR accused of being "wreckers," or saboteurs of communism, in the 1930s and later.

Putin, Vladimir (990): President of Russia elected in 2000 and prime minister as of 2008; he has worked to reestablish Russia as a world power through control of the country's resources and military capabilities.

realism (748): An artistic style that arose in the mid-nineteenth century and was dedicated to depicting society realistically without romantic or idealistic overtones.

Realpolitik (721): Policies developed after the revolutions of 1848 and initially associated with nation building; they were based on realism rather than on the romantic notions of earlier nationalists. The term has come to mean any policy based on considerations of power alone.

Reform Act of 1884 (787): British legislation that granted the right to vote to a mass male citizenry.

Reform Bill of 1832 (681): A measure passed by the British Parliament to increase the number of male voters by about 50 percent and give representation to new cities in the north; it set a precedent for widening suffrage.

restoration (669): The epoch after the fall of Napoleon, in which the Congress of Vienna aimed to "restore" as many regimes as possible to their former rulers.

Robespierre, Maximilien (631): A lawyer from northern France who, as leader of the Committee of Public Safety, laid out the principles of a republic of virtue and of the Terror; his arrest and execution in July 1794 brought an end to the Terror.

romanticism (598): An artistic movement of the late eighteenth and early nineteenth centuries that glorified nature, emotion, genius, and imagination.

Rousseau, Jean-Jacques (594): One of the most important philosophes (1712–1778); he argued that only a government based on a social contract among the citizens could make people truly moral and free.

Rushdie, Salman (1013): Immigrant British author, whose novel *The Satanic Verses* (1988) led the ayatollah Ruhollah Khomeini of Iran to issue a fatwa calling for Rushdie's murder.

Russification (728): A program for the integration of Russia's many nationality groups that involved the forced learning of the Russian language and the practice of Russian Orthodox religion as well as the settlement of ethnic Russians among other nationality groups.

samizdat (962): A key form of dissident activity across the Soviet bloc in which individuals reproduced government-suppressed publications by hand and passed them from reader to reader, thus building a foundation for the successful resistance of the 1980s.

Sand, George (697): The pen name of French novelist Amandine-Aurore-Lucile Dupin Dudevant (1804–1876), who showed her independence in the 1830s by dressing like a man and smoking cigars. The term *George-Sandism* became an expression of disdain for independent women.

Schlieffen Plan (839): The Germans' strategy in World War I that called for attacks on two fronts—concentrating first on France to the west and then turning east to attack Russia.

Scott, Sir Walter (675): A prolific author (1771–1832) of popular historical novels; he also collected and published traditional Scottish ballads and wrote poetry.

Second International (785): A transnational organization of workers established in 1889, mostly committed to Marxian socialism.

Seven Years' War (605): A worldwide series of battles (1756–1763) between Austria, France, Russia, and Sweden on one side and Prussia and Great Britain on the other.

socialism (706): A social and political ideology, originating in the early nineteenth century, that advocated the reorganization of society to overcome the new tensions created by industrialization and restore social harmony through communities based on cooperation.

Solidarity (977): A Polish labor union founded in 1980 by Lech Walesa and Anna Walentynowicz that contested Communist Party programs and eventually succeeded in ousting the party from the Polish government.

South African War (818): The war (1899–1902) between Britain and the Boer (originally Dutch) inhabitants of South Africa for control of the region; also called the Boer War.

soviets (846): Councils of workers and soldiers first formed in Russia in the Revolution of 1905; they were revived to represent the people in the early days of the 1917 Russian Revolution.

stagflation (971): The combination of a stagnant economy and soaring inflation; a period of stagflation occurred in the West in the 1970s as a result of an OPEC embargo on oil.

Stalin, Joseph (878): Leader of the USSR who, with considerable backing, formed a brutal dictatorship in the 1930s and forcefully converted the country into an industrial power.

Terror (631): The policy established under the direction of the Committee of Public Safety during the French Revolution to arrest dissidents and execute opponents in order to protect the republic from its enemies.

Thatcher, Margaret (973): Prime minister of Britain (1979–1990) who set a new tone for British politics by promoting neoliberal economic policies and criticizing poor people, union members, and racial minorities as worthless, even harmful citizens.

Thermidorian Reaction (638): The violent backlash against the rule of Robespierre that dismantled the Terror and punished Jacobins and their supporters.

Third Republic (787): The French government that succeeded Napoleon III's Second Empire after its defeat in the Franco-Prussian War of 1870–1871. It lasted until France's defeat by Germany in 1940.

total war (836): A war built on the full mobilization of soldiers, civilians, and technology of the nations involved. The term also refers to a highly destructive war of ideologies.

Truman Doctrine (919): The policy devised by U.S. president Harry Truman to limit communism after World War II by countering political crises with economic and military aid.

United Nations (UN) (934): An organization set up in 1945 for collective security and for the resolution of international conflicts through both deliberation and the use of force.

urbanization (692): The growth of towns and cities due to the movement of people from rural to urban areas, a trend that was encouraged by the development of factories and railroads.

Vatican II (937): A Catholic Council held between 1962 and 1965 to modernize some aspects of church teachings (such as condemnation of Jews), to update the liturgy, and to promote cooperation among the faiths (i.e., ecumenism).

war guilt clause (852): The part of the Treaty of Versailles that assigned blame for World War I to Germany.

Warsaw Pact (921): A security alliance of the Soviet Union and its allies formed in 1955, in retaliation for NATO's admittance of West Germany.

Weimar Republic (851): The parliamentary republic established in 1919 in Germany to replace the monarchy.

welfare state (927): A system (developed on both sides during the cold war) comprising government-sponsored social programs to provide health care, family allowances, disability insurance, and pensions for veterans and retired workers.

Zionism (817): A movement that began in the late nineteenth century among European Jews to found a Jewish state.

Additional Credits

Chapter 18, page 590: "Denis Diderot, 'Encyclopedia' (1755)." From *Denis Diderot, The Encyclopedia: Selections*, edited and translated by Stephen J. Gendzier. Harper & Row Publishers, Inc. 1967, copyright Stephen J. Gendzier. Reprinted by permission of Stephen J. Gendzier. **Page 594:** "Jean-Jacques Rousseau, *Émile* (1762)." From *Women, the Family, and Freedom: The Debate in Documents,* Volume 1, *1750–1880*, edited by Susan Groag Bell and Karen M. Offen. Copyright © 1983 by the Board of Trustees of the Leland Stanford Junior University. All rights reserved. Used with the permission of Stanford University Press, www.sup.org. **Page 594:** "Madame de Beaumer, Editorial in *Le Journal des Dames.*" From *Women, The Family, and Freedom: The Debate in Documents,* Volume 1, *1750–1880*, edited by Susan Groag Bell and Karen M. Offen. Copyright © 1983 by the Board of Trustees of the Leland Stanford Junior University. All rights reserved. Used with the permission of Stanford University Press, www.sup.org.

Chapter 19, page 645: "Anne-Louise-Germaine de Staël, *Considerations on the Main Events of the French Revolution* (1818)." From *An Extraordinary Woman: Selected Writings of Germaine de Staël*, edited by Vivian Folkenflik. Copyright © 1987 Columbia University Press. Reprinted with permission of the publisher.

Chapter 20, page 666: "Benjamin Constant, Spokesman for the Liberal Opposition to Napoleon." From "Further Reflections on Usurpation" in *Constant: Political Writings*, edited and translated by Biancamaria Fontana. Copyright © 1988 by Cambridge University Press. Reprinted with the permission of Cambridge University Press.

Chapter 21, page 713: "Alexis de Tocqueville Describes the June Days in Paris (1848)." From Alexis de Tocqueville, *Recollections: The French Revolution of 1848*, edited by J. P. Mayer and A. P. Kerr, translated by George Lawrence. Copyright © 1986 by Transaction Publishers. Reprinted by permission of the publisher.

Chapter 23, page 764: "An African King Describes His Government." From *Report and Proceedings with Appendices of the Government Commission on Native Laws and Customs, Cape of Good Hope Parliamentary Paper, G4*, 1883, Part 1, 523–30, excerpted in William H. Worger, Nancy L. Clark, and Edward A. Alpers, eds. *Africa and the West: A Documentary History*, 2nd ed., vol. 1, *From the Slave Trade to Conquest, 1441–1905* (New York: Oxford University Press, 2010), 208, 209. Copyright © 2001, 2010 by William H. Worger, Nancy L. Clark, and Edward A. Alpers. By permission of Oxford University Press. **Page 778:** "The Government View." Quoted in Julianna Puskas, "Consequences of Overseas Migration for the Country of Origin: The Case of Hungary," in *Roots of the Transplanted,* vol. 1, *Late 19th Century East Central and Southeastern Europe*, edited by Dirk Hoerder and Inge Blank (Boulder: East European Monographs, 1994), 397. Copyright © 1994 by Dirk Hoerder and Inge Blank. Reprinted by permission of Dirk Hoerder. **Page 778:** "Migration Defended." From H. Arnold Barton, *A Folk Divided: Homeland Swedes and Swedish Americans, 1840–1940* (Carbondale: Southern Illinois University Press, 1994), 72–73, 137. Copyright © 1994 by the Board of Trustees, Southern Illinois University. Reprinted by permission of the publisher. **Page 779:** "The Perils of Migration." Quoted in Frantisek Bielik, Horst Hogh, and Anna Stvrtecka, "Slovak Images of the New World: 'We Could Pay Off Our Debts,'" in *Roots of the Transplanted,* vol. 1, *Late 19th Century East Central and Southeastern Europe*, edited by Dirk Hoerder and Inge Blank (Boulder: East European Monographs, 1994), 388. Copyright © 1994 by Dirk Hoerder and Inge Blank. Reprinted by permission of Dirk Hoerder. **Page 782:** "Henrik Ibsen, From *A Doll's House*." From *A Doll's House/Ghost/An Enemy of the People/Rosmersholm* by Henrik Ibsen and newly translated by Michael Meyer. Copyright © 1966 by Michael Meyer. Copyright renewed 1994 by Michael Meyer. Reprinted by permission of Harold Ober Associates Incorporated.

Chapter 24, page 817: "Leon Pinsker Calls for a Jewish State." From Robert Chazan and Marc Lee Raphael, eds., *Modern Jewish History: A Source Reader* (New York: Schocken Books, 1974). Copyright © 1974. Reprinted by permission of Marc Lee Raphael. **Page 823:** "Turkish Nationalism." Mehmed Emin, "Going to Battle," from Robert G. Landen, ed., *The Emergence of the Modern Middle East: Selected Readings* (New York: Van Nostrand Reinhold Company, 1970), 120. Copyright © 1970. Reprinted by permission. **Page 824:** "Vietnamese Resistance and the Importance of Becoming Modern." Excerpted from Phan Boi Chau, "The New Vietnam" (1907), as quoted in Truong Buu Lam, *Colonialism Experienced: Vietnamese Writings on Colonialism, 1900–1931*. Copyright © by the University of Michigan 2000. Reprinted by permission of the publisher.

Chapter 25, page 847: "Outbreak of the Russian Revolution." From Eduard Dune, *Notes of a Red Guard*, translated and edited by Dianne Koenker and S. A. Smith. Copyright © 1933 by Dianne Koenker and S. A. Smith. Reprinted by permission of the University of Illinois Press. **Page 865:** "Memory and Battlefield Tourism." From Vera Brittain, *Testament of Youth*. Copyright © 1978, Virago Press. Extracts from Vera Brittain are reproduced by permission of Mark Bostridge and T. J. Brittain-Catlin, literary executors for the Vera Brittain Estate, 1970.

Chapter 26, page 877: "A Family Copes with Unemployment." From Marie Jahoda, Paul Lazarsfeld, and Hans Zeisel, *Marienthal: The Sociography of an Unemployed Community*, translated by John Reginall and Thomas Elsaesser (Chicago: Aldine, Atherton, 1933; repr., 1971), pps. 87–88. Copyright © 2002 Transaction Publishers. Reprinted by permission of Transaction Publishers. **Page 882:** "An Author Opposes Nazism." From Lion Feuchtwanger, "How Do We Struggle against a Third Reich?" January 21, 1931, in *The Weimar Republic Sourcebook*, edited by Anton Kaes, Martin Jay, and Edward Dimendberg. Copyright © 1994. Reprinted by permission of the University of California Press. **Page 883:** "A Professor against Hitler." From Victor Klemperer, *I Will Bear Witness: A Diary of the Nazi Years, 1933–1941*, translated by Martin Chalmers. Copyright © 1998 by Martin Chalmers. Used by permission of Random House, Inc. **Page 883** "Praise for Nazis" and "Hitler in Prayers." From Claudia Koonz, *Mothers in the Fatherland: Women, the Family, and Nazi Politics*. Copyright © 1987 by Claudia Koonz. Reprinted by permission of St. Martin's Press, Inc. **Page 892:** "The Greater East Asia Co-Prosperity Sphere." Excerpted from "Draft of Basic Plan for Establishment of Greater East Asia Co-Prosperity Sphere" in *Sources of Japanese Tradition*, compiled by Ryusaku Tsunoda, William Theodore de Bary, and Donald Keene (New York: Columbia University Press, 1958), 802–3, 805. Copyright © 1958 by Ryusaku Tsunoda, William Theodore de Bary, and Donald Keene. Reprinted with permission of the publisher.

Chapter 28, page 966: "Criticizing White Feminism (The Combahee River Collective Statement)." From *Feminism in Our Time: The Essential Writings, World War II to the Present*, edited by Miriam Schneir (New York: Vintage, 1994), 177–79. Copyright © 1994 Vintage. Reprinted by permission of Monthly Review Foundation. **Page 966:** "Criticizing Socialism." From *Women and Russia: Feminist Writings from the Soviet Union*, edited by Tatyana Mamonova. Copyright © 1984 by Tatyana Mamonova. Reprinted by permission of Beacon Press, Boston. **Page 967:** "Comparing the Situation of European and African Women." From Awa Thiam, *Black Sisters, Speak Out: Feminism and Oppression in Black Africa*, translated by Dorothy S. Blair. Copyright © 1986 by Awa Thiam. Reprinted by permission of Pluto Press. **Page 975:** "Margaret Thatcher's Economic Vision." From a speech given by Margaret Thatcher to the Conservative Party Conference, Brighton, October 10, 1980. Copyright © Margaret Thatcher Foundation. All Rights Reserved. Reprinted by permission of the Margaret Thatcher Foundation, info@margaretthatcher.org. **Page 978:** "A Citizen's Experience of Gorbachev's Reforms." From a letter by Z. I. Kupriyanova, January 1988. Reprinted with the permission of Simon & Schuster, Inc., and Ed Victor Ltd. Literary Agency from Christopher Cerf and Marina Albee, *Small Fires: Letters from the Soviet People to* Ogonyok *Magazine, 1987–1990*. Copyright © 1990 by Christopher Cerf and Marina Albee. All rights reserved.

Chapter 29, page 1010: "The View from Everyday Life" and "Too Much Islamic Architecture." From Jennifer Ehrlich, "Liberal Netherlands Grows

Less So on Immigration," *Christian Science Monitor*, December 19, 2003. Copyright © 2003. Reprinted by permission of Jennifer Ehrlich. **Page 1010:** "Opposing Immigration and Turkey's Membership in the European Union." Geert Wilders quoted in " 'Turkey in the EU? Never!' " *Expatica*, October 5, 2004, http://www.expatica.com/nl/news/news_focus/turkey-in-the-eu-never-12536_60600.html. Reprinted by permission of Expatica Communications. **Page 1010:** "A Student's Thoughts on Muslims in the Netherlands." Loubna el Morabet quoted in "Muslims Quietly Take Wilders' Abuse" by Sheila Kamerman and Dirk Vlasblom, Radio Netherlands Worldwide Africa Desk, March 26, 2010, http://www.rnw.nl/africa/article/muslims-quietly-take-wilders-abuse-0. **Page 1011:** "An Evaluation of Dutch Values." Funda Müjde, from "Holland," posted on the Funda Müjde Web site: http://www.fundam.nl/english/fundas-column-telegraaf-daily-newspaper-04.htm. Reprinted by permission of Müjde Productions Amsterdam.

Index

A note about the index:
Names of individuals appear in bold face; biographical dates are included for major historical figures.
Letters in parenthesis following pages refer to:
(i) illustrations, including photographs and artifacts
(f) figures, including charts, graphs, and tables
(m) maps
(b) boxed features (such as "Contrasting Views")

Abandoned children, Napoleonic Civil Code and, 657
Abdul Hamid II (Ottoman Empire), 823–824
Abolitionism, 592, 701
Abortion, 604, 800
  Napoleonic Civil Code and, 657
  in Soviet Union, 880
Absolutism, in France, 610
Abstract expressionism, 943
Academies, learned societies and, 601
Acquired immunodeficiency syndrome (AIDS). *See* AIDS
Activism
  anticolonial, 877–878
  by citizens, 964–969
  civil rights, 964
  in colonies after World War I, 859
  by homosexuals, 964
  against industrial growth, 1000
  NGOs and, 999
  in 1968, 965–969
  in Poland, 977–978
  in Prague Spring, 967–969
  reaction against, 969
  by students, 964, 966–967
  by women, 811, 964–965
  by workers, 784, 810–811, 966–967
Act of Union (Britain), in 1801, 705
Adams, John, on French Revolution, 643
Addis Ababa, Ethiopia, 891
"Address on Abolishing the Slave Trade," 641*(b)*
Adenauer, Konrad (1876–1967), 924
Administration. *See* Government
Adrianople, Treaty of (1829), 677
Advertising, cold war culture and, 941
Afghanistan
  British in, 765, 766–767
  refugees from, 1008
  Soviet war in, 976, 977
  Taliban in, 1005
Africa. *See also* Egypt; North Africa; Slavery; specific locations
  Berlin Conference (1884–1885) and, 762
  communism in, 930
  decolonization of (1951–1990), 934*(m)*
  drought and famine in, 770, 1002
  economic development in, 1003
  European colonization of, 762–765, 763*(m)*
  European missionaries in, 768
  German colonialism in, 759
  Great Depression in, 876–877
  imperialism in, 762–764, 763*(m)*, 818–819, 819*(m)*
  Italy and, 818, 891
  malaria in, 770
  in 1914, 819*(m)*
  resistance to colonialism in, 824
  before World War I, 825
  World War I and, 837
  World War II and, 902, 903*(m)*
African Americans
  civil rights and, 938, 962, 964
  emancipation of, 938
  jazz and, 865
Africans
  European views of, 592
  as slaves, 670
Aggression. *See also* Invasions; Violence; Wars and warfare
  in 1930s, 890
Agrarianism, in Germany, 814–815
Agribusiness, international, 956–957
Agricultural revolution, in 18th century, 687
Agriculture. *See also* Collective farming; Farms and farming
  in Africa, 764–765
  in eastern Europe, 858
  in Egypt, 761
  in Great Depression, 875–876
  innovations in, 610, 770
  labor for, 690
  population and, 695
  Soviet, 880, 917
  technical planners in, 956–957
Aïda (Verdi), 720*(i)*, 744
AIDS (disease), 977, 1002–1003
Airbus, 956, 956*(m)*
Air force, German, 852, 896
Airlift, in Berlin, 921
Airplanes
  in World War I, 841*(i)*
  in World War II, 896
Air pollution. *See also* Pollution
  industrialization and, 691
Akhmatova, Anna, 929
Albania
  fascism in, 879
  in First Balkan War, 827
Albanian Muslims, in Kosovo, 990
Albert (England), 736, 738*(b)*, 738*(i)*, 739–740
  arts and, 749
Alcohol and alcoholism
  in Russia, 1002
  in Soviet Union, 976
  temperance societies and, 699
Aldrin, Edwin "Buzz," 952
Alexander I (Russia, r. 1801–1825), 676
  conservatism of, 670
  Holy Alliance and, 670
  Napoleon and, 661, 664
  Poland and, 679
  reforms of, 662
Alexander II (Russia, r. 1855–1881), 725, 726–727, 728–729, 791
Alexander Nevsky (movie), 881
Alexandra (Russia), 846
Algeria
  France and, 695, 701–702, 745, 761
  torture in, 935*(b)*
  in World War II, 904
Alliances. *See also* Allies; specific alliances
  World War I and, 790, 825, 836–837
Allies
  denazification by, 923
  World War I and, 836, 840*(m)*, 850
  World War II and, 897, 902, 904, 907, 917
All Quiet on the Western Front (Remarque), 863, 885
al-Qaeda, 1003, 1005
  Madrid bombings by, 1005
Alsace
  France and, 852
  Germany and, 770
  World War I and, 837
Amar, Jules, 835, 842, 857, 864
American Historical Association, 804
American Indians. *See* Native Americans
American Revolution, 612–614
  French finances after, 623
American Temperance Society, 699
Americas, slavery in, 701
Amiens, Treaty of (1802), 661
Amritsar massacre (1919), 859
Anarchists and anarchism, 746
  assassinations and, 811
Anglo-French Declaration (November 7, 1918), 854*(b)*
Animals
  city sanitation and, 694
  Society for the Prevention of Cruelty to Animals and, 699
Anna Karenina (Tolstoy), 791
Annam, in Union of Indochina, 766
Anschluss (merger), 894
Antarctica, 592

Anthony, Susan B. (1820–1906), 811
Anthropology, 960
Anticlericalism, French Revolution and, 670
Anticolonialism, 877–878
Anti-Corn Law League, 705
Antiglobalism, 999
Anti-immigrant politicians, 1009
Antimonarchists, in Spain, 892–894
Anti-Semitism
in Austria-Hungary, 815–816
in Baltic region, 990
in former Soviet Union, 993
in France, 788, 814, 814*(i)*
toward Freud, 803*(i)*
in Germany, 814–815, 881
in Great Depression, 876
of Hitler, 868, 881, 885
in Hungary, 888
mass politics and, 813–817
in Russia, 813–814
in Soviet Union, 917, 969
World War I and, 845
World War II and, 915
Antislavery movement, natural rights and, 592
Antiwar protest, 969
Appeasement, of Hitler, 894–895
Appliances. *See also* Consumers and consumerism
after World War I, 862
April Theses (Russia), 847
Arab-Israeli wars (1967, 1973), 971
Arab world. *See also* Islam; Middle East
European-occupied lands and, 761–762
Middle East politics and, 932–933
Muslims and, 931
wars with Israel, 971
Architecture
in England, 736
in France, 655
Islamic in Netherlands, 1010
medievalism in 1800s and, 696
postmodern, 1014–1015
after World War I, 864
Archives (historical), about cold war, 918*(b)*, 918*(i)*
Arctic region, pack ice decline in, 1000
Argentina, Falkland war and, 974
Aristocracy. *See also* Nobility
after 1848 revolutions, 715
in Great Britain, 736–737
in Russia, 727–728
upper class and, 775
Armed forces. *See also* Military; Navy; Soldiers; Wars and warfare
in France, 638–640
German, 852
Grand Army of Napoleon, 659–661
in Japan, 890, 897
Prussian, 606–607, 733, 734
school sports and, 781
Armenia and Armenians
in Ottoman Empire, 842
strikes by, 821
in Tajikistan, 990
Armistice, in World War I, 850
Arms and armaments. *See also* Weapons
growth in (1890–1914), 828*(b)*, 828*(f)*
Arms race
in cold war, 925*(f)*
before World War I, 827
Armstrong, Louis (1900–1971), 865
Armstrong, Neil, 952
Art(s). *See also* Architecture; Sculpture; specific arts and artists
in cold war, 943
in Communist culture, 943
cultural identity and, 722
decorative, 783
in Enlightenment, 602
in France, 633–634
in Germany, 647
imperialism, industry, and, 781–783
industrial society and, 696–701
modern, 807–809
in Nazi Germany, 885
in Nigeria, 765*(i)*
politics and, 808–809
pop art and, 959*(i)*
postmodern, 1014–1015
realism in, 748–751, 750*(i)*
romanticism in, 672*(i)*, 672–675, 674*(i)*, 675*(i)*
on serfs, 726
Soviet, 881
Soviet dissident (1960s and 1970s), 963*(b)*, 963*(i)*
in technocratic society, 959–960
of upper classes, 776
after World War I, 863
Article 231, of Treaty of Versailles, 852
Articles of Confederation (U.S.), 614
Artillery, 827
Artisans, 777–778
workshops of, 745–746
Art nouveau, 809
Aryans, in Nazi Germany, 884, 885
Ashes and Diamonds (film), 939*(i)*
Asia. *See also* specific locations
AIDS in, 1003
communism in, 930
drought and famine in, 770
economic recovery in, 1008
end of empires in, 931–932
European missionaries in, 768
Great Depression in, 876
imperialism in, 765–766, 820, 820*(m)*
influence of, 986
Japanese expansionism in, 890
Russian expansion in, 765–766, 766*(m)*
soldiers in World War I from, 841–842
U.S. national debt financed by, 1007
in Western consumer economy, 1010
women in, 1007
Assassinations
by anarchists, 811
in Europe (1970s–1980s), 972
Assemblies, in France, 610
Assembly line, in United States, 860
Assembly of Notables (France), 623–624
Association for the Taxation of Financial Transactions and Aid to Citizens (ATTAC), 999
Astronomy, in 1930s, 889
Aswan Dam, 933*(i)*
Atatürk. *See* Kemal, Mustafa
Atheists, 591
Atlantic Charter, 907
Atomic age, society during, 943–944
Atomic bomb, 905*(i)*, 905–907. *See also* Nuclear weapons
purposes of U.S. use, 918*(b)*
Soviet, 924
Atomic power, 953
Attlee, Clement (1883–1967), 924
Au Coin de la Rue (department store), 774*(i)*
Auerstädt, battle at (1806), 661
Auschwitz-Birkenau extermination and labor camp, 873, 898–899
Austerlitz, battle of (1805), 661
Australia
exploration of, 592
after World War I, 857
Austria. *See also* Austria-Hungary; Habsburgs
Anschluss with Germany, 894
Belgium and, 622
Bosnia and Herzegovina occupied by, 790
Congress of Vienna and, 668, 669*(m)*
Crimean War and, 724
Dollfuss in, 888
economy in, 975–976
France and, 629, 724
German Confederation and, 669
Germany and, 733, 894
in Great Depression, 877*(b)*
in Holy Alliance, 670
Holy Roman Empire and, 662
iron in, 689
Italy and, 675–676, 712, 713–714
Lombardy and, 730–731
Metternich and, 668–669
Napoleon and, 640, 661
Polish partition and, 640
Prussia and, 733
reforms in, 608, 609
Russia and, 724, 726
Austria-Hungary, 736*(m)*
anti-Semitism in, 815–816
authoritarianism in, 789–791
in Central Powers, 836
ethnic groups in (c. 1900), 815
Francis Joseph and, 735–736
Germany and, 791, 837
industrialization in, 771
nationalism in, 815, 844
Poland and, 852
after World War I, 853*(m)*
World War I and, 827, 828–830, 829*(i)*, 846
Austrian Empire, nationalism in, 703, 713–714
Austrian Netherlands, 669, 669*(m)*
France and, 639, 653
revolt in, 620, 621
Austro-Hungarian Empire. *See* Austria-Hungary
Authoritarianism. *See also* Dictators
in Austria-Hungary, 789–791
fascist, 879*(b)*
in Russia, 813–814
after World War I, 869
Authority. *See* Political power
Autocracy, in Russia, 715, 729
Auto-Emancipation (Pinsker), 817*(b)*
Automobiles and automobile industry
invention of, 769
Smart car and, 1000*(i)*, 1001
in United States, 860
Avant-garde arts, 808
in Soviet Union, 881
after World War I, 862
Avatar (film), 1014
Aviation. *See* Airplanes
Axis powers, 892, 896, 902. *See also* Nazis and Nazism
Allied postwar prosecution of leaders, 923
end in Europe, 903–905

Ba'al Shem Tov (Israel ben Eliezer) (c. 1700–1760), 598
Babi Yar (Yevtushenko), 962
Baby boom, after World War II, 917
Baker, Josephine (1906–1976), 865
Baku, strikes in, 821
Bakunin, Mikhail (1814–1876), 746
Balance of power
  after Congress of Vienna, 669*(m)*, 669–670
  Crimean War and, 724–725
  in Europe, 646*(m)*
  among imperial nations, 859
  in 1970s and 1980s, 970–980
Balkan region
  in c. 1878, 790
  1908–1914, 826*(m)*
  cities in, 800
  crises before World War I, 826–827
  family system in, 801
  nationalism in, 676, 676*(m)*, 789, 825
  violence in, 988–989
Ballot Act (England, 1872), 787
Baltic region
  anti-Semitism in, 990
  Nazi attack on, 897
  Nazi-Soviet Pact and, 895
  Polish Corridor and, 852
  Russia and, 896
Balzac, Honoré de (1799–1850), 696
Bandung Convention, 935
Bangalore, 1011
Banks and banking, economic crisis (1997) and, 1008
Barbed wire, 770
Barcelona, 892, 893*(i)*
Barnard, Christiaan, 954
Baroque, 602
Barry, J. D., 764*(b)*
Barth, Karl, 889
Basque nationalism, 998
Basques, 972
Bastille, 624–625, 625*(i)*
Bastille Day (France), 625
Batavian Republic, 640
Bathing, 741
Batista, Fulgencio, 944
Battlefronts, in World War I, 839–842
Battle of the Nations (1813), 664
Battles. *See* specific battles and wars
Baudelaire, Charles-Pierre, 748–749
Bauhaus, 864
Bavaria, 713
Baxter, George (1804–1867), 716*(i)*
Bazán, Emilia Pardo, 783
Beatles, 939, 959
Beauharnais, Eugène de, 657
Beaumarchais, Pierre-Augustin Caron de (1732–1799), 612
Beaumer, Madame de, 594–595*(b)*
Beautification, of cities, 739
Beauvoir, Simone de, 938, 938*(i)*
Beccaria, Cesare (1738–1794), 608, 674
Becquerel, Antoine (1852–1908), 806
Beer Hall Putsch, 858, 868
Beethoven, Ludwig van (1770–1827), 602, 674
Beggars, 604
Beijing, Tiananmen Square riots in, 978
Beirut, 1005
Belarus, Russia and, 993
Belgian Congo, 762*(i)*
Belgium, 620
  Africa and, 762, 762*(i)*
  constitutional monarchy in, 679
  cultural differences in, 998
  end of empire in, 934
  Germany and, 836, 896
  independence of, 622, 679
  industrialization in, 690
  Napoleon in, 665
  railroads in, 688–689
  revolutions of 1848 and, 715
  voting rights in, 788
  in World War I, 839
Belgrade, 800
Beloved (Morrison), 1013
Ben Bella, Ahmed (Algeria), 933
Benefits
  for veterans, 861
  for workers, 886
Ben Eliezer, Israel. *See* Ba'al Shem Tov
Beneš, Edvard (1884–1948), 919
Bentham, Jeremy (1748–1832), 705
Benz, Karl, 769
Bergen-Belsen concentration camp, 937
Berlin
  airlift in, 921
  blockade of, 921
  expansion to 1914, 789*(m)*
  population of, 685
  rebuilding of, 800
  women clearing postwar, 923*(i)*
Berlin Conference (1884–1885), 762, 819
Berlin Wall (1961), 937, 944
  fall of (1989), 979
Bernadette (Saint). *See* Soubirous, Bernadette
Berthier, Alexandre, 655
Berthollet, Claude, 655
Betrothed, The (Manzoni), 674
Bible
  Darwin on, 752
  literal truth of, 960
Bible groups, 698
Bicycles, 781
  lanes for, 1001
Bicycle Thief, The (film), 943
Bicycle Wheel (Duchamp), 808*(i)*
Big bang theory, 953
Big-game hunting, 775, 776*(i)*
Big Three, in World War II, 907
Bilbao, Spain, Guggenheim Museum in, 1014–1015
Bildung, 811
Bill of Rights, in United States, 614
Binet, Alfred, 803
Bin Laden, Osama, 1003, 1005
Biology, revolution in, 953–954
Birth(s), illegitimate, 694
Birth control, 780, 800
  in France, 964
  in Great Depression, 876
  in Soviet Union, 880
Birth control pill, 953, 954, 964
Birthrate
  drop in, 800
  in England, 690
  in Great Depression, 876
  growth as global issue, 1001–1002
  in Soviet bloc, 958
  in Soviet Union, 880–881
  after World War II, 917
Bismarck, Otto von (1815–1898), 717, 721, 729, 732
  Africa and, 762
  colonialism of, 818–819
  German unification and, 731–735
  Kulturkampf and, 751
  power politics and, 789–790
  William II and, 791
Black and Tans, 859
"Black is beautiful," 964
Black Panthers, 964
"Black power," 964
Blacks. *See* African Americans; Slavery
Black Shirts (Italy), 867*(i)*, 868
Black Skin, White Masks (Fanon), 938
Blake, William (1757–1827), 675*(i)*
Blanc, Louis (1811–1882), 707
Blast furnaces, 770
Blitzkrieg ("lightning war"), 896
Blockades
  of Berlin, 921
  of Cuba, 944
Blood sports, 699
Bloody Sunday (Ireland), 972
"Bloody Sunday" (Russia, 1905), 821
Blue Angel, The (film), 888
Blum, Léon, 887n, 888
Bobbies (London police), 680
Boers, 763, 818
Boer War (1899–1902), 818
Bohemia
  Austria and, 789
  industrialization in, 690
Bolívar, Simon (1783–1830), 677–678, 679*(i)*
Böll, Heinrich, 940
"Bollywood" films, 1014
Bolshevik Revolution (Russia), 847–848, 866
Bolsheviks, 811
  Poland and, 851–852
  resistance to, 865–866
  show trials of, 880
Bombs and bombings. *See also* Atomic bomb; Nuclear weapons
  of Dresden and Tokyo, 897
  in Ireland, 972
  terrorist, 1005, 1006*(i)*
  in World War I, 838
  in World War II, 896–897
Bomb shelter, 943*(i)*
Bonald, Louis de, on social order, 670
Bonaparte family. *See also* Napoleon I Bonaparte
  Caroline (1782–1839), 657
  Jerome (1784–1860), 661
  Joseph (1768–1844), 657, 664
  Louis (1778–1846), 657
  Lucien (1775–1840), 653
Bond, James (character), 942, 943
Bon Marché, 774
Book(s). *See also* Literature; Printing
  in Enlightenment, 597, 603
Book of Laughter and Forgetting, The (Kundera), 969
Book of the New Moral World, The (Owen), 707
Borders
  in Congress of Vienna, 669
  Italian, 731
  of Korea, 931
  of United States, 737
Borkowska, Teofila, 778*(b)*

Borodino, battle at (1812), 664
Bosnia, 826
  Austrian occupation of, 790
  as independent republic, 990
Bosnia-Herzegovina, 826, 828
  civil war in, 988
Bosnian Serbs, 988
Boston Female Moral Reform Society, 699
Boston Tea Party (1773), 613
Boulanger, Georges (1837–1891), 788
Boulton, Matthew, 687
Boundaries. *See* Borders
Bourbon family (France), 670, 788
Bourgeois, aristocracy and, 775
Bourgeoisie, 600. *See also* Middle class
Bové, José, 999
Boxer Uprising (China), 822*(i)*, 822–823
Bradbury, Ray, 942
Brain drain, 957, 969, 992–993
Brando, Marlon, 939
Brandt, Willy (1913–1992), 961
Braque, Georges (1882–1963), 808
Braun, Eva, 904–905
Brazil, 677
  economy in, 1003, 1007, 1008
Breast feeding, 780
Brest-Litovsk, Treaty of (1918), 848
Bretons, 998
Brezhnev, Leonid (1909–1982), 961
Brezhnev Doctrine, 979
BRICs (Brazil, Russia, India, and China), 1006
Britain. *See also* British Empire; England (Britain); Great Britain
  battle of, 896, 897
  emigration from, 776
Britannia (suffrage paper), 842
British and Foreign School Society, 699
British East Africa, independence in, 933
British Empire, 761
  Anglo-Indian polo team and, 781*(i)*
  India and, 743–744, 765
  World War I and, 837
British-French Concorde, 955–956
British Isles. *See* Britain; England (Britain)
Broken Eggs (Greuze), 603*(i)*
Brontë, Charlotte (1816–1855), 697
Brown, Louise (1978–), 954–955, 955*(i)*
Browning, Elizabeth Barrett (1806–1861), 696
Brown Shirts, in Germany, 858
Brown v. Board of Education (1954), 938
Brunswick, duke of, 629
Bucharest, 800
Buda, working classes in, 694
Budapest, 998
  fighting in World War II, 904*(i)*
Buffer zone, after World War II, 917
Buildings. *See* Architecture
Bulatov, Eric, 963*(b)*, 963*(i)*
Bulgakov, Mikhail, 1013
Bulgaria
  as Axis power, 896
  communism in, 919
  economy in, 997–998
  in EU, 997
  fascism in, 879
  migration from, 858
  Ottomans and, 789
  Russia and, 790
  before World War I, 827
  in World War II, 904
Bulgarians, nationalism of, 824
Bullbaiting, 699
Bundesrat (Germany), 734
Burden, The (Daumier), 750*(i)*
Bureaucracy
  expansion of, 741
  Napoleon and, 655–657
  Nazi use of, 596*(b)*
  reforms in, 607–608
  in Russia, 866
  in Soviet Union, 879
  transnational, 927
Burke, Edmund (1729–1799), 644*(b)*, 670
Burma
British colonialism in, 765*(m)*
  in World War II, 897
Burschenschaften (student societies), 676
Bush, George W., Taliban in Afghanistan and, 1005
Business. *See also* Commerce; Trade and trade routes
  expansion of, 768
  forms of, 772
  global, 998
  in Great Depression, 874–875
  mergers in, 986
  revolution in, 772–775
Byron, Lord (George Gordon, 1788–1824), 672, 676

Cabet, Étienne (1788–1856), 707
Cabinet of Doctor Caligari (film), 863
Cage, John, 960
Cairo, 761
Calas, Jean, 591–592
Calcutta (Kolkata), cotton exports from, 690
Calendar
  in French Republic, 635
  in Russia, 846n
California, 737
Calvinism, in France, 592
Cambodia
  in Union of Indochina, 766
  U.S. invasion of, 969
Cambridge University, women's education at, 742–743
Cameroons, 762
  German colonies in, 819
Camus, Albert, 937
Canada
  cession to Britain, 606
  self-determination for, 702
  self-government by, 739
  welfare state in, 927
  after World War I, 857
Canals, 740
Cancino, Fernandez Luis, 679*(i)*
Canning, 770
Canton system, 606
Cape Colony (southern Africa), 818
Capital (financial), in England, 687
Capital-intensive industry, 772
Capitalism
  Marx on, 746
  Stalin on, 920
Capitalist countries, as first world, 914
Caporetto, battle at, 849
Carbonari (Italy), 671, 675, 676
Carbon dioxide, atmospheric pollution and, 1000
Car-free zones, 1001
Caribbean region
  France in, 661
  immigrants to Europe from, 935, 936*(i)*
  slave revolts in, 641–643, 642*(m)*
Carlsbad Decrees, 676
Carnegie, Andrew, 770
Caroline (England), 679, 680
Carson, Rachel, 1000
Cartels, 772
  after World War I, 860
Carter, Jimmy, 972
Cartoons, political, 643*(i)*
Cartwright, Edmund, 687
Casino Royale (Fleming), 942
Cassatt, Mary, 783, 784*(i)*
Castlereagh, Robert (1769–1822), 668, 670
Castro, Fidel (1926–), 944
Catherine II ("the Great") (Russia, r. 1762–1796), 586*(i)*, 587–588, 606
  nobility and, 600
  Poland and, 622
  Pugachev rebellion and, 611
  reforms by, 608, 609
Catholicism. *See* Roman Catholicism
Cavour, Camillo di (Italy, 1810–1861), 721, 729, 730
Ceaușescu, Nicolae, 980
Censorship
  in France, 623, 678
  in Italian provinces, 703
  under Metternich, 676
  in Nazi Germany, 885
  in World War II, 900
Census, 741
Centers of influence, 986
Central America, female workers in, 1007
Central Europe
  Nazi conquest of, 894–896
  in 1930s, 888
  political trends in, 811
  power politics in, 788–791
  after World War I, 858
Central Intelligence Agency (CIA), 944
Central Powers (World War I), 836, 840, 849
Central Short Time Committee (Britain), 691–692
Cereal grains. *See* Grain
Cetshwayo (Zulu king), 764*(b)*
Cézanne, Paul (1839–1906), 808
CFCs. *See* Chlorofluorocarbons
Chamberlain, Neville (1869–1940), 894
Chamber of Deputies (France), 670–671, 887
Chamber of Peers (France), 670
Chambord, comte de, 788
Chaplin, Charlie (1889–1977), 863, 888
Charitable foundations, 999
Charity(ies), 604
  women and, 699, 700
Charles IV (Spain, r. 1788–1808), 664
Charles X (France, r. 1824–1830), 678
Charles Albert (Piedmont-Sardinia, r. 1831–1849), 675, 712
Charter of the Nobility (Russia), 600, 611
Chartism, 708–709
Chateaubriand, François-René de (1768–1848), 658
Châtelet, Émilie du (1706–1749), 589–590
Chávez, César (1927–1993), 964
Chechnya, 990, 992
  Russia and, 993, 994*(i)*
Cheka (Russian secret police), 848
Chelmno, extermination camp at, 898

Chernobyl catastrophe, 999–1000
Childbearing, in welfare state, 941
Childbirth, improvements in, 954
Child labor, industrial, 691, 691*(i)*
Child marriage, in India, 744
Children
abandonment of, 604
in concentration camps (c. 1945), 899*(i)*
in Enlightenment, 605
as factory workers, 691
in Great Depression, 876
mortality of, 604
in Romania, 980*(i)*
in Sunday school, 699
in Sweden, 886
thalidomide and, 954*(i)*
in upper class, 775
in workforce, 773
Chile
economy in, 1007
uprising in (1989), 978
China
Boxer Uprising in, 822–823
civilian casualties in World War II, 898
civil war in, 745
Communists in, 931
Cultural Revolution in, 970
economy in, 1006
English trade and, 765
Europeans and, 745
gunboats in, 770
imperialism in, 765, 766–767
Japan and, 837, 890
Nixon in, 970
opium trade and, 702
Russia and, 765, 993
socialism in, 823
Soviet Union and, 961
Tiananmen Square uprising in (1989), 978–979
as U.S. creditor, 1007
workers in, 1007
Chirac, Jacques, 975
Chlorine gas, 838
Chlorofluorocarbons (CFCs), 1000
Cholera, 694, 739
spread of (1826–1855), 694*(m)*
Chopin, Frédéric (1810–1849), 697
Christian Democrats
in cold war, 961
in Italy, 924, 972
Christianity. *See also* Missions and missionaries; Roman Catholicism; specific groups
in India, 671*(i)*
missionaries and, 768
Christian Social Party (Austria-Hungary), 815
Christmas Carol, The (Dickens), 697
Church(es)
in Enlightenment, 608–609
reforms of, 937
revivalism and, 598–599
Church and state
in Enlightenment, 591–592
in France, 654
in Germany, 751
Churchill, Randolph, 775
Churchill, Winston (1874–1965), 775, 896, 907, 917, 932
CIA. *See* Central Intelligence Agency
CIS. *See* Commonwealth of Independent States
Cisalpine Republic, 640
Cities and towns. *See also* Urban areas; Urbanization
car-free zones in, 1001
cholera in, 694, 694*(m)*
global, 998
industrialization and, 685
order in, 739–740
overcrowding and disease in, 693–694
Paris Commune and, 745–746
population growth in, 800
Citizens and citizenship. *See also* Democracy; Voting and voting rights
activism and, 964–969
global, 984*(i)*
for immigrant workers, 936
Civic nationalism, 729
Civil Code (Napoleon), 652, 657–658, 700
land ownership and, 695
Louis XVIII and, 670
women under, 658
Civil Constitution of the Clergy (France, 1790), 628
Civil disobedience, in India, 877
Civilians
after World War I, 860–862
in World War I, 842, 844–845
after World War II, 923, 923*(i)*
in World War II, 897–900, 900–902
Civilization(s). *See also* Culture; Geography; Western world
"clash" of, 986
imperialism and, 767–768
Civil rights
for French Protestants, 592
movements for, 938
women and, 965
Civil Rights Act (U.S., 1964), 962
Civil rights movement (U.S.), 962, 964
Civil service. *See* Bureaucracy
Civil war(s)
in Bosnia-Herzegovina, 988
in China, 745
in France, 636, 747
in Russia, 848–849, 849*(m)*
in Spain (1936–1939), 892–894, 893*(i)*, 893*(m)*
in United States, 737–739
Clair, René, 888
Clandestine workers, 936
Classes. *See also* Aristocracy
city renovation and, 739
clothing and, 656*(b)*, 656*(i)*
differences among, 700*(i)*
fashions and, 700
imperial society and, 775–780
Marx on, 746
middle class and, 600–603
nobility and, 599–600
struggle among, 713*(b)*
working class, 690–691
Classical music, 602–603, 960
Classicism, romanticism and, 672
Class struggle, Paris Commune as, 748
Clemenceau, Georges (1841–1929), 852
Clement XIV (Pope, r. 1769–1774), 610
Clergy
in France, 623, 654
in French Revolution, 637–638
in Germany, 751
Methodist, 598–599
Shi'ite, 1003–1004
Clermont Tonnerre, Stanislas de (1757–1792), 627*(b)*
Climate, pollution and, 1000
Cloning, 953–954
Clothing, 687. *See also* Textiles and textile industry
class and, 700
Napoleonic revolution in, 656*(b)*, 656*(i)*
of upper class, 775–776
World War I and, 845, 861
Clown, The (Böll), 940
Coal and coal industry
cartels in, 772
German, after World War I, 852, 856
industrialization and, 689
output of, 690*(f)*
strikes in England (1926), 859
Cochin China, 744
in Union of Indochina, 766
Codes (military), World War II and, 896
Codes of law. *See* Law(s); Law codes
Cohabitation, 958
Coitus interruptus, 800
Cold war, 914. *See also* Superpowers
arms race in, 925*(f)*
consumerism in, 939
culture of, 942–943
decolonization in, 930–936
emerging nations in, 933*(i)*, 933–935
historians on, 918*(b)*
origins of, 917–920
Pasternak and, 913
protests against, 961–969
space race and, 952–953
world during (c. 1960), 945*(m)*
Cole, Thomas (1801–1848), 696
Collaborators, in World War II, 922–923
Collage, 808
Collective action, 784–785
Collective farming. *See also* Collectivization
propaganda for, 928*(i)*
in Russia, 992
Soviet, 880, 917, 928–929
Collective security, 853. *See also* Alliances
after World War I, 856
Collectivists, 707
Collectivization. *See also* Collective farming
in China, 931
in Soviet bloc, 898
Colleges. *See* Universities and colleges
Colonies and colonization
in Africa, 759, 762–765, 763*(m)*
British India and, 743*(m)*, 743–744
British in Malay peninsula and Burma, 765*(m)*
European in Africa, 762–765
global North vs. South and, 1003
imperialism and, 701
of Napoleon, 661–662
in 1930s, 890
resistance to, 822–825, 877
revolts in 1820s, 675
revolutions by North American, 612–614
revolutions in French colonies, 640–643
traumatized peoples in, 938
violence of, 762*(i)*
World War I and, 837, 854, 859
after World War II, 908
Colossus (computer), 951
Combahee River Statement (1977), 966*(b)*
COMECON. *See* Council for Mutual Economic Assistance

Commerce. *See also* Business; Trade and trade routes
in Continental System, 662–663
digitization and, E-3
in European-controlled Africa, 762
in Germany, 961
industrial innovation and, 769–771
migration and, 776–777
Committee of Public Safety (France), 631–633, 634, 636, 637, 638
Common Market (Europe), 923, 925–926, 995
England, Ireland, and Denmark in, 961
as European Union, 986, 995–996
manufacturing in, 956
Spain in, 975
United States and, 970
Common Sense (Paine), McCarthy and, 924
Commonwealth of Independent States (CIS), 990, 991*(m)*
Communes. *See also* Paris Commune
in Paris, 745, 746*(m)*, 746–747, 747*(i)*
Communications
global, 1012
global technology and, E-1
in late 1800s, 761
satellites for, 951, 953
Communism, 707–708. *See also* Communist Party
arts and, 943
in China, 931
collapse in Europe (1989–1990), 981*(m)*
collapse in Soviet bloc, 976–980
collective farming under, 928*(i)*
in Czechoslovakia, 949
in eastern Europe, 919–920
in France, 887–888
utopia of, 865–867
Communist China. *See* China
Communist (Third) International (Comintern), 849
Communist Manifesto, The (Marx and Engels), 707–708, 708*(b)*
Communist Party
in Europe after World War II, 924
in Indochina, 878
in Russia, 848, 866, 919, 990
Communities
worker activities in, 786
on World Wide Web, 1009
Compulsory education, 742
Computers, 951–952
Internet and, 1009
Comte, Auguste (1798–1857), 701, 753
Concentration camps
Kikuyus in, 933
as memorials, 901
Nazi, 873, 884, 898–900, 899*(i)*, 899*(m)*
in South African (Boer) War, 818
survivors of, 915–916
Concert of Europe, 668
end of, 722–724
Concerts, 602
Concorde aircraft, 955–956
Condition of the Working Class in England, The (Engels), 692, 707
Condoms, 695, 800
Confederacy (United States South), 737–739
Confederation of the Rhine, 662, 668
Confessions (Rousseau), 598
Congo, 762
immigrants from, 985, 1008
Congress kingdom, Poland and, 679
Congress of Vienna (1814–1815), 667–670, 668*(i)*, 669*(m)*, 724
conservatism after, 670–671
Conscription. *See* Military draft
Conservation, of energy, 971–972
Conservatism
challenges to, 672
after Congress of Vienna, 670–671
in 1980s, 972
after revolutions of 1848, 715
Conservative Party (England), 736, 827, 973
Considerations on France (Maistre), 645*(b)*
Considerations on the Main Events of the French Revolution (de Staël), 645*(b)*
Constant, Benjamin (1767–1830), 666–667*(b)*
Constantine (Russia), 676
Constitution
in France, 626, 628, 629, 630, 653
in Poland, 622
in Sweden, 612
in United States, 614
Constitutionalism, Enlightenment and, 596–597
Constitutional monarchy
in Belgium, 679
in France, 628
in Italy, 813
in Spain, 973
Consulate (France), 653–654
Consumer economy, global, 1010–1011
Consumers and consumerism
in cold war, 939, 941
department stores and, 774*(i)*, 774–775
in Soviet bloc, 929–930
after World War I, 861–862
after World War II, 917, 923
young people and, 959
Continental Congress, First and Second, 613
Continental Europe
industrialization of, 690
liberalism in, 706
Napoleon in, 660–661
railroads and, 689
Continental System, 662–663
Contraception, 695. *See also* Birth control
oral, 953, 954
Contrasts (Pugin), 696
Convention. *See* National Convention (France)
Cook, James (1728–1779), 592
Co-Prosperity Sphere, Japanese, 892*(b)*
Corday, Charlotte (1768–1793), 635–636
Córdoba, 975
Corinne (de Staël), 658
Corn Laws (Britain), repeal of, 705–706
Coronation, of Napoleon I, 654, 655*(i)*
Coronation of Napoleon and Josephine (David), 655*(i)*
Corporate state, in fascist Italy, 868
Corporations
limited-liability, 772
multinational, 955–956
Corps législatif (France), 723
Corroded Metals (rock band), 1009
Corruption, in Russia, 990
Corsica and Corsicans, 998
Cortes (Spain), 675
Cosmonauts, 930, 952
Cossacks, 611, 611*(i)*
Cost of living
in cities, 998
in World War I, 845*(f)*
Cotton and cotton industry. *See also* Textiles and textile industry
in Egypt, 761
India and, 690
industrialization and, 687
in United States, 690
Council for Mutual Economic Assistance (COMECON), 929
Council of Five Hundred (France), 653
Council of State (France), 654
Counterrevolutionaries, in Russian civil war, 848
Countryside. *See* Rural areas
Coups
in Austria, 888
in France, 654
Courbet, Gustave, 749
Court (royal)
in England, 600
in France, 597
painting in, 602
Courts (legal), in France, 609–610
Cracow, 640
Crafts, industrialization and, 770
Craft unions, 785
Cream separator, 770
Credit, collapse of, 1007–1008
Crick, Francis, 939–940, 953
Crime and criminals, poverty and, 604
Crime and Punishment (Dostoevsky), 749
Crimean War (1853–1856), 722–723, 724*(m)*, 724–726
Mediterranean region and, 744
nurses in, 725*(i)*
photography in, 738*(b)*, 738*(i)*
Crimes against humanity
by Milosevic, 987n, 990
Nuremberg trials and, 923
Critique of Pure Reason, The (Kant), 597
Croatia, 988
independence of, 850, 990
nationalism and, 703
Serbs murdered in, 989
Croats. *See also* Yugoslavia
nationalism and, 703, 714, 844
in Yugoslavia, 920
Crops
in Egypt, 761
failures of, 709–710
Cross-cultural contact. *See* Culture; Trade and trade routes
Cross in the Mountains, The (Friedrich), 674
Crouching Tiger, Hidden Dragon (film), 1012
Cruikshank, George (1792–1878), 697
"Cry of the Children, The" (Browning), 696
Crystal Palace (1851), 716*(i)*, 716–717
Cuba
Castro in, 944
Spain and, 677
United States and, 818
Cuban missile crisis (1962), 914, 937, 944, 944*(m)*
Cubism, 808, 810
Cult(s)
of Lenin, 867
of the offensive, 838–839
of personality, 929
Cultivation. *See* Agriculture; Crops; Farms and farming
Cult of Reason (France), 634–635
Cult of the Supreme Being (France), 634–635
Cultural Revolution (China, 1960s), 970

Culture. *See also* Art(s); Intellectual thought; Popular culture; Society
in Belgium, 998
in cold war, 942–943
debates over future, 863–865
in Digital Age, E-4–E-5
education and, 742
Enlightenment styles of, 601–603
in former Soviet bloc, 1013–1014
French republican, 633–634
global, 1011–1015
imperial society and, 775–783
Irish, 813
in mid-1800s, 698
in nation-states, 722
in Nazi Germany, 885
in 1930s, 888–889
non-Western, 767–768, 1012–1013
popular, 940*(b)*
in Russia, 866
of social order, 748–753
and society in Enlightenment, 599–605
Stalinism and, 929
television and, 951
U.S. dominance of, 1014
after World War II, 937–938, 939–943
Curie, Marie (1867–1934), 806–807, 807*(i)*
Curie, Pierre (1859–1906), 806–807, 807*(i)*
Currency
euro as, 995, 995*(i)*
in Sweden, 886
Cybulski, Zbigniew, 939*(i)*, 941*(i)*
Cyprus
economic protests on, 1007*(i)*
in EU, 996
Czartoryska, Zofia, 590
Czech language, in Bohemia, 789
Czechoslovakia
anti-Soviet movement in, 965
collapse of communism in, 979–980
Communists in, 919
in Little Entente, 856, 856*(m)*
Nazi Germany and, 894
Prague Spring and, 967–969
refugees after World War I, 858
rural family in, 800*(i)*
Slovak Fascist Party in, 888
after World War I, 852, 858
Czech people, 815. *See also* Bohemia
independence of, 850
nationalism and, 703, 844
self-determination for, 713
Czech Republic
in EU, 996
fertility rates in, 1002
foreign investment in, 996

Dachau concentration camp, 884, 901
Dada movement, 863
Daguerre, Jacques (1787–1851), 698, 698*(i)*
Daguerreotype, 698, 698*(i)*
Daily life. *See* Lifestyle
Daladier, Édouard (1884–1970), 894
Dalai Lama, 1012
Dalmatian coast, Austria and, 669*(m)*
Dance, 809–810
Danes. *See also* Denmark
self-determination for, 713
Danton, Georges-Jacques (1759–1794), 635, 637
Danubian principalities, 677
Darwin, Charles (1809–1882), 752, 781
Das Kapital (Marx), 746
Daumier, Honoré, 711*(i)*, 750*(i)*
David, Jacques-Louis (1748–1825), 633–634, 650*(i)*, 655*(i)*, 657*(i)*
Davis, Angela, 965
Dawes Plan (1924), 856
Day-care centers, 927
D-Day (June 6, 1944), 905
Dean, James, 939
Death(s), from influenza pandemic (1918–1919), 850*(f)*
Debt, in Germany after World War I, 856
Debussy, Claude (1862–1918), 809–810
Decembrist Revolt (Russia), 676
De-Christianization, in revolutionary France, 633, 634–635
Declaration of Independence (United States, 1776), 613*(b)*
Enlightenment ideals in, 588
Declaration of the Rights of Man and Citizen (France), 626–627, 627*(b)*
Decolonization
of Africa (1951–1990), 934*(m)*
of Belgium, 934
during cold war, 930–936
Dutch, 934
Decorative arts, 783
Defense
cold war spending on, 944
before World War I, 827
Deficits, trade, 772
De Gaulle, Charles (1890–1970), 924
Algerian independence and, 934
on English words in France, 1014
nuclear power and, 953, 961
strikes and, 967
on television, 951
World War II and, 897, 902
Degeneration (Nordau), 803
De Gouges, Olympe (1748–1793), 627, 633
Deists, 591
De Kooning, Willem, 943
Delacroix, Eugène (1798–1863), 674, 674*(i)*
Delhi, 743
Demilitarization, of Rhineland, 856
Demilitarized zone (Rhineland), Nazi troops in, 891
Democracies (democratic countries), in 1930s, 886–889
Democracy
in early United States, 588
economic, 857
Soviets and, 917–919
Democratic Party (Germany), 856*(i)*
Demography, censuses and, 741
Demoiselles d'Avignon, Les (Picasso), 808
Demonstrations. *See* Activism; Protest(s); Revolts and rebellions
Denationalization, 1008
Denazification, after World War II, 923
D'Enghien, duke (France), 654
Denmark
in Common Market, 961
German invasion of, 896
population growth in, 800
Prussia and, 733
voting rights in, 788
welfare state in, 927*(i)*
Dentists, 928
Department stores, 774*(i)*, 774–775
Dépôts de mendicité, 604
Depression (economic). *See* Great Depression
De Sica, Vittorio, 943
Despotism, enlightened, 605
De Staël, Anne-Louise-Germaine (1766–1817), 645*(b)*, 658, 659, 664
Détente policy, 970, 974
Devaluation, of Swedish currency, 886
Diamonds, in Africa, 763
Diary of a Young Girl (Frank), 937
Dickens, Charles, 696–697, 748
Dictators and dictatorships. *See also* Authoritarianism
in Nazi Germany, 874
ousting of (1970s), 973
in Soviet Union, 874
after World War I, 874
Diderot, Denis (1713–1784), 589, 590*(b)*, 597
on Jews, 609
on legal reform, 592
Diem, Ngo Dinh, 932
Dien Bien Phu, battle of (1954), 932
Diet (food). *See also* Food(s)
crop failures and, 709
Dietrich, Marlene, 888
Digital Age
society in, E-2
West during, E-1–E-6
world in new millennium, E-3*(m)*
Dior, Christian, 940
Diplomacy
at Congress of Vienna, 668*(i)*, 668–670
in Germany, 789
in 1970s, 970
Peace of Paris and, 856–857
after World War I, 856–857
before World War I, 828, 829
Directory (France), 638
Napoleon and, 653
Disabilities, thalidomide and, 954*(i)*
Disarmament, after World War I, 856
Discrimination, against colonial peoples, 930
Disease. *See also* Health
AIDS, 977, 1002–1003
cholera, 694, 694*(m)*
control of, 1002
germ theory of, 740
global, 986, 1002–1003
malaria as, 770
tuberculosis, 694
urbanization and, 693–694
Disraeli, Benjamin (1804–1881), 736, 790
Dissident artists, in Soviet Union, 962
Divided Heaven (Wolf), 962
Divorce, 801
Civil Code of Napoleon and, 658
in France, 635, 711
in Soviet Union, 881
Divorcers, The (Daumier), 711*(i)*
Dix, Otto, 843*(b)*, 843*(i)*
DNA, 953–954
Doctors. *See also* Medicine
numbers of, 928
Doctors Without Borders, 999
Doctor Zhivago (novel and movie), 912*(i)*, 913, 943
Dollfuss, Engelbert, 888
Doll's House, A (Ibsen), 782, 782*(b)*, 811
Domesticity
in cold war, 940–941
women and, 700–701

Domestic system, 687
Dominion of Canada, 739. *See also* Canada
Doré, Gustave (1832–1883), 702*(i)*
Dostoevsky, Fyodor, 749, 791
Double Helix, The (Watson), 939
Double standard, sexual, 775
Draft. *See* Military draft
Dreadnought, HMS (ship), 827
Dreams of My Russian Summers (Makine), 1014
Dresden, bombing of, 897
Dreyfus, Alfred (1859–1935), 814, 814*(i)*
Dreyfus Affair (France), 814
Drinking water, in Africa, 1002
Drought, in Africa and Asia, 770, 1002
Drug culture, 964
Drugs, to cure AIDS, 1003
Drunkenness, temperance movements and, 699
Dual Alliance, 790
Dual Monarchy, 736, 815, 826
Dubček, Alexander, 967–968, 979–980
Du Bois, W. E. B. (1868–1963), 854
Duchamp, Marcel, 808*(i)*
Duchy of Warsaw, 661, 668
  as Poland, 669*(m)*
Duma (Russia), 821, 846
Dunkirk, 896
Dutch. *See also* Boers; Dutch Republic; Netherlands
  Africa and, 762–763
  Belgian independence from, 679
  colonies of, 859, 890
  decolonization and, 934
  end of empire, 934
  evaluation of values, 1011*(b)*
  globalization and, 1010*(b)*
  imperialism of, 762–763
  Japan and, 745
  Napoleon and, 664
Dutch Patriot Revolt (1787), 621–622
Dutch Republic. *See also* Dutch; Holland; Netherlands
  American Revolution and, 614
  Congress of Vienna and, 669, 669*(m)*
  France and, 639, 639*(m)*
  in Netherlands, 669, 669*(m)*
  protests in, 620–622
  revolts in, 620
Dynasties. *See* Kings and kingdoms; Monarchs and monarchies; specific dynasties and rulers

East Africa
  German colonies in, 819
  independence in, 933
  resistance to Germany in, 824
  World War I and, 837
East Asia
  economies of, 1006–1007
  Japan and, 820, 890
  U.S. and Soviet interests in, 931
East Berlin, fall of Berlin Wall and, 979
Easter Monday (1916), Irish protests on, 846
Eastern Europe. *See also* specific locations
  brain drain from, 957, 969
  communism in, 919, 976–980, 981*(m)*
  and Communist disintegration in 1989, 978–980
  economic recovery in, 928–930
  education in, 699
  EU members from, 996–998
  families in, 800
  farmers in, 876
  father's role in, 801
  Havel on, 997*(b)*
  industrialization in, 690
  landowners in, 695
  modern arts in, 808–809
  in 1930s, 888
  in 1990s, 987*(m)*
  political trends in, 811
  power politics in, 791
  prostitutes from, 1008
  refugees to western Europe from, 915
  revolution of 1848 in, 714*(i)*
  Soviets and, 919–920, 923
  in Western consumer economy, 1010
  after World War I, 858
Eastern front, in World War I, 839
East Germany, 921
  flight from, 979, 981*(m)*
  West German trade with, 961
East India Company (Britain), 702, 743, 761
East Prussia
  Polish Corridor and, 852
  in World War I, 839
Ebert, Friedrich (1871–1925), 851, 852
Ebola virus, 1003
Ecce Homo (Grosz), 864*(i)*
Ecce Homo (Nietzsche), 864*(i)*
Economic democracy, 857
Economic development loans, 1003
Economic planning, in Soviet Union, 879
Economics, supply-side, 973
Economist, The (periodical), 705–706
Economy. *See also* Agriculture; Farms and farming; Great Depression; Labor; Trade and trade routes; Wealth
  in Austria, 975–976
  crisis in 1870s–1890s, 771–772
  in Digital Age, E-2–E-4
  in eastern Europe, 997–998
  in England, 771, 888, 973–974
  in Enlightenment, 603–604
  fascism and, 868
  in former Soviet Union, 992
  in France, 624, 771, 888, 975
  in Germany, 771, 789, 920
  global, 986, 1006–1008
  global networks and, 1009–1011
  global organizations and, 999
  in Great Depression (1930s), 874–878
  in Greece, 996
  growth of German and American, 770–771
  in Hungary, 888
  imperialism and, 701–702
  in Japan, 859
  in Korean War, 925
  liberals on, 705
  Marx on, 746
  Napoleon and, 662
  of Nazi Germany, 884–885
  non-Western, 986
  oil crisis and (1970s), 971–972
  of Pacific region, 1006*(m)*, 1006–1007
  Peace of Paris and, 855–856
  protests and, 1007*(i)*
  in Russia, 990
  Smith on, 593
  Soviet, 878–880, 976
  in Spain, 975
  top fifteen (2010), 1016*(m)*
  in United States, 771, 916–917, 974
  in western Europe, 974–975
  after World War I, 855–856, 857, 858, 860
  after World War II, 924–925
  World War II production and, 900–902
  worldwide collapse of (1997), 1007–1008
Ecosystems, destruction of, 1000
ECSC. *See* European Coal and Steel Community
Ecumenism, Vatican II and, 937
Edict of Nantes (1598), revocation of, 592
Education. *See also* Higher education; Philosophy; Schools; Universities and colleges
  in Austria, 609
  in eastern Europe, 929
  in France, 788
  in French Revolution, 635
  integration in United States, 938
  Napoleon on, 658
  for poor people, 699–700
  in postindustrial age, 957–958
  professionalization and, 742–743
  in Prussia, 609
  reform of, 742
  Rousseau on, 594*(b)*, 595
  in Russia, 609, 866
  of women, 658
Educational television, 951
Edward VII (England, r. 1901–1910), 805*(i)*
EEC. *See* European Economic Community
Efficiency experts, in Russia, 866
Ego, 804
Egypt
  agriculture in, 761
  England and, 761*(m)*, 825, 837
  government overturned in, E-4
  independence of, 932–933
  Napoleon and, 653
  Sadat and, 974*(i)*
  Saint-Simonians in, 707
  Suez Canal and, 744–745
  West and, 720*(i)*
  after World War I, 859
  in World War II, 904
Egyptian-Israeli peace accord, 974*(i)*
Eiffel Tower, 769
Einstein, Albert (1879–1955), 807
Eisenhower, Dwight (1890–1969), 905
Eisenstein, Sergei, 863, 881
Elba, island of, 665
Elections, in Germany (1932), 882–883
Electricity, 769, 769*(i)*
Electronic media
  in Digital Age, E-1
  wars, peace, politics, and, E-4
Electroworld, in Budapest, 998
Elektra (Strauss), 810
Eliot, George (Mary Ann Evans), 748
Eliot, T. S., 864
Elites. *See also* Aristocracy
  in Enlightenment, 599–600
  French Revolution and, 646–647
  imperial, 775
  middle class as, 600–603
Elizabeth (Russia, r. 1741–1762), 605–606
Ellis, Havelock, 802
Ellison, Ralph, 962
Emancipation
  of Russian serfs, 726–727
  of U.S. slaves, 938
Emancipation Proclamation (U.S., 1863), 737

Embargo
on exports to Japan, 890
on oil, 971
Emerging economies
in India, 1008
in Pacific region, 1007–1008
in South Africa, 1008
Emerging nations, in cold war, 933*(i)*, 933–935
Emigration, 695. *See also* Immigrants and immigration; Migration
European (1870–1890), 777*(f)*
rural, 692–693
Émile (Rousseau), 593*(i)*, 594*(b)*, 595
Emin, Mehmed, 823*(b)*
Empires. *See also* Classes; Imperialism; specific empires
arts and, 783
in Asia, 931–932
costs and profits of, 767
culture and, 781–783
in France, 734
imperialism and, 759–760, 761–768
industry, technology, and, 768–775
society and, 775–783
World War I and, 836–837, 852
Employment. *See also* Women; Workforce
industrial, 690–692
in service sector, 956
Ems telegram (Bismarck), 734
Enabling Act (Germany), 884
Encyclopedia (Diderot, ed.), 589, 590*(b)*
Energy. *See also* Oil and oil industry
Einstein on, 807
electricity as, 769
in 1980s, 972
nuclear, 914
Engels, Friedrich (1820–1895), 692, 707–708, 708*(b)*
Engines, steam, 686–687
England (Britain). *See also* Britain; Great Britain; Ireland; Parliament (England)
Africa and, 762
American Revolution against, 612–614
British Empire of, 761
Canada and, 606
Catholicism in, 681
colonies of, 837, 890
Common Market and, 926, 961
at Congress of Vienna, 668
Crimean War and, 724–725
Crystal Palace in, 716*(i)*, 716–717
economy after World War I, 855
Egypt and, 761*(m)*, 825, 932–933
examination system in, 742
factory workers in, 690
Falkland war and, 974
France and, 662–663
French Revolution and, 636
Holy Alliance and, 670
India and, 743–744, 931
Industrial Revolution in, 686–689
industrial slowdown in, 770
Iraq oil and, 854–855*(b)*
Ireland and, 787, 813
Irish Republican Army and, 972
Japanese in, 998
landed gentry in, 600
landowners in, 695
liberalism in, 705, 812–813
in Malay peninsula and Burma (1826–1890), 765*(m)*
manufacturing in, 689
Methodists in, 671
Monroe Doctrine and, 678
Munich Pact and, 894
Napoleon and, 653, 660, 661, 662
Nazis and, 896–897
in 1930s, 887–888
nobility in, 600
opium and, 702, 702*(i)*, 702*(m)*
political reforms in, 786–787
poor law in (1834), 699
population of, 687
racism in, 800
railroads in, 685, 688–689
Reform Bill of 1832 in, 679–681
reforms in, 736–737
resistance to, 614*(i)*, 614–615
revolutions of 1848 and, 715
Russia and, 790
in 1780, 615*(m)*
in Seven Years' War, 605–606
slave trade and, 701
southern Africa and, 763*(m)*, 763–764, 818
textile industry in, 690
Thatcher in, 973–974, 974*(i)*
woman suffrage in, 811, 812
workday limits in, 691
after World War I, 854*(b)*, 858–859
in World War I, 845–846
after World War II, 907, 915, 924
in World War II, 897, 904
English language, spread of, 1014
Enlightened despots, 605
Enlightenment, 587–615
cultural styles in, 601–603
Declaration of Independence and, 588
France and, 589–591, 597
French Revolution and, 626
in Germany, 597
Hitler and, 596*(b)*
individual and society during, 592–596
intellectual thought in, 588–592
Kant on, 596*(b)*
nobility during, 599–600
rebellions against state power in, 610–614
religion in, 608–609
science in, 589*(i)*
secularism in, 592
society and culture in, 599–605
spread of, 596–597
women in, 590–591, 594–595*(b)*
Entente Cordiale, 825, 827, 836
Entertainment, popular, 604
Entrepreneurs, in United States, 770
Environment
activism for, 1000
global, 986
global warming and, 1000
pollution of, 999–1000
suburbs and, 928
Epidemics. *See also* Disease
AIDS as, 1002–1003
cholera, 694, 694*(m)*
in cities, 739
global, 986
influenza (1918–1919), 850, 850*(f)*
Equal Employment Opportunity Commission (EEOC), 962
Equality. *See also* Gender and gender issues; Rights
in France, 627
in Poland, 858
in Russia, 866
U.S. civil rights movement and, 964
Equiano, Olaudah, 592
Eriksen, Vigilius, 586*(i)*
Erikson, Erik, 804*(b)*
Eroica Symphony (Beethoven), 674
Esquivel, Laura, 1012–1013
Essay contests, in Enlightenment, 601
Esterházy family, 603
Estonia, 848
in EU, 996
independence of, 990
Nazi-Soviet Pact and, 895
Ethiopia
drought and poverty in, 1002
Italy and, 818, 891
struggle for (1896), 818*(m)*
Ethnic cleansing, 988–989
Ethnic Germans, 815
Ethnicity and ethnic groups
in Austria-Hungary, 736, 815, 837
in Austrian Empire, 703
in Balkans, 826–827
in former Soviet Union, 990
in Hungary, 714, 888
minorities after World War I, 858
in Ottoman Empire, 823–824
racism toward, 800–801
in Russia, 728–729, 766*(m)*, 821
in Yugoslavia, 987–990
Ethnography, 960
EU. *See* European Union
Eugenics, 801
Eugénie (France, r. 1853–1871), 723, 723*(i)*, 724
Euro, 995, 995*(i)*
European Coal and Steel Community (ECSC), 925–926
European Common Market, 923
European Community (EC), Greece in, 996
Europe and Europeans. *See also* Eastern Europe; Western Europe
in 1780, 615*(m)*
in 1799, 646*(m)*
in 1815, 669*(m)*
in 1830, 680*(m)*
in 1850, 717*(m)*
in 1871, 755*(m)*
in c. 1890, 793*(m)*
in 1914, 831*(m)*
in 1920s, 857–862
in 1929, 869*(m)*
in 1945, 909*(m)*
China and, 745
collapse of communism in (1989–1990), 981*(m)*
Common Market in, 925–926
Congress of Vienna and, 668–670, 669*(m)*
denazification of, 923
economy in smaller states, 975–976
emigration of workers from, 776–778
EU in, 995–996
fertility rates in, 1001–1002
French Revolution and, 633
global crises before World War I, 797–798
Green Party in, 1000
high-tech industries in, 1006
immigrants to, 935–936
industrialization in, 688, 689*(m)*
Kellogg-Briand Pact and, 856–857
languages in 19th-century Europe, 704*(m)*
migration within, 777

Europe and Europeans (*continued*)
Muslims in, 1008
after Napoleon, 667–672
protests in 1960s in, 964
railroads in, 688
recovery after World War II, 922–930
resistance to Nazis in, 902–903
smart cars in, 1000*(i)*
television and, 950–951
temporary workers in, 935
terrorism in, 972
views on French Revolution, 643–647
welfare state in, 927
after World War I, 850–857
World War I and, 835–851
World War II and, 894–905, 903*(m)*, 907–908, 914–915
World War II impact on, 916*(m)*
European Economic Community (EEC), 926, 994–995. *See also* Common Market
European Federation of Green Parties, 1001*(b)*
European Green Party, 1001*(b)*
European Union (EU)
Common Market as, 986, 995–996
drawbacks to membership in, 996
Dutch opposition to Turkish membership in, 1010*(b)*
eastern European members of, 996–998
economic collapse and, 1008
former Soviet bloc members of, 995
membership in, 987*(m)*, 996–997
in 2011, 996*(m)*
Evangelicals and Evangelicalism, 599
"Evil empire," Soviet Union as, 974
Evolution, Darwin on, 752, 753*(i)*
Examination system, in England, 742
Exchange. *See* Trade and trade routes
Existentialism, 937–938
Expansion
European, 743
French, 638–640, 639*(m)*, 744–745
imperialist, 761–768
industrial power and, 768
Japanese, 817, 890, 891*(m)*
by Nazi Germany (1933–1939), 895*(m)*
Russian in Asia, 765–766, 766*(m)*
of United States (1850–1870), 737*(m)*
Exploration, by Cook, 592
Exports. *See also* Trade and trade routes
Japanese, 890
trade deficits and, 772
Expressionism, 808–809
Extermination camps, Nazi, 898, 899*(m)*, 899–900

Fabian Society, 780
Facebook, protests and, E-4
Factories
computers in, 951–952
in Great Depression, 876
power looms in, 687
in Russia, 771
scientific management in, 860
in Soviet Union, 879
steam engines in, 686–687
workday limits for, 691
workers in, 690–692
after World War II, 925
Factory Act (Britain, 1833), 691
Fahrenheit 451 (Bradbury), 942
Falange Party (Spain), 893
Falkland Islands, war over (1982), 974
Families
agricultural, 695
allowances to, 927
birth control and, 780
Civil Code of Napoleon and, 657
Czech, 800*(i)*
in eastern Europe, 801
as factory workers, 690
in French Revolution, 635
in postindustrial age, 958–959
in Soviet Union, 881
in Sweden, 886–887
after World War I, 861
Family allowance, in Sweden, 886
Famines, 770
in Africa, 1002
in Ireland, 709*(i)*, 709–710
Fanon, Frantz, 938
Farms and farming. *See also* Agriculture; Collective farming; Land; Peasants; Rural areas
free trade and, 772
in Great Depression, 875–876
population and, 800
postindustrial, 956
Fascism, 879*(b)*. *See also* Nazis and Nazism (Germany)
in Italy, 867–868
in Spain, 893, 893*(i)*
Fascist Party (Italy), 867–868
Fashion, 940, 941
Fashoda, Sudan, 825
Fathers. *See* Children; Families
Fathers and Sons (Turgenev), 749
Fauves (painters), 807–808
Fawcett, Millicent Garrett (1847–1929), 811
Feinstein, Charles H., 693
Females. *See* Women
Feminine Mystique, The (Friedan), 965
Feminism. *See also* Women
debates in, 966–967*(b)*
environmentalism and, 967*(b)*
in France, 715
in 1960s and 1970s, 964–965, 965*(i)*
reforms of marriage and, 801
in World War I, 842
Fencing, 770
Ferdinand I (Austrian Empire, 1835–1848), 714
Ferdinand VII (Spain, r. 1808 and 1814–1833), 664, 675
Fertility
in European countries, 1001–1002
in former Soviet Union, 1002
in Great Depression, 876
social reforms and, 780
Fertilizers, 770
Festivals
French republican, 633–634
in French revolutionary calendar, 635
Feuchtwanger, Lion, 882*(b)*
Feudalism, end of French, 626
Fields, Gracie, 888, 889*(i)*
Fighting "Téméraire" Tugged to Her Last Berth to Be Broken Up, The (Turner), 696, 697*(i)*
Filipinos, 818. *See also* Philippines
Films, 862–863
global, 1014
Italian, 943
in 1930s, 888
about resistance, 937
on television, 951
transnational, 1012
after World War I, 862–863
in World War II, 900
"Final Solution," World War II and, 898. *See also* Holocaust
Finances, in France, 623
Finland
economic development in, 925
woman suffrage in, 811–812, 812*(i)*
Fireside chats, by Roosevelt, Franklin D., 886, 887*(i)*
First Balkan War (1912), 826*(m)*, 827
First Consul, Napoleon as, 653–654
First Continental Congress (U.S.), 613
First Estate (France), 624, 625*(i)*
First Fascist Program (Italy), 879
First International, 785
First Moroccan Crisis (1905), 825
First Partition of Poland (1772), 607, 607*(m)*
First Reich (Germany), 884
First Republic (France), 630
First world, 914
First World War. *See* World War I
Five-year plans, in Soviet Union, 878–880
Flappers, 862*(i)*
Flaubert, Gustave, 748, 749
Fleming, Ian, 942
Fleurs du mal, Les (Baudelaire), 748
Floods, global ice melting and, 1000
Floor Burger (Oldenburg), 959*(i)*
Flour War (France, 1775), 610–611
Flu. *See* Influenza epidemic
Flying shuttle, 687
Folk motifs, 783, 960
Folktales, 674
Food(s). *See also* Crops; Diet (food)
canning of, 770
production and distribution of, 695
riots over, 610–611, 625
in World War I, 845
Food-processing firms, 860
Forced labor. *See also* Slavery
German in Soviet Union, 920
Ford, Henry, 862
Ford Foundation, 999
Ford Motor Company, 860
Foreign aid
to Soviet Union, 917
after World War II, 919
Foreign investment, 996
in eastern Europe, 996
Foreign trade, German, 961
Foreign workers, worldwide, 1008–1009
Formosa. *See* Taiwan
Fossil fuels
pollution and, 1000
reducing dependence on, 1001
Fouché, Joseph (1759–1820), 654
Foundling hospitals, 604
Fourier, Charles (1772–1837), 706, 707
Fourteen Points (1918), 846, 852, 854*(b)*
Fourth Republic (France), 924, 934
Four-year plan (Germany), 884
France. *See also* French Revolution; Paris; Second Empire
Africa and, 762
Algeria and, 695, 701–702, 745
American Revolution and, 613
anticolonial activism and, 878
anti-Semitism in, 788

Asia and, 765
birth control in, 964–965
Bretons, Corsicans, and, 998
civil war in, 636, 747
in cold war, 961
colonies of, 890
at Congress of Vienna, 668
constitutional monarchy in, 628
constitutions in, 626, 628, 629, 630, 653
Continental System and, 662–663
Crimean War and, 724–725
division of (1940), 896*(m)*
divorce in, 711*(i)*, 801
Dreyfus Affair in, 814, 814*(i)*
economy in, 624, 855, 888, 975
education in, 699
Enlightenment in, 588, 597
expansion by, 744–745
family allowances in, 927
First Republic in, 630
Flour War in (1775), 610–611
Fourth Republic in, 924
Freemasons in, 601
Germany and, 837, 896
imperialism by, 761, 766, 767
independence for colonies of, 933–934
Indochina and, 766, 824–825
industry and business in, 771
inflation in (1973), 971
intellectual thought in, 658
Iraq oil and, 854–855*(b)*
Italian unification and, 730–731
Jews in, 788
landowners in, 695
Little Entente and, 856
McDonald's in, 999
mergers in, 955
Mexico and, 739
migration for work in, 604
Morocco and, 825
Muslims in, 1008
mutual aid societies in, 709
in 1930s, 887–888
nobility in, 600, 623, 655–657, 678
nuclear energy in, 953
Paris Commune and, 745, 746*(m)*, 746–747
parlements in, 609–610
peasants in, 636
Popular Front in, 886
Prussia and, 639–640
railroads in, 724
religion in, 671–672
resistance to Nazis in, 902
revolutions of 1848 and, 710–711, 715
Roman Catholicism in, 628, 654, 671
science in, 658
Second Empire in, 734, 787
Second Republic in, 711
serfs in, 609
1789–1791, 629*(m)*
in Seven Years' War, 605–606
slave trade and, 701
Spain and, 664, 675
student protests in, 966–967
Third Republic in, 787–788
Tunisia and, 761
women in, 710, 711*(i)*, 857
after World War I, 854*(b)*, 858
in World War I, 837*(i)*, 840*(m)*, 846
after World War II, 924
in World War II Allies, 897

Francis Ferdinand (Austria, 1863–1914), 828
Francis Joseph (Austrian Empire, r. 1848–1916), 714, 733, 789
Austro-Hungarian Empire and, 735–736
Vienna and, 739
Franco, Francisco (1892–1975), 893, 894, 973
Franco-Prussian War (1870–1871), 724, 733–734, 734*(b)*, 770
Frank, Anne (1929–1945), 937
Frankenstein (Shelley), 651, 672*(i)*, 673
Frankfurt, parliament, in 1848, 713
Frederick II the Great (Prussia, r. 1740–1786), 605
nobility and, 600
reforms by, 609
Frederick William I (Prussia, r. 1713–1740), 606
Frederick William III (Prussia, r. 1797–1840), 662
Frederick William IV (Prussia, r. 1840–1860), 712
Free Corps (Dutch Patriots), 622
Freedom(s). *See also* Rights
in France, 626, 654
individual, 596
Rousseau and, 594
in United States, 614, 626, 924
Freedom of Information Act (1966, 1974), 918
Free French, 897, 902, 924
Free market, cartels, trusts, and, 772
Free-market proposals, 593, 610
Freemasons, 600–601
Free Woman, The (newspaper), 707
Freikorps (Germany), 851
French Academy of Science, 807
French and Indian War. *See* Seven Years' War
French Empire, under Napoleon, 659–666, 660*(m)*
French Republics, 633–635, 654–655
French Revolution (1787–1800), 619–620
Burke on, 644*(b)*
contemporary perspectives on, 644–645*(b)*
criticisms of, 670
de-Christianization in, 633, 634–635
Declaration of Rights in, 626–627, 627*(b)*
fall of Bastille and, 624–626, 625*(i)*
Freemasons and, 601
origins of (1787–1789), 623–626
politicization of daily life in, 635
postrevolutionary period and, 651–672
Terror in, 631–638
warfare during, 633, 637, 638–640
women in, 627, 635–636, 636–637
women's march to Versailles in, 618*(i)*
worldwide reactions to, 643–647
French Revolution (1830), 678–679
Freud, Sigmund (1856–1939), 797, 798, 803*(i)*, 803–805, 816
Friedan, Betty, 965
Friedland, battle at (1807), 661
Friedrich, Caspar David (1774–1840), 673–674
Front for National Liberation (FNL, Algeria), 933–934
Fuels, fossil, 1000
Führer, Hitler as, 882
Fuseli, Johann Heinrich, 672*(i)*

Gaelic language, 704–705
Gagarin, Yuri (1934–1968), 930, 952
Galicia, 704, 839, 840
Gamberros ("hooligans," Spain), 939
Game laws, in England, 600

Gandhi, Mohandas K. ("Mahatma," 1869–1948), 877, 878*(i)*
assassination of, 931
U.S. civil rights movement and, 938
García Márquez, Gabriel, 1012
Garibaldi, Giuseppe (1807–1882), 712, 730*(m)*, 731
Gasoline engine, 769
Gay liberation movement, 964
Gays. *See* Homosexuality
Gaza, 971, 1005
Gdańsk shipyards, 977
Gehry, Frank, 1014–1015
Gender and gender issues. *See also* Men; Woman suffrage; Women
class and, 700
in French Revolution, 627
Freud on, 804
in Great Depression, 876
in Nazi Germany, 885
neutrality in Digital Age, E-2
in religion, 751
after World War I, 861
before World War I, 798–799
General, The (Orlov), 963*(b)*, 963*(i)*
General Maximum (France), 633
General School Ordinance (Austria), 609
General strike (England, 1926), 859, 860
General will, Rousseau's concept of, 596
Generation gap, 940, 958–959
Genetics
DNA and, 953–954
research in, 956
Geneva Conference (1954), 932, 962
Genius of Christianity (Chateaubriand), 658
Genlis, Stéphanie de (1746–1830), 603
Genoa, 670
Genocide, 986. *See also* Holocaust
in Africa, 1003
ethnic cleansing as, 988–989
in World War II, 896, 922
Gentry, in England, 600
Geoffrin, Marie-Thérèse (1699–1777), 590, 591*(i)*, 622
Geography, of France, 629*(m)*
George III (England, r. 1760–1820), 612
George IV (England, r. 1820–1830), 679–680
George V (England), 839
German Confederation, 669, 669*(m)*, 733
German Empire
of Bismarck, 734–735
after World War I, 853*(m)*
German Federal Republic, West Germany as, 924
German language, in Austria-Hungary, 735
German people, in Czechoslovakia, 894
Germany. *See also* East Germany; Nazis and Nazism (Germany); West Germany; World War I; World War II
Africa and, 762
anti-Semitism in, 814–815
arts in, 863
Austria and, 733
birthrate drop in, 800
in Central Powers, 836
in cold war, 961
colonial resistance to, 824
consolidation of, 661–662, 662*(i)*
Democratic Party in, 856*(i)*
division of, 920–922, 921*(m)*
economy in, 770–771, 789, 855–856

Germany (*continued*)
end of World War I and, 850
Enlightenment in, 597
fall of Berlin Wall and, 979
in Great Depression, 877*(b)*
headscarf controversy in, 1009*(i)*
immigration from, 695
imperialism by, 818–819
Jesuit expulsion from, 751
Morocco and, 825
Napoleon and, 661–662
nationalism and, 703, 715
nobility in, 600
opera in, 749
Paris Peace Conference and, 852–853
Poland and, 852, 896
as political entity, 597
population growth in, 800
postwar economy in, 920
power politics in, 789
racism in, 676, 800
railroads in, 689
renaissance in, 647
reparations after World War II, 920
Russia and, 856
Social Democrats in, 789, 810, 815, 827, 851
Spanish Civil War and, 893*(m)*, 894
unification of, 703, 712–713, 731–735, 733*(m)*
World War I and, 829–830, 839, 845–846, 848, 858
after World War II, 907, 915
before World War II, 890–894
World War II surrender by, 905
Germ theory of disease, 740
Gerome, Jean-Léon, 723*(i)*
Gestapo, 884, 898
Ghana, 933
Giacometti, Alberto, 907*(i)*
Gibbon, Edward (1737–1794), 597
Gillray, James (1756–1815), 643*(i)*
Giolitti, Giovanni (1842–1928), 813
Girls. *See* Mothers; Women
Girondins (France), 631, 632, 637
Girton (Cambridge University), 742
Give Us Liberty (film), 888
Gladstone, William (1809–1898), 784, 786
Glasnost (openness), 977, 978*(b)*
Glenn, John, 952
Global communication technology, E-1
Global culture, 1011–1015
Globalization, 986. *See also* Immigrants and immigration; Migration
of cities, 998
of communications, 1012
of culture, 1011–1015
Dutch and, 1010*(b)*
economic, 1008–1011
efforts to block, 999
Islam, West, and, 1003–1005
migration and, 984*(i)*, 985–986
nation-state and, 994–999
North vs. South and, 1003
pollution and, 999–1001
population, health, disease, and, 1001–1003
of tourism, 1012, 1012*(i)*
use of term, 988*(b)*
world challenges and, 999–1008
world economy and, 1006–1008
Global networks, economy and, 1009–1011
Global organizations, 999
Global war, World War II as, 890
Global warming, 1000
Goering, Hermann (1893–1946), 884
Goethe, Johann Wolfgang von (1749–1832), 598, 673
"Going to Battle" (Emin), 823*(b)*
Golan Heights, 971
Gold Coast, 764
independence of, 933
Gömbös, Gyula, 888
Gomley, Margaret, 691
Gonne, Maud (1866–1953), 813
Gorbachev, Mikhail, 950, 970, 976–977, 977*(i)*
experience of glasnost under, 978*(b)*
fall of Soviet Union and, 979, 990
Gorbachev, Raisa, 977*(i)*
Gordon, George, 612
Gordon riots (London), 612
Goulash communism, 929
Government. *See also* Kings and kingdoms; Monarchs and monarchies; Society
of Bolshevik Russia, 847–849
business and, 768
constitutionalism in, 596–597
economic role of, 974
in Europe after World War II, 922
expansion of, 741–742
of former Soviet Union, 992
of France, 724
of Germany, 851, 881
labor strikes and, 785
Napoleon and, 662
NGOs and, 999
of Poland, 679
of postrevolutionary France, 670–671
in postwar Europe, 923–927
professionalization of, 742
public welfare reforms and, 699–700
of Russia, 727
Smith on, 593
of Soviet Russia, 848–849
Swedish programs and, 886
television funded by, 951
totalitarian, 878–885
view of migration by, 778*(b)*
in World War I, 842–844
Goya y Lucientes, Francisco José de (1746–1828), 663*(i)*
Grain
free trade in, 610
shortages of, 609
Granada, 975
Grand Alliance. *See also* Allies
World War II and, 897, 907
Grand Army (France), 659–661
life in, 659–660
retreat from Moscow by, 664
"Grand tours," of Europe, 601
Graphic arts, 783
Great Awakening, 598, 599*(i)*, 671
second, 671
Great Britain. *See also* Britain; England (Britain)
creation of, 705
Great Depression (1930s), 874–878
democracies in, 886–889
in England, 887
in France, 887–888
in Germany, 872*(i)*, 881
in non-Western countries, 876–878
society in, 876
in Sweden, 886
in United States, 874–875
Great Dictator, The (film), 888
Greater East Asia Co-Prosperity Sphere, 890, 892*(b)*
Great Exhibition (England), 716*(i)*
Great Fear (France, 1789), 626, 626*(m)*
Great Reforms, in Russia, 726–727, 728–729
Great Society, 962
Great War. *See* World War I
Greece
Communists in, 919
dictator ousted in, 973
EU and, 996
fascism in, 879
independence from Turks, 676–677, 677*(i)*
migration from, 858
revolt in 1820s, 675
before World War I, 826, 827
before World War II, 894
Green Armies, 865
Greenhouse effect, 1000
Green Party
in Europe, 1000, 1001*(b)*
in Germany, 1000
transnational, 1001*(b)*
Gregorian calendar, in Russia, 846n
Greuze, Jean-Baptiste, 603*(i)*
Grosz, George (1893–1959), 863, 864*(i)*
Groupies, 959
Grozny, Chechnya, 993
Grundy, Sydney, 801*(i)*
Guadalcanal, battle at, 905
Guadeloupe, 606*(m)*, 643
Guam, 818
in World War II, 897
Guernica (Picasso), 894
Guggenheim Museum (Bilbao), 1015
Guilds, in Europe, 609
Guillotin, Joseph-Ignace (1738–1814), 632*(i)*
Guillotine, 631–632, 632*(i)*
Gulag, in Soviet Union, 880, 929, 969
Gulag Archipelago, The (Solzhenitsyn), 969
GUM store (Moscow), 993*(i)*
Gunboats, 770
Gustavus III (Sweden, r. 1771–1792), 611–612, 647
Gypsies. *See* Roma; Sinti people

Habsburgs (Habsburg dynasty). *See also* Holy Roman Empire
nationalism and, 703
World War I and, 852
Haiti. *See also* St. Domingue
AIDS in, 1003
uprising in (1989), 978
Hall of Mirrors (Versailles), German Empire proclaimed at, 734
Hamas forces, 1004*(m)*
Handicapped, Nazis and, 885
Handloom weavers, 688
Hard Times (Dickens), 748
Hasidism, 598
Haussmann, George Eugène (1809–1891), 739
Havel, Václav, 979, 997*(b)*, 1012
Hawaii, United States and, 818
Haydn, Franz Joseph (1732–1809), 602, 603
Headscarf, controversy over, 1009*(i)*
Head Start, 962
Health. *See also* Disease; Medicine; Public health
in cities, 739–741
as global issue, 1002–1003
national health care programs and, 928

Heart transplant, 954
Heisenberg, Werner, 889
Helsinki accords (1975), 970
Helvetic Republic, 640
Hemingway, Ernest, 861
Herder, Johann Gottfried, 729
Hervier, Louis Adolphe, 712*(i)*
Herzegovina. *See also* Bosnia-Herzegovina
  Austrian occupation of, 790
Herzen, Alexander (1812–1870), 706
Herzl, Theodor (1860–1904), 816–817, 817*(b)*
Heterosexuality
  patriotic nature of, 803
  after World War I, 861
Hezbollah, 1004*(m)*, 1005
Hierarchy. *See also* Classes
  in Napoleonic France, 657
Hieroglyphs (Egypt), 653
High culture, in cold war, 943
Higher education. *See also* Universities and colleges
  in postindustrial age, 958
  for women, 742–743
High-tech industries, 1006
Hillesum, Etty, 873
Himmler, Heinrich (1900–1945), 884
Hindenburg, Paul von (1847–1934), 839
Hindus (India), 671–672, 960, 1007
  Indian independence and, 931
  and Muslims, 823
Hip-hop music, 1012
Hirohito (Japan, r. 1926–1989), 890, 897
Hiroshima, bombing of, 905*(i)*
Hispaniola, 641. *See also* Haiti; St. Domingue
History and historians, on cold war, 918*(b)*
History of the Decline and Fall of the Roman Empire (Gibbon), 597
Hitler, Adolf (1889–1945), 862, 874. *See also* Holocaust; Nazis and Nazism
  assassination attempts against, 903
  expansion by, 890–892
  Great Depression and, 872*(i)*
  Japan and, 890
  on Masonic lodges, 596*(b)*
  Munich Pact (1938) and, 894
  Mussolini and, 868
  rise of, 881–883
  Russia and, 664
  on street activism, 882–883*(b)*
  suicide by, 904–905
  after World War I, 858
Hitler Youth, 885
Hobson, J. A., 818
Ho Chi Minh (1890–1969), 878, 932
Hohenlinden, battle of (1800), 661
Holland, France and, 657
"Hollow Men, The" (Eliot), 864
Holocaust, 898–900
  literature about, 937
  Middle East politics and, 932
Holocaust Museum (Washington, D.C.), 901
Holstein, 733
Holy Alliance, 670
Holy Land. *See* Israel; Palestine
Holy Roman Empire
  in 1799, 646*(m)*
  Austria as, 662
  German Confederation as, 669
Home front, in World War I, 842–845
Home rule, for Ireland, 787, 813
Homo Sapiens (Pelevin), 1014
Homosexuality, 802
  activism and, 964
  AIDS and, 1003
  in 18th century, 604–605
  Nazis and, 899–900
Hong Kong, 702
  as colony, 931
  as Pacific tiger, 1006
Hoover, Herbert, 886
Horses, in cities, 694
Hospitals, foundling, 604
Hostage crisis, in Iran, 972
House, Edward (1856–1924), 825
Households
  relationships in, 958
  work in, 958
Houses of Parliament (England), rebuilding of, 696
Housewives, protests by, 785
Housing. *See also* Architecture
  economic collapse (1997) and, 1007
  in England, 887
  in France, 961
  in Sweden, 976
  upper-class, 775–776
  World War I and, 861, 861*(i)*
  after World War II, 916–917, 928
Hubble, Edwin, 889, 953
Hugenberg, Alfred, 881
Hugo, Victor (1802–1885), 667*(b)*
Human rights
  Helsinki accords on (1975), 970
  race and, 938
Hume, David (1711–1776), 591, 592
Hundred Days, of Napoleon, 665
Hungarian Revolution (1956), 930
Hungary. *See also* Austria-Hungary
  agriculture in, 928–929
  in Austria-Hungary, 735–736
  as Axis power, 896
  collapse of communism in, 979
  Communists in, 919
  in EU, 996
  foreign investment in, 996
  free-market practices in, 992
  Magyars in, 858
  market system in, 961–962
  nationalism and, 703, 714, 815
  in 1930s, 888
  public health in, 741–742
  reforms in, 706
  revolt in (1956), 930
  Russia and, 714
  social issues in, 741–742
  Soviets and, 919
  uprisings in (1956), 964
  after World War I, 852
  in World War I, 840
  in World War II, 904
Hunger. *See* Famines
Huns (Germans), in World War I, 842
Hunter's Sketches, A (Turgenev), 726
Huskisson, William (1770–1830), 685
Hydroelectricity, 771
Hygiene. *See also* Sanitation
  in Russia, 866
  after World War I, 861–862

Iberia. *See* Portugal; Spain
Ibsen, Henrik, 782, 782*(b)*, 811
Ice, melting of, 1000
I Ching (Chinese Book of Changes), 960
Id, 804
Ideal Marriage: . . . (van de Velde), 861
Identity
  cultural, 722
  in global cities, 998
  national, 674
  nationalism and, 729
  Russian, 749
  sexual, 801–802
  social, E-2
Ideology. *See also* Liberals and liberalism; Utilitarianism
  communism as, 707–708
  of domesticity and separate spheres, 700, 701
  after French Revolution, 686
  liberalism as, 705–706
  nationalism as, 703–705
  socialism as, 706–707
IKEA furniture, 998
Illegal immigrants, unemployment and, 986
Illegitimate children, in European cities, 694
Illiteracy, 742
Illness. *See* Disease; Health; Medicine
IMF. *See* International Monetary Fund
Immaculate Conception, 751
Immigrants and immigration. *See also* Migration
  in Digital Age, E-5
  from Europe, 758*(i)*
  to Europe, 935–936
  European workers as, 776–778, 935–936, 936*(i)*
  to Israel, 932
  Muslim in Netherlands, 1010*(b)*
  in Sweden, 976
  urbanization and, 692–693
  as workers, 935–936
  worldwide, 985–986
Immunosuppressants, 954
Imperialism, 759–760
  in Africa, 762–764, 763*(m)*, 819*(m)*
  arts and, 781–783
  in Asia, 765–766, 820*(m)*
  challenges to, 817–825
  in China, 765, 767
  "civilizing" nature of, 767–768
  colonialism and, 701
  by Dutch, 762–763
  economic and political, 701–702
  in Egypt, 761
  by England, 761, 762, 763–764, 765, 818
  by France, 761, 766, 767
  by Germany, 762, 818–819
  in India, 765
  by Italy, 818
  by Japan, 766, 820
  migration and, 776–777
  missionary activity and, 672
  new imperialism, 761–768
  in 1920s, 859
  in 1930s, 890–892
  overthrow of, 931
  paradoxes of, 766–767
  by Russia, 765–766
  of Spain, 818
  of United States, 818
  by Western nations, 760
Imports. *See also* Slavery
  trade deficits and, 772
Impressionism, 783
Income tax, 741

Independence. *See also* American Revolution; Revolution(s)
in Africa, 933–934
of Belgium, 622, 679
for colonial peoples, 877, 930–936
Irish, 813
in Latin America, 677–678, 678*(m)*
regional, 998
Independence movements
in cold war, 930–936
in India, 823
India
Amritsar massacre in (1919), 859
anti-colonialism in, 877
British control of, 702, 743–744, 761, 765
cloth exports and, 690
economy in, 1007
France and, 606, 606*(m)*
French Revolution and, 643
Gandhi in, 877, 878*(i)*
imperialism in, 765
independence for, 930–931
missionaries in, 671*(i)*, 671–672
nationalists in, 823
railroads in, 688
Russia and, 993
World War I and, 837, 857
World War II and, 902
Indiana (Sand), 697, 698*(i)*
Indian National Congress, 765, 823, 931
Indian Rebellion (1857), 743, 743*(m)*, 744*(i)*
Indians. *See* Native Americans
Individuals, roles in society, 592–596
Indochina. *See also* Vietnam
cold war in, 931–932
France and, 766, 824–825
in 1954, 932*(m)*
Union of (1893), 766, 766*(m)*
after World War I, 878
Indochinese Communist Party, 878
Indonesia
independence in, 935
after World War I, 859
in World War II, 897
Industrialization, 685–686. *See also* Factories; Industrial Revolution
cities and, 685
Crystal Palace exhibition and, 716*(i)*, 716–717
in Europe, 688, 689*(m)*
factory workers and, 690–692
population and, 800
proto-, 687
railroads and, 684*(i)*, 685, 689
in Russia, 821
urbanization and, 692–695
Industrial Revolution, 686–695. *See also* Industrialization
in England, 686–689
"second," 769–770
Industrial technology, reproduction and, 800
Industry
activism against, 1000
arts and, 781–783
capital-intensive, 772
in eastern Europe, 858
empires and, 768–775
in England, 974
expansion of, 760, 769–771
in former Soviet Union, 992
in Great Depression, 876
innovation in, 769–771
in Japan, 766, 931, 1006
painting and, 783
Soviet, 917
in World War II, 900
Infanticide
in 18th century, 604
in European cities, 694
Napoleonic Civil Code and, 657
Infant mortality, 691
decline of, 695, 928
Inflation
European aristocrats and, 600
in former Soviet Union, 992
in Germany, 856, 856*(i)*, 858
in 1980s, 972
oil crisis and, 971
in United States, 974
in West, 971
in West Germany, 974
in World War I, 846
Influenza epidemic, of 1918–1919, 850, 850*(f)*
Information
sharing via digital media, E-4–E-5
from television, 951
Information age, 950–952
Infrastructure, after World War II, 925
Inheritance, in France, 635
Innovation. *See also* Intellectual thought; Inventions
economic crises and, 772
industrial, 769–771
Inquiry into the Nature and Causes of the Wealth of Nations, An (Smith), 593
Insourcing, 1010
Installment buying, 862
Intellectual thought. *See also* Art(s); Literature; Philosophy
academies and, 601
in Digital Age, E-4–E-5
in Enlightenment, 588–592, 599
on French Revolution, 647
in Germany, 647
Napoleon and, 658
on postmodernism, 1015
realism and, 748–751
in technocratic society, 959–960
Intelligence tests, 803
Intelligentsia, in Russia, 821
Intelsat I (satellite), 953
Interesting Narrative of the Life of Olaudah Equiano, The (Equiano), 592
International agreements, after World War I, 856–857
International Court of Justice. *See* World Court
International Monetary Fund (IMF), 999, 1003
International organizations, global, 999
Internationals
First, 785
Second, 785, 786, 810
International trade. *See* Trade and trade routes
International Woman Suffrage Alliance (1904), 811
International Women's Day, 846
International Zionist Congress (1897), 817
Internet, 1009
Digital Age, E-2
global network and, E-3*(m)*
outsourcing, insourcing, and, 1010
Interpretation of Dreams, The (Freud), 803–804
Interventionism, by United States, 919
Invasions
of Iraq, 1005
of Russia, 664
Inventions. *See also* Technology
industrial, 685, 686–687
Investment. *See also* Business; Finances
in eastern Europe, 996
In vitro fertilization, 954–955, 955*(i)*
Iran. *See also* Khomeini, Ayatollah Ruhollah
economy in, 1007
refugees in, 1008
religious uprising in, 972
terrorism in, 972
after World War I, 859, 878
Iran-Iraq War, refugees from, 1008
Iraq. *See also* Iraq War
oil in, 854–855*(b)*
Iraq war (2003–), 1005
refugees from, 1008
Ireland. *See also* Northern Ireland
in Common Market, 961
computer literacy in, 1009–1010
Easter uprising in (1916), 846
England and, 813
famine in, 709*(i)*, 709–710
home rule for, 787, 813
immigration from, 695
IRA terrorism in, 972
Irish Free State and, 859, 859*(m)*
nationalism in, 704–705
in Western consumer economy, 1010
after World War I, 858–859
Irish Free State (1921), 859*(m)*
Irish National Theater, 813
Irish Republican Army (IRA), 972, 973*(i)*
Iron and iron industry
railroads and, 689
in United States, 770
Islam, 960. *See also* Arab-Israeli wars; Middle East; Muslims; Oil
influence of, 986
in Iran, 972
radical, 1003–1005
Island-hopping strategy, in World War II, 905
Israel. *See also* Jews and Judaism; Palestine
creation of state (1948), 932, 932*(m)*
Egyptian peace accord with, 974*(i)*
Palestine conflict with, 1004*(m)*, 1004–1005
Six-Day War (1967) and, 971, 971*(m)*
Yom Kippur War (1973) and, 971
Italy. *See also* Papacy; Rome
in 1848, 711–712, 712*(m)*, 714
Africa and, 762, 818
Austria and, 713–714
clandestine workers in, 936
consolidation of, 662*(i)*
constitutional monarchy in, 813
Ethiopia invaded by, 891
fascism in, 867–868
fertility rate in, 1001–1002
films in, 943
Freemasons in, 601
imperialism by, 818
independence for northern, 998
industrialization in, 771
Japan as ally of, 897
kingdom of, 662
landowners in, 695
Manzoni on, 674
Napoleon and, 640
nationalism in, 671, 703, 711–712

at Paris Peace Conference, 852
railroad in, 684*(i)*
Red Brigades in, 972
republic in, 924
revolt in 1820s, 675, 678*(m)*
revolt in 1830s, 679
Spanish Civil War and, 893*(m)*, 894
unification of, 675, 712, 724, 730*(m)*, 730–731
unrest before World War I, 813
voting rights in, 788
women in, 857
in World War I, 836, 849
after World War II, 915
before World War II, 890–894
Ivanhoe (Scott), 675

J'accuse (Zola), 814
Jacobin Clubs (France), 630, 638
in French-annexed territories, 639
Jacobs, Aletta (1851–1929), 780, 844
Jahn, Friedrich Ludwig (1778–1852), 676
Jane Eyre (Brontë), 697
Japan
atomic bombing of, 905–907
Bolsheviks and, 849
China and, 837
civilians in World War II and, 898
economy in, 1006
expansion by, 817, 890, 891*(m)*
Greater East-Asia Co-Prosperity Sphere and, 890, 892*(b)*
high-tech industries in, 1006
impact on painting, 784*(i)*
imperialism by, 766, 820
Kellogg-Briand Pact and, 856–857
Korea and, 766, 820
Meiji Restoration in, 745
military in government of, 890
modernization in, 745, 766, 767*(i)*
Pearl Harbor attack by, 897
reindustrialization of, 931
Russo-Japanese War and, 818, 820
Sino-Japanese War and, 820
surrender in World War II, 907
U.S. national debt and, 1007
war with Russia, 818
after World War I, 857, 859
World War I and, 836
World War II and, 897, 905–907, 906*(m)*
Jaruzelski, Wojciech, 978
Jazz (Morrison), 1013
Jazz, after World War I, 861, 865
Jazz Age, Twenties as, 857–862, 865
Jefferson, Thomas (1743–1826)
Declaration of Independence and, 613*(b)*, 626
on French Revolution, 643
Jena, battle at (1806), 661
Jerome, Jeanette, 775
Jesuits, 610, 671
in Germany, 751
Jewish Museum (Berlin), 901*(i)*
Jewish State, The (Herzl), 817
Jews and Judaism. *See also* Anti-Semitism; Israel; Zionism
blamed for economic hardship, 876
emigration by, 776, 916
in Enlightenment, 601, 609
in France, 788
French Revolution and, 646–647
in German Enlightenment, 597
Hitler and, 873
Holocaust and, 898–900
mass politics and, 813–817
Middle East politics and, 932
migration in 19th century, 816*(m)*
Nazis and, 885
in Netherlands, 873
in Palestine, 816–817, 817*(b)*, 890
in Russia, 791
secularization and, 751
in Soviet Union, 917, 969
violence against, 791, 792*(i)*
World War I and, 845
after World War II, 915
Job Corps, 962
Jobs. *See* Employment; Labor; Workers
John XXIII (Pope, r. 1958–1963), 937
Johnson, Lyndon B. (1908–1973), 962, 964
Joliot-Curie, Irene, 807*(i)*
Jordan, Israel and, 971
Joseph II (Austrian and Holy Roman Emperor, r. 1780–1790), 607, 608*(i)*, 609
Josephine (France), 655*(i)*, 657
Joseph the Provider (Mann), 889
Journal des Dames, Le (periodical), 594–595*(b)*
Journalism, mass, 786
Journalists, in post-Soviet Russia, 994*(i)*
Joyce, James, 864
Juan Carlos (Spain), 973
Judaism. *See* Jews and Judaism
Judicial system. *See* Courts (legal); Law(s)
Julian calendar, in Russia, 846n
June Days (France), 711, 713*(b)*, 715
Jünger, Ernst, 863
Junkers (Prussia), 610
Bismarck and, 732
Justice, Beccaria on, 608
Jutland, battle at, 839

Kádár, János, 961–963
Kafka, Franz, 864
Kamikaze tactics, World War II and, 905
Kancheli, Giya, 1014
Kandinsky, Wassily (1866–1944), 809
Kant, Immanuel (1724–1804), 589, 596*(b)*, 597, 647
Kay, John, 687
Keep Smiling (film), 888
Kellogg-Briand Pact (1928), 856–857
Kemal, Mustafa ("Atatürk," 1881–1938), 877–878
Kennedy, John Fitzgerald (1917–1963), 943–944
assassination of, 962
Cuban missile crisis and, 918
Kent State University, antiwar protest at, 969
Kenya
independence of, 933
World War I and, 837
Kerensky, Aleksandr (1881–1970), 847–848
KGB, 990
Russian security after, 991
Khomeini, Ayatollah Ruhollah, 972, 1003, 1013
Khrushchev, Nikita (1894–1971), 918, 929–930, 933*(i)*, 961
Cuban missile crisis and, 944, 944*(m)*
Kielce, Poland, Jews killed in, 915
Kikuyu people, 933
King, Martin Luther Jr. (1929–1968), 938, 965
Kingdom of the Serbs, Croats, and Slovenes, 852, 858. *See also* Yugoslavia
Kingdom of the Two Sicilies, 712*(m)*
Kings and kingdoms. *See also* Empires; specific locations and rulers
in Africa, 764*(b)*
in France, 628–631
Kipling, Rudyard (1865–1936), 818, 860
Kissinger, Henry, 970
Klemperer, Victor, 883*(b)*
Kleptocracies, 1003
Kohl, Helmut, 974
Kokoschka, Oskar (1886–1980), 809
Kolkhoz (Soviet collective farms), 880
Kollontai, Aleksandra (1872–1952), 866
Kollwitz, Käthe (1867–1945), 834*(i)*, 863
Korea. *See also* Korean War; South Korea
Japan and, 766, 820
Soviets and, 907
Korean War (1950–1953), 931, 931*(m)*
economic growth during, 925
Kościuszko, Tadeusz (1746–1817), 640
Kosovo, Albanian Muslims in, 990
Kossuth, Lajos (1802–1894), 706, 714
Kosygin, Alexei (1904–1980), 961
Kotzebue, August von (1761–1819), 676
Krasikov Street (Bulatov), 963*(b)*, 963*(i)*
Kristallnacht, 885
Kronstadt revolt, 865
Kulak, in Russia, 880
Kulturkampf, 751, 789
Kundera, Milan, 969, 1013
Kurile Islands, Soviets and, 907
Kyoto Protocol, 1001

Labor. *See also* Slavery; Workforce
African, 764–765
agricultural, 690
Civil Code of Napoleon and, 658
computers and, 951–952
immigrants as, 777
organization of, 709
outwork and, 779–780
political theorists and, 745
power of, 810–811
in Russia, 771
Smith on, 593
temporary workers in Europe and, 935
as working class, 691
Labor camps, Nazi, 898
Labor parties, 961
Labor strikes. *See* Strikes
Labor unions, 691, 745, 784–785
in England, 680
in Germany, 884
women and, 707
after World War I, 860
Labour Party (England), 780, 887, 924, 973
Lady of the Lake, The (Scott), 675
Lafayette, Marie-Joseph (Marquis de, 1757–1834), 626, 630
Laissez-faire, 593
Lakes, pollution of, 1000
Lamb, Ann, 701
Lamballe, princess of, 630
Land
in eastern Europe, 928–929
in Russia, 727
after World War I, 875
Land and Liberty group (Russia), 791
Land Freedom Army (Mau Mau), 933

Land grants, in Russia, 727
Landowners, in Russia, 727
Langer, William, 804*(b)*
Languages
in Austria-Hungary, 735
English, 1014
Gaelic, 704–705
of 19th-century Europe, 704*(m)*
after World War I, 857
Laos, in Indochina, 766
Larrey, Dominique-Jean (1766–1842), 658
Las Cases, Emmanuel de (1766–1842), 666*(b)*
Latin America. *See also* specific locations
abolition of slavery in, 701
communism in, 930
economic development in, 1003
Great Depression in, 876
literature in, 1012–1013
migration to, 779*(b)*
revolts in 1820s, 675
wars of independence in, 677–678, 678*(m)*
Latvia
economy in, 997–998
in EU, 996
independence of, 990
Nazi-Soviet Pact and, 895
Law(s). *See also* Law codes; specific laws
women's work regulated by, 780–781
Law codes, Civil Code of Napoleon and, 652, 657–658, 670, 700
Law of Indemnity (France, 1825), 678
Law of Sacrilege (France, 1825), 678
Lawrence, D. H., 861
Lay Down Your Arms (Suttner), 811
League of Nations, 853–854
aggressors and, 890
Ethiopia and, 891
Germany and, 856, 891
Japan and, 859
Japanese invasion of Manchuria and, 890
Locarno Treaty and, 856
racial equality and, 877
United States and, 887
Learned societies, 601
Learning. *See* Education; Intellectual thought
Lebanon, Israeli attack on, 1005
Lebensraum (living space), 891, 896
Legal systems. *See* Law(s)
Legion of Honor, 657
Legislation. *See* Law(s)
Legislatures. *See* Assemblies
Leibniz, Gottfried Wilhelm (1646–1716), 590
Leisure
of middle class, 781
of upper class, 775
Lem, Stanislaw, 952
Lemonnier, Anicet Charles, 591*(i)*
Lenin, V. I. (1870–1924), 810, 827–848, 849*(i)*, 918*(b)*
NEP and, 865–866
Worker Opposition and, 866
Leningrad, 866. *See also* Petrograd; St. Petersburg
deaths during siege of, 902
Nazi attack on, 897
Leo XIII (Pope), 751
Leopold (Saxe-Coburg), as Belgian king, 679
Leopold II (Belgium, r. 1865–1909), 762, 762*(i)*
Leopold II (Holy Roman Emperor, r. 1790–1792), 608*(i)*, 609, 622
Lesbians. *See* Homosexuality
Lessing, Gotthold (1729–1781), 597
Lesueur brothers, 628*(i)*
Letter, The (Cassatt), 783, 784*(i)*
Letters on Education (Macaulay), 595*(b)*
Levi, Primo, 899
Lévi-Strauss, Claude, 960
Lewis, Sarah, 700
Liberal Party (England), 736, 786, 812
Liberals and liberalism
in Austria, 789
in Britain, 705
in economics and politics, 705–706
French rejection of, 788
in Hungary, 706
in Italy, 676
revising, 812–813
Liberty, French Revolution and, 634, 634*(i)*
Libeskind, Daniel, 901*(i)*
Libraries, in Enlightenment, 603
Libya, Italy and, 818
Liebknecht, Karl (1871–1919), 851
Life expectancy
of Manchester workers, 691
in Russia, 1002
Life of Insects, The (Pelevin), 1014
Lifestyle
in eastern Europe, 993, 997–998
economic change and, 779–780
in former Soviet Union, 992–993
in Great Depression, 876
Irish, 813
in Nazi extermination camps, 899–900
in postindustrial age, 958–959
private life and, 798–799
in Soviet Union, 917, 976
in United States, 916–917
in World War I, 842–845
after World War II, 936–944
in World War II, 900–902
Ligeti, György, 969
Lighting, electric, 769*(i)*
Like Water for Chocolate (Esquivel), 1012–1013
Limited liability corporation, 772
Lincoln, Abraham (1809–1865), 737–739
Lindsay, Norman, 843*(b)*, 843*(i)*
"Lines Composed a Few Miles above Tintern Abbey" (Wordsworth), 673*(b)*
Lissitsky, Eli, 866*(i)*
Lister, Joseph, 740
Literacy. *See also* Illiteracy
education and, 742
of lower classes, 604
Nazi suspicion of, 898
newspapers and, 786
in Russia, 866
Literature. *See also* Poets and poetry
in Enlightenment, 603
French, 658
about Holocaust and resistance, 937
Latin American, 1012–1013
in 1930s, 888–889
realist novels and, 748–749
Russian, 749
in Soviet bloc, 962
Lithuania. *See also* Poland-Lithuania
in EU, 996
independence of, 990
Nazi-Soviet Pact and, 895
Russia and, 607, 848
Little Entente, 856*(m)*
Liverpool and Manchester Railway Line, 685
Living standards, in global South, 1003
Lloyd George, David (1863–1945), 852
Loans
economic development, 1003
IMF, 999
Locarno, Treaty of, 856
Locke, John (1632–1704), 596, 746
liberalism and, 705
Lombardy, 730
Austria and, 669*(m)*
London. *See also* England (Britain)
Crystal Palace in, 716*(i)*, 716–717
overcrowding in, 693
population of, 685
poverty in, 694–695
riots in, 612
sanitation in, 693
Treaty of (1915), 852, 867
London Society for Effecting the Abolition of the Slave Trade, 701
Long-distance trade. *See* Trade and trade routes
Lorentz, Alcide, 698*(i)*
Lorraine
France and, 852
Germany and, 770
World War I and, 837
Louis XV (France, r. 1715–1774), 610
Louis XVI (France, r. 1774–1792), 610, 612, 630*(i)*
civil rights of Protestants and, 609
end of monarchy and, 628–631
execution of, 631, 631*(i)*
French government under, 623–631
war of, 629
Louis XVII (France, d. 1795), 623*(i)*, 665
Louis XVIII (France, r. 1814–1824), 665, 670
Louis, A., guillotine and, 632
Louisiana, Napoleonic Civil Code in, 658
Louisiana Territory, 660*(m)*, 661
Louis-Philippe (France, r. 1830–1848), 678, 701, 706, 710
Love in the Time of Cholera (García Márquez), 1012
Low Countries. *See also* Austrian Netherlands; Belgium; Dutch; Dutch Republic; Netherlands
protests in, 620–622
in 1787, 622*(m)*
Lower classes. *See also* Classes
middle-class fears and, 694–695
Ludd, Ned (fictitious figure), 688
Luddites, 688
Ludendorff, Erich (1865–1937), 839, 858
Ludin, Fereshta, headscarf of, 1009*(i)*
Ludwig of Bavaria, as Otto I (Greece), 677
Lueger, Karl (1844–1910), 815
Luftwaffe, 896
Lusitania (ship), 839
Luther, Martin (1483–1546), psychohistory and, 804*(b)*
Luxembourg, 620
Germany and, 837
in World War I, 839
Luxemburg, Rosa (1870–1919), 851
Lycées, 658, 742
Lynchings, in 1930s, 886
Lyon
in French Revolution of 1787–1800, 636
in French Revolution of 1830, 678

Maastricht Treaty (1994), 995
Mabuse, Peter, 716*(i)*
Macaulay, Catharine Sawbridge (1731–1791), 595*(b)*, 603
Macaulay, Thomas Babington (1800–1859), 681, 705
MacDonald, Ramsay (1866–1937), 858–859, 887
Macedonia, in First Balkan War, 827
Macedonians, nationalism of, 824
Machine guns, 770
Machines, 687
  computers and, 951–952
Madame Bovary (Flaubert), 748
Madame Butterfly (Puccini), 810
Madrid, al-Qaeda train bombings in, 1005, 1006*(i)*
Mafia, Russian, 992
Magical realism, in literature, 1012–1013
Magyarization, 815
Magyars, nationalism of, 703, 706, 714
Mahan, Alfred Thayer (1840–1914), 827
Mainz, 639
Maistre, Joseph de (1753–1821), 645*(b)*
Makine, Andrei, 1014
Malaria, 770, 1002
Malaya, in World War II, 897
Malay peninsula, British colonialism in, 765*(m)*
Male suffrage, 630, 788
Malta, 701
  in EU, 996
Management
  in postindustrial society, 956
  scientific, 860
  white-collar services and, 773
Manchester, 691
  growth of, 692
  sanitation in, 694
Manchuria
  Japan and, 890
  Soviets and, 907
  Trans-Siberian Railroad in, 820
Mandate system
  revolts against, 859
  after World War I, 854
Mandela, Nelson, 1007, 1012
Manet, Édouard, 749, 750*(i)*
Manhattan Project, 905
"Manifesto of the 'Green Women'" (1975), 967
Mann, Thomas, 888–889
Manonova, Tatyana, 966*(b)*
Manufacturing
  in England, 689
  in Europe, 860
  expansion of, 760
  in Germany, 689
  multinational, 955–956, 956*(m)*
  steel in, 769
Manzoni, Alessandro (1785–1873), 674
Mao Zedong (1893–1976), 931, 970
Maquis (French partisans), 902
Marat, Jean-Paul (1743–1793), 632, 635–636
Marconi, Guglielmo, 863
Marengo, battle of (1800), 661
Maria Carolina (Naples), 608*(i)*
Maria Theresa (Austria, r. 1740–1780), 608*(i)*
Marie-Antoinette (1755–1793), 608*(i)*, 612, 623, 623*(i)*, 629
Marie-Louise (Austria), 657, 665
Marienthal, Germany, 877*(b)*
Marijuana, 964
Maritime exploration. *See* Exploration
Market(s)
  Napoleon and, 662
  online, 1009
  in Russia, 771*(i)*
  Smith, Adam, and, 593
  after World War I, 857
Market economy
  in former Soviet Union, 992–993
  in Russia, 990
Market system, in Hungary, 961–962
Marne River, battle at, 839
Marriage
  child, 744
  cohabitation and, 958
  in Nazi Germany, 885
  reforms of, 800, 801
  in Soviet Union, 880–881
Marriage of Figaro, The (Beaumarchais), 612
Married Love (Stopes), 861
"Marseillaise, La" (French anthem), 633
Marshall, George C. (1880–1959), 919
Marshall Plan (1947), 919, 920*(i)*, 925
Martinique, 606*(m)*, 643
Marx, Karl (1818–1883), 692, 707–708, 708*(b)*, 745
  on Paris Commune, 748
  Rousseau's influence on, 596
Marxism, 746
  German, 810
  Russian, 811, 821, 848–849
  women and, 786
  worker activism and, 784
Masons and Masonic lodges, 596*(b)*, 600–601
Massacre at Chios (Delacroix), 674
Massacres, in Srebrenica, 989
Masses
  culture for, 862–865
  dictators and, 865–868
  Hitler on, 882
  Mill on, 753
  in Russia, 866
  after World War I, 862
Mass journalism, 786
Mass politics, 783–791, 810–817
Master and Margarita, The (Bulgakov), 1013
Mastersingers of Nuremberg, The (Wagner), 749
Masturbation, 605
Matchgirls, in London, 784–785
Materialism, 746
Maternity benefits, 927
Matisse, Henri (1869–1954), 808
Matrix Reloaded, The (film), 1014
Mau Mau, 933
May 1, as holiday, 786
Mayakovsky, Vladimir, 866
Mazzini, Giuseppe (1805–1872), 703, 712
McCarthy, Joseph, and McCarthyism, 924
McDonald's, protests against, 999
Mechanics Institutes, 699
Mechanized loom, 687
Media
  Hitler and, 882
  mass culture and, 862
  Spanish-language television as, 1014
Medical experiments, in concentration camps, 899
Medical schools, women in, 743
Medicine. *See also* Childbirth
  atomic science and, 914
  in France, 658
  heart transplants and, 954
  in India, 744
  national health programs and, 928
  professionalization of, 742
  social reform and, 780
  Western, 1002
Mediterranean region
  in 1871, 755*(m)*
  imperialism in, 761–762
  Suez Canal and, 724, 744–745, 761, 761*(m)*
Meiji Restoration (Japan), 745, 766
Mein Kampf (Hitler), 868, 882
Meir, Golda, 932
Men. *See also* Fathers; Gender and gender issues
  in cold war, 940
  in Great Depression, 876
Mendel, Gregor (1822–1884), 752
Mendelssohn, Moses (1729–1786), 597
Mensheviks, 811
Mental illness, 803–805
Mercantilism, Smith on, 593
Mercy, A (Morrison), 1013
Mergers, 955
  business, 986
  after World War I, 860
Mesopotamia, British-French division of oil in, 854–855*(b)*
Methodism, 598–599, 671
Metternich, Klemens von (1773–1859), 668–669, 670, 676, 703
Mexican Americans, protests by, 964
Mexican-American War, 737
Mexico
  France and, 739
  United States and, 737
Mickiewicz, Adam (1798–1855), 703–704
Middle class. *See also* Bourgeoisie; Classes
  education for, 742
  as elite, 600–603
  Enlightenment and, 599
  fears of, 694–695
  in France, 623
  leisure of, 781
  nobility intermarriage with, 600
  painting and, 602
  in Soviet Union, 961
  student rejection of values, 964
  women in, 685–686, 801–803
Middle East. *See also* Arab world
  foreign workers in, 1008
  independence and, 855*(b)*, 932–933
  oil and, 932, 970–971, 971*(i)*
  radical Islam in, 1004
  in 21st century, 1004*(m)*
  U.S. national debt financed by, 1007
  after World War I, 854–855*(b)*
Middlemarch (Eliot), 748
Midway Island, battle at, 905
Migrants
  global, 984*(i)*
  money sent home by, 1008
  opportunities for, 776–777
  prosperous, 998
Migration. *See also* Immigrants and immigration; Refugees
  to cities, 692–693
  defenses of, 777–778*(b)*
  in Digital Age, E-5
  European, 776–778
  experiences of, 778–779*(b)*

Migration (*continued*)
from former Soviet Union, 992–993
global, 986, 1008–1009
Jewish (19th century), 816*(m)*
political and economic reasons for, 779*(b)*
view of those left behind, 778*(b)*
for work, 603–604
after World War I, 858
Milan, nationalism in, 712
Militance. *See also* Activism
by blacks, 964
Islamic, 972
Militant nationalism, in Balkans, 817, 825
Militaristic nationalism, 729
Military. *See also* Armed forces
in Prague, 714
Prussian, 734
reform in Russia, 727
Soviet, 976
before World War I, 827–828
Military cemeteries, 860
Military draft
in French Revolution, 631, 633
World War I and, 827, 842
Military spending, 925*(f)*
after Korean War, 931
in United States, 1006–1007
Military technology, in World War I, 838–839
Mill, Harriet Taylor, 753, 811
Mill, John Stuart (1806–1873), 753, 811
Mill on the Floss, The (Eliot), 748
Milosevic, Slobodan, 987–988, 990
Mines Act (Britain, 1842), 691
Mines and mining
child labor in, 691*(i)*
disasters in China, 1007
in England, 859
in World War I, 845–846
Minorities
in Austria-Hungary, 735
Napoleon and, 662
rights for, in France, 627*(b)*
after World War I, 858
Mir (Russian community), 727, 771
Missiles
Cuban missile crisis and, 914, 937, 944, 944*(m)*
space age and, 952–953
Missions and missionaries
in China, 745
in Enlightenment, 609
European, 768
in India, 671*(i)*, 671–672
Mitteleuropa, 826
Mitterrand, François, 975
Mobility. *See* Immigrants and immigration; Migration; Social mobility
Mobilization, World War I and, 829–830, 842–844
Modern, use of term, 798, 799*(b)*
Modernism, 806
in music and dance, 809–810
in painting, 807–809
Modernity
Enlightenment and, 592–593
scientific and irrational in, 806–810
use of term, 799
World War I and, 797–798
Modernization, in Japan, 745, 766, 767*(i)*
Modern Times (film), 888
Moldavia, 725
Monarchism
in Austria-Hungary, 789
in France, 787–788
Spanish Civil War and, 892–894
Monarchs and monarchies. *See also* Kings and kingdoms; specific locations and rulers
dual monarchy and, 736
in France, 670–671, 678–679
in Spain, 664
Monetarists, Thatcher and, 973
Money, lending in late 1860s, 761
Monks and monasteries. *See* Religious orders
Monroe, James, 678
Monroe Doctrine (1823), 678
Montenegro
rebellion in, 789
before World War I, 826
Montesquieu, baron of (Charles-Louis de Secondat) (1689–1755), 608
Montessori, Maria, 802, 802*(i)*
Montgolfier brothers, 589*(i)*
Monuments, museums and, 901*(b)*
Morality, in literature, 888–889
Moral reform societies, 698, 699
Morocco, 825, 933
in World War II, 904
Morris, May (1862–1938), 783
Morris, William (1834–1896), 783
Morrison, Toni, 1013, 1013*(i)*
Mortality. *See also* Death(s)
child, 604
Moscow
market in, 771*(i)*
Napoleon and, 664, 665*(b)*
Nazis and, 897
uprisings in, 821
Mostar Bridge, destruction of, 989, 989*(i)*
Mothers. *See also* Children; Families; Women
in workforce, 958
Mountain (French political faction), 631, 632
Movies. *See* Films
Mozart, Wolfgang Amadeus (1756–1791), 602–603
Mrs. Dalloway (Woolf), 864
Müller-Otfried, Paula, 883*(b)*
Multinational corporations, 955–956
Multinationalism, in Austria-Hungary, 815
Munch, Edvard (1863–1944), 796*(i)*, 809
Munich Pact (1938), 894
Munitions, before World War I, 827
Münter, Gabriele (1877–1962), 809
Murat, Joachim (1767–1815), 657
Museum(s), 775, 901*(b)*
on Holocaust, 901
Jewish Museum (Berlin) and, 901*(i)*
nation building and, 740*(i)*
Music
baroque, 602
classical, 602–603
jazz and, 865
in postindustrial age, 960
in post-Soviet bloc, 1014
revolt in, 809–810
romantic, 674
transnational, 1012
Muslim League, 823, 931
Muslims. *See also* Islam
Bosnian, 988
in Europe, 1008
in European-occupied lands, 761–762
in French Algeria, 934
as immigrants, 1010
in India, 743, 823
Indian independence and, 931
in Netherlands, 1010–1011*(b)*
in Russia, 866
in Soviet Central Asia, 987
in Yugoslavia, 920
Mussolini, Benito (1883–1945), 862, 867*(i)*, 867–868
death of, 904
expansion by, 891
fascism and, 879*(b)*
Japan and, 890
Munich Pact and, 894
Mutual aid societies, in France, 709
Myrdal, Alva (1902–1986), 886
Mysticism, Jewish, 598

NAACP. *See* National Association for the Advancement of Colored People
NAFTA. *See* North American Free Trade Agreement
Nagasaki, bombing of, 905–907
Nagy, Imre, 930
Names, in France, 635
Nanking, Treaty of (1842), 702
Naples
France and, 657
kingdom of, 662
rebels in, 679
Napoleon I Bonaparte (France, r. 1799–1815), 640, 650*(i)*, 651–667, 657*(i)*
conquests by, 659–664
Continental System and, 662–663
coronation of, 654, 655*(i)*
defeat of, 664–666
deposing of, 665
in Egypt, 653
as First Consul, 653–654
French Empire of, 659–666, 660*(m)*
Hundred Days of, 665
impact of, 661–664
on own legacy, 666*(b)*
resistance to, 663–664
Russia and, 664–665
on St. Helena, 666
at Waterloo, 665–666
Napoleon II (France), 711
Napoleon III (France, 1808–1873), 711, 722, 723*(i)*, 723–724
Crimean War and, 724–726
Germany and, 724, 734
Italian unification and, 730–731
United States and, 739
Napoleon Crossing the Alps at St. Bernard (David), 650*(i)*
Napoleonic Code. *See* Civil Code (Napoleon)
Napoleonic Empire, 659–666, 660*(m)*
Napoleonic wars, 653–654
Nasser, Gamal Abdel (1918–1970), 933, 933*(i)*
Nation(s). *See also* State (nation)
Battle of the (1813), 664
fragmentation of, 998
National Aeronautics and Space Administration (NASA), 930
National Assembly (France), 624, 626, 627*(b)*, 628, 711
National Association for the Advancement of Colored People (NAACP), 938

National Congress of the Chechen People, 993
National Convention (France), 630–631, 632, 635, 636–637, 638
National debt, in United States, 1007
National Front Party (France), 975
National Guard, in France, 626, 636, 711, 747
National health programs, 928
National identity. *See* Identity
Nationalism, 677, 703–705
  in Algeria, 933–934
  anti-French, 647
  anti-Semitism and, 813
  artistic criticisms of, 808
  in Austria-Hungary, 815, 844
  in Balkans, 676, 676*(m)*, 789, 825
  Basque, 998
  Egyptian, 761
  in England, 974
  ethnic, 815
  in France, 633
  in Germany, 712–713, 715, 814–815
  in India, 823
  in Indochina, 824–825, 859, 931–932
  in Ireland, 704–705
  in Italy, 671, 703, 711–712
  Jewish, 816–817
  Magyar, 706, 714
  in 1970s, 972–973, 973*(m)*
  in Poland, 703–704
  population and, 800
  regional, 998
  romantic, 674–675
  in Russia, 704
  in Spain, 664
  of student societies, 676
  Turkish, 823–824
  uses of term, 729
  in Yugoslavia, 987
Nationalist Party (China), 823
Nationality. *See also* Ethnicity and ethnic groups; Minorities
  EU membership and, 997
  in Russia, 715
  after World War I, 858
Nationalization
  of Russian factories, 848
  of Suez Canal, 933
National minorities. *See* Minorities
National order, religion and, 751
National Socialists (Germany). *See* Nazis and Nazism
National states. *See* State (nation)
National workshops, in Paris, 710
Nation building, 729–739. *See also* Unification
  abroad, 743
  arts and, 751
  Austria-Hungary and, 735–736
  education and, 742–743
  in Italy, 813
  museums and, 740*(i)*
  in North America, 737–739
  social order for, 739–748
  women as "republican mothers" in, 731*(i)*
Nation-states, 722. *See also* State (nation)
  in Digital Age, E-5
  in global age, 994–999
  nation building and, 729–739
Native Americans, on reservations, 737
NATO. *See* North Atlantic Treaty Organization
Natural History of Religion, The (Hume), 591
Natural law, 589
Natural resources
  in Latin America, 1003
  in United States, 770
Natural rights, 589
  antislavery movement and, 592
  Rousseau on, 594
Natural sciences, 752–753
  social sciences and, 753
Navarino Bay, battle at, 677
Navy
  English, 653
  French, 653
  World War I and, 827, 839
Nazis and Nazism (Germany), 868, 872*(i)*, 884*(i)*, 975. *See also* Fascism; Hitler, Adolf
  Austria and, 888, 894
  Blitzkrieg by, 896
  central Europe conquered by, 894–896
  division of opinion about, 882–883*(b)*
  economic and social programs of, 884–885
  German casualties in World War II, 903
  growth of (1933–1939), 895*(m)*
  Hitler and, 874, 881–885
  Holocaust and, 898–900
  invasion of Poland by, 896
  Japan as ally of, 897
  Jews and, 885
  Nuremberg Laws and, 885
  postwar dealings with, 922–923
  in postwar mainstream, 937
  resistance to, 902*(i)*, 902–905
  Russia and, 895–896, 897
  Stalin on, 920
Nazi-Soviet Pact (1939), 895–896, 897
Near East. *See* Mesopotamia; Middle East
Necker, Jacques (1732–1804), 625, 658, 659*(i)*
Nelson, Horatio (1758–1805), 653
Neoclassical arts and architecture, 601–602, 602*(i)*
Neoliberalism, 974
Nestlé, 860
Netherlands, 669*(m)*. *See also* Dutch
  Congress of Vienna on, 668
  German invasion of, 896
  Islamic architecture in, 1010
  Muslims in, 1010–1011*(b)*
  Napoleon and, 662
  Nazi conquest of, 873
  revolutions of 1848 and, 715
  voting rights in, 788
Neuroses, in 20th-century society, 805
Neutrality, in World War I, 839, 840*(m)*
New Caledonia, 592
New Deal (United States), 886
New Economic Policy (NEP), 865–866
New Harmony, Indiana, 706
New Heloise, The (Rousseau), 595
New imperialism, 761–768
New Lanark, Scotland, 706
"New look," in cold war fashion, 940, 941*(i)*
"New man," after World War I, 866*(i)*
Newnham (Cambridge University), 742
Newspapers, 862
  increase in, 611
  mass, 786
Newton, Isaac (1642–1727), 590
Newtonian System of the Universe Digested for Young Minds, The ("Tom Telescope"), 605
New unionism, 785
New woman, 801–803
New Woman, The (Grundy), 801*(i)*
New Zealand, 592, 702
NGOs. *See* Nongovernmental organizations
Nice, 639, 670, 730
Nicholas I (Russia, r. 1825–1855), 676, 706, 714, 715, 724
Nicholas II (Russia, r. 1894–1917), 813–814
  Russian Revolution of 1905 and, 821, 821*(m)*
  Russian Revolution of 1917 and, 846–847
  World War I and, 830, 842
Nietzsche, Friedrich (1844–1900), 802, 806, 864*(i)*
Nigeria, 765*(i)*, 930
  economy in, 1007
  independence of, 933
Nightingale, Florence (1820–1910), 725, 741
Nightmare, The (Fuseli), 672*(i)*
Night of Broken Glass. *See* Kristallnacht
Night of the Long Knives (Nazi Germany), 884
1984 (Orwell), 908, 942
Nixon, Richard (1913–1994), 969, 970
Nkrumah, Kwame (1909–1972), 933
Nobel, Alfred, dynamite and, 827
Nobel Prize
  to Curie, Marie, 807, 807*(i)*
  to Morrison, Toni, 1013, 1013*(i)*
  for Peace, 811, 1012
Nobility. *See also* Aristocracy
  arts and, 602
  in Austria, 610
  in Enlightenment, 599–600
  in France, 623, 655–657, 678
  in French Revolution, 637
  reforms and, 609
  in Russia, 727–728
Nongovernmental organizations (NGOs), 999, 1003
Nonviolent resistance, in civil rights movement, 938
Non-Western world
  economies of, 1016*(m)*
  Western consumer economy and, 1010
Nordau, Max (1849–1923), 803
North, Marianne, 760*(i)*
North (global), vs. South (global), 1003, E-3*(m)*
North (U.S.), 737–739
North Africa
  European workers from, 935
  in World War II, 904
North America
  Freemasons in, 601
  Great Awakening in, 598, 599*(i)*
  migration to, 776, 777
  nation building in, 737–739
  revivalism in, 598
  revolution in, 612–614
  in Seven Years' War, 606*(m)*
North American Free Trade Agreement (NAFTA), 995
North Atlantic Treaty Organization (NATO), 921
  French withdrawal from, 961
  Kosovo and, 990
North Briton (newspaper), 612
Northern Ireland
  rapprochement with Ireland and, 975
  violence in, 972, 973*(i)*
  after World War I, 859
North German Confederation, 733

North Vietnam, 962, 969. *See also* Vietnam
Norway, German invasion of, 896
Novels. *See also* Literature
realist, 748–749
social conditions in (1800s), 696–697
Nuclear age, 914
lifestyle and culture in, 936–944
Nuclear energy, 914, 953
Nuclear power
Chernobyl catastrophe and, 977, 999–1000
in France, 961
plants, 953
Nuclear weapons, test-ban treaty and, 944
Nuremberg Laws (Germany, 1935), 885
Nuremberg trials, 923
Nursing, in Crimean War, 725, 725*(i)*, 726*(b)*

Obama, Barack, 1005
Occupation (military)
French, 639
of Germany, 920–922, 921*(m)*
of postwar Europe, 915
of U.S. South, 739
Occupation (jobs), postindustrial, 957*(f)*
O'Connell, Daniel (1775–1847), 705
Oil and oil industry
crisis in (1970s), 971–972
in Middle East, 932
prices (1955–1985), 972*(f)*
United States and, 770, 970–971
West's dependence upon, 859, 971–972
after World War I, 854–855*(b)*, 878
Okinawa, Japan and, 766
Old Curiosity Shop, The (Dickens), 697
Oldenburg, Claes, 959*(i)*, 959–960
Oligarchs, in Russia, 990
Oliver Twist (Dickens), 697
Olympia (Manet), 749, 750*(i)*
Once Upon the River Love (Makine), 1014
On Crimes and Punishments (Beccaria), 608
One Day in the Life of Ivan Denisovitch (Solzhenitsyn), 930
One Hundred Years of Solitude (García Márquez), 1012
On Germany (de Staël), 658
On Liberty (Mill), 753
Online marketplace, 1009
Online transactions, E-3–E-4
On the Origin of Species (Darwin), 752
OPEC. *See* Organization of Petroleum Exporting Countries
Open City (film), 943
Open Society Foundation, 999
Opera, 720*(i)*, 721
in Enlightenment, 603
realism in, 749
Operation Vittles, 921
Opium
in London, 702*(i)*
trade in, 702
Opium War (1839–1842), 702, 702*(m)*, 745
Optimism, in Digital Age, E-5
Orange, house of, 621, 622
Orange Free State, 818
Order (organization), after protests of 1968, 969
Organization of Labor (Blanc), 707
Organization of Petroleum Exporting Countries (OPEC), 971
Organizations, global, 999
Orlando (Woolf), 863, 864
Orlov, Boris, 963*(b)*, 963*(i)*
Orthodox Christianity
religious toleration of, 609
in Russia, 715, 728–729
Orwell, George (1903–1950), 888, 908, 942
Ostpolitik, 961
Otto I (Greece, r. 1832–1862), 677
Ottoman Empire. *See also* Ottoman Turks; Turkey
Balkans and, 826*(m)*
Crimean War and, 724*(m)*, 724–725
European powers and, 745
Russia and, 765
Slav rebellion in, 789
World War I and, 836, 852, 853*(m)*, 854*(b)*, 859, 877–878
Young Turks in, 823–824
Ottoman Turks. *See also* Ottoman Empire
Greek independence from, 676–677, 677*(i)*
Outsourcing
in eastern Europe, 997–998
to Ireland, 1009–1010
Outwork, 770, 779–780
Owen, Robert (1771–1858), 706–707
Oxford University, 742
Oxygen, depletion of, 1000
Ozone layer, 1000

Pacific Ocean region
economies of, 1006–1007
uprisings in 1989, 978
World War II and, 897, 905–907, 906*(m)*
Pacific tigers, 1006*(m)*, 1006–1007
Pacifism, women and, 811
Pact of Steel (1939), 894
Paestum, 601
Paine, Thomas (1737–1809), 644–645*(b)*, 924
Painting. *See also* Art(s)
in cold war, 943
industry and, 783
middle class and, 602
realistic, 749
romantic, 673–674, 696
Pakistan, 931
Palach, Jan, 948*(i)*, 949, 968, 979
Pale of Settlement (Russia), 791
Palermo, rebels in, 679
Palestine
Israeli conflict with, 1004*(m)*, 1004–1005
Jews in, 816–817, 817*(b)*, 890, 916
partition of, 932, 932*(m)*
Pan-Arabic world, 1003
Pandemics. *See also* Disease; Epidemics
influenza, 850, 850*(f)*
Pankhurst, Christabel, 842
Pankhurst, Emmeline (1858–1928), 812, 842
Pan-Slavism, 736, 789
Papacy. *See also* Pope; Roman Catholicism; specific popes
Rome and, 734
Papal States, 712*(m)*
Napoleon and, 640
Paradigm shift, scientific, 807
Paramilitary, in France, 887
Paris. *See also* France; Peace of Paris
de Gaulle and, 961
department store in, 774*(i)*
fighting in (1830), 678
Haussmannization in, 739
overcrowding in, 693
parlement of, 623–624
population of, 685
rebuilding of, 724
revolution of 1848 and, 710, 712*(i)*
September massacres in, 630
sewers of, 741*(i)*
terrorist bombing in, 1005
Treaty of (1856), 606, 725
Paris Commune (1871), 745, 746*(m)*, 746–747, 747*(i)*
Paris Peace Conference (1919–1920), 852–854, 854–855*(b)*
Parks, Rosa, 938
Parlements (France), 609–610, 611
Parliament. *See also* Parliament (England)
in Spain, 675
Parliament (England), 612–613, 696
Parliament Bill (England, 1911), 812
Parnell, Charles Stewart (1846–1891), 787, 787*(i)*
Pärt, Arvo, 960
Partisans
in France, 902
in Yugoslavia, 920
Partitions. *See also* Zones of occupation
of India, 931
of Palestine, 932
of Poland, 607, 607*(i)*, 607*(m)*, 640, 640*(m)*
Pasternak, Boris (1890–1960), 912*(i)*, 913, 917, 930
Pasteur, Louis, 740
Pasteurization process, 740
Pastoral Symphony (Beethoven), 674
Paternalism, in Civil Code of Napoleon, 657–658
Patriarchy, feminists on, 966–967*(b)*
Patriotic Women's Club, The (Lesueur), 628*(i)*
Patriots
Dutch, 621–622
French, 625–626
Polish, 622
Paul (Russia, r. 1796–1801), 662
Paul VI (Pope, r. 1963–1978), 960
Pavlov, Ivan (1849–1936), 803
Paxton, Joseph (1801–1865), 716*(i)*
Peace
digitization and, E-4
after World War I, 851–857, 853*(m)*
Peace accords, Egyptian-Israeli, 974*(i)*
Peacekeeping
in former Yugoslavia, 990
by UN in Kosovo, 990
Peace of Paris (1919–1920), economic and diplomatic consequences of, 852–857, 855–857, 868
Pearl Harbor, Japanese attack on, 897
Peasant Party (Poland), 919
Peasants. *See also* Serfs and serfdom
aristocratic rights and, 600
Belgian independence and, 622
in China, 931
collectivization and, 928–929
in France, 623, 626, 636
French Revolution and, 646–647
industrialization and, 690
in Italy, 712
in mid-1800s, 695
in Prussia, 662
in Russia, 726–727, 766*(m)*, 771, 821–822, 866
Peel, Robert (1788–1850), 680, 706
Pelevin, Victor, 1014

Pelletier, Fernande, 956–957
Pennsylvania, terrorist attack and, 1005
Pensions
in former Soviet Union, 993
for veterans, 861, 927
Pentagon, terrorist attack on, 1005
Pentateuch. *See* Torah
People of color, after World War II, 938
People's Charter, 708–709
People's Republic of China, 931. *See also* China
People's Will (Russia), 791
Perestroika (restructuring), 976, 977
Persia
as Iran, 878
Russia and, 765
Pest (city), working classes in, 694
Pétain, Henri Philippe, 896
Peter and the Wolf (Prokofiev), 881
Peter III (Russia, r. 1762), 605–606, 611
Peterloo massacre, 680
Peters, Carl, 759, 762
Petrograd, 842. *See also* St. Petersburg
as Leningrad, 866
revolts in, 846
Peugeot, Armand (1849–1915), 769
Philanthropy. *See* Charity(ies)
Philippines
Japanese attack on, 897
United States and, 818
uprising in (1989), 978
in World War II, 897
Philosophes, 588, 589, 592
Philosophical and Political History of European Colonies and Commerce in Two Indies (Raynal), 592
Philosophical Dictionary (Voltaire), 591
Philosophy
existential, 937–938
of Kant, 597
Phonographs, 862
Photography, 698, 698*(i)*, 738*(b)*, 738*(i)*
Physicians. *See* Doctors; Medicine
Physics, in 1930s, 889
Physiocrats, 609, 610
Picasso, Pablo (1881–1973), 808, 904
Piedmont, 675, 679. *See also* Piedmont-Sardinia
Piedmont-Sardinia, 670, 675, 712, 712*(m)*, 721, 729
Pieds noirs (Algeria), 934
Pietism, 598, 671
Pill, the (oral contraceptive), 953, 954, 964
Pilsudski, Jozef, 858
Pinsker, Leon (1821–1891), 816, 817*(b)*
Pitt, William (1759–1806), 633
Pius VI (Pope, r. 1775–1799), 628
Pius VII (Pope, r. 1800–1823), 654, 655*(i)*
Pius IX (Pope, r. 1846–1878), 712, 751
Pius XI (Pope, r. 1922–1939), 889
Plague, The (Camus), 937
Planck, Max (1858–1947), 807
Playboy magazine, 940
Plebiscites, in France, 654
Poets and poetry
romanticism in, 672–673
after World War I, 864
Pogroms
Jewish emigration and, 776
against Jews, 791, 792*(i)*
Poison gas, 838
Poisson, Jeanne-Antoinette. *See* Pompadour, marquise de
Poland. *See also* Poland-Lithuania
Bolsheviks and, 851–852
collapse of communism in, 979
communism in, 919
Congress of Vienna and, 669, 669*(m)*
duchy of Warsaw as, 669*(m)*
ethnic minorities in, 858
in EU, 996
extermination and labor camps in, 898–899
farming in, 929
foreign investment in, 996
free-market practices in, 992
Freemasons in, 601
German invasion of (1939), 874, 896
independence movement in, 622
Jews killed in, 916
land in, 875–876
Little Entente and, 856
Nazis and, 897, 898–899
Nazi-Soviet Pact and, 895
partitions of, 607, 607*(i)*, 607*(m)*, 640, 640*(m)*
protests in (1956), 930
refugees from, 922*(i)*
resistance in World War II, 902
revolts in, 620, 621, 679
Russia and, 728
Solidarity movement in, 977–978
World War I and, 840, 852, 856
World War II and, 894, 904, 907
Poland-Lithuania. *See also* Lithuania; Poland
partition of Poland and, 607
Police
in London, 680
in Russia, 810
Polish Corridor, 852
Polish Legion, 703–704
Polish people
nationalism and, 703–704
self-determination for, 713
Political cartoons, by Gillray, 643*(i)*
Political parties, workers in, 785–786, 810
Political power
in rural areas, 695
of state, 605–610, 610–614
Political prisoners, in Dachau, 901
Politics and political systems
in Digital Age, E-4
in England (Britain), 736–737
in French Revolution, 635
in Great Depression, 876
imperialism and, 701–702
liberalism and, 705–706
mass, 783–791, 810–817
in mid-1800s, 695
Napoleon III and, 724
nationalism and, 703–705
in Nazi Germany, 883–884
in Soviet Union, 880
television and, 951
Western European participation in, 786–787
workers in, 784–786
in World War I, 842, 846
after World War II, 914–922
Politkovskaya, Anna, 994*(i)*
Polke, Sigmar, 960
Pollock, Jackson, 943
Pollution
as global issue, 999–1001
industrialization and, 691
Polo, Anglo-Indian team in, 781*(i)*
Polonium, 806–807
Pommier, Amédée, 695
Pompadour, marquise de (Jeanne-Antoinette Poisson, 1721–1764), 591
Poniatowski, Stanislaw August (Poland, r. 1764–1795), 622
Poor laws, England (1834), 699
Poor people. *See also* Poverty
education for, 699–700
in Enlightenment, 603–604
reforms for, 699–700
Pop art, 959*(i)*, 959–960
Pope. *See also* Papacy; specific popes
Napoleon and, 640
Popular culture, 604
in cold war, 940*(b)*
Popular Front
in France, 886, 887–888
in Spain, 893
Population. *See also* Agriculture; Food(s)
censuses and, 741
city overcrowding and, 692–693
of England, 687
of Europe (1850), 717*(m)*
of European workers, 935
as global issue, 1001–1002
in Ireland, 709–710
of Soviet Union, 880–881
in Sweden, 886
urban, 692
of western Europe, 915
world growth of (1950–2010), 1002*(f)*
after World War I, 858
before World War I, 799–801
Populists, in Russia, 791
Portici, Italy, 684*(i)*
Portraits, of royal courts, 602
Portugal
Africa and, 762
American colonies of, 677
dictator ousted in, 973
France and, 664
inflation in (1973), 971
slave trade and, 701
Positivism, 753, 806
Possessed, The (Dostoevsky), 791
Postindustrial age
education in, 957–958
music in, 960
occupational structure in (1984), 957*(f)*
religion in, 960
social science in, 960
society and culture in, 955–981
technology in, 950–955
Postindustrial skills, 1009
Postmodernism, 1014–1015
Postwar period, after World War II, 913–944
Potato famine (Ireland), 709–710
Potemkin (battleship), 821
Potemkin (film), 863
Potsdam, World War II meeting at, 907
Pottery. *See* Art(s)
Poverty. *See also* Poor people
in cities, 694–695
in Enlightenment, 603–604
industrialization and, 686
social issues and, 741
social reforms and, 780
U.S. programs for, 962
Power (energy). *See* Energy

Power (political). *See* Political power
Power politics, in central and eastern Europe, 788–791
Prague
  Slav congress in, 714
  student activism in, 964
Prague Spring, 967–969, 968*(i)*
Pravda (Soviet newspaper), 880, 990
Presley, Elvis, 939, 941*(i)*
Press. *See* Media; Newspapers
Price, Richard (1723–1791), 643
Price(s), in France, 624
Price controls, in France, 609
Princes. *See also* Nobility
  in Germany, 713
Princip, Gavrilo, 828, 829*(i)*
Printing, 786
Prison(s)
  camps, in Soviet Union, 880, 929
  reforms of, 705
  Soviet Gulag as, 880, 929
Prisoners of war, after World War II, 915
Private life, before World War I, 798–799
Private property, in Russia, 848
Privatization, in former Soviet Union, 992
Production, Marx on, 746
Professions, 742–743
  women in, 743
Project Head Start, 962
Prokofiev, Sergei, 881
Proletkult (Russia), 866
Propaganda
  in fascist Italy, 868
  by Hitler, 881–882
  in Soviet Union, 917
  in World War I, 842, 843*(b)*, 843*(i)*, 862
  in World War II, 902
Property, Proudhon on, 707, 745
Property rights, Civil Code of Napoleon and, 657–658
Prosperity, in European states, 975–976
Prostheses, Amar, Jules, and, 835, 842, 857, 864
Prostitution
  in former Soviet Union, 992
  industrialization and, 685, 686
  international sex rings and, 1008
  regulation of, 741
Protective Association, 706
Protest(s)
  in cold war, 948*(i)*, 949, 961–969
  economic crisis and, 1007*(i)*
  Facebook and, E-4
  in France, 887, 966–967
  at Kent State, 969
  in Low Countries, 620–622
  in 1960s, 964–969
  in Soviet bloc, 930
  student, 965–966
  by workers, 784–785
  against World War I, 845–846
  worldwide (1989), 978–980
Protestants and Protestantism. *See also* Edict of Nantes
  in France, 609
  Irish Republican Army and, 972
  in postindustrial age, 970
  religious toleration and, 609
  revivalism and, 598
Proto-industrialization, 687
Proudhon, Pierre-Joseph (1809–1865), 707, 745–746
Provinces, in France, 629*(m)*
Provisional Government (Russia), 846–848
Prussia. *See also* Germany
  Bismarck and, 732
  Congress of Vienna and, 668, 669*(m)*
  Dutch and, 622
  France and, 629, 630, 639, 661, 724
  Franco-Prussian War and, 720
  Frankfurt parliament and, 713
  Freemasons in, 601
  German unification and, 731–735
  in Holy Alliance, 670
  industrialization in, 690
  landowners in, 695
  Napoleon and, 661
  nationalism in, 703
  peasants in, 662
  Poland and, 640
  reforms in, 607–608, 662
  revolt in, 712
  schools in, 609
  in Seven Years' War, 606
  Spain and, 733–734
  William I of, 732*(i)*
Psychoanalysis, 803–805
Psychohistory, 804–805*(b)*
Psychology, 960
Public health, 740
  reforms in, 739–741
Public opinion, 611–612
Public relations, before World War I, 827
Puccini, Giacomo (1858–1924), 810
Puerto Rico, 677
  United States and, 818
Pugachev, Emelian (1742–1775), rebellion led by, 611, 611*(m)*
Pump priming, 884, 886
  England and, 888
Punjab, tiger hunting in, 776*(i)*
Purges, by Stalin, 880, 930
Pushkin, Alexander (1799–1837), 676
Putin, Vladimir, 990–992
  Chechnya and, 993, 994*(i)*
Putting-out system, 687, 690

Qadaffi, Muammar, 1003
Qing Empire (China), 745
  Boxer Uprising and, 822–823
Quakers, 701
Quantum theory, 807
Queen(s). *See* Kings and kingdoms; Monarchs and monarchies; specific rulers
Queen Caroline Affair, 679–680
Quinine, 770

Race and racism
  in Austria-Hungary, 815–816
  Darwin on, 753
  fascism and, 879
  in Great Depression, 876
  human rights and, 938
  in Japan, 890
  nationalism and, 729
  in Nazi Germany, 884, 885
  in political parties, 1009
  population and, 800–801
  in United States, 739, 886
  in World War II, 897, 902
Radetzky, Joseph (1766–1858), 714
Radicalism, in Islam, 1003–1005
Radio, 862, 863
  in cold war, 941
  in World War II, 900
Radioactive waste, disposal of, 957
Radioactivity, 807, 999–1000
Radium, 806–807
Railroads, 686, 688–689
  emigration and, 777
  in England, 685
  expansion of, 769
  in France, 724
  in Hungary, 706
  in Italy, 684*(i)*
  Piedmontese, 730
  in Russia, 695
  in United States, 688
Rain, Steam, and Speed: The Great Western Railway (Turner), 696
Rain forests, clearing of, 1000
Rapallo, Treaty of (1922), 856
Rasputin, Grigori, 846
Rational thought, modernization and, 799
Rauschenberg, Robert, 959
Raw materials
  consumerism and, 774–775
  imperialism and, 761
  for industrialization, 687
Raynal, Guillaume (1713–1796), 592
Reactors, nuclear, 953
Reading. *See also* Literacy
  in Enlightenment, 603
Reagan, Ronald, 974, 977
Reaganomics, 974
Realism, 748
  in arts, 748–751, 750*(i)*
Realpolitik, 721–722, 731, 970
  in England, 737
  German unification and, 731–735
Reason
  in Enlightenment, 592–593
  in France, 626–628
  in German Enlightenment, 597
  limits of, 598–599
Rebellions. *See* Revolts and rebellions
Rebel Without a Cause (film), 939
Recessions. *See also* Economy; Great Depression
  in 1970s, 971
Recovery. *See* Europe, recovery after World War II
Red Army (Russia), 848, 849
Red Army faction, in West Germany, 972
Red Brigades, in Italy, 972
Reds, in Russia, 848
Red Sea, Suez Canal and, 724
Red Shirts (Italy), 731, 731*(i)*
"Red Terror" (France), 638
Reform Act (England, 1884), 787
Reform and reformers
  in Austria, 609
  in churches, 937
  in cold war, 948*(i)*, 949–950
  of education, 742
  in England, 736–737, 786–787
  Enlightenment and, 588
  in France, 678
  industrialization and, 685
  by Johnson, Lyndon, 962
  limits of, 609–610
  of marriage, 801
  middle-class fears and, 694–695
  Napoleonic, 662

in 1980s, 972–976
in Poland, 622
for poor, 699–700
of prisons, 705
in Prussia, 662
in public health, 739–741
in Russia, 662, 726–729, 821–822
slavery and, 701
social, 696–701, 780–781
in Soviet Union, 961–962, 976
state power and, 605–610
Reform Bills (England)
in 1832, 679–681
Second (1867), 736
Refrigeration, 770
Refugees
migration of, 1008
Polish, 922*(i)*
after World War II, 907, 915
Regional differences, activism for regional independence and, 998
Reich (Germany), 734
Reichstag (Germany), 734–735, 810, 846, 881
burning of (1933), 883
rebuilding of, 1015, 1015*(i)*
Reinsurance Treaty (1887), 790, 791
Relief programs. *See* Social welfare
Religion(s). *See also* Christianity; Islam; Jews and Judaism; specific groups
in Austria, 609
in Balkan region, 826–827
Civil Code of Napoleon and, 657
Congress of Vienna and, 670
in Enlightenment, 591, 608–609
European missionaries and, 768
in France, 634, 671–672, 814
imperialism and, 761
independence movements and, 930–931
in Ireland, 813
Napoleon and, 654, 662
national order and, 751
in 1930s, 889
in postindustrial age, 960
revivalism and, 598–599
in school curriculum, 742
social reform and, 699, 780
spread of Western, 761
in technocratic society, 959–960
Religious orders, women's, 751
Religious Society of Friends. *See* Quakers
Religious toleration
in Enlightenment, 609
in EU, 1011*(b)*
in France, 627
Remarque, Erich Maria, 863, 885
Reparations
German, after World War I, 852–853
after World War II, 920
Repatriation, after World War II, 923*(i)*
Repression
liberal reforms and, 706
of Soviet arts, 962
Reproduction
decline in, 800
scientists on, 752–753
Reproduction technology, 954–955
Reproductive rights, 964–965
Republic(s)
former Soviet, 990
in former Yugoslavia, 988
in France, 630, 633–635, 654–655, 711
in Italy, 924
Rome (city) as, 712
soviet, 851
in Spanish America, 677–678
in United States, 614
Republicanism, in France, 788
"Republican mothers," 731*(i)*
Republican Party (U.S.), 737
Republicans, in Spain, 893–894
"Republic of letters," 588–589
Research
genetic, 956
scientific, 740, 958
in social sciences, 960
Reservations, native Americans on, 737
Resistance
to colonialism, 822–825
to French Revolution, 635–636
in India to British, 743*(m)*
to Napoleon I, 663–664
to Nazis, 902–905, 923, 937
Resolution of the Syrian Congress at Damascus (July 2, 1919), 855*(b)*
Resources. *See also* Natural resources
imperialism and, 761
in World War II, 900–902
Restoration, of European balance, 669
Reunification. *See also* Unification
of Germany, 979*(i)*
of Vietnam, 969
Revisionism, 810
Revivals and revivalism, 598–599, 671
Revolts and rebellions
by Austrian Netherlands against France, 653
in British India, 743, 743*(m)*
in central Europe, 712–714
in 1820s, 675–678
by ethnic groups in Russia, 728
in France, 626, 626*(m)*, 636
in Galicia, 704
in India (1857), 743, 743*(m)*, 744*(i)*
in Italy, 679
in name of liberty, 620
by Paris Commune, 747
in Poland, 679, 977–978
Pugachev Rebellion, 611, 611*(m)*
by Russian peasants, 726
by Russian youth, 728
in St. Domingue, 641*(b)*, 641–643, 642*(m)*
by Slavs against Turks, 789
against Soviets (1956), 930
against state power, 610–614
after World War I, 851–852
Revolution(s). *See also* French Revolution; Revolts and rebellions
American, 612–614
Atlantic, 620
in business, 772–775
in clothing, 656, 656*(i)*
in 1820s, 678*(m)*
of 1848, 686, 709–711, 710*(m)*, 712*(i)*, 714*(i)*, 715
in French colonies, 640–643
in Hungary (1956), 930
in Italy, 711–712
of 1989, 978–980
in North America, 612–614
Paris Commune and, 747
in Russia (1905), 821, 821*(m)*
in Russia (1917), 846–849
use of term, 621*(b)*
after World War I, 851
in Yugoslavia, 920, 920*(m)*
Revolutionary era (1787–1789), 620–631
Revolutionary Tribunal (France), 633, 637, 638
Revolutionary War in America. *See* American Revolution
Rhineland
demilitarization of, 856
German invasion of, 891
Rhine River region, after World War I, 852
Rhodes, Cecil (1853–1902), 763
Rhodesia, 930
Rich people. *See* Wealth
Rifles, 770
Riga, 740
Rights. *See also* Natural rights
of European aristocrats, 600
in France, 626–628
for minorities, 627*(b)*
for women, 627, 753
Rights of Man, The (Paine), 644–645
Right wing, in Germany, 815
Ring of the Nibelungen, The (Wagner), 749
Riots
civil rights, 965–966
food, 610–611, 625
in France, 887
in London, 612
in 1981, 974
Stonewall (U.S.), 964
Risorgimento (Italy), 729
Rite of Spring, The (Stravinsky), 809
Roads and highways. *See* Automobiles and automobile industry; Transportation
Roaring Twenties, 857–862
Robespierre, Maximilien (1758–1794), 631–638
Rob Roy (Scott), 675
Rock-and-roll music, culture of, 939, 941*(i)*, 959
Rockefeller, John D., 770, 772
Rockefeller Foundation, 999
Rocket (railroad engine), 685
Rockets, space age and, 952–953
Rococo style, 602
Roehm, Ernst, 884
Roland, Jeanne (1754–1793), 631, 633
Rolling Stones, 958*(i)*, 1012
Roma (gypsies), 1009
Nazis and, 885, 899–900
Roman Catholicism. *See also* Missions and missionaries; Papacy
charities and, 699
in England, 681
Enlightenment and, 597, 608–609
in France, 628, 654, 671
in Germany, 889
in Ireland, 972
in Italy, 868
religion, national order, and, 751
in Spain, 664
Vatican II and, 937
women's orders in, 751
in World War II, 902
Romania, 725
as Axis power, 896
collapse of communism in, 980
communism in, 919
economy in, 997–998
in EU, 997
fascism in, 879
homeless children in, 980*(i)*
in Little Entente, 856, 856*(m)*

Romania (*continued*)
refugees after World War I, 858
before World War I, 826
before World War II, 894
in World War II, 904
Romanians, 815
nationalism of, 714
Romanov dynasty, end of, 846, 849
Romanticism, 598
in arts, 672*(i)*, 672–675, 674*(i)*, 675*(i)*
social question and, 696
Romantic nationalism, 674–675, 729
Rome (city), 731
France and, 657
growth of, 771
Italy and, 731
as part of Italy, 734
as republic, 712
Treaty of (1957), 926
Rome–Berlin Axis, 892
Rommel, Erwin, 904
Ronaldo (Brazilian soccer player), 1012
Roosevelt, Eleanor (1884–1962), 886, 887*(i)*
Roosevelt, Franklin Delano (1882–1945), 886, 887*(i)*
declaration of war on Japan by, 897
embargo on Japanese exports by, 890
World War II and, 907
Roosevelt, Theodore (1858–1919), 818
on family planning, 800
Rosetta stone, 653
Rossbach, battle at, 605
Rossellini, Roberto, 943
Rousseau, Jean-Jacques (1712–1778), 588, 591*(i)*, 593*(i)*, 594–596, 597
Émile, 593*(i)*, 594*(b)*
romanticism and, 598
on society, 594–596
Royal courts. *See* Court (royal)
Royal Dutch Shell, 860
Royalists, in France, 654
Royalty. *See* Kings and kingdoms; Monarchs and monarchies
Ruhr River region, 856, 891
Rural areas. *See also* Farms and farming
cholera in, 694, 694*(m)*
in Great Depression, 876
Great Fear in France, 626, 626*(m)*
industrialization and, 686
migration from, 777
power in, 695
Rushdie, Salman, 1013
Russia. *See also* Russian Republic; Soviet Union
Asia and, 765
Austria and, 724, 726
authoritarianism and anti-Semitism in, 813–814
Baltic region and, 896
Bulgaria and, 790
civil war in (1917–1922), 848–849, 849*(m)*
concert of Europe and, 722–723
Congress of Vienna and, 668, 669*(m)*
Crimean War and, 724–726
Decembrist Revolt in, 676
economy in, 990, 1007
education in, 609
Freemasons in, 601
Germany and, 836, 856
Hitler and, 664
Hungary and, 714
imperialism by, 765–766
industrialization in, 690, 771, 821
international politics and, 993–994
Jews in, 609, 813–814, 816*(m)*
land in, 727
liberalism in, 706
life expectancy in, 1002
literature in, 749
Lithuania and, 607
market in, 771*(i)*
Marxism in, 811, 821
migration from, 858
movies from, 863
Napoleon I and, 660*(m)*, 661, 664–665, 665*(b)*
nationalism in, 704
nobility in, 600
Poland and, 622, 640, 728, 852
political power in, 695
power politics in, 788
railroads in, 695
reforms in, 608, 662
revolt in 1820s, 675
revolutions of 1848 and, 715
serfs in, 726–727, 727*(i)*
socialism in, 810–811
toxic wastes in, 1000
Turkey and, 677, 789–790
universal suffrage in, 848
unrest in, 791
urban water supplies in, 740
women in, 821
workers' parties in, 810
World War I and, 829, 839, 840, 865–867
Russian Empire, 821–822
after World War I, 853*(m)*
Russian Mafia, 992
Russian Orthodox church
Slavophiles and, 704
women in, 751
Russian Republic, 990. *See also* Russia; Soviet Union; Soviet Union (former)
Russian Revolution (1905), 821, 821*(m)*
Russian Revolution (1917), 810
of March, 846
outbreak of, 847*(b)*
Russification
under Alexander II (Russia), 728–729
Stolypin and, 822
Russo-Japanese War (1904–1905), 818, 820
Ruthenians, 815
Rwanda, 1003
migration from, 1008

SA. *See* Stürmabteilung
Saar basin, 852
Sachs, Nelly (1891–1970), 937
al-Sadat, Mohammed Anwar, 974*(i)*
Saddam Hussein, 1003
St. Domingue. *See also* Haiti
Napoleon and, 661
revolt in, 641*(b)*, 641–643, 642*(m)*
St. Giles, London, 693
St. Helena, Napoleon on, 666
St. Petersburg. *See also* Leningrad; Petrograd
Decembrist Revolt and, 676
St. Peter's Fields, Manchester, political meeting in, 680
Saint Phalle, Niki de, 942*(i)*, 960
Saint-Simon, Henri de (Count) (1760–1825), 706
Sakhalin Islands, Soviets and, 907
Salome (Strauss), 810
Salons, 590–591, 591*(i)*
SALT I. *See* Strategic Arms Limitation Treaty
Salvation, Wesley on, 598
Samizdat culture, 962
Samurai tradition, 766
Sand, George (Amandine-Aurore-Lucile Dupin Dudevant, 1804–1876), 697, 698*(i)*
Sanitation
in cities, 739, 800
in India, 744
urban, 693–694
Sans-culottes (French workers), 624, 630, 638
Sanssouci (Frederick the Great's palace), 602
San Stefano, Treaty of (1878), 790
Sarajevo, Francis Ferdinand assassinated in, 828, 836
SARS (severe acute respiratory syndrome), 1003
Sartre, Jean-Paul, 937, 938*(i)*
Satanic Verses, The (Rushdie), 1013
Satellites (artificial)
communications, 953, 1012
Sputnik as, 930
Satellite states. *See* Soviet bloc; Soviet Union
Sati (widow's self-immolation), 671–672, 744
Satyagraha (Gandhi), 938
Saudi Arabia
Britain and, 932
economy in, 1007
Savage Mind, The (Lévi-Strauss), 960
Savoy, 639, 670, 730
Saxony
Congress of Vienna and, 668, 669*(m)*
industrialization in, 690
Scandinavia. *See also* specific locations
economic development in, 925
industrialization in, 771
modern arts in, 808–809
Schiller, Friedrich, 674
Schleswig, 733
Schlieffen Plan, 839, 839*(m)*
Schnittke, Alfred, 1014
Schoenberg, Arnold (1874–1951), 810
Scholars and scholarship. *See also* History and historians; Intellectual thought
Catholic, 751
Schools. *See also* Education
attendance at, 742
in Austria, 609
compulsory education and, 742
in French Revolution, 635
Napoleon on, 658
professionalization and, 742–743
sports in, 781
Schreiner, Olive, 783
Schumacher, E. F. "Fritz," 1000
Schuman, Robert, 925–926, 926*(b)*
Schuman Plan on European Unity (1950), 926*(b)*
Schutzstaffel (SS), in Nazi Germany, 884, 897
Science(s). *See also* Astronomy; Medicine; Technology
biology and, 953–954
in Enlightenment, 589*(i)*
gender stereotypes and, 700–701
industrialization and, 687
Napoleon and, 658
in 1930s, 889
public health and, 740
reproductive technology and, 953–955
revolution in, 806–807
of "self," 803–805
in Soviet Union, 958

Scientific management, productivity and, 860
Scott, Walter (1771–1832), 675
Scream, The (Munch), 796*(i)*, 809
Sculpture, Soviet dissident, 963*(b)*, 963*(i)*
Seacole, Mary (1805–1881), 726*(b)*
Sears, Roebuck, 774
SEATO. *See* Southeast Asia Treaty Organization
Secession, from Yugoslavia, 988
Secondary education
  expansion of, 742
  in France, 658
Second Continental Congress, 613
Second Empire (France), 734, 787
Second Estate (France), 624, 625*(i)*
Second Great Awakening, 671
"Second" Industrial Revolution, 769–770
Second International, 785, 786, 810
Second Moroccan Crisis (1911), 825
Second of May, The, 1808 (Goya), 663*(i)*
Second Partition of Poland (1793), 640, 640*(m)*
Second Reform Bill (England, 1867), 736
Second Reich (Germany), 884
Second Republic (France), 711
Second Sex, The (Beauvoir), 938n
Second Vatican Council (Vatican II), 937
Second world, 914
Second World War. *See* World War II
Secret police, in Russia, 791, 821, 848
Secular culture, 937
Secularism, in Enlightenment, 592
Secularization, 751
Security Council (UN), Korean War and, 931
Sedition laws, in World War I, 842
Segregation
  civil rights movement and, 938
  in public facilities, 962
Seigneurial dues, 600
Sejm (Polish parliament), 858
Selective breeding, of people, 801
"Self," science of, 803–805
Self-determination, in central Europe, 713–714
Self-government, by Canada, 739
Self-immolation, of Jan Palach (Czechoslovakia), 948*(i)*, 949
Self-interest, Smith on, 593
Sen, Amartya, 1008
Senegal, immigrants from, 984*(i)*
Separate spheres ideology, 700, 701
Separatism, Basque, 998
September 11, 2001, terrorist attacks, 1005, 1005*(i)*
September massacres, in Paris, 630
Serbia, 990
  Bosnia and, 826
  rebellion in, 789
  before World War I, 826, 827
  World War I and, 828–829
Serbs. *See also* Yugoslavia
  Albanian Muslims attacked by, 990
  Bosnian Muslims massacred by, 988
  Croatia and, 989
  in former Yugoslavia, 987–990
  Kingdom of the, 852, 858
  nationalism and, 703, 714, 824, 844
  in Yugoslavia, 920
Serfs and serfdom. *See also* Slavery
  in Enlightenment, 609
  industrialization and, 690
  Napoleon and, 662
  in Poland, 622, 640
  in Russia, 600, 611, 695, 726–727, 727*(i)*
Servants, in upper-class homes, 775
Service-based global organizations, 999
Service industries
  personnel in, 956
  spread via Internet, 1009
  workers in urban slums, 998
Services, white-collar, 773–774
Seurat, Georges, 783
Sevastopol, 725
Seven Years' War (1756–1763), 605–606, 606*(m)*, 623
Sewage and sewage systems, in Paris, 740, 741*(i)*
Sex and sexuality. *See also* Gender and gender issues; Homosexuality
  changes in, 604–605
  in cold war, 940
  reproduction and, 752–753
  reproduction technology and, 954–955
  sexual revolution and, 959, 964
  social classes and, 775
  after World War I, 861
"Sexology," 802
Sex rings, 1008
Sexual identity, 801–803
Sexual Inversion (Ellis), 802
Shah of Iran, 1003
Shamanism, Freud on, 803*(i)*
Shelley, Mary (1797–1851), 651, 672*(i)*, 673
Shelley, Percy Bysshe (1792–1822), 651
Shell shock, in World War I, 842
Shi'ite Muslims, 1003–1004
Ships and shipping
  ice pack and, 1000
  reduction after World War I, 856
  World War I and, 827, 859
Shipyard Sally (film), 889*(i)*
Shopping
  in former Soviet Union, 993*(i)*
  malls in eastern Europe, 998
Show trials, in Soviet Union, 880
Siberia
  Japanese ouster from, 849
  Russia and, 821
Sicily
  migrants from, 776
  in World War II, 904
"Sick man of Europe," Ottoman Empire as, 724
Sieyès, Emmanuel-Joseph (1748–1836), 624, 655
Sikhs, 931
Silent Spring (Carson), 1000
Silesia, 606
Simyonov, Yulian, 942
Sinai, 971
Singapore, 702
  as Pacific tiger, 1006
  in World War II, 897
Sinn Féin (Ireland), 813
Sino-Japanese War (1894), 820
Sinope, battle at, 724
Sinti people, Nazis and, 885, 899–900
Six Acts (Britain), 680
Six-Day War (1967), 971
Skepticism, French Revolution and, 670
Slav congress (Prague), 714
Slave labor, in World War II, 900
Slavery. *See also* Serfs and serfdom
  abolition of, 592, 701
  in United States, 737–739
Slave trade, 615*(m)*
  address on abolishing, 641*(b)*
  Congress of Vienna and, 670
  Latin American abolition of, 677
Slavophiles (Russia), 704
Slavs, Nazis and, 885, 899–900
Slovak Fascist Party, 888
Slovakia, in EU, 996
Slovaks, 714, 815
  independence of, 850
  Prague Spring and, 967–969
Slovenes, 714. *See also* Yugoslavia
  nationalism of, 844
Slovenia, 988
  in EU, 996
  foreign investment in, 996
Slumdog Millionaire (film), 1014
Slums, 998
  clearance in England, 887
Small Is Beautiful (Schumacher), 1000
Smallpox, 1002
Smart car, 1000*(i)*, 1001
Smith, Adam (1723–1790), 593
Smith, Zadie, 1013
Smuggling, Continental System and, 663
Social classes. *See* Classes
Social Contract, The (Rousseau), 595, 596
Social Darwinism, 753
  on mental decline, 803
  wealth and, 775
Social Democrats, in Germany, 789, 810, 815, 827, 851
Social hierarchies. *See* Classes
Socialism, 706–707
  in China, 823
  critiques of, 966*(b)*
  in Germany, 810
  Marx on, 746
  origins of, 706–707
  in Russia, 810–811
  women and, 707
  after World War I, 851
Socialist countries, as second world, 914
Socialist parties, 961
Socialist realism, 881, 962
Social mobility, after World War II, 915
Social order, 721–722
  culture of, 748–753
  nation building through, 739–748
  religion and, 751
Social sciences, 753, 960
Social Security Act (U.S., 1935), 886
Social welfare
  in Italy, 813
  Popular Front and, 888
  in Sweden, 886–887
  in United States, 886
Society. *See also* Art(s); Civilization(s); Classes; Religion
  arts and industrial, 696–701
  in atomic age, 943–944
  in Austria, 975–976
  and culture in Enlightenment, 599–605
  in Digital Age, E-2
  in England, 974
  in Enlightenment, 592–596, 603–605
  in France, 975
  in Germany, 974–975
  global (21st century), 1008–1015
  in Great Depression, 876
  ideologies in, 686
  imperial, 775–783
  industrialization and, 685–686
  in Nazi Germany, 884–885
  in novels, 696–697

Society (*continued*)
postindustrial, 955–959
realist novel and, 748
reforms of, 696–701, 780–781
in Russia, 990
in Soviet Union, 880–881
in Sweden, 976
in United States under Reagan, 974
after World War I, 860–862
before World War I, 798–806
after World War II, 915–916
Society for the Prevention of Cruelty to Animals, 699
Society of Friends. *See* Quakers
Society of Jesus. *See* Jesuits
Society of Revolutionary Republican Women (France), 636–637
Society of Supporters of the Bill of Rights (England), 612
Society of the Friends of Blacks, 641, 641*(b)*
Society of the Righteous and Harmonious Fist. *See* Boxer Uprising
Society of United Irishmen, 646
Sociology, 753, 960
Sofia, 800
Solaris (novel and film), 952
Solar system, space exploration and, 953
Soldiers. *See also* Armed forces; Military; Veterans
artificial limbs for, 835
colonial, in World War I, 841–842
in Crimean War, 725, 725*(i)*
in Napoleon's army, 665*(b)*
World War I and, 840–842, 841*(i)*, 842*(i)*, 843*(b)*, 857, 860
Solidarity movement, 977–978
Solzhenitsyn, Aleksandr, 930, 969
Somalia, 1003
drought and poverty in, 1002
Somme, battle at the, 840
Sony Corporation, videocassettes and, 951
Sophie (Austria), 828
Sorrows of Young Werther, The (Goethe), 598
Soubirous, Bernadette (St. Bernadette of Lourdes), 751
South (U.S.), 737–739
South (global), vs. North (global), 1003, E-3*(m)*
South Africa
African migrants in, 1008
economy in, 1007
uprising in (1989), 978
South African (Boer) War (1899–1902), 818
South America
migration to, 777
in Western consumer economy, 1010
South Asia, British rule in, 743–744
Southeast Asia, Nixon and, 969
Southeast Asia Treaty Organization (SEATO), 931
Southern Africa, imperialism in, 762–763, 763*(m)*
South Korea
female workers in, 1007
as Pacific tiger, 1006
South Vietnam, 962, 969. *See also* Vietnam
Southwest Africa, German colonies in, 819
Southwest region, in United States, 737
Soviet bloc. *See also* Eastern Europe
arts in, 962
birthrate in, 958
collapse of communism in, 976–979, 980*(m)*
creation of, 929
postindustrial work life in, 956
scientific applications in, 957–958
World War II and, 898
Soviet Central Asia, Muslims in, 987
Soviet republics, 851
Soviets (councils), 846–847, 865
Soviet Union. *See also* Russia; Soviet Union (former); Superpowers
anti-Semitism in, 917, 969
Asian interests of, 931
atomic bomb of, 924
in cold war, 914, 961–962
collapse of, 976–977, 986–987, 990–994
creation of, 866–867
dissident art in 1960s and 1970s, 963*(b)*, 963*(i)*
economy in, 878–880
expansion of, 930
vs. fascist state, 879
five-year plans in, 878–880
German partition and, 920–922, 921*(m)*
Germans in, 920, 922
historical evidence about cold war, 918
human rights in, 970
industry in, 917
internal problems in, 970
Jews in, 917
Nazi attack on (1941), 897
Nazi-Soviet Pact and, 895
Prague Spring and, 968*(i)*, 968–969
Reagan and, 974
reforms in, 976–977
scientific research in, 958
secret archives of, 918*(b)*, 918*(i)*
society in, 880–881
Spanish Civil War and, 894
Stalin in, 874, 878–881
television in, 951
in UN, 934–935
U.S. test-ban treaty with, 944
after World War II, 907, 915, 916–917
in World War II, 897, 900, 904
Soviet Union (former). *See also* Russia; Soviet Union
Chechnya and, 990
countries of (c. 2000), 991*(m)*
culture in, 1013–1014
fertility rates in, 1002
lifestyle in, 992–993
market economy in, 992–993
nations in EU, 995
politics and, 993–994
Space exploration, 930, 952
moon landing and, 952
Space race, 952–953
Spain. *See also Cortes* (Spain); Spanish Civil War (1936–1939)
al-Qaeda train bombings in Madrid, 1005, 1006*(i)*
American colonies of, 677–678
American Revolution and, 613–614
Basques in, 972
constitutional monarchy in, 973
economy in, 975
fertility rate in, 1001–1002
France and, 657, 663*(i)*, 664, 675
liberalism rejected in, 788
Prussia and, 733–734
revolt in 1820s, 675
slave trade and, 701
terrorist attacks in (2004), 1005, 1006*(i)*
voting rights in, 788
Spanish America. *See* Latin America
Spanish-American War (1898), 818
Spanish Civil War (1936–1939), 892–894, 893*(i)*, 893*(m)*
Spanish-language television, 1014
Spencer, Herbert (1820–1903), 753
Spending, military, 925*(f)*, 931, 944, 1006–1007
Spheres of influence. *See also* Colonies and colonization
Soviet bloc as, 929–930
Spinning jenny, 687
Spontaneous ovulation, 753–754
Sports, 604
polo as, 781*(i)*
popular blood, 699
team, 781
after World War I, 862
Sputnik, 930
Srebrenica, 989, 990
SS. *See* Schutzstaffel
Stadholder (Dutch official), 621, 639, 669
Stagflation, in England, 974
Stalin, Joseph (1879–1953), 862, 866–867, 874
cold war and, 918*(b)*
death of, 929–930
eastern Europe and, 919–920
on Nazism, 920
Nazi-Soviet Pact and, 895–896
purges by, 880
Spanish Civil War and, 894
totalitarianism of, 878–881
after World War II, 917
World War II and, 907
Stalingrad, battle of (1942–1943), 903–904
Stalinism, 917, 929
Stamp Act (Britain, 1765), 614*(i)*
Standard of living
of working class, 692–693*(b)*, 693*(f)*, 760
in World War I, 845
after World War II, 914, 922, 928
Standard Oil Trust, 772
State (nation). *See also* Church and state; Nation-state
French, 654
power of, 605–610
rebellions against, 610–614
reforms sponsored by, 607–608
Statue of Liberty (New York), 634*(i)*
Statues. *See* Sculpture
Status. *See* Classes
Steam engines, 686–687
in continental Europe, 690
in England, 689
Steamships
emigration and, 777
in Great Britain, 689
Steel, 769, 770
Stephenson, George (1781–1848), 685, 688
Sterilization, 801
"Still Life" (Daguerre), 698*(i)*
Stock, in business, 772
Stock market, crash in 1929, 873–874
Stolypin, Pyotr (1863–1911), 821–822
Stonewall riot, 964
Stopes, Marie, 861
Storm troopers. *See* Stürmabteilung
Stowe, Harriet Beecher, 726
Stranger, The (Camus), 937
Strasbourg, EU parliament in, 995

Strategic Arms Limitation Treaty (SALT I), 970
Strategic Defense Initiative (SDI), 974
Strauss, Richard (1864–1949), 810
Stravinsky, Igor (1882–1971), 809
Strikes, 709, 745–746, 784–785. *See also* Labor
  in England (1926), 859, 860
  in France, 966–967
  by women, 784
Structuralism, 960
Students
  activism by, 964
  antiwar protests by, 969
Stürmabteilung (SA, "storm troopers"), 883, 884
Subjection of Women, The (Mill), 753
Submarine warfare, in World War I, 839, 845–846
Sub-Saharan Africa
  AIDS in, 1003
  European workers from, 935
  independence after World War II, 933–935
  World War I and, 837
Suburbs, after World War II, 928
Succession, to Napoleon I, 657
Sudan, 1003
  conflict in, 825
  drought and poverty in, 1002
Sudetenland, 894
Suez Canal, 720*(i)*, 724, 744–745, 761, 761*(m)*, 837, 931–932
  crisis over (1956), 931
Suffrage. *See* Voting and voting rights
Suffragists, 798, 811–812, 860
Suicide bombers
  Chechen, 993
  Palestinian, 1004–1005
Sukarno, Achmed (1901–1970), 935
Sun Also Rises, The (Hemingway), 861
Sunday schools, 698, 699
Sunni Muslims, 1004*(m)*
Sun Yat-sen (China, 1866–1925), 822–823
Superego, 804
Superpowers. *See also* Cold war; Soviet Union; United States
  Indochina and, 932
  order after 1968 and, 969
  on postwar Germany, 920
  after World War II, 914, 916–922
Superstores, 998
Supply-side economists, Thatcher and, 973
Surrender, after World War I, 852
Suttner, Bertha von (1843–1914), 811
Suu Kyi, Aung San, 1012
Suzuki, Ichiro, 1012
Sweden
  birthrate drop in, 800
  economy in, 925, 976
  emigration from, 776
  income tax in, 741
  in 1930s, 886–887
  reforms in, 611–612
  service workers in, 956
  society in, 976
  voting rights in, 788
  women in, 801, 965
Swine flu, 1003
Switzerland, France and, 640
Syllabus of Errors, The (Pius IX), 751
Synagogues, Nazi destruction of, 885
Syndicalists, 811
Synthetics, after World War II, 925
Syphilis, 741
Syria, Israel and, 971
Syrian Congress, Resolution of (1919), 855*(b)*
System of Positive Politics . . . (Comte), 753
Széchenyi, Stephen (1791–1860), 706, 714

T4 project, 885, 898
Taaffe, Edouard von (1833–1895), 789
Taiping ("Heavenly Kingdom" movement), 745
Taiwan
  female workers in, 1007
  as Pacific tiger, 1006
Tajikistan, 990
Tajik people, 990
Taliban, 1005
Talleyrand, Charles Maurice de (1754–1838), 669
Tanks, 838
Tanzania, World War I and, 837
Tariffs, 772
  Napoleon and, 662
Tatars, strikes by, 821
Taxation
  in France, 623, 624, 628
  income tax, 741
  international, 999
  of peasants, 600
Taylor, Frederick (1856–1915), 860
Taylor, Harriet, 811
Tea Act (Britain, 1773), 613
Teachers, women as, 743
Team sports, 781
Technical education, 742, 958
Technical planners, in agriculture, 956–957
Technocratic society, art, ideas, and religion in, 959–960
Technocrats, 926–927
Technology, 741*(i)*. *See also* Science(s)
  arts and, 864–865
  in Digital Age, E-3, E-5
  environment and, 1000
  in postindustrial age, 950–955
  reproduction, 954–955
  spread of, 768–775
Technology bubble, economic collapse and, 1007–1008
Technopoles, Soviet, 961
"Teddy boys" (England), 939
Teenagers, in postindustrial society, 959
Teheran, hostage crisis in, 972
Telecommunications, 950
Telephone operators, in Berlin, 773*(i)*
Television, 941, 950–951
Temperance movement, 698, 699
Ten Days That Shook the World (film), 863
"Tennis court oath" (France), 624
Tennyson, Alfred, Lord (1809–1892), 700
Tereshkova, Valentina, 952, 952*(i)*
Terror (France), 631–638
Terrorism
  Basque renunciation of, 998
  in Digital Age, E-4
  by French military, 934
  in Germany, 974
  global, 986
  in Nazi Germany, 883–884
  in 1980s, 972–973
  from 1980s into 2000s, 1005, 1006*(i)*
  Palestinian suicide bombers and, 1004–1005
  in Russia, 994*(i)*
  of September 11, 2001, 1005
  in Spain, 1005, 1006*(i)*
Test-ban treaty, 944
Tet offensive (1968), 965
Texas, U.S. annexation of, 737
Textiles and textile industry
  in England, 686–687, 688, 690
  industrialization of, 686–687, 770
  women in, 811
Thailand, economic collapse in, 1007
Thaim, Awa, 967*(b)*
Thalidomide, impact on children, 954*(i)*
Thatcher, Margaret, 970, 973–974, 974*(i)*
Theory of Harmony (Schoenberg), 810
Thermidorian Reaction (France), 638
Thévenin, Charles, 625*(i)*
Think tanks, 999
Third Estate (France), 624, 625*(i)*
Third International, 849
Third Partition of Poland (1795), 640, 640*(m)*
Third Reich (Germany), 881n, 884
Third Republic (France), 787–788
Third Section (Russian political police), 676
Third world, 914
  imperialism overthrown in, 931
Three Emperors' League, 789, 790
Three Guineas (Woolf), 889
"Three Principles of the People" (Sun Yat-sen), 822–823
Tiananmen Square, riots in, 978, 1012
Tigers, hunting of, 776*(i)*
Tilak, B. G. (1856–1920), 823
Tilsit, Treaties of, 661
Tin, 770
Tito (Josip Broz) (1892–1980), 920
Tocqueville, Alexis de (1805–1859), 691, 711, 713*(b)*
Togoland, German colonies in, 819
Toilets, public, 740–741
Tokyo, 766
  bombing of, 897
Toleration. *See* Religious toleration
Tolstoy, Leo (1828–1910), 722, 791
Tonkin, in Union of Indochina, 766
Torah, violence against Jews and, 792*(i)*
Tories (England), 681, 736
Torture
  in Algeria, 935*(b)*
  French abolition of, 653
  Voltaire on, 592
Totalitarianism
  in Europe, 878–885
  French Revolution and, 620
Total war. *See also* World War I; World War II
  cold war and, 914
  World War I as, 836, 857
Tour de France, 781
Tourism, 760*(i)*
  global, 1012, 1012*(i)*
Toussaint L'Ouverture, François Dominique (1743–1803), 642*(i)*, 642–643
Towns. *See* Cities and towns; Urban areas
Toxic waste, 1000
Trade and trade routes. *See also* Commerce
  deficits in, 772
  in c. 1890, 793*(m)*
  English, 689
  imperialism and, 765
  with Japan, 745
  liberals on, 705
  Smith on, 593
Trade unions. *See* Labor unions
Transgaz (Czech Republic), 996

Transnational culture, of black immigrants, 1012
Transportation. *See also* Canals; Railroads
farming and, 772
in late 1800s, 761
Trans-Siberian Railroad, 765–766, 771, 820
Transvaal, 818
Transylvania, nationalism and, 703
Trasformismo policy (Italy), 813
Travel, by Russian, 727
Travels in Icaria (Cabet), 707
Treaties. *See also* specific treaties
after Congress of Vienna, 670
after World War I, 852–853
Trench warfare, in World War I, 839, 840–841, 841*(i)*
Trials, in Soviet Union, 880
"Trickle-down prosperity," 973–974
Tricolor (French flag), 635, 788
Triple Alliance, 790, 825, 836
Tristan, Flora (1801–1844), 707
Troops. *See* Armed forces; Military; Soldiers
Trotsky, Leon (1879–1940), 848, 849*(i)*, 867
Truman, Harry S. (1884–1972), 906*(m)*, 907, 917
Truman Doctrine, 919
"Trumpet Calls, The" (Lindsay), 843*(b)*, 843*(i)*
Trusts, 772
Tsars (Russia), autocracy of, 715, 729
Tsushima Strait, battle of, 820
Tuberculosis, 694
Tuileries palace, 630
Tunisia
French occupation of, 761
government overturned in, E-4
Turgenev, Ivan, 726, 749
Turgot, Jacques (1727–1781), 610
Turkey. *See also* Ottoman Empire; Ottoman Turks
Armenians in, 842
Communists in, 919
Dutch opposition to, 1010
EU and, 996
migration from, 858
nationalism in, 823*(b)*, 823–824
Russia and, 677, 789–790
women in, 877–878
workers in Germany from, 975
after World War I, 877–878
before World War II, 894
Young Turks in, 823–824
Turks. *See* Ottoman Empire; Ottoman Turks; Turkey
Turner, Joseph M. W. (1775–1851), 674, 696, 697*(i)*
Twenties, Europe in, 857–862
"Two Islands, The" (Hugo), 667*(b)*
2001: A Space Odyssey (film), 952, 969
Typesetting, 786
Typhoid, 739–740
Tz'u-hsi (Empress) (Cixi, China, 1835–1908), 822

U-boats. *See* Submarine warfare
Ukraine
fertility rates in, 1002
Nazi attack on, 897
Russia and, 848, 993
Ulm, battle at (1805), 661
Ulster, 859, 859*(m)*
Ultra (British code-breaking group), 896
Ultras (French ultraroyalists), 671
Ulysses (Joyce), 864
UN. *See* United Nations
Unbearable Lightness of Being, The (Kundera), 969
Uncle Tom's Cabin (Stowe), 726
Unconscious, use of term, 805
Unemployment
in 1848, 710
in Germany, 884
in Great Depression, 875, 875*(i)*, 877*(b)*, 886
illegal immigrants and, 986
in 1980s, 972
after World War I, 857
Unification. *See also* Berlin; Berlin Wall; Germany; Reunification
of Germany, 703, 712–713, 731–735
of Italy, 712, 724, 729–730, 730*(m)*
Union (United States North), 737–739
Union of Soviet Socialist Republics (USSR). *See* Soviet Union
Unions. *See* Labor unions
United Nations (UN)
creation of, 907, 914
embargo against Bosnian Muslims, 988
Korean War and, 931
newly independent nations in, 934–935
United States. *See also* Superpowers
AIDS in, 1003
artists in, 864–865
Asian interests of, 931
citizen activism in 1960s, 964–966
civil rights in, 938
in cold war, 914
Constitution and Bill of Rights in, 614
cotton industry in, 690
cultural dominance by, 1014
democracy after World War II, 924
dominance by, 986
economy in, 770–771, 860, 916–917
expansion of (1850–1870), 737*(m)*
French Revolution and, 643
German partition and, 920–922, 921*(m)*
Great Depression in, 874–875, 886
high-tech industries in, 1006
historical evidence about cold war, 918*(b)*
Israel and, 971
Japanese attack on (1941), 897
Jewish migration to, 816
Kellogg-Briand Pact and, 856–857
Kyoto Protocol and, 1001
Middle East and, 932
migrants to, 777
national debt of, 1007
nation building in, 737–739
railroads in, 688
reaction against activism, 969
Reagan in, 974
revolution in, 612–614
Saint-Simonians in, 707
service workers in, 956
Spanish-American War and, 818
television in, 941
temperance movement in, 699
in UN, 934–935
welfare state in, 886, 927
woman suffrage in, 811
after World War I, 857
in World War I, 839, 846
after World War II, 916–917
in World War II, 897
Universal Exhibition (Manet), 749
Universal Exposition (Paris, 1889), 769
Universal suffrage
male, 630
in Russia, 848
Universities and colleges. *See also* Education; Higher education
Great Awakening and, 598
protests in (1960s), 965–966
Upper class, 775. *See also* Aristocracy; Classes; Elites; Nobility
Urban areas. *See also* Cities and towns
cholera in, 694, 694*(m)*
cost of living in, 998
industrialization and, 685
movement to, 777, 929
order in, 739–740
workers in, 760
Urbanization, 692–695
Crystal Palace as view of, 716–717
European (1750–1800), 601*(b)*, 601*(f)*
in France, 746–747
industrial, 692–695
USSR. *See* Soviet Union
Utilitarianism, 705
Utopia, communist, 865–867

Vaccines, 1002
Vallain, Jeanne-Louise, 634*(i)*
Values
in Digital Age, E-4
Dutch, 1011*(b)*
rejection of middle-class, 964
Western, 937–938
Van de Velde, Theodor, 861
Van Gogh, Vincent, 783
Vatican II, 937, 960
Velvet revolution, in Czechoslovakia, 980
Vendée Rebellion (1793), 636, 636*(m)*
Venereal disease, 741
Venetia, 731
Austria and, 669*(m)*
Italy and, 731
Verdi, Giuseppe, 720*(i)*, 721, 731, 744, 749
Verdun, battle at, 840
Versailles
German Empire proclaimed at, 735
women's march to, 618*(i)*, 627
Versailles Treaty, 852, 890–891
Veterans
radio for, 863
after World War I, 857, 860–861
after World War II, 927
Vichy France, 896
Victor Emmanuel II (Italy, r. 1861–1878), 721, 730*(m)*
Victor Emmanuel III (Italy, r. 1900–1946), 867
Victoria (England, r. 1837–1901), 736, 738*(b)*, 738*(i)*
as empress of India, 743
Victorian epoch, 736
"Victorian" woman, 700–701
Victory over the Sun: The New Man (Lissitsky), 866*(i)*
Video recorders, 951, 1012
Vienna
Kunsthistorisches Museum in, 740*(i)*
Napoleon and, 661
rebuilding of, 735, 739
uprising of 1848 in, 714
Vietcong, 964

Viet Minh, 932
Vietnam. *See also* Indochina; Vietnam War
France and, 744–745, 766
Vietnam War (1954–1975), 962*(m)*, 962–964
Nixon and, 969
Tet offensive in, 965
Vigée-Lebrun, Marie-Louise-Elizabeth (1755–1842), 602, 623*(i)*, 659*(i)*
Villages. *See* Cities and towns; Urban areas
Vilnius, 640
Violence. *See also* Wars and warfare
in Balkans, 988–989
of colonization, 762*(i)*
in eastern Europe, 993
in French Revolution, 620, 626
in 1960s activist movements, 965–969
for upward mobility, 915–916
after World War II, 915–916
Virtue, French republic of, 633–635
Visual arts, 959–960. *See also* Art(s)
Vladivostok, Trans-Siberian Railroad to, 771
Voice of America, 943
Volksgemeinschaft, in Germany, 884
Voltaire (François-Marie Arouet) (1694–1778), 590, 591*(i)*, 592, 597
Catherine II and, 588
as deist, 591
Von Bülow, Frieda, 759, 762
Voting and voting rights. *See also* Suffragists
in France, 628, 630, 678
in Italy, 788
in Russia, 848
in western Europe, 788
women and, 784, 811–812
after World War I, 857
Voyages of exploration. *See* Exploration
Vranitsky, Franz, 975–976

Wagner, Richard, 749
Wajda, Andrzej, 939*(i)*
Walentynowicz, Anna, 977
Walesa, Lech, 977, 979
Wallachia, 725
Wallenberg, Raoul (1912–1947), 902
Walter, Jakob (1788–1864), 665*(b)*
Wannsee, Germany, extermination of Jews and, 898
War and Peace (Tolstoy), 791
War guilt clause, 852–853
Warhol, Andy, 959
War of Independence (United States). *See* American Revolution
War of Italian Unification, 724
Wars and warfare. *See also* Armed forces; Civil war(s); specific battles and wars
digitization and, E-4
French Revolution and, 633, 637, 638–640
for German unification, 733–734
in late 18th century, 605–607
for Latin American independence, 677–678
Napoleonic, 653–654
nation building and, 729–739
in 21st century, 1008
U.S. global power through, 986
Warsaw, 640
duchy of, 661, 668
Warsaw Ghetto, 898*(i)*
Warsaw Pact, 921
Hungary and, 930
Washington Conference (1921), 856, 859
"Waste Land, The" (Eliot), 864
Waste materials
human, 693–694
radioactive, 957
toxic, 1000
Water
for drinking, in Africa, 1002
in urban areas, 693–694, 740
Watergate scandal, 970
Waterloo, battle of (1815), 665
Watson, James, 939–940, 953
Watt, James (1736–1819), 686–687
Wealth and wealthy
from factories, 691
in global cities, 998
in Russia, 990, 992
Smith on, 593
upper class and, 775–776
Wealth gap, 695
North/South, E-3*(m)*
Weapons. *See also* Arms race; Technology
industrial technology and, 770
before World War I, 827
in World War I, 837, 838–839
World War II production of, 900*(f)*
Weapons of mass destruction, Iraq and, 1005
Weaving, industrialization and, 687, 688
Weber, Max (1864–1920), 806
Wedgwood, Josiah (1730–1795), 601–602
Weimar Republic (Germany), 858, 860, 868, 881
Welfare and welfare state, 801. *See also* Social welfare
childbearing and, 941
in cold war, 961
in Denmark, 927*(i)*
in England, 973
in Europe, 975
reforms in, 699–700
television programming in, 951
in United States, 886
after World War II, 914
Wellington, Arthur Wellesley (Duke of, 1769–1852), 665, 681
Wells, H. G. (1866–1946), 797
Wesley, John (1703–1791), 598–599, 671
Wesleyans. *See* Methodism
West. *See* Western world
West Africa, independence in, 933
West Berlin, fall of Berlin Wall and, 979
Western civilization. *See* Western world
Western Europe
vs. eastern Europe, 993
economic development in, 925
political participation in, 786–788
voting rights in, 788
after World War I, 858–859
after World War II, 915–916, 923–927
Western front, in World War I, 840*(m)*
Westernization
in Japan, 766
of Russia, 704
of Turkey, 877–878
Western world. *See also* Europe and Europeans; World War I; World War II
culture from beyond, 1012–1013
in digital world, E-5
in c. 1890, 793*(m)*
fertility rate in, 1001–1002
globalization in, 985–986, 1010–1011
global migration and, 1008–1009
imperialism by, 760
Islamic radicalism and, 1003–1005
non-Western cultures and, 767–768
reforms in 1980s, 972–976
restoring values in, 937–938
Soviet cultural and scientific meetings with, 961
woman suffrage in, 857*(f)*
West Germany
Allied zones merged as, 920–921
creation of, 920–921
East German trade with, 961
economy of, 921, 925
female employment in, 927
as German Federal Republic, 924
government of, 924
Green Party in, 1000
inflation in (1973), 971
Kohl in, 974
Red Army faction in, 972
West Indies, 606*(m)*
Westphalia, kingdom of, 661
"What Is Enlightenment?" (Kant), 596*(b)*
What Is Property? (Proudhon), 707
What Is the Third Estate? (Sieyès), 624
Whigs (England), 681, 736
White-collar service sector, 773–774
workers in, 956
Whitefield, George (1714–1770), 599*(i)*
Whites
black criticism of feminism by, 966*(b)*
in Russia, 848, 849
White supremacists, 1009
White Teeth (Smith), 1013
"White Terror" (France), 638
Wilde, Oscar (1854–1900), 802, 802*(i)*
Wild One, The (film), 939
Wilkes, John (1727–1797), 612–613
William (Netherlands), 679
William I (Prussia and Germany, r. 1861–1888), 732, 732*(i)*, 734, 789
William II (Germany, r. 1888–1918), 791, 802–803, 805*(i)*, 810, 815
flight from Germany, 850
World War I and, 825, 829, 839
Wilson, Woodrow (1856–1924), 825
Fourteen Points of, 846, 852, 854*(b)*
League of Nations and, 853–854
World War I and, 839
Windischgrätz, Alfred von (1787–1862), 714
Winter Palace (St. Petersburg), 821
Wolf, Christa, 962
"Wolf-Man" (Freud's patient), 797, 798
Wollstonecraft, Mary (1759–1797), 651
Woman suffrage, 709, 711, 798, 811–812, 860
in Finland, 811, 812*(i)*
in France, 711
in West, 857*(f)*
World War I and, 842, 857, 860
Women. *See also* Feminism; Gender and gender issues; Woman suffrage; Women's rights
in Africa, 933
in Asia, 1007
birth control and, 780
books for, 603*(i)*
charitable work and, 699, 700
Civil Code of Napoleon and, 658, 700
Darwin on, 753
domesticity and, 700–701
education for, 658, 742
in 18th century, 604
employment of, 927–928
Enlightenment and, 590–591, 594–595*(b)*

Women (*continued*)
European and American compared, 967*(b)*
as factory workers, 691
in France, 710, 711*(i)*
in French Revolution, 618*(i)*, 627, 636–637
gender stereotypes and, 700–701
George-Sandism and, 697
in Great Depression, 876
in Italy, 868
literacy of, 604
as Methodists, 671
middle-class, 685–686
in Nazi Germany, 885
new woman and, 801–803
in Paris Commune, 747
as philosophes, 589–590
in professions, 743
Proudhon on, 745
religion and, 751
resistance by (World War II), 902–903
after revolutions of 1848, 715
rights of, 627, 753
in Russia, 821, 866
socialism and, 707
social sciences and, 753
Soviet, 881, 917
in Turkey, 877–878
university education for, 801
in upper class, 775
voting and, 784
welfare state and, 927
in white-collar service sector, 773*(i)*, 773–774
in workers' political parties, 785–786
in workforce, 780–781, 798, 857, 925, 941, 942*(f)*, 958
workhouses and, 699
after World War I, 861–862
in World War I, 860
in World War II, 900
Women in Love (Lawrence), 861
Women's movement, 964–965
Women's Paradise (Zola), 781
Women's rights, suffrage and, 811–812
Women's Social and Political Union (WSPU), 812
Woolf, Virginia, 863, 889
Wordsworth, William (1770–1850), 642, 673, 673*(b)*
Workday, limits on, 691
Worker Opposition (Russia), 866
Workers. *See also* Labor
in Asia, 1007
Civil Code of Napoleon and, 658
clandestine, 936
in 1870s–1890s, 784–786
in England (1926), 859, 860
in Europe, 935–936, 936*(i)*
in France, 678
government inquiries about, 691
industrial, 690–692
political theorists and, 745
in postindustrial society, 956–957
poverty of, 694–695
in Russia, 771, 821
scientific management in, 860
in slums, 998
in Soviet Union, 879–880
in United States, 860
urban, 760
women as, 701, 707
Workforce
children in, 773
in Sweden, 976
temporary in Europe, 935
women in, 773–774, 781–782, 798, 857, 927–928, 941, 942*(f)*, 958
in World War I, 844*(i)*, 845
after World War II, 925
Workhouses, 604, 699
Working class, 690–691
education for, 742
political parties and, 785–786
reforms for, 780–781
socialist view of, 708–709
standard of living of, 692–693*(b)*, 693*(f)*
unions, strikes, and, 784–785
women in, 707
Workplace, regulation of, 781
Workshops, Proudhon on, 745–746
World. *See also* Economy; Globalization
in cold war (c. 1960), 945*(m)*
World Bank, 999
economic development loans by, 1003
World Court, Milosevic and, 990
World's fair, of 1867, 749
World Trade Center, destruction of, 1005
World Trade Organization (WTO), 999
World War I (1914–1918)
armistice in, 850
Balkan crises before, 826–827
battlefronts in, 839–842
battles in, 840, 840*(m)*
casualties in, 840, 868
colonial soldiers in, 841–842
cost of living in, 845*(f)*
ending of, 849–851
Europe after, 851–857
Europe at outbreak of, 836–839
in France, 840*(m)*
Germany after, 852–853
as Great War, 835
home front in, 842–845
Middle East after, 854–855*(b)*
mobilization for, 829–830
naval war in, 839
outbreak of, 828–830
peace after, 851–857, 853*(m)*
protests against, 845–846
psychohistorians on, 805*(i)*
society after, 860–862
soldiers in, 840–842, 841*(i)*
submarine warfare in, 845
as total war, 826
trench warfare in, 839, 840
United States in, 846
weapons in, 838
workforce in, 844*(i)*, 845
World War II (1939–1945), 874, 896–908
in Africa, 903*(m)*
battles in, 903*(m)*, 904*(i)*, 905
civilians in, 897–900
end of empires after, 931–935
in Europe, 894–905, 896–897, 903*(m)*
Europe after, 907–908
events leading to, 825–830, 890–892
genocide in, 896
as global war, 890
impact on Europe, 916*(m)*
imperialism preceding, 890–892
legacy of, 907–908
lifestyle after, 936–944
national production during, 900–902
Nazis after, 922–923
in Pacific region, 897, 905–907, 906*(m)*
postwar period after, 913–944
weapons production in, 900*(f)*
western rebirth after, 923–927
World Wide Web, communities on, 1009
Wounded Soldier (Dix), 843*(b)*, 843*(i)*
Wretched of the Earth, The (Fanon), 938
WTO. *See* World Trade Organization

Xenophobia, 676
Xhosa people, 762

Yalta meeting (1945), 907
Yataro, Iwasaki, 766
Yeats, William Butler, 813, 864
Yeltsin, Boris, 977, 990
Yevtushenko, Yevgeny (1933–), 962
Yom Kippur War (1973), 971
Young Bosnians, 829*(i)*
Young Ireland, 704
Young Italy, 703
Young Man Luther (Erikson), 804*(b)*
Young people
in cold war, 939
as consumers, 959
generation gap and, 958–959
Young Plan (1929), 856
Young Turks, 823–824
Ypsilanti, Alexander, 676
Y Tu Mamá También (film), 1014
Yugoslavia, 852
breakup of, 981*(m)*, 987–990
in Little Entente, 856, 856*(m)*
refugees after World War I, 858
resistance to Soviets in, 919–920, 920*(m)*
Yugoslavia (former). *See also* Yugoslavia
Serbs in, 987–990
in c. 2000, 989
Yukos Oil Company (Russia), 992
Yurdakul. *See* Emin, Mehmed

Zadruga (Balkan family system), 801
Zanzibar, Germans in, 759
Zasulich, Vera, 791
Zemstvos (Russian councils), 727, 821
Zhenotdel (Women's Bureau, Russia), 866
Zhukov, Georgy (Marshal), 929
Zionism, 816*(m)*, 817, 916
Zographos, Panagiotis, 677*(i)*
Zola, Émile, 781–782, 814
Zollverein (customs union), 703
Zones of occupation, in Germany, 920–922, 921*(m)*
Zulu people, 762, 764*(b)*

Elevation
Feet
Meters
Over 13,120
Over 4,001
6,561–13,120
2,001–4,000
1,641–6,560
501–2,000
661–1640
201–500
0–660
0–200
Below sea level
Below sea level
National capital
Major city
0
150
300 miles
0
150
300 kilometers
N
W
E
S
NORTHERN IRELAND
SCOTLAND
Glasgow
Edinburgh
Belfast
Dublin
IRELAND
Cork
UNITED KINGDOM
Liverpool
Birmingham
WALES
ENGLAND
Thames R.
London
North Sea
Bergen
NORWAY
Oslo
SWEDEN
Stockholm
Göteborg
Aarhus
DENMARK
Copenhagen
Baltic Sea
Kaliningrad
Gdansk
NETHERLANDS
Amsterdam
Rotterdam
Antwerp
Brussels
BELGIUM
Elbe R.
Berlin
Vistula R.
POLAND
English Channel
GERMANY
Rhine R.
Frankfurt
Oder R.
Prague
Cracow
CZECH REP.
Brno
ATLANTIC OCEAN
Paris
Seine R.
Luxembourg
LUXEMBOURG
Loire R.
LIECHTENSTEIN
Munich
Vienna
Danube R.
SLOVAKIA
Bratislava
Zürich
Vaduz
Bern
SWITZERLAND
Innsbruck
AUSTRIA
Budapest
Graz
HUNGARY
Bay of Biscay
FRANCE
Lyon
ALPS
Milan
SLOVENIA
Ljubljana
Zagreb
Rhône R.
Po R.
CROATIA
Belgrade
San Marino
SAN MARINO
BOSNIA AND HERZEGOVINA
Oporto
ANDORRA
Andorra la Vella
PYRENEES
Ebro R.
Marseille
MONACO
APENNINES
Adriatic Sea
Split
Sarajevo
PORTUGAL
Madrid
Barcelona
Corsica
Podgorica
Lisbon
SPAIN
Rome
ITALY
MONTENEGRO
Tirana
ALBANIA
Naples
Seville
BALEARIC IS.
Sardinia
Tyrrhenian Sea
Gibraltar (Br.)
Ionian Sea
Palermo
Algiers
Sicily
Tunis
Rabat
Valletta
MALTA
MOROCCO
TUNISIA
Mediterranean
ALGERIA
Tripoli
LIBYA

FINLAND
Helsinki
St. Petersburg
Tallinn
ESTONIA
Pärnu
Riga
elgava
LATVIA
LITHUANIA
Kaunas
USSIA
Vilnius
Minsk
BELARUS
Warsaw
Brest
Gomel
Moscow
RUSSIAN FEDERATION
URAL MTS.
Ural R.
Volga R.
KAZAKHSTAN
Kharkiv
Kiev
UKRAINE
Dnieper R.
CARPATHIAN MTS.
Miskolc
MOLDOVA
Chisinau
Tiraspol
Odessa
Cluj
Timisoara
ROMANIA
Bucharest
Danube R.
Black Sea
CAUCASUS MTS.
Caspian Sea
Baku
GEORGIA
Tbilisi
ARMENIA
Yerevan
AZERBAIJAN
SERBIA
Pristina
KOSOVO
BULGARIA
Sofia
Plovdiv
Skopje
MACEDONIA
Istanbul
Salonica
Ankara
TURKEY
Aegean Sea
GREECE
Izmir
Athens
Tehran
IRAN
Tigris R.
SYRIA
Baghdad
Nicosia
Crete
CYPRUS
Beirut
Damascus
LEBANON
IRAQ
Euphrates R.
Sea
ISRAEL
Tel Aviv
Amman
Jerusalem
Kuwait City
KUWAIT
JORDAN
Alexandria
SAUDI ARABIA
Cairo
EGYPT
Nile R.

80°N
60°N
40°N
20°N
0°
Equator
20°S
40°S
60°S
80°S
160°W
140°W
120°W
100°W
80°W
60°W
40°W
20°W
Greenland (Den.)
Alaska (U.S.)
ICELAND
CANADA
UNITED KINGDOM
IRELAND
FRANCE
SPAIN
PORTUGAL
UNITED STATES
Azores (Port.)
ATLANTIC OCEAN
Madeira (Port.)
MOROCCO
Canary Is. (Sp.)
Western Sahara (Mor.)
BAHAMAS
DOMINICAN REPUBLIC
HAITI
Puerto Rico (U.S.)
MEXICO
Hawaii (U.S.)
CUBA
JAMAICA
ST. KITTS AND NEVIS
ANTIGUA AND BARBUDA
MAURITANIA
CAPE VERDE
BELIZE
Guadeloupe (Fr.)
DOMINICA
HONDURAS
Martinique (Fr.)
ST. VINCENT AND THE GRENADINES
SENEGAL
MALI
GUATEMALA
ST. LUCIA
BARBADOS
GAMBIA
EL SALVADOR
NICARAGUA
GRENADA
GUINEA-BISSAU
TRINIDAD AND TOBAGO
COSTA RICA
GUYANA
VENEZUELA
GUINEA
SURINAME
PANAMA
SIERRA LEONE
French Guiana (Fr.)
PACIFIC OCEAN
COLOMBIA
LIBERIA
CÔTE D'IVOIRE
Galápagos Is. (Ec.)
ECUADOR
BURKINA FASO
GHANA
BRAZIL
SAMOA
PERU
TONGA
BOLIVIA
PARAGUAY
Easter I. (Chile)
CHILE
URUGUAY
ATLANTIC OCEAN
0
1,500
3,000 miles
0
1,500
3,000 kilometers
ARGENTINA
Falkland Is. (U.K.)

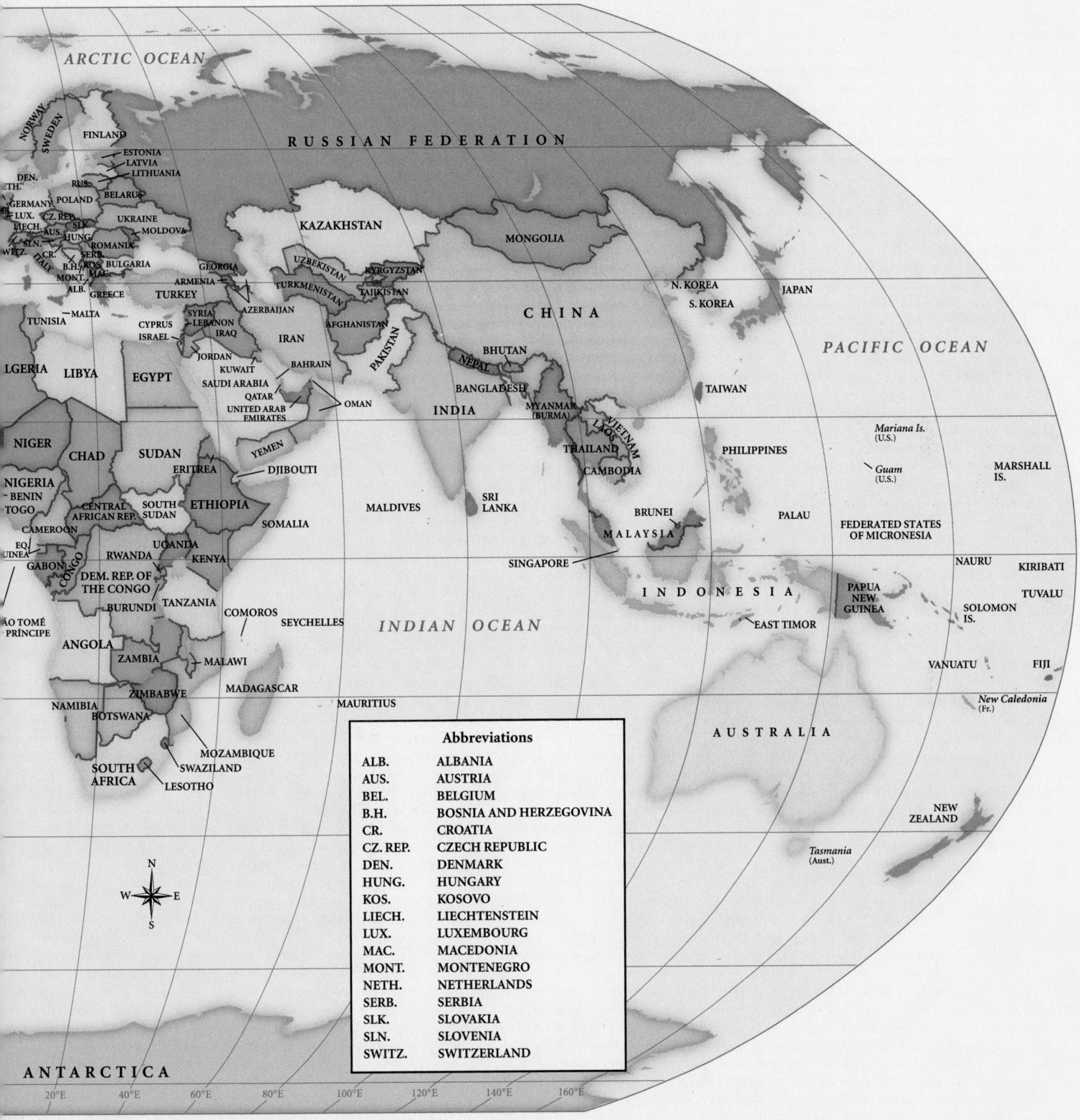
ARCTIC OCEAN
RUSSIAN FEDERATION
NORWAY
SWEDEN
FINLAND
ESTONIA
LATVIA
LITHUANIA
DEN.
NETH.
RUS.
BELARUS
GERMANY
POLAND
LUX.
CZ. REP.
LIECH.
SLK.
AUS.
UKRAINE
MOLDOVA
HUNG.
SLN.
ROMANIA
SWITZ.
CR.
SERB.
ITALY
B.H.
KOS.
BULGARIA
MONT.
MAC.
ALB.
GREECE
MALTA
TUNISIA
KAZAKHSTAN
MONGOLIA
GEORGIA
ARMENIA
TURKEY
UZBEKISTAN
KYRGYZSTAN
TURKMENISTAN
TAJIKISTAN
AZERBAIJAN
SYRIA
LEBANON
CYPRUS
ISRAEL
IRAQ
IRAN
AFGHANISTAN
PAKISTAN
JORDAN
KUWAIT
BAHRAIN
SAUDI ARABIA
QATAR
UNITED ARAB EMIRATES
OMAN
YEMEN
LIBYA
EGYPT
NIGER
CHAD
SUDAN
ERITREA
DJIBOUTI
NIGERIA
BENIN
TOGO
CENTRAL AFRICAN REP.
SOUTH SUDAN
ETHIOPIA
SOMALIA
CAMEROON
EQ. GUINEA
GABON
CONGO
UGANDA
RWANDA
KENYA
DEM. REP. OF THE CONGO
BURUNDI
TANZANIA
COMOROS
SEYCHELLES
ANGOLA
ZAMBIA
MALAWI
ZIMBABWE
MADAGASCAR
NAMIBIA
BOTSWANA
MAURITIUS
MOZAMBIQUE
SWAZILAND
SOUTH AFRICA
LESOTHO
ANTARCTICA
CHINA
N. KOREA
S. KOREA
JAPAN
PACIFIC OCEAN
BHUTAN
NEPAL
BANGLADESH
INDIA
MYANMAR (BURMA)
LAOS
VIETNAM
THAILAND
CAMBODIA
TAIWAN
PHILIPPINES
Mariana Is. (U.S.)
Guam (U.S.)
MARSHALL IS.
MALDIVES
SRI LANKA
BRUNEI
MALAYSIA
PALAU
FEDERATED STATES OF MICRONESIA
SINGAPORE
NAURU
KIRIBATI
INDONESIA
PAPUA NEW GUINEA
TUVALU
SOLOMON IS.
EAST TIMOR
INDIAN OCEAN
VANUATU
FIJI
New Caledonia (Fr.)
AUSTRALIA
NEW ZEALAND
Tasmania (Aust.)
N
W
E
S
20°E
40°E
60°E
80°E
100°E
120°E
140°E
160°E
Abbreviations
ALB. ALBANIA
AUS. AUSTRIA
BEL. BELGIUM
B.H. BOSNIA AND HERZEGOVINA
CR. CROATIA
CZ. REP. CZECH REPUBLIC
DEN. DENMARK
HUNG. HUNGARY
KOS. KOSOVO
LIECH. LIECHTENSTEIN
LUX. LUXEMBOURG
MAC. MACEDONIA
MONT. MONTENEGRO
NETH. NETHERLANDS
SERB. SERBIA
SLK. SLOVAKIA
SLN. SLOVENIA
SWITZ. SWITZERLAND

About the authors

Lynn Hunt (Ph.D., Stanford University) is Eugen Weber Professor of Modern European History at the University of California, Los Angeles. She is the author or editor of several books, including most recently *Bernard Picart and the First Global Vision of Religion; The Book That Changed Europe: Picart and Bernard's Religious Ceremonies of the World; Measuring Time, Making History;* and *Inventing Human Rights.*

Thomas R. Martin (Ph.D., Harvard University) is Jeremiah O'Connor Professor in Classics at the College of the Holy Cross. He is the author of *Ancient Greece* and *Sovereignty and Coinage in Classical Greece* and is one of the originators of *Perseus: Interactive Sources and Studies on Ancient Greece* (www.perseus.tufts.edu). He is currently conducting research on the career of Pericles as a political leader in classical Athens as well as on the text of Josephus's *Jewish War.*

Barbara H. Rosenwein (Ph.D., University of Chicago) is professor of history at Loyola University Chicago. She is the author or editor of several books including *A Short History of the Middle Ages* and *Emotional Communities in the Early Middle Ages.* She is currently working on a general history of the emotions in the West.

Bonnie G. Smith (Ph.D., University of Rochester) is Board of Governors Professor of History at Rutgers University. She is the author or editor of several books including *The Oxford Encyclopedia of Women in World History; The Gender of History: Men, Women and Historical Practice;* and *Ladies of the Leisure Class.* Currently she is studying the globalization of European culture and society since the seventeenth century.

About the cover image

Vasili Semenovich Sadovnikov (1800–79), *The Unveiling of the Nicholas I Memorial in St. Petersburg,* 1857

This grand statue of Nicholas I of Russia (r. 1825–1855), who died in 1855, depicts the former tsar as a majestic knight on a rearing horse. Created by French-born architect Auguste de Montferrand and commissioned by Nicholas's successor and son, Alexander II, the statue was considered a feat of design. In contrast to his father's regime, Alexander's reign heralded a new age of Great Reforms, the most significant of which was his emancipation of almost fifty million Russian serfs.